THE NAVAL INSTITUTE GUIDE TO THE

Ships and Aircraft of the U.S. Fleet

EIGHTEENTH EDITION

THE NAVAL INSTITUTE GUIDE TO THE

Ships and Aircraft of the U.S. Fleet

Norman Polmar

Samuel Loring Morison, Senior Researcher—Ships
Richard R. Burgess, Senior Researcher—Aviation
Julie Olver, Managing Editor

Naval Institute Press
Annapolis, Maryland

ISBN-10: 1-59114-685-2
ISBN-13: 978-1-59114-685-8

Printed in the United States of America on acid-free paper ∞
12 11 10   9 8 7 6

For
Rae Morgan
and
Edward L. (Ned) Beach

✯ ✯ ✯ ✯ ✯

Friends of the Naval Institute
and of Mine

Contents

The nuclear-propelled special-mission submarine JIMMY CARTER (SSN 23) departing on initial sea trials in November 2004. Like most U.S. Navy ships of recent construction, the three submarines of the SEAWOLF (SSN 21) class were far over cost estimates, which is a major factor in the current debates over future Navy ship construction. The JIMMY CARTER is configured for special operations, including deep-ocean search and recovery and serving as a mother ship for underwater vehicles. (General Dynamics/Electric Boat)

PREFACE

As this edition of *Ship and Aircraft* goes to press, the U.S. Navy is undergoing probably the most extensive changes since the post–World War II era. A decade and a half ago, the U.S. Navy underwent major reductions—from a fleet of some 550 ships at the end of the Cold War to about 450 only three years later.

By the time of the terrorist attacks on the United States by fundamentalist Muslims in September 2001, the Navy was fighting to maintain a 300-ship fleet. In the years since those events, the fleet has declined slightly and is the smallest force since 1917. Even more significant have been the changes in the direction of the Navy—an effort to initiate a true "transformation," to use the current Pentagon terminology.

The Navy is initiating new ship types, especially the Littoral Combat Ship (LCS) and the Maritime Prepositioning Force (Future) (MPF[F]) ships. Also noteworthy, the Navy is acquiring a Swedish GOTLAND-class submarine on loan for Anti-Submarine Warfare (ASW) training. The acquisition of this advanced, nonnuclear submarine is remarkable in view of the previous (successful) efforts by the nuclear submarine community to prevent the U.S. Navy from acquiring such craft for ASW training. After some ten years of benign neglect, ASW in the littoral is on the verge of a renaissance, of sorts, and the need to understand the worldwide submarine threat to U.S. and allied forces "transformed" Navy thinking about training realities.

Several new aircraft are described in this volume. Among them are the EA-18G "Growler," the long-awaited replacement for the EA-6B Prowler electric countermeasures aircraft, and the Multimission Maritime Aircraft (MMA), the long-delayed replacement for the P-3C Orion maritime patrol/ASW aircraft. There also are new weapons and sensors.

But a true transformation transcends just ships and aircraft. Admiral Vern Clark, Chief of Naval Operations since July 2000, has directed that unmanned vehicles—air, surface, and undersea—be developed and employed wherever possible. In addition, in developing a dogma for a Concept of Operations (CONOPS) for the 21st century, Admiral Clark has directed the development of a "family of systems"—under the label "Sea Power 21"—consisting of Sea Strike, Sea Shield, and Sea Base. These form the basis for future platform, systems, and technology developments.

Less clear is the "linking" concept of FORCEnet, the underpinning of network-centric warfare: Command, Control, and Communications (C^3) and Intelligence, Surveillance, and Reconnaissance (ISR). Beyond the linking aspects of FORCEnet, it could become the key factor in "information warfare"—exploiting U.S. strengths and potential enemy weaknesses in the C^3/ISR areas.

"Sea Power 21" also promotes new deployment practices and personnel rotation policies, e.g., Sea Swap (see Chapter 9).

These efforts, it is hoped, will enable the U.S. Navy to contribute effectively to the ongoing war against terrorism—in reality World War III. This volume describes the ship and aircraft, and their associated weapons, as well as the naval services that will man them in the coming years.

Many individuals and organizations have provided assistance in producing this book. First and foremost, I am in debt to Julie Olver, managing editor of the Naval Institute *Proceedings* and *Naval History* magazines, who was responsible for editing this edition.

Samuel Loring Morison, researcher par excellence, and Richard Burgess, managing editor of *Sea Power* magazine, have spent many hours researching ship and aircraft data for this edition, and have replied to my interminable questions.

Others who made contributions to this edition include: Journalist 2nd Class Dan Ball, *Naval Aviation News*; Major Matt Boykin, Marine Corps Combat Development Center; Christopher P. Cavas, senior correspondent, *Defense News*; Steve Daskal, purveyor and interpreter of Internet information; Janet M. Gottfredsen, communications and public relations, Lockheed Martin; Robbie Harris, Lockheed Martin; Kenneth Hoffman, editor, *Minewarnews*; Comdr. Glen King, public affairs officer, Naval Special Warfare Command; Neil King, Lockheed Martin; Fred Lash, congressional and public affairs, Naval Sea Systems Command; Edward H. Lundquist, director of communications for the Center for Security Strategies and Operations of Anteon Corp.; Ted Minter, who has double-checked me on many, many ship facts; Gordon I. Peterson, senior technical writer for the Coast Guard's Integrated Deepwater System; Lt. Herlinda Rojas, public affairs officer, Mine Warfare Command; Lt.(jg) Ken Shade, pubic affairs, Naval Reserve Forces Command; William S. Tuttle, public relations, Sikorsky/United Aircraft; Edward J. Walsh, public affairs, Office of Naval Research; Edward C. Whitman, senior editor, *Undersea Warfare*; and John Whipple, publications director for the Center for Security Strategies and Operations at Anteon Corp.

Several "desk people" at the Navy's Office of Information (CHINFO) have been helpful in tracking down facts and figures: Lt. Comdr. Danny Hernandez, Lt. Pauline Pimentel, and Lt. Jason Salata.

I have borrowed heavily from the analysis and writings of Eric Labs of the Congressional Research Service; Ron O'Rourke of the Congressional Budget Office; and Dr. Scott C. Truver, group vice president, Anteon Corp., who also is a friend and confidant. Eric Wertheim, editor of *Combat Fleets of the World,* and A. D. Baker III, his predecessor, have shared much of their research and observations with me.

In this computer era, several web sites have been consulted, especially the work of John Pike, and the databases of Federation of American Scientists, Global Security Organization, and Periscope produced by the United Communications Group.

Similarly, I have drawn heavily from several journals, in addition, of course, to the Naval Institute *Proceedings*. These have been primarily *Navy Times, Naval Aviation News, The Hook* (Tailhook Association), *Sea Power* (Navy League of the United States), and *Naval Forces*.

Several photographers have provided a veritable stream of photographs of U.S. ships and aircraft. Beyond those that appear in the book, their other photos are an invaluable source of intelligence on shipboard weapons and electronics. These professionals are: Dr. Giorgio Arra, Leo Van Ginderen, Jürg Kürsener, Peter B. Mersky, Stefan Terzibaschitsch, Mike Wilson, and W. Michael Young.

Of course, a majority of the photographs are official U.S. Navy. Where known, the photographers are credited. All users of photographs from the Navy's web site—Navy NewsStand—must be in debt to Christopher Madden of CHINFO and his most-helpful staff.

Much well-deserved praise must go to the publishing professionals at the Naval Institute. This is the first edition of this book published under the leadership of Tom Wilkerson, publisher, and Mark Gatlin, director of the Naval Institute Press. Both of these professionals have been supportive of this reference work and its author. This edition of *Ships and Aircraft* was produced by the splendid efforts of several members of the Naval Institute staff: Jennifer (Till) Wallace, photo researcher; Karen Eskew, Faith Stewart, and Donna Doyle, who were responsible for design and layouts; Gordon W. Keiser, senior editor of *Proceedings,* for editing and "transportation"; and Liese Doherty and Jaci Day, who provided invaluable help on the book.

Several members of the Naval Institute marketing staff have taken considerable time and trouble with this project—Susan Artigiani, Tom Harnish, Judy Heise, Maureen Peterson, Janice Smith, and, especially, Brian Walker.

Finally, Fred H. Rainbow, director of periodicals and seminars at the Naval Institute, initiated a new method of book design and production to produce this edition. His continued help and support, as well as his long-time friendship, have been invaluable.

Work on the next edition of *Ships and Aircraft* begins immediately. Additions, corrections, comments, and photographs should be addressed to the undersigned in care of the Naval Institute or at the following e-mail address: wordsmh@aol.com

NORMAN POLMAR

The first shipboard installation of the AN/SLY-2(V) fixed-array radar is in the missile cruiser PHILIPPINE SEA *(CG 58). The antenna is fitted on the starboard side of the ship's after deckhouse; the ship's aft-facing AN/SPY-1 radar antenna is at far left, above the helicopter hangar. New electronic systems are being developed for the future Navy, although their viability for the war against terrorism is not certain. (U.S. Navy)*

CHAPTER 1

State of the Fleet

Sailors aboard the carrier THEODORE ROOSEVELT (CVN 71) pose questions to Chief of Naval Operations Admiral Vern Clark while the carrier operates in support of U.S. forces in Iraq. Admiral Clark has initiated far-reaching changes in the Navy and has garnered high-level support for his policies. (U.S. Navy/Eric A. Clement)

The United States is fighting World War III. Unlike the last "hot" wars fought by the United States in Korea and Vietnam, the current conflict against terrorism spawned by Muslim extremism affects almost every country. In addition, there is no clear or neat end in sight; there is no "light at the end of the tunnel," to employ that infamous term uttered during the Vietnam War.[1]

It is difficult to determine when and where this new world war began. Was it the abortive attempt to blow up the World Trade Center in 1993; the attack on the U.S. barracks known as Khobar Towers in Saudi Arabia in 1996; the car bombing of two U.S. embassies in Africa in 1998; the attack on the USS COLE (DDG 67) in 2000; or the devastating assault on the World Trade Center and Pentagon on 11 September 2001?[2]

For the U.S. Navy, the questions quickly became what roles naval forces would play in this global conflict and what kinds and numbers of ships and aircraft would be required to fulfill those roles. And could they be funded within likely budget allocations?

Soon after the demise of the Soviet Union and end of the Cold War, the U.S. Navy adopted a new strategy centered on the support of operations ashore. This later was refined to include U.S. naval dominance in the littoral or offshore waters, especially in those areas where U.S. forces were required to operate ashore. Subsequently, in 2004, Secretary of Defense Donald Rumsfeld directed a new strategic doctrine for the armed forces: Combat forces were to respond to crisis or combat situations anywhere in the world within 10 days. The crisis or conflict was to be resolved within 30 days, after which the committed forces should be reconstituted within 30 days and ready for transfer to another crisis or combat area. This 10–30–30 strategy replaced the two-and-half conflict, one-plus-one, and other recent strategic concepts that sought to guide the development, structure, and operations of U.S. armed forces.

---

1 An excellent exposition of this subject was presented by former Secretary of the Navy John Lehman at the U.S. Naval Institute's Naval History Symposium at Annapolis, Maryland, 31 March 2004. His remarks were published as "'Our Enemy Is Not Terrorism," U.S. Naval Institute *Proceedings* (May 2004), pp. 52–54. Mr. Lehman was a member of the National Commission on Terrorist Attacks Upon the United States (the "9/11 Commission").

2 Similarly, it was difficult to determine precisely when World War II began—with the Japanese assaults on China in the 1930s; Hitler's invasion of Poland in 1939; or Japan's attack on Pearl Harbor and U.S. bases in the Philippines in December 1941?

In response to those and earlier requirements, Chief of Naval Operations Admiral Vern Clark has produced a series of initiatives or "pillars" under the umbrella of "Sea Power 21":[3]

• *Sea Strike*: Expanded power projection that employs networked sensors, combat systems, and warriors to amplify the offensive impact of naval forces. This includes increased operational tempo, reach, and effectiveness.

• *Sea Shield*: Naval capabilities related to homeland defense, sea control in specific areas, the defense of naval forces in littoral areas, and the projection of air and missile defenses overland.

• *Sea Basing*: Enhanced operational independence and support for joint forces provided by networked, mobile, and secure platforms operating in the maritime domain.

• *ForceNet*: Overarching integration of warriors, sensors, and weapons into a fully netted combat force, fully integrated with the planned Global Information Grid of the Department of Defense.

In all these areas, Admiral Clark is seeking to (1) reduce manning requirements, and (2) increase the use of unmanned vehicles—air, surface, and undersea.

Almost all aspects of the Navy are being affected by these new Department of Defense and Navy strategies. The service's leadership believes they will arrest and then reverse the post–Cold War trend of fleet decline. The Navy in early 2005 was to have just under 300 ships, compared to approximately 545 when the Cold War ended in 1991—a 45 percent decline in less than 15 years.

Admiral Clark has stated a goal of 375 surface ships and submarines, although there are unofficial reports he has backed off that total. The number 310 often is mentioned in Pentagon hallways. Add to that the 65 Littoral Combat Ships (LCS) being advocated by Admiral Clark and the total comes to 375. But it is unlikely that in the current budget environment the Navy can attain a fleet of 375 ships, even if a large number of LCS is funded.

For example, to maintain 300 ships, the Navy must build an average of 10 ships per year. The Fiscal Year (FY) 2001–2005 ship-

TABLE 1-1. FORCE STRUCTURE

	FY 2003	FY 2004	FY 2005
Fleet ballistic missile submarines	16	14	14
Guided missile submarines	—	—	2
Attack submarines	54	54	55
Aircraft carriers	12	12	12
Surface combatants	106	103	100
Amphibious warfare ships	36	35	36
Mine warfare ships	17	17	17
Combat logistics ships	34	34	33
Support ships	19	19	19
Total	296	292	290

building programs have averaged just 5½ ships.[4] And although the 30-year shipbuilding program presented to Congress by the Navy in 2003, discussed in this volume, calls for a future building rate of from 7 to 14 ships per year (the latter for FY 2009–2018), this rate is unobtainable given the probable fiscal conditions of the foreseeable future, even with a significant number of those ships being of the LCS type. Indeed, even the near-term ship program presented to Congress as part of the FY 2005 budget may be unattainable, especially with the delay in the DD(X) program announced shortly after the budget was presented and the desirability of delaying procurement of the MPF(F) future maritime prepositioning ships. (See Table 1-1.)

Clearly, a realistic and White House/Congress-supported, long-range shipbuilding plan is needed.

---

3 The U.S. Naval Institute *Proceedings* published a series of articles in 2003–2004 by senior officers addressing aspects of "Sea Power 21"; also see Adm. Vern Clark, USN, "Persistent Combat Power," U.S. Naval Institute *Proceedings* (May 2003), pp. 46–48.

4 The 5½ ships include the first two LCSs, which were funded with research and development funds, and not shipbuilding funds.

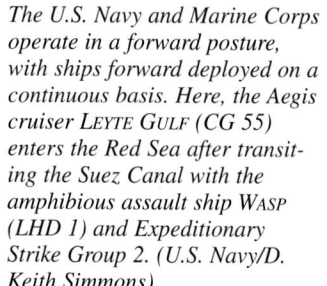

The U.S. Navy and Marine Corps operate in a forward posture, with ships forward deployed on a continuous basis. Here, the Aegis cruiser LEYTE GULF (CG 55) enters the Red Sea after transiting the Suez Canal with the amphibious assault ship WASP (LHD 1) and Expeditionary Strike Group 2. (U.S. Navy/D. Keith Simmons)

SHIPS

Submarines: The need for 14 ballistic missile submarines (SSBNs) with a combined loadout of 336 missiles is being questioned in some quarters of government in view of the current world situation—World War III being waged mainly against nonnational terrorist groups and the demonstrated reluctance of the United States to employ nuclear weapons.[5] The SSBN force, operated under the two-crew construct, has an at-sea availability well over 50 percent.

With the end of the Cold War, construction of Trident SSBNs was halted at 18 submarines. By the start of the 21st century, the Navy had decided—based on strategic arms agreements—to reduce that force from 18 to 14. Even with this cut, a reduction in the numbers of warheads in Trident missiles, and possibly going to a single-crew operating procedure, there likely will be a further decrease in SSBNs by the end of this decade, based on a combination of arms control issues, lack of credible strategic attack scenarios, and political considerations. Numbers from 10 to 12 SSBNs are said to be "floated" in discussions,[6] although there appears to be a lack of supporting analysis for these additional cuts.

The reduction of SSBN force levels from 18 to 14 led the nuclear submarine community, or "union," to advocate converting those first four available Trident submarines to combination cruise missile/Special Operations Forces (SOF) transport submarines (SSGNs). The conversions, which will provide the four SSGNs to the fleet in 2007–2008, are being hailed as "transformational," but that term, which has been in vogue as justification for new programs, does not accurately apply here (see Appendix F). The SSGNs will introduce no new capabilities to the fleet—existing attack submarines can launch Tomahawk cruise missiles, and in the past, the Navy has operated specialized SOF transport submarines (converted from SSBNs). Indeed, combining those capabilities in a single hull could cause mission conflicts, as discussed in Chapter 10.

Rather, the principal value of the SSGN appears to be its ability to clandestinely shift a large number of cruise missiles (154) into a forward area, and to remain in the area without external support (e.g., air defense, replenishment ships) for two or three months.

With respect to attack submarines (SSNs), the Navy's force level has declined from 95 at the end of the Cold War to approximately 55. However, the current construction rate of one submarine per year of the VIRGINIA (SSN 774) class is not enough to maintain that number and will mean a force reduction to about 40 SSNs by 2012. Several efforts by the submarine community to increase building rates to two or even three SSNs per year have not been approved by the Navy's leadership or by the Department of Defense, although two SSNs are shown in the planned FY 2009 procurement plan.

Efforts to increase procurement have failed in spite of periodic recounting by the submarine leadership of a requirement for 68 SSNs by 2015 and 76 by 2025.[7] These numbers are based on a Joint Chiefs of Staff study of the requests put forward by U.S. combatant commanders (formerly known as unified commanders-in-chief),[8] the largest portion of which were based on Intelligence, Surveillance, and Reconnaissance (ISR) operations. Opponents of an increase in SSNs quickly note that "periscopes cannot see over the hill," a criticism of their overland ISR effectiveness. On a day-to-day basis, little of the large volumes of intelligence being passed

---

5 The U.S. government apparently has given strong consideration to the employment of nuclear weapons on three occasions since the 1945 bombings of Hiroshima and Nagasaki—in response to Chinese entry in the Korean War in 1950, to support the French in Indochina in 1954, and during the Cuban Missile Crisis of 1962. Reportedly, there was no consideration of employing nuclear weapons in the Vietnam War.

6 By comparison, in 2004, the Russian Navy had 14 operational SSBNs, with 232 ballistic missiles; two other SSBNs may be employed for research and tests.

7 Adm. F. L. Bowman, USN, Director, Naval Nuclear Propulsion, "Remarks at Corporate Benefactors Day," *The Submarine Review* (April 2002), pp. 14–15.

8 The regional combatant commanders, who employ but do not procure military forces, invariably ask for "more" weapons than are politically or fiscally possible to procure.

The nuclear-propelled attack submarine VIRGINIA (SSN 774) returns to the Electric Boat yard where she was built following her July 2004 sea trials. The VIRGINIA class is in series production in an awkward and expensive, two-yard construction effort developed for political reasons. (General Dynamics/ Electric Boat)

to U.S. commanders in Afghanistan and Iraq is provided by submarines. In addition, critics note that submarines are limited in their ability to communicate while at high speed and at depth.

Indeed, in 2004, accounts began to surface of both Navy and congressional "studies" that indicated a smaller SSN force—the number 37 was cited—might be in the offing. Two proposals have been raised to compensate for such reductions: employing "sea swap"—the rotation of crews to deployed ships—and increasing the number of submarines forward based at Guam (now three).

Regardless of the numbers of SSNs, the submarine force must try to increase the ratio of time deployed. While most surface ships have a deployment ratio of roughly 1-in-3, submarines are closer to 1-in-6, i.e., only 9 of about 55 submarines were forward deployed at any given time in 2004.[9] Revised maintenance cycles and longer periods between refueling for newer submarines (because of their 30-year fuel cores) could improve this.

Submarines are useful tools in both crises and conflicts, but their *relative* effectiveness in the current war against terrorism and the requirements in terms of numbers as well as types will be further questioned and analyzed in the coming years. Despite these questions, the VIRGINIA appears to be an excellent post–Cold War SSN design, especially in view of her large swimmer lockout chamber, reconfigurable torpedo room, and 12 vertical-launch tubes for Tomahawk missiles.

Aircraft Carriers: Seemingly inviolate is the number of large aircraft carriers in the fleet—12, a number that dates from the mid-1990s. Aircraft carriers demonstrated their value in the U.S. invasions of both Afghanistan (2002) and Iraq (2003). In the former operation, there were no airfields available to U.S. forces within tactical air range when the conflict began. In addition to the carriers operating standard naval aircraft, the KITTY HAWK (CV 63), after sending most of her air wing ashore, served as a floating base for Army special forces and their brood of helicopters. Although some land bases were available to U.S. air forces in the Gulf States during the invasion of Iraq, severe restrictions on operations from bases in Turkey and Saudi Arabia made the availability of carriers far more important than in the 1991 Gulf War.

Under the so-called Fleet Response Plan, efforts are under way to revise the standard forward-deployment cycle for naval forces—historically 1-in-3—to provide more flexibility. A particular goal is enabling a surge of aircraft carriers during crises periods. Previous efforts to significantly alter deployment cycles have not been successful over the long term; still, during Operation Summer Pulse 2004 in June–July 2004, the Navy was able to deploy seven carriers for a brief period (some were forward deployed at the time, and one was transiting from Norfolk to San Diego).[10]

Construction of nuclear-propelled aircraft carriers (CVN) continues at a rate to sustain the 12-ship force level, with an approximately 50-year platform service life. After construction of ten carriers of the basic NIMITZ (CVN 68) design, the Navy and the Department of Defense have agreed to request authorization of a greatly improved NIMITZ-class carrier in the FY 2007 budget. That ship will cost in excess of $12 billion, more than twice that of the last CVN to be built. That amount does include the substantial outlays for research and development necessary for a lead ship; still, the new carrier—the CVN 78—will carry no more aircraft or munitions and will not go faster or have a greater endurance than her predecessor. The principal advantage, if achieved, will be the reduction in crew size—the goal is some 800 men and women. But reductions of that magnitude, i.e., 50 percent of the ship's crew, are highly unlikely.

Surface combatants: The surface combatant force—cruisers, destroyers, and frigates—also is being reduced in number. But in this category, the Navy is, in many respects, demonstrating the most innovative—some would say transformational—policies and programs.

The five oldest ships of the Aegis cruiser force, completed between 1983 and 1987, now are being discarded. With probable service lives of at least 30 years, these ship still are highly effective for anti-air, anti-surface, and anti-submarine operations, but they have Mk 26 twin-arm missile launchers instead of the Vertical Launching Systems (VLS) of the 22 improved Aegis cruisers. Thus, rather than spending funds to update and man those ships, the Navy is cutting its cruiser force to 22 ships.

There is no shortfall of Aegis warships. The Navy has plans for 62 Aegis destroyers of the ARLEIGH BURKE (DDG 51) class, and further delays in the follow-on DD(X) program *should* see additional BURKEs being procured. Indeed, a lack of definition in the mission of the DD(X), issues of cost, and lingering questions over the cancellation of its predecessor, the ZUMWALT (DD 21) class of land-attack destroyers, all are expected to cause delays in or at least a stretching out of the DD(X) program.

Through all the indecision of the past few years about the future of surface combatants, the procurement of the ARLEIGH BURKE-class destroyers has continued at the rate of three per year, an endorsement of the value of such surface combatants.

In the future, some or all of the Aegis cruisers also will be tasked with Ballistic Missile Defense (BMD), providing the sea-based component of theater/regional defenses against such missiles. The BMD mission will be the primary justification for a new class of cruiser-type ships, if the class is pursued.

Although there is little controversy over the need for major surface combatants, the Littoral Combat Ship (LCS) is a most controversial program. Strongly endorsed by Admiral Clark, the LCS is intended to operate in coastal/regional areas, primarily to carry out anti-submarine warfare (ASW) against diesel-electric and Air-Independent Propulsion (AIP) submarines; to protect friendly forces against "swarming" small craft attackers; and to conduct forward mine clearance. Other missions being considered are support of Special Operations Forces and fire support for raiding and special operations.

Admiral Clark envisions large numbers of these craft, up to 65, with interchangeable mission modules proving unprecedented flexibility in their operations. A "down-select" among the various contractor proposals in May 2004 provided two basic hull designs for initial production. Criticism—in Congress and by the Congressional Budget Office—has centered on the lack of analysis to support the LCS concept and numbers. Within the Navy, there are opponents who see the program as taking funds from other surface combatant programs. In addition, there is the historic U.S. Navy bias against corvette-size, "non-blue-water" combatants.

Nevertheless, of all combatant programs being pursued or advocated at this time, the LCS may be the only one that truly qualifies as a "transformational" warship.

Amphibious Warfare: Another area of uncertainty is amphibious warfare. Among amphibious warships, the LHA/LHD helicopter

9 Adm. F. L. Bowman, USN, Director, Naval Nuclear Propulsion, statement at Naval Submarine League symposium, Alexandria, Va., 9 June 2004.
10 The carriers were:
CV 63 KITTY HAWK
CVN 65 ENTERPRISE
CV 67 JOHN F. KENNEDY
CVN 73 GEORGE WASHINGTON
CVN 74 JOHN C. STENNIS
CVN 75 HARRY S. TRUMAN
CVN 76 RONALD REAGAN

One-half of the Navy's amphibious assault ships operate together in the Persian Gulf during 2003 operations against Iraq. These helicopter/STOVL carriers have demonstrated great flexibility. Led by the TARAWA (LHA 1), flagship of Task Force 51, from left are the BONHOMME RICHARD (LHD 6), KEARSARGE (LHD 3), BATAAN (LHD 5), SAIPAN (LHA 2), and BOXER (LHD 4). (U.S. Navy/Larry S. Carlson)

carriers continue to demonstrate their value and flexibility. Their use as bases for Marine helicopters and AV-8B Harrier attack aircraft and the promise that the Joint Strike Fighter (JSF) can operate from their flight decks highlight a continuing need for these "pocket aircraft carriers."[11]

The Navy's long-standing force of 12 amphibious groups, each capable of transporting a Marine Expeditionary Unit (MEU) of some 2,000 troops, will undergo reduction and/or restructuring in the near future. The decision to cutback the number of amphibious transport docks (LPD) being procured and the development of the sea basing concept bring into question the entire Navy–Marine Corps amphibious assault program.

Also, certain so-called connector programs—the means of getting troops and equipment to the beach—are being reviewed. These include the Expeditionary Fighting Vehicle (EFV)—recently changed from the Advanced Amphibian Assault Vehicle (AAAV), a name change intended to imply that the new "amphibious tractor" is a transformational system—as well as the highly effective air cushion landing craft (LCAC). The planned replacement utility landing craft (LCU[R]) has been canceled.

SEA BASING

The Navy's response to Secretary Rumsfeld's 10-30-30 strategy will be centered in large part on Admiral Clark's sea basing concept. Derived in part from the Maritime Prepositioning Ships (MPS) initiated in the early 1980s, the plan provides for a large operating base that can be established rapidly (within ten days) in a forward area, some 25–100 miles offshore of the objective.

This sea base will consist of Maritime Prepositioning Force (MPF) ships and, most likely, amphibious and replenishment ships. It will not be centered on "floating islands" or the Mobile Offshore Base Systems (MOBS), although some proponents in the Department of Defense and industry continue to propose the latter (see Chapter 13). Indeed, there are promoters of a sea base large enough to support operations by C-130 Hercules cargo aircraft.[12]

The MPF ships will differ greatly from current MPS ships in that they will be larger and will (1) have facilities for troops to come aboard at sea, be berthed, and "marry up" with their equipment; (2) be able to put those troops ashore in a combat environment; (3) provide command and control, medical, and resupply

functions; (4) reembark troops after the operation for rehabilitation and the reconditioning or replacement of their equipment, with additional supplies and equipment brought on board; and (5) move with the sea base to another location, with the embarked forces ready for combat within 30 days. Thus, the MPF ships will be more complex (and more expensive) than the MPS ships.

Although the MPF ships will not be capable of operating C-130 Hercules conventional aircraft, a variety of fixed-wing Vertical Takeoff and Landing (VTOL) aircraft, including AV-8B Harriers and MV-22 Ospreys, as well as helicopters, will operate from the sea base. Hopefully, the potential for eventual operation of larger VSTOL aircraft, including a Bell quad-rotor aircraft that could be the size of a later Hercules, will be incorporated in the MPF design.

Several ship designs for the MPF program were being developed as this edition of *Ships and Aircraft* went to press. Among them are several with large aviation facilities (i.e., full or near-full flight decks). One of the more interesting concepts is the Maersk S-class container ship, extensively modified to operate VSTOL aircraft and helicopters. That modification was developed as an offshore aviation base under a government contract following the success of the carrier KITTY HAWK as a SOF helicopter platform during the Afghan invasion of 2002 (see Chapter 24).

AIRCRAFT

Major changes are under way for carrier-based aircraft. The Grumman F-14 Tomcat, an outstanding fighter-attack aircraft, is being rapidly retired. It still is effective, but maintenance costs are significantly higher than for the McDonnell Douglas F/A-18 Hornet, and cost arguably is the principal factor in today's decision making. In the near future, all carriers will have four F/A-18 strike-

---

11 The LHA/LHDs can operate 20 Harriers, plus a few helicopters. These ships are more than twice as large as the two small helicopter carriers employed successfully in the Falklands conflict of 1982, operating Harriers and helicopters.

12 In 1963, Lt. James H. Flatley III, USN, flying a KC-130F made numerous touch-and-go and full-stop landings, and takeoffs from the carrier FORRESTAL (CV 59). No arresting gear or catapults were used, and the KC-130F had a maximum weight of 120,000 pounds. Such flights, however, were deemed not practical on an operational basis.

Four Marine Corps MV-22 Osprey tilt-rotor aircraft rest at the Naval Air Station, Patuxent River, Maryland, during their test and evaluation. The STOVL aircraft will provide more effective transport of troops and cargo than the current CH-46E Sea Knight and offers the promise of an effective platform for several other missions. (U.S. Navy)

fighter squadrons, and those squadrons will be both Navy and Marine Corps, as Admiral Clark and Commandant of the Marine Corps General Michael W. Hagee seek to completely integrate carrier aviation.

While long-range planning calls for the Lockheed Martin F-35 Joint Strike Fighter eventually to replace the F/A-18, the JSF program is being delayed. It will be well after 2015 before that aircraft enters naval service in sufficient numbers to fill carrier squadrons.[13]

Simultaneously, carrier-based ASW capabilities are being reduced precipitously. The Lockheed S-3 Vikings, long without an ASW capability but still useful for surveillance and tanking, are being discarded. This leaves the MH-60R Seahawk helicopter as the only carrier-based ASW aircraft. However, as indicated by the M prefix, these are multimission aircraft, and the few embarked in carriers will be required to perform a plethora of missions, reducing their ASW proficiency.

Carriers also embark the venerable, albeit undated, Grumman E-2C Hawkeye Airborne Early Warning (AEW) aircraft and the Grumman EA-6B Prowler electronic attack/countermeasures aircraft. The last are from both Navy and Marine Corps squadrons and perform electronic warfare activities in support of both naval and Air Force operations. The E-2Cs will undergo additional upgrades. The EA-18G variant of the Hornet is being procured to replace the EA-6B. It is expected that Unmanned Aerial Vehicles (UAVs) will carry part of the electronic attack/countermeasures burden.

A major question for future consideration is how the Bell-Boeing MV-22 Osprey could fit into carrier operations. That flexible tilt-rotor aircraft is belatedly in production for the Marine

Corps and Air Force, the latter for Special Operations Forces. In the past, AEW and ASW roles have been proposed for a carrier-based V-22. While there is no movement in that direction at this writing, the operational success of that aircraft in Marine Corps and Air Force service could reopen such considerations.

A final carrier aircraft issue is tankers. When the Navy retired the last of the Grumman A-6 Intruder attack aircraft in 1996, the very useful KA-6D tankers also were discarded. The Air Force was charged with providing tanker support for Navy–Marine Corps forces—when its tankers are available.

Subsequently, S-3B Vikings, denuded of their ASW gear, became useful surrogate tankers. With the beaching of the Vikings, F/A-18 Hornets carrying "buddy" refueling stores will be the only carrier-based tankers. This arrangement suffers from the limited fuel for transfer carried by Hornets and the reduction of a carrier's strike-fighter forces when planes are allocated to the tanker role.

The Navy has belatedly decided on a replacement for the venerable P-3 Orion maritime patrol aircraft, which entered naval service in its original configuration in 1962. The Multimission Maritime Aircraft (MMA) will be the successor to the current P-3C and possibly to the EP-3E Electronic Intelligence (ELINT) aircraft. Admiral Clark has said he intends to procure the Army's Aerial Common Sensor (ACS) aircraft as a replacement for the EP-3E.

---

13 Variants of the F-35 JSF are planned for the U.S. Air Force and Royal Navy, as well as for the U.S. Navy and Marine Corps; several other nations are expressing interest in the aircraft.

Boeing's proposal for the MMA, which is to have an "all-jet" (turbofan) configuration, was accepted in 2004. The other MMA competitor was Lockheed, which had provided the Navy with patrol-type aircraft since 1941—the PBO Hudson, PV Ventura and Harpoon, P2V/P-2 Neptune, and P3V/P-3 Orion.

Rotary-wing aircraft: The MV-22 Osprey is in production for the Marine Corps, and the Air Force is buying the CV-22 variant for SOF operations. The multirole MH-60R Seahawk and MH-60S Knighthawk also are in production, replacements for the SH-60 Seahawk, UH-46 Sea Knight, and possibly MH-53E Sea Dragon helicopters. If the "necking down" of the helicopter force includes loss of the MH-53Es, which are employed for mine countermeasures and vertical replenishment, the Navy will suffer a significant loss in capabilities.

In the offing is the CH-53X, a long-needed replacement for the Marine Corps' CH-53E Super Stallion heavy-lift helicopter. With a maximum lift of some 15 tons, the H-53E series is the most powerful helicopter in the West. The replacement—which should become the CH-53F—will have greater lift and range capabilities.

A decision will be made shortly—after the 2004 presidential election—on procurement of the VXX presidential transport helicopter. This will replace the long-serving VH-3 Sea King. The Navy's delay in selection makes it appear that the Lockheed Martin-led team's US101, a variant of the Agusta-Westland EH-101 will be the winner. The Sikorsky-Vought team's S-92 is the alternative. The EH-101 already is in military service in several other counties.

Unmanned Aerial Vehicles: UAVs will have an increasing role in naval operations. The Navy and, especially, the Marine Corps are using and evaluating a large number of UAVs, including the Pioneer, first acquired by the Navy in the mid-1980s. These vehicles are being employed in a variety of roles, and the development of Unmanned Combat Air Vehicles (UCAV) could see them aboard carriers to carry out fighter and strike missions.

In particular, the high-priority LCS will carry UAVs for several of its missions. Also significant is the Broad-Area Maritime Surveillance (BAMS) program, which will provide a very-long-range/high-endurance unmanned aircraft. Unfortunately, the Navy has been slow in pursuing this program. A prime candidate for the BAMS role is the Northrop Grumman/Teledyne Ryan Aeronautical Global Hawk, which has been operational since 2003.

Because of the significance of UAVs in the future fleet, a separate chapter describes these vehicles (see Chapter 29).

SAILORS AND MARINES

The "global war on terrorism" has been strenuous for all the armed forces. The Navy, already forward deployed on a 1-in-3 basis when the buildup for the invasion of Afghanistan began in 2002, started deploying on a wartime basis. Thousands of reservists were called to active duty, both to support the fleet and to provide security for the massive Navy base structure. The latter proved particularly difficult because of the collocation of major naval facilities and civilian areas, especially locations such as San Diego, where the base complexes are open to civilian water traffic.

At the same time, Admiral Clark began looking for ways to reduce Navy manpower. Some of the numerous experiments in crew reductions have been successful, but certainly not all. Other ploys, such as Sea Swap, have reported initial success, but the long-term problems of such methods have yet to be determined.

At this writing, Navy recruitment and retention remain high, meeting most goals, even in the always difficult category of submarine enlisted men and junior officers. The long-term effects of the demanding aviation and surface ship deployment schedule also have yet to be determined.

The Marine Corps has been at the forefront of the assaults on Afghanistan and Iraq, and Marine security forces have had a key role in the security of naval bases in the United States and abroad and of U.S. naval ships, including forward-operating MPS ship-

U.S. warships that forward deploy have been armed with light automatic weapons, and their crews have been specially trained—and in some instances, augmented by special teams—to repel terrorist attacks. Here, sailors on the carrier GEORGE WASHINGTON (CVN 73) fire a .50-caliber machine gun M2 during an exercise in the Persian Gulf. (U.S. Navy/ Michael D. Blackwell II)

Marines have been employed as ground combat troops and on special operations in Afghanistan and Iraq, while maintaining afloat deployments and exercises in other areas. These Marine reservists from the 4th Reconnaissance Battalion are handling a rubber craft aboard the Polish minelayer/landing ship POZNAN while training in the Baltic Sea. (U.S. Navy/George Sisting)

ping. Indeed, during those operations, Marines were employed virtually interchangeably with Army units.

While Marines have performed as expected and admirably, they have lacked some of the equipment for long-duration ground operations, such as heavy trucks and tanks. Possibly more significant, this employment again has raised the question of whether Marines should be maintained as a "separate army," with almost one-third the number of active divisions as the U.S. Army (although Army strength is being significantly increased).[14] This situation will be further confused under the sea base concept, which is intended to support amphibious and land operations by Army units as well as by Marines.

At this time, the Marine Corps is being increased in size, while the Navy is undergoing a personnel reduction.

SHIPBUILDING INDUSTRY

The Navy is the primary customer for ship construction and repair in the United States. In fact, two of the largest U.S. shipyards, the

General Dynamics/Electric Boat yard in Groton, Connecticut, and Newport News Shipbuilding in Virginia build only naval ships.

The existing U.S. shipbuilding industry can build, overhaul, and repair a fleet of 375 ships without too much difficulty. The only significant problem is ensuring qualified labor is available at the right time at the proper place. The inability of the U.S. government to commit to long-term, steady rate ship construction both exacerbates the labor problem and greatly increases shipbuilding costs.

Submarine construction costs appear to be particularly high ($2-plus billion per unit of the VIRGINIA class, developed as a lower-cost alternative to the SEAWOLF/SSN 21 program). One of the "artificial" factors contributing to the high SSN costs is the joint construction of the VIRGINIA class by Newport News and Electric Boat, with the resulting transfer of people, submarine components,

---

14 In 2004, the Army had 10 active divisions with 33 combat brigades, which is being increased to 48; there are 5 equivalent reserve divisions (15 combat brigades). The Marine Corps has 3 active and 1 reserve division.

The shape of things to come: The High Speed Vessels (HSV) JOINT VENTURE (HSV-X1) and SPEARHEAD (TSV-1X), both now under Army operational control, are highly effective theater transports. The Army and Navy may procure additional ships of this type, but built in U.S. shipyards. All four HSVs now in U.S. military service were constructed in Australia. (U.S. Navy/Joseph Krypel)

TABLE 1-2. FUTURE-YEAR AIRCRAFT PROCUREMENT

Aircraft Type	FY 2005	FY 2006	FY 2007	FY 2008	FY 2009
F-35 JSF	—	—	2	16	40
F/A-18E/F	42	38	30	24	20
EA-18G	—	4	12	18	22
E-2C	2	2	2	4	4
Multimission Maritime Aircraft	—	—	—	—	8
Aircraft Common Sensor	—	—	—	2	2
KC-130J Hercules	4	4	4	4	5
C-40A Clipper	1	3	3	—	—
C-37	1	—	—	—	2
T-48	1	3	3	7	—
T-45	8	5	—	—	—
T-6A Texan	—	—	24	46	48
MV-22	8	15	29	30	33
VXX (presidential transport hel.)	5	—	3	4	—
MH-60R	8	15	21	31	31
MH-60S	15	26	30	30	40
CH-53X	—	—	—	3	5
BAMS UAV	—	—	2	4	4
Totals	95	115	165	225	264

TABLE 1-3. FUTURE-YEAR SHIPBUILDING PROGRAM

Ship Type	FY 2005	FY 2006	FY 2007	FY 2008	FY 2009
SSN 774	1	1	1	1	2
CVN 78	—	—	1	—	—
DD(X)	1	—	2	2	3
DDG 79	3	—	—	—	—
LCS 1	1	2	1	3	6
LHA(R)	—	—	—	1	—
LPD 17	1	1	1	1	1
T-AKE 1	2	2	1	—	—
T-AOE(X)	—	—	—	—	2
T-AVB 5	—	—	—	—	1
MPF(F)	—	—	1	—	2
Totals	9	6	8	8	17

and data between the yards. Data compatibility was the most significant (albeit not most expensive) aspect of the joint effort. More economical *and competitive* approaches were possible, but the Navy's submarine community sought and obtained this awkward arrangement for political reasons.

As Appendix B indicates, during the post–Cold War era, the Navy's shipbuilding program has osculated significantly. While some $20 billion per year is planned for ship construction in the later years of this decade, for a number of reasons such expenditures seem unlikely.

The U.S. shipbuilding industry continues to be plagued by the lack of effective long-range planning by the Navy, Department of Defense, and Congress. Continual changes in procurement plans and delays in funding, coupled with shipyard problems, have led to higher than planned costs and building delays. The SAN ANTONIO (LPD 17), shown under construction, is far behind schedule and far over budget. (U.S. Navy)

CHAPTER 2

Glossary

A Navy SEAL observes Special Operations Forces operations in the hills of eastern Afghanistan. Naval forces had important roles in Afghanistan operations despite that nation's distance from the sea. On his back, the sailor has an M4 carbine, a shortened version of the M16 rifle, with a special sight and illuminator. (U.S. Navy/Tim Turner)

The following are abbreviations and terms that appear in multiple chapters. More esoteric abbreviations relevant to only one or two chapters are not provided here, but are addressed within the specific chapters, especially those related to aviation, aircraft, weapons, and sensors.

AA	Anti-Aircraft
AAM	Air-to-Air Missile
AAW	Anti-Air Warfare
ABL	Armored Box Launcher
AN/	prefix for U.S. military electronic equipment; in this volume, the AN/ is omitted, thus, only the subsequent three-letter designations are used (e.g., BQS-6 vice AN/BQS-6); originally AN indicated Army–Navy
APSRON	Afloat Prepositioning Ships Squadron
ARG	Amphibious Ready Group; now ESG
ASROC	Anti-Submarine Rocket
ASUW	Anti-Surface Warfare
ASW	Anti-Submarine Warfare
beam	extreme width of hull
bhp	brake horsepower (for diesel engines)

BPDMS	Basic Point Defense Missile System
cal	caliber: (1) the diameter of a gun's bore; U.S. naval guns with diameters of less than 1 inch (25.4 mm) are measured in calibers—fractions of an inch, as .50 caliber-or millimeters (mm) (2) the nominal length of the gun's bore expressed in multiples of its bore; thus, a 76-mm/62-cal gun has a bore or inner barrel length of 4,712 mm or approximately 185 1/2 inches (4.7 m)
CBR	Chemical–Biological–Radiological
CIWS	Close-In Weapon System
COD	Carrier Onboard Delivery
comm.	commissioned
	Note: Some Navy ships are given administrative commissionings at their building yards, being placed "In Commission Special"; their formal commissionings are then held later in politically important locations. The latter dates are listed in this volume.
COTS	Commercial-off-the-Shelf [electronics]
CSG	Carrier Strike Group; formerly CVBG
CVBG	Carrier Battle Group; now CSG

decomm.	decommissioned
displacement	*light*: displacement of ship and all machinery without crew, provisions, fuel, munitions, other consumables, or aircraft
	standard: displacement of ship fully manned and equipped, ready for sea, including all provisions, munitions, and aircraft, but without fuels
	full load: displacement of ship complete and ready for service in all respects, including all fuels (aviation as well as ship)
DoD	Department of Defense
DP	Dual Purpose (for use against air and surface targets)
draft	maximum draft of ship at full load, including fixed projections beneath the keel (e.g., sonar dome)
DWT	Deadweight Tonnage (ship's carrying capacity)
ECM	Electronic Countermeasures
EO	Electro-Optical
ERGM	Extended-Range Guided Munition
ESG	Expeditionary Strike Group; formerly ARG
ESM	Electronic Surveillance Measures
EW	Electronic Warfare
extreme width	maximum width at or about a carrier's flight deck, including fixed projections (e.g., gun tubs)
FBM	Fleet Ballistic Missile
FCS	Fire Control System
FLIR	Forward-Looking Infrared
FRAM	Fleet Rehabilitation and Modernization
FY	Fiscal Year; from 1 October of the calendar year until 30 September of the following year (since June 1976; previously, from 1 July through 30 June)
GFCS	Gunfire Control System
GRT	Gross Registered Tons (ship's tonnage measured in total cubic contents, expressed in units of 100 cubic feet or 2.83 m³)
hp	horsepower
HSV	High Speed Vessel
HY	High Yield (steel)
IOC	Initial Operational Capability
IR	Infrared
ISR	Intelligence/Surveillance/Reconnaissance
LAMPS	Light Airborne Multi-Purpose System (helicopter)
LASH	Lighter Aboard Ship
lbst	pounds static thrust
length	*waterline*: length measured at the waterline (generally the same as between perpendiculars [bp])
	overall: maximum length overall
Mach	speed of sound at sea level
MAD	Magnetic Anomaly Detection
MarAd	Maritime Administration
MCLWG	Major Caliber Lightweight Gun
MCM	Mine Countermeasures
MEB	Marine Expeditionary Brigade
MEF	Marine Expeditionary Force
MEU	Marine Expeditionary Unit
Mk	Mark
Mod	Modification
MPF	Maritime Prepositioning Force
MPS	(1) Maritime Prepositioning Ship (2) Maritime Prepositioning Squadron
MSC	Military Sealift Command (changed from Military Sea Transportation Service in 1970)

MSTS	Military Sea Transportation Service (established 1 October 1949); changed to MSC in 1970
NDRF	National Defense Reserve Fleet
nm	nautical mile (1.852 km)
NOAA	National Oceanic and Atmospheric Administration
NRF	Naval Reserve Force
NSSM	NATO Sea Sparrow Missile
NVR	Naval Vessel Register[1]
personnel	Billets Authorized (BA), the term used to indicate approved and funded manpower requirements for a ship or unit. The term "manning," used in previous editions of *Ships and Aircraft*, indicates a number of personnel at a specific activity time. The terms "crew" and "complement" traditionally refer to a given ship or unit's manning, but no longer are official terms used in U.S. Navy manpower or personnel planning.
psi	pounds per square inch (kg/cm2) (boiler pressure)
RAST	Recovery Assistance, Securing, and Traversing System
RCOH	Refueling/Complex Overhaul
reactors	the first letter of the reactor designation indicates the platform (A = aircraft carrier, C = cruiser, D = frigate [DL/DLG], S = submarine); the numeral indicates the sequence of the reactor design by the manufacturer (who is indicated by the second letter, i.e., G = General Electric, W = Westinghouse)
RFA	Royal Fleet Auxiliary (British)
RPV	Remotely Piloted Vehicle; now UAV
RRF	Ready Reserve Fleet
SAG	Surface Action Group
SAM	Surface-to-Air Missile
SAR	Search and Rescue
SCB	Ships Characteristics Board's sequential numbering of Navy ship designs reaching the advanced planning stage; numbered in a single sequential series from 1947 (SCB No. 1 was the NORFOLK/CLK 1, later DL 1) through 1964 (SCB No. 252 was the FLAGSTAFF/PGH 1); from 1964 on numbered blocks:
	001-009 cruisers
	100 carriers
	200 destroyers/frigates
	300 submarines
	400 amphibious
	500 mine warfare
	600 patrol
	700 auxiliary
	800 service craft
	900 special purpose
	The latter numbers have suffixes indicating the fiscal year of prototype, e.g., 400.65 being the LCC of fiscal year 1965 design.
SEABEE	Sea Barge
SEAL	Sea–Air–Land (team)
shp	shaft horsepower
SLBM	Submarine-Launched Ballistic Missile
SLEP	Service Life Extension Program
SOF	Special Operations Forces

---

1 The official U.S. Navy list of ships and craft owned by the Navy.

SOSUS	Sound Surveillance System	
SRBOC	Super Rapid-Blooming Offboard Chaff	
SSM	Surface-to-Surface Missile	
status	**AA**	Atlantic Active
	AR	Atlantic Reserve
	GL	Great Lakes (Coast Guard)
	ICIR	In Commission, In Reserve
	NRF	Naval Reserve Force
	PA	Pacific Active
	PR	Pacific Reserve
	R&D	Research and Development
	ROS	Reduced Operating Status
	RRF	Ready Reserve Force
	TRA	Training
	Yard	Undergoing major overhaul/conversion
STOL	Short Take-Off and Landing	
STOVL	Short Take-Off/Vertical Landing[2]	
str.	stricken (from the Naval Vessel Register)	
SUBROC	Submarine Rocket	
SURTASS	Surveillance Towed Array Sensor System	
SWATH	Small Waterplane-Area Twin Hull (ship)	
TACAN	Tactical Air Navigation	
TACTAS	Tactical Towed Array Sonar	
TAS	Target Acquisition System	
TASM	Tomahawk Anti-Ship Missile	

TASS	Towed Array Sonar System
TLAM	Tomahawk Land-Attack Missile
TUAV	Tactical Unmanned Aerial Vehicle
UAV	Unmanned Aerial Vehicle (formerly Remotely Piloted Vehicle [RPV])
UNREP	Underway Replenishment
URG	Underway Replenishment Group
USCGC	U.S. Coast Guard Cutter
USNS	U.S. Naval Ship
USS	U.S. Ship
USV	Unmanned Surface Vehicle
UUV	Unmanned Undersea Vehicle (formerly Unmanned Underwater Vehicle)
VDS	Variable Depth Sonar
VERTREP	Vertical Replenishment
VLA	Vertical Launch ASROC
VLS	Vertical Launching System
VOD	Vertical Onboard Delivery
VSTOL	Vertical/Short Take-Off and Landing
VTUAV	Vertical Tactical Unmanned Aerial Vehicle

---

2 The term "VSTOL," for Vertical/Short Take-Off and Landing, was used by the Marine Corps until early 1995, when the less accurate term "STOVL" was adopted by Headquarters, Marine Corps.

A heavily laden air cushion landing craft carries troops and vehicles of the 24th Marine Expeditionary Unit ashore in Kuwait from the amphibious assault ship KEARSARGE *(LHD 3). Although the United States has not carried out an opposed amphibious landing since 1950, L-type ships have been invaluable in combat, crisis, and peacekeeping operations. (U.S. Navy/Kenny Swartout)*

CHAPTER 3

Ship Classifications

A CV, CVN, and AOE conduct an underway replenishment operation in the Atlantic: The oil-burning carrier JOHN F. KENNEDY (CV 67) takes on ordnance from the replenishment ship SEATTLE (AOE 3) while the nuclear-propelled carrier ENTERPRISE (CVN 65) participates in the evolution through vertical replenishment. Their designations date to a 1920 classification scheme. (U.S. Navy/Joshua Karsten)

U.S. Navy ships and most small craft are classified by type, and then by sequence within that type. The list of classifications is issued periodically, updating a system that was established in 1920.

The following are those classifications on the current Secretary of the Navy Instruction "Classification of Naval Ships and Craft," which was last revised in 1993. Letter prefixes to these basic symbols are used to indicate:

F   being constructed for foreign government
T-   assigned to Military Sealift Command (formerly Military Sea Transportation Service)
W   Coast Guard cutter or boat

The suffix N generally is used to denote nuclear-propelled ships. For service craft, however, the suffix N indicates a non-self-propelled version of a similar self-propelled craft. The prefix letter W in the list indicates Coast Guard cutters and boats. In fact, these classifications are not included in the Navy list of classifications.

There are many inconsistencies in the current classification list. The suffix letter X—which does not appear in the classification list—is used unofficially to indicate new designs or classes, as DDX, LHDX, AKX, and ARX. Some more-formal designations exist for several years in official documents and usage before they appear in the ship classification instruction, as MSH (added to the list in 1982), LHD (added in 1983), and AKE (not yet on the list).

Parentheses are not used in ship designations.

In the following list, ships are arranged in the order of the current Navy instruction on classifications; some levels of subcategorization are deleted for purposes of readability. Note that combat logistics ships are listed—as combat ships—ahead of mine warfare ships and separate from other auxiliary ships.

WARSHIP CLASSIFICATIONS

Aircraft Carrier Type
    CV   Multipurpose aircraft carrier
    CVN   Multipurpose aircraft carrier (nuclear propulsion)

Surface Combatant Type
    BB   Battleship
    CG   Guided missile cruiser
    CGN   Guided missile cruiser (nuclear propulsion)
    DD   Destroyer
    DDG   Guided missile destroyer
    FF   Frigate
    FFG   Guided missile frigate
    FFT   Frigate (Reserve Training)

Submarine Type
    SSN   Submarine (nuclear propulsion)
    SSBN   Ballistic missile submarine (nuclear propulsion)

OTHER COMBATANT CLASSIFICATIONS

Patrol Ships

PHM	Patrol combatant missile (hydrofoil)

Amphibious Warfare Type Ships

LHA	Amphibious assault ship (general purpose)
LHD	Amphibious assault ship (multipurpose)
LPD	Amphibious transport dock
LPH	Amphibious assault ship (helicopter)
LKA	Amphibious cargo ship
LSD	Dock landing ship
LST	Tank landing ship
LCC	Amphibious command ship

Combat Logistics Type Ships

AE	Ammunition ship
AF	Store ship
AFS	Combat store ship
AO	Oiler
AOE	Fast combat support ship
AOR	Replenishment oiler

Mine Warfare Type Ships

MSO	Minesweeper, ocean
MCM	Mine countermeasures ship
MCS	Mine countermeasures support ship
MHC	Minehunter, coastal

Coastal Defense Type Ships

PC	Patrol, coastal

AUXILIARY CLASSIFICATIONS

Mobile Logistic Type Ships

AD	Destroyer tender
AR	Repair ship
AS	Submarine tender

Support Type Ships

ARS	Salvage ship
ASR	Submarine rescue ship
ATF	Fleet ocean tug
ATS	Salvage and rescue ship
ACS	Auxiliary crane ship
AG	Auxiliary general
AGDS	Deep submergence support ship
AGF	Miscellaneous command ship
AGFF	Auxiliary general frigate
AGM	Missile range instrumentation ship
AGOR	Oceanographic research ship
AGOS	Ocean surveillance ship
AGS	Surveying ship
AGSS	Auxiliary research submarine
AH	Hospital ship
AK	Cargo ship
AKB	Auxiliary cargo barge/lighter ship
AKF	Auxiliary cargo float-on/float-off ship
AKR	Vehicle cargo ship
AOG	Gasoline tanker
AOT	Transport oiler
AP	Transport
ARC	Cable repairing ship
AVB	Aviation logistic support ship
AVT	Auxiliary aircraft landing training ship

COMBATANT CRAFT CLASSIFICATIONS

Patrol Type Craft

PB	Patrol boat
PCF	Patrol craft (fast)
PTF	Fast patrol craft
ATC	Mini armored troop carrier
PBR	River patrol craft

Amphibious Warfare Type Craft

LCAC	Landing craft, air cushion
LCM	Landing craft, mechanized
LCPL	Landing craft, personnel, large
LCU	Landing craft, utility
LCVP	Landing craft, vehicle, personnel
LWT	Amphibious warping tug
SLWT	Side loadable warping tug
LSSC	Light SEAL support craft
MSSC	Medium SEAL support craft
SDV	Swimmer delivery vehicle[1]
SWCL	Special warfare craft, light
SWCM	Special warfare craft, medium

SUPPORT CRAFT CLASSIFICATIONS

Dry Docks (non-self-propelled)

AFDB	Large auxiliary floating dry dock
AFDL	Small auxiliary floating dry dock
AFDM	Medium auxiliary floating dry dock
ARD	Auxiliary repair dock
ARDM	Medium auxiliary repair dry dock
YFD	Yard floating dry dock

Tugs (self-propelled)

YTB	Large harbor tug
YTL	Small harbor tug
YTM	Medium harbor tug

Tankers (self-propelled)

YO	Fuel oil barge
YOG	Gasoline barge
YW	Water barge

Lighters and Barges (self-propelled)

CSP	Causeway section, powered
YF	Covered lighter
YFR	Refrigerated covered lighter
YFU	Harbor utility craft
YG	Garbage lighter

(non-self-propelled)

CSNP	Causeway section, nonpowered
YC	Open lighter
YCF	Car float
YCSS	Cargo semisubmersible barge
YCV	Aircraft transportation lighter
YFN	Covered lighter
YFNB	Large covered lighter
YFNX	Lighter (special purpose)
YFRN	Refrigerated covered lighter
YFRT	Range tender

---

1 Generally referred to as SEAL delivery vehicle.

YGN	Garbage lighter
YOGN	Gasoline barge
YON	Fuel oil barge
YOS	Oil storage barge
YSR	Sludge removal barge
YWN	Water barge

Other Craft

(self-propelled)

DSRV	Deep submergence rescue vehicle
DSV	Deep submergence vehicle
NR	Submersible research vehicle (nuclear propulsion)
YAG	Miscellaneous auxiliary service craft
YFB	Ferry boat or launch
YM	Dredge
YP	Patrol craft, training
YSD	Seaplane wrecking derrick
YTT	Torpedo trials craft

(non-self-propelled)

APL	Barracks craft
YD	Floating crane
YDT	Diving tender
YFND	Dry dock companion craft
YFP	Floating power barge
YHLC	Salvage lift craft, heavy
YLC	Salvage lift craft, light
YMN	Dredge
YNG	Gate craft
YPD	Floating pile driver
YR	Floating workshop
YRB	Repair and berthing barge
YRBM	Repair, berthing and messing barge
YRDH	Floating dry dock workshop (hull)
YRDM	Floating dry dock workshop (machine)
YRR	Radiological repair barge
YRST	Salvage craft tender

Unclassified Miscellaneous

IX	Unclassified miscellaneous unit

COAST GUARD CUTTERS AND BOATS

The designations currently in use for Coast Guard cutters and boats:

WAGB	Icebreaker
WAGO	Oceanographic cutter
WHEC	High Endurance Cutter (multimission; 30–45 days at sea without support)
WIX	Training cutter
WLB	Offshore buoy tender (full sea-keeping capability; medium endurance)

WLI	Inshore buoy tender (short endurance)
WLIC	Inland construction tender (short endurance)
WLM	Coastal buoy tender (medium endurance)
WLR	River buoy tender (short endurance)
WLV	Light Vessel
WMEC	Medium Endurance Cutter (multimission; 10–30 days at sea without support)
WPB	Patrol Boat (multimission; 1–7 days at sea without support)
WSES	Surface Effect Ship

The Coast Guard uses the term "icebreaker" for a variety of vessels with the following categories:

Type A	late GLACIER (WAGB 4)
Type B	MACKINAW (WAGB 83) and late Wind (WAGB) class
Type C	Bay (WTGB 140) class
Type D	medium harbor tugs (WYTM)
Type E	small harbor tugs (WYTL)
Type P	Polar (WAGB) class

MARITIME ADMINISTRATION

The following are Maritime Administration design classifications; they were developed in the late 1930s by the Maritime Commission. They currently are assigned only to auxiliary/sealift ships; during World War II the escort aircraft carriers, frigates, and tank landing ships designed by the Maritime Commission also had these design classifications.

The first letter-number series indicates ship type with the adjacent letter indicating size (e.g., C4)

C	Cargo
P	Passenger
R	Refrigerator (reefer)
S	Special type
T	Tanker
VC	Victory-Cargo

The second letter-number series indicates propulsion:

M	Motor (diesel)
ME2	Motor; 2 shafts (diesel)
MET	diesel-electric; 2 shafts
S	Steam
S2	Steam; 2 shafts
SE	turbo-electric
SE2	turbo-electric; 2 shafts
ST	Steam; 2 shafts

The third letter-number series indicates specific ship design, usually beginning with A1 or 1; later designs have lower-case letters, as 1b.

CHAPTER 4

Defense Organization

Joint operations are the catchword of today's U.S. armed forces. Here, a U.S. Army MH-47 Chinook, modified to support special operations, approaches the flight deck of the KITTY HAWK (CV 63) as the carrier prepared to serve as a forward base for Army helicopter operations in Afghanistan. Part of Carrier Air Wing 5 (tail code NF) remained on board during the operations. (U.S. Navy/Todd Frantom)

The United States has a unified defense establishment responsible for the conduct of military operations—in peace and in war—in support of the National Security Strategy. The basic structure was established in 1947 and has undergone several major modifications during the Cold War and, subsequently, during the current war against terrorism.

The president—under the provisions of the U.S. Constitution—is Commander-in-Chief of the U.S. armed forces. The Secretary of Defense and the Chairman of the Joint Chiefs of Staff are the principal military advisors to the president. In addition, by statute, the president is assisted by an advisory body known as the National Security Council (NSC) that provides advice on a broad range of national security and intelligence matters. Chaired by the president, the NSC includes as permanent members the vice president, the Secretaries of Defense, State, and Treasury, the Chairman of the Joint Chiefs of Staff, and the Director of Central Intelligence. The official who coordinates NSC activities and directs its staff activities is known as the president's National Security Advisor.

The National Command Authorities (NCA) was the traditional term for the president and Secretary of Defense, together with their duly deputized alternates or successors. It was used to signify the constitutional authority to direct the armed forces and, especially, to release nuclear weapons. No one else in the U.S. chain of command had the authority to take the latter action. In 2002, Secretary of Defense Donald Rumsfeld abolished the term NCA and directed that the terms president and Secretary of Defense, as appropriate, be used in its place.

The principal components of the defense establishment are:
• Department of Defense
• Joint Chiefs of Staff and Joint Staff
• military departments and their subordinate services
• unified combatant commands

Four of the U.S. military services are within the Department of Defense. The fifth, the U.S. Coast Guard, is part of the Department of Homeland Security; that service has responsibilities to both departments (see Chapter 32).

DEPARTMENT OF DEFENSE

The Department of Defense is headed by the Secretary of Defense, a member of the president's cabinet and of the National Security Council. By custom the Secretary of Defense is a civilian.[1]

The principal deputies to the Secretary of Defense are the Deputy Secretary and four Under Secretaries. There are eight Assistant Secretaries of Defense (ASD) and other civilian officials at that level who report directly to the Secretary and Deputy Secretary. The four Under Secretaries, in turn, are supported by 23 persons at the Deputy Under Secretary (DUS) and ASD levels (see Figure 4-1).[2]

The large staff that supports these officials is the Office of the Secretary of Defense (OSD). There are approximately 465 military personnel and 1,560 civilians assigned to OSD. In addition, there are 15 separate agencies under the Secretary of Defense that support the Department of Defense and the military services. These agencies generally perform functions that affect all U.S. military activities. Of these agencies, eight are headed by military officers (indicated by asterisks) and seven by civilians:

- Defense Advanced Research Projects Agency
- Defense Commissary Agency*
- Defense Contract Audit Agency
- Defense Contract Management Agency
- Defense Finance and Accounting Service
- Defense Information Systems Agency*
- Defense Intelligence Agency*
- Defense Legal Services Agency
- Defense Logistics Agency*
- Defense Security Cooperation Agency*
- Defense Threat Reduction Agency
- Missile Defense Agency* (formerly the Ballistic Missile Defense Organization)
- National Imagery and Mapping Agency* (formerly the Defense Mapping Agency)
- National Security Agency*
- National Security Service

The Defense Intelligence Agency (DIA), in addition to performing intelligence analysis for OSD, serves as the intelligence staff for the Joint Chiefs of Staff (the equivalent of a J-2 staff). The National Security Agency (NSA) performs electronic intercept and cryptological activities to support the entire U.S. intelligence community, as well as the defense establishment. That agency also supervises the cryptologic activities of the Army, Navy, Marine Corps, and Air Force.

Historical: Congress established the War Department in 1789 and the Navy Department in 1798 (see Chapter 5). These two departments administered the U.S. armed services, with the Navy Department responsible for both the Navy and the Marine Corps. The secretaries of these two departments reported directly to the president and were members of the president's cabinet.

This arrangement continued until the National Security Act of 1947, which became effective on 18 September 1947, creating the National Military Establishment and the National Security Council and Joint Chiefs of Staff.[3] The Departments of the Army, Navy, and Air Force were established as cabinet-level departments, with the newly created post of Secretary of Defense functioning primarily as coordinator of these military departments.

The 1949 amendments to the National Security Act established the Secretary of Defense as the principal assistant to the president on defense matters and changed the National Military Establishment to the Department of Defense (DoD). These amendments also made the three military departments subordinate to DoD and removed their secretaries from cabinet level. Subsequent actions by various Secretaries of Defense have taken away many of the deci-

Secretary of Defense Donald Rumsfeld, served November 1975–January 1977 and since January 2001. (DoD/R. D. Ward)

sion-making prerogatives of the military departments and assigned them to OSD and to various defense agencies.

The Defense Reorganization Act of 1958 established a new chain of command from the president and Secretary of Defense to the unified and specified commanders-in-chief, who were given "full operational command" over the forces assigned to them. However, the Secretary of Defense could delegate operational control over forces to the Joint Chiefs of Staff when he deemed it appropriate. Previously, the military departments had acted as the executive agencies for the control of their respective forces.

Table 4-1 shows the armed forces personnel authorized for fiscal year (FY) 2005 (beginning 1 October 2004). Note that the Navy Department now has a significantly larger active-duty personnel strength than either the Army or the Air Force. The Army and Marine Corps are being increased in size, and the Navy is being reduced by some 35,000 officers and enlisted personnel.

Table 4-1. DEPARTMENT OF DEFENSE MANPOWER, Fall 2004*

Service	Active Duty	Reserve and National Guard	Civilians
Army	493,800	555,000	236,675**
Navy	377,370	87,800 }	181,375
Marine Corps	175,600	40,080 }	
Air Force	379,100	182,600	158,200
DoD agencies	—	—	672,900
Totals	1,425,870	865,480	1,249,150

* Numbers are rounded.
** Includes 24,618 civil engineers and 107 with military cemeteries.

While there are five military services, there are seven reserve components: the Army, Navy, Marine Corps, Air Force, and Coast Guard reserve organizations and the Army and Air National Guard. The National Guard organizations are under state control during peacetime but can be called into federal service at the direction of the president. (The Coast Guard Reserve totals some 9,000 men and women, just under 20 percent of Coast Guard strength.)

---

1 The exception was General of the Army George C. Marshall, who was Chief of Staff of the U.S. Army during World War II (from September 1939 to November 1945). He subsequently served as both Secretary of State (1947–1949) and Secretary of Defense (1950–1951).

2 One assistant to each DUSD is designated as Principal Deputy Under Secretary of Defense (PDUSD).

3 The definitive work on organization changes of this period is Dr. Steven L. Rearden, *The Formative Years 1947–1950*, vol. 1 of *History of the Office of the Secretary of Defense* (Washington, D.C.: Office of the Secretary of Defense, 1984).

Figure 4-1. Office of the Secretary of Defense

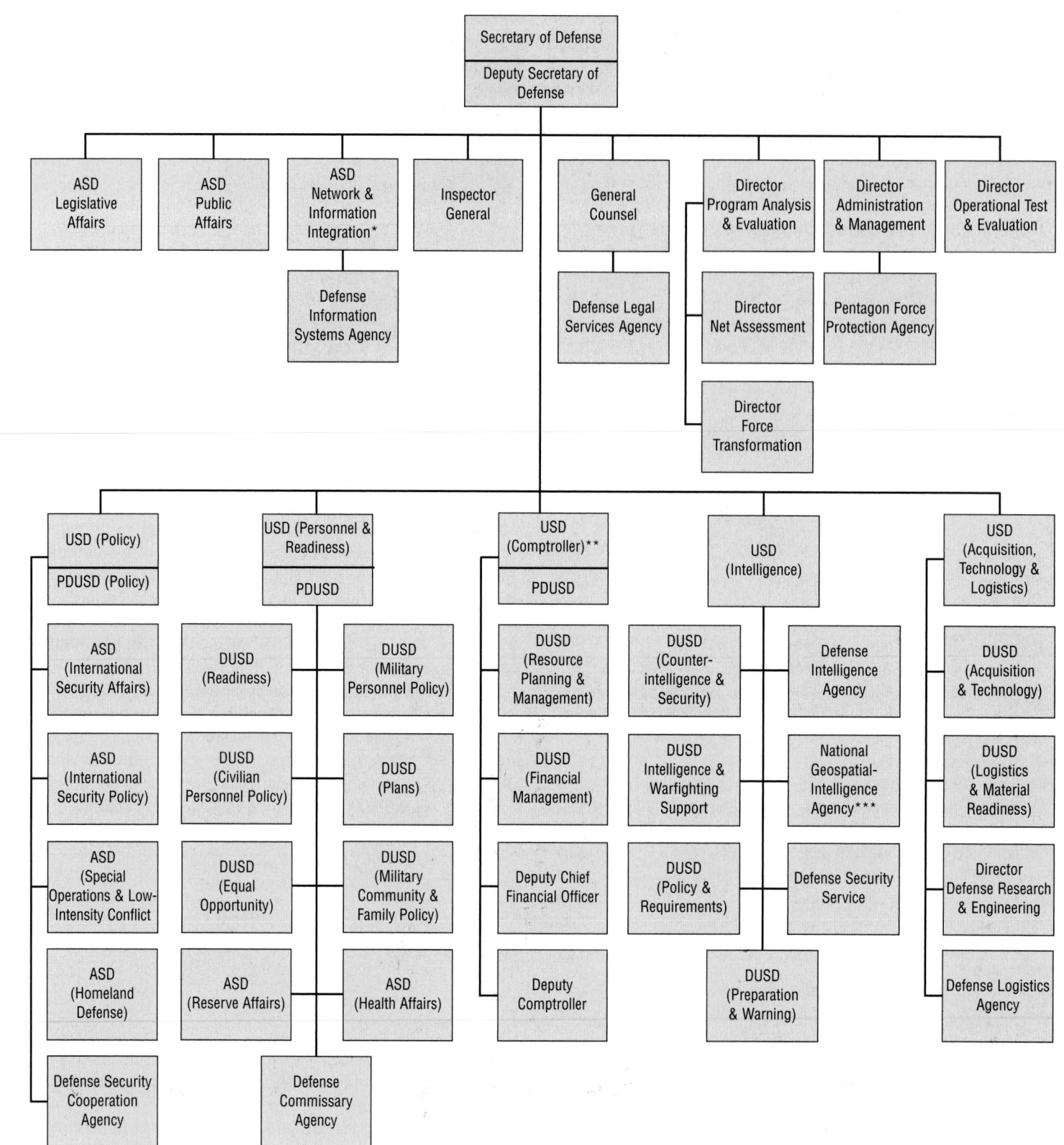

* Also DoD Chief Information Officer
** Also Chief Financial Officer, DoD
*** Formerly National Imagery and Mapping Agency
ASD = Assistant Secretary of Defense
DUSD = Deputy Under Secretary of Defense
PDUSD = Principal Deputy Under Secretary of Defense
USD = Under Secretary of Defense

JOINT CHIEFS OF STAFF

The Joint Chiefs of Staff (JCS) consists of the Chairman, Vice Chairman, and the military chiefs of the Army, Navy, Air Force, and Marine Corps. The Chairman and the Vice Chairman are four-star officers (i.e., general or admiral), as are the military service chiefs.

The Goldwater–Nichols Act of 1986 reduced the role of the members of the JCS but increased the authority of the Chairman, the senior U.S. military officer.[4] The Chairman of the Joint Chiefs became the principal military advisor to the president, and the Secretary of Defense heads the Joint Staff. Significantly, under Goldwater–Nichols, the Chairman of the JCS is in the chain of command between the president and Secretary of Defense and the unified commanders.

The Joint Staff consists of seven directorates that perform military staff functions for the Joint Chiefs and to some extent for the unified commands. The staff directorates are:
- J-1 Manpower and Personnel
- J-2 Intelligence
- J-3 Operations
- J-4 Logistics
- J-5 Strategic Plans and Policy
- J-6 Command, Control, Communications, and Computer Systems
- J-7 Operational Plans and Interoperability
- J-8 Force Structure, Resources, and Assessment

The directors of the JCS staff directorates are three-star officers (i.e., lieutenant general or vice admiral). Their staffs are comprised mostly of military officers from all services. There are approximately 1,200 military personnel and 185 civilians assigned to the Joint Staff.

The J-2 does not have a major staff as do the other directorates; rather, the DoD/JCS intelligence function is carried out by the DIA.

Unlike the former Soviet General Staff and the senior military staffs of some other nations, the officers assigned to the Joint Staff are not professional staff officers but are assigned for two- or three-year periods from their services, often without having any prior staff experience or education.

Historical: President Franklin D. Roosevelt and British Prime Minister Winston Churchill decided at their wartime meeting in Washington, D.C., during December 1941–January 1942 to create the Anglo–American Combined Chiefs of Staff. The British com-

ponent already existed as the Chiefs of Staff Committee; there was no comparable U.S. body of senior military officers.

Without specific executive action or congressional legislation, the senior U.S. military officers met as a body for the first time with their British colleagues on 23 January 1942, to form the Combined Chiefs of Staff. At the time, the term "Joint Chiefs of Staff" was used for the Americans, although some members were not the chiefs of their services. This JCS initially consisted of the Chief of Naval Operations; Commander-in-Chief, U.S. Fleet; Army Chief of Staff; and Chief of the Army Air Forces.[5] The position of Chief of Naval Operations was combined with that of Commander-in-Chief, U.S. Fleet, in March 1942, giving the JCS three members. In July 1942, retired Admiral William D. Leahy was recalled to active duty and appointed Chief of Staff to the Commander-in-Chief (Roosevelt) and became de facto Chairman of the JCS. The JCS membership remained at those four men for the remainder of the war.

The JCS served as both the U.S. component of the Combined Chiefs of Staff and the executive body for the direction of U.S. military forces during the war.

The JCS was formally established by the National Security Act of 1947, but the position of chairman was not authorized until the 1949 amendments. Thereafter, the chairmanship rotated, in no particular order, among the Army, Navy, and Air Force.[6] Some, but not all, of the chairmen were former chiefs of their services.

Initially, the Commandant of the Marine Corps sat with the JCS only when specifically invited to discuss Marine Corps issues, and without a formal vote. The Commandant was authorized to sit with the JCS and vote on those issues of direct interest to the Marine Corps in 1952, and in 1979, was made a full member of the JCS.

---

4 Named after Sen. Barry Goldwater (Arizona) and Rep. Bill Nichols (Alabama).
5 The Chief of the Army Air Forces was changed to Commanding General in March 1942.
6 Four of the 16 Chairmen of the Joint Chiefs of Staff since 1942 have been naval officers:
Fleet Adm. William D. Leahy   June 1942–Mar 1949
Adm. Arthur W. Radford   Aug 1953–Aug 1957
Adm. Thomas H. Moorer   July 1970–June 1974
Adm. William J. Crowe Jr.   Oct 1985–Sep 1989
Adm. Leahy's official position was Chief of Staff to the president; he served as the de facto Chairman of the JCS.

The Joint Chiefs of Staff: from left, Vice Chairman Gen. Peter Pace, USMC; Chairman Gen. Richard B. Myers, USAF; Adm. Vern Clark, USN; Gen. John P. Jumper, USAF; Gen. Michael W. Hagee, USMC; and Gen. Peter J. Schoomaker, USA. The Chiefs of Staff no longer have the important role and prestige they enjoyed since the JCS was informally established in 1942. (JCS/Salli Sobsey)

The position of Vice Chairman was established in 1987, dictated by Goldwater–Nichols. Previously, when the Chairman was absent, the other members served in his place by rotation. In addition to being a stand-in for the Chairman, the Vice Chairman chairs the powerful Joint Requirements Oversight Council (JROC), which controls acquisition of weapon systems for the military services.

MILITARY DEPARTMENTS

There are three military departments within the Department of Defense—Army, Navy, and Air Force. Each is headed by a civilian Secretary, Under Secretary, and several Assistant Secretaries. These are civilian positions, although, on occasion, professional officers have been appointed as Assistant Secretaries, and within the Navy, the Chief of Naval Operations has served as acting Secretary.

Reporting directly to the civilian secretary is the chief of the service, who is the senior military officer of that department (except for officers assigned as Chairman and Vice Chairman of the JCS, who rank above the service chiefs). There are two military services within the Navy Department, the Navy and the Marine Corps.

The military departments are responsible for the training, provision of equipment, and administration of their services. They do not direct military operations; that function was taken away by the Defense Reorganization Act of 1958. The influence and prerogatives of the military departments have varied considerably in recent years based on the personality, influence, and attitudes of the service secretaries and, to a lesser degree, on the service chiefs.

Historical: The Second Continental Congress on 14 June 1775 authorized the first increment of national troops, with their officers responsible to Congress. The U.S. Constitution of 1789 provided that the president be Commander-in-Chief of the Army and the Navy, his powers over them exclusive, limited only "by their nature and by the principles of our institutions." On 7 August 1789, Congress created the War Department, but not a Navy Department.

The U.S. Navy originated with General George Washington's decision in 1775 to dispatch vessels to prey on British shipping. In October of that year, the Continental Congress established a Naval Committee to acquire and fit out vessels for naval operations. (The following month, it established the Marine Corps.)

At the conclusion of the American Revolution in 1783, the weak and almost bankrupt Congress ordered the Navy be disbanded. Although the Constitution directed Congress "to provide and maintain a navy," a separate Navy Department was not considered necessary and naval affairs—such as they were—were included under the jurisdiction of the War Department. Not until the Navy Act of 1794, which authorized the procurement of six frigates, was the Navy reestablished.[7] Not until 30 April 1798 did Congress create the Navy Department.

The 1949 amendments to the National Security Act removed the secretaries of the three military departments from the cabinet and placed them under the supervision of the Secretary of Defense.

UNIFIED COMBATANT COMMANDS

Almost all U.S. operating forces are assigned to unified combat commands, which plan for military operations, direct exercises and combat operations, and have operational control of specifically assigned U.S. forces. The 1958 reorganization of the Department of Defense established the chain of command of the operating forces from the National Command Authorities—the president and Secretary of Defense—directly to the commanders, then called commanders-in-chief, of the unified and specified commands. At that time, *unified* commands had components from two or more military services, while *specified* commands contained forces from

a single service (e.g., the Strategic Air Command, which consisted solely of Air Force components).

The Goldwater–Nicholas Act of 1986 greatly strengthened the role and authority of the unified commanders. Commenting on the act and its influence on the Persian Gulf conflict of 1991, journalist Michael R. Gordon and retired Marine Lieutenant General Bernard (Mick) Trainor, also a distinguished journalist, wrote in *The General's War* that the Goldwater-Nichols Act

> also strengthened the role of the chairman of the JCS and of field commanders. As a result, [JCS Chairman Colin L.] Powell wielded power and influence beyond that exercised by previous chairmen. His fellow members of the Joint Chiefs were relegated to onlookers who simply provided the forces. As for [General Norman] Schwarzkopf [Commander-in-Chief, Central Command], he was king of his domain. During the war, no serious attempt was made by any of the services to go around Schwarzkopf. A service chief could not even visit the Gulf without his permission.[8]

There currently are nine unified commands, all of which contain forces from two or more of the military services. Five of the unified commands are responsible for specific geographic areas, and four have worldwide functional areas of responsibility (see Figure 4-2). The unified command structure is not fixed by law or regulation, and the number of commands and their respective responsibilities periodically are changed at the direction of the president and Secretary of Defense. For example, in the aftermath of the terrorist attacks on the United States on 11 September 2001, DoD established the Northern Command, primarily to enhance U.S. military capabilities for the defense of the continental United States.

Of the geographic commands, Northern Command (NORTH-COM), Joint Forces Command (JFCOM), Pacific Command (PACOM), and European Command (EUCOM) have major forces assigned to them; Central Command (CENTCOM) and Southern Command (SOUTHCOM) primarily have planning, command, and control elements on a permanent basis, with specific forces assigned to them by other unified commands during an exercise, a crisis, or in wartime. For example, prior to the Iraqi invasion of Kuwait in August 1990, CENTCOM was a planning staff of several hundred men and women in the United States. When Operation Desert Shield was initiated, CENTCOM took command of the buildup, with more than 500,000 U.S. military personnel with large numbers of ships, aircraft, and ground units assigned. Subsequently, CENTCOM, in coordination with the commander of Saudi forces, directed Operation Desert Storm, the 1991 assault on Iraq and occupied Kuwait.

CENTCOM also controlled the buildups, invasions, and follow-up combat operations in Afghanistan and Iraq in 2002–2004.

Still, in 1993, in a report to the Secretary of Defense on the roles, missions, and functions of the armed forces, General Powell, then JCS Chairman, lamented,

> The unified command structure works well overseas, where CINCs with a geographic area of responsibility effectively direct the forces assigned to them from the Services in accomplishing a wide range of missions. . . .
> But unification has never been achieved in the United States to the same degree as overseas. While forces based in the United States are assigned, by law, to one CINC, many are assigned to overseas CINCs and have limited opportunities to train jointly with the overseas-based forces they would join for military operations in crisis or war.[9]

---

7 These six frigates included the CONSTITUTION and CONSTELLATION; see Chapter 25.

8 Michael R. Gordon and Lt. Gen. Bernard E. Trainor, USMC (Ret.), *The General's War: The Inside Story of the Conflict in the Gulf* (Boston: Little, Brown, 1995), p. 471.

9 Chairman, Joint Chiefs of Staff, "1993 Report on the Roles, Missions, and Functions of the Armed Forces," 10 February 1993, p. III-3.

Figure 4-2. National Defense Command Structure

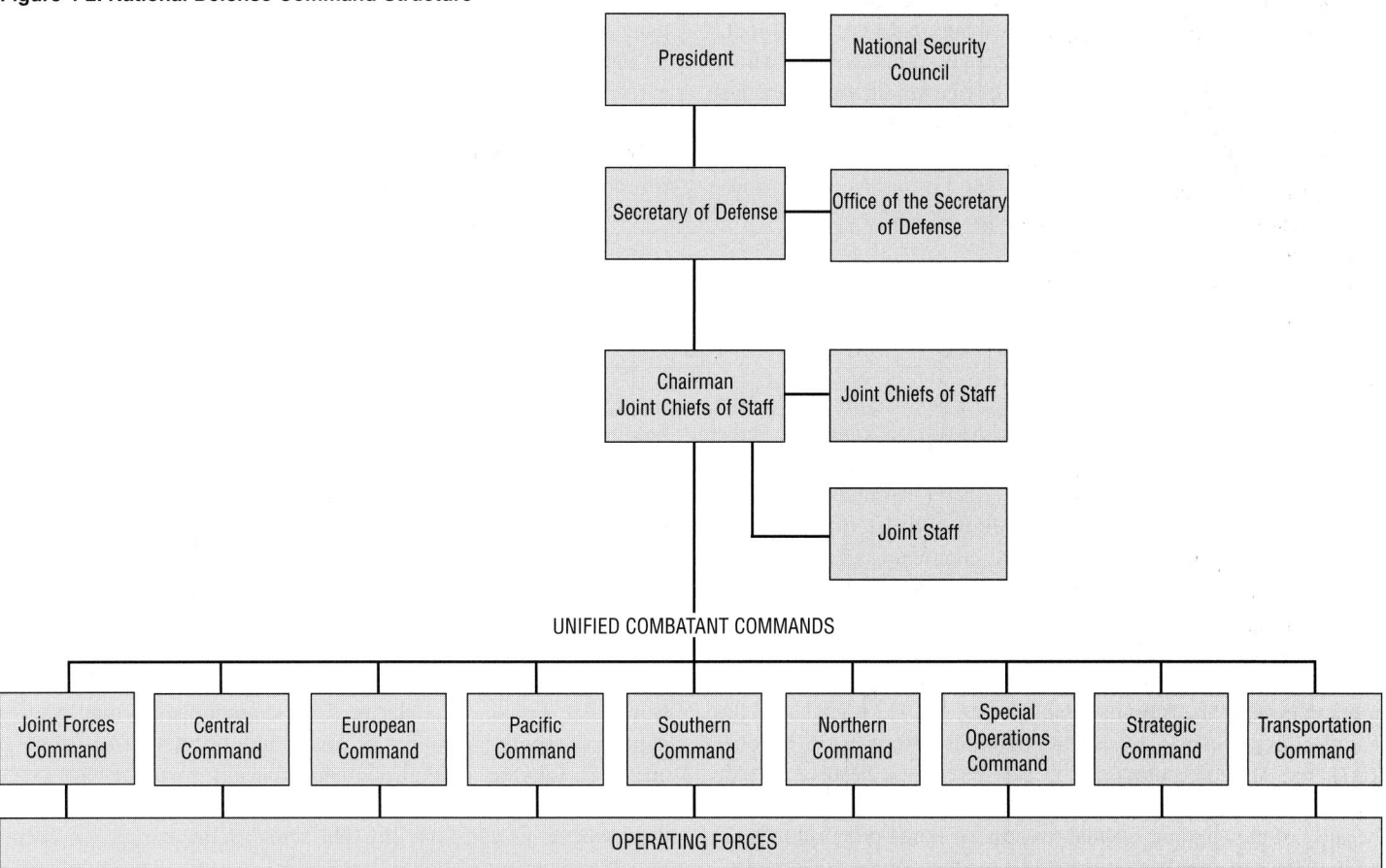

Twice before, the Joint Chiefs of Staff had attempted to establish a single command to oversee military forces in the United States: In 1961, the U.S. Strike Command (STRICOM) was activated to provide unified control over Army and Air Force units based in the United States, with responsibility to train forces, develop joint doctrine, and plan for and execute contingency operations as ordered. Subsequently, STRICOM also was given geographic responsibility for contingency planning for the Middle East, South Asia, and Africa south of the Sahara. General Powell noted, "In attempting to fulfill its functional responsibilities as trainer and provider of forces, STRICOM frequently collided with the Services' authority under Title X [U.S. code] to organize, train, and equip forces."[10]

In 1971, STRICOM was replaced by the Readiness Command (REDCOM), which had the same training and readiness functions but no geographic areas of responsibility. REDCOM, according to Powell, experienced some of the same resistance from the military services as did its predecessor. Still, over time, REDCOM was given additional responsibilities, including a requirement to plan for and provide Joint Task Force (JTF) headquarters for operations in areas that were not assigned to existing unified commands. What began as REDCOM's Rapid Deployment JTF eventually grew into a new unified combat command—CENTCOM, established in 1983. With headquarters at MacDill Air Force Base in Tampa, Florida, CENTCOM was given responsibility for Southwest Asia and related areas. REDCOM was abolished in 1987.

Subsequently, the Atlantic Command (LANTCOM) was reorganized on 1 October 1993 as the U.S. Atlantic Command (USACOM) to prepare essentially all U.S. continental combat forces for overseas deployment. Significantly, USACOM did not control Pacific Fleet forces based on the U.S. West Coast; those forces—including Marine Forces Pacific—continued to come under PACOM. Although there has been increased emphasis on "universal" doctrine and structure for U.S. forces, differences in geogra-

phy, allies, commander personalities, and other factors made operations in the Pacific very different from those in the European–Atlantic and other regions.

LANTCOM/USACOM again was reorganized with the establishment of the JFCOM on 7 October 1999 to control all U.S. forces in the Atlantic area and to serve as the DoD agent for joint warfighting experimentation—the creation and exploration of new combat concepts—and provide military assistance to civilian authorities for consequence management of Weapons of Mass Destruction (WMD).[11] At the same time, responsibility for U.S. military operations in selected waters around Africa and Europe was transferred from JFCOM to EUCOM and CENTCOM, effective 1 October 2000.

From the start of the unified and specified command structure, their commanders were known as Commanders-in-Chief (CinC), a title that dates within the U.S armed forces to General George Washington.[12] Thus, the Commander-in-Chief, European Command, was known as CinCEUCOM.

However, on 24 October 2002, Secretary Rumsfeld directed that the term "CinC" be dropped for the unified commands and subordinate organizations (as the Atlantic and Pacific Fleets) and in its place the term "combatant commander" be used for all appropriate military commanders. Only the president would henceforth be known as Commander-in-Chief.

All the unified combatant commands are led by four-star officers. (There have been no specified commands since the U.S. Forces Command was disestablished in 1993.) Historically, some

---

10 Chairman, Joint Chiefs of Staff, "1993 Report on the Roles, Missions and Functions of the Armed Forces," p. III-3.
11 WMD are chemical, biological, and nuclear weapons.
12 Washington was named CinC of the Continental Army on 15 June 1775, the day before the Battle of Bunker Hill.

unified commander positions rotated among the services and some were assigned to officers of only one or two of the services.

Two "firsts" in the combatant commands significant to the U.S. Marine Corps have occurred during Mr. Rumsfeld's current tenure as Secretary of Defense (from January 2001). Previously, Marine officers have held unified commands only in CENTCOM and its predecessor organizations, and once in USACOM. In January 2003, Marine General James L. Jones became head of EUCOM, a post that previously had been held only by Army and Air Force officers.[13] And in July 2004, General James E. Cartwright became head of the Strategic Command, again the first Marine to hold that position, which had been held only by Air Force and Navy officers since its establishment in 1992.

At the end of 2004, of the nine unified combatant commands, one was held by an Army general, two by Air Force generals, three by Marine generals, and three—Joint Forces Command, Northern Command, and Pacific Command—by Navy admirals. (By comparison, when the 17th Edition of *Ships and Aircraft* was published in 2001, there was one unified command under an Army general, three under Air Force generals, three under Navy admirals, and one under a Marine general.)

An Air Force general officer was nominated in the fall of 2004 to become Commander, U.S. Pacific Command, a position held for more than 62 years, from its establishment in 1942 (then called the Pacific Oceans Area), by a Navy admiral. However, in October 2004, the Air Force officer, who was serving as head of the Air Force Material Command, asked that his nomination be withdrawn because of the ongoing scandal over an Air Force proposal to lease and then buy tanker aircraft from the Boeing Company. Accordingly, the Navy admiral commanding the Pacific Command would remain in that post into 2005.

Coast Guard forces operating in forward areas report to the appropriate unified commander.

The current unified commands are:

Central Command: CENTCOM has area responsibility for the Middle East (less Israel, Lebanon, Syria), southwest Asia (Afghanistan, Iran, Pakistan), the Persian Gulf and Arabian Sea, northwest Africa (Egypt, Eritrea, Ethiopia, Kenya, Somalia, Sudan), and the central Asian states of the former Soviet Union (Kazakhstan, Kyrgyzstan, Tajikistan, Turkmenistan, Uzbekistan).

The Central Command directed U.S. military operations during the buildup and war in the Persian Gulf area in 1990–1991 and subsequently directed strikes against Iraq (including Operation Desert Fox and in the northern and southern "no-fly zones"). CENTCOM again directed the buildup and combat operations beginning in 2002 in Afghanistan and Iraq.

The service component commands under CENTCOM are:
• Air Forces
• Army Forces
• Marine Forces
• Naval Forces (including the Fifth Fleet)
• Special Operations Forces
CENTCOM is the direct successor to the U.S. Rapid Deployment Force (see above).
Headquarters: MacDill Air Force Base, Tampa, Florida.
Established: January 1983.
Commander: Central Command has always been headed by an Army or Marine officer.
European Command: EUCOM's area of responsibility includes all of western Europe, portions of the Middle East (Israel, Lebanon, Syria), the Western Slavic and Caucasus states of the former Soviet Union (Armenia, Azerbaijan, Belarus, Georgia, Moldova, Ukraine), most of Africa, and the Mediterranean. The Combatant Commander, European Command, also serves as the NATO

Supreme Allied Command Europe (SACEUR). The 1999 campaign against Serbia was directed by SACEUR.

The service component commands under EUCOM are:
• Air Forces Europe
• Army Europe
• Naval Forces Europe (including the Sixth Fleet)
• Special Operations Forces
Headquarters: Stuttgart-Vaihingen, Germany.
Established: March 1947.[14]
Commander: The European Command was headed by an Army or Air Force officer until January 2003, when Marine General James L. Jones became the combatant commander.
Joint Forces Command: JFCOM has geographic responsibility for the North and South Atlantic areas, less the Caribbean and South American coastal areas. The Commander, JFCOM, is also NATO Supreme Allied Commander Atlantic, one of two major NATO military commands, with responsibility for NATO operations in the North Atlantic area. (Until 1985, he also served as CinC, U.S. Atlantic Fleet).

The Joint Forces Command—which replaced USACOM—is the largest U.S. unified command, with responsibility for the readiness of most military forces within the continental United States. Its principal mission is to develop joint force "packages" of Army, Navy, Air Force, and Marine Corps components that can be deployed rapidly to overseas areas and operate effectively on arrival in forward areas. Under this concept, major service commands in the United States report to JFCOM for training and deployment; in addition, JFCOM remains the unified or operational commander for the Atlantic Fleet, as well as responsible for its readiness and training.

The service component commands under JFCOM are:
• Air Forces
• Atlantic Fleet (including the Second Fleet)
• Army Forces Command
• Marine Forces (II Marine Expeditionary Force)
• Special Operations Forces
Headquarters: Norfolk, Virginia.
Established: 1 December 1947 as Atlantic Command; 1 October 1993 as U.S. Atlantic Command; and 7 October 1999 as JFCOM.
Commander: From its establishment until 1994, Commander-in-Chief, USACOM/LANTCOM, has been a Navy officer, except for 1994–1997, when Marine General John J. Sheehan served in this position.
Northern Command: NORTHCOM was established following the 11 September 2001 attacks to provide a central command organization for all Department of Defense activities concerned with homeland defense and to provide a focal point for military relationship with civil authorities.

NORTHCOM's specific mission is to:

conduct operations to deter, prevent, and defeat threats and aggression aimed at the United States, its territories and interests within the assigned area of responsibility; and as directed by the President or Secretary of Defense, provide military assistance to civil authorities including consequence management operations.

The Northern Command's area of responsibility includes the air, land, and sea approaches and encompasses the continental United States, Alaska, Canada, Mexico, and the surrounding water out to approximately 500 nm (925 km). It also includes the Gulf of Mexico, Puerto Rico, and the U.S. Virgin Islands. NORTHCOM

---

13 Gen. Jones had served as Commandant of the Marine Corps from 1999 to 2002.
14 From March 1947 until July 1952, this position was Commander-in-Chief, Europe (CinCEUR), largely a U.S. Army command and only nominally a unified command.

also is responsible for security cooperation and the coordination of area defenses with Canada and Mexico.

(Hawaii and U.S. territories and possessions in the Pacific remain the responsibility of the Pacific Command.)

The commander of NORTHCOM is double-hatted as Commander, North American Aerospace Command (NORAD); see below.

NORTHCOM's civil support mission includes domestic disaster relief operations during fires, hurricanes, floods, and earthquakes. Support also includes counterdrug operations and managing the damage of a terrorist event employing a weapon of mass destruction. The command provides assistance to a lead federal agency when tasked by DoD.

Major military service forces are not assigned to NORTHCOM. The Atlantic Fleet is assigned to provide training and advisory functions.

The command's counternarcotics efforts are undertaken by Joint Task Force (JTF) 6, headquartered at Biggs Army Airfield, Fort Bliss, Texas. JTF-6 is comprised of approximately 160 soldiers, sailors, Marines, airmen, and DoD civilian specialists. The task force provides DoD counterdrug support to federal, regional, state, and local law enforcement agencies throughout the continental United States.

When directed, JTF-6 also provides operational, training, and intelligence support to domestic agencies' efforts in combating terrorism. Since its inception in 1989, JTF-6 has provided support to more than 430 federal, regional, state, and local law enforcement agencies and counterdrug task forces.

NORTHCOM's Joint Task Force Civil Support (JTF-CS) provides command and control for DoD forces that operate in support of the lead federal agency managing the consequences of a chemical, biological, radiological, nuclear, or high-yield explosive incident in the United States. Headquartered at Fort Monroe in Hampton, Virginia, JTF-CS began operations in October 1999.

The JTF-CS consists of approximately 160 military and civilian personnel under the command of a National Guard general officer.

In addition, the Joint Force Headquarters–National Capital Region was established on 22 September 2004 to deter and respond to terrorist activities in the Washington, D.C., area. Subordinate to NORTHCOM, the command will include the Army's Military District of Washington, the Naval District of Washington, and certain Air Force, Marine Corps, and Coast Guard components. The command's headquarters, located at Fort Leslie J. McNair in Washington, D.C., will number about 60 military and civilian personnel.

Headquarters: Peterson Air Force Base, Colorado Springs, Colorado.

Established: 1 October 2002.

Commander: The first combatant commander of NORTHCOM was an Air Force general officer. He was succeeded in November 2004 by Navy Admiral Timothy J. Keating.

Pacific Command: PACOM has the largest geographic area of the unified commands, with responsibility for the Pacific and Indian Ocean areas less the Arabian Sea and for most of the non-Russian portions of the Asian mainland, Australia, and New Zealand.

The CinC PACOM, also was CinC Pacific Fleet, until 1958.

The service component commands under PACOM are:
• Army Forces
• Marine Forces (I and III Marine Expeditionary Forces)
• Pacific Air Forces
• Pacific Fleet (including the Third and Seventh Fleets)
• Special Operations Forces

Headquarters: Camp H. M. Smith, Oahu, Hawaii.

Established: January 1947.

Commander: From its establishment in 1947, PACOM has been commanded by a Navy officer; in 2004, an Air Force officer was nominated to head the command, but he subsequently withdrew his name from consideration.

Southern Command: SOUTHCOM is responsible for operations in Central and South America, including coastal waters, and the Caribbean and Gulf of Mexico.

An Alaskan Air National Guard KC-135R Stratotanker refuels an F/A-18F Super Hornet from Strike Fighter Squadron 41. The Navy squadron was participating in exercise Cooperative Cope Thunder 2004. With the demise of dedicated carrier-based tanker aircraft, the Air Force is responsible for providing tanker support to naval aviation. (USAF/Joshua Strang)

The command was known as the Caribbean Command (CinC CARIB) until June 1963.

The service component commands under SOUTHCOM are:
• Air Forces
• Army Forces
• Naval Forces (Surface Group 2)
• Special Operations Forces

Headquarters: Miami, Florida. SOUTHCOM headquarters previously was located at Quarry Heights, Panama City, Panama; in 1995, it moved to the Coast Guard facility at Richmond Heights in Dade County, Florida, near Miami. (As part of the Panama Canal Treaty, all U.S. military forces had to leave Panama by 31 December 1999, including SOUTHCOM's approximately 700 headquarters personnel.)

Established: November 1947.

Commander: Southern Command historically has been commanded by an Army officer; however, the current commander is Marine General Charles E. Wilhelm.

Space Command: SPACECOM was disbanded on 1 October 2002, and its responsibilities and activities were transferred to the U.S. Strategic Command. SPACECOM had jurisdiction over U.S. activities and forces in space, including the monitoring of foreign space activities. In 1999, SPACECOM also was given responsibility for DoD computer network defense—monitoring and attempting to stop cyber intrusions.

The Army, Navy, and Air Force Space Commands were the principal components of SPACECOM.

Headquarters: Peterson Air Force Base, Colorado Springs, Colorado.

Established: September 1985.

Commander: SPACECOM had always been commanded by an Air Force officer.

Special Operations Command: SOCOM directs U.S. special forces activities throughout the world through the subordinate commanders of the geographic unified commands. SOCOM differs from all other unified commands in that it has major budget planning and manpower management responsibilities that are similar to those of the military services.

Its component commands, with published numbers of personnel in the components in parentheses, are:
• Air Force Special Operations Command (11,600)
• Army Special Operations Command (29,400)
• Naval Special Warfare Command (6,300)
• Marine Corps Detachment 1 (see below)

The Marine component—initially 86 men—was established on 20 June 2003. Previously, the Marine Corps shunned the formation of a special operations component, believing that any Marine unit was capable of such operations. Indeed, all deploying Marine Expeditionary Units (MEU) are Special Operations Capable (SOC).

In addition, within SOCOM there is a Joint Special Operations Command of some 700 personnel, which includes both planning teams and operational units.

Headquarters: MacDill Air Force Base, Tampa, Florida.

Established: April 1987.

Commander: The CinC/commander of SOCOM has been an Army officer since SOCOM's establishment, except for 2001–2003, when it was an Air Force general.

Strategic Command: All U.S. land-based and sea-based strategic forces are assigned to STRATCOM. The Strategic Air Command (SAC), a specified command with only Air Force components, was abolished in 1992, and most of its resources were assigned to the newly formed Strategic Command. Also incorporated into the

Strategic Command was the Joint Strategic Target Planning Staff (JSTPS), a multiservice agency that planned the laydown of U.S. strategic weapons and various Navy activities related to strategic missile submarine operations.[15] On 1 October 2002, U.S. SPACE-COM was disbanded and its responsibilities and activities were transferred to the Strategic Command.

Thus, STRATCOM is the command and control entity for all U.S. strategic forces and controls military space operations, computer network operations, information operations, strategic warning and intelligence assessments, and strategic planning.

Components include the newly established (2004) Air Force Strategic Command and Navy Task Forces 134 and 144 (i.e., Pacific and Atlantic Fleet submarine forces).

Headquarters: Offutt Air Force Base, Nebraska.

Established: June 1992.

Commander: STRATCOM had been headed by Air Force and Navy officers until July 2004, when Marine General James E. Cartwright became its head.

Transportation Command: All nontactical U.S. military air and sea transport resources are assigned to the Transportation Command (TRANSCOM). Its component commands are:
• Air Force Air Mobility Command
• Navy Military Sealift Command
• Army Military Transportation Management Command

Headquarters: Scott Air Force Base, Illinois.

Established: July 1987.

Commander: TRANSCOM has always been commanded by an Air Force officer.

In addition to the nine unified commands, there are several sub-unified commands and combined commands that have important roles in U.S. defense strategy. Two of these commands are unique and warrant special attention.

U.S. Forces Korea: U.S. Forces Korea (USFK), a subordinate command of PACOM, is the joint headquarters through which U.S. combat forces would be sent to the Combined Forces Command, the binational command that has operational control over U.S. and Republic of Korea (ROK) forces in South Korea.

The Commander, USFK, is a U.S. Army general and also serves as Commander, Combined Forces Command, with a four-star ROK Army general as his deputy.

In addition, the Commander, USFK, serves as CinC, United Nations Command, and represents the United Nations Security Council on the Korean Peninsula.

North American Aerospace Defense Command: The North American Aerospace Defense Command (NORAD) is a binational, combined command of Canadian and U.S. forces. The command is responsible for aerospace warning and air defense control for North America.

The Commander, U.S. Northern Command, also serves as Commander, NORAD, and in the latter role has responsibilities to both the U.S. president and the Canadian prime minister. The previous commander, Air Force General Ralph E. Eberhart, has stated that expanding NORAD to include Mexico is under consideration. He said it might not happen soon but is, "someday, going to make sense."[16] Admiral Keating, who became head of Northern

---

15 Despite some writers stating that the new U.S. Strategic Command combined the separate Air Force and Navy strategic commands, in fact, the Navy never had a strategic command; naval strategic forces—carrier-based aircraft and ballistic missile submarines—were assigned to the Atlantic, Pacific, and European unified commands and their subordinate Navy fleets.

16 William B. Scott, "Expanding Norad," *Aviation Week & Space Technology* (13 September 2004), p. 62.

Command in November 2004, is the first non-Air Force officer to command NORAD.

NORAD's command center is located in Cheyenne Mountain, an underground base that is the centralized collection facility for the worldwide system of sensors.

There currently are no U.S. specified commands. Previously, there were three: Strategic Air Command and Military Airlift Command (MAC), both comprised of Air Force personnel, and Forces Command, comprised of Army personnel. SAC and MAC (previously the Military Air Transport Service) were disestablished in 1992, with most of their components transferred in part to the new Strategic Command and Transportation Command, respectively.

Forces Command (FORCECOM), which was responsible for all U.S. Army forces (active and inactive) in the United States, became the Army's component command of the U.S. Atlantic Command (now Joint Forces Command). Established in July 1987, Forces Command was disestablished as a specified command in 1993.

Historical: The official history of the U.S. Joint Chiefs of Staff states, "The surprise attack [on Pearl Harbor] indicated dramatically the difficulties inherent in coordinating responsibility for defense of the whole Hawaiian area. It likewise made President Roosevelt and his advisors determine that there be no uncertainty as to responsibility for protection of the Panama Canal."[17]

Consequently, on 12 December 1941, in a meeting with the president, U.S. military leaders established the first unified commands: all U.S. military forces in the Hawaiian area were placed under the Commander in Chief, Pacific Fleet, and those in the Panama area under the CinC, Panama (an Army Air Forces officer).

Subsequent U.S. unified commanders also were Allied commanders, with responsibility for directing U.S. and British forces in a specific area (with some other Allied forces being present in some commands). The complexity of strategic bombing operations against Germany (including coordination with the British bombers) and later Japan led to the JCS establishing U.S. Strategic Air Forces in Europe and U.S. Strategic Air Forces in the Pacific. These were all-Army Air Force commands that were operationally outside the control of the respective Allied commanders and, in reality, the first U.S. specified commands.

Unified and specified commanders were in a sort of limbo after World War II, as the military departments tended to direct operations of their forces within specific geographic areas. The 1958 defense reorganization gave the unified commands responsibility for all military forces and operations within a specific area and established specified commands when the component forces were all from one service.

JOINT TASK FORCES

Periodically, unified joint task forces are organized within unified commands for specific operations. In 1989, several JTFs were established to help combat the influx of illegal drugs into the United States. There are three such JTFs engaged in counternarcotic operations:

Unified/Specified Command	Task Force	Area
U.S. Atlantic Command	JTF-4	U.S. East Coast, Caribbean
U.S. Pacific Command	JTF-5	U.S. West Coast
U.S. Northern Command	JTF-6	U.S.–Mexican border

These task forces serve as their respective commands' counternarcotic coordinators, with forces from all military services, including the Coast Guard, assigned. The JTFs also coordinate activities with other unified and service commands, and with other government agencies. Coast Guard flag officers currently serve as Commander, JTF-4, with headquarters in Key West, Florida, and Commander, JTF-5, with headquarters in Alameda, California.

Historical: The first joint task force of the post–World War II era was JTF-1, established in 1946 to conduct the multiservice atomic bomb tests at Bikini atoll in July 1946. Task forces are nonpermanent organizations, formed and disestablished as required.

17 Grace Person Hayes, *The History of the Joint Chiefs of Staff in World War II: The War against Japan* (Annapolis, Md.: Naval Institute Press, 1982), p. 29.

Figure 4-3. U.S. Unified/Combatant Commands

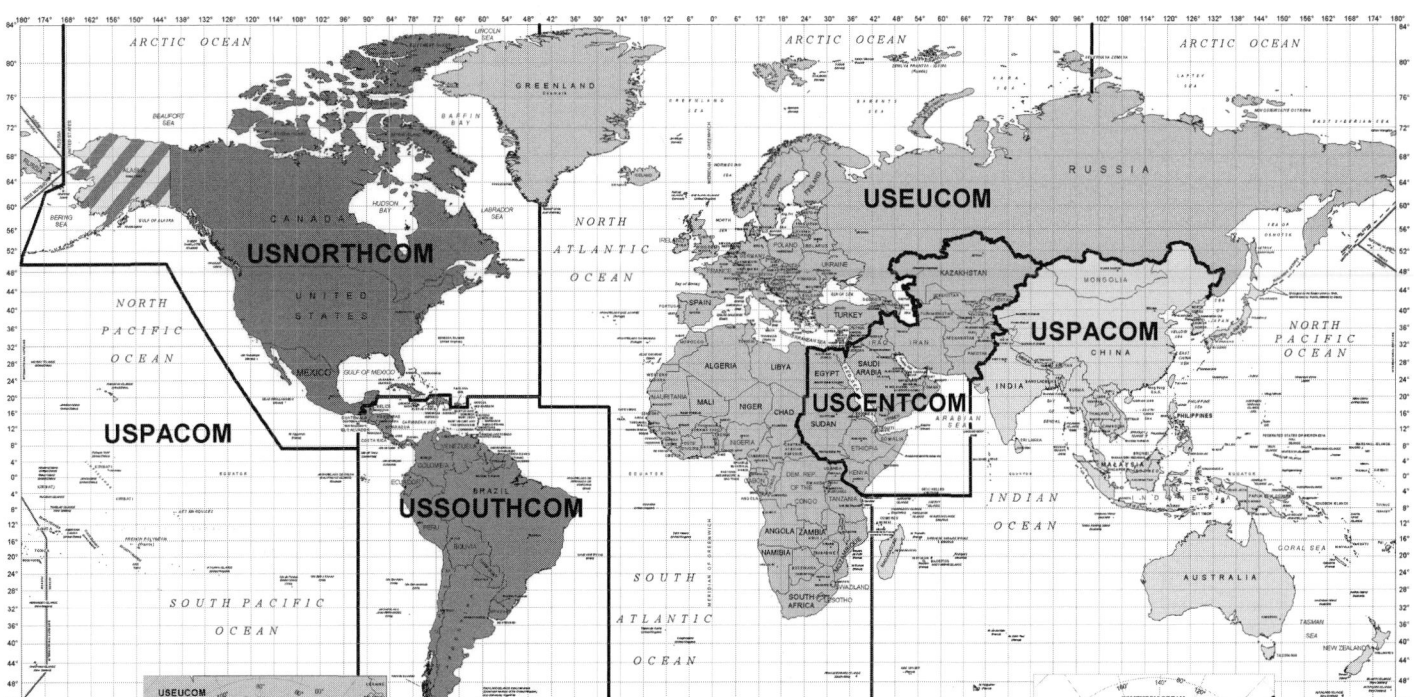

CHAPTER 5

Navy Organization

A Navy search team returns to the Aegis cruiser LEYTE GULF (CG 55) during operations in the Gulf of Oman. The Navy is responsible for providing trained and ready forces to be employed throughout the world by unified commanders. At the time this photo was taken in 2004, the LEYTE GULF was a component of Task Force 150, a multinational force operating in the Middle East to counter terrorist-related activities at sea. (U.S. Navy/Bart Bauer)

Under Department of Defense instructions, the Navy Department is directed to:

Prepare forces and establish reserves of manpower, equipment, and supplies for the effective prosecution of war and military operations short of war and planning for the expansion of peacetime components to meet the needs of war.

Maintain in readiness mobile reserve forces, properly organized, trained, and equipped for employment in emergency.

Provide adequate, timely, and reliable intelligence and counterintelligence for the Military Department and other Agencies as directed by competent authority.

Recruit, organize, train, and equip interoperable forces for assignment to the Combatant Commands.

Prepare and submit budgets for their respective departments; justifying before the Congress budget requests as approved by the president; and to administer the funds made available for maintaining, equipping, and training the forces of their respective departments, including those assigned to Combatant Commands. The budget submissions to the Secretary of Defense by the Military Departments shall be prepared on the basis, among other things, of the recommendations of Commanders of the Combatant Commands and of

service component commanders of forces assigned to Combatant Commands.

Conduct research; develop tactics, techniques, and organization; and develop and procure weapons, equipment, and supplies essential to the fulfillment of the functions assigned in this Directive.

Develop, garrison, supply, equip, and maintain bases and other installations, including lines of communication, and provide administrative and logistics support for all forces and bases, unless otherwise directed by the Secretary of Defense.

Provide, as directed, such forces, military missions, and detachments for service in foreign countries as may be required to support the national interests of the United States.[1]

The Navy does not directly control operating forces, except as specifically assigned by the president, Secretary of Defense,

---

1 Department of Defense Directive, "Functions of the Department of Defense and Its Major Components," No. 5100.1, 1 August 2002. This is the latest iteration of the "roles and missions" statement originally developed at the so-called Key West conference, chaired by Secretary of Defense James Forrestal, in March 1948.

Chairman of the Joint Chiefs of Staff, or commanders of unified combatant commands (see Chapter 4).

To carry out the above functions, the Navy is part of a dual command structure: (1) an administrative structure that originates with the Secretary of the Navy and the Chief of Naval Operations, and (2) an operational structure that originates with the unified commanders. This configuration fulfills the institutional need for civilian control and the balancing of service interests by enabling the Navy to support deployed forces without intervening in combat operations directed by the unified command system and relieves the fleet and task force commanders from the administrative and procurement workload that otherwise would distract them from their primary task—the command of combat forces.

The Navy has long had a bilinear organization, with squadron and later fleet commanders and, after 1942, the Chief of Naval Operations exercising military command over the operating forces, and the Secretary of the Navy, through civilian assistants and the chiefs of the various bureaus and agencies, directing business, research and development, procurement, and support activities. Responsibility for military command of operating forces subsequently has been transferred to the unified commands.

OPERATIONAL ORGANIZATION

The operating forces of the Navy and Marine Corps—like those of the Army and Air Force—are subordinate to unified commands. Most naval forces are assigned to the naval component commanders of three unified commands; their basic command structure is shown in Figure 5-1.

Unified Command	Naval Component	Operating Fleet
U.S. Joint Forces Command	Atlantic Fleet	Second Fleet
U.S. Central Command	Naval Forces Central Command	Fifth Fleet
U.S. European Command	Naval Forces Europe	Sixth Fleet
U.S. Pacific Command	Pacific Fleet	Third Fleet
		Seventh Fleet
U.S. Northern Command	Atlantic Fleet	—

Commander, Naval Forces Central Command, is a vice admiral, and the other three naval component commanders are full admirals; all have shore-based staffs.[2] (The Commander, U.S. Naval Forces Central Command, has the additional duty of Commander, Fifth Fleet.) Several major naval commanders are "double-hatted" as NATO commanders.

The Commander, Atlantic Fleet, serves as component commander for the newly established U.S. Northern Command. In this case, the naval component primarily provides advisory and training functions and does not provide ships or aircraft on a regular basis as do the naval components under the other unified commands.

The Atlantic and Pacific Fleets have similar structures, with subordinate "type" commanders who are responsible for the administration and support of specific ship/aircraft types (see Figure 5-2). The senior-ranking type commander also is the senior officer of that "community"—i.e., aviation, surface, submarines—with administrative control over all commands within the community, and is senior to the director of the corresponding warfare "desk" in the Office of the Chief of Naval Operations. The exception to this arrangement is the Director, Naval Nuclear Propulsion (in Washington, D.C.), a submariner and a full admiral, with an eight-year tenure. He thus is the de facto head of all submarine activities.

The submarine force type commanders also are operational commanders. All major type commanders are vice admirals, except the Commander, Submarine Force Pacific Fleet, who is a rear admiral.

Figure 5-1. Operational Chain of Command

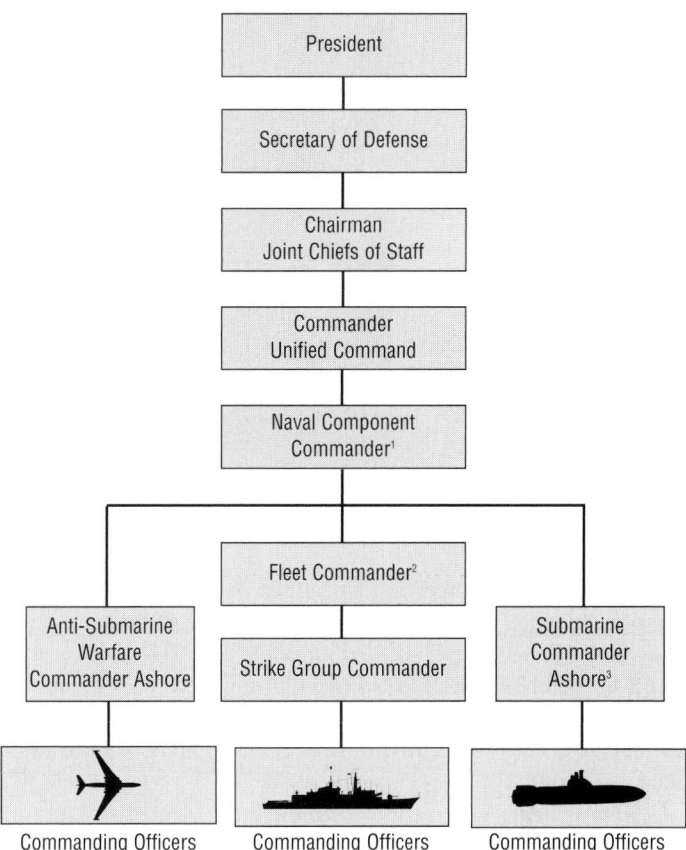

[1]Nominally Commander, U.S. Atlantic Fleet, Pacific Fleet, or Naval Forces Europe
[2]Nominally numbered fleet commander
[3]Nominally Commander, Submarine Force Atlantic Fleet, or Submarine Force Pacific Fleet

Figure 5-2. Fleet Command Structure

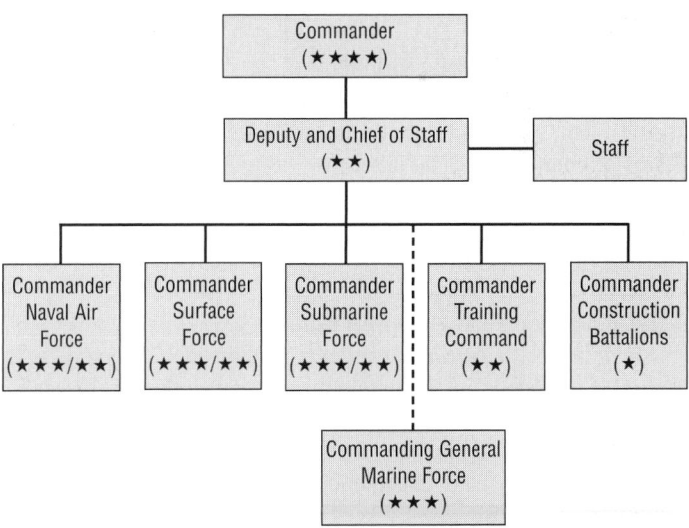

Until 2004, the Atlantic and Pacific Fleet commanders were Commanders-in-Chief (CinC).

Chief of Naval Operations Admiral Vern Clark on 1 October 2000 established the position of Commander, Fleet Forces Command, as the Navy's senior fleet commander, to sponsor the "transformation" (modernization) of the fleet and to align training and doctrine within both the Atlantic and Pacific Fleets. The

---

2 All active duty U.S. Navy admirals and Marine Corps generals are listed, with their current positions, in the May issue of the U.S. Naval Institute *Proceedings* (Naval Review issue) and the January issue of *Sea Power* (Navy League of the United States).

Secretary of the Navy Gordon R. England, served May 2001– January 2003 and since September 2003. (U.S. Navy/Nathanael T. Miller)

Commander, Fleet Forces Command, is double-hatted as Commander, Atlantic Fleet, using largely the same staff for both positions. Indeed, Admiral Clark told reporters the Atlantic Fleet was being "subsumed" by Fleet Forces Command and could be absorbed by the senior organization at a future date.[3] Various Navy documents already make use of the term Fleet Forces Command in place of Atlantic Fleet.

Atlantic Fleet. The Commander, Atlantic Fleet, functions in both the administrative and tactical chains of command. Until 1986, the position of CinC Atlantic Fleet was an additional duty of the CinC Atlantic Command, who also was the NATO Supreme Allied Commander Atlantic. Secretary of the Navy John Lehman separated the command and fleet positions to establish an additional four-star position for flag officers.

The Second Fleet is the major operational component of the Atlantic Fleet.

Headquarters: Norfolk, Virginia.

Pacific Fleet: Like Commander, Atlantic Fleet, the Commander, Pacific Fleet, functions in both the administrative and operational chains of command. In the latter role (as a naval component commander), he is responsible for naval operations in the Pacific and Indian Ocean areas.

The principal operating commands are the Third and Seventh Fleets.

Headquarters: Pearl Harbor, Hawaii.

Naval Forces Central Command: Commander, Naval Forces Central Command, is the component commander of the U.S. Central Command (CENTCOM), responsible for naval activities in the Arabian Sea, Persian Gulf, Red Sea, and portions of the Indian Ocean. Previously, the Commander, Middle East Force, a rear admiral, commanded naval forces in the area under the aegis of CENTCOM. During the 1990–1991 naval buildup and conflict in the Gulf, the Commander, Seventh Fleet, exercised command of naval forces in the region as the CinCCENT naval component commander.

The naval component commander was upgraded to vice admiral in 1992 and given the additional designated as Commander, Fifth Fleet, in 1995 (see below). The Deputy Commander, Naval Forces Central Command, a rear admiral, is at CENTCOM headquarters at MacDill Air Force Base, near Tampa, Florida.

Headquarters: Bahrain.

Naval Forces Europe: The Commander, Naval Forces Europe, is responsible for U.S. naval operations in the European area, including the Sixth Fleet in the Mediterranean Sea. The commander simultaneously holds the NATO position of Commander, Allied Forces Southern Europe, responsible to the NATO Supreme Allied Commander, Europe.

The Commander, Naval Forces Europe, does not have administrative responsibilities for support of U.S. naval forces in Europe, those functions being under the cognizance of the Commander, Atlantic Fleet.

Headquarters: Naples, Italy

The numbered fleet commanders are vice admirals. Their staffs normally are "split" between the fleet flagship and a component ashore.

Second Fleet: Operating in the Atlantic area, the Second Fleet serves as the NATO strike force, is responsible for anti-submarine operations in the Atlantic, and, increasingly, has operational requirements in the Caribbean and off Central America. Most ships of the Second Fleet rotate at regular intervals to the Sixth Fleet in the Mediterranean and to the Fifth Fleet in the Persian Gulf area.

Fleet headquarters: Norfolk, Va.

Flagship: MOUNT WHITNEY (LCC 20).

Third Fleet: The Third Fleet operates in the Eastern Pacific and rotates ships to the Seventh Fleet in the Western Pacific–Indian Ocean areas and to the Fifth Fleet. The Third Fleet originally had an Anti-Submarine Warfare (ASW) orientation, derived from its origins as Anti-Submarine Force Pacific. The growth of Soviet naval capabilities in the Pacific during the 1980s led to an increase in carrier battle force operations in the Third Fleet, with regular North Pacific operations, some within air strike range of Russian bases in Siberia.

Fleet headquarters: Naval Air Station North Island (San Diego), California. (Fleet headquarters were shifted from Ford Island in Pearl Harbor to San Diego in August 1991.)

Flagship: The CORONADO (AGF 11), nominally Third Fleet flagship, was temporarily assigned to the Seventh Fleet in 2004.

Fifth Fleet: The Commander, Naval Forces Central Command, is also Commander, Fifth Fleet, that position having been established on 1 July 1995. The fleet has no ships permanently assigned. Rather, ships from other fleets that deploy into the area are assigned to the Fifth Fleet. There are up to 15 active Navy/Military Sealift Command ships in the CENTCOM area at any given time, plus about 25 Maritime Prepositioning Ships (MPS) and Afloat Prepositioning Ships (APS), most of which are anchored at Diego Garcia.

Various task forces are activated within Fifth Fleet, depending on the ships in the area. For example, TF 50 (Naval Expeditionary Force) is activated when a Carrier Battle Group (CVBG) and Amphibious Ready Group (ARG) are in the area; TF 51 (Amphibious Force) is activated when there is an ARG but no carrier. The normal commanders of these forces retain command, but are assigned to the Fifth Fleet in addition.

Commander, Task Force 53 (Logistics Force), has a permanent staff at Bahrain. He also serves as Commander, Service Force, for Naval Forces Central Command and has control of all underway replenishment ships, tenders, tugs, and the MPS/APS ships in the area.

Four mine countermeasures ships are now homeported at Mina' Sulman, Bahrain. Their crews are rotated from the United States by air every six months (see Chapter 22). The LA SALLE (AGF 3) previously was flagship of Commander, Middle East Force, based at Mina' Sulman.

Headquarters: Bahrain.

3 William H. McMichael, "No More 'Atlantic Fleet'?" *Navy Times* (27 October 2003), p. 12.

Sixth Fleet: The Sixth Fleet operates in the Mediterranean Sea and has both U.S. and NATO responsibilities, the latter as NATO Striking and Support Forces, Southern Europe. Several NATO allies provide direct support to the Sixth Fleet in terms of shore bases and ASW and reconnaissance forces.

A submarine tender and the fleet flagship are homeported in the Mediterranean, the SIMON LAKE (AS 33) at La Maddalena, Italy, and the LA SALLE at Gaeta, Italy. Most Sixth Fleet ships and aircraft squadrons are on rotation from the Atlantic Fleet; those units normally spend 6 months in transit and operating in the Mediterranean and Persian Gulf areas and 12 months in their home port and in Atlantic operations.

Fleet headquarters: Gaeta, Italy.

Fleet flagship: LA SALLE.

Seventh Fleet: The Seventh Fleet has broad responsibilities for naval operations in the Western Pacific and Indian Ocean areas—from the Kamchatka Peninsula of Russian Siberia to the Indian Ocean. Thus, the Seventh Fleet has complex and wide-ranging mission requirements with only limited allied support available. The aircraft carrier KITTY HAWK (CV 63), a cruiser-destroyer group, an amphibious group, and two mine countermeasures ships are homeported in Japan.

During the Persian Gulf operations of 1990–1991 (Operations Desert Shield and Desert Storm), the Commander, Seventh Fleet, became the naval component commander for Central Command.

Fleet headquarters: Yokosuka, Japan.

Flagship: The BLUE RIDGE (LCC 19) is assigned as Seventh Fleet flagship.

Historical: The U.S. Navy's numbered fleets were established from 1942 onward within the U.S. Atlantic and Pacific Fleets. Those in the Atlantic–Mediterranean area were given even numbers; those in the Pacific area received odd numbers. The U.S. numbered fleets are/were:

First Fleet: Established in the Eastern Pacific as the First Task Fleet in 1947; changed to the First Fleet in 1950. Disestablished in 1973.

Second Fleet: Established for operations in the North Atlantic as the Second Task Fleet in 1947; changed to Second Fleet in 1950.

Third Fleet: Established in 1943 for operations in the Western Pacific. The Third Fleet generally shared naval forces with the Fifth Fleet; while one fleet commander and his staff were at sea operating against the Japanese, the other commander and staff would be ashore at Pearl Harbor, Hawaii, planning the next operation. Disestablished in 1946, Third Fleet was reestablished in 1973 for operations in the Eastern Pacific, the initial staff and operating components being based on Anti-Submarine Force Pacific.

Fourth Fleet: The former U.S. South Atlantic Force, renamed in 1943. Disestablished in 1946.

Fifth Fleet: Established in 1944 for operations in the Western Pacific. Disestablished in 1946, and reestablished in 1995 for operations in the Persian Gulf–Indian Ocean area.

Sixth Fleet: Established as the Sixth Task Fleet in 1948 for operations in the Mediterranean. Changed to Sixth Fleet in 1950.

Seventh Fleet: Formed in 1943 to provide naval support to operations by General Douglas MacArthur (and called "MacArthur's Navy"). From 1949 to 1950, it was designated Seventh Task Fleet, after which it was renamed Seventh Fleet.

Eighth Fleet: Established in 1943 to conduct operations in the Mediterranean. Disestablished in 1946.

Ninth Fleet: Designation not used.

Tenth Fleet: A "paper" fleet established in the Navy Department on 20 May 1943 to coordinate Atlantic area ASW under the direct command of the Chief of Naval Operations and CINC U.S. Fleet, Admiral Ernest J. King.[4]

Eleventh Fleet: Designation not used.

Twelfth Fleet: Established in 1943, with headquarters in London, as the U.S. Navy's planning staff for European operations. Disestablished in 1946.

ADMINISTRATIVE ORGANIZATION

The administrative organization of the Navy begins with the Secretary of Defense and proceeds through the Secretary of the Navy and the Chief of Naval Operations (CNO), as shown in simplified form in Figure 5-3. The CNO is double-hatted as both the uniformed head of the Navy and a member of the Joint Chiefs of Staff.

The Secretary of the Navy and the CNO essentially are managers supporting the unified commanders. They are responsible for logistics, maintenance, personnel management, procurement of naval systems and supplies, and research and development.

To accomplish these tasks, the Secretary and the Chief of Naval Operations each have staff organizations, with the Secretary's comprised mostly of civilians and the CNO's mostly of naval personnel. The Secretary of the Navy (SECNAV) organization is shown in

Figure 5-3. Administrative Chain of Command

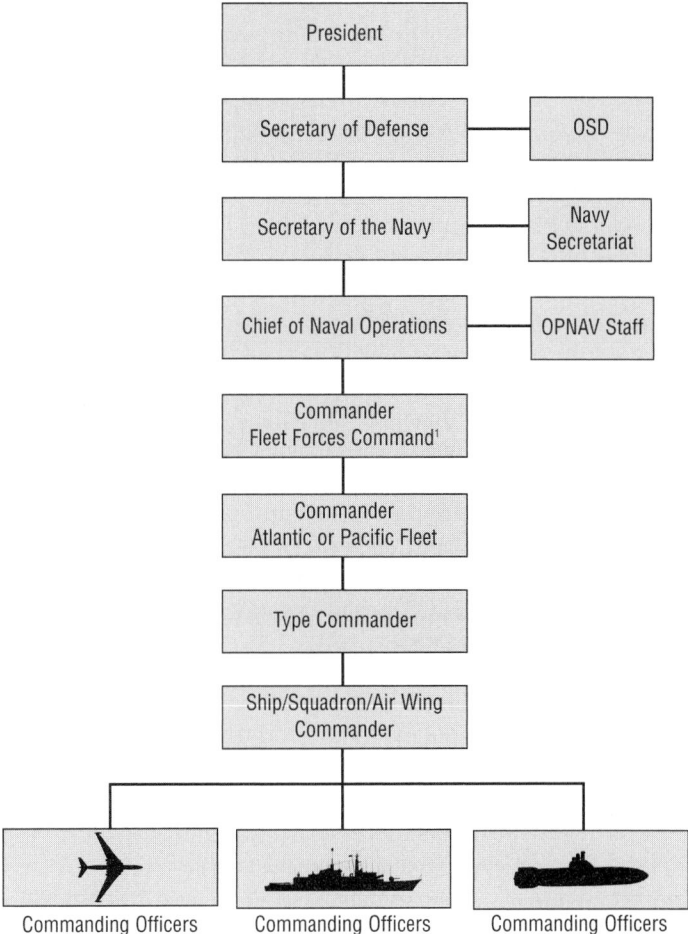

¹Currently also Commander, U.S. Atlantic Fleet

---

4 The Battle of the Atlantic essentially was won in May 1943, almost simultaneous with setting up the Tenth Fleet. The delay was caused largely by Admiral King wishing to keep direct control of the ASW campaign and the bitter controversy between the Army Air Forces and the Navy over the control of land-based maritime patrol aircraft.

Figure 5-4; several active-duty naval officers hold positions within SECNAV.[5]

SECNAV officials handle Marine Corps as well as Navy matters within their areas of responsibility, and several Marine officers serve in the Navy secretariat as well as in senior positions in the Office of the Chief of Naval Operations (OPNAV).

Beyond the SECNAV and OPNAV staffs, there are several separate Navy commands:
- Bureau of Medicine and Surgery (★★★)
- Bureau of Naval Personnel (★★★)
- Naval Air Systems Command (★★★)
- Naval Data Automation Command (captain)
- Naval Education and Training Command (★★★)
- Naval Facilities Engineering Command (★★★)
- Naval Intelligence Command (captain)
- Naval Meteorology and Oceanography Command (★)
- Military Sealift Command (★★★)
- Naval Networks and Space Operations Command (★)
- Naval Network Warfare Command (★★★)
- Naval Personnel Development Command (★★★)
- Naval Reserve Forces Command (★★)
- Naval Safety Center (★★)
- Naval Sea Systems Command (★★★)
- Naval Security Group Command (★★)
- Naval Space Command (★)
- Naval Special Warfare Command (★)
- Naval Supply Systems Command (★★)
- Naval Telecommunications Command (captain)
- Naval Warfare Development Command (★★)
- Navy Exchange Service Command (★★)
- Navy Recruiting Command (★★)
- Office of Naval Research (★★)
- Space and Naval Warfare Systems Command (★★)

The commanders of several of these commands are double-hatted. For example, the vice admiral serving as the Chief, Bureau of Medicine and Surgery, also is the Director of Naval Medicine and serves on the OPNAV staff as the Surgeon General of the Navy (N093). The head of the Office of Naval Research is the Chief of Naval Research, a rear admiral; he also serves as the Director, Test and Evaluation and Technology Requirements, in OPNAV (N091).

The Naval Space Command is a naval component of the U.S. Strategic Command (formerly the U.S. Space Command), and the Naval Special Warfare Command is the naval component of the U.S. Special Operations Command.

The CNO has several deputies and assistants and a large staff historically known as the Office of the Chief of Naval Operations. The most far-reaching reorganization of U.S. Navy headquarters in almost 50 years, announced on 22 July 1992, changed the OPNAV staff in an effort to eliminate the so-called platform barons, the vice admirals who directed the submarine, surface, and air communities, or "unions." The reorganization also eliminated several flag billets, including four vice admirals, and reduced the headquarters staff by about 150 military and civilian positions.

These changes were made, according to the Navy's statement to Congress, because

> the dramatic changes that have taken place and are continuing to take place in the world situation have dictated a reduction in the force structure of the U.S. Navy. This reduction also requires that the Navy review how its command and administrative structure is organized. Navy leadership has recognized for some time the need to have a tighter, leaner headquarters organization, better tailored and coordinated to deal with [Department of Defense] and [Joint Chiefs of Staff] as well as operational staffs.[6]

Figure 5-4. Office of the Secretary of the Navy

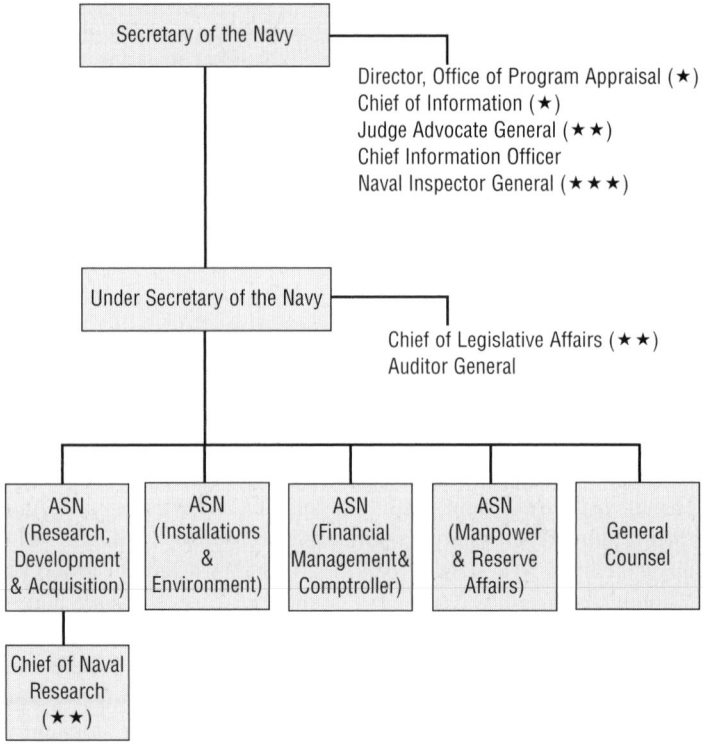

However, the reorganization also reflected a long-standing desire by Department of Defense officials, as well as senior Army and Air Force officers, to bring the Navy's executive staff "into line" with the other services. The reorganization brings the Navy into closer alignment with the staff of the Joint Chiefs, as well. The principal subordinates to the CNO and their N-series OPNAV codes are shown in Figure 5-5.

The concept of the platform barons, who sought to control their respective communities as fiefdoms, dates to August 1943, when the Deputy CNO (DCNO) for air was established with responsibility for "the preparation, readiness and logistic support" of naval aviation. Surface and submarine warfare matters were directed by a single DCNO, who also had general sponsorship responsibilities for aviation ships (aircraft carriers and seaplane tenders). However, in 1971, then-CNO Admiral Elmo R. Zumwalt, in response to pleading for "equality" by Admiral H. G. Rickover, then head of naval nuclear propulsion, and by the submarine community, established a separate DCNO (OP-02) for submarine warfare. Zumwalt believed "setting up the DCNO for Submarines made it easier to deal with the submarine community and with Rickover."[7] This move, in turn, led to OP-03 becoming the DCNO for surface warfare and initiated two decades of intra-Navy competition as the platform barons competed for resources, political position, and even flag billets. Beyond the competitive aspects, the new arrangement made it easy for non-platform-specific programs, such as mine warfare, to "fall through the cracks"—to become lost or underfunded.

Secretary of the Navy Sean O'Keefe, in announcing the 1992 changes, stressed, "One of my primary concerns is ending rivalries and jealousies between the various key warfare fighting communi-

---

5 The rank of military incumbents are shown: ★ = rear admiral (lower half); ★★ = rear admiral; ★★★ = vice admiral; ★★★★ = admiral.

6 Memorandum from Capt. J. R. McCleary, USN, subject: "Reorganization of the Naval Headquarters Staff," 22 July 1992.

7 Adm. H. G. Rickover, USN, head of naval propulsion from 1948 until 1982.

Figure 5-5. Office of the Chief of Naval Operations

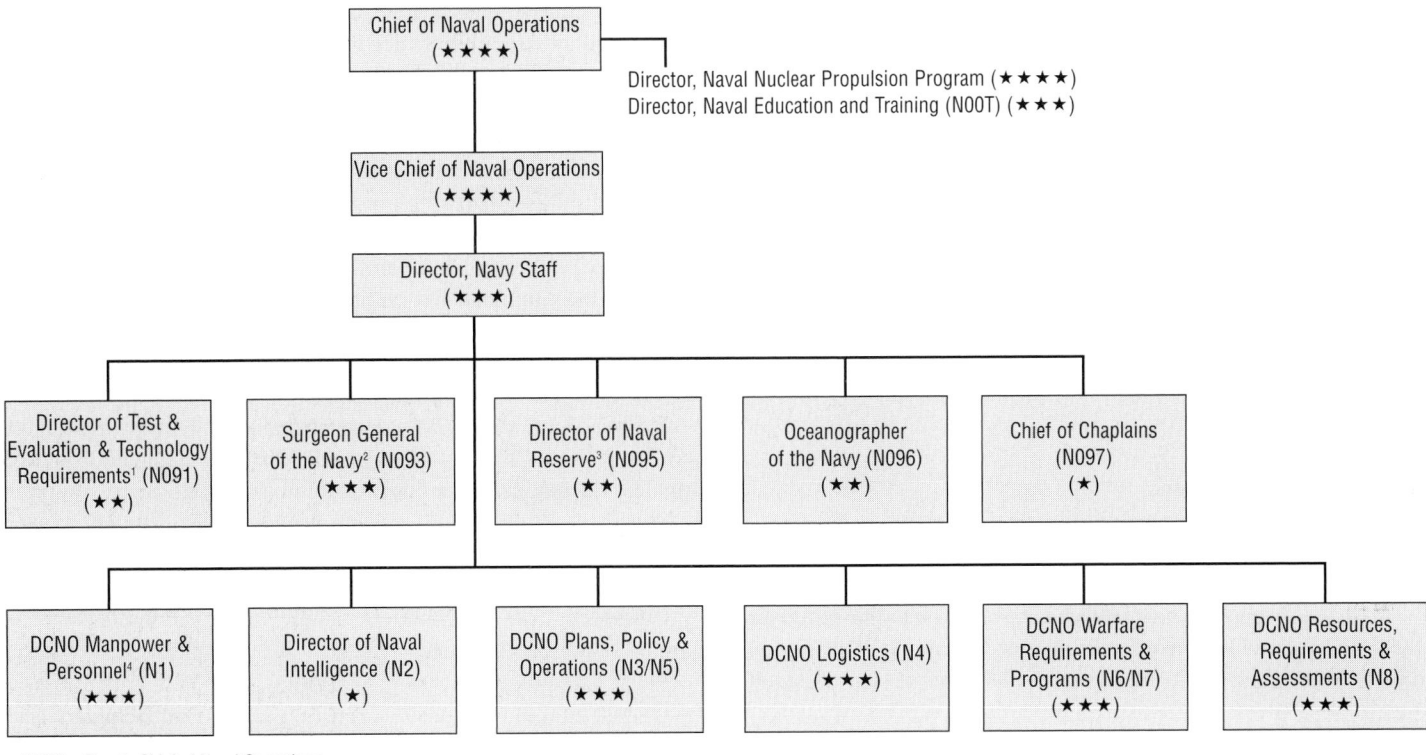

Chief of Naval Operations (★★★★)

Director, Naval Nuclear Propulsion Program (★★★★)
Director, Naval Education and Training (N00T) (★★★)

Vice Chief of Naval Operations (★★★★)

Director, Navy Staff (★★★)

| Director of Test & Evaluation & Technology Requirements[1] (N091) (★★) | Surgeon General of the Navy[2] (N093) (★★★) | Director of Naval Reserve[3] (N095) (★★) | Oceanographer of the Navy (N096) (★★) | Chief of Chaplains (N097) (★) |

| DCNO Manpower & Personnel[4] (N1) (★★★) | Director of Naval Intelligence (N2) (★) | DCNO Plans, Policy & Operations (N3/N5) (★★★) | DCNO Logistics (N4) (★★★) | DCNO Warfare Requirements & Programs (N6/N7) (★★★) | DCNO Resources, Requirements & Assessments (N8) (★★★) |

DCNO = Deputy Chief of Naval Operations
[1] Also Chief of Naval Research
[2] Also Chief of Bureau of Medicine and Surgery
[3] Also Chief of Naval Research and Director, Naval Reserve Force
[4] Also Chief of Bureau of Naval Personnel

ties in the Navy. . . . We believe there can be no jealousy among the fingers of a strong fist. This Navy reorganization will begin the process of bringing our warfare fighters together into a tighter, stronger fist."[8]

Unfortunately, the reorganization missed the opportunity to return ASW and mine warfare programs to realistic staff levels, especially considering their increasing importance for potential operations in littoral areas. They should have been placed at the same level within N8 as the air, surface, and subsurface offices. Subsequently, the ASW office was elevated to the one-star level (N74). Mine warfare remains subsumed in the Expeditionary Warfare Directorate (N75), with the Director, Surface Warfare (N76) as platform sponsor.

---

8 Secretary of the Navy Sean O'Keefe, press conference, Pentagon, 22 July 1992.

A prototype Fire Scout Tactical Unmanned Aerial Vehicle (TUAV) turns up on the deck of an amphibious ship. This "bird" has Marine markings. The Fire Scout, with a helicopter configuration, lacks the stealth and certain other features that could be important in UAV operations; however, the need for a near-term vehicle for use from the Littoral Combat Ship (LCS) led the Navy to adopt it. (U.S. Navy)

From a viewpoint of ships and aircraft programs, the DCNO for Warfare Requirements and Programs (N7) and the DCNO for Resources, Requirements, and Assessments (N8) are the most significant OPNAV offices. Their principal subordinate divisions and branches are:

DCNO for Warfare Requirements and Programs (N7)
- N70 Warfare Integration
- N74 Anti-Submarine Warfare
- N75 Expeditionary Warfare[9]
- N76 Surface Warfare
- N77 Submarine Warfare
- N78 Air Warfare
- N79 Naval Training and Education

DCNO for Resources, Requirements, and Assessments (N8)
- N80 Programming
- N81 Assessment
- N82 Fiscal Management
- N83/N81D JROC Requirements and CinC Liaison[10]
- N89 Special Programs
- N8C Quadrennial Defense Review

Historical: The first American naval vessel was the schooner HANNAH, which sailed on orders from General George Washington in early September 1775. The HANNAH and other vessels, manned by sailors from the maritime areas, particularly Salem, Marblehead, and Beverly, Massachusetts, were intended to embarrass the British and capture gunpowder for use by Washington's forces.[11]

The Continental Navy was founded on 13 October 1775, when the Continental Congress established a naval committee to acquire and fit out vessels for sea and to write appropriate regulations. The following month, the committee purchased two sailing ships and two brigs, and, subsequently, two sloops and two schooners. Esek Hopkins, brother of the Rhode Island member of the Naval Committee, was appointed Commander-in-Chief of the Fleet.

When the American Revolution ended, the central government saw no need for a fleet and had no means to fund one. By 1785, all U.S. warships had been disposed of. The War Department handled all "naval" matters during this period.

Events of the early 1790s demonstrated a need for a fleet, and the Navy Act of 27 May 1794 provided for the acquisition of six frigates. Each frigate was constructed in a separate port:[12]

Ship	Launched	Builder Location
CHESAPEAKE (36 guns)	1799	Norfolk, Va.[13]
CONGRESS (36 guns)	1799	Portsmouth, N.H.
CONSTELLATION (36 guns)	1797	Baltimore
CONSTITUTION (44 guns)	1797	Boston
PRESIDENT (44 guns)	1799	New York
UNITED STATES (44 guns)	1797	Philadelphia

(The CONSTITUTION survives, in active commission, at the Charlestown Naval Shipyard, Boston. See Chapter 25.)

The Navy Department was formally established by an act of Congress on 30 April 1798, and the first Secretary of the Navy, Benjamin Stoddart, was installed on 18 June. As established, the Secretary of the Navy exercised direct control over the Navy's shore establishment, as well as over the operating forces.

From 1842 onward, Congress established a series of bureaus to provide effective procurement of ships and supplies, to manage personnel, and to operate shore activities. These bureaus, commanded by naval officers, reported directly to the Secretary of the Navy. This organizational concept continues today, with the original bureaus having evolved into the modern systems commands and bureaus. However, the systems commands and bureaus now report directly to the Secretary of the Navy *and* the CNO.

The position of Aide for Operation was established in 1890 to provide a flag officer (rear admiral) on the staff of the Secretary of the Navy. This officer was responsible for ship operations, as well as training, planning, intelligence, and logistics, and was to recommend officer appointments. In 1915, as a result of the war in Europe, the position was change to Chief of Naval Operations with the rank of full admiral, the first appointee being Admiral William S. Benson.

However, the CNO did not direct naval forces afloat. Rather, various squadron and, from 1906, fleet commanders exercised command of ships, with their commands based on geographic areas. In 1919, the position of Commander-in-Chief, U.S. Fleet

Crewmen work on the first Advanced SEAL Delivery System (ASDS) during operations off Hawaii, where the lead craft is being tested. The craft's periscope and communications mast fold rather than retract. The ASDS offers the promise of effective clandestine submarine operations; however, the program is stalled because of costs and technical problems. (U.S. Navy)

---

9 The Director, Expeditionary Warfare, is a Marine major general.

10 JROC = Joint Requirements Oversight Council; also the CinC title has been changed to Commander [Unified Combatant Command]; the OPNAV title had not been changed when this edition went to press.

11 The best single volume history of the U.S. Navy is E. B. Potter and Fleet Adm. Chester W. Nimitz, USN, *Sea Power: A Naval History* (Annapolis, Md.: Naval Institute Press, 1981)

12 These ships are best described in Howard I. Chapelle, *The History of the American Sailing Navy: The Ships and Their Design* (New York: Bonanza Books, 1949).

13 At the time called Gosport.

(CinCUS), was established as overall commander of U.S. naval forces afloat. The CinCUS—pronounced "sink us"—reported to the Secretary of the Navy, independent of the CNO.

The positions of CNO and CinCUS remained separate until Admiral Ernest J. King—who had become Commander-in-Chief, U.S. Fleet, in December 1941—also was named Chief of Naval Operations in March 1942. From that time on, the CNO had de facto command of operational forces afloat in addition to being the Navy member of the Joint Chiefs of Staff. The position of Commander-in-Chief, U.S. Fleet (whose acronym King had changed to ComInCh—pronounced com-INCH), was abolished in October 1945, immediately after World War II.

There have been continuous organizational changes within the Navy. Among the more significant, in 1963, the separate technical bureaus were incorporated under a central Naval Material Command headed by the Chief of Naval Material (a full admiral). This increased the influence of the CNO over the bureaus. In 1966, the Secretary of the Navy placed the Naval Material Command (and its subordinate system commands) directly under the CNO, giving him full responsibility for material, personnel, and medical support of the operating forces. Also during this period, the techni-

cal bureaus were redesignated as systems commands—air, ship, ordnance, electronic, supply, etc.

The intermediate administrative organization of the Naval Material Command was abolished in 1985 by Secretary of the Navy Lehman. Under his revisions, the Secretary and the CNO exercise joint direction of the six systems commands—at the time the Naval Air Systems Command, Naval Sea Systems Command, Space and Naval Warfare Systems Command, Naval Facilities Engineering Command, and Naval Supply Systems Command.

The Bureau of Naval Personnel and the Bureau of Medicine and Surgery had remained outside the Naval Material Command. Their titles survived until 1978 and 1982, when the organizations were renamed, respectively, Naval Military Personnel Command and Naval Medical Command. Those awkward and bureaucratic titles survived only until 1989, when their traditional bureau names were restored.[14]

---

14 The Bureau of Personnel was created in October 1942, evolving from the Bureau of Navigation (1862) and the predecessor Bureau of Ordnance and Hydrography (1842); the Bureau of Medicine and Surgery was one of the five bureaus originally established by Congress in August 1842.

The submarine tender EMORY S. LAND *(AS 39) provides support for the destroyer* COLE *(DDG 67) at La Maddalena, Italy. The* LAND *is one of only two tender-type ships that remain in U.S. naval service. The demise of AD/AS/AR-type ships has led to increased reliance on overseas port facilities; the Sea Swap program (see Chapter 9) could exacerbate this situation as ships remain forward deployed for a year or more. (U.S. Navy/Wesley Marquis)*

Major U.S. Navy–Marine Corps Installations

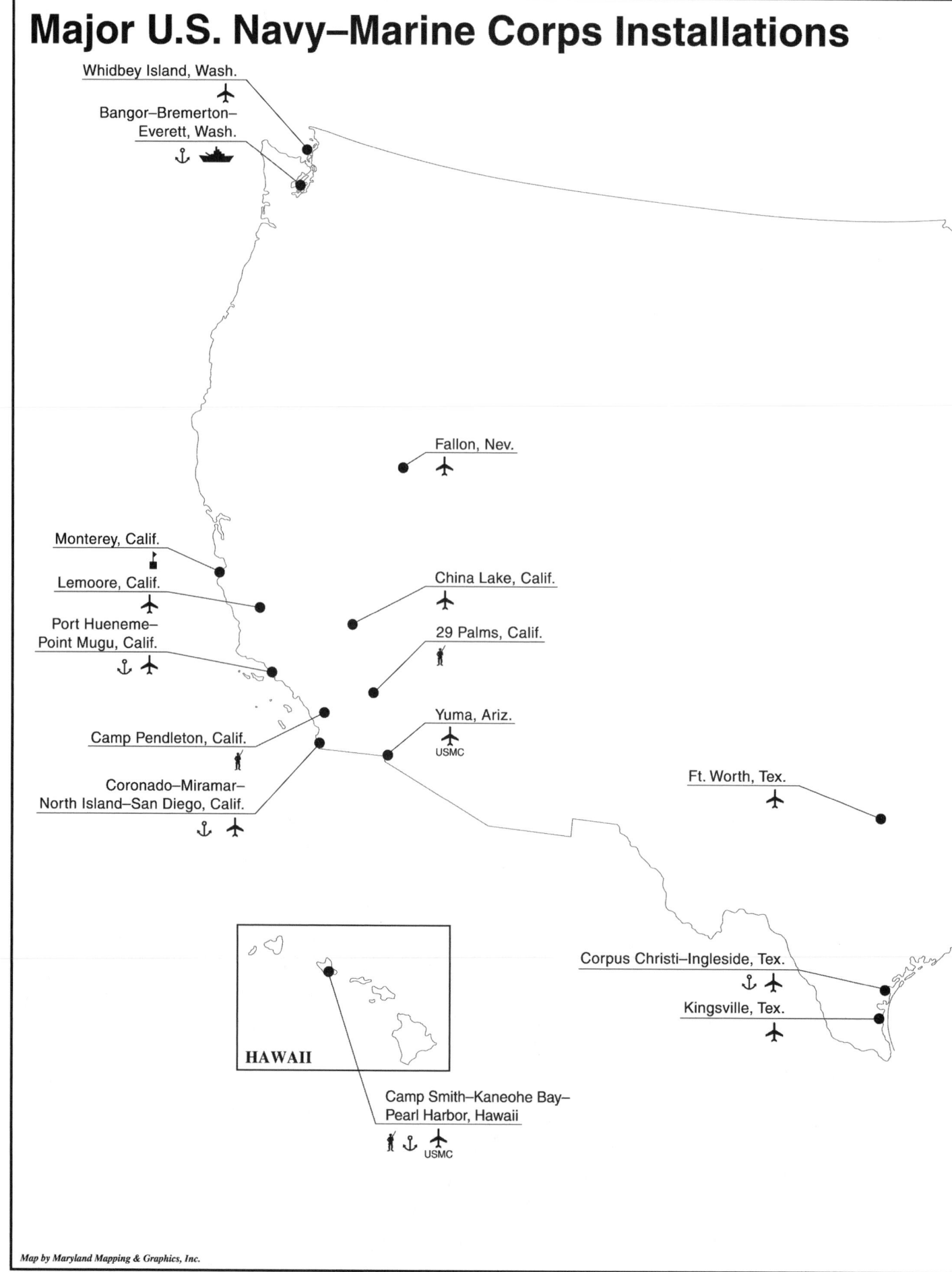

Whidbey Island, Wash.

Bangor–Bremerton–
Everett, Wash.

Fallon, Nev.

Monterey, Calif.

Lemoore, Calif.

China Lake, Calif.

Port Hueneme–
Point Mugu, Calif.

29 Palms, Calif.

Yuma, Ariz.
USMC

Camp Pendleton, Calif.

Ft. Worth, Tex.

Coronado–Miramar–
North Island–San Diego, Calif.

HAWAII

Corpus Christi–Ingleside, Tex.

Kingsville, Tex.

Camp Smith–Kaneohe Bay–
Pearl Harbor, Hawaii
USMC

Map by Maryland Mapping & Graphics, Inc.

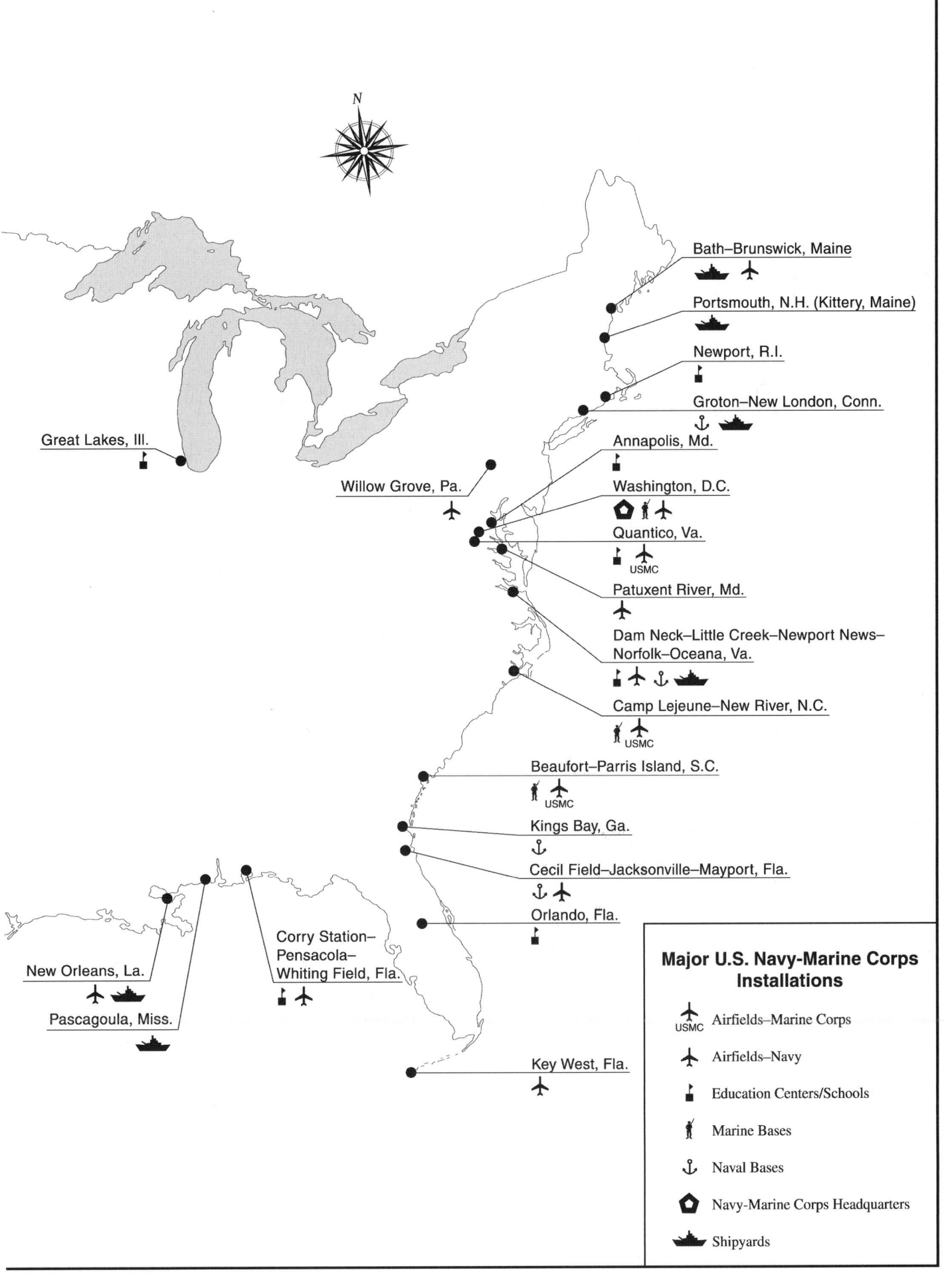

Bath–Brunswick, Maine

Portsmouth, N.H. (Kittery, Maine)

Newport, R.I.

Groton–New London, Conn.

Great Lakes, Ill.

Annapolis, Md.

Willow Grove, Pa.

Washington, D.C.

Quantico, Va.
USMC

Patuxent River, Md.

Dam Neck–Little Creek–Newport News–
Norfolk–Oceana, Va.

Camp Lejeune–New River, N.C.
USMC

Beaufort–Parris Island, S.C.
USMC

Kings Bay, Ga.

Cecil Field–Jacksonville–Mayport, Fla.

Orlando, Fla.

New Orleans, La.

Corry Station–
Pensacola–
Whiting Field, Fla.

Pascagoula, Miss.

Key West, Fla.

**Major U.S. Navy-Marine Corps
Installations**

Airfields–Marine Corps
USMC

Airfields–Navy

Education Centers/Schools

Marine Bases

Naval Bases

Navy-Marine Corps Headquarters

Shipyards

CHAPTER 6

Fleet Organization

Cruisers, destroyers, frigates, aircraft carriers, and submarines have been integrated into Carrier Strike Groups (CSG). Crewmen of the carrier KITTY HAWK (CV 63) walk the flight deck searching for debris that could be ingested into aircraft engines while the cruiser CHANCELLORSVILLE (CG 62) sails in company during operations in the Pacific. An EA-6B Prowler, S-3B Viking, and F/A-18 Hornet of Carrier Air Wing 5 are visible in this 2004 photo. (U.S. Navy/Lamel J. Hinton)

The Navy's fleet organization continues to change in the wake of the reduction in air, surface, and submarine forces following the end of the Cold War and the shifts in deployment policies initiated under Chief of Naval Operations Admiral Vern Clark's "Sea Power 21" concepts. The latest changes were announced in September 2004, when the Cruiser–Destroyer Groups (CruDesGru) and Carrier Groups (CarGru) were redesignated Carrier Strike Groups (CSG).

The carrier groups were changed to CSGs with the same organizational designations; the CruDesGru numbers were changed to:

Former	Current
CruDesGru-1	CSG-15
CruDesGru-2	CSG-10
CruDesGru-3	CSG-9
CruDesGru-5	CSG-11
CruDesGru-8	CSG-12
CruDesGru-12	CSG-14

Accordingly, there now are 14 CSGs—1 through 12, 14, and 15.

The CSG organization moves group commanders to positions more closely aligned with the manner in which their forces train and deploy. CruDesGru and CarGru commanders and their staffs now are under the numbered fleet commanders, as well as under their type commanders. However, the change causes some confusion as not all CSGs will include aircraft carriers.

Similarly, in 2003, Amphibious Groups (PhibGru) were redesignated as Expeditionary Strike Groups (ESG). The ESGs will include surface combatants and, possibly, attack submarines and amphibious ships. The PhibGru-to-ESG designations remained the same.

Each CSG nominally consists of an aircraft carrier and two missile cruisers, all located at the same base when possible. This has been done less frequently as the size of the fleet has been reduced and with the limited numbers of ports at which carriers are based.

As noted in Chapter 5, all naval forces are assigned to both administrative and operational commands. The operational organizations are based primarily on task forces/groups. The Task Force (TF) and Task Group (TG) organizations listed in this chapter under the commanders of the Atlantic and Pacific Fleets are mainly for contingency operations; exceptions include the respective submarine force commanders, who have both operational and administrative roles. TF organizations are employed for exercises, forward deployment operations, and in war.

Naval administrative organizations are asymmetrical; the hierarchy, organization, and composition of units vary within the fleets and from fleet to fleet. Ship squadrons that do not have ships assigned usually are operational command staffs that control forward deployed forces or training workups or ships undergoing maintenance and overhaul.

The Western Hemisphere Group of the Atlantic Fleet, established in 1995, deploys ships for four- and five-month operations, such as Caribbean operations and the South American training exercise UNITAS.

The following tables provide a breakdown of naval organizations and nominal ship assignments as of 2004. The fleet organization is in a state of flux because of several factors, among them fleet reductions (such as the accelerated retirement of destroyers of the SPRUANCE/DD 963 class) and the structuring of the CSGs and ESGs.

Ships assigned to type commanders are indicated under the administrative organizations. Such assignments change regularly as new ships are commissioned, older ships are stricken, and ships are reassigned for overhaul or modernization. Specific aircraft carriers and fleet flagships are identified. The fleet flagships (⚓) are listed under their administrative commands; see Chapter 19 for operational details.

The ships listed are active unless indicated as in the Naval Reserve Force (NRF). Headquarters locations or flagship home ports are indicated, although all ships of a command may not be at the same port.

The Marine Force organizations are described in Chapter 7. The Naval Special Warfare Command is address in Chapter 21 and Mine Warfare Command in Chapter 22. Details of aviation organizations, both land-based and carrier-based wings and squadrons, are described in Chapter 27.

PACIFIC FLEET

TF 10	Temporary Operations Force
TF 11	Training Force
TF 12	Anti-Submarine Force
TF 14	Submarine Force
TF 15	Surface Force
TF 16	Maritime Defense Zone[1]
TF 17	Naval Air Force
TF 18	Sealift Forces
TF 19	Fleet Marine Force[2]
TF 91	Naval Forces Alaska

THIRD FLEET

TF 30	Battle Force
TF 31	Command and Coordination Force
TF 32	Ready Force
TF 33	Combat Logistics Support Force
TF 34	Submarine Force
TF 35	Surface Combatant Force
TF 36	Amphibious Force
TF 37	Carrier Strike Force
TF 39	Landing Force[2]
TF 150	Maritime Interception Operations[3]

Two MCMs are assigned to the Third Fleet and based in Bahrain (also listed under Mine Warfare Command).

SEVENTH FLEET

TF 70	Battle Force
TF 71	Command and Coordination Force
TF 72	Patrol and Reconnaissance Force
TF 74	Submarine Force
TF 75	Surface Combatant Force
TF 76	Amphibious Force
TF 79	Landing Force[2]
LCC	BLUE RIDGE (⚓ Seventh Fleet) Yokosuka, Japan[4]

CARRIER STRIKE GROUPS

Carrier Strike Group 1	North Island, Calif.
Carrier Strike Group 3	Alameda, Calif.
CVN CARL VINSON	Bremerton, Wash.
1 CG	San Diego, Calif.
Carrier Strike Group 5	Yokosuka, Japan
CV KITTY HAWK	Yokosuka, Japan
Carrier Strike Group 7	North Island, Calif.
CVN JOHN C. STENNIS	San Diego, Calif.
1 CG	
1 FFG	
Carrier Strike Group 15	San Diego, Calif.
CVN RONALD REAGAN	San Diego, Calif.
2 CG	
1 FFG	
Carrier Strike Group 9	San Diego, Calif.
CVN ABRAHAM LINCOLN	Everett, Wash.
4 CG	
2 DDG	
1 FFG	
Carrier Strike Group 11	San Diego, Calif.
CVN NIMITZ	North Island, Calif.
1 CG	San Diego, Calif.

1 Commanded by a Coast Guard officer.
2 Commanded by a Marine officer.
3 TF 150 is composed of ships from several nations at any given time, with the TF commander alternating among those navies. The TF patrols the Arabian Sea area seeking to interdict the shipment of terrorist-related materials. The nations that have provided ships to TF 150 are: Australia, Canada, France, Germany, Great Britain, Italy, Japan, Pakistan, Spain, New Zealand, and the United States.
4 The LCC BLUE RIDGE recently completed overhaul in Japan.

NAVAL AIR FORCE PACIFIC	**North Island, Calif.**
Carrier Air Wing 2	Miramar, Calif.
Carrier Air Wing 5	Yokosuka, Japan
Carrier Air Wing 9	Lemoore, Calif.
Carrier Air Wing 11	Miramar, Calif.
Carrier Air Wing 14	Miramar, Calif.
Air Early Warning Wing	Miramar, Calif.
Electronic Attack Wing	Whidbey Island, Wash.
Fleet Air Western Pacific	Atsugi, Japan
Helicopter Tactical Wing	North Island, Calif.
Helicopter Anti-Submarine Wing	North Island, Calif.
Helicopter Anti-Submarine Light Wing	North Island, Calif.
Patrol and Reconnaissance Force	Kaneohe Bay, Hawaii
PATRECONWING-10	Whidbey Island, Wash.
PATRECONWING-1	Kamiseya, Japan
Sea Control Wing	North Island, Calif.
Strategic Communications Wing 1	Tinker AFB, Okla.
Strike-Fighter Wing Pacific	Lemoore, Calif.

NAVAL SURFACE FORCE PACIFIC	**Coronado, Calif.**
1 LSD	
Destroyer Squadron 1	
1 FFG	
Destroyer Squadron 7	
5 DDG	
1 FFG	
Destroyer Squadron 15	Yokosuka, Japan
3 CG	
2 DDG	
2 FFG	
Destroyer Squadron 17	San Diego, Calif.
Destroyer Squadron 21	San Diego, Calif.
2 DDG	
1 FFG	
Destroyer Squadron 23	San Diego, Calif.
4 DDG	
2 FFG	
Surface Group Pacific Northwest	Everett, Wash.
Destroyer Squadron 9	Everett, Wash.
1 DDG	
Surface Group Mid-Pacific	Pearl Harbor, Hawaii
1 ARS	
Destroyer Squadron 31	Pearl Harbor, Hawaii
5 DDG	
2 FFG	
Expeditionary Strike Group 1	White Beach, Okinawa
Amphibious Squadron 11	Sasebo, Japan
1 LHD ESSEX	
1 LPD	
2 LSD	
2 MCM (also listed under Mine Warfare Command)	
LHA BELLEAU WOOD	San Diego, Calif.
1 LPD	San Diego, Calif.
2 LSD	San Diego, Calif.
Amphibious Squadron 5	San Diego, Calif.
Amphibious Squadron 7	San Diego, Calif.
Expeditionary Strike Group 3	San Diego, Calif.
LHA PELELIU	
LHA TARAWA	
LHD BOXER	
LHD BONHOMME RICHARD	
5 LPD	
3 LSD	
Amphibious Squadron 1	
Amphibious Squadron 3	
Naval Beach Group 1	Coronado (San Diego), Calif.
Amphibious Construction Battalion 1	
Assault Craft Units 1, 5	
Beachmaster Unit 1	
Logistic Group Western Pacific	Singapore
Surface Group Pacific Northwest	Everett, Wash.
2 AOE	
Naval Surface Group Mid-Pacific	Pearl Harbor, Hawaii
2 ARS[5]	

SUBMARINE FORCE PACIFIC	**Pearl Harbor, Hawaii**
Submarine Squadron 1	Pearl Harbor, Hawaii
5 SSN	
Submarine Squadron 3	Pearl Harbor, Hawaii
6 SSN	
Submarine Squadron 7	Pearl Harbor, Hawaii
5 SSN 3	
Submarine Squadron 11	San Diego, Calif.
7 SSN	
1 ARDM	
Submarine Group 7	Yokosuka, Japan
1 AS	Guam
Submarine Squadron 15	Guam
3 SSN	
Submarine Group 9	Bangor, Wash.
Submarine Development Squadron 7	Bangor, Wash.
1 AGSS	San Diego, Calif.
1 DSRV (submersible)	North Island, Calif.
1 DSV (submersible)	San Diego, Calif.
Submarine Squadron 17	Bangor, Wash.
6 SSBN	
4 SSGN[6]	
Submarine Development Squadron 19	Bangor, Wash.[7]

FLEET ASW COMMAND	**San Diego, Calif.**[8]
TRAINING COMMAND PACIFIC	**San Diego, Calif.**
3RD NAVAL CONSTRUCTION BRIGADE	**Pearl Harbor, Hawaii**
Mobile Construction Battalions 3, 4, 5, 40	Port Hueneme, Calif.
Underwater Construction Team 2	Port Hueneme, Calif.

ATLANTIC FLEET

TF-40	Naval Surface Force
TF-41	Naval Air Force
TF-42	Submarine Force
TF-43	Training Command
TF-44	Coast Guard Forces[1]
TF-45	Marine Force[2]
TF-46	Mine Warfare Force
TF-47	Naval Construction Battalions
TF-49	Poseidon Operational Test Force
TF-80	Naval Patrol and Protection of Shipping
TF-81	Sea Control and Surveillance Force
TF-82	Amphibious Task Force
TF-83	Landing Force[2]
TF-84	ASW Task Force
TF-85	Mobile Logistic Support Force
TF-86	Patrol Air Task Force
TF-87	Tactical Development and Evaluation and Transit Force
TF-88	Training Force
TF-89	Maritime Defense Zone[1]
TF-134	Naval Forces Caribbean
TF-137	Eastern Atlantic
TF-138	South Atlantic Force
TF-139	Multilateral Special Operations Force
TF-142	Operational Test and Evaluation Force

SECOND FLEET

TF-20	Battle Force
TF-21	Sea Control and Surveillance Force
TF-22	Amphibious Force
TF-23	Landing Force[2]
TF-24	ASW Task Force
TF-25	Mobile Logistics Support Force
TF-26	Patrol Air Force
TF-28	Caribbean Contingency Force

---

5 One ship, the SAFEGUARD (ARS 50), is homeported in Japan.
6 Undergoing conversion.
7 Established 1 July 2003 to provide operational/administrative support for the JIMMY CARTER (SSN 23) when that special mission sub becomes operational in 2005.
8 Established 8 April 2004.

The Navy's newest submarine, the VIRGINIA (SSN 774), commissioned in October 2004, is assigned to Submarine Group 2 at Groton, Connecticut. When she becomes fully operational and ready to deploy, she will be assigned to a submarine squadron. Civilian tugs from the Moran firm ease her into Norfolk. (U.S. Navy/Andy Zask)

CARRIER STRIKE GROUPS

Carrier Strike Group 2	Norfolk, Va.
CVN HARRY S. TRUMAN	
Carrier Strike Group 4	Norfolk, Va.
CVN THEODORE ROOSEVELT	Norfolk, Va.
2 CG	Norfolk, Va.
Carrier Strike Group 6	Mayport, Fla.
CV JOHN F. KENNEDY	Mayport, Fla.
2 CG	
Carrier Strike Group 8	Norfolk, Va.
Carrier Strike Group 10	Norfolk, Va.
CVN GEORGE WASHINGTON	Norfolk, Va.
Carrier Strike Group 12	Norfolk, Va.
CVN DWIGHT D. EISENHOWER	Norfolk, Va.
2 CG	
Carrier Strike Group 14	Mayport, Fla.
CVN ENTERPRISE	Norfolk, Va.
2 CG	

NAVAL AIR FORCE ATLANTIC — **Norfolk, Va.**

Carrier Air Wing 1	Oceana, Va.
Carrier Air Wing 3	Oceana, Va.
Carrier Air Wing 7	Oceana, Va.
Carrier Air Wing 8	Oceana, Va.
Carrier Air Wing 17	Cecil Field, Fla.
Airborne Early Warning Wing	Norfolk, Va.
Fighter Wing	Oceana, Va.
Fleet Air Mediterranean	Naples, Italy
Fleet Air Caribbean (on standby status)	
Helicopter Anti-Submarine Wing	Jacksonville, Fla.
Helicopter Anti-Submarine Light Wing	Mayport, Fla.
Helicopter Tactical Wing	Norfolk, Va.
Patrol and Reconnaissance Force	Norfolk, Va.
PATRECONWING-5	Brunswick, Maine
PATRECONWING-11	Jacksonville, Fla.
Sea Control Wing	Cecil Field, Fla.
Strike-Fighter Wing	Oceana, Fla.

NAVAL SURFACE FORCE ATLANTIC — **Norfolk, Va.**

Surface Warfare Development Group	
Destroyer Squadron 2	Norfolk, Va.
3 DDG	
1 FFG	
Destroyer Squadron 18	Norfolk, Va.
4 DDG	
1 FFG	
Destroyer Squadron 22	Norfolk, Va.
3 DDG	
1 FFG	
Destroyer Squadron 24	Mayport, Fla.
3 DDG	
2 FFG	

Destroyer Squadron 26	Norfolk, Va.
4 DDG	
1 FFG	
Destroyer Squadron 28	Norfolk, Va.
1 CG	
3 DDG	
1 FFG	
Surface Group 2	Mayport, Fla.
Destroyer Squadron 6	Pascagoula, Miss.
2 CG (being decommissioned)	
4 FFG	
Destroyer Squadron 14	Mayport, Fla.
7 FFG	
Surface Group 4	
Surface Group 6	
Surface Group Mediterranean	
AGF LA SALLE (⚓ Sixth Fleet) Gaeta, Italy	
Western Hemisphere Group	
5 CG	
5 FFG	
Combat Logistics Squadron 2	Norfolk, Va.
2 AOE	
2 ARS	
2 ARS	
Expeditionary Strike Group 2	Norfolk, Va.
LHD BATAAN	
LHD IWO JIMA	
6 LSD	
Amphibious Squadron 2	Norfolk, Va.
Amphibious Squadron 4	Norfolk, Va.
Amphibious Squadron 6	Norfolk, Va.
Amphibious Squadron 8	Little Creek, Va.
LCC MOUNT WHITNEY (⚓ Second Fleet)	Norfolk, Va.
LHA NASSAU	
LHA SAIPAN	
LHD KEARSARGE	
LHD WASP	
5 LPD	
Naval Beach Group 2	
Beach Master Unit 2	
Amphibious Construction Battalion 2	
Assault Craft Unit 2	
Assault Craft Unit 4	
Naval Inshore Underwater Group 2	

MINE WARFARE COMMAND   **Ingleside, Texas**
   Mine Countermeasures Squadron 1   Ingleside, Texas
      3 MCM[9]
      1 MCM (NRF)
      4 MHC (NRF)
   Mine Countermeasures Squadron 2   Ingleside, Texas
      2 MCM
      4 MCM (NRF)
      3 MHC (NRF)
   Mine Countermeasures Squadron 3   Ingleside, Texas
      3 MCM[10]
      1 MCM (NRF)
      2 MHC[11]
      3 MHC (NRF)

SUBMARINE FORCE ATLANTIC   **Norfolk, Va.**
   Submarine Squadron 6   Norfolk, Va.
      6 SSN
   Submarine Squadron 8   Norfolk, Va.
      6 SSN
   Submarine Group 2   Groton, Conn.
      3 SSN
      1 ARDM
     Submarine Squadron 2   Groton, Conn.
       5 SSN
       NR-1
     Submarine Squadron 4   Groton, Conn.
       5 SSN
     Submarine Development Squadron 12 Groton, Conn.
       5 SSN
   Submarine Group 8   Naples, Italy
      1 AS   La Maddalena, Italy
     Submarine Squadron 22   La Maddalena, Italy

Submarine Group 10   Kings Bay, Ga.
   Submarine Squadron 16
      4 SSBN
   Submarine Squadron 20
      4 SSBN

TRAINING COMMAND ATLANTIC   **Norfolk, Va.**
   2nd NAVAL CONSTRUCTION BRIGADE   Little Creek, Va.
   Mobile Construction Battalions 1, 7, 13,
     14, 20, 21, 23, 24, 26, 27, 74, 133
   Underwater Construction Team 1

FIFTH FLEET   Bahrain

TF 50	Naval Expeditionary Force
TF 51	Amphibious Force
TF 53	Logistics Force

Destroyer Squadron 50/Middle East Force Surface Action Group

SIXTH FLEET   Gaeta, Italy

TF 60	Battle Force
TG 60.1	Battle Group
TG 60.2	Battle Group[2]
TF 61	Amphibious Force
TF 62	Landing Force[2]
TF 63	Service Force
TF 66	ASW Force
TF 67	Maritime Surveillance and Reconnaissance Force
TF 68	Special Operations Force
TF 69	Attack Submarine Force

AGF LA SALLE (⚓ Sixth Fleet) homeported in Gaeta, Italy

---

9 Two MCMS are assigned to the Seventh Fleet and based in Japan.
10 Two MCMs are assigned to the Third Fleet and based in Bahrain.
11 Both MHCs are assigned to the Third Fleet and based in Bahrain.

Task Force 150, a multinational force operating in the Arabian Sea area, is comprised of warships from Australia, Canada, France, Germany, Great Britain, Italy, Pakistan, New Zealand, Spain, and the United States. Third in line is the Aegis cruiser LEYTE GULF (CG 55). (U.S. Navy/Bart Bauer)

CHAPTER 7

Marine Forces

Marines on the march in the Middle East. In the fall of 2004, some 25,000 Marines and sailors were in Iraq attempting to pacify the country and help establish a democratic government. Marines were employed as ground combat troops in Operation Iraqi Freedom, having been brought ashore in "administrative landings" in Kuwait. (U.S. Marine Corps/Mauricio Campino)

The Marine Corps is a separate service within the Department of the Navy. Its primary mission is to provide the unified combatant commanders and the Atlantic and Pacific Fleets with combat ready air-ground task forces to conduct amphibious operations.

The Marine Corps' operating forces consist of:
- Marine Corps Forces
- Marine Corps Security Forces at naval installations in the United States and aboard
- Security guard detachments at U.S. embassies and consulates
- Counterterrorist forces

The commanders of Marine Corps Forces (MARFOR) Atlantic and Pacific serve as the Marine Corps component commanders to their respective combat commanders and also may serve as commanding generals of Fleet Marine Force (FMF) Atlantic or Pacific. In addition, in their roles as Commanding General FMF Atlantic and Pacific, they serve as "type" commanders within the Atlantic and Pacific Fleets, respectively.

The current Marine Corps strength of 176,200 active-duty personnel—plus 98,955 reservists—compares to a post–Vietnam War peak of approximately 200,000 active-duty men and women in the late 1980s. The U.S. Marine Corps is, by a significant margin, the largest such force in the world.[1] And teamed with the Navy's Expeditionary Strike Groups (ESGs)—formerly Amphibious

Ready Groups (ARGs)—the Corps is the world's foremost amphibious assault force by both qualitative and quantitative measures.

Table 7-1. MARINE CORPS STRENGTH (30 June 2004)

	Officers	Enlisted	Total
Active duty	19,050	157,150	172,200
Reserve Units	3,470	36,190	39,660
Individual Reserves	3,410	55,885	59,295

However, the Marine Corps has not undertaken an opposed amphibious assault in more than a half-century, since the landing at Inchon, Korea, in September 1950. Instead, it largely has been engaged as a conventional ground force. This has been especially true with its participation in the U.S. invasions of Afghanistan in 2002 and of Iraq in 2004.

---

1 At the time of the demise of the Soviet Union in December 1991, the Soviet Naval Infantry or marines consisted of some 18,000 troops. However, in the late 1980s, four motorized rifle divisions of the Soviet Ground Forces had been transferred to the Navy and, with the Naval Infantry and Navy-controlled Coastal Missile–Artillery Force (some 14,000 troops), formed the Coastal Defense Force within the naval establishment. Major marine organizations are maintained by China, Taiwan, Vietnam, South Korea, Thailand, and Britain.

General Michael W. Hagee, USMC, Commandant of the Marine Corps since January 2003. (U.S. Navy/Johnny Bivera)

During Operation Enduring Freedom—the Afghanistan assault—the Marines entered the country entirely by air, and their close air support initially came from carriers operating in the Persian Gulf, flown by Navy and Marine Corps carrier-based squadrons supported by Air Force tankers.

In Operation Iraqi Freedom—the Iraqi campaign—the I Marine Expeditionary Force (MEF), based on the 1st Marine Division, conducted 26 days of sustained combat operations. It executed four major river crossings, fought ten major engagements, and destroyed eight Iraqi divisions before stopping at Tikrit, almost 500 miles (805 km) inland. Their "jumping off" point was Kuwait. Similarly, the 26th Marine Expeditionary Unit (MEU) was inserted into northern Iraq by air from amphibious ships in the Eastern Mediterranean, a distance of almost 1,200 miles (1,930 km).

Despite the duration and distances inland of these operations, their support was derived primarily from ships, with the Marine combat service support units demonstrating great flexibility and resourcefulness. While there were intermittent shortages of rations and equipment, the Marines were able to "continue the march" into the heart of Iraq.

But the Marine assault in Iraq did demonstrate the inability of Marines to carry out sustained ground combat operations with organic resources. In Operation Iraqi Freedom, the I MEF consumed more than six million gallons of JP-8 vehicle fuel per month. This was possible because of the availability a major base in Kuwait with a suitable ground source of bulk fuel throughout the operation; also, the Marines made use of civilian truck transportation for moving fuel from Kuwait to the 1st Force Service Support Group's mobile replenishment sites.

Significantly, neither the Afghanistan nor Iraq operations involved amphibious landings. The Marines did not undertake an amphibious assault in Operation Desert Storm—the 1991 Gulf War—either. Separate from the 76,000 Marines ashore when that war began on 17 January 1991, there were 17,000 Marines on board 31 amphibious ships in the Persian Gulf. (Another 5,000 were embarked in amphibious ships in the eastern Mediterranean.) Although Iraqi troops occupied the Kuwaiti coast as well as the small Iraqi coastline, the Marines made only administrative landings on coalition-held beaches.

At no time during Desert Storm was serious consideration given to an amphibious assault. Coupled with the absence of amphibious landings in the 2003–2004 assaults, this begs a reexamination of the entire concept of over-the-beach operations by the Corps. Indeed, with the promise of air assaults conducted at greater distances from the beach by the MV-22 Osprey and the proposed CH-53X heavy-lift helicopter, the probability of a waterborne assault in the foreseeable future appears to be virtually nil.

If the sea base concept is pursued (see Chapter 24), the distance from future at-sea "platforms" to the objective will be far greater than the maximum 25 miles (40-km) amphibious ships can now operate from the beach. Even that distance appears to be too great for realistic operation by the new amphibian assault vehicles, the Expeditionary Fighting Vehicles (EFVs). Thus, all assault forces would reach the beach by air. (Air cushion landing craft [LCACs] are not assault vehicles, but are employed for logistics support.)

While across-the-beach is the traditional rational for "amphibious" forces, the U.S. Marine Corps must look to its many other exemplary characteristics and capabilities for its future viability.

SECURITY AND COUNTERTERRORISM

The Marine Corps provides security force detachments at various ammunition storage sites, major bases in the United States and overseas, the U.S. Naval Academy in Annapolis, Maryland, and U.S. embassies and consulates abroad.

At the start of the 21st century, the Marine Corps has been assigned increasing roles in security and counterterrorism operations. It activated the 4th Marine Expeditionary Brigade (Anti-Terrorism)—designated 4th MEB(AT)—on 29 October 2001 to coordinate its efforts to deter, detect, defend against, and respond to acts of domestic and international terrorism.[2] Beyond normal security and force protection, the brigade provides unified commands with specialized anti-terrorist forces, as appropriate.

Headquartered at Camp Lejeune, North Carolina, with almost 5,000 Marines and sailors assigned, the brigade's components include:

Marine Corps Security Guard Battalion. The Security Guard Battalion, with headquarters at Quantico, Virginia, provides Marine security services at some 140 U.S. embassies, consulates, and missions in more than 100 countries. The battalion is organized into a headquarters company, nine "line" companies, and a security guard school. The line companies have regional responsibilities:

	Headquarters	*Area*
Company A	Frankfurt, Germany	former Soviet bloc countries
Company B	Nicosia, Cyprus	North Africa, Middle East
Company C	Bangkok, Thailand	Far East, Asia, Australia
Company D	Ft. Lauderdale, Fla.	South America
Company E	Frankfurt, Germany	Western Europe
Company F	Pretoria, South Africa	Sub-Sahara Africa
Company G	Abidjan, Cote d'Ivoire	Western Africa
Company H	Frankfurt, Germany	Eastern Europe
Company I	Ft. Lauderdale, Fla.	Central America, Caribbean, Canada (Ottawa)

More than 1,100 men and women are assigned to the battalion.

The current security guard program has its origins in a December 1948 agreement between the State Department and the Marine Corps. However, Marines have worked with and protected U.S. diplomats in overseas locations since the beginnings of the nation.

Marine Corps Security Force Battalion. The Security Force Battalion, with headquarters at Norfolk, Virginia, provides security companies for U.S. naval facilities and supports two Fleet Anti-terrorism Security Team (FAST) companies. The latter units, first

---

2 The 4th Brigade of Marines originally was activated as part of the 2nd Army Division in 1917; the unit fought in France and was deactivated in 1919. It was activated periodically for crises and conflicts from 1961 to 1992.

established in 1987, provide specially trained security/anti-terror-ism teams to forward areas or locations within the United States as directed by the Commander, Fleet Forces Command, and the Commandant of the Marine Corps. (There have been references to a 3rd FAST Company, but no information on the unit is available publicly.)

The 1st FAST Company is based at Norfolk, and the 2nd FAST Company is at nearby Yorktown, Virginia. Each company has a per-sonnel strength of 321 organized into a headquarters, a weapons platoon, and seven guard platoons. Elements of both FAST compa-nies have been deployed overseas in response to crises and terror-ist acts.

The security companies are located at
• Bangor, Washington
• Guantanamo Bay, Cuba
• Keflavik, Iceland
• Kings Bay, Georgia
• London, England
• Manama, Bahrain
• Naples, Italy
• Patuxent River, Maryland
• Rota, Spain

In addition, security detachments are located at a number of "barracks" in the United States and overseas. The Marine barracks in Washington also provides security and honor guards for the White House, provides parades and music for Washington-area events, provides security for the nearby Washington Navy Yard, and supports the Marine Corps Schools at Quantico.

There also is a security force training company at Chesapeake, Virginia.

The battalion has more than 2,300 Marine Corps and Navy per-sonnel assigned.

(A Pacific Security Force Battalion had been established with headquarters at Mare Island, California. That unit has been dises-tablished, with the Atlantic battalion now having worldwide responsibilities.)

Chemical, Biological Incident Response Force. Personnel of this unit are specially trained to respond to terrorist use of chemical or biological agents and weapons. The unit is the Department of Defense's premier complete incident response force; it is capable of providing agent detection and identification, casualty search and rescue, personnel decontamination, emergency medical care, and stabilization of contaminated personnel.

Since its establishment in February 1996, the force has support-ed 12 national special security events, including the Atlanta Olympics, two presidential inaugurations, and every State of the Union address. The force also participated in Operation Noble Eagle, responding to biological threats in the Longworth and Hart office buildings in Washington, D.C.

Anti-Terrorism Battalion. This is the 3rd Battalion, 8th Marine Regiment, which has undergone specialized training, including urban conflict and enhanced marksmanship. The battalion, based at Camp Lejeune, has more than 700 Marine and Navy personnel assigned.

One other specialized Marine organization warrants attention here: Marine Corps Detachment 1, which was established on 20 June 2003 as a "proof of concept" for Marine special operations forces. The detachment initially had 86 men assigned.

Previously, the Marine Corps had shunned the formation of a special operations component, believing that all Marine units were capable of such operations. Indeed, all deploying MEUs are Special Operations Capable (SOC), having undergone specialized security, hostage rescue, and anti-terrorism training prior to for-ward deployment.

Figure 7-1. NOTIONAL MAGTF STRUCTURE

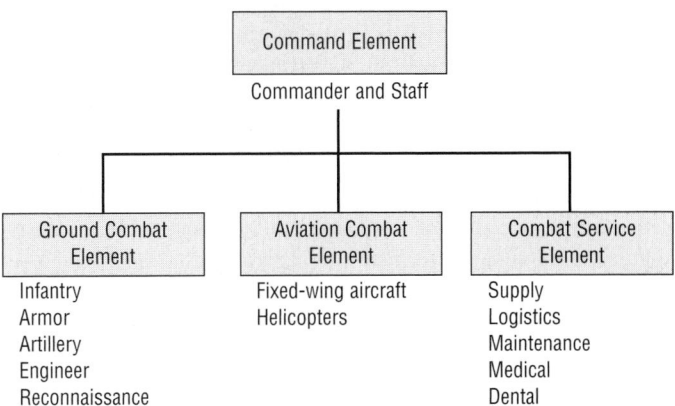

Detachment 1 was stood up at Camp Pendleton, California, and was transferred to the operational control of the U.S. Special Operations Command in December 2003. It has since deployed to the U.S. Central Command's area of operations (i.e., the Middle East) with a Navy special warfare component.

The Marine Corps no longer provides Marine security detach-ments on board U.S. Navy ships. The last detachment was in the carrier GEORGE WASHINGTON (CVN 73) and departed the ship on 3 April 1998. It consisted of one officer and 25 enlisted Marines; prior to the early 1990s force reductions, Marine carrier detach-ments numbered two officers and 64 enlisted men.

Marines had been on board U.S. warships virtually without interruption from the Corps' founding in 1775. During the 20th century, Marine security detachments were found on board aircraft carriers, battleships, the larger cruisers (CA/CAG/CB/CL/CLG), and some submarine tenders, the last to provide security for nuclear warheads in submarine-launched ballistic missiles.

MARINE FORCES

The Marine Forces (MARFOR) Atlantic and Pacific are organized as Marine Air-Ground Task Forces (MAGTF) and are employed either as a component of naval expeditionary forces or as part of joint or combined forces.

From 1933 to 1994, the Marines assigned to fleets were desig-nated the Fleet Marine Force (FMF); they provided the tactical and support organizations for amphibious operations. Following Operations Desert Shield and Desert Storm in the Persian Gulf, in July 1994, the term FMF was dropped in favor of Marine Forces. During the Gulf campaign, the Marines ashore in Saudi Arabia became the Marine component of the Central Command (CENT-COM), on an equal basis with the Army, Air Force, and Navy com-ponents. (The Marine forces afloat in the Gulf were under the Navy component commander.)

The Marine Corps is a "combined arms" force possessing armor and heavy artillery, infantry units, and a large tactical air arm, including fixed-wing aircraft and helicopters. It is the only such service with its own air arm, except for a small number of helicopters and light fixed-wing aircraft flown by the British and Russian marines. (The U.S. Marine Corps aviation structure is described in Chapter 27, and Marine Corps aircraft are listed in Chapter 28).

The Marine Corps is organized into three ground divisions and three aircraft wings[3], with a large combat support force formed

---

3 The Marine Corps strength of three active divisions and three active aircraft wings is specified in legislation, the only service with that peculiarity.

into three service support groups. The Marine Corps Reserve consists of an additional division, aircraft wing, and support group. Since the start of World War II, the Marine Corps has followed a basic triangular organization, with each division having three infantry regiments (plus an artillery regiment); each infantry regiment having three rifle battalions; and each battalion having three rifle companies (plus a weapons company).[4]

The combined arms regiments established in the early 1990s have been replaced by a third infantry regiment, with tanks and light armored vehicles formed into separate battalions.

Marine divisions are believed to be the world's largest; the 1st Marine Division (the largest) has a strength of 20,231 Marines and 1,455 Navy personnel. Figures 7-2 through 7-4 show the nominal division organization. Total personnel varies among the division and component units because of differing organizations, especially artillery regiments, and personnel shortfalls in some units.

Marine divisions generally are considered to be "mechanized" combat units. Each has a single tank battalion with 58 M1A1 Abrams tanks mounting 120-mm guns. The division's light armored vehicle battalion has 116 wheeled light armored vehicles, 16 of which mount anti-tank missiles. The Marines also employ AAV-series tracked amphibious vehicles for battlefield transport; however, those vehicles are limited to the role of armored personnel carriers (see Chapter 20).

The three Marine artillery regiments (10th, 11th, and 12th Marines) were reorganized in late 1992, with each regiment assigned three or four direct support battalions, and each battalion having three firing batteries with six M198 155-mm towed howitzers. In the mid-1990s, the artillery regiments again were reorganized to better support MEU deployments; two regiments have four artillery battalions and the 12th Marine Regiment has only two (18 howitzers per battalion).

In addition to the 155-mm howitzers, each MEF has available 48 M101A1 105-mm towed howitzers for use in special contingencies where the 16,000-pound (7,258-kg) M198s are not suitable. The present plan is to retain the M198s in artillery battalions until the Marine Corps receives the lightweight 155-mm howitzer LW 155, which weighs less than 9,000 pounds (4,082 kg).[5] The LW 155—with the little used military designation M777—will replace all Marine M198s, with an initial operational capability expected in 2005 and total replacement accomplished within three years.

In addition, the Marine Corps is acquiring the High-Mobility Artillery Rocket System (HIMARS). This system is mounted on the chassis of a five-ton truck and carries a six-pack of Multiple Launch Rocket System (MLRS) rockets. The MLRS missile weighs about 675 pounds (306 kg), including a 200-pound (91-kg) warhead. Its range, with guided projectiles available, is out to 37 miles (60 km).

HIMARS, originally deployed in 1983, is in service with the U.S. Army and several other nations. The Marine Corps, which earlier rejected the MLRS, will field one battery in 2005–2006, with one active battalion and one reserve battalion planned to enter service about 2007.

Today, Marine divisions and wings can be considered primarily as administrative structure, as Marine units deploy in MAGTF formations; see below.

Marine divisions have minimal organic combat service support. What they have is provided by a Force Service Support Group (FSSG) assigned to each division/wing MEF or to four MEUs simultaneously. Each FSSG has a nominal strength of 7,951 Marines and 1,208 Navy personnel, although changes are being made in the support structure, as well as in the Marine combat organizations (see Figure 7-5).

Figure 7-2. MARINE CORPS DIVISION*

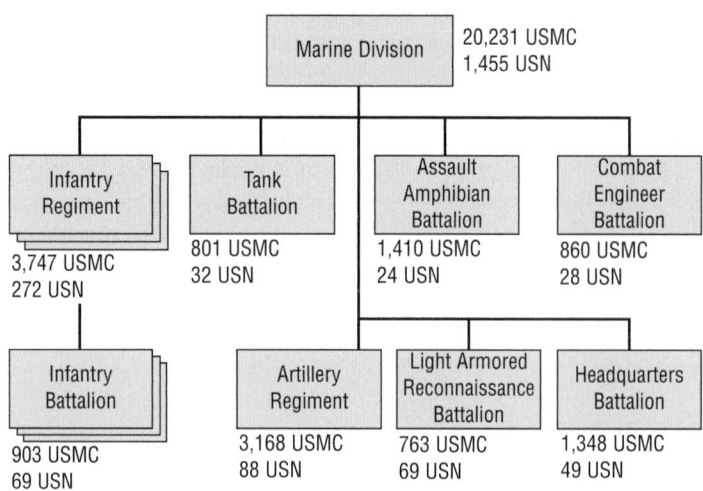

* Based on 1st Marine Division

Figure 7-3. MARINE INFANTRY BATTALION

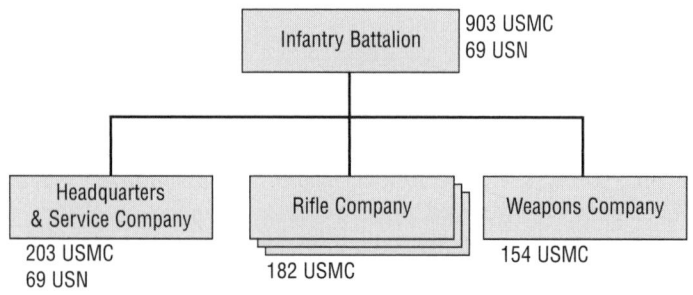

Figure 7-4. NOMINAL ARTILLERY REGIMENT

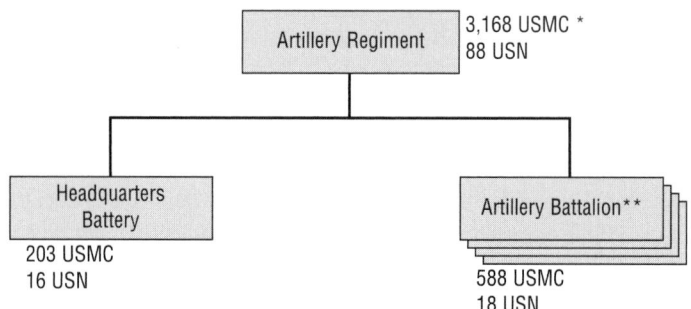

* Includes non-headquarters support components.

** The 10th and 11th Marine Regiments each have four artillery battalions; the 12th Marine Regiment has two battalions.

The Marine Corps does not have medical, dental, or chaplain personnel, but relies on the Navy to provide these services. These Navy personnel are fully integrated into Marine units and, when in the field, dress in Marine uniform. In turn, Marine representatives are assigned to all appropriate Navy staffs, including those of the Secretary of the Navy and the Office of the Chief of Naval Operations (OPNAV). A Marine major general serves as Director, Expeditionary Warfare, in OPNAV (code N85), and the lieutenant general who serves as Deputy Chief of Staff for Aviation at Marine

---

4 In 1988–1989, eight Marine battalions, designated as MEU(SOC), were provided with a fourth rifle company. However, the drawdown of Marine strength forced a reduction to three rifle companies in those battalions during 1991.

5 The M198 can be helicopter lifted only by the CH-53E Super Stallion, the largest helicopter in the West. The LW 155 howitzer can be lifted by the CH-46E Sky Knight and CH-53D Sea Stallion helicopters, as well as by the CH-53E.

Figure 7-5. FORCE SERVICE SUPPORT GROUP

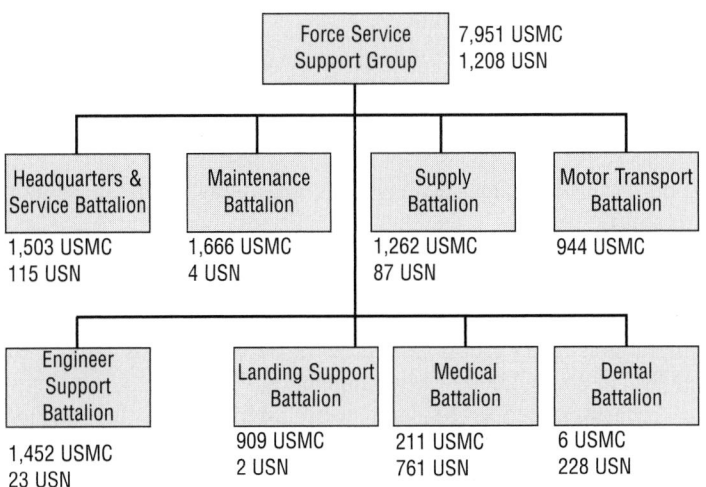

Headquarters also is assigned as Principal Advisor, Marine Aviation (code N88M), to the Director of Air Warfare Division in OPNAV.

MARINE AIR-GROUND TASK FORCES

The Marine Forces are the amphibious assault component of what now are called Naval Expeditionary Forces—Marine assault units, amphibious ships, supporting carrier task forces, and other forces required to project U.S. military power by sea.

The combined arms MAGTF—pronounced "*MAG*-taf"—can be tailored to the size and composition required to meet a broad range of operational requirements and for transport by various methods. There are three generic types of MAGTFs:
• Marine Expeditionary Unit (MEU)
• Marine Expeditionary Brigade (MEB)
• Marine Expeditionary Force (MEF)
During the 1980s, some MEUs underwent special training and qualifications to be designated as special operations capable. All deploying MEUs now are SOC qualified and are considered capable of carrying out six missions: amphibious raids, security opera-

tions (e.g., of an embassy), Noncombatant Evacuation Operations (NEO), direct action, humanitarian/civic assistance, and Tactical Recovery of Aircraft and Personnel (TRAP).

Each MAGTF has four fundamental elements that are drawn from the ground divisions, aircraft wings, and support groups as needed; those elements are shown in Table 7-2 and Figure 7-1.

The buildup of MAGTFs from the component "building blocks" is not linear. For example, while a Marine regiment and aircraft group are the ground and air elements of a MEB, a division–wing team cannot form three MEBs because of the shortfall of command and support units. Thus, the Marine Corps—with three divisions and three wings—can effectively deploy two MEFs or perhaps four MEBs, plus some smaller units.

The MAGTFs, when established in the late 1970s, were not intended to be permanent organizations but were to be "task organized for a specific mission and, after completion of that mission, . . . dissolved."[6] In the 1980s, however, they took on an increasingly permanent structure. The shift came in large part because of commitments to "marrying" Marine combat units with weapons and material in Maritime Prepositioning Ships (MPS) deployed in various ocean areas and prepositioned ashore in Norway. The permanent assignment of MAGTFs to specific prepositioned equipment and to specific geographic areas has reduced the flexibility of Marine units.

During 1992, as a consequence of force level reductions and lessons learned in Desert Shield/Desert Storm, the Marine Corps began to reform its MAGTF structure. There currently are 14 permanent MAGTF command elements—3 MEFs, 4 MEBs, and 7 MEUs, including the 4th MEB(AT), which is not a "line" organization.

The standing MEUs are:
• *Camp Pendleton, California*
  11th, 13th, 15th
• *Camp Lejeune, North Carolina*
  22nd, 24th, 26th
• *Okinawa*
  31st

---

6 Commanding General, Marine Corps Development and Educational Command, *Marine Air-Ground Task Force Doctrine* (FMFM 0-1) (Quantico, Va., June 1978), p. 1-5.

Table 7-2. MARINE AIR-GROUND TASK FORCE ORGANIZATIONS

	Marine Expeditionary Force (MEF)	Marine Expeditionary Brigade (MEB)	Marine Expeditionary Unit (MEU)
Total personnel*	1,000–4,000	4,000–18,000	30,000–60,000
Commander	colonel	brigadier general	lieutenant general
Ground combat element	infantry battalion	infantry regiment	one or more divisions
Aviation combat element	composite squadron (helicopters + STOVL)	aircraft group	aircraft wing
Combat service support element	MEU service support group	brigade service support group	force service support group
Self-sustainment capability	15 days	30 days	60 days
Amphibious lift	4–6 ships	21–26 ships	approx. 50 ships
Major equipment	5 tanks	17 tanks	70 tanks
	8 155-mm howitzers	24 155-mm howitzers	108 155-m howitzers
	8 81-mm mortars	6 8-inch (203-mm) howitzers	12 8-inch (203-mm) howitzers
	9 60-mm mortars	24 81-mm mortars	72 81-mm mortars
	32 Dragon anti-tank launchers	27 60-mm mortars	81 60-mm mortars
	8 TOW anti-tank launchers**	96 Dragon anti-tank launchers	288 Dragon anti-tank launchers
	12 assault amphibian vehicles	48 TOW anti-tank launchers	144 TOW anti-tank launchers
	5 Stinger SAM teams	47 assault amphibian vehicles	208 assault amphibian vehicles
	6 fixed-wing aircraft (STOVL)	36 light armored vehicles	147 light armored vehicles
	~20 helicopters	6 Hawk SAM launchers	24 Hawk SAM launchers
		15 Stinger SAM teams	75 Stinger SAM teams
		~75 fixed-wing aircraft	~150 fixed-wing aircraft
		~100 helicopters	~150 helicopters

* Varies with tactical situation, level of combat, etc.

** Additional TOW launchers are mounted on AH-1 SeaCobra helicopters.

The MEUs are sized to be carried by a Navy Amphibious Squadron (PhibRon), which, when combined with the MEU and other naval forces, forms an ESG.

MARINE FORCE MOBILITY

Mobility is a principle of naval operations and is a key characteristic of the FMF. There are several aspects to FMF mobility:

Forward afloat forces. Marine units normally are afloat in amphibious ships in forward areas—one in the Mediterranean area and one in the Pacific–Indian Ocean area. At times, additional MEUs or larger formations are at sea, in transit to relieve forward-deployed MEUs or for exercises. As a crisis begins to evolve, the afloat MEUs, like other naval forces, can be dispatched to the problem area without intruding on foreign territory or air space.

Amphibious assault. The Marines have a significant amphibious assault capability employing helicopters, landing craft, and vehicles from the Navy's amphibious ships. The existing amphibious force has a theoretical lift capacity of the assault echelon of approximately one MEF, i.e., a reinforced division and the helicopter and STOVL portions of an aircraft wing.[7] (The "assault echelon" is the portion of the force that makes the actual landing—about two-thirds of the troops, one-half the vehicles, and one-quarter of the cargo of the unit.)

Recent reductions in the fleet have meant a decline in lift capacity to only 2½ MEBs, i.e., reinforced regiments.

Maritime prepositioning. Three squadrons of maritime prepositioning ships are forward deployed, one in the Atlantic, one off Diego Garcia in the Indian Ocean, and one off the Mariana Islands in the Western Pacific. Each carries weapons, vehicles, equipment, munitions, and provisions for a MEB (see Chapter 8). These ships can be sent into a port to be "married" with Marines flown into the area by transport aircraft. While this force does not have the ability to make a forcible entry—it requires a friendly port or sheltered unloading area and nearby airfield—the viability of the MPS concept was demonstrated in Operation Desert Shield in August 1991 and in the buildup for the invasion of Iraq in 2003.

Airlift. Marines, like other light combat forces, can be airlifted into an area by transport aircraft. The Marine Corps has a small force of C-130 Hercules transport-tanker aircraft, but a sizeable troop commitment would require the use of U.S. Air Force transport aircraft.

Aircraft carriers. In 1992, the U.S. Atlantic Command began examining the feasibility of putting Marine *ground* combat troops aboard large-deck carriers. The reported rationale for such a move was to:
• Better justify large-deck carriers by giving them an assault capability
• Provide more fleet flexibility by being able to rapidly embark a Marine assault force in a carrier
• Provide an assault capability in an area without deploying an amphibious ready group, i.e., three to five amphibious ships with a MEU of some 2,000 Marines embarked.

Accordingly, 538 Marines were embarked in the carrier THEODORE ROOSEVELT (CVN 71) in mid-January 1993 for a month of at-sea training and workup. Designated as a Special-Purpose Marine Air-Ground Task Force (SPMAGTF), the group consisted of a rifle company (190 men) from the 3rd Battalion, 6th Marines; a command staff and various detachments, including an 18-man reconnaissance platoon; and a heavy helicopter squadron (HMH-362) with a component from a utility and attack helicopter squadron (HMLA-167) with six CH-53 Sea Stallion and four UH-1N Huey helicopters.[8]

Following the month-long workup, on 11 March 1993, the ROOSEVELT battle group departed Norfolk, steaming for the Mediterranean and a six-month deployment as a component of the Sixth Fleet. Aboard the carrier—in addition to the 638 Marines—was Carrier Air Wing (CVW) 8. To make space for the Marines and their helicopters, CVW 8 left on the beach anti-submarine squadron VS-24 with the wing's S-3B Vikings. In addition, Marine squadron VMFA-312 with F/A-18C Hornets was embarked in the carrier in place of CVW-8's second F-14 Tomcat squadron.

The loss of the Vikings was of particular concern to some Navy

---

7 The term VSTOL, for Vertical/Short Take-Off and Landing, was used by the Marine Corps until early 1995, when the term STOVL was adopted by Headquarters, Marine Corps.
8 The aviation personnel totaled about 230 men.

Marines on patrol: (left) Troops from the 15th Marine Expeditionary Unit patrol the streets of Nasiriyah, Iraq; (right) fellow "leathernecks" pass through a dry creek bed while searching caves in Khowst, Afghanistan. Marines are at the forefront in the war against terrorism, with other units serving afloat and ashore around the world. (U.S. Marine Corps/Brian L. Wickliffe, Justin M. Mason)

planners, not only because of their anti-submarine prowess, but also because of their effectiveness for general surveillance and their value as tankers for extending the range of the Hornets. The two latter roles could have been of particular importance as the ROOSEVELT operated in the Adriatic Sea area, supporting efforts to stop the racial fighting in the former Yugoslavia.

Although the Atlantic Command had at one point envisioned the Marines aboard the ROOSEVELT as a substitute for an ARG, in fact, an ARG with a MEU embarked also was deployed in the Med. But the focus was on the ROOSEVELT and the 600-man SPMAGTF.

The deployment identified a number of problems with Marines aboard large-deck carriers (see 17th Edition/pages 43–44). There were benefits and lessons learned, but they were far outweighed by the costs and disadvantages, and the concept was not continued.

MARINE AVIATION

The Marine Corps has a large aviation component, with some 900 aircraft in the active force, most in three aircraft wings, and some 200 aircraft in the reserve force, assigned to a single aircraft wing.

All Marine aviators are trained by the Naval Air Training Command, a joint Navy–Marine Corps organization.

There is an increasing move to merge Navy and Marine Corps aviation on an operational basis. For example, most aircraft carriers are being provided with a Marine F/A-18 Hornet squadron, and a Navy F/A-18 squadron normally is forward deployed with Marine Aircraft Group 12 at Iwakuni, Japan.[9]

The interchange of Navy–Marine F/A-18 squadrons is in part in compensation for the reduction in total Navy and Marine F/A-18 units from the current 64 to 59 within the next few years. Some analysts, however, question the efficacy of this interchange, as Navy and Marine aviation units have some different roles and missions, although their aircraft and weapons are similar. For example, according to one press report:

Instead of practicing carrier landings and doing air wing training, the

Marines maintain an M1A1 Abrams main battle tank in Kuwait. The Marine Corps—like the Army—is moving toward "lighter" units, especially with a British-developed 155-mm howitzer replacing the "overweight" M198 howitzer.(U.S. Marine Corps/Kevin C. Quihuis Jr.)

VFA-97's pilots participated in a mini-Combined Arms Exercise with a Marine battalion at the Marine Corps Air Ground Combat Center in Twenty-nine Palms, Calif., in March [2004].[10]

MARINE FORCES RESERVE

The Marine Forces Reserve (formerly Marine Corps Reserve) consists of the 4th Marine Division, 4th MAW, and 4th FSSG. These units generally parallel active units in organization, but in some categories they have older equipment and lack several service support components. Based on command problems during the reserve call-up in Desert Shield and Desert Storm, the Marine Corps in 1992 reorganized its reserves under one command structure. The Marine Forces Reserve oversees the training, equipping, and leadership of the Marine reserve components.

---

9 The first Navy squadron to deploy was VFA-97, which reached Iwakuni in September 2004 for a six-month deployment.
10 Christopher Munsey, "Navy Pilots Get a Taste of Leatherneck Training," *Navy Times* (27 September 2004), p. 18.

An AV-8B Harrier lands aboard the amphibious assault ship BATAAN (LHD 5) in the Red Sea during Operation Iraqi Freedom. The ship operated two squadrons of Harriers—24 aircraft—during the operation, as did the BONHOMME RICHARD (LHD 6). At the same time, the KEARSARGE (LHD 3) and SAIPAN (LHA 2) had all-helicopter air groups, demonstrating the flexibility of sea-based Marine aviation. (U.S. Navy/Jonathan Carmichael)

Table 7-3. MARINE CORPS BASING

ACTIVE COMPONENTS
Beaufort, S.C.
   Marine Aircraft Group 31
Camp H. M. Smith, Hawaii
   Headquarters Marine Force Pacific
Camp Lejeune, N.C.
   Headquarters II Marine Expeditionary Force
   2nd Marine Division
      2nd, 6th, 8th Marine Regiments (infantry)
      10th Marine Regiment (artillery)
      2nd Tank Battalion
      2nd Assault Amphibian Battalion
      2nd Combat Engineer Battalion
      2nd Light Armored Reconnaissance Battalion
   2nd Force Service Support Group
   2nd Marine Aircraft Wing
   2nd Marine Expeditionary Brigade
   4th Marine Expeditionary Brigade (AT)
   Marine Transport Squadron (VMR) 1
Camp Pendleton, Calif.
   Headquarters I Marine Expeditionary Force
   1st Marine Division
      1st, 5th Marine Regiments (infantry)
      11th Marine Regiment (artillery)
      1st Combat Engineer Battalion
      3rd Assault Amphibian Battalion
   1st Force Service Support Group
   Marine Aircraft Group 39
Cherry Point, N.C.
   Marine Aircraft Group 14
Japan
   Marine Aircraft Groups 12, 36
Kaneohoe, Hawaii
   3rd Marine Regiment (infantry)
   1th Marine Regiment (artillery)
   Marine Aircraft Group 24
Miramar, California
   Marine Aircraft Groups 11, 16

New River, N.C.
   Marine Aircraft Groups 26, 29
Norfolk, Va.
   Headquarters Marine Force Atlantic
Okinawa
   Headquarters III Marine Expeditionary Force
      (Camp Courtney)
   Headquarters I Marine Aircraft Wing
   3rd Marine Division
      4th Regiment (infantry)
   3rd Marine Expeditionary Brigade
   31st Marine Expeditionary Unit
   3rd Force Service Support Group
Twenty-nine Palms, Calif.
   7th Marine Regiment (infantry)
   3rd Tank Battalion
   3rd Amphibious Assault Battalion
Yuma, Ariz.
   Marine Aircraft Group 13

RESERVE COMPONENTS
Dallas, Texas
   14th Marine Regiment (artillery)
Fort Worth, Texas
   Marine Aircraft Group 41
Kansas City, Mo.
   24th Marine Regiment
New Orleans, La.
   Headquarters Marine Forces Reserve
   4th Marine Division
   4th Force Service Support Group
Overland Park, Kan.
   Reserve Support Command
San Rafael, Calif.
   23rd Marine Regiment
Worcester, Mass.
   25th Marine Regiment

As of 1 March 2004, the Marine Corps Reserve was more than 98,000 strong—59 percent (58,571) in the Individual Ready Reserve, and 41 percent (40,235) assigned to reserve units, either as drilling members or Active Reserve Marines, or in the training pipeline for units.

Marine reservists (other than Active Reserve Marines) have training sessions on a weekly or monthly basis and for two weeks during the summer. The latter periods include participation in exercises with active units in the United States and overseas.

Following the events of 11 September 2001, there have been wide-scale call-ups of Marine reservists. Through 1 April 2004, there have been 27,389 reserve activations in response to both internal and joint operational requirements. During the peak of Operation Enduring Freedom and Operation Iraqi Freedom, the Marine Corps had 21,316 reservists on active duty. These call-ups included reserve aviation units. As of 18 March 2004, there were 5,125 reserve Marines on active duty in worldwide operations.

Marine reservists also have been employed in efforts to halt illegal immigration along the U.S. border with Mexico. And in 2004, 335 Marines reservists volunteered to deploy to participate in Operation UNITAS, the joint U.S.–South American naval exercise.

Historical. The Marine Corps was established on 10 November 1775 by the Continental Congress, with two battalions of troops raised who were "good seamen, or so acquainted with maritime affairs as to be able to serve to advantage by sea, when required." Subsequently, Marines have fought in almost all U.S. conflicts.

The Corps reached a peak strength of 485,000 men and women during World War II, with six divisions and five aircraft wings (plus numerous separate squadrons).

During the 1950s, the United States began maintaining battalion landing teams (and later MEUs) afloat, embarked in amphibious ships, in the Mediterranean, Western Pacific, and, at times, in the Caribbean and Persian Gulf areas.

The Marine Corps always has been a separate service within the Navy Department. Its senior officer is the Commandant, with the rank of full general. He is a member of the Joint Chiefs of Staff (JCS) and is responsible for the readiness and training of the Marine Corps; he does not have operational command of Marine combat forces except as assigned by the JCS or Secretary of Defense.

CHAPTER 8

Military Sealift Command

The Military Sealift Command (MSC) carries out a multiplicity of tasks for the Navy and other military services and for defense agencies. Here, in preparation for operations in Iraq, the maritime prepositioning ship CPL LOUIS J. HAUGE, JR. (T-AK 3000) unloads Marine light armored vehicles in a Persian Gulf port. All MSC ships are civilian manned, although many have military security detachments, and some command ships have composite Navy–civilian crews. (U.S. Navy/Aaron Pineda)

Sealift is the term used for the movement of weapons and materiel to forward areas by sea. The Military Sealift Command (MSC) operates a variety of ships in support of the Department of Defense and the military services. The Commander, MSC, is a vice admiral, with headquarters at the Washington Navy Yard in Washington, D.C. Under a dual-command concept, he reports both to the Navy chain of command and to the unified Transportation Command, as well as to the Navy's fleet commanders, serving as a "type" commander for MSC-operated ships (see Figure 8-1).

There are five MSC area commands—each headed by a Navy captain—located in Norfolk, Virginia; San Diego, California; Naples, Italy; Yokohama, Japan; and Bahrain.[1] Smaller, subarea commands are located at other ports. These commands manage ship charters, cargo assignments, scheduling, and planning in their respective areas.

The MSC has more than 9,000 military and civilian personnel worldwide. As of 31 August 2004, these consisted of:
- 627 active-duty Navy personnel (144 officers, 483 enlisted)
- 1,017 civil service employees ashore
- 4,085 civil service employees afloat
- 3,420 civilian mariners under contract

In addition, there are 1,377 Naval Reserve personnel in MSC reserve units.

---

1 At the end of the 1991 Gulf War, MSC saw the need to establish a permanent office in the Persian Gulf area to coordinate operations, maintenance, and planning. In April 1992, the MSC Office Southwest Asia was established. It received the designation Task Force 53 from the Commander, Naval Forces, Central Command, and in February 1999, was elevated to the fifth MSC area command.

Vice Admiral David L. Brewer III, U.S. Navy, Commander, Military Sealift Command, since August 2001. (U.S. Navy)

Figure 8-1. MSC COMMAND RELATIONSHIPS

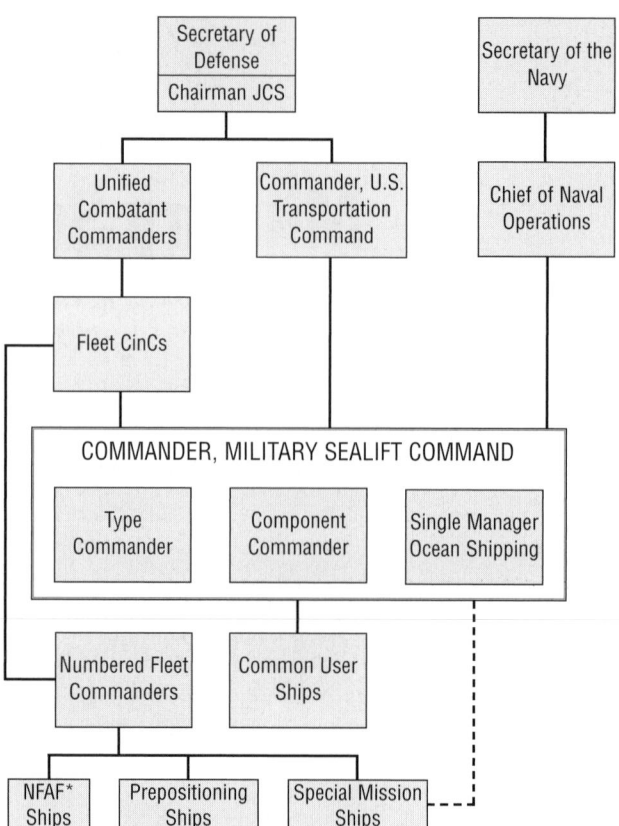

* NFAF = Naval Fleet Auxiliary Force

The MSC currently operates some 125 ships. All are civilian manned—although many have Navy communications and/or technical personnel on board (see Chapters 23, 24, and 25)—or are under long-term charter to commercial firms. In addition, a large number of Navy-owned ships are laid up under various programs, although some these vessels are activated periodically for exercises or to handle special cargo requirements.

The ships are managed by MSC ship programs; these are designated PM (for Program Manager):

- PM 1 Naval Fleet Auxiliary Force (NFAF)
- PM 2 Special Mission Ships
- PM 3 Prepositioning Ships
- PM 4 Ship Introduction

All MSC ships with Navy designations have the prefix T-. Navy-owned ships have USNS, for United States Naval Ship, before their names; other ships have the prefix SS (Steamship), MV (Motor Vessel), or RV (Research Vessel).

NAVAL FLEET AUXILIARY FORCE

The MSC currently operates 38 naval auxiliary ships that provide direct support to the fleet. These ships are described in Chapter 23.

The current NFAF consists of 33 underway replenishment ships (AE/AFS/AO/AOE types) and the Navy's five operational fleet tugs (ATF).[2] These ships are operated by civil service mariners, and some have small Navy detachments on board to provide communications and to support ordnance handling and helicopter operations.

In addition, the Navy's two hospital ships, the MERCY (T-AH 19) and COMFORT (T-AH 20), which are maintained in reduced operating status, can be fully activated, crewed, and ready for deployment with MSC operating crews. These are considered both auxiliary and sealift ships, the latter because of their probable deployment to support forward-deployed U.S. ground forces (as in the 1991 Gulf War). In addition, the hospital ships periodically are activated for forward deployment in peacetime to provide their hospital facilities to other nations.

(Although the Navy's two aviation support ships [AVB] are considered by the MSC to be prepositioning ships rather than auxiliary ships, because of their ability to support the Marine forces they are listed with other fleet auxiliary ships in Chapter 23.)

The Navy's four salvage ships of the SAFEGUARD (ARS 50) class are expected to be transferred to the MSC as NFAF ships.

SPECIAL MISSION SHIPS

The MSC provides and operates ships to support specialized military activities, especially oceanographic and hydrographic sur-

veys, undersea surveillance, acoustic research, missile range instrumentation, and the collection of telemetry intelligence against foreign missile tests. Currently, 23 ships operated by the MSC are in this category. Of these, 17 are naval auxiliary ships (AGM/AGOR/AGOS/AGS/ARC types). This is a major reduction from the end of the Cold War era, when there were 20 T-AGOS/SURTASS ocean surveillance ships and a large number of research ships in MSC service. (Only four T-AGOS sonar surveillance ships remain in service in that role.)

Also in this category are the high-speed vessel SWIFT (HSV 2) and five service craft that provide specialized services for the Navy.

The MSC provides onboard support for the fleet flagships BLUE RIDGE (LCC 19) and CORONADO (AGF 11). This includes MSC civil service mariners providing navigation, deck, engineering, laundry, galley, cleaning, and other services.

Special mission ships are both government-owned and chartered, and they are operated by either civil service mariners or contract employees. These ships and craft embark both Navy and civilian scientists and technicians in addition to their civilian crews.

PREPOSITIONING SHIPS

There currently are 37 prepositioning ships operated by the MSC. These ships are kept forward deployed with equipment, weapons, provisions, potable water, fuels, and other materiel for the Army, Navy, Marine Corps, and Air Force.

There are several categories of prepositioning ships. Most of these ships—described in Chapter 24—are specialized cargo ships that have been extensively converted or built specifically for the prepositioning role. In particular, they are configured for handling

---

2 The only Navy-manned underway replenishment ships are four fast combat support ships of the SACRAMENTO (AOE 1) class.

heavy military vehicles, containerized cargo, and break-bulk cargo. They are supplemented by standard cargo ships and tankers.[3]

Historical. The forward-deployed or prepositioning concept was introduced on a large scale by Secretary of Defense Robert S. McNamara in the mid-1960s, when he proposed a force of 30 Fast Deployment Logistic (FDL) ships be constructed in addition to a force of long-range transport aircraft. Congress refused to fund the FDL ships, but the aircraft were developed as the C-5 Galaxy program. The Department of Defense did modify several cargo ships and tank landing ships (LSTs) that then were forward deployed carrying supplies and munitions, including nuclear weapons.

SEALIFT

The MSC sealift program is responsible for the fleet of tankers and dry cargo ships that carry cargo for all Department of Defense agencies and military services. Most of these ships are U.S.-flag commercial vessels chartered to carry specific cargoes; however, the MSC does own four tankers and has long-term charters for two tankers and 20 dry cargo ships.

For surge sealift, in peacetime, crisis, or war, the MSC looks first to the charter market. If suitable U.S.-flag ships are not available, it can activate Fast Sealift Ships (FSS) or Ready Reserve Force (RRF) ships.

Fast Sealift Ships (FSS). These are the world's fastest oceangoing cargo ships, acquired in the 1980s specifically to carry Army tanks, armored personnel carriers, and other combat vehicles and trucks. There are eight of these 33-knot, roll-on/roll-off ships, which combined can carry the equipment of an Army heavy (mechanized) division.

The FSS ships are kept in U.S. ports and can be activated and under way in four days. (It will take the Army at least that long to transport, by rail, the vehicles from their home bases to ports of embarkation.)

Ready Reserve Force (RRF). This is a fleet of some 70 reserve ships maintained and crewed by the Maritime Administration that can be activated in 4, 5, 10, or 20 days.[4] These ships include roll-on/roll-off cargo ships, break-bulk ships, barge carriers, auxiliary crane ships, tankers, and two small troop ships. The last are employed as state maritime training ships.

Several RRF ships provide unique capabilities for handling bulky, oversize military equipment. The shortage of roll-on/roll-off ships in U.S. commercial services makes the RRF especially valuable. When activated, the RRF ships come under the operational control of the MSC.

These ships are laid up at various U.S. ports.

SHIP INTRODUCTION

This MSC program is responsible for overseeing ship acquisitions, including the transfer of auxiliary ships from active Navy to MSC status, new ship construction, and conversions and modifications of merchant-type ships.

This program also manages the Department of Defense national defense features program that seeks to provide features in U.S.-flag merchant ships that would make them useful for military sealift, such as reinforced roll-on/roll-off ramps, strengthened vehicle decks, and heavy cargo cranes.

Historical. The Military Sealift Command was established in response to an August 1949 directive by the Secretary of Defense making the Secretary of the Navy the single manager for ocean transportation within the defense establishment. Previously, four separate government agencies (including the Army and Navy) controlled oceangoing merchant ships.

The Military Sea Transportation Service (MSTS), based on the Naval Ocean Transport Service (NOTS), was established within the Navy on 1 October 1949. The following year, oceangoing cargo ships and transports of the Army Transportation Corps were transferred to the MSTS. Through 1950, additional Army ships

---

3 Tankers differ from oilers (or fleet oilers) in that the former are point-to-point petroleum carriers while the latter are rigged for the underway replenishment of ships at sea.

4 The Maritime Administration is an agency of the Department of Transportation; it was under the Department of Commerce from its establishment in 1950 until transferred to Transportation in 1981.

MSC-operated replenishment ships operate in forward areas to support Navy strike groups, as the USNS Supply *(T-AOE 6) shows during an Underway Replenishment (UNREP) of the missile cruiser* Vella Gulf *(CG 72). Munitions and provisions are transferred by helicopter to ships both alongside and miles away. But these UNREP ships are unarmed and hence a vulnerable component of naval operations. (U.S. Navy/Konstandinos Goumenidis)*

were transferred to the Navy agency. By 1950, the Army had transferred to Navy–MSTS control:

- 4 AF refrigerated cargo ships
- 13 AK cargo ships
- 3 AKL light cargo ships
- 5 AKV aircraft cargo ships
- 41 AP transports
- 1 APC coastal transport
- 1 ATA auxiliary tug
- 1 LST tank landing ship
- 2 YO fuel oil barges

Many of these ships and craft had been built for the Navy and subsequently transferred to the Army.

Under the aegis of the MSTS, some of these ships were manned by Navy crews (and designated USS) and others by civilian mariners (designated USNS). Other Navy ships were assigned to the MSTS with Navy crews. Initially, only the civilian-manned ships had the prefix T- added to their designations; this later was extended to include Navy-manned ships assigned to the MSTS. Some of the Navy-manned ships were armed. The last Navy crews went ashore in the 1960s, after which all ships were manned by civil service civilian or contract civilian crews.

The MSTS was renamed Military Sealift Command on 1 August 1970 to bring the name in line with the Air Force's Military Airlift Command (MAC).[5] The Military Airlift Command, however, was a specified command within the defense establishment, while the MSC remained a Navy command, reporting to the Chief of Naval Operations.[6]

On 1 July 1987, the unified U.S. Transportation Command (TRANSCOM) was established, with the MSC and the MAC as its principal components. The Commander, MSC, is a component commander of TRANSCOM.

MSC replenishment ships operate both Navy-manned MH-60S Knighthawk helicopters and civilian/contractor-operated SA 330J Puma helicopters. This Puma, from the UNREP ship SPICA *(T-AFS 9), is having a cargo sling attached during operations with the carrier* JOHN F. KENNEDY *(CV 67) in the Arabian Sea. (U.S. Navy/Joshua Karsten)*

---

5 The Air Force's Military Air Transport Service (MATS) was renamed Military Airlift Command on 1 January 1966; it was replaced on 1 June 1992 by the Air Mobility Command [AMC]. The AMC is responsible for both tactical and strategic airlift as well as aerial refueling operations.

6 A specified command was an organization under the Secretary of Defense/Chairman, Joint Chiefs of Staff, that was comprised mostly of personnel and resources from a single military service.

The heavily laden USNS BENAVIDEZ *(T-AKR 306) is one of a flotilla of large cargo-type ships employed to preposition or transport military equipment. All have major Roll-On/Roll-Off (RO/RO) capabilities, reflecting the enormous numbers of vehicles used by the U.S. Army and Marine Corps. Other ships are configured to carry specialized munition loads. (U.S. Navy/Paul Farley)*

CHAPTER 9

Naval Personnel

Sailors are the U.S. Navy's most important "component." Despite the arduous and extended operations in Afghanistan and Iraq, as well as forward deployments in other areas, Navy recruiting and reenlistment rates are very high. There is more concern over officer retention, with major problems in several officer categories. These men and women are undergoing inspection at Fleet Activities Sasebo, Japan. (U.S. Navy/Jonathan R. Kulp)

The decline of U.S. Navy personnel strength since the end of the Cold War was arrested in the late 1990s as the service sought to halt the reduction of the fleet at about 300 ships. At the start of the war against terrorism, however, Chief of Naval Operations Admiral Vern Clark opted to reduce Navy manpower by as many as 39,000 men and women and redirect the money saved to fund recapitalization efforts.[1]

The Navy plans to cut 7,900 active duty personnel during Fiscal Year (FY) 2005 to reach a year-end goal of 365,000. The reductions will come through the decommissioning of older ships, mili-

tary-to-civilian job conversions, more efficient manning, organizational realignment, and the elimination of duplicative jobs.

During the past year, the Navy has retained sailors at near historic rates, while, according to the Chief of Naval Personnel,

> focusing even more on the quality of both those we keep on the rolls and those we bring in through recruiting. Such efforts have combined to allow us to dramatically reduce accession goals. This, in turn, has

---

1 The planned 600-ship fleet of the Reagan administration would have required some 622,000 personnel for full manning.

Admiral Vern Clark, USN, Chief of
Naval Operations since July 2000.
(U.S. Navy/Johnny Bivera)

saved literally millions of dollars in training replacement personnel
while preserving knowledge, skills, abilities, and leadership experience within our ranks.

In 2003, we exceeded all aggregate retention goals for the third
straight year; our recruiters . . . met our annual active enlisted acces-
sion goal for the fifth straight year.[2]

To date, improving economic conditions and an emphasis on
higher recruit quality have not hurt overall Navy recruiting efforts.
Recruit quality is measured primarily by the percentage of high
school graduates, the number of recruits scoring in categories
I-IIIA or the top half on the Armed Forces Qualification Test
(AFQT), and the number of recruits possessing prior college experience. In FY 2003, the Navy accessed 94.3 percent high school
graduates, a significant improvement from the previous year's 91.9
percent and well above the Department of Defense (DoD) minimum standard of 90 percent. The Navy acquired 65.7 percent category I-IIIA recruits against a DoD minimum standard of 60 percent, and achieved a 40 percent increase in the percentage of
recruits with college experience. This situation occurred in spite of
an increase in Operational Tempo (OPTEMPO), or deployment
time, as the Navy has played key roles in the 2002 invasion of
Afghanistan and the 2003 invasion of Iraq.

Retention successes have enabled the Navy to reduce the acces-
sion rate over the past several years, but the service remains aware
that prevailing winds could change quickly, necessitating a sudden
surge in recruiting goals. Economic conditions that have proved
favorable to Navy retention and high recruiting rates are not
expected to continue. The 6.4 percent national unemployment rate
of June 2003 had decreased to 5.7 percent by December 2003 and
was projected to continue declining over the next two years.

The Navy, like the other military services, offers a variety of
other programs to provide incentive for skilled personnel to
remain in the service. Assignment Incentive Pay (AIP) is attract-
ing qualified sailors to hard-to-fill duty stations. AIP allows sailors
to bid for additional monetary compensation in return for service
at these locations, which in turn enhances combat readiness by
permitting market forces to distribute sailors to where they are
most needed. Less than a year after the pilot program began in
June 2003, more than 1,100 AIP bids had been processed, with
238 sailors receiving an average of $245 extra pay each month and
challenging duty assignments being filled without the forced
assignment of personnel.

The Navy also has a Selective Reenlistment Bonus (SRB) to
help retain enlisted personnel. This is used for sailors with critical
skills and has been a useful, albeit expensive, tool.

At the same time, turnover is required to maintain a reasonable
age spread among personnel. Careful management is required as
Navy manpower is reduced by some 39,000 men and women.

Also, under a program instituted by the Navy in the fall of 2004,
Chief Petty Officers (CPO) have assumed the role of division officers aboard the missile destroyer DECATUR (DDG 73). Chiefs serving as leading chief petty officers have moved into division officer
duties in 19 of DECATUR's 23 divisions. According to Rear Admiral
Terry Etnyre, Commander, Naval Surface Force, Atlantic Fleet,
"Chief petty officers are the backbone of the Navy, and allowing
them more responsibility in this pilot program will develop lessons
for potential future applications. The surface Navy is not doing
away with division officers and not trying to solve a problem. We
are interested in utilizing our enlisted talent in a new way in this
experiment."

These CPOs report directly to the department heads on the ship.
Four first-tour division officers are remaining in those positions.

"This will help keep an emphasis on professional leadership
growth for chiefs in seagoing billets, as opposed to multiple similar [leading] CPO jobs in their careers," said Etnyre. "It's an experiment many of us are interested in seeing the results of." The program is scheduled to last for one full personnel assignment cycle—
approximately two years—including an overseas deployment.

As enlisted personnel depart the service, the Navy is seeking to
retain some in civilian status. According to the Chief of Naval
Personnel, "After investing in sailors' career development for many
years, it makes sense to encourage them to continue contributing to
Navy as a civilian employee. In doing so, we retain the knowledge,
skills, and abilities they acquired through years of service and specialized training in the Navy."[3]

In addition, the Navy is transferring many uniformed jobs to the
civil sector. For example, in 2004–2005, the Navy is converting
1,768 officer and enlisted medical billets to civilian jobs.[4] This is in
line with the DoD policy of replacing military medical personnel
with civilians wherever possible. All are occurring at medical commands and facilities in the continental United States. No overseas
or deployable commands are affected.

A Navy spokesman said the enlisted medical conversions are
1,000 hospital corpsmen and 236 dental technicians, or about 4.4
percent of the 27,770 total billets in the two ratings. With respect
to officers, 532 billets will convert to civilian positions, i.e., 4.8
percent of the 11,109 personnel in the Navy's four medical sub-
communities. There are 187 Medical Service Corps officers, 158
Medical Corps (i.e., physicians), 103 Dental Corps, and 84 Nurse
Corps.

After this first wave of transfers is complete, the Navy still will
have 3,643 "nonreadiness" medical billets that have been identified as candidates for future conversion in the military-to-civilian
program.

Another issue with respect to enlisted personnel is the specter of
reinstatement of the draft. When conscription ended in 1973, the
U.S. armed forces became an all-volunteer force. So far, the
George W. Bush administration and the U.S. military leadership
have resisted returning to the draft because (1) recruiting for all
services is providing approximately the number of personnel
required, (2) a draft probably would require the induction of more
personnel than currently authorized, and (3) a draft would require
an enlarged basic training base, with inherent increases in costs for
facilities and training personnel. In addition, reinstating the draft
would raise the social issue of whether women would be included.

2 Vice Adm. Gerald L. Hoewing, USN, Chief of Naval Personnel and Deputy
  Chief of Naval Operations for Manpower and Personnel, testimony before the
  House Armed Services Committee, 24 March 2004.
3 Vice Adm. Hoewing, testimony before the House Armed Services Committee,
  24 March 2004.
4 Mark D. Faram, "Navy to Transfer 1,772 Medical Jobs to Civilians over the
  Next Year," Navy Times (4 October 2004), p. 17.

OFFICER PERSONNEL

Retention of officer personnel is a more complex issue, as each warfare and specialist community has a different set of goals and criteria for retention. Critical categories—pilots and submariners—receive large bonus payments for their commitments, also skewing analysis of the officer situation. For example, continuation pay for nuclear-qualified submarine officers who sign on for four or five additional years is $25,000 per year, in addition to their standard pay and submarine service pay. (Those signing on for three years rate $22,000 per year.) Still, shortages continue in the submarine and aviation officer categories.

In the surface warfare community, the shortage of department heads (lieutenants, lieutenant commanders) led to a massive assignment of extra junior officers (JOs) to surface ships in 2003–2004, to provide a "breeding ground" for department heads. Thus, a ship requiring 15 junior officers might have 20 or 25, in the hope that from that pool sufficient candidates could be sent to department head school. Obviously, such a surplus of JOs reduced their individual responsibilities as well as opportunities for realistic on-the-job training, while creating overcrowded conditions in "officers country" in those ships.

The submarine community appears to be especially vulnerable to officer shortfalls. Inadequate junior officer retention means demanding sea tours must be extended for still-serving officers in order to meet safety and readiness requirements. Excessively long department head tours, in turn, adversely impact junior officer retention, creating a downward spiral. At the same time, these officers, many graduates of prestigious colleges and having exceptional nuclear training, are in great demand in the civilian world.

This situation has again raised the issue of a two-track career system for the submarine community: nuclear engineering specialists and nonengineers, with the latter serving in the weapons, communications, and other nonengineering billets. The U.S. Navy had manned its submarines with both "non-nukes" and "nukes" until 1988, when the non-nuclear trained personnel were sent ashore, and all U.S. submarines now have all nuclear-trained officers (except for the research submarine DOLPHIN/AGSS 555).

Meanwhile, the Navy's officer corps is suffering from a succession of commanding officers (COs) being relieved of duty. As this edition of *Ships and Aircraft* went to press, more than a score had been "fired" within the past year. These have included surface, aviation, and submarine officers, most from afloat commands—including three aircraft carrier COs, and both Naval Academy and non-academy graduates. They have been lieutenant commanders up to vice admiral. The causes have included collisions at sea, sexual misconduct, misspending government funds, and several "relieved for cause" with no further explanation made to the public. There has been no recognizable pattern to any aspect of these firings.[5]

The situation has led to concern throughout the Navy, but there are no obvious or universal answers to this important and frustrating situation.

Table 9-1. NAVY STRENGTH (30 June 2004)

	Officers	Enlisted	Total
Active duty	55,592	316,783	372,375
FTS*	1,493	11,991	13,484
Reserve Units	15,833	51,902	67,735
USNA Midshipmen**	—	—	3,146

* FTS = Full Time Support; formerly Training and Administration of Reserves (TAR).
** U.S. Naval Academy. The academy had graduated 990 midshipmen on 28 May 2004. The class of 2008 is not included in this number. Thus, normal midshipmen strength is just over 4,000.

FLAG OFFICERS

The Navy continues to have fewer flag officers than there are general officers in the Army and Air Force. Table 9-2 shows the number of active-duty flag and general officers in the armed forces on 30 June 2004. As of that date, the Air Force had the highest ratio of generals to total force; the Army and Navy were about equal; and the Marine Corps had the lowest ratio. Of course, the Marine Corps

---

5 Two of the submarine commanding officers were relieved of duty during the past few years for actions that took place when squadron commanders were embarked in the submarines; the squadron commanders also were relieved.

Many Navy jobs are far "below decks," such as lighting off a boiler in the carrier JOHN F. KENNEDY (CV 67) during operations in the Persian Gulf. Machinist Mate 3rd Class Mahmoud Rayan and his colleagues work long, hard hours and, despite efforts such as Sea Swap, their deployment schedules are subject to frequent change. (U.S. Navy/William Hiembuch)

Table 9-2. FLAG & GENERAL OFFICER STRENGTH (30 June 2004)

	Navy	Marine Corps	Army	Air Force
General/Admiral	9	4	11	12
Lt. Gen./Vice Adm.	32	15	38	41
Maj. Gen./Rear Adm. (Upper Half)	69	21	102	81
Brig. Gen./Rear Adm. (Lower Half)	107	41	149	139
Totals	217	81	300	273

Table 9-3. FLAG OFFICER ASSIGNMENTS (30 June 2004)

	Admiral	Vice Admiral	Rear Admiral	Rear Adm.(LH)
Office of the Chief of Naval Operations	2	4	12	18
Naval activities afloat*	3	7	17	26
Systems Commands and Bureaus	1	3	3	10
Naval activities ashore**	7	32	28	
Unified, joint, allied commands	3	6	7	16

* Includes fleet commanders and staffs, and Military Sealift Command billets.
** Includes type commanders and subordinate commands.

receives all medical, dental, and chaplain support from the Navy, alleviating the need for flag officers in those categories. While a few Marine general officers service in the Office of the Chief of Naval Operations (OPNAV), those positions support both Navy and Marine Corps programs.

The overall number of admirals in all grades has declined since the end of Cold War, as the number of Navy formations (groups, wings, etc.) has declined. Since June 2004, the number of Navy four-star admirals has declined as unified combatant commands previously led by Navy admirals have gone to officers of other services.

The distribution of unrestricted line admirals on active duty in June 2004 is shown in Table 9-2. Such a list is, of necessity, somewhat arbitrary. Many officers, for example, are double-hatted: the admiral who serves as Commander, U.S. Naval Forces Europe, also serves as Commander, Allied Forces Southern Europe, a NATO command. Similarly, the vice admiral who serves as Chief of Naval Personnel (i.e., head of the Bureau of Naval Personnel), also holds the position of Deputy Chief of Naval Operations for Manpower and Personnel (N1) on the OPNAV staff.

Still, certain observations can be made: The two OPNAV admiral billets are the Chief of Naval Operations (CNO) and the Vice CNO. The admiral within the systems commands is the Director, Naval Nuclear Propulsion, certainly an inflated rank for the officer responsible primarily for nuclear reactor development and nuclear personnel training.[6]

The six other full admirals in the Navy in June 2004 were evenly divided between Navy commands (Commander, Fleet Forces Command; Commander, Naval Forces Europe; Commander, Pacific Fleet) and unified commands (Commander, U.S. Strategic Command; Commander, U.S. Pacific Command; Supreme Allied Commander, Transformation). The Supreme Allied Commander, Transformation, the NATO billet that formerly was Supreme Allied Commander, Atlantic (SACLant), also serves as Commander, U.S. Joint Forces Command, formerly the U.S. Atlantic Command (LantCom).

Historical: The Continental Congress named Esek Hopkins as commander-in-chief of the fleet in December 1775, a rank he held for a year. On 15 November 1776, it established four Navy flag ranks: Admiral, Vice Admiral, Rear Admiral, and Commodore.

These were the flag ranks in the Royal Navy at that time. But no officers were commissioned in those grades until 1862, apparently for fear of imitating the Royal Navy. The courtesy title of commodore was used by an officer commanding a squadron of ships. The honorific was retained until death but brought no extra pay.

Boatswain's Mate 3rd Class Michelle Atwell aboard the harbor tug MUSKEGON *(YTB 763) helps rig a line to assist the missile cruiser* COWPENS *(CG 63) at Naval Base Yokosuka, Japan. While many Navy jobs are considered high tech, a number still require muscle and traditional sailing skills. (U.S. Navy/Alan Warner)*

In 1857, Congress changed the designation "commodore" to "flag officer" and allowed each squadron commander to display the flag of vice admiral or rear admiral, the former for those having served 20 years or more as a captain, the latter for those with less than 20 years. Two years later, Charles Stewart was designated as senior flag officer.

With the size and importance of fleets in the Civil War, on 16 July 1862 Congress created the rank of rear admiral, to be held by not more than nine officers on active duty. Subsequently, Congress instituted the ranks of admiral and vice admiral for specific individuals in recognition of their wartime service.

The rapid growth of navies at the turn the century called for the appointment of more admirals. As early as March 1899, Congress divided the rear admiral list into upper and lower halves, although commodore periodically was reinstated in wartime. George Dewey, hero of the Battle of Manila Bay (1898), was promoted to Admiral of the Navy in 1903, a rank created especially for him by Congress and to date from March 1899. Dewey remained on active duty in that rank until his death in 1917.[7]

---

6 This position was established at the four-star level in 1973 when the incumbent, Admiral H. G. Rickover, was promoted to full admiral. On Rickover being relieved of duty in January 1982, Congress established the position at the four-star level with a legislated eight-year tenure.

7 Adm. Dewey never wore insignia above the rank of admiral (four stars).

The "temporary" ranks of admiral and vice admiral were thereafter assigned to officers on the basis of their positions; they reverted to rear admirals on leaving the four-star jobs. By 1941, the CNO, Commander-in-Chief, U.S. Fleet, and commanders of the Atlantic, Pacific, and Asiatic Fleets were full admirals.

During World War II, the massive size of the U.S. armed forces and the need to deal with British contemporaries led Congress to authorize five-star ranks in November 1944; for the Navy, this meant that four officers would be promoted to fleet admiral. In order of precedence, they were William D. Leahy, Chief of Staff to the president (and de facto Chairman of the Joint Chiefs of Staff); Ernest J. King, Commander-in-Chief, U.S. Fleet *and* Chief of Naval Operations; and Chester W. Nimitz, Commander-in-Chief, Pacific Ocean Areas, and Commander-in-Chief, Pacific Fleet. Disagreements between Secretary of the Navy James Forrestal and Admiral King led to the fourth officer not being named to five-star rank until December 1945. He was William F. (Bull) Halsey.[8]

With the death of Admiral Nimitz in 1966, the rank of fleet admiral ceased to exist.

WOMEN IN THE NAVY

Women in the Navy, especially in seagoing positions, continues to be an issue. Currently, the Navy prohibits women from serving in some 33,000 positions, about 25,000 of which are aboard submarines. The others are in the SEALs and in jobs that directly support Marine combat forces (i.e., medical, dental, chaplain, and liaison personnel assigned to Marine combat units).[9]

Women comprise just under 15 percent of the Navy's personnel strength. That is similar to the Army's percentage, but slightly lower than that of the Air Force (19 percent). The service with the lowest percentage of women on active duty is the Marine Corps (6 percent). Until her retirement on 1 October 2004, the senior female U.S. military officer was a Navy vice admiral. All services have female flag and general officers, with the Navy having three rear admirals and five lower-half rear admirals when this edition went to press.

Essentially all types of surface ships now have women in their crews, as do seagoing and land-based aviation squadrons. The obvious exception is submarines, although in 1999, then-Secretary of the Navy Richard Danzig raised that issue, stating:

> Congress and political power are changing. More and more, we see the role of women increasing in that regard. As that is the case, realistically, if the submarine force remains a white male bastion, it will wind up getting less and less support when it requires resources, when it has troubles.[10]

Mr. Danzig's speech came a few weeks after a Pentagon advisory group on women's issues—the Defense Advisory Committee on Women in the Services—asked the Navy why its new submarines of the VIRGINIA (SSN 774) class were not being designed to accommodate women. The committee also raised the question of the feasibility of women serving in existing U.S. submarines.[11]

Indicating that Trident missiles submarines of the OHIO (SSBN 726) class were the primary candidates for near-term integration of women, Mr. Danzig admitted, "There are realities here that are difficult," but pointed out that there were difficulties in integrating women into naval aviation as well as in surface ships. Mr. Danzig noted, "I am not animated by some feeling of affirmative action or political correctness. I am animated by the fundamental perception that we are a democracy. The character of our country is changing. As the character of the country changes, so must the character of our military."

What some observers considered a first step in integrating women in submarines occurred during the summer of 1999, when for two days at a time, five Trident submarines took women to sea. As part of the summer training program for Naval Reserve Officer Training Corps (NROTC) students, the SSBNs each embarked nine female cadets, with a total of 144 women going to sea in the submarines that summer. Such distaff cruises have continued.

The Navy's leadership—submariners and nonsubmariners—have emphatically opposed women aboard submarines. Proponents are quick to point out that Australia and some Scandinavian navies have gender-integrated submarine crews and have designed their subs to provide some privacy. However, those navies with women serving in submarines have different missions for their undersea forces, with boats typically deploying on patrols of only a few weeks. In addition, the social structures of those countries are quite different from that of the United States; for example, toilets can be shared by both sexes aboard foreign ships without difficulty.

Modifying warships—surface ships or submarines—to accommodate women is expensive, and submarines, even Trident submarines, already have cramped quarters. Some "hot bunking," the sharing of some bunks, is required aboard attack submarines (SSNs).[12] The assignment of women to SSBNs or SSNs most likely will reduce the ratio of toilet facilities (heads) available to enlisted men because of the imbalance in crew proportions and the physical layout and number of heads.

Historical. Women have long served at sea in U.S. Navy hospital ships and transports. Since 1979, they also have been assigned to noncombatant ships and craft, mostly tenders, repair ships, and fleet oilers. The aircraft carrier DWIGHT D. EISENHOWER (CVN 69) was the first U.S. Navy warship to deploy with women, departing Norfolk, Virginia, on 20 October 1994 with 367 female officers and enlisted personnel on board. The ship deployed for six months, operating in the Mediterranean–Adriatic areas.

The first woman to head a Navy aircraft squadron took command of Electronic Warfare Squadron (VAQ) 34 in July 1990, and in December 1990, the first woman took command of a U.S. Navy ship, the salvage ship OPPORTUNE (ARS 41). Subsequently, female commanding officers have been named to other types of ships, including destroyers and amphibious ships.[13]

SEA SWAP PROGRAM

Concern over reducing personnel while at the same time fully manning an albeit reduced fleet has led the Navy to put in force two major initiatives. The first was to significantly reduce ship

---

8 Four U.S. Army officers were promoted to General of the Army in December 1944: George C. Marshall, Chief of Staff of the Army; Douglas MacArthur, Commander-in-Chief, Southwest Pacific Area; Dwight D. Eisenhower, Supreme Allied Commander Europe; and Henry (Hap) Arnold, head of the Army Air Forces. In September 1950, the Chairman of the Joint Chiefs of Staff, Omar Bradley, was promoted to General of the Army.

9 SEAL = Sea-Air-Land.

10 Secretary Danzig speech to Naval Submarine League, Arlington, Va., 4 June 1999.

11 The committee—known as DACOWITS—was established in 1951 to assist the armed forces in recruiting quality women for military service. The role of DACOWITS has since evolved into advising the Secretary of Defense on all policies related to women in the armed forces.

12 The cost of adding female facilities aboard surface ships has been estimated at $5,000 for each female berth; it is between $200,000 and $400,000 per female in submarines; see Andrea Stone, "Navy Says Subs Should Keep Hatches Closed to Women," *Navy Times* (27 September 1999), p. 14.

13 Lt. Comdr. Darlene M. Iskra took command after the OPPORTUNE after the ship's previous commanding officer was taken off in a medical emergency; the ship had an all-male crew at the time.

manning requirements. For example, the never-built land-attack destroyer ZUMWALT (DD 21 program) had a design goal of a crew of 75 plus a helicopter detachment of 21—fewer than 100 personnel per ship.

Similarly, under the "Smart Ship" program, ships in service carried out experimental programs that capitalized on automation to cut crew numbers. While major reductions in personnel were made for deployments, the maintenance requirements, watchstanding schedules, and other issues greatly reduced the effectiveness of such efforts.

Subsequently, under Admiral Clark, the Navy has instituted the second initiative—Sea Swap. Long transit times from continental U.S. ports to the Persian Gulf, which took up to six weeks each way, were creating considerable "nonproductive" time for deploying ships. Accordingly, under Sea Swap, the San Diego-based destroyer HIGGINS (DDG 76) and the Pearl Harbor-based FLETCHER (DD 992) were deployed to the Persian Gulf in 2002, but instead of returning home after six months, their crews were replaced by crewmen from other San Diego-based ships flown into Singapore and Australia. Similar crew trades occurred every six months until 2004.

The HIGGINS returned to San Diego in April 2004 after being deployed for 18 months. In late May, the FLETCHER arrived at San Diego after 22 months away. Sea Swap—with four "swaps" per ship—had increased by one-third the number of days the warships were effectively at sea, according to the Navy-sponsored Center for Naval Analyses.

As this edition went to press, there were mixed reactions to Sea Swap. According to the San Diego *Union-Tribune*,

> The experiment's architect, Vice Admiral Timothy LaFleur, has trumpeted the trial's success, saying Sea Swap reduced lengthy transits from the West Coast and increased the time warships could stay on duty off Iraq by one-third.
>
> "I think that's a real win for us," LaFleur said.
>
> But a survey of participating sailors by a Navy-funded think tank found the crews had a negative attitude about Sea Swap and predicted morale would drop and more sailors would leave the service rather than reenlist.
>
> Complaints included the loss of liberty port calls and the additional training and work required under Sea Swap.
>
> The Navy disputed claims that retention has suffered and called for further study of reenlistment rates.[14]

A key factor is morale—the sense a sailor has about "his" or "her" ship. Under Sea Swap, sailors know they will be on board for about six months and then likely will never serve in that ship again. Hence, there is little incentive to take special care of the ship because she is not theirs. This will require enhanced monitoring of the ships' condition, with additional recordkeeping.

A second series of Sea Swap trials involving East Coast-based destroyers was scheduled to follow.

A plan to swap Marines and sailors assigned to amphibious ships is in the preliminary stages, although "amphibs" would present the additional problem of handling embarked Marine aircraft. Aircraft maintenance is completely different from ship maintenance and may require a different swap schedule and different handling of flight and maintenance personnel. For the two-destroyer crew swap program, only the FLETCHER had helicopters on board. They were kept on board for up to 12 months, after which they were replaced, carried to and from the ship by Air Force C-5 Galaxy transports. After careful inspections of the SH-60B helicopters, it was decided to keep them deployed for more than 12 months.

While some observers compare Sea Swap with the strategic missile submarine manning program, which since 1960 has had

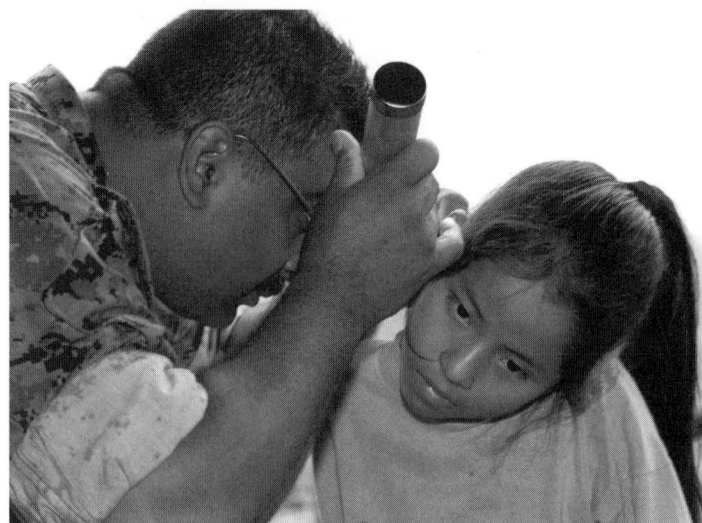

Sailors carry out humanitarian missions throughout the world, both preplanned and in response to natural disasters. Naval Reserve Lieutenant Anthony Edwards, with the Marine Corps Reserve's 4th Force Support Group, is shown in Peru, where U.S. naval forces provide medical assistance as part of the UNITAS multinational exercises. (U.S. Navy/Dave Fliesen)

alternating Blue and Gold crews for each submarine, the procedures are totally different. The two SSBN crews are assigned to a single submarine, and when ashore, the alternating crew is training and preparing for the next deterrent patrol of that submarine.

More successful has been the replacement of crews of coastal patrol ships (PC) and mine warfare ships (MCM, MHC). Those are significantly smaller crews, usually rotating from the same continental U.S. home ports.

NAVAL RESERVE

Efforts are under way to further integrate the Naval Reserve and the active naval forces. This is occurring in large part because of the major use of reservists following the 11 September 2001 terrorist attacks—mainly for security of naval installations—and for the 2003 invasion of Iraq. Since September 2001, more than 4,500 Naval Reserve officers some 18,500 enlisted personnel have been mobilized. (By comparison, a total of 21,109 reservists were activated in 1990–1991 for Operations Desert Storm and Desert Shield.)

For Operation Iraqi Freedom, 12,046 Naval Reservists served on active duty. They included Strike-Fighter Squadron (VFA) 201, based at Fort Worth, Texas, the first reserve "tail hook" squadron to deploy on board a carrier since the Korean War.

VFA-201, flying F/A-18A Hornets, was activated on 7 October 2002 for one year to deploy with Carrier Air Wing 8 aboard the USS THEODORE ROOSEVELT (CVN 71). The squadron took the place of active squadron VFA-102, which was in transition to the F/A-18F. After completing a short-notice workup, VFA-201 was integrated with the active air wing and during Operation Iraqi Freedom flew 224 combat sorties and delivered 125 tons of bombs and missiles.

Also activated was reserve Helicopter Combat Search and Rescue/Special Warfare Support Squadron (HCS) 5, based at Naval Air Station North Island (San Diego). Called to active duty in

---

14 James W. Crawley, "Sea Swap Program May Hurt Retention," *San Diego Union-Tribune* (2 August 2004). Vice Adm. LaFleur is Commander, Naval Surface Force, Pacific Fleet.

Figure 9-1. NAVAL RESERVE STRUCTURE

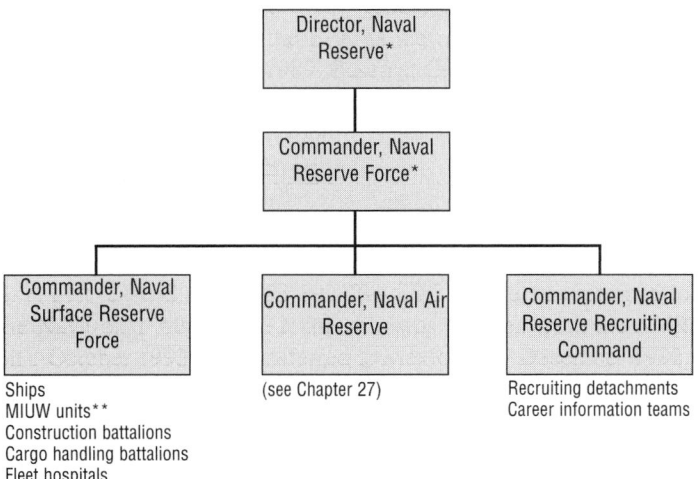

Ships
MIUW units**
Construction battalions
Cargo handling battalions
Fleet hospitals
Naval Reserve centers

(see Chapter 27)

Recruiting detachments
Career information teams

* Same individual "double-hatted"
** MIUW = Mobile Inshore Undersea Warfare

March 2003, the squadron was deployed to Iraq, where it provided support to Navy and other-service forces. Reserve squadron HCS-4, based at Norfolk, was scheduled to relieve HCS-5 in Iraq. Both squadrons fly HH-60H Seahawk helicopters.

Other Naval Reserve activations during Operation Iraqi Freedom included:
• 362 men and women mobilized to augment the staff of Commander, Fifth Fleet, the naval component commander for Commander, U.S. Central Command
• 478 personnel from cargo handling battalions mobilized for the movement of cargo from bases in the United States and overseas to the Persian Gulf area
• 548 Naval Reservists recalled to support the National Naval Medical Center in Bethesda, Maryland, in part replacing active-duty personnel embarked in the hospital ship COMFORT (T-AH 20)
• 843 reservists activated to provide support to Marine Forces during the war, including 592 enlisted hospital corpsmen assigned to provide battlefield medical support to Marine units

The Naval Reserve is undergoing restructuring to ensure compatibility with changes being made in the Navy. For example, with the restructuring that came with establishment of the Fleet Forces Command, the Reserve assigned both the Commander, Naval Reserve Force, in Washington, D.C., and the Commander, Naval Reserve Forces Command, in New Orleans, Louisiana, with additional duty to the Commander, Fleet Forces Command, in Norfolk.

In addition, while the basic Naval Reserve program provides for 48 drill days per year (over 12 weekends) and 12 days of annual training, other options are being considered. A pilot program was initiated in 2004 under which reservists in certain specialty fields could spend 32 days on active training. The reservists in this program still would be required to spend two drills per quarter at their reserve centers, taking care of paperwork and other administrative tasks.[15]

The Naval Reserve has two principal categories of personnel:
• *Selected Reserve.* Full-Time Support (FTS), formerly called Training and Administration of Reserves (TAR); Naval Reserve Force units (ships, aircraft, and specialized units); and a few hundred individuals

• *Individual Ready Reserve.* Individuals, usually men and women who have been separated from active duty

With respect to total reserve personnel, the Naval Reserve end strength requested in the FY 2005 defense budget is 83,400, a decrease of 2,500 from FY 2004. This is due primarily to the shifting of Naval Coastal Warfare units into the active force, the decommissioning of a fleet hospital, and medical program billet reductions as a result of force restructuring.

At present, no homeland defense/homeland security mission has been assigned to the Naval Reserve. The Assistant Secretary of Defense for Reserve Affairs and the Assistant Secretary of Defense for Homeland Defense are conducting a study to determine the appropriate role of reserve components in these areas. Specific roles could include harbor defense, port security, maritime surveillance and tracking, and maintenance of shipping channels. Some of these are now the responsibility of the Coast Guard.

The Naval Reserve Force currently operates 20 warships, all of which have composite active–reserve crews.

Frigates
FFG 28 BOONE (Mayport, Fla.)
FFG 29 STEPHEN W. GROVES (Pascagoula, Miss.)
FFG 38 CURTS (San Diego, Calif.)
FFG 39 DOYLE (Mayport, Fla.)
FFG 42 KLAKRING (Mayport, Fla.)
Mine countermeasures ships
MCM 1 AVENGER
MCM 2 DEFENDER
MCM 3 SENTRY
MCM 4 CHAMPION
MCM 11 GLADIATOR
MHC 51 OSPREY
MHC 52 HERON
MHC 53 PELICAN
MHC 54 ROBIN
MHC 55 ORIOLE
MHC 56 KINGFISHER
MHC 57 CORMORANT
MHC 58 BLACK HAWK
MHC 59 FALCON
MHC 62 SHRIKE

All reserve-manned mine warfare ships are based at Ingleside, Texas.

The Naval Air Force Reserve, with some 230 aircraft, currently is organized into 34 squadrons (asterisks indicate ship-based units):
Fixed-wing aircraft
1 VAQ Electronic attack squadron*
2 VAW Airborne early warning squadrons
3 VFA Strike-fighter squadrons*
2 VFC Fighter composite squadrons
7 VP Patrol squadrons
14 VR Fleet logistic support squadrons
Helicopters
1 HC Helicopter combat support squadron
2 HCS Helicopter combat search and rescue/special warfare support squadrons
1 HS Helicopter Anti-submarine Warfare (ASW) squadron*
1 HSL Light helicopter ASW squadron*
Details of the Naval Air Force Reserve organization and squadron locations are provided in Chapter 27. Reserve personnel also augment active-duty squadrons.

---

15 See Christopher Munsey, "Navy Offers Month-long Reserve Drill," *Navy Times* (27 September 2004), p. 21.

Historical. The naval reserve concept can be traced to the American Revolution, when several of the colonies employed armed merchant ships to resist British military activities within their state's waters. By the time of the signing of the Declaration of Independence in July 1776, 11 colonies had some form of navy.

During the next century, there were various forms of state volunteers, and a volunteer force was established in the Union Navy during the Civil War. Then, beginning in 1888, several states established naval components as part of their state militias. These naval militias were intended for harbor and coastal defense; they had no federal standing, and rules for applicants and level of competence varied considerably.

Beginning in 1891, the Navy offered to allow state militias to participate in some fleet exercises, and there soon followed federal cooperation in a number of training areas. Two years later, the training ship NEW HAMPSHIRE (launched in 1864, although laid down 45 years earlier!) was transferred from the Navy to the New York State Naval Militia.

By the eve of the Spanish–American War of 1898 there were more than 4,000 men in state naval militias. When the conflict erupted, the militias were used to patrol the coasts (there was a perceived threat of a Spanish assault), and thousands more militiamen were taken into the Navy. Their outstanding service led to Navy Department recommendations for the creation of a national Naval Reserve. This was opposed—mostly by state interests—until 1914, when Congress passed legislation that largely placed the naval militias under the supervision of the Navy Department. In time of war, they would become part of the Navy (as the state National Guard units would become part of the Army). A year later, in 1915, the U.S. Naval Reserve was established, to be comprised of men honorably discharged from the active Navy.

With U.S. entry into World War I in April 1917, the militias were mobilized as the National Naval Volunteers, with almost the total strength of slightly more than 10,000 men coming onto active duty in the Navy. By September 1917, their ranks had grown to almost 17,000 men. These volunteers were consolidated with the Naval Reserve in July 1918, creating the basis of the current U.S. Naval Reserve organization. (California, Illinois, and New York continue to maintain state naval forces, whose members also are in the Naval Reserve.)

The Naval Reserve had major roles in World War II, the Korean War, the Vietnam War, the 1991 war in the Persian Gulf, and the 2003 invasion of Iraq, as well as in periodic operations in which reserve ships and aircraft squadrons joined active naval forces in humanitarian, peacekeeping, and combat operations.

Naval Reserve squadrons, especially maritime patrol (VP) and logistics (VR), regularly operate overseas in support of naval operations. These P-3C Orions from VP-66, based at Naval Air Station Willow Grove, Pennsylvania, are at NAS Keflavik, Iceland, participating in a multinational anti-submarine exercise. (U.S. Navy/Mark O'Donald)

CHAPTER 10

Strategic Missile Submarines

Several crewmen work on the deck of the Trident missile submarine RHODE ISLAND as she cruises on the surface—a very rare activity for an SSBN. The Navy's 14 Trident submarines are the most potent and the most survivable component of U.S. strategic offensive forces. (2003, U.S. Navy / B. L. Keller)

The U.S. Navy operated 14 Trident strategic missile submarines (SSBNs) of the OHIO class in early 2005. That number, based on U.S.-Russian nuclear arms agreements, carry a total of 336 Submarine-Launched Ballistic Missiles (SLBMs), providing the majority of the ballistic missiles and nuclear Reentry Vehicles (RVs) of the U.S. nuclear arsenal.

Another four OHIO-class submarines have been taken out of the strategic role and are being converted to combination cruise missile and transport/special forces submarines (SSGNs; see chapter 11). All earlier SSBNs have been retired (including those converted to transport submarines) and have been discarded.

The 18 Trident missile submarines were completed from 1981 to 1997; each carried 24 SLBMs. The first eight OHIO-class SSBNs were armed with the Trident C-4 missile; the ten subsequent submarines had D-5 missiles. With the four oldest OHIO-class submarines being converted to SSGNs, the four others with the C-4 missile have been upgraded to launch the D-5.

The Trident D-5 has greater range and accuracy than the C-4 and can deliver 75 percent more payload. It is considered the only "hard kill" strategic weapon in the U.S. arsenal, i.e., having the yield and accuracy to destroy hardened silo Intercontinental Ballistic Missiles (ICBMs) and certain other protected targets.

The D-5 missiles carry two types of RVs and warheads: The Mk 4 RV has eight W76 warheads, each with a yield estimated at 100 kilotons; the Mk 5 RV has eight W88 warheads with estimated yields of 475 kilotons. The exact inventory mix is not known, but only an estimated 400 of the Mk 5 were built before production ended in 1989. Thus, most Trident D-5 missiles have the Mk 4/W76 payload.[1]

An estimate of nuclear weapons currently assigned to U.S. operational forces is provided in table 10-1. The Trident missiles are the only nuclear weapons currently in Navy service. An estimated 320 Tomahawk Land-Attack Missiles-Nuclear (TLAM-Ns) with the W88-0 warhead are at storage sites in the United States for naval use; however, the lack of realistic training for their use and handling makes their effective future employment by the Navy doubtful. No Navy or Marine Corps aircraft currently are capable of carrying nuclear weapons.

U.S. NUCLEAR FORCES

In January 2002, the Department of Defense revealed plans to change U.S. nuclear policy and to further reduce the nation's nuclear weapons arsenal. The alterations reflected recommendations of the Nuclear Posture Review completed in late 2001.[2]

The new policy marks a significant shift from Cold War thinking, including a change to the infamous concept of a U.S. nuclear

---

1 All nuclear weapons data are based on Robert S. Norris, Hans M. Kristensen, and Joshua Handler, "U.S. Nuclear Forces, 2003," *The Bulletin of the Atomic Scientists* (May/June 2003), pp. 73-76, with updates from Mr. Norris.

2 J. D. Crouch, Assistant Secretary of Defense for International Security Policy, et al., press conference, Pentagon, 9 January 2002.

forces "triad," a term apparently coined about 1970 by Major General Glenn Kent, a leading Air Force strategic planner, and quickly encouraged "throughout the Air Force to help explain the continuing need for a manned strategic bomber."[3] A new triad is being proposed in which nuclear forces—ICBMs, SLBMs, and manned bombers—form a "mini-triad" within a broader nuclear policy structure, augmented by a national missile defense system and highly responsive conventional forces. All will be linked by upgraded command-and-control, intelligence, and planning activities.

At the same time, the U.S. nuclear arsenal is being reduced from more than 7,000 nuclear weapons in 2004 to about 3,800 by 2007, and to between 1,700 and 2,200 nuclear weapons by 2012. Assistant Secretary of Defense J. D. Crouch, in the briefing of the Nuclear Posture Review in January 2002, said many of the removed warheads would be kept in reserve as a "responsive force," able to be installed in missiles within weeks or months. Crouch explained that the Nuclear Posture Review—mandated by Congress—reflected the current security environment. The Cold War provided in the Soviet Union "basically a known, single ideological opponent. . . . We relied not exclusively, but very heavily on our offensive nuclear forces, and we had a threat-based approach to nuclear planning . . . the focus was on the Soviet Union . . . [and] everything else was sort of a lesser included case."

Today, the world is very much changed, explained Crouch. Accordingly, the United States should deploy the lowest number of nuclear weapons consistent with the new security requirements of the United States, its allies, and friends. Further, the reductions will be achieved unilaterally, without the requirement for Cold War–style treaties. Fewer nuclear weapons will mean greater emphasis on highly responsive, advanced conventional weapons.

When the Cold War ended in 1991, the United States had some 20,000 nuclear weapons in service. President George H. W. Bush, on 27 September 1991, announced a massive cutback in U.S. nuclear weapons, tactical and strategic, a decision that led to the current 7,000-plus inventory. Most of these weapons are strategic, with the Minuteman III ICBMs, Trident D-5 SLBMs, and B-52H Stratofortress and B-2 Spirit long-range bombers scheduled to be kept in service at least until 2020.

Table 10-1. ACTIVE U.S. NUCLEAR WEAPON SYSTEMS, 2004

Weapon	Operational[*]	Launchers/ Missiles/ Bombers	Total Warheads
ICBM Minuteman III	1970	500	1,200
ICBM Peacekeeper MX	1986	40	500
SLBM Trident II D-5	1990	336	1,920
Bomber B-2 Spirit	1994	16**	800***
Bomber B-52H Stratofortress	1961	56**	860#
Fighter F-15E Eagle##	1988	~650	(see notes)
Fighter F-16 Fighting Falcon##	1980		

*   Oldest configuration now operational.

**   Primary inventory, i.e., number of aircraft assigned for nuclear/conventional strike missions.

*** B61 and B83 bombs; the B61 also is carried by the F-15E and F-16, as well as by NATO tactical aircraft. Another 500 B61s are in reserve.

\#   Air-launched cruise missiles (ALCMs).

\#\#   Fighter-bombers based in Europe and the United States.

The MX Peacekeeper ICBM force is being retired; the MX targets will be covered in part by the additional Trident D-5 missiles. In addition, the 500 Minuteman III missiles are being downloaded to one RV per missile. This reconfiguration to single warheads is to be accomplished by 2007. Thus, the SSBN/SLBM nuclear force is becoming an even more important component of U.S. nuclear forces.

There currently are no new types of SSBNs or SLBMs under development in the United States. The Navy's 30-year shipbuilding plan submitted to Congress in 2003 does call for a future SSBN construction program to replace the Ohio class (see below).

Production of Trident D-5 missiles for U.S. submarines is continuing through at least 2013. This will support the four submarines (SSBN 730–733) being converted to carry the D-5 missile and the four British Trident-armed submarines of the Vanguard class, as well as continued firing of test and training weapons.[4] The total Trident D-5 procurement now is planned at 568 missiles (see chapter 31). In addition, some older missiles will be upgraded to support Ohio-class submarine deployments through 2042; these will carry the designation D-5A.

On top of the force cutbacks, the operating tempo of the remaining 14 Trident submarines has been reduced, although no action has been taken on proposals that the force shift from the historic two-crew operating concept to a single crew. This shift could result in considerable financial savings, but single crewing also would severely reduce Trident submarine time at sea and mean less flexibility in scheduling deterrent patrols.[5]

The Navy has conducted a demonstration firing of a Trident D-5 missile configured for carrying a conventional, high-explosive warhead. The concept was suggested by the Navy's Strategic Systems Project Office as a means of striking time-sensitive, heavily defended, high-value targets. Such a weapon could enable the Navy to retain the four nonstrategic submarines for a conventional role. However, there could be significant problems with the deployment of conventionally armed SLBMs, such as a nation's early warning system indicating that U.S. ballistic missiles were being fired with no way of knowing the intended target or whether the weapons were nuclear or conventional. Further, existing treaties and their missile counts would have to be modified. Thus, employing Trident SSBNs in a conventional strike role is highly unlikely.

The last of 41 earlier Polaris–Poseidon ballistic missile submarines completed from 1959 to 1967, the Kamehameha, has been decommissioned and stricken. The Kamehameha was one of four SSBNs modified to serve as transport/special operations submarines (see chapter 11). Two other retired SSBNs, the Daniel Webster and Sam Rayburn, are retained as immobilized Moored Training Ships (MTS) for nuclear propulsion operators at Charleston, South Carolina. During their operational careers, these 41 submarines were armed in succession with Polaris missiles (41 submarines), Poseidon missiles (31), and Trident C-4 missiles (12).

The dismantling of a nuclear-propelled submarine requires more than a year. Because U.S. Navy nuclear-propelled ships, by law, must have personnel on board until the reactor is permanently closed down and the fuel removed, on deactivation nuclear ships and submarines are placed "In Commission, In Reserve" (ICIR). Once a ship has been placed in ICIR status she cannot be returned to service. After the reactor shutdown requirements have been met, the ships are officially decommissioned and, in recent years, stricken on the same date, usually some six to eight months after the ICIR date. In particular, SSBNs are cut into sections to meet disarmament treaty stipulations.

3 Letter to the author from Col. Charles D. Cooper, USAF, Office of Public Affairs, Department of the Air Force, 5 February 1981.

4 The four Royal Navy SSBNs each carry 16 Trident D-5 missiles, which are armed with British-produced W76-type warheads. Only sufficient missiles for three submarines are being procured—58 missiles, including test, training, and spare weapons. British SSBNs go on patrol with some empty tubes. (Previous plans provided for the British procurement of 65 missiles.)

5 The only other nations that now maintain continuous SSBN/SLBM patrols are Britain and France; Russian SSBN/SLBM patrols have been sporadic, with no strategic missile submarines at sea at certain times.

The reactors are "defueled" and removed from the submarines along with other radioactive and hazardous material. The reactors then are "temporarily" buried at Hanford, Washington. Submarines decommissioned on the East Coast are defueled and then towed to Puget Sound for the removal and burial of their reactor compartments and scrapping of the submarines. The submarines are stripped of any material that may be of use in the fleet.

The average cost of decommissioning, defueling, and partially dismantling a nuclear-powered submarine in FY 1999 dollars was $32 million for an SSBN and $26 million for an SSN.

Builders: The Electric Boat Division of General Dynamics in Groton, Connecticut, built all 18 of the Trident submarines and 17 of the 41 U.S. Polaris–Poseidon submarines. The Polaris submarine program was a spectacular U.S. submarine construction effort: 41 submarines completed in just 7½ years following a highly compressed development period. (In addition to the Polaris submarines, the Navy completed 17 other nuclear-propelled submarines during that period, an average of almost 8 per year.)

Names: The 41 Polaris strategic missile submarines completed from 1959 to 1967 were named for "famous Americans," although, in fact, several honored men who were never in the American colonies or the United States.

The subsequent Trident submarines, completed from 1981 to 1997, are named for states of the Union. Previously, state names were assigned to battleships and, later, to guided missile cruisers (CGN 36–41) and attack submarines (SSN 22 and 774–). An exception to this naming convention was made on 27 September 1983, when the SSBN 730 was named for the late Senator Henry M. (Scoop) Jackson, long-time supporter of nuclear and defense programs.

Operational: The Trident SSBN force is based at Bangor, Washington, for patrols in the North Pacific, and at Kings Bay, Georgia, for patrols in the North Atlantic.

As of June 2004, U.S. ballistic missile submarines have completed 3,632 deterrent patrols:

1,245	Polaris
1,182	Poseidon
397	Trident C-4 backfit in older submarines
481	Trident C-4 in OHIO-class submarines
327	Trident D-5 in OHIO-class submarines

This number does not include the 41 deterrent patrols conducted by five Regulus-armed cruise missile submarines in the North Pacific from 1959 to 1964.[6]

The pioneer GEORGE WASHINGTON conducted the first ballistic missile patrol, departing on 15 November 1960, carrying 16 Polaris A-1 missiles. The boat was at sea on that initial patrol for 67 consecutive days, remaining submerged for 66 days, 10 hours—an underwater endurance record.

Table 10-2. STRATEGIC MISSILE DEPLOYMENTS

Missile	First Patrol Begun	Last Patrol Completed
Polaris A-1	GEORGE WASHINGTON 15 Nov 1960	ABRAHAM LINCOLN 14 Oct 1965
Polaris A-2	ETHAN ALLEN 26 June 1962	JOHN MARSHALL 9 June 1974
Polaris A-3	DANIEL WEBSTER 28 Sep 1964	ROBERT E. LEE 1 Oct 1981*
Poseidon C-3	JAMES MADISON 31 Mar 1971	KAMEHAMEHA and ULYSSES S. GRANT** 1 Oct 1991
Trident C-4	FRANCIS SCOTT KEY 20 Oct 1979	MICHIGAN 15 Dec 2003
Trident D-5	TENNESSEE 29 Mar 1990	(missile in service)

* The date the ROBERT E. LEE was taken off alert; she was still at sea at the time, but Polaris patrols officially ended on 1 October 1981.

** The KAMEHAMEHA and ULYSSES S. GRANT were taken off alert on this date; although the submarines still were at sea, returning to port on 15 and 16 October 1981, respectively, their deterrent patrols officially ended on 1 October 1991.

Personnel: SSBNs are manned by two complete crews, designated Blue and Gold. While one crew is at sea, the other is engaged in training (mostly with system simulators), leave, medical treatment, and other shore activities. The normal deployment patrol (with one crew) has been up to 70 days.

Secretary of the Navy Richard Danzig on 3 June 1999 proposed that consideration be given to assigning women to submarine crews; the Trident SSBNs are the principal candidates for mixed-manning because of their size and accommodations. However, no action has been taken to enable women to serve in submarines. (Female midshipmen from the U.S. Naval Academy have made orientation cruises on Trident Submarines.)

---

6 The operational Regulus submarines were the TUNNY (SSG 282), BARBERO (SSG 317), GRAYBACK (SSG 574), GROWLER (SSG 577), and HALIBUT (SSGN 586). They deployed with the Regulus I surface-launched cruise missile in the northwest Pacific area from September 1959 to July 1964.

When on the surface with a pair of tugs, even a large Trident submarine appears diminutive, like the PENNSYLVANIA, shown here arriving at Kings Bay, Georgia, the Atlantic area Trident base. Her two periscopes are fully extended in this view. (2002, U.S. Navy / Brian Nokell)

ADVANCED STRATEGIC MISSILE SUBMARINE

The Navy's 30-year shipbuilding plan submitted to Congress in 2003 lists the procurement of an SSBN(X) ballistic missile submarine, beginning in the period FY 2019–2023, with ten addi-tional submarines listed for authorization at the rate of one per year. Options that have been put forth include a variant of the VIRGINIA (SSN 774) class, or a new design based on the existing OHIO class.

14 STRATEGIC MISSILE SUBMARINES: OHIO CLASS

Number	Name	FY	Builder	Start	Laid down	Launched	Commissioned	Status
SSBN 730	HENRY M. JACKSON	77	General Dynamics/Electric Boat	28 Feb 1978	19 Jan 1981	15 Oct 1983	6 Oct 1984	**PA**
SSBN 731	ALABAMA	78	General Dynamics/Electric Boat	6 Apr 1979	27 Aug 1981	19 May 1984	25 May 1985	**PA**
SSBN 732	ALASKA	78	General Dynamics/Electric Boat	12 Oct 1979	9 Mar 1983	12 Jan 1985	25 Jan 1986	**PA**
SSBN 733	NEVADA	80	General Dynamics/Electric Boat	17 Feb 1981	8 Aug 1983	14 Sep 1985	16 Aug 1986	**PA**
SSBN 734	TENNESSEE	81	General Dynamics/Electric Boat	15 Jan 1982	9 June 1986	13 Dec 1986	17 Dec 1988	**AA**
SSBN 735	PENNSYLVANIA	83	General Dynamics/Electric Boat	29 Nov 1982	2 Mar 1987	23 Apr 1988	9 Sep 1989	**PA**
SSBN 736	WEST VIRGINIA	84	General Dynamics/Electric Boat	21 Nov 1983	18 Dec 1987	14 Oct 1989	20 Oct 1990	**AA**
SSBN 737	KENTUCKY	85	General Dynamics/Electric Boat	13 Aug 1985	18 Dec 1987	11 Aug 1990	13 July 1991	**PA**
SSBN 738	MARYLAND	86	General Dynamics/Electric Boat	22 Mar 1986	18 Dec 1987	10 Aug 1991	13 June 1992	**AA**
SSBN 739	NEBRASKA	87	General Dynamics/Electric Boat	6 June 1987	18 Dec 1987	15 Aug 1992	10 July 1993	**AA**
SSBN 740	RHODE ISLAND	88	General Dynamics/Electric Boat	23 Apr 1988	—	17 July 1993	9 July 1994	**AA**
SSBN 741	MAINE	89	General Dynamics/Electric Boat	4 Apr 1989		16 July 1994	29 July 1995	**AA**
SSBN 742	WYOMING	90	General Dynamics/Electric Boat	27 Jan 1990	—	15 July 1995	13 July 1996	**AA**
SSBN 743	LOUISIANA	91	General Dynamics/Electric Boat	15 May 1991	—	27 July 1996	6 Sep 1997	**AA**

Displacement:	16,764 tons standard	ASW weapons:	Mk 48 ADCAP torpedoes
	18,750 tons submerged	Radars:	BPS-15A surface search on SSBNs 730-740
Length:	560 feet (170.7 m) overall		BPS-16 surface search on SSBNs 741-743
Beam:	42 feet (12.8 m)	Sonars:	BQQ-6 or BQQ-10 ARCI bow mounted passive
Draft:	361/4 feet (11.05 m)		TB-29 towed array
Propulsion:	2 steam turbines (General Electric); approx.		BQR-19 active navigation
	35,000 shp; 1 shaft		BQS-13 active
Reactors:	1 S8G pressurized-water (General Electric)		BQS-15 under ice
Speed:	approx 25 knots surface	Fire control:	1 CCS Mk 2 Mod 3
	approx. 25 knots submerged		1 Mk 98 missile FCS
Personnel:	160 (15 officers + 145 enlisted) in SSBNs 730–733		1 Mk 118 torpedo FCS
	159 (15 officers + 144 enlisted) in SSBNs 734–743	EW systems:	WLR-8(V)5
Missiles:	24 tubes for Trident D-5 SLBMs		WLR-10
Torpedo tubes:	4 21-inch (533-mm) tubes angled Mk 68		WLY-1

These are the largest submarines to be built in the United States. They are surpassed in size by only the Soviet Typhoon-class (Project 941) SSBNs, which displace more than twice as much, and Oscar-class (Project 949) SSGNs.[7] The OHIO was laid down nine years after completion of the previous U.S. strategic missile submarine, the WILL ROGERS.

Incorporation of the D-5 missile in SSBNs 734–736 resulted in a one-year delay in their construction; the SSBN 737 and later submarines were ordered as D-5 ships (see *Missiles* notes).

Four ships of this class have been removed from the strategic role and converted to combination cruise missile and transport/special forces submarines and redesignated SSGNs (see chapter 11).

Class: The Trident program originated with the Department of Defense-sponsored STRAT-X study of 1967–1968 to determine future strategic weapon requirements. The study recommended two land-based and two sea-based strategic systems, with one of the latter being the Underwater Long-Range Missile System (ULMS). The ULMS evolved into the Trident system, the name being changed to Trident on 16 May 1972. (One land-based strategic offensive system also was initiated, the MX land-based missile.)

The Trident program lagged considerably behind the schedule established when the weapon system was approved for development in May 1972. The lead submarine was funded in FY 1974, with a plan to construct an initial series of ten Trident SSBNs at an annual rate of 1-3-3-3, with the last boats to be completed by 1982.

The first Trident submarine was ordered on 25 July 1974, with a planned delivery of 30 April 1979. However, the shipyard agreed to attempt to make delivery in December 1977 because of the program's high priority. Subsequent delays caused by the Navy's man-agement of the project, design changes, and problems at the shipyard resulted in late deliveries of the early submarines, with authorizations for the initial series of ten covering a ten-year period instead of four years.

By the early 1980s, Navy planning called for a class of 24 OHIO-class SSBNs (to be assigned hull numbers 726–749). These were to replace the 41 Polaris–Poseidon submarines. The 1972 SALT I strategic arms limitation agreement with the Soviet Union required the decommissioning of the Polaris A-3 submarines THEODORE ROOSEVELT and ABRAHAM LINCOLN to compensate for the OHIO entering service—the first U.S. SSBNs to be decommissioned.

The OHIO-class submarines were designed for 30-year service lives. Subsequent changes in operational/maintenance cycles and reevaluation have increased that to 44 years.

Builders: Note that four submarines of this class were laid down at the Electric Boat yard on the same date. The last four submarines did not have formal keel layings.

During the mid-1980s, Secretary of the Navy John Lehman gave consideration to constructing some Trident submarines at Newport News Shipbuilding because of the submarine construction backlog and higher-than-expected costs at Electric Boat; in the event, all were built at Electric Boat.

Design: SCB No. 304.74. These are the largest submarines to be built in the West, their size having been determined by their missile battery and reactor plant. They are reported to have a 985-foot (300-m) operating depth.

---

7 The Typhoons have a submerged displacement of 48,000 tons; the Oscar Is displace 22,500 tons submerged, the later units (Oscar II) being slightly larger.

The OHIO-class submarines have a conservative design, with the bow sonar dome and angled torpedo tubes similar to later attack submarine designs.

The Trident submarines have comfortable crew accommodations. Three logistic hatches—in the forward (control–accommodation section), center (missile), and after (engineering) compartments—have escape trunks that can be removed when in port to provide large, six-foot (1.8-m) diameter resupply and repair openings. These permit the rapid transfer of supply pallets, equipment replacement modules, and even machinery components, significantly reducing replenishment and maintenance time. (Standard U.S. submarine hatches are 26 inches/0.66 m in diameter.)

Electronics: The 14 submarines being retained as strategic missile platforms are being fitted with the BQQ-10 Acoustic Rapid COTS Insertion (ARCI) sonar update. See information on the AUGUSTA (SSN 710) in chapter 11. The first SSBN to receive ARCI was the ALASKA in the fall of 2000.

Engineering: The S8G reactor plant originally was intended to provide up to 60,000 shp, having been based on an early 1970s design for a large, high-speed cruise missile submarine. Its actual horsepower is publicly reported as being in excess of 30,000 shp.

A land-based prototype of the OHIO plant was installed at West Milton, New York.

Reportedly, the OHIO exceeded the ship's design goals for self-quieting, and at low speeds (i.e., when using natural convection rather than pumps for the circulation of pressurized water in the primary loop) may be the quietest U.S. nuclear submarine constructed, except possibly for the SEAWOLF (SSN 21) class.

Missiles: The first eight submarines were completed with a Trident C-4 missile capability. Beginning with the ninth ship, they were fitted with the Trident D-5. The D-5 missile has been backfitted into SSBNs 730–733: the first two ships in 2000–2001, and the second two in 2004–2005.

The OHIO fired the first Trident C-4 to be launched from this class on 17 January 1982. The TENNESSEE launched the first D-5 missile from a submarine on 21 March 1989; that missile failed. The first successful Trident D-5 submarine launch (again from the TENNESSEE) occurred on 2 August 1989.

These submarines will be refitted with the improved Mk 4 fire control system.

Operational: The OHIO made the first operational patrol of this class, from 1 October 1982 to 10 December 1982.

The first squadron of OHIO-class submarines, Submarine Squadron (SubRon) 17, activated on 1 January 1981, operates in the Pacific, based at Bangor, Washington. SubRon 16 operates in the Atlantic, based at Kings Bay, Georgia. It was the second squadron, in service from 18 October 1963 until its deactivation on 25 June 1994. It was reactivated as a Triden SSBN squadron on 7 August 1997. SubRon 20 manages SSBN overhuals and maintenance at Kings Bay.

With the withdrawal of four Trident submarines for conversion to SSGNs and the upgrading of all submarines to a D-5 missile configuration, the Navy had planned a "balanced" force, with seven boats in each ocean area. However, it now appears there will be eight SSBNs in the Atlantic and six in the Pacific. The KENTUCKY and PENNSYLVANIA shifted to the Pacific in late 2002, sailing around South America rather than transiting the Panama Canal.

These submarines are designed to conduct 70-day patrols followed by 25-day overhaul/replenishment periods, during which time the alternating Blue/Gold crews change over. Under this schedule the submarines undergo a lengthy overhaul and reactor refueling every ten years.

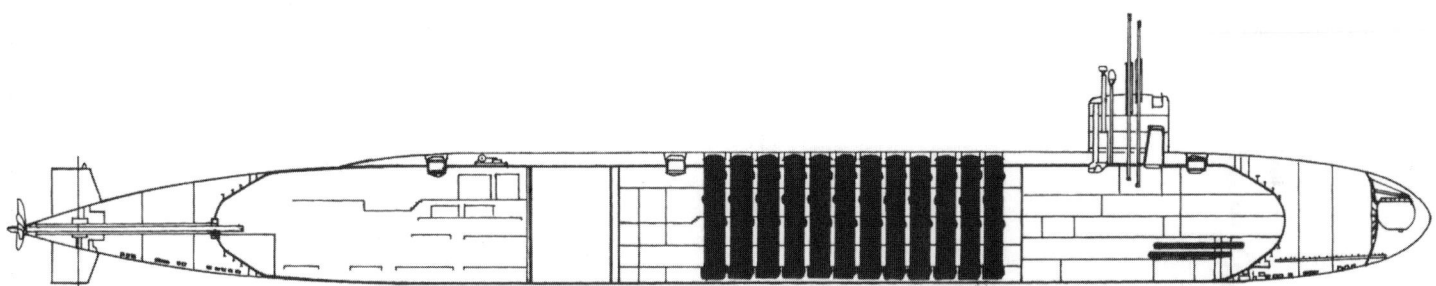

USS OHIO (Drawing from Cold War Submarines © *A. D. Baker III)*

An aerial view of the Trident submarine NEVADA under way in the Atlantic reveals the long, low lines of the OHIO design, which contrasts sharply with the much higher "turtleback" designs of Soviet Delta-class SSBNs and the massive Typhoon SSBN. (1999, Leo Van Ginderen)

The ALASKA *entering a missile loading dock. Her 24 missile hatch coverings, aft of the sail, fold flush with the deck and are visible only from specific angles. The largest submarines built in the West, the* OHIO *SSBNs are smaller than the Soviet-built Oscar SSGNs and Typhoon SSBNs. (1998, U.S. Navy / Gene Royer)*

The FLORIDA *off the Atlantic coast. Her BPS-15 series radar is behind her cockpit; behind that are her two periscopes and, with mottled camouflage, two OE-207 series antenna masts. Retracted into the after portion of the sail is her BRN-3 antenna mast and snorkel induction mast. (2002, U.S. Navy / B. L. Keller)*

The OHIO *in dry-dock at the Puget Sound Naval Shipyard (Washington) shows the circular hull cross section of Trident SSBNs. The bow is devoted to her sonar dome, with torpedo tubes angled out, two per side, aft of the dome; they are not visible here. (2003, U.S. Navy)*

The Moored Training Submarines DANIEL WEBSTER (left) and SAM RAYBURN are immobilized at Charleston, South Carolina, to train nuclear propulsion operators. Nuclear propulsion training also is given at land-based reactor sites. (U.S. Navy)

Table 10-3. BALLISTIC MISSILE SUBMARINES

Number	Name	Comm.	Notes
GEORGE WASHINGTON class (5)			
SSBN 598	GEORGE WASHINGTON	1959	decomm. 25 Jan 1985; str. 30 Apr 1986
SSBN 599	PATRICK HENRY	1960	decomm. 25 May 1984; str. 16 Dec 1985
SSBN 600	THEODORE ROOSEVELT	1961	decomm. 28 Feb 1981; str. 1 Dec 1982
SSBN 601	ROBERT E. LEE	1960	decomm. 1 Dec 1983; str. 30 Apr 1986
SSBN 602	ABRAHAM LINCOLN	1961	decomm. 28 Feb 1981; str. 1 Dec 1982
ETHAN ALLEN class (5)			
SSBN 608	ETHAN ALLEN	1961	decomm. 31 Mar 1983; str. 2 Apr 1983
SSBN 609	SAM HOUSTON	1962	decomm./str. 6 Sep 1991
SSBN 610	THOMAS A. EDISON	1962	decomm. 1 Dec 1983; str. 30 Apr 1986
SSBN 611	JOHN MARSHALL	1962	decomm./str. 22 July 1992
LAFAYETTE class (31)			
SSBN 616	LAFAYETTE	1963	decomm./str. 12 Aug 1991
SSBN 617	ALEXANDER HAMILTON	1963	decomm./str. 23 Feb 1993
ETHAN ALLEN class (continued)			
SSBN 618	THOMAS JEFFERSON	1963	decomm. 24 Jan 1985; str. 30 Apr 1986
LAFAYETTE class (continued)			
SSBN 619	ANDREW JACKSON	1963	decomm./str. 31 Aug 1989
SSBN 620	JOHN ADAMS	1964	decomm./str. 24 Mar 1989
SSBN 622	JAMES MONROE	1963	decomm./str. 25 Sep 1990
SSBN 623	NATHAN HALE	1963	decomm./str. 31 Mar 1986
SSBN 624	WOODROW WILSON	1963	decomm./str. 1 Sep 1994
SSBN 625	HENRY CLAY	1964	decomm./str. 5 Nov 1990
SSBN 626	DANIEL WEBSTER	1964	decomm./str. 30 Aug 1990; to MTS
SSBN 627	JAMES MADISON	1964	decomm./str. 20 Nov 1992
SSBN 628	TECUMSEH	1964	decomm./str. 23 July 1993
SSBN 629	DANIEL BOONE	1964	decomm./str. 18 Feb 1994
SSBN 630	JOHN C. CALHOUN	1964	decomm/str. 28 Mar 1994
SSBN 631 1992	ULYSSES S. GRANT	1964	decomm./str. 12 June
SSBN 632	VON STEUBEN	1964	decomm./str. 26 Feb 1994
SSBN 633	CASIMIR PULASKI	1964	decomm./str. 7 Mar 1994
SSBN 634	STONEWALL JACKSON	1964	decomm./str. 23 Dec 1987
SSBN 635	SAM RAYBURN	1964	decomm./str. 31 July 1989; to MTS
SSBN 636	NATAHANAEL GREENE	1964	decomm./str. 31 Jan 1987
SSBN 640	BENJAMIN FRANKLIN	1965	decomm./str. 23 Nov 1993
SSBN 641	SIMON BOLIVAR	1965	decomm./str. 8 Feb 1995
SSBN 642	KAMEHAMEHA	1965	decomm./str. 2 Apr 2002
SSBN 643	GEORGE BANCROFT	1966	decomm./str. 21 Sep 1993
SSBN 644	LEWIS AND CLARK	1965	decomm./str. 1 Aug 1992
SSBN 645	JAMES K. POLK	1966	decomm./str. 8 July 1999
SSBN 654	GEORGE C. MARSHALL	1966	decomm./str. 24 Sep 1992
SSBN 655	HENRY L. STIMSON	1966	decomm./str. 5 May 1993
SSBN 656	GEORGE WASHINGTON CARVER	1966	decomm./str. 18 Mar 1993
SSBN 657	FRANCIS SCOTT KEY	1966	decomm./str. 2 Sep 1993
SSBN 658	MARIANO G. VALLEJO	1966	decomm./str. 9 Mar 1995
SSBN 659	WILL ROGERS	1967	decomm./str. 12 Apr 1993
SSBN 726– 743	OHIO class		

Ballistic missile submarines are numbered in the same series as attack/special-purpose submarines (see chapter 11 for SSN hull numbers). The GEORGE WASHINGTON class was converted during the design/construction stage from attack submarines of the SKIPJACK (SSN 585) class. The ETHAN ALLEN-class submarines were the first U.S. SSBNs designed from the outset as ballistic missile ships.

Eight early SSBNs were briefly reclassified and employed as attack submarines in 1980–1982: SSN 598, 599, 601, 608–611, and 618. They had limited effectiveness in the SSN role because of their sonar, noise levels, and number of torpedoes.

Four ex-missile submarines were converted to transport special operations forces: The JOHN MARSHALL and SAM HOUSTON were extensively converted in 1984–1986 to transport submarines to carry SEALs or other special forces; they were decommissioned in 1991–1992. They were replaced by the JAMES K. POLK and KAMEHAMEHA, converted in 1992–1993; they were decommissioned in 1999 and 2002, respectively. The KAMEHAMEHA was in commission for more than 36 years, longer than any other U.S. nuclear submarine. (See chapter 11 for details on transport submarines.) The SAM HOUSTON also was employed in the mid-1980s as a test platform for the UQQ-2 Surveillance Towed Array Sonar System (SURTASS); the SURTASS is carried by T-AGOS surveillance ships (see chapter 23).

The SAM RAYBURN and DANIEL WEBSTER were modified (and immobilized) to serve as moored training ships for nuclear propulsion plant operators. Their propellers were removed and their missile tubes filled with concrete. They are officially listed as "floating equipment" by the Navy and are moored at Charleston, South Carolina.

CHAPTER 11

Submarines

Crewmen line the deck and gangway of the LOUISVILLE, moored at the submarine base at Pearl Harbor, Hawaii. Submarine crews are among the elite of the Navy because of their selection process and training. When this photo was taken, the LOUISVILLE had just received the Battle Efficiency "E" award. (2004, U.S. Navy/Corwin M. Colbert)

The U.S. Navy's attack submarine force in early 2005 consists of 54 nuclear-propelled submarines. In addition, one diesel-electric research submarine, the DOLPHIN (AGSS 555), is in service (see chapter 12).[1]

One extensively modified submarine of the SEAWOLF class is under construction (the JIMMY CARTER), as are the first submarines of the VIRGINIA class. Both classes have been highly controversial. In addition to new construction nuclear-propelled attack submarines (SSNs), the Navy is converting four Trident-armed OHIO (SSBN 726)-class platforms to combination cruise missile and transport/special forces submarines (SSGNs). These submarines, which were retired from the strategic missile role in 2002–2004, are deemed attack submarines and are discussed below.

The attack submarine force has been reduced precipitously since the end of the Cold War—from almost 100 SSNs in 1991 to an approved force level of 55 today. This smaller number has been recommended under various Department of Defense studies, beginning with the *Report of the Bottom-Up Review* of October 1993.[2] The Trident SSGN conversions will be counted against the SSN force level under current Department of Defense policies.

The U.S. submarine community has stated a requirement for 68 SSNs by 2015 and 76 by 2025, based on a Joint Chiefs of Staff study of the requirements put forward by the U.S. regional commanders (formerly known as unified commanders-in-chief).[3] However, these regional commanders, who are responsible for employing forces but do not procure military forces, invariably ask for more weapons than are politically or fiscally possible to procure. Also, the principal rationale for the additional SSNs is Intelligence, Surveillance, and Reconnaissance (ISR) missions, including the landing of Special Operations Forces (SOF) on hostile beaches.

The Navy's long-range shipbuilding plan calls for an increase in SSN construction from one to two submarines per year beginning with the Fiscal Year (FY) 2007 shipbuilding program. However, congressional support for the increase will depend to a large degree on the success of the VIRGINIA (commissioned in 2004) and ship/program costs. To achieve the proposed force of 76 submarines by 2025, the Navy would have to have authorization of an average of three submarines per year, clearly an impossible goal. Without this increase in the building rate, the number of SSNs in commission eventually will decline to some 30 units, based on an SSN service life expectancy of 30 years.

Several alternatives have been put forward for obtaining more mission capability from a 55-submarine force. These alternatives

---

1 The Navy also holds one older diesel-electric submarine, also suitable for the research role, the ex-USS TROUT (SS 566); see Chapter 12.
2 The *Report of the Bottom-Up Review*, commissioned by Secretary of Defense Les Aspin, recommended a force of 45–55 submarines. The subsequent Quarterly Defense Review recommended a force of 50 SSNs.
3 Adm. F. L. Bowman, USN, Director, Naval Nuclear Propulsion, "Remarks at Corporate Benefactors Day," *The Submarine Review* (April 2002), pp. 14–15.

have been addressed in a recent study by the Congressional Budget Office (CBO):[4]

- Use the four ex-Trident SSGNs to perform missions identified by the Joint Chiefs of Staff study (i.e., ISR).
- Use more than one crew to operate some SSNs (as now done with Trident SSBNs).
- Base additional SSNs on Guam, beyond the three planned by the Navy, thus reducing submarine transit times to their operational areas.[5]

CRUISE MISSILE/TRANSPORT SUBMARINES

The SSGN concept provides considerable promise for a versatile and effective warship. With four SSGNs (each manned by two, alternating crews), it will be possible to keep two missile submarine forward deployed on a continuous basis.

However, many questions related to the SSGN concept remain. Today, Tomahawk Land-Attack Missiles (TLAM) are carried primarily in cruisers and destroyers, with smaller numbers in attack submarines fitted with Vertical Launching Systems (VLS). A TLAM loadout of 154 missiles is carried in perhaps three or four cruisers and destroyers in a battle group. Those surface warships carry out many tasks beyond land attack, including anti-air warfare, anti-surface warfare, patrol and interdiction, and gunfire support. Would an area or fleet commander be willing to give up those three or four ships for a single SSGN, or would he want the SSGN in addition?

The land-attack mission often requires a large amount of communications and data-link traffic. This will be true especially with the planned Tactical Tomahawk, a quick-reaction missile that can be retargeted while in flight. Could an SSGN maintain its clandestine posture and still handle the communications requirement? In addition, when a TLAM is launched today, planners attempt to avoid both friendly and enemy ships, and perhaps certain geographic areas on the first leg of the missile's flight. Data for this flight profile are fed into the missile shortly before launch, based on the launch ship's own radar/electronic intercept data, as well as on external data sources. Again, in certain situations, this requirement could be difficult for cruise missile submarines.

SOF personnel currently are transported in attack submarines, with several boats of the Los Angeles class modified to carry either a single dry deck shelter or an Advanced SEAL Delivery System (ASDS) vehicle (see Chapter 12 for names). The now-building submarine Jimmy Carter and the Virginia class also will be capable of embarking a dry deck shelter or ASDS, and later units will have "convertible" torpedo rooms for rapid conversion to support SOF personnel, with enlarged lock-out hatches and storage space for their equipment.

Thus, there will be significant support available for SOF operations even without the Trident SSGN conversions. Indeed, some submarine officers believe the attack submarines—although their SOF capacity is smaller—will be far more effective than SSGNs: (1) with more platforms available, SSNs will permit greater geographic coverage; (2) it will be easier to maneuver and "hide" an SSN than an SSGN of almost 17,000 tons displacement, about twice that of an attack submarine; and (3) while the SSGNs will accommodate 66 SOF personnel, most operations require smaller numbers, from a few to perhaps a dozen people to be put ashore or taken off. Indeed, with one exception, neither U.S. nor Soviet submarines carried out operational clandestine landings of more than a dozen men during the entire Cold War.

There also is concern from some Navy planners over whether the SSGNs, while carrying SEAL teams or other special operations forces, would be able to perform their land-attack missions.

The SOF-carrying submarine might have to leave her assigned missile launch "box" or required operating area to carry out the SOF assignment, and vice versa, if both roles must be conducted simultaneously.

TRANSPORT SUBMARINES

All specialized transport submarines have been discarded. The last, the Kamehameha, was decommissioned in 2002, leaving a gap of four years until the first Ohio-class SSGN conversion joins the fleet. The Kamehameha and three other ex-Polaris SSBNs converted to serve in the SOF transport role had had their 16 missile tubes demilitarized and were fitted to carry and support some 60 SEALs or other special forces troops. (See 17th Edition/pages 86–88.)

Previously, the Navy employed converted/modified diesel-electric submarines in the transport role. The non-nuclear submarines were given special amphibious designations; not so the nuclear submarines, which were changed from SSBN to SSN.

The following submarines had special transport roles:

Table 11-1. TRANSPORT SUBMARINES

Number*	Former	Name	Transport
APS 1	SM 1	Argonaut	1942–1943**
APSS 282	SS/SSG 282	Tunny	1966–1969
SSP 313	SS 313	Perch	1948–1959
SSP 315	SS 315	Sealion	1948–1969
APSS 574	SSG 574	Grayback	1969–1984
SSN 609	SSBN 609	Sam Houston	1986–1991
SSN 611	SSBN 611	John Marshall	1984–1992
SSN 642	SSBN 642	Kamehameha	1992–2002
SSN 645	SSBN 645	James K. Polk	1993–1999

* The designations APSS, SSP, and LPSS were used for specialized transport submarines during the Cold War era; several of these submarines were reclassified within that series.

** The Argonaut was sunk by Japanese surface ships on 26 February 1943.

SPECIAL MISSION SUBMARINES

The Navy has discarded the Parche, an extensively converted Sturgeon-class SSN configured for ocean search-and-recovery operations. Her mission will be taken over by the Jimmy Carter, albeit after a two-year gap in that capability in the fleet. (The Parche is described in the 17th Edition/pages 85–86.) The Jimmy Carter incorporates a number of advanced features for carrying out a variety of specialized missions.

Previously, the Navy had employed the converted submarines Seawolf (SSN 575) and Halibut (SSGN/SSN 567) in the ocean search-and-recovery role. Those submarines gained public notoriety when it was revealed they had been employed to "tap" into Soviet seafloor communications cables. A former employee of the National Security Agency, Ronald Pelton, disclosed those clandestine operations to the Soviets in January 1980.[6] The Halibut also was employed to tow a seafloor camera system to locate the remains of a Soviet Golf II-class (Project 629A) SSB that sank in the North Pacific in 1968.[7]

All Sturgeon and earlier attack submarines have been stricken. The converted Parche was the last, taken out of service in 2003; the last "straight" Sturgeon-class SSN was the L. Mendel Rivers, taken out of service in early 2001. Submarines of the stan-

4 Eric J. Labs, *Increasing the Mission Capability of the Attack Submarine Force* (Washington, D.C.: Congressional Budget Office, March 2002).

5 Those SSNs are the City of Corpus Christi, Houston, and San Francisco.

6 See Sherry Sontag and Christopher Drew, *Blind Man's Bluff: The Untold Story of American Submarine Espionage* (New York: PublicAffairs, 1998), pp. 158–83.

7 See Roger C. Dunham, *Spy Sub* (Annapolis, Md.: Naval Institute Press, 1996). This is a lightly disguised fictional account of the Halibut's search operation by a crew member.

dard LOS ANGELES class now are being decommissioned and stricken to attain the authorized force level of 55 SSNs.

Nuclear-propelled submarines cannot be laid up in reserve for possible future reactivation because of the measures necessary for shutting down their reactor plants and removing possibly radioactive components. (See Chapter 10 [*Operational* notes] for details of nuclear submarine deactivation/disposal.)

Several submarines of the ETHAN ALLEN and GEORGE WASHINGTON classes served briefly in the SSN role during the 1980s; they were not successful as SSNs because of their relatively high self-noise levels, limited sonar capability, and few torpedo reloads.

All diesel-electric combat submarines have been discarded from the U.S. Navy; the diesel-electric research submarine DOLPHIN remains in service. Several proposals have been made for the U.S. Navy to procure non-nuclear submarines, particularly designs fitted with Air Independent Propulsion (AIP) to supplement the diesel-electric propulsion plant. Such submarines could carry out some missions as well as nuclear units, among them anti-submarine training (against non-nuclear submarine targets), special operations in low-threat areas, and research and development. However, non-nuclear submarine construction has been strongly opposed by the U.S. submarine community's leadership, as has construction of conventional submarines in U.S. shipyards for foreign navies. (In 1994, the Litton/Ingalls yard obtained U.S. State Department permission to explore the construction and/or fitting out of submarines in the United States for the Egyptian Navy. That effort was aborted after strong objections by the nuclear submarine community. Previously, the yard was involved in the procurement—albeit not construction—of German-built submarines for the Israeli Navy. The Israeli and South Korean Navies also had attempted to construct nonnuclear submarines in the United States.)

The last U.S. Navy diesel-electric attack submarine was the BLUEBACK, stricken in 1990 after 31 years of service.[8]

Builders: Two U.S. shipyards construct submarines: General Dynamics/Electric Boat, successor to the John P. Holland Torpedo Boat Company, which can trace its construction lineage for the U.S. Navy to 1900, when the Navy commissioned the HOLLAND (SS 1) as its first official submarine; and Newport News Shipbuilding, which first built submarines in 1905–1906, completing five craft designed by Simon Lake for the Russian Navy. Northrop Grumman Corporation's acquisition of Newport News Shipbuilding was announced on 8 November 2001.

Electric Boat completed its first nuclear submarine, the NAUTILUS, in 1955; the first Newport News-built nuclear submarine was the SHARK of 1961.

In the 1960s, at the height of the Navy's Polaris submarine construction program, there were seven U.S. shipyards building nuclear-propelled submarines:

• General Dynamics/Electric Boat Company (Connecticut)
• General Dynamics/Quincy (Massachusetts)
• Ingalls Shipbuilding (Mississippi)
• Mare Island Naval Shipyard (California)
• Newport News Shipbuilding (Virginia)
• New York Shipbuilding (New Jersey)
• Portsmouth Naval Shipyard (Maine)

Classification: Beginning in 1920 with the USS HOLLAND, all U.S. submarines have been assigned hull numbers in a single series, with ten exceptions: the SEAWOLF class (SSN 21–23) and the seven small/midget undersea craft listed at the end of this chapter (SSK, SST, and SSX types).

Names: Attack submarines have had several name sources. The Navy's first submarine was named for its designer, Irish immigrant–schoolteacher John P. Holland, who was living when the craft was accepted by the Navy in 1900. Subsequent U.S. submarines were given fish names until 1911, when class letters and numerals were assigned (e.g., A-2). This scheme continued until 1931, at which time fish names again were used (in addition to a scheme of class letter designations and hull numbers).

After World War II, the class letter–number names again were used for the small K (hunter-killer) and T (training) submarines, but these subsequently were given fish names. Postwar submarines continued the use of fish and other marine-life names until 1971, when Vice Admiral H. G. Rickover, then head of the Navy's nuclear propulsion program, instituted the practice of naming attack submarines for deceased members of Congress who had supported nuclear programs—he is reputed to have observed, "Fish don't vote." Four SSNs were so named: the GLENARD P. LIPSCOMB, L. MENDEL RIVERS, RICHARD B. RUSSELL, and WILLIAM H. BATES.

The naming source for attack submarines was changed in 1974 to city names, with the first being the LOS ANGELES. However, on 9 May 1983, then-Secretary of the Navy John Lehman directed that the SSN 705 be named HYMAN G. RICKOVER, for Admiral Rickover, whom he had helped force to leave the Navy in January 1982. (This was only the second recent U.S. Navy ship to be named for a living person, the first being the carrier CARL VINSON/CVN 70.) Lehman's action was intended to prevent Congress from naming an aircraft carrier for Rickover.

The SSN 21 reverted to a fish name, SEAWOLF, but the SSN 22 carries a state name, CONNECTICUT, and the SSN 23 is named JIMMY CARTER, the only attack submarine to be named for a president. In the late 1990s, when Secretary of the Navy John Dalton named the CONNECTICUT and JIMMY CARTER, state names were carried by battleships, cruisers, and strategic missile submarines; president names were being assigned to aircraft carriers.

Operational: The primary peacetime SSN missions are intelligence collection, observation of potentially hostile surface ships and submarines, and anti-submarine training for air, surface, and submarine forces. One or two SSNs normally deploy overseas with each carrier battle group.

In wartime, the primary mission of U.S. attack submarines is to operate against enemy "attack" and strategic missile submarines, as well as to carry out anti-surface warfare, land attack (with Tomahawk), and mining operations.

During the 1991 Gulf War, two LOS ANGELES-class SSNs fired TLAMs against targets in Iraq. Those 12 missiles, 4 percent of the 288 Tomahawks launched in that conflict, were fired primarily for "public relations" purposes, although the launchings were valuable to test the concept. Subsequently, submarines have fired TLAMs in several crises and conflicts, against targets in Afghanistan, Sudan, and Yugoslavia. During Operation Allied Force, the 1999 NATO strikes against Yugoslavia, 321 TLAMs were launched by U.S. surface ships and submarines and the British SSN SPLENDID.[9] Submarines accounted for 25 percent of the launches.

During Operation Iraqi Freedom (March–April 2003), almost 800 Tomahawks were launched by surface ships and submarines.

---

8 Her sister ship BARBEL was in commission for 30.9 years and the BONEFISH for 29.2 years, longer than all nuclear-propelled submarines except the KAMEHAMEHA (SSBN 642), in commission more than 46 years.

9 HMS SPLENDID was the first British warship armed with Tomahawk missiles. The Royal Navy initially procured 65 TLAMs; additional missile have been ordered with British submarines participating in the TLAM strikes of the second Gulf War in 2003.

Thirty percent were fired by 12 U.S. and 2 British SSNs. The USS SAN JUAN launched 27 TLAMs, the most of any submarine.

Payload: All U.S. combat submarines (SSBN/SSN), except for the SEAWOLF class, have 21-inch (533-mm) torpedo tubes. This diameter has been the standard in U.S. submarines since the AA-2 (SS 60) completed in 1922. The SEAWOLF introduced 26½-inch (670-mm)-diameter torpedo tubes to U.S. submarines.[10] Though the class carries the 21-inch Mk 48 ADCAP (Advanced Capability) torpedo, the larger-diameter tubes permit quiet, "swim-out" launch.

The Tomahawk land-attack missile is launched from standard 21-inch torpedo tubes and from the Vertical Launching System, which also has 21-inch-diameter launch tubes.

The limitation in the launch envelope caused by this historical reliance on the 21-inch tube led the Defense Science Board Task Force on Submarines of the Future, convened in 1998 and chaired by John Stenbit, to call for greatly increase submarine payloads and alternative means of launching weapons and other payloads.[11] The task force report, published in June 1998, noted:

> The next generation SSN must be a highly capable warship with rapid response capability:
> • It should have flexible payload interfaces with the water, not torpedo tubes, VLS and other special purpose interfaces.
> • It should not constrain the ship and size of weapons, auxiliary vehicles, and other payloads when they are used.

The Stenbit task force was particularly concerned that existing SSN weapon launchers were limited to 21-inch-diameter torpedo tubes, 21-inch VLS tubes, and smaller-diameter countermeasure ejectors.[12] By comparison, Soviet–Russian "attack" submarines have both 21-inch and 26½-inch torpedo tubes plus—in some units (SSG/SSGN)—large-diameter missile launching tubes.

Both the Defense Science Board's report and a briefing for industry sponsored by the Navy and the Defense Advanced Research Projects Agency (DARPA) on 10 December 1998 stressed that the VIRGINIA program should continue and evolve: "We should not stop an effective program until we have a superior replacement," and "We need to get comfortable with the 'flexible interface with the water,' and we need to design and test it."

The next-generation SSN should be a large, nuclear submarine, the task force concluded: "We need to cover the world from the U.S. [at] high transit speed, [with] independent logistics, and endurance," and "We need to have flexible payloads." This dictates a large submarine with a hull 33–39 feet [10–11.9 meters] in diameter. However, this submarine must be a "combat" ship, and not simply a "mother" to long-range weapons, sensors, submersibles, and other systems.

While the task force recommended against the United States developing diesel submarines, it noted:

> Just because we choose not to build diesels, we must learn from the development of such ships for
> • Technology infusion
> • Threat understanding
> • Operational development
> • Training and tactics for close range engagements

The OHIO-class SSGN conversions will have inserts in most of their Trident ballistic missile tubes to accommodate seven TLAMs.

Personnel: Most but not necessarily all personnel assigned to a submarine deploy with the craft; several might be left ashore for family, medical, or educational reasons. Still, with rare exceptions, U.S. attack submarines do not have sufficient berths for all enlisted men, and bunk sharing ("hot bunking") is required. The SEAWOLF, for example, is short 12 bunks. When a full load of torpedo/weapons is not being carried, additional temporary bunks can be fitted in the torpedo room.

Weapons: All operational U.S. attack submarines carry the Mk 48 ADCAP torpedo for use against surface ships and submarines. They also can carry the Tomahawk missile, launched from standard torpedo tubes or, in the Improved LOS ANGELES and VIRGINIA classes, from 12 VLS tubes.

The Improved LOS ANGELES and later submarines also can launch the Mk 67 Submarine-Launched Mobile Mine (SLMM), carried in place of torpedoes.

Harpoon anti-ship missiles previously carried by U.S. submarines have been beached.

The Sea Lance Anti-Submarine Warfare (ASW) Stand-Off Weapon (SOW) was canceled. Ostensibly, it was to have been a replacement for the outdated Submarine Rocket (SUBROC), an ASW weapon that carried a nuclear depth bomb. SUBROC, launched from 21-inch submarine torpedo tubes, was taken out of service in 1989. With the loss of the Sea Lance, no ASW stand-off weapon is available to U.S. submarines. (The Sea Lance was to have carried both a nuclear depth bomb and the Mk 50 conventional, lightweight torpedo as warheads, with the latter having development priority.)

The Tomahawk Land-Attack Missile–Nuclear (TLAM-N) was taken out of service in 1992. It could be launched by both surface ships and attack submarines, and 57 LOS ANGELES-class submarines were so configured. Today, some 320 TLAM-Ns remain in storage, and a Portable Launching System (PLS) has been developed to support placing these missiles on board specific SSNs, if necessary. The PLS, first delivered to the Navy in FY 1999, consists of a laptop computer that connects to the submarine's weapon control system to permit TLAM-N checkout and launching. The capability to deploy TLAM-N missiles in submarines, however, will be limited by the requirement to train personnel in handling and launching these weapons.[13]

The four oldest Trident strategic missile submarines have been removed from the SSBN role and are being converted to combination cruise missile/special operations transports.

Table 11-2. SUBMARINE FORCE LEVELS (EARLY 2005)

Type	Class/Ship	Comm.	Active*	Building**
SSGN 726	Converted OHIO	2006–	—	4***
SSN 774	VIRGINIA	2004–	1	5
SSN 23	JIMMY CARTER	2005	—	1
SSN 21	SEAWOLF	1997–1998	2	—
SSN 751	Improved LOS ANGELES	1988–1996	23	—
SSN 688	LOS ANGELES	1976–1989	28	—

* Some submarines are in the process of "standing down" in preparation for being decommissioned and stricken.
** Submarines authorized through FY 2004.
***Four submarines undergoing conversion.

---

10 The actual internal diameter is 30 inches (762 mm), but there are fixed skids that reduce the useable diameter to 26½ inches.

11 Office of the Secretary of the Navy (Assistant Secretary for Research, Development, and Acquisition), Defense Advanced Research Projects Agency, and Chief of Naval Operations (Submarine Warfare Division), "Memorandum of Agreement: A Project to Revise the Payloads and Sensors of Attack Submarines," 19 August 1998.

12 The exception being the three SEAWOLF-class submarines; each has eight 26½-inch torpedo tubes.

13 See Lt. Michael Kostiuk, USN, "Removal of the Nuclear Strike Option from United States Attack Submarines," *The Submarine Review* (January 1998), pp. 85–90.

4 CRUISE MISSILE AND SPECIAL FORCES TRANSPORT SUBMARINES: CONVERTED "OHIO" CLASS

Number	Name	FY	Builder	Start	Laid down	Launched	Comm.	Conversion Start	Conversion Complete	Status
SSGN 726	OHIO	74	General Dynamics/Electric Boat	19 July 1974	10 Apr 1976	7 Apr 1976	11 Nov 1981	15 Nov 2003	2006	Conversion
SSGN 727	MICHIGAN	75	General Dynamics/Electric Boat	15 Aug 1975	4 Apr 1977	26 Apr 1980	11 Sep 1982	1 Nov 2003	2006	Conversion
SSGN 728	FLORIDA	75	General Dynamics/Electric Boat	27 Feb 1976	9 June 1977	14 Nov 1981	18 June 1983	28 June 2003	2006	Conversion
SSGN 729	GEORGIA	76	General Dynamics/Electric Boat	17 Jan 1977	7 Apr 1979	6 Nov 1982	11 Feb 1984	1 Jan 2004	2007	Conversion

Displacement:	16,764 tons standard	ASW weapons:	Mk 48 torpedoes
	18,750 tons submerged	Radars:	BPS-15J surface search
Length:	560 feet (170.7 m) overall	Sonars:	BQQ-6 bow mounted passive
Beam:	42 feet (12.8 m)		BQR-15 towed array; being replaced by TB-29A thin-line
Draft:	36¼ feet (11.05 m)		towed array
Propulsion:	2 steam turbines (General Electric); approx. 35,000 shp;		BQR-19 active navigation
	1 shaft		BQS-13 active
Reactors:	1 S8G pressurized-water (General Electric)		BQS-15 under ice
Speed:	approx. 25 knots surface	Fire control:	1 CCS Mk 2 Mod 3
	approx. 25 knots submerged		1 Mk 98 missile Fire Control System (FCS)
Personnel:	160 (15 officers + 145 enlisted)		1 Mk 118 torpedo FCS
Troops:	66 (14 officers + 52 enlisted)	EW systems:	BLQ-10
Missiles:	22 tubes of 7 TLAMs (154); see *Conversion* notes		WLR-8(V)5
Torpedo tubes:	4 21-inch (533-mm) tubes Mk 68 (angled)		WLR-10

The OHIO began her SSGN conversion/refueling in FY 2003, the FLORIDA and MICHIGAN in FY 2004, and the GEORGIA in FY 2005. The OHIO is scheduled to be fully operational in June 2007 and all four submarines by 2008. The OHIO and MICHIGAN are being converted at the Puget Sound Naval Shipyard (Washington), and the FLORIDA and GEORGIA at the Norfolk Naval Shipyard (Virginia).

Classification: Previous U.S. nuclear-propelled submarines assigned the guided missile classification were the USS HALIBUT (SSGN 587) and SSGNs 594–596 and 607; the latter four submarines were built as ASW submarines of the THRESHER class after cancellation of the Regulus II missile program in 1958. (Several U.S. diesel-electric submarines, both conversions and new construction, were designated SSG.)

The four OHIO conversions were changed to SSGN in 2004.

Conversion: The SSGN conversion will permit multiple configurations that can be changed out either in the submarines' home ports or in selected overseas ports. All variants would have berthing, messing, and equipment spaces for 66 special operations forces personnel and their gear. Former Trident launch tubes No. 1 and 2 would be permanently modified for five-man SOF lock-in/lock-out and for attaching ASDS vehicles and Dry Deck Shelters (DDS). The remaining 22 ex-Trident missile tubes would be modified to accept modules/canisters that could store and launch seven TLAMs or other strike missiles. However, if the ASDS or DDS is mounted, not all tubes could be used for missiles. The three configurations are:

• Maximum strike—launch tubes No. 3–24 each could have "seven-pack" missile canisters; all 154 missiles could be fired in six minutes.

• Strike/SOF—launch tubes No. 5–24 could be loaded with 140 missiles; launch tubes No. 3 and 4 could be loaded with SOF stowage canisters; two ASDS vehicles could be carried.

• Strike/SOF—launch tubes No. 7–24 could be loaded with 126 missiles; launch tubes No. 5 and 6 could remain empty or be loaded with additional SOF equipment; other tubes would be blocked by two DDSs.

Additional temporary bunks and hot bunking could provide accommodations for up to 100 SOF personnel for short periods.

The submarines eventually will be capable of supporting, launching, and recovering Unmanned Undersea Vehicles (UUVs) and possibly Unmanned Aerial Vehicles (UAVs).

Cost: The Navy had estimated the following aggregate costs for the four SSGN conversions in FY 1998 dollars:

Development and conversion	$ 1.994 billion
Refueling (reactor cores)	$ .440 billion
Total	$ 2.434 billion

By mid-2003, the estimated cost was $3.8 billion. Final costs were expected to be significantly higher than estimated.

Missiles: These submarines will carry TLAM Block III and Tactical Tomahawk (TACTOM) missiles. The FLORIDA (while configured as an SSBN) became the first strategic missile submarine to launch a tactical missile (see *Operational* notes).

Operational: The FLORIDA launched the first Tomahawk missile from an OHIO-class submarine on 14 January 2003 during operations in the Gulf of Mexico (Operation Giant Shadow). A second launch, on 16 January, also saw the submarine firing an instrumented Block III missile. For both tests, the missile was launched from a Multiple All-up-rounds Canister (MAC) in a configuration similar to the tightly packed, seven-missile cluster of Tomahawk missiles planned for SSGN tubes.

The SSGNs will be based at the Trident home ports of Kings Bay, Georgia, and Bangor, Washington.

Personnel: It is proposed that the SSGNs have two alternating crews, as when they were Trident SSBNs. The Navy is keeping the same Billets Authorized as these ships had as SSBNs until they have begun fleet operations.

Table 11-3. SSGN CONFIGURATION OPTIONS

Configuration	SOF Troops	Land-Attack Missiles	Tubes for SOF Storage	ASDS/DDS
Maximum Strike	66	154	0	0
Strike/SOF (2 ASDS)	66	140	2	2
Strike/SOF (2 DDS)	66	126	4	2

An artist's conception of a Trident SSBN as converted to a cruise missile/transport submarine (SSGN). In this view, the SSGN has a dry deck shelter and an Advanced SEAL Delivery System vehicle aft of the sail structure; three Tomahawks are being launched from the submarine's large missile battery. (U.S. Navy)

A Tomahawk missile streaks from the water after being launched from the Trident submarine FLORIDA off the Bahamas during Operation Giant Shadow. The FLORIDA, still an SSBN at the time, is now being converted to an SSGN. She launched two instrumented, unarmed TLAMs during the exercise in January 2003. (2003, U.S. Navy)

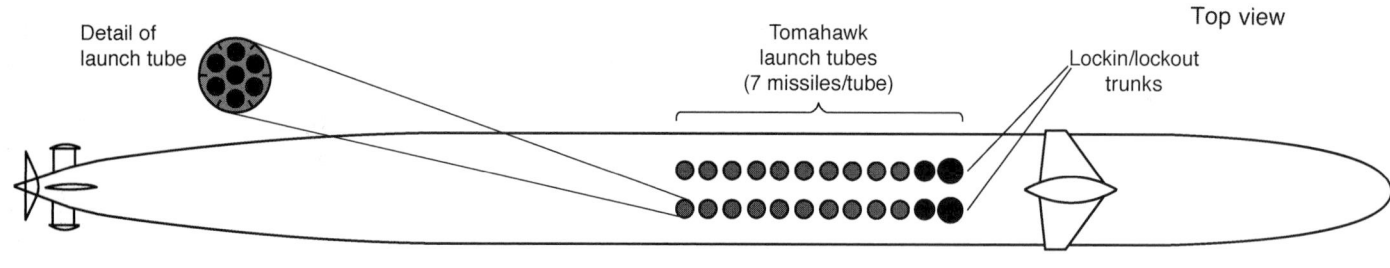

Detail of launch tube

Tomahawk launch tubes (7 missiles/tube)

Lockin/lockout trunks

Top view

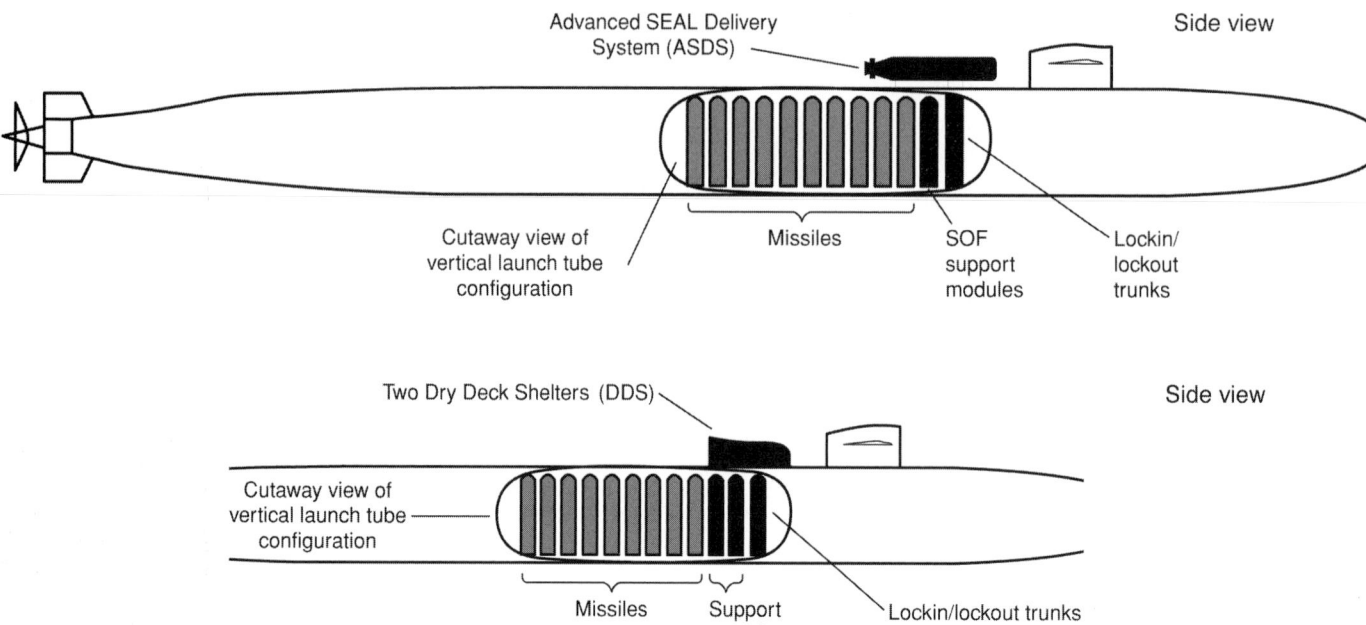

Advanced SEAL Delivery System (ASDS)

Side view

Cutaway view of vertical launch tube configuration

Missiles

SOF support modules

Lockin/ lockout trunks

Two Dry Deck Shelters (DDS)

Side view

Cutaway view of vertical launch tube configuration

Missiles

Support modules

Lockin/lockout trunks

SSGN strike/transport configurations.

The OHIO undergoing conversion to an SSGN at the Puget Sound Naval Shipyard. The hatches of her missile tubes are open, as the tubes are being modified to each launch seven Tomahawk land-attack missiles. (2004, U.S. Navy)

(1 + 29) NUCLEAR-PROPELLED ATTACK SUBMARINES: "VIRGINIA" CLASS

Number	Name	FY	Builder	Started	Laid Down	Launched	Christened	Comm.	Status
SSN 774	VIRGINIA	98	General Dynamics/Electric Boat	15 Aug 1997	2 Sep 1999	7 Aug 2003	16 Aug 2003	23 Oct 2004	**AA**
SSN 775	TEXAS	99	Northrop Grumman/Newport News	8 Sep 1998	12 July 2002	2005	31 July 2004	2005	Building
SSN 776	HAWAII	01	General Dynamics/Electric Boat	26 Oct 1999	27 Aug 2004			2006	Building
SSN 777	NORTH CAROLINA	02	Northrop Grumman/Newport News	2 Mar 2001	22 May 2002			2007	Building
SSN 778	NEW HAMPSHIRE	03	General Dynamics/Electric Boat	5 Aug 2002				2009	Building
SSN 779	NEW MEXICO	04	Northrop Grumman/Newport News	14 Mar 2003				2010	Building
SSN 780	....	05	General Dynamics/Electric Boat	4 Aug 2004				2011	Planned
SSN 781	....	06	Northrop Grumman/Newport News					2012	Planned
SSN 782	....	07	General Dynamics/Electric Boat					2013	Planned
SSN 783	....	07	Northrop Grumman/Newport News S					2013	Planned
SSN 784–803	20 ships	08–18						2014	Planned

Displacement:	7,800 tons submerged
Length:	377 feet (114.94 m) overall
Beam:	34 feet (10.37 m)
Draft:	
Propulsion:	2 steam turbines; approx. 25,000 shp; 1 shaft/propulsor
Reactors:	1 S9G pressurized-water (General Electric)
Speed:	25+ knots
Personnel:	134 (14 officers + 120 enlisted)
Missiles:	TLAMs launched from torpedo tubes and VLS
	12 vertical launch tubes for TLAMs

Torpedoes tubes:	4 21-inch (533-mm) tubes angled (27 weapons)
ASW weapons:	Mk 48 ADCAP torpedoes
Radars:	surface search
Sonars:	BQG-5A lightweight Wide Aperture Array (WAA)
	BQQ-6 bow mounted active/passive (spherical)
	BQQ-10 Acoustic Rapid COTS Insertion (ARCI) sonar update
	minehunting sonar
	TB-29A thin-line towed array
EW systems:	BLD-1
	ULR-21

The development of a lower-cost SSN was initiated in 1988–1990 in response to the increasing costs of the SEAWOLF class, as well as to questions about that submarine's roles and missions. The Navy's goal for the program was to develop a multimission attack submarine that was (1) substantially less expensive than the SEAWOLF design, (2) capable of maintaining U.S. undersea superiority against a reduced but continuing Russian submarine effort, (3) more capable than the SEAWOLF and improved LOS ANGELES classes for operations in littoral areas, and (4) better able than the SEAWOLF and improved LOS ANGELES designs to incorporate major new submarine technologies as they became available.

The result is the VIRGINIA-class submarines, being constructed jointly by the Electric Boat and Newport News shipyards, with assembly and completion being alternated between the yards. (The assembly/completion yard is listed as "builder" in the class table.) This is a unique arrangement in submarine construction, with no precedent in U.S. or foreign experience. The scheme was developed to ensure continued survivability of both shipyards in the submarine construction business, but it has led to higher costs, increased construction times, and questions about legal liability. Another option that would have ensured the same result but with more efficient construction would have been to alternative the submarine contracts between the two yards.

The Navy hopes to increase the building rate to two submarines per year beginning with the FY 2008 program. On 14 August 2003, the Navy announced a contract award for a "block-buy" for one VIRGINIA-class SSN each year from FY 2003 through FY 2006, and two submarines in 2007, pending congressional authorization and appropriation. However, through 2004, the Department of Defense and the Navy's leadership have refused to approve a two-per-year SSN construction rate for the foreseeable future.

The unit numbers in the class table are based on the Navy's 30-year shipbuilding plan presented to Congress in 2003.

Note that the VIRGINIA has a keel-laying date. That ceremony was reintroduced to U.S. submarine construction with that submarine. All of the submarine "keels" are put down at the Electric Boat plant at Quonset Point, Rhode Island.

Builders: The Navy originally planned for Electric Boat to build all submarines of this class, which would have forced Newport News Shipbuilding out of submarine construction. Congressional action forced the Navy to accept the participation of both yards. Subsequently, with the Navy's strong encouragement, the two yards proposed and initiated a joint construction program, with each yard having responsibility for specific portions: Newport News Shipbuilding builds the bow, stern, sail, and habitability sections, auxiliary machinery, and weapons handling spaces of all units; Electric Boat builds the pressure hull, command-and-control spaces, engine room, and main propulsion unit raft for all units.[14] The yards also will alternate building reactor plant modules and performing final outfitting, testing, and delivery.

Cost: In 1994, the Navy estimated that the lead submarine would cost about $3.4 billion (including about $1.1 billion in nonrecurring design costs) and the fifth and follow-on submarines each would cost $1.54 *billion* (in FY 1998 dollars).[15] The 1994 study prepared for the Navy estimated the following costs for the first three units:

FY 1998	NSSN No. 1	$2.237 billion
FY 2000	NSSN No. 2	$1.843 billion
FY 2001	NSSN No. 3	$1.746 billion
Nonrecurring costs		$4.681 billion

By mid-2004, the estimated cost for all ships of the class was an average of more than $2 billion per submarine.

Design: The VIRGINIA-class submarines are expected to have an acoustic signature (self-radiated noise) of the same level as the SEAWOLF design. This is in contrast to the long-held U.S. Navy belief that the larger the submarine, the quieter the submarine.[16]

The VIRGINIA torpedo room will be configured for the rapid removal of weapon stowage and handling equipment to facilitate the use of the submarine as a special forces (SEAL) transport or

14 The Royal Navy developed the concept of "rafting" propulsion machinery in the Ton-class minesweepers built in the 1950s and 1960s, isolating the machinery from the hull to reduce vulnerability to acoustic mines. This arrangement did not affect the noise-generating machinery, but decreased sound transmission through the hull into the water. This concept was selected for the U.S. THRESHER class in April 1957 and has been used in all subsequent U.S. nuclear-powered submarines.

15 Nonrecurring costs are for design, research and development, etc.

16 See Rear Adm. W. J. Holland Jr., USN (Ret), "Diesel Boats Again?" U.S. Naval Institute *Proceedings* (June 1996), p. 13, and subsequent commentary, especially N. Polmar, "New Approach to Submarines," U.S. Naval Institute *Proceedings* (August 1996), pp. 87–88, and Holland (December 1996), pp. 23–24.

possibly for other specialized roles. To further support special forces, one escape hatch will have a nine-man lock-in/lock-out trunk. The sail will house an Electronic Surveillance Measures (ESM) mast, multifunction communication masts, and two Photonics masts for improved imaging functions. The Photonics masts are nonpenetrating and replace the conventional (pressure-hull-penetrating) periscopes. The system provides several high-resolution color cameras that send visual images to large-screen displays in the ship's control room. Enhanced infrared and low-level-light image-enhancement features are provided. The mast also includes an infrared-laser range finder.

The pressure hull is being fabricated of HY-100 steel.

In response to criticisms of the NSSN/VIRGINIA design as too conservative, the Navy developed a series of "technology insertion possibilities" for the class, whereby new technologies could be incorporated into successive units. An impressive list of 72 possible technology insertions/improvements was presented by the Navy to Congress in 1997 to help justify the VIRGINIA design. Fourteen of those—19 percent—were payload technologies, new weapons such as the Tomahawk upgrades, the Navy Tactical Missile System (NTACMS), and unmanned vehicles. And most, if not all, of the technology insertions could as easily be incorporated into the earlier SEAWOLF or even LOS ANGELES SSN designs. In addition, because of cost increases, few major changes will be made to successive flights of the VIRGINIA class.

Electronics: Space and weight are to be reserved for possible installation of a lightweight Wide Aperture Array (WAA) sonar, considered by the U.S. Navy to be the optimum acoustic sensor for use against the diesel-electric submarine threat in littoral waters.

The VIRGINIA is rolled out of her building hall at the Electric Boat yard prior to her launching and christening. Her hull form is similar to previous U.S. SSNs; she has a "fillet" at the forward foot of her sail to improve her hydrodynamic characteristics. (2003, General Dynamics/Electric Boat)

These submarines will be fitted with the BQQ-10 Acoustic Rapid Commercial-off-the-Shelf Insertion (ARCI) sonar, an upgrade to the BQQ-6.

Engineering: The reactor core (fuel) for these submarines is expected to last their 30-year service lives.

Historical: In 1990, Chief of Naval Operations Admiral Frank B. Kelso II proposed a lower-cost SSN, initially given the project name "Centurion" (to reflect a submarine for the year 2000[17]). The designation was changed in 1993 to New Attack Submarine (originally NSSN, then briefly NAS, but changed back to NSSN); the lead submarine was given a state name in late 1998 (see *Name* notes).[18]

The Navy originally announced plans to construct two or three Centurions per year to maintain a force level of some 80 attack submarines. On 19 March 1991, Secretary of the Navy H. Lawrence Garrett III testified before Congress that

> the Navy face[s] a long-term problem of maintaining an adequate force of first-line ships when the [SSN] 688 class begins to be retired. As part of an overall effort to seek economies in all our ships and aircraft, I have recently directed the Chief of Naval Operations . . . to begin studies for a new submarine that would incorporate the technologies developed for SSN 21 and new technologies, in a smaller, less expensive platform as an option when the LOS ANGELES class submarines reach the end of their service lives after the year 2000. . . . The proposed new submarine will complement the SEAWOLF in the multimission environment of the twenty-first century. While the SEAWOLF design strongly emphasizes ASW capability against the very best projected Soviet submarines, this new submarine design will emphasize capability in other kinds of contingencies. Both of these ships will allow us to maintain an adequate force level as we move past the year 2010.

Through mid-1991 the Navy maintained that the Centurion/NSSN would be a *complement* to the SEAWOLF rather than a successor. In late June 1991, however, there were reports that the SEAWOLF procurement would cease about the year 2000 to permit acceleration of the new, lower-cost attack submarine.

On 28 August 1992, the Under Secretary of Defense for Acquisition approved concept definition studies for the new attack submarine with the Defense Acquisition Board (DAB) directing the Navy to keep the cost of the Centurion SSN program at $1 billion or less per submarine and to examine a variety of attack submarine alternatives (including conventional submarines). The alternatives listed in the directive were largely ignored by Navy planners (see 16th Edition/page 65).

As a result of the DAB review, on 12 January 1994, the Navy was directed to study several nuclear-propelled attack submarine concepts and their impact on the industrial base. On 1 August 1994, the DAB approved Phase I design efforts focused on the authorization of a lead ship in FY 1998.

However, on 9 December 1994, Secretary of Defense William J. Perry announced a series of budget cutbacks, among them a delay of construction of the third NSSN until FY 2002. The Navy had proposed a building rate of almost two units per year from 2001 onward, for a tentative total of 30 NSSNs through fiscal 2014. Some program proposals had addressed up to 45 units.

Missiles: Tomahawk missiles can be launched from the torpedo tubes in this class. All have 12 vertical launch tubes for Tomahawk missiles fitted forward, between the pressure hull and sonar sphere.

Torpedoes: The VIRGINIAS will stow fewer weapons in the torpedo room/tubes than can the SEAWOLF class.

---

17 There has never been a U.S. Navy ship with the name Centurion. The Royal Navy has had nine ships named CENTURION since 1650, including two battleships.

18 The term NAS was being used within the Department of Defense at the time for National Aerospace Plane.

The VIRGINIA *emerging from her building hall shows the long hull of the submarine and the diminutive sail (fairwater) structure. Her pump-jet propulsor is shrouded. Adjacent to her lower rudder is a pod for streaming her towed-array sonar. Building sheds are on her deck. (2003, General Dynamics/Electric Boat*

The VIRGINIA *under construction at the Electric Boat yard. Her 12 vertical launch TLAM tubes are visible immediately aft of her sonar dome. The bow fairing that covers the dome had not yet been installed when this photo was taken. Note the scale from workmen in the photo. (2003, U.S. Navy)*

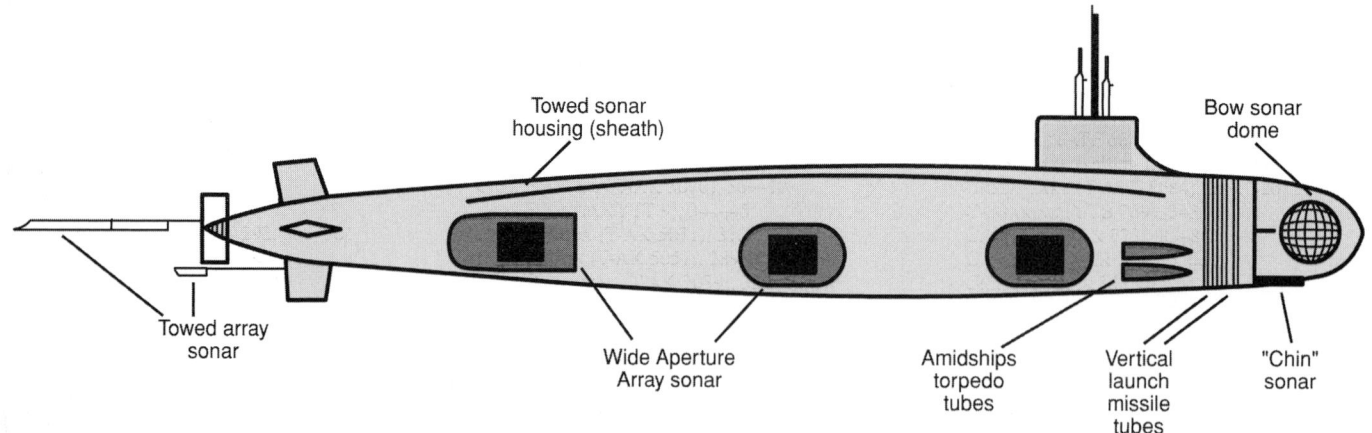

The VIRGINIA-*class SSNs have a straightforward design. The use of a Photonics mast alleviates the need for the sail structure to be directly above the control room, as required in submarines with conventional periscopes. (Chris Nazelrod)*

(1) NUCLEAR-PROPELLED SPECIAL MISSION SUBMARINE: MODIFIED "SEAWOLF" CLASS

Number	Name	FY	Builder	Start	Launch	Comm.	Christened	Status
SSN 23	JIMMY CARTER	92/96	General Dynamics/Electric Boat	12 Dec 1995	13 May 2004	early 2005	5 June 2004	Building

Displacement:		Missiles:	TLAMs launched from torpedo tubes
Length:	380 ⅓ feet (115.9 m) overall	Torpedo tubes:	8 26½-inch (670-mm) tubes angled (50 weapons)
Beam:		ASW weapons:	Mk 48 ADCAP torpedoes
Draft:		Radars:	BPS-16 surface search
Propulsion:	2 steam turbines (General Electric); approx. 40,000 shp;	Sonars/Fire control:	BSY-2 with bow-mounted transducers
	1 shaft/propulsor		BQG-5D hull-mounted WAAs
Reactors:	1 S6W pressurized-water (Westinghouse)		BQS-24 navigation/ice-avoidance
Speed:	15 knots surface		TB-16D towed array
	approx. 30 knots submerged		TB-29A thin-line towed array
Personnel:	144 (15 officers + 129 enlisted)	EW systems:	BLD-1D/F
Troops:	50 SEALs		WLQ-4(V)1

The JIMMY CARTER was ordered as the third submarine of the SEAWOLF class. In 1999, the Navy directed Electric Boat to complete the submarine as a special mission submarine to replace the PARCHE for deep-ocean search, research, and recovery operations. She also will have an enhanced SOF capability.

The modifications have added approximately 40 months to the construction timeline for the submarine, which originally was scheduled for delivery as a "straight" SSN on 31 December 2001. (The Navy had estimated the design change would add only some 15 months to construction time.)

The JIMMY CARTER will be assigned to Submarine Development Squadron 19 and based at Bangor, Washington.

See SEAWOLF-class entry for other program data.

Cost: The SEAWOLF-class submarines are the most costly ever constructed. Precise data have not been made publicly available by the Navy, but in the mid-1970s, the estimated cost for a 29-ship SEAWOLF program was $38 billion (then-year dollars).

In 1988, the Navy estimated that construction of 29 submarines at an eventual production rate of three or four per year would cost $36 billion. The Secretary of the Navy's cost ceiling for the program (in fiscal 1985 dollars) was $1.6 billion for the lead ship and $1 billion for the fifth and later ships, excluding the cost of constructing the ninth and later ships with HY-130 steel. (These estimates could not take into account the welding problems and resulting delays.) In addition, the development cost of the BSY-2 was estimated at $1 billion.

The SSN 21 total cost was estimated at $718 million (fiscal 1987 dollars) at the time of contract award; in mid-1994, the esti-

mated cost of the submarine was in excess of $1.1 billion. The SSN 22 cost was estimated at $689 million (fiscal 1991) at the time of contract award.

The fiscal 1991 defense appropriation provided $2.4 billion to build the SSN 23 and to cover advanced procurement items for follow-on SEAWOLFs. On 18 January 1994, Chief of Naval Operations Admiral Kelso, in his briefing "Restructuring Naval Forces," stated that $900 million already had been spent on the SSN 23 and that $1.5 billion was required to complete her—an estimated total of $2.4 billion. This was prior to the decision to complete the SSN 23 to a modified design, which the Navy estimates will add $887 million to the ship's cost.

In 1999, knowledgeable sources placed the total cost of the SEAWOLF program at almost $16 billion for three submarines. At that time, the JIMMY CARTER had not yet been completed.

Design: The JIMMY CARTER is being lengthened by a wide-diameter amidships section. The submarine will be fitted to carry either a DDS or ASDS vehicle plus Remote Operating Vehicles (ROVs). There will be dedicated berthing for SOF personnel, as well as stowage space for their equipment.

Names: The SSN 23 introduced a new name source to attack submarines: former (and living) presidents. Jimmy Carter was the first U.S. Naval Academy graduate to be elected president, and he served in a diesel sub before entering nuclear school. He left the Navy before reporting to a nuclear submarine, but he still was able to campaign as a "nuclear engineer" during his presidential bid.

The JIMMY CARTER *emerges from the building hall at the Electric Boat yard. The submarine, enlarged for her special mission role, is now the U.S. Navy's largest SSN. The submarine should properly be designated SSAGN. (General Dynamics/Electric Boat)*

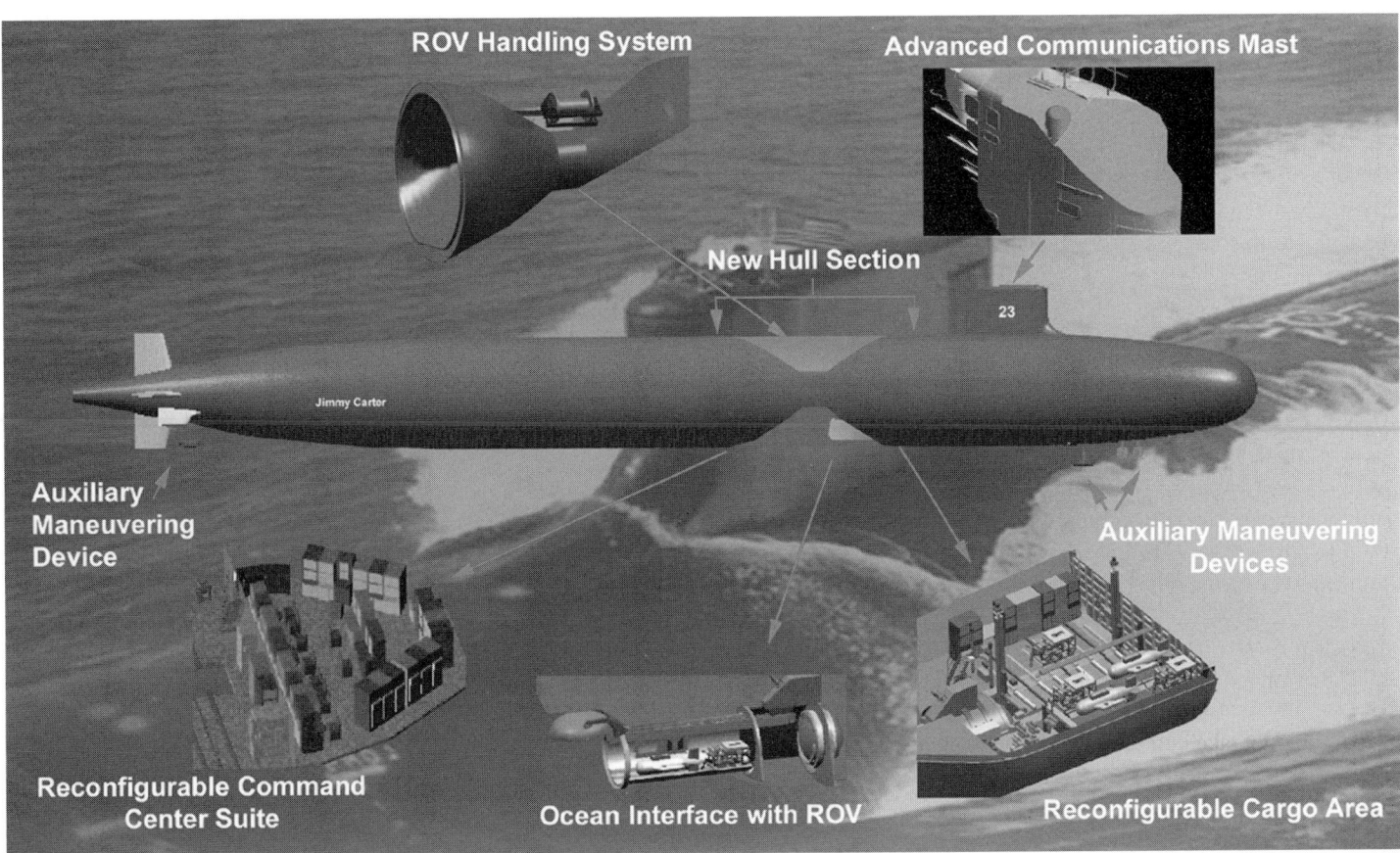

The JIMMY CARTER *(U.S. Navy)*

2 NUCLEAR-PROPELLED ATTACK SUBMARINES: "SEAWOLF" CLASS

Number	Name	FY	Builder	Started	Launched	Comm.	Status
SSN 21	SEAWOLF	89	General Dynamics/Electric Boat	25 Oct 1989	24 June 1995	19 July 1997	**AA**
SSN 22	CONNECTICUT	91	General Dynamics/Electric Boat	14 Sep 1992	1 Sep 1997	11 Dec 1998	**AA**

Displacement:	7,460 tons surface		Missiles:	TLAMs launched from torpedo tubes
	9,137 tons submerged (see *Design* notes)		Torpedo tubes:	8 26½-inch (670-mm) tubes angled (50 weapons)
Length:	353 feet (107.6 m) overall		ASW weapons:	Mk 48 ADCAP torpedoes
Beam:	40 feet (12.2 m)		Radars:	BPS-16 surface search
Draft:	36 feet (10.98 m)		Sonars/Fire control:	BSY-2 with bow-mounted transducers
Propulsion:	2 steam turbines (General Electric); approx. 40,000 shp;			BQG-5D hull-mounted Wide Aperture Arrays (WAAs)
	1 shaft/propulsor			BQS-24 navigation/ice-avoidance
Reactors:	1 S6W pressurized-water (Westinghouse)			TB-16D towed array
Speed:	15 knots surface			TB-29A thin-line towed array
	35 knots submerged (see *Engineering* notes)		EW systems:	BLD-1D/F
Personnel:	138 (14 officers + 124 enlisted)			WLQ-4(V)1

The SEAWOLF was developed as a follow-on to the LOS ANGELES class with the primary mission of anti-submarine operations against advanced Soviet nuclear-propelled submarines. The SEAWOLF was the most controversial U.S. warship program of the 1980s and early 1990s. Her construction time was unprecedented for nuclear submarines, as were the delays until she could undertake at-sea operations.

The Navy originally planned to construct about 30 submarines of this class, to be authorized in fiscal years 1989–2000: one in FY 1989, two each in FY 1991 and 1992, and an average of 3.3 ships annually in the following years. Subsequent controversy over the design, the issue of concurrent BSY-2 system development and submarine construction, and high costs led to reductions in the program. On 13 August 1990, as a result of a four-month Department of Defense major warship and threat review, the SEAWOLF procurement was reduced to 12 submarines and the production rate was cut to three submarines every two years (i.e., 1.5 per year). The six-year defense plan submitted to Congress in February 1991 reduced the planned procurement rate to one SSN per year through FY 1995; after that there would be a two–one–two–one schedule starting in FY 1996.

In September 1991, Chief of Naval Operations Admiral Kelso said he expected only one SEAWOLF per year to be constructed until the lead Centurion SSN was authorized, indicating that he did not anticipate a total program of more than seven or eight SEAWOLFs. In January 1992, the Department of Defense announced that the entire SEAWOLF program would be canceled with only the first unit to be completed. The funds voted by Congress for the SSN 22 and SSN 23 were to be rescinded.

The SEAWOLF became a political issue when, during the presidential primary campaign of 1992, then-Governor Bill Clinton told Connecticut voters he would continue production of the SEAWOLF class beyond the first unit. Primary candidate Paul Tsongas observed that Clinton, a Democrat, was supporting a defense program that even the Republican president did not wish to continue.

Lobbying by the Navy's nuclear submarine community and support by congressional representatives, especially from Connecticut, led the administration to reverse its proposal to halt the program with one submarine. Thus, two additional submarines were funded.

The SSN 21 delivery originally was scheduled for November 1994; it was delayed by at least six months (to May 1995) because of changes in the BSY-2 system configuration.[19] On 1 August 1991, the Navy announced that massive weld failures had been discovered in the hull that would delay the lead submarine at least into 1996. The cracks in the welding, which were first discovered in June 1991, required the replacement of all welds. The SEAWOLF contract was increased by $58,825,590 to cover the cost of the corrections.

During the SEAWOLF sea trials of 3–4 July 1997, the submarine's flank sonar arrays were damaged. This led to a further delay, with her commissioning in May 1997—two and a half years behind the original schedule.

Funding for the SSN 22, authorized in fiscal 1991, was retained by Congress with an additional $540,200,000 to be used for either the third SEAWOLF or some other project to preserve the submarine construction base.

The SSN 23 originally was authorized in 1992, but the George H. W. Bush administration withheld the funds pending studies of alternative submarine programs. The fiscal 1996 defense budget requested additional funding for the third SEAWOLF to keep the submarine production line at Electric Boat "hot" until the planned New Attack Submarine (NSSN) could be authorized in fiscal 1998. The interval between the second SEAWOLF (1991 authorization) and the third (1996) was probably the longest interval between submarine authorizations in U.S. Navy history.

Builders: On 9 January 1989, a fixed-price, incentive-plus-fee contract to build the lead submarine of the SEAWOLF class was awarded to Electric Boat. Construction began on 25 October 1989. The submarine's completion was delayed by several problems, including welding of the HY-100 steel.

The Navy awarded a contract for the SSN 22 to Electric Boat on 3 May 1991. Four days later, Newport News Shipbuilding filed a lawsuit protesting the decision, basing its case on a congressional mandate to preserve a two-yard submarine construction capability.[20] On 31 August 1991, a federal judge voided the contract award with Electric Boat and directed that the Navy recompete the contract for the second SEAWOLF. It again was awarded to Electric Boat.

Subsequently, in 1995, the Newport News shipyard proposed that it could build the New Attack Submarine (i.e., VIRGINIA class) without the Navy having to build the SSN 23 to "bridge" the construction gap between the SSN 22 and the New Attack Submarine, as would be required at Electric Boat. This was possible because Newport News has a broader business base than Electric Boat, including the Navy's carrier construction and refueling program, deactivating nuclear cruisers, commercial ship construction and overhaul, and possibly frigate construction for other navies. Bill Fricks, president of the Newport News yard, told a congressional committee in April 1995 that by taking over the nuclear submarine program, Newport News could save the Navy $2 billion in the pro-

---

19 The first *Naval Sea Systems Command Monthly Progress Report* issued after the construction contract was awarded listed the SSN 21 projected launch date as 28 January 1994 and completion on 26 May 1995.

20 On 7 May 1991, the Navy terminated a contract with Newport News Shipbuilding to participate in the design of the Centurion. This was one day after Newport News filed its suit challenging the selection of Electric Boat to build the second SEAWOLF. Navy officials denied the two events were linked.

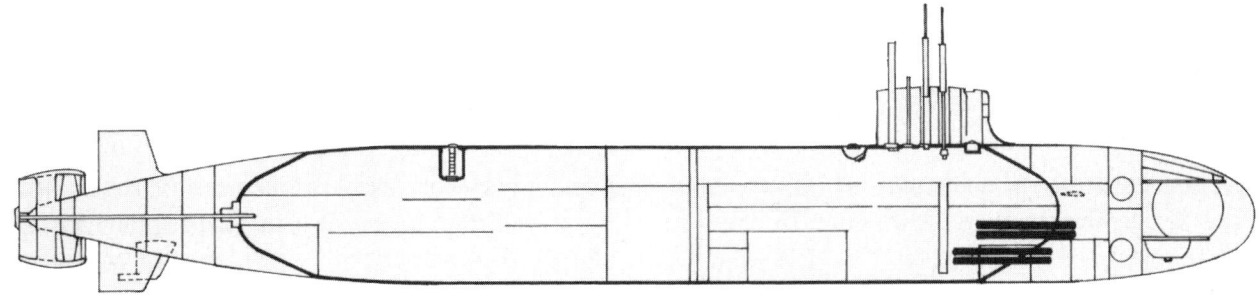

Seawolf (Drawing from Cold War Submarines © *A. D. Baker III)*

curement of the first five VIRGINIA SSNs and another $7–$10 billion over the life of the program of up to 45 submarines.

In the event, construction of all three submarines of the class was awarded to Electric Boat.

Class: The decision to construct a new SSN class was taken in July 1982. This followed a Navy decision one year earlier not to construct a new SSN (see 13th Edition/page 54). When the SEAWOLF was conceived in 1982, the SSN force level goal was increased from 90 to 100 submarines.[21] But from the outset of the SEAWOLF effort, it was apparent from even a cursory look at the program that it would be impossible to maintain a 100 SSN force with procurement of the SEAWOLF because of the submarine's high cost.

Classification: The Navy designated this class as SSN 21, indicating an attack submarine for the 21st century. The subsequent use of that designation as the SEAWOLF's hull number and the sequential numbering of the two other units of the class repeat the hull numbers of three previous U.S. submarines (completed in 1912–1913):

SS 21 BARRACUDA (also F-2)
SS 22 PICKEREL (also F-3)
SS 23 SKATE (also F-4)

As these submarines were numbered in the same series as U.S. nuclear submarines, the use of SSN 21, 22, and 23 is a violation of Secretary of the Navy policy and instructions on ship classifications.

Cost: See JIMMY CARTER entry.

Design: The basic SEAWOLF design, established in 1982–1983, emphasized: (1) improved machinery, (2) quieting, and (3) improved combat systems, both sensors and additional weapons.

The SEAWOLF is considered the first "top-to-bottom" U.S. attack submarine design since the SKIPJACK of the late 1950s. The SEAWOLFs are slightly faster than the LOS ANGELES class and have more torpedo tubes and more internally stowed weapons; there are no Tomahawk launch tubes external to the pressure hull, as in the later units of the LOS ANGELES class. The design provides for a smaller length-to-beam ratio than in previous U.S. attack submarine classes. A six-surface tail configuration is used with the single propeller shaft common to U.S. SSNs since the late 1950s, but the propeller is a circular shroud or duct similar to the installation in some British TRAFALGAR-class SSNs and (on a smaller scale) the Mk 48 torpedo. The submarines have bow-mounted diving planes (vice sail-mounted), which retract into the bow for under-ice operations.

According to Electric Boat, "The SEAWOLF will be less detectable at high speed than a LOS ANGELES-class SSN sitting at the pier" and is the "world's quietest submarine." Both statements were made before the SEAWOLF was launched.[22]

The submerged displacement (9,137 tons) listed in the table is just shy of the 9,150-ton limit imposed by the Secretary of the Navy about 1986. The actual submerged displacement is approxi-

mately 9,300 tons, some 150 tons of which is the water trapped in the bow sonar dome, which in most submarines is normally flooded and closed when the submarine is at sea. In this class, however, to keep within the secretary's ceiling, the sonar dome is "open" to the sea when flooded.

The ninth and subsequent units were to have had HY-130 steel vice the HY-100 steel used in the earlier SEAWOLF-class submarines. All U.S. submarines from the THRESHER through the LOS ANGELES class were constructed of HY-80 steel.[23] (HY-100 steel originally was proposed for the LOS ANGELES class.)

Electronics: These submarines have the BSY-2 combat system, previously known as SUBACS, for Submarine Advanced Combat System (see Chapter 29 for characteristics). The BQG-5D WAA system has three rectangular arrays fitted to each side of the submarine's hull.

Changes in the design of the BSY-2 caused redesign of portions of the SEAWOLF. In addition to the large bow spherical array, there are three WAA panels along each side of the submarine.

Engineering: The maximum submerged speed has been officially stated to be 35 knots, making the SEAWOLF class faster than any previous U.S. submarine design. The SEAWOLF is reported to have a maximum "acoustic speed"—the speed at which the submarine can transit while maintaining a sufficiently low noise level to still employ passive sonar with a narrow-band capability—in excess of 20 knots (a comparative Soviet speed was reported at 6–8 knots for submarines built in the 1980s).

Immediately after the SEAWOLF's sea trials of 3–4 July 1997, Admiral Bruce DeMars, head of naval nuclear propulsion, declared the SEAWOLF had gone faster than any previous U.S. submarine.[24] Unofficial reports credited her with 37 knots. However, the trials were not conducted over a measured mile, full instrumentation was not mounted in the submarine, nor was her anechoic coating installed.

Names: With the SSN 21, the Navy reverted to the practice of using fish names for submarines. The name SEAWOLF was chosen for the lead submarine of the class in 1986 with the assumption that the existing SEAWOLF (SSN 575) would be stricken by the time the new craft was launched; indeed, the SSN 575 was stricken on 10 July 1987.

The first SEAWOLF (SS 28), later renamed H-1, ran aground in 1920 off San Margarita Island, California; four men died. The sub-

---

21 Ninety attack submarines was the Navy's force goal from 1973 to 1981; that goal was never achieved. Before that, the force goal was 120 attack submarines, both diesel-electric and nuclear.

22 "Seawolf," on the reverse of an artist's concept prepared by General Dynamics/Electric Boat Division [n.d.].

23 HY-80 was used in the SKIPJACK class, but the THRESHER was the first to have a complete HY-80 pressure hull, permitting a deeper operating depth.

24 Adm. Bruce DeMars, USN, press conference, New London, Conn., 5 July 1996. Previously, the fastest U.S. submarine unquestionably was the research submarine ALBACORE (AGSS 569).

marine sank as she was refloated. The second (SS 197) was sunk in late 1944 by U.S. anti-submarine forces. There were no survivors. She had made 12 successful war patrols in 1942–1944. The third SEAWOLF (SSN 575) was the nation's second nuclear submarine.

The second submarine of this class was named CONNECTICUT. State names had been used for the 18 Trident missile submarines of the OHIO class and, before that, for guided missile cruisers and battleships. The last U.S. ship named CONNECTICUT (BB 18) was stricken in 1923. The state name was assigned to the SSN 22 through the efforts of the Connecticut congressional delegation, to honor the state where one of the two surviving submarine building yards is located. (Subsequently, the SSN 774 was named to honor the home state of the other submarine construction yard, VIRGINIA.)

Operational: The SEAWOLF was operational from August 1997 to July 1998, carrying out trials, evaluations, and limited exercises; she returned to the Electric Boat yard in July 1998 for a 14-month post-shakedown availability. The work included application of anechoic coating to the submarine.

The SEAWOLF did not undertake her first deployment until June–December 2001—an unprecedented interval of four years from completion to first deployment. When she did deploy to the North Atlantic and Mediterranean in 2001, she had TLAMs on board, but she was not certified to launch them until after the CONNECTICUT completed her TLAM firing trials in September 2001.

The CONNECTICUT steamed to the Arctic in May 2001 and made one surfacing at the North Pole. Subsequently, the SEAWOLF undertook an Arctic cruise.

Torpedoes: The Navy originally planned to place the torpedo tubes in the bow, where they would be less vulnerable to water flow problems during weapon launches at high speed. Following tests, the launch tubes were retained in the angled position used in all designs since the TULLIBEE and THRESHER classes. Firing tests, however, demonstrated the feasibility of firing high-speed torpedoes from amidship tubes, and the SEAWOLF design was modified accordingly.

The SEAWOLF at high speed on the surface during the NATO anti-submarine exercise Odin One in the North Sea area. The Navy Department has released very few photos of the SEAWOLF and her sister ship, the CONNECTICUT. Even fewer probably will be available of the third ship of the class, the JIMMY CARTER. (2003, U.S. Navy)

The CONNECTICUT being a assisted by a commercial tug while departing her home port of New London, Connecticut. The three submarines of this class all have different name sources, testimony to the Navy's confusion and the political influence on naming Navy ships. (2003, U.S. Navy/Woody Paschall)

23 NUCLEAR-PROPELLED ATTACK SUBMARINES: IMPROVED "LOS ANGELES" CLASS

Number	Name	FY	Builder	Laid Down	Launched	Comm.	Status
SSN 751	SAN JUAN	83	General Dynamics/Electric Boat	16 Aug 1985	6 Dec 1986	6 Aug 1988	**AA**
SSN 752	PASADENA	83	General Dynamics/Electric Boat	20 Dec 1985	12 Sep 1987	11 Feb 1989	**PA**
SSN 753	ALBANY	84	Newport News Shipbuilding	22 Apr 1985	13 June 1987	7 Apr 1990	**AA**
SSN 754	TOPEKA	84	General Dynamics/Electric Boat	13 May 1986	23 Jan 1988	21 Oct 1989	**PA**
SSN 755	MIAMI	84	General Dynamics/Electric Boat	24 Oct 1986	12 Nov 1988	30 June 1990	**AA**
SSN 756	SCRANTON	85	Newport News Shipbuilding	29 Aug 1986	3 July 1989	26 Jan 1991	**AA**
SSN 757	ALEXANDRIA	85	Newport News Shipbuilding	19 June 1987	23 June 1990	29 June 1991	**AA**
SSN 758	ASHEVILLE	85	Newport News Shipbuilding	9 Jan 1987	24 Feb 1990	28 Sep 1991	**PA**
SSN 759	JEFFERSON CITY	85	Newport News Shipbuilding	21 Sep 1987	17 Aug 1990	29 Feb 1992	**PA**
SSN 760	ANNAPOLIS	86	General Dynamics/Electric Boat	15 June 1988	18 May 1991	11 Apr 1992	**AA**
SSN 761	SPRINGFIELD	86	General Dynamics/Electric Boat	29 Jan 1990	4 Jan 1992	9 Jan 1993	**AA**
SSN 762	COLUMBUS	86	General Dynamics/Electric Boat	7 Jan 1991	1 Aug 1992	24 July 1993	**PA**
SSN 763	SANTA FE	86	General Dynamics/Electric Boat	9 Sep 1991	12 Dec 1992	8 Jan 1994	**PA**
SSN 764	BOISE	87	Newport News Shipbuilding	25 Aug 1988	23 Mar 1991	7 Nov 1992	**AA**
SSN 765	MONTPELIER	87	Newport News Shipbuilding	19 May 1989	23 Aug 1991	13 Mar 1993	**AA**
SSN 766	CHARLOTTE	87	Newport News Shipbuilding	17 Aug 1990	3 Oct 1992	16 Sep 1994	**PA**
SSN 767	HAMPTON	87	Newport News Shipbuilding	2 Mar 1990	28 Sep 1991	6 Nov 1993	**AA**
SSN 768	HARTFORD	88	General Dynamics/Electric Boat	27 Apr 1992	4 Dec 1993	10 Dec 1994	**AA**
SSN 769	TOLEDO	88	Newport News Shipbuilding	6 May 1991	28 Aug 1993	24 Feb 1995	**AA**
SSN 770	TUCSON	88	Newport News Shipbuilding	15 Aug 1991	19 Mar 1994	9 Sep 1995	**PA**
SSN 771	COLUMBIA	89	General Dynamics/Electric Boat	21 Apr 1993	24 Sep 1994	9 Oct 1995	**PA**
SSN 772	GREENEVILLE	89	Newport News Shipbuilding	28 Feb 1992	17 Sep 1994	16 Feb 1996	**PA**
SSN 773	CHEYENNE	90	Newport News Shipbuilding	6 July 1992	1 Apr 1995	13 Sep 1996	**PA**

Displacement:	6,300 tons standard, except SSNs 771–773 6,330 tons 7,147 tons submerged, except SSNs 771–773 7,177 tons	Sonars:	BQQ-5C/D multifunction bow mounted (being upgraded to BQQ-5E) or BQQ-10 ARCI sonar update
Length:	360 feet (109.7 m) overall		BQR-15 towed array
Beam:	33 feet (10.1 m)		BQR-26 in some units
Draft:	32 feet (9.75 m)		BQS-13 active
Propulsion:	2 steam turbines; approx. 30,000 shp; 1 shaft		BQS-15 under ice/mine detection
Reactors:	1 S6G pressurized-water (General Electric)		BSY-1 combat system
Speed:	22 knots surface approx. 33 knots submerged		TB-23 and/or TB-29 towed array; TB-29A thin-line towed array being fitted
Personnel:	143 (14 officers + 129 enlisted)	Fire control:	1 CCS Mk 2 Mod 2
Missiles:	TLAMs launched from torpedo tubes 12 vertical launch tubes for TLAMs		1 Mk 117 torpedo FCS
Torpedo tubes:	4 21-inch (533-mm) tubes angled Mk 67 (25 weapons)	EW systems:	BRD-7 direction finder
ASW weapons:	Mk 48 ADCAP torpedoes		WLR-8(V)
Radars:	BPS-15H surface search		WLR-9
			WLR-12

These are Improved LOS ANGELES-class submarines with Tomahawk vertical launch missile tubes, minelaying and under-ice capabilities, and improved machinery quieting. Submarines of this class are expected to have service lives of 33 years.

See the LOS ANGELES-class entry for additional information and notes on these submarines.

Class: The LOS ANGELES class is the world's largest series of nuclear-propelled submarines, with 62 units completed. The "final" program was for 65 units, but the Navy did not request funds for the last four, instead supporting the SEAWOLF program; however, Congress authorized one of those LOS ANGELES-class submarines (SSN 773).

Except for the Soviet diesel-electric Whiskey class (236 units completed 1949–1957) and Foxtrot class (62 built for Soviet service plus 17 for foreign navies, 1958–1973), this also is the largest class of submarines built since World War II by any nation.

Electronics: These submarines are fitted with the BSY-1 sonar/fire control "combat system." Major problems were encountered in late 1986 in installing the initial system in the SSN 751, resulting in a completion delay for the submarine.

The ASHEVILLE was fitted in March 1995 with a "chin"-mounted High-Frequency (HF) sonar for shallow-water tactical operations.

The BQQ-10 ARCI provides an update to the BQQ-5/BQQ-6/BSY-1 sonars (see *Electronics* notes for the LOS ANGELES class).

Engineering: The first half of this class has fuel cores that require replacement after about 15 years, i.e., one-half the submarine's operating life. The second half of the class has 30-year cores. The SSN 768 and later units have improved quieting features.

Missiles: Tomahawk missiles can be launched from the torpedo tubes in this class. All have 12 vertical launch tubes for Tomahawk missiles fitted forward, between the pressure hull and sonar sphere, in space previously used for ballast tanks.

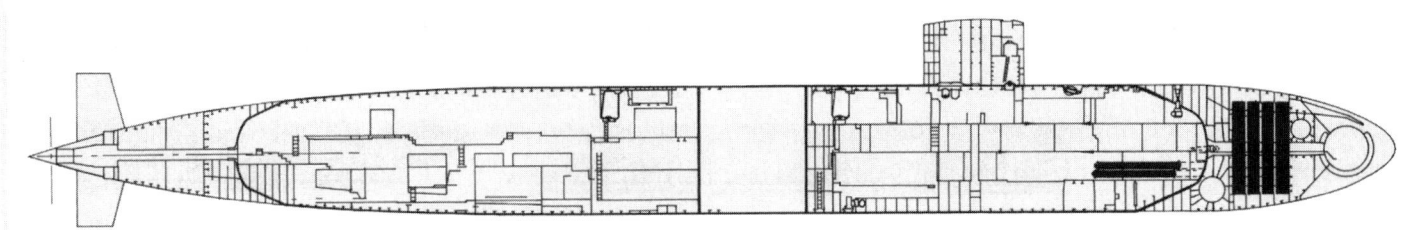

TOLEDO (Improved LOS ANGELES Class) (Drawing from Cold War Submarines © *A. D. Baker III)*

The ASHEVILLE at high speed off the coast of San Diego. The Improved LOS ANGELES-class SSNs have retractable bow diving planes, a feature that was abandoned by the U.S. Navy starting with the SKIPJACK class designed in the 1950s. (2003, U.S. Navy/Thomas C. Peterson)

The GREENEVILLE operating off Hawaii with the first Advanced SEAL Delivery System vehicle. The 65-foot minisub can be carried by the GREENEVILLE and the CHARLOTTE. Eventually, the four converted Trident SSGNs also will be configured to carry these vehicles, although their arrival in the fleet has been slowed. (2003, U.S. Navy)

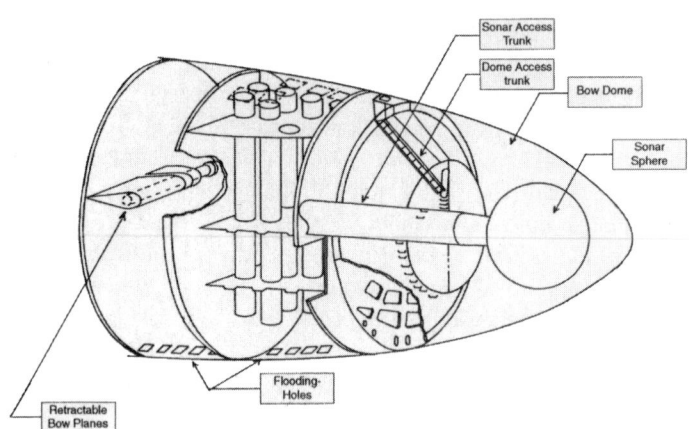

Bow section of a VLS-configured LOS ANGELES-class submarine. (Drawing from Cold War Submarines *© A. D. Baker III)*

The view looking forward from the sail of the OKLAHOMA CITY shows the open hatches of the submarine's 12 vertical launch Tomahawk missile tubes. These weapons were added without any increase in the submarine's dimensions or reduction in torpedo loadout. (U.S. Navy)

28 NUCLEAR-PROPELLED ATTACK SUBMARINES: "LOS ANGELES" CLASS

Number	Name	FY	Builder	Laid Down	Launched	Comm.	Status
SSN 688	LOS ANGELES	70	Newport News Shipbuilding	8 Jan 1972	6 Apr 1974	13 Nov 1976	**PA**
SSN 689	BATON ROUGE	70	Newport News Shipbuilding	18 Nov 1972	26 Apr 1975	25 June 1977	decomm./str. 13 Jan 1995
SSN 690	PHILADELPHIA	70	General Dynamics/Electric Boat	12 Aug 1972	19 Oct 1974	25 June 1977	**AA**
SSN 691	MEMPHIS	71	Newport News Shipbuilding	23 June 1973	3 Apr 1976	17 Dec 1977	**AA**
SSN 692	OMAHA	71	General Dynamics/Electric Boat	27 Jan 1973	21 Feb 1976	11 Mar 1978	decomm./str. 5 Oct 1995
SSN 693	CINCINNATI	71	Newport News Shipbuilding	6 Apr 1974	19 Feb 1977	10 June 1978	decomm./str. 29 July 1996
SSN 694	GROTON	71	General Dynamics/Electric Boat	3 Aug 1973	9 Oct 1976	8 July 1978	decomm./str. 7 Nov 1997
SSN 695	BIRMINGHAM	72	Newport News Shipbuilding	26 Apr 1975	29 Oct 1977	16 Dec 1978	decomm./str. 22 Dec 1997
SSN 696	NEW YORK CITY	72	General Dynamics/Electric Boat	15 Dec 1973	18 June 1977	3 Mar 1978	decomm./str. 30 Apr 1997
SSN 697	INDIANAPOLIS	72	General Dynamics/Electric Boat	19 Oct 1974	30 July 1977	5 Jan 1980	decomm./str. 22 Dec 1998
SSN 698	BREMERTON	72	General Dynamics/Electric Boat	6 May 1976	22 July 1978	28 Mar 1981	**PA**
SSN 699	JACKSONVILLE	72	General Dynamics/Electric Boat	21 Feb 1976	18 Nov 1978	16 May 1981	**AA**
SSN 700	DALLAS	73	General Dynamics/Electric Boat	9 Oct 1976	28 Apr 1979	18 July 1981	**AA**
SSN 701	LA JOLLA	73	General Dynamics/Electric Boat	16 Oct 1976	11 Aug 1979	24 Oct 1981	**PA**
SSN 702	PHOENIX	73	General Dynamics/Electric Boat	30 July 1977	8 Dec 1979	19 Dec 1981	decomm./str. 29 July 1998
SSN 703	BOSTON	73	General Dynamics/Electric Boat	11 Aug 1978	19 Apr 1980	30 Jan 1982	decomm./str. 1 Sep 1999
SSN 704	BALTIMORE	73	General Dynamics/Electric Boat	21 May 1979	13 Dec 1980	24 July 1982	decomm./str. 10 July 1998
SSN 705	CITY OF CORPUS CHRISTI	73	General Dynamics/Electric Boat	4 Sep 1979	25 Apr 1981	8 Jan 1983	**PA**
SSN 706	ALBUQUERQUE	74	General Dynamics/Electric Boat	27 Dec 1979	13 Mar 1982	21 May 1983	**AA**
SSN 707	PORTSMOUTH	74	General Dynamics/Electric Boat	8 May 1980	18 Sep 1982	1 Oct 1983	**PA**
SSN 708	MINNEAPOLIS-SAINT PAUL	74	General Dynamics/Electric Boat	20 Jan 1981	19 Mar 1983	17 Mar 1984	**AA**
SSN 709	HYMAN G. RICKOVER	74	General Dynamics/Electric Boat	24 July 1981	17 Aug 1983	8 Sep 1984	**AA**
SSN 710	AUGUSTA	74	General Dynamics/Electric Boat	1 Apr 1982	21 Jan 1984	19 Jan 1985	**AA**
SSN 711	SAN FRANCISCO	75	Newport News Shipbuilding	26 May 1977	27 Oct 1979	24 Apr 1981	**PA**
SSN 712	ATLANTA	75	Newport News Shipbuilding	17 Aug 1978	16 Aug 1980	6 Mar 1982	decomm./str. 1 Sep 1999
SSN 713	HOUSTON	75	Newport News Shipbuilding	29 Jan 1979	21 Mar 1981	25 Sep 1982	**PA**
SSN 714	NORFOLK	76	Newport News Shipbuilding	1 Aug 1979	31 Oct 1981	21 May 1983	**AA**
SSN 715	BUFFALO	76	Newport News Shipbuilding	25 Jan 1980	8 May 1982	5 Nov 1983	**PA**
SSN 716	SALT LAKE CITY	77	Newport News Shipbuilding	26 Aug 1980	16 Oct 1982	12 May 1984	**PA**
SSN 717	OLYMPIA	77	Newport News Shipbuilding	31 Mar 1981	30 Apr 1983	17 Nov 1984	**PA**
SSN 718	HONOLULU	77	Newport News Shipbuilding	10 Nov 1981	24 Sep 1983	6 July 1985	**PA**
SSN 719	PROVIDENCE	78	General Dynamics/Electric Boat	14 Oct 1982	4 Aug 1984	27 July 1985	**AA**
SSN 720	PITTSBURGH	79	General Dynamics/Electric Boat	15 Apr 1983	8 Dec 1984	23 Nov 1985	**AA**
SSN 721	CHICAGO	80	Newport News Shipbuilding	5 Jan 1983	13 Oct 1984	27 Sep 1986	**PA**
SSN 722	KEY WEST	80	Newport News Shipbuilding	6 July 1983	20 July 1985	12 Sep 1887	**PA**
SSN 723	OKLAHOMA CITY	81	Newport News Shipbuilding	4 Jan 1984	2 Nov 1985	9 July 1988	**AA**
SSN 724	LOUISVILLE	81	General Dynamics/Electric Boat	16 Sep 1984	14 Dec 1985	8 Nov 1986	**PA**
SSN 725	HELENA	82	General Dynamics/Electric Boat	28 Mar 1985	28 June 1986	11 July 1987	**PA**
SSN 750	NEWPORT NEWS	82	Newport News Shipbuilding	3 Mar 1984	15 Mar 1986	3 June 1989	**AA**

Displacement:	SSN 688–699:	6,080 tons standard		ASW weapons:	Mk 48 ADCAP torpedoes
		6,927 tons submerged		Radars:	BPS-15H surface search
	SSN 700–715:	6,130 tons standard		Sonars:	BQQ-5 multifunction bow mounted (BQQ-5E in later and updated units)
		6,977 tons submerged			
	SSN 716–718:	6,165 tons standard			BQR-15 towed array
		7,012 tons submerged			BQR-26 in some submarines
	SSN 719–750:	6,255 tons standard			BQS-13 active
		7,102 tons submerged			BQS-15 under ice/mine detection
Length:	360 feet (109.7 m) overall				TB-16 (BQQ-5A) or TB-23 (BQQ-5D) towed array in later and updated units; TB-29A thin-line towed array being fitted
Beam:	33 feet (10.1 m)				
Draft:	32 feet (9.75 m)			Fire control:	SSN 688–719: 1 CCS Mk 2 Mod 0
Propulsion:	2 steam turbines; approx. 30,000 shp; 1 shaft				SSN 719–725, 750: 1 CCS Mk 2 Mod 1
Reactors:	1 S6G pressurized-water (General Electric)				1 Mk 117 torpedo FCS
Speed:	approximately 33 knots submerged			EW systems:	BRD-7 direction finder
Personnel:	143 (14 officers + 129 enlisted)				WLR-8(V)
Missiles:	TLAMs launched from torpedo tubes				WLR-9
Torpedo tubes:	4 21-inch (533-mm) tubes angled Mk 67 (25 weapons)				WLR-12

These are large attack submarines, originally developed to counter the Soviet Victor fast-attack submarines that were first completed in 1967–1968.

The LOS ANGELES submarines are about five knots faster than the previous U.S. STURGEON class, the higher speed being their principal advantage over that earlier design (see *Engineering* notes). However, the LOS ANGELES class is about one-half again as large in terms of displacement and considerably more expensive (see *Cost* notes). Also, the original LOS ANGELES design lacked under-ice and minelaying capabilities, both vital for modern submarine warfare. The SSN 756 and later units have a minelaying capability.

The SAN JUAN and later units are considered an "improved" design (see previous listing).

In response to congressional pressure, in 1989 the MEMPHIS was assigned as a Research-and-Development (R&D) platform, although she retained her combat capabilities. She was modified for the role in the mid 1990s, but a short time later reverted to a standard SSN. She kept her SSN designation while employed in R&D activities.

The CITY OF CORPUS CHRISTI and the SAN FRANCISCO were homeported in Guam in late 2002, with the HOUSTON following in 2004. These are the first U.S. nuclear-propelled ships to be based outside the United States. This "forward basing" reduces the ships'

The sail of the BALTIMORE at high speed, with all periscopes and masts retracted. Aft of her diminutive cockpit are fitted her BPS-15H radar, twin BRA-34 antenna masts, side-by-side Type 8 and Type 18 periscopes, a BRD-7 antenna mast, and the large snorkel induction mast. (1996, U.S. Navy/Chris Vickers)

transit times to operational areas in the Western Pacific and Persian Gulf regions. Along with the submarine tender FRANK CABLE (AS-40), the SSNs at Guam are part of Submarine Squadron 15, which was reactivated on 23 September 2001 to command submarine activities at Guam.

Class: There originally were 39 "straight" LOS ANGELES-class submarines plus the 23 improved submarines.

Classification: Submarine hull numbers 726–749 were reserved for additional Trident SSBNs.

Conversion: During her mid-1990s refit for the R&D role, the MEMPHIS received numerous modifications, which added some 50 tons to her displacement. The modifications included: (1) Glass-Reinforced Plastic (GRP) turtleback aft of the sail to accommodate ROVs and UUVs; (2) winch, drum, and other fittings for towing experimental acoustic arrays; (3) vertical surfaces at the ends of her horizontal (stern) stabilizers to support sonar arrays; approximately 1 foot, 4 inches (4.27 m) high and 4 feet, 6 inches (1.37 m) wide; (4) fiber-optic database; (5) 58 standardized equipment racks for additional electronic test gear; and (6) oversize logistics hatch to facilitate equipment installation and removal.

The MEMPHIS began operating as an "interim" R&D platform in August 1989, providing an at-sea test platform for DARPA, the Navy, and industry. One of the first projects to be evaluated in the MEMPHIS was a nonpenetrating Photonics periscope (i.e., mounted on a flexible cable employing fiber optics).

Design: SCB No. 303. These are large SSNs, the increase in size over the STURGEON class being primarily to accommodate installation of the larger, more-capable S6G reactor plant in an effort to regain the speed lost in the PERMIT and STURGEON classes.

They were designed to be constructed of HY-100 steel; however, they were built with HY-80. The ALBANY and TOPEKA have some hull sections of HY-100 that served as materials test beds for the SEAWOLF class; they have not encountered the welding problems sustained by the later submarine.

The LOS ANGELES-class also has improved sonar and fire control systems (that were being retrofitted to the STURGEON class) com-

pared to previous attack submarines. They are not fitted to carry mines, nor are they configured for under-ice operations; these shortcomings are corrected in the Improved LOS ANGELES class.

These submarines originally had berthing for only 95 enlisted men; the remainder used sleeping bags in available spaces or hot bunked. Berthing has been added, but the ships are considered to be quite crowded in comparison with earlier SSNs.

Electronics: The early submarines were fitted with the Mk 113 (analog) fire control system and could carry the Tomahawk missile; those with the Mk 117 (digital) cannot carry the SUBROC. All have been refitted with the Mk 117.

The AUGUSTA was fitted with the BQQ-10 ARCI sonar system in 1997. This is an upgrade to the BQQ-5/BQQ-6/BSY-1 "legacy" sonars. The entire submarine force is scheduled to receive the update by 2005.

Engineering: The first half of this submarine class has 15-year fuel cores (i.e., one-half the expected operational life of the submarine); later units have 30-year fuel cores. According to official Navy statements, with this class, "the speed threshold which had been established by SKIPJACK 18 years earlier was finally surpassed."

Missiles: Tomahawk missiles can be launched from the torpedo tubes in this class. The ATLANTA was the first SSN to deploy with Tomahawk, in November 1983.

Names: Most of the earlier submarines of this class carry names previously borne by cruisers; many later names were carried by lesser warships (e.g., frigates).

The SSN 705 originally was named CORPUS CHRISTI for the Texas port city. That name previously was borne by the frigate PF 44 (launched in 1943) and the seaplane tender ALBEMARLE (AV 5), which was converted to a helicopter repair ship (ARVH 1) during the Vietnam War and renamed CORPUS CHRISTI BAY (she was operated by the Military Sealift Command for the Army). After protests from Catholic groups, the SSN 705 name was changed to CITY OF CORPUS CHRISTI on 10 May 1982.

The SSN 708 honors Minnesota's "twin cities," which actually are Minneapolis–St. Paul (vice *Saint* Paul).

The SSN 709 was named for Admiral H. G. Rickover, longtime head of the U.S. Navy's nuclear propulsion program, on 4 March 1983. The move was, in part, an effort to preempt congressional pressure to name an aircraft carrier for the controversial admiral.

The SSN 719 was named PROVIDENCE in September 1983 to honor the state of Rhode Island after the ballistic missile submarine RHODE ISLAND (SSBN 730) was renamed HENRY M. JACKSON.

The SSN 757 originally was named ASHEVILLE; her name was changed to ALEXANDRIA on 27 February 1987. The SSN 764 originally was named HARTFORD and the SSN 768 BOISE; they swapped names on 3 March 1989.

Operational: The LOUISVILLE and PITTSBURGH launched TLAMs against targets in Iraq during the 1991 Gulf War. The latter fired the first "war shot" against an enemy by a U.S. submarine since World War II. The LOUISVILLE fired eight missiles and the PITTSBURGH four—4 percent of the 288 fired in the Gulf War.

The AUGUSTA suffered an underwater collision with a Soviet nuclear-propelled strategic missile submarine in the North Atlantic in October 1986. Repairs to the AUGUSTA cost $2.7 million.

The BATON ROUGE collided with a Russian nuclear-propelled submarine in the Barents Sea on 11 February 1992. U.S. officials said the incident occurred in international waters, beyond the 12-nm (22.2-km) territorial zone recognized by the United States; Russian officials said it was off Murmansk, within their territorial waters. Neither ship was reported to have serious damage and there were no injuries. However, the Navy placed the BATON ROUGE In Commission, In Reserve, on 11 January 1993, for subsequent disposal.

The LA JOLLA operating off the coast of Kyushu, Japan, with the rescue submersible MYSTIC (DSRV 1) mounted on her after deck during an exercise with the Japanese Maritime Self-Defense Force. The DSRV can be carried and operated from several U.S. and foreign submarines modified to support it. (2002, JMSDF)

The LA JOLLA at Pearl Harbor with a Dry Deck Shelter (DDS) fitted aft of her sail. The DDS can be used to carry Swimmer Delivery Vehicles or rigid-hull inflatable boats and to lock out and recover SEALs and other swimmers. (2004, U.S. Navy/Corwin M. Colbert)

The stern aspect of the MEMPHIS departing Suda Bay, Crete, a major air and naval base in the Mediterranean that has long been used by U.S. naval forces. The large diving planes distinguish the older LOS ANGELES-class SSNs from the improved units, which are fitted with retractable bow planes. (2003, U.S. Navy/Paul Farley)

Table 11-4. POST–WORLD WAR II SUBMARINES

Number	Name	Comm.	Notes
	K-1 class		
SS 551	BASS		ex-SSK 2 (see below)
SS 552	BONITA		ex-SSK 3 (see below)
SS 553	(Norwegian KINN)		offshore procurement
SS 554	(Danish SPRINGEREN)		offshore procurement
	DOLPHIN type		
AGSS 555	DOLPHIN	1968	
SS 556–562	not used		
	TANG class (6)		
SS 563	TANG	1951	to Turkey 1980
SS 564	TRIGGER	1952	to Italy 1973
SS 565	WAHOO	1952	str. 1983 (scrapped)
SS 566	TROUT	1952	to Iran 1978 (not transferred; retained by U.S. government)
SS 567	GUDGEON	1952	to Turkey 1983
SS 568	HARDER	1952	to Italy 1974
	ALBACORE type		
AGSS 569	ALBACORE	1953	str. 1980 (museum)
AGSS 570			completed as SST 1
	NAUTILUS type		
SSN 571	NAUTILUS	1954	decomm. 1980 (museum)
	SAILFISH class (2)		
SSR 572	SAILFISH	1956	stricken 1978
SSR 573	SALMON	1956	stricken 1977
	GRAYBACK class (2)		
SSG 574	GRAYBACK	1958	stricken 1984
	SEAWOLF type		
SSN 575	SEAWOLF	1957	stricken 1987
	DARTER type		
SS 576	DARTER	1956	stricken 1990
	GRAYBACK class (continued)		
SSG 577	GROWLER	1958	stricken 1980 (museum)
	SKATE class (4)		
SSN 578	SKATE	1957	stricken 1986
SSN 579	SWORDFISH	1958	stricken 1989
	BARBEL class (3)		
SS 580	BARBEL	1959	stricken 1990
SS 581	BLUEBACK	1959	stricken 1990
SS 582	BONEFISH	1959	stricken 1989
	SKATE class (continued)		
SSN 583	SARGO	1958	stricken 1988
SSN 584	SEADRAGON	1959	stricken 1986
	SKIPJACK class (6)		
SSN 585	SKIPJACK	1959	stricken 1990
	TRITON type		
SSRN 586	TRITON	1959	to SSN 1961; stricken 1986
	HALIBUT type		
SSGN 587	HALIBUT	1960	to SSN 1965; stricken 1986
	SKIPJACK class (continued)		
SSN 588	SCAMP	1961	stricken 1988
SSN 589	SCORPION	1960	sunk 27 May 1968
SSN 590	SCULPIN	1961	stricken 1990
SSN 591	SHARK	1961	stricken 1990
SSN 592	SNOOK	1961	stricken 1986
	THRESHER class (14)		
SSN 593	THRESHER	1961	sunk 10 Apr. 1963
SSN 594	PERMIT	1962	decomm./str. 23 July 1991
SSN 595	PLUNGER	1962	decomm./str. 2 Feb 1990
SSN 596	BARB	1963	decomm./str. 20 Dec 1989
	TULLIBEE type		
SSN 597	TULLIBEE	1960	decomm./str. 18 June 1988
SSBN 598–602			see Chapter 10
	THRESHER class (continued)		
SSN 603	POLLACK	1964	decomm./str. 1 Mar 1989
SSN 604	HADDO	1964	decomm./str. 12 June 1991
SSN 605	JACK	1967	decomm./str. 11 July 1990
SSN 606	TINOSA	1964	decomm./str. 15 Jan 1992
SSN 607	DACE	1964	decomm./str. 2 Dec 1988
SSBN 608–611			see Chapter 10
	THRESHER class (continued)		
SSN 612	GUARDFISH	1966	decomm./str. 4 Feb 1992
SSN 613	FLASHER	1966	decomm./str. 14 Sep 1992
SSN 614	GREENLING	1967	decomm./str. 18 Apr 1994
SSN 615	GATO	1968	decomm./str. 26 Apr 1996
SSBN 616–620			see Chapter 10
	THRESHER class (continued)		
SSN 621	HADDOCK	1967	decomm./str. 7 Apr 1993
SSBN 622–636			see Chapter 10
	STURGEON class (37)		
SSN 637	STURGEON	1967	decomm./str. 1 Aug 1994
SSN 638	WHALE	1968	decomm./str. 25 June 1996
SSN 639	TAUTOG	1968	decomm./str. 31 Mar 1997
SSBN 640–645			see Chapter 10
	STURGEON class (continued)		
SSN 646	GRAYLING	1969	decomm./str. 18 July 1997
SSN 647	POGY	1971	decomm./str. 11 June 1999
SSN 648	ASPRO	1969	decomm./str. 3 Mar 1995
SSN 649	SUNFISH	1969	decomm./str. 28 Mar 1997
SSN 650	PARGO	1968	decomm./str. 14 Apr 1995
SSN 651	QUEENFISH	1966	decomm./str. 8 Nov 1991
SSN 652	PUFFER	1969	decomm./str. 12 July 1996
SSN 653	RAY	1967	decomm./str. 16 Mar 1993
SSBN 654–659			see Chapter 10
	STURGEON class (continued)		
SSN 660	SAND LANCE	1971	decomm./str. 7 Aug 1998
SSN 661	LAPON	1967	decomm./str. 8 Aug 1992
SSN 662	GURNARD	1968	decomm./str. 28 Apr 1995
SSN 663	HAMMERHEAD	1968	decomm./str. 5 Apr 1995
SSN 664	SEA DEVIL	1969	decomm./str. 16 Oct 1991
SSN 665	GUITARRO	1972	decomm./str. 29 May 1992
SSN 666	HAWKBILL	1971	decomm./str. 15 Mar 2000
SSN 667	BERGALL	1969	decomm./str. 6 June 1996
SSN 668	SPADEFISH	1969	decomm./str. 11 Apr 1997
SSN 669	SEAHORSE	1969	decomm./str. 17 Aug 1995
SSN 670	FINBACK	1970	decomm./str. 28 Mar 1997
	NARWHAL type		
SSN 671	NARWHAL	1969	decomm./str.1 July 1999
	STURGEON class (continued)		
SSN 672	PINTADO	1971	decomm./str. 26 Feb 1998
SSN 673	FLYING FISH	1970	decomm./str. 16 May 1996
SSN 674	TREPANG	1970	decomm./str. 1 June 1999
SSN 675	BLUEFISH	1971	decomm./str. 31 May 1996
SSN 676	BILLFISH	1971	decomm./str. 1 July 1999
SSN 677	DRUM	1972	decomm./str. 30 Oct 1995
SSN 678	ARCHERFISH	1971	decomm./str. 31 Mar 1998
SSN 679	SILVERSIDES	1972	decomm./str. 21 July 1994
SSN 680	WILLIAM H. BATES	1973	decomm./str. 11 Feb 2000
SSN 681	BATFISH	1972	decomm./str. 17 Mar 1999
SSN 682	TUNNY	1974	decomm./str. 13 Mar 1998
SSN 683	PARCHE	1974	decomm./str. 30 Sep 2003
SSN 684	CAVALLA	1973	decomm./str. 30 Mar 1998
	GLENARD P. LIPSCOMB type		
SSN 685	GLENARD P. LIPSCOMB	1974	decomm./str. 11 July 1990
	STURGEON class (continued)		
SSN 686	L. MENDEL RIVERS	1975	decomm./str. 10 May 2001
SSN 687	RICHARD B. RUSSELL	1975	decomm./str. 24 June 1994
SSN 688–725	LOS ANGELES class		
SSBN 726–749			see Chapter 10
SSN 750–773	LOS ANGELES class		
SSN 774–	VIRGINIA class		

U.S. submarine programs reached hull number SS 562 during World War II, with hulls 526–562 canceled late in the war. Subsequently, five of these numbers were assigned to postwar submarines, three U.S. submarines and two U.S.-financed foreign-built submarines (offshore procurement); two others, to be built in Portugal (SS 556) and Norway (SS 557), were canceled in 1961.

The last war-built submarine on the Naval Vessel Register was the transport submarine SEALION (LPSS 315), decommissioned and laid up in 1970 and stricken in 1977. The last active submarine of World War II construction was the TIGRONE (AGSS 419), which was decommissioned and stricken on 1 July 1975 (correction from 17th Edition).

Note the large number of submarine designs developed and built from the late 1940s into the early 1960s. This was a period of highly innovative thinking in the submarine community, in part arising from the search for new roles for submarines and exploration of the potential impact of emerging technologies on submarine warfare. In particular, the research submarine ALBACORE introduced many of the features found in subsequent undersea craft; in many respects, she was the beginning of the modern submarine era.

The three units of the BARBEL class were the last diesel-electric combat submarines built in the United States and the last in U.S. Navy service. They were the first combat submarines to incorporate the ALBACORE's "tear-drop" high-speed hull design. The BARBEL recently was sunk as a target, on 30 January 2001.

The GRAYBACK and GROWLER were similar ships, although their dimensions differed slightly. They carried the Regulus land-attack guided/cruise missile. The GRAYBACK was reconfigured as a transport submarine (redesignated LPSS); she was succeeded in that role by nuclear-propelled submarines (see Chapter 10).

The pioneering nuclear-propelled submarine NAUTILUS survives as a memorial/museum at Groton, Connecticut. She was commissioned on 30 September 1954, but did not get under way until 3 January 1955. The NAUTILUS was decommissioned on 3 March 1980, after being defueled and modified at the Mare Island Naval Shipyard, Vallejo, California. In 1985, she was towed to Groton and formally transferred to private control on 6 July 1985, for use as a museum.[25] She remains on the Naval Vessel Register as "floating equipment."

The special-purpose nuclear submarines TRITON and HALIBUT were redesignated as SSNs after being withdrawn from their specialized roles as radar picket and guided/cruise missile (Regulus) platforms, respectively. The SEAWOLF, HALIBUT, and PARCHE were modified for deep-ocean search-and-recovery operations; they carried out special "spy" missions, including tapping into Soviet seafloor communication cables.

The SSNs 594–596 and 607 were ordered as SSGNs to carry the Regulus II guided missile. They were reordered as THRESHER-class SSNs on 15 October 1959 following cancellation of the Regulus II.

The THRESHER was lost on post-overhaul sea trials off New England on 10 April 1963 with all 112 naval personnel and 17 civilians on board. This was the world's first nuclear submarine loss and the worst submarine disaster on record in terms of lives lost.

The SCORPION was lost with all 99 men on board on 27 May 1968 some 400 nm (741 km) southwest of the Azores. She was transiting to Norfolk following a deployment in the Mediterranean.

Table 11-5. HUNTER-KILLER SUBMARINES

Number	Name/Renamed	Comm.	Notes
SSK 1	K 1 / BARRACUDA	1951	to SST 3
SSK 2	K 2 / BASS	1951	to SS 551/str. 1965
SSK 3	K 3 / BONITA	1952	to SS 552/str. 1965

These purpose-built SSKs were small hunter-killer submarines, intended to lie in wait to intercept Soviet submarines off their home ports and in narrow waterways. Several hundred were to have been produced in time of war.

Originally assigned K-number "names," these submarines were given fish names in 1955. The BASS and BONITA were reclassified SS in 1959 for use in the training role; the BARRACUDA was changed to SST in 1959 for the training role.

In addition to these built-for-the-purpose SSKs, the nuclear-propelled TULLIBEE was built as an SSKN (although designated SSN 597). Seven war-built GATO (SS 212)-class diesel submarines were converted to hunter-killer submarines in the 1950s and redesignated SSK with their SS hull numbers (214, 240–244, 246).

Table 11-6. TRAINING SUBMARINES

Number	Name/Renamed	Comm.	Notes
SST 1	T 1 / MACKEREL	1953	str. 1973
SST 2	T 2 / MARLIN	1953	str. 1973 (museum)
SST 3	BARRACUDA (ex-K 1)	1951	str. 1973

The SST 1 and 2 were small submarines developed for training and target use. The MACKEREL was ordered as AGSS 570 and completed as the SST 1. Originally assigned T-number "names," the three were given fish names in 1956.

The BARRACUDA was changed from SSK 1 to SST 3 after operating as a hunter-killer submarine. She later was reclassified SS-T3 as a force-level adjustment, and then changed back to SST 3.

Table 11-7. MIDGET SUBMARINES

Number	Name	In Service	Notes
SSX 1	X-1	1955	str. 1973

The U.S. Navy's lone midget submarine was the X-1, which was based on British X-craft submersibles. She had a closed-cycle/hydrogen-peroxide-diesel propulsion system. The SSX 1 was placed In Service vice In Commission, with an officer-in-charge.

She is on display at the Submarine Museum at the Naval Submarine Base New London in Groton, Connecticut.

---

25 The Navy had decided to moor the ship at the Washington Navy Yard in the nation's capital. However, President Carter directed that she be moored at New London.

CHAPTER 12

Research Submarines and Submersibles

Crewmen of the USS LA JOLLA (SSN 701) lower the national ensign as the attack submarine departs Sasebo, Japan, carrying the rescue submersible MYSTIC. The LA JOLLA and MYSTIC were participating the submarine rescue exercise Pacific Reach 2002, conducted by ships and submarines of several Pacific Rim navies. (2002, U.S. Navy/Wes Eplen)

The U.S. Navy operates one dedicated diesel-electric research submarine, the DOLPHIN; one nuclear-propelled research "submersible," the NR-1; and one rescue submersible, the MYSTIC; plus a number of small, SEAL delivery vehicles, including the new Advanced SEAL Delivery System (ASDS), which in several respects resembles a midget submarine.[1] Several unmanned submersibles are operated in a number of naval roles. These are classified as Large Scale Vehicles (LSVs), Unmanned Underwater Vehicles (UUVs), and Remotely Operated Vehicles (ROVs).

An additional research submersible owned by the Navy—the ALVIN—is operated by a civilian research institution.

The former diesel-electric combat submarine TROUT also is retained by the Navy. There have been several efforts to reactivate her, with a civilian contract crew, to carry out research-and-development work; however, the submarine community has strongly opposed the reactivation of the non-nuclear submarine.

Classification: The Navy's first deep-diving craft, the bathyscaph TRIESTE, did not have a hull number. When rebuilt as the TRIESTE II with a more hydrodynamic float and other features, she was designated X-1 and, subsequently, as DSV (Deep Submergence Vehicle) 1.[2]

The DSV 2 through DSV 4 are listed below; the DSV 5 was the unmanned, tethered vehicle NEMO.[3]

Related vehicles designations are DSRV (Deep Submergence Rescue Vehicle), with two having been built, and the aborted DSSV (Deep Submergence Search Vehicle). The latter was assigned to two 20,000-foot-capable vehicles designed in the 1970s but not built.

---

1 SEAL = Sea, Air, Land (team).
2 The original TRIESTE is at the Navy Museum at the Navy Yard, Washington, D.C.; the TRIESTE II is at the Naval Undersea Museum at Keyport, Washington.
3 On display at San Diego.

Operational: Submarine Development Squadron 5 at Point Loma (San Diego), California, operates the research submarine DOLPHIN and the rescue submersible MYSTIC. The latter is based at the Deep Submergence Unit at Naval Air Station (NAS) North Island (San Diego). A number of unmanned vehicles and two Submarine Rescue Chambers (SRCs) also are based at NAS North Island.

The special missions submarine JIMMY CARTER (SSN 23) also will be assigned to Submarine Development Squadron 5, established on 1 July 2003, at Bangor, Washington. The squadron's mission is to provide operational and administrative support for the JIMMY CARTER, "undersea research and development, unmanned undersea vehicles and off hull sensors tactical development."

Submarine Squadron 2 at the Naval Submarine Base New London (Groton, Connecticut) operates the nuclear submersible NR-1, as well as several attack submarines. The NR-1 is based at the Portsmouth Naval Shipyard in Kittery, Maine.

Personnel: The manning data provided in the individual submersibles' entries are for the actual number of operating personnel on board these submersibles. The following list shows the number of Navy personnel assigned to each craft, including maintenance and relief operators.

	Total	Officers	Enlisted
NR-1	35	4	31
MYSTIC	20	3	17

1 RESEARCH SUBMARINE: "DOLPHIN"

Number	Name	FY	Builder	Laid Down	Launched	Comm.	Status
AGSS 555	DOLPHIN	61	Portsmouth Naval Shipyard	9 Nov 1962	8 June 1968	17 Aug 1968	Yard

Displacement:	860 tons standard	Operating depth:	3,000 feet (915 m)
	950 tons submerged	Personnel:	48 (4 officers + 44 enlisted) + 5 scientists
Length:	165 feet (50.3 m) overall	Torpedo tubes:	removed
Beam:	19 5/12 feet (5.9 m)	Radars:	SPS-53 navigation (portable)
Draft:	16 feet (4.9 m)	Sonars:	BQR-2 passive (bow mounted)
Propulsion:	2 diesel engines (General Motors 12V71); 850 bhp		BQS-15 active
	1 electric motor (Elliott); 1,650 shp; 1 shaft	Fire control:	none
Speed:	7.5 knots surface		
	15 knots submerged		

The DOLPHIN is an experimental, deep-diving submarine, and the last non-nuclear submarine to be built by the U.S. Navy. She has operated at greater depths than any other operational U.S. submarine.

Design: SCB No. 207. The DOLPHIN has a constant-diameter pressure hull with an outside diameter of approximately 15 feet (4.57 m) and hemisphere heads at both ends. The submarine has a stepped sail, with the radar antenna, Ultra High Frequency (UHF) antenna, and single periscope mounted on the upper (rear) step, and the lights, whip antenna, Very Low Frequency (VLF) loop antenna, and searchlight mounted on the lower step. There are internal and external mounting points for equipment.

An improved rudder design and other features permit maneuvering without conventional submarine diving planes. There are minimal penetrations of the pressure hull (e.g., only one access hatch) and built-in safety systems that automatically surface the submarine in an emergency. The single experimental torpedo tube origi-

nally fitted was removed in 1970. The DOLPHIN has been modified to test HY-130 steel components.

Electronics: Various experimental sonars have been fitted in the DOLPHIN. Her original bow sonar, which had four arrays that could be extended at 90° angles to the submarine's bow–stern axis, has been removed.

Engineering: Submerged endurance is approximately 24 hours; her sea endurance is about 14 days.

Operational: The DOLPHIN's activities have supported research in air–submarine laser communications, deep submergence, sonar, oceanography, and ASW.

The DOLPHIN was badly damaged by fire and flooding while operating some 100 nm off San Diego on 21 May 2002. Only minor injuries were suffered by the crew, who were forced to abandon the submarine after bringing her to the surface. The DOLPHIN was towed back into San Diego. She has been rehabilitated and will return to service in 2005.

The deep-diving DOLPHIN is the only nonnuclear submarine currently in U.S. naval service. The craft has carried out a variety of research activities in connection with communications, sonar, weapons, and other areas. Few photos are taken of Navy research craft and submersibles. (U.S. Navy)

1 DIESEL-ELECTRIC ATTACK SUBMARINE: "TANG" CLASS

Number	Name	FY	Builder	Launched	Comm.	Status
ex-SS 566	TROUT	48	General Dynamics/Electric Boat	21 Aug 1951	27 June 1952	str. 19 Dec 1978; see text

Displacement:	2,100 tons standard		Operating depth:	700 feet (213 m)
	2,700 tons submerged		Personnel:	88 (8 officers + 80 enlisted)
Length:	287 feet (87.5 m) overall		Torpedo tubes:	8 21-inch (533-mm) tubes; 6 Mk 43 bow + 2 Mk 44 stern
Beam:	27 1/6 feet (8.3 m)		Torpedoes:	26
Draft:	19 feet (5.8 m)		Radars:	
Propulsion:	3 diesel engines (Fairbanks Morse) 4,500 bhp		Sonars:	BQS-4
	2 electric motors (Westinghouse); 5,600 shp; 2 shafts			BQG-4 Passive Underwater Fire Control System (PUFFS)
Speed:	16 knots surface		Fire control:	Mk 10 torpedo FCS
	16 knots submerged			

The TROUT is the last diesel-electric attack submarine retained by the U.S. Navy. Decommissioned and stricken on 19 December 1978 and sold to Iran, the TROUT (and two sister ships) was retained by the U.S. government after the overthrow of the Shah in early 1979. The two other submarines, the TANG and GUDGEON, were transferred to Turkey (see table 11-4). The TROUT was maintained at the Philadelphia Naval Shipyard, then at Newport, Rhode Island, before being towed to Key West in July 1997. Officially stricken, she was maintained by the Naval Air Warfare Center's Aircraft Division until 2004 when she was towed top the Philadelphia Naval Shipyard pending disposal.

The TROUT is not operational and is considered "floating equipment"; however, maintenance and preparations for getting her under way have begun (a timetable had not been developed when this edition went to press). Plans are to use the TROUT as an underwater acoustic target for research and development, operational testing, and anti-submarine warfare training in the lower Florida Keys. The rehabilitation is being undertaken by Naval Reservists.

The interest in an ASW target by the U.S. Navy—albeit not by the submarine community—stems from the U.S. Navy attack submarine force being all nuclear, with the LOS ANGELES (SSN 688) class the "smallest" attack submarines now in service. The SSNs cannot effectively simulate diesel-electric submarine targets for anti-submarine forces. They are too large, have very different signatures from the typical submarines operated by Third World navies, and are operated quite unlike the submarines the United States could be fighting in a future conflict.

In addition, the current force level goal of 55 SSNs provides too few submarines for training air and surface ASW forces, especially for reserve frigates and maritime patrol aircraft, which have low priority for submarine target time. The shortfall in SSNs for operational taskings has been well publicized of late, and ASW training falls relatively low on the list of assignments.[4]

Class: Six submarines of the TANG class were completed in 1951–1952; see Table 11-4 for disposition.

Design: SCB-2A. This design incorporates many features of the German Type XXI, the most advanced submarine design of World War II.

The TROUT's keel was laid down on 1 December 1949.

4 See Lt. Comdr. Carey Matthews, USNR, "Anti-Sub Warfare Calls for 2 Russian Diesels," *Navy Times* (26 February 1996), p. 33; Lt. Jack Shriver, USN, "Developing Real Anti-Diesel Tactics," *The Submarine Review* (April 1998), pp. 90–94; N. Polmar, "Realistic ASW Training," U.S. Naval Institute *Proceedings* (December 1999), pp. 86–87; and commentary on the last article by Comdr. Dennis K. Fargo, USN (Ret.), and Michael Wheeler, U.S. Naval Institute *Proceedings* (February 2004), pp. 20, 22–24, 26–27.

The former USS TROUT alongside a pier at Key West, Florida. The TROUT, out of service since 1978, could be employed—probably with a civilian crew—as a useful research and limited ASW target submarine, in the opinion of many naval specialists. (2003, Naval Air Warfare Center, Key West)

SUBMERSIBLES

1 NUCLEAR-PROPELLED RESEARCH SUBMERSIBLE: "NR-1"

Number	Name	FY	Builder	Laid Down	Launched	In Service	Status
NR-1	(unnamed)	—	General Dynamics/Electric Boat	10 June 1967	25 Jan 1969	27 Oct 1969	**AA**

Displacement:	365.5 tons surface		Reactors:	1 pressurized-water
	393 tons submerged		Speed:	4.5 knots surface
Length:	136 feet (41.46 m) waterline			3.5 knots submerged
	145¾ feet (44.44 m) overall		Endurance:	210 man-days nominal
	96½ feet (29.3 m) pressure hull			330 man-days maximum
Beam:	12½ feet (3.8 m)		Operating depth:	3,000 feet (915 m[5])
Draft:	15½ feet (4.6 m)		Personnel:	11 operators + 2 scientists
Propulsion:	turbo-electric drive with outboard electric motors; 2 propellers			

The NR-1 originally was built as a test platform for a small submarine nuclear power plant, but she often has been employed as a deep-ocean research and recovery vehicle. Following the end of the Cold War in 1991, she has been employed extensively in nonnaval scientific and historical research activities.

In explaining the craft's importance, Admiral H. G. Rickover, then head of the Navy's nuclear propulsion program, told a congressional committee, "You will be looking at a development that I believe will be as significant for the United States as was the NAUTILUS" (SSN 571).[6] Rickover planned to construct a series of these craft, hence the designation NR-1.

The veil of secrecy surrounding the NR-1 was partially lifted on 18 April 1965, when President Lyndon Johnson announced the development of the craft. The White House release, citing the severe endurance and space limitations of existing research submersibles, stated:

> The development of a nuclear propulsion plant for a deep submergence research vehicle will give greater freedom of movement and much greater endurance of propulsion and auxiliary power. This capability will contribute greatly to accelerate man's exploration and exploitation of the vast resources of the ocean.[7]

Beyond her nuclear plant, which gives her a theoretical unlimited underwater endurance, the NR-1's most remarkable feature is her operating depth of 3,000 feet (915 m). This is far greater than that of the U.S. Navy's combat submarines, and while it is not as great as the Navy's other manned research submersibles, their underwater endurance is only a few hours.

The Knolls Atomic Power Laboratory in Schenectady, New York, designed the reactor, and the submersible was designed and subsequently built by the Electric Boat yard in Groton. The NR-1 was launched on 25 January 1969, underwent initial sea trials in August, and was placed in service on 27 October of that year. The Deep Submergence Systems Project (DSSP), the Navy's management office for the NR-1, was not allowed to publicize the craft except to reiterate what was said in President Johnson's statement (which had been prepared by Rickover's office). The launch photo of the NR-1 even had the craft's fixed mast and television camera blacked out. (The camera was provided in place of conventional periscopes.)

The NR-1 is in service vice in commission and is commanded by an officer-in-charge rather than a commanding officer. She is towed and supported by the support ship CAROLYN CHOUEST, a leased commercial tender.

Class: A Hull Test Vehicle (HTV) originally was proposed as the NR-2 in 1976 by Admiral Rickover, but was never built (see 16th Edition/page 322).

Classification: NR-1 indicates Nuclear Research vehicle, although the craft is listed as a submersible research vehicle in the Naval Vessel Register.

Cost: The craft was funded as a nuclear-propulsion project rather than as new ship construction. As proposed, the Atomic Energy Commission (now Department of Energy) was to pay for the research and development of the reactor plant and the Navy for the deep-ocean research vehicle. Admiral Rickover estimated he could produce the craft for $30 million, the amount available in the management fund of the Navy's Polaris project, which at the time was managing such deep-ocean programs. He stressed to Congress that the NR-1—except for the propulsion plant—would employ existing technology and equipment.

The cost of the NR-1 at launch in 1969 was $67.5 million, plus $19.9 million for oceanographic equipment and sensors and $11.8 million for research and development—a total of $99.2 million. The Navy has never revealed "final" cost figures for the craft. Cost, however, seemed irrelevant in view of the unprecedented capabilities of the NR-1 to carry out research and ocean-engineering work.[8]

Design: The NR-1, largely resembling a conventional submarine, is fabricated of HY-80 steel. She is fitted with two large wheels that permit her to roll and rest on the ocean floor. The retractable tires are normal truck tires, with inner tubes filled with alcohol.

In addition to her twin screws, which provide a submerged speed of 3.5 knots, the craft has paired ducted thrusters forward and aft to provide a high degree of maneuverability. Extensive external lights, viewing ports, close-range sonars, a remote-controlled mechanical arm, and a recovery cage provide considerable capabilities. The craft carries 22,000 pounds (9,980 kg) of expendable lead shot to provide emergency buoyancy.

Three bunks are provided; crew endurance is limited to a maximum of 30-day missions. There is a warming oven for frozen foods and a hot-drink dispenser.

The NR-1's principal operational limitation is her deployment mobility. Because of her slow speeds, she must be towed to her operating area, either by a surface ship or (underwater) by a nuclear submarine. Her surface towing speed is up to six knots; submerged it is just under four knots.

Electronics: The NR-1 is provided with forward and side-looking sonars; a Doppler sonar is provided to measure over-bottom speed. A BQN-13 rescue pinger beacon is installed.

---

5 The Navy officially lists the NR-1 operating depth as 2,375 feet; however, Navy statements continually cite a 3,000-foot capability.

6 Adm. H. G. Rickover, USN (Ret), in *Naval Nuclear Propulsion Program—1967–68, Hearings before the Joint Committee on Atomic Energy, Congress of the United States* (Washington, D.C.: Joint Committee on Atomic Energy, Congress, 1968), p. 30.

7 Untitled White House press release (Austin, Texas), 18 April 1965.

8 For a discussion of the trials and tribulations of NR-1 funding, see Capt. William M. Nicholson, USN (Ret.), "Truth Is in the Eye of the Beholder," *Naval Institute Proceedings* (June 1995), pp. 10–11.

Engineering: The craft was first refueled during an extensive yard period from November 1990 to November 1992; she is scheduled to be refueled in 2012, based on the 20-year service life of her reactor core.

Operational: The major NR-1 activities of the Cold War era still are classified. Undoubtedly, she was employed to help maintain the Navy's Sound Surveillance System (SOSUS) and other seafloor installations; she probably also was used to help recover objects that fell to the ocean floor—Soviet as well as American.

Some of the NR-1's exploits were publicized. For example, in 1976, she played a key role in recovering an F-14 Tomcat fighter armed with a then-new Phoenix missile that rolled off the deck of the carrier JOHN F. KENNEDY (CV 67) and came to rest at a depth of 1,960 feet (598 m). In 1986, the NR-1 participated in the search for wreckage of the crashed space shuttle *Challenger* off Cape Kennedy, Florida.

A few NR-1 exploits were acknowledged only reluctantly. In 1970, for example, she participated in installation of the NATO-sponsored, eight-nation Azores Fixed Acoustic Range (AFAR). Obviously, a large number of civilians as well as military personnel ashore and afloat were cognizant of the NR-1's participation. When she entered Ponta Delgada in the Azores, many civilians in the port saw and probably photographed her. Still, Rickover objected strongly to the craft being mentioned in press releases or public documents related to AFAR.

With the end of the Cold War, the role of the NR-1 has changed. The Navy, with fewer classified deep-ocean missions, has made the remarkable craft available for civilian scientific and exploration work. In the spring of 1996, the NR-1 operated off Key Largo, Florida, to support the Jason Project VII, an educational program for youth. In the summer and early fall of 1996, she deployed to Norway to support a government request to survey fjords, harbors, shipwrecks, and other undersea obstructions.

From June to late August 1997, the NR-1 operated in the eastern Mediterranean, where, at the behest of the Israeli Navy, she searched unsuccessfully for the wreckage of the submarine DAKAR, lost in January 1968 while en route from Britain to Israel. The NR-1's Mediterranean deployment also included exploring the wreck of the BRITANNIC, sister ship of the TITANIC, and searching for Roman wrecks. The latter effort included 19 dives for a total of 403 hours submerged, with 294 hours actually engaged in search, excavating, and recovery operations. Employing a conventional submersible for this work would have required thousands of hours because of the extra time needed to dive and return to the surface to recharge batteries.

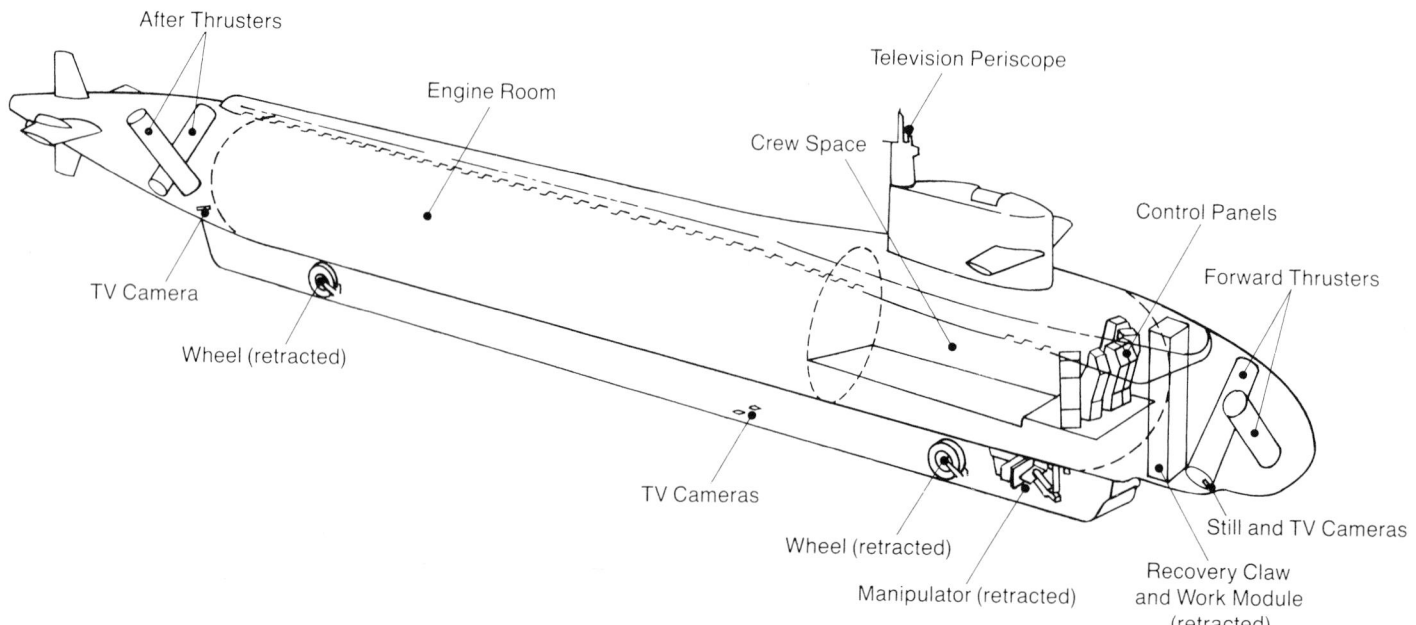

Nuclear-Propelled Submersible NR-1.

The NR-1 at sea—under tow. The nuclear-propelled submersible normally is towed to operating areas by a surface ship or, submerged, by an attack submarine. When developed by Admiral Hyman Rickover, the NR-1 was envisioned as the first of a series of such undersea craft; in the event, she was a one-of-a-kind submersible. (Giorgio Arra)

Details of the NR-1's sail structure, with a crewman standing on her starboard sail-mounted diving plane. The submarine has a fixed mast with a television-like optical system. Note the towing gear fitted to her bow. (U.S. Navy)

1 DEEP SUBMERGENCE RESCUE VEHICLE: "MYSTIC" CLASS

Number	Name	Launched	Completed	Status
DSRV 1	MYSTIC	24 Jan 1970	6 Aug 1971	Operational
DSRV 2	AVALON	1 May 1971	28 July 1972	Inactive 1 Sep 2000

Builders:	Lockheed Missiles and Space Co., Sunnyvale, California
Weight:	37 tons
Length:	49⅔ feet (15 m) overall
Diameter:	8 feet (2.4 m)
Propulsion:	1 electric motor, 15 shp, 1 propeller mounted in control shroud (see *Engineering* notes)
Speed:	4 knots
Operating depth:	5,000 feet (1,524 m)
Crew:	3 + 24 rescuees

The DSRVs were developed after the loss of the submarine THRESHER (SSN 593) in 1963 to provide the capability for rescuing survivors from submarines disabled on the ocean floor above their hull collapse depths. The DSRV design provides a long-range, all-weather rescue capability.[9]

After lengthy tests and evaluation, both DSRVs were declared fully operational in late 1977.

The AVALON was scheduled to be taken out of service on 1 September 2000; however, the loss of the Soviet submarine KURSK on 12 August 2000 delayed this action. The MYSTIC is scheduled to be taken out of service about 2005. Subsequently, submarine rescue will be conducted with rescue chambers based on surface ships, i.e., the same scheme used by the U.S. Navy from the late 1930s until the availability of these DSRVs (see below).

Class: Initially, 12 rescue vehicles were planned, each able to carry 12 survivors. When vehicle capability was increased to 24 survivors, the proposed number of DSRVs was reduced to six. In the event, only two units were built.

The DSRVs were developed by the Navy's Deep Submergence Systems Project, which also had responsibility for the nonpropulsion aspects of the NR-1 and had planned a set of DSSVs with a 20,000-foot operating capability. They were designed but never funded or built.

---

9 The term "rescue" is for the use of external means to remove survivors from a stricken submarine; the term "escape" refers to the survivors of a stricken submarine reaching the surface without external assistance.

The MYSTIC mated to the USS LA JOLLA departs Sasebo for a multinational rescue exercise. The five active U.S. submarines that can accommodate the dry deck shelter also can carry the DSRV. The skirt beneath the MYSTIC, which is removed for air and road transport, is mated to the submarine's after hatch. (2002, U.S. Navy/Wes Eplen)

Costs: The estimated construction cost of the DSRV 1 was $41 million, and the DSRV 2 cost $23 million. The total development, construction, test, and initial support costs for these craft have run in excess of $220 million. However, some of the funding was a "cover" for classified deep-ocean research and recovery projects.

Design: The DSRV consists of three interconnected personnel spheres, each 7½ feet (2.3 m) in diameter, constructed of HY-140 steel, encased in a fiberglass-reinforced plastic shell. The MYSTIC originally was certified only to 3,500 feet for technical reasons; this subsequently was increased to 5,000 feet.

The forward sphere contains the vehicle's controls and is manned by the pilot and copilot; the center and after spheres can accommodate 24 survivors and a third crewman.

The DSRVs can mate with all U.S. submarines except the DOLPHIN and NR-1. They were configured to be launched and recovered by a submerged attack submarine or by a submarine rescue ship of the PIGEON (ASR 21) class. After launching, the DSRV can descend to the disabled submarine, "mate" with one of the submarine's escape hatches, take on board up to 24 survivors, and return to the "mother" submarine or ASR. The submersible can be air transported in a C-141 or C-5 cargo aircraft, and ground transported by a special trailer.

It is fitted with a remote-control manipulator.

Electronics: The DSRVs are fitted with elaborate search and navigation sonars, closed-circuit television, and optical viewing devices for locating a disabled submarine and mating with the stricken craft's escape hatches.

Engineering: The DSRVs have a single propeller driven by a 15-hp electric motor for forward propulsion. The propeller is in a rotating control shroud, which alleviates the need for rudders and diving planes (which could interfere with a rescue mission). Four ducted thrusters—two vertical and two horizontal, each powered by a 7½-hp electric motor—provide precise maneuvering. The craft has an endurance of five hours at a speed of four knots.

Names: Names were assigned in 1977.

Operational: The DSRV rapid-deployment concept has been tested periodically using U.S. and British nuclear-propelled submarines for support. The operational DSRV is maintained in a high state of readiness, ready to be flown to a port, loaded on board a submarine, and transported to the site of a submarine casualty anywhere in the world within 72 hours.

A DSRV is loaded into an Air Force C-5B Galaxy transport during a rescue exercise. The rescue vehicles were designed specifically for rapid deployment to a port in the vicinity of a submarine disaster, where they would be loaded on specially modified "mother" submarines or surface ships. (U.S. Navy)

The MYSTIC and AVALON on wheeled dollies, ready for road or air transportation. The MYSTIC (left) has a modified sonar installed in her bow. The openings near the crafts' bows are for their ducted thrusters, which permit precise maneuvering for underwater submarine mating. (U.S. Navy)

RESEARCH SUBMERSIBLES: MODIFIED "ALVIN" CLASS

The submersible TURTLE (DSV 2) was taken out of service on 1 October 1977 and the SEA CLIFF (DSV 4) on 1 April 1998; the latter craft then was transferred to the Woods Hole Oceanographic Institution on 30 June 1998.

See 16th Edition/page 325 for characteristics.

1 RESEARCH SUBMERSIBLE: "ALVIN" CLASS

Number	Name	Launched	Completed	Status
DSV 2	ALVIN	5 June 1964	1965	Academic

Builders:	General Mills Inc., Minneapolis, Minnesota
Weight:	16 tons
Length:	22½ feet (6.9 m) overall
Beam:	8 feet (2.4 m); 12 feet (3.7 m) over propeller pods
Speed:	2 knots
Operating depth:	13,124 feet (4,000 m)
Crew:	1 + 2 scientists

The ALVIN is operated by the Woods Hole Oceanographic Institution, Woods Hole, Massachusetts, for the Office of Naval Research, which sponsored construction of the craft.

The ALVIN accidentally sank in 5,050 feet (1,540 m) of water on 16 October 1968, when her sphere flooded (there were no casualties). She was raised in August 1969, refurbished from May 1971 to October 1972, and became operational in November 1972. (The research ship MIZAR/T-AGOR 11 and the commercial submersible ALUMINAUT effected the salvage.)

Classification: Classified DSV 2 on 1 June 1971.

Design: As built, the ALVIN had a single, 7-foot (2.1 m) diameter pressure sphere made of HY-100 steel, which gave her a 6,000-foot (1,828.8 m) operating depth. She was refitted with a titanium sphere in 1971–1972, which increased her capabilities. She is fitted with a remote-control manipulator.

Engineering: A single stern propeller is fitted for forward propulsion; two pod-mounted propellers driven by separate electric motors rotate for maneuvering. No through thrusters are fitted. Endurance is one hour at 2.5 knots and eight hours at 1 knot.

Operational: In 1988, the ALVIN aided in the location and photographing of the sunken ocean liner TITANIC.

The venerable ALVIN continues to serve as a very useful research tool. Here being lifted aboard a landing ship, the ALVIN shows her skids for bottom sitting, ducted propeller, and small maneuvering propellers fitted amidships. Two of her viewing ports are evident. (U.S. Navy)

SEAL DELIVERY VEHICLES

The Navy has two types of SEAL Delivery Vehicles (SDVs): The first "dry" passenger Advanced SEAL Delivery System (ASDS) is now operational, and there are about 15 "wet" SDVs that can be carried into forward areas in hangars fitted to attack or special forces transport submarines.[10]

The Navy Special Warfare organization, which operates SEAL units, is shown in chapter 21.

1 + 5 ADVANCED SEAL DELIVERY SYSTEMS

Number	Completed	Status
ASDS No. 1	Aug 2001	Operational
ASDS No. 2	FY 2009	Planned
ASDS No. 3	FY 20011	Planned
ASDS No. 4	FY 20012	Planned
ASDS No. 5	FY 20013	Planned
ASDS No. 6	FY 20014	Planned

Builders:	Northrop Grumman Ocean Systems, Annapolis, Maryland
Displacement:	55 tons (dry)
Length:	65 feet (19.8 m) overall
Beam:	6¾ feet (2.06 m)
Height:	8¼ feet (2.5 m)
Propulsion:	1 electric motor; 67 hp; 1 propeller + 4 thrusters
Speed:	8 knots
Range:	125+ nm (230+ km)
Crew:	2 (1 officer + 1 enlisted) + 8 SEALs

These are advanced SDVs that can carry SEALs in a dry environment, providing a "lock-out" capability.

Each of the four proposed cruise missile and transport/special forces submarines converted from OHIO (SSBN/ SSGN 726)-class submarines can carry two ASDS vehicles. The attack submarines CHARLOTTE (SSN 766) and GREENEVILLE each can carry a single ASDS.[11]

Reportedly, the Navy has a requirement for 11 of the new vehicles, although only 6 currently are planned for construction.[12] The construction of ASDS No. 1 was significantly behind schedule, and the entire program appears to have a low priority in the Navy, and there have been some efforts to cancel the entire program because of technical problems.

It has been proposed that the new ASDS could be used for submarine rescue. Capable of mating with specific submarine escape hatches, the ASDS has an operating depth of a little more than 200 feet, which is relatively shallow, but certainly useful in some situations if the ASDS crew is properly trained and some additional equipment is fitted to the vehicle.[13] (The vehicle's collapse depth is equal to that of an SSN.)

The lead vehicle was estimated to cost $230 million.[14] That figure obviously includes some program start-up costs.

Design: The ASDS has three compartments—the forward control compartment, amidships lock-in/lock-out chamber, and after SEAL compartment. Top and bottom hatches are provided to the lock-in/lock-out chamber for both ingress and egress to the vehicle.

Among the craft's several unusual features are the "folding" communications mast and periscope. The craft is not large enough

---

10 Officially *Swimmer* Delivery Vehicle on the basis of Secretary of the Navy Instruction 5030.1L, "Classification of Naval Ships and Craft." However, they invariably are referred to as SEAL Delivery Vehicles.
11 The GREENEVILLE was the test submarine for the ASDS vehicle.
12 See N. Polmar, The U.S. Navy, "Projecting Our SEALS," U.S. Naval Institute *Proceedings* (September 2001), pp. 87–88.
13 A useful exposition on this subject is Frederick M. Cancilliere, "Update on UUV Technology," *The Submarine Review* (July 1995), pp. 75–82.
14 See Gregg K. Kakesako, "Minisub at Pearl Will Carry SEALS Close to Targets," *Star-Bulletin* (Honolulu), 6 May 2000; based on interview with Comdr. Joe Fallone, USN, program manager.

to be fitted with conventional telescoping devices.

The vehicle can be carried by a C-5 Galaxy or C-17 Skytrain transport aircraft.

Engineering: Electric motors power the main propulsor, a shrouded propeller. Four small, trainable thrusters—two forward and two aft—provide precise maneuvering and hover capabilities. These are needed for mating operations with submarines.

Personnel: The pilot is a submarine officer and the copilot a SEAL officer. Up to 16 SEALs can be transported without their diving/breathing gear and weapons.

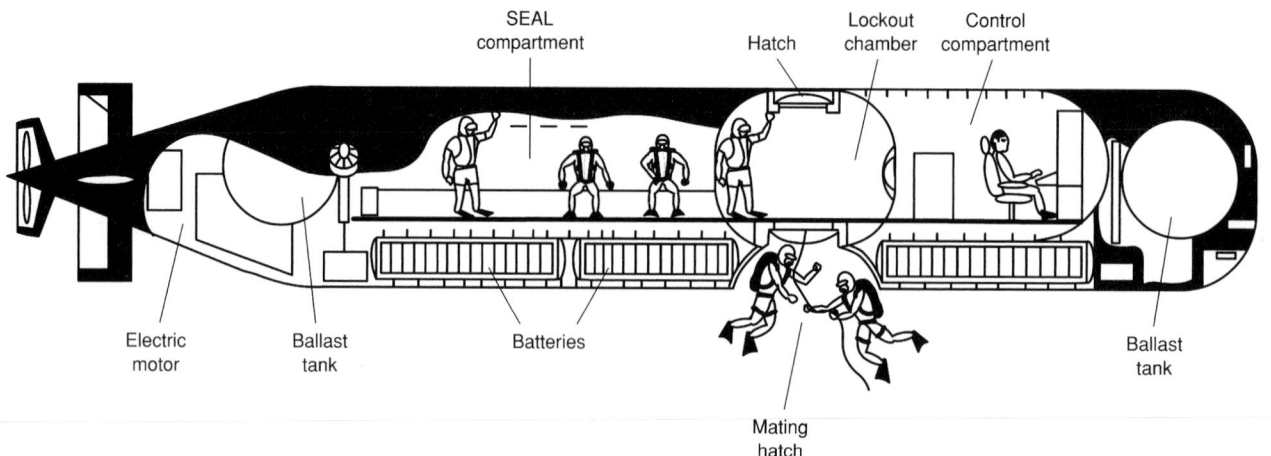

The ASDS vehicle has three compartments: control, lockout, and passenger–cargo area. Capable of being carried to forward areas by modified SSNs or the new SSGNs, the submersible will provide the potential for clandestine missions in the littoral areas. (Chris Nazelrod)

SEALs atop the low-lying ASDS vehicle during trials in Hawaiian waters. The craft's folding (nonperiscoping) periscope and electronics mast are in the raised position. Delays, battery problems, and cost increases have placed the program in jeopardy. (U.S. Navy)

The first ASDS vehicle on the deck of an SSN during trials. Carrying DDS, ASDS, and DSRV payloads prevents attack submarines from operating at high speed, and causes some increases in flow noises. However, the submarines are able to operate at their maximum depth. (U.S. Navy)

In the forward area, the ASDS vehicle will anchor in the water column to enable SEALs to exit and enter from the bottom hatch to the lockout chamber. Unlike earlier SDVs, the new craft provides a dry, heated environment for the SEALs or other swimmers. (U.S. Navy)

APPROX. 15 SEAL DELIVERY VEHICLES: SDV Mk VIII TYPE

There are about 15 older SEAL delivery vehicles that can be carried into forward areas in dry deck shelter hangars fitted to attack or special operations submarines. These Mk VIII Mod 1 fiberglass "wet" vehicles can carry eight SEALs wearing individual self-contained breathing apparatus, one of whom pilots the vehicle.

The vehicles are all upgrades of earlier SDVs, with improved propulsion and electronics equipment. The use of more efficient packaging has increased their capacity from six to eight SEALs.

A follow-on SDV program was canceled in 1992 because of cost overruns and schedule slippage. That craft was being built by the UNISYS Corp. The ASDS program was developed in its place.

Electronics: A Doppler sonar is provided that displays speed, distance traveled, heading, altitude, and other piloting functions.

Propulsion: The SDVs are propelled by 18-hp electric motors with rechargeable silver–zinc batteries.

A Mk VIII Mod 1 SDV being lowered into the water. The pilot's compartment is open and the passenger compartment's covers are closed. A swimmer is at the port quarter. These craft are carried in the DDS mounted on attack submarines. (U.S. Navy)

A Mk VIII Mod 0 SDV, showing the pilot and passenger compartments open. The acoustic "window" in the bow has been deleted in the conversions to the Mod 1 configuration. The craft has a six-blade propeller powered by battery-supplied electric motors. (U.S. Navy)

Members of SEAL Team 2 conduct exercises with a Mk VIII Mod 1 SDV during operations in the Caribbean. These "wet" submersibles, long the standard war horse of SEALS, have severely limited range and capabilities. (1997, U.S. Navy/Andy McKaskle)

DRY DECK SHELTERS

Dry Deck Shelters (DDSs) are used to house SEAL delivery vehicles and swimmers—each can accommodate a single SDV or 20 SEALs. They are mounted on the afterdecks of specially configured attack (SSN) and cruise missile/transport (SSGN) submarines, the latter carrying one DDS and the former two. The submarines retain their full suite of weapons and sensors for operations as attack submarines (although there is some loss of speed), but they have special fittings, modifications to their air systems, and other features to enable them to carry the shelters. The DDS can be used to transport and launch an SDV or to "lock out" combat swimmers.

A DDS can be installed aboard a submarine in about 12 hours and is air transportable. The DDS lower hatch is installed over the submarine's after hatch to permit free passage between the submarine and the DDS while the submarine is underwater and approaching the objective area. Then, with the submarine still submerged, the SEALs can exit the DDS and ascend to the surface, bringing with them equipment and rubber rafts, or they can mount an SDV and travel underwater several miles to their objective area.

The DDS has an internal pressure of one atmosphere and can be carried to the test depth of the submarine.

The Navy has six DDSs, the first built by Electric Boat and the remainder by Newport News Shipbuilding. The prototype was delivered in 1982 and the remainder in 1987–1991. The shelters are 38 feet long (11.6 m) and have a maximum diameter of 9 feet (2.8 m), and weigh 30 tons. Each has a lock-out chamber built into its forward end, with hatches to the hangar portion of the DDS and to connect to the submarine's escape trunk. Three DDSs have right-hand doors and three have left-hand doors, to facilitate mounting two shelters side by side on an SSGN.

Five existing LOS ANGELES (SSN 688)-class submarines are fitted to carry a single DDS:

- SSN 688   LOS ANGELES
- SSN 690   PHILADELPHIA
- SSN 700   DALLAS
- SSN 701   LA JOLLA
- SSN 715   BUFFALO

In addition, submarines of the VIRGINIA (SSN 774) class and the special mission submarine JIMMY CARTER will be configured to carry a single DDS.

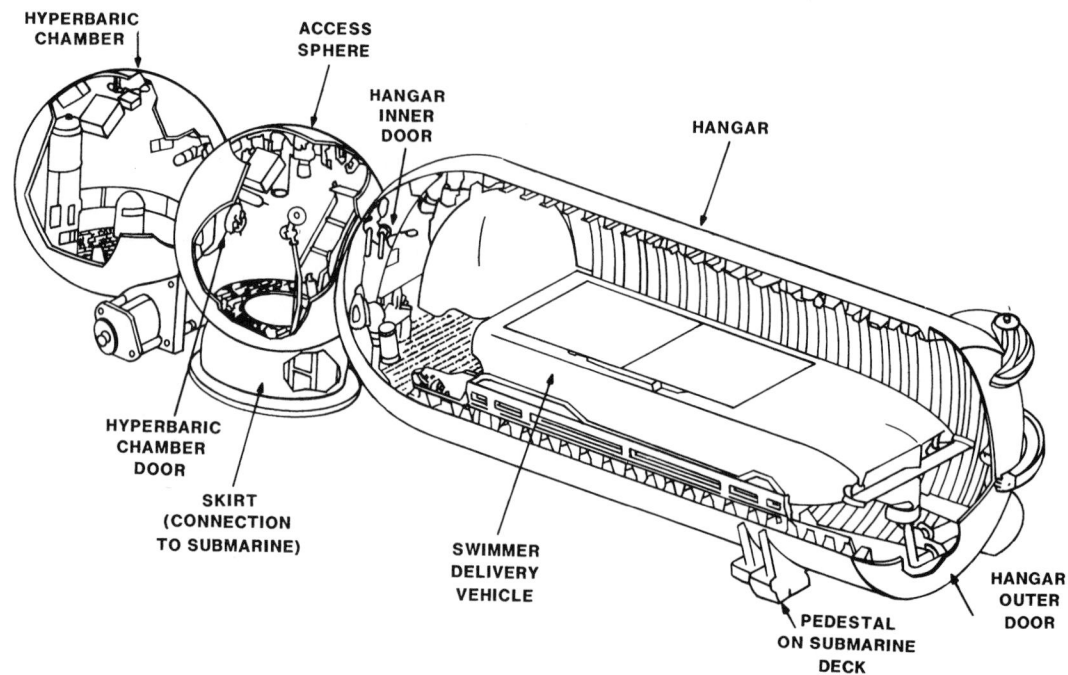

A single Dry Deck Shelter (DDS) can be carried by five existing attack submarines. The Trident SSGN conversions and the specially configured JIMMY CARTER (SSN 23) also will be capable of carrying the DDS.

A DDS mounted on the USS ARCHERFISH (SSN 678) with the door open. An extending, ladder-like rack holds the SDV or a rigid hull inflatable boat; it extends out from the hangar for launching the craft. (1996, Leo Van Ginderen)

A DDS with a portion of the covering removed to reveal the small hyperbaric chamber, the access sphere (center), and the hangar. These shelters can be transferred from one submarine to another at a shipyard or by a floating crane. (U.S. Navy)

A DDS is lifted from the SEAL transport submarine SAM HOUSTON (SSN 609) during her brief tenure as a special operations submarine. In addition to the mountings for the DDS, the modified submarines have racks on deck for gasoline storage for use by rigid hull inflatable boats. (U.S. Navy)

LARGE SCALE VEHICLES

Two unmanned Large Scale Vehicles (LSVs) are employed by the Navy to test and evaluate advanced submarine designs and features. They operate in Lake Pend Oreille, Idaho, where the Navy has an instrumented test range. The operating depth of the LSVs is not known; the lake has a maximum depth of 1,150 feet (350 m).

Except during transit and in emergency situations, the craft are controlled by onboard computers programmed before each test run. They are monitored by operators in a shore facility and the tender that tows them. An earlier (unnumbered) LSV named KAMLOOPS represented the hull form of the STURGEON (SSN 637) design.

Names: Kamloops and Kokanee are trout found in Lake Pend Oreille; Cutthroat is a salmon found in the lake.

1 LARGE SCALE TEST VEHICLE: "CUTTHROAT" TYPE

Number	Name	Completed	Status
LSV 2	CUTTHROAT	2001	Operational

Builders:	Newport News Shipbuilding and Electric Boat
Displacement:	196 tons
Length:	111 feet (33.84 m) overall
Beam:	10 feet (3.05 m)
Draft:	
Propulsion:	direct-drive electric motor; 3,000 shp; 1 shaft
Speed:	
Crew:	unmanned

This is the Navy's second submersible formally classified as an LSV; it was developed to simulate the VIRGINIA hull design and control features. It is a 0.294-scale model of the submarine.

Hull sections were built at both submarine yards, and then integrated by Newport News Shipbuilding. Construction began in September 1998, with Newport News producing the forward hull, sail, and systems/components for the forward section of the vehicle; Electric Boat built the after hull, propulsion plant, and steering and diving controls. The sections were shipped by truck to Bayview for final assembly.

The CUTTHROAT is the world's largest autonomous, unmanned submarine.

She was funded in FY 1997.

Design: The CUTTHROAT is more modular than the KOKANEE, enabling modifications—including radical hull changes—to be made with less impact to other systems on the craft. The LSV 2 has a significantly lower self-generated noise level than the LSV 1.

The LSV CUTTHROAT is a large, unmanned submersible employed to test the configuration and hydrodynamic characteristics of the Virginia (SSN 774)-class design. This model and the LSV KOKANEE are tested on a deep lake in Idaho. (U.S. Navy)

1 LARGE SCALE TEST VEHICLE: "KOKANEE" TYPE

Number	Name	Completed	Status
LSV 2	KOKANEE	1988	Operational

Builders:	Southwest Research Institute, San Antonio, Texas
Displacement:	155 tons
Length:	88⅝ feet (27.1 m) overall
Beam:	10⅛ feet (3.1 m)
Draft:	9½ feet (2.9 m)
Propulsion:	direct-drive electric motor; 3,000 shp; 1 shaft
Speed:	
Crew:	unmanned

The KOKANEE is a submarine-design test vehicle operated in Lake Pend Oreille by the acoustic research detachment of the David Taylor Research Center (DTRC) at Carderock, Maryland. The craft, a one-quarter scale model of the SEAWOLF (SSN 21), has been employed to test variations of submarine propulsors and hydrodynamic features. The submersible also was modified to test an advanced sail structure for use in the VIRGINIA class.

The LSV concept was proposed by Dr. M. M. Sevik of DTRC in 1972 as an extension of the center's model testing program. The construction contract was awarded in February 1984. The completed vehicle was transported by train from San Antonio to Bayview in October 1987 and was dedicated at ceremonies there on 7 March 1988.

Cost: Construction cost of the KOKANEE was $65 million.

Design: The KOKANEE has a conventional submarine configuration with a modified sail or fairwater structure (which can be removed). The forward portion of the submarine contains electric storage batteries; the after portion has the DC electric motor and auxiliary machinery, as well as data recorders, guidance, and navigation equipment.

Engineering: The KOKANEE has lead-acid batteries. Her endurance is approximately six hours for medium-power runs and two or three hours for full-power runs.

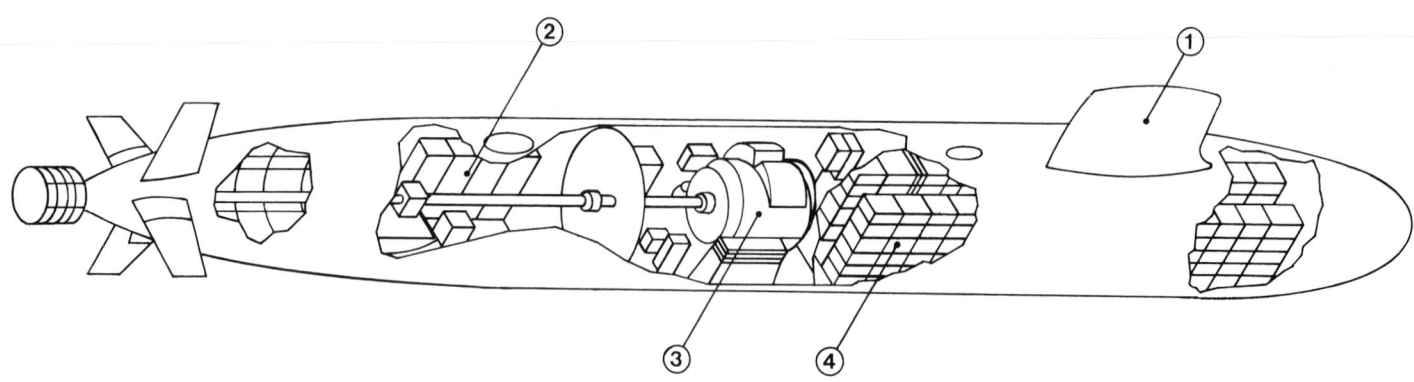

Large Scale test Vehicle KOKANEE
(1) Removable sail (fairwater); (2) Data recorders and navigation equipment; (3) DC electric motor; (4) Batteries. (William Clipson)

The LSV KOKANEE immediately after surfacing from a test run in lake Pend Oreille, Bayview, Idaho. The submersible has been used for hydrodynamic tests of the SEAWOLF (SSN 21) design. The craft's hull is gray and the sail structure is red. (U.S. Navy)

UNMANNED UNDERSEA VEHICLES

The U.S. Navy is developing a series of autonomous Unmanned Undersea Vehicles (UUVs). The submarine UUV programs are described below. Surface-launched UUVs, being developed primarily for the mine countermeasures role, are described in Chapter 22.

A Seahorse UUV, normally surface launched and recovered, was launched from one of the Trident submarine FLORIDA's (SSBN 728) ballistic missile tubes during Operation Giant Shadow in January 2003 (see Chapter 11). It was recovered by the surveying ship MARY SEARS (T-AGS 65), which served as a surrogate command-and-control center for the FLORIDA. Giant Shadow evaluated SSGN concepts; the FLORIDA is one of four Trident submarines being converted to that configuration.

The Navy's primary UUV operational command is Submarine Development Squadron 5, with most UUVs assigned to a detachment based at Bangor, Washington.

History: The Navy and the Defense Advanced Research Projects Agency (DARPA) initiated a joint advanced-technology UUV program in 1986. Through this effort, DARPA has developed two prototypes for test bed/mission hardware demonstrations. One vehicle took the first mission package—a tactical acoustic decoy system developed by Martin Marietta—to sea in 1990 and has since been transferred to the Navy for testing. According to a Navy spokesman, the initial payoff for this UUV would be increased submarine survivability, but it also would pave the way for UUV application to a number of classified submarine scenarios.

The **Near-term Mine Reconnaissance System** (NMRS) provides the initial autonomous UUV capability to U.S. submarines. It is capable of limited mine detection, classification, and localization. The NMRS integrates forward-looking sonar for obstacle avoidance and initial search capability with an improved AQS-14 side-scan sonar for target classification. It can be launched and recovered from standard 21-inch (533-mm) torpedo tubes in LOS ANGELES-class submarines or from a dry deck shelter.

At-sea tests of the NMRS were conducted in 1998 from the research ship KNORR (AGOR 15). The program is considerably behind schedule; the prototype operational system, scheduled for delivery in FY 1998, was delivered in 2003. The NMRS was developed by Northrop Grumman Ocean Systems, Annapolis, Maryland.

The **BLQ-11 Long-term Mine Reconnaissance System** (LMRS) was to be the successor to the NMRS for use from submarines of the LOS ANGELES and VIRGINIA classes. It provides clandestine mine reconnaissance with detection and limited classification. It also can be launched from standard torpedo tubes or a DDS. Its autonomous endurance is more than 40 hours.

The first system was delivered in 2003; it is scheduled to enter service in FY 2005. The LMRS was developed by Boeing, Anaheim, California.

The **Mission Reconfigurable UUV** is an outgrowth of the LMRS program and was scheduled to begin development in FY 2004. The Navy expects this system to have "plug and play" sensor packages for a variety of Intelligence/Surveillance/Reconnaissance (ISR) missions employing electromagnetic and electro-optical sensors as well as acoustic systems.

SUBMARINE RESCUE SYSTEMS

The U.S. Navy is in the process of updating its submarine rescue capability with the procurement of the Submarine Rescue Diving and Recompression System (SRDRS). Despite its atrocious title, the system gives promise of an effective and highly mobile means

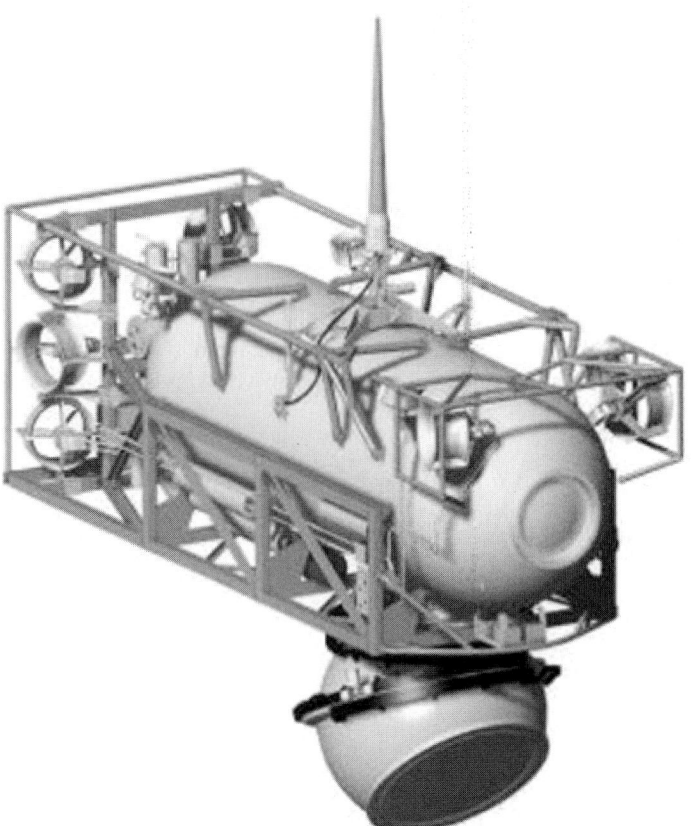

The manned, tethered ROV component of the Submarine Rescue Diving and Recompression System (SRDRS) showing the main pressure chamber, rotating mating skirt, and small, rotating propeller devices. Being surface-supported, the SRDRS cannot be used to rescue submariners in heavy weather or under ice. (Phoenix International)

of rescuing survivors from submarines disabled in relatively shallow water, i.e,. down to the current U.S. submarine collapse depth of some 2,000 feet. The SRDRS was developed to replace the Navy's long-serving deep submergence rescue vehicles MYSTIC and AVALON.

A tethered and manned ROV based on the Australian Navy's Remora vehicle is the primary component of the new rescue system. It will dive to the stricken submarine and be able to maneuver into position to mate with the submarine's forward or after escape hatch. An articulated "skirt" beneath the ROV will permit it to mate with a disabled submarine lying at a significant angle— 45° to the horizontal will be the minimum angle; 60° the goal. The vehicle will be self-sufficient with regard to electrical power and air, with the tether to guide it back to the surface ship. As it reaches the surface, the ROV will be lifted out of the water and onto the decompression chambers by a shipboard crane.

The ROV will be controlled from the surface ship; its operator will have comprehensive displays of the in situ environment from sonar and television cameras on the ROV. The vehicle will have two crewmen on board to provide on-scene evaluation of the situation and to help submarine survivors enter the ROV. The threshold number of survivors who can be accommodated is 12, with a goal of 15.

The surface ship component of the SRDRS will be a ship of opportunity carrying the extensive support/control/decompression facility. This facility is designed to fit on board a variety of merchant and naval ships, with minimum demands on the ship for services. Indeed, the SRDRS will have its own control room, maintenance shop, winch, air, power, deep-sea mooring gear, and other equipment. All components—including the ROV—will be sized to fit in the standard container "envelope," i.e., 8 x 8 x 20 feet (2.4 x 2.4 x 6.1 m).

Perhaps the most important component of the shipboard SRDRS is the two decompression chambers, each able to treat 33 survivors, bringing them up to surface pressure from a six-atmosphere environment. Such high-pressure situations occur in a stricken submarine as water leaks into the pressure hull, compressing the remaining air, or when high-pressure air is intentionally introduced into the hull to stop incoming water. Without proper decompression, the survivors would suffer "bends," an often crippling or even fatal disease.

After taking on survivors, the rescue ROV is brought aboard ship, where it can mate with a module fitted between the two decompression chambers, enabling survivors, under pressure, to move directly into either chamber. Obviously, one of the shortfalls of the system is that it can decompress a maximum of only some 81 survivors at a time—66 men in the two chambers plus perhaps 15 in the ROV itself.

(With the DSRV system, more survivors could have been decompressed using the entire forward compartment of the "mother" submarines. The now-discarded PIGEON-class submarine rescue ships had large decompression chambers to which the DSRVs could mate.)

In an effort to ensure the SRDRS can reach a disabled submarine anywhere in the world within 72 hours, the Navy is identifying several hundred ships of opportunity that could accommodate

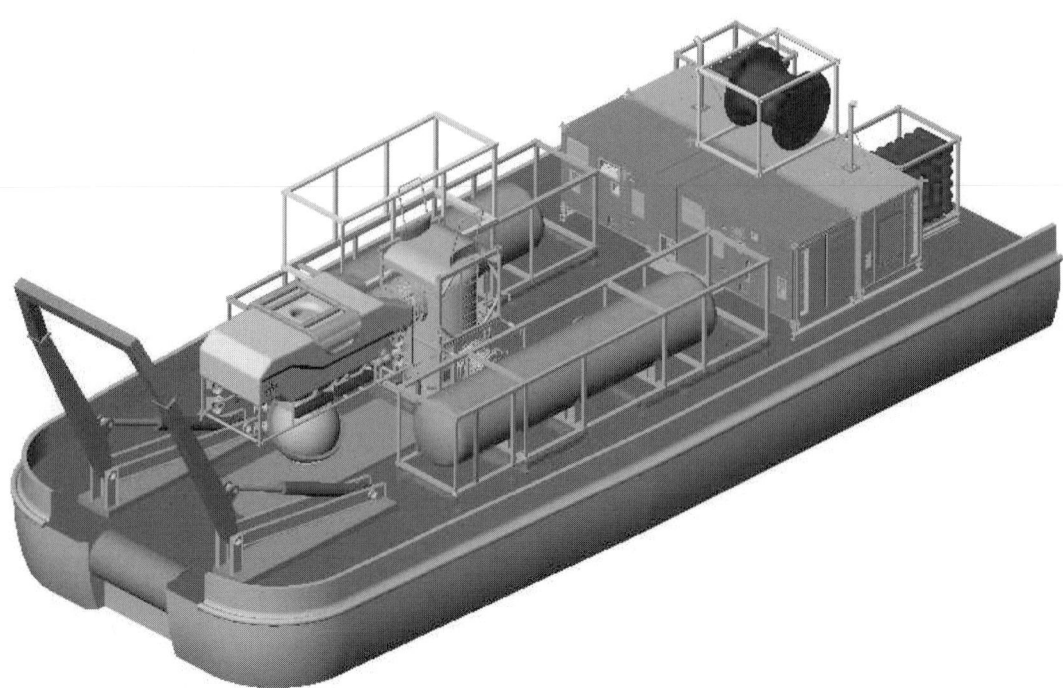

A drawing of the SRDRS arrangement on a surface ship. The major components are the rescue ROV handling crane, the ROV (forward of the crane), and the transfer structure, the last fitted between the two decompression chambers. All components are air transportable and can be installed on commercial ships. (Phoenix International)

An artist's impression of the rescue ROV mounted on a disabled submarine's escape trunk. Two men are shown passing through the mating skirt into the ROV's main pressure chamber, which has seating for 12 to 15 survivors. (Phoenix International)

the system. Probably based at Naval Air Station North Island, now home of the DSRVs, the SRDRS would be flown to a port near the downed submarine, trucked to pierside, and then loaded aboard ship. Several sets of steel SRDRS "templates" would be prepositioned around the world. In the event of a submarine disaster with survivors, the ship of opportunity would be identified and a set of templates flown to a port and placed aboard. Laid out on her deck, the templates mark the locations for all SRDRS components. Thus, as the containers arrive on the pier, they can be hoisted aboard and bolted or lashed in the proper position with minimum loss of time.

The ability to use ships of opportunity is a major advantage over the DSRV system, which can be operated from only a few mother submarines—eight U.S., four British, and one French undersea craft. However, being submarine-supported gave the DSRV an all-weather and under-ice capability not possible with surface ship supports. It is planned for the SRDRS system to be useable from surface ships in at least sea state 4, with a goal of sea state 7.

Under current planning, the Navy will procure one SRDRS with two ROVs. This will ensure that one vehicle is always available when the other is undergoing maintenance.

The U.S. Navy submarine community believes the fleet will have a viable and affordable rescue capability with the availability of the SRDRS from about 2006 onward.

The SRDRS will be supplemented by two McCann-type Submarine Rescue Chambers (SRC). The McCann chamber was developed in the 1930s and was used to pulled 33 survivors from the sunken submarine SQUALUS (SS 192) in 1939.[15] This was the U.S. Navy's only submarine rescue operation. The SRCs, which require diver support, can function to a depth of 850 feet (259 m).

In addition, the Navy is procuring the British-developed Submarine Escape and Immersion Equipment (SEIE) to provide enhanced escape capabilities to U.S. submariners. These full-body suits include thermal protection and have built-in life rafts. They provide a realistic capability for escape from depths to 600 feet (183 m) and for survival on the surface. Heretofore, the possibility of submarine crewmen escaping successfully from such a depth, as well as their survival on the surface (without immediate support), was speculative at best.

Thus, the SRDRS, SRC, and SEIE are expected to provide the best combination of affordable and effective features for saving survivors of disabled submarines.

Navymen prepare a McCann Submarine Rescue Chamber (SRC) on the merchant ship KENDRICK at Singapore for exercise Pacific Reach. The Navy maintains two SRCs, which can be flown to a rescue site and placed aboard a naval or merchant ship. Use of the SRC requires precise mooring and support by divers. (2000, U.S. Navy/Terry Cosgrove)

15 The SQUALUS subsequently was salvaged and was recommissioned in 1940 as the USS SAILFISH (SS 192).

CHAPTER 13

Aircraft Carriers

Sailors man the flight deck of the aircraft carrier ENTERPRISE *as she approaches the pier at her home port of Norfolk, Virginia. The "Big E" and her strike group were returning from a six-month deployment, which included participation in Operations Iraqi Freedom and Enduring Freedom. (2004, U.S. Navy/Sondra Howett)*

Aircraft carriers remain the backbone of U.S. conventional naval forces. The U.S. carrier force in early 2005 consists of 12 operational carriers—10 nuclear-propelled ships (CVNs) and 2 conventional, oil-burning ships (CVs).

The Navy has had 12 carriers in commission since 1984; for the decade prior, that number had varied from 13 to a peak of 15 (in 1991). Since 1980, however, beginning with the SARATOGA, one carrier has been out of service undergoing major overhaul/modernization (including refueling for nuclear-propelled ships). This process takes from two to three and a half years, effectively reducing carrier strength by one, despite the Navy officially keeping the ship in commission. The overhaul/modernization extends the effective service life of the carrier by approximately 30–45 years.

When the DWIGHT D. EISENHOWER completed her overhaul/refueling in late 2004, she was not followed into the yard by the CARL VINSON, as had been planned. Rather, on 9 October 2003, the Navy Department announced that the latter carrier's three-year over-

haul/refueling would be postponed at least 12 months to create a more manageable workflow at the nation's shipyards.

The CARL VINSON, homeported in Bremerton, Washington, was scheduled to steam to Newport News, Virginia, to begin her overhaul/refueling in November 2004. The delay will keep the carrier at Newport News from Fiscal Year (FY) 2006 to the beginning of FY 2009, when the carrier THEODORE ROOSEVELT now is scheduled to enter the yard for overhaul/refueling. The "slack" in work at Newport News will be taken up by the FY 2005 maintenance work on the GEORGE WASHINGTON, which the Navy has rescheduled from the Norfolk Naval Shipyard to the Newport News yard.

One nuclear-propelled carrier is under construction, the GEORGE H. W. BUSH, the tenth ship of the NIMITZ class. A follow-on class of nuclear-propelled carriers is planned, with the lead ship, the CVN 78, planned for authorization in FY 2007 and becoming operational in 2014. Additional CVNs of that improved design are planned for procurement at the rate of about one every five years for the foreseeable future. (There would be a six-year interval between authorization of the GEORGE H. W. BUSH and the CVN 78 if the latter ship is authorized in FY 2007.)

No conventional carriers currently are laid up in reserve—mothballed—as "mobilization assets." The INDEPENDENCE and the RANGER were laid up in 2003, with the just-retired CONSTELLATION scheduled to replace the RANGER, when the decision was made not to continue to hold them. The feasibility of reactivating those ships was highly questionable because of their outdated equipment, large manning requirements, and the approximately one year required to bring them back to active status.

The KITTY HAWK was employed for several months in 2001 primarily as a floating base for Special Operations Forces (SOF) during the U.S. assault on Afghanistan. Following her successful employment in that role, the Department of Defense considered converting the CONSTELLATION to a specialized SOF-support ship, but no action was taken. Obviously, employing an LHA/LHD-type ship would be more efficient from a cost and manning viewpoint.

As demonstrated on several occasions in the past, a large aircraft carrier can be adapted rapidly to other roles. The DWIGHT D. EISENHOWER, for example, embarked 1,800 troops of the Army's 10th Mountain Division and their helicopters on short notice for the U.S. invasion of Haiti in September 1994. Earlier that same year, the GEORGE WASHINGTON had embarked soldiers of the 75th Special Forces Group and their helicopters during Fleet Exercise 2-94.

In addition, in 1993, a Marine task force with 538 Marines (including 227 aviation personnel) and ten helicopters deployed to the Mediterranean in the carrier THEODORE ROOSEVELT. A similar deployment subsequently was undertaken in the AMERICA. But those efforts attempted to merge an "attack carrier" with an "amphibious ship"—unsuccessfully.[1]

The JOHN F. KENNEDY was designated as an "operational reserve/training" ship from 1994 to 2000, but in reality she operated and deployed as a standard carrier with reserve personnel making up a small fraction of her crew (see next page). In September 1999, the Navy decided to stop the pretense and change the ship's status from Naval Reserve Force (NRF) to active.

A force of 15 active carriers is required to provide essentially full-time presence in three key regions where naval presence is considered important by the Department of Defense—the Mediterranean, the Western Pacific, and the Indian Ocean/Persian Gulf. A 12-carrier force can provide full-time presence in one region, with a minimum of two-month "gaps" in presence in the other two. With 11 operational carriers—the actual number available—the gap increases, and even this amount of coverage is possible only by homeporting a carrier in Japan, currently the KITTY HAWK.

The Navy no longer operates a dedicated pilot Carrier Qualification (CARQUAL) training ship (AVT). The FORRESTAL was to have replaced the venerable LEXINGTON (CV/AVT 16), an ESSEX/HANCOCK-class carrier completed in 1943, which served in the pilot training role from 1963 to 1990. Instead, the FORRESTAL was decommissioned as part of the post–Cold War cutback of naval forces (the ship already had been reclassified AVT 59). The LEXINGTON had succeeded the ANTIETAM (CV/AVT 36), the first large-deck dedicated training carrier, which served in that role from 1957 to 1962. Basic pilot training in carrier landings now is carried out aboard aircraft carriers as they are available.

All World War II–built carriers of the MIDWAY and ESSEX/ HANCOCK classes have been retired, the last being the MIDWAY, which was decommissioned in 1992 after 46½ years of service.

In addition to the ships described in this chapter, the Navy operates 12 large helicopter carriers called amphibious assault ships (LHA/LHD); these ships are described in Chapter 19. All of the ear-lier LPH-type helicopter carriers have been stricken, including the INCHON (MCS 12, ex-LPH 12), which lately had been employed as a mine warfare support ship; see Chapter 22.

Aircraft: The composition of carrier air wings is described in Chapter 27. Nominal wing strength is provided in this chapter based on a composition of one fighter squadron (VF) and three strike fighter squadrons (VFA), plus electronic attack (VAQ), airborne early warning (VAW), and sea control (VS) fixed-wing aircraft and anti-submarine (HS) and special operations (HC) helicopters.

Builders: Newport News Shipbuilding in Newport News, Virginia, is the only U.S. shipyard now constructing large aircraft carriers. That yard built four of the eight oil-burning "super carriers" completed since 1955 (CV 59, 61, 66, 67), as well as all nuclear-propelled carriers. The acquisition of Newport News by Northrop Grumman Corporation was announced on 8 November 2001.

The New York Shipbuilding Corp., in Camden, New Jersey, built one super carrier now in service, the KITTY HAWK.

The Northrop Grumman Ship Systems/Ingalls Shipyard in Pascagoula, Mississippi, constructs all of the Navy's carrier-type amphibious ships of approximately 45,000 tons (LHA/LHD).

Design: Displacements of carriers have been continuously increased as new equipment has been added during overhauls and modernization. The data below have been updated for this edition.

Electronics: No U.S. aircraft carriers are fitted with sonar.

Marines: Aircraft carriers no longer carry permanent Marine Corps security detachments. The last detachment was in the carrier GEORGE WASHINGTON; the 26-Marine unit departed the ship when she returned from deployment on 3 April 1988, ending a more than 200-year tradition of Marines serving in major U.S. warships. (Previously, Marine detachments also were carried on board battleships and larger cruisers, i.e., CA, CAG, CB, CL, CLG, and the larger CG-type ships.)

Marine carrier detachments consisted of 2 officers and 64 enlisted men until 1993. On 28 May 1993, the Chief of Naval Operations approved a Marine Corps proposal to reduce the size of the detachments, and by June 1993, all carrier detachments numbered 1 officer and 25 enlisted men.

Marine aircraft squadrons now serve aboard aircraft carriers (as well as on helicopter carriers) on a regular basis. Marine attack (AV-8B Harrier), electronic attack (EA-6B Prowler), and fighter-attack (F/A-18) aircraft are carrier capable, and all Marines aviators are trained in carrier operations.

Guns: The Mk 15 Phalanx Close-In Weapon Systems (CIWS) are being replaced in all active carriers by Rolling Airframe Missile (RAM) launchers (see below). In addition, all carriers are fitted with several hand-operated .50-caliber machine guns intended for protection against small craft, although the effectiveness of such weapons against high-speed suicide craft is questionable.

Missiles: All active carriers are being fitted with two Mk 49 RAM launchers to replace the three or four Mk 15 CIWSs previously carried. Also fitted are two Mk 29 NATO Sea Sparrow launchers. The SPQ-9B radar is installed with the RAM, comprising, with the NATO Sea Sparrow, the Surface Ship Defense System (SSDS) Mk 2. The SSDS Mk 2 also is being fitted in amphibious assault ships (LHA/LHD).

The SSDS Mk 2 installations in all active carriers are expected to be completed by 2005.

Names: U.S. aircraft carriers traditionally were named for older American warships and battles, with the exception of the first carri-

---

1 See N. Polmar, "Marines on Carriers—Con and Con," *U.S. Naval Institute Proceedings* (August 1993), pp. 105–6.

er, named LANGLEY (CV 1) for aviation pioneer Samuel P. Langley.[2] In 1945, the CVB 42 was named for President Franklin D. Roosevelt, who had died in office. She was followed in 1954 by the CVA 59, named for the first Secretary of Defense, James Forrestal, who committed suicide soon after leaving office; and the CVA 67, named in 1964 for President John F. Kennedy, assassinated while in office.

Subsequently, the Navy named the CVN 68 for Fleet Admiral Chester W. Nimitz, who died in 1966. From that point on, the naming of carriers became totally a political offering (see *Name* notes in the NIMITZ-class entry). And, beginning with the CARL VINSON, several carriers have been named for living persons, a practice previously abhorred in the United States.

Operational: From the late 1940s into the late 1980s, the Navy attempted to operate two carriers forward in the Mediterranean and three, then two, in the Western Pacific–Indian Ocean region. With the remaining carriers in transit to or from deployment areas, engaged in fleet exercises or other types of training, or in overhaul, there was a 1:3 deployment cycle, which meant a ship was forward deployed for about 6 months at a time, within an 18-month period. The longer deployments necessitated by the various crises since the Vietnam War invariably resulted in lower retention rates, a critical factor in an all-volunteer, high-tech service. Also, the 1:3 cycle did not take into account carriers undergoing long-term modernization.

The crises and conflicts of the early 1980s, especially the Soviet invasion of Afghanistan (1979) and the Iran–Iraq War (1980–1988), led to more flexible carrier deployment patterns—called FLEX-OPS. Carriers were withdrawn from some areas and required to spend more time at sea to provide for multicarrier exercises or to support special operations, as in the continuing crisis in Lebanon, the invasion of Grenada in October 1983, operations against Libya in 1986, Operations Desert Shield/Desert Storm (the first Gulf War, 1990–1991), the invasion of Afghanistan in 2001, and the second Gulf War in 2003. Carrier deployments thus significantly exceeded the nominal ratio of 6 months' deployment to 12 months in transit, overhaul, in port, and/or local operations.

Table 13-1. CARRIER FORCE LEVELS (EARLY 2005)

Number	Class/Ship	Comm.	Active	Building*	Notes
CVN 68	NIMITZ	1975–	9	1	nuclear-propelled
CV 67	JOHN F. KENNEDY	1968	1	—	conventional propulsion
CVN 65	ENTERPRISE	1961	1	—	nuclear-propelled
CV 63	KITTY HAWK	1961	1	—	conventional propulsion

* Carriers authorized through FY 2004.

The situation was exacerbated in the 1990s because of the general concern for the Indian Ocean area in the wake of the Gulf War and subsequently by the war on terrorism, with its extensive carrier-based operations in Afghanistan and Iraq. The steaming distances from U.S. ports to the Indian Ocean and Persian Gulf require on the order of five carriers to maintain one ship in the area.

Personnel: Aircraft carriers have a very high percentage of women in their crews—approximately 20 percent, i.e., some 500 personnel. This does not include women in embarked air wings.

Torpedo countermeasures: Aircraft carriers are fitted with the SLQ-25 Nixie, an advanced towed noisemaker.

The revelation in the mid-1980s of several unexpected Soviet submarine and torpedo developments led to a new emphasis on torpedo countermeasures. The Surface Ship Torpedo Decoy System (SSTDS) was initiated (see Chapter 32) and has been fitted to most active aircraft carriers. Some carriers have been fitted with 12.75-inch (324-mm) Mk 32 torpedo tubes (in triple mounts) for launching modified Mk 46 torpedoes to counter the Russian Type 65-80 and other wake-homing torpedoes.

---

2 The most notable exception to the traditional naming scheme was the SHANGRI-LA (CV 38), named by the Navy after journalists asked where the Doolittle bombers that struck Tokyo and other Japanese cities in April 1942 had flown from. President Franklin D. Roosevelt replied "Shangri-La," referring to the mythical Asian kingdom in James Hilton's novel *Lost Horizon*. The Doolittle bombers had flown from the carrier HORNET (CV 8). Shangri-La also was the name given to the presidential retreat in Maryland, later renamed Camp David.

The hangar deck of the JOHN F. KENNEDY is void of aircraft as the ship loads munitions from the replenishment ship SEATTLE (AOE 3) and the carrier ENTERPRISE prior to a six-month deployment to the Mediterranean. All will be stowed in the ship's massive magazines before the air wing comes on board. (2004, U.S. Navy/Anthony Riddle)

NEXT-GENERATION AIRCRAFT CARRIERS

The U.S. Navy initiated a program in 1996 to develop a totally new carrier design—given the designation CVX, for an aircraft carrier of undetermined characteristics. The CVX, according to the Navy's then-Director of Air Warfare, Rear Admiral Dennis V. McGinn, was being designed on a "clean sheet of paper" and would "feature improved characteristics in selected areas, such as launch and recovery equipment, flight deck layout, C4I [Command, Control, Communications, Computers, and Intelligence] systems, information networks and propulsion systems . . . [and] features that will make them more affordable to operate."[3]

The CVX was to be the U.S. Navy's next-generation aircraft carrier, a major divergence from previous designs. The first ship of the new class was to be funded in FY 2006 and to join the fleet about 2013 (to replace the ENTERPRISE). The CVX also promised a more efficient warship, capable of handling advanced aircraft at a faster operating cycle, with more efficient aircraft arming techniques (especially requiring less manpower), lower detection signatures (and hence enhanced survivability), overall decreased manning requirements, and significantly lower construction, operating, and modernization costs.

These and other advanced carrier concepts were being studied by the Navy and at the Carrier Innovation Center of Newport News Shipbuilding. The center also was examining non-nuclear propulsion concepts for the ship, primarily gas turbines, which would be cheaper (even including fuel) and require fewer crewmen with less specialized training than would a nuclear propulsion plant.

But within a few months, this "entirely new class" was canceled because of funding shortfalls. Although the Navy never announced a total development and design cost for the CVX, the FY 1999 defense program indicated planned expenditures of just over $1 billion.

The Navy never adequately planned for CVX development costs, and never advised Congress of the total funding requirements. Despite this, Navy leadership continued to promote the CVX concept. Indeed, this stance continued in public even after Chief of Naval Operations Admiral Jay L. Johnson announced early in 1998 that the CVX would definitely have nuclear propulsion, a direct contradiction of the "clean sheet" concept.

Johnson's decision ostensibly was based on the draft study *CVX Feasibility* prepared by the Naval Research Advisory Committee (NRAC) in 1997, which stated that "for maximum availability, the ship should have a nuclear power plant."[4] But the Navy's powerful nuclear propulsion community, led by Admiral Frank (Skip) Bowman, already had decided that nuclear power was "a given" for the CVX, according to a leading defense writer.[5] According to Bowman, "Without this endurance and flexibility [provided by nuclear-propelled carriers], we would be hard put to do what we are doing today."

While the NRAC draft study said nuclear propulsion provides the "sustained high speed sprint capability . . . necessary if CVX is to be available for rapidly evolving crises," a comprehensive study published in June 1994 by the Greenpeace organization—*Aircraft Carriers: The Limits of Nuclear Power*—concluded:

> The cost of nuclear power is not justified in peacetime or in wartime, in terms of useful military capability. Nuclear ships are more expensive, less available, and only comparable in generating and sustaining air operations. They operate as part of integrated and increasingly joint military missions close to land, and nuclear-powered carriers are not used any differently than their conventional counterparts.[6]

The Greenpeace report was based largely on an analysis of three U.S. Navy claims for nuclear-propelled carriers:[7]

- virtually unlimited range at maximum speed
- ability to remain on-station indefinitely without refueling
- greater storage capacity for combat consumables, such as bombs and jet fuel

Using Navy data, it concluded that during the Vietnam and Persian Gulf wars, the period between the two conflicts, and the operation of carriers in crisis response as well as deployments in general, operations have not matched the promises or expectations of nuclear propulsion:

> Nuclear-powered carriers do not transit faster to a region, remain longer on-station, or drop significantly more ordnance or launch more aircraft sorties than do conventionally powered carriers. In fact the Navy itself does not appear to distinguish between nuclear and conventional carriers in its operational planning or crisis preparation.[8]

The Greenpeace paper made additional points against nuclear-propelled carriers: (1) they require more shipyard time, with a related reduction in at-sea time; (2) the costs associated with their uranium fuel cores—from design through disposal—are significant but barely factored in program costs; (3) political liabilities associated with nuclear carriers place limitations on foreign port calls, overseas basing, and transit through certain straits and canals; and (4) all nuclear-propelled escort ships (DLGN/CGN) have been discarded, further reducing the potential effectiveness of nuclear carriers (see Chapter 15).

(Not mentioned in the Greenpeace report is the increased cost of nuclear-trained engineering personnel compared to personnel for fossil-fuel ships. Also, with the demise of the nuclear cruiser force, promotion and command opportunities for those men and women are reduced significantly, which will have an adverse impact on their recruitment, retention, and cost.)

Despite Admiral Johnson's acquiescence to the nuclear propulsion community, the CVX program continued to be underfunded by the Navy. Then, in spring 1999, Congress cut almost $100 million from CVX development. A Navy official later was reported as saying, "We just cannot afford the investment needed to achieve the hoped for long-term savings."[9]

Thus, the "first" CVX was scuttled by the Navy.

The next carrier, subsequently named GEORGE H. W. BUSH, has been described by the Navy as a "transition" ship between the NIMITZ design and the CVX, a term still used as a public relations device. The CVN 77 will incorporate some new features, continuing the tradition of incremental improvements to carriers.

Not only does this approach negate the original clean-slate CVX concept earlier espoused by the Navy's leadership, but it also ignores the highly innovative study undertaken by the Center for Naval Analyses (CNA) and the Naval Sea Systems Command (NAVSEA) in early 1995. The CNA–NAVSEA effort proposed six design concepts for the CVX (their basic characteristics were described in the 16th Edition/pages 89–90). While most of these

---

3 Rear Adm. McGinn, Director, Naval Air Warfare, Office of the Chief of Naval Operations, *Naval Aviation: Forward Air Power . . . From the Sea* (1998), p. 30. Also see N. Polmar, "Carrier Questions—and Some Answers," U.S. Naval Institute *Proceedings* (April 1998), pp. 103–4.

4 NRAC, comprised of 14 civilian businessmen, engineers, and scientists, and 1 physician, is the principal advisory body to the Secretary of the Navy.

5 Tom Philpott, "Bowman Sees a Smaller Fleet More Reliant on Nuclear Power" (syndicated column Military Update), 6 November 1997.

6 Hans M. Kristensen, William M. Arkin, and Joshua Handler, *Aircraft Carriers: The Limits Of Nuclear Power* (Washington, D.C.: Greenpeace, June 1994). Also see N. Polmar, "Nuclear Carrier Questions," U.S. Naval Institute *Proceedings* (September 1994), pp. 121–22.

7 "Navy Kicks off Campaign to Sell CVN-76 Carrier to Congress," *Inside the Navy* (12 March 1994), pp. 7–8.

8 Kristensen, et al., *Aircraft Carriers*, p. 3.

9 "Navy Takes New Look at CVX Plan, Cost," *Navy News & Undersea Technology* (1 June 1998), p. 1.

designs would carry significantly fewer aircraft than a NIMITZ-class CVN, other, larger carrier concepts also have been suggested. For example, in the late 1990s, the Naval Surface Warfare Center Carderock (Maryland) Division undertook a series of excellent studies of future aircraft carriers. But all so-called radical concepts have been steadfastly rejected by the Navy.

MOBILE OFFSHORE BASE

Another "aircraft carrier" concept that continues to receive support from some officials of the Department of Defense is the Mobile Offshore Base (MOB). A MOB is a large, mobile sea base, made up of modular components that are towed to the crisis area and assembled at sea.

These platforms—referred to in the Bottom-Up Review as "floating islands"—would be capable of handling from 150 to almost 300 aircraft, depending on type, including C-130 Hercules and possibly C-17 Skytrain transports, as well as large amounts of dry and liquid cargoes. Although not directly comparable to aircraft carriers, MOBs could reduce the requirement for carriers in some areas where ample time, resources, and security are available to deploy and assemble the platforms.

These platforms would be non-self-propelled. One CNA study addressed a MOB concept comprising six modules assembled to form a platform 3,000 feet (914.6 m) long and 300 feet (91.46 m) wide. Another concept being developed by McDermott International and Babcock & Wilcox provides for a platform 4,925 feet (1,502 m) long and 500 feet (152 m) wide. This design has five separate modules to be towed to and assembled at the remote location. The assembled displacement at operating draft would be 1,700,000 tons. Massive amounts of cargo could be transported and stored in the individual sections.

The MOB concept would be the largest floating structure ever built. However, with the available offshore drilling platform and related technology and the use of subcomponents, there is considered to be little risk in the construction of the platform.

A MOB also could be used to rearm surface ships and submarines and to refuel surface ships.

In 2001, the Institute for Defense Analysis, a Pentagon- sponsored think tank, said a MOB would be less cost-effective than nuclear-propelled carriers or high-speed cargo ships for projecting U.S. military power into distant regions. By one estimate, one MOB module would cost about $1.5 billion, meaning a set of modules 5,000 feet long could cost $8 billion.[10]

Critics also have cited the loss to explosion of a huge floating oil platform off Brazil in 2001 to warn that such massive structures, filled with ammunition and fuel, are too vulnerable to accidents at sea and enemy attacks.

Supporters point out that MOB-type platforms would complement, not replace, aircraft carriers. The Department of Defense is sponsoring ongoing studies of the MOB concept, and the Navy's 30-year shipbuilding plan submitted to Congress in 2003 has $100 million in FY 2008 and $900 million in FY 2009 for construction of a mobile offshore base. However, these funds may have been inserted as a "place holder" to ensure Navy participation in the project should the Department of Defense continue to show interest.

From 2003 onward, the MOB concept has received less support because of the efforts of Chief of Naval Operations Admiral Vern Clark to develop the "Sea Base" concept (see Chapters 1 and 24).

---

10 Pat Towell, "'Mobile Offshore Base' Proposal Has Slew of Powerful Opponents," *Congressional Quarterly Weekly* (15 February 2003).

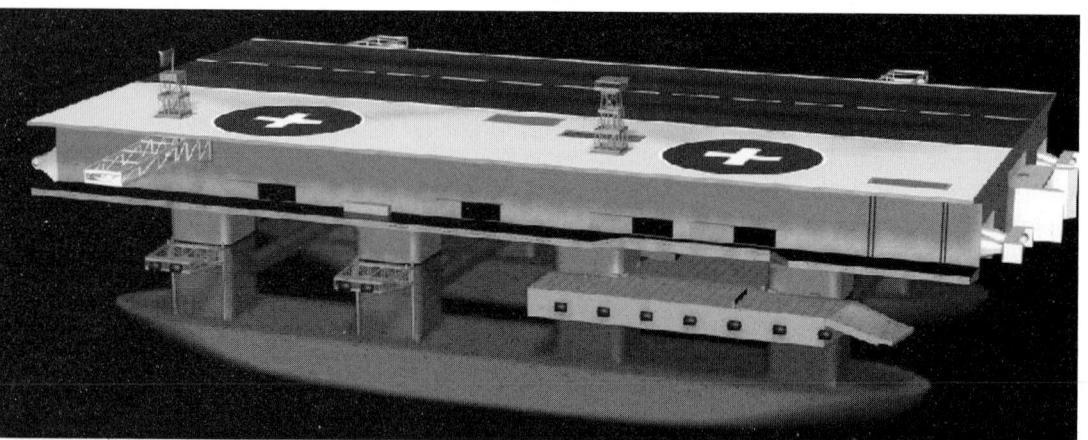

An artist's view of one of the five semisubmersible base units—each 1,000 feet (305 m) long—that would be assembled to form the Mobile Offshore Base (MOB). The assembled MOB could provide an operating and support base for aircraft. However, in many respects, the Sea Base concept has overtaken the MOB. (McDermott International)

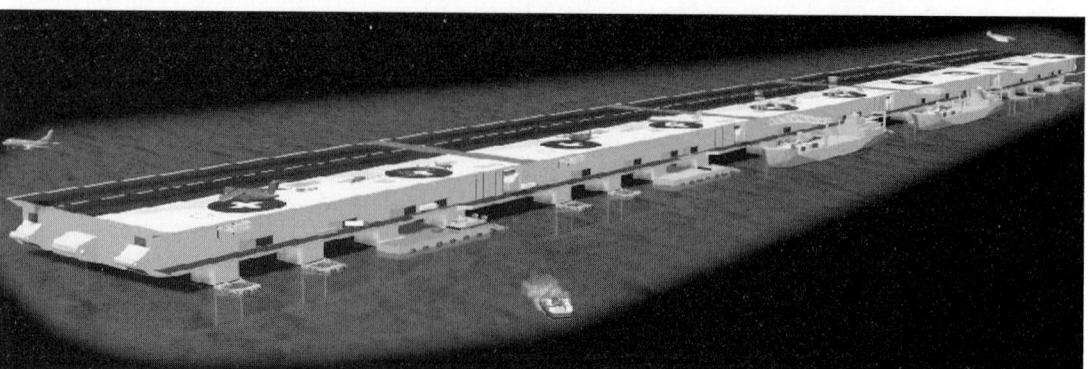

The Mobile Offshore Base (MOB) has been considered by the Department of Defense as a means of supporting aviation and staging operations at sea when land bases are not available. The shortcomings of the MOB include its lack of mobility and the time required to deploy and assemble. (McDermott International)

(1+) NUCLEAR-PROPELLED AIRCRAFT CARRIERS: IMPROVED "NIMITZ" CLASS

Number	Name	FY	Builder	Laid Down	Launched	Comm.	Status
CVN 78	....	07	Northrop Grumman/Newport News Shipbuilding, Va.			2014	Planned

Displacement:	100,000+ tons full load		Aircraft:	approx. 70
Length			Catapults:	4 electromagnetic
Beam:			Elevators:	3 deck edge
Draft:			Missiles:	2 8-cell NATO Sea Sparrow launchers Mk 29
Propulsion:				2 21-cell RAM launchers Mk 49
Reactors:	2 A5W pressurized-water reactors		Guns:	none
Speed:	approx. 30 knots		Radar:	
Range:			Fire Control:	
Personnel:				

This is an improved NIMITZ-class design, with a number of advances planned to increase operational efficiency and reduce manning requirements. The ship is expected to become operational in 2016.

Class: The Navy's 30-year shipbuilding plan presented to Congress in 2003 lists the following CVN procurement during five-year periods:

2004–2008	1 CVN comm. 2014
2009–2013	1 CVN comm. 2018
2014–2018	1 CVN comm: 2023
2019–2023	1 CVN
2024–2028	2 CVN
2029–2033	1 CVN

Cost: The unofficial estimate for development and construction of the CVN 78 is approximately $12 billion, or twice the cost of the last NIMITZ-class ships.

Classification: The ship initially was referred to as CVX and then CVN 21 in official documents (with CVNX being used briefly). By 2003, the designation CVN 78 was widely accepted. The Navy's carrier program office stresses that CVN 21 was a program designation, not a hull number, unlike with the SEAWOLF (SSN 21) class.

Design: The CVN 78 will have an improved flight deck arrangement (with increased deck space) and a new-design superstructure, located farther aft than in NIMITZ-class ships. Aircraft capacity and ship speed will be similar to the NIMITZ class. The introductions of some of the following improvements will be spread over several ships (including the CVN 77).

Aircraft operating features will include the provision of three or four electromagnetic catapults, replacing the steam catapults used in U.S. aircraft carriers since the early 1950s.[11]

Three (rather than four) elevators will be fitted. Only three aircraft arresting wires will be fitted (as in CVN 76 and 77), rather than the four in other U.S. carriers. The No. 4 wire will be deleted—very few aircraft "catch" that wire during flight operations—which will reduce costs. Three (rather than four) bomb elevators are provided, plus a utility elevator between the two starboard elevators.

The bridge structure probably will incorporate fixed-antenna, phased-array radars and phased-array communication antennas.

Personnel: Chief of Naval Operations Admiral Clark had cited hoped-for personnel reductions on the order of 50 percent compared with the NIMITZ-class manpower requirements. About one-half that number is the set goal for the CVN 78, i.e., a reduction of some 800 billets.

Propulsion: A new reactor plant is being designed for the CVN 78. A large electrical-generation plant is planned, with all possible auxiliary steam equipment being converted to electric (e.g., galley and laundry equipment, hot water heaters, and air heating systems). Of course, electric drive is necessary to permit the use of electromagnetic catapults.

The combination of advanced reactor and zonal electric distribution systems is expected to increase the power-generation capacity of the CVN 78 some 300 percent over the NIMITZ class.

---

11 The catapults are designated Electo-Magnetic Aircraft Launching System (EMALS).

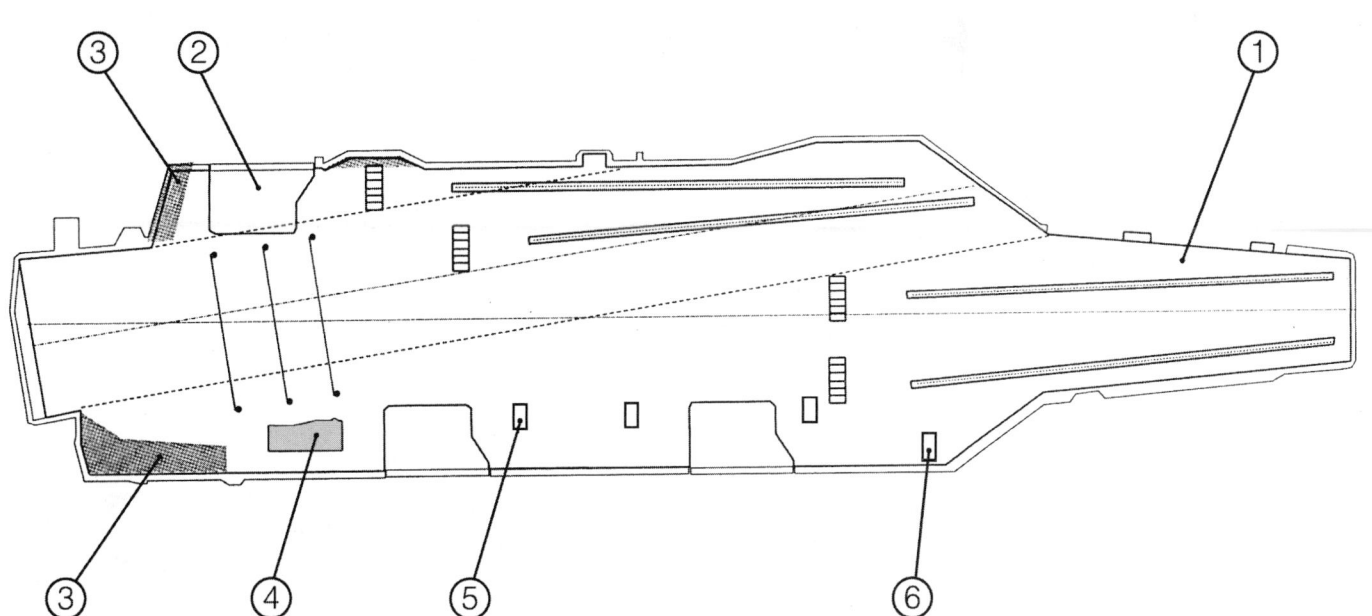

Aircraft Carrier CVN 78
1. Catapults (4) 2. Elevators (3) 3. Flight deck extensions 4. Island structure 5. Bomb elevators (3) 6. Utility elevator

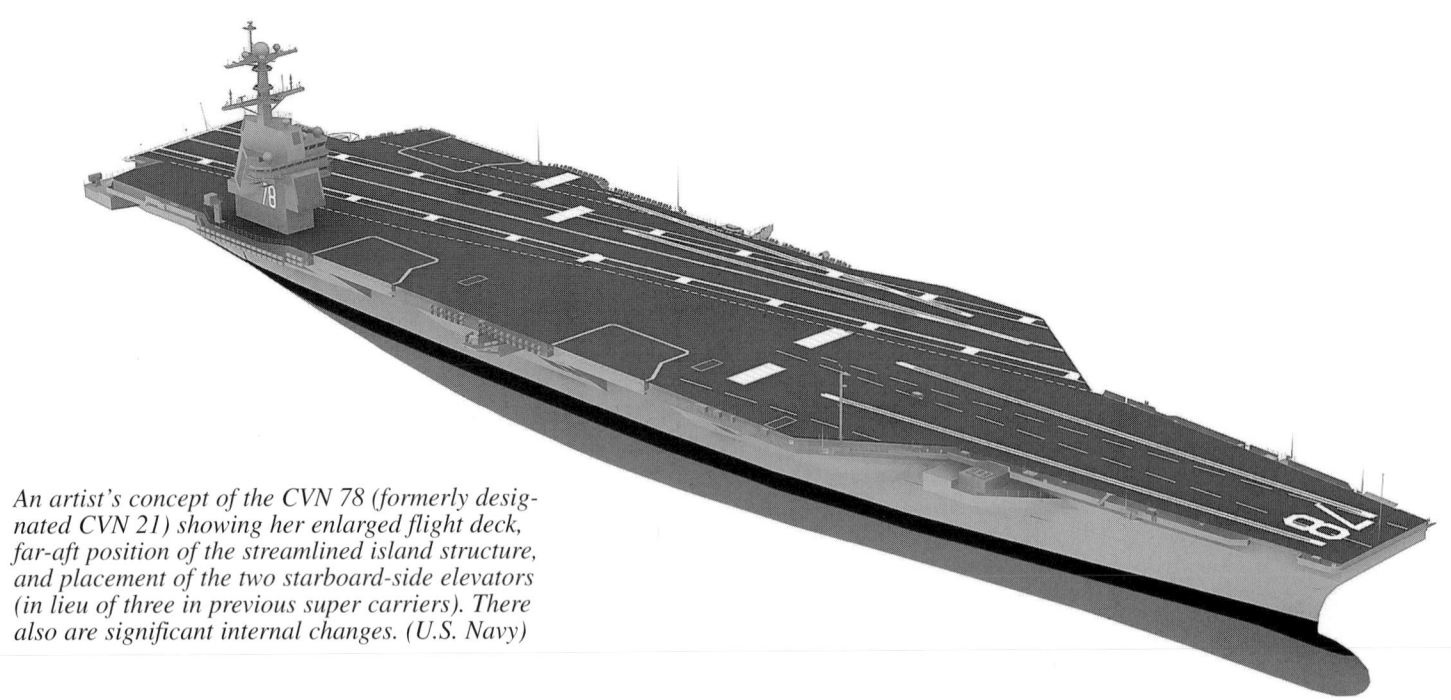

An artist's concept of the CVN 78 (formerly designated CVN 21) showing her enlarged flight deck, far-aft position of the streamlined island structure, and placement of the two starboard-side elevators (in lieu of three in previous super carriers). There also are significant internal changes. (U.S. Navy)

9 + 1 NUCLEAR-PROPELLED AIRCRAFT CARRIERS: "NIMITZ" CLASS

Number	Name	FY	Builder	Laid Down	Launched	Comm.	Status
CVN 68	NIMITZ	67	Newport News Shipbuilding, Va.	22 June 1968	13 May 1972	3 May 1975	**PA**
CVN 69	DWIGHT D. EISENHOWER	70	Newport News Shipbuilding, Va.	15 Aug 1970	11 Oct 1975	18 Oct 1977	**AA**
CVN 70	CARL VINSON	74	Newport News Shipbuilding, Va.	11 Oct 1975	15 Mar 1980	13 Mar 1982	**PA**
CVN 71	THEODORE ROOSEVELT	80	Newport News Shipbuilding, Va.	31 Oct 1981	27 Oct 1984	25 Oct 1986	**AA**
CVN 72	ABRAHAM LINCOLN	83	Newport News Shipbuilding, Va.	3 Nov 1984	13 Feb 1988	11 Nov 1989	**PA**
CVN 73	GEORGE WASHINGTON	83	Newport News Shipbuilding, Va.	25 Aug 1986	21 July 1990	4 July 1992	**AA**
CVN 74	JOHN C. STENNIS	88	Newport News Shipbuilding, Va.	13 Mar 1991	13 Nov 1993	2 Dec 1995	**PA**
CVN 75	HARRY S. TRUMAN	88	Newport News Shipbuilding, Va.	29 Nov 1993	7 Sep 1996	25 July 1998	**AA**
CVN 76	RONALD REAGAN	95	Northrop Grumman/Newport News Shipbuilding, Va.	12 Feb 1998	10 Mar 2001	12 July 2003	**PA**
CVN 77	GEORGE H. W. BUSH	01	Northrop Grumman/Newport News Shipbuilding, Va.	6 Sep 2003	2006	2008	Building

Displacement:	*Light*	*Full load*
CVN 68	77,264 tons	100,020 tons
CVN 69	78,837 tons	101,635 tons
CVN 70	78,434 tons	101,264 tons
CVN 71	80,777 tons	104,581 tons
CVN 72	81,451 tons	104,263 tons
CVN 73	81,364 tons	104,178 tons
CVN 74	80,506 tons	103,314 tons
CVN 75	81,069 tons	103,877 tons
CVN 76	78,621 tons	101,429 tons
CVN 77	102,000 tons	

Length:	1,040 feet (317.2 m) waterline	
CVN 68	1,115 feet (339.94 m) overall	
CVN 69, 70	1,098 feet (334.76 m) overall	
CVN 71–76	1,092 feet (332.93 m) overall	
CVN 77	approx. 1,100 feet (335.37 m) overall	
Beam:	134 feet (40.85 m)	
Flight deck	252 feet (76.83 m)	
Draft:	CVN 68–70 37 feet (11.3 m)	
	CVN 71–76 38½ feet (11.7 m)	
Propulsion:	4 steam turbines (General Electric); 280,000 shp; 4 shafts	
Reactors:	2 pressurized-water A4W (Westinghouse)	
Speed:	30+ knots	

Personnel:	*Total*	*Officers*	*Enlisted*
CVN 68	3,157	160	2,997
CVN 69	2,878	162	2,716
CVN 70	3,159	160	2,999
CVN 71	3,163	161	3,002
CVN 72	3,166	160	3,006
CVN 73	3,163	161	3,002
CVN 74	3,163	161	3,002
CVN 75	3,155	161	2,994
CVN 76	3,154	161	2,993

Flag:	approx. 60 (25 officers + 35 enlisted) when embarked
Air wing:	approx. 1,700
Aircraft:	approx. 70
Catapults:	4 steam Mk 13-1 in CVN 68–71
	4 steam Mk 13-2 in CVN 72 and later ships
Elevators:	4 deck edge (85 x 52 feet/25.9 x 15.85 m); 130,000-lb (58,500-kg) capacity
Missiles:	2 8-cell NATO Sea Sparrow launchers Mk 29
	2 21-cell RAM missile launchers Mk 49
Guns:	or 3 or 4 20-mm Phalanx CIWS Mk 15 (multi-barrel)
Radars:	SPQ-9B track-while-scan in ships with RAM
	SPS-48E 3-D air search
	SPS-49(V)5 air search
	SPS-64(V)9 navigation
	SPS-67(V)1 surface search
	Mk 23 Target Acquisition System (TAS)
Sonars:	none
Fire control:	3 Mk 91 missile FCS
EW systems:	SLQ-25A Nixie torpedo countermeasures
	SLQ-32(V)4

These are the largest warships ever built, the first to exceed 100,000 tons full load displacement. Nine are in commission, with one more under construction. Details vary, as improvements have been made in virtually every succeeding ship (see *Design* notes).

The NIMITZ class represents the longest production run of a basic ship design by any Navy—the interval between completion of the lead ship and the planned completion of the last being 33 years. (The preliminary design of the NIMITZ began in 1964.) Except for the U.S. helicopter carriers of the similar TARAWA (LHA 1) and WASP (LHD 1) classes (i.e, 12 ships), the NIMITZ class also is the largest number of aircraft carriers built to the same basic design since World War II .

Armament: The CVNs 68, 69, and 76 have been fitted with the Ship Self-Defense System (SSDS) Mk 2.

Class: A program to construct the first three CVNs of the NIMITZ class was approved by Secretary of Defense Robert S. McNamara during the Vietnam War to replace the three MIDWAY-class carriers and provide a force of 12 large carriers (i.e., CV 59–64, 66, and 67 and CVN 65 and 68–70). The ships were delayed during construction by labor strikes and schedule problems at the Newport News yard. The NIMITZ was seven years from keel laying to commissioning, compared to less than four years for the more complex (eight-reactor) ENTERPRISE.

The RONALD REAGAN was authorized in fiscal 1995, seven years after the CVN 75, the longest interval between authorizations in this class. She was funded after the Cold War ended, having been put forward by the Clinton administration and approved by Congress with relatively little debate and only minor opposition—true testimony to the aircraft carrier's efficacy. The "periodic" construction of large carriers followed, as the United States continued to require tactical aviation in distant areas. Note that two NIMITZ-class ships were authorized in FY 83 and 88, a unique achievement of the Reagan administration's naval buildup under the guidance of Secretary of the Navy John Lehman.

Classification: The NIMITZ and DWIGHT D. EISENHOWER were ordered as attack aircraft carriers (CVAN); they were changed to multimission aircraft carriers (CVN) on 30 June 1975. The CARL VINSON and later ships were ordered as CVNs.

Design: SCB No. 102. The general arrangement of these ships is similar to the previous KITTY HAWK class with respect to flight deck, hangar, elevators, and island structure (e.g., the island structure is aft of the No. 1 and No. 2 elevators, with the No. 4 elevator on the port side, aft of the angled deck and opposite the No. 3 elevator on the starboard side). The angled deck is canted 9° 3' to port and is 796⅔ feet (242.9 m) long. The hangar deck is 684 feet (208.5 m) long, 108 feet (32.9 m) wide, and 26½ feet (8.1 m) high.

The CVN 71 and later ships incorporate improved magazine protection and modular construction techniques that helped to reduce construction time; the CVN 73 and later ships have improved topside ballistic protection; and the CVN 74 and later units were constructed with HSLA-100 steel. There also have been incremental improvements in the ships' electrical and electronics systems.

"Full load" is maximum displacement after underway replenishment at sea of full ordnance and aviation fuel capacity (previously referred to as "combat load"). Payload includes approximately 2,900 tons of aviation ordnance and up to 3.5 million gallons (13.2 million liters) of jet fuel (JP-5).

The RONALD REAGAN and GEORGE H. W. BUSH have only three arresting wires as compared to the four fitted in all other U.S. carriers now in service. In carrier operations the fourth wire was rarely used; procurement and maintenance savings will accrue from the deletion. (Earlier ships will retain their four wires.)

The island structures of the REAGAN and BUSH have higher overheads for more efficient running of distribution systems (heat, air conditioning, electrical piping, wave guides, etc.); this configuration eliminates one deck level. In addition, the two ships' island and mast designs are different, to provide additional growth margin and improved survivability for internal cables and wave guides, and to support new antenna arrangement. (The REAGAN island's 010 level is 52½ feet/16 m above the flight deck; in previous ships the 011 level was 54½ feet/16.6 m above the flight deck.)

Details differ based on individual ships' configuration with respect to maintenance facilities, electronic systems, etc.

Electronics: Several carrier-landing systems are provided: SPN-42A carrier-controlled approach in CVN 68–71; SPN-43C marshalling in all ships; SPN-44 landing aid in the CVN 71 and later ships; two SPN-46 air traffic control in the CVN 72 and later ships.

Periodic proposals to provide these ships with the SPY-1 radar have been turned down on the basis of cost.

Engineering: These carriers have only two reactors, compared to eight in the first nuclear carrier, the ENTERPRISE. The fuel cores in the early ships were estimated to have a service life of at least 13 years (800,000–1,000,000 nm/1,481,000–1,850,350 km); the later cores have been pushed out to 25 years. This means the later ships would be refueled only once during a service life of 45–50 years. See *Modernization* notes.

The CVN 77 may have the improved A5W reactor plant.

Guns: The CVN 68 and 69 had three Mk 15 Phalanx CIWS; four CIWS were installed in later ships. These were removed with the installation of Mk 49 RAM launchers.

Missiles: The CVN 68 and 69 were built with the Sea Sparrow Mk 25 missile launchers (with Mk 115 fire control system); they were rearmed with NATO Sea Sparrow system.

Modernization: The NIMITZ was the first ship of the class to undergo the Refueling/Complex Overhaul (RCOH) process, with the subsequent ships following in order. The process, which includes the only nuclear refueling of the ships during their service, is expected to provide a 45–50-year service life.

All ROCHs are undertaken at the Newport News shipyard; the dates for the CVN 70 and later ships are based on a 2004 schedule.

Ship	Start of RCOH	Completion of RCOH
CVN 68	29 May 1998	28 June 2001
CVN 69	21 May 2001	Oct 2004
CVN 70	2005	2006
CVN 71	2009	2012
CVN 72	2012	2015
CVN 73	2015	2018
CVN 74	2018	2022

The DWIGHT D. EISENHOWER's RCOH was estimated to cost approximately $1.5 billion; the estimated cost of the CARL VINSON's RCOH is $3.2 billion.

Names: The CVN 68 remembers one of four admirals to hold five-star rank. The Navy's three other Fleet Admirals—William D. Leahy, Ernest J. King, and William F. Halsey—were remembered by guided missile frigates.[12] There were two other ships named for five-star officers: the Polaris submarine SSBN 654 named GEORGE C. MARSHALL, for the World War II Army chief of staff and later the Secretary of State and Secretary of Defense; and the missile range instrumentation ship GEN. H. H. ARNOLD (T-AGM 9), honoring the World War II commander of the Army Air Forces.[13] Thus, of nine five-star officers in the U.S. armed forces, seven have been honored by U.S. ships; only Generals of the Army Omar Bradley and Douglas MacArthur have been slighted.

The CVN 69 was named for General/President Dwight D. Eisenhower. Originally named EISENHOWER, the ship was renamed DWIGHT D. EISENHOWER on 23 May 1970 at White House direction.

The CVN 71–73 and 75–77 honor former presidents, three of whom previously had ballistic missile submarines named for them: THEODORE ROOSEVELT (SSBN 600), ABRAHAM LINCOLN (SSBN 602), and GEORGE WASHINGTON (SSBN 598). The CVN 72 and CVN 73 were named prior to their start, in part to preempt potential congressional pressure to name one of those ships for Admiral H. G. Rickover (the SSN 709 was named for the admiral).

The CVN 70 and 74 were named for, respectively, the long-time chairman of the House Armed Services Committee and major supporter of the U.S. naval buildup in the eve of World War II, and a Navy supporter who served in the House of Representatives from 1947 to 1988.

---

12 Frigates, i.e., DLG, later redesignated CG or DDG.
13 The T-AGM 9 was built as the troop transport GEN R. E. CALLAN (AP 139).

The CVN 75 originally was named UNITED STATES, after one of the six sailing frigates authorized by Congress in 1794 and the first to be launched; the other ships in that series included the frigates CONSTITUTION and CONSTELLATION. The second UNITED STATES was a battle cruiser (CC 6) laid down in 1920 but canceled; sister ships were completed as the carriers LEXINGTON (CV 2) and SARATOGA (CV 3). The next UNITED STATES was the first "super carrier" (CVA 58), laid down in April 1949 and promptly canceled, leading to the carrier-versus-B-36 controversy. On 2 February 1995, the CVN 75 was renamed for the 33rd president.

The CVN 77 was named while George W. Bush was president.

Operational: The CARL VINSON shifted to the Pacific Fleet in 1983, the NIMITZ in 1987, the ABRAHAM LINCOLN in 1990, the JOHN C. STENNIS in 1999, and the RONALD REAGAN in 2004.

Personnel: Aircraft carriers were the first U.S. combatant ships to have women assigned as permanent crew members, with the DWIGHT D. EISENHOWER the first to deploy with women. She departed Norfolk, Virginia, on 20 October 1994 with 367 female officers and enlisteds on board. The ship deployed for six months, operating in the Mediterranean–Adriatic areas.

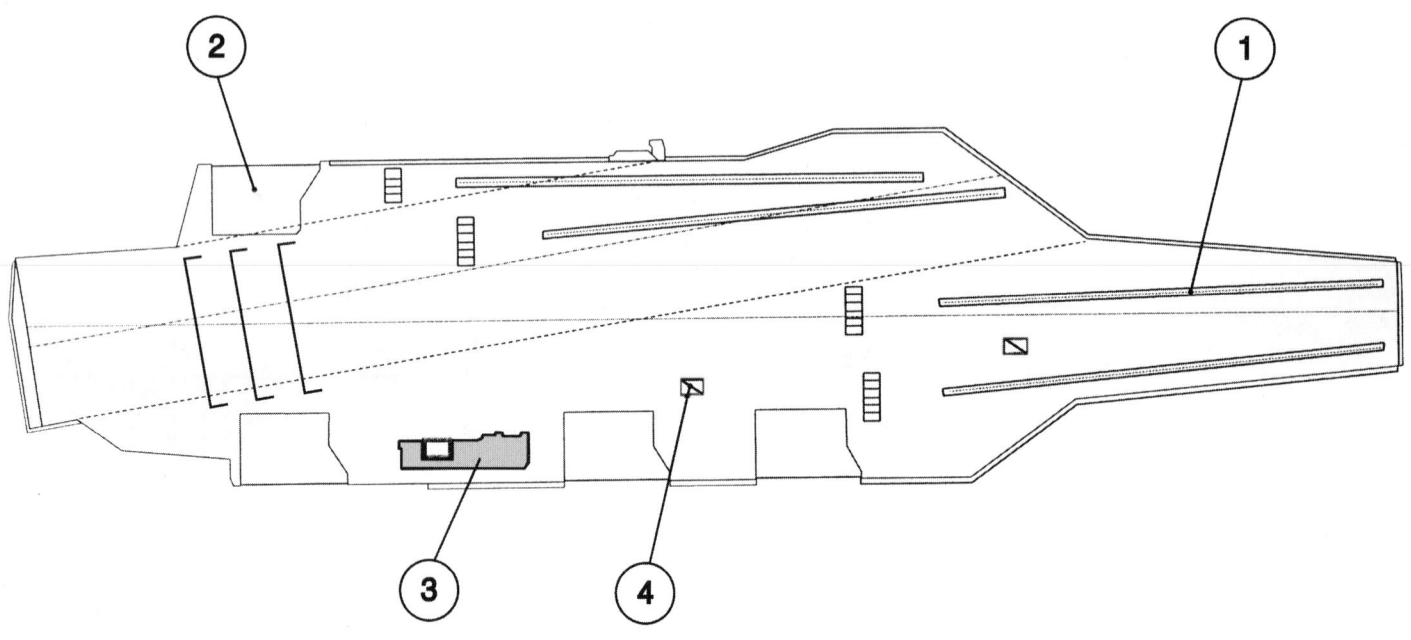

Aircraft Carrier GEORGE H. W. BUSH
1. Catapults (4) 2. Elevators (4) 3. Island structure 4. Bomb elevators (3)

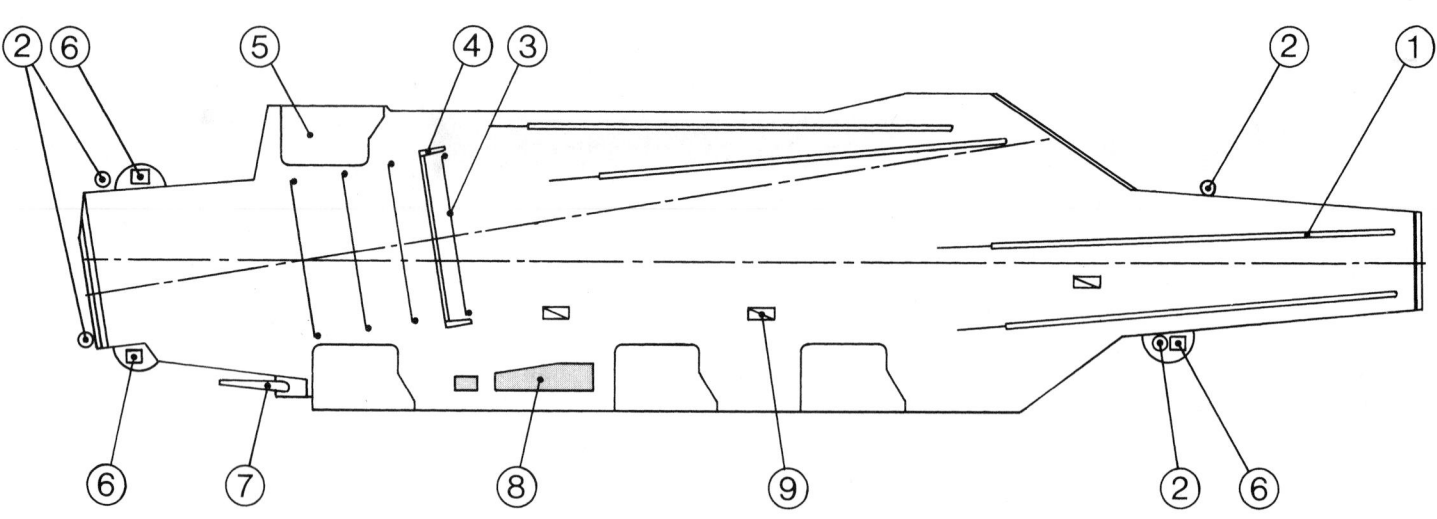

Aircraft Carrier GEORGE WASHINGTON
1. Catapults (4) 2. Phalanx CIWS (4) 3. Arresting wires (4) 4. Barricade 5. Elevators (4) 6. NATO Sea Sparrow (3) 7. Aircraft crane 8. Island structure 9. Bomb elevators (3) (William Clipson)

An F/A-18C Hornet streaks over the CARL VINSON. The massive island structure is topped with an SPS-48E 3-D radar antenna and communications antenna domes; the radar mast aft of the island carries the SPS-49 long-range air search radar. A mobile wrecking crane is parked between the island and radar mast. (2004, U.S. Navy/Chris M. Valdez)

The HARRY S. TRUMAN during training operations off the Virginia coast. There are three F-14 Tomcats and an F/A-18 Hornet on the port-side deck-edge elevator (just forward of the large communications dome); there is a NATO Sea Sparrow missile launcher above a Phalanx CIWS on the port quarter. (2004, U.S. Navy/Christopher B. Stoltz)

The HARRY S. TRUMAN, deployed in the Mediterranean, being approached by the replenishment ship SPICA (T-AFS 9) as the ships begin an Underway Replenishment (UNREP) evolution. Helicopters from both ships will supplement the "high-line" transfer of fuel, stores, and munitions. Fifty-two aircraft of Carrier Air Wing 3 are visible. (2003, U.S. Navy/John L. Beeman)

The JOHN C. STENNIS cruises off Southern California with Carrier Air Wing 14 on board. The ship's two angled-deck steam catapult tracks are visible; F/A-18 Hornets are parked over the two forward catapult tracks. (2004, U.S. Navy/Joshua Ward)

The GEORGE WASHINGTON during an Underway Replenishment (UNREP) evolution with the fast combat support ship SUPPLY (T-AOE 6) in the Persian Gulf. MH-60S Knighthawks also are participating. Cargo helicopters are carried by Navy- and civilian-manned UNREP ships. (2004, U.S. Navy/Robert Brooks)

The CARL VINSON steaming at slow speed in the Western Pacific. The ship's three starboard-side elevator openings are visible, two forward and one aft of the island structure. The CVN 78 design moves the island structure farther aft and dispenses with the aftermost starboard elevator. (2003, U.S. Navy/Inez Lawson)

The NIMITZ entering Pearl Harbor, assisted by civilian tugs, while en route to a Western Pacific deployment. The NIMITZ, the first of her class, was completed in 1975. In many ways, she is based on the design of the first super carrier, the canceled UNITED STATES (CVA 58), designed just after World War II. (2003, U.S. Navy/ Benjamin David Glass)

1 AIRCRAFT CARRIER: "JOHN F. KENNEDY" TYPE

Number	Name	FY	Builder	Laid Down	Launched	Comm.	Status
CV 67	JOHN F. KENNEDY	63	Newport News Shipbuilding, Va.	22 Oct 1964	27May 1967	7 Sep 1968	**AA**

Displacement:	60,760 tons light	Elevators:	4 deck edge (85 x 52 feet/25.9 x 15.9 m) 130,000-lb
	82,760 tons full load		(58,500 kg) capacity
Length:	990 feet (301.9 m) waterline	Missiles:	2 8-cell NATO Sea Sparrow launchers Mk 29
	1,073 feet (327.13 m) overall		2 21-cell RAM launchers Mk 49
Beam:	128½ feet (39.2 m)	Guns:	removed
Flight deck:	252 feet (76.8 m)	Radars:	SPQ-9B track-while-scan
Draft:	37 feet (11.3 m)		SPS-48E 3-D air search
Propulsion:	4 steam turbines (General Electric); 280,000 shp;4 shafts		SPS-49(V)5 air search
Boilers:	8 1,200 psi (83.4 kg/cm2) (Foster-Wheeler)		SPS-64(V)9 surface search
Speed:	33 knots		SPS-67(V)1 surface search
Range:	12,000 nm (22,225 km) at 20 knots		Mk 23 Target Acquisition System (TAS)
Personnel:	3,030 (143 officers + 2,887 enlisted)	Sonars:	none
Flag:	approx. 60 (25 officers + 35 enlisted) when embarked	Fire control:	3 Mk 91 missile FCS
Air wing: approx.	1,700	EW systems:	SLQ-32(v)4
Aircraft: approx.	70		WLR-1H
Catapults:	3 steam C13 + 1 steam C13-1		WLR-11

The ship is similar to the KITTY HAWK class (i.e., Improved FORRESTAL design). Construction of the JOHN F. KENNEDY was delayed because of lengthy debates over whether the carrier should have nuclear or conventional propulsion.

The JOHN F. KENNEDY was changed from active status to the Naval Reserve Force (NRF) on 1 October 1994 and from September 1995 served as an "operational reserve/training carrier," providing carrier landing training for pilots while maintaining the capability to deploy as an operational carrier on short notice. However, fleet requirements led to the ship serving as a fully operational carrier, deploying on a regular basis. In addition, the "experiment" in partial reserve manning was unsuccessful, and on 1 October 2000, she reverted to active status; see *Personnel* notes. This was the first time an aircraft carrier had been assigned to the NRF and homeported in Mayport, Florida (previous AVT training carriers were based at Pensacola, Florida).

The ship probably will replace the KITTY HAWK as the Japan-based carrier about 2008. The current planned retirement date for the JOHN F. KENNEDY is 2018, with her nominal replacement the CVN 79.

Classification: The "JFK" originally was an attack aircraft carrier (CVA); the ship was changed to CV on 1 December 1974.

Design: SCB No. 127C. See KITTY HAWK class for general design notes.

The hangar deck is 688 feet (209.75 m) long, 106 feet (32.3 m) wide, and 25 (7.6 m) feet high. The angled deck is canted 11° to port and is 754 feet (229.9 m) long. The JOHN F. KENNEDY's stack is angled out to starboard to help carry exhaust gases away from the approach path to the flight deck.

Electronics: Several carrier-landing systems are provided: SPN-35 blind-landing approach radar, SPN-41 landing aid, SPN-42 carrier-controlled approach, SPN-43C marshalling, and two SPN-46 air traffic control.

The JOHN F. KENNEDY has a bow sonar dome, but no sonar was ever installed.

Missiles: The JOHN F. KENNEDY originally had three Sea Sparrow Mk 25 launchers and Mk 115 FCS.

Modernization: After the Secretary of Defense in early 1991 canceled the planned Service Life Extension Program (SLEP) for the JOHN F. KENNEDY, Congress placed language in the FY 1991 supplemental appropriation to force the SLEP to be undertaken at the Philadelphia Naval Shipyard.[14] However, Congress voted only $405 million for the work—about half the estimated cost of a SLEP—so the Navy instead undertook a two-year Comprehensive Overhaul (COH) modernization (vice about three years for a SLEP).

The JOHN F. KENNEDY arrived at the Philadelphia yard on 13 September 1993, modernization work began on 13 September 1993, and work was completed on 15 September 1995. Cost of the ship's modernization was $491 million.

Personnel: As an NRF/training carrier, the JFK initially was to embark some 600 reserve personnel (about 20 percent of the crew),

The JOHN F. KENNEDY's island structure is dominated by the ship's angled funnel, intended to remove stack gas from the approach path for aircraft. The tower aft of the island mounts the ship's SPS-48E 3-D search radar. There is a Phalanx CIWS just forward of the funnel. (2004, U.S. Navy/Chris Weibull)

with most serving on board the ship for their annual two weeks' active duty for training. It was quickly decided that such assignments would be prohibitively expensive.

Subsequently, the carrier was to embark 277 Naval Reservists for a period of one year. However, after screening reservists' qualifications against billets, the Navy accepted only 115 for service aboard the JOHN F. KENNEDY, and only 68 of those reported for duty in March 1999. In addition, some 300 Navy Training and Administration of Reserves (TAR) personnel were assigned to the ship. (TARs are full-time reserve personnel.)

---

14 The Philadelphia yard was closed in 1996.

The JOHN F. KENNEDY departs Naval Station Mayport, Florida, for trials after a ten-month maintenance period. Completing such work away from major shipyard facilities has been judged to provide more operational time for carriers. The "JFK" was the last non-nuclear super carrier built by the United States. (2003, U.S. Navy/Greg Curry)

The JOHN F. KENNEDY and the replenishment ship SEATTLE (AOE 3) conduct an ammunition onload as the carrier prepares for deployment to the Mediterranean. Crated bombs and missiles are stacked on the ship's flight deck. The carrier ENTERPRISE, returning from deployment, also was transferring munitions to the "JFK." (2004, U.S. Navy/Joshua Karsten)

1 NUCLEAR-PROPELLED AIRCRAFT CARRIER: "ENTERPRISE" TYPE

Number	Name	FY	Builder	Laid Down	Launched	Comm.	Status
CVN 65	ENTERPRISE	58	Newport News Shipbuilding, Va.	4 Feb 1958	24 Sep 1960	25 Nov 1961	**AA**

Displacement	75,865 tons light	Catapults:	4 steam C13-1
	93,445 tons full load	Elevators:	4 deck edge (85 x 52 feet/25.9 x 15.9 m); 130,000-lb
Length:	1,040 feet (317.07 m) waterline		(58,500-kg) capacity
	1,088 feet (331.70 m) overall	Missiles:	2 8-cell NATO Sea Sparrow launchers Mk 29
Beam:	133 feet (40.5 m)	Guns:	3 20-mm Phalanx CIWS Mk 15 (3 multibarrel)
Flight deck:	248⅓ feet (75.7 m)	Radars:	SPS-48E 3-D air search
Draft:	39 feet (11.9 m)		SPS-49(V)5 air search
Propulsion:	4 steam turbines (Westinghouse); approx. 280,000 shp;		SPS-64(V)9 navigation
	4 shafts		SPS-67(V)1 surface search
Reactors:	8 pressurized-water A2W (Westinghouse)		Mk 23 Target Acquisition System (TAS)
Speed:	33 knots	Sonars:	none
Personnel:	3,335 (171 officers + 3,164 enlisted)	Fire control:	3 Mk 91 missile FCS
Flag:	approx. 60 (25 officers + 35 enlisted) when embarked	EW systems:	SLQ-32(V)4
Air wing:	approx. 1,700		WLR-1H
Aircraft:	approx. 70		

The ENTERPRISE was the world's second nuclear-propelled surface warship and the largest and most expensive warship at the time of construction. Her estimated construction cost was $444 million.

The ship operated in the Pacific from 1965 until early 1990. On 16 March 1990, she arrived at Norfolk in preparation for a three-year refueling/modernization at Newport News Shipbuilding (see *Modernization* notes). She resumed operations with the Atlantic Fleet in 1995.

The "Big E" is scheduled to be retired in 2013, being replaced by the CVN 78.

Class: Congress provided $35 million in the fiscal 1960 budget for long-lead-time nuclear components for a second aircraft carrier of this type; however, the Eisenhower administration (1953–1961) deferred the project. The next nuclear carrier, the NIMITZ, was not ordered until 1967, almost ten years after the ENTERPRISE, with two oil-burning carriers constructed in the interim.

Classification: Originally classified as an attack aircraft carrier (CVAN), the ENTERPRISE was changed to a multimission carrier (CVN) on 30 June 1975.

Design: SCB design No. 160. The ENTERPRISE was built to a modified KITTY HAWK design, but in her original configuration, she had a distinctive island structure because of the arrangement of her "billboard" radar antennas (see *Electronics* notes).

Her hangar deck is 860 feet (262.2 m) long, 107 feet (32.6 m) wide, and 25 feet (7.6 m) high. The angled deck is 755⅝ feet (230.4 m) long and canted 10° to port.

Electronics: The ENTERPRISE and the cruiser LONG BEACH (CGN 9) were the only ships fitted with the Hughes SPS-32 and SPS-33 fixed-array radars. The radars were difficult to maintain and were replaced during the ENTERPRISE's 1979–1981 modernization with conventional SPS-48 and SPS-49 radars, with a new island structure installed.

Carrier-landing systems provided are the SPN-41 landing aid, SPN-43C marshalling, and two SPN-46 air traffic control.

Engineering: At the time of her construction, the ENTERPRISE was estimated to have a cruising range of more than 200,000 nm (370,400 km) without refueling. On her initial set of fuel cores, the ship traveled 207,000 nm (383,365 km).

The two-reactor A1W prototype of the ENTERPRISE propulsion plant was constructed at Arco, Idaho.

Missiles: As built, the ENTERPRISE had neither defensive missiles nor guns, the planned Terrier system having been deleted from the design because of cost. Late in 1967, she was fitted with two Sea Sparrow Mk 25 launchers. During her 1979–1982 overhaul, the NATO Sea Sparrow Mk 29 launchers were installed, as were the Phalanx CIWS.

Modernization: The ENTERPRISE underwent RCOH modernization and nuclear refueling at Newport News Shipbuilding; she arrived at the yard on 12 October 1990 and work began on 8 January 1991. (Her nuclear plant was shut down at the Norfolk Naval Base on 15 August 1990, and she was towed to the Newport News yard.)

The ENTERPRISE carried out initial post-overhaul sea trials on 27–30 September 1994. After additional at-sea operations, the carrier returned to Newport News and completed fitting out on 6 December 1994. A post-overhaul yard period followed; she returned to the fleet in July 1995.

The refueling was expected to provide cores with service lives of about 20 years, i.e., until about 2115.

Operational: During August–October 1964, the ENTERPRISE, the cruiser LONG BEACH, and the frigate BAINBRIDGE (DLGN 25/CGN 25) formed all-nuclear Task Force 1. The ships steamed around the world, traveling 32,600 nm (60,375 km) in 64 days, including time for port visits in several countries. They took on no fuel or provisions during the cruise, except for special food for a kangaroo that was picked up in Australia.

The ENTERPRISE shifted to the Pacific Fleet in 1965 and in November of that year began flying air strikes against North Vietnam, becoming the first nuclear ship to enter combat. She remained in the Pacific until 1990, when she returned to the Atlantic in preparation for overhaul at Newport News Shipbuilding.

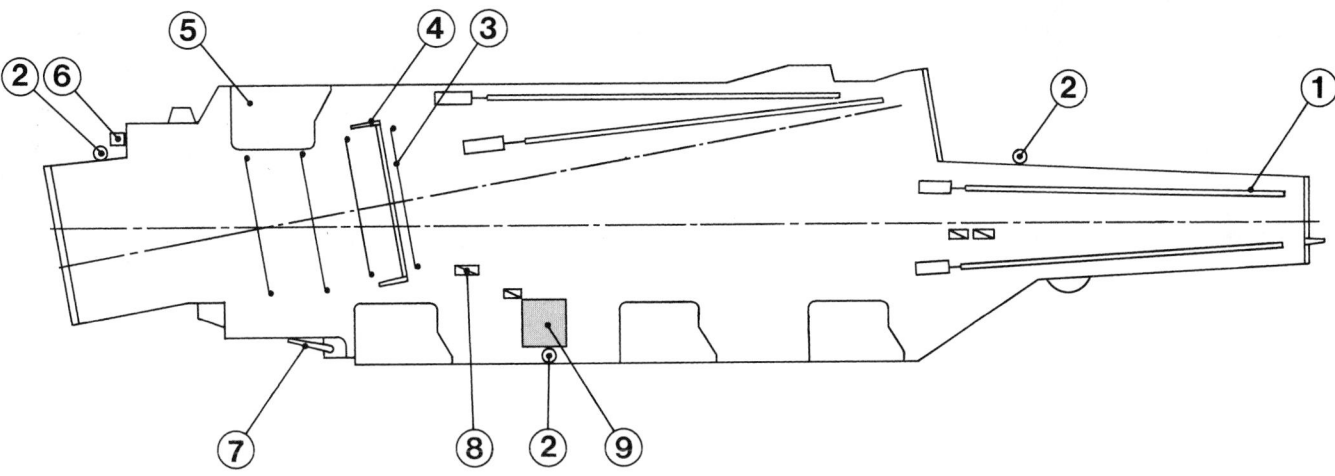

Aircraft Carrier ENTERPRISE
1. Catapults (4) 2. Phalanx CIWS (4) 3. Arresting wires (4) 4. Barricade 5. Elevators (4) 6. NATO Sea Sparrow (3) 7. Aircraft crane 8. Bomb elevators (4) 9. Island structure (William Clipson

The island structure of the ENTERPRISE *with a mobile wrecking crane parked behind. The large radar antennas are for the SPS-48E (left) and SPS-49. The "Big E" and the nuclear-propelled cruiser* LONG BEACH *(CGN 9) were built with the massive SPS-32/ SPS-33 "billboard" radars. Their removal left the Enterprise with a diminutive island structure. (2004, U.S. Navy/Joshua Karsten)*

Stern aspect of the ENTERPRISE *during operations in the Atlantic. Munitions are stacked on her flight deck; her air wing is ashore. (2003, U.S. Navy/Douglas M. Pearlman)*

The carrier ENTERPRISE *and the Aegis cruiser* GETTYSBURG *(CG 64) refuel from the replenishment ship* DETROIT *(AOE 6) in the Arabian Sea. Even nuclear carriers require replenishment every few days, especially during combat operations, of aviation fuel, munitions, and provisions. (2003, U.S. Navy/Douglas M. Pearlman)*

1 AIRCRAFT CARRIER: "KITTY HAWK" CLASS

Number	Name	FY	Builder	Laid Down	Launched	Comm.	Status
CV 63	KITTY HAWK	56	New York Shipbuilding, Camden, N.J.	27 Dec 1956	21 May 1960	29 Apr 1961	**PA**
CV 64	CONSTELLATION	57	New York Naval Shipyard, Brooklyn,N.Y.	14 Sep 1957	8 Oct 1960	27 Oct 1961	decomm. 6 Aug 2003; str. 2 Dec 2003
CV 66	AMERICA	61	Newport News Shipbuilding, Va.	9 Jan 1961	1 Feb 1964	23 Jan 1965	decomm./str. 9 Aug 1996

Displacement:	61,107 tons light		Elevators:	4 deck edge (85 x 52 feet/25.9 x 15.9 m) 130,000-lb
	81,953 tons full load			(58,500 kg) capacity
Length:	990 feet (301.9 m) waterline		Missiles:	2 8-cell NATO Sea Sparrow launchers Mk 29
	1,069 feet (325.91 m) overall			2 21-cell RAM launchers Mk 49
Beam:	129¹½ feet (39.6 m)		Guns:	removed
Flight deck:	282 feet (85.98 m)		Radars:	SPQ-9B track-while-scan
Draft:	37 feet (11.3 m)			SPS-48E 3-D air search
Propulsion:	4 steam turbines (General Electric); 280,000 shp; 4 shafts			SPS-49(V)5 air search
Boilers:	8 1,200 psi (83.4 kg/cm2) (Foster-Wheeler)			SPS-64(V)9 surface search
Speed:	33 knots			SPS-67(V)1 surface search
Range:	12,000 nm (22,225 km) at 20 knots			Mk 23 Target Acquisition System (TAS)
Personnel:	3,160 (148 officers + 3,012 enlisted)		Sonars:	none
Flag:	approx. 60 (25 officers + 35 enlisted) when embarked		Fire control:	3 Mk 91 missile FCS
Air wing:	approx. 1,700		EW systems:	SLQ-29 (SLQ-17 + WLR-8)
Aircraft:	approx. 70			WLR-1H
Catapults:	4 steam C13			WLR-11

This class has a modified FORRESTAL configuration with improved elevator and flight deck arrangements. The JOHN F. KENNEDY is similar in design. Construction of the KITTY HAWK was delayed because of shipyard problems. The above data are for the KITTY HAWK.

The KITTY HAWK is homeported in Yokosuka, Japan. Her planned retirement date is 2008, with the JOHN F. KENNEDY probably replacing her as the Japan-based carrier.

The CONSTELLATION is retained a mobilization asset; she is laid up at Bremerton, Washington.

Builders: The KITTY HAWK is the last U.S. aircraft carrier to be built by a shipyard other than Newport News Shipbuilding.

Class: There were three ships in the KITTY HAWK class; the JOHN F. KENNEDY officially is a single ship "type." All four of these carriers often were grouped with the FORRESTAL class in force-level discussions.

The AMERICA was decommissioned and stricken after only 31.5 years of service because of the high maintenance and overhaul costs caused by the thinner hull plating and other cost-reduction methods employed in her construction.

Classification: These ships originally were attack aircraft carriers (CVA). Two ships were changed to multimission carriers (CV) when modified to operate Anti-Submarine Warfare (ASW) aircraft, the KITTY HAWK on 29 April 1973 and the JOHN F. KENNEDY on 1 December 1974. The CONSTELLATION was changed to CV on 30 June 1975, prior to being modified.

Design: SCB No. 127 (KITTY HAWK). These ships are larger than the FORRESTAL class and have an improved flight deck arrangement, with two elevators forward of the island structure and the port-side elevator on the stern quarter rather than at the forward end of the angled flight deck.

The hangar deck in the KITTY HAWK is 740 feet (225.6 m) long, 101 feet (30.8 m) wide, and 25 feet (7.6 m) high. Her angled deck is 722⁷⁄₁₂ feet (220.3 m) long and canted 11° to port.

Electronics: Several carrier-landing systems are provided in these ships: SPN-35 blind-landing approach radar, SPN-41 landing aid, SPN-42 carrier-controlled approach, SPN-43C marshalling, and two SPN-46 air traffic control.

Missiles: All three ships were built with two Terrier missile launchers (Mk 10 Mod 3 on starboard quarter and Mk 10 Mod 4 on port quarter) with SPQ-55B missile control "searchlight" radars.

Modernization: The KITTY HAWK was modernized under the SLEP upgrade at the Philadelphia Naval Shipyard. She arrived at the yard on 7 April 1987, the modernization began on 28 January 1988, and work was completed on 31 August 1991. SLEP added an estimated 15 years to the ship's nominal 30-year service life.

Operational: The KITTY HAWK is the Navy's forward-based carrier at Yokosuka, Japan, having replaced the INDEPENDENCE, which was homeported there from September 1991 to July 1998. The KITTY HAWK arrived at Yokosuka on 11 August 1998, after trading air wings with the INDEPENDENCE at Pearl Harbor on 18 July 1998.

The KITTY HAWK departed Yokosuka on 30 September 2001 to support U.S. operations in Afghanistan carrying a large contingent of Special Operations Forces (SOF). Carrier Air Wing 5 provided several F/A-18C Hornet strike fighters and a small number of EA-6B Prowler and E-2C Hawkeye support aircraft. The ship also embarked the Army's 160th Special Operations Regiment with MH-47, MH-53, and MH-60 helicopters and some 1,000 SOF personnel from Army, Navy, and Air Force units. The KITTY HAWK operated in the Persian Gulf, carrying out intensive operations in support of the U.S. assault on Afghanistan. She departed the Gulf area on 8 December 2001 and returned to Yokosuka on the 23rd.

The KITTY HAWK tests her washdown system while operating in the Philippine Sea. The system covers her flight deck and island structure with high-pressure water and aqueous film-forming foam for protection against nuclear, chemical, and biological attacks. All major U.S. warships have such washdown systems. (2004, U.S. Navy/Jason R. Williams)

The KITTY HAWK during flight operations in the Philippine Sea. She is the oldest warship in active service; the only older U.S. warship in commission is the sailing frigate CONSTITUTION, which was commissioned in 1798 (see Chapter 25). (2004, U.S. Navy/William H. Ramsey)

The sister ships Constellation *and* Kitty Hawk *steam together a few months before the "Connie" was decommissioned. At the time, both carriers were operating in the Persian Gulf in support of U.S. military operations in Iraq. (2003, U.S. Navy/Timothy Smith)*

AIRCRAFT CARRIERS: "FORRESTAL" CLASS

Number	Name	Comm.	Status
CV 59	FORRESTAL	1 Oct 1955	decomm./str. 10 Sep 1993
CV 60	SARATOGA	14 Apr 1956	decomm./str. 30 Sep 1994
CV 61	RANGER	10 Aug 1957	decomm. 10 July 1993; str. 8 Mar 2004
CV 62	INDEPENDENCE	10 Jan 1959	decomm. 30 Sep 1998; str. 8 Mar 2004

The FORRESTAL class was the world's first aircraft carrier design to be constructed from the keel up after World War II and the first class of "super carriers." The ships were intended specifically to operate heavy and high-performance turbojet attack aircraft, especially nuclear-armed planes capable of striking the Soviet Union.

In 2004, the SARATOGA became a museum–memorial at San Diego, California.

See 17th Edition/pages 122–24 for characteristics.

Class: The FORRESTAL made her last operational deployment in mid-1991, after which she was to become the Navy's pilot landing training ship. Instead, she was decommissioned and stricken in 1993, prior to undertaking that role (the FORRESTAL was changed from CV to AVT on 4 February 1992).

Classification: All were completed as attack carriers (CVA), although the FORRESTAL and SARATOGA were ordered as large carriers (CVB). They were changed to multimission aircraft carriers (CV) to operate S-3A Viking ASW aircraft and SH-3 Sea King ASW helicopters—the FORRESTAL and RANGER on 30 June 1975 (prior to modification), the SARATOGA on 30 June 1972, and INDEPENDENCE on 28 February 1973.

Design: SCB No. 80. This class incorporated many design features of the aborted carrier UNITED STATES. The original design provided for an axial (straight) flight deck. The FORRESTAL was modified during construction to incorporate the British-developed angled flight deck. Details of these ships differed considerably.

Guns: These were the last U.S. aircraft carriers built with major gun armament. As built, all ships had eight 5-inch/54-cal DP Mk 42 single guns, mounted in pairs on sponsons, both sides, forward and aft.

Operational: The INDEPENDENCE was last homeported in Yokosuka, Japan, having replaced the MIDWAY as the only U.S. aircraft carrier based overseas. The INDEPENDENCE arrived at Yokosuka on 11 September 1991, after trading air wings with the MIDWAY at Pearl Harbor on 15 July 1991. In turn, the INDEPENDENCE was replaced by the KITTY HAWK.

Table 13-2. POST-WORLD WAR II AIRCRAFT CARRIERS

Number	Name	Comm.	Notes
	MIDWAY class (3)		
CVB 41	MIDWAY	1945	decomm. 11 Apr 1992; str. 17 Mar 1997
CVB 42	FRANKLIN D. ROOSEVELT	1945	stricken 1972
CVB 43	CORAL SEA	1947	decomm./str. 30 April 1990
CVB 44	(unnamed)		canceled 1943
CVB 56, 57	(unnamed)		canceled 1945
	UNITED STATES class[15]		
CVA 58	UNITED STATES		canceled 1949
CVA 59–62	FORRESTAL class		
CVA 63, 64	KITTY HAWK class		
CVAN 65	ENTERPRISE		
CVA 66	KITTY HAWK class (cont.)		
CVA 67	JOHN F. KENNEDY		
CVN 68	NIMITZ class		

The three war-built ships of the MIDWAY class were completed as "large" carriers (CVB), changed to attack carriers (CVA) in 1952, and then to multipurpose carriers (CV) in 1975. They were prominent ships in U.S. Cold War operations. Three additional MIDWAY-class carriers were canceled in 1945. The CV 45–55 were canceled ships of the ESSEX (CV 9) class. (See 16th Edition/pages 103–4 for MIDWAY-class characteristics.)

The MIDWAY was the last World War II-era warship in commission in the U.S. Navy. She was based at Yokosuka, Japan, from 1973 until 1991, the first U.S. carrier ever to be based in a foreign country. (Another U.S. carrier was planned for homeporting in Pireaus, Greece, in the early 1970s, but that proposal was dropped because of problems within the Greek military government.)

The UNITED STATES was a "heavy" aircraft carrier (CVA); she was authorized in fiscal 1948 and laid down at Newport News Shipbuilding on 18 April 1949, but was canceled on 23 April 1949. Although never completed, her design was the progenitor of the FORRESTAL and subsequent large U.S. aircraft carriers. The ship was to have had a standard displacement of 65,000 tons and 80,000 tons full load. Four ships of this class of large carriers, intended primarily to operate nuclear strike aircraft, were planned, with the lead ship to be completed on 1 July 1952.

Several aircraft carriers are retained as memorials/museums; see Appendix D.

---

15 Most Navy planning documents of the time postulated four ships of this design.

The aircraft carrier MIDWAY, the longest-serving carrier in U.S. Navy history, is shown being maneuvered to her final resting place in San Diego. The ship will serve as both a museum and a memorial. Naval Air Station North Island, home port to several aircraft carriers, is in the background. (2004, U.S. Navy/Arlo K. Abrahamson)

The ENTERPRISE steams through the North Atlantic, participating in Operation Summer Pulse 2004—the simultaneous deployment of seven carrier strike groups. This was the first major deployment under the so-called Fleet Response Plan, which seeks to replace standard fleet deployments with more flexible capabilities. (2004, U.S. Navy/Joshua Kinter)

CHAPTER 14

Battleships

Manned but definitely not ready for sea: Sailors from the carrier THEODORE ROOSEVELT (CVN 71) man the rails of the battleship WISCONSIN during her 60th anniversary commemoration at Norfolk, Virginia. Although still on the Naval Vessel Register, the ship is unsuitable for reactivation. (2004, U.S. Navy/Aaron Burden)

The Navy retains two battleships in reserve, the IOWA and the WISCONSIN. They currently are scheduled to be stricken from the Naval Vessel Register (NVR) in 2007.

The two battleships have been retained by congressional edict, driven by the pleas of individuals and members of Congress who believe the dreadnoughts, built with 1930s technology, can have a role in the 21st century.

The battleship era in the U.S. Navy was thought to have ended on 12 January 1995, when the four ships of the IOWA class were stricken from the NVR. Those four ships had been the world's last operational battleships, all having been returned to active service during the Reagan administration as part of the buildup to a 600-ship fleet under the leadership of Secretary of the Navy John Lehman.

The 1995 decision to strike the four ships came after the Navy's senior officers realized there was no practical role for the ships in future naval operations, while the cost and problems of reactivating the 57,700-ton warships were considered prohibitive. The official strike notice declared they were being disposed of "due to the expenditure necessary to ensure continued, reliable service; the costs of which would be disproportionate to the ships' value."[1]

But the battleship advocates mobilized and took up arms, ably abetted by several "air power" advocates. This strange alliance came about as both groups opposed the development of the Arsenal Ship, advocated in the early 1990s by then–Chief of Naval Operations Admiral Jeremy M. (Mike) Boorda. The Arsenal Ship gave promise of providing effective long-range strike and support for troops ashore, a role earlier fulfilled by battleships. For their part, air power advocates saw the Arsenal Ship's strike missiles as competition for manned strategic bombers. (See Appendix E.)

As a result of a campaign in the press and letters to Congress, on 29 June 1995, the Senate Armed Services Committee voted 17 to 3 to direct the Navy to retain the two Iowa-class battleships in best condition in mothballs on the NVR. The language of the Senate amendment to the Fiscal Year (FY) 1996 defense authorization act directed: "The Secretary of the Navy shall list on the Naval Vessel Register, and maintain on such register, at least two of the Iowa class battleships that were stricken from the register in February [sic] 1995."

Further, the amendment proposed that the Secretary maintain two Iowas until the Navy had an "operational surface fire support capability that equals or exceeds the fire support capability that the Iowa class battleships . . . would, if in active service, be able to provide for Marine Corps amphibious assaults and operations ashore." The Senate report of 8 July 1995 also observed that the four battleships were the Navy's "only remaining potential source of around-the-clock accurate, high-volume, heavy fire support."

Significantly, the leadership of the Marine Corps did not make strong protests when the battleships were stricken, nor were they particularly vocal in supporting retention of the ships.

The Navy did not reinstate the two ships until 30 December 1997, when, under congressional pressure, a memo to do so was promulgated, signed by Chief of Naval Operations Admiral Jay Johnson on 21 January 1998, and by Secretary of the Navy John H. Dalton on 12 February 1998.

Thus, two dreadnoughts are back in the Navy. Navy–Marine Corps planning for future amphibious assaults—there has not been an opposed landing by U.S. Marines since Inchon, Korea, in September 1950—calls for assault forces to be launched from over the horizon, from as far as 50 nm (92.65 km) to perhaps 25 nm (46.3 km) offshore. The availability of helicopters, the MV-22 Osprey, and the Air-Cushion Landing Craft (LCAC) permit the longer assault ranges. In addition, there is an increased threat to ships operating closer inshore from mines and anti-ship missiles, the latter launched from shore cover.

An Iowa-class battleship's 16-inch (406-mm) guns have a maximum range of 27 nm (50 km). This range makes the battleship irrelevant for gunfire support unless she can be brought close inshore. In view of the damage sustained by a U.S. helicopter carrier and Aegis cruiser from mines in the 1991 Gulf War, and the

two cruise missiles fired against a battleship in that conflict, naval commanders should be reluctant to bring such "high-value" and high-visibility targets close inshore. Even steaming a few miles offshore, the battleship's guns could be irrelevant, as current amphibious doctrine calls for using helicopters and MV-22s to land assault troops far inshore, away from coastal defenses and closer to their objectives. Programs considered in the late 1980s to develop extended-range munitions for the battleships' 16-inch guns have not been pursued.

Naval surface fire support is discussed in Chapter 31.

Battleships reactivated in the 1980s each carried 32 Tomahawk missiles, but a modified destroyer of the SPRUANCE (DD 963) class, while retaining all other weapons and systems, could carry 61 vertical-launch missiles for land attack.

The other problem with the battleships is the cost of reactivating and operating them. During the Reagan administration, the cost of reactivating the four ships totaled some $1.66 billion. The estimated cost in 1999 of bringing back two ships was about $650 million, according to official statements, but such numbers appear too low in comparison with the 1980s reactivation costs.[2]

Reactivation/modernization of the battleships would take 18–24 months, assuming shipyard facilities were available. In addition, the ships would have to be provided with modern (compatible) radars, electronic countermeasures, communications, and other equipment, which may or may not be readily available.

Finding a crew could be even more difficult. Currently, there are no U.S. Navy personnel qualified in the 16-inch or the 5-inch/38-cal guns, the Mk 13 fire control systems, 600-pound steam plants, or many of the other systems fitted in the battleships. Each ship would require a crew of some 1,600 men (and women, if funds were available for modifying berthing quarters). Additional crewmen in training, transit, and other assignments would push the total manning requirements for two battleships to about 3,500—enough personnel to operate about ten modern missile destroyers.

Once reactivated, up to six months of at-sea crew training would be necessary for the battleships to be ready for combat. Thus, the Iowa and Wisconsin could take approximately two years from the order being given until they would be available to the fleet.

Classification: The U.S. Navy's first two steel battleships, the Texas and the Maine (both completed in 1895), were not assigned hull numbers. The U.S. Navy classification scheme of 1920 established the designation BB for battleships, with ships in existence at that time being so designated. The Indiana (also completed in 1895) became BB 1.

The Iowa class reached hull number BB 66 (the canceled Kentucky). The subsequent, never-started Montana class was assigned hull numbers BB 67–71.

---

1 Vice Adm. W. A. Earner, USN, Deputy Chief of Naval Operations (Logistics), letter to Secretary of the Navy, subject: "Striking of Iowa Class Battleships," 5 January 1995. Secretary of the Navy John H. Dalton approved the recommendation to dispose of the ships on 12 January 1995.
2 Statement of Secretary of the Navy Richard Danzig to Congress, 26 March 1999; the statement estimated the cost of reactivating the Iowa at $221,300,000 and the Wisconsin $430,000,000.

2 BATTLESHIPS: "IOWA" CLASS

Number	Name	Builder	Laid Down	Launched	Comm.	Status
BB 61	Iowa	New York Navy Yard, Brooklyn, N.Y.	27 June 1940	27 Aug 1942	22 Feb 1943	AR; decomm. 26 Oct 1990
BB 62	New Jersey	Philadelphia Navy Yard, Pa.	16 Sep 1940	7 Dec 1942	23 May 1943	decomm. 8 Feb 1991; str. 4 Jan 1999
BB 63	Missouri	New York Navy Yard, Brooklyn, N.Y.	6 Jan 1941	29 Jan 1944	11 June 1944	decomm. 31 Mar 1992; str. 12 Jan 1995
BB 64	Wisconsin	Philadelphia Navy Yard, Pa.	25 Jan 1941	7 Dec 1943	16 Apr 1944	AR; decomm. 30 Sep 1991

Displacement:	48,425 tons standard		Guns:	9 16-inch (406-mm) 50-cal Mk 7 (3 triple)
	57,350 tons full load			12 5-inch (127 mm) 38-cal DP Mk 28 (6 twin)
Length:	860 feet (262.3 m) waterline			4 20-mm Phalanx CIWS Mk 16 (4 multibarrel)
	887¼ feet (270.6 m) overall		Radars:	LN-66 navigation in BB 61
Beam:	108 ⅛ feet (33.0 m)			SPS-49 air search
Draft:	38 feet (11.6 m)			SPS-64(V) in BB 64
Propulsion:	4 steam turbines (General Electric in BB 61;			SPS-67 surface search
	Westinghouse in BB 64); 212,000 shp; 4 shafts		Sonars:	none
Boilers:	8 600 psi (41.7 kg/cm2)(Babcock & Wilcox)		Fire control:	4 Mk 37 GFCS with Mk 25 radar
Speed:	33 knots (see *Engineering* notes)			2 Mk 38 gun directors with Mk 13 radar
Range:	15,000 nm (27,780 km) at 15 knots			1 Mk 40 gun director with Mk 26 radar
Personnel:	approx. 1,570 (70 officers + 1,500 enlisted)			1 SQQ-9 in BB 61
Marines:	55 (2 officers + 53 enlisted)		EW systems:	SLQ-25 Nixie torpedo countermeasures
Helicopters:	landing area			SLQ-32(V)3
Missiles:	16 Harpoon SSM (4 quad canisters Mk 141)			
	32 Tomahawk TASM/TLAM (8 quad ABL Mk 143)			

The Iowa and Wisconsin are the world's only battleships remaining in naval service, albeit laid up in reserve. Originally a class of four ships, all were modernized and recommissioned as part of the naval buildup under the Reagan administration.

The recommissioning of the Wisconsin in 1988 marked the first time all four battleships had been in commission since 1955. All have since been retired; when they were stricken from the NVR on 12 January 1995, it was the first time since 1895 that there were no battleships in the U.S. Navy. Congress subsequently forced the Navy to reinstate two ships, and on 12 February 1998, the New Jersey and Wisconsin were reinstated on the NVR. However, because of interest by the New Jersey congressional delegation in making the New Jersey a memorial/museum, she was again stricken on 4 January 1999, with the Iowa reinstated in her place on the same date. This was done despite damage to the Iowa's No. 2 16-inch turret (it was inoperative) and the additional time and cost that would be required to reactive that ship.

The above data reflect the state of the Iowa and Wisconsin at the time of their decommissioning in 1990–1991.

The Iowa initially was in mothballs at Newport, Rhode Island. She was towed to Suisun Bay, California, near San Francisco, pending possible emplacement at that city as a museum. The Wisconsin is at Norfolk, Virginia, and although listed as a reserve "mobilization asset" while on the NVR, she already has become a museum ship, open to the pubic, as part of the Nauticus Museum complex. The Missouri is a memorial at Pearl Harbor, moored next to the remains of the sunken battleship Arizona (BB 39). She was opened to the public on the 55th anniversary of her launching, 29 January 1999. The New Jersey is moored as a museum at Camden, New Jersey. Some battleship supporters had wanted her permanently anchored off the Statue of Liberty in New York Harbor, in effect making her part of that national monument. However, the organization sponsoring the ship decided Bayonne would be a better location. This led advocates for placing the ship at Camden to fire a legal salvo for possession of the ship, and the New Jersey subsequently was sent to Camden.

There are several other "modern" battleships and one dreadnought-era battleship preserved in the United States (see Appendix D). Only one foreign steel battleship is preserved, the Japanese pre-dreadnought Mikasa (completed in 1902) at Yokosuka.

Aircraft: These ships were built with two rotating stern catapults and an aircraft crane for handing floatplanes. Three aircraft normally were embarked for scouting and gunfire spotting. The catapults were beached during the Korean War and the ships were assigned utility helicopters. During the Vietnam War, the New Jersey also flew QH-50C "snoopy dash" drones for gunfire spotting.

The Iowa deployed in 1987 with five Pioneer surveillance drones (with a control system that included the radome mounted on the second funnel). The other three later were fitted to operate the Pioneer, with the Missouri and Wisconsin flying the drones for gunfire spotting during the 1991 Gulf War.

One or two utility helicopters normally are embarked. No elevators or aircraft support facilities are provided.

Class: Completed in 1943–1944, the Iowas were the world's last battleships to be built, although two ships under construction in the same period were completed after World War II, the British Vanguard (laid down in 1941 and completed in 1946) and the French Jean Bart (laid down in 1939 and completed in 1952).

The U.S. dreadnoughts were exceeded in size and firepower only by the Japanese sister ships Yamato and Musashi, both completed and sunk during World War II. Those ships displaced some 70,000 tons full load and had a main battery of nine 18.1-inch (460-mm) guns. (Both were sunk by U.S. carrier-based aircraft.)

The U.S. Navy originally ordered six ships of the Iowa class. However, the Illinois (BB 65) was canceled on 11 August 1945 when 22 percent complete; and construction of the Kentucky (BB 66) was suspended on 17 February 1947 when 72.1 percent complete. The Kentucky was canceled on 22 January 1950 (although the hull was not stricken from the NVR until 9 June 1958). In the early 1950s, the Navy intended to complete the Kentucky as a guided missile ship carrying the Terrier missile system, but no work was undertaken on that project.

In the post–World War II period, there were occasional proposals to recommission the Iowas, as well as to convert/modify them for such specialized roles as guided missile ships (anti-air warfare [AAW] role with Terrier/Talos missiles), fleet command ships, ballistic missile monitors (carrying Polaris submarine-launched ballistic missiles), and commando/assault ships.

Five larger battleships of the Montana class (BB 67–71) were ordered on 9 September 1940, but none was laid down, and the program was canceled on 21 July 1943. They were to have mounted four triple 16-inch gun turrets, displace 58,000 tons standard, and be 903 feet (275.3 m) long. Construction of the Midway (CVB 41)-class aircraft carriers and other priority naval construction programs, as well as the ascendancy of carrier-based aircraft over the battleship gun, brought about the end of the Montana class.

There was speculative press mention of a "super Montana" class of some 80,000 tons mounting 20-inch (508-mm) guns with the hull numbers BB 72–78; in fact, no battleships beyond the MONTANAS were formally considered by the U.S. Navy.

Design: The design of these ships was constrained by the requirement to transit the Panama Canal (its lock width is 110 feet/33.5 m).

Armor protection was intended to protect vital areas of the ship from enemy shells fired by guns up to 16 inches. The Class A steel armor belt tapers vertically from 307 mm to 41 mm. There is a lower armor belt of 343 mm aft of the No. 3 main battery turret to protect the propeller shafts (within the hull). Turret faces have 432 mm of armor, turret tops 184 mm, turret backs 305 mm, barbettes up to 295 mm, second armor deck 152 mm, conning tower sides 439 mm, and conning tower top 184 mm.

Electronics: During their 1980s reactivation, the ships were fitted with a cruiser (CG/CGN) communications suite; the WISCONSIN had the most-capable communications suite of the four ships. However, they lacked the Naval Tactical Data System (NTDS), except for the Link 11 receiver, and certain other electronic features of modern surface combatants.

Engineering: All of these ships achieved 35 knots in service.

Guns: As built during World War II, in addition to the main battery of nine 16-inch guns, these ships carried 20 5-inch/38-cal guns (twin), up to 80 40-mm AA guns (quad), and almost 60 20-mm anti-aircraft (AA) guns (twin and single). The 20-mm weapons were removed after the war, and the number of 40-mm guns was successively reduced. (The NEW JERSEY carried only nine 16-inch and 20 5-inch guns during her brief Vietnam reactivation.)

Postwar plans to provide twin 3-inch/50-cal AA mounts in place of the quad 40-mm mounts were abandoned.

Four of the original ten 5-inch/38-cal twin gun mounts were removed during the ships' 1980s reactivation. Four Phalanx Gatling-type guns also were provided for anti-ship missile defense.

Missiles: During the 1970s, there was a proposal to provide the IOWAS with the Aegis/SPY-1 AAW weapon system. However, it was written off as too costly and was not reconsidered when the ships were recommissioned in the early 1980s. When reactivation plans were being prepared in the 1980s, the Navy intended to fit the Sea Sparrow Point Defense Missile System (PDMS). However, it was determined the system could not withstand the overpressure when the 16-inch guns were fired.

Modernization: When reactivated, these ships underwent a limited modernization, including installation of updated communications and radar equipment and sewage holding tanks and habitability features. The defensive Phalanx Close-in Weapon System as well as Harpoon and Tomahawk offensive missiles were fitted.

A Phase II modernization was to have included additional Tomahawks fired from vertical launchers, removal of the after 16-inch gun turret, and other upgrades. This proposal was dropped in 1983. (Also proposed was fitting a flight deck aft for Vertical/Short Take-Off and Landing [VSTOL] aircraft operations.)

There have been several proposals to fit these ships as numbered fleet flagships, but they have not been so modified or employed.

The IOWA and WISCONSIN were modernized at the Avondale and Litton/Ingalls shipyards.

Operational: All four ships of the class saw extensive combat in the later stages of World War II, mainly as AAW defense ships for fast carriers; in the Korean War (1950–1953), they served primarily as shore bombardment ships. They also served as fleet and force flagships in those conflicts.

The MISSOURI, named for the home state of President Harry S. Truman, was the scene of the Japanese surrender ceremony in Tokyo Bay on 2 September 1945, officially marking the end of World War II. Three ships were mothballed after the war, and the MISSOURI was retained in partial commission as a training ship.

The NEW JERSEY arriving at Philadelphia, pending her move to Camden, New Jersey, for permanent mooring. The battleship was at Bremerton, Washington, when the political decision was made to make her a memorial–museum ship in New Jersey, necessitating towing her through the Panama Canal to the East Coast—at taxpayers' expense. (1999, U.S. Navy/John F. Williams)

During her 1968–1969 reactivation for the Vietnam War, the NEW JERSEY made one deployment to the Western Pacific. She was on the "gun line" off South Vietnam for 120 days, during which time she fired 5,688 rounds of 16-inch ammunition and 14,891 5-inch rounds. (The NEW JERSEY fired a total of 6,200 main-battery rounds in her 1968–1969 commission, including test and training; by comparison, she fired 771 rounds from 1943 to 1948, and 6,671 during her participation in the Korean War and midshipmen cruises from 1950 to 1957.)

The NEW JERSEY deployed to the Western Pacific in June 1983, but shortly after her arrival in the Far East she was ordered to stand off Central America, and on 12 September 1983, she transited the Panama Canal into the Caribbean. Later that month she made a hurried trip across the Atlantic to operate off the coast of war-torn Lebanon. The NEW JERSEY fired her 16-inch guns against shore targets near Beirut for the first time on 14 December 1983.

The IOWA suffered an explosion in her No. 2 16-inch gun turret on 19 April 1989, while operating some 330 nm (610 km) off Puerto Rico. One officer and 46 enlisted men in the turret and below-deck projectile-handling spaces were killed in the explosion and flash fire; 11 sailors in lower powder magazines escaped without harm, and those spaces were partially flooded to prevent a powder explosion, which most likely would have destroyed the ship. The damaged gun—center gun of No. 2 turret—was not repaired before the ship was mothballed.

The Navy's investigations concluded the most probable cause of the disaster was a sabotage–suicide effort by a sailor in the turret. However, subsequent investigation, mainly by Sandia National Laboratories, concluded the "foreign materials" the Navy had found in the damaged turret were normal to battleship turrets, and that the powder bags had been overrammed against the projectile, making them overly sensitive. This led to an official Navy apology to the family of the sailor who had been implicated.

The parts needed to rehabilitate the IOWA's No. 2 turret have been procured, with the cost of the repairs estimated at about $8 million. The ships' other guns are in good condition. (Barrel relining generally is needed after firing some 1,500 rounds per barrel.) There are plenty of shells and powder available: three "shipfills" per ship (i.e., 1,280 16-inch rounds) plus powder, and enough ammunition for two years of training.

The WISCONSIN and MISSOURI participated in Operation Desert Storm in January–February 1991. Operating in the Persian Gulf,

the MISSOURI fired 759 16-inch rounds and launched 28 Tomahawk cruise missiles, and the WISCONSIN fired 319 16-inch rounds and launched 24 missiles. (Thus, 18 percent of the 288 Tomahawks launched in the conflict were from the two battleships.)

During their 1980s reactivation period, the four battleships fired the following numbers of 16-inch rounds (Desert Storm included):

IOWA	2,034
NEW JERSEY	2,983
MISSOURI	2,602
WISCONSIN	1,408

The last ship to decommission, the MISSOURI, was present at Pearl Harbor on 7 December 1991 to help commemorate the 50th anniversary of the Japanese attack that caused U.S. entry into World War II. Subsequently, she steamed into the Long Beach Naval Shipyard (California) on 21 December 1991 for deactivation. She was decommissioned there on 31 March 1992 and then towed to the Bremerton Naval Shipyard (Washington) for storage until the decision was made by the Secretary of the Navy to permanently moor her at Pearl Harbor.

Personnel: The NEW JERSEY recommissioning in 1982 marked the first time that Marines had served in a U.S. battleship since the Korean War. The World War II manning of this class was 2,500–2,900 men per ship.

Table 14-1. "IOWA" CLASS ACTIVE SERVICE

Number	Name	World War II	Korean War	Vietnam War	600-Ship Fleet
BB 61	IOWA	22 Feb 1943–24 Mar 1949	25 Aug 1951–24 Feb 1958	—	28 Apr 1984–26 Oct 1990
BB 62	NEW JERSEY	23 May 1943–30 June 1948	21 Nov 1950–21 Aug 1957	6 Apr 1968–17 Dec 1969	28 Dec 1982–8 Feb 1991
BB 63	MISSOURI	11 June 1944 ◄————————► 26 Feb 1955		—	10 May 1986–31 Mar 1992
BB 64	WISCONSIN	16 Apr 1944–1 July 1948	3 Mar 1951–8 Mar 1958	—	22 Oct 1988–30 Sep 1991

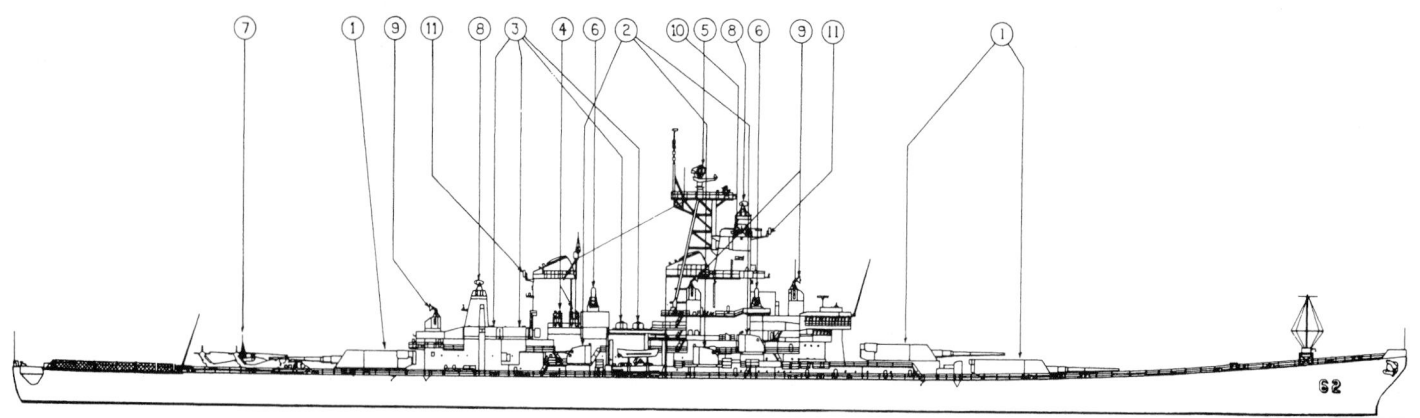

Battleship NEW JERSEY
1. 16-inch triple gun turret (3) 2. 5-inch twin gun mounts (6) 3. Tomahawk quad box launcher (8) 4. Harpoon quad canister launcher (4) 5. SPS-49(V)5 air search radar 6. Phalanx CIWS (4) 7. Helicopter landing and parking areas 8. Mk 38 gunfire control radar (2) 9. Mk 37 gunfire control radar (4) 10. SLQ-32 (V3) electronic countermeasures (2) 11. OE-28 antenna for WSC-3 satellite communications (2) Note: The drawing omits the unmanned aerial vehicle control radome antenna atop the after funnel and the SPQ-9A gunfire control radar above the upper bridge. (A. D. Baker III)

The dreadnought MISSOURI, moored at Ford Island in Pearl Harbor, Hawaii. The "Mighty Mo" is moored in "battleship row," immediately aft of the USS ARIZONA (BB 39) memorial. The MISSOURI and WISCONSIN are considered in the best material condition of the four IOWA-class ships. (2003, U.S. Navy/Yesenia Rosas)

The Iowa *moored at Newport, Rhode Island, with the carrier* Forrestal *(CV 59). There are drives by several communities around the United States to preserve virtually all available battleships and aircraft carriers as museums–memorials. Although impressive, battleships are dwarfed by aircraft carriers, as well as by maritime prepositioning ships. (1999)*

The plan arrangement of the Wisconsin *is evident as she enters the Norfolk Naval Shipyard (Portsmouth), Virginia, before being moored at the Nauticus maritime center in downtown Norfolk. The site of her permanent mooring, opposed by many residents, makes her the dominate feature of the Norfolk skyline. (1995, U.S. Navy/Robert J. Sitar)*

The Missouri *entering Pearl Harbor, Hawaii, at the end of her final voyage. All four* Iowa*-class battleships will become museums–memorials. They will bring to eight the number of battleships preserved in the United States, not including the remains of the* Arizona *(BB 39) and* Utah *(BB 31/AG 16) at Pearl Harbor. (1998, U.S. Navy/Kerry Baker)*

CHAPTER 15

Cruisers and Destroyers

With most of her crew manning the rail, the Aegis cruiser THOMAS S. GATES gets under way from Pascagoula, Mississippi. Cruisers and destroyers are highly capable and highly versatile warships, which the Navy is struggling to adapt for conflicts in littoral waters and to support operations ashore beyond missile strikes. (2004, U.S. Navy/Stacey Byington)

The U.S. Navy currently has an approved force level of 116 major surface combatants—cruisers, destroyers, and frigates. As of early 2005, however, the Navy had 26 cruisers and 51 destroyers in active service in addition to frigates. Two ex-destroyers are employed as test-and-development ships (see Chapter 25). The frigate force, which is shrinking rapidly, is described in Chapter 16.

The improved ARLEIGH BURKE class is in series production—the only major surface combatant under construction for the U.S. Navy

when this edition went to press, although the first of a new class of destroyers, designated DD(X), is in development. The DD(X), with a full load displacement of some 14,000 tons, should properly be classified as a cruiser. It is significantly larger than the TICONDEROGA class, the only ships now in U.S. service classified as cruisers.[1]

---

1 The TICONDEROGAS originally were classified as destroyers, beginning with DD 47.

The so-called Land Attack Destroyer (DD 21)—part of the Surface Combatant (SC) 21 program of the early 1990s—has been canceled. The lead ship, named for the late Admiral Elmo R. Zumwalt, had not yet been ordered when the entire program was terminated, a decision made primarily for political reasons, as the program was considered too closely related to the Clinton administration.

The SC 21 program envisioned a family of warships ranging in size from an austere, 4,000-ton frigate-sized Sea Dominance combatant to a large, 20,000-ton, "high-end," multimission Power Projection Ship, which evolved into the DD 21. Two other concepts were for a Large Capacity Missile Ship that, at some 20,000 tons, would perform arsenal-ship, land-attack, and strike tasks in direct support of forces ashore, and a 10,000-ton New Design Full Capacity Combatant to replace the TICONDEROGA-class cruisers and, eventually, the ARLEIGH BURKE-class destroyers.

The DD 21 was partially reborn in the DD(X) program, a much less ambitious effort with respect to firepower and the scope of the program (see below).

Meanwhile, older cruisers and destroyers are being retired far short of their predicted 30-year service lives: the four KIDD-class DDGs and most of the SPRUANCE-class DDs now have been stricken. The latter ships fitted with 61-cell Vertical Launching Systems (VLS) were particularly valuable as they had two 5-inch guns and could embark (and hangar) two SH-60B Seahawk helicopters. Although lacking the Aegis anti-air systems of the 28 early ARLEIGH BURKE-class destroyers, their large Tomahawk battery, 5-inch guns, and Anti-Submarine Warfare (ASW) systems (i.e., two helicopters) provided superior capabilities.

In addition, the first five TICONDEROGA-class Aegis cruisers, armed with two Mk 26 missile systems (88 missiles) rather than VLS (122 missiles), are being retired in 2004–2006. (Taiwan has expressed great interest in obtaining some of these ships.)

The roles and to some degree the configurations of cruisers and destroyers are essentially the same. The blurring of lines between the two categories can be seen in the TICONDEROGAS having the same hull and propulsion plant and some of the same combat systems as the destroyers of the SPRUANCE and KIDD classes, and essentially the same anti-air system as the ARLEIGH BURKE class. The term "cruiser" now indicates the ship is commanded by a captain (rather than a commander, as are destroyers).[2]

U.S. cruisers and destroyers currently have two principal roles: (1) defending surface naval forces, and (2) strikes against shore targets. These roles will be expanded with the Theater Ballistic Missile Defense (TBMD) and possibly National Missile Defense (NMD) capabilities being provided to some TICONDEROGA-class ships and a planned CG(X) cruiser class.

All U.S. guided missile cruisers (CG) and destroyers (DDG) now in service, except for the early ships of the TICONDEROGA class, are fitted with VLS missiles, providing considerable weapons flexibility and firepower. Further, all CG/DDG ships have the Aegis/SPY-1 radar and weapons control system.

---

2 Three other navies now have warships rated as cruisers in their active fleets: Italy has the VITTORIO VENETO (9,500 tons); Russia has one nuclear-propelled KIROV-class ship (approximately 26,000 tons), with three additional units laid up, and three SLAVA-class ships (11,280 tons); and Peru has the ALMIRANTE GRAU (12,165 tons), a former Dutch ship. Ukraine has an unfinished SLAVA-class cruiser, reported to be about 94 percent complete. No nation is currently building cruisers.

The Aegis destroyer HIGGINS fires a Standard SM-2 surface-to-air missile during a fleet exercise. Aegis cruisers and destroyers have the most potent anti-air/missile capability of any land- or sea-based system. Aegis now is being expanded to provide a ballistic missile intercept capability. (2002, U.S. Navy/Rebecca J. Moat)

The Aegis cruiser VELLA GULF heels to port while making a tight turn during operations in the Mediterranean Sea. The Aegis cruisers were built on SPRUANCE-class destroyer hulls, an astute transformation effort that placed Aegis in the fleet long before it could have been operational under other options. (2004, U.S. Navy/Jason R. Zalasky)

The only U.S. cruisers now in active commission are the TICONDEROGA class, which originally were designated as destroyers. In most respects, these ships are the most capable surface combatants afloat today. Their Aegis combat system is undoubtedly the best anti-air missile system in service with any navy, and the ships also have the most capable ASW suite available in the U.S. Navy, the same as in the SPRUANCE-class destroyers.

The 18 conventional cruisers of the LEAHY and BELKNAP classes have been discarded. Those ships, graceful in appearance and capable warships for their time, were decommissioned with the end of the Cold War (as were the Navy's nuclear-propelled cruisers; see below). Their lack of Aegis/VLS and high maintenance requirements made them obvious candidates for rapid disposal.

Builders: All U.S. cruisers and destroyers now in service were built by Bath Iron Works in Maine, now owned by General Dynamics, and Litton's Ingalls Shipbuilding yard at Pascagoula, Mississippi, now owned by Northrop Grumman. The keel-laying dates for the Ingalls-built ships mark the start of erection of the first module on the horizontal building position at the yard; the ships are lowered into the water on a floating dock (launching) and are formally christened at later dates.

Guns: All active cruisers and destroyers have 5-inch (127-mm) guns. No "gun ships" remain in commission; the last two heavy cruisers (CA), armed with 8-inch (203-mm) guns, have been stricken. At the start of the battleship recommissioning program in the early 1980s, there were proposals to reactivate the two surviving heavy cruisers, the DES MOINES (CA 134) and SALEM (CA 139), instead of or in addition to the battleships. The Navy rejected those proposals, preferring the larger guns of the more-impressive IOWA (BB 61)-class dreadnoughts. (The two mothballed heavy cruisers were stricken on 9 July 1991 and 12 July 1991, respectively.)

A 15-inch/62-cal Mk 45 Mod 4 gun with a longer range and fitted for firing advanced munitions is now being installed on Improved ARLEIGH BURKE-class destroyers; the DD(X) will have the more-capable 155-mm Advanced Gun System (AGS). The latter weapon replaces the 175-mm gun and Vertical-Launch Gun (VLG) at one point planned for the DD 21 class. The 8-inch (203-mm) Major Caliber Lightweight Gun (MCLWG), at one time proposed for the entire SPRUANCE class, was terminated. The MCLWG was evaluated successfully ashore and at sea in the destroyer HULL in 1975–1979.

In the offing is an electromagnetic rail gun suitable for surface combatants with electric drive, as the planned DD(X) (see Chapter 30).

Beginning in the 1980s, cruisers have been fitted with .50-cal machine guns and Mk 38 25-mm Bushmaster "chain" guns for close-in defense against small craft. This armament is especially important for ships deploying into the Persian Gulf area. The weapons are sometimes shifted from ship to ship as they forward deploy; accordingly, they are not listed under the specific class entries.

Engineering: All U.S. cruisers and destroyers have aircraft-type gas turbine propulsion. The planned DD(X) will have electric drive with gas turbine prime movers.

Names: U.S. cruisers traditionally had been named for major U.S. cities, with the exception of the CANBERRA (CA 70, later CAG 2), which was named for an Australian cruiser sunk in 1942 while operating with U.S. forces. From 1971 to 1978, six cruisers (DLGN/CGN 36–41) were assigned state names. From 1981, cruisers have been named for famous U.S. battles, although even this scheme was corrupted when the CG 51 was named for a deceased Secretary of the Navy and Secretary of Defense.

U.S. destroyers traditionally have been named for naval heroes and leaders, including deceased Secretaries of the Navy, admirals, and inventors. In 1998, the DDG 80 was named ROOSEVELT, honoring President Franklin D. Roosevelt and—to be politically correct—his wife, Eleanor. She is the first "first lady" to have a Navy ship named in her honor. (The 32nd president previously was honored by the carrier FRANKLIN D. ROOSEVELT/CVB 42, which was on the Naval Vessel Register from 1945 to 1972.)

In recent years, past presidents have been honored by aircraft carriers (CV/CVN) and strategic missile submarines (SSBN), plus one attack submarine, the JIMMY CARTER (SSN 23). Both the DDG 80 and SSN 23 were named by Secretary of the Navy John Dalton (1993–1998).

Operational: Three cruisers and three destroyers (as well as two frigates) are homeported in Yokosuka, Japan. They are part of the KITTY HAWK (CV 63) battle group.

Personnel: The numbers of officers and enlisted personnel assigned to ships within a given class vary slightly, based on modifications to the ship, equipment installed, etc. Average ship personnel within each class is provided below. Efforts are being made to reduce manning on all surface combatants, with some ships being employed as trial ships for more drastic reductions through "smart manning."

Table 15-1. CRUISER–DESTROYER FORCE LEVELS (EARLY 2005)

Number	Class/Ship	Comm.	Active	Building*	Reserve
CG 52	Improved TICONDEROGA	1986–1994	22	—	—
CG 47	TICONDEROGA	1983–1987	2	—	3
DDG 79	Improved ARLEIGH BURKE	2000–	16	18	—
DDG 51	ARLEIGH BURKE	1991–1999	28	—	—
DD 963	SPRUANCE	1975–1983	2	—	4

* Ships authorized through fiscal 2004.

AEGIS COMBAT SYSTEM

The Aegis combat system (Mk 7) is the Navy's primary anti-air/anti-missile warfare system, now provided in U.S. cruisers and destroyers and several Japanese and Spanish warships.[3] It is the most advanced anti-air system in existence, land-based or naval. During the development of Aegis, a National Security Council study identified "the high priority need of the U.S. Navy for adequate defense against an increasingly sophisticated Soviet anti-ship missile threat."[4] The study went on to report that "the deployment of the Aegis system would offset a primary deficiency in fleet capabilities."

The Aegis system includes the SPY-1 radar, Mk 99 fire control directors (which incorporate the SPG-62 radar), and related computers, displays, weapon control consoles, and power sources.

With conventional, rotating radar antennas, targets are "painted" once each rotation or scan to provide a single positional datum point. Several scans—perhaps requiring 10–30 seconds—are required to establish course, speed, altitude, and rate of change of the target. In the Aegis system, each of the four SPY-1 fixed antennas or arrays covers over 90° in azimuth from the horizon to zenith as the ship rolls up to 30° and pitches up to 10°. These arrays are about 12½ feet (3.8 m) across with 4,480 energy-radiating elements fixed into each antenna "face." Computers schedule

---

3 In Greek mythology Aegis was the name of the shield of Zeus.
4 Quoted in Rear Adm. Wayne E. Meyer, USN, and Capt. Bart Dalla Mura, USN, "Aegis," U.S. Naval Institute *Proceedings* (February 1977), p. 97. Adm. Meyer was head of the Aegis program from 1970 to 1983.

the pencil-like search beams from the Aegis arrays to seek out targets; when a beam dwells on a target, the computers schedule several additional beams against the target within a second of initial detection. Thus, a continuous track of the target can be established before a conventional radar antenna could complete a single rotation.

The SPY-1 accordingly functions as both a search radar and a fire control radar, alleviating the time and possible target track loss of a "handover" process between conventional radars. (See Chapter 31 for additional details.)

A land-based, partial prototype of the Aegis combat system was installed at the (then) RCA facility at Moorestown, New Jersey, and shipboard trials were conducted on the missile test ship NORTON SOUND (AVM 1, ex-AV 11).

The Aegis program office in the Naval Sea Systems Command has established its own classification of Aegis ships with variations known as "baselines." The following are the principal baseline characteristics; note that there are some system overlaps in the TICONDEROGA-class cruisers.

Baseline 0:
CG 47, 48   SPY-1A radar
              Mk 26 launchers
              UYK-7/UYK-20 computers
              SH-2F LAMPS I helicopter

Baseline 1:
CG 49–51   SPY-1A radar
              Mk 26 launchers
              UYK-7/UYK-20 computers
              SH-60B LAMPS III helicopter

Baseline 2:
CG 52–58   VLS/Tomahawk
              SQQ-89 ASW system

Baseline 3:
CG 59–64   SPY-1B radar
              improved communications
              Joint Tactical Information Distribution System
                (JTIDS)
              UYK-43 computers

Baseline 4:
CG 65–73   SPY-1B(V) radar
              SQS-53C sonar
              UYK-43/44 computers
DDG 51–67   SPY-1D radar
              SQQ-89(V)4 sonar suite
              UYK-43/44 computers

Baseline 5:
DDG 68–78   SPY-1D radar
              SLQ-32(V)3 EW suite
              SM-2 Block IV missile
              JTIDS (DDG 72–78 only)
              Combat Direction Finding (DF)

Baseline 6:
DDG 79–90   SPY-1D(V) littoral mod
              helicopter hangar
              Evolved Sea Sparrow Missile (ESSM)
              Theater Ballistic Missile Defense
              Cooperative Engagement Capability (CEC)
              UYK-70 displays

Baseline 7:
DDG 91–112   Tomahawk Fire Control System (FCS) upgrade
              Theater-Wide TBMD
              SQQ-89(V)14 or 15 sonar suite

The planned upgrade/conversion of Aegis cruisers CG 52–73 will provide a common baseline for all 22 ships. The first ship to be upgraded will be the CAPE ST. GEORGE.

Outside the U.S. Navy, Aegis has been installed in four Japanese destroyers of the KONGO class and is being fitted in four Spanish frigates of the ÁLVARDO DE BAZÁN class. The Japanese Maritime Self-Defense Force is planning a follow-on DDG class equipped with Aegis. In addition, in 2002, the South Korean Navy selected the Aegis system for its new KDX III-class DDGs.

Taiwan has sought to procure U.S.-built Aegis DDGs, but that request has been turned down by the U.S. government, primarily because of political pressure from China. Instead, Taiwan will receive the four KIDD-class DDGs.

History: Aegis evolved from the Typhon anti-aircraft combat system, development of which was begun in 1958 to defend against advanced Soviet aircraft and air-to-surface missiles. Typhon, however, was canceled in 1963 because of technical difficulties and the high cost of the system, which was intended for large, nuclear-propelled "frigates" (DLGN).[5]

The follow-on Advanced Surface Missile System (ASMS) made use of some Typhon technology and sought to use existing missiles—the Terrier, Tartar, and their descendent SM series. Although development was slower than expected, ASMS became the basis for the Aegis combat system, whose development formally began in December 1969.

BALLISTIC MISSILE DEFENSE

The United States formally withdrew from the Anti-Ballistic Missile (ABM) Treaty with Russia on 13 June 2002.[6] That same day, the cruiser LAKE ERIE conducted a test of the sea-based, midcourse Standard SM-3 missile, designed to intercept ballistic missiles midway in their trajectories. Cruisers and destroyers fitted with the Aegis combat system will have a major role in U.S. development of ballistic missile defense systems.

The proliferation of ballistic missile technology—with more than 20 nations now having some form of ballistic or cruise missiles—has sparked renewed interest in missile defense. In response, the Department of Defense is sponsoring the development of both Theater Air and Missile Defense (TAMD) and National Missile Defense (NMD) programs.

The emphasis in this weapons area is on TAMD systems to protect forward-deployed U.S. forces, as well as allied and friendly forces. The plan envisions time-phased acquisition of multitier, interoperable missile defense systems to provide in-depth defense against theater ballistic and cruise missiles. Within this program, the so-called lower-tier systems to defeat short-range ballistic missiles have the highest priority. The Navy's Area Defense System and the Army's Patriot Advanced Capability 3 (PAC-3) and are the principal lower-tier programs.[7] (The Air Force also is developing an

---

5 The missile test ship NORTON SOUND (AVM 1, ex-AV 11) was fitted with components of the Typhon system and, subsequently, with portions of the later Advanced Surface Missile System/Aegis combat system.

6 The ABM treaty, originally between the USSR and United States, limited the countries to two ABM sites, one at their respective capitals and one at a second site. The USSR fully deployed ABM systems around Moscow and Leningrad (St. Petersburg). The United States operated a Safeguard ABM system at Grand Forks, North Dakota, from 1 October 1975 until February 1976—133 days! (Some Safeguard radar was incorporated into the North American Air Defense Command's warning and assessment network).

7 The PAC-3 development effort suffered numerous failures and setbacks before scoring two successful intercepts of target missiles in 1999. Obviously, the program requires the development and deployment of new radars and fire control systems, and the establishment of new missile-defense units.

airborne laser defense program, with five long-endurance aircraft being proposed to provide two aircraft on 24-hour patrols in a theater; a modified Boeing 747-400 is laser platform.)

The Navy's area defense system will use a reconfigured SPY-1 radar and an upgraded version of the Standard Missile (SM-2 Block IV-A) in existing Aegis warships. This system promises to provide a high degree of effectiveness in detecting and intercepting ballistic and cruise missile threats in forward coastal areas. Low-rate initial production of Block IV-A missiles began in Fiscal Year (FY) 2000 to support development and operational testing prior to a limited operational capability being achieved in FY 2003.

Current planning provides for the procurement of 1,500 ship-launched Block IV-A missiles with a new infrared seeker, an adjunct forward-looking fuze, and an improved autopilot. Although the DDG 68 and later ships of the ARLEIGH BURKE class will be armed with this missile, Navy documents indicate that only the DDG 79–112 of this class (34 ships) will have a theater ballistic missile defense capability.

(A lower-tier program in development as a follow-on to the Pac-3 is the Medium Extended Air Defense System [MEADS] being pursued cooperatively with Germany and Italy. This is planned as a highly mobile missile defense system for use with ground troops. The use of components of the PAC-3 program is expected to reduce costs and development time. However, Congress denied the entire $48.5 million asked for by the Clinton administration in the FY 2000 budget request, apparently because of the lack of support by senior military officers.)

Upper-tier missile defense systems—the Terminal High-Altitude Area Defense (THAAD) and Navy Theater-Wide (NTW) systems—are intended to intercept incoming ballistic missiles at high altitudes, permitting the defense of larger areas. NTW builds on the Aegis combat system, as well as the Navy Area Defense system. Developmental testing of both THAAD and NTW is planned through 2001. The Navy tests include a specialized Aegis-controlled lightweight exoatmospheric projectile.

Both systems will be examined after tests, and based on that assessment, the Department of Defense will allocate resources. The objective will be to field an upper-tier defensive system between 2007 and 2010. (Deployment of such a system could force opponents to rely more on cruise missiles, forcing the deployment of a an extensive cruise missile defense system.)

In 1999, a proposal was put forward to give four TICONDEROGA-class ships an NTW capability consisting of an upgraded Aegis combat system with a high-powered discriminator radar, and 20 SM-3 versions of the Standard missile per ship. The plan provided for the initial test ship to become operation by 2006, and a fully operational ship to be available the following year. However, whether the Navy will assign ships as specialized missile defense ships is not clear. (In the late 1960s, the Navy proposed a Sea-Based Anti-Ballistic Missile Intercept System [SABMIS] with dedicated missile ships.[8])

The SM-3 is an evolved SM-2 Block IV-A booster and sustainer motor supplemented by a third-stage rocket motor and a fourth-stage kinetic kill vehicle. The kill vehicle is guided by an infrared focal plane array seeker.

The National Missile Defense program is in response to the possibility that in the future a rogue nation might possess Intercontinental Ballistic Missiles (ICBMs) that could threaten the United States. This possibility, according to the Secretary of Defense, was underscored by the August 1998 attempt by North Korea to launch a satellite on a Taepo Dong 1 (TD-1) missile.[9] The test, which demonstrated some important aspects of ICBM development, most notably multistage separation, also indicated North Korea's continued interest in developing a long-range missile capa-

bility. While the U.S. intelligence community expected a TD-1 launch for some time, it did not anticipate that the missile would have a third stage or that it would be used to attempt to place a satellite in orbit. And, of course, in 2003 the North Korean regime announced that, despite earlier multinational agreements, it was proceeding with the development of nuclear weapons.

Accordingly, an NMD program is being funded for research and development. On 29 June 1999, President Bill Clinton signed the National Missile Defense Act, which makes it U.S. policy to deploy an NMD system as soon as it becomes technologically feasible. The system being developed would have as its primary mission the defense of the United States—all 50 states—against a small number of intercontinental missiles. It would not be capable of defending against a large-scale missile attack.

An initial operational capability is proposed for FY 2003. The Department of Defense official in charge of NMD has said it would be unlikely for a sea-based system using the SM-3 missile to be at sea before 2010 or 2011, adding, "The most practical and effective NMD role for a Navy Theater-Wide system would be to supplement land-based NMD."[10] The NMD most likely would be a land- or space-based system. The Air Force has proposed a space-based laser system for this role.

COOPERATIVE ENGAGEMENT CAPABILITY

The Cooperative Engagement Capability (CEC) is a program to improve battle group Anti-Air Warfare (AAW) and Theater Air Defense (TAD) capabilities by integrating the radar data of several ships and aircraft into a single, real-time, fire-control-quality composite track picture available to all participating ships and aircraft. By simultaneously distributing multiple platforms' radar data on airborne threats to each ship within the battle group, CEC extends the range at which a ship can engage hostile missiles to well beyond the radar horizon, significantly improving area, local, and self-defense capabilities. Operating under the direction of a designated commander, CEC will enable a battle group or joint force to act as a single defensive combat system.

The initial CEC operational capability was declared in FY 1996 after a series of tests involving the Aegis cruisers ANZIO and CAPE ST. GEORGE, the aircraft carrier ENTERPRISE (CVN 65), the amphibious assault ship WASP (LHD 1), and P-3C Orion patrol aircraft. The Navy put to sea additional operational CEC systems in 1998 in the Aegis cruisers HUE CITY and VICKSBURG, the carrier JOHN F. KENNEDY (CV 67), and four E-2C Hawkeye radar aircraft. However, the CEC installations in the ANZIO and CAPE ST. GEORGE caused major computer crashes and the ships were inoperative for some 16 months while the problems were corrected.

The total CEC-capable force in 2007 is expected to consist of 12 aircraft carriers, 65 Aegis cruisers and destroyers, 12 non-Aegis destroyers, 12 LHA/LHD-type amphibious ships, and 23 LPD/LSD-type amphibious ships, plus E-2C Hawkeye and P-3C Orion aircraft.

8 See N. Polmar, "Ballistic Missile Defense . . . From the Sea," U.S. Naval Institute *Proceedings* (June 2003), pp. 86–87.

9 Secretary of Defense William S. Cohen, *Annual Report to the President and the Congress* (Washington, D.C.: 1999), p. 74. In the 1998 flight test, the TD-1 missile traveled 3,400 nm (6,300 km); unofficial estimates contend that a three-stage version of the TD-series could travel 4,900 nm (9,080 km) with a nuclear warhead.

10 John Harvey, Deputy Assist Secretary of Defense for Nuclear Forces and Missile Defense Policy, 26 July 1999, quoted in Keith J. Costa, "Citing Secret Study, DoD Official Says Navy NMD Role Unlikely by 2005," *Inside Missile Defense* (11 August 1999), pp. 18–19.

NUCLEAR-PROPELLED SURFACE COMBATANTS

All nine nuclear-propelled cruisers (CGN) have been stricken, some significantly before the end of their postulated 30-year service lives. Their limited weapons systems (none was fitted Aegis, VLS, or an ASW helicopter capability) and the high cost of nuclear refueling led to their premature disposal. The decommissioning of the nuclear cruiser force means the Navy's nuclear-propelled aircraft carriers operate with only oil-burning screening ships.

The nine cruisers and their ages at decommissioning are indicated below; see Table 15-2 for their commissioning and decommissioning dates.

CGN 9	Long Beach	37.9 years
CGN 25	Bainbridge	33.9 years
CGN 35	Truxtun	28.3 years
CGN 36	California	25.5 years
CGN 37	South Carolina	24.8 years
CGN 38	Virginia	18.2 years
CGN 39	Texas	15.8 years
CGN 40	Mississippi	19.0 years
CGN 41	Arkansas	17.7 years

The Reagan administration had included a nuclear-propelled cruiser in the last year of the FY 1983–1987 shipbuilding plan, but that ship "slipped" into oblivion. According to Navy officials, the ship was placed in the long-range program for "planning purposes" and was not be pursued in subsequent shipbuilding programs.

Other than the Long Beach, the Navy's nuclear-propelled cruisers were large destroyer or frigate (DLGN)-type ships that had been reclassified as cruisers in 1975. The Long Beach was the only new-construction cruiser built by the U.S. Navy in the post–World War II period.

A planned strike cruiser (CSGN), developed in 1973–1974 as an enlarged carrier escort ship intended specifically to carry the Aegis combat system, was an outgrowth of the DLGN concept. It was to have had a full-load displacement of more than 17,000 tons. Up to four CSGNs were considered necessary to screen each carrier.

The cost of the lead strike cruiser in FY 1976 was estimated at $1.371 billion; she was to have been completed in December 1983. After the ship was ignored by Congress, Naval Sea Systems Command hurriedly developed a strike cruiser Mk II design retaining the same armament but with a flight deck, presenting a superficial similarity to the Soviet Kiev-class Vertical Take-Off and Landing (VTOL) carriers. (See 13th Edition/pages 136–37 for details.)

The Typhon combat system, precursor to Aegis, was to be fitted in large, nuclear-propelled frigates (DLGN). These ships were to displace some 12,000 tons full load in their largest configuration. The lead ship was planned for the FY 1963 shipbuilding program.

The Navy's nuclear propulsion community had long sought all-nuclear escorts for aircraft carriers—up to four cruiser-type ships of 10,000 tons or more for each nuclear carrier. Advocacy by Admiral H. G. Rickover, then head of naval nuclear propulsion, led Congress to specify in the FY 1975 Defense legislation that all future major combatants world have nuclear propulsion (Title VIII of the FY 1975 Military Appropriation Authorization Act, Public Law 93-365, 88 Statue 408).

In the event, the last U.S. nuclear-propelled cruiser was authorized in FY 1975. All subsequent major combatants (cruisers and destroyers) have been gas-turbine propelled. The only other nation to construct nuclear-propelled surface combatants has been the Soviet Union, completing four ships of the 28,000-ton Kirov class from 1980 to 1996.

See 16th Edition/pages 115–19 for final CGN characteristics.

A line of surface combatants during a joint British–American exercise with the San Jacinto leading the Mitscher, frigate Hawes (FFG 53), and other ships. While most U.S. warship programs have been wrapped in controversy, the production of Aegis warships—cruisers and, subsequently, destroyers—has continued unabated. (2002, U.S. Navy/Isaac Merriman)

CRUISERS

ADVANCED MISSILE CRUISERS

The Navy is planning a class of advanced missile cruisers, currently designated CG(X), to replace the TICONDEROGA-class ships and to provide enhanced ballistic missile defense capabilities, theater and possibly national. The design will be based on the DD(X).

The Navy's 30-year shipbuilding plan presented to Congress in 2003 lists 24 ships authorized for construction during FY 2014–2033. The lead ship is planned for authorization in FY 2014, with commissioning in 2018.

The CG(X) proposal replaces the "21st century air defense cruisers" (CG 21 design) announced by the Navy in January 2000.

At that time, the Navy's 30-year shipbuilding plan reflected a class of 27 advanced air defense ships to provide a one-for-one replacement of the TICONDEROGA-class Aegis cruisers.

Electronics: The CG(X) will have an S-band main search/missile engagement radar.[11] *Missiles*: The CG(X) will be armed with a significantly larger missile battery than the DD(X). The cruise will carry the Extended-Range Active Missile (ERAM) SM-6 variant of the Standard missile.

---

11 The ship will have the Solid-State ESPY (SS-SPY) radar now in development. This will be a multifunction, phased-array radar capable of search, detection, and tracking of air surface targets, and of supporting missile engagement. (See Chapter 31.)

22 GUIDED MISSILE CRUISERS: IMPROVED "TICONDEROGA" CLASS

Number	Name	FY	Builder	Laid down	Launched	Christened	Comm.	Status
CG 52	BUNKER HILL	82	Litton/Ingalls, Pascagoula, Miss.	11 Jan 1984	11 Mar 1985	19 Apr 1985	20 Sep 1986	**PA**
CG 53	MOBILE BAY	82	Litton/Ingalls, Pascagoula, Miss.	6 June 1984	22 Aug 1985	12 Oct 1985	21 Feb 1987	**PA**
CG 54	ANTIETAM	83	Litton/Ingalls, Pascagoula, Miss.	15 Nov 1984	14 Feb 1986	19 Apr 1986	6 June 1987	**PA**
CG 55	LEYTE GULF	83	Litton/Ingalls, Pascagoula, Miss.	18 Mar 1985	20 June 1986	11 Oct 1986	26 Sep 1987	**AA**
CG 56	SAN JACINTO	83	Litton/Ingalls, Pascagoula, Miss.	24 July 1985	14 Nov 1986	24 Jan 1987	23 Jan 1988	**AA**
CG 57	LAKE CHAMPLAIN	84	Litton/Ingalls, Pascagoula, Miss.	3 Mar 1986	3 Apr 1987	25 Apr 1987	12 Aug 1988	**AA**
CG 58	PHILIPPINE SEA	84	Bath Iron Works, Maine	8 May 1986	12 July 1987	—	18 Mar 1989	**AA**
CG 59	PRINCETON	84	Litton/Ingalls, Pascagoula, Miss.	15 Oct 1986	25 Sep 1987	17 Oct 1987	11 Feb 1989	**PA**
CG 60	NORMANDY	85	Bath Iron Works, Maine	7 Apr 1987	19 Mar 1988	—	9 Dec 1989	**AA**
CG 61	MONTEREY	85	Bath Iron Works, Maine	19 Aug 1987	23 Oct 1988	—	16 June 1990	**AA**
CG 62	CHANCELLORSVILLE	85	Litton/Ingalls, Pascagoula, Miss.	24 June 1987	15 July 1988	23 July 1988	4 Nov 1989	**PA**
CG 63	COWPENS	86	Bath Iron Works, Maine	23 Dec 1987	11 Mar 1989	—	9 Mar 1991	**PA**
CG 64	GETTYSBURG	86	Bath Iron Works, Maine	17 Aug 1988	22 July 1989	—	22 June 1991	**AA**
CG 65	CHOSIN	86	Litton/Ingalls, Pascagoula, Miss.	22 July 1988	1 Sep 1989	14 Oct 1989	12 Jan 1991	**PA**
CG 66	HUE CITY	87	Litton/Ingalls, Pascagoula, Miss.	20 Feb 1988	1 June 1990	21 July 1990	14 Sep 1991	**AA**
CG 67	SHILOH	87	Bath Iron Works, Maine	1 Aug 1989	8 Sep 1990	—	18 July 1992	**PA**
CG 68	ANZIO	87	Litton/Ingalls, Pascagoula, Miss.	21 Aug 1989	2 Nov 1990	10 Nov 1990	2 May 1992	**AA**
CG 69	VICKSBURG	88	Litton/Ingalls, Pascagoula, Miss.	30 May 1990	2 Aug 1991	12 Oct 1991	14 Nov 1992	**AA**
CG 70	LAKE ERIE	88	Bath Iron Works, Maine	6 Mar 1990	13 July 1991	—	24 July 1993	**PA**
CG 71	CAPE ST. GEORGE	88	Litton/Ingalls, Pascagoula, Miss.	19 Nov 1990	10 Jan 1992	13 June 1992	12 June 1993	**AA**
CG 72	VELLA GULF	88	Litton/Ingalls, Pascagoula, Miss.	22 Apr 1991	30 May 1992	25 July 1992	18 Sep 1993	**AA**
CG 73	PORT ROYAL	88	Litton/Ingalls, Pascagoula, Miss.	20 Nov 1991	20 Nov 1992	5 Dec 1992	9 July 1994	**PA**

Displacement:	8,910 tons standard	ASW weapons:	VLA (ASROC) in some ships
	9,466 tons full load		6 12.75-inch (324-mm) torpedo tubes Mk 32
Length:	532⅔ feet (162.4 m) waterline		(2 triple) for Mk 46 and Mk 50 torpedoes
	567 feet (172.9 m) overall	Radars:	SPS-49(V)6/7/8 air search
Beam:	55 feet (16.75 m)		SPS-55 surface search
Draft:	31½ feet (9.6 m)		SPS-64(V)9 navigation
Propulsion:	4 gas turbines (General Electric LM 2500); 80,000 shp;		CG 52–58: (4) SPY-1A multifunction
	2 shafts		CG 59–73: (4) SPY-1B multifunction
Speed:	30+ knots	Sonars:	CG 52–55: SQS-53A bow mounted
Range:	6,000 nm (11,110 km) at 20 knots		CG 56–67: SQS-53B bow mounted
Personnel:	approx. 379 (29 officers + 350 enlisted)		CG 68–73: SQS-53C bow mounted
	+ 21-man LAMPS detachment (6 officers + 15 enlisted)		SQR-19 TACTAS
Helicopters:	2 SH-60B Seahawk LAMPS III	Fire control:	1 Mk 7 Aegis combat system
Missiles:	2 61-cell VLS for Standard-MR SM-2/Tomahawk/VLA		1 Mk 86 Gunfire Control System (GFCS) with SPQ-9A radar
	(ASROC) (122 weapons) Mk 41 Mod 0		4 Mk 99 missile directors with SPG-62 radar
	8 Harpoon SSM Mk 141 (2 quad canisters)		1 Mk 116 ASW FCS
Guns:	2 5-inch (127-mm) 54-cal DP Mk 45 (2 single)		SQQ-89(V)3 ASW system in CG 54–73
	2 20-mm Phalanx CIWS Mk 15 (2 multibarrel)		SWG-1 (Harpoon)
	several light machine guns or cannon		SWG-3 (Tomahawk)
		EW systems:	SLQ-25 Nixie
			SLQ-32(V)3

These later TICONDEROGA-class cruisers differ from the first five in having the Vertical Launching System for missiles. The VLS permits them to carry Tomahawks, providing a land-attack capability, as well as more missiles of all types than the earlier ships (122 compared to 88). These ships are scheduled to receive a major

upgrade beginning in FY 2006 (see *Modernization* notes).

Like the earlier TICONDEROGAS, these are the world's most capable Anti-Air Warfare (AAW) ships, developed to provide carrier battle group defense against aircraft and anti-ship missiles. In addition, the ships have major ASW capabilities.

The Ingalls-built ships were launched from a floating dock; their christening—public relations—ceremonies were held at later dates.

The CHANCELLORSVILLE, COWPENS, and VINCENNES are home-ported in Yokosuka, part of the KITTY HAWK carrier battle group.

See TICONDEROGA class for additional design data.

Class: This is numerically the largest cruiser class built by any Navy in the post–World War II period. The only other cruiser class of comparable size was the 27-ship CLEVELAND (CL 55) class built for the U.S. Navy, completed 1942–1945 (another 9 were completed as small aircraft carriers [CVL]).

When conceived, the TICONDEROGA class was intended to complement the nuclear-propelled strike cruiser (CSGN), which also was to be fitted with the Aegis AAW system. However, Congress refused to fund the strike cruiser and only the conventionally propelled Aegis ships were built. The Aegis system subsequently was fitted in the ARLEIGH BURKE-class destroyers.

Design: These ships were the ultimate development of the basic SPRUANCE design. In all, 62 ships were built to that design:

31	DD	SPRUANCE class
4	DDG	KIDD class
5	CG	TICONDEROGA class (Mk 26 launchers)
22	CG	Improved TICONDEROGA class (VLS launchers)

Electronics: The SHILOH is the first—and at this writing, the only—cruiser to be fitted with Area Air Defense Command

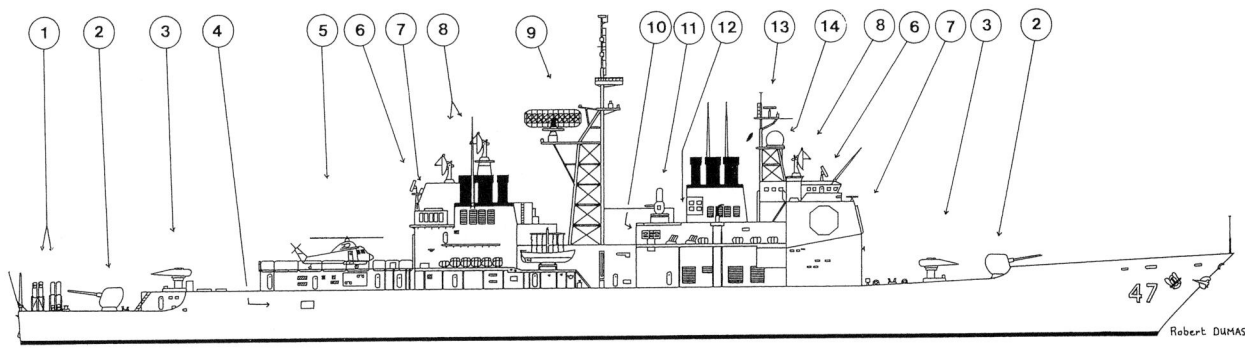

Guided Missile Cruiser TICONDEROGA (top)

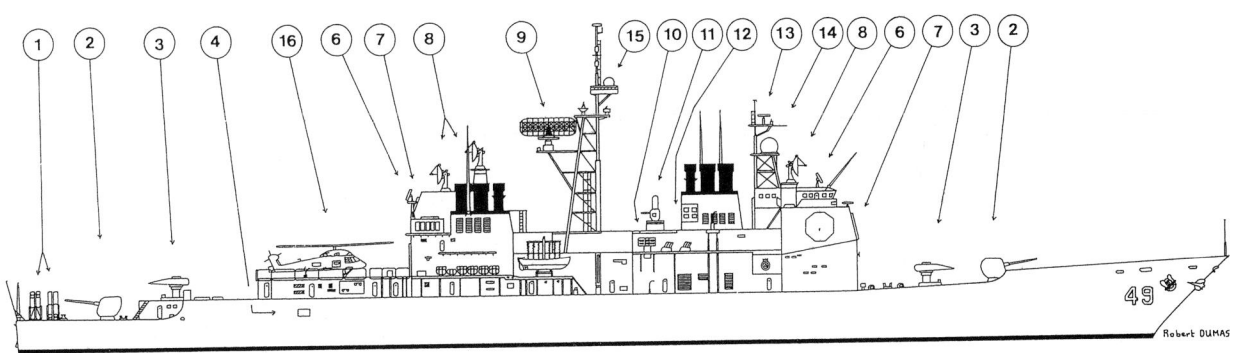

Guided Missile Cruiser VINCENNES (center)

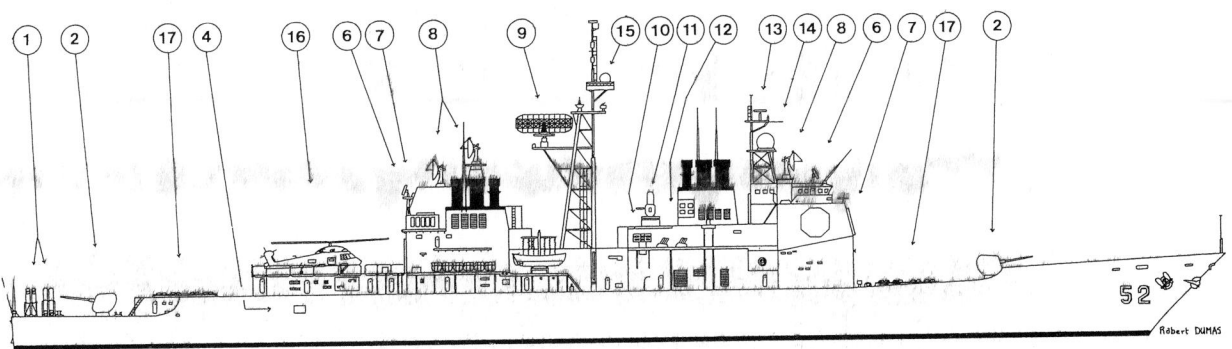

Guided Missile Cruiser BUNKER HILL (bottom)

1. Harpoon missile canisters (8) 2. 5-inch DP single gun mount Mk 45 (2) 3. Surface-to-air missile launcher Mk 26 4. 12.75-inch triple torpedo tubes Mk 32 5. SH-2F LAMPS I helicopter (2) 6. OE-82 satellite communications antenna (2) 7. SPY-1 fixed-array radar antenna (4) 8. SPG-62 radar illuminator (4) 9. SPS-49(V)6 air search radar 10. SLQ-32(V)3 electronic countermeasures (2) 11. Phalanx close-in weapon system Mk 15 (2) 12. SRBOC decoy-launcher Mk 36 (4) 13. SPS-55 surface search radar 14. SPQ-9A surface/gunfire control radar 15. SPS-64(V)9 navigation radar 16. SH-60B LAMPS III helicopter (2) 17. Vertical launching system Mk 41 (2) Note: SH-2F LAMPS I helicopter no longer in service. (Robert Dumans)

(AADC) system, an analysis and display system employing "six degrees of freedom" modeling capability with a "three-dimensional" tactical operations display system. Additional cruiser installations have been delayed because of cost constraints.

The command ships BLUE RIDGE (LCC 19) and MOUNT WHITNEY (LCC 20) also have the AADC system.

Missiles: The VLS provides these ships with a Tomahawk launch capability. The BUNKER HILL was the first U.S. naval ship—other than the missile test ship NORTON SOUND and experimental surface effect ship SES-100B—to launch a missile at sea from a VLS installation, on 20 May 1986.

Some of these ships will be fitted with the Navy's sea-based Theater Ballistic Missile Defense system, which will employ the Standard SM-3 missile as a forward, high-altitude interceptor against theater ballistic missile attacks. The LAKE ERIE and PORT ROYAL are the first ships fitted with TBMD capabilities, to conduct at-sea systems tests, help develop doctrine and tactics, and train personnel. The LAKE ERIE was test ship for the Standard SM-3.

Modernization: All 22 ships of this class are planned for the cruiser conversion program. All ships (now Aegis Baseline 2, 3, or 4) will be upgraded to a common Aegis baseline. Included in the conversions are:
• Cooperative Engagement Capability
• Evolved Sea Sparrow Missile
• Mk 34 Gun Weapons System
• Phalanx Block 1B CIWS
• Shipboard Advanced Radar Target Identification System (SARTIS)
• SPQ-9B radar

• SQQ-89A(V)15 sonar suite

Other improvements will enhance survivability, reduce topside weight, reduce maintenance costs, and cut manning requirements through automation.

The first ship to be converted will be the CAPE ST. GEORGE—the last ship completed—beginning in 2006; the last conversion is to be completed in 2014.

Names: Most of these ship names remember World War II–era aircraft carriers of the ESSEX (CV 9) and INDEPENDENCE (CVL 22) classes (also see WASP/LHD 1 class amphibious ships). The CG 66 is the second U.S. warship to be named for a battle of the Vietnam War; the PELELIU (LHA 5) originally was named DA NANG, but that ship was renamed on 15 February 1978, after the fall of the Republic of South Vietnam to communist forces.

The CG 69 originally was PORT ROYAL; this was changed while the ship was under construction.

Operational: During the first Gulf War, on 18 February 1991, the PRINCETON struck a bottom-laid influence mine that damaged the ship (a second mine was detonated by the explosion). She had to be towed to port, although at no time was she in danger of sinking and most of her combat systems remained operational. (The ship could have proceeded under her own power, but the commanding officer decided on the tow to avoid strain on her hull until an examination could be made in a dockyard.) Repairs were made during a seven-week "availability" at Dubai in the United Arab Emirates followed by a two-month yard period in the United States.

The ANTIETAM during exercises off the coast of California. Aegis cruisers are easily identified by their massive superstructure and two masts. The SPY-1 fixed-array antennas are mounted on the forward superstructure "block" (facing forward and to starboard) and after "block" (facing aft and to port). (2004, U.S. Navy/John DeCoursey)

The VELLA GULF broadside during a training evolution in the Atlantic. Despite their bulky superstructures, there is a certain glamour to their appearance. The unmanned 5-inch gun mounts are relatively small; the quad canisters for Harpoon anti-ship missiles are visible on the fantail. (2003, U.S. Navy/Joan Kretschmer)

The LAKE CHAMPLAIN showing the plan perspective of an Aegis cruiser. Note the relatively unimpressive VLS installations aft of the forward 5-inch gun mount and aft of the helicopter deck. The superstructure is topped with a mass of antennas and antenna domes. (2003, U.S. Navy/Jayme Pastoric)

The stern aspect of the ANTIETAM while operating with a carrier battle group. The after portion of the superstructure houses the twin hangars for LAMPS helicopters. Adjacent to the 5-inch gun mounts there are vertical replenishment spots marked on the deck both forward and aft. (2003, U.S. Navy, Karen B. Elterman)

3 GUIDED MISSILE CRUISERS: "TICONDEROGA" CLASS

Number	Name	FY	Builder	Laid down	Launched	Christened	Comm.	Status
CG 47	TICONDEROGA	78	Litton/Ingalls, Pascagoula, Miss.	21 Jan 1980	25 Apr 1981	16 May 1981	22 Jan 1983	decomm./str. 30 Sep 2004
CG 48	YORKTOWN	80	Litton/Ingalls, Pascagoula, Miss.	19 Oct 1981	17 Jan 1983	16 Apr 1983	4 July 1984	AR; decomm 3 Dec 2004
CG 49	VINCENNES	81	Litton/Ingalls, Pascagoula, Miss.	20 Oct 1982	14 Jan 1984	18 Apr 1984	6 July 1985	**PA**
CG 50	VALLEY FORGE	81	Litton/Ingalls, Pascagoula, Miss.	14 Apr 1983	23 June 1984	29 Sep 1984	11 Jan 1986	decomm./str. 30 Aug 2004
CG 51	THOMAS S. GATES	82	Bath Iron Works, Maine	31 Aug 1984	14 Dec 1985	—	22 Aug 1987	**AA**

Displacement:	CG 47, 48: 7,019 tons light		2 20-mm Phalanx CIWS Mk 15 (2 multibarrel)
	CG 49–51: 7,014 tons light		several light machine guns or cannon
	CG 47, 48: 9,589 tons full load	ASW weapons:	6 12.75-inch (324-mm) torpedo tubes Mk 32 (2 triple) for
	CG 49–51: 9,407 tons full load		Mk 46 and Mk 50 torpedoes
Length:	532⅔ feet (162.4 m) waterline	Radars:	SPS-49(V)6/7/8 air search
	567 feet (172.9 m) overall		SPS-53 surface search
Beam:	55 feet (16.75 m)		SPS-55 surface search
Draft:	31½ feet (9.6 m)		SPS-64(V)9 navigation
Propulsion:	4 gas turbines (General Electric LM 2500);80,000 shp;		(4) SPY-1A multifunction
	2 shafts	Sonars:	SQS-53A bow mounted
Speed:	30+ knots		SQR-19 towed array
Range:	6,000 nm (11,110 km) at 20 knots	Fire control:	1 Mk 7 Aegis combat system
Personnel:	approx. 351 (26 officers + 325 enlisted)		1 Mk 86 GFCS with SPQ-9A radar
	+ 21-man LAMPS detachment (6 officers + 15 enlisted)		4 Mk 99 missile directors with SPG-62 radar
	in CG 49–51		1 Mk 116 ASW FCS
Helicopters:	2 SH-60B Seahawk LAMPS III in CG 49–51		SWG-1 (Harpoon)
Missiles:	2 twin Mk 26 Mod 1 launchers for Standard-MR SM-2		SWG-3 (Tomahawk)
	(88 weapons)	EW systems:	SLQ-25A Nixie
	8 Harpoon SSM Mk 141 (2 quad canisters)		SLQ-32(V)3
Guns:	2 5-inch (127-mm) 54-cal DP Mk 45 (2 single)		

These first five TICONDEROGA-class ships have Mk 26 twin-arm missile launcher in lieu of the more-capable VLS in the later 22 ships.

The Ingalls-built ships are launched from a floating dock; their christening—public relations—ceremonies are held at later dates. The ships were considered for the cruiser conversion program, to provide them with updated electric and weapon systems, as well as modernization of their hull, propulsion, and electrical systems, but in 2003, the Navy decided not to upgrade the ships, and all five will be retired in 2004–2006.

ASW weapons: As completed, these ships fired the Anti-Submarine Rocket (ASROC) from their forward Mk 26 launcher; that weapon is no longer in service.

Classification: This class was changed from guided missile destroyers (DDG, with same hull numbers) to guided missile cruisers on 1 January 1980, to better reflect the ships' capabilities and cost.

Design: SCB No. 226. These ships are based on the SPRUANCE design, employing the same hull and propulsion plant. The superstructure has been enlarged to accommodate the Aegis/SPY-1 equipment, with two fixed-array radar antennas on the forward deckhouse, facing forward and to starboard, and two on the after deckhouse, facing aft and to port. Internal changes include limited armor plating for the magazine and critical electronic spaces, increases in the ship's service generators from three 2,000 kw to three 2,500 kw, additional accommodations, and additional fuel tanks.

During construction, the design was changed to provide higher exhaust stacks and a bow bulwark, the latter required to reduce water over the bow as a result of the greater draft compared to the SPRUANCE class.

The VINCENNES and later ships have tripod (vice quadrapod) lattice masts, reducing topside weight by some nine tons.

Electronics: All ships have the SQR-17 sonar data processor. The SQS-53 series + SQR-19 sonars comprise the SQQ-89(V)3 suite.

Helicopters: These ships have the Recovery Assistance, Securing, and Traversing (RAST) helicopter-hauldown system (see OLIVER HAZARD PERRY/FFG 7 class). The sizes of the twin helicopter hangars in these ships vary; they are approximately 39 feet (11.9 m) long, 26½–29 feet (8.1–8.8 m) wide, and 14⅓–15½ feet (4.35–4.7 m) high.

The first two ships of this class carried the SH-2F LAMPS I helicopter, now discarded; the CG 49–51 were fitted to carry the SH-60B Seahawk LAMPS III.

Names: The CG 51 is named for a deceased Secretary of the Navy and Secretary of Defense. (Other Secretaries of the Navy are remembered by destroyers and cruisers, the former having been named for secretaries when they were built as DLG "frigates" in the destroyer family. The only other Secretaries of Defense to have had Navy ships named in their honor were James V. Forrestal, also a former Secretary of the Navy, and George C. Marshall.)

Operational: The VINCENNES shot down an Iranian commercial airliner on 3 July 1988 over the southern Persian Gulf. All 290 passengers and crew were killed. The VINCENNES's combat information center had identified the target as probably an Iranian F-14 Tomcat making a dive on the ship. Two Standard missiles were fired.

The THOMAS S. GATES *going to sea. The ship's forward Mk 26 Standard missile launcher is visible between the forward 5-inch gun and the superstructure. Twin-arm missile launchers first went to sea in U.S. warships in 1955 in the converted Terrier cruiser* BOSTON *(CAG 1). (2004, U.S. Navy/Stacey Byington)*

The VINCENNES *pulls away from the carrier* KITTY HAWK *(CV 63) after an underway replenishment in the Western Pacific. One hangar bay on the* VINCENNES *is open. The Mk 26 Standard missile launcher elevates to the vertical position for reloading from the below-deck, circular magazine. (2004, U.S. Navy/Bo J. Flannigan)*

Table 15-2. GUIDED MISSILE CRUISERS

Number	Name	Missile Comm.	Notes
BALTIMORE-class conversions (2)			
CAG 1	BOSTON (ex-CA 69)	1955	reverted to CA 69; str. 1973
CAG 2	CANBERRA (ex-CA 70)	1956	reverted to CA 70; str. 1978
CLEVELAND-class conversions (6)			
CLG 3	GALVESTON (ex-CL 93)	1958	stricken 1973
CLG 4	LITTLE ROCK (ex-CL 92)	1960	changed to CG 4; str. 1977
CLG 5	OKLAHOMA CITY (ex-CL 91)	1960	changed to CG 5; str. 1982
CLG 6	PROVIDENCE (ex-CL 82)	1959	changed to CG 6; str. 1978
CLG 7	SPRINGFIELD (ex-CL 66)	1960	changed to CG 7; str. 1978
CLG 8	TOPEKA (ex-CL 67)	1960	stricken 1973
LONG BEACH type			
CGN 9	LONG BEACH (ex-CLGN/CGN 160)	1961	decomm./str. 1 May 1995
BALTIMORE/OREGON CITY-class conversions (3)			
CG 10	ALBANY (ex-CA 123)	1962	stricken 1985
CG 11	CHICAGO (ex-CA 136)	1964	stricken 1984
CG 12	COLUMBUS (ex-CA 74)	1962	stricken 1976
CG 13	(undesignated)		conversion canceled
CG 14	BREMERTON (CA 130)		conversion canceled
CG 15	ROCHESTER (CA 124)		conversion canceled
LEAHY class (9)			
CG 16	LEAHY (ex-DLG 16)	1962	decomm./str. 1 Oct 1993

Number	Name	Missile Comm.	Notes
CG 17	HARRY E. YARNELL (DLG 17)	1963	decomm./str. 29 Oct 1993
CG 18	WORDEN (ex-DLG 18)	1963	decomm./str. 10 Oct 1993
CG 19	DALE (ex-DLG 19)	1962	decomm./str. 23 Sep 1994
CG 20	RICHMOND K. TURNER (ex-DLG 20)	1964	decomm./str. 30 June 1995
CG 21	GRIDLEY (ex-DLG 21)	1963	decomm./str. 21 Jan 1994
CG 22	ENGLAND (ex-DLG 22)	1962	decomm./str. 21 Jan 1994
CG 23	HALSEY (ex-DLG 23)	1963	decomm./str. 28 Jan 1994
CG 24	REEVES (ex-DLG 24)	1964	decomm./str. 12 Nov 1993
BAINBRIDGE type			
CGN 25	BAINBRIDGE (ex-DLGN 25)	1962	decomm./str. 13 Sep 1996
BELKNAP class (9)			
CG 26	BELKNAP (ex-DLG 26)	1964	decomm./str. 15 Mar 1995
CG 27	JOSEPHUS DANIELS (ex-DLG 27)	1965	decomm./str. 22 Jan 1994
CG 28	WAINWRIGHT (ex-DLG 28)	1966	decomm./str. 10 Nov 1993
CG 29	JOUETT (ex-DLG 29)	1966	decomm./str. 28 Jan 1994
CG 30	HORNE (ex-DLG 30)	1967	decomm./str. 4 Feb 1994
CG 31	STERETT (ex-DLG 31)	1967	decomm./str. 24 Mar 1994
CG 32	WILLIAM H. STANDLEY (ex-DLG 32)	1966	decomm./str. 11 Feb 1994
CG 33	FOX (ex-DLG 33)	1966	decomm./str. 15 Apr 1994
CG 34	BIDDLE (ex-DLG 34)	1967	decomm./str. 30 Nov 1993
TRUXTUN type			
CGN 35	TRUXTUN (ex-DLGN 35)	1967	decomm./str. 11 Sep 1995

Number	Name	Missile Comm.	Notes
CALIFORNIA class (2)			
CGN 36	CALIFORNIA (ex-DLGN 36)	1974	decomm./str. 9 July 1999
CGN 37	SOUTH CAROLINA (DLGN 37)	1975	decomm./str. 30 July 1999
VIRGINIA class (4)			
CGN 38	VIRGINIA (ex-DLGN 38)	1976	decomm./str. 10 Nov 1994
CGN 39	TEXAS (ex-DLGN 39)	1977	decomm./str. 16 July 1993
CGN 40	MISSISSIPPI (ex-DLGN 40)	1978	decomm./str. 28 July 1997
CGN 41	ARKANSAS	1980	decomm./str. 7 July 1998
CGN 42	(undesignated)		canceled
CG 43–46	not used		
CG 47–73	TICONDEROGA (ex-DDG 47) class		

World War II cruiser programs reached hull number CL 159 (hulls 154–159 were canceled in 1945). All heavy (CA), light (CL), and anti-aircraft (CLAA) cruisers were numbered in the same series. One unfinished cruiser hull was completed after the war as the command ship NORTHAMPTON. Begun as the heavy cruiser CA 125, she was suspended in 1945 when 56.2 percent complete; she was reordered in 1948 and completed as a tactical command ship (CLC 1) in 1953; changed to a national command ship (CC 1) in 1962. She was stricken in 1977.

The guided missile cruiser classifications were established in 1952 to reflect the specialized weapons and AAW roles of these ships. Only one new-construction cruiser was built by the U.S. Navy after World War II, the LONG BEACH, ordered as CLGN 160, changed to CGN 160, and completed as CGN 9. The LONG BEACH was the world's first nuclear-propelled surface warship. (The Soviet nuclear-propelled icebreaker LENIN was completed in 1959.) She also was the world's first warship to be built with guided missiles as the main battery, carrying two Terrier surface-to-air launchers forward and a Talos surface-to-air launch aft. No guns were fitted as built (subsequently, two 5-inch/38 DP guns and, later, two Phalanx CIWS were installed).

Eleven war-built cruisers were converted to a missile configuration (CAG 1, 2, CLG 3–8, CG 10–12): Three heavy cruisers of the BALTIMORE class were converted to all-missile configurations (CG), and two other cruisers of the class with 8-inch (203-mm) guns and six CLEVELAND-class cruisers with 6-inch (152-mm) guns were converted to a combination gun–missile configuration (CAG and CLG, respectively). All have been stricken, the last being the OKLAHOMA CITY, decommissioned in 1979 and stricken in 1982. The two CAGs lost their missile systems and reverted to CA designations during the Vietnam War; four of the CLGs were changed to CG in 1975, although they retained 6-inch and 5-inch (127-mm) guns forward.

Three additional conversions of this kind were canceled because of increasing costs. The conversions and further new cruiser construction were halted in favor of the smaller and comparatively less expensive "frigates" (DLG/DLGN), which could carry most of a cruiser's missile armament.

A total of nine nuclear-propelled cruisers and frigates were built (the seven frigates were reclassified as cruisers in 1975). All have been stricken.

In all, 25 guided missile frigates (DLG/DLGN) were changed to cruisers; the ARKANSAS was ordered as CGN 41.

The LEAHY-class ships were "double-end" Terrier/Standard-Extended Range (ER) missile cruisers with surface-to-air missile launchers forward and aft. They were the smallest U.S. Navy ships to be classified as cruisers in the post–World War II era. The BELKNAP-class ships were "single-end" Terrier/Standard-ER guid-

ed missile cruisers. After suffering major damage in a collision with the carrier JOHN F. KENNEDY (CV 67), the BELKNAP was rebuilt in 1978–1980 and configured as Sixth Fleet flagship; she served in that role until 1995.

Recent expenditures of cruisers as target ships include the WORDEN on 17 June 2000; the DALE on 6 April 2000; the REEVES on 1 June 2001; and the WAINWRIGHT on 13 June 2002.

Table 15-3. HUNTER-KILLER CRUISERS

Number	Name	Notes
CLK 1	NORFOLK	completed as DL 1
CLK 2	NEW HAVEN	deferred 1949; canceled 1951

The U.S. Navy established the classification of hunter-killer cruiser (CLK) in 1949 for a planned class of 12 small cruisers intended for ASW operations against high-speed submarines. Only the lead ship, the NORFOLK, was completed; she was reclassified as a frigate (DL) while under construction. She was employed mainly in ASW test and evaluation, and was decommissioned in 1970 and stricken in 1973.

Table 15-4. FRIGATES/GUIDED MISSILE FRIGATES

Number	Name	Comm.	Notes
NORFOLK type			
DL 1	NORFOLK (ex-CLK 1)	1953	stricken 1973
MITSCHER class (4)			
DL 2	MITSCHER (ex-DD 927)	1953	converted to DDG 35
DL 3	JOHN S. MCCAIN (ex-DD 928)	1953	converted to DDG 36
DL 4	WILLIS A. LEE (ex-DD 930)	1954	stricken 1972
DL 5	WILKINSON (ex-DD 930)	1954	stricken 1974
DLG 6–15	FARRAGUT class		changed to DDG 37–46
DLG 16–24	LEAHY class		changed to CG 16–24
BAINBRIDGE type			
DLGN 25	BAINBRIDGE	1962	changed to CGN 25
DLG 26–34	BELKNAP class		changed to CG 26–34
TRUXTUN type			
DLGN 35	TRUXTUN	1967	changed to CGN 35
DLGN 36–37	CALIFORNIA class		changed to CGN 36–37
DLGN 38–40	VIRGINIA class		changed to CGN 38–40

The frigate classification (DL) was established in 1951 for large destroyer-type ships designed to operate with fast carrier forces. Initially intended as highly capable ASW platforms, with the deployment of missile systems, these ships (DLG/DLGN) have emphasized anti-air warfare, although some also had the most-capable contemporary ASW systems (i.e., large sonar, helicopter, ASROC).

The hunter-killer cruiser NORFOLK was completed as the DL 1, and four MITSCHER-class ships ordered as destroyers were completed as DL 2–5. These ships were built with an all-gun armament plus the Weapon Alfa ASW rocket launcher and other ASW weapons. The DL 6–8 were changed to DLG in 1956, i.e., before keel laying.

The all-gun and missile-armed frigates were numbered in the same series; in the cruiser, destroyer, and destroyer escort/frigate categories, missile and nonmissile ships were assigned hull numbers in separate series.

The frigate classification was abolished on 30 June 1975, and the new frigate classification FF/FFG was established to indicate smaller escort ships (formerly DE/DEG). The FARRAGUT class of DLGs was reclassified as destroyers (DDG); the other DLG/DLGN ships became cruisers (CG/CGN).

DESTROYERS

ADVANCED DESTROYER DESIGN: DD(X)

Units	FY	Comm.	Status
1 ship	05	2013	Planned
1 ship	06		Planned
1 ship	07		Planned
2 ships	08		Planned
3 ships	09		Planned
8 ships per year	10–13		Planned
8 ships per year	14–18		Planned

Displacement:	approx. 14,000 tons full load
Length:	approx. 600 feet (183.0 m) overall
Beam:	approx. 79 feet (24.0 m)
Draft:	approx. 27½ feet (8.4 m)
Propulsion:	4 gas turbines (Rolls-Royce MT30); 100,000+ shp; electric drive; 2 shafts
Speed:	30+ knots
Range:	
Personnel:	approx. 125–175
Helicopters:	1 or 2 MH-60R Seahawk 3 Vertical Take-off Unmanned Aerial Vehicles (VTUAVs)
Missiles:	Peripheral VLS for Standard–Medium Range (MR) SM-2/TLAM (approx. 80 missiles)
Guns:	2 155-mm Advanced Gun Systems (AGS) 2 57mn/70-cal Mk110
ASW weapons:	
Radars:	SPY-3 multifunction S-VSR
Sonar:	
Fire Control:	

The DD(X) is the planned follow-on to the ARLEIGH BURKE class as the Navy's primary surface combatant.

On 29 April 2002, the Navy announced that the so-called Gold Team, led by Northrop Grumman's Ingalls shipyard, would be the lead design agent for the DD(X) program. The contract for $2.9 billion was for the design, construction, and test of 11 major subsystems of the ship. The Gold Team also includes Raytheon, Boeing, Lockheed Martin, and Bath Iron Works as subcontractors. (Bath is owned by the General Dynamics Corp., which was the leader of the losing Blue Team.)

Construction of the lead ship was not included in the award. This is a departure from the aborted ZUMWALT/DD 21 program, whose contract award would have included design and construction of the lead ship, series production, service-life maintenance, and other cost-reduction features. Significant from the ship design viewpoint, although the DD(X) and DD 21 are approximately the same size, the DD 21 was planned to carry more missile cells and fewer personnel.

Design: The DD(X) design has a wave-piercing, tumblehome hull configuration and a block, low-radar-cross-section superstructure.

Engineering: A land-based test facility for one-half the DD(X) propulsion plant is being built.

Guns: The initial ships will have two Advanced Gun Systems with a reported 600-round magazine per gun.

Missiles: The ship will have "peripheral" VLS cells rather than the centerline "blocks" configuration of the Mk 41 VLS.

The peripheral VLS—also referred to as the Advanced VLS (AVLS)—differs from the Mk 41 in having four-cell modules installed along the perimeter of the ship's deck rather than in the standard, centrally placed VLS battery. According to the AVLS development team of Northrop Grumman, United Defense, and Raytheon, this arrangement will reduce the ship's vulnerability to a single missile, shell, or bomb hit.

But with the peripheral VLS, the ship will lose the modular, centerline "footprint" of the Mk 41 launcher package. The Mk 41 was developed specifically to replace the Mk 26 missile launcher and 88-round missile magazine in Aegis cruisers. Twenty-two of the 27 ships of the TICONDEROGA class have the Mk 41 VLS with 61-cell launchers forward and aft in place of Mk 26 systems. Subsequently, 61-cell launchers were installed forward in 24 destroyers of the SPRUANCE class, replacing the ASROC "box" launcher and magazine in those ships.

This modular replacement capability provides the potential for the Mk 41 VLS battery in turn to be replaced by a more-advanced weapons "module," such as the electromagnetic rail gun or a laser weapon system, when it becomes available. These weapons systems are practical for the electric-drive DD(X) and CG(X). This swap could not be done with the AVLS, which will consist of rows of missiles cells along the sides of the ship.

The peripheral VLS offers some advantages over the conventional VLS arrangement, primarily a slightly larger (28-inch/710-mm) launch cell and, reportedly, enhanced survivability against a missile hit. With respect to the latter, combat experience in World War II, Vietnam, and the Falklands and the 1987 attack on the USS STARK (FFG 37), as well as numerous missile trials, demonstrate that even a single missile hit almost always will cripple—if not sink—a warship. The peripheral installation, accordingly, is of questionable value with respect to enhancing ship survivability in the opinion of some Navy officials.

Propulsion: All previous U.S. Navy gas-turbine destroyers, as well as the TICONDEROGA-class cruisers, had General Electric LM 2500 turbines. DD(X) will be the first modern U.S. warship with all-electric drive and an integrated power architecture.[12] (DD 21 also was to have been propelled by electric drive and have an integrated power architecture.) Employing electric drive is expected to:
• reduce ship costs
• reduce ship signatures, especially noise
• reduce fuel consumption
• reduce maintenance requirements
• reduce manpower requirements
• increase available power for sensors and weapons

The key element of an integrated power architecture is a single-source generator for all of the ship's power requirements, including propulsion. The primary power source for the DD(X) will be gas turbines. However, instead of a reduction gear to convert the turbine power into useable (propulsive) power as in previous cruisers and destroyers, the DD(X) engine will power an electric generator. The electricity produced is then carried by cable to a motor drive. The use of a cable eliminates the requirement for the gas turbines to be aligned with propeller shafts, permitting considerable flexibility in ship design. In addition, the turbine can continually be operating at its most fuel efficient speed, with the motor drive making changes in shaft turns/speed.

---

12 A perceptive look at the potential for "electric ships" is Dr. Scott C. Truver, "Origins of the All-Electric Navy," U.S. Naval Institute *Proceedings* (October 1999), pp. 50–57. The U.S. Navy's first large electric-drive surface ship was the collier JUPITER (AC 3), commissioned in 1913. That ship later was converted to the Navy's first aircraft carrier, the USS LANGLEY (CV 1). Subsequently the Navy constructed the battleship NEW MEXICO (BB 40) and the large aircraft carriers LEXINGTON (CV 2) and SARATOGA (CV 3) with turbo-electric drive (employing steam turbines). During World War II a large number of destroyer escorts (DE) were built with turbo-electric and diesel-electric drive. Since World War II no major surface warships were built with electric drive until the DD 21/DD(X) programs.

The DD(X) will combine features of the ill-fated Zumwalt *DD 21 design, a tumblehome-hull design, a peripheral VLS, and twin 155-mm gun systems. This drawing shows the planned peripheral or Advanced Vertical Launching System (AVLS) along the sides of the deck both forward and amidships. (Northrop Grumman Ship Systems and Raytheon)*

A quarter view of the DD(X) showing the ship's large helicopter deck and hangar. The DD(X) will operate manned MH-60R Seahawk helicopters and VTUAVs. The class is expected to be constructed at Northrop Grumman's Ingalls shipyard at Pascagoula and by Bath Iron Works. (U.S. Navy)

LAND-ATTACK MISSILE DESTROYERS: "ZUMWALT" CLASS

The Zumwalt class of 30-plus land-attack destroyers—given the program designation DD 21—was canceled in 2001. Department of Defense officials cited the large size of the ship, although it probably would have been only a small percentage larger than the replacement DD(X).

The lead ship was to be authorized in FY 2004 and placed in commission in 2008; follow-on ships were to reach the building rate of three per year, i.e., the DDG 51 rate. The design featured a large number of vertical-launch missiles and long-range guns for land attack/fire support and a very small crew (i.e., a manning goal of 74 plus a 21-man helicopter detachment).

Designs up to 20,000 tons were considered, although a ship of some 15,000–17,000 tons appeared most likely.

The DD 21 program replaced the DD(V) program, which had sought to determine the characteristics for a new guided missile destroyer intended to begin construction in the FY 1998 shipbuilding program. In the event, it was decided to continue construction of the Arleigh Burke class (Flight IIA) into the 21st century.

Cost: The Navy's cost goal was $750 million per ship by the fifth unit. With two shipyards expected to produce the DD 21 class,

that cost goal would have applied to hull no. 9 or 10. The first few ships were to cost approximately $1.5 billion per unit.

Electronics: It was never decided whether the ship would have the Aegis/SPY-1 or a lesser air defense combat system. See entry for Multi-Function Radar (MFR) in Chapter 31.

Personnel: The manning goal for the DD 21 was 95 officers and enlisted personnel, including a 21-man helicopter detachment (for two SH-60 helicopters). The Navy's Program Executive Office (PEO) for DD 21 had said manning might have exceeded the target if: (1) the cost of automation exceeded the cost of maintaining a larger crew; (2) appropriate workload-reduction technology was unavailable; (3) the Navy manpower or training situation changed; or (4) holdover shipboard technology, such as the Link 16 system, required additional personnel.

Missiles: The Navy's VLS goal for the DD 21 was 256 cells.

Although other missile-launch systems had been proposed, the DD 21 undoubtedly would have had the Mk 41 VLS, as no alternatives were expected to be available by the time construction was to have begun.

Names: The lead ship was named on 4 July 2001 for the Chief of Naval Operations from 1970 to 1974.

IMPROVED "ARLEIGH BURKE" CLASS (FLIGHT III)

The so-called Flight III was a proposed enhancement of the Arleigh Burke design, the principal changes being provision of a two-helicopter hangar and reduced radar and infrared signatures. This variant would have displaced 10,722 tons full load; weapons

and sensors would have been similar to the basic Burke class except for provision of an improved SPY-1 radar (designated SPY-1E in some publications). Development of this design was halted in favor of the DD 21/SC 21 program.

17 + 17 GUIDED MISSILE DESTROYERS: IMPROVED "ARLEIGH BURKE" CLASS (FLIGHT IIA)

Number	Name	FY	Builder	Laid Down	Launched	Christened	Comm.	Status
DDG 79	OSCAR AUSTIN	94	Bath Iron Works, Maine	9 Oct 1997	7 Nov 1998	—	19 Aug 2000	**AA**
DDG 80	ROOSEVELT	95	Litton/Ingalls, Pascagoula, Miss.	15 Dec 1997	10 Jan 1999	23 Jan 1999	14 Oct 2000	**AA**
DDG 81	WINSTON S. CHURCHILL	95	Bath Iron Works, Maine	7 May 1998	17 Apr 1999	—	10 Mar 2001	**AA**
DDG 82	LASSEN	95	Northrop Grumman/Ingalls, Pascagoula, Miss.	24 Aug 1998	16 Oct 1999	6 Nov 2000	21 Apr 2001	**PA**
DDG 83	HOWARD	96	Bath Iron Works, Maine	9 Dec 1998	20 Nov 1999	—	20 Oct 2001	**PA**
DDG 84	BULKELEY	96	Northrop Grumman/Ingalls, Pascagoula, Miss.	10 May 1999	21 June 2000	24 June 2000	8 Dec 2001	**AA**
DDG 85	MCCAMPBELL	97	Bath Iron Works, Maine	5 July 1999	2 July 2000	—	17 Aug 2002	**PA**
DDG 86	SHOUP	97	Northrop Grumman/Ingalls, Pascagoula, Miss.	13 Dec 1999	22 Nov 2000	24 Feb 2001	22 June 2002	**PA**
DDG 87	MASON	97	Bath Iron Works, Maine	20 Jan 2000	23 June 2001	—	12 Apr 2003	**AA**
DDG 88	PREBLE	97	Northrop Grumman/Ingalls, Pascagoula, Miss.	22 June 2000	1 June 2001	9 June 2001	9 Nov 2002	**PA**
DDG 89	MUSTIN	98	Northrop Grumman/Ingalls, Pascagoula, Miss.	15 Jan 2001	12 Dec 2001	15 Dec 2001	26 July 2003	**PA**
DDG 90	CHAFEE	98	Bath Iron Works, Maine	12 Apr 2001	2 Nov 2002	—	18 Oct 2003	**PA**
DDG 91	PINCKNEY	98	Northrop Grumman/Ingalls, Pascagoula, Miss.	16 July 2001	26 June 2002	29 June 2002	24 May 2004	**PA**
DDG 92	MOMSEN	99	Bath Iron Works, Maine	16 Nov 2001	19 July 2003	9 Aug 2003	28 Aug 2004	**PA**
DDG 93	CHUNG-HOON	99	Northrop Grumman/Ingalls, Pascagoula, Miss.	14 Jan 2002	15 Dec 2002	11 Jan 2003	18 Sep 2004	**PA**
DDG 94	NITZE	99	Bath Iron Works, Maine	20 Sep 2002	3 Apr 2004	17 Apr 2004	2005	Building
DDG 95	JAMES E. WILLIAMS	00	Northrop Grumman/Ingalls, Pascagoula, Miss.	15 July 2002	28 June 2003	28 June 2003	11 Dec 2004	**AA**
DDG 96	BAINBRIDGE	00	Bath Iron Works, Maine	7 May 2003	13 Nov 2004	—	2005	Building
DDG 97	HALSEY	00	Northrop Grumman/Ingalls, Pascagoula, Miss.	13 Jan 2003	9 Jan 2004		2005	Building
DDG 98	FORREST SHERMAN	01	Northrop Grumman/Ingalls, Pascagoula, Miss.	7 Aug 2003	2004		2005	Building
DDG 99	FARRAGUT	01	Bath Iron Works, Maine	2004	2005		2006	Building
DDG 100	KIDD	01	Northrop Grumman/Ingalls, Pascagoula, Miss.	2004	2005		2006	Building
DDG 101	GRIDLEY	02	Bath Iron Works, Maine	2004	2006		2007	Building
DDG 102	SAMPSON	02	Bath Iron Works, Maine	2005	2006		2007	Building
DDG 103	TRUXTUN	02	Northrop Grumman/Ingalls, Pascagoula, Miss.	2005	2006		2007	Building
DDG 104	STERETT	03	Bath Iron Works, Maine	2005	2007		2008	Building
DDG 105	DEWEY	03	Northrop Grumman/Ingalls, Pascagoula, Miss.	2006	2007		2008	Building
DDG 106	....	03	Bath Iron Works, Maine	2006	2007		2008	Building
DDG 107	....	04	Northrop Grumman/Ingalls, Pascagoula, Miss.	2007	2008		2009	Building
DDG 108	....	04	Bath Iron Works, Maine	2007	2008		2009	Building
DDG 109	....	04	Bath Iron Works, Maine	2007	2009		2009	Building
DDG 110	....	05	Northrop Grumman/Ingalls, Pascagoula, Miss.	2008	2009		2010	Building
DDG 111	....	05	Bath Iron Works, Maine	2008	2009		2010	Building
DDG 112	....	05	Bath Iron Works, Maine	2008	2010		2011	Building

Displacement:	9,217 tons full load	ASW weapons:	VLA (ASROC)
Length:	509 feet (155.18 m) overall		6 12.75-inch (324-mm) torpedo tubes Mk 32 (2 triple) for
Beam:	59 feet (18.0 m) waterline		Mk 46 and Mk 50 torpedoes
	66½ feet (20.4 m) extreme	Radars:	SPS-64(V)9 navigation
Draft:	30½ feet (9.3 m)		SPS-67(V)3 surface search
Propulsion:	4 gas turbines (General Electric LM 2500-30);100,000 shp;		(4) SPY-1D multifunction in DDG 79–90
	2 shafts		(4) SPY-1D(V) multifunction in DDG 91–112
Speed:	31 knots	Sonars:	SQS-53C(V)1 bow mounted
Range:	4,400 nm (8,150 km) at 20 knots	Fire control:	3 Mk 99 illuminators with SPG-62 radar
Personnel:	approx. 315 (22 officers + 293 enlisted)		1 Mk 116 ASW control system
	+ 21-man LAMPS detachment (6 officers + 15 enlisted)		1 Mk 160 GFCS
Helicopters:	2 SH-60R LAMPS III		SQQ-89(V)10 ASW system
Missiles:	96-cell VLS for Standard-MR SM-2/Tomahawk/VLA		SWG-3 (Tomahawk)
	(ASROC) Mk 41 Mod 0	EW systems:	SLQ-25A Nixie
Guns:	1 5-inch (127-mm) 54-cal DP Mk 45 in DDG 79–80;		SLQ-32(V)3 in DDG 79–84; (V)2 in DDG 85–90
	1 5-inch (127mm) 62-cal. DP Mk 45 Mod 4 in later ships		SLY-2 in DDG 91 and later ships
	2 20-mm Phalanx CIWS Mk 15 (2 multibarrel)		

These are improved ARLEIGH BURKE-class ships, the most significant differences being six additional vertical-launching missile cells and full facilities for supporting two SH-60B Seahawk helicopters. The Flight IIA ships, however, are larger and do not have Harpoon canisters (as do all other active cruisers and destroyers).

The delay in construction and then cancellation of the DD 21 class caused an increase in the size of this class, and several additional changes were made because of delays in the DD(X) program. The latest available information is reflected in the class table. Construction is expected to end with the FY 2005 program.

Builders: The MASON was the last major warship to be constructed in the United States (at Bath Iron Works) on an inclined building way. Subsequent ships built at the Bath yard have been constructed on horizontal assembly positions and lowered into the water by a launching dock. All ships of the ARLEIGH BURKE, KIDD, and TICONDEROGA classes built at Litton/Ingalls (now Northrop Grumman/Ingalls) were assembled on a horizontal assembly line.

Design: In addition to the added VLS cells and helicopter facility, the Flight IIA ships have the two after SPY-1 radar "faces" mounted one deck (8 feet/2.4 m) higher than in the earlier ships to improve line-of-sight performance over the after end of the ship. The after superstructure has been extended to accommodate the dual hangar, and the transom extended, accounting for the greater length, to accommodate the stern helicopter deck.

They have limited steel and Kevlar armor for critical spaces.

Electronics: Beginning with the DDG 91, the SPY-1D radar is a modified variant (V modification) to enhance performance in littoral areas (i.e., against background land clutter).

The SQS-53C sonar has been fitted with the Kingfisher modification, i.e., (V)1 modification, for mine detection. The SQR-19 TACTAS towed array found in earlier ships will not be fitted in these ships, although it could be "reconstituted" if necessary.

Guns: The WINSTON S. CHURCHILL and later units mount the 5-inch/62-cal gun. The gun fires Extended Range Guided Munition (ERGM) rounds (see Chapter 31).

Helicopters: The Recovery Assist, Secure, and Traverse (RAST) system is being fitted in these ships. The helicopter hangar doors are an accordion type, folding upward.

Missiles: The self-loading feature of the two VLS batteries has been deleted in these ships, permitting 32 VLS cells forward and 64 cells aft, for a total of 96 weapons.

The eight-canister Harpoon missile battery found in all other U.S. cruisers and destroyers has been deleted from these ships as a weight-saving measure. However, they could be mounted at a future date between the funnels.

Names: The DDG 81 originally was named WINSTON CHURCHILL; it was changed on 3 August 1998. The DDG 94 was named for Ambassador Paul H. Nitze, former Secretary of the Navy and Under Secretary of Defense, on his 94th birthday.

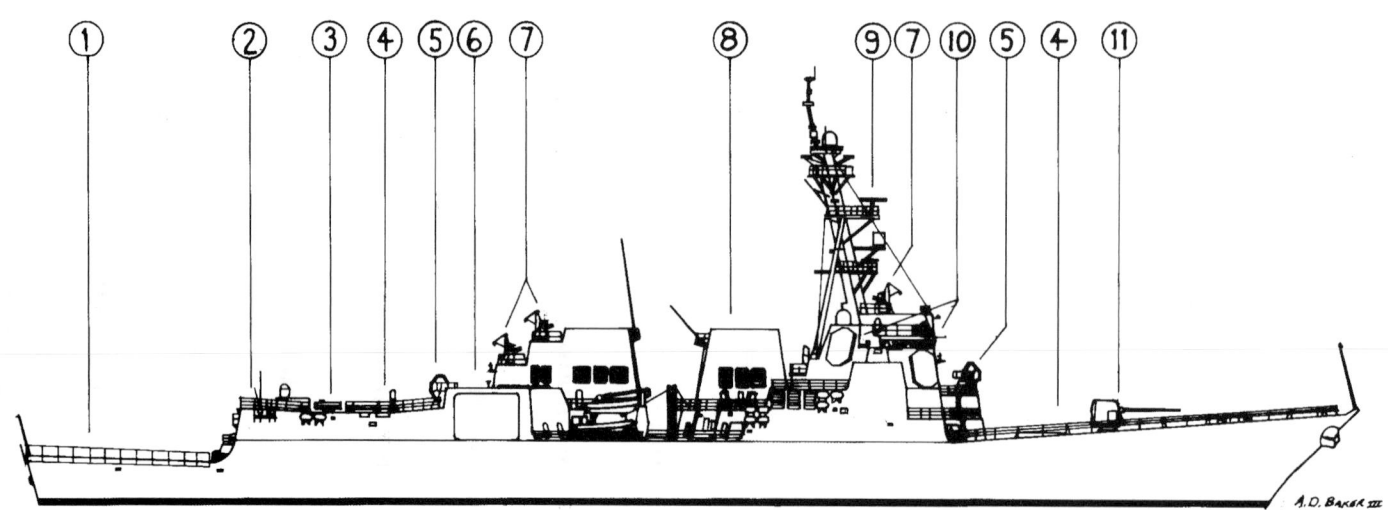

Guided Missile Destroyer Pinckney
1. Helicopter deck 2. Helicopter hangars 3. 12.75-inch triple torpedo tubes Mk 32 4. Vertical launching system Mk 41 (2) 5. SLY-2 electronic warfare system 6. Hangar for WLD-1 remote minehunting system 7. SPG-62 radar illuminator (3) 8. SRBOC decoy launcher Mk 36 (4) 9. SPS-67(V)4 surface search radar 10. SPY-1D(V) fixed-array radar antenna (4) 11. 5-inch DP single gun mount Mk 45 (A. D. Baker III)

The ROOSEVELT during launch-and-recovery operations with an SH-60B Seahawk LAMPS III helicopter. The twin hangars are outboard of the after Mk 41 vertical-launch missile battery. There are two rigid hull inflatable boats stowed on the starboard side. (Litton/Ingalls Shipbuilding)

The BULKELEY in the Persian Gulf, typical of the Improved ARLEIGH BURKE-class destroyers. She has twin Satellite Communication (SATCOM) antenna domes atop her superstructure; there is a Phalanx CIWS immediately forward of the bridge. The stem anchor is evident. (2004, U.S. Navy/Brien Aho)

The DONALD COOK under way in the Mediterranean Sea. There is a vertical replenishment spot marked forward. The later ARLEIGH BURKE-class ships have a twin hangar for H-60 helicopters, a feature missing in the earlier ships of this design. This was a major shortcoming, as lack of a helicopter hangar prevents effective operation of UAVs as well as helicopters. (2002, U.S. Navy/Michael W. Pendergrass)

The destroyer LASSEN heels to port as the ship executes a sharp turn during operations in the Philippine Sea. These ships retained the same armament as the earlier ARLEIGH BURKE-class destroyers while incorporating a two-helicopter hangar in their design. (2003, U.S. Navy/Dustin Howell)

28 GUIDED MISSILE DESTROYERS: "ARLEIGH BURKE" CLASS (FLIGHTS I/II)

Number	Name	FY	Builder	Laid Down	Launched	Christened	Comm.	Status
DDG 51	Arleigh Burke	85	Bath Iron Works, Maine	6 Dec 1988	16 Sep 1989	—	4 July 1991	**AA**
DDG 52	Barry	87	Litton/Ingalls, Pascagoula, Miss.	26 Feb 1990	10 May 1991	8 June 1991	12 Dec 1992	**AA**
DDG 53	John Paul Jones	87	Bath Iron Works, Maine	8 Aug 1990	26 Oct 1991	—	18 Dec 1993	**PA**
DDG 54	Curtis Wilbur	89	Bath Iron Works, Maine	12 Mar 1991	16 May 1992	—	19 Mar 1994	**PA**
DDG 55	Stout	89	Litton/Ingalls, Pascagoula, Miss.	12 Aug 1991	16 Oct 1992	24 Oct 1992	13 Aug 1994	**AA**
DDG 56	John S. McCain	89	Bath Iron Works, Maine	3 Sep 1991	26 Sep 1992	—	2 July 1994	**PA**
DDG 57	Mitscher	89	Litton/Ingalls, Pascagoula, Miss.	12 Feb 1992	7 May 1993	15 May 1993	10 Dec 1994	**AA**
DDG 58	Laboon	89	Bath Iron Works, Maine	24 Mar 1992	20 Feb 1993	—	18 Mar 1995	**AA**
DDG 59	Russell	90	Litton/Ingalls, Pascagoula, Miss.	27 July 1992	20 Oct1993	23 Oct 1993	20 May 1995	**PA**
DDG 60	Paul Hamilton	90	Bath Iron Works, Maine	24 Aug 1992	24 July 1993	—	27 May 1995	**PA**
DDG 61	Ramage	90	Litton/Ingalls, Pascagoula, Miss.	4 Jan 1993	11 Feb 1994	23 Apr 1994	22 July 1995	**AA**
DDG 62	Fitzgerald	90	Bath Iron Works, Maine	9 Feb 1993	29 Jan 1994	—	14 Oct1995	**PA**
DDG 63	Stethem	90	Litton/Ingalls, Pascagoula, Miss.	10 May 1993	17 June 1994	16 July 1994	21 Oct 1995	**PA**
DDG 64	Carney	91	Bath Iron Works, Maine	3 Aug 1993	23 July 1994	—	13 Apr1996	**AA**
DDG 65	Benfold	91	Litton/Ingalls, Pascagoula, Miss.	27 Sep 1993	9 Nov 1994	12 Nov 1994	30 Mar 1996	**PA**
DDG 66	Gonzalez	91	Bath Iron Works, Maine	3 Feb 1994	17 Dec 1994	18 Feb 1995	12 Oct 1966	**AA**
DDG 67	Cole	91	Litton/Ingalls, Pascagoula, Miss.	28 Feb 1994	10 Feb 1995	8 Apr 1995	8 June 1996	**AA**
DDG 68	The Sullivans	92	Bath Iron Works, Maine	27 July 1994	12 Aug 1995	—	19 Apr1996	**AA**
DDG 69	Milius	92	Litton/Ingalls, Pascagoula, Miss.	8 Aug 1994	1 Aug 1995 28	Oct 1995	23 Nov 1996	**PA**
DDG 70	Hopper	92	Bath Iron Works, Maine	23 Feb 1995	6 Jan 1996	—	6 Sep 1997	**PA**
DDG 71	Ross	92	Litton/Ingalls, Pascagoula, Miss.	10 Apr 1995	22 Mar 1996	20 Apr 1996	28 June 1997	**AA**
DDG 72	Mahan	92	Bath Iron Works, Maine	17 Aug 1995	29 June 1996	—	14 Feb 1998	**AA**
DDG 73	Decatur	93	Bath Iron Works, Maine	11 Jan 1996	10 Nov 1996	—	29 Aug 1998	**PA**
DDG 74	McFaul	93	Litton/Ingalls, Pascagoula, Miss.	26 Jan 1996	18 Jan 1997	12 Apr 1997	25 Apr 1998	**AA**
DDG 75	Donald Cook	93	Bath Iron Works, Maine	9 July 1996	3 May 1997	—	21 Aug 1998	**AA**
DDG 76	Higgins	93	Bath Iron Works, Maine	14 Nov 1996	4 Oct 1997	—	24 Apr 1999	**PA**
DDG 77	O'Kane	94	Bath Iron Works, Maine	8 May 1997	28 Mar 1998	—	23 Oct 1999	**PA**
DDG 78	Porter	94	Litton/Ingalls, Pascagoula, Miss.	2 Dec 1996	12 Nov 1997	15 Nov 1997	20 Mar 1999	**AA**

Displacement:	DDG 51: 6,624 tons light
	later units: 6,682 tons light
	DDG 51: 8,315 tons full load
	later units: 8,373 tons full load
Length:	465⅝ feet (142.0 m) waterline
	504½ feet (153.8 m) overall
Beam:	59 feet (18.0 m) at waterline
	66¹¹⁄₁₂ feet (20.4 m) extreme
Draft:	30⅞ feet (9.3 m)
Propulsion:	4 gas turbines (General Electric LM 2500-30); 100,000 shp; 2 shafts
Speed:	31 knots
Range:	4,400 nm (8,150 km) at 20 knots
Personnel:	approx. 320 (22 officers + 298 enlisted) + 21-man LAMPS detachment (6 officers + 15 enlisted)
Helicopters:	landing deck only
Missiles:	90-cell VLS for Standard-MR SM-2/Tomahawk/VLA (ASROC) Mk 41 Mod 0 8 Harpoon SSM Mk 141 (2 quad canisters)
Guns:	1 5-inch (127-mm) 54-cal DP Mk 45 2 20-mm Phalanx CIWS Mk 15 (2 multibarrel)
ASW weapons:	VLA (ASROC) 6 12.75-inch (324-mm) torpedo tubes Mk 32 (2 triple) for Mk 46 and Mk 50 torpedoes
Radars:	1 SPS-64(V)9 navigation 1 SPS-67(V)3/4 surface search (4) SPY-1D multifunction
Sonars:	SQS-53C(V)1 bow mounted SQR-19B TACTAS towed array
Fire control:	3 Mk 99 illuminators with SPG-62 radar 1 Mk 116 ASW control system 1 Mk 160 GFCS SQQ-89(V)4 ASW system SWG-1 (Harpoon) SWG-3 (Tomahawk)
EW systems:	SLQ-25A Nixie SLQ-32(V)2 in DDG 51–67 SLQ-32(V)3 in DDG 68–78

These destroyers emphasize AAW capabilities and were intended to complement Aegis cruisers of the Ticonderoga class in the air/ missile defense of carrier battle groups. Initial plans for a more-advanced radar and propulsion plant for these ships were dropped in favor of the propulsion plant in the CG 47/DDG 993/DD 963 classes and a derivative of the CG 47 Aegis radar.

The production DDG 51 units were planned to cost approximately 75 percent of a CG 47-class cruiser. The significant differences in the weapons and sensors for the DDG 51 from the CG 47 are:

- three vice four missile illuminators
- 90 vice 122 VLS missiles
- no helicopter hangar
- no AAW commander/coordination facilities

The lead ship of the class was completed 21 months behind schedule; the original contract with Bath Iron Works stipulated delivery in October 1989. The Navy says the delays were caused by: (1) a 90-day labor strike at Bath Iron Works, (2) corrections to government-furnished information for the main reduction gear, (3) Navy changes to engine room piping, (4) extension of the combat system testing program, and (5) limitations of Bath's design and production capacity.

The John S. McCain is homeported in Yokosuka, a component of the Kitty Hawk battle group.

Builders: In the late 1980s, Congress attempted to open construction of the Arleigh Burke class to a third shipyard, the most probable candidates being Todd Pacific Shipyards at Long Beach, California, and Avondale Shipyards at New Orleans, Louisiana. Because of the low production rate envisioned at that time, however, the Navy limited construction to two yards.

Class: Original Navy planning provided for 50–60 advanced missile destroyers to be authorized in FY 1985–1994 to replace about the same number of older cruisers and destroyers. The Carter administration proposed the construction of 49 ships of this class, while the Reagan administration (1981) initially envisioned a program of 63 ships.

The DDG 51–71 (21 ships) are Flight I and the DDG 72–78 (7 ships) are Flight II. The later ships have a number of combat capability improvements, such as the Joint Tactical Information Distribution System (JTIDS), Tactical Data Information Exchange Subsystem (TADIX), the upgraded SLQ-32(V)3, and the Standard-MR Block IV missile. The later ships also have the ability to refuel and rearm helicopters (see below).

Classification: The initial Navy study, conducted in 1979, leading to the preliminary design of this ship used the designation DDX and subsequently DDGX. (Of the various design/capability options developed in the study, subtype 3A was selected for development as the DDG 51.)

Cost: Early cost estimates stipulated $550 million per ship (FY 1982 dollars) for the 6,000-ton ship in series production. Subsequently, in February 1983, the Secretary of the Navy established a cost ceiling of $1.1 billion for the lead ship and $700 million each for ships no. 6–10. In early 1987, the Navy estimated the lead ship would cost $1.048 billion in FY 1983 dollars and the later ships $677 million.

Design: From the outset, these ships were directed by the Chief of Naval Operations to be smaller and less expensive than the DDG/CG 47 design. Early design concepts envisioned a ship as small as 6,000 tons full load displacement.

These are the first U.S. destroyers of post–World War II construction with steel superstructures, a decision made as a result of the cruiser BELKNAP's collision with an aircraft carrier in 1975 (and not after the loss of the British destroyer SHEFFIELD to an Argentine-launched Exocet air-to-surface missile in the 1982 conflict in the Falklands). The steel construction provides increased resistance to blast overpressure, fragment, and fire damage, plus Electromagnetic Pulse (EMP) protection. The ships have 130 tons of Kevlar armor plating to protect vital spaces.

This is the first class of U.S. Navy ships to be built with the so-called Level III collective protection features against Chemical–Biological–Radiological (CBR) attack. This provides the maximum protection possible within a ship, including in berthing, medical, and control spaces. (The second class to be so fitted is the Supply/AOE 6 class.)

The ships have been designed with a significantly reduced radar cross section over previous destroyer-type ships.

Early designs provided for a 61-foot (18.6-m) beam; it was subsequently reduced to 59 feet (18 m).

The DECATUR was the Navy's first environmentally friendly "green ship," having an onboard paper pulper, plastics processor, and other equipment to help reduce, store, and recycle materials from metal to paper.

Electronics: A derivative of the CG 47 Aegis system is provided, with all four SPY-1D radar faces mounted on a single, forward deckhouse.

The SQS-53C sonar has been fitted with the Kingfisher modification, i.e., (V)1 modification, for mine detection.

Engineering: Essentially the same propulsion plant as in the CG 47/DD 963/DDG 997 classes is fitted in this class. At congressional urging, the Navy looked into the possibility of a Rankin regenerative system to enhance the efficiency of the gas turbines, but that system required too much internal volume to be practical for the class.

The ARLEIGH BURKE reportedly attained 32 knots on sea trials with 103,000 shp. The sustained horsepower for these ships is approximately 90,000 shp.

Guns: The original DDGX proposal called for a gun armament of only two Phalanx CIWS. Subsequently, a single 76-mm OTO Malera Mk 75 gun was provided in the design, and later the single 5-inch/54 cal Mk 45 was dictated, in addition to the two CIWS.

Helicopters: These ships have large helicopter landing areas on their fantails and a Vertical Replenishment (VERTREP) position forward; however, no hangars are provided and helicopters normally will not be deployed in these ships. The DDG 52 and later ships have the RAST hauldown system, plus helicopter refueling and rearming capabilities (adding 58 tons to full load displacement).

Names: In 1983, the not-yet-started DDG 51 was named for Admiral Arleigh Burke, the Chief of Naval Operations from 1955 to 1961. This was the second U.S. ship in recent years to be named for a living person, the first being the CARL VINSON (CVN 70).

The DDG 52 originally was named JOHN BARRY; it was changed to BARRY on 1 February 1988, back to JOHN BARRY on 9 May 1988, and again back to BARRY on 8 December 1989—further testimony to the confusion in the U.S. Navy ship naming process.

The DDG 68 is named for the five Sullivan brothers, killed on 12–13 November 1942 when the light cruiser JUNEAU (CLAA 52) was sunk by Japanese forces. Only ten men from a crew of 700 survived. The destroyer DD 537 previously carried the name.

The DDG 70 is named for Rear Admiral Grace M. Hopper, a pioneer in developing computer languages. This is only the second U.S. warship to be named for a woman, the first being the HIGBEE (DD 806), honoring the second commandant of the Navy Nurse Corps (1911–1922) and first woman to be awarded the Navy Cross.

Operational: The destroyer COLE was heavily damaged by terrorists in an explosive-laden suicide boat in the port of Aden, Yemen, on 12 October 2000. She was in transit from her home port of Norfolk, Virginia, to the Persian Gulf and had entered Aden for a brief refueling stop. As the ship was taking on fuel from a "dolphin," or refueling pier, in the center of the harbor, a small craft, apparently operated by two men, came alongside and exploded.

The blast tore a hole approximately 30 x 40 feet (9.1 x 12.2 m) in the port side of the hull; 17 sailors were killed and 39 injured. The COLE was transported back to the United States on the Norwegian heavy-lift ship BLUE MARLIN and underwent repairs at the Litton/Ingalls Shipyard from December 2000 to April 2002, at a cost of $250 million.

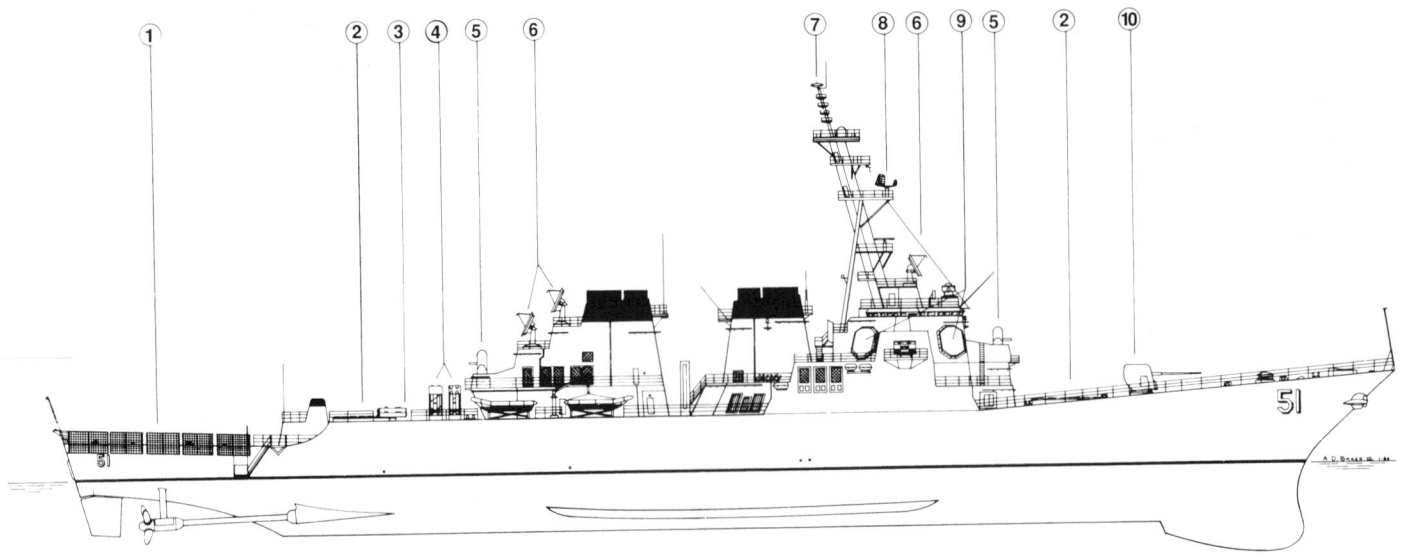

Guided Missile Destroyer ARLEIGH BURKE
1. Helicopter deck 2. Vertical launching system Mk 41 (2) 3. 12.75-inch triple torpedo tubes Mk 32 4. Harpoon missile canisters (8) 5. Phalanx close-in weapon system Mk 15 (2) 6. SPG-62 radar illuminator (3) 7. Tactical aircraft control system URN-20 8. SPS-67(V)3 surface search radar above SPS-64(V) navigation radar 9. SPY-1D fixed-array radar 10. 5-inch DP single gun mount Mk 45 (A. D. Baker III)

The rehabilitated COLE *working up in the Atlantic for a deployment to the Mediterranean Sea. The angled hull and funnels of the* ARLEIGH BURKE *class are evident here; the center stern opening is for the SLQ-25 Nixie torpedo countermeasures device. (2003, U.S. Navy/ Douglas M. Pearlman)*

The O'KANE in the Persian Gulf during Operation Iraqi Freedom. The diminutive 5-inch single Mk 45 gun mount is forward; the original ARLEIGH BURKE design provided for only 20-mm Phalanx close-in weapon systems. The Harpoon canisters are mounted just aft of the second funnel and after Phalanx CIWS. (2003, U.S. Navy/Alan J. Baribeau)

The McFAUL under way as part of the WASP (LHD 1) Expeditionary Strike Group (ESG). Surface combatants and attack submarines now operate with amphibious ships to form ESGs in an effort to increase fleet flexibility. The McFAUL flies an oversize battle flag. (2004, U.S. Navy/David K. Simmons)

GUIDED MISSILES DESTROYERS: "KIDD" CLASS

Number	Name	Comm.	Status
DDG 993	KIDD	1981	decomm./str. 12 Mar 1998; to Taiwan
DDG 994	CALLAGHAN	1981	decomm./str. 31 Mar 1998; to Taiwan
DDG 995	SCOTT	1981	decomm./str. 10 Dec 1998; to Taiwan
DDG 996	CHANDLER	1982	decomm./str. 23 Sep 1999; to Taiwan

These were "double-end" Standard-ER guided missile destroyers built on SPRUANCE-class hulls. They were considered highly effective, but for fiscal reasons they were retired after 16½–17½ years of service in the U.S. Navy.

Six ships originally were ordered by Iran. They were assigned destroyer hull numbers by the U.S. Navy (DD 993–998); see Table 15-6. After the Shah of Iran was deposed in the Islamic revolution,

the four ships actually built went to the U.S. Navy with DDG designations, but with their DD-series hull numbers. The remaining two were canceled, and one of their hull numbers subsequently was reassigned to the 31st SPRUANCE-class ship.

After being decommissioned, the quartet were offered to the Greek Navy, but that transfer was aborted for political reasons. The government of Taiwan, after failing to obtain U.S. Aegis destroyers, in early 2001 agreed to the purchase of all four ships at a reported price of $732 million, which subsequently was reduced by 15 percent because of Taiwanese Navy budget limitations. All were sold to Taiwan in 2003 with delivery at a later date. Standard–ER SM-2 Block IIIA and Harpoon missiles will be provided for the ships.

See 16th Edition/pages 128–30 for characteristics.

6 DESTROYERS: "SPRUANCE" CLASS

Number	Name	FY	Builder	Laid Down	Launched	Comm.	Status
DD 963	SPRUANCE	70	Litton/Ingalls, Pascagoula, Miss.	27 Nov 1972	10 Nov 1973	20 Sep 1975	AR; decomm. 24 Sep 2004
DD 964	PAUL F. FOSTER	70	Litton/Ingalls, Pascagoula, Miss.	6 Feb 1973	23 Feb 1974	21 Feb 1975	decomm. 27 Mar 2003; str. 6 Apr 2004 (test ship)
DD 965	KINKAID	70	Litton/Ingalls, Pascagoula, Miss.	19 Apr 1973	25 May 1974	10 July 1976	decomm. 7 Jan 2003; str. 6 Apr 2004
DD 966	HEWITT	71	Litton/Ingalls, Pascagoula, Miss.	23 July 1973	24 Aug 1974	25 Sep 1976	decomm. 19 July 2001; str.5 June 2002
DD 967	ELLIOT	71	Litton/Ingalls, Pascagoula, Miss.	15 Oct 1973	19 Dec 1974	22 Jan 1977	decomm. 2 Dec 2003; str. 6 Apr 2004
DD 968	ARTHUR W. RADFORD	71	Litton/Ingalls, Pascagoula, Miss.	14 Jan 1974	1 Mar 1975	16 Apr 1977	decomm. 18 Mar 2003; str. 6 Apr 2004 (test ship)
DD 969	PETERSON	71	Litton/Ingalls, Pascagoula, Miss.	29 Apr 1974	21 June 1975	9 July 1977	decomm. 4 Oct 2002; str. 6 Nov 2002
DD 970	CARON	71	Litton/Ingalls, Pascagoula, Miss.	1 July 1974	24 June 1975	1 Oct 1977	decomm. 15 Oct 2001; str. 5 June 2002
DD 971	DAVID R. RAY	71	Litton/Ingalls, Pascagoula, Miss.	23 Sep 1974	23 Aug 1975	19 Nov 1977	decomm. 28 Feb 2002; str. 6 Nov 2002
DD 972	OLDENDORF	72	Litton/Ingalls, Pascagoula, Miss.	27 Dec 1974	21 Oct 1975	4 Mar 1978	decomm. 20 June 2003; str. 6 Apr 2004
DD 973	JOHN YOUNG	72	Litton/Ingalls, Pascagoula, Miss.	17 Feb 1975	7 Feb 1976	20 May 1978	decomm. 30 Sep 2002; str. 6 Nov 2002
DD 974	COMTE DE GRASSE	72	Litton/Ingalls, Pascagoula, Miss.	4 Apr 1975	26 Mar 1976	5 Aug 1978	decomm./str. 5 June 1998
DD 975	O'BRIEN	72	Litton/Ingalls, Pascagoula, Miss.	9 May 1975	8 July 1976	3 Dec 1977	decomm./str. Sep 2004
DD 976	MERRILL	72	Litton/Ingalls, Pascagoula, Miss.	16 June 1975	1 Sep 1976	11 Mar 1978	decomm./str. 26 Mar 1998
DD 977	BRISCOE	72	Litton/Ingalls, Pascagoula, Miss.	21 July 1975	18 Dec 1976	3 June 1978	decomm. 2 Oct 2003; str. 6 Apr 2004
DD 978	STUMP	72	Litton/Ingalls, Pascagoula, Miss.	22 Aug 1975	21 Mar 1977	19 Aug 1978	decomm./str. 22 Oct 2004
DD 979	CONOLLY	74	Litton/Ingalls, Pascagoula, Miss.	29 Sep 1975	3 June 1977	14 Oct 1978	decomm./str. 18 Sep 1998
DD 980	MOOSBRUGGER	74	Litton/Ingalls, Pascagoula, Miss.	3 Nov 1975	23 July 1977	16 Dec 1978	AR; decomm. 15 Dec 2000
DD 981	JOHN HANCOCK	74	Litton/Ingalls, Pascagoula, Miss.	16 Jan 1976	28 Sep 1977	10 Mar 1979	AR; decomm. 16 Oct 2003
DD 982	NICHOLSON	74	Litton/Ingalls, Pascagoula, Miss.	20 Feb 1976	29 Nov 1977	12 May 1979	decomm. 20 Dec 2000; str. 6 Apr 2004
DD 983	JOHN RODGERS	74	Litton/Ingalls, Pascagoula, Miss.	12 Aug 1976	25 Feb 1978	14 July 1979	decomm./str. 4 Sep 1998
DD 984	LEFTWICH	74	Litton/Ingalls, Pascagoula, Miss.	12 Nov 1976	8 Apr 1978	25 Aug 1979	decomm./str. 27 Mar 1998
DD 985	CUSHING	74	Litton/Ingalls, Pascagoula, Miss.	2 Feb 1977	17 June 1978	20 Oct 1979	**PA**
DD 986	HARRY W. HILL	75	Litton/Ingalls, Pascagoula, Miss.	1 Apr 1977	10 Aug 1978	17 Nov 1979	decomm./str. 29 May 1998
DD 987	O'BANNON	75	Litton/Ingalls, Pascagoula, Miss.	24 June 1977	25 Sep 1978	15 Dec 1979	**AA**
DD 988	THORN	75	Litton/Ingalls, Pascagoula, Miss.	29 Aug 1977	14 Nov 1978	16 Feb 1980	AR; decomm. 25 Aug 2004
DD 989	DEYO	75	Litton/Ingalls, Pascagoula, Miss.	14 Oct 1977	20 Jan 1979	22 Mar 1980	decomm. 6 Nov 2003; str. 6 Apr 2004
DD 990	INGERSOLL	75	Litton/Ingalls, Pascagoula, Miss.	16 Dec 1977	10 Mar 1979	12 Apr 1980	decomm./str. 24 July 1998
DD 991	FIFE	75	Litton/Ingalls, Pascagoula, Miss.	6 Mar 1978	1 May 1979	31 May 1980	decomm. 28 Feb 2003; str. 6 Apr 2004
DD 992	FLETCHER	75	Litton/Ingalls, Pascagoula, Miss.	24 Apr 1978	16 June 1979	12 July 1980	decomm./str. Oct 2004
DD 997	HAYLER	78	Litton/Ingalls, Pascagoula, Miss.	22 Oct 1980	27 Mar 1982	5 Mar 1983	decomm./str. 6 Apr 2004

Displacement:	7,410 tons light
	9,250 tons full load
Length:	528½ feet (161.25 m) waterline
	563⅙ feet (171.7 m) overall
Beam:	55 feet (16.8 m)
Draft:	29 feet (8.8 m)
Propulsion:	4 gas turbines (General Electric LM 2500); 86,000 shp; 2 shafts
Speed:	32.5 knots
Range:	6,000 nm (11,112 km) at 20 knots
	3,300 nm (6,112 km) at 30 knots
Personnel:	approx. 325 (21 officers + 304 enlisted)
	+ 21-man LAMPS detachment (6 officers + 15 enlisted)
Helicopters:	2 SH-60B Seahawk LAMPS III
Missiles:	1 8-cell NATO Sea Sparrow launcher Mk 29
	1 21-cell RAM launcher Mk 49
	8 Harpoon SSM Mk 141 (2 quad canisters)
	30-cell VLS for Tomahawk/VLA(ASROC) Mk 41 Mod 0
Guns:	2 5-inch (127-mm) 54-cal DP Mk 45 (2 single)
	2 25-mm Bushmaster cannon Mk 38 (2 single) in some ships
	2 20-mm Phalanx CIWS Mk 15 (2 multibarrel)
	4 machine guns 50-cal/M2
ASW weapons:	6 12.75-inch (324-mm) torpedo tubes Mk 32 (2 triple) for Mk 46 and Mk 50 torpedoes
Radars:	Mk 23 Target Acquisition System (TAS) in most ships
	SPS-40B/C/D/E air search
	SPS-53 or SPS-64(V)9 or LN-66 navigation
	SPS-55 surface search
	SPS-64(V)9 navigation
Sonars:	SQS-53B bow mounted
	SQR-19A/B TACTAS towed array in most ships
Fire control:	1 Mk 86 GFCS with SPG-60 and SPQ-9A radars
	1 Mk 91 missile FCS
	1 Mk 116 ASW FCS
	SQQ-89(V)1 ASW system
	SWG-1 (Harpoon)
	SWG-3 (Tomahawk)
EW systems:	SLQ-25A Nixie
	SLQ-32(V)3
	SLQ-34 Classic Outboard direction finder in several ships

The 31-ship SPRUANCE class originally was built as specialized ASW ships. They since have been provided with an anti-ship capability with the Harpoon missile and, subsequently, most ships with a long-range anti-ship/land-attack capability with the Tomahawk missile. (These were the only ships rated as destroyers to carry the Tomahawk.) Seven ships had Armored Box Launchers (ABL) mounted forward of the bridge for eight Tomahawk missiles; the 24 other ships had 61-cell VLS fitted forward of the bridge (replacing the ASROC launcher and magazine). The ABLs were removed in the mid-1990s, prior to the ships being decommissioned in 1998.

Only one ship remains active, the STUMP; her decommissioning is tentatively scheduled for September 2005. Several of the eight decommissioned ships will be retained in mothballs as mobilization assets, but probably one-half will be discarded in the near term.

The PAUL F. FOSTER has been converted to a Self-Defense Systems Test Ship (SDSTS) to replace the ex-DECATUR (DDG 31). She remains on the Naval Vessel Register (NVR) as "floating equipment"; see Chapter 25. The ARTHUR W. RADFORD has been transferred to the Northrop Grumman Systems/Ingalls shipyard for conversion to a test ship for DD(X) systems, including electric propulsion systems, radars, sonars, and the Advanced Gun System. The ship has been stricken from the NVR.

After being decommissioned, the FIFE was held in standby status for four months in the event that the 2003 war in Iraq warranted the ship being recommissioned.

ASW weapons: As built, these ships had a Mk 16 ASROC launcher forward of the bridge (with reload capability); it was removed with the installation of VLS. It subsequently also was removed from ships with ABL Tomahawk launchers.

Builders: The entire SPRUANCE class was contracted with a single shipyard to facilitate design and mass production. A contract for the development and production of 30 ships was awarded on 23 June 1970 to a new yard established by the Ingalls Shipbuilding Division of Litton Industries at Pascagoula, Mississippi. Labor and technical problems delayed the construction of these ships. The 31st ship was placed under contract in 1979 (see *Class* notes).

Class: The SPRUANCE-class destroyers were developed as replacements for the large number of World War II–built general purpose destroyers of the ALLEN M. SUMNER (DD 692) and GEARING (DD 710) classes that reached the end of their service lives in the mid-1970s. In addition to these 31 ships, four similar ships were ordered with the Mk 26/Standard AAW missile system for the Iranian Navy, but they were completed as the U.S. KIDD class, accounting for hull numbers DD 993–996.

An additional ship of the SPRUANCE class was ordered on 29 September 1979 (DD 997). One of two authorized (one funded) by Congress, she came with a proviso; in the wording of the Senate Committee on Armed Services, "The committee does not intend for these funds to be used for acquisition of two standard DD 963-class destroyers; rather, it is the committee's intention that these ships be the first element in a new technology approach to the problems of designing surface escorts. The standard [DD] 963 class design should be modified to substantially increase the number of helicopter aircraft carried." This modification also would have permitted the eventual operation of VSTOL aircraft. However, the Navy chose to build the ship as a standard SPRUANCE, and no additional ships were funded by Congress. (The ship initially was listed as DDH 997 in Navy working papers.)

The JOHN HANCOCK and MOOSBRUGGER were the first VLS-configured ships to be decommissioned and stricken, both in late 2000.

Additional ships will be discarded as improved ARLEIGH BURKE-class destroyers join the fleet.

The HAYLER was sunk as a target on 12–13 November 2004.

Design: SCB No. 224. The original concept for this class provided for an AAW missile version (DXG), as well as the ASW version (DX); these became the KIDD and SPRUANCE classes, respectively.

The SPRUANCE design provided for the subsequent installation of additional weapon systems, specifically, the Mk 26 missile launcher (and later the Mk 41 VLS) forward, with removal of the ASROC launcher, and aft, with removal of the Sea Sparrow launcher (see *Missiles* notes). In addition, the forward 5-inch gun could have been replaced by the now-canceled 8-inch Mk 71 MCLWG.

The Mk 16 ASROC launchers (8 cells) have been removed. They could be automatically reloaded, with a vertical magazine providing 16 reloads. The Sea Sparrow launcher is reloaded "by hand," with a total of 24 Sea Sparrow missiles carried.

The ARTHUR W. RADFORD was fitted with an Advanced Enclosed Mast/Sensor (AEM/S) structure in place of her mainmast during a refit at Norfolk Naval Shipyard in 1997. Built by Litton/Ingalls, the mast is fabricated of nonmetallic material and envelopes the normal suite of radar and communications antennas; it is 93 feet (28.3 m) high and, at its widest point, 31 feet (9.4 m) in diameter.[13] The mast reduces the ship's radar cross section and improves sensor performance. The project cost $23 million.

Electronics: As built, these ships had the SLQ-32(V)2; it later was upgraded to (V)3 configuration.

The Mk 23 TAS is not provided in the DD 985, 988, and 992.

Original plans were for these ships to have the SQS-35 Independent Variable Depth Sonar (IVDS) in addition to a bow-mounted SQS-53. The IVDS was deleted because of the effectiveness of the SQS-53. The Navy subsequently decided to fit these ships with the SQR-19 TACTAS; of the remaining ships, the SQR-19 is not fitted in the DD 985 and 988. The STUMP was fitted with the engineering development model of the SQS-53C sonar; the MOOSBRUGGER was refitted with the SQS-53B sonar and was the first Navy ship to have the SQQ-89 system. Four ships were fitted with the SQR-15 TASS; it had been removed by 1992.

Engineering: These were the first U.S. Navy major surface combatants to have gas-turbine propulsion as their main propulsion. Gas turbines previously were installed in Navy patrol combatants (PGM/PG 84 class) and in the Coast Guard HAMILTON (WHEC 715) class and some cutters of the RELIANCE (WMEC 615) class.

The SPRUANCE-class ships have four LM 2500 gas turbines, which are modified TF39 aircraft turbofan engines. One engine can propel the ships at about 19 knots, two engines at about 27 knots, and three and four engines can provide speeds in excess of 30 knots. The engines have a maximum rating of 86,000 shp; 80,000 shp is the sustained rating.

Guns: Bushmaster "chain guns" are fitted in some ships when they forward deploy, especially to the Persian Gulf area. Also fitted are .50-caliber machine guns.

Helicopters: The twin helicopter hangars in these ships vary in size; they are 49–54 feet (14.9–16.5 m) long, 21–23½ feet (6.4–7.2 m) wide, and at least 16 feet (4.9 m) high.

Missiles: The Mk 41 VLS installation replaced the ASROC launcher and magazine. The VLS can launch vertical-launch ASROCs, as well as Tomahawk missiles.

All active ships have RAM launchers fitted on their fantails. The DAVID R. RAY in the late 1980s evaluated the RAM Ex-31 (now Mk 49) launcher; subsequently, the launcher was fitted on the fantail of two ships, the OLDENDORF and JOHN YOUNG (and removed from the DAVID R. RAY). The only other U.S. warships to be fitted with the RAM system are aircraft carriers and amphibious ships.

---

13 The mast is fabricated of 5-inch (127-mm)-thick sandwiches of circuit boards and Polyvinyl Chloride Foam (PVC) with a hollow core; the mast's sides are flat to reduce radar reflections. The mast provides access to all installed electronics through an enclosed ladder.

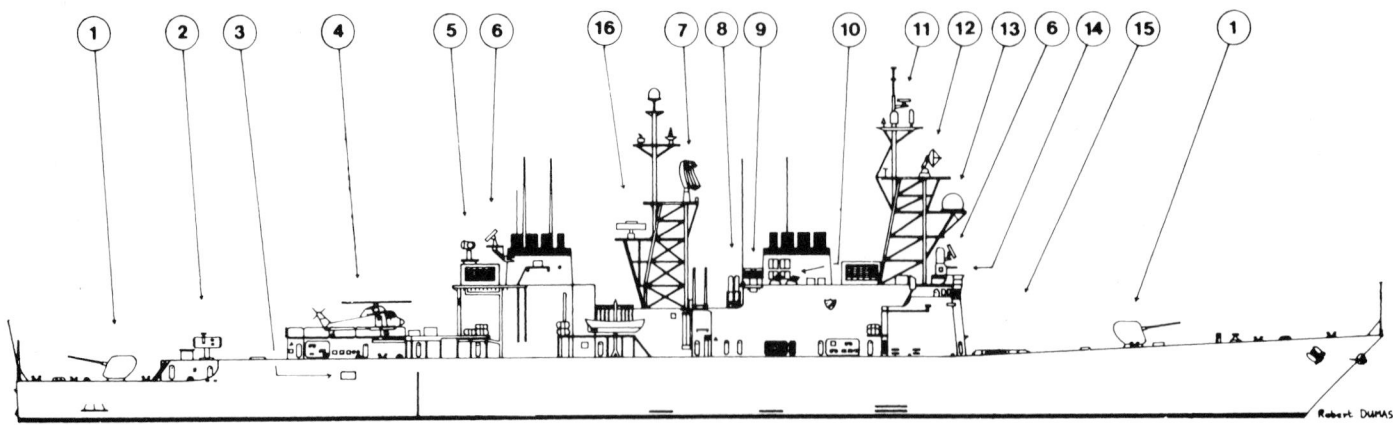

Destroyer SPRUANCE
1. 5-inch DP single gun mount Mk 45 2. NATO Sea Sparrow missile launcher Mk 29 3. 12.75-inch triple torpedo tubes Mk 32 4. LAMPS helicopter. 5. Mk 91 Mod 0 radar director for Sea Sparrow missiles 6. OE-82 satellite communication antennas (2) 7. SPS-40 air search radar 8. Harpoon missile canisters (8) 9. SLQ-32(V)2 electronic countermeasures 10. SRBOC decoy launcher (4) 11. SPS-55 surface search radar 12. SPG-60 gun/missile control radar 13. SPQ-9A gunfire control radar 14. 20-mm Phalanx close-in weapon system (2) 15. Vertical launching system Mk 41 16. Mk 23 TAS radar (Robert Dumas)

The FLETCHER *in the Persian Gulf flying a large national ensign. The ship's forward Phalanx CIWS is visible atop the bridge, as is the after Phalanx CIWS, on the port side. (2002, U.S. Navy/ Brien Aho)*

The destroyer THORN *while operating with the* ENTERPRISE *(CVN 65) battle group. There is an SH-60B Seahawk on her flight deck; the NATO Sea Sparrow missile launcher, after 5-inch DP gun mount, and RAM launcher are visible, as are the ship's massive array of antennas, common to all U.S. warships. (2003, U.S. Navy/Aaron Peterson)*

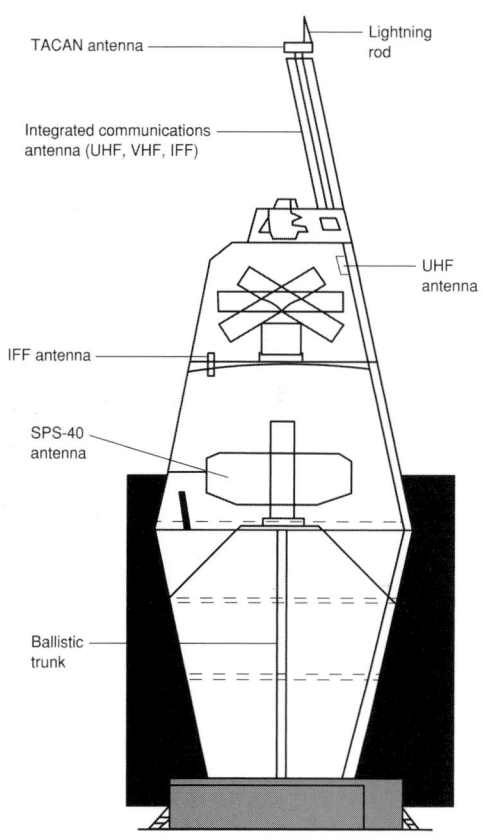

TACAN antenna

Lightning rod

Integrated communications antenna (UHF, VHF, IFF)

UHF antenna

IFF antenna

SPS-40 antenna

Ballistic trunk

Advanced Enclosed Mast/Sensor (AEM/S) fitted in the ARTHUR W. RADFORD *(Chris Nazelrod)*

The CUSHING *sailing in heavy weather while operating in the South China Sea. The ship is one of several surface combatants homeported at Yokosuka, Japan, to support the* KITTY HAWK, *the Navy's only overseas-based aircraft carrier. (2001, U.S. Navy/Dennis Cantrell)*

The ARTHUR W. RADFORD, *now a test ship for DD(X) systems, was fitted with an Advanced Enclosed Mast/Sensor (AEM/S) structure in place of her mainmast. The AEM/S was intended to reduce the ship's radar cross section and enhance radar performance. (2002, U.S. Navy/Summer M. Anderson)*

The FLETCHER barely under way in the Persian Gulf during Exercise Arabian Shark 2000. The U.S. Navy has kept a continuous presence in the Persian Gulf since 1949, with major forces deployed there for the conflicts of 1991 and 2003. (2000, U.S. Navy/David J. Weideman

Table 15-5. GUIDED MISSILE DESTROYERS

Number	Name	Comm.	Notes
	GYATT type		
DDG 1	GYATT (ex-DD 712)	1956	str. as DD 712 in 1969 (see text)
	CHARLES F. ADAMS class (23)		
DDG 2	CHARLES F. ADAMS	1960	decomm./str. 20 Nov 1992
DDG 3	JOHN KING	1961	decomm. 30 Mar 1990; str. 12 Jan 1993
DDG 4	LAWRENCE	1962	decomm. 30 Mar 1990; str. 16 May 1990
DDG 5	CLAUDE V. RICKETTS	1962	decomm. 31 Oct 1989; str.1 June 1990
DDG 6	BARNEY	1962	decomm. 17 Dec 1990; str. 20 Nov 1992
DDG 7	HENRY B. WILSON	1960	decomm. 2 Oct 1989; str. 26 Jan 1990
DDG 8	LYNDE MCCORMICK	1961	decomm. 1 Oct 1991; str. 20 Nov 1992
DDG 9	TOWERS	1961	decomm. 1 Oct 1990; str. 1 Oct 1990
DDG 10	SAMPSON	1961	decomm. 24 June 1991; str. 20 Nov1992
DDG 11	SELLERS	1961	decomm. 31 Oct 1989; str. 20 Nov 1992
DDG 12	ROBISON	1961	decomm. 1 Oct 1991; str. 20 Nov 1992
DDG 13	HOEL	1962	decomm. 1 Oct 1990; str. 20 Nov 1992
DDG 14	BUCHANAN	1962	decomm. 1 Oct 1991; str. 20 Nov 1992
DDG 15	BERKELEY	1962	decomm. 1 May 1992; str. 30 Sep 1992
DDG 16	JOSEPH STRAUSS	1963	decomm. 1 Feb 1990; to Greece
DDG 17	CONYNGHAM	1963	decomm. 29 Oct 1990; str. 30 May 1991
DDG 18	SEMMES	1962	decomm. 12 Sep 1991; to Greece
DDG 19	TATNALL	1963	decomm. 18 Jan 1991; str. 12 June 1993
DDG 20	GOLDSBOROUGH	1963	decomm./str. 29 Apr 1993; to Australia
DDG 21	COCHRANE	1964	decomm. 1 Oct 1990; str. 20 Nov 1992
DDG 22	BENJAMIN STODDERT	1964	decomm. 20 Dec 1991; str. 20 Nov 1992
DDG 23	RICHARD E. BYRD	1964	decomm. 27 Apr 1990; to Greece
DDG 24	WADDELL	1964	decomm. 1 Oct 1992; to Greece
DDG 25–27			built for Australia
DDG 28–30			built for West Germany
	Converted FORREST SHERMAN class (4)		
DDG 31	DECATUR (ex-DD 936)	1956	str. 1988 (test ship)
DDG 32	JOHN PAUL JONES (ex-DD 932)	1956	str. 1986
DDG 33	PARSONS (ex-DD 949)	1959	str. 1984
DDG 34	SOMERS (ex-DD 947)	1959	str. 1988
	Converted MITSCHER class (2)		
DDG 35	MITSCHER (ex-DL 2)	1968	str. 1978
DDG 36	JOHN S. MCCAIN (ex-DL 3)	1969	str. 1978
	FARRAGUT class (10)		
DDG 37	FARRAGUT (ex-DLG 6)	1960	decomm. 31 Oct 1989; str. 20 Nov 1992
DDG 38	LUCE (ex-DLG 7)	1961	decomm. 1 Apr 1991; str. 20 Nov 1992
DDG 39	MACDONOUGH (ex-DLG 8)	1961	decomm. 23 Oct 1992; str. 30 Nov 1992
DDG 40	COONTZ (ex-DLG 9)	1960	decomm. 2 Oct 1989; str. 6 May 1993
DDG 41	KING (ex-DLG 10)	1960	decomm. 28 Mar 1991; str. 20 Nov 1992
DDG 42	MAHAN (ex-DLG 11)	1960	decomm. 15 June 1993; str. 15 June 1993
DDG 43	DAHLGREN (ex-DLG 12)	1961	decomm. 31 July 1992; str. 20 Nov 1992
DDG 44	WILLIAM V. PRATT (ex-DLG 13)	1961	decomm. 30 Sep 1991; str. 20 Nov 1992
DDG 45	DEWEY (ex-DLG 14)	1959	decomm. 31 Aug 1990; str. 20 Nov 1992
DDG 46	PREBLE (ex-DLG 15)	1960	decomm. 15 Nov 1991; str. 20 Nov 1992
DDG 47–50	TICONDEROGA class		changed to CG 47–50
DDG 51–112	ARLEIGH BURKE class		

The guided missile destroyer classification was established in 1956. The first DDG was the GEARING-class destroyer GYATT (DD 712), fitted with a twin Terrier SAM launcher aft, replacing the ship's after 5-inch twin gun mount. Two twin 5-inch/38-cal gun mounts were retained forward. The GYATT became DDG 712 on 3 December 1956 and DDG 1 on 23 April 1957; she reverted to DD 712 on 1 October 1962 with the removal of her missile system.

All subsequent DDGs were fitted with the smaller Tartar (later Standard-MR) missile system until the FARRAGUT-class frigates armed with the Terrier/Standard-ER missile were reclassified as destroyers in 1975. The ten FARRAGUT-class frigates were single-end missile ships; the first three ships were ordered as all-gun frigates (DL 6–8); the COONTZ was the first ship ordered as a DLG. All were changed from DLG to DDG in 1975.

Six CHARLES F. ADAMS-class DDGs built for Australia and West Germany in U.S. shipyards were assigned U.S. hull numbers.

Four all-gun destroyers of the FORREST SHERMAN class and two frigates of the MITSCHER class were converted to DDGs with the installation of a Mk 13 Tartar launcher aft; gun armament was retained forward.

The TICONDEROGA was ordered as DDG 47. She was reclassified as a cruiser in 1980.

Four guided missile destroyers recently were sunk as targets:

Ship	*Date*
BUCHANAN	14 June 2000
JOHN PAUL JONES	31 Jan 2001
LYNDE MCCORMICK	24 Feb 2001
TOWERS	9 Oct 2002

Table 15-6. POST-WORLD WAR II DESTROYERS

Number	Name	Comm.	Notes
DD 927–930	Mitscher class		completed as DL 2–5
	Forrest Sherman class (18)		
DD 931	Forrest Sherman	1955	stricken 27 July 1990
DD 932	John Paul Jones	1956	to DDG 32; stricken 1985
DD 933	Barry	1956	to floating equipment 1983; museum
DD 934	(ex-Japanese Hanazuki)		war prize
DD 935	(ex-German T-35)		war prize
	Forrest Sherman class (continued)		
DD 936	Decatur	1956	to DDG 31; str. 1988; retained as test ship until 2004
DD 937	Davis	1957	stricken 27 July 1990
DD 938	Jonas Ingram	1957	stricken 1983
DD 939	(ex-German Z-39)		war prize
	Forrest Sherman class (continued)		
DD 940	Manley	1957	stricken 1 June 1990
DD 941	Du Pont	1957	stricken 1 June 1990
DD 942	Bigelow	1957	stricken 1 June 1990
DD 943	Blandy	1957	stricken 27 July 1990
DD 944	Mullinnix	1958	stricken 26 July 1990
DD 945	Hull	1958	stricken 1983
DD 946	Edson	1958	stricken 1989
DD 947	Somers	1959	to DDG 34
DD 948	Morton	1959	stricken 7 Feb 1990
DD 949	Parsons	1959	to DDG 33
DD 950	Richard S. Edwards	1959	stricken 7 Feb 1990
DD 951	Turner Joy	1959	stricken 13 Feb 1990
DD 952–959	Charles F. Adams class		completed as DDG 2–9
DD 960	(Japanese Akizuki)		Offshore Procurement (OSP)
DD 961	(Japanese Terusuki)		OSP
DD 962	(ex-British Charity)		to Pakistan 1958 (Shah Jahan)
DD 963–992	Spruance class		
	Kidd class		
DD 993	(Iranian Kourosh)		completed as U.S. DDG 993
DD 994	(Iranian Daryush)		completed as U.S. DDG 994
DD 995	(Iranian Ardeshir)		canceled 1976
DD 996	(Iranian Nader)		completed as U.S. DDG 995
DD 997	(Iranian Shapour)		canceled 1976; hull number reassigned to Spruance class
	Spruance class (continued)		
DD 997	Hayler		
	Kidd class (continued)		
DD 998	(Iranian Anoushirvan)		completed as U.S. DDG 996

U.S. World War II destroyer programs reached hull number DD 926 (with hulls DD 891–926 being canceled in 1945). Many ships built during the war subsequently were reclassified as escort destroyers (DDE), hunter-killer destroyers (DDK), radar picket destroyers (DDR), and experimental destroyers (EDD). One Gearing-class ship was converted to a missile configuration (DDG 712) to evaluate the Terrier system in a destroyer-size ship; she subsequently was changed to DDG 1 (and reverted to DD 712 in 1962 when the Terrier launcher was beached). All except the missile ship conversions retained their DD hull numbers in their new roles.

As indicated in table 15.6, several war prizes and foreign-built ships had DD-series hull numbers, as did one British destroyer transferred to Pakistan with U.S. funds.[14] Two destroyers built in Japan with U.S. funds for the Japanese Maritime Self-Defense Force under the Offshore Procurement (OSP) program also had U.S. hull numbers.

The Forrest Sherman class was halted at 18 ships in favor of building the Charles F. Adams-class DDGs, which had a similar design with a Mk 11 or Mk 13 missile launcher aft in place of two 5-inch/54-cal gun mounts. The Barry is retained as a museum ship, being reclassified as "floating equipment" in 1983; since 2 February 1984, she has been permanently moored at the Washington Navy Yard, adjacent to the Navy Museum. The Barry is manned by one officer and 15 enlisted active-duty Navy personnel.

The Edson was transferred to the Intrepid (CVS 11) Sea-Air Museum in New York City on 30 June 1989. The Jonas Ingram, stripped of weapons and radars, served as a test hulk at the Philadelphia Naval Shipyard; she was sunk as a target in 1988. The Mullinnix was sunk as a target in 1992.

The stricken Decatur served as a test hulk for the Ship Self-Defense System (SSDS), operating out of the Naval Surface Warfare Center Port Hueneme Division, California. She has been replaced by the Paul F. Foster.

The Somers served as a target hulk for the Naval Air Weapons Center at Point Mugu, California; she was sunk as a target on 22 July 1998. Other destroyers recently sunk as targets were:

	Date
Caron	4 Dec 2003
Bigelow	2 Apr 2003
Merrill	1 Aug 2003
John Young	13 Apr 2004

Of the several ships transferred to other navies, the Goldsborough went to Australia to supply spare parts to support other ships and the Richard E. Byrd went to Greece for the same purpose.

---

14 While three Axis destroyers were given DD numbers, U.S. warship designations were not assigned to the Japanese battleship Nagato, Japanese light cruiser Sakawa, German heavy cruiser Prinz Eugen, and several German and Japanese submarines acquired after World War II. The German CA was assigned the designation IX 300 (sunk in Bikini atomic bomb tests of 1946 along with the Nagato and Sakawa). The German supply ship Conecuh became the IX 301 and saw U.S. Navy service as the AO/AOR 110.

CHAPTER 16

Frigates

Crewmen man the rail of the frigate REUBEN JAMES *as she moors at the ship's home port of Pearl Harbor after a deployment to the Middle East, which included participation in Operation Iraqi Freedom. With the Mk 13 missile launcher removed, these ships have lost much of their military effectiveness. (2003, U.S. Navy)*

The frigate has become one of the least important U.S. Navy warships in the post–Cold War era, although they still are widely deployed and used. As of early 2005, the Navy had 22 frigates in active service and another 8 assigned to the Naval Reserve Force (NRF), all of the OLIVER HAZARD PERRY class. The NRF ships have composite active–reserve crews.

Although the date for retirement of the last Navy frigates has been delayed, all probably will be discarded by the early 2020s. In the interim, removal of the Mk 13 Standard/Harpoon missile launcher has left these ships without effective anti-air or anti-ship capabilities, except that their SH-60 Seahawk helicopters could carry the Penguin anti-ship missile. Indeed, deletion of the Mk 13 system means these ships should properly be designated FF rather than FFG. The missile systems were removed as a cost-saving measure.

No frigate-type ships are under construction or proposed for the U.S. Navy. However, the Littoral Combat Ship (LCS) will carry out some missions traditionally assigned to frigates.

During the Cold War, the U.S. Navy built frigates in large numbers to help counter the Soviet submarine threat. The frigate force peaked in 1985 with 115 ships in service (94 active and 21 NRF ships). Their numbers were reduced precipitously with the collapse of the Soviet Union.

U.S. frigates have been primarily Anti-Submarine Warfare (ASW) ships, with the OLIVER HAZARD PERRY class also providing limited Anti-Air Warfare (AAW) defense to amphibious and replenishment groups and convoys, as well as an anti-ship capability. Despite the higher speed and missile capabilities of these ships, they still are not capable of serving as effective escorts for carrier battle groups in wartime. The removal of their Mk 13 missile system limits them to the ASW and general peacetime patrol–interdiction roles.

The Navy had plans to install the Rolling Airframe Missile (RAM) as a replacement for the Mk 13, but that project has been dropped because of costs and the relatively limited remaining service life of these ships.

With Navy force levels holding steady at between 110 and 116 surface combatants (cruisers, destroyers, frigates), the emphasis will be on the more-capable cruisers and destroyers. The argument can be—and has been—made that frigates in fact *should* have an important role in post–Cold War naval operations because of the value of such ships in exercises and operations with coalition partners, many of whom operate frigates as their major warships, and because of the value of frigate-size warships in littoral operations.[1] The planned LCS, however, could supersede the frigate in this respect.

During the late 1970s, the Navy proposed the construction of a class of small frigates (design designation FFX) for use by the Naval Reserve Force. These ships were intended to augment the OLIVER HAZARD PERRY-class frigates in the ASW role in low-threat areas. Some 12 ships were planned, with the lead ship intended for authorization in Fiscal Year (FY) 1984. For several reasons, the FFX class was not started. Subsequently, the NRF was provided with frigates of the KNOX and OLIVER HAZARD PERRY classes to replace its aging destroyers of the GEARING (DD 710) class.

In the mid-1980s, the Navy began design of an advanced frigate for construction in the 1990s to replace the KNOX and earlier frigate classes. That effort was canceled in 1986 by the Deputy Chief of Naval Operations (Surface Warfare) because of the large size of those designs.

Classification: This type of warship was officially classified as "escort vessel" (DE) from its inception in the U.S. Navy in 1941, although the DE type invariably was called "destroyer escort"—often in official publications. Only in the early 1950s, as the Soviet submarine threat emerged and DE production began to accelerate, were these ships generally referred to as escort vessels. (At that time, the term "frigate" was applied to large destroyer-type ships given the DL/DLG/DLGN designation.)

Subsequently, missile-armed escort ships were designated DEG, and the escort research ship GLOVER became AGDE. All escort ships were changed to "frigate" (FF/FFG/AGFF) on 30 June 1975.

Guns: Beginning during the 1990–1991 crisis and war in the Persian Gulf, several OLIVER HAZARD PERRY-class frigates were fitted with .50-cal machine guns and Mk 38 25-mm Bushmaster "chain" guns for close-in defense against small craft. The weapons

The ELROD at high speed while operating with the GEORGE WASHINGTON (CVN 73) carrier battle group in the Atlantic. Although intended for the convoy and amphibious group escort role, the OLIVER HAZARD PERRY-class frigates have proved to be highly versatile warships—until they beached their Mk 13 missile launchers. (2004, U.S. Navy/Brien Aho)

are shifted from ship to ship as they forward deploy; accordingly, they are not listed under the specific class entries.

These are the only U.S. Navy ships that mount the OTO Melara 76-mm gun; the now-discarded hydrofoil missile ships of the PEGASUS (PHM 1) class also mounted the weapon. It still is fitted in U.S. Coast Guard cutters (and numerous foreign ships).

Beginning in 2002, all active frigates have been upgraded to the Phalanx Block 1B Close-In Weapon System (CIWS) and the Mk 53 Nulka decoy system.

Names: The frigate ship type evolved from the World War II–era destroyer escort (DE), and frigates thus have destroyer-type names honoring American naval officers, heroes, and inventors. The HAROLD E. HOLT remembers the deceased Australian prime minister who supported U.S. policies in the Vietnam War.

Personnel: Note that in the NRF ships, active duty personnel outnumber reservists.

---

1 See Capt. Donald Loren, USN, "(Not Quite) The (Almost) End of the Frigate," U.S. Naval Institute *Proceedings* (October 1996), p. 41.

30 FRIGATES: "OLIVER HAZARD PERRY" CLASS

Number	Name	FY	Builder	Laid Down	Launched	Comm.	Status
FFG 7	OLIVER HAZARD PERRY	73	Bath Iron Works, Maine	12 June 1976	25 Sep 1976	17 Dec 1977	decomm. 20 Feb 1997; str. 3 May 1999
FFG 8	McINERNEY	75	Bath Iron Works, Maine	16 Jan 1978	4 Nov 1978	15 Dec 1979	**AA**
FFG 9	WADSWORTH	75	Todd Shipyards, San Pedro, Calif.	13 July 1977	29 July 1978	28 Feb 1980	decomm. 28 June 2002; str. 23 July 2002; to Poland 2002
FFG 10	DUNCAN	75	Todd Shipyards, Seattle, Wash.	29 Apr 1977	1 Mar 1978	24 May 1980	decomm. 17 Dec 1994; str. 5 Jan 1998; to Turkey 1998
FFG 11	CLARK	76	Bath Iron Works, Maine	17 July 1978	24 Mar 1979	9 May 1980	decomm./str. 15 Mar 2000; to Poland 2000
FFG 12	GEORGE PHILIP	76	Todd Shipyards, San Pedro, Calif.	14 Dec 1977	16 Dec 1978	15 Nov 1980	decomm. 15 Mar 2003; to Poland 2005
FFG 13	SAMUEL ELIOT MORISON	76	Bath Iron Works, Maine	4 Dec 1978	14 July 1979	11 Oct 1980	decomm. 10 Apr 2002; str. 23 July 2002; to Turkey 2002
FFG 14	SIDES	76	Todd Shipyards, San Pedro, Calif.	7 Aug 1978	19 May 1979	30 May 1981	decomm./str. 28 Feb 2003; to Portugal 2005
FFG 15	ESTOCIN	76	Bath Iron Works, Maine	2 Apr 1979	3 Nov 1979	10 Jan 1981	decomm./str. 3 Apr 2003; to Turkey 2003
FFG 16	CLIFTON SPRAGUE	76	Bath Iron Works, Maine	30 July 1979	16 Feb 1980	21 Mar 1981	decomm. 2 June 1995; str. 4 Sep 1997; to Turkey 1997
FFG 19	JOHN A. MOORE	77	Todd Shipyards, San Pedro, Calif.	19 Dec 1978	20 Oct 1979	14 Nov 1981	decomm./str. 1 Sep 2000; to Turkey 2000
FFG 20	ANTRIM	77	Todd Shipyards, Seattle, Wash.	21 June 1978	27 Mar 1979	26 Sep 1981	decomm. 8 May 1996; str. 4 Sep 1997; to Turkey 1997
FFG 21	FLATLEY	77	Bath Iron Works, Maine	13 Nov 1979	15 May 1980	20 June 1981	decomm. 11 May 1996; to Turkey 1997
FFG 22	FAHRION	77	Todd Shipyards, Seattle, Wash.	1 Dec 1978	24 Aug 1979	16 Jan 1982	decomm./str. 31 Mar 1998; to Egypt 1998
FFG 23	LEWIS B. PULLER	77	Todd Shipyards, San Pedro, Calif.	23 May 1979	15 Mar 1980	17 Apr 1982	decomm./str. 18 Sep 1998; to Egypt 1998
FFG 24	JACK WILLIAMS	77	Bath Iron Works, Maine	25 Feb 1980	30 Aug 1980	19 Sep 1981	decomm./str. 13 Sep 1996; to Bahrain 1996
FFG 25	COPELAND	77	Todd Shipyards, San Pedro, Calif.	24 Oct 1979	26 July 1980	7 Aug 1982	decomm./str. 18 Sep 1996; to Egypt 1996
FFG 26	GALLERY	77	Bath Iron Works, Maine	17 May 1980	20 Dec 1980	5 Dec 1981	decomm./str. 14 June 1996; to Egypt 1996
FFG 27	MAHLON S. TISDALE	78	Todd Shipyards, San Pedro, Calif.	19 Mar 1980	7 Feb 1981	13 Nov 1982	decomm. 27 Sep 1996; str. 20 Feb 1998; to Turkey 1999
FFG 28	BOONE	78	Todd Shipyards, Seattle, Wash.	27 Mar 1979	16 Jan 1980	15 May 1982	**NRF-A**
FFG 29	STEPHEN W. GROVES	7	Bath Iron Works, Maine	16 Sep 1980	4 Apr 1981	17 Apr 1982	**NRF-A**
FFG 30	REID	78	Todd Shipyards, San Pedro, Calif.	8 Oct 1980	27 June 1981	19 Feb 1983	decomm./str. 25 Sep 1998; to Turkey 1999
FFG 31	STARK	78	Todd Shipyards, Seattle, Wash.	24 Aug 1979	30 May 1980	23 Oct 1982	decomm./str. 7 May 1999
FFG 32	JOHN L. HALL	78	Bath Iron Works, Maine	5 Jan 1981	24 July 1981	26 June 1982	**AA**
FFG 33	JARRETT	78	Todd Shipyards, San Pedro, Calif.	11 Feb 1981	17 Oct 1981	2 July 1983	**PA**
FFG 34	AUBREY FITCH	78	Bath Iron Works, Maine	10 Apr 1981	17 Oct 1981	9 Oct 1982	decomm. 12 Dec 1997; str. 3 May 1999
FFG 36	UNDERWOOD	79	Bath Iron Works, Maine	3 Aug 1981	6 Feb 1982	29 Jan 1983	**AA**
FFG 37	CROMMELIN	79	Todd Shipyards, Seattle, Wash.	30 May 1980	1 July 1981	18 June 1983	**PA**
FFG 38	CURTS	79	Todd Shipyards, San Pedro, Calif.	1 July 1981	6 Mar 1982	8 Oct 1983	**NRF-P**
FFG 39	DOYLE	79	Bath Iron Works, Maine	23 Oct 1981	22 May 1982	21 May 1983	**NRF-A**
FFG 40	HALYBURTON	79	Todd Shipyards, Seattle, Wash.	26 Sep 1980	13 Oct 1981	7 Jan 1984	**AA**
FFG 41	McCLUSKY	79	Todd Shipyards, San Pedro, Calif.	21 Oct 1981	18 Sep 1982	10 Dec 1983	**NRF-P**
FFG 42	KLAKRING	79	Bath Iron Works, Maine	19 Feb 1982	18 Sep 1982	20 Aug 1983	**NRF-A**
FFG 43	THACH	79	Todd Shipyards, San Pedro, Calif.	6 Mar 1982	18 Dec 1982	17 Mar 1984	**PA**
FFG 45	DE WERT	80	Bath Iron Works, Maine	14 June 1982	18 Dec 1982	19 Nov 1983	**AA**
FFG 46	RENTZ	80	Todd Shipyards, San Pedro, Calif.	18 Sep 1982	16 July 1983	30 June 1984	**PA**
FFG 47	NICHOLAS	80	Bath Iron Woks, Maine	27 Sep 1982	23 Apr 1983	10 Mar 1984	**AA**
FFG 48	VANDEGRIFT	80	Todd Shipyards, Seattle, Wash.	13 Oct 1981	15 Oct 1982	24 Nov 1984	**PA**
FFG 49	ROBERT G. BRADLEY	80	Bath Iron Works, Maine	28 Dec 1982	13 Aug 1983	11 Aug 1984	**AA**
FFG 50	JESSE L. TAYLOR	81	Bath Iron Works, Maine	5 May 1983	5 Nov 1983	1 Dec 1984	**AA**
FFG 51	GARY	81	Todd Shipyards, San Pedro, Calif.	18 Dec 1982	19 Nov 1983	17 Nov 1984	**PA**
FFG 52	CARR	81	Todd Shipyards, Seattle, Wash.	26 Mar 1982	26 Feb 1983	27 July 1985	**AA**
FFG 53	HAWES	81	Bath Iron Works, Maine	22 Aug 1983	17 Feb 1984	9 Feb 1985	**AA**
FFG 54	FORD	81	Todd Shipyards, San Pedro, Calif.	16 July 1983	23 June 1984	29 June 1985	**PA**
FFG 55	ELROD	81	Bath Iron Works, Maine	21 Nov 1983	12 May 1984	6 July 1985	**AA**
FFG 56	SIMPSON	82	Bath Iron Works, Maine	27 Feb 1984	31 Aug 1984	9 Nov 1985	**NRF-A**
FFG 57	REUBEN JAMES	82	Todd Shipyards, San Pedro, Calif.	19 Nov 1983	8 Feb 1985	22 Mar 1986	**PA**
FFG 58	SAMUEL B. ROBERTS	82	Bath Iron Works, Maine	21 May 1984	8 Dec 1984	12 Apr 1986	**AA**
FFG 59	KAUFFMAN	83	Bath Iron Works, Maine	8 Apr 1985	29 Mar 1986	21 Feb 1987	**AA**
FFG 60	RODNEY M. DAVIS	83	Todd Shipyards, San Pedro, Calif.	8 Feb 1985	11 Jan 1986	9 May 1987	**NRF-P**
FFG 61	INGRAHAM	84	Todd Shipyards, San Pedro, Calif.	30 Mar 1987	25 June 1988	5 Aug 1989	**PA**

Displacement:	2,769 tons light, except 3,210 tons for ships with LAMPS III modification
	3,658 tons full load, except 3,900–4,100 tons for ships with LAMPS III modification
Length:	413 feet (125.9 m) waterline
	445 feet (135.6 m) overall, except 455¼ feet (138.8 m) for ships with LAMPS III modification
Beam:	45 feet (13.7 m)
Draft:	21¹¹⁄₁₂ feet (6.7 m)
Propulsion:	2 gas turbines (General Electric LM 2500); 40,000 shp; 1 shaft
Speed:	29 knots (sustained; see *Engineering* notes)
Range:	5,000 nm (9,260 km) at 18 knots
	4,200 nm (7,778 km) at 20 knots
Personnel:	active ships—approx. 218 (16 officers + 202 enlisted) + 21-man LAMPS detachment (6 officers + 15 enlisted)
	NRF ships—approx. 135 active (10 officers + 125 enlisted) + 100 reserve (7 officers + 93 enlisted)
Helicopters:	1 or 2 SH-60B Seahawk LAMPS III in FFG 8, 28, 29, 32, 33, 36–61
Missiles:	removed

Guns:	1 76-mm/62-cal AA Mk 75
	1 20-mm Phalanx CIWS Mk 15 (multibarrel)
ASW weapons:	6 12.75-in (324-mm) torpedo tubes Mk 32 (2 triple) for Mk 46 torpedoes; provision for Mk 50 torpedoes in 13 ships (see *ASW Weapons* notes)
Radars:	SPS-49(V)4 air search, except SPS-49(V)5 in FFG 50, 51, 53, 55, 56, 61
	SPS-55 surface search
Sonars:	SQS-56 keel mounted
	SQR-19 TACTAS towed array, except none in FFG 51, 52, 54
Fire control:	1 Mk 13 weapon direction system
	1 Mk 92 weapons FCS except Mk 92 Mod 6 CORT in FFG 36, 47, 48, 50–55, 57, 59, 61
	1 STIR radar
	SQQ-89(V)2 ASW system
	SYS-2(V)2 Integrated Automatic Detection and Tracking (IADT) system in FFG 50 and FFG 61
EW systems:	SLQ-25A Nixie in FFG 36, 47, 51–53, 55, 57–60
	SLQ-32(V)2, except SLQ-32(V)5 with Sidekick in FFG 29, 32, 36, 40, 45–59, 61

This is the third-largest class of major surface warships to be built by any nation since World War II, with 51 ships completed for the U.S. Navy between 1977 and 1989; additional ships for foreign navies were built in the United States and in other countries (see *Class* notes). The Soviet SKORYY class of destroyers was larger, with 72 ships completed between 1950 and 1954, and the U.S. ARLEIGH BURKE (DDG 51) class currently is planned at 62 ships.

The OLIVER HAZARD PERRY class was initiated in the early 1970s—together with the planned Sea Control Ship (SCS)—to provide a viable capability for defending Sea Lines of Communications (SLOC) against Soviet air and submarine attacks. After the cutbacks in the DX/DXG program (i.e., SPRUANCE/DD 963) class, the FFG 7 class also was looked on as a replacement for destroyers of the GEARING (DD 710) class being retired.

These frigates lack the large, hull-mounted active/passive sonar and Anti-Submarine Rocket (ASROC) launcher of previous U.S. frigate classes. However, their towed arrays and ability to support two large, LAMPS III helicopters make them useful ASW ships. In addition, they have a surface-to-air missile system, a feature lacking in all but six of the previous U.S. post–World War II frigates (see Table 16-1).[2] And, despite their relatively light construction, according to the reference work *Combat Fleets of the World*, "the soundness of the design has permitted the expansion [of capabilities], and the ships have proven remarkably sturdy."[3]

Twenty-one ships have been decommissioned through the end of 2004. Many of these have been transferred to foreign navies, including the first U.S. warships ever to be transferred to Poland.

Eight ships are assigned to the Naval Reserve Force:

		Date Transferred	*Home Port*
FFG 28	BOONE	30 Sep 1998	Mayport, Fla.
FFG 29	STEPHEN W. GROVES	30 Sep 1997	Pascagoula, Miss.
FFG 38	CURTS	30 Sep 1998	San Diego, Calif.
FFG 39	DOYLE	1 Oct 2002	Mayport, Fla.
FFG 41	McCLUSKY	1 Oct 2002	San Diego, Calif.
FFG 42	KLAKRING	1 Oct 2002	Mayport, Fla.
FFG 56	SIMPSON	1 Oct 2002	Mayport, Fla.
FFG 60	RODNEY M. DAVIS	1 Oct 2002	San Diego, Calif.

The GARY and VANDEGRIFT are homeported in Yokosuka, Japan, as part of the KITTY HAWK (CV 63) battle group.

ASW Weapons: The only ship-mounted ASW weapons are Mk 32 torpedo tubes; the SH-60B helicopters are these frigates' primary ASW weapon. These are the first U.S. surface combatants built without ASROC since that weapon became available in the early 1960s.

Thirteen ships—FFG 40, 43, 46, 47, 50–56, 58, 59—are fitted with the Flexible Universal Storage System (FUSS) to permit the storage of Penguin air-to-surface missiles and Mk 50 torpedoes (in addition to Mk 46 torpedoes).

Class: Early U.S. Navy planning provided for approximately 75 ships of this class. Shipbuilding programs of the early 1970s reduced the number of units to be built in "later" years, in part because of the planned FFX, a smaller frigate intended specifically for NRF operation (see below).

The Carter administration's second five-year plan, for FY 1982–1986, deleted all FFG 7 construction after one ship in the 1983 program. However, the Reagan administration's shipbuilding program put forward in January 1982 provided for 12 additional FFGs in FY 1983–1987. Congress approved the two ships in the FY 1983 budget, but the Reagan administration's subsequent five-year plan (FY 1984–1988) deleted further construction, thus halting the FFG 7 program at 50 ships. Congress subsequently funded one additional ship (FFG 61) in the FY 1984 budget specifically for construction at the Todd San Pedro yard.

Todd Seattle built four ships of this class for the Australian Navy (given the U.S. designations FFG 17, 18, 35, and 44), delivered from 1980 to 1983. Additional ships of this design have been constructed in Australia (two), Spain (seven), and Taiwan (seven) for their respective navies. Thus, the total number of ships built to the OLIVER HAZARD PERRY design is 71.

Classification: When conceived, these ships were designated "patrol frigates" (PF), a designation previously applied to a series of smaller, World War II–era ships (PF 1–102) and postwar coastal escorts that were constructed specifically for foreign transfer (PF 103–108). The OLIVER HAZARD PERRY was designated PF 109 until 30 June 1975, when she was changed to "frigate" FFG 7.

The removal of their Mk 13 missile launchers beginning in 2003 should have resulted in the ships being changed to FF.

Design: SCB design No. 261. During their design phase, Chief of Naval Operations Admiral Elmo R. Zumwalt placed constraints on the ships' cost, displacement, and crew size:

• $50 million in then-year dollars
• 3,530 tons full load
• 185 crew (17 officers + 168 enlisted)

---

2 The point-defense missile systems fitted in a number of previous frigates did have a limited anti-air capability, but they were intended primarily to defeat incoming Styx-type anti-ship cruise missiles.

3 A. D. Baker III, *Combat Fleets of the World 1998-1999* (Annapolis, Md.: Naval Institute Press, 1998), p. 1028.

All three parameters were exceeded, although the design did arrest the upward trend in frigate (DE/FF) cost, size, and manning.

Note the short interval between the OLIVER HAZARD PERRY's keel laying and launching; this was due to modular construction. Fabrication of her modules actually began on 17 December 1974. These ships were designed for modular assembly to facilitate mass production. All major components were tested at sea or in land facilities before completion of the lead ship. Space and weight were reserved for fin stabilizers, which were installed during construction in FFG 36 and later units.

Early designs provided for a single hangar aft with twin funnels ("split" by the hangar). The design was revised to provide separate, side-by-side hangars to accommodate two SH-60B helicopters (see *Helicopters* notes). The hangars vary in size; they are approximately 41–46 feet (12.5–14 m) long, 13⅔–16 feet (4.2–4.9 m) wide, and 13½–15½ feet (4.1–4.7 m) in height. In addition to the fantail landing area, the ships have a Vertical Replenishment (VERTREP) area forward.

Electronics: The Separate Target Illumination Radar (STIR) is a modified SPG-60 radar. The Sperry Corporation had lobbied Congress and the Navy to install a phased-array radar in the later ships of this class, with a backfit to the earlier ships, but the Navy considered the cost prohibitive.

The INGRAHAM was completed with an improved combat system referred to as CORT (Coherent Receiver/ Transmitter) developed by Sperry/Unisys. It consists of the Mk 92 Mod 6 fire control system with the SYS-2(V)2 automatic tracking system. The ship's SPS-49(V)5 digital radar has enhanced Electronic Countermeasures (ECM) capabilities. A similar CORT refit followed in 11 other ships.

The Sidekick ECM installation provides an active countermeasures capability to the otherwise passive SLQ-32(V)2; suites so modified are redesignated SLQ-32(V)5.

The first ship to be built with the SQR-19 was the ELROD, with the array to be backfitted in the earlier ships completed with the SQR-18A. The limited capabilities of the hull-mounted SQS-56 forces these ships to rely primarily on the towed array for effective ASW.

The Kingfisher modification to the SQS-26 sonar provides for enhanced mine detection.

The FFG 9, 31, 32, 36, 38, 42, 43, 47–55, and 57–61 have been fitted with a passive countermeasures system (formerly Outlaw Bandit) to reduce their ship's radar cross section to enhance survivability.

Engineering: These ships have two LM 2500 gas turbine main propulsion engines and can attain 25 knots on one engine. On trials, some ships reportedly reached 36 knots. The maximum rated horsepower is 41,000; the sustained shp is shown in the above data table.

The ships have two 350-hp electric-drive, retractable auxiliary propulsion pods for precise maneuvering; they also provide a "come-home" capability at 6 knots in the event of main propulsion failure. They are fitted with four 1,000-kilowatt diesel ship's service generators, and thus lack the elaborate silencing of the SPRUANCE-class destroyers, which have gas turbine generators.

Guns: Early designs addressed a variety of guns for these ships, among them a twin 35-mm rapid-fire gun in place of the later 76-mm gun and CIWS. These are the first U.S. surface combatants built since the early 1960s without a 5-inch gun.

The FORD was the first U.S. ship fitted with the Mk 15 Block 1B CIWS.

Helicopters: These were the first U.S. ships fitted with a helicopter haul-down system, the Recovery, Assistance, Securing, and Traversing (RAST) system. The MCINERNEY was modified to serve as test ship for RAST and conducted FFG sea trials with the SH-60B in 1981. The system permits the recovery of helicopters with the ship rolling through 28° and pitching up to 5°. RAST was backfitted in those ships completed prior to the JESSE L. TAYLOR that

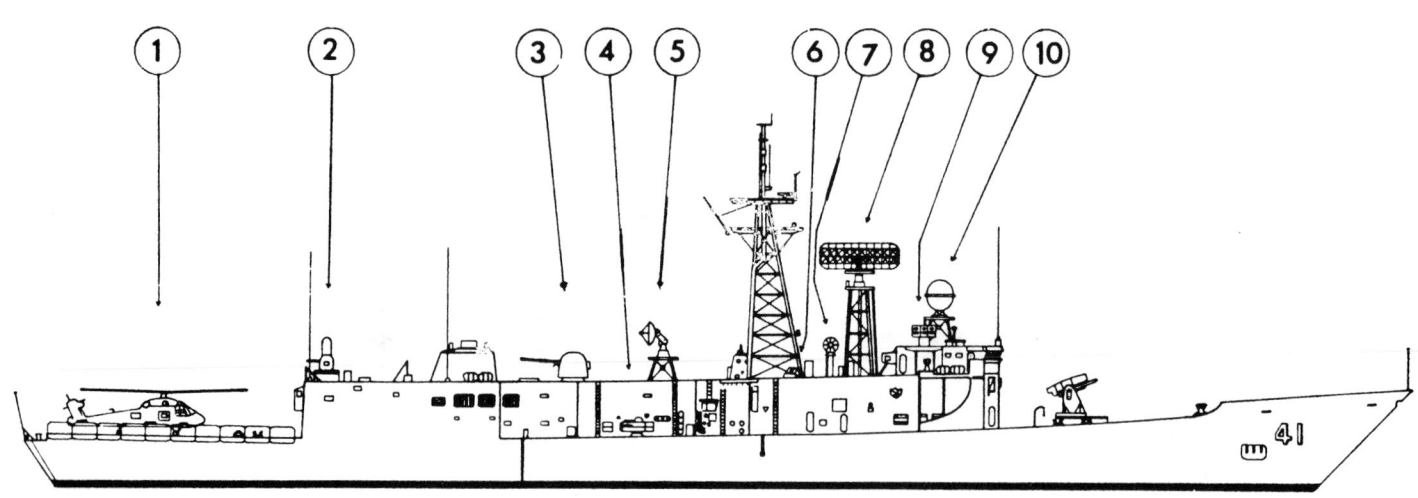

Frigate MCCLUSKY
1. SH-60B LAMPS III helicopter 2. Phalanx close-in weapon system Mk 15 3. 76-mm AA gun mount Mk 75 4. 12.75-inch triple torpedo tubes Mk 32 5. Separate Target Illumination Radar (STIR) fire control radar 6. Super Rapid-Blooming Offboard Chaff (SRBOC) decoy launcher Mk 36 (2) 7. OE-82 satellite communications antenna (2) 8. SPS-49(V)4/5 air search radar 9. SLQ-32(V)2 electronic countermeasures (2) 10. Mk 92 fire control radar (Robert Dumas)

have LAMPS III capability, and that ship became the first to be completed with the system.

Early NRF ships were fitted to operate the SH-2G LAMPS I helicopter.

The DOYLE served as trials ship for the Canadair CL-227 Sentinel unmanned aerial reconnaissance vehicle, a peanut-shaped Vertical Take-Off and Landing (VTOL) aircraft.

Personnel: The original complement was to be 179 (12 officers + 167 enlisted); this was increased to 185 (17 officers + 168 enlisted) by the time the design was completed.

Missiles: As built, all ships had a single Mk 13 Mod 4 launcher for Standard-MR surface-to-air missiles and Harpoon anti-ship missiles (40 weapons). The launchers were deleted from the 29 surviving U.S. ships in 2003.

Operational: While operating in the Persian Gulf on the night of 17 May 1987, the STARK was struck by two Exocet missiles launched by an Iraqi Mirage F1 aircraft that had mistaken the frigate for an Iranian ship. The STARK suffered 37 dead when one

of the missile warheads detonated, and unexpended fuel in both missiles set fires and caused heavy damage. Her crew fought fires for 24 hours, and at one point the accumulation of water on board from fire-fighting efforts caused the ship to list 16°. (The STARK was able to return to the United States under her own power and underwent repairs at the Litton/Ingalls yard from November 1987 to August 1988, at an estimated cost of $90 million.)

The SAMUEL B. ROBERTS struck an Iranian-laid mine in the Persian Gulf on 14 April 1988. The ship suffered a 22-foot (6.7 m) gash in the side, a 9-foot (2.7 m) tear in the bottom, and a cracked superstructure. Her gas turbines were knocked from their mountings, and there was heavy flooding. Ten sailors were injured, but there were no fatalities. (After emergency repairs, on 1 July 1988, the crippled SAMUEL B. ROBERTS departed the Gulf on board the Dutch-flag heavy-lift ship MIGHTY SERVANT 2. The frigate was brought back to the United States and underwent repairs at Bath Iron Works from October 1988 to October 1989, at an estimated cost of $37.5 million.)

The CROMMELIN departs Pearl Harbor, passing Ford Island and the battleship ARIZONA (BB 39) memorial. The Mk 13 launcher was fitted forward of the bridge structure. Note how the amidships hangars extend the full width of the ship. There are two lattice masts atop the forward superstructure. (2004, U.S. Navy/Dennis C. Cantrell)

Crewmen muster on the helicopter deck of the REUBEN JAMES in Pearl Harbor. The twin helicopter hangars are evident, with the control station between them; a Phalanx close-in weapon system is mounted above the hangar structure. The safety net around the helicopter deck folds down for flight operations. (2003, U.S. Navy/Dennis Cantrell)

The jumbled superstructure of the JARRETT is evident as the frigate refuels from the helicopter carrier PELELIU (LHA 5) during operations in the Indian Ocean. A rigid hull inflatable boat is visible on the JARRETT's port side, mounted above the triple 12.75-inch torpedo tubes. (2003, U.S. Navy/Joshua L. Pritekel)

Table 16-1. GUIDED MISSILE ESCORTS/FRIGATES

Number	Name	Comm.	Notes
Brooke class (6)			
DEG 1	Brooke	1966	decomm. 16 Sep 1988; to Pakistan 1989
DEG 2	Ramsey	1967	decomm. 1 Sep 1988; str. 13 Sep 1994
DEG 3	Schofield	1968	decomm. 8 Sep 1988; str. 13 Sep 1994
DEG 4	Talbot	1967	decomm. 30 Sep 1988; to Pakistan 1989
DEG 5	Richard L. Page	1967	decomm. 30 Sep 1988; to Pakistan 1989
DEG 6	Julius A. Furer	1967	decomm. 10 Nov 1988; to Pakistan 1989

These ships were built as guided missile escorts (DEG); they were reclassified as guided missile frigates (FFG) in 1975.

The Brooke-class frigates were identical to the Garcia class except for a Mk 22 single-arm launcher for Tartar/Standard-MR missiles in place of the second 5-inch gun. Additional ships of this configuration were planned but not built because of the significantly higher costs of the missile variants compared to the all-gun ASW frigates and the ships' limited magazine capacity (16 missiles).

The Talbot conducted at-sea tests of the gun, fire control, and sonar systems for the Oliver Hazard Perry class.

The four ships loaned to Pakistan were returned to U.S. custody and stricken; note that the Talbot was stricken before "title" was returned to the United States:

	Returned	*Stricken*
Brooke	2 Jan 1994	2 Jan 1994
Talbot	11 Dec 1993	29 Nov 1993
Page	15 Jan 1994	15 Jan 1994
Furer	11 Dec 1993	2 Jan 1994

The Ramsey was sunk as a target on 15 June 2000.

Table 16-2. POST–WORLD WAR II ESCORTS/FRIGATES

Number	Name	Comm.	Notes
Dealey class (13)			
DE 1006	Dealey	1954	to Uruguay 1972
DE 1007–1013	French frigates		OSP
Dealey class (continued)			
DE 1014	Cromwell	1954	stricken 1972
DE 1015	Hammerberg	1955	stricken 1973
DE 1016–1019	French frigates		OSP
DE 1020	Italian frigate		OSP
Dealey class (continued)			
DE 1021	Courtney	1956	stricken 1973
DE 1022	Lester	1957	stricken 1973
DE 1023	Evans	1957	stricken 1973
DE 1024	Bridget	1957	stricken 1973
DE 1025	Bauer	1957	stricken 1973
DE 1026	Hooper	1958	stricken 1973
DE 1027	John Willis	1957	stricken 1972
DE 1028	Van Voorhis	1957	stricken 1972
DE 1029	Hartley	1957	to Colombia 1972
DE 1030	Joseph K. Taussig	1957	stricken 1972
DE 1031	Italian frigate		OSP
DE 1032	Portuguese frigate		OSP
Claud Jones class (4)			
DE 1033	Claud Jones	1959	to Indonesia 1974
DE 1034	John R. Perry	1959	to Indonesia 1973
DE 1035	Charles Berry	1959	to Indonesia 1974
DE 1036	McMorris	1960	to Indonesia 1974
Bronstein class (2)			
DE 1037	Bronstein	1963	decomm. 13 Dec 1990; str. 4 Oct 1991; to Mexico 1993
DE 1038	McCloy	1963	decomm. 14 Dec 1990; str. 4 Oct 1991; to Mexico 1993
DE 1039	Portuguese frigate		OSP
Garcia class (10)			
DE 1040	Garcia	1964	decomm./str. 31 Jan 1989; to Pakistan 1989
DE 1041	Bradley	1965	decomm. 30 Sep 1988; to Brazil 1989; str. 24 Jan 2001
DE 1042	Portuguese frigate		OSP
Garcia class (continued)			
DE 1043	Edward McDonnell	1965	decomm. 30 Sep 1988; str. 15 Dec 1992
DE 1044	Brumby	1965	decomm. 31 Mar 1989; to Pakistan 1989; str. 1 July 1994
DE 1045	Davidson	1965	decomm. 8 Dec 1988; to Brazil 1989; str. 24 Jan 2001
DE 1046	Portuguese frigate		OSP
Garcia class (continued)			
DE 1047	Voge	1966	decomm. 1 Aug 1989; str. 15 Dec 1992
DE 1048	Sample	1968	decomm. 23 Sep 1988; to Brazil 1989; str. 24 Jan 2001
DE 1049	Koelsch	1967	decomm. 31 May 1989; to Pakistan 1989; str. 1 July 1994
DE 1050	Albert David	1968	decomm. 18 Sep 1989; to Brazil 1989; str. 24 Jan 2001
DE 1051	O'Callahan	1968	decomm. 20 Dec 1988; to Pakistan 1989; str. 29 Nov 1993
Knox class (46)			
DE 1052	Knox	1969	decomm. 14 Feb 1992; str. 11 Jan 1995
DE 1053	Roark	1969	decomm. 14 Dec 1991; str. 11 Jan 1995
DE 1054	Gray	1970	decomm. 30 Sep 1991; str. 11 Jan 1995
DE 1055	Hepburn	1969	decomm. 20 Dec 1991; str. 11 Jan 1995
DE 1056	Connole	1969	decomm./to Greece 30 Aug 1992; str. 11 Jan 1995
DE 1057	Rathburne	1970	decomm. 14 Feb 1992; str. 11 Jan 1995
DE 1058	Meyerkord	1969	decomm. 14 Dec 1991; str. 11 Jan 1995
DE 1059	W. S. Sims	1970	decomm. 6 Sep 1991; str. 11 Jan 1995; to Turkey 1998 (parts)
DE 1060	Lang	1970	decomm. 12 Dec 1991; str. 11 Jan 1995
DE 1061	Patterson	1970	decomm. 30 Sep 1991; str. 11 Jan 1995
DE 1062	Whipple	1970	decomm. 14 Feb 1992; str. 11 Jan 1995; to Mexico 2001
DE 1063	Reasoner	1971	decomm./to Turkey 28 Aug 1993; str. 11 Jan 1995
DE 1064	Lockwood	1970	decomm./str. 27 Sep 1993
DE 1065	Stein	1972	decomm. 19 Mar 1992; str. 11 Jan 1995; to Mexico 1998
DE 1066	Marvin Shields	1971	decomm. 2 July 1992; str. 11 Jan 1995; to Mexico 1998
DE 1067	Francis Hammond	1970	decomm. 2 July 1992; str. 11 Jan 1995
DE 1068	Vreeland	1970	decomm. 30 June 1992; to Greece 1992; str. 11 Jan 1995
DE 1069	Bagley	1972	decomm. 30 Sep 1991; str. 11 Jan 1995
DE 1070	Downes	1971	decomm. 5 June 1992; str. 11 Jan 1995
DE 1071	Badger	1970	decomm. 20 Dec 1991; str. 11 Jan 1995
DE 1072	Blakely	1970	decomm. 15 Nov 1991; str. 11 Jan 1995
DE 1073	Robert E. Peary	1972	decomm. 7 Aug 1992; to Taiwan 1992; str. 11 Jan 1995
DE 1074	Harold E. Holt	1971	decomm. 2 July 1992; str. 11 Jan 1995
DE 1075	Trippe	1970	decomm./to Greece 30 July 1992; str. 11 Jan 1995
DE 1076	Fanning	1971	decomm./to Turkey 31 July 1992; str. 11 Jan 1995
DE 1077	Ouellet	1970	decomm. 6 Aug 1993; str. 11 Jan 1995

(continued next page)

(continued from previous page)

Number	Name	Comm.	Notes
DE 1078*	JOSEPH HEWES	1971	decomm./to Taiwan 30 June 1994; str. 11 Jan 1995
DE 1079*	BOWEN	1971	decomm./to Turkey 3 June 1994; str. 1 1Jan 1995
DE 1080	PAUL	1971	decomm. 14 Aug 1992; str. 11 Jan 1995; to Turkey 1998 (parts)
DE 1081	AYLWIN	1971	decomm. 15 May 1992; to Taiwan 1998; str. 11 Jan 1995
DE 1082	ELMER MONTGOMERY	1971	decomm./stricken 30 June 1993; to Turkey 1993
DE 1083	COOK	1971	decomm. 30 Apr 1992; to Taiwan 1994; str. 11 Jan 1995
DE 1084*	MCCANDLESS	1972	decomm./to Turkey 20 June 1994; str .11 Jan 1995
DE 1085*	DONALD B. BEARY	1972	decomm./to Turkey 20 May 1994; str. 11 Jan 1995
DE 1086	BREWTON	1972	decomm. 2 July 1992; to Taiwan 1992; str. 11 Jan 1995
DE 1087	KIRK	1972	decomm./to Taiwan 6 Aug 1993; str. 11 Jan 1995
DE 1088	BARBEY	1972	decomm. 20 Mar 1992; to Taiwan 1994; str. 11 Jan 1995
DE 1089*	JESSE L. BROWN	1973	decomm. 27 July 1994; str. 11 Jan 1995; to Egypt 1994
DE 1090*	AINSWORTH	1973	decomm./to Turkey 27 May 1994; str. 11 June 1995
DE 1091	MILLER	1973	decomm. 15 Oct 1991; str. 11 Jan 1995; to Turkey 1998 (parts)
DE 1092	THOMAS C. HART	1973	decomm./to Turkey 30 Aug 1993; str. 11 Jan 1995
DE 1093	CAPDANNO	1973	decomm./to Turkey 30 July 1993; str. 11 Jan 1995
DE 1094	PHARRIS	1974	decomm. 15 Apr 1992; str. 11 Jan 1995; to Mexico 2000
DE 1095*	TRUETT	1974	decomm. 30 July 1994; to Thailand 1994; str. 11 Jan 1995
DE 1096	VALDEZ	1974	decomm. 16 Dec 1991; str. 11 Jan 1995; to Taiwan 1998
DE 1097*	MOINESTER	1974	decomm. 28 July 1994; str. 11 Jan 1995; to Egypt 1998; canceled
DE 1098–1107	KNOX class		
FF 1098	GLOVER (ex-AGDE 1)	1965	decomm. 15 June 1990; to MSC; str. 20 Nov 1992 (see text)

*Redesignated as training frigate (FFT).

U.S. World War II destroyer escort programs reached hull number DE 1005 (DE 801–1005 were canceled in 1943). After the war, 43 destroyer escorts were converted to radar picket escorts (DER)—7 for the tactical fleet role and 36 for strategic early warning of a Soviet bomber attack against the continental United States. Three were modified to an escort control (DEC) configuration to support amphibious landings. These 46 ships retained their original DE hull numbers in their new roles. (During the war, 96 DEs were converted to high-speed transports, designated in the series APD 37–139; the APD 1–36 were converted World War I–era destroyers.)

The first postwar DEs were envisioned as successors to the war-built, steel-hulled submarine chasers (PC/PCE). With the start of the postwar programs in the early 1950s, these ships were reclassified as ocean escorts (DE), partly to avoid confusion with escort destroyers (DDE). In 1975, all existing U.S. escort vessels (DE/DEG/DER) were reclassified as frigates (FF/FFG/FFR).

U.S. hull numbers were assigned to 17 ships built in Europe with U.S. funding through the Offshore Procurement (OSP) program. Thirteen U.S. ships of the DEALEY design (DE 1006, 1014, 1015, 1021–1030) were completed between 1954 and 1957, and ships of the CLAUD JONES design (DE 1033–1036) were competed in 1959–1960. Both of these designs were intended for mass production in wartime, especially by small shipyards. Significantly, while the massive World War II–era DE program included large numbers of diesel-propelled ships, in the postwar era only the four ships of the CLAUD JONES class were diesel; the rest were steam/geared powered until the advent of the OLIVER HAZARD PERRY class (gas turbine).

Many war-built and Cold War–era frigates have been transferred to other nations. Those transferred before being stricken from the Naval Vessel Register (NVR) were on lease. They subsequently were either formally sold to the countries or returned to U.S. custody (in place) and disposed of. Three KNOX-class frigates were transferred to Turkey in 1998 at no cost to be cannibalized for spare parts.

The Navy "cleaned house" on 11 January 1995, striking 43 frigates from the NVR, many in foreign service, others decommissioned in the United States.

The two-ship BRONSTEIN class (DE 1037, 1038) introduced several new ASW capabilities to U.S. frigates—drone helicopters, ASROC, and large SQS-26 bow-mounted sonar. They were armed with 3-inch guns. The subsequent BROOKE, GARCIA, and KNOX classes had 5-inch guns, and the OLIVER HAZARD PERRY class returned to smaller-caliber, 76-mm weapons.

Of the GARCIA class, the O'CALLAHAN was returned from Pakistan on 14 November 1993; the GARCIA on 13 November 1994; and the BRUMBY and KOELSCH on 19 August 1994. All four were stricken on the same dates.

The KNOX class, with 46 ships completed, was the largest class of surface combatants to be constructed in the West after World War II until 51 PERRY-class frigates. The KNOX DE/FFs were criticized for their large size (comparable to World War II–era destroyers) with only a single propeller shaft and limited AAW and anti-surface warfare (ASUW) capabilities. The latter limitation was partially corrected with the Harpoon missile fired from the ASROC launcher.

Eight KNOX-class ships were redesignated FFT (same hull numbers) in 1991 for the purpose of training reserve crews; they are indicated by asterisks in the above table. The scheme was short-lived, with the ships retaining their FFT designations until transferred or stricken. See 15th Edition/ pages 147–49 for details.

The GLOVER was built as an experimental frigate with a modified propeller configuration. She was commissioned in 1965 as the AGDE 1; subsequently changed to AGFF 1 and then FF 1098; then decommissioned and again assigned to the research role with the auxiliary designation T-AGFF 1 on 15 June 1990, being operated from that date by the Military Sealift Command.

Four frigates were recently sunk as targets:

	Sunk
HEPBURN	4 June 2002
RATHBURNE	5 July 2002
HAROLD E. HOLT	10 July 2002
DOWNES	15 Aug 2003

The ELROD going to sea to join the guided missile destroyers RAMAGE (DDG 61) and ROSS (DDG 71) to form an independent surface strike group. Considering the firepower and sensors of the two Aegis destroyers, the contributions of the nonmissile frigate to such a group are limited. (2004, U.S. Navy/Greg Roberts)

The SIMPSON passes the Statue of Liberty in New York Harbor as part of a parade of ships which the frigate was serving with the NATO STANDING NAVAL FORCE ATLANTIC. She was one of the last frigates to have the standard missile launcher Mk 13 visible here forward of the ship's bridge in the vertical, loading position. (2004, U.S. Navy/Steven J. Weber)

CHAPTER 17
Littoral Combat Ships

Small crews, innovative design, and a high degree of stealth will be traits of the Littoral Combat Ships (LCS). This is an artist's depiction of the head-on view of the General Dynamics–Bath Iron Works design for the LCS. The General Dynamics–Bath and Lockheed Martin teams each will build one Flight 0 ship. (General Dynamics)

The Navy is planning to construct a large class of Littoral Combat Ships (LCS). The Navy's annual program guide—"Vision . . . Presence . . . Power"—bases the LCS requirement on the need to overcome anti-access threats in littoral waters, especially "quiet diesel submarines armed with a variety of anti-ship weapons, mines, and attacks by small surface craft."[1] The guide goes on to say,

One element of the future "surface combatant family of ships," with its open-systems architecture design, modular weapons and sensor systems, and a variety of manned and unmanned vehicles, the LCS will be optimized to combat these anti-access threats in the littoral.[2]

1 Adm. Vern Clark, USN, "Vision . . . Presence . . . Power . . ." (Washington, D.C.: Department of the Navy, 2003), p. 114.
2 Clark, "Vision . . . Presence . . . Power . . .," pp. 114–15.

The Lockheed Martin LCS design provides for a conventional, high-speed monohull. There is a gun mount forward and a Rolling Airframe Missile (RAM) launcher amidships, atop the large helicopter/unmanned aerial vehicle hangar. A variety of hull forms were proposed by the six original LCS competitors. (Lockheed Martin)

The LCS program was initiated by Chief of Naval Operations Admiral Vern Clark as a means of building the Navy's force level, as well as to provide a needed capability for littoral operations. He has called for a force of some 60 littoral combat ships, to be added to then-planned fleet of 315 ships for a total of 375 surface ships and submarines. (Although Admiral Clark had consistently cited 60 units, the Navy's 30-year shipbuilding plan provided to Congress in 2003 lists only 56 LCSs to be constructed through 2019.)

In 2003, Admiral Clark made the design and procurement of the littoral combat ship the Navy's number one program priority for the next fiscal year. During a session with newspaper reporters on 1 May, he said the LCS would be "filling a role that is not being met today."[3] He sought to have funding for long-lead components for the first LCS in the Fiscal Year (FY) 2004 budget, with lead ship construction beginning in 2005. Series production would follow.

The LCS program offers the Navy the opportunity to have a more significant role in the littoral and regional operations that are expected to be the hallmark of the U.S. Navy for the foreseeable future. The concept holds promise as a multipurpose platform that can (1) operate in the important area between amphibious group or carrier battle groups—which are expected to operate some 50 miles or more offshore—and the beach; and (2) operate in coastal areas where there is a need for a "warship," but not the larger Aegis cruisers and destroyers that are the majority of the Navy's surface combatants.

In addition, the LCS appears to fit more closely the definition of "transformational" being proffered by Department of Defense officials than most other Navy platforms, whose sponsors have sought to declare their programs transformational to justify them in the budget process.[4] Indeed, the LCS offers the Navy an opportunity to carry out certain forward operations with a less expensive platform and far less personnel than is possible today.

Thus, there appears to be a valid requirement for the LCS. The most recent endorsement comes from two retired flag officers who have held major fleet commands as well as key surface warfare positions, and who are known for their innovative outlooks, Vice Admirals Henry Mustin and Douglas Katz.[5] They concluded, "LCS must be built, and built now, even faster than the current plan."

However, there is significant opposition to the LCS program. During a congressional hearing on 3 March 2004, Senator Edward Kennedy, the ranking minority member of the Senate Armed Services Committee's Seapower subcommittee, stated:

As far as I can tell, the Navy spent very little time figuring out whether the LCS system was the best way to deal with the threats. Why should we leap into a 50- or 60-ship program without the analysis that shows the LCS is the most effective way to deal with the problem?

Vice Admiral John B. Nathman, Deputy Chief of Naval Operations for Warfare Requirements and Programs, countered that the Navy has spent the past year and a half putting "a great amount of rigor and work into our analysis." He continued, "There is some very compelling analysis about the value of LCS."

Unfortunately, the existing ship design and procurement procedures of the Department of the Navy and the Department of Defense work against acceleration of LCS acquisition. Also, past experience has shown that new warship concepts that incorporate new hull configurations, new propulsion, and new weapons and other systems invariably encounter unforeseen difficulties.

The LCS design provides for mission modules of approximately 140 tons to carry out specialized missions. The first "packages" to be developed will be Anti-Submarine Warfare (ASW), Mine Countermeasures (MCM), and Anti-Surface Warfare (ASUW), to counter attacks by large numbers of small boats ("swarming"). ASUW also includes defense against hostile small craft armed or possibly loaded with explosives for suicide operations and perhaps attacking in large numbers. The ASW mission will be oriented against Air Independent Propulsion (AIP) and diesel submarines operating in littoral areas. A fire-support module to work with SEALs and raiding parties also is being considered.

In addition, the Commander, Naval Special Forces Command, has said there probably will be an LCS module to support SEALs. That package, he explained, will likely be "an undersea support module that could support diving operations as well as SEAL delivery vehicle operations or something of that nature."[6]

3 Dale Eisman, "Navy Leader Makes Case for New Ships Designed to Speed Quietly to Hot Spots," *The Virginian-Pilot* (2 May 2002), p. 1.

4 See Gen. Richard B. Myers, USAF, "Understanding Transformation," U.S. Naval Institute *Proceedings* (February 2003), pp. 38–41; reprinted in the volume as Appendix F.

5 Vice Adm. Henry C. Mustin, USN (Ret.), and Vice Adm. Douglas J. Katz, USN (Ret.), "All Ahead Flank for LCS," U.S. Naval Institute *Proceedings* (February 2003), pp. 30–33.

6 B. C. Kessner, "Navy Special Warfare Input, Possible Module for LCS," *Defense Daily* (3 July 2003), p. 1.

All modules would rely heavily on unmanned systems. In September 2003, the Navy listed the planned mission modules (see Table 17-1) for the first two units. These are considered Flight 0 ships; the subsequent Flight 1 and later ships would have some more advanced systems.

Table 17-1. Potential LCS Mission Modules

Task	Systems
MCM	1 MH-60 Seahawk helicopter with airborne MCM systems 3 RQ-8 Fire Scout Vertical Take-off Unmanned Aerial Vehicles (VTUAVs) WLD-1 Remote Minehunting System (RMS) AQS-20 minehunting sonar Organic Airborne and Surface Influence Sweep (OASIS) system Airborne Laser Mine Detection System (ALMDS) Rapid Airborne Mine Clearance System (RAMICS) Advanced Mine Neutralization System (AMNS) Battle Space Preparation Autonomous Underwater Vehicles (BPAUV) man-portable Remote Environmental Monitoring Units (REMUS)
ASW	1 MH-60R Seahawk helicopter with ASW sensors and weapons 3 Fire Scout VTUAVs 2 Spartan Scout-type boats with ASW package Advanced Deployable System (ADS) (sonar array) periscope-detecting radar potential RMS fitted with ASW sensors
ASUW	1 MH-60R Seahawk helicopter with rockets, guns, missiles RQ-8 Fire Scout VTUAVs with night-vision systems, infrared thermal imaging, rockets, guns, missiles 2 Spartan Scout-type boats with electro-optical infrared camera, gun system, possibly Hellfire or Javelin missiles vertical-launch missiles

In theory, the mission modules will be interchangeable and able to be replaced in a forward area. It is highly unlikely, however, that "spare" modules would be available. Rather, an LCS probably would deploy and operate with the same package until entering a shipyard for a major overhaul, at which time the on-board module would be available for transfer to another ship. (This assumes the module itself would not require overhaul/modification/updating while the LCS is in the yard.)

Cost: Probably the principal unknown in the LCS program is cost. The LCS is envisioned as a "low-cost" warship, with estimates for production units ranging from $100 million to $500 million. (By comparison, an improved ARLEIGH BURKE/DDG 51-class Aegis destroyer costs about $1 billion and a VIRGINIA/SSN 774-class nuclear-powered attack submarine just over $2 billion.) However, design and startup costs could be relatively high, in part because the U.S. Navy has had little successful experience in developing small combatants (i.e., warships smaller than frigates). The mission modules, initially of three types, also could add significantly to costs.

Design: Vice Admiral Timothy LaFleur, the Navy's senior surface warfare officer, has observed that the small crews and the use of composite materials may make it difficult to keep an LCS afloat if she is hit by enemy fire. The Navy has a tradition of fighting to save stricken ships and then bringing them back into service, he said, and LCS sailors no doubt would continue it. But the admiral also acknowledged that the new ships might be equipped with systems to facilitate a quick escape for the crew in the event of serious damage, much as aircraft ejection seats and parachutes allow pilots and airmen to get away when necessary.[7]

Historical. The concept of a small, high-capability warship for the modern U.S. Navy was first voiced in the late 1990s by Vice Admiral Arthur K. Cebrowski, at the time president of the Naval War College, and retired Captain Wayne P. Hughes, at the Naval Postgraduate School.[8] The Cebrowski–Hughes concept—originally called streetfighter—was immediately rejected by the mainstream surface Navy, which feared it would be competition for the next-generation surface combatant, then the DD 21 land-attack destroyer. However, the streetfighter concept gained support in the George W. Bush administration as Secretary of Defense Donald Rumsfeld sought "transformational" systems that could equip the military to better respond to post–Cold War operational requirements.[9]

Subsequently, one naval officer writing on the subject—calling it a "guerrilla warfare ship"—has listed these missions for the ship:
- littoral battlespace domination
- maritime embargo
- precision engagement
- surface and subsurface surveillance and choke-point traffic monitoring
- interdiction of littoral traffic
- commerce raiding
- special forces delivery and extraction
- protection of the amphibious assault lines of communications, which will extend over the horizon[10]

---

7 Dale Eisman, "Navy Steps Up Schedule for 'Littoral Combat Ships,'" *Norfolk Virginian-Pilot* (15 January 2003).

8 See, for example, Vice Adm. A. K. Cebrowski, USN, and Capt. Wayne P. Hughes Jr., USN (Ret.), "Rebalancing the Fleet," U.S. Naval Institute *Proceedings* (November 1999), pp. 31–34.

9 After retiring from active duty in October 2001, Adm. Cebrowski was appointed Director of the Office of Force Transformation within the Department of Defense.

10 Lt. Comdr. Dave Weeks, USNR, "A Combatant for the Littorals," U.S. Naval Institute *Proceedings* (November 1999), p. 27.

The General Dynamics–Bath LCS design is based on the trimaran hull-form demonstrated in the British research vessel TRITON, *completed in 2001. The trimaran design offers a broad amidships deck combined with high speed. (General Dynamics)*

The General Dynamics–Bath LCS design shown in rough seas, with one H-60 series helicopter on her flight deck and a second having just taken off. The LCS designs provide for modular "mission packages" that can be swapped out to vary the ships' combat capabilities. (General Dynamics)

(56) LITTORAL COMBAT SHIPS

Units	FY	Comm.	Status
1 ship	05	2008	Planned
1 ship	06	2009	Planned
3 ships	08	2011–2012	Planned
4 ships	09		Planned
5 ships per year	10–18		Planned
2 ships	19		Planned

Builders:	General Dynamics (GD)
	Lockheed Martin (LM)
Displacement:	GD: 2,633 tons full load
	LM: 2,794 tons full load
Mission module:	GD: 206.7 tons
	LM: 211.6 tons
Length:	GD: 416⅔ feet (127.04 m) overall
	LM: 378 feet (115.24 m) overall
Beam:	GD: 99⅔ feet (30.4 m)
	LM: 57½ feet (17.5 m)
Draft:	GD: 14⅘ feet (4.51 m)
	LM: 12⅘ feet (3.9 m)
Propulsion:	2 gas turbines; 2 shafts (see *Engineering* notes)
Speed:	approx. 45 knots
Range:	GD: 4,300 nm at 20 knots cruise
	1,940 nm at 46 knots sprint
	LM: 3,550 nm at 18 knots cruise
	1,150 nm at 45 knots sprint
Personnel:	approx. 15–50 ship's company + mission specialists
Helicopters:	1 MH-60R Seahawk
	up to 3 RQ-8 Fire Scout VTUAVs
Missiles:	mission modules, plus probably 21-cell Rolling Airframe Missile launcher Mk 49
Guns:	1 20-mm Phalanx Close-In Weapon System
	or 1 57-mm/70-cal cannon Mk 110
ASW weapons:	mission modules
Radars:	air search
	surface search
Sonars:	mission modules
Fire control:	mission modules

The characteristics in the data table are core features that will be found in each LCS. Different modules will provide weapons, sensors, and other equipment for specific mission requirements. The first two ships are considered Flight 0; the third and later ships are Flight 1. The two builders indicated each will construct one Flight 0 ship.

Builders: The Navy in early 2003 invited six U.S. consortiums to participate in a design/concept competition for the littoral combat ship. In August 2003, three were selected to develop a preliminary LCS design:

• General Dynamics with Bath Iron Works, Austal USA, Bender Shipbuilding, and Tampa Bay Shipbuilding ($8,900,000)

• Lockheed Martin Naval Electronics & Surveillance Systems with Bollinger Shipyards and Marinette Marine ($9,993,359)

• Raytheon Company, Integrated Defense Systems with Atlantic Marine Alabama Shipbuilding ($9,996,124)

The teams eliminated in that first round of competition were Northrop Grumman; Textron with Halter Marine; and Titan Corp. with Nichols Brothers.

On 27 May 2004, two of the teams were selected—led by Lockheed Martin and General Dynamics—each to build one of the Flight 0 prototype ships.

Cost: The overall LCS program with up to 60 ships has been estimated at $15–$20 billion, including development costs and the procurement of mission modules.

Engineering: The Flight 1 ships are planned to have electric drive.

Personnel: The above data reflect the Navy's objective of a 15-man crew for the LCS, with a maximum of 50 personnel. In addition, each mission module will have technicians assigned who will come aboard the ship in addition to the standard LCS manning. In theory, the mission module will include berthing and messing space for the additional personnel.

A modified rigid hull inflatable boat configured as an unmanned Spartan Scout craft approaches the cruiser GETTYSBURG *(CG 64). The LCS will make use of Unmanned Surface Vehicles (USVs) for various missions. Although crewmen are aboard the Spartan in this photo, the craft was under remote control. (2003, U.S. Navy/Justin McGarry)*

CHAPTER 18

Command Ships

Crewmen crowd the bow of the command ship MOUNT WHITNEY as she enters her home port of Norfolk, Virginia, after a seven-month deployment. Command ships are adorned with communications antenna domes; SLQ-32(V)3 antennas are visible on the ship's bridge wings. (2003, U.S. Navy/ Thomas Coffelt)

The U.S. Navy has four fleet-level command ships in active service: The MOUNT WHITNEY, flagship of the Second Fleet in the Atlantic; the CORONADO, flagship of the Third Fleet in the Eastern Pacific; the LA SALLE, flagship of the Sixth Fleet in the Mediterranean; and the BLUE RIDGE, flagship of the Seventh Fleet in the Western Pacific.

The CORONADO and BLUE RIDGE have composite Navy-civilian service crews, the latter personnel under the Military Sealift Command. Each ship has a Navy captain in command, with a chief mate in charge of the civilian mariners who provide the ships' mess, laundry, and other house keeping functions as well as providing the ships' engineering personnel. The CORONADO adopted this manning concept in 2003 and the BLUE RIDGE in 2004.

All four ships are overage—the LA SALLE has been in service for more than 40 years and the three other command ships about 35 years. Plans to construct a new series of joint command ships (JCC) have been abandoned (see below).

From the end of World War II until the 1970s, U.S. numbered fleets generally had cruisers for flagships, but the cruisers now in service do not have major flag facilities and accommodations. The last specially configured cruiser-flagship, the BELKNAP (CG 26), was partially converted in 1978–1980 to accommodate a portion of the Sixth Fleet staff, while retaining full missile cruiser capability. She was decommissioned in 1995.

The four battleships of the IOWA (BB 61) class reactivated in the 1980s at times embarked flag officers and served as limited command ships, although they were not fitted to serve as major flagships.

Classification: The BLUE RIDGE and MOUNT WHITNEY retain their LCC amphibious command ship designation in the fleet command ship role; the miscellaneous flagships (AGF) retain their previous LPD hull numbers with the AGF designation.

Names: Amphibious command ships (AGC/LCC) traditionally have been assigned the names of American mountains and mountain ranges. The AGFs retain their amphibious ship names.

JOINT COMMAND AND CONTROL SHIPS

A program for several joint command and control ships (JCC) was initiated in the late 1990s as a potential replacement for the four existing command ships. The JCC, sometimes referred to as the JCC(X), would provide a platform for joint command-and-control functions in forward areas.

The first phase of the Navy JCC study, completed in spring 2000, was to determine whether the required capabilities could be provided by systems other than command ships. The alternatives assessed included relying on land-based facilities (in both the United States and forward areas); using a mix of existing ships, such as aircraft carriers, amphibious ships, and cruisers; or employing some combination of these approaches.

Pending completion of this initial study, the Department of Defense programmed funds to acquire two joint command and control ships, one each in fiscal years (FY) 2004 and 2005. It was envisioned that two follow-on ships would be requested in FY 2006 and FY 2007, and that the first unit could be operational as early as 2007.

However, in a major policy shift, Defense budget planners did not include preliminary funding for the JCC in the proposed DoD budget for FY 2003, effectively killing the development of a specialized platform. Chief of Naval Operations Admiral Vern Clark's executive council has reviewed the ship and mission package concepts, and—apparently in lieu of the single-mission platform—recommended several multimission alternatives.

Among the more promising options was reported to be the Maritime Prepositioning Force–Future (MPF–F), envisioned as a follow-on to the current fleet of leased and purchased prepositioned cargo ships (see Chapter 24). The MPF–F is expected to be developed by 2009. The new class of MPF–F ships would continue the program of forward-deployment afloat of ground combat and support material that can be "married" to troops flown into the forward area. Such a ship could carry a JCC module that could be manned by command, communications, and staff personnel flown in, in time of crisis. Obviously, unlike with a command team already embarked in a ship, there would be "dead time" while the team is moved to the forward area and then transported to the host ship.

Alternatively, the next generation of cruisers, amphibious helicopter carriers, or even large-deck carriers could have JCC facilities built in.

2 AMPHIBIOUS COMMAND SHIPS: "BLUE RIDGE" CLASS

Number	Name	FY	Builder	Laid Down	Launched	Comm.	Status
LCC 19	BLUE RIDGE	65	Philadelphia Naval Shipyard	27 Feb 1967	4 Jan 1969	14 Nov 1970	**PA**
LCC 20	MOUNT WHITNEY	66	Newport News Shipbuilding, Va.	8 Jan 1969	8 Jan 1970	16 Jan 1971	**AA**

Displacement:	16,790 tons light 18,646 tons full load	Flag:	LCC 19: 257 (72 officers + 185 enlisted) LCC 20: 296 (82 officers + 214 enlisted)
Length:	579 1½ feet (176.8 m) waterline 636 ⅚ feet (194.0 m) overall	Helicopters: Missiles:	landing area only (see *Helicopter* notes) removed
Beam:	82 feet (25.0 m)	Guns:	2 25-mm Bushmaster cannon Mk 38 (2 single)
Extreme width:	108 feet (32.9 m)		2 20-mm Phalanx CIWS Mk 15 (2 multibarrel)
Draft:	28 ⅚ feet (8.8 m)		4 12.7-mm machine guns (4 single)
Propulsion:	1 steam turbine (General Electric); 22,000 shp; 1 shaft	Radars:	SPS-40E air search
Boilers:	2 600 psi (41.7 kg/cm2) (Foster Wheeler)		SPS-48C 3-D search
Speed:	22 knots		SPS-64(V)9 navigation
Range:	13,500 nm (25,000 km) at 16 knots		SPS-65(V)1 surface search
Personnel:	LCC 19: 622 (35 officers + 587 enlisted)	Fire control:	removed
	LCC 20: 576 (36 officers + 540 enlisted)	EW systems:	SLQ-25A Nixie
			SLQ-32(V)3

These are large command ships, the only U.S. Navy ships to be designed from the outset for the amphibious command ship role. The Navy's earlier command ships, most built to merchant ship specifications, could not operate with the 20-knot amphibious ships built from the 1960s onward. Both of these ships are now employed as fleet flagships.

The BLUE RIDGE is homeported in Yokosuka, Japan, having relieved the cruiser OKLAHOMA CITY (CG 5) in October 1979 as flagship of the Seventh Fleet. The MOUNT WHITNEY is based at Norfolk, Virginia, having relieved the cruiser ALBANY (CG 10) as flagship of the Second Fleet in January 1981.

The above data for the BLUE RIDGE reflect her configuration and personnel in late 2003.

Class: A third ship of this class (AGC 21) was planned—to have been configured for service as both an amphibious flagship and fleet flagship—but was canceled.

Classification: These ships originally were classified as amphibious force flagships (AGC); they were changed to amphibious command ships (LCC) on 1 January 1969.

Design: SCB No. 400. The hull and propulsion machinery are similar to that of the IWO JIMA (LPH 2)-class helicopter carriers.

The command ship facilities originally provided in this class were for a Navy amphibious task force commander and a Marine assault force commander and their staffs. Their designed flag/staff accommodations were for 200 officers and 500 enlisted men.

The ships have large open deck areas to allow for optimum antenna placement. There is a helicopter landing area aft, but no hangar. (A small vehicle hangar is serviced by an elevator.) Davits provide stowage for five landing craft (LCPL/LCVP type) plus a ship's launch.

Engineering: Maximum sustained speed is 20 knots.

Guns: The early designs for this ship provided for six 3-inch/50-cal Anti-Aircraft (AA) Mk 33 guns in twin mounts. Two pair forward of the bridge structure in enclosed gun houses were fitted, but the third pair on the forecastle was not installed. The two 3-inch mounts were removed in 1992.

Phalanx Close-In Weapon Systems (CIWS) were long scheduled for installation in these ships. Two CIWS were provided in the BLUE RIDGE in 1985, mounted forward on a small deckhouse fitted on the main deck and a sponson at the stern (increasing length approximately 16 feet/4.9 m); the same installation was fitted the in MOUNT WHITNEY in 1987.

Helicopters: A UH-3H Sea King is usually assigned to each ship.

Missiles: Two 8-tube Sea Sparrow Basic Point Defense Missile System (BPDMS) launchers were fitted abaft of the bridge structure in 1974. They were removed from both ships in 1992, as were the two Mk 115 missile fire control systems.

Operational: In addition to their staffs, both ships carry Marine communications detachments on a permanent basis.

The BLUE RIDGE entering Yokosuka, Japan. Successors to the amphibious force flagships (AGC) of World War II, the BLUE RIDGE and MOUNT WHITNEY are in need of replacement, but no LCCs are now planned for construction. (2004, U.S. Navy/Alan Warner)

The MOUNT WHITNEY, steaming off the Horn of Africa, exercises her washdown system, intended to counter the effects of nuclear, biological, and chemical attacks. The large, open decks are required to reduce the mutual interference of the ship's large array of communications antennas. (2003, U.S. Navy/George Kusner)

The BLUE RIDGE at Yokosuka. The LCCs have large, open gallery decks for small boat stowage; there is a large helicopter flight deck aft, but no hangar has been provided. The ships now are armed with Phalanx close-in weapon system mounts forward and aft. Earlier they had 3-inch guns and then Sea Sparrow missiles. (2004, U.S. Navy/Alan Warner)

AMPHIBIOUS COMMAND SHIPS

Amphibious command ships—originally called amphibious force flagships—reached hull number AGC 18 during World War II.

Fourteen C2-type merchant ships were completed as command ships (AGC 1–3, 5, 7–17); one transport was converted to that role (AGC 4), as was one small seaplane tender, the BISCAYNE (AGC 18, ex-AVP 11). In addition, six large Coast Guard cutters of the Secretary class were reconfigured as flagships in 1944–1945, but only one was reclassified, the DUANE (AGC 6, ex-WPG 33). After the war, the six ships, rated as 327-foot (99.7-m) cutters by the Coast Guard, reverted to multimission ships.

Five surviving C2-type ships were changed from AGC to LCC on 1 January 1969. The last war-era AGC to see active naval service was the ELDORADO (AGC/LCC 11), decommissioned in 1973.

The civilian yacht WILLIAMSBURG, which served as a gunboat (PG 56) from 1941 to 1945, was assigned as the presidential yacht after World War II, and redesignated AGC 369 on 10 November 1945.[1] She served in that role for Presidents Harry S. Truman and (for one cruise) Dwight D. Eisenhower. The WILLIAMSBURG was decommissioned in 1953 and stricken in 1962; she then was employed as a civilian oceanographic research ship from 1962 to 1986.

The WILLIAMSBURG is now at San Francisco and efforts are under way to preserve her.

---

1 Reportedly, AGC 369 was President Truman's license plate number when county commissioner in Missouri before being elected to the U.S. Senate.

1 MISCELLANEOUS FLAGSHIP: CONVERTED "AUSTIN" CLASS

Number	Name	FY	Builder	Laid Down	Launched	Comm.	Status
AGF 11 (ex-LPD 11)	CORONADO	64	Lockheed Shipbuilding & Construction., Seattle	3 May 1965	30 July 1966	23 May 1970	**PA**

Displacement:	11,050 tons light	Helicopters:	1 UH-3H Sea King
	16,912 tons full load	Missiles:	none
Length:	568 ¾ feet (173.4 m) overall	Guns:	2 20-mm Phalanx CIWS Mk 15 (2 multibarrel)
Beam:	84 feet (25.6 m)		2 12.7-mm machine guns (2 single)
Draft:	23 ⅞ feet (7.2 m)	Radars:	SPS-10F surface search
Propulsion:	2 steam turbines (De Laval); 24,000 shp; 2 shafts		SPS-40E air search
Boilers:	2 600 psi (41.7 kg/cm2) (Foster Wheeler)		SPS-64(V)9 navigation
Speed:	21 knots	Fire control:	local control only
Range:	7,700 nm (14,260 km) at 20 knots	EW systems:	SLQ-32(V)2
Personnel:	see text		WLR-1H intercept
Flag:	200–300		

The CORONADO was built and served as an amphibious ship until 1980, when she was modified to serve as a temporary flagship to permit the Middle East flagship LA SALLE to undergo a lengthy overhaul at the Philadelphia Naval Shipyard. After her own overhaul in 1983–1984, she became flagship of the Sixth Fleet in August 1985, replacing the destroyer tender PUGET SOUND (AD 38). She was home ported in Gaeta, Italy.

In June 1986, with the BELKNAP assigned as Sixth Fleet flagship, the CORONADO departed the Mediterranean and the following month shifted to the Pacific to become flagship for Commander, Third Fleet (then based at Pearl Harbor). Prior to breaking his flag in the CORONADO on 26 November 1986, the Commander, Third Fleet, had flown his flag ashore since the end of World War II.

The ship next deployed to the Persian Gulf, arriving in January 1988 to serve as interim flagship for Commander, U.S. Middle East Force, for most of that year. She returned to Pearl Harbor in November 1988 to resume duties as Third Fleet flagship.

In August 1991, with the Commander, Third Fleet, embarked, the CORONADO, shifted her home port to North Island Naval Air Station at San Diego, California. Later, as the piers at North Island became too crowded because of carrier operations, she shifted her home port to the adjacent submarine base at Point Loma.

The CORONADO subsequently was assigned as temporary flagship for the Seventh Fleet while the BLUE RIDGE underwent an overhaul at Yokosuka. In November 2003, the Third Fleet staff officially moved ashore to Point Loma (San Diego), although most staff elements had moved ashore earlier.

The ship's manning then was changed from all-Navy to a composite Navy–civilian crew, the latter under the aegis of the Military Sealift Command. Whereas the ship previously was manned by 481 naval personnel, the composite crew consists of 117 Navy and 153 civilian personnel, a total of 270. The Navy men and women operate the ship's combat information center, communications, electronic warfare, weapons, and helicopter control functions. The civilian mariners are responsible for basic shipboard functions such as navigation, propulsion, and auxiliary machinery operation, maintenance and repair, and laundry facilities. (In addition, some 200–300 Seventh Fleet flag personnel are embarked at any given time.)

The CORONADO departed San Diego on 5 March 2004 and arrived at Yokosuka on 24 March 2004. She returned to San Diego on 3 November 2004 to again serve as the flagship for the Third Fleet.

Classification: The CORONADO's classification changed from LPD 11 to AGF 11 on 1 October 1980.

Conversion: The CORONADO's telescoping hangar is 49½ feet (15.1 m) long, and 18½ feet (5.6 m) wide, and 17⅔ feet (5.4 m) high; it expands to a length of about 75 feet (22.9 m). The ship retained a docking well until her 1997–1998 overhaul, when the well deck was rebuilt to provide additional flag working space and accommodations.

Design: SCB No. 187C. See the AUSTIN (LPD 4) listing in Chapter 18 for additional details. The ship is similar to but larger than the LA SALLE.

Guns: Phalanx CIWS have been installed on an extension of the bridge structure, forward to port, and amidships, on the starboard side. The two 3-inch/50-cal Mk 33 AA twin gun mounts previously carried in the AGF role were removed in the early 1990s.

Operational: In October 2000, the Secretary of the Navy established the Sea-Based Battle Lab in the CORONADO (in addition to her serving as flagship for the Third Fleet). The ship was modified with more than 16,000 feet² (1,485 m²) of reconfigurable space for testing and evaluating prototype systems and software for naval Command, Control, and Communications (C^3).

The CORONADO's extensive modifications for her role as a fleet flagship are evident in this bow view, which shows her port-side appendages and the mass of antenna domes that cover her enlarged superstructure. (2004, U.S. Navy/Novia E. Harrington)

The CORONADO, showing her enclosed stern, helicopter flight deck, and partially open helicopter hangar. Hidden in the superstructure clutter are two Phalanx close-in weapon system mounts. The two AGFs have limited space and facilities for the role of numbered fleet flagships. (2004, U.S. Navy/John E. Woods)

The CORONADO during an underway replenishment with the oiler TIPPECANOE (T-AO 199) while serving as Seventh Fleet flagship. The CORONADO's large, "two spot" helicopter deck is evident; unlike the LCCs, the two AGFs have helicopter hangars. (2004, U.S. Navy/John E. Woods)

1 MISCELLANEOUS FLAGSHIP: CONVERTED "RALEIGH" CLASS

Number	Name	FY	Builder	Laid down	Launched	Comm.	Status
AGF 3 (ex-LPD 3	LA SALLE	61	New York Naval Shipyard, Brooklyn	2 Apr 1962	3 Aug 1963	22 Feb 1964	**AA**

Displacement:	8,040 tons light	Flag:	223 (72 officers + 151 enlisted)
	14,650 tons full load	Helicopters:	1 UH-3H Sea King
Length:	500 feet (152.4 m) waterline	Missiles:	none
	521¾ feet (159.0 m) overall	Guns:	2 25-mm Bushmaster cannon Mk 38 (2 single)
Beam:	84 feet (25.6 m)		2 20-mm Phalanx CIWS Mk 15 (2 multibarrel)
Draft:	22 feet (6.7 m)		2 12.7-mm machine guns (2 single)
Propulsion:	2 steam turbines (De Laval); 24,000 shp; 2 shafts	Radars:	SPS-10F surface search
Boilers:	2 600 psi (41.7 kg/cm2) (Babcock & Wilcox)		SPS-40E air search
Speed:	21.6 knots (20 knots sustained)		SPS-64(V)9 navigation
Range:	9,600 nm (17,780 km) at 16 knots	Fire control:	local control only
	16,500 nm (30,558 km) at 10 knots	EW systems:	SLQ-32(V)3
Personnel:	493 (25 officers + 468 enlisted)		WLR-1H

The LA SALLE was converted from an amphibious ship specifically to serve as flagship for Commander, U.S. Middle East Force (now Commander, U.S. Naval Forces, Central Command). In November 1994, she replaced the cruiser BELKNAP as flagship of the Sixth Fleet in the Mediterranean. She is homeported at Gaeta, Italy.

Class: The LA SALLE was one of three amphibious transport docks of the RALEIGH (LPD 1) class.

Classification: She was built as LPD 3 and served as an amphibious ship until 1 July 1972, when she was to AGF 3.

Conversion: The ship was converted to a flagship in 1972, with command and communication facilities, a helicopter hangar, and additional air conditioning. The amidships hangar is 47½ feet (14.6 m) long, 18½ feet (5.5 m) wide, and 19⅓ feet (5.9 m) high.

Design: SCB No. 187A.

Guns: Phalanx CIWS have been installed amidships, port and starboard. The two 3-inch/50-cal Mk 33 AA twin gun mounts previously mounted as an AGF have been deleted.

Operational: The LA SALLE operated in the Persian Gulf–Indian Ocean area from 1972 to 1980, when she was relieved by the CORONADO. She underwent an extensive overhaul at the Philadelphia Naval Shipyard from December 1980 to September 1982, after which she in turn relieved the CORONADO as flagship of the Middle East Force on 16 June 1983 at Mina' Sulman, Bahrain. She served in that role during the 1991 Persian Gulf War, shifting to the Mediterranean in late 1994. She is homeported Gaeta, Italy.

In 1984, in response to mining of the Red Sea by a Libyan merchant ship, the LA SALLE operated RH-53D Sea Stallion mine countermeasure helicopters.

Prior to the conversion of the LA SALLE, the flagships of the Commander, Middle East Force, had been small seaplane tenders of the BARENGAT (AVP 10) class from the time that command was established in the late 1940s (see 17th Edition/page 170).

The LA SALLE while serving as Sixth Fleet flagship during operations in the Mediterranean Sea. Older and smaller than the CORONADO, her flag spaces and accommodations are crowded. Her helicopter hangar is offset to port. (2003, U.S. Navy/Christopher B. Stoltz)

CHAPTER 19

Amphibious Warfare Ships

Marines from the 26th Marine Expeditionary Unit (MEU) on the flight deck of the Iwo JIMA prepare to board helicopters for a flight to Monrovia, Liberia, to support peacekeeping operations. Amphibious ships are useful across a broad range of "ops"—from assault to peacekeeping and disaster relief activities. (2003, U.S. Navy/ Christian N. Knoell)

The U.S. Navy's amphibious lift in early 2005 consists of 35 ships in active service. Four additional amphibious-type ships are employed as command ships for fleet commanders and are not available to provide amphibious lift (see Chapter 18). In addition, five older amphibious ships (LKA) are maintained in reserve to off-set the rapid retirement of older "amphibs" and delays in the SAN ANTONIO-class dock landing ship program.

Procurement of the SAN ANTONIO-class LPDs, vital for the Navy to maintain 12 Expeditionary Strike Groups (ESGs) of three ships each, was cut back abruptly in 2004. Chief of Naval Operations Admiral Vern Clark announced that probably 8 LPDs would be procured rather than the planned 12. This reduction, in turn, is expected to decrease the number of ESGs available for amphibious assault. This change in amphibious ship procurement and possibly force structure relates directly to the development of the Maritime Prepositioning Force (MPF), a new concept in projecting ground forces overseas that evolved from the Maritime Prepositioning Squadrons (MPS) developed in the early 1980s (see Chapter 24).

The Navy's long-range, 30-year shipbuilding plan previously had called for a 36-ship amphibious force capable of supporting 12 ESGs. Initiated in 2003, the ESGs replace the Amphibious Ready Groups (ARG). Each ESG contains the three amphibious ships of the ARG, plus surface combatants, one or two attack submarines (SSN), and land-based maritime patrol aircraft (P-3C Orions). These enhancements are expected to enable them to carry out "sea strike" missions in lesser-threat environments that do not require the participation of aircraft carriers.

The amphibious assault capabilities of the ESG and ARG are identical: a Marine Expeditionary Unit (MEU)—basically a reinforced rifle battalion and composite helicopter–AV-8B Harrier squadron. Total MEU strength is just over 2,000 Marines (see Chapter 7). The standard ESG/ARG carries helicopters, three landing craft (LCU), three air cushion landing craft (LCAC), and amphibious assault vehicles (AAV—"amphibious tractors") that can land the combat components of the MEU.

In the later stages of the Cold War, the U.S. Navy–Marine Corps requirement for amphibious lift was 60-plus ships capable of carrying the assault elements of a Marine Expeditionary Force (MEF) plus a Marine Expeditionary Brigade (MEB). In 1991—when the Soviet Union collapsed—the Navy had 60 amphibious ships in active commission, plus three Naval Reserve Force (NRF) ships.

The post–Cold War requirement initially was for sufficient amphibious ships to lift the assault elements of three MEBs; it subsequently was reduced to two and a half MEBs, and even that goal cannot be achieved with the cutback in the LPD construction program. This is a significantly lesser lift capability than the previous MEF + MEB requirement, because a MEF, in addition to having the rough equivalent of three MEBs as ground combat elements, contains numerous command, combat support, and other support components.

Thus, since the mid-1990s, the Navy's amphibious lift capacity has been less than two and a half MEBs, *if* essentially all amphibious ships were available—a total lift capacity of perhaps 25,000 troops. This is a theoretical capability, however, as it is impossible to assemble more than perhaps three ESG/ARGs in a given area in less than perhaps two to three months. (During the five-month buildup for the Persian Gulf conflict of January 1991, the Navy assembled 31 amphibious ships embarking a MEB plus a separate MEU—a total of some 17,000 troops.)

The ESGs were to be standardized at three ships:
• 1 LHA/LHD (amphibious assault ship)
• 1 LPD (dock landing ship)
• 1 LSD (dock landing ship)
Obviously, the cutback in LPD production to eight ships—and possibly fewer—will require a reduction in the number of ESGs and/or a revision of their composition. For example, an ESG with only a helicopter ship (LHA/LHD) would carry a reduced MEU, deleting the tanks, assault amphibian vehicles, a rifle company, and other components of a standard MEU. Other ESGs could have one LHA/LHD and three LSDs, the latter providing the lift capacity of one LSD and one LPD. And, of course, perhaps eight ESGs could have the "model" three-ship configuration.

Normally, two or three ESG/ARGs are forward deployed: one in the Atlantic–Mediterranean area, one in the Persian Gulf–Indian Ocean area, and one in the Western Pacific area. The other ESG/ARGs ships are in transit, working up (with MEUs), or in overhaul. One ARG (four ships) is forward based in Sasebo, Japan.

During 2003, the last U.S. tank landing ship (LST) was discarded. Since the LST was introduced in the U.S. Navy on 14 December 1942 with the commissioning of the LST 1 , a total of 1,096 LSTs were built in the United States through 1972 (see below).

Table 19-1. AMPHIBIOUS WARFARE SHIPS (EARLY 2005)

Type	Class/Ship	Comm.	Active	Reserve	Building*
LHD 8	Improved Wasp	2007	—	—	1
LHD 1	Wasp	1989–2001	7	—	—
LHA 1	Tarawa	1976–1980	5	—	—
LPD 17	San Antonio	2005–	—	—	6
LPD 4	Austin	1965–1971	11	—	—
LSD 49	Harpers Ferry	1995–1998	4	—	—
LSD 41	Whidbey Island	1985–1992	8	—	—
LKA 113	Charleston	1968–1970	—	5	—

* Ships authorized through FY 2004.

Aircraft: A standard LHA/LHD "air wing" consists of a Marine composite squadron of 18 CH-46 Sea Knights, 4 CH-53 Sea Stallions, and 4 AH-1W SeaCobra helicopters, plus a couple of UH-1N Huey command/utility helicopters.

These ships regularly operate AV-8B Harrier Short Take-off and Vertical Landing (STOVL) fixed-wing attack aircraft. They also can operate Unmanned Aerial Vehicle (UAV)-type aircraft.

No catapults or arresting gear is fitted in the LHA/LHD-type ships. There have been proposals to modify these ships with ski ramps to enhance the takeoff capabilities of STOVL aircraft (as in British STOVL and vertical/short take-off and landing ships), but the Navy's aviation community has steadfastly refused to seriously consider such proposals.

Builders: The acquisition of the Litton/Ingalls Shipyard at Pascagoula, Mississippi, by Northrop Grumman Ship Systems was completed on 21 December 2000.

Guns: Beginning in the 1980s, LSD- and LPD-type amphibious ships were fitted with .50-cal/7.62-mm machine guns, 25-mm Mk 38 Bushmaster "chain" guns, and 20-mm cannon for close-in defense against small craft; this armament suite was especially important for ships deploying into the Persian Gulf.

The 3-inch/50-cal (76-mm) guns have been removed from all surviving amphibious ships, except for the five CHARLESTON-class LKAs, all in reserve. Similarly, the 5-inch/54-cal (127-mm) guns have been removed from the TARAWA-class LHAs.

Historical: There have been three major "spurts" of amphibious ship construction since World War II. The first, during the Korean War, produced the LSD 28 and LST 1156 classes (23 ships); the second, in the Kennedy and Johnson administrations of the early 1960s, produced the LCC 19, LHA 1, LKA 112, LPD 12, LSD 36, and LST 1179 classes (49 ships).

The third postwar amphibious ship buildup was part of the Reagan administration's program in the 1980s for a 600-ship fleet. This effort began with the WHIDBEY ISLAND, the first amphibious ship authorized for the U.S. Navy in a decade. That ship was funded by Congress in Fiscal Year (FY) 1981 over the objections of the Carter administration. When the Reagan administration entered the White House in January 1981, amphibious ship construction was accelerated. This third burst included the WASP, WHIDBEY ISLAND, and HARPERS FERRY classes. Eighteen ships of these three classes were funded in the FY 1984–1993 shipbuilding programs.

Table 19.2 shows the nominal lift capacity of current amphibious ships.

Names: Amphibious assault ships (LPH/LHA) are named for battles fought by Marines; the LHD series, however, carries the names of World War II–era aircraft carriers, which in turn were named for Navy ships and battles.

Amphibious transport docks (LPD) are named for cities that honor explorers and pioneers.

Dock landing ships (LSD) carry the names of historic sites and cities.

Amphibious cargo ships (LKA) were named for counties.

Operational: Amphibious Group 1 (PHIBGRU 1)/Amphibious Squadron 11 (PHIBRON 11) has as its core the four amphibious ships—one LHD, one LPD, and two LSDs—homeported in Sasebo, Japan. (These are the only U.S. "amphibs" based overseas.) The squadron initially was activated in July 1966 and at the time was comprised of seven ships homeported in Long Beach, California, with the VALLEY FORGE as flagship. The squadron was "reactivated" on 30 September 1992 to provide a forward-deployed PHIBRON in the Far East.

PHIBRON 11 embarks the 31st Marine Expeditionary Unit, which is based on Okinawa.

Amphibious Group 1 controls amphibious operations for the Seventh Fleet, the Commander PHIBGRU-1 also serving as Commander Task Force 76.

Table 19-2. NOMINAL AMPHIBIOUS LIFT CAPABILITIES

Class	Troops	Vehicle space (square feet)	Cargo space (cubic feet)	Helicopter spots*	LCAC spots**
LHD 1	1,685	20,900	109,000	46	3
LHA 1	1,710	25,400	105,900	41	1
LPD 17	720	25,000	25,000	6	2
LPD 4	***	12,000	40,000	4	1
LSD 49 CV	400	16,600	50,700	2	2
LSD 41	450	13,500	5,100	0	4
LKA 113	210	32,900	66,100	0	—

* Hangar and flight deck capacity (CH-46E equivalents) for ships that normally embark helicopters.
** Docking well capacity.
***LPD 6, 14, 15 can accommodate 930 troops; LPD 7–10, 12, 13 can accommodate 840 troops, the reduction to provide space for flag accommodations.

A Marine CH-53E Super Stallion passes over the amphibious assault ship BOXER during operations in the Persian Gulf. Additional CH-53Es are on the BOXER's flight deck, as are CH-46E Sea Knight helicopters; her stern gate is partially lowered. (2004, U.S. Navy/ Christopher Elmini)

(9) AMPHIBIOUS ASSAULT SHIPS: LHA(R) PROGRAM

Units	FY	Comm.	Status	Units	FY	Comm.	Status
1 ship	07	2014	Planned	1 ship	19		Planned
1 ship	10		Planned	2 ships	24–28		Planned
1 ship	13		Planned	2 ships	29–33		Planned
1 ship	16		Planned				

Displacement:	approx. 50,000 tons full load		Aircraft:	AV-8B Harrier STOVL
Length:	921 feet (280.7 m) overall		30+	MV-22 Osprey VTOL
Beam:	116 feet (35.4 m)			CH-53E Sea Stallion helicopters
Extreme width:			Elevators:	2 deck edge
Draft:			Missiles:	21-cell RAM launchers Mk 49
Propulsion:	2 gas turbine; 70,000 shp; 2 shafts		Guns:	20-mm Phalanx CIWS Mk 15 (3 multibarrel)
Speed:	20+ knots		Radars:	
Range:			Fire Control:	
Personnel:			EW Systems:	
Troops:	2,000			

The above are planning characteristics provided by the Naval Sea Systems Command. The definitive configuration of the ship had not been determined when this edition of *Ships and Aircraft* went to press.

The Navy's 30-year shipbuilding plan provided to Congress in 2003 lists ten ships as replacements for current amphibious assault ships. Designated LHA(R)—R for replacement—the ships initially will replace the early LHAs as they begin to reach the ends of their expected service lives between 2011 and 2015. (The LHD 8 will replace the first LHA.)

The most probable configuration for the LHA(R) will be the "LHD-Plug-Plus," the basic LHD 8 design, lengthened and possibly widened to accommodate the F-35 Joint Strike Fighter, nomi-

nal replacement for the AV-8B Harrier STOVL aircraft; the MV-22 Osprey, replacement for the CH-46 Sea Knight; and other features. The ship would displace about 50,000 tons full load. Most significant, the LHA(R) will *not* have a docking well. This will provide more space for the support of F-35/JSV and MV-22 operations.

However, more radical configurations also have been proposed, especially the so-called Dual Tram Line design, which calls for a ship of some 69,000 tons full-load displacement. That ship could simultaneously operate both STOVL aircraft and helicopters, which is not possible with the other LHA/LHD designs. Cost was estimated in FY 2003 dollars at $4.1 billion for the lead ship and $2.8 billion for follow-on ships. The first LHA(R) is listed in the FY 2007 shipbuilding plan at a cost of $3.1 billion.

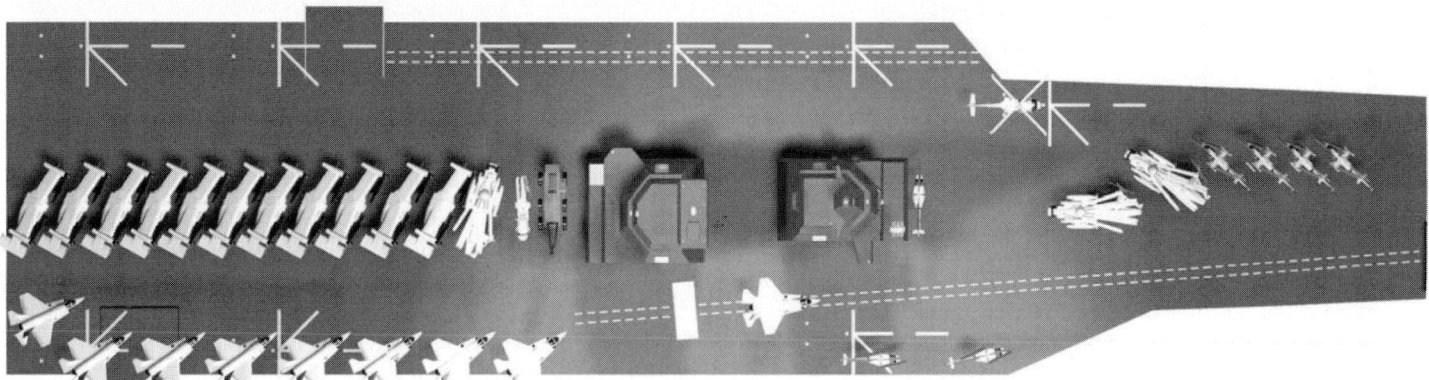

The Dual Tram Line design for a future helicopter/STOVL carrier. The large ship—estimated at 69,000 tons—would operate helicopters and MV-22 Osprey STOVL aircraft from the port side, and the F-35 Joint Strike Fighter from the starboard side. The ship would have centerline island structures. (U.S. Navy)

(1) AMPHIBIOUS ASSAULT SHIP: IMPROVED "WASP" CLASS

Number	Name	FY	Builder	Laid Down	Launched	Comm.	Status
LHD 8	MAKIN ISLAND	02	Northrop Grumman/Ingalls Shipbuilding, Pascagoula, Miss.	14 Feb 2004	2006	2007	Building

Displacement:	approx. 45,000 tons full load	Missiles:	2 21-cell RAM launchers Mk 49
Length:	778 feet (237.2 m) water line	Guns:	2 20-mm Phalanx CIWS Mk 15 (3 multibarrel)
	844 feet (257.32 m) overall		8 .50-cal machine guns M2HB (8 single)
Beam:	106 feet (32.32 m)	Radars:	Mk 23 Target Acquisition System (TAS)
Extreme width:	110 feet (33.54 m)		SPS-48E 3-D air search
Draft:			SPS-49(V)5 air search
Propulsion:	2 gas turbines (General Electric LM 2500+); 70,000 shp; 2		SPS-64(V)9 navigation
shafts			SPS-67(V)3 surface search
Speed:	20+ knots	Fire control:	2 Mk 91 missiles FCS
Range:			1 SYS-2(V)3 weapon control system
Personnel:		EW systems:	SLQ-25A Nixie
Troops:	approx. 2,000		SLQ-32(V)3
Aircraft:	approx. 40 STOVL and helicopters		SRS-1 combat D/F
Elevators:	2 deck edge (50 x 45 feet | 15.2 x 13.7 m)		

This eighth ship of the WASP class introduces gas-turbine propulsion and other features to the design. See the WASP-class entry for additional commentary and notes. No additional ships of this class are planned as the Navy moves toward the LHA(R) class.

Cost: Congress appropriated $880 million in design and material procurement for the LHD 8, including $460 million in the FY 2001 budget; $420 million was appropriated in FY 1999 and 2000. The total cost is estimated at $1.8 billion.

7 AMPHIBIOUS ASSAULT SHIPS: "WASP" CLASS

Number	Name	FY	Builder	Laid Down	Launched	Christened	Comm.	Status
LHD 1	Wasp	84	Litton/Ingalls Shipbuilding, Pascagoula, Miss.	30 May 1985	4 Aug 1987	19 Sep 1987	6 July 1989	**AA**
LHD 2	Essex	86	Litton/Ingalls Shipbuilding, Pascagoula, Miss.	20 Mar 1989	7 Jan 1991	16 Mar 1991	17 Oct 1992	**PA**
LHD 3	Kearsarge	88	Litton/Ingalls Shipbuilding, Pascagoula, Miss.	6 Feb 1990	26 Mar 1992	16 May 1992	16 Oct 1993	**AA**
LHD 4	Boxer	89	Litton/Ingalls Shipbuilding, Pascagoula, Miss.	8 Apr 1991	13 Aug 1993	13 Aug 1993	11 Feb 1995	**PA**
LHD 5	Bataan	91	Litton/Ingalls Shipbuilding, Pascagoula, Miss.	22 June 1994	15 Mar 1996	18 May 1996	20 Sep 1997	**AA**
LHD 6	Bonhomme Richard	93	Litton/Ingalls Shipbuilding, Pascagoula, Miss.	18 Apr 1995	14 Mar 1997	14 Mar 1997	15 Aug 1998	**PA**
LHD 7	Iwo Jima	96	Litton/Ingalls Sh.ipbuilding, Pascagoula, Miss.	12 Dec 1997	25 Mar 2001	25 Mar 2001	30 June 2001	**AA**

Displacement:	28,233 tons light	Elevators:	2 deck edge (50 x 45 feet / 15.2 x 13.7 m)
	40,535 tons full load	Missiles:	2 8-cell NATO Sea Sparrow missile launchers Mk 29
Length:	777⅝ feet (237.1 m) waterline		2 21-cell RAM launchers Mk 49
	844 feet (257.3 m) overall	Guns:	4 25-mm Bushmaster cannon Mk 38 (4 single),
Beam:	106 feet (32.3 m) waterline		except 3 guns in LHD 5–7
Extreme width:	140 feet (42.7 m)		3 20-mm Phalanx CIWS Mk 15 (3 multibarrel),
Draft:	26⅔ feet (8.1 m)		except 2 guns in LHD 5–7
Propulsion:	2 steam turbines; 77,000 shp; 2 shafts		4 .50-cal machine guns M2HB (8 single)
Boilers:	2 600 psi (41.7 kg/cm²) (Combustion Engineering)	Radars:	Mk 23 Target Acquisition System (TAS)
Speed:	24 knots (22 knots sustained)		SPS-48E 3-D air search
Range:	9,500 nm (17,594 km) at 20 knots		SPS-49(V)5 air search
Personnel:	LHD 1 1,142 (61 officers + 1,081 enlisted)		SPS-64(V)9 navigation
	LHD 2 1,149 (61 officers + 1,088 enlisted)		SPS-67(V)3 surface search
	LHD 3–5, 7 1,142 (62 officers + 1,080 enlisted)	Fire control:	2 Mk 91 missiles FCS
	LHD 6 1,129 (62 officers + 1,067 enlisted)		1 SYS-2(V)3 weapon control system
Troops:	1,700	EW systems:	SLQ-25A Nixie
Aircraft:	amphibious role: approx. 30 CH-46 Sea Knight and CH-53		SLQ-32(V)
	Sea Stallion helicopters + 6 AV-8B Harrier STOVL		SRS-1 combat D/F
	carrier role: approx. 20 AV-8B Harrier STOVL + 6 SH-60 ASW		
	helicopters		

These ships and the similar Tarawa class are the world's largest amphibious ships. The only larger ships to have been employed in this role were the converted fleet carriers of the Essex (CV 9) class.

The Wasp class initially was purposed as helicopter-carrying amphibious ships that would be smaller and less costly than the Tarawa class. In the event, the basic LHA design was adopted with the following principal differences: (1) increased Harrier STOVL aircraft support capability; (2) movement of the stern elevator to the starboard side of the flight deck; (3) redesign of the docking well to accommodate three LCACs, and with an LPD/LSD stern gate rather than the sectional, "split" gate of the LHA; and (4) changes in the self-defense armament.

The Essex is homeported in Sasebo, Japan; she is flagship for Amphibious Force Seventh Fleet, Amphibious Group 1, Amphibious Squadron 11, and Task Force 76.

The massive island structure of the Essex shows the ship's large pole masts (replacing lattice masts of the LHA); the ship's SPS-48E 3-D radar antenna is forward on the superstructure, the reverse of the LHA arrangement. Encapsulated life rafts line the side of the big ship. (2003, U.S. Navy/Novia E. Harrington)

Classification: During the preliminary design stage, these ships were designated LHDX. They should have been designated sequentially in the LHA series, as the differences in the two types are minor and they have the same role.

Cost: The Bonhomme Richard is officially listed as an FY 1993 ship, although only advanced funds were provided in FY 1993 ($303.1 million); the majority of the funds ($893.8 million) were provided in FY 1994. The ship also required outfitting and post-delivery funding, for a total cost in excess of $1.2 billion.

Design: The basic configuration of these ships is similar to the Tarawa class; however, they have less vehicle storage and bulk cargo space, but carry more aircraft, and the arrangement of the docking well permits more air cushion landing craft (three) to be embarked; alternatively, the well can accommodate 12 LCM(6)s or 6 LCM(8)s or 2 LCU 1610s. The LHDs also have communications and certain command spaces moved into the hull (vice island structure in the LHAs) for better protection.

Medical facilities include beds for 600 patients and six operating rooms and extensive dental facilities.

Electronics: These ships are fitted with SPN-35A marshalling and SPN-43B and SPN-47 aircraft approach/control systems.

Engineering: Maximum horsepower is indicated in the above data table; the sustained shp is 70,000.

Missiles: The Rolling Airframe Missile (RAM) launchers were added to the first six ships after completion; one of the (three) original CIWS mounts was deleted with the missile installation.

Names: These ships honor World War II–era fleet carriers (CV/CVL) and, in some cases, earlier Navy ships. The Wasp recalls both the CV 7, sunk in 1942, and her namesake, the CV 18.

The Bonhomme Richard is named for the carrier CV 31—although that ship was the Bon Homme Richard—and the original frigate Bonhomme Richard, commanded by John Paul Jones in 1779 during her heroic battle with the British frigate Serapis.

The Iwo Jima is named for the U.S. Navy's first helicopter carrier (LPH 2) and the penultimate U.S. amphibious assault of World War II.

Troops: An additional 190 troops to the 1,700 indicated above can be embarked for transits of several days.

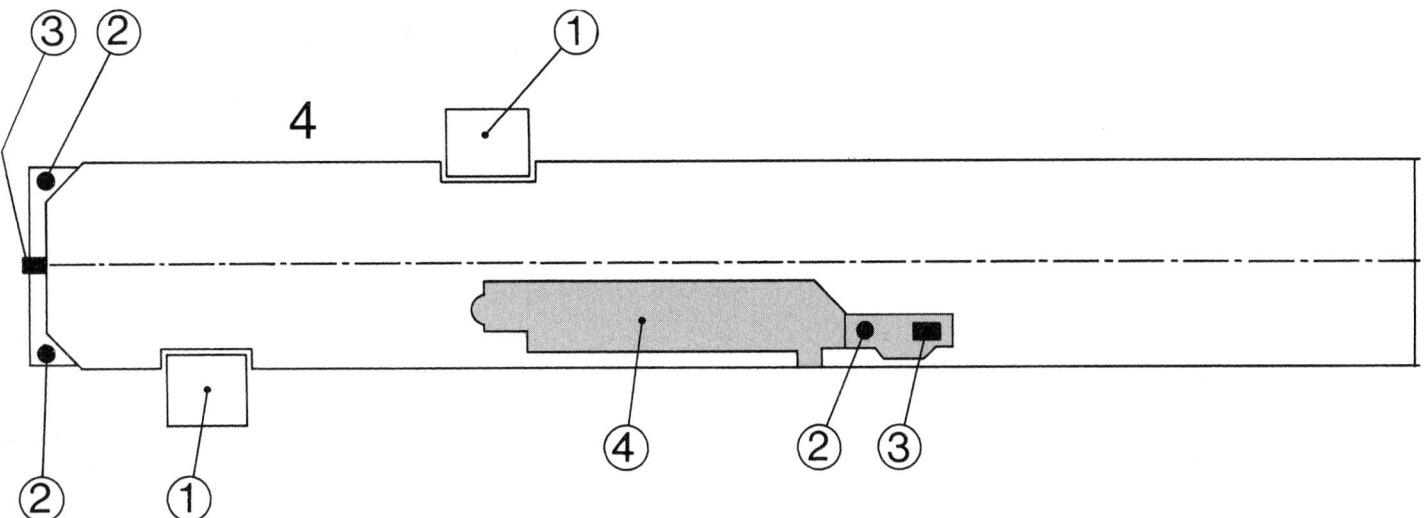

*Amphibious Assault Ship W*ASP
1. Deck-edge elevator (2). 2. Phalanx close-in weapon system Mk 15 (3). 3. NATO Sea Sparrow missile launcher Mk 29 (2) 4. Island structure. Note: The drawing omits the Rolling Airframe Missile (RAM) launchers.

*The W*ASP *takes on nearly 65,000 gallons of fuel during an underway replenishment from the USNS S*UPPLY *(T-AOE 6) during operations in the Arabian Sea. A variety of helicopters are parked on the W*ASP*'s flight deck, and four AV-8B Harriers are parked on her starboard quarter (adjacent to the deck-edge elevator). (2002, U.S. Navy, Teresa Ellison)*

Light Armored Vehicles (LAVs) are among the vehicles loaded on an LCAC within the massive docking well of the BONHOMME RICHARD. Docking well ships normally carry preloaded LCACs and LCUs; on return trips to the "amphib," vehicles are loaded into landing craft from the large garage levels. (2003, U.S. Navy/Christian Hansen)

Assault Amphibian Vehicles (AAVs) from the 3rd Amphibious Assault Battalion enter the flooded docking well of the BONHOMME RICHARD during training operations off the California coast. A Phalanx close-in weapon system is visible at left and a Rolling Airframe Missile launcher at right, above the entrance to the docking well. (2004, U.S. Navy/Jennifer Swader)

5 AMPHIBIOUS ASSAULT SHIPS: "TARAWA" CLASS

Number	Name	FY	Builder	Laid down	Launched	Christened	Comm.	Status
LHA 1	TARAWA	69	Litton/Ingalls Shipbuilding, Pascagoula, Miss.	15 Nov 1971	1 Dec 1973	1 Dec 1973	29 May 1976	**PA**
LHA 2	SAIPAN	70	Litton/Ingalls Shipbuilding, Pascagoula, Miss.	21 July 1972	18 July 1974	20 July 1974	15 Oct 1977	**AA**
LHA 3	BELLEAU WOOD	70	Litton/Ingalls Shipbuilding, Pascagoula, Miss.	5 Mar 1973	11 Apr 1977	11 June 1977	23 Sep 1978	**PA**
LHA 4	NASSAU	71	Litton/Ingalls Shipbuilding, Pascagoula, Miss.	13 Aug 1973	21 Jan 1978	28 Jan 1978	28 July 1979	**AA**
LHA 5	PELELIU	71	Litton/Ingalls Shipbuilding, Pascagoula, Miss.	12 Nov 1976	25 Nov 1978	6 Jan 1979	3 May 1980	**PA**

Displacement:	33,536 tons light	Elevators:	1 deck edge (50 x 34 feet / 15.2 x 10.3 m)
	39,967 tons full load		1 stern (59¾ x 34¾ feet / 18.2 x 10.6 m)
Length:	777⅔ feet (237.1 m) waterline	Missiles:	2 21-cell RAM launchers Mk 49
	833¾ feet (254.2 m) overall		4 25-mm Bushmaster cannon Mk 38 (4 single)
Beam:	106 feet (32.3 m)	Guns:	2 20-mm Phalanx CIWS Mk 15 (2 multibarrel)
Extreme width:	132 feet (40.2 m)		3 .50-cal machine guns M2HB (3 single)
Draft:	26 feet (7.9 m)	Radars:	Mk 23 Target Acquisition System (TAS)
Propulsion:	2 steam turbines (Westinghouse); 77,000 shp; 2 shafts		SPS-40E air search
Boilers:	2 600 psi (41.7 kg/cm²) (Combustion Engineering)		SPS-48E 3-D air search
Speed:	24 knots (22 knots sustained)		SPS-64(V)9 navigation
Range:	10,000 nm (18,520 km) at 20 knots		SPS-67(V)3 surface search
Personnel:	LHA 1, 2, 4 1,103 (61 officers + 1,042 enlisted)	Fire control:	1 Mk 86 GFCS with SPG-60 and SPQ-9A radars
	LHA 3, 5 1,105 (61 officers + 1,044 enlisted)		2 Mk 115 missile FCS
Troops:	1,700		1 SWY-2 weapon control system (RAM)
Aircraft:	approx. 30 CH-46 Sea Knight and CH-53 Sea Stallion	EW systems:	SLQ-25A Nixie
	+ 6 AV-8B Harrier STOVL		SLQ-32(V)3

The TARAWA-class ships combine the capabilities of several types of amphibious ships in a single hull. In addition, these ships periodically have operated large numbers of AV-8 Harrier STOVL aircraft and OV-10 Bronco Short Take-Off and Landing (STOL) aircraft.

It has been suggested that when the LHA 1 is replaced by the LHD 8, the older ship could be converted to a mine countermeasures support ship; however, her large manning requirements and operating costs make that proposal impractical.

Class: Nine ships of this class originally were planned in the early 1960s. The Navy announced on 20 January 1971 that LHA 6–9 would not be constructed (they were formally canceled on 9 February 1971).

Design: SCB No. 410. Special features of this class include an 18-foot (5.5-m) section of the mast that is hinged to permit passage under bridges; a 5,000-square-foot (450-m²) training and acclimatization room to permit troops to exercise in a controlled environment; the vehicle storage decks connected by ramps to the flight deck and docking well; and five cargo elevators to move equipment between the holds and flight deck. Extensive command and communications facilities are provided for an amphibious force commander.

The hangar deck is 820 feet (250 m) long and 78 feet (27.8 m) wide, with a 20-foot (6.1-m) overhead.

The stern docking well is 268 feet (81.7 m) long and 78 feet (23.8 m) wide and can accommodate 4 LCU 1610 landing craft or 7 LCM(8)s or 17 LCM(6)s or 45 AAV/LVTP-7 amphibian vehicles. Because of the arrangement of the docking well, only one LCAC can be carried. In addition, 35 amphibian vehicles can be carried on the third deck of an LHA.

Extensive medical facilities are provided, including three operating rooms and bed space for 300 patients.

Electronics: SPN-35 aircraft marshalling and SPN-43B approach/control systems are fitted. The ships' radars have been upgraded.

Engineering: Maximum horsepower is indicated in the class table; the sustained shp is 70,000. A 900-hp through-tunnel thruster is fitted in the forward part of the hull to assist in maneuvering while launching landing craft.

The ships' boilers are the largest ever manufactured in the United States.

Guns: As built, these ships were armed with three single 5-inch (127-mm) guns. One gun and one Sea Sparrow launcher were removed from each ship in the early 1990s to provide space for the UAV control station. The two other guns were deleted in the late 1990s.

Missiles: These ships originally had two Sea Sparrow Basic Point Defense Missile System (BPDMS) Mk 25 launchers (one in LHA 2) controlled by two Mk 71 directors with Mk 115 radars. These have been replaced by two RAM launchers, beginning with the PELELIU and BELLEAU WOOD having been refitted in 1992.

Names: The PELELIU originally was named DA NANG; she was renamed on 15 February 1978, i.e., after the Republic of (South) Vietnam had fallen to communist forces.

Operational: The NASSAU evaluated the "sea control" configuration for these ships during a 1981 deployment, when she successfully operated 19 AV-8A Harrier STOVL aircraft. That same year, the TARAWA made the first extended deployment of an amphibious ship with Harriers on board, carrying 6 AV-8A aircraft during a deployment to the Western Pacific. Subsequent studies showed that an LHA in the sea control role could effectively operate 20 Harriers plus 4–6 SH-60B LAMPS III helicopters.

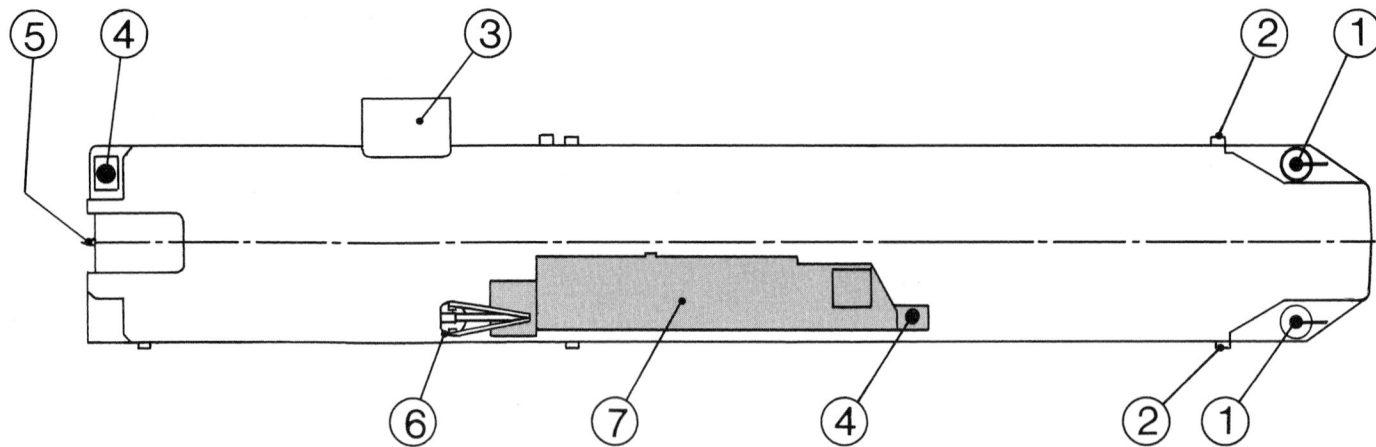

Amphibious Assault Ship TARAWA
1. Former position of 5-inch/54-cal. dual-purpose single gun mounts (2) 2. Positions of 25-mm Bushmaster cannon (4) 3. Deck-edge elevator 4. Phalanx close-in weapon system Mk 15 (2). 5. Stern elevator 6. Aircraft crane 7. Island structure. Note: The drawing omits the Rolling Airframe Missile launchers.

The massive island structure of the SAIPAN *is topped by two lattice masts, the after one supporting the SPS-48E 3-D radar antenna. The low structure forward of the island covers entry to vehicle ramps and cargo elevators. (2004, U.S. Navy/Courtney Torgrude)*

The SAIPAN *with several CH-46E Sea Knights forward and a CH-53E Super Stallion near the port deck-edge elevator. A Phalanx close-in weapon system and Rolling Airframe Missile launcher on the forward end of the superstructure are lost amid the clutter of antenna domes. (2004, U.S. Navy/Courtney Torgrude)*

The PELELIU *approaches a pier at San Diego after a six-and-a-half-month deployment. She deployed with an LPD, LSD, guided missile destroyer, and frigate to form Expeditionary Strike Group (ESG) 1. The term "ESG" denotes an expanded Amphibious Ready Group (ARG), augmented with surface combatants and, possibly, submarines and land-based aircraft. (2004, U.S. Navy/Ted Banks)*

The SAIPAN with her flight deck clear of aircraft as the ship undergoes training off the Atlantic coast in preparation for deployment. Her port deck-edge elevator is in a similar location to those of LHDs, but there is a stern elevator in place of the LHD's starboard deck-edge elevator. (2004, U.S. Navy/ Gary L. Johnson)

A busy day for the TARAWA in the Persian Gulf: an LCU backs out of the ship's docking well while a CH-53E Super Stallion heads away from the ship toward shore. Another CH-53E overhangs the portside of the flight deck. There is a Phalanx close-in weapon system on the port quarter and a Rolling Airframe Missile launcher on the starboard quarter. (2003, U.S. Navy/Taylor Goode)

Table 19-3. AMPHIBIOUS ASSAULT SHIPS

Number	Name	LPH Comm.	Notes
	Converted COMMENCEMENT BAY class		
LPH 1	BLOCK ISLAND (ex-CVE 106)		conversion canceled
	Iwo JIMA class (7)		
LPH 2	Iwo JIMA	1961	decomm. 14 July 1993; str. 24 Sep 1993
LPH 3	OKINAWA	1962	decomm./str. 17 Dec 1992
	Converted ESSEX class (3)		
LPH 4	BOXER (ex-CV 21)	1959	stricken 1969
LPH 5	PRINCETON (ex-CV 37)	1959	stricken 1970
	Converted CASABLANCA class		
LPH 6	THETIS BAY (ex-CVE 90)	1956	stricken 1966
	Iwo JIMA class (continued)		
LPH 7	GUADALCANAL	1963	decomm./str. 31 Aug 1994
	Converted ESSEX class (continued)		
LPH 8	VALLEY FORGE (ex-CV 45)	1961	stricken 1970
	Iwo JIMA class (continued)		
LPH 9	GUAM	1965	decomm./str. 25 Aug 1998
LPH 10	TRIPOLI	1966	decomm./str. 15 Sep 1995
LPH 11	NEW ORLEANS	1968	decomm. 1 Oct 1997; str. 23 Oct 1998
LPH 12	INCHON	1970	converted to MCS 12

The LPH was the predecessor to the Navy's current LHA/LHD amphibious ships. The latter added a "wet" docking well to the basic aircraft carrier (CV/CVE) configuration of the LPH. The LPH classification for amphibious assault ships was established in 1955. (The U.S. Navy designation LPH has *never* signified "Landing Platform Helicopter," as appears in some publications.) The World War II–era escort carrier BLOCK ISLAND was to have been LPH 1, but her conversion was canceled. Three large aircraft carriers of the ESSEX class subsequently were modified to LPHs, as was the escort carrier THETIS BAY. The THETIS BAY had been designated as a helicopter assault carrier (CVHA 1) at the start of her 1955–1956 conversion, but she was changed to LPH to avoid confusion and budget competition with CV-type aircraft carriers.

The three ESSEX LPHs previously were designated CV/CVA/CVS. In addition to this trio of ships, the TARAWA (CVS 40) operated extensively with Marine helicopters in the late 1950s.

The IWO JIMA class represented an improved World War II–type escort carrier design with accommodations for a Marine battalion and a helicopter squadron. These ships also operated Harrier STOVL aircraft. Unlike the Royal Navy's commando carriers from the 1960s and the later TARAWA/WASP classes, the LPHs did not carry landing craft, except that LCVP davits were provided in the INCHON. The GUAM served as an interim Sea Control Ship (SCS) in 1971–1972. Several of the ships have been employed in the mine countermeasures role, operating CH-53/MH-53/RH-53 helicopters.

After being stricken, the OKINAWA, GUAM, and GUADALCANAL were transferred to the National Defense Reserve Fleet (NDRF). The GUAM was sunk as a target on 16 October 2001, and the OKINAWA was sunk as a target on 6 June 2002.[1] The INCHON was converted to a mine countermeasures support ship (see Chapter 22)

See 16th Edition/pages 157–59 for LPH 2 class characteristics.

(8) AMPHIBIOUS TRANSPORT DOCKS: "SAN ANTONIO" CLASS

Number	Name	FY	Builder	Laid Down	Launched	Christened	Comm.	Status
LPD 17	SAN ANTONIO	96	Northrop Grumman/Avondale, New Orleans	9 Dec 2000	12 July 2003	19 July 2003	2005	Building
LPD 18	NEW ORLEANS	99	Northrop Grumman/Avondale, New Orleans	14 Oct 2002	18 Nov 2004	20 Nov 2004	2006	Building
LPD 19	MESA VERDE	00	Northrop Grumman/Avondale, New Orleans	25 Feb 2003	2004		2006	Building
LPD 20	GREEN BAY	00	Northrop Grumman/Avondale, New Orleans	7 Aug 2003	2005		2006	Building
LPD 21	NEW YORK	03	Northrop Grumman/Avondale, New Orleans	10 Sep 2004			2007	Building
LPD 22	SAN DIEGO	04	Northrop Grumman/Avondale, New Orleans					Building
LPD 23	ANCHORAGE	05	Northrop Grumman/Avondale, New Orleans					Planned
LPD 24	ARLINGTON	06	Northrop Grumman/Avondal.e, New Orleans					Planned

Displacement:	24,900 tons full load	Guns:	2 30-mm Bushmaster II cannon Mk 44 (2 single)
Length:	684 feet (208.5 m) overall		2 12.7-mm machine guns Mk 26 (2 single)
Beam:	105 feet (31.9 m)	Radars:	Mk 23 Target Acquisition System (TAS)
Draft:	23 feet (7.0 m)		SPS-48E 3-D air search (in initial units; new D-band radar in later ships)
Propulsion:	4 turbocharged diesel engines; 40,000 shp; 2 shafts		SPS-64(V)9 navigation
Speed:	25 knots maximum; 22 knots sustained		SPS-67(V)3 surface search
Range:		Fire control:	1 SPQ-9B radar
Personnel:	361 (28 officers + 333 enlisted)		1 SWY-2 weapon control system (RAM)
Troops:	720	EW systems:	SLQ-25A Nixie
Helicopters:	1 or 2 (see *Helicopter* notes)		SLQ-32(V)3
Missiles:	2 21-cell RAM launchers Mk 49 (see *Missile* notes)		

The LPD is a development of the dock landing ship (LSD) design, which had its origins in World War II; the LPD design provides for increased troop and vehicle capacity and a relatively small docking well. These ships have fixed helicopter decks above the docking well (the LSDs have removable decks over the docking well). They carry Marines into forward areas and unload them by landing craft and vehicles carried in their docking wells, and by helicopters provided mainly from amphibious assault ships.

The LPD 17 class is described by the Navy as the functional replacement for 41 older ships: 11 LPDs, 5 LSDs, 20 LSTs, and 5 LKAs. The class was designated LX during the design phase.

The Navy's 1996 competition for the "winner-take-all" contract for these ships was won by a consortium led by Avondale Shipyards and Bath Iron Works; accordingly, eight ships were to be built at the Avondale yard and four at the Bath yard. However, massive delays in the lead ship construction and major cost increases led the Navy and the shipyards to transfer all the LPD contracts to the Avondale facility.

Under the original schedule, all 12 ships were to have been completed between 2003 and 2008. The lead ship, with a contract award date of 17 December 1996, initially was scheduled for completion in September 2002.

Class: The Navy originally proposed a program of 27 LX-type ships to operate with 17 LSD and 15 LHA/LHD to provide a MEF + MEB lift capability of 59 ships; however, the reduced amphibious lift goals have led to a 12-ship LX/LPD 17 program.

---

1 The OKINAWA was sunk with Mk 48 ADCAP torpedoes by the USS PORTSMOUTH (SSN 707).

Design: Compared to the previous LPD 4 class, these ships are considerably larger—i.e., 32 percent in full load displacement—and have more vehicle storage space, at the cost of reduced bulk cargo space. They can accommodate two LCACs in the docking well, compared to one in the earlier ships.

The LPD 17 class will have a 24-bed medical facility with two operating rooms.

Another 100 troops beyond the 720 listed in the above data table can be accommodated for periods of several days.

Helicopters: Two helicopter landing spots are provided. The hangar, built into the after superstructure, can accommodate one CH-53E or two CH-46 helicopters, or one MV-22 Osprey STOVL aircraft.

Missiles: The forward RAM launcher is on the port side of the forward superstructure; the amidships RAM launcher is on the starboard side of the after structure.

Space and weight are reserved for possible future installation of the Evolved Sea Sparrow Missile (ESSM) in a vertical-launch system (modified Mk 41 with 16 launch cells) just forward of the superstructure.

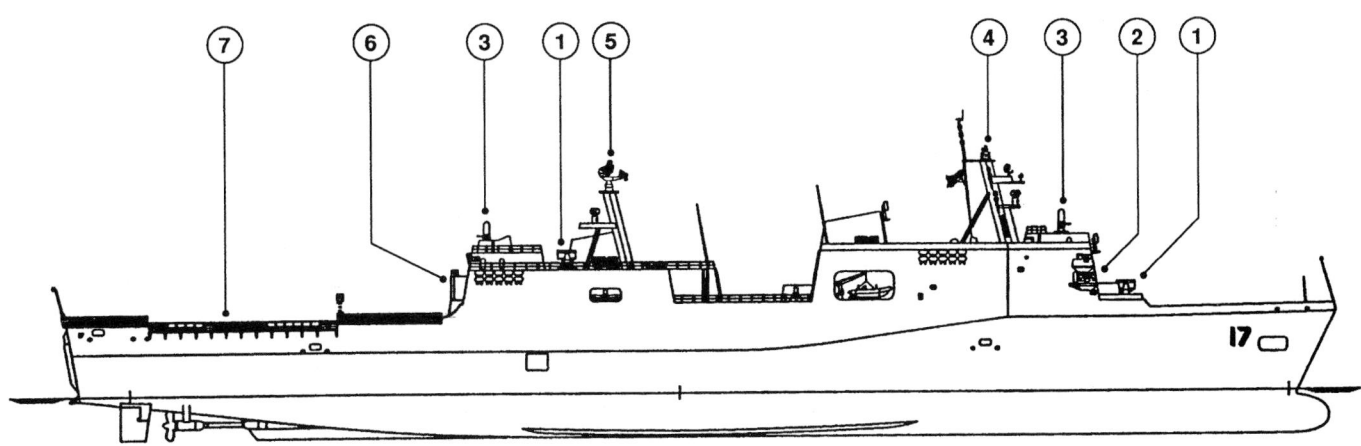

Amphibious Transport Dock San Antonio *(Early mast configuration)*
1. Rolling Airframe Missile launcher Mk 49 (2) 2. SLQ-32(V)3 electronic countermeasures (2) 3. Phalanx close-in weapon system Mk 15 (2) 4. SPS-64(V)9 navigation radar. 5. SPS-49(V)5 air search radar. 7. Helicopter/ STOVL flight deck.

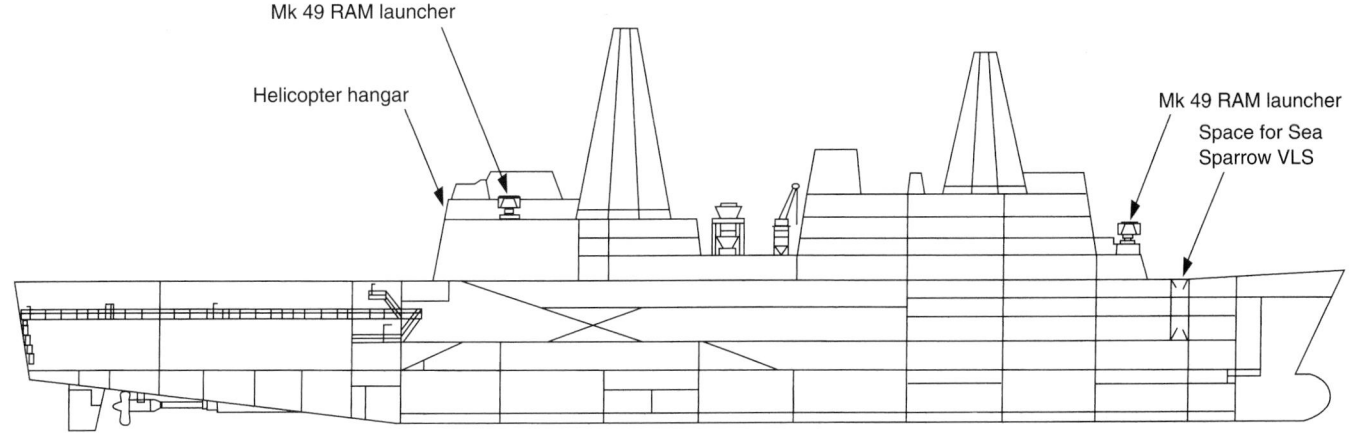

Amphibious Transport Dock San Antonio

The San Antonio *immediately after being christened on 19 July 2003. Note the bulbous bow configuration, normally submerged when the ship is at standard displacement. The massive superstructure has some features to help reduce the ship's radar cross section. (2003, Northrop Grumman Corp.)*

An artist's depiction of the SAN ANTONIO *with the early mast configuration. She will be the largest amphibious ship built in the United States except for the LHA/LHD helicopter/STOVL carriers. The* SAN ANTONIO *retains the basic LPD/LSD design that dates from World War II. The hangar, however, is an integral part of the superstructure. (U.S. Navy)*

11 AMPHIBIOUS TRANSPORT DOCKS: "AUSTIN" CLASS

Number	Name	FY	Builder	Laid Down	Launched	Commissioned	Status
LPD 4	AUSTIN	62	New York Naval Shipyard, Brooklyn	4 Feb 1963	27 June 1964	6 Feb 1965	**AA**
LPD 5	OGDEN	62	New York Naval Shipyard, Brooklyn	4 Feb 1963	27 June 1964	19 June 1965	**PA**
LPD 6	DULUTH	62	New York Naval Shipyard, Brooklyn	18 Dec 1963	14 Aug 1965	18 Dec 1965	**PA**
LPD 7	CLEVELAND	63	Ingalls Shipbuilding, Pascagoula, Miss.	30 Nov 1964	7 May 1966	21 Apr 1967	**PA**
LPD 8	DUBUQUE	63	Ingalls Shipbuilding, Pascagoula, Miss.	25 Jan 1965	6 Aug 1966	1 Sep 1967	**PA**
LPD 9	DENVER	63	Lockheed Shipbuilding & Construction, Seattle	7 Feb 1964	23 Jan 1965	26 Oct 1968	**PA**
LPD 10	JUNEAU	63	Lockheed Shipbuilding & Construction, Seattle	23 Jan 1965	12 Feb 1966	12 July 1969	**PA**
LPD 12	SHREVEPORT	64	Lockheed Shipbuilding & Construction, Seattle	27 Dec 1965	25 Oct 1966	12 Dec 1970	**AA**
LPD 13	NASHVILLE	64	Lockheed Shipbuilding & Construction, Seattle	14 Mar 1966	7 Oct 1967	14 Feb 1970	**AA**
LPD 14	TRENTON	65	Lockheed Shipbuilding & Construction, Seattle	8 Aug 1966	3 Aug 1968	6 Mar 1971	**AA**
LPD 15	PONCE	65	Lockheed Shipbuilding & Construction, Seattle	31 Oct 1966	30 May 1970	10 July 1971	**AA**

Displacement:	9,128 tons light		Troops:	LPD 6, 14, 15 930
	16,585–17,595 tons full load			LPD 7–10, 12, 13 840
Length:	568¾ feet (173.4 m) overall		Flag:	90 in LPD 7–10, 12, 13
Beam:	84 feet (25.6 m)		Helicopters:	1 CH-46 Sea Knight
Draft:	23–23½ feet (7.0–7.2 m)		Missiles:	none
Propulsion:	2 steam turbines (De Laval); 24,000 shp; 2 shafts		Guns:	2 25-mm Bushmaster cannon Mk 38 (2 single)
Boilers:	2 600 psi (41.7 kg/cm²) (Foster Wheeler, except Babcock & Wilcox in LPD 5, 12)			2 20-mm Phalanx CIWS Mk 15 (2 multibarrel)
				8 .50-cal machine guns M2HB (8 single)
Speed:	21 knots		Radars	SPS-10F surface search
Range:	7,700 nm (14,260 km) at 20 knots			SPS-40B air search, except SPS-40E in LPD 13
Personnel:	LPD 6 372 (24 officers + 348 enlisted)			SPS-64(V)9 navigation
	LPD 7–9 378 (25 officers + 353 enlisted)		Fire control:	removed
	LPD 10, 12, 13 378 (24 officers + 354 enlisted)		EW systems:	SLQ-25A Nixie
	LPD 14 373 (24 officers + 349 enlisted)			SLQ-32(V)1
	LPD 15 373 (25 officers + 348 enlisted)			

These ships are enlarged versions of the previous RALEIGH-class LPDs.

The JUNEAU is homeported at Sasebo, Japan.

Aircraft: These ships have deployed with up to six CH-46 Sea Knights embarked for short-term operations. They are rated as able to deploy with up to four cargo helicopters (CH-46 or CH-53), but this can be done only with a helicopter carrier in company to provide maintenance and other support on a sustained basis.

Builders: The DULUTH was completed at the Philadelphia Naval Shipyard after the closing of the New York Naval Shipyard; she was reassigned to the Philadelphia shipyard on 24 November 1965.

Class: An additional ship of this class (LPD 16) was provided in the FY 1966 shipbuilding program, but construction was deferred in favor of the LHA program, and the ship officially was canceled on 25 February 1969.

The CORONADO (LPD 11) was modified for use as a flagship in 1980 and reclassified AGF 11.

Design: The LPD 6–10 are SCB No. 187B; the LPD 11–13 are No. 187C, which was changed to No. 402 for the LPD 14 and 15 under the new SCB numbering scheme.

The LPD 7–10, 12, and 13 are configured as amphibious squadron flagships and have an additional bridge level, plus flag berthing space and communications equipment. The docking well in these ships is 168 feet (51.2 m) long and 50 feet (15.2 m) wide; it can accommodate 1 LCAC, or 1 LCU and 3 LCM(6)s, or 9 LCM(6)s, or 4 LCM(8)s, or 28 AAV/LVTP-7 amphibian vehicles. In addition, 2 LCM(6)s or 4 LCVP/LCPLs normally are carried on the helicopter deck; up to 16 amphibian vehicles can be parked on the main deck.

One 30-ton-capacity crane and six 4-ton cranes are provided.

Guns: As built these ships had eight 3-inch (76-mm)/50-cal Anti-Aircraft (AA) Mk 33 guns in twin mounts. Two mounts were removed in the late 1970s and two in the early 1990s. They had Mk 56 and Mk 63 Gunfire Control System (GFCS).

Helicopters: These ships have a fixed flight deck with two landing spots above the docking well. All are fitted with hangars, which vary from 58 to 64 feet (17.7 to 19.5 m) in length, 18½ to 24 feet (5.6 to 7.3 m) in width, and 17½ to 19 feet (5.3 to 5.8 m) in height. The hangars have extensions that can expand to provide a length of approximately 80 feet (24.4 m).

Modernization: A Service Life Extension Program (SLEP) was developed for these ships to permit them to operate 10–15 years beyond their nominal 30-year service lives. In addition to general improvements, they were to be fitted with the SPS-67 radar in place of the SPS-10 and modified to carry two LCACs; their aviation capabilities also were to be improved. However, budget constraints and congressional opposition caused cancellation of the program.

The DUBUQUE shows the antenna-studded superstructure of a modern amphibious ship. The two-bridge configuration of a flagship is evident. The ship's two Phalanx close-in weapon system mounts are visible—forward of the bridge structure on the port side, and amidships, atop the superstructure, on the starboard side. (2003, U.S. Navy/Jennifer Swader)

The DUBUQUE departs San Diego. She is loaded with Marine helicopters, including several AH-1W SeaCobra gunships. Life raft canisters line the sides of the superstructure. The LPD design is similar to the LSD except that in the former the flight deck is an integral part of the hull. (2003, U.S. Navy/Gregory Badger)

The OGDEN—with sailors and Marines lining the rail—heads to sea. The expanding helicopter hangar is visible on her flight deck, as is the ship's large boat crane. The massive gate to the ship's wet well conceals the several landing craft within the ship. (2003, U.S. Navy/Alan D. Monyelle)

Table 19-4. AMPHIBIOUS TRANSPORT DOCKS

Number	Name	Comm.	Notes
RALEIGH class (3)			
LPD 1	RALEIGH	1962	decomm. 13 Dec 1991; str. 25 Jan 1992
LPD 2	VANCOUVER	1963	decomm. 31 Mar 1992; str. 8 Apr 1997
LPD 3	LA SALLE	1964	converted to AGF 3
LPD 4–16	AUSTIN class		
LPD 17–24	SAN ANTONIO class		

The RALEIGH was transferred to the NDRF on 23 July 1992. She was retained for use as a nondestructive target by the Atlantic Fleet, but finally was sunk as a target on 4 December 1994.

The VANCOUVER was transferred to the NDRF in 2001.

The LA SALLE served in the amphibious role until converted to a miscellaneous flagship in 1972.

(12) ADVANCED DOCK LANDING SHIPS

Units	FY	Comm.	Status
4 ships	19–23		Planned
5 ships	24–28		Planned
3 ships	29–33		Planned

The Navy's 30-year shipbuilding plan provides an LSD(X) program to replace the current LSD force. No details exist.

4 DOCK LANDING SHIPS: "HARPERS FERRY" CLASS

Number	Name	FY	Builder	Laid Down	Launched	Comm.	Status
LSD 49	HARPERS FERRY	88	Avondale Industries, New Orleans	15 Apr 1991	16 Jan 1993	7 Jan 1995	**PA**
LSD 50	CARTER HALL	90	Avondale Industries, New Orleans	11 Nov 1991	2 Oct 1993	30 Sep 1995	**AA**
LSD 51	OAK HILL	91	Avondale Industries, New Orleans	21 Sep 1992	11 June 1994	8 June 1996	**AA**
LSD 52	PEARL HARBOR	93	Avondale Industries, New Orleans	27 Jan 1995	24 Feb 1996	30 May 1998	**PA**

Displacement:	11,894 tons light	Helicopters:	landing area
	16,695 tons full load	Missiles:	2 21-cell RAM launchers Mk 49
Length:	580 feet (176.8 m) waterline	Guns:	2 25-mm Bushmaster cannon Mk 38 (2 single)
	609¾ feet (185.8 m) overall		2 20-mm Phalanx CIWS Mk 15 (2 multibarrel)
Beam:	84 feet (25.6 m)		6 .50-cal machine guns M2HB (6 single)
Draft:	19¾ feet (6.0 m)	Radars:	1 SPS-49(V)5 air search
Propulsion:	4 diesel engines (Colt-Pielstick 16 PC2.5V400); 41,600 6hp; 2 shafts		1 SPS-64(V)9 navigation
			1 SPS-67(V)1 surface search
Speed:	22 knots	Fire control:	1 SWY-2 weapon control system in LSD 49
Range:	approx. 8,000 nm (14,816 km) at 20 knots	EW systems:	SLQ-25A Nixie
Personnel:	307 (19 officers + 288 enlisted)		SLQ-32(V)2
Troops:	400		

These ships are similar to the WHIDBEY ISLAND-class LSDs, but with a smaller docking well to provide space for increased troop, vehicle, cargo, and helicopter capacity. Some Navy planning documents refer to the class as LSD 41CV, for *Cargo Variant*.

An additional 100 troops beyond the 400 listed in the above data table can be embarked for short durations (i.e., several days).

Class: The Navy originally planned a class of six ships, but the LSD 53 and LSD 54 were canceled. The LSD 52 originally was funded in FY 1992, but the funds were rescinded by the George H. W. Bush administration; Congress again funded the ship in FY 1993.

Design: The docking well is 180 feet (54.9 m) by 50 feet (15.2 m); it can accommodate two LCACs or one LCU or four LCM(8)s or nine LCM(6) landing craft.

A 30-ton-capacity crane is provided; an 8-ton cargo elevator is fitted to service the helicopter deck.

Engineering: Maximum horsepower is given in the data table; sustained horsepower is 34,600.

Names: LSDs are named for historic sites. Harpers Ferry, West Virginia, was site of a government arsenal that insurrectionist–abolitionist John Brown captured in 1859, a prelude to the American Civil War.

The LSD 52 remembers the site of the Japanese surprise attack on the U.S. Fleet on 7 December 1941, and not the attack itself.

A small salvage craft rests in the docking well of the HARPERS FERRY in the port of Sasebo, Japan. Future docking well ships may be "dry" rather than "wet" as air cushion landing craft and amphibious vehicles do not require wet wells. (2004, U.S. Navy/ Jonathan R. Kulp)

The HARPERS FERRY seen head-on reveals the massive, block-like superstructure of the ship. The forward Phalanx close-in weapon system is located on the centerline, just below the bridge; above the bridge, below the lattice mast, is a 21-cell Rolling Airframe Missile launcher. (2003, U.S. Navy/Chuck Bell)

The HARPERS FERRY and her sister ships are outwardly similar to the previous WHIDBEY ISLAND class, but there are significant internal changes. Here, the PEARL HARBOR returns to her home port of San Diego after supporting Operation Iraqi Freedom. (2003, U.S. Navy/ Mahlon K. Miller)

8 DOCK LANDING SHIPS: "WHIDBEY ISLAND" CLASS

Number	Name	FY	Builder	Laid Down	Launched	Comm.	Status
LSD 41	WHIDBEY ISLAND	81	Lockheed Shipbuilding, Seattle	4 Aug 1981	10 June 1983	9 Feb 1985	**AA**
LSD 42	GERMANTOWN	82	Lockheed Shipbuilding, Seattle	5 Aug 1982	29 June 1984	8 Feb 1986	**PA**
LSD 43	FORT MCHENRY	83	Lockheed Shipbuilding, Seattle	10 June 1983	1 Feb 1986	8 Aug 1987	**PA**
LSD 44	GUNSTON HALL	84	Avondale Industries, New Orleans	26 May 1986	27 June 1987	22 Apr 1989	**AA**
LSD 45	COMSTOCK	85	Avondale Industries, New Orleans	27 Oct 1986	16 Jan 1988	3 Feb 1990	**PA**
LSD 46	TORTUGA	85	Avondale Industries, New orleans	23 Mar 1987	15 Sep 1988	17 Nov 1990	**AA**
LSD 47	RUSHMORE	86	Avondale Industries, New Orleans	9 Nov 1987	6 May 1989	1 June 1991	**PA**
LSD 48	ASHLAND	86	Avondale Industries, New Orleans	4 Apr 1988	11 Nov 1989	9 May 1992	**AA**

Displacement:	12,434 tons standard		Helicopters:	landing area
	15,745 tons full load		Missiles:	2 21-cell RAM launchers Mk 49
Length:	580 feet (176.8 m) waterline		Guns:	2 25-mm Bushmaster cannon Mk 38 (2 single)
	609⅚ feet (185.8 m) overall			2 20-mm Phalanx CIWS Mk 15 (2 multibarrel)
Beam:	84 feet (25.6 m)			6 .50-cal machine guns M2HB (6 single)
Draft:	19⅔ feet (6.0 m)		Radars:	SPS-64(V)9 navigation
Propulsion:	4 diesel engines (SEMT-Pielstick 16 PC2.5 V400);			SPS-49(V)1 air search in LSD 41–45; (V)5 in LSD 46–48
	41,600 bhp; 2 shafts			SPS-67(V)1 surface search
Speed:	22 knots		Fire control:	1 SWY-2 weapon control system (RAM)
Range:	8,000 nm (14,816 km) at 20 knots		EW systems:	SLQ-25A Nixie
Personnel:	310 (19 officers + 291 enlisted)			SLQ-32(V)1
Troops:	560			

These ships were built to replace the THOMASTON-class LSDs and to provide increased lift for air cushion landing craft.

The FORT MCHENRY and GERMANTOWN are homeported in Sasebo, Japan.

Class: Navy planning in the early 1980s called for nine or ten ships of this class to replace the LSD 28 class; the number subsequently was increased to 12 through the FY 1988 shipbuilding program. However, the decision was made in the mid-1980s to instead produce eight LSD 41s and six LSD 41 cargo variants (HARPERS FERRY class).

Design: The docking well is 440 feet (134.1 m) long and 50 feet (15.2 m) wide; it can accommodate 4 LCACs, or 3 LCU or 10 LCM(8) or 21 LCM(6) landing craft, or 64 AAV/LVTP-7 amphib-

ian vehicles. In addition, several LCVP/LCPL-type landing craft normally are carried on deck.

The ships are fitted with one 60-ton-capacity crane and one 20-ton crane. No helicopter hangar or support facilities are provided.

Engineering: These are the first U.S. ships powered by medium-speed diesel engines. Of French design, the diesels are produced in the United States under license by the Fairbanks Morse Division of Colt Industries. Maximum horsepower is given in the above data table; sustained horsepower is 33,600.

Missiles: These ships have been fitted with the RAM system. The WHIDBEY ISLAND conducted trials with the system (one launcher) in June 1993 using radar inputs from the Phalanx VPS-2 search and track radar.

The FORT MCHENRY *with equipment of the 31st Marine Expeditionary Unit on her flight deck during training exercises in the Western Pacific. Aft of the superstructure are the ship's twin funnels (outboard of the docking well) and large boat crane. (2002, U.S. Navy/Gary B. Granger)*

The stern aspect of the COMSTOCK shows the helicopter superdeck of the LSD design. The helicopter deck can be removed for LCUs carrying outsize cargo to enter the ship's docking well. The safety rail folds down for flight operations. (2004, U.S. Navy/Bre' N. Cameron-Smith)

The radically different LPD/LSD superstructures are evident in this view of the JUNEAU (left) and FORT MCHENRY moored together at the White Beach naval facility on Okinawa. The "amphibs" homeported at Sasebo support the 3rd Marine Division based on Okinawa. (2003, U.S. Navy/Anthony J. Pugliani)

DOCK LANDING SHIP: "ANCHORAGE" CLASS

Number	Name	Comm.	Notes
LSD 36	ANCHORAGE	1969	decomm. 1 Oct 2003; str. 8 Mar 2004
LSD 37	PORTLAND	1970	decomm. 4 Aug 2003; str. 8 Mar 2004
LSD 38	PENSACOLA	1971	decomm./str. 30 Sep 1999; to Taiwan 1999
LSD 39	MOUNT VERNON	1972	decomm. 25 July 2003; str. 8 Mar 2004
LSD 40	FORT FISHER	1972	decomm./str. 27 Feb 1998

These versatile LSDs were part of the large amphibious ship construction program of the early 1960s and were to supplement the LPDs/LHAs by carrying additional landing craft to the assault area.

Table 19-5. POST–WORLD WAR II DOCK LANDING SHIPS

Number	Name	Comm.	Notes
THOMASTON class (8)			
LSD 28	THOMASTON	1954	decomm. 1984; str. 24 Feb 1992
LSD 29	PLYMOUTH ROCK	1954	decomm. 1983; str. 24 Feb 1992
LSD 30	FORT SNELLING	1955	decomm. 1984; str. 24 Feb 1992
LSD 31	POINT DEFIANCE	1955	decomm. 1983; str. 24 Feb 1992
LSD 32	SPIEGEL GROVE	1956	decomm. 1989; str. 13 Dec 1989
LSD 33	ALAMO	1956	decomm. 28 Sep 1990; to Brazil 1990; str. 24 Jan 2001
LSD 34	HERMITAGE	1956	decomm. 1989; to Brazil 1989; str. 24 Jan 2001
LSD 35	MONTICELLO	1957	decomm. 1985; str. 24 Feb 1992
LSD 36–40	ANCHORAGE class		
LSD 41–48	WHIDBEY ISLAND class		
LSD 49–52	HARPERS FERRY class		

After the tank landing ship, the dock landing ship was in many respects the most innovative amphibious ship developed during World War II. Establishing the basic design for future LSD/LPD classes, the ASHLAND (LSD 1), completed in 1943, had a large superstructure forward and a docking well that took up most of her hull, with machinery fitted in the side walls of the dock. The wartime program embraced LSD 1–27, with the LSD 9–12 being built for Britain.

The SPIEGEL GROVE was transferred to the state of Florida in 2001 to be sunk off the coast as an artificial reef.

TANK LANDING SHIPS: "NEWPORT" CLASS

Number	Name	Comm.	Status
LST 1179	NEWPORT	1969	decomm. 1 Oct 1992; str./to Mexico 13 July 2001
LST 1180	MANITOWOC	1970	decomm. 30 June 1993; to Taiwan 1995; str. 23 July 2002
LST 1181	SUMTER	1970	decomm. 30 Sep 1993; to Taiwan 1995; str. 23 July 2002
LST 1182	FRESNO	1969	decomm. 8 Apr 1993; str. 2003
LST 1183	PEORIA	1970	decomm. 28 Jan 1994; str. 6 Nov 2002
LST 1184	FREDERICK	1970	decomm./str./to Mexico 5 Oct 2002
LST 1185	SCHENECTADY	1970	decomm. 15 Dec 1993; str. 13 July 2001
LST 1186	CAYUGA	1970	decomm./to Brazil 26 Aug 1994; str. 23 July 2002
LST 1187	TUSCALOOSA	1970	decomm. 18 Feb 1994; str. 2003
LST 1188	SAGINAW	1971	decomm./str. 28 June 1994; to Australia 1994
LST 1189	SAN BERNARDINO	1971	decomm./str. 30 Sep 1995; to Chile 1995
LST 1190	BOULDER	1971	decomm. 28 Feb 1994; str. 2003
LST 1191	RACINE	1971	decomm. 2 Oct 1993; str. 2003
LST 1192	SPARTANBURG COUNTY	1971	decomm./str. 16 Dec 1994; to Malaysia
LST 1193	FAIRFAX COUNTY	1971	decomm./str. 17 Aug 1994; to Australia 1994
LST 1194	LA MOURE COUNTY	1971	decomm./str. 17 Nov 2000
LST 1195	BARBOUR COUNTY	1972	decomm. 30 Mar 1992; str. 13 July 2001
LST 1196	HARLAN COUNTY	1972	decomm. 14 Apr 1995; to Spain 1995; str. 23 July 2002
LST 1197	BARNSTABLE COUNTY	1972	decomm. 29 June 1994; to Spain 1994; str. 23 July 2002
LST 1198	BRISTOL COUNTY	1972	decomm./str. 29 July 1994; to Morocco 1994

The 20 ships of the NEWPORT class represented the ultimate design in landing ships that could be "beached." However, they generally unloaded onto pontoon causeways. They departed from the traditional LST bow-door design to obtain a hull design for a sustained speed of 20 knots.

A number of these ships served in the Naval Reserve Force. The decommissionings and shifts of those ships to the NRF in 1992–1995 marked the first time since 1942 that there had not been LSTs in the active U.S. amphibious force. The disposal of the last units in 2003 marked the first time no LSTs have been on the Naval Vessel Register (NVR).

Several ships have been transferred to other navies. The LST 1193 departed Little Creek, Virginia, en route to Australia on 15 August 1994 as a U.S. Navy ship carrying a combined U.S. (150) and Australian (20) crew; she was decommissioned and stricken en route to Sydney. In Australian service, she and the LST 1188 were converted in 1995–2000 to serve as training and helicopter support ships; they support Army Black Hawk helicopters, as well as Navy S70B-2 Seahawk helicopters, the latter flown from Australian frigates of the OLIVER HAZARD PERRY (FFG 7) design.

Seven additional ships of this design planned for the FY 1971 shipbuilding program were canceled.

See 17th Edition/pages 188–89 for characteristics.

Operational: The LA MOURE COUNTY, in NRF status since 1995, was participating the UNITAS exercise off Caleta Cifuncho Bay, Chile, when on 12 September 2000, in darkness and fog, she ran aground. She was operating with the Chilean LST VALDIVIA (the former USS SAN BERNARDINO), which pulled her off the rocks. The LA MOURE COUNTY suffered massive damage to her hull and propulsion plant. She was towed to Talcahuano by a Chilean icebreaker. Her damage was evaluated as too costly to repair, and she was sunk as a target on 10 July 2001.

Table 19-6. POST–WORLD WAR II TANK LANDING SHIPS

Number	Name	Comm.	Notes
TALBOT COUNTY class (2)			
LST 1153	TALBOT COUNTY	1947	stricken 1973
LST 1154	TALLAHATCHEE COUNTY	1949	converted to AVB 2
LST 1155	(unnamed)		canceled 1946
TERREBONNE PARISH class (15)			
LST 1156	TERREBONNE PARISH	1952	to Spain 1971
LST 1157	TERRELL COUNTY	1954	to Greece 1977
LST 1158	TIOGA COUNTY	1953	stricken 1973
LST 1159	TOM GREEN COUNTY	1953	to Spain 1972
LST 1160	TRAVERSE COUNTY	1953	to Peru 1984
LST 1161	VERNON COUNTY	1953	to Venezuela 1973
LST 1162	WAHKIAKUM COUNTY	1953	stricken 1973
LST 1163	WALDO COUNTY	1953	to Peru 1984
LST 1164	WALWORTH COUNTY	1953	to Peru 1984
LST 1165	WASHOE COUNTY	1953	to Peru 1984
LST 1166	WASHTENAW COUNTY	1953	converted to MSS 2
LST 1167	WESTCHESTER COUNTY	1954	to Turkey 1974
LST 1168	WEXFORD COUNTY	1954	to Spain 1971
LST 1169	WHITFIELD COUNTY	1954	to Greece 1977
LST 1170	WINDHAM COUNTY	1954	to Turkey 1973
DE SOTO COUNTY class (7)			
LST 1171	DE SOTO COUNTY	1958	to Italy 1972
LST 1172	(unnamed)		canceled 1955
LST 1173	SUFFOLK COUNTY	1957	stricken 1989
LST 1174	GRANT COUNTY	1957	to Brazil 1973
LST 1175	YORK COUNTY	1957	to Italy 1972
LST 1176	GRAHAM COUNTY	1958	converted to AGP 1176
LST 1177	LORAIN COUNTY	1958	stricken 1989
LST 1178	WOOD COUNTY	1959	stricken 1989
LST 1179–1198	NEWPORT class		

From December 1942 to June 1945, a total of 1,052 LSTs were completed for the U.S. Navy (numbered LST 1–1152, with 100 units being canceled). All were of the same basic design. Three larger, improved LSTs with steam-turbine propulsion were ordered late in the war; two were completed, the LST 1153 and LST 1154. (All other U.S. LSTs have had diesel propulsion.)

The TALLAHATCHEE COUNTY was converted to an advanced aviation base ship (AVB 2), to provide support for patrol planes operating from remote airfields in the Mediterranean. (Earlier, the ALAMEDA COUNTY/LST 32 had served as the AVB 1.) The designation AVB subsequently was assigned to two merchant ships converted to support Marine aviation deployments overseas (see Chapter 23).

The TERREBONNE PARISH-class LSTs were of the Navy's first post–World War II tank landing ship design. All were in Navy service until decommissioned in 1970, except the WALWORTH COUNTY, which was decommissioned in 1971; the LST 1158, 1160, and 1162–1165 then served with the Military Sealift Command in 1972–1973 (designated T-LST).

The WASHTENAW COUNTY was reclassified as a "minesweeper special" (MSS 2) and used as a pressure-mine countermeasures craft in North Vietnamese waters (stricken in 1973).

The DE SOTO COUNTY class was the last LST design with traditional bow doors and ramp, and superstructure aft. The GRAHAM COUNTY, converted to a gunboat support ship (AGP 1176) to service the ASHEVILLE (PG 84)-class ships, operated in the Mediterranean. The WOOD COUNTY was to support the PEGASUS (PHM 1)-class hydrofoil missile craft, but her conversion was canceled in 1977; she was to have been designated AGHS 1178.

5 AMPHIBIOUS CARGO SHIPS: "CHARLESTON" CLASS

Number	Name	FY	Comm.	Status
LKA 113	CHARLESTON	65	14 Dec 1968	AR
LKA 114	DURHAM	65	24 May 1969	PR
LKA 115	MOBILE	65	29 Sep 1969	PR
LKA 116	SAINT LOUIS	65	22 Nov 1969	PR
LKA 117	EL PASO	65	17 Jan 1970	AR

Builders:	Newport News Shipbuilding and Dry Dock, Va.
Displacement:	10,000 tons light
	20,700 tons full load
Length:	549¾ feet (167.6 m) waterline
	576 feet (175.6 m) overall
Beam:	62 feet (18.9 m)
Draft:	27½ feet (8.5 m)
Propulsion:	1 steam turbine (Westinghouse); 22,000 shp; 1 shaft
Boilers:	2 600 psi (41.7 kg/cm2) (Combustion Engineering)
Speed:	20 knots
Range:	9,600 nm (17,800 km) at 16 knots
Personnel:	approx. 363 (25 officers + 338 enlisted)
Troops:	approx. 225
Helicopters:	landing area only
Missiles:	none
Guns:	6 3-inch (76-mm) 50-cal AA Mk 33 (3 twin),
	except 4 guns in LKA 113, 117
	2 20-mm Phalanx CIWS Mk 15 (2 multibarrel) in LKA 113, 117
Radars:	LN-66 navigation, except SPS-64(V)9 in LKA 115
	SPS-10F surface search
Fire control:	local control only for 3-inch guns
EW systems:	SLQ-25A Nixie in LKA 117
	SLQ-32(V)1

These ships carry heavy equipment and supplies for amphibious assaults. They are configured for rapid unloading of equipment into landing craft and helicopters.

During 1979–1981, four of the ships were shifted to the NRF; they were returned to active Navy service in the early 1980s to improve amphibious readiness in response to the crises in the Persian Gulf, Lebanon, and Caribbean areas. All were decommissioned in 1992–1994.

The plan to assign the LKA 115 and 117 to the Military Sealift Command (MSC) in Reduced Operating Status (ROS) was can-

celed because of funding limitations. They were to have been manned with 50-man nucleus crews and capable of being reactivated within five days.

All five ships are in Category B reserve, suitable for activation within 180 days. The LKA 113, 115, and 117 are at Philadelphia; the LKA 114 and 116 are at Pearl Harbor.

The LKA 113 was transferred to the NDRF on 29 September 1992, but returned to the NVR on 31 May 1994.

		Returned to	
	To NRF	Active Fleet	Decomm.
LKA 113	21 Nov 1979	18 Feb 1983	27 Apr 1992
LKA 114	1 Oct 1979	1 Oct 1982	25 Feb 1994
LKA 115	1 Sep 1980	30 Sep 1983	4 Feb 1994
LKA 116	—	—	2 Nov 1992
LKA 117	1 Mar 1981	1 Oct 1982	21 Apr 1994

Classification: These ships were ordered as attack cargo ships (AKA). The CHARLESTON was changed to LKA on 14 December 1968; the others were changed on 1 January 1969.

Design: SCB No. 403. This is the first class of ships designed specifically for this role; all previous ships of the AKA/LKA type were converted from or built to merchant designs.

These ships have a large helicopter landing area aft, but no hangar or maintenance facilities. There are two 78-ton-capacity booms, two 40-ton booms, and eight 15-ton booms.

The ships normally carried as deck cargo 4 LCM(8)s, 5 LCM(6)s, 2 LCVPs, and 2 LCPLs.

Engineering: Maximum horsepower is shown in the class table; sustained shp is 19,250.

Guns: As built, four 3-inch twin gun mounts were installed. One mount was removed from each ship, as was the Mk 56 GFCS in 1977–1978. Subsequently, a second 3-inch twin mount was removed for the installation of the CIWS in two ships.

Two Phalanx CIWS are fitted in two of these ships. One CIWS is fitted forward, to port of the remaining forward 3-inch gun mount, and the other is fitted on the superstructure in place of the starboard 3-inch gun mount.

Table 19-7. POST–WORLD WAR II AMPHIBIOUS CARGO SHIPS

Number	Name	Comm.	Notes
Mariner class			
AKA 112	TULARE	1956	(see text)
LKA 113–117	CHARLESTON class		

The TULARE was acquired by the Navy while under construction as a Mariner-class merchant ship (C4-S-1a). Built as AKA 112, she was changed to LKA 112 on 1 January 1969. The TULARE was decommissioned in 1981 and placed in the NDRF, reinstated on the NVR in 1984, and again stricken on 31 August 1992.

In addition to the three Mariner-class amphibious ships listed here as cargo ship and attack transports, two other ships of that class became support ships for the Polaris program (AG 153, AG 154). One ship of this design remains on the NVR as a missile range instrumentation ship, the OBSERVATION ISLAND (T-AGM 23).

Table 19-8. POST–WORLD WAR II ATTACK TRANSPORTS

Number	Name	Comm.	Notes
Mariner class			
APA 248	PAUL REVERE	1958	stricken/to Spain 1980
APA 249	FRANCIS MARION	1961	stricken/to Spain 1980

Attack transports carried troops and landing craft. Both ships were acquired while under construction as Mariner-class cargo ships. Initially designated APA, they were changed to LPA on 1 January 1969.

CHAPTER 20

Landing Craft and Vehicles

Sailors and Marines crowd the LCU 1634 as the craft approaches the beach at Iwo Jima. This friendly landing was part of the 58th anniversary of the savage battle for that Pacific island in World War II. LCUs continue to be important for amphibious operations because of their large payloads. (2003, U.S. Navy/Wes Eplen)

The U.S. Navy operates several hundred landing craft. All landing craft are operated by Navy personnel. The expeditionary fighting vehicles and assault amphibian vehicles (formerly amphibious tractors) are operated by the Marine Corps and are described in the latter section of this chapter.

The larger air cushion landing craft (LCAC) and utility landing craft (LCU) are identified by hull numbers. The smaller landing craft are identified by the ship, unit, or base to which they are assigned.

Numerous LCUs have been transferred to other navies, reclassified, or stricken. Other LCU-type ships serve as a test support craft (IX), ferry boats (YFB), and harbor utility craft (YFU); they are described in Chapter 25. The U.S. Army operates several LCUs in the same designation series as the Navy craft, as well as mechanized landing craft (LCMs) (see Chapter 35).

The amphibious forces also operate warping tugs (LWT), which are used to move pontoon causeways in amphibious areas. They can be transported to forward areas by amphibious ships.

Additional small craft employed in amphibious operations are listed in Chapter 21, "Patrol and Special Warfare Craft."

Operational: In the Pacific Fleet, Naval Beach Group 1, based at the Naval Amphibious Base Coronado (San Diego), California, has Assault Craft Unit (ACU) 1, which operates conventional landing craft, and ACU-5 at Camp Pendleton, California, which operates LCACs. In the Atlantic Fleet, Naval Beach Group 2 at Little Creek (Norfolk), Virginia, has ACU-2 for conventional landing craft and ACU-4 for LCACs.

Personnel: The total personnel assigned to assault craft units, including their detachments, are:

Unit	Total	Officers	Enlisted
ACU-1	305	9	296
ACU-2	298	11	287
ACU-4	608	23	585
ACU-5	671	29	642

LANDING CRAFT

HEAVY-LIFT LANDING CRAFT AIR CUSHION

The Navy is considering a further Service Life Extension Program (SLEP) for existing LCACs, to provide a Heavy-Lift Landing Craft Air Cushion (HLCAC). In the HLCAC configuration the craft could carry 144 tons of cargo, i.e., double the SLEP capability of 72 tons.

The HLCAC conversion would lengthen the LCAC by approximately 37 feet (11.3 m), for a total length of 124½ feet (37.95 m), and add two gas turbines, for a total of six.

Research and development efforts related to the HLCAC began in Fiscal Year (FY) 2004, and the first conversion has been scheduled for FY 2008. Current planning calls for two LCACs to be replaced by one HLCAC.

91 AIR CUSHION LANDING CRAFT: LCAC TYPE

Number	FY	In service	Assignment	Number	FY	In service	Assignment	Number	FY	In service	Assignment
LCAC 1	82	14 Dec 1984	ACU-5	LCAC 32	86	1 May 1991	ACU-5	LCAC 63	91	30 Sep 1993	ACU-5
LCAC 2	82	22 Feb 1986	ACU-5	LCAC 33	86	4 June 1991	ACU-5	LCAC 64	91	27 Oct 1993	ACU-5
LCAC 3	82	9 June 1986	ACU-5	LCAC 34	89	31 May 1992	ACU-5	LCAC 65	91	24 Nov 1993	ACU-5
LCAC 4	83	13 Aug 1986	ACU-5	LCAC 35	89	31 May 1992	ACU-5	LCAC 66	91	31 Dec 1993	NCSL*
LCAC 5	83	26 Nov 1986	ACU-5	LCAC 36	89	1 May 1992	ACU-4	LCAC 67	91	25 Feb 1994	ACU-4
LCAC 6	83	1 Dec 1986	ACU-5	LCAC 37	89	31 July 1991	ACU-4	LCAC 68	91	25 Mar 1994	ACU-4
LCAC 7	84	18 Mar 1987	ACU-4	LCAC 38	89	6 Sep 1991	ACU-4	LCAC 69	91	29 Apr 1994	ACU-4
LCAC 8	84	3 June 1987	ACU-4	LCAC 39	89	30 Sep 1991	ACU-4	LCAC 70	91	5 June 1994	ACU-4
LCAC 9	84	26 June 1987	ACU-4	LCAC 40	89	5 Nov 1991	ACU-4	LCAC 71	91	21 June 1994	ACU-4
LCAC 10	84	4 Sep 1987	ACU-4	LCAC 41	89	27 Nov 1991	ACU-4	LCAC 72	91	28 July 1994	ACU-5
LCAC 11	84	7 Dec 1987	ACU-4	LCAC 42	89	20 Dec 199	ACU-5	LCAC 73	92	28 Sep 1994	ACU-5
LCAC 12	84	23 Dec 1987	ACU-4	LCAC 43	89	21 Feb 1992	ACU-5	LCAC 74	92	10 Nov 1994	ACU-5
LCAC 13	85	30 Sep 1988	ACU-5	LCAC 44	89	29 Feb 1992	ACU-5	LCAC 75	92	6 Jan 1995	ACU-5
LCAC 14	85	3 Nov 1988	ACU-5	LCAC 45	89	26 Mar 1992	ACU-5	LCAC 76	92	14 Feb 1995	ACU-5
LCAC 15	85	20 Sep 1988	ACU-4	LCAC 46	89	8 May 1992	ACU-4	LCAC 77	92	31 Mar 1995	ACU-4
LCAC 16	85	4 Nov 1988	ACU-5	LCAC 47	89	24 June 1992	ACU-5	LCAC 78	92	23 May 1995	ACU-4
LCAC 17	85	1989	ACU-5	LCAC 48	89	17 July 1992	ACU-5	LCAC 79	92	20 July 1995	ACU-4
LCAC 18	85	1989	ACU-5	LCAC 49	90	16 Oct 1992	ACU-4	LCAC 80	92	23 Aug 1995	ACU-5
LCAC 19	85	May 1990	ACU-4	LCAC 50	90	28 Feb 1993	ACU-4	LCAC 81	92	25 Oct 1995	ACU-5
LCAC 20	85	Sep 1990	ACU-4	LCAC 51	90	June 1993	ACU-4	LCAC 82	92	13 Dec 1995	SLEP
LCAC 21	85	1990	ACU-4	LCAC 52	90	2 Sep 1992	ACU-5	LCAC 83	92	29 Feb 1996	SLEP
LCAC 22	86	Nov 1990	ACU-5	LCAC 53	90	10 July 1992	ACU-5	LCAC 84	92	25 Apr 1996	SLEP
LCAC 23	86	15 June 1991	ACU-5	LCAC 54	90	30 Oct 1992	ACU-4	LCAC 85	93	25 July 1996	SLEP
LCAC 24	86	1 Mar 1990	ACU-5	LCAC 55	90	30 Nov 1992	ACU-4	LCAC 86	93	26 Sep 1996	SLEP
LCAC 25	86	29 June 1990	ACU-4	LCAC 56	90	8 Jan 1993	ACU-5	LCAC 87	93	20 Nov 1996	SLEP
LCAC 26	86	July 1990	ACU-4	LCAC 57	90	26 Feb 1993	ACU-5	LCAC 88	93	20 Feb 1997	SLEP
LCAC 27	86	24 Aug 1990	ACU-4	LCAC 58	90	31 Mar 1993	ACU-5	LCAC 89	93	15 Apr 1997	SLEP
LCAC 28	86	12 Oct 1990	ACU-4	LCAC 59	90	30 Apr 1993	ACU-5	LCAC 90	93	24 Oct 1997	SLEP
LCAC 29	86	18 Dec 1990	ACU-5	LCAC 60	90	4 June 1993	ACU-4	LCAC 91	93	19 Dec 2000	SLEP
LCAC 30	86	19 Dec 1990	ACU-5	LCAC 61	91	30 July 1993	ACU-5				
LCAC 31	86	27 Feb 1991	ACU-5	LCAC 62	91	31 Aug 1993	ACU-5				

* Naval Coastal Systems Laboratory, Panama City, Florida

Builders:	Bell-Aerospace/Textron Marine Systems, New Orleans, except LCAC 15–23, 34–36, 49–51 by Avondale Gulfport Marine, La.	Propulsion/lift:	4 gas turbines (Avco-Lycoming TF-40B); 15,820 shp; 2 shrouded propellers, 2 bow thrusters/4 centrifugal lift fans
Displacement:	102.2 tons light	Speed:	50 knots maximum on cushion
	169 tons full load		40+ knots with payload on cushion in sea state 2
	184 tons overload		30+ knots with payload on cushion in sea state 3
Length:	81 feet (24.7 m) overall (structure)		25 knots maximum on hull
	87½ feet (26.8 m) on cushion	Range:	200 nm (370 km) at 40 knots with payload
Beam:	43⅔ feet (13.3 m) (structure)	Crew:	5 (enlisted)
	47 feet (14.3 m) on cushion	Troops:	24
Draft:	3 feet (0.9 m) structure	Guns:	(see notes)
		Radars:	navigation

These landing craft are the first advanced-technology surface ships to be produced in series by the U.S. Navy. They carry heavy vehicles and cargo from amphibious ships onto the beach at higher speeds and for longer distances than can conventional landing craft.

LCACs are assigned to assault craft units, with several ACU-5 craft being based at Sasebo, Japan. Ten LCACs are in reserve—Reduced Operating Status (ROS); several are undergoing SLEP; and the LCAC 66 is employed for test and evaluation.

Note the very late delivery of the last unit (see *Modernization* notes).

Builders: Lockheed Shipyard in Seattle, Washington, originally was the second source for LCAC construction; however, beginning in June 1988, that firm divested itself of shipbuilding activities and the Gulfport Marine division of Avondale Industries took over the

Lockheed contracts.

Class: The original Navy–Marine Corps plan was to acquire 107 LCACs to support an amphibious assault force of one Marine Expeditionary Force (MEF) plus one Marine Expeditionary Brigade (MEB). In early 1984, the Department of Defense announced a plan for "at least 90" units, although the 107 force-level goal was listed in official documents through FY 1991. The FY 1993 DoD budget request provided for the final 7 LCACs, for a total of 91 units.

Design: The Navy began development of air-cushion craft in 1960. The LCAC design is based on the JEFF(B), one of two competitive prototypes delivered to the Navy in 1977.

The LCAC has a modular design, which facilitates construction, maintenance, and damage repairs. The craft are fully "skirted";

they are amphibious and can clear land obstacles up to 4 feet (1.2 m) high. Bow and stern ramps are fitted. The cargo deck area is 81 feet (24.7 m) x 27 feet (8.2 m), totaling 1,809 square feet (162.8 m²).

The design payload is 120,000 pounds (54,545 kg), with a maximum overload of 150,000 pounds (68,182 kg). The LCAC initially could accommodate one M1 tank or four Light Armored Vehicles (LAV) or three AAV7/LVTP-7 amphibian vehicles (two AAVs if appliqué armor is fitted) or two M198 155-mm towed howitzers.

The control compartment is located on the starboard side. It has an aircraft-type cockpit, with the operator seated on the far right, the engineer in the center, and the navigator on the left.

Design problems occurred in the early units; operational tests revealed that the craft shipped water that could cause electrical shorts and interrupt operations. The Navy did not request additional units in the FY 1987–1988 budgets to allow time for the five completed units to undergo additional testing so modifications could be developed. The early craft have been modified.

All units were built with composite (ceramic tile) armor for the control station module. The LCAC 34 and later units have one engine on each side armored, and the LCAC 61 and subsequent units have additional engine armor. Armor, modular arrangement, and redundancy provide a relatively high degree of survivability.

Electronics: The modified LN-66 is combined with a Unisys-developed system to provide multiple functions.

Engineering: The gas turbines are fitted in modules, two per side. The clutch/gearbox system permits a high degree of flexibility. Two engines normally are employed for propulsion and two for lift; under emergency conditions one engine can provide propulsion and one can provide lift. The craft have a high degree of maneuverability and can turn 180° within their own length.

The propellers are four-blade, 11¾-foot (3.6-m) diameter, reversible, each fitted with two rudders; the lift fans are 5¼ feet (1.6 m) in diameter.

Guns: No armament is fitted; however, three mounting positions are provided: one for a 7.62-mm M60 machine gun and two for 7.62-mm M60 or .50-cal M2HB machine guns or 40-mm Mk 19 grenade launchers.

The LCAC 66 conducted trials in 1966 with a 30-mm GAU-13 Gatling gun fitted in a GAU-5 pod; its purpose was to provide organic suppression fire to landing forces.

Mine countermeasures: In December 1993, the Navy decided to provide a packaged Mine Countermeasures (MCM) capability for use by LCACs. Operational test and evaluation began with the reconfigured LCAC 66 in February 1994 at Panama City, Florida. Fitted with MCM gear, this craft is referred to as a multipurpose air-cushion vehicle (MCAC). Subsequently, 16 M58 modular lane-sweeping MCM packages were procured, with the first delivered in mid-1993. These packages permit an LCAC to employ the same countermeasures sleds used by MH-53E MCM helicopters. Towing speed for these systems is 25 knots. The AQS-14 mine-hunting sonar also can be fitted.

The LCAC also can be configured as a platform for the Shallow-water Assault Breaching (SABRE) line charge system. Each LCAC can carry nine SABRE line-explosive launchers and two Distributed Explosive Technology (DET) explosive net-array launchers. These would be employed to clear mined beach areas for LCACs and possibly amphibian vehicles to come ashore.

(The Royal Navy conducted mine countermeasures trials with the 55-ton BH7 Mk 2 hovercraft [pennant P 235] in 1983. An enlarged, specialized BH7 Mk 20 configured for the MCM role—using U.S. helicopter equipment—was designed but not procured.)

Modernization: Modifications are required for these craft to carry the improved (and heavier) M1 Abrams tanks now in Marine Corps service. The older LCACs require rehabilitation, and a SLEP began in FY 2000 to extend the service lives of 74 units from 20 to 30+ years.

The SLEP process, being carried out at Textron Marine and Land Systems in New Orleans, Louisiana, gives the LCACs increased reliability and reduced maintenance requirements by providing state-of-the-art components, improved engines, and increased fuel capacity. The SLEP Phase 1 modernization is to complete by 2010, to coincide with introduction of the Expeditionary Fighting Vehicle (EFV), formerly the Advanced Amphibious Assault Vehicle (AAAV). Through 2016, as part of SLEP Phase 2, other upgrades will be provided, including (1) open architecture based on Commercial-off-the-Shelf (COTS) equipment that will permit easier navigation and communications upgrades; (2) engine upgrades to the ETF-40B configuration to provide greater lift, especially in hot environments, reduced fuel consumption, reduced maintenance requirements, and reduced lift "footprint"; (3) replacement of the "buoyancy box" to reduce corrosion and "fatigue"; and (4) a deeper skirt, which will reduce drag to increase overwater performance and reduce skirt maintenance. It is not known how these SLEP efforts will relate to the planned HLCAC program.

The LCAC 91 was built to SLEP Phase 1 standards, hence the delay in her completion.

Operational: Each LCAC is commanded by a craftmaster, a chief petty officer, who also pilots the craft; the other crewmen are the engineer, navigator, load master, and deck seaman.

The LCACs are assigned in approximately equal numbers to ACU-4 at Little Creek, and ACU-5 at Camp Pendleton. ACU-4 was established in 1987 and ACU-5 in 1983.

The LCACs can be carried in the following amphibious ships: LHD (3 per ship), LHA (1 per ship), LPD 17 (2 per ship), LPD 4 (1 per ship), LSD 49 (2 per ship), and LSD 41 (4 per ship).

Seventeen LCACs were deployed on board amphibious ships participating in Operation Desert Storm in January–February 1991. All were "mission-ready" and operated in day and night exercises and administrative (noncombat) landings with 100 percent availability. (This was precisely one-half the number of LCACs in service at the time.)

Three LCACs normally are embarked in each Expeditionary Strike Group (ESG) or Amphibious Ready Group (ARG).

The LCAC 84 "flies" toward the beach at Kuwait as the amphibious assault ship KEARSARGE (LHD 3) unloads troops and vehicles of the 2nd Marine Expeditionary Brigade (MEB). There is a Light Armored Reconnaissance Vehicle (LARV) ahead of several "hum-vee" utility vehicles. (2002, U.S. Navy/Gregg L. Snaza)

A Marine Light Armored Reconnaissance Vehicle (LARV) rolls down the rear ramp of an LCAC in Kuwait, during Operation Enduring Freedom. There are twin rudders mounted on the propeller housings. The bow–stern ramp arrangement allows vehicles to drive through the LCACs when they are being loaded in a well-deck amphibious ship. (2003, U.S. Navy/Arlo K. Abrahamson)

Men of an Explosive Ordnance Demolition (EOD) team drag their rubber boat onto the rear ramp of an LCAC after having been dropped into the Adriatic Sea from a helicopter during an exercise. The team, based aboard the amphibious ship KEARSARGE, was supporting Operation Allied Force. (1999, U.S. Navy/Seth Rossman)

Marines from Battalion Landing Team 2/3 (2nd Battalion, 3rd Regiment) come ashore from the LCAC 47 at Barking Sands, Kauai (Hawaii), on an exercise. Despite their lack of stealth, LCACs have been invaluable in the ship-to-shore movement of troops and vehicles. (2002, U.S. Navy/Jane Campbell)

(19) UTILITY LANDING CRAFT (REPLACEMENT)

Units	FY	Completed	Status
2 ships	05	2007	Planned
3 ships	06		Planned
3 ships	07		Planned
3 ships	08		Planned
3 ships	09		Planned
3 ships	10		Planned
2 ships	11		Planned

A 19-unit replacement LCU class is planned, although in 2004, the reconsideration of amphibious force levels and construction programs and the Sea Basing concept made further LCU procurement questionable. Earlier, the Navy had planned for 35 new LCUs, to be delivered from 2005 through 2012. The revision will mean one or, at most, two of these valuable craft will be embarked in an ESG/ARG. The planned SLEP-modified LCAC/HLCAC will compensate for the LCU reduction.

The new LCU will be capable of lifting up to 225 tons of cargo, i.e., three M1A1 tanks or (for short trips) 400 combat-loaded troops. Maximum speed will be between 20 and 25 knots in sea state 3. It will be configured for independent operations up to ten days, with a range of 1,000 nm.

Issues being addressed in the LCU design include enhanced navigation for over-the-horizon operations, armor, and Chemical-Biological-Radiological (CBR) protection. The craft will have bow thrusters for maneuverability.

38 UTILITY LANDING CRAFT: "LCU 1610" CLASS

Number	Assignment	Number	Assignment	Number	Assignment
LCU 1616	ACU-1	LCU 1644	ACU-2	LCU 1658	ACU-2
LCU 1617	ACU-1	LCU 1645	ACU-2	LCU 1659	ACU-2
LCU 1619	ACU-1	LCU 1646	ACU-1	LCU 1660	ACU-2
LCU 1624	ACU-1	LCU 1647	Naval Air Warfare Center,	LCU 1661	ACU-2
LCU 1627	ACU-1		Ft. Lauderdale, Fla.	LCU 1662	ACU-2
LCU 1629	ACU-1	LCU 1648	ACU-1	LCU 1663	ACU-2
LCU 1630	ACU-1	LCU 1649	ACU-2	LCU 1664	ACU-2
LCU 1631	ACU-1	LCU 1650	ACU-2	LCU 1665	Fleet Activities Sasebo, Japan
LCU 1632	ACU-1	LCU 1651	ACU-1	LCU 1666	ACU-1
LCU 1633	ACU-1	LCU 1653	ACU-2	135CU8501	reserve training; Buffalo, N.Y.
LCU 1634	ACU-1	LCU 1654	ACU-2		(ex-LCU 1680)
LCU 1635	ACU-1	LCU 1655	ACU-2	135CU8502	reserve training; Tampa, Fla.
LCU 1641		LCU 1656	ACU-2		(ex-LCU 1681)
LCU 1643	ACU-2	LCU 1657	ACU-2		

Builders:	Defoe Shipbuilding, Bay City, Wisc.: LCU 1646–1666	Draft:	6½ feet (2.1 m)
	General Ship & Engine Works, East Boston: LCU 1627, 1631–1635	Propulsion:	4 diesel engines (General Motors Detroit 6-71); 1,200 bhp, except LCU 1646 and later units 4 General Motors 12V71N,
	Gunderson Bros, Portland, Ore: LCU 1616–1619, 1623, 1624		1,700 bhp; 2 Kort-nozzle propellers
	Marinette Marine, Wisc.: LCU 1643–1645	Speed	11 knots
	Moss Point Marine, Escatawpa, Miss.: LCU 1680, 1681	Range:	1,200 nm (2,222 km) at 8 knots with payload
	Southern Shipbuilding, Slidell, La.: LCU 1626, 1629, 1630	Crew:	6 (enlisted), except LCU 1680, 1681 14 (2 officers +
Displacement:	190 tons light		12 enlisted)
	390 tons full load, except LCU 1680, 1681 404 tons	Troops:	8
Length:	134¾ feet (41.1 m) overall	Guns:	2 20-mm cannon or 2 .50-cal machine guns M2 (2 single)
Beam:	29¾ feet (9.1 m)	Radars:	SPS-69 Pathfinder navigation

These are improved LCUs, with 15 units (LCU 1610–1624) completed in 1959–1960 and the remainder from 1967 to 1976, except the LCU 1680 and LCU 1681 in 1987.

Class: This class originally consisted of hull numbers 1610–1624 and 1627–1681.

The LCU 1680 and LCU 1681 were built to a modified design.

The LCU 1667–1679 went to the U.S. Army.

The LCU 1621, 1623, and 1628 have been converted to auxiliary swimmer delivery vehicles (ASDV) to support diving operations, and others became service craft (YFU); both types are described in Chapter 25.

The LCU 1624 and LCU 1641 were expended as targets on 4 May 2002. The LCU 1613 was stricken in 1993, LCU 1652 in 1998 (after grounding), and LCU 1614 in 2001.

Classification: Two LCUs assigned to Naval Reserve training activities have hull registry numbers.

Design: The LCU 1610–1624 were SCB No. 149; the LCU 1627 and later units were SCB No. 149B (new series SCB No. 406).

These LCUs have a "drive-through" configuration with bow and stern ramps, and a small, starboard-side island structure housing controls and accommodations. Previous LCU/LCT-type landing craft had a small deck structure aft. They are welded-steel construction; the mast folds down for entering well decks of amphibious ships.

Cargo capacity is one M1 tank or up to about 190 tons of cargo or, for short distances, 350–400 troops.

Engineering: The LCU 1621 had vertical shafts fitted with vertical-axis, cycloidal, six-blade propellers. All other units have Kort-nozzle propellers. The LCU 1680 and 1681 were built with improved engines; they have been backfitted in the LCU 1646 and later units.

Guns: Weapons are not normally fitted in these craft.

Operational: Most LCUs are assigned to Assault Craft Units 1 and 2, as indicated in the class table.

The LCU 1641 is used as a training minelayer; she is fitted with a stern mine rail and a recovery crane.

Marines pack the LCU 1631 as the troops are transported from the South Korean port of Pohang to the amphibious ship ESSEX (LHD 2) following a joint–combined exercise on the Korean peninsula. The LCU's mast and radar are lowered to enable the craft to enter the ESSEX's docking well. (2002, U.S. Navy/Gary B. Granger)

The LCU 1654 backs away from the amphibious ship WASP (LHD 1) with Marines of the 22nd Marine Expeditionary Unit (MEU) during operations in the Persian Gulf. The current LCUs have both a bow ramp and a stern gate, enabling "drive through" operations. (2004, U.S. Navy/Keith Simmons)

Trucks come ashore in Kuwait from the LCU 1664 as the 24th Marine Expeditionary Unit (MEU) prepares for operations in Iraq in support of Operation Iraqi Freedom. While most assault troops are landed by helicopter, most of their heavy weapons, most vehicles, and stores come ashore by LCACs and LCUs. (2003, U.S. Navy/Joe Krypel)

The white-painted LCU 1647, assigned to support and research duties with the Naval Air Warfare Center's detachment at Key West, Florida. A heavy crane is fitted aft. Three other extensively modified LCUs support combat swimmer operations (see Chapter 25). (U.S. Navy)

The LCU 1660 enters the flooded well deck of the amphibious ship SAIPAN (LHA 2) during operations off the Atlantic coast. The LHA's monorail system for handing cargo is visible in the overhead of the docking well. The LCU replacement program is unlikely to be pursued. (2004, U.S. Navy/Courtney Torgrude)

1 UTILITY LANDING CRAFT: "LCU 1466" CLASS

Number	Assignment
LCU 1590 (ex-Army SPOTSYLVANIA)	Mobile Diving and Salvage Unit 2

Displacement:	180 tons light
	360 tons full load
Length:	119 feet (39.0 m) overall
Beam:	34 feet (10.4 m)
Draft:	6 feet (1.8 m)
Propulsion:	3 geared diesel engines (Gray Marine 64 YTL); 675 bhp;
	3 shafts
Speed:	8 knots
Range:	700 nm (1,300 km) at 7 knots with payload
Crew:	
Troops:	(see notes)
Guns:	removed
Radars:	navigation

The LCU 1590 is the lone survivor in U.S. Navy service of a large series of LCUs. She now serves as a diving tender and support craft for Mobile Diving and Salvage Unit 2, but because the craft retains her LCU designation, she is included here.

The ex-LCU 1486/YFU 50 survives as a workboat designated 119WB8501.

Class: This class covered hull numbers LCU 1466–1609, with 14 units (LCU 1594–1607, completed in 1955) constructed in Japan under the Offshore Procurement (OSP) program for foreign service. Other ships of this design were built for the U.S. Army.

Numerous U.S. units were transferred to other nations; others became service craft (YFU).

Classification: The LCU 1466–1503 were ordered as utility landing ships (LSU) on 31 October 1951; they were reclassified as LCUs on 15 April 1952.

Design: SCB No. 25. These craft have a deckhouse-aft configuration.

Guns: All were built with gun "tubs" on either side of the bridge structure for .50-cal machine guns or 20-mm cannon.

POST–WORLD WAR II TANK LANDING CRAFT

The tank landing craft designs LCT(1), (2), (3), and (4) were British. The first U.S. design was the LCT(5), with LCT 1–500 being completed in 1942; many were transferred to Great Britain.

An LCU 1466-class landing craft carries three Marine M48 Patton tanks (with turrets turned to the rear) during a landing exercise. Many of these craft were operated by the Army as well as by the Navy. They have only a bow ramp; twin 20-mm cannon are fitted on either side of the bridge. (U.S. Navy)

The LCT(6) followed, with LCT 501–1465 being completed in 1943–1944; a few went to Britain and six became coastal mine hunters, designated AMc(U) 1–6.[1] The LCT(6) design had an "island" structure on the port side, introducing the "drive-through" configuration to landing craft. The U.S. LCT(7) nos. 1501–1830 were oceangoing craft, completed as medium landing ships (LSM/LSMR). The British LCT(8) was a similar, oceangoing craft.

In 1949, the surviving LCT(6)s were reclassified as utility landing ships (LSU) with their LCT hull numbers. Landing craft nos. 1466–1503 were ordered in 1951 as LSUs but were changed to LCU in May 1952. Subsequent LCUs follow in sequence, bypassing the numbers initially assigned to the LCT(7) series.

---

1 AMc(U) = minesweeper, coastal (underwater locator).

29 MECHANIZED LANDING CRAFT: LCM(8) Mk 3, Mk 5

Weight:	34 tons light
	121 tons full load
Length:	73⁷⁄₁₂ feet (22.4 m) overall
Beam:	21 feet (6.4 m)
Draft:	4½ feet (1.4 m) aft
Propulsion:	4 diesel engines (General Motors Detroit 6-71); 1,300 bhp; 2 shafts (see *Engineering* notes)
Speed:	12 knots
Range:	150 nm (278 km) at 12 knots
Crew:	5 (enlisted)
Guns:	none (see *Guns* notes)

These are standard landing craft intended to carry vehicles and cargo. Their capacity is 58 tons of cargo or light vehicles. No accommodations are provided in these or other LCM-type craft.

Most of these craft are assigned to Assault Craft Units 1 and 2. For LCM and smaller units, both active and laid-up craft are totaled.

Engineering: Most have four General Motors (GM) 6-71 diesels; a few have two of the larger GM 12V71 diesels. The last 20 units (delivered 1991–1992) have GM 8V92N engines.

Guns: A pair of .50-cal machine guns can be fitted.

25 MECHANIZED LANDING CRAFT: LCM(8) Mk 2, Mk 4

Weight:	36.5 tons light
	106.75 tons full load
Length:	74½ feet (22.6 m) overall
Beam:	21½ feet (6.4 m)
Draft:	4½ feet (1.4 m)
Propulsion:	4 diesel engines (General Motors); 1,300 bhp; 2 shafts
Speed:	12 knots
Range:	150 nm (278 km) at 12 knots
Crew:	5 (enlisted)
Guns:	none

These are aluminum versions of the steel-hulled LCM(8) originally developed for use with the Charleston (LKA 113)-class amphibious cargo ships (Mk 2). Subsequently, additional units were ordered for use aboard maritime prepositioning ships (Mk 4).

Cargo capacity is 65 tons of cargo or light vehicles.

Engineering: Some units have been refitted with Kort nozzles.

An LCM(8) assigned to the Naval Amphibious Base in Coronado (San Diego). The bow-ramp configuration varies in these craft. The mast mounts a navigation light. (Giorgio Arra)

An LCM(8) from Assault Craft Unit 2 operating off Norfolk. A glass-windowed cover is installed over the conning position. LCMs and smaller craft are identified by their parent ship, base, or unit. (Giorgio Arra)

19 MECHANIZED LANDING CRAFT: LCM(6) TYPE

Weight:	26.7 tons light
	62.35 tons full load
Length:	56 feet (17.1 m) overall
Beam:	14⅓ feet (4.4 m)
Draft:	3⅞ feet (1.2 m)
Propulsion:	2 diesel engines (Gray Marine 64HN9 or General Motors 8V71); 625 bhp; 2 shafts
Speed:	12 knots
Range:	130 nm (240 km) at 9 knots
Crew:	5 (enlisted)
Guns:	none

Additional units serve in various support roles. Numerous LCMs of this type were converted to riverine combat craft during the Vietnam War. Of the above total, about ten normally are carried aboard amphibious ships.

Of welded steel construction, they can carry 34 tons of cargo or, for short distances, 120 troops.

Engineering: The above horsepower and speed are for the General Motors engines; those with Gray Marine have 450 bhp and can make 10 knots.

A short-hull LCM(6) traveling at high speed. (Giorgio Arra)

An LCM(6) modified to serve as a tender at the Naval Surface Warfare facility in Florida. A life raft canister is fitted alongside the pilothouse. (Giorgio Arra)

106 LANDING CRAFT PERSONNEL LIGHT (LCPL): Mk 11, Mk 12, Mk 13

Weight:	10 tons full load
Length:	36 feet (11.0 m) overall
Beam:	13 feet (4.0 m)
Draft:	3½ feet (1.1 m)
Propulsion:	1 diesel engine (General Motors 8V71); 350 bhp; 1 shaft (see *Engineering* notes)
Speed:	17 knots
Range:	150 nm (278 km) at 15 knots
Crew:	3 (enlisted)
Guns:	none (see *Guns* notes)

These small landing craft are used for passenger transport and for the control of other landing craft. About 100 currently are carried in amphibious ships, with the remainder assigned to shore activities.

LCPLs are built of fiberglass-reinforced plastic. They carry 17 passengers or two tons of cargo.

Engineering: The later LCPLs have Cummins lightweight engines fitted.

Guns: During the Vietnam War several LCPLs were armed with one or more .50- and .30-cal machine guns and employed for inshore patrol (some with a navigation radar fitted).

LANDING CRAFT VEHICLE AND PERSONNEL (LCVP)

All LCVPs have been discarded. The design of these 36-foot (10.9 m) landing craft dates back to the Higgins craft of World War II. See 17th Edition/page 199 for characteristics.

LANDING VEHICLES

Assault Amphibian Vehicles (AAV) are used by the Marine Corps for assault landings and for subsequent movement ashore. The Marine Corps currently operates 1,323 assault amphibian vehicles of the AAV7 series. Most of these are troop carriers (AAVP7), but 106 are configured as command vehicles (AAVC7) and 64 as recovery/repair vehicles (AAVR7).

The Expeditionary Fighting Vehicle (EFV)—previously designated Advanced Assault Amphibian Vehicle (AAAV)—is under development. According to the official Marine Corps web site (www.usmc.mil), the 10 September 2003 designation change was made "in keeping with the U.S. Marine Corps cultural shift from a 20th century force defined by amphibious operations to a 21st Century force focusing on a broadened range of employment concepts and possibilities across a spectrum of conflict."

Increasingly, the Marines have employed AAVs—previously designated tracked landing vehicles (LVT)—on land, as well as for ship-to-shore movement. The AAV/LVT is limited as an armored personnel carrier because of (1) its high noise level, (2) the height of the vehicle, (3) its treads, which are susceptible to damage during heavy land use, (4) its slow speed over certain terrain, and (5) its light armor. Also, there is no effective method of protecting the troops in the AAV7 vehicles from CBR weapons attack.

The Marine Corps has three battalions and two smaller units that operate amphibian tractors:

• 1st Armored Assault Battalion on Okinawa to support the 3rd Marine Division (two amphibian companies)
• 2nd Assault Amphibian Battalion at Camp Lejeune, North Carolina, to support the 2nd Marine Division (four amphibian companies)
• 3rd Assault Amphibian Battalion at Camp Pendleton, California (three amphibian companies)
• Company D, 3rd Assault Amphibian Battalion, at Twenty Nine Palms, California
• Detachment A, 3rd Assault Amphibian Battalion (two platoons), at Kaneohoe Bay, Hawaii

The battalion on Okinawa is designated as an *armored* unit, with two tank companies in addition to the amphibian companies. The standard amphibian battalion has a total of 1,166 personnel and 208 amphibian vehicles—187 AAVP7s, 15 AAVC7s, and 6 AAVR7s.

The 2nd and 3rd Battalions each is capable of simultaneously lifting the assault elements of a Marine Expeditionary Brigade (i.e., reinforced regiment), while the 1st Battalion can provide lift for a Marine Expeditionary Unit (i.e., reinforced battalion).

There are another 327 AAVs forward deployed on board the maritime prepositioning ships. Additional AAVs are assigned to the Marine Corps Reserve and are in the pipeline for maintenance, training, etc.

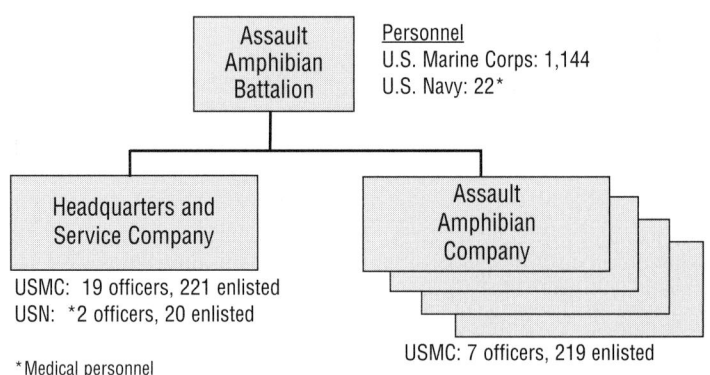

Figure 20-1. MARINE ASSAULT AMPHIBIAN BATTALION

Splash! An AAVP7 splashes from the well deck of the amphibious ship JUNEAU *(LPD 10) during a landing exercise by the 31st Marine Expeditionary Unit (MEU) off the coast of Tok Sok Ri, South Korea. Despite the development of the Expeditionary Fighting Vehicle (EFV), the AAVP7 will be the principal Marine "amtrac." (2002, U.S. Marine Corps/James Davis)*

The service life of the present AAV7 "family" of vehicles was expected to end in the mid-1980s. However, when they failed to gain approval for a follow-on amphibian vehicle, the Marines embarked on an extensive Service Life Extension Program for existing vehicles (with modified vehicles receiving the designation suffix A1).

There have been two previously proposed successors to the AAV7/LVTP-7, the landing assault vehicle (LVA), initiated in 1973 and canceled in 1979, followed by the advanced tracked landing vehicle, designated LVT(X). The aborted LVT(X), which was cancelled in 1985, is described in the 13th Edition/page 212.

Classification: The AAV7 series initially was designated landing vehicle tracked, personnel (LVTP)-7. The term "AAV" was adopted in the 1970s as a "sexy" designation for the next generation of assault amphibian vehicle.

Modernization: The AAV7 SLEP included the following changes:
• An electric-drive turret mounting a 40-mm Mk 19 grenade launcher as well as the older but more reliable .50-cal M2 machine gun, to replace the existing gun turret, which mounted a single .50-cal M85 machine gun.
• An advanced mine-clearing system that fires explosive "snakes" to detonate ground mines. The system—including a possible later version with fuel-air explosive—can be installed on top of a tractor.
• A limited CBR alarm and protection system.
• Appliqué steel armor that can be bolted on the vehicle by the crew. This P-900 armor will defeat 14.7-mm gunfire. The armor weighs 3,500 pounds (1,591 kg), which the vehicle can easily handle—in fact, the weight actually improves the water stability of the craft. A lighter, improved armor is in development.
• A bow plane that extends when the craft is in the water to reduce the tendency to push down into seas.
• An automatic fire sensor and suppression system to reduce the possibility of fuel fires in the troop compartment.
• Improved transmission and suspension.
• A magnetic heading device.

These improvements add weight to the vehicle, but this is not a concern because of the craft's great payload. More critical is space, with the changes reducing the troop capacity to perhaps 21 riflemen; if crew-served weapons, such as mortars, are carried, the troop capacity is even less.

EXPEDITIONARY FIGHTING VEHICLES

Weight:	64,000 pounds (29,030 kg) empty
	74,000 pounds (33,566 kg) fully loaded
Length:	27⅝ feet (8.48 m) on land
	37 feet (11.28 m) in water
Width:	12 feet (3.66 m)
Height:	10 feet (3.05 m)
Propulsion:	1 diesel engine (MTU MT883 Ra-523); 2,700 hp in water mode, 850 hp in land mode; <u>tracked running gear on land</u>
	2 23-inch (584-m) diameter waterjets in water
Speed:	<u>45 mph on land</u>
	20 knots in 3 foot (0.91 m) waves
	25 knots maximum

Range:	400 miles (643 km) on land
	65 miles (105 km) in water
Crew:	3 (enlisted)
Troops:	18
Guns:	1 30-mm Bushmaster II cannon Mk 44
	(200 rounds ready + 400 stowed)
	1 7.62-mm machine gun M240
	(800 rounds ready + 1,600 stowed)

Development of an Expeditionary Fighting Vehicle (EFV), formerly designated Advanced Amphibian Assault Vehicle (AAAV), "remains our primary developmental research effort," according to the Commandant of the Marine Corps.[2] This development program seeks to provide a high-speed tracked vehicle to move assault troops from amphibious ships beyond the horizon to inland objectives. The Marine Corps envisions a so-called high-speed sea craft with the land mission capabilities of the U.S. Army's Bradley Armored Fighting Vehicle.

The Marine Corps plans to procure 1,013 EFVs to replace just over 1,300 AAV7s. Two groups, United Defense (formerly FMC Corporation's Ground Systems Division, which built all AAV7s) and General Dynamics' Land Systems Division teamed with AAI Corp., competed for the development contract. Following tests with demonstration vehicles, General Dynamics was selected to produce 15 prototype EFVs—13 troop carriers and 2 command-and-control vehicles. Full-scale production is to begin in FY 2006, with a unit price of more than $8 million and a total program price—for development and procurement—estimated at some $9 billion.

The first EFV/AAAV prototype was delivered in August 1999.

Initial operational capability for the EFV is planned for 2008, with all vehicles fielded by 2014.

Classification: These vehicles were changed from AAV to Expeditionary Fighting Vehicle on 10 September 2003.

Design: The General Dynamics–AAI design has a planing hull. The team has produced three EFV technology test beds under contract to the Navy, with the last—called a Propulsion System Demonstrator (PSD)—achieving a planing speed of 25 mph (40 km/h) for 33 nm (61 km) in trials, with a top speed of 45 mph (72.4 km/h). Vehicle weight was 57,000 pounds (25,855 kg). The craft had a Cummins VTA 903T diesel engine and (for high water speed) a General Electric LM 120/T700/TC7 gas turbine engine. Such a combat vehicle, with a crew of three, could carry 15 troops.

The EFV will have the Global Positioning System (GPS), Forward-Looking Infrared (FLIR), and night-vision devices for navigating, targeting, and intelligence collection. In place of troops the vehicle can carry 5,130 pounds (2,327 kg) of cargo.

Guns: The 25-mm cannon and 7.62-mm machine gun are coaxially mounted in a turret atop the vehicle.

---

2 Gen. A. M. Gray, USMC, testimony before the House Armed Services Committee, 21 February 1991.

An Expeditionary Fighting Vehicle (EFV) prototype at high speed. The EFV provides significant performance advantages over the AAVP7 series, but its role in future amphibious operations is open to question. The EFV is intended to operate ashore as an armored personnel carrier (General Dynamics Land Systems)

Another view of a prototype Expeditionary Fighting Vehicle (EFV) at high speed, clearly showing the bow planing panel. The twin stacks at the after end of the vehicle will not be fitted in operational vehicles. Still, the EFV is expected to have significant heat and wake signatures when at high speed. (U.S. Marine Corps)

A prototype Expeditionary Fighting Vehicle (EFV) operating as an armored fighting vehicle ashore. The designation change from AAAV to EFV was made in 2003 to help justify the vehicle as being "expeditionary," part of the Navy–Marine Corps transformation to the post–Cold War era. (General Dynamics Land Systems)

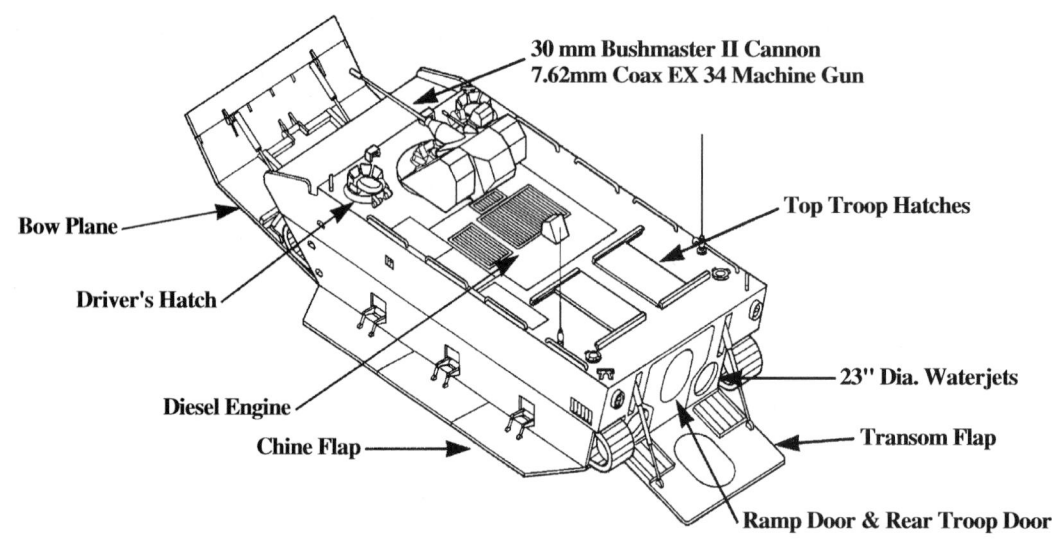

Expeditionary Fighting Vehicle

925 PERSONNEL VEHICLES: AAVP7A1 SERIES (formerly LVTP-7)

Weight:	38,450 pounds (17,477 kg) empty
	50,350 pounds (22,886 kg) loaded
Length:	26 feet (7.9 m) overall
Width:	10¾ feet (3.3 m)
Height:	10¼ feet (3.1 m)
Draft:	5⅚ feet (1.7 m)
Propulsion:	turbo-supercharged diesel engine (Cummins VT400); 400 hp; tracked running gear on land
	2 waterjets in water (3,025 lbst each)
Speed:	40 mph maximum, 20–30 mph cruise on land
	8.4 mph maximum, 8 mph cruise in water
Range:	300 miles at 25 mph on land
	approx. 55 miles at 8 mph in water
Crew:	3 (enlisted)
Troops:	18
Guns:	1 .50-cal machine gun M2
	1 40-mm grenade launcher Mk 19

The AAVP7 is a full-tracked, amphibian vehicle, providing an over-the-beach capability for landing troops and equipment through heavy surf. It is the world's only vehicle capable of operating in rough seas and plunging surf (up to ten feet high). Several hundred have been modernized and are designated AAV7A1 (see

Modernization notes). These vehicles were designed and manufactured by the Ordnance Division of FMC Corporation, San Jose, California. They also are used by the marine forces of Argentina, Brazil, Italy, South Korea, Spain, and Thailand.

Armament: The LVTP-7 was designed to mount a 20-mm cannon coaxially with a machine gun; however, because of development problems, the cannon was deleted. The current .50-cal machine gun is comounted with a 40-mm grenade launcher in a 360° powered turret; the turret holds 200 .50-cal rounds and 98 40-mm rounds. A mine-clearance kit can be fitted for clearing beach obstacles. This consists of a rack launcher firing three 350-foot-long explosive line charges. Detonation is controlled by wire from within the vehicle.

Class: The prototypes for the LVTP-7 design were 15 LVTPX-12 vehicles delivered to the Marines in 1967–1968. These were followed by a production run of 965 LVTP-7s delivered from 1970 to 1974, plus the specialized LVTC and LVTR vehicles described below. In addition, one LVTE-7 prototype of an assault engineer/mine-clearance vehicle was delivered in 1970, but none were series produced. Additional vehicles have been produced for use by the maritime prepositioning forces.

Design: The LVTP-7 was designed to replace the LVTP-5 series amtracs and offered increased land and water speeds and more range, with less vehicle weight. In lieu of troops, the newer vehicle can carry 10,000 pounds (4,545 kg) of cargo. The LVTP-7 has a rear door and ramp for loading/unloading troops and cargo; it can turn 360o within its own length on land or in water.

Modernization: The SLEP-upgraded vehicles were designated LVTP-7A1 prior to the change to AAV7A1. The first updated vehicles were delivered to the Marine Corps on 24 October 1983.

A AAV7 carrying Marines of the 31st Marine Expeditionary Unit departs the amphibious ship FORT MCHENRY *(LSD 43) during an exercise off the coast of South Korea. The top of the troop/cargo compartment can be opened when the vehicle is operating ashore. (2004, U.S. Navy/David Ham)*

An AAVP7 partially submerges as it leaves the well deck of the amphibious ship BONHOMME RICHARD *(LHD 6) during an exercise off Camp Pendleton, California. A machine gun and grenade launcher are comounted in the turret on vehicle's right side. (2004, U.S. Navy/Jennifer Rivera)*

A column of AAVP7s during an exercise at the Coronado Naval Amphibious Base near San Diego. These troops, from the 1st Marine Division were engaged in some of the early fighting in Iraq during Operation Iraqi Freedom. Note the high profile of these vehicles when on land. (2003, U.S. Marine Corps/Bill Lisbon)

79 COMMAND VEHICLES: AAVC7A1 SERIES (FORMERLY LVTC-7)

Weight:	40,187 pounds (18,267 kg) empty
	44,111 pounds (20,050 kg) loaded
Crew:	12 (3 vehicle crew, 5 radiomen, 4 unit commander and staff)
Troops:	none
Guns:	1 7.62-mm machine gun M60D

Except as indicated above, the AAVC7 command vehicles' characteristics are similar to those of the basic AAV7 series. Eighty-five of these vehicles originally were procured for use as command vehicles in amphibious landings. Additional units were procured in the 1980s.

These vehicles are fitted with radios, cryptographic equipment, and telephones. Seventy-seven of the original vehicles are being modernized to the 7A1 configuration.

53 RECOVERY VEHICLES: AAVR7A1 SERIES (FORMERLY LVTR-7)

Weight	47,304 pounds (21,502 kg) empty
	49,853 pounds (22,660 kg) loaded
Crew:	5 (3 vehicle crew, 2 mechanics)
Troops:	none
Guns:	1 7.62-mm machine gun M60D

Except as indicated above, the characteristics of the AAVR7A1 recovery/repair vehicles are similar to the AAV7 series. Sixty of these vehicles originally were procured for the recovery of damaged amtracs during amphibious landings. Additional units were procured during the 1980s.

They are fitted with a 6,000-pound (2,727-kg) capacity telescoping boom-type crane and 30,000-pound (13,636-kg) pull winch, plus maintenance equipment.

POST–WORLD WAR II AMPHIBIAN TRACTORS

The U.S. Marine Corps procured 18,620 amtracs of various LVT/ LVTA models during World War II. The first postwar LVT design produced for the Corps was the LVTP-5 troop carrier and its derivatives: the LVTH-6, mounting a 105-mm howitzer; the LVTE-1 engineer vehicle; the LVTC-1 command vehicle; and the LVTR-1 recovery vehicle. A total of 1,332 of these vehicles were manufactured between 1951 and 1957.

This series was followed by the LVT-7 (now AAV7) series.

AMPHIBIOUS WARPING TUGS

The Navy operates several of these craft, which are fabricated from pontoon sections. They are used to ferry material from amphibious and Maritime Prepositioning Ships (MPS) to shore, to install amphibious fuel and water transfer systems, and to maneuver and support causeways. One warping tug (SLWT) and three or four powered causeway sections (CSP) are carried by many MPS vessel.

The tugs are operated by Amphibious Construction Battalions (ACB) under Commanders, Naval Beach Group 1 (Coronado, California) and Naval Beach Group 2 (Norfolk, Virginia).

21 SIDE LOADABLE WARPING TUGS

Builders:	Oregon Iron Works, Klackamas, Ore.
Displacement:	100 tons light
Length:	80 feet (24.38 m) overall
Beam:	22 feet (6.71 m)
Draft:	
Propulsion:	2 diesel engines (General Motors Detroit Diesel 6V92); 860 bhp; all-azimuth propulsors
Speed:	5 knots
Range:	
Crew:	

These units were delivered in 1994–1995. Each consists of 36 sections that can be easily taken apart and reassembled.

3 SIDE-LOADABLE WARPING TUGS

Number	Number	Number
SLWT 4013	SLWT 4014	SLWT 4015

Builders:	PACECO, Gulfport, Miss.
Weight:	110 tons loaded
Length:	84 feet (25.6 m) overall
Beam:	21¼ feet (6.48 m)
Draft:	2⅔ feet (0.8 m)
Propulsion:	2 turbocharged diesel engines (Detroit Diesel 8V71TI; 850 bhp; 2 waterjet propulsion units with 360° rotating nozzles with 12,500 lbs (5,625 kg) thrust
Speed:	8.5 knots
Range:	75 nm (140 km)
Crew:	8 (enlisted)

These side-loadable warping tugs are modular, consisting of 33 replaceable pontoon "cans" that are bolted together, plus three engine modules, a small control station, and an A-frame lifting device. They can be connected as "pushers" to from one to six unpowered pontoon causeways to form barge ferries; each causeway can carry 100 tons of containerized cargo or vehicles. Without the A-frame and with minor modifications, these craft are designated as causeway section, powered (CSP); that designation is now found on the Navy's ship classification list (see Chapter 3).

The SLWT has a double-drum, diesel-powered A-frame/winch (turbocharged Detroit Model 4-53T) with a lifting capacity of 12 tons. It is fitted with 1,120-pound (504-kg) stern anchor. Fuel capacity is 625 gallons (2,375 liters).

Classification: In the fleet, these craft are (incorrectly) referred to as side-loading warping tugs (SLWT).

An SLWT-type warping tug making speed in San Diego harbor. (1999, William Michael Young)

The SLWT 35 pushing two pontoon causeways. These "tugs" and pontoon causeways are necessary for unloading Maritime Prepositioning Ships (MPS) in remote areas. (1982, U.S. Navy/Tom Hollinberger)

1 AMPHIBIOUS WARPING TUG

Number	
LWT 1 (also 85WT681)	

Builders:	Campbell Machine Works, San Diego, Calif.
Weight:	61 tons light
Length:	85 feet (25.9 m) overall
Beam:	22 feet (6.7 m)
Draft:	6'1½ feet (2.1 m)
Propulsion:	2 diesel engines (General Motors Detroit Diesel 8V71); 420 bhp; 2 steerable propellers
Speed:	9 knots
Range:	
Crew:	6 (enlisted)

Two units of this aluminum-construction design were delivered in 1970 The LWT 2 (85WT682) has been discarded, but this unit has been retained.

4 SELF-PROPELLED JOINT MODULAR LIGHTERS

Builders:	Baltimore Marine Industries, Maryland
Displacement:	
Length:	40 feet (12.19 m) overall
Beam:	8 feet (2.44 m)
Draft:	
Propulsion:	1 diesel engine (Cummins QSK19); 760 bhp; 1 waterjet
Speed:	
Range:	
Personnel:	

These craft serve as tugs for pontoon-like modules used for unloading maritime prepositioning ships and merchant ships, including operations of the Army's Joint Logistics Over-the-Shore (JOTS) program. A total of 60 units were procured in 2000, but only these four units are self-propelled. The non-self-propelled units are moved by tugs.

A self-propelled joint modular lighter. (2000, Kurt Greiner)

The SLWT 35 from Amphibious Construction Battalion 1 serves as a pusher for pontoon causeways; Marine trucks are parked on the causeways. (1992, U.S. Navy/Tom Hollinberger)

Warping tugs handle pontoon barges as the Seabee ship CAPE MAY (T-AKR 5063) unloads Army trucks during an exercise near Puerto Castilla, Honduras. (2004, U.S. Navy/C. Warner)

CHAPTER 21

Patrol and Special Warfare Craft

Crewmen of CYCLONE-class coastal patrol ships, wearing "camis," which have become a Navy utility uniform, are addressed by the Commander, Amphibious Group 2, Rear Admiral Michael P. Nowakowski, at Little Creek. Small combatants such as the CYCLONES have never been popular in the U.S. Navy. (2002, U.S. Navy/Kelley Anderson)

The role of special warfare craft in the U.S. Navy has increased significantly in the post–Cold War era with the Navy's emphasis on littoral warfare and special operations forces. This role has been further enhanced following the terrorist events of 11 September 2001 and the need for increased U.S. port security.

The largest Navy ships in this category are the CYCLONE-class coastal patrol ships (PC), which when laid down beginning in 1991, were the first major patrol craft to be built for the U.S. Navy

in more than a decade. The Navy's leadership has not supported the operation of these ships and on several occasions has attempted to discard them; for several years, the craft were funded by the U.S. Special Operations Command.

During 1998, the Navy gave serious consideration to the transfer up to one-half of the CYCLONE class to the Coast Guard, which would have operated the ships in support of both the U.S. Special Operations Command and Coast Guard requirements. The Navy also planned to transfer several to other countries, including Colombia, Egypt, and the Philippines. In the event, the PCs—except for the CYCLONE—were retained in Navy service under the control/funding of the U.S. Special Operations Command.

In 2002–2003, in the aftermath of terrorist attacks on the World Trade Center and Pentagon, the Department of Defense directed the transfer of the ships from Commander, Naval Special Warfare Command, a subordinate organization of the U.S. Special Operations Command, to the Atlantic and Pacific Fleet commanders for use in anti-terrorism force protection for Navy ships and other maritime homeland security roles. The nine PCs in the Atlantic Fleet were transferred on 1 October 2002, and the four PCs in the Pacific Fleet were transferred on 17 March 2003. Within the fleet organizations, they are assigned to the respective Naval Surface Force commanders.

Finally, in the fall of 2004, five units of the class were transferred to the Coast Guard. The ships are on four-year loan, which is a nominal duration, and they may be operated by the Coast Guard for a shorter or longer period. The Navy retains maintenance responsibility for the ships.

There is no Navy interest in a successor large patrol ship or craft, in part because of the planned Littoral Combat Ship (LCS), which could carry out some coastal patrol/anti-submarine functions. The LCS also might have a SEAL (Sea-Air-Land forces) support mission module (see Chapter 17).

The CYCLONE class was the Navy's third post–World War II "large" patrol series of ships to be built. The Navy's six hydrofoil missile craft (PHM) have been discarded, most after little more than a decade of operational service. Designed as Cold War attack craft to counter Soviet warships in coastal areas (such as the Aegean Sea), they were never forward deployed and spent virtually all of their service in the Caribbean area engaged in anti-drug operations. Also discarded have been the earlier ASHEVILLE-class patrol gunboats (PGM/PG) constructed in the 1960s. Those ships participated in offshore patrol operations during the Vietnam War.

The 14-ship CYCLONE class followed a series of U.S. Navy failures during the 1980s to develop patrol/special warfare craft. The earlier efforts had the design designations PBM, PCM, SWCM (Sea Viking), SWCX, and PXM, the last being a hydrofoil patrol craft. The Navy evaluated several advanced technology combat craft in the 1960s and produced several hundred coastal and riverine patrol and support craft. Those, too, have been discarded, except for a few craft operated by Special Boat Unit 22 (see below).

During the Vietnam War, the lack of a capability in small combatant craft forced the Navy to procure Norwegian-built fast patrol boats and to adopt commercial designs for naval use. The Navy subsequently sought to keep abreast of small craft design, and during the early 1980s, U.S. yards delivered a series of Navy-designed missile craft (PCG/PGG types) to Saudi Arabia, as well as smaller inshore and riverine combat craft to several other countries.

Many older patrol and SEAL support craft have been discarded.

Armament: No anti-submarine weapons are carried by U.S. patrol craft.

Classification: The smaller, unnamed patrol boats and craft are individually designated by hull length, hull type, calendar year of construction, and consecutive hull number of that type built during the year. Thus, 68PB842 indicates the second 68-foot PB-type craft built in 1984. The first two letters in this scheme generally are used in the designation:

PB   patrol boat
RP   river patrol boat

Operational: All Navy special warfare craft except for the PC coastal patrol ships are assigned to the Naval Special Warfare Command, which is the naval component of the U.S. Special Operations Command (see Chapter 4). The major Navy special warfare forces are located at the Naval Amphibious Base Coronado (San Diego), California, and the Naval Amphibious Base Little Creek (Norfolk), Virginia. (See Figure 21-1.)

NAVAL SPECIAL WARFARE COMMAND

The Naval Special Warfare (NSW) Command has approximately 5,400 active-duty personnel, including 2,450 SEALs and 600 special warfare combatant craft crewmen. NSW also can call on the services of some 1,200 reservists, including approximately 325 SEALs, 125 combatant craft crewmen, and 775 support personnel. The number of active-duty SEALs is being increased.

Most NSW units are based at Coronado and Little Creek. Four Naval Special Warfare Groups direct the Navy's SEAL teams, Naval Special Warfare Units (NSWU), SEAL Delivery Vehicle (SDV) teams, and Special Boat Teams (SBT).

The NSWUs with multiple components and capabilities are deploying components, including SEAL teams and boat units. They deploy on a six-month rotation, generally supporting deploying surface forces. They include command and control faculties to operate in forward areas. Units also are permanently deployed at Stuggart, Germany (NSWU-2); Rota, Spain (NSWU-10); Guam (NSWU-1); and Bahrain (NSWU-3). NSWU-4 was at Roosevelt Roads, Puerto Rico; that unit was decommissioned in 2003 following the closure of nearby Vieques Island to Navy live-fire exercises.

The SEAL delivery vehicle teams are specially trained SEALs and support personnel who operate and maintain delivery vehicles,

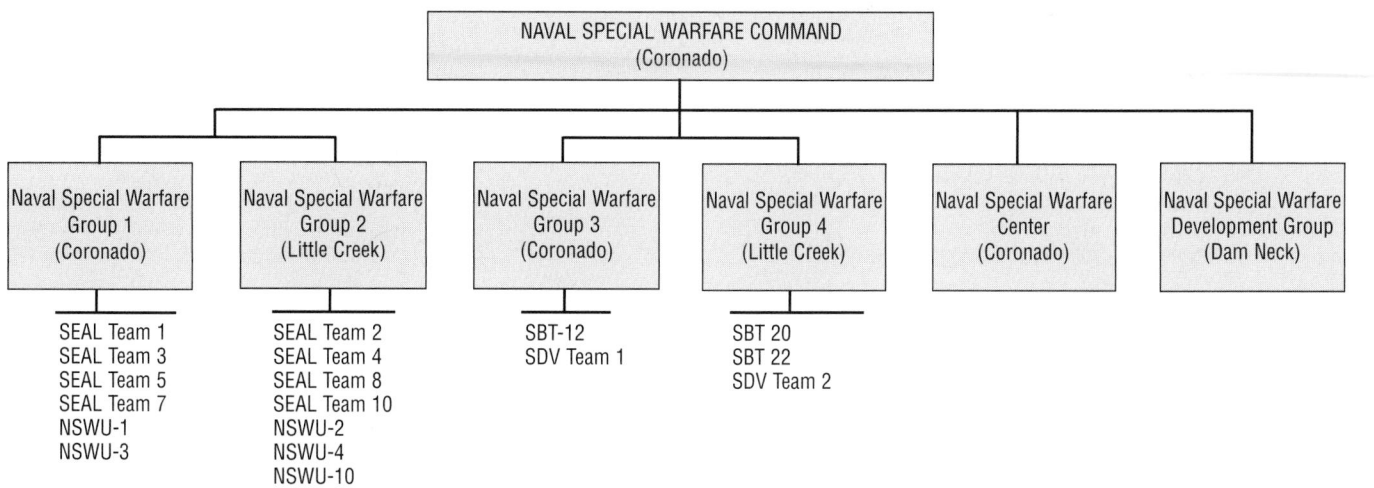

Figure 21-1. NAVAL SPECIAL WARFARE COMMAND

Dry Deck Shelters (DDS), and the Advanced Seal Delivery System (ASDS) (see Chapter 12). SDV Team 1 is based at Pearl Harbor, Hawaii, and SDV Team 2 is at Little Creek.

The previous Special Boat Squadrons (SBS) transitioned into a component of the NSWGs in Fiscal Year (FY) 2003.

The SEAL team is the basic unit of naval special warfare. The team table of organization provides for up to eight 16-man platoons, each commanded by a lieutenant. The platoons are divided into two 8-man squadrons. The platoons generally undertake independent operations, including sabotage, demolition, intelligence collection, hydrographic survey, and the training and advising of friendly military forces. SEAL teams and squads can be inserted into an operational area by helicopter, surface craft, or submarines, or by parachuting from aircraft.

The Naval Special Warfare Development Group at Dam Neck, Virginia, formerly was SEAL Team 6. This group is responsible for U.S. counterterrorist activities in the maritime environment, including hostage rescue. The group also manages the test, evaluation, and development of technology applicable to these forces.

The Naval Special Warfare Center at Coronado serves as the "schoolhouse" for basic and advanced special warfare training, including SEAL training.

Naval small craft also are operated by the Naval Reserve, which has two major subordinate commands, Naval Coastal Warfare Group 1 at San Diego and Naval Coastal Warfare Group 2 at Norfolk. The groups control a large number of reserve Harbor Defense Commands (HDC), Inshore Boat Units (IBU), Mobile Inshore Undersea Warfare Units (MIUWU), and Naval Coastal Warfare Squadrons (NCWRons). These units are located at reserve centers throughout the United States. (See Figure 21-2.)

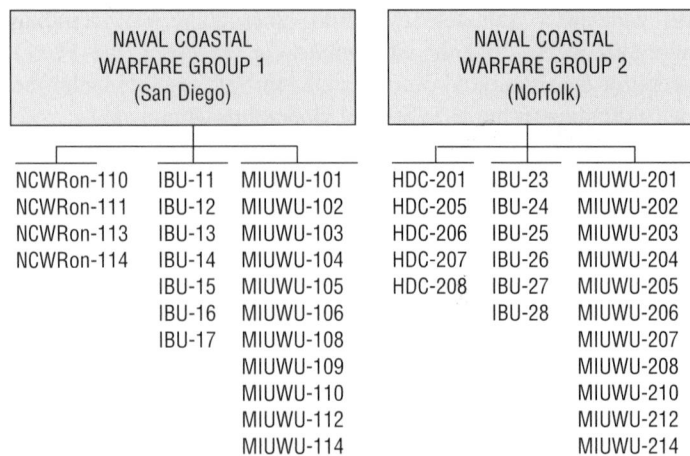

Figure 21-2. NAVAL RESERVE FORCES

Naval special warfare forces are being enlarged, and there have been several organizational changes during the past few years, including the establishment of Naval Special Warfare Groups 3 and 4. The latest change when this edition of *Ships and Aircraft* went to press was the redesignation of HDC Units 110, 111, 113, and 114 to Naval Coastal Warfare Squadrons 30, 31, 33, and 34, respectively. That change was effective 25 May 2004.

Historical: The Naval Special Warfare Command was commissioned on 16 April 1987 at the Naval Amphibious Base Coronado (San Diego) as the naval component of the U.S. Special Operations Command headquartered in Tampa, Florida.

Operational: Navy SEALs were among the first U.S. troops on the ground in the invasions of Afghanistan (2001) and Iraq (2003).

8 COASTAL PATROL SHIPS: "CYCLONE" CLASS

Number	Name	FY	Laid down	Launched	Comm.	Status
PC 1	CYCLONE	90	22 June 1991	1 Feb 1992	7 Aug 1993[1]	(see text); to Philippines 2003
PC 2	TEMPEST	90	30 Sep 1991	4 Apr 1992	21 Aug 1993	to Coast Guard 2004
PC 3	HURRICANE	90	20 Nov 1991	6 June 1992	15 Oct 1993	**PA**
PC 4	MONSOON	90	15 Feb 1992	10 Oct 1992	22 Jan 1994	to Coast Guard 2004
PC 5	TYPHOON	90	15 May 1992	3 Mar 1993	12 Feb 1994	**AA**
PC 6	SIROCCO	90	20 June 1992	29 May 1993	11 June 1994[2]	**AA**
PC 7	SQUALL	90	17 Feb 1993	28 Aug 1993	4 July 1994	**PA**
PC 8	ZEPHYR	90	6 Mar 1993	3 Dec 1993	15 Oct 1994	to Coast Guard 2004
PC 9	CHINOOK	91	16 June 1993	6 Feb 1994	28 Jan 1995	**AA**
PC 10	FIREBOLT	91	17 Sep 1993	10 June 1994	10 June 1995	**AA**
PC 11	WHIRLWIND	91	4 Mar 1994	9 Sep 1994	1 July 1995	**AA**
PC 12	THUNDERBOLT	91	9 June 1994	2 Dec 1994	7 Oct 1995	**AA**
PC 13	SHAMAL	91	22 Sep 1994	3 Mar 1995	27 Jan 1996	to Coast Guard 2004
PC 14	TORNADO	96	25 Aug 1998	7 June 1999	24 June 2000	to Coast Guard 2004

Builders:	Bollinger Shipyards, Lockport, La.	Personnel:	28 (4 officers + 24 enlisted)
Displacement:	331 tons full load	Troops:	9 (SEALs or other passengers)
Length:	157 5/12 feet (48.0 m) waterline	Missiles:	hand-held Stinger point-defense missile launchers
	170 1/2 feet (52.0 m) overall	Guns:	2 25-mm Bushmaster cannon Mk 38 (2 single)
Beam:	25 feet (7.6 m)		4 .50-cal machine guns M2HB (2 twin)
Draft:	7 7/8 feet (2.4 m)		2 7.62-mm machine guns M60 (2 single)
Propulsion:	4 diesel engines (Paxman Valenta 16VRP-200);		2 40-mm grenade launchers Mk 19 (2 single)
	13,400 bhp; 4 shafts	Radars:	2 Sperry RASCAR 2500 surface search (S and X bands)
Speed:	35 knots	Sonars:	Wesmar side-scanning (HF)
Range:	2,000 nm (3,700 km) at 12 knots	EW systems:	APR-39A(V)1 radar warning receiver

These are small combatants intended for coastal interdiction and the support of special operations forces, primarily Navy SEALs. They were specifically intended as replacements for the Navy's overage PB Mk III craft. The CYCLONE class was "designed to cost," hence a readily available foreign design was adopted. According to the reference work *Combat Fleets of the World*, these ships "have limited endurance for their size, and their combat systems and

ammunition allowance do not compare well with those of similar ships in most other navies."[3]

---

1 The CYCLONE was the first Navy ship commissioned at the U.S. Naval Academy.
2 The SIROCCO was commissioned at the Washington Navy Yard. She was the first U.S. Navy ship to be placed in commission at the yard since 1879.
3 A. D. Baker III, *Combat Fleets of the World 1998-1999* (Annapolis, Md.: Naval Institute Press, 1998), p. 1031.

In anticipation of completion of the TORNADO, the CYCLONE was decommissioned and stricken on 28 February 2000 and transferred to the Coast Guard the following day. Most of her Navy crew was transferred to the TORNADO. According to unofficial reports, the CYCLONE was transferred to avoid the Navy having to stand up another PC crew.

The Coast Guard did not activate the CYCLONE; she was towed to the Coast Guard Yard in Curtis Bay, Maryland, and remained there until transferred to the Philippine Navy on 6 March 2003. The ship had been in active U.S. Navy service for six and a half years.

In 1998, the THUNDERBOLT was commissioned as a Coast Guard cutter for a six-month operational evaluation; she was returned to Navy. Six of these ships (the PC 2–4 and 10–12) were placed under Coast Guard tactical control for homeland security missions with Navy crews and Coast Guard Law Enforcement Detachments (LED) on 5 November 2001; the seven others were placed under Coast Guard tactical control on 27 December 2001. However, permanent transfers were not made because of Coast Guard funding limitations, and the ships later were reassigned from the overall control/funding of the U.S. Special Operations Command to the Atlantic and Pacific Fleet commanders (see above).[4]

Five units were decommissioned on 30 September 2004 and transferred to the Coast Guard on 1 October 2004. They retain their Navy designations with the Coast Guard W prefix (see Chapter 32). The CYCLONE was not assigned a hull number after her transfer.

The Pacific Fleet PCs are based at Naval Air Station North Island (San Diego), California, and the Atlantic Fleet PCs are at the Naval Amphibious Base Little Creek (Norfolk), Virginia.

Armament: These ships were to be fitted with the Stabilized Weapon Platform System (SWPS), installed on the fantail. The SWPS could launch a variety of missiles, including the Hellfire, Stinger, and Hydra-70, with a comounted 25-mm or 30-mm cannon, a television camera, laser rangefinder and designator, and Forward-Looking Infrared (FLIR) sensor. The system was not installed.

The CYCLONE-class ammunition allowance is:

Stinger missile launcher	6 ready missiles
25-mm cannon	2,000 rounds
.50-cal machine gun	2,000 rounds
7.62-mm machine gun	2,000 rounds
grenade launcher	1,000 rounds

Builders: The building yard previously was named Bollinger Machine Shop & Shipyard.

Class: The Navy planned to construct 16 of these ships when the program was defined in the late 1980s; by the time the lead ship was ordered, the program had been reduced to 13 units.

Bollinger was awarded a contract for the construction of eight ships, with an option for five additional units, on 3 August 1990; the five-ship option was exercised on 19 July 1991.

In the Fiscal Year (FY) 1996 budget, without a Navy request, Congress funded $20 million for advance procurement of another ship of the CYCLONE class. Although not included in the Department of Defense shipbuilding plan, the ship was fully funded in FY 1997 as a political benefit for the shipyard area.

Classification: These ships originally were designated PBC, for patrol boat, coastal. They were changed to PC, for patrol, coastal, on 25 July 1991; however, that classification does not appear on the 1993 Secretary of the Navy instruction listing ship classifications.

The classification PC originated in World War I as the *hull number* for a series of 110-foot (33.5-m) wood-hull submarine chasers given *names* in an SC series. Beginning in 1940, a series of steel-hull submarine chasers was built with PC designations, and in October 1942, all wood-hull sub chasers were given SC hull numbers.

---

4 Each ship costs approx $3 million per year to operate.

Twin .50-caliber machine guns have been fitted to the bridge wings of the CYCLONE class. With other automatic weapons, the ships have potent firepower for close-in engagements. Seaman Electronics Technician Robert Tetzlaff stands lookout as the CHINOOK operates in the Persian Gulf. (2003, U.S.Navy/William F. Gowdy)

A 25-mm Bushmaster cannon is fitted forward in the CYCLONE class. This weapon is in wide use as a secondary battery in numerous other Navy ships, as well as aboard Coast Guard cutters. A 30-mm version has been developed. Engineman 3rd Class Edward Bessette scans the horizon from the CHINOOK. (2003, U.S. Navy/William F. Gowdy)

The World War II steel-hull program reached hull number PC 1603 (completed in 1944); most were 173-foot (52.7-m) oceangoing craft designated PC, although the PCE-PCS-SC types shared the same numbering series. Postwar ships with PC-PCE designations built in U.S. and foreign shipyards, all for use by foreign navies, took the series to PC 1646; the PC 1647 and 1648 were canceled. Thus, the new-construction CYCLONE-class PCs should properly have begun with hull no. 1649—not PC 1.

Design: The PC hull/propulsion design is based on the Vosper Thornycroft-built missile craft of the RAMADAN class constructed for Egypt (six units completed 1981–1982), Oman (four units completed 1982–1989), and Kenya (two units completed 1987).

The U.S. ships have steel hulls with aluminum superstructures; 1-inch (25-mm) appliqué armor is fitted to portions of the superstructure to protect against small arms fire. Endurance is ten days.

A single 20-foot (6.1-m) Rigid Hull Inflatable Boat (RHIB) normally is carried by each PC. The TORNADO was completed with a stern ramp to facilitate the handling of RHIBS; the MONSOON, SHAMAL, TEMPEST, and ZEPHYR subsequently were modified with a similar ramp.

Electronics: The ships have two Mk 52 chaff/decoy launchers. An Identification Friend or Foe (IFF) transponder is fitted but no interrogator.

Names: These ships are named for weather elements.

Operational: These ships initially were placed "In Commission, Special," at the Bollinger yard to permit Navy crews to take the ships to ports where they were placed in "In Commission, Full," the formal commissioning ceremony (listed above).

The first four ships of the class participated in the U.S. occupation of Haiti in 1994; the MONSOON ran aground during coastal patrol activities. During the operations off Haiti, the boats carried

The TORNADO, prior to transfer to the Coast Guard, with her stern gate open, showing the improved rigid hull inflatable boat recovery system fitted in some of these ships. High-speed recovery reduces the exposure of the PC as well as SEALs to enemy fire. (2000, Bollinger Shipyards)

up to 25 SEALs while on multiday patrols.

The first overseas deployment of this class began on 21 April 1995, when the TYPHOON and SIROCCO departed Norfolk for operations in the Baltic and Mediterranean Seas.

The CHINOOK and FIREBOLT deployed to the Persian Gulf in January 2003 and participated in Operation Iraqi Freedom (2003). They remain in the Gulf, with replacement crews being flown out from the United States, drawn from other Atlantic Fleet PCs.

Personnel: Originally intended to be commanded by lieutenants, in fact these ships are commanded by lieutenant commanders.

The CHINOOK in the Persian Gulf. The coastal patrol ships, of an outdated design, are non-stealthy craft. The CHINOOK has the improved stern configuration with handling gear for rigid hull inflatable boats. The lead ship of the class has been transferred to the Philippine Navy. The U.S. Navy periodically has sought to discard the PCs. (2003, U.S. Navy/William F. Gowdy)

The FIREBOLT off Yorktown, Virginia. The bulky, squared superstructure and lattice mast contribute to the ship's large radar cross section. The FIREBOLT has a crane at the stern for handling rigid hull inflatable boats. The PCs have a splinter camouflage paint scheme, the only U.S. ships now with a camouflage motif. (1999, U.S. Navy/William H. Clarke)

The TEMPEST escorting the carrier HARRY S. TRUMAN (CVN 75) as the flattop departs Naval Station Norfolk for operations off the Atlantic coast. The Coast Guard shares such escort functions with the Navy at various U.S. ports and shipyards. (2003, U.S. Navy/Danny Ewing Jr.)

GUIDED MISSILE CRAFT: EX-SOVIET TARANTUL I CLASS

The former East German missile craft HIDDENSEE is now a museum/exhibition ship at Battleship Cove in Fall River, Massachusetts. Completed in 1995, the ship was built in the Soviet Union for service in the East German Navy. She was transferred to the U.S. Navy in 1992 for trials and evaluation.

Listed as "floating equipment" and designated 185NS9201, the craft was operated by the Naval Air Warfare Center at Patuxent River, Maryland, until 18 April 1996. She was transferred to Battleship Cove on 20 October 1996.

The HIDDENSEE was a Tarantul I-class missile craft; see 16th Edition/page 194 for characteristics.

PATROL COMBATANTS—MISSILE (HYDROFOIL): "PEGASUS" CLASS

Number	Name	Comm.	Notes
PHM 1	PEGASUS	1977	
PHM 2	HERCULES	1983	
PHM 3	TAURUS	1981	Decommissioned and stricken
PHM 4	AQUILA	1982	30 July 1993
PHM 5	ARIES	1983	
PHM 6	GEMINI	1983	

These were high-speed, heavily armed missile craft, originally intended to conduct sea control operations in restricted seas. However, from their completion, they were employed primarily in anti-drug operations in the Caribbean area.

Class: This design was one of several new warship types initiated by Admiral Elmo R. Zumwalt when he was Chief of Naval Operations (1970–1974). A class of 30 craft was planned. When Zumwalt left office, the Navy's leadership reduced the program to only the prototype; however, congressional pressure led to the first "flight" of six ships, already funded, being completed.

See 15th Edition/pages 197–98 for characteristics.

2 + ? SEMI-SUBMERSIBLE SEAL CRAFT

Number	Name	Completed	Status
71NS0301	Sealion 1	Jan 2003	Trials
	Sealion 2	2004	Trials

Builders:	Oregon Iron Works, Clackamas, Ore.
Displacement:	
Length:	71 feet (21.65 m) overall
Beam:	
Draft:	
Propulsion:	2 diesel engines; 2 waterjets
Speed:	40+ knots
Crew:	3 (enlisted)
Troops:	8 (SEALs)
Guns:	none

These are technology demonstration craft for high-speed, semisubmersible SEAL delivery craft. The name SEALION has been corrupted into an acronym for SEAL Insertion, Observation, and Neutralization.

The existing craft were limited in size for transport in a C-17 cargo aircraft. The Navy is evaluating that restriction for future SEALION-type craft.

The craft are being evaluated by Naval Special Warfare Group 4 at Norfolk, Virginia. No decision has been made concerning the construction of additional units of this general design.

Design: The design provides for a high-speed craft that, when approaching an objective, can slow and partially submerge through the use of ballast tanks. Only a few inches of the hull and minimal superstructure are above the surface in the partially submerged configuration.

The craft has a low radar cross section and low heat and wake signatures when operating in a stealth mode.

Two RHIBs can be carried.

There are no berthing, mess, or head facilities in the craft.

The SEALION 1 at high speed. This technology demonstration craft can reach speeds in excess of 40 knots as a fast planing craft; at slow speeds, the craft can ballast down until there are only a few inches of freeboard. Eight SEALs and two rigid hull inflatable boats can be carried, exiting through a large stern door. (2004, U.S. Navy)

SEA SPECTRE PATROL BOATS

Two PB Mk III Sea Spectre patrol boats are retained for use as gun system trials craft. (See Chapter 25.)

20 SPECIAL OPERATIONS CRAFT: Mk V TYPE

Builders:	Trinity-Halter Marine, Gulfport, Miss.
Displacement:	approx. 75 tons full load
Length:	82 feet (25.0 m) overall
Beam:	17 feet (5.18 m)
Draft:	5 feet (1.52 m)
Propulsion:	2 diesel engines (MTU 16V396 TE94); 4,770 hp; 2 waterjets
Speed:	50+ knots
Range:	600 nm (1,112 km) at 35 knots
Crew:	5 (enlisted)
Troops:	16 (SEALs or other passengers)
Guns:	combinations of .50-cal machine guns M2HB, 7.62-mm machine guns M60E, and 40-mm grenade launchers Mk 19
Radars:	navigation

The Trinity-Halter design won the Navy's competition against the Peterson Builders' Mk V Sea Stalker design for a special warfare craft (see 16th Edition/pages 188–89).

These craft support special operations forces: insertion and extraction (primarily of SEALs), and limited coastal patrol and interdiction operations. They entered service from 1995 to 1999.

Design: These craft are fabricated of aluminum. Up to four

The stern of a Mk V special operations craft showing the Rigid Hull Inflatable Boat (RHIB) recovery ramp and stowage position. Several RHIBs can be carried. (1999, Leo Van. Ginderen]

combat rubber raiding craft can be carried, launched over a stern ramp. The Mk Vs can be air transported by C-5 Galaxy aircraft (two craft plus their support equipment).

Operational: Twelve Mk V craft are assigned to Special Boat Squadron 1 at Coronado and eight to Special Boat Squadron 2 at Little Creek.

A Mk V special operations craft at high speed during operations in the Persian Gulf area. This craft has four twin .50-caliber machine guns mounted amidships. Formerly assigned to special boat squadrons, the craft now are assigned to Naval Special Warfare Groups 3 and 4. (2003, U.S. Navy/Arlo K. Abramhamson)

The after aspect of a Mk V special operations craft, with a rigid hull inflatable boat being carried on the stern. This craft has tripod pintels for mounting machine guns or Mk 19 grenade launchers. Up to 16 SEALs can be carried for short periods. (1999, Leo Van Ginderen)

17 SMALL UNIT RIVERINE CRAFT (SURC)

Builders:	SadeBoats International, Port Orchard, Ore.
Weight:	
Length:	39 feet (11.9 m) overall
Beam:	
Draft:	¾ feet (0.23 m)
Propulsion:	2 inboard gasoline engines; 880 hp; 2 waterjets
Speed:	35 knots
Range:	300 nm (555 km)
Crew:	2 (enlisted)
Troops:	13
Guns:	machine guns and grenade launchers
Radars:	commercial navigation

Procurement of the Small Unit Riverine Craft (SURC) is under way as a replacement for the Marine rigid raider craft (see below). Raytheon Integrated Defense Systems is the prime contractor for the SURC.

The first two SURCs were delivered in early 2004, with 17 planned for delivery by early 2005. The SURCs initially are being operated by the Small Craft Company, Headquarters and Support Battalion, 2nd Marine Division, at Camp Lejeune, North Carolina. The final production numbers were not established when this edition of *Ships and Aircraft* went to press

Design: The hull is Glass-Reinforced Plastic (GRP). The craft can remain afloat as a survival platform when filled with water.

The SURC is air transportable by CH-53D and CH-53E helicopters, with a goal of also being sling-carried by an MV-22 Osprey Short Take-off/Vertical Landing (STOVL) aircraft. It can be carried internally by a variety of transport aircraft.

70+ RIGID HULL INFLATABLE BOATS (RHIB)

Builders:	United States Marine, New Orleans, La.
Weight:	17,400 lbs (7,893 kg)
Length:	35¹⁄₂ feet (10.95 m) overall
Beam:	10⁷⁄₁₂ feet (3.23 m)
Draft:	2¹⁄₁₂ feet (0.89 m)
Propulsion:	2 turbocharged diesel engines (Caterpillar 3126); 940 bhp; 2 waterjets
Speed:	45 knots maximum
	33 knots sustained
Range:	200 nm (370 km) at 33 knots
Crew:	3 (enlisted)
Troops:	8 SEALs
Guns:	(see notes)
Radars:	Furuno 841 navigation

These craft are employed by SEALs for ship-to-shore insertion/extraction and are carried by some surface combatants for security and merchant ship inspection functions. They are faster, quieter, and have a greater range than previous boats; also, troops being carried are subjected to less spray than in previous boats. An entire SEAL squad can be transported in these craft.

Design: The RHIB hull is a deep V fabricated of fiberglass and Kevlar.

Guns: Two mounts are provided for machine guns or grenade launchers.

A graphic showing the new Small Unit Riverine Craft (SURC) with an open cockpit and three machine guns fitted. (U.S. Marine Corps)

An early SURC—with covered cockpit—during trials at Camp Lejeune, North Carolina. This craft has two gun pintels forward and a machine gun fitted aft. It features low-noise engines, shallow draft, and a Global Positioning System (GPS). (U.S. Marine Corps/Jerad W. Alexander)

A Rigid Hull Inflatable Boat (RHIB) from the amphibious ship SHREVEPORT *(LPD 12) during an exercise in the Arabian Sea. Note the twin-arm mast that mounts the craft's radome and other antennas. The after section of the RHIB can be rigged with seats for troops or with gun mounts. (2001, U.S. Navy/David C. Mercil)*

Naval Special Warfare combat craft crewmen man the .50-caliber machine guns mounted forward and aft on this rigid hull inflatable boat as it moves at slow speed in the Persian Gulf area. (2003, U.S. Navy/ Arlo K. Abrahamson)

A RHIB carries special boat team personnel during operations in the Persian Gulf area, where they are used extensively for patrol and to board and search merchant ships. There are machine guns forward and aft, the latter on the fantail, behind the bench seating. (2003, U.S. Navy/Michael J. Pusnik Jr.)

32 RIVERINE ASSAULT CRAFT: STINGER TYPE

Builders:	SeaArk Marine, Monticello, Ark. (14 units)
	Swiftships, Morgan City, La. (18 units)
Weight:	7.5 tons full load
Length:	34½ feet (10.64 m)
Beam:	9¼ feet (2.82 m)
Draft:	2⅙ feet (0.66 m)
Propulsion:	2 diesel engines (BTA5.9M2); 600 bhp; 1 waterjet
Speed:	38 knots maximum
	34.5 knots sustained
Range:	
Crew:	4 (enlisted)
Troops:	8 SEALS
Guns:	2 .50-cal machine guns M2HB
	2 7.62-mm machine guns M60 (see notes)
Radars:	SPS-69 navigation

These "Stinger"-type riverine patrol craft replaced the older PBR type, which dated to the Vietnam War (see below). They were delivered from 1990 to 1994. They can carry four Combat Rubber Raiding Craft (CRRC).

Design: These craft are aluminum. Four weapon mountings are provided; Mk 19 grenade launchers also can be fitted.

Stinger at high speed with men posing at the craft's two .50-caliber machine guns. These craft are distinguished by their low cockpits and low-mounted radome. (1990, SeaArk Marine)

5 RIVERINE PATROL BOATS (PBR): Mk 2 TYPE

Builders:	Uniflite, Bellingham, Wash.
Displacement:	7.5 tons light
	8.9 tons full load
Length:	32 feet (9.75 m) overall
Beam:	11⅔ feet (3.6 m)
Draft:	2⁷⁄₁₂ feet (0.8 m)
Propulsion:	2 diesel engines (General Motors 6V53 or
	6V53T or 4-53N); 430 bhp; 2 waterjets
Speed:	24 knots
Range:	150 nm (278 m) at 23 knots
Crew:	4 or 5 (enlisted)
Missiles:	none
Guns:	1 60-mm mortar Mk 4 in some units
	1 25-mm Bushmaster cannon Mk 38
	1 .50-cal machine gun
	1 40-mm grenade launcher Mk 19
Radars:	navigation

These heavily armed craft were developed for riverine warfare in Vietnam. All are operated by the Naval Reserve Force. These craft are assigned to Special Boat Unit 22 for Naval Reserve training.

Class: More than 500 PBRs were built in 1965–1973, with most transferred to South Vietnam after being used by the U.S. Navy. Additional units were built for the U.S. Navy in the early 1980s (with General Motors [GM] 4-53N diesel engines). Subsequently,

replacement hulls have been procured commercially for refit and replacement of existing boats in a one-for-one "swap." The newer boats are being provided with GM 6V53T engines.

The 31RP66108, 31RP7023, and 31RP9999—not included in the above type totals—are at the Naval Historical Center at the Washington Navy Yard.

Design: These craft have fiberglass hulls and ceramic armor. They can be transported in C-5 Galaxy cargo aircraft.

Engineering: The waterjet propulsion enables the boats to operate in shallow and debris-filled water with a very high degree of maneuverability.

One of the few surviving riverine patrol boats, a type that was used widely in the riverine operations of the Vietnam War. There are gun shields aft for mounting machine guns. (1988, Giorgio Arra)

Another view of a riverine patrol boat Mk 2 under way in San Francisco Bay. The Coast Guard aids-to-navigation boat 55101 is in the background. (1988, Giorgio Arra)

18 INTERIM RIGID INFLATABLE BOATS (IRIB)

Builders:	Novamarine and Bollinger Shipyards, Lockport, La.
Weight:	
Length:	30 feet (9.14 m)
Beam:	9 feet (2.74 m)
Draft:	2 feet (0.61 m)
Propulsion:	2 diesel engines (Iveco); 600 bhp; 2 waterjets
Speed:	30+ knots
Range:	
Crew:	2 (enlisted)
Troops:	8 SEALs
Guns:	1 7.62-mm machine gun M60
	or 1 40-mm grenade launcher Mk 19
Radars:	Furuno 1731 navigation

These were considered interim craft, pending production of the more-capable RHIB. The original contract with Novamarine was canceled when that firm went bankrupt, and a replacement contract was placed with Bollinger. The RIBs were delivered in 1992–1993.

The craft have been criticized as having too little freeboard, and the program was canceled after 18 units were completed.

Design: These craft have fiberglass-coated hulls with Hypalon-coated, nylon inflated sponsons.

Approx. 120 MARINE RIGID RAIDER CRAFT

Builders:	Boston Whaler, Rockport, Mass.
Weight:	approx. 2,400 lbs
Length:	22⅓ feet (6.81 m)
Beam:	7⁵⁄₁₂ feet (2.26 m)
Draft:	1½ feet (0.46 m)
Propulsion:	2 outboard motors
Speed:	35 knots
Range:	135 nm (250 km) at 32 knots
Crew:	1 (enlisted)
Troops:	10
Guns:	1 7.62-mm machine gun M60
Radars:	commercial navigation

These craft are widely used by deployed (afloat) Marine units. They replaced the Zodiac rigid inflatable boats. The rigid raider craft has performed marginally as a riverine craft because of its limited payload, slow speed, lack of self-protection, and excessive noise signature. In addition, the craft are beyond their expected ten-year service lives.

They were delivered beginning in 1998.

Design: The craft are built of Glass-Reinforced Plastic (GRP).

COMBAT RUBBER RAIDING CRAFT (CRRC)

Weight:	265 pounds (120 kg)
Length:	15⁵⁄₁₂ feet (4.7 m) overall
Beam:	6¼ feet (1.9 m)
Draft:	2 feet (0.61 m)
Propulsion:	2 outboard gasoline engines; 140 hp
Speed:	approx. 20 knots
Range:	60+ nm (111 km)
Manning:	1 (enlisted)
Troops:	8
Guns:	none
Radars:	none

Inflatable Combat Rubber Raiding Craft (CRRC) are used for clandestine insertion/extraction of SEAL forces. They can be carried and launched from submarines and aircraft, as well as from surface ships and craft. The RHIBs are superior in performance.

An 18-gallon (68-liter) fuel bladder is fitted to the craft.

A Novmarine-built interim rigid inflatable boat under way off San Diego. The mast–radar arrangement on the Bollinger boats differ from this configuration. (1999, W. Michael Young)

Nine Marines and their gear crowd a combat rubber raiding craft (CRRC) during an exercise in New River Inlet, North Carolina. These troops are from the 2nd Battalion, 2nd Marines, part of the 24th Marine Expeditionary Unit (2002, U.S. Marine Corps/Jeff Sisto)

A rigid raider craft's Marines check out a machine gun mounted on the bow. Another gun is mounted aft, behind the mast-supported radome. The twin outboard motors are just visible. (1998, Department of Defense)

Marines recover a combat rubber raiding craft (CRRC) aboard a nuclear-propelled submarine during an exercise. The craft's outboard motor is visible. (1994, U.S. Marine Corps/Robert A. Berry)

This rigid raider craft (left) is patrolling San Diego Bay, carrying several swimmers in wet suits seated amidships. The craft's foremast mounts navigation lights and a loudspeaker. (2000, W. Michael Young)

PATROL BOATS

These craft are employed primarily for anti-terrorist patrols around U.S. naval bases and other facilities in the United States and overseas. Many of these craft are manned by Naval Reservists. The Coast Guard shares this mission. Beyond the craft listed here, small numbers of several additional designs are in service.

3 KINGSTON DESIGN

Builders:	Willard Marine, Anaheim, Calif.
Displacement:	5.5 tons full load
Length:	32½ feet (9.76 m) overall
Beam:	8¼½ feet (2.7 m)
Draft:	1⅚ feet (0.55 m)
Propulsion:	2 diesel engines (Cummins 6BTA); 710 bhp; 2 waterjets
Speed:	30+ knots
Range:	210 nm (390 km)
Crew:	5 (enlisted)
Guns:	up to 3 7.62-mm machine guns M60 (single)

These craft, placed in service in 2001, are assigned to Naval Coastal Warfare Group 1 at San Diego for harbor patrol.

They have an aluminum hull encased in a rigid inflatable collar and an aluminum cabin.

Service craft numbers 32IB0001–32IB0003 are assigned.

A 32-foot Kingston-design patrol boat operating in the Persian gulf area. A 7.62-mm machine gun M60 is mounted forward and two more are fitted aft. (2003, U.S. Navy/Arlo K. Abrahamson)

A 32-foot Kingston patrol boat in San Diego harbor. These craft have a rigid inflatable collar fitted around their hulls; there is a diving platform aft. (2001, W. Michael Young)

2 COASTAL RUNNER DESIGN

Builders:	Glacier Bay Cats, Monroe, Wash.
Displacement:	2.38 tons light
Length:	30 feet (7.92 m) overall
Beam:	8½ feet (2.59 m)
Draft:	1⅚ feet (0.56 m)
Propulsion:	2 gasoline outboard engines (Yamaha 150HDPI); 300 hp
Speed:	30+ knots
Range:	100 nm (185 km) at 29 knots
Crew:	2 or 3 (enlisted)
Guns:	2 7.62-mm machine guns M60 (2 single)

These craft are based at Norfolk and Groton, Connecticut, to escort submarines.

They have a commercial catamaran design and are built of GRP. The Navy took delivery in 2001 and 2002.

A 30-foot Coastal Runner catamaran. These patrol craft are used to escort submarines in transit to open water. (2001, Glacier Bay Cats)

22 INSHORE PATROL BOATS

Builder:	Workskiff, Burlington, Wash.
Displacement:	2 tons full load
Length:	27 feet (8.23 m) overall
Beam:	8½ feet (2.6 m)
Draft:	2⅓ feet (0.71 m)
Propulsion:	2 gasoline outboard engines; 300 hp
Speed:	30+ knots
Range:	
Crew:	4 (enlisted)
Guns:	2 7.62-mm machine guns M60 (2 single)

These craft, numbered 8MIB9401–8MIB9422, are assigned to Naval Coastal Warfare Groups 1 and 2.

They are built of aluminum.

A 27-foot inshore patrol boat surveys the waters of Souda Bay, Crete. In the background are the submarine tender EMORY S. LAND (AS 39) and a SPRUANCE (DD 963)-class destroyer. (2003, U.S. Navy/John Gaffney)

A 27-foot inshore patrol boat makes a high-speed turn in the waters off Fujairah, United Arab Emirates. Assigned to Inshore Boat Unit 25, the reserve-manned craft mounts three machine guns. (2004, U.S. Navy/Jason Trevett)

A 24-foot harbor security boat in the Persian Gulf. (1991, U.S. Navy)

4 RAIDER DESIGN

Builder:	NAPCO International, North Miami, Fla.
Displacement:	2 tons light
	3 tons full load
Length:	22⅕ feet (6.81 m) overall
Beam:	7⁵⁄₁₂ feet (2.26 m)
Draft:	2⅚ feet (0.86 m)
Propulsion:	2 gasoline outboard engines (Evinrude or Johnson); 280 hp
Speed:	40 knots
Range:	165 nm (305 km) at 40 knots
	220 nm (405 km) at 30 knots
Crew:	3 (enlisted)
Guns:	2 .50-caliber machine guns M2 (2 single)

These are modified Boston Whaler hulls fabricated of GRP.

They were placed in service in 1986.

58 HARBOR SECURITY BOATS (HSB)

Builder:	Peterson Builders, Sturgeon Bay, Wisc.
Displacement:	2.5 tons light
	3.8 tons full load
Length:	24 feet (7.3 m) overall
Beam:	7½ feet (2.3 m)
Draft:	5⅕ feet (1.6 m)
Propulsion:	2 diesel engines (Volvo Penta AGAD 41A); 2 outboard drives
Speed:	22.5 knots
Range:	
Crew:	4 (enlisted)
Guns:	(see notes)

These craft are employed for harbor patrol at various bases, shipyards, and forward operating areas. They are constructed of aluminum. No armament normally is provided, but light machine guns can be mounted.

Class: Originally, 75 craft were in this series, numbered 24HS8701–24HS8750 and 24HS8801–24HS8825. All were constructed in 1988–1989.

A 22½-foot modified Boston Whaler configured as a patrol boat with a machine gun mounted on the bow operates in the Persian Gulf area. (2003, U.S. Navy/Brien Aho)

Stern aspect of a harbor security boat in the Persian Gulf patrolling against floating mines and swimmers. (1991, U.S. Navy)

CHAPTER 22

Mine Countermeasures Ships and Craft

Manpower is still a requirement in the modern U.S. fleet, evidenced here as Mineman 2nd Class Christine Beal guides an SLQ-48 mine neutralization vehicle onto its cradle. This vehicle is used in exercises at the Mine Warfare Training Center, Ingleside, Texas. (U.S. Navy / Chris Desmond)

The U.S. Navy's leadership continues to be mostly ambivalent about mine warfare. In the 1990s, the Navy attempted to discard most Mine Countermeasures (MCM) ships, but was stopped by the Secretary of Defense. Subsequently, when the Littoral Combat Ship (LCS) program was initiated, one of the primary mission modules for the LCS was for littoral MCM (see Chapter 17). Efforts are being made to develop "organic" MCM systems that can be carried by surface combatants, amphibious ships, and submarines—primarily for mapping and marking hostile minefields—but such systems require constant training and maintenance, activities that could detract from the platform's primary missions. Similarly, the issue of specialist versus nonspecialist operators for such organic systems has not been fully resolved and also could have an impact on effectiveness.

Periodic proposals to discard most or all MH-53E Sea Dragon MCM helicopters have been aborted (see Chapter 28).

In spite of the surface and airborne MCM force developed late in the 20th century, as well as new MCM devices that have entered service, questions remain about the fundamental ability of the U.S. Navy to cope with modern mine warfare. U.S. Navy limitations

were illuminated by the mining of the super tanker BRIDGETON in the first convoy escorted by U.S. forces in the Persian Gulf in 1987 during the Iraq–Iran conflict, the mining of the U.S. frigate SAMUEL B. ROBERTS (FFG 58) in the Gulf in 1988, and the damage inflicted by mines on the helicopter carrier TRIPOLI (LPH 10) and the Aegis cruiser PRINCETON (CG 59) in the Persian Gulf conflict of 1991.

According to the U.S. Navy's official history of the 1991 Persian Gulf conflict, *Shield and Sword*, the commanding officer of one Aegis cruiser, Captain Steve Woodall, said, "I could make [an Iraqi] airplane a memory . . . [but] the most appreciable threat to us [was] just hitting a mine."[1] The result was ludicrous: Aegis cruisers—the most advanced surface warships afloat—with sailors perched on their bows with binoculars, searching the water for mines!

The problems of locating and destroying Iraqi mines, the superiority of foreign mine countermeasures ships, the complications

---

1 Dr. Edward J. Marolda and Dr. Robert J. Schneller Jr., *Shield and Sword: The United States Navy and the Persian Gulf War* (Washington, D.C.: Naval Historical Center, 1998), p. 205.

caused by the unclear "command–control picture," and the short-comings of the command staff for the U.S. mine countermeasures group led General Norman Schwarzkopf to declare that the Navy's "very, very antiquated mine-sweeping fleet . . . frankly, just could not get the job done."[2] Vice Admiral Stanley Arthur, commander of U.S. naval forces in the Gulf, concluded, "Everybody in the world had better minesweepers out there than I did."[3]

Thus, even with the demise of the Soviet Union as a major military power, sea mines remain a major threat to U.S. and other nations' maritime operations. The Department of Defense report on the Persian Gulf conflict stated:

> Operation Desert Shield and Desert Storm highlighted the dangers that sea mines pose to naval forces. Mines will continue to pose a difficult problem. Refocusing our national defense strategy away from the European theater and toward regional contingencies has exposed a gap in U.S. mine warfare capability that our European allies were previously expected to fill.[4]

Most of the MCM conditions that existed in 1991 exist today.

No additional mine countermeasures ships are planned by the U.S. Navy, the emphasis now being on so-called organic MCM capabilities and the planned LCS with an MCM module. The current force of 26 MCM ships falls short of providing the Navy's minimum goal for mine countermeasures capabilities, which, as stated in 1991, was 45 new MCM/MHC ships, plus helicopters. (Studies of wartime requirements indicate a need for at least 60 mine countermeasures ships, with the high end of estimates in the hundreds, much too large a force for U.S. peacetime budgets—or interest.)

In response to these shortfalls, difficulties, and criticisms, the U.S. Navy began development of several organic MCM systems that can be carried by warships into forward areas, obviating the need for specialized MCM ships. The systems for submarines are listed in Chapter 12, and those for surface ships and aircraft are listed at the end of this chapter.

The Navy's conventional MCM force has completed its long-delayed modernization, with new ships and helicopters (MH-53E) entering the fleet. This latest buildup was initiated under the Reagan–Lehman naval program of the early 1980s. After an almost 30-year hiatus in the series production of minesweepers, two new ship classes were initiated, the AVENGER-class MCM ships and the CARDINAL-class air-cushion mine hunters (MSH). Both encountered major construction problems, with the CARDINAL class being canceled and the OSPREY class (MHC), adopted from the Italian LERICI design, being built in its place.

(All U.S. minesweepers of the MSO and MSC types built during the Korean War era have been stricken, although many continue to serve in other navies. The smaller MSB and Craft of Opportunity Program [COOP] mine countermeasure craft also are gone, with a single exception.)

In addition, air-cushion landing craft (LCAC) can be employed to undertake mine countermeasures operations in shallow water (see Chapter 20).

The helicopter carrier INCHON (LPH 12) was converted to an MCM support ship in 1995–1996. There had long been a need for such a ship to enhance the effectiveness and on-station time of forward deployed MCM forces, both surface ships and helicopters. The INCHON now has been discarded; in her place, the Navy is evaluating a High Speed Vessel (HSV) and can employ larger helicopter carriers (LHA/LHD) on an ad hoc basis, although the use of those amphibious ships can be undertaken only at the cost of further reducing the Navy's limited amphibious assault capabilities.

Two Airborne MCM squadrons are operational, Helicopter Mine Countermeasures Squadron (HM) 14 at Naval Station Norfolk, Virginia, and HM-15 at Naval Air Station (NAS) Corpus Christi, Texas.[5] Both squadrons fly the MH-53E Sea Dragon helicopter, with 12 aircraft per squadron.

The MH-53E is scheduled for eventual replacement by the MH-60S Knighthawk. The latter helicopter does not have the lift capacity, endurance, or night-flying capabilities of the MH-53E. Still, the Navy points to economic benefits in the "necking down" to only two helicopter types in the fleet—the MH-60R Blackhawk and MH-60S. (The Marine Corps will continue to fly the similar CH-53E Super Stallion and its eventual replacement, now designated CH-53X.)

Reserve MCM helicopter squadrons HM-18 and HM-19 have been disestablished, with their personnel integrated into the active-duty squadrons. Also disestablished is reserve Light Helicopter Anti-Submarine Squadron (HSL) 94 at NAS Willow Grove, Pennsylvania, which flew the SH-2G LAMPS I helicopter fitted with the airborne laser mine detection system.

Similarly, HM-12, the MCM readiness/transition training squadron was disestablished, with the Marine Corps now being responsible for all H-53 pilot and air crew training. (See Chapter 27 for details of MCM helicopter squadrons.)

These MCM forces have the primary mission of clearing U.S. waters and strategic choke points and clearing paths for amphibious assaults. The helicopters have a limited night-flying capability and limited detection capabilities against bottom-laid mines.

Almost all surface minesweepers and one of the two helicopter MCM squadrons are based at the mine warfare complex at NAS Corpus Christi and the adjacent base at Ingleside, Texas. The headquarters for the Mine Warfare Command is located at the air station.

The move to Ingleside began shortly after the Navy's May 1991 announcement that all MCM forces would be relocated there. In a report to the Secretary of the Navy issued on 27 December 1991, the General Accounting Office attacked the Navy's plan, criticizing the Navy for not spending enough time analyzing the issue and indicating that the costs of the relocation could be prohibitive. (The Mine Warfare Command and several mine warfare ships previously were based at Charleston, South Carolina.)

The move to Ingleside was commended by the Navy in 1992 as improving efficiency, but other criticism arose, based primarily on (1) removing mine warfare ships and people from the major fleet operating bases, thus inhibiting the exchange of ideas; (2) making exercises with the fleet more difficult and costly; and (3) increasing transit distances to and from forward operating areas, a significant factor for the relatively low-speed MCM forces.

Subsequently, the Navy has based two MCMs at Sasebo, Japan, and two MCMs are forward based at Bahrain in the Persian Gulf. Proposals to base MCMs in Astoria, Oregon, and Pearl Harbor, Hawaii, have not been pursued.

Mine countermeasures: The MCM and MHC classes both use hull-mounted Variable Depth Sonar (VDS) as their primary means of mine detection and the cable-controlled SLQ-48 Mine Neutralization System (MNS) for examining and clearing mines (see the description at end of this chapter).

Names: The larger minesweepers have adjectives as names, and smaller units have bird names. The use of bird names dates to World War I and was continued for most U.S. minesweepers until the 1950s, except that the larger, destroyer–minesweepers (DMS series) retained their destroyer names.

---

2 *Shield and Sword*, p. 263.
3 *Shield and Sword*, p. 263.
4 Department of Defense, Conduct of the Persian Gulf Conflict (Washington, D.C.: July 1991), p. 6-9.
5 NAS Norfolk was changed from a separate naval air station to a detachment of NAS Oceana, Virginia, in 1998.

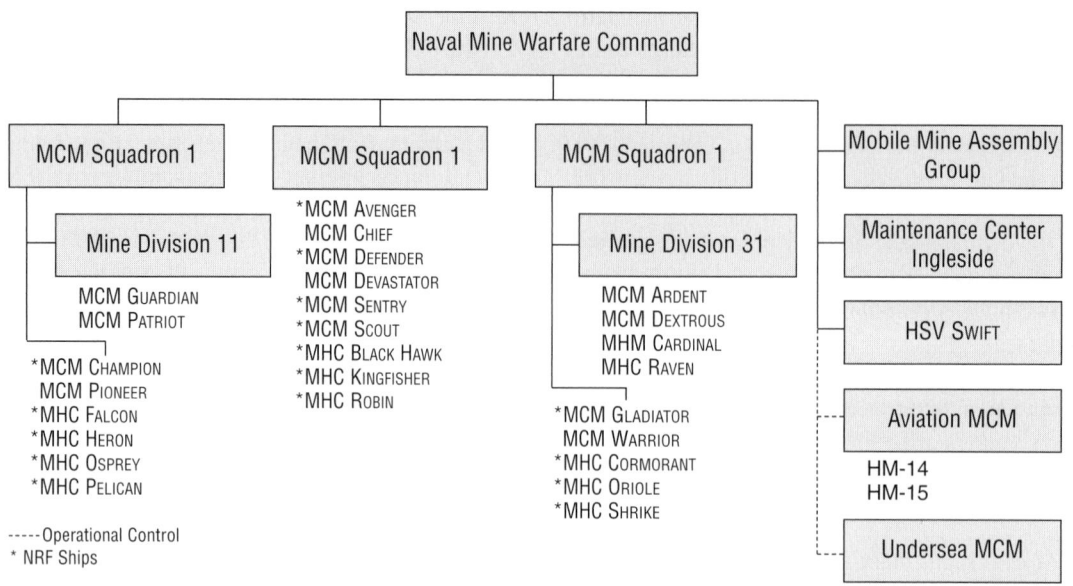

Figure 22-1. Mine Warfare Command

Operational: U.S. minesweepers escorted Kuwaiti tankers and other merchant ships in the Persian Gulf in the late 1980s during the Iran–Iraq conflict, and again in 1990–1991 during Desert Shield/Desert Storm operations. The Navy sent four MSOs, as well as MSBs, to the Persian Gulf in 1988, and the AVENGER, GUARDIAN, and three MSOs into the Gulf in 1990–1991.

The entire U.S. Navy surface ship/craft MCM force originally was scheduled to be operated by the Naval Reserve Force (NRF). However, following the mine countermeasures effort in Operation Desert Storm, the Defense Department and Navy decided to retain ten of the AVENGER-class ships in the active fleet. Five of those large MCM ships and ten of the smaller OSPREY-class ships are operated by the NRF with composite active–reserve crews.

Personnel: The two MCMs based in Bahrain, the ARDENT and DEXTROUS, were engaged in crew rotations from 1996 to 2000 with four other MCMs at Ingleside. That program was canceled for efficiency and cost reasons.

A form of the Navy's Sea Swap program was being developed in 2004 for the two MCMs and possibly the two MHCs based at Bahrain, the CARDINAL and RAVEN. Details had not been worked out when this edition of *Ships and Aircraft* went to press.

Table 22-1. MINE WARFARE SHIPS (EARLY 2005)

Type	Ship/Class	Comm.	Active	NRF
HSV-2	SWIFT	2003	1*	—
MCM 1	AVENGER	1987–1994	9	5
MHC 51	OSPREY	1992–1999	2	10

* Available on a part-time basis.

MINE COUNTERMEASURES SUPPORT SHIPS

1 INTERIM MINE COUNTERMEASURES SUPPORT SHIP: HSV TYPE

Number	Name	Launched	In service	Status
HSV-2	SWIFT	29 July 2003	15 Aug 2003	**AA**

The high speed vessel SWIFT is operated jointly by the Atlantic Fleet and the Naval Mine Warfare Command on lease from the Australian firm INCAT. She was built specifically for the U.S. Navy, her design reflecting initial lessons learned in the construction of the HSV 1X and TSV 1X, also leased by the Department of Defense and both currently operated by the U.S. Army.

Thus the SWIFT has two home ports, Norfolk, Virginia, and Ingleside, Texas, and is manned by two, alternating crews.

Five MCM ships are moored together at the mine warfare complex in Ingleside, Texas. The ships were nested in a "Mediterranean moor"—their sterns to the pier—in anticipation of a tropical storm striking the Texas coast. The GLADIATOR is closest to the camera. (2003, U.S. Navy/Sean Janusheske)

The ship has been highly successful in her role as an interim MCM support ship. (See Chapter 24 for characteristics.)

MINE COUNTERMEASURES SUPPORT SHIP: "IWO JIMA" CLASS

The former MCS INCHON, converted from an IWO JIMA (LPH 2)-class helicopter carrier, was decommissioned and stricken on 20 June 2002, after a fire caused $10 million in damage while she was undergoing an overhaul. She was scheduled to be sunk as a target.

The INCHON was the largest ship ever to carry a mine warfare designation. She could embark an MCM squadron commander and his staff and could provide alongside services for four MCM/MHC-type ships, as well as supporting her embarked helicopters.

A Rigid Hull Inflatable Boat (RHIB) engaged in mine clearing operations approaches the high speed vessel SWIFT during an exercise off the Hawaiian Islands. The SWIFT's stability, larger cargo deck, and large stern opening, with a 13-ton-capacity crane on the port quarter, facilitates the handling of RHIBs and MCM equipment. (2004, U.S. Navy/Richard J. Brunson)

The INCHON was the last LPH-type ship in U.S. Navy service (see 17th Edition/pages 218–19).

Table 22-2. MINE WARFARE COMMAND AND SUPPORT SHIPS

Number	Name	Comm.	MCS Comm.	Former*
MCS 1	CATSKILL	1944	1967	LSV 1, CM 6, AP 106
MCS 2	OZARK	1944	1967	LSV 2, CM 7, AP 107
MCS 3	OSAGE	1944	—	LSV 3, AN 3, AP 108
MCS 4	SAUGUS	1945	—	LSV 4, AN 4, AP 109
MCS 5	MONITOR	1944	—	LSV 5
MCS 6	ORLEANS PARISH	1945	(1952)	LST 1069
MCS 7	EPPING FOREST	1943	1962	LSD 4
MCS 8–11	not used			
MCS 12	INCHON	1970	1996	LPH 12

* AP = transport; CM = minelayer; LPH = amphibious assault ship; LSD = dock landing ship; LST = tank landing ship; LSV = vehicle landing ship

The designation MCS, for mine countermeasures ship, was established in 1956; it subsequently was changed to mine warfare command and support ship, and then to mine countermeasures support ship. The CATSKILL and OZARK were converted in 1963–1967; their near sister ships LSV 3–5 were not converted and remained laid up in "mothballs" while carrying the MCS designation.

The ORLEANS PARISH supported minesweepers from 1952 to 1960, being redesignated MCS 6 in 1959. After serving in the mine warfare role, she was transferred to the Military Sea Transportation Service (MSTS) in 1966 (redesignated T-LST 1069) for use as a cargo ship and sold to the Philippines in 1976.

The INCHON should have been designated MCS 8. However, the Navy again exhibited its disregard for classification procedures by retaining her LPH number with her new designation.

MINE COUNTERMEASURES SHIPS

(14) ADVANCED MINE COUNTERMEASURES SHIPS

Units	FY	Comm.	Status
8 ships	14–18		Planned
6 ships	19–23		Planned

The Navy's 30-year shipbuilding plan presented to Congress in 2003 includes the construction of 14 advanced mine countermeasures ships, designated MCM(X), to be authorized in the years indicated above. No characteristics for these ships have been developed.

The high speed vessel SWIFT slows to refuel the mine warfare ship AVENGER during a RIMPAC exercise off the Hawaiian Islands. The SWIFT has demonstrated the feasibility of employing a ship of this design to support MCM operations. However, at this time, there are no plans for a dedicated MCM support ship. (2004, U.S. Navy/Michelle R. Hammond)

14 MINE COUNTERMEASURES SHIPS: "AVENGER" CLASS

Number	Name	FY	Builders	Laid down	Launched	Comm.	Status
MCM 1	AVENGER	82	Peterson Builders, Sturgeon Bay, Wisc.	3 June 1983	15 June 1985	12 Sep 1987	**NRF-A**
MCM 2	DEFENDER	83	Marinette Marine, Marinette, Wisc.	1 Dec 1983	4 Apr 1987	30 Sep 1989	**NRF-A**
MCM 3	SENTRY	84	Peterson Builders, Sturgeon Bay, Wisc.	8 Oct 1983	20 Sep 1986	6 Oct 1990	**NRF-A**
MCM 4	CHAMPION	84	Marinette Marine, Marinette, Wisc.	28 June 1984	15 Apr 1989	8 Feb 1991	**NRF-A**
MCM 5	GUARDIAN	84	Peterson Builders, Sturgeon Bay, Wisc.	8 May 1985	20 June 1987	16 Dec 1989	**PA**
MCM 6	DEVASTATOR	85	Peterson Builders, Sturgeon Bay, Wisc.	9 Feb 1987	11 June 1988	6 Oct 1990	**AA**
MCM 7	PATRIOT	85	Marinette Marine, Marinette, Wisc.	31 Mar 1987	15 May 1990	13 Dec 1991	**PA**
MCM 8	SCOUT	85	Peterson Builders, Sturgeon Bay, Wisc.	8 June 1987	20 May 1989	15 Dec 1990	**AA**
MCM 9	PIONEER	85	Peterson Builders, Sturgeon Bay, Wisc.	5 June 1989	25 Aug 1990	7 Dec 1992	**AA**
MCM 10	WARRIOR	86	Peterson Builders, Sturgeon Bay, Wisc.	25 Sep 1989	8 Dec 1990	30 Dec 1992	**AA**
MCM 11	GLADIATOR	86	Peterson Builders, Sturgeon Bay, Wisc.	7 May 1990	29 June 1991	4 June 1993	**NRF-A**
MCM 12	ARDENT	90	Peterson Builders, Sturgeon Bay, Wisc.	22 Oct 1990	16 Nov 1991	18 Sep 1993	**AA**
MCM 13	DEXTEROUS	90	Peterson Builders, Sturgeon Bay, Wisc.	11 Mar 1991	20 June 1992	9 July 1994	**AA**
MCM 14	CHIEF	90	Peterson Builders, Sturgeon Bay, Wisc.	19 Aug 1991	12 June 1993	5 Nov 1994	**AA**

Displacement:	1,195 tons light	Speed:	13.5 knots
	1,312 tons full load	Range:	2,500 nm (4,630 km) at 10 knots
Length:	212¾ feet (64.85 m) waterline	Personnel:	MCM 1–4, 11: 36 active (5 officers + 31 enlisted) + 53
	224¼ feet (68.4 m) overall		reserve (3 officers + 50 enlisted)
Beam:	38¹¹⁄₂ feet (11.9 m)		others: 83 (7 officers + 76 enlisted)
Draft:	11¼ feet (3.4 m)	Guns:	2 .50-cal machine guns M2HB (2 single)
Propulsion:	MCM 1, 2: 4 diesel engines (Waukesha L-1616); 2,280 bhp;	Radars:	SPS-55 surface search
	2 shafts		SPS-64(V)9 navigation
	MCM 3–14: 4 diesel engines (Isotta-Fraschini	Sonars:	MCM 2–9: SQQ-30 mine detection
	ID36 SS 6V-AM); 2,600 bhp; 2 shafts (see notes)		MCM 1, 10–14: SQQ-32 mine detection
	2 low-speed motors (Hansome); 400 shp (geared to		
	propellers)		

These are relatively large mine countermeasures ships intended to locate and destroy mines that cannot be countered by conventional minesweeping techniques.

The AVENGER class suffered a number of design and construction problems. The first two ships were fitted with American engines from existing stocks; they were installed improperly and subsequent tests revealed a potential fire hazard from lubricating oil leaking through the turbocharger into the exhaust stack. This engine design had been blamed for a series of fires in previous minesweepers. The Italian engines planned for the later MCMs initially failed in their endurance tests, passing only after major modifications.

The MCMs also are overweight—one of two planned DC generators for sweep gear and mine hunting had to be deleted because of space/weight constraints, and the ships have had electronic interference problems. During Operation Desert Storm in 1991, the AVENGER suffered continuous problems with both main engines and her generator as she hunted mines in the Persian Gulf. There are indications that her acoustic signature was greater than expected.

The AVENGER was ordered on 29 June 1982, becoming the first large minesweeper under construction for the U.S. Navy since the ASSURANCE (MSO 521) was completed 25 years earlier. The AVENGER was almost two years behind her original contract schedule; the follow-on ships also were late.

Five of these ships have been transferred to NRF status, with nine retained in active service. The last to become an NRF ship was the GLADIATOR, on 1 October 2000.

The GUARDIAN and PATRIOT are based at Sasebo, Japan; the ARDENT and DEXTROUS are based at Bahrain in the Persian Gulf. All other ships are based at Ingleside, Texas.

Class: The Navy originally planned a two-year "program gap" between the Fiscal Year (FY) 1982 lead ship and the four ships in FY 1984. Subsequently, the Navy sought to accelerate the program with four ships in FY 1983. Congress, citing problems with the MCM design, instead funded only one ship in FY 1983 and directed the Navy to develop a second source shipyard (i.e., Marinette).

The DEXTEROUS, one of two MCMs forward based at Bahrain in the Persian Gulf. Most U.S. mine warfare ships normally are found at the mine warfare complex at Ingleside, Texas, a considerable distance from U.S. fleet bases and probable operating areas. (2003, U.S. Navy/Brien Aho)

Design: The MCM design is similar to previous MSO classes. Their hulls are constructed of fiberglass-sheathed wood (laminated oak framing, Douglas fir planking and deck sheathing with reinforced fiberglass covering). One or two MNS vehicles can be carried in addition to conventional sweep gear.

The MCM concept has undergone several changes in the past two decades, having originally been proposed in the late 1970s as an oceangoing ship to protect U.S. strategic missile submarines against Soviet deep-ocean mines. A Small Waterplane Area Twin Hull (SWATH) design was considered for that first concept to provide improved seakeeping in northern waters; the MCMs would have operated in pairs, towing a sweep gear between them. Nineteen of these ships were proposed, to have displaced 1,640 tons and with a length of 265 feet (80.8 m).

Electronics: These craft are fitted with the SSN-2(V) precise navigation system and SYQ-13 navigation/command system; the improved SYQ-15 is to replace the latter system.

Early ships were fitted with the SQQ-30 variable-depth minehunting sonar. This equipment, an upgraded SQQ-14, has severe limitations and is replaced in later ships by the SQQ-32. The Navy planned to backfit the SQQ-32 into the earlier ships, and in 1990, the AVENGER was hurriedly refitted with the engineering development model of the SQQ-32 for operations in the Persian Gulf. Deployed to the Gulf (with several MSOs), the AVENGER detected the first Manta bottom mine to be discovered, but the ship then suffered mechanical and power-generation problems and was forced to withdraw from the mined area.

Engineering: All ships have four very-low-magnetic-signature diesel engines for propulsion; electrical power for minesweeping gear is provided by gas turbines. The low-speed motors are geared to the propellers. A 350-hp bow thruster is fitted for precise maneuvering. Maximum minehunting speed is five knots.

Congress directed that the MCM 10–14 would have American-made diesel engines; however, in the event, foreign engines were procured.

Names: Navy publicity at the time of the commissioning of the CHIEF stated that the ship "was named CHIEF in honor of the chief petty officers" of the Navy. In reality, the ship was named (on 3 July 1990) along with several other MCMs to "commemorate the service of World War II minecraft that saw significant service. . . .

The AVENGER *at San Diego during a four-month training deployment from her home port of Ingleside, Texas. The large reel for the SQS-32 mine detection sonar is visible forward of the bridge. Floats or "pigs" for streaming minesweeping gear are visible at her stern. (2004, U.S. Navy/Johansen Laurel)*

The AVENGER*'s port aspect shows her stowage for three rigid hull inflatable boat-type craft on that side. These ships are too slow and lack weapons for employment as effective patrol/anti-submarine warfare craft, a capability of some World War II–era minesweepers as well as Soviet postwar MCM ships. (2004, U.S. Navy/Michelle R. Hammond)*

CHIEF (MCM 14) commemorates CHIEF (AM 315), [which] earned five battle stars in World War II." The AM-315 was named for "the head or leader of a group," according to the U.S. Naval History Center.

Operational: The first overseas deployment of this class was by the AVENGER, sent to the Persian Gulf for Operations Desert Shield and Desert Storm; she was transported to the area by a heavy-lift ship, along with three MSOs.[6] The AVENGER returned to the United States in June 1991 (under her own power).

OCEAN MINESWEEPERS: "ACME" CLASS

Number	Name	Comm.	Notes
MSO 508	ACME	1956	decomm. 1970; str. 1976
MSO 509	ADROIT	1957	decomm. 12 Dec 1991; str. 8 May 1992
MSO 510	ADVANCE	1958	decomm. 1970; str. 1976
MSO 511	AFFRAY	1958	decomm./str. 31 Dec 1992

This was an improved ocean minesweeper design, based on the earlier AGILE and AGGRESSIVE classes. The four ships built for the U.S. Navy have been stricken; the ADROIT and AFFRAY were assigned to the NRF in their later years. Seven additional ships (MSO 512–518) were built for allied navies.

The ADROIT participated in Operation Desert Storm (1991).

See 15th Edition/pages 213–14 for characteristics.

OCEAN MINESWEEPERS: "AGILE" AND "AGGRESSIVE" CLASSES

Number	Name	Comm.	Notes
MSO 427	CONSTANT	1954	decomm. 30 Sep 1992; str. 9 Mar 1994
MSO 433	ENGAGE	1954	decomm. 30 Dec 1991; str. 20 Apr 1992
MSO 437	ENHANCE	1954	decomm. 13 Dec 1991; str. 21 Feb 1992
MSO 438	ESTEEM	1954	decomm./str. 20 Sep 1991
MSO 439	EXCEL	1955	decomm. 30 Sep 1992; str. 28 Mar 1994
MSO 440	EXPLOIT	1954	decomm. 16 Dec 1993; str. 28 Mar 1994
MSO 441	EXULTANT	1954	decomm. 30 June 1993; str. 9 Mar 1994
MSO 442	FEARLESS	1955	decomm. 23 Oct 1990; str. 28 Oct 1990
MSO 446	FORTIFY	1954	decomm. 31 Aug 1992; str. 9 Mar 1994
MSO 448	ILLUSIVE	1955	decomm. 30 Mar 1990; str. 1 June 1990
MSO 449	IMPERVIOUS	1955	decomm. 12 Dec 1991; str. 18 Mar 1992
MSO 455	IMPLICIT	1954	decomm./to Taiwan 30 Sep 1994; str. 29 Nov 1994
MSO 456	INFLICT	1954	decomm. 30 Mar 1990; str. 23 May 1990
MSO 464	PLUCK	1954	decomm. 29 Nov 1990; str. 16 Jan 1991
MSO 488	CONQUEST	1955	decomm./str. 29 June 1994; to Taiwan 1994
MSO 489	GALLANT	1955	decomm./str. 29 Apr 1994; to Taiwan 1994
MSO 490	LEADER	1955	decomm. 12 Dec 1991; str. 18 Mar 1992
MSO 492	PLEDGE	1956	decomm./str. 31 Jan 1994 to Taiwan 1994

All ocean minesweepers of the massive Korean War-era program have been discarded. Fifty-eight ships of this design were built for the U.S. Navy (MSO 421–449, 455–474, 488–496); another 27 ships were built for allied navies (MSO 450–454, 475–487, 498–507, with the MSO 497 being canceled).

The above list contains those ships stricken since 1990. All but the LEADER were assigned to the NRF prior to their disposal.

All three ships of the similar ABILITY class (MSO 519–521) built for the U.S. Navy have been discarded. The MSO 522 of that design was built for foreign use.

See 15th Edition/pages 214–15 for characteristics.

---

6 The four mine warfare ships were carried by the Dutch heavy-lift ship SUPER SERVANT 3, which departed Norfolk on 29 August 1990 and arrived at Bahrain on 3 October 1990. The use of a heavy-lift ship saved debilitating wear and tear on the MCM ships and crews during the long transit.

The port side of the RAVEN shows the amidships location of the ship's mast and her short funnel. She carries two machine guns; Soviet-era mine countermeasures ships were heavily armed. (2004, U.S. Navy/Daniel E. Smith)

12 COASTAL MINEHUNTERS: "OSPREY" CLASS

Number	Name	FY	Builder	Start*	Launched	Comm.	Status
MHC 51	Osprey	86	Intermarine USA, Savannah, Ga.	16 May 1988	23 Mar 1991	20 Nov 1993	**NRF-A**
MHC 52	Heron	89	Intermarine USA, Savannah, Ga.	7 Apr 1989	21 Mar 1992	6 Aug 1994	**NRF-A**
MHC 53	Pelican	89	Avondale Industries, New Orleans, La.	6 May 1991	27 Feb 1993	18 Nov 1995	**NRF-A**
MHC 54	Robin	90	Avondale Industries, New Orleans, La.	28 Jan 1992	11 Sep 1993	11 May 1996	**NRF-A**
MHC 55	Oriole	90	Avondale Industries, New Orleans, La.	8 May 1991	22 May 1993	16 Sep 1995	**NRF-A**
MHC 56	Kingfisher	91	Avondale Industries, New Orleans, La.	24 Mar 1992	18 June 1994	26 Oct 1996	**NRF-A**
MHC 57	Cormorant	91	Avondale Industries, New Orleans, La.	8 Apr 1992	21 Oct 1995	12 Apr 1997	**NRF-A**
MHC 58	Blackhawk	92	Intermarine USA, Savannah, Ga.	12 May 1992	27 Aug 1994	11 May 1996	**NRF-A**
MHC 59	Falcon	92	Intermarine USA, Savannah, Ga.	3 Apr 1993	3 June 1995	8 Feb 1997	**NRF-A**
MHC 60	Cardinal	92	Intermarine USA, Savannah, Ga.	1 Feb 1994	9 Mar 1996	18 Oct 1997	**PA (Gulf)**
MHC 61	Raven	93	Intermarine USA, Savannah, Ga.	4 May 1994	28 Sep 1996	5 Sep 1998	**PA (Gulf)**
MHC 62	Shrike	93	Intermarine USA, Savannah, Ga.	1 Aug 1995	24 May 1997	31 May 1999	**NRF-A**

* These ships did not have a formal keel laying.

Displacement:	803 tons light	Speed:	12 knots
	918 tons full load	Range:	2,500 nm (4,630 km) at 12 knots
Length:	174⅙ feet (53.1 m) waterline	Personnel:	MHC 60, 61: 51 (5 officers + 46 enlisted)
	187¾ feet (57.25 m) overall		others: 34 active (2 officers + 32 enlisted) + 21 reserve
Beam:	35¹¹⁄₂ feet (10.95 m)		(3 officers + 18 enlisted)
Draft:	9½ feet (2.9 m)	Guns:	2 .50-cal machine guns M2HB (2 single)
Propulsion:	2 diesel engines (Isotta-Fraschini ID36 SS 6V-AM)1,160 bhp;	Radar:	SPS-64(V)9 navigation
	2 cycloidal propellers	Sonar:	SQQ-32 mine detection
	2 180-shp hydraulic motors for quiet operation		

These ships are intended for harbor clearance, port breakout, and deep-water coastal mine countermeasures. This class was developed in place of the canceled CARDINAL class of air-cushion mine hunters.

The CARDINAL and RAVEN were transferred from Ingleside to the Persian Gulf in July–August 2000 on board the merchant ship BLUE MARLIN. The two MHCs now are homeported at Manama, Bahrain, along with two larger MCMs, forming Mine Division 31.

The OSPREY and SHRIKE were transferred to the NRF on 1 October 2000 and 1 April 2000, respectively. The CARDINAL and RAVEN are the only MHCs in active commission; all others are assigned to the NRF and are based at Ingleside, Texas.

Class: Congress added one ship to the George H. W. Bush administration's request for two MHCs each in the FY 1992 and 1993 programs, reflecting the increased concern over the U.S. Navy's mine countermeasures capabilities. Still, only 12 MHCs have been procured, although the initial program called for 17 ships. The follow-on, enlarged MHC(V) program was canceled in 1991.

Classification: The MHC designation originated in the early 1950s as AMC(U), for mine vessel underwater locator. Those ships were intended to locate and plot mines for subsequent destruction by minesweepers. The BITTERN (MHC 43), completed in 1957, was built for the purpose on a 144-foot (43.9-m) MSC hull with a full-load displacement of 350 tons; the planned series production of similar MHCs was canceled, and the hull numbers MHC 44 and 45 were allocated to conversions (see below).

The AMC(U) 1–10 were converted LCT(6)s; the AMC(U) 7–11 and 15–42 were converted LSI(L)s; the AMC(U) 12 and 13 were converted coastal survey ships (AGSC), which in turned had been converted from YMS motor minesweepers; the AMC(U) 14 was a converted AMC, originally built as a PCS/PC; and the MHC 44, 45, and AMC(U) 46–50 were converted YMS minesweepers.

The designation AMC(U) was changed to coastal minehunter (MHC) on 7 February 1955.

Design: The Italian Navy procured four similar ships of the LERICI class, completed in 1985; additional ships were built in Italy for Malaysia and Nigeria. The U.S. design is slightly larger to accommodate U.S. sonars, the MNS, and navigation gear; also, a different propulsion system is provided.

These are the first U.S. Navy ships to be constructed of Glass-Reinforced Plastic (GRP), a material long used in foreign mine

The RAVEN steaming in the Persian Gulf. She is one of two MHCs based at Bahrain. The Gulf area is highly vulnerable to mining by small craft, an act that could impede the flow of Middle East petroleum to several countries. (2004, U.S. Navy / Daniel E. Smith)

countermeasures craft. These are the world's largest MCM ships to be constructed entirely of GRP. The hull is a solid, continuous monocoque structure, with no longitudinal or transverse framing.

The ships are fitted with the SYQ-13 tactical navigation/command system. One MNS vehicle is carried.

At-sea endurance is 15 days.

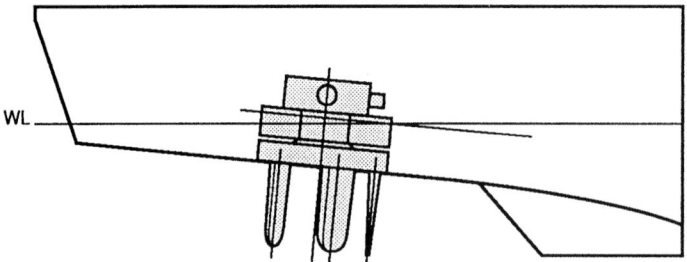

A diagram of the Voith Schneider propeller arrangement in the OSPREY-*class ships. This arrangement provides a high degree of maneuverability.*

Engineering: They have a 180-shp bow thruster.

1 SWATH MINESWEEPING BOAT

Number	Name	Completed	Status
MHS 1	SWATH 1	May 1998	Operational

Builders:	Swath Ocean Systems, National City, Calif.
Weight:	
Length:	40 feet (12.19 m) overall
Beam:	18 feet (5.49 m)
Draft:	
Propulsion:	2 diesel engines; 2 shafts
Speed:	
Range:	
Crew:	
Guns:	none
Radars:	navigation

A SWATH-configured minehunting boat, the craft can handle a tethered Remotely Operated Vehicle (ROV) over the stern.

The craft is officially designated 40MC9601; both the designation MHS (minehunting SWATH) and name SWATH 1 are unofficial.

Design: The craft is of aluminum construction and can be air transported in a C-5 Galaxy transport.

Electronics: She is fitted with a Klein 5500 multibeam, side-scanning, high-frequency sonar and a Simrad SM 2000 mine-avoidance high-frequency sonar.

Operational: The craft is assigned to Explosive Ordnance Disposal Mobile Unit 7 at San Diego, California.

In April 2000, the SWATH 1 was flown to Thailand to participate in an exercise.

POST–WORLD WAR II MINESWEEPERS

A large number of minesweepers of various types were built by the U.S. Navy after World War II, beginning with the massive ocean minesweeper (AM/MSO) and coastal minesweeper (AMS/MSC) series in the early 1950s. During the 1960s, numerous smaller riverine sweep craft were developed for use in the Vietnam War (all of which have been discarded, as have all previous ships and craft).

MINESWEEPING BOATS

The Navy's long-serving minesweeping boats (MSB) built in the 1960s all have been removed from the MCM role, the last in 1993.

This series embraced hull numbers MSB 5–54, with the MSB 24 not built and MSB 29 being an enlarged design. (The MSB 1–4 were Army craft acquired in 1946.) The ex-MSB 17 remains in ser-

The RAVEN, *like other U.S. Navy ships, is inundated with communications antennas. The two circular antennas atop her bridge structure are OE-82 satellite antennas. (2004, U.S. Navy/Brien Aho)*

SWATH 1 *(2001, George Schneider)*

SWATH 1 *(1999, W. Michael Young)*

vice in a utility role for U.S. naval forces in the Panama Canal Zone (redesignated 57UB753). Many units served in the Vietnam War.

CRAFT OF OPPORTUNITY PROGRAM
The Navy developed the Craft of Opportunity Program (COOP) in the 1980s to provide a mine countermeasures capability for U.S. ports, employing fishing craft and small patrol-type craft. The COOP effort has been discarded. The Navy had sought to cancel the program in 1990, but Congress continued to fund it for several years. The Navy has disposed of all COOP craft, the last being the CT-15, ex-YP 662. Built in 1959, she previously was a Naval Academy seamanship training craft.

Classification: Note that CT (for COOP Trainer) was not an "official" designation; a hyphen is used in the designation. Several CT numbers were used twice.

UNMANNED CATAMARAN MINESWEEPERS
The Swedish-built, radio-controlled catamaran minesweepers GERRY and PEGGY have been discarded. The U.S. Navy purchased them from the Swedish Navy just after the outbreak of the Gulf War in early 1991. They were employed that year in Persian Gulf operations. Several of these craft are in Swedish service.

See 17th Edition/page 207 for characteristics.

The U.S. Navy employed drone minesweepers in riverine operations during the Vietnam War.

UNMANNED SURFACE SYSTEMS

Submarine-operated MCM systems are discussed in Chapter 12. The following systems are listed in alphabetical order.

Battlespace Preparation Autonomous Underwater Vehicle (BPAUV). The BPAUV is an unmanned, untethered anti-mine vehicle that travels along a preset course after launch, mapping mines and other obstacles in its path. The vehicle can be employed for bottom mapping and bathymetric and hydrographic surveys, as well as for mine hunting. The data are recorded and downloaded after recovery. The vehicle can be carried and launched by a variety of ships and even fishing craft and RHIBs.

Developed and built by Bluefin Robotics (Cambridge, Massachusetts), the BPAUV has a low-drag fairing with a single, articulated, ducted propeller. Side-scanning sonar and other sensors are fitted. Operating depth is 900 feet (270 m).

Four vehicles were delivered by mid-2004.

Weight:	483 lb (220 kg) dry
	798 lb (360 kg) wet
Length:	10⅙ feet (3.1 m)
Diameter:	21 inches (533 mm)

The minehunter FALCON recovers a Battlespace Preparation Autonomous Underwater Vehicle (BPAUV) after a test run. Once on board the MHC, the data collected by the vehicle will be downloaded into the ship's computers; that data then can be shared with other platforms. (2003, U.S. Navy)

Propulsion:	1 electric motor
Speed:	

Mine Neutralization System. One SLQ-48 Mine Neutralization System vehicle is carried on board ships of the AVENGER and OSPREY classes. Formerly called the Mine Neutralization Vehicle (MNV), the device is controlled and powered through a 3,500-foot (1,067-m) cable. A closed-circuit television and close-range sonar provide viewing of objects detected by shipboard sonar; the sonar range against mines is approximately 1,000 yards (915 m). The vehicle can then cut cables for moored mines or plant a small explosive charge to detonate bottom mines; the two charges carried by the MNS each have 85 pounds (38.5 kg) of high explosives.

The Navy took delivery of 67 systems from Honeywell (subsequently Alliant Techsystems) from 1987 to 1995. The SLQ-48 was used extensively in the Persian Gulf during Operation Desert Storm in 1991.

Weight:	2,750 lb (1,247 kg)
Length:	12½ feet (3.8 m)
Width:	3 feet (0.9 m)
Height:	3 feet (0.9 m)
Propulsion:	2 electric motors; 30 hp
Speed:	6 knots

Naval Special Warfare Semi-autonomous Hydrographic Reconnaissance Vehicle (SAHRV). The SAHRV is one of a family of "small" UUVs. This vehicle would be used by SEALs from small ships and craft to determine the presence of mines and other threats.

The first system, developed by Woods Hole Oceanographic Institution, was delivered in FY 2003.

SLQ-37 Magnetic/Acoustic Influence Sweep System. Installed in the AVENGER class, the SLQ-37 consists of a Mk 5 "straight-tail" magnetic sweep combined with the earlier Mk 4(V) and/or Mk 6(B) acoustic sweeps. This system can be configured several ways to counter specific types of minefields.

SLQ-38 Mechanical Cable-Cutting Sweeps. Mechanical or "Oropesa" wire sweeps of various types are fitted in the AVENGER class to counter moored buoyant (cable) mines. The SLQ-38 can be rigged from one or both sides of an MCM, or can be used in conjunction with a second MCM.

Wire cable cutters cut the mooring cable and the mine is destroyed by gunfire when it bobs to the surface. During normal, one-ship operations, the SLQ-38 can sweep a path 250 yards (228.6 m) wide; a two-MCM sweep can cover 500 yards (457 m).

Very Shallow Water (VSW) Mine Countermeasures. This UUV will be used to map near-shore areas for mines and other underwater obstacles.

An SLQ-48 mine neutralization vehicle is lowered into the sea. These vehicles are carried by both MCM and MHC mine countermeasures ships. (Alliant Techsystems)

An operational capability is planned for FY 2005.

WLD-1 Remote Mine-hunting System (RMS). RMS provides surface ships with an organic mine reconnaissance capability. The RMS vehicle is a semiautonomous, semisubmersible vehicle that tows an AQS-20A mine reconnaissance sonar. It is launched and recovered by surface ships. Engineering challenges included achieving a high sortie rate with reliable launch and recovery techniques even in high sea states.

In FY 1997, the RMS concept was successfully demonstrated by a prototype system operated from the destroyer CUSHING (DD 985) in an Arabian Gulf exercise. The first operational WLD-1(V)3 system was delivered to the fleet in FY 2000. It was developed by Lockheed Martin, Syracuse, N.Y.

The above-water projection of the WLD-1 RMS. (U.S. Navy)

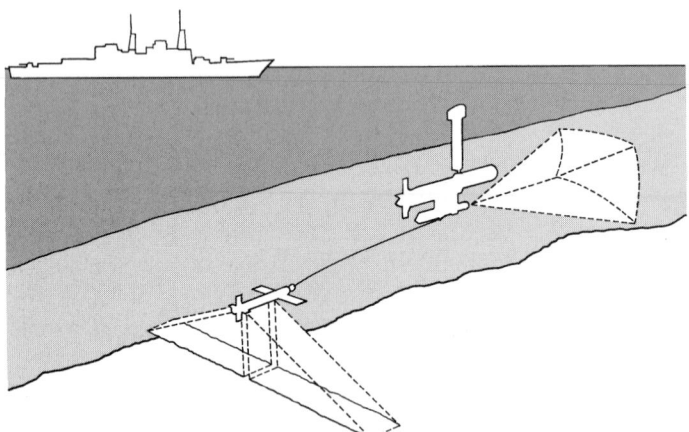

A diagram showing the operational procedure for the WLD-1 RMS. The device is shown here towing the side-scanning sonar. It is controlled by a destroyer several miles away.

The WLD-1 RMS with the towed side-scanning sonar stowed under the vehicle. (Lockheed Martin)

A mock-up of the WLD-1 RMS is put through handling tests on the destroyer PINCKNEY (DDG 91). Six DDGs are scheduled to receive the RMS during 2004–2005. (2003, U.S. Navy/Neil Gibbons)

AIRBORNE MCM SYSTEMS

These systems are deployed from MH-60 Seahawk and MH-53E Sea Dragon MCM helicopters; see Chapter 28.

Airborne Laser Mine Detection System (ALMDS). ALMDS is an electro-optical mine-detection system using an aircraft-mounted laser to detect floating and anchored mines. This capability was successfully demonstrated during an operational assessment in 1995 (employing an SH-2F LAMPS I helicopter). An interim contingency capability was developed employing Naval Reserve SH-2G LAMPS I helicopters, which have now been discarded.

The program goal is to integrate the ALMDS into the HH-60 and SH-60 Seahawk force.

The prime contractor for the contingency system is Kaman Corp.

Airborne Mine Neutralization System (AMNS). The AMNS is an expendable, remotely operated mine neutralization device that will be compatible with MH-60S Knighthawk helicopters.

The AMNS currently is in the engineering and manufacturing development phase, employing off-the-shelf technologies to the extent possible. The system is scheduled to become operational late in 2003. The prime contractors are Lockheed Martin and Atlas (Germany).

ALQ-141 Acoustic System. This airborne mine countermeasures system is an underwater towed body providing electronic countermeasures to counter new mine threats. The towed device and associated electronics have distinct surveillance and sweep-to-detonate modes.

A Mk 2(G) Acoustic Sweep. The device—also called "rattle bars"—consists of parallel pipes or bars, towed broadside-on, at speeds from four to ten knots. This produces a Bernoulli effect between the bars, causing them to bang together to produce medium- to high-frequency acoustic energy.

The A Mk 2(G) was used by helicopters during Operation End Sweep in North Vietnam in 1973 and in Operation Desert Storm in the Persian Gulf in 1991.

AN 37U Mechanical Sweep. This is a variable-depth towed mechanical sweep system capable of countering moored mines in both deep and shallow water.

AQS-14 Sonar. This is an active, helicopter-towed minehunting sonar developed for the earlier RH-53D Sea Stallion helicopter. It is a multibeam, side-looking sonar with electronic beam-forming. The system consists of three parts: a stabilized underwater vehicle, an electromechanical tow cable, and a console in the helicopter. The underwater vehicle, almost 10 feet (3 m) long, can be maintained at a fixed depth above the sea floor or below the surface; the thin, coaxial cable is armored and nonmagnetic. The sonar information is presented on two continuous "waterfall" acoustic displays.

The system became operational in 1984, and its first operational use came in August of that year during Operation Intense Look, the Red Sea/Gulf of Suez mine crisis.[7]

Mk 103 Mechanical Sweep. This helicopter-towed system for sweeping bottom-moored mines consists of a tow wire, sweep wires (with explosive-actuated cutters), floats, a depressor, and float pendants (for visual location of the floats). This is similar to the conventional sweep gear long used by surface mine hunters.

Mk 104 Acoustic Sweep. This airborne system consists of a cavitating disk within a venturi tube, driven by two self-rotating disks. The Mk 104 is towed behind a helicopter or can be attached to the Mk 105 sled to provide a combination acoustic/magnetic system.

Weight:	180 lb (81.65 kg)
Length:	49 inches (1.2 m)
Width:	26 inches (660 mm)
Height:	35 inches (890 mm)

7 Beyond mine hunting, the AQS-14 was used successfully from helicopters in January 1992 to locate cyanide containers on the ocean floor.

The helicopter-towed ASQ-14 sonar. An MH-53E Sea Dragon helicopter is in the background; note the handling fitted to the helicopter's rear ramp. (U.S. Navy)

Mk 105 Magnetic Sweep. The Mk 105 is a helicopter-towed hydrofoil sled. It is fitted with a gas turbine generator to power its magnetic sweep gear. The sled typically is towed at 20–25 knots, about 450 feet (137 m) behind the helicopter; it becomes foilborne at about 13 knots. Twin magnetic tails consisting of open-electrode magnetic sweeps about 600 feet (183 m) long are towed behind the sled. A combination of influence sweeps can be achieved by the addition of a Mk 104 or an A Mk 2(G) acoustic system to the sweep array (see Mk 106).

The vehicle is launched and recovered from a surface ship or shore base, hooked to a hovering helicopter. The helicopter can refuel the sled during a mission.

Operational since 1970, the Mk 105 was used during Operation End Sweep in 1973, the Suez Canal sweeps of 1974–1975, and in Operation Desert Storm in 1991. The system is being upgraded for improved reliability and performance. The following are sled characteristics:

	original	*upgraded*
Weight:	5,907 lb (2,679 kg)	7,259 lb (3,293 kg) dry
	748 lb (339 kg)	1,741 lb (790 kg) fuel
Length:	27½ feet (8.38 m)	
Width:	11½ feet (3.5 m) at float	
	16½ feet (5.0 m) at top foil tip	

Mk 106 Acoustic/Magnetic Sweep. The Mk 106 is a helicopter-towed acoustic/magnetic sweep consisting of the Mk 105 sled and a Mk 104 attached to one of the magnetic tails. The Mk 106 com-bination was used extensively during MCM operations in the Red Sea and Gulf of Suez.

Shallow Water Influence Minesweeping System (SWIMS). This is a self-contained, high-speed, shallow-water magnetic influence sweeping device developed in the 1990s.

The SWIMS is 10-feet (3.05m) long and 20 inches (508 mm) in diameter, and can be transported and deployed by an MH-53E helicopter. The system emulates the magnetic signatures of the platforms in transit through an assault area, as well as conducts generic minesweeping operations. Designed to operate in shallow water at speeds up to 40 knots, it can be towed as a single unit or in tandem.

SPU-1W Magnetic Orange Pipe (MOP). The MOP is a magnetized pipe filled with styrofoam for buoyancy that causes magnetically activated mines to detonate. A modern version of the World War II–era "iron rail" sweep, the MOP was conceived as a precursor sweep mechanism for helicopters during Operation End Sweep in North Vietnamese waters. Mines laid there by U.S. naval aircraft were so sensitive that they would have destroyed the Mk 105 sleds towed by helicopters. The MOP also was used to sweep waters too shallow for the Mk 105 sled.

A single helicopter can tow up to three MOPs in tandem to enhance sweep effectiveness.

Weight:	1,000 pounds (453.6 kg)
Length:	30 feet (9.15 m)
Diameter:	10¾ inches (273 mm)

Sailors from Helicopter Mine Countermeasures Squadron 15 work on a Mk 105 minesweeping sled. The gas turbine engine on the sled provides electrical power for the sled's magnetic and acoustic signature generation to detonate mines. (2002, U.S. Navy/Marc Boyd)

A Mk 105 sled from squadron Helicopter Mine Countermeasures Squadron 15 is prepared for towing by an MH-53E helicopter. The squadron was operating from the helicopter carrier KEARSARGE (LHD 3) at the time. (2002, U.S. Navy/Angel Roman-Otero)

An MH-53E Sea Dragon from Helicopter Mine Countermeasures Squadron 14 pulls a Mk 105 magnetic sled during MCM operations near the mouth of the Khawar Abd Allah River that separates Iraq and Iran. The three-engine MH-53E helicopter, the largest in the West, is scheduled to be replaced in the MCM role by the multipurpose MH-60S Knighthawk. (2003, U.S. Navy/Brien Aho)

MARINE MAMMAL SYSTEMS

The U.S. Navy has developed a fully operational minehunting capability employing trained bottlenose dolphins and sea lions. Part of the Navy's Marine Mammal Systems (MMS), it is used when hardware is inadequate or personnel safety is an issue. Dolphins are used because of their exceptional biological sonar, which is unmatched by hardware sonars in detecting objects in the water column and on the ocean floor. Sea lions are used because of their highly sensitive underwater directional hearing and low-light-level vision. Both mammals are trainable for tasks and capable of repetitive diving.

All mammals are assigned to the Navy's Explosive Ordnance Disposal (EOD) Group 1 and the subordinate Naval Special Clearance Team 1 and EOD Mobile Unit 3 at San Diego, except MMS Mk 6, which is assigned to EOD Mobile Unit 6 at Charleston, South Carolina. MMS Mk 4, 7, and 8 are under the operational control of Commander, Mine Warfare Command, at Ingleside. About 40 marine mammals are in "naval service."

Each "system" has four to eight mammals, an officer-in-charge, and several enlisted personnel. The mammal units can be transported by aircraft, helicopter, and land vehicles, and can be maintained on board an amphibious ship. For example, in the multinational RIMPAC '94 exercise, dolphins and their supporting personnel and equipment were based on the amphibious ship JUNEAU (LPD 10). The mammals—two Mk 4 dolphins and four Mk 7 dolphins—lived in specially designed saltwater pools kept in the ship's docking well. Operating one at a time, the dolphins then swam to the operating area, accompanied by their handlers riding in small boats.

The MMS mammals also have been used for waterfront security, including during the 1996 Republican Convention in San Diego.

The current systems are:

Mk 4: A four-dolphin searching detachment that detects and marks the location of moored mines.

Mk 5: A four sea lion exercise-mine recovery unit that operates training mines fitted with acoustic pingers. The sea lions can locate these mines in depths to 1,000 feet (305 m) and attach a recovery device. These sea lions were used in the Persian Gulf in 2003.

Mk 6: A six-dolphin and swimmer detection detachment that can detect and mark the location of an intruder in an area. The system was used in Vietnam in 1970–1971 and in the Persian Gulf in 1987–1988 and again in 2003.

Mk 7: A dolphin mine-search system that can detect and mark the locations of mines on and buried in the ocean floor. The system is configured specifically to support amphibious operations.

Mk 8: Another dolphin team; no details of this system are publicly available.

A dolphin from the Mk 6 system "talks" with a handler during operations in the Persian Gulf. The acoustic prowess of marine animals is invaluable in littoral naval operations. (2003, U.S. Navy/Veronica Birmingham)

"Zak," a 375-pound sea lion of the Mk 5 system leaps into a rigid hull inflatable boat during a harbor-patrol training session at Bahrain. Sea lions and dolphins are trained to locate swimmers and suspicious objects in port and harbor areas. (2003, U.S. Navy/Bob Houlihan)

During Persian Gulf operations, the docking well of the amphibious ship GUNSTON HALL (LSD 44) is used to house holding pens for nine dolphins, as well as other gear for mine clearance units from the Australia, Britain, and the United States. (2003, U.S. Navy/Brien Aho)

CHAPTER 23

Auxiliary Ships

Boatswain's mates aboard the carrier ENTERPRISE (CVN 65) handle a line during an Underway Replenishment (UNREP) with the combat support ship DETROIT during Operation Summer Pulse 2004. UNREP permits Navy surface ships to range far and wide, without dependence on land bases. (2004, U.S. Navy/Alex J. Recalde)

Auxiliary ships provide support to the "fighting fleet" and special services to the Navy and other U.S. military services. There are a large number of different types of specialized auxiliary ships in U.S. naval service; most are operated by the Military Sealift Command's (MSC) Naval Fleet Auxiliary Force with civilian crews, but Navy communications personnel and other specialists are assigned to some MSC ships. Only nine auxiliary ships listed in this chapter are manned by active-duty Navy crews: three replenishment ships (AOE), four salvage ships (ARS), and two submarine tenders (AS).

Sealift ships—although nominally considered to be auxiliary ships—are described in Chapter 24.

Like other components of the Navy, the roster of auxiliary ships has been slashed in the post–Cold War reductions. In particular, the tender force has been all but eliminated; only 2 submarine tenders remain in active service, compared to 9 destroyer tenders and 11 submarine tenders in commission in 1990.

A new class of Underway Replenishment (UNREP) ships with the designation AKE is under construction. No other auxiliary ships are under construction except for sealift ships (see Chapter 24).

Almost all of the large numbers of auxiliary ships built in the 1940s and 1950s have been discarded from active naval service. Several civilian auxiliary ships under charter to the Navy are listed under service craft (see Chapter 25).

Classification: Auxiliary ships are listed in this chapter in alphabetical order according to type classification. The U.S. Navy arranges auxiliary ships according to function, under the categories:

1. Combat Logistic Type Ships—ships that have the capability to provide underway replenishment to fleet units.[1]
   a. Underway Replenishment: AE, AFS, AO, AOE
2. Mobile Logistic Type Ships—ships that have the capability to provide underway replenishment to fleet units and/or provide direct material support to other deployed units operating far from home base.
   a. Material Support: AS
3. Support Type Ships—ships designed to operate in the open ocean in a variety of sea states to provide general support to either combatant forces or shore-based establishments. (Includes smaller auxiliaries that, by the nature of their duties, rarely leave inshore waters.)
   a. Fleet Support: ARS, ATF
   b. Other Auxiliaries: ACS, AG, AGF, AGM, AGOR, AGOS, AGSS, AH, AK, AKB, AKR, AOG, AOT, AP, ARC, AVB

Although overly simplistic, this scheme does attempt to indicate the types of support the various auxiliaries provide to the fleet. This Navy scheme was initiated in 1978.

Three ships officially classified as auxiliaries are listed elsewhere in this volume and are not included in Table 23-1: two miscellaneous command ships (AGF) in Chapter 18 and one auxiliary submarine (AGSS) in Chapter 12.

Guns: Most Navy-manned auxiliaries have a minimal armament of 20-mm Gatling guns for close-in self-defense.

No active auxiliary ships retain the 5-inch/38-cal (127-mm) guns that populated such ships from the late 1930s onward, or the 3-inch/50-cal (76-mm) guns that were common in auxiliary ships from the early 1940s.

None of the ships operated by the MSC is armed.

Missiles: The Navy-manned AOE replenishment ships are the only U.S. Navy auxiliary ships armed with guided missiles.

Names: The historical naming scheme for auxiliary ships, like those for combatants, has undergone a considerable degree of corruption during the past few years, mainly for political purposes. See comments under various auxiliary ship headings.

Operational: Auxiliary ships are operated by the active Navy and the MSC, the latter with civil service or contractor civilian

Sailors line a hangar bay of the ENTERPRISE *during an UNREP with the* DETROIT. *UNREPs demand large numbers of sailors to handle lines and stores; efforts to reduce carrier manning will have to consider these requirements, which were exacerbated with the shift of many UNREP ships to the Military Sealift Command with smaller crews. (2004, U.S. Navy/Jason W. Pfiester)*

crews. Navy communications or specialist detachment are assigned to some MSC-manned ships.

Ships assigned to the MSC-Reduced Operating Status (ROS) are laid up in reserve, in four- or five-day readiness for reactivation. They have cadre crews of a few civilian maintenance personnel.

Auxiliary ships no longer are assigned to the Naval Reserve Force (NRF), which previously manned several salvage ships (ARS) with composite active–reserve crews.

Several Navy ships are on loan to academic institutions conducting naval research projects. The Maritime Administration (MarAd) holds title to all state maritime academy training ships, most of which are former U.S. Navy ships.

The MSC ships have the prefix "USNS," for U.S. Naval Ship, and the prefix "T-" is appended to their hull numbers.

Status: Navy ships are decommissioned; Military Sealift Command (civilian-manned) ships taken out of service are placed Out of Service, In Reserve (OSIR).

---

1 These are officially considered warship/combatant ships.

Table 23-1. AUXILIARY SHIPS (EARLY 2005)

Type		Active				Reserve	Building*
		Total	Navy	MSC	Academic		
AD	Destroyer tenders	—	—	—	—	2	—
AE	Ammunition ships	6	—	6	—	1	—
AFS	Combat stores ships	6	—	6	—	2	—
AG	Miscellaneous auxiliaries	1	—	1	—	—	—
AGM	Missile range instrumentation ships	2	—	2	—	—	—
AGOR	Oceanographic research ships	7	—	—	7	—	—
AGOS	Ocean surveillance ships	5	—	4	—	1	—
AGS	Surveying ships	8	—	8	—	—	—
AH	Hospital ships	—	—	—	—	2	—
AKE	Dry cargo/ammunition ships	—	—	—	—	—	6
AO	Oilers	14	—	13	—	3	—
AOE	Fast combat support ships	7	3	4	—	1	—
ARC	Cable ships	1	—	1	—	—	—
ARS	Salvage ships	4	4	—	—	—	—
AS	Submarine tenders	4	2	—	—	2	—
ATF	Fleet tugs	7	—	5	2**	—	—
AVB	Aviation logistic ships	—	—	—	—	2	—

* Ships authorized through FY 2004.
** Ships on commercial loan.

AUXILIARY CRANE SHIPS

The auxiliary crane ships (ACS) are listed with sealift ships (Chapter 24). The Navy's one previous ship in this general category was the ex-battleship KEARSARGE (BB 5, redesignated IX 16 and then AB 1). Completed in 1900, the KEARSARGE was converted in 1920, being fitted with a 250-ton-capacity crane and hull blisters to provide more stability; she was non-self-propelled. In 1941, she was renamed CRANE SHIP NO. 1 when the name KEARSARGE was assigned to the carrier CV 12 (subsequently renamed HORNET) and then to the CV 33. The CRANE SHIP NO. 1 was stricken in 1955 and sold for scrap.[2]

DESTROYER TENDERS

Destroyer tenders have served the U.S. Navy from 1898 (the USS DIXIE/AD 1) until 1996, when the last active ship was decommissioned. These ships provided all manner of support to destroyers and other surface ships.

Names: Destroyer tenders were named for geographic areas, except for the SAMUEL GOMPERS, which honored a labor leader.

---

2 An excellent description of the CRANE SHIP NO. 1 is A. D. Baker III, "Historic Fleets," *Naval History* (August 2004), pp. 12, 15.

2 DESTROYER TENDERS: "SAMUEL GOMPERS" CLASS

Number	Name	FY	Launched	Comm.	Status
AD 37	SAMUEL GOMPERS	64	14 May 1966	1 July 1967	decomm. 27 Oct 1995; str. 7 Apr 1999
AD 38	PUGET SOUND	65	16 Sep 1966	27 Apr 1968	AR; decomm. 27 Jan 1996
AD 41	YELLOWSTONE	75	27 Jan 1979	28 June 1980	decomm. 31 Jan 1996; str. 7 Apr 1999
AD 42	ACADIA	76	28 July 1979	6 June 1981	PR; decomm. 16 Dec 1994
AD 43	CAPE COD	77	2 Aug 1980	17 Apr 1982	decomm. 29 Sep 1995; str. 7 Apr 1999
AD 44	SHENANDOAH	79	6 Feb 1982	15 Aug 1983	decomm. 13 Sep 1996; str. 7 Apr 1999

Builders:	AD 38: Puget Sound Naval Shipyard, Wash.	Boilers:	2 600 psi (41.7 kg/cm2)(Combustion Engineering)
	AD 42: National Steel & Shipbuilding, San Diego, Calif.	Speed:	20 knots (18 knots sustained)
Displacement:	AD 38: 13,600 tons light	Range:	
	AD 42: 13,318 tons light	Personnel:	AD 38: 625 (42 officers + 583 enlisted)
	AD 38: 20,500 tons full load		AD 42: 631 (47 officers + 584 enlisted)
	AD 42: 20,224 tons full load	Helicopters:	landing area (see *Design* notes)
Length:	620 feet (189.02 m) waterline	Guns:	2 40-mm grenade launchers Mk 19 (2 single)
	643⅜ feet (196.3 m) overall		4 20-mm cannon Mk 67 (2 single) in AD 38;
Beam:	85 feet (25.9 m)		2 guns in AD 42
Draft:	22½ feet (6.9 m)	Radars:	LN-66 navigation
Propulsion:	2 steam turbines (De Laval); 20,000 shp; 1 shaft		SPS-10 surface search

These were the Navy's only destroyer tenders designed and built after World War II. They were configured to support modern surface combatants, including ships with nuclear and gas turbine propulsion. They are similar to the L. Y. SPEAR-class submarine tenders.

The PUGET SOUND and ACADIA are being maintained in reserve, one on each coast. In addition, the YELLOWSTONE, CAPE COD, and SHENANDOAH (all three in strike status) were assigned to the National Defense Reserve Fleet (NDRF) on 6 February, 29 September, and 2 November 2000, respectively.

The SAMUEL GOMPERS was sunk as a target on 21 July 2003.

Class: The AD 39 was authorized in the Fiscal Year (FY) 1969 shipbuilding program but was canceled prior to the start of construction because of cost overruns in other new ship programs. The

AD 40 was authorized in FY 1973 but was not built. An AD 45 was planned for the FY 1980 program but was not funded. Two additional tenders planned for FY 1987 and 1988 were deleted from the five-year program of January 1984.

The AD 41 and later ships are officially considered the YELLOWSTONE class; they are similar and hence combined in this entry.

Design: The SAMUEL GOMPERS was SCB No. 244; subsequent ships were No. 700 in the new SCB series.

A landing platform and hangar for Drone Anti-Submarine Helicopters (DASH) were provided in the AD 37 and AD 38. The later ships had helicopter decks only.

The ships have two 30-ton-capacity and two 6½-ton cranes.

The PUGET SOUND is one of only two destroyer tenders retained in reserve, the survivors of a once numerous auxiliary type. Her massive hull contains repair shops and provisions, parts, and munitions stowage, as well as accommodations for a crew of skilled mechanists and artisans. (1991, Giorgio Arra)

The PUGET SOUND—*like other tender-type ships—has large cranes for handling parts, provisions, and munitions for her brood. Large side ports open to provide direct access to ships moored alongside. Note her squared-off stern and stern anchor. (1991, Giorgio Arra)*

Guns: As built, the AD 37 and AD 38 had a single 5-inch/38-cal Dual Purpose (DP) gun forward with a Mk 56 Gunfire Control System (GFCS); this armament was removed. Plans to install NATO Sea Sparrow missile launchers in these ships were dropped.

Operational: The PUGET SOUND served as flagship of the U.S. Sixth Fleet from May 1980 to October 1985, when she was relieved by the command ship CORONADO (AGF 11). While serving as the Sixth Fleet flagship, the PUGET SOUND was homeported at Gaeta, Italy. As fleet flagship, she carried some 225 flag personnel.

Table 23-2. DESTROYER TENDERS

Number	Name	Comm.	Notes
	DIXIE class (5)		
AD 14	DIXIE	1940	str. 1982
AD 15	PRAIRIE	1940	decomm./str. 26 Mar 1993
	C3-S1-N2 type		
AD 16	CASCADE	1943	str. 1974
	DIXIE class (continued)		
AD 17	PIEDMONT	1944	str. 1982; to Turkey 1982
AD 18	SIERRA	1944	decomm./str. 29 Oct 1993
AD 19	YOSEMITE	1944	decomm./str. 27 Jan 1994
	C3 cargo type (2)		
AD 20	HAMUL (ex-AK 20)		str. 1963
AD 21	MARKAB (ex-AK 31)		to AR 23
AD 22–25	KLONDIKE class		modified C3 design
AD 26–31	SHENANDOAH class		modified C3 design
AD 32	NEW ENGLAND (ex-AS 28)		canceled 1945
AD 33	SHENANDOAH class		canceled 1945
AD 34	ALCOR (ex-AR 10, AG 34)		str. 1946
AD 35, 36	SHENANDOAH class		(AD 35 canceled 1945)
AD 37–44	SAMUEL GOMPERS class		

World War II destroyer tenders reached hull number AD 36, with the AD 32, 33, and 35 being canceled at the end of World War II. The AD 32 was to have been a one-of-a-kind tender. Several of the war-built ships served into the 1990s, hence they are listed above. During their very long careers, these ships were modernized to support surface warships fitted with Anti-Submarine Rockets (ASROC), improved electronics, nuclear propulsion, etc.

Three destroyer tenders were reclassified as repair ships: the KLONDIKE (AD 22) to AR 22 in 1960, MARKAB (AD 21) to AR 23 in 1959, and GRAND CANYON (AD 28) to AR 28 in 1971.

AMMUNITION SHIPS

These ships carry a vast variety of munitions for surface combatants and aircraft carriers. They are capable of underway replenishment of warships.

Names: Ammunition ships carry the names of explosives and volcanoes.

AMMUNITION SHIPS: MODIFIED "KILAUEA" CLASS

The planned ammunition ships of the modified KILAUEA class (AE 36–40) were deferred in favor of construction of additional AOE-type replenishment ships. The lead ship initially was planned for the FY 1986 shipbuilding program, but the ships were delayed continually. When the program was halted, one ship was planned for FY 1991, one for FY 1992, two for FY 1993, and one for FY 1994.

These ships were to have been slightly larger than the KILAUEA class, with gas turbine propulsion (two LM 2500s) (see 14th Edition/ pages 250–51 for characteristics).

7 AMMUNITION SHIPS: "KILAUEA" CLASS

Number	Name	FY	Launched	Comm.	to MSC	Status
T-AE 26	KILAUEA	65	9 Aug 1967	10 Aug 1968	1 Oct 1980	**MSC-P**
T-AE 27	BUTTE	65	9 Aug 1967	29 Nov 1968	3 June 1996	**MSC-A**
T-AE 28	SANTA BARBARA	66	23 Jan 1968	11 July 1970	30 Sep 1998	MSC-ROS
AE 29	MOUNT HOOD	66	17 July 1968	1 May 1971	—	decomm./str. 13 Aug 1999
T-AE 32	FLINT	67	9 Nov 1970	20 Nov 1971	4 Aug 1995	**MSC-P**
T-AE 33	SHASTA	67	3 Apr 1971	26 Feb 1972	1 Oct 1997	**MSC-P**
T-AE 34	MOUNT BAKER	68	23 Oct 1971	22 July 1972	18 Dec 1996	**MSC-A**
T-AE 35	KISKA	68	11 Mar 1972	16 Dec 1972	1 Aug 1996	**MSC-P**

Builders:	AE 26, 27: General Dynamics, Quincy, Mass.	Speed:	22 knots (20 knots sustained)
	AE 28: Bethlehem Steel, Sparrows Point, Md.	Range:	18,000 nm (33,336 km) at 11 knots
	AE 32–35: Ingalls Shipbuilding, Pascagoula, Miss.		10,000 nm (18,520 km) at 20 knots
Displacement:	9,238 tons light	Personnel:	125 civilian, except 133 in T-AE 32, + 21–26 Navy (1–4
	19,937 tons full load		officers + 20–22 enlisted) + helicopter det.
Length:	563⅝ feet (171.9 m) overall	Helicopters:	2 UH-46 Sea Knight
Beam:	81 feet (24.7 m)	Guns:	removed
Draft:	27¹¹⁄₂ feet (8.5 m)	Radars:	SPS-10F surface search
Propulsion:	3 steam turbines (General Electric); 22,000 shp; 1 shaft		SPS-64(V)9 navigation
Boilers:	3 600 psi (41.7 kg/cm2) (Foster Wheeler)	EW systems:	removed

These are high-capability underway replenishment ships, fitted with the Fast Automatic Shuttle Transfer (FAST) system for the rapid transfer of missiles and other munitions.

Seven of these were taken out of Navy commission and transferred to the Military Sealift Command for operation by civilian crews, with Navy communications and helicopter detachments. The KILAUEA subsequently was taken out of MSC service on 1 October 2000 to become the first MSC fleet auxiliary in ROS; she has since been reactivated. The SANTA BARBARA is now similarly laid up in ROS (scheduled for reactivation in 45 days).

The MOUNT HOOD was decommissioned and stricken without being transferred to the MSC (as had been planned for 1998); she has been scrapped.

Design: SCB No. 703. The KILAUEA design provides for the ship's main cargo spaces forward of the superstructure and a helicopter landing area aft. A hangar approximately 50 feet (15.2 m) long, 15½–17½ feet (4.7–5.3 m) wide, and 16⅔–17¾ feet (5.1–5.4 m) high is built into the superstructure. Cargo capacity is approximately 6,500 tons.

Guns: As built, the ships had eight 3-inch/50-cal Mk 33 guns in twin mounts with two Mk 56 GFCS. Their armament was reduced during the late 1970s; the Navy-manned ships lost their last two 3-inch gun mounts in the late 1980s with two Phalanx Close-in Weapon Systems (CIWS) were installed.

On transfer to the MSC, the ships were totally disarmed, and their SLQ-25 Nixie and SLQ-32(V)1 electronic systems were removed (seven ships).

The large helicopter deck and twin hangars of the KILAUEA class are evident in this view of the SHASTA. Cargo handling/UNREP gear is mounted forward and aft, as well as amidships. All UNREP ships in U.S. service are operated by MSC, except for three AOEs. (2002, U.S. Navy/Bob Meeker)

The KISKA in the Persian Gulf during an UNREP with an aircraft carrier during Operation Iraqi Freedom. An SH-60 Seahawk, taken from its anti-submarine duties, is lifting ordnance from the KISKA's helicopter deck. Vertical replenishment is a key component of UNREP operations. (2003, U.S. Navy/John P. Curtis)

The MOUNT BAKER slowly approaches a pier at Souda Bay, Crete. The Greek port has been invaluable for U.S./NATO operations in the Mediterranean area. When Navy manned, the MOUNT BAKER carried 3-inch/50-cal guns and, later, Phalanx Close-In Weapon System (CIWS) mounts. (2004, U.S. Navy/Paul Farley)

The SPICA maneuvers near the carrier HARRY S. TRUMAN (CVN 75). The three British-built combat stores ship have two hangars in their after superstructures. The helicopter on her deck is a French-built SA 330J Puma, one of several under Navy contract to support UNREP operations. (2003, U.S. Navy/John L. Beeman)

Table 23-3. AMMUNITION SHIPS

Number	Name	Comm.	Notes
Suribachi class (5)			
AE 21	Suribachi	1956	decomm. 2 Dec 1994; str. 12 Dec 1996
AE 22	Mauna Kea	1957	decomm. 30 June 1995; str. 12 Dec 1996
AE 23	Nitro	1959	decomm. 28 Apr 1995; str. 14 Aug 1995
AE 24	Pyro	1959	decomm. 31 May 1994; str. 8 Apr 1997
AE 25	Haleakala	1959	decomm./str. 10 Dec 1993
AE 26–29	Kilauea class		
AE 30	Virgo (ex-AKA 20)	1943	str. 1971
AE 31	Chara (ex-AKA 58)	1944	str. 1972
AE 32–35	Kilauea class		

The AE program of World War II reached hull number AE 19. The AE 20 was a C1-A (diesel) cargo ship (AK 22), which was changed to attack cargo ship (AKA 5) in 1943, reverted to AK 22 in 1944, and changed to AE in 1948. The later AE 30 and 31 also were former attack cargo ships; their heavy booms for lifting vehicles and landing craft facilitated their use as ammo ships. They both were stricken as AKAs in 1960–1961, then reinstated on the Naval Vessel Register (NVR) in 1965 and recommissioned as AEs in 1966.

The Suribachi class (AE 21–25) was designed specifically for underway replenishment of munitions; the three later ships also were referred to as the Nitro class (the AE 21 and AE 22 were SCB No. 114; AE 23–25 were SCB 114A). The Mauna Kea was transferred to the NRF in 1979 and the Pyro in 1980; however, the heavy operating tempo in the Indian Ocean–Persian Gulf areas led to their being returned to the active fleet in 1982.

The Nitro and Pyro (both in strike status) were assigned to the NDRF on 9 February and 17 August 2000, respectively.

STORE SHIPS

These ships carried refrigerated stores and general cargo for the underway replenishment of ships at sea; they generally were referred to as "reefers." Their role in the fleet was taken over by the more versatile AFS/AOE/AOR types.

World War II–era store ships reached hull number AF 47. All postwar ships were based on merchant designs. Most were of the R series, indicating refrigerated holds; for example, the R2 was the reefer variant of the C2 design. By 1990, all had been stricken except one ship of the R3-S-4a type.

STORE SHIPS: "RIGEL" CLASS

Number	Name	Comm.	To MSC	Status
T-AF 58	Rigel	1955	23 June 1975	decomm. 9 Sep 1992; str. 16 May 1994
AF 59	Vega	1955	—	str. 1977

The Rigel was the last store ship in naval service. She and her sister ship Vega were the Navy's largest reefers and only designed-for-the-purpose store ships, being built to a modified R3-S-4a merchant design. They were similar to the AE 21 design.

COMBAT STORES SHIPS

These ships combined the capabilities of early store ships (AF), stores-issue ships (AKS), and aviation store ships (AVS), carrying refrigerated and dry stores, as well as parts and other cargo, for underway replenishment of ships at sea. They do not carry bulk petroleum products as do the AOE/AOR replenishment ships.

Names: British-built combat stores ships are named for celestial bodies; U.S.-built ships have city names, except that the Mars honors the Roman god of war.

3 COMBAT STORES SHIPS: EX-BRITISH STORES SUPPORT SHIPS

Number	Name	Launched	Completed	U.S. In Service	Status
T-AFS 8	Sirius	7 Apr 1966	22 Dec 1966	17 Jan 1981	**MSC-A**
T-AFS 9	Spica	22 Feb 1967	21 Mar 1967	4 Nov 1981	**MSC-P**
T-AFS 10	Saturn	16 Sep 1966	10 Aug 1967	30 Sep 1984	**MSC-A**

Builders:	Swan Hunter & Wighman Richardson, Wallsend-on-Tyne (England)	Propulsion:	1 turbocharged diesel engine (Wallsend-Sulzer 8RD76); 12,700 bhp; 1 shaft
Displacement:	9,010 tons light 16,792 tons full load	Speed:	19 knots
		Range:	27,500 nm (50,930 km) at 12 knots
Length:	489⅝ feet (149.35 m) waterline 523¼ feet (159.5 m) overall		11,000 nm (20,372 km) at 19 knots
		Personnel:	103 civilian + 26 Navy (4 officers + 22 enlisted) + helicopter det.
Beam:	72 feet (22.0 m)	Helicopters:	2 UH-46 Sea Knight
Draft:	25½ feet (7.8 m)	Radars:	2 navigation

These ships are former Royal Navy replenishment ships acquired by the U.S. Navy because of the increased logistics demands of maintaining two carrier battle groups in the Persian Gulf–Indian Ocean area following the crises and conflicts in that region that began with the Iranian Revolution of 1979. The ships previously were operated as Royal Fleet Auxiliary (RFA) ships with civilian crews.

With the purchase of the third British ship, the Navy dropped plans to construct an additional AFS of the Mars class under the FY 1987 shipbuilding program.

Class: This was a class of three ships, their British names being Lyness, Tarbatness, and Stromness, respectively. The Lyness

originally was acquired by the U.S. government on a one-year bare-boat charter on 17 January 1981, at which time she was placed in U.S. service (renamed Sirius); she was acquired by the Navy on 1 March 1982.

The Tarbatness was acquired on time charter on 30 September 1981; that was changed to a bare-boat charter on 4 November 1981, and at that time she was placed in U.S. service (renamed Spica). She was acquired by the Navy on 30 September 1982.

The Stromness was acquired on 1 October 1983 (renamed Saturn).

The Sirius and Spica were purchased under the FY 1982 program at a total cost of $37 million. The Saturn was purchased in

FY 1984 for $13 million (plus $3.1 million in spare parts for the entire class).

Helicopters: The SATURN conducted flight tests with the SA 330J Puma as a Vertical Replenishment (VERTREP) helicopter off the Virginia coast on 20–21 December 1999. The Puma now is employed aboard these ships in the VERTREP role because of the shortfall in Navy UH-46 Sea Knight and, subsequently, MH-60S Knighthawk helicopters. The Pumas are operated by a commercial helicopter services firm.

Modernization: In U.S. service, the ships have been modernized with improved communication and UNREP facilities, plus automated data processing. All have been fitted with twin helicopter hangars.

The SATURN shows the unusual appearance of these British built ships, with the funnel isolated from the forward and after superstructures. Here, a CH-46D Sea Knight operates from the ship. The Navy also uses the massive MH-53E Sea Dragon for UNREP, although those aircraft are scheduled for replacement by the MH-60S Knighthawk. (2002, U.S. Navy/Alta I. Cutler)

The SPICA approaches the carrier JOHN F. KENNEDY during UNREP operations in the Mediterranean. Civilian-piloted SA 330J Puma cargo helicopters are operating from the SPICA. (2002, U.S. Navy/Jim Hampshire)

5 COMBAT STORES SHIPS: "MARS" CLASS

Number	Name	FY	Launched	Comm.	to MSC	Status
T-AFS 1	Mars	61	15 June 1963	21 Dec 1963	1 Feb 1993	OSIR 18 Feb 1998; PR
AFS 2	Sylvania	62	15 Aug 1963	11 July 1964	—	decomm. 26 May 1994; str. 5 Jan 1995
T-AFS 3	Niagara Falls	64	26 Mar 1966	29 Apr 1967	23 Sep 1994	**MSC-A**
AFS 4	White Plains	65	23 July 1966	23 Nov 1968	—	decomm. 17 Apr 1995; str. 24 Aug 1995
T-AFS 5	Concord	65	17 Dec 1966	27 Nov 1968	15 Oct 1992	**MSC-P**
T-AFS 6	San Diego	66	13 Apr 1968	24 May 1969	11 Aug 1993	OSIR 10 Dec 1997; AR
T-AFS 7	San Jose	67	12 Dec 1969	23 Oct 1970	2 Nov 1993	**MSC-A**

Builders:	National Steel & Shipbuilding, San Diego, Calif.	Speed:	21 knots
Displacement:	9,200–9,400 tons light	Range:	18,000 nm (33,336 km) at 11 knots
	16,070 tons full load		10,000 nm (18,520 km) at 20 knots
Length:	529⅞ feet (161.5 m) waterline	Personnel:	136 civilian + 26 Navy (4 officers + 22 enlisted)
	580⅝ feet (177.1 m) overall		+ helicopter det.
Beam:	79 feet (24.1 m)	Helicopters:	2 UH-46 Sea Knight
Draft:	24 feet (7.3 m)	Guns:	removed
Propulsion:	2 steam turbines (De Laval, except Westinghouse in AFS 6);	Radars:	LN-66 navigation
	22,000 shp; 1 shaft		SPS-10 surface search
Boilers:	3 600 psi (41.7 kg/cm2) (Babcock & Wilcox)		

These are large, built-for-the-purpose underway replenishment ships combining the capabilities of store ships (AF) and stores-issue ships (AKS). All ships of this class originally were in active Navy service; six were transferred to MSC operation with civilian crews (the SYLVANIA and WHITE PLAINS were decommissioned while in active Navy service). During modification for MSC operation, their cargo handling capabilities were enhanced (e.g., additional cargo elevators).

The SYLVANIA (while in strike status) was assigned to the NDRF on 12 September 2000. The WHITE PLAINS was sunk on 4 July 2002 as a target for South Korean warships (off the coast of Southern California).

Class: Three additional ships of this class originally were planned in the FY 1977–1978 shipbuilding programs; they were not requested by the administration in those years.

Design: The AFS 1–3 were SCB No. 208; the later ships were No. 705 in the later SCB series. These ships have five cargo holds

(one refrigerated) with a combined 7,000-ton cargo capacity. A large helicopter deck is fitted, with a hangar 46¾–51 feet in length and 16–23 feet wide.

Electronics: When Navy manned, these ships had the SLQ-32(V)1 Electronic Countermeasures (ECM) system and SLQ-25 Nixie towed acoustic torpedo decoy.

Engineering: Two boilers normally are used for full-power steaming with the third shut down for maintenance.

Guns: These ships were completed with four 3-inch twin gun mounts, with one pair of mounts forward and a second pair aft of the funnel. Two mounts were deleted from all ships but the WHITE PLAINS during the late 1970s; all ships lost their Mk 56 GFCS, as well as their SPS-40 air-search radar.

The WHITE PLAINS carried eight 3-inch guns into the mid-1980s when she beached two twin mounts in favor of two Phalanx CIWS. The other ships were to be similarly rearmed. All guns were removed for MSC service (i.e., from all ships except the SYLVANIA).

The stern aspect of the SAN JOSE shows the large helicopter deck of these ships and the two-hangar after superstructure. Like all other civilian-manned, MSC-operated UNREP ships, their 3-inch/50-cal guns and Phalanx CIWS have been removed. The flight deck is cluttered with packets to be lifted by helicopter. (2003, U.S. Navy/Jason T. Poplin)

The SAN JOSE pulls alongside the carrier NIMITZ (CVN 68) during UNREP operations in the South Pacific. At the time, the NIMITZ was en route to the Persian Gulf to participate in Operation Iraqi Freedom. (2003, U.S. Navy/Timothy Sosa)

The NIAGARA FALLS is one of three MARS-class combat stores ships still in service, all civilian manned under the MSC. Originally a class of seven Navy-manned ships, the others fell to post–Cold War cutbacks. The new T-AKE design will replace the surviving ships. (2002, U.S. Navy/Michael J. Pusnik Jr.)

MISCELLANEOUS AUXILIARIES

The HAYES is in naval service under the designation miscellaneous auxiliary. A second—the infamous deep-ocean salvage ship GLOMAR EXPLORER (AG 193)—remains on the NVR in a loan status, being used by a commercial firm as a deep-sea drilling platform.

1 SOUND TRIALS SHIP: "HAYES"

Number	Name	FY	Launched	Comm.	Status
T-AG 195 (ex-T-AGOR 16)	HAYES	67	2 July 1970	21 July 1971	**MSC-A**

Builders:	Todd Shipyards, Seattle, Wash.	Propulsion:	diesel-electric (3 Caterpillar 3516 geared diesels);
Displacement:	2,329 tons light		5,400 shp; 2 shafts
	4,037 tons full load	Speed:	12 knots
Length:	220 feet (67.1 m) waterline	Range:	6,000 nm (11,112 km) at 12 knots
	246⅚ feet (75.1 m) overall	Personnel:	19 civilian + 30 technicians
Beam:	75 feet (22.9 m)	Helicopters:	no facilities
Draft:	22 feet (6.7 m)	Radars:	Raytheon TM 1650/6X navigation
			Raytheon TM 1660/12S navigation

The HAYES is a catamaran, built specifically for use as an oceanographic research ship. She has been converted to an acoustic research ship to replace the sound barge MONOB ONE (YAG 61) in support of noise measuring of nuclear-propelled submarines. In her new role the HAYES can transport, deploy, and retrieve acoustic arrays and conduct acoustic research. She is operated by an MSC civilian crew.

Following service as an oceanographic research ship (T-AGOR 16), the HAYES was laid up from 1983 until her conversion to a sound trials ship began in 1989. The conversion was completed and she was returned to service on 19 June 1992.

The HAYES operates in the Exuma Sound in the Bahama Islands under sponsorship of the David Taylor Research Center. She is homeported at Port Canaveral, Florida.

Classification: The ships was changed from T-AGOR 16 to T-AG 195 on 20 March 1989.

Conversion: The HAYES was to have been converted to a sound trials ship under a contract awarded on 20 February 1987 to Tacoma Boatbuilding Co. in Tacoma, Washington. Conversion began on 27 August 1989, but the contract was terminated, and the ship was towed to the Puget Sound Naval Shipyard on 1 December 1990 for completion. She was placed in MSC service in 1992.

Design: SCB No. 726. The HAYES has two hulls, each with a 24-foot (7.3-m) beam, spaced 27 feet (8.2 m) apart, for an overall ship beam of 75 feet (22.9 m). Berthing and messing spaces are located in the forward superstructure "block," and the laboratories are located aft.

The catamaran design provides a stable work platform with a large, open deck area; also, a centerline well makes it possible to lower research equipment into the sheltered water between the two hulls. Some seakeeping problems were encountered in the design, and it has not been repeated. In particular, the HAYES suffered excessive pitching in her AGOR role and was not considered particularly successful as a seagoing research ship.

The HAYES was built simultaneously with the catamaran submarine rescue ships of the PIGEON (ASR 21) class. This design differs considerably from the Small Waterplane Area Twin Hull (SWATH) design employed for ocean surveillance ships (AGOS); see below.

Electronics: The ship conducts noise measurements with a towed array, with a towing speed of 3–10 knots.

Engineering: The AG conversion included providing a high degree of automation in the engineering spaces; the original four high-speed diesel engines driving controllable-pitch propellers were replaced. An auxiliary 165-hp diesel engine is provided in each hull to permit a "creeping" speed of 2–4 knots with main propulsion shut down.

NAVIGATION RESEARCH SHIP: CONVERTED OILER

Number	Name	Acquired by Navy	T-AGM in service	Notes
T-AG 194	VANGUARD	1947	1966	OSIR 30 Mar 1998; to NDRF 12 June 1998

This ship was built as a merchant tanker (MISSION SAN FERNANDO); she was acquired by the Navy in 1947 and placed in service as a fleet oiler (AO 122) with the Naval Transportation Service. She was transferred to the Military Sea Transportation Service (MSTS) when that agency was created in 1949 (changed to T-AO 122). Subsequently, she was in and out of service as the oiler/tanker requirements changed: to the NDRF in 1955; stricken on 22 June 1955; reacquired by the Navy on 21 June 1956; stricken and returned to the NDRF on 4 September 1957; reacquired by the Navy on 28 September 1964 for conversion to T-AGM 19 and renamed MUSCLE SHOALS. She was renamed VANGUARD in 1965.

The HAYES supports the research and development of advanced acoustic sensors, as well as submarine noise suppression efforts. Catamaran hulls have not been efficient for most large, oceangoing ship designs. (1992, courtesy Capt. David W. Muir/USNS HAYES)

The HAYES, following extensive conversion to a sound trials ship, meets the very stringent self-generated noise levels required to measure other ships' self-generated noises specified in Navy noise reduction programs. (1992, courtesy Capt. David W. Muir/USNS HAYES)

Later employed as a navigation test ship for Trident strategic missile submarines, her designation was changed to T-AG 194 in 1980.

The three AGMs of this type—Maritime Administration T2-SE-A2—were the largest of the 23 range instrumentation ships operated by the United States.

The VANGUARD will be stricken in the near future.

See 16th Edition/pages 218–19 for characteristics.

1 HEAVY LIFT SHIP: "GLOMAR EXPLORER"

Number	Name	Launched	Completed	Status
AG 193	GLOMAR EXPLORER	1 Nov 1972	July 1973	loan

Builders:	Sun Shipbuilding and Dry Dock, Chester, Pa.
Displacement:	63,300 tons full load
Tonnage:	39,705 deadweight tons (DWT)
	27,445 gross registered tons (GRT)
	18,511 tons net
Length:	556½½ feet (169.8 m) waterline
	618¾ feet (188.7 m) overall
Beam:	115⅝ feet (35.3 m)
Draft:	46½½ feet (14.3 m)
Propulsion:	diesel-electric (5 Nordberg diesel engines; 6 General Electric motors); 13,200 shp; 2 shafts
Speed:	10.8 knots
Range:	
Personnel:	approx. 180 civilian
Helicopters:	landing area
Radars:	2 navigation

The GLOMAR EXPLORER was built and operated by the Central Intelligence Agency specifically to lift the remains of a Soviet Golf-class (Project 629) ballistic missile submarine that sank in the mid-Pacific in 1968. The ship lifted the forward portion of the submarine from a depth of 3 miles (4.8 km) in 1974 in a clandestine operation given the code name Operation Jennifer. (The ship's cover story was that it was conducting a seafloor mining operation under the aegis of millionaire Howard Hughes through the Summa Corporation for his firm Global Marine Development.)

The ship was acquired by the Navy on 30 September 1976 and placed on the NVR; she was transferred to MarAd on 17 January 1977 and laid up in the NDRF in Suisun Bay, California.

Subsequent Navy efforts to sell the ship failed, and in 1978 she was leased to Global Marine Development, Inc., for a commercial seafloor mining venture; she was to be operated by Lockheed Missiles and Space Company in that role. However, that lease was terminated and the ship was returned to Navy control on 25 April 1980 and reassigned to MarAd on the same date.

In late 1979, the Navy planned to provide the ship to the National Science Foundation as a deep-sea drilling ship. After modification, she was to have the capability to drill into the earth at an operating depth of approximately 15,000 feet (4,573 m). That project was not funded.

Since 2 July 1996, the ship has been on loan to Chevron U.S.A. Production Company. In August 1998, she drilled to a record 7,718 feet (2,353 m) on an initial exploratory test well in the Gulf of Mexico's Atwater Valley Block No. 118, about 175 nm (324 km) southeast of New Orleans. The ship remains on the NVR.

Classification: When acquired by the Navy in 1976, the GLOMAR EXPLORER was assigned hull number AG 193.

Cost: The cost of the ship at the time of construction was estimated at $350 million. Certain related equipment and the cost of the HMB-1 submersible barge plus personnel brought the total project cost to an estimated $550 million.

Design: The ship was designed specifically to lift the sunken Golf-class submarine from a depth of 16,500 feet (5,030 m), employing a heavy-lift system including a grappling claw that could be attached to the ship clandestinely by a submersible barge (designated HMB-1). Reportedly, the barge also would have been used to hide the Soviet submarine had the entire 330-foot (100.6-m) hull been salvaged. In the event, the portion salvaged could be accommodated in a large underwater hangar, or "moon pool," within the GLOMAR EXPLORER.

Engineering: Three bow and two stern thrusters are fitted, with an automatic position-keeping system to permit precise maneuvering or holding directly over an object on the ocean floor.

Name: As built, the ship was named HUGHES GLOMAR EXPLORER. Although no Navy name was ever assigned, she is listed in the NVR and other official documents as the GLOMAR EXPLORER.

Operational: The GLOMAR EXPLORER arrived at the submarine lift site on 4 July 1974 and during the month-long operation lifted the forward portion of the submarine. The amidships section containing three SS-N-5 ballistic missiles with nuclear warheads was not salvaged. However, torpedoes were recovered, including two reported to have nuclear warheads. The remains of the submarine were studied within the GLOMAR EXPLORER, then cut apart and packaged for further analysis or jettisoned.

This was the deepest and most complex salvage operation ever undertaken by any nation.

The GLOMAR EXPLORER as configured for deep-ocean lift for the highly classified Project Jennifer. The ship has since been modified and currently is employed as a deep-sea drilling ship. The associated HMB-1 submersible barge is being used to support the SEA SHADOW project (see Chapter 25).

SONAR TRIALS SHIP: "GLOVER"

The GLOVER was authorized as a miscellaneous auxiliary (AG 163), was completed in 1965 as an escort research ship (AGDE 1), and was reclassified as a frigate research ship (AGFF 1) on 30 June 1975. She was used primarily for research into the 1970s, after which the ship became an operational frigate, being reclassified FF 1098 on 1 October 1979 (assigned the hull number of a canceled KNOX/FF 1052-class frigate).

She was again changed to AGFF and designated T-AGFF 1 on 15 June 1990 as a sonar trials ship; she was reconfigured as trials ship for the wide-aperture array sonar and placed in MSC service on 15 June 1991. The forward 5-inch gun mount was retained—making her the only MSC-operated warship.

The GLOVER was placed out of service on 28 September 1992 and transferred to the NDRF on that date; she was stricken on 18 August 1994.

MISCELLANEOUS AUXILIARIES

A variety of ships were designated as miscellaneous auxiliaries to fulfill a number of auxiliary and research functions. At the end of World War II, the AG series had reached hull number 120. In the postwar period, the series reached AG 195, plus two ocean mine-sweepers that served as miscellaneous auxiliaries with their MSO hull numbers: the ALACRITY (MSO/AG 520) and the ASSURANCE (MSO/AG 521).

Of the AG-series ships on the NVR in 1990, the hydrographic research ship KINGSPORT (T-AG 164) was stricken on 31 January 1984 and laid up in the James River (Virginia) group of the NDRF; she was *again* stricken on 20 August 1990 as a result of a Navy records error and later sold for scrap. The small surveying ship S. P. LEE (T-AG 192) was loaned to the U.S. Geological Survey in February 1974; the ship was carried on the NVR in a lease status until taken out of service on 1 August 1992. She was stricken on 1 October 1992 and transferred to Mexico on 7 December 1992.

INTELLIGENCE COLLECTION SHIPS

The U.S. Navy converted ten cargo hulls to intelligence collection ships in the 1960s, with plans for a larger force of these platforms to supplement aircraft, submarines, and surface warships employed in that role.[3] The conversions were to be the equivalent of the large force of Soviet intelligence collection ships (AGI).

Intended for the collection of Signals Intelligence (SIGINT), these ships were manned by Navy personnel but operated under the aegis of the National Security Agency, with some civilian specialists on board. Their "cover" was the collection of oceanographic and other environmental information—they were designated AGER for environmental research ship or AGTR for technical research ship—but their real role was readily apparent from their operations and electronic antennas. The ships carried a minimal armament of machine guns and small arms.

Three FS/AKL-type cargo ships (AGER 1–3) were converted to this role, as were five larger ships of the Liberty and Victory classes (AGTR 1–5).[4] Two smaller cargo-type ships also were employed by the U.S. government in the intelligence role in the 1960s, the PRIVATE JOSEPH E. VALDEZ (AG 169) and SERGEANT JOSEPH E. MULLER (AG 171).

The U.S. specialized intelligence ship program was abandoned after the Israeli attack on the LIBERTY (AGTR 5) in 1967 and the capture of the PUEBLO (AGER 2) by North Korea in 1968. The PUEBLO remains listed as active, in commission, on the NVR, although she has been interned since being captured on 23 January 1968 while some 12 nm (22.2 km) off the coast of Wonsan in international waters. The ship remains at Wonsan, having been opened in 1995 for selective tourist visits.

One former repair ship also served in the intelligence collection role: the SPHINX (ARL 24, ex-LST 963). She was the last of several score LSTs converted to various types of repair and support ships to be operated by the U.S. Navy. Completed in 1944, she was in service from 1944 to 1947, 1950 to 1956, and again from 1967 to 1971 as an ARL. The SPHINX was recommissioned in 1985 for employment as an intelligence collection ship to operate off Central America to intercept radio and radar emissions from Marxist Nicaragua. The ship was decommissioned and stricken on 19 June 1989 and transferred to the NDRF on 15 June 1990. On 2 December 2002, she was transferred to Veterans Park Museum, Dunkirk, New York, for use as a museum.

DEEP SUBMERGENCE SUPPORT SHIPS

The hybrid missile test/support ship POINT LOMA (T-AGDS 2) was taken out of MSC service and stricken on 1 October 1993; she was transferred to the NDRF on 4 October 1993.

The POINT LOMA was built as an Arctic cargo ship, fitted with a docking well; she originally was named POINT BARROW and designated T-AKD 1. As an AGDS, she supported the deep-diving bathyscaph TRIESTE II.

See 15th Edition/pages 233–34 for characteristics.

(The previous TRIESTE II support ship, the modified floating dry dock WHITE SANDS/ARD 20, was briefly assigned the hull number AGDS 1.)

MISSILE RANGE INSTRUMENTATION SHIPS

The Navy and Air Force converted 23 merchant-type ships and one surveillance ship to serve as missile range instrumentation ships to support various U.S. research, space, and missile programs. Two remain in naval service, the OBSERVATION ISLAND and the INVINCIBLE.

A list of the 24 range instrumentation ships appears in Table 23-4.

In December 2003, the Navy awarded Raytheon Company a $1.04 billion contract to replace the existing Cobra Judy system in the OBSERVATION ISLAND with a long-loiter, ballistic missile data collection capability in support of international treaty verification, as well as for intelligence collection. The Raytheon-led team will design, build, integrate, and test a dual-band (S- and X-band) radar suite and provide engineering and management support for procurement of the Cobra Judy replacement ship. Northrop Grumman is the principal teammate for the project.

Names: Missile range instrumentation ships (AGM) have been named from a variety of sources, including cities, "ranges" (RANGE SENTINEL/T-AGM 22), and missile projects (REDSTONE/T-AGM 20). Some of the ships previously "owned" by the Air Force honor generals (GENERAL H. H. ARNOLD/T-AGM 9). The OBSERVATION ISLAND retains the name assigned when she supported the Polaris program.

3 See N. Polmar, "American Spy Ships," U.S. Naval Institute *Proceedings* (October 2003), pp. 117–18.

4 The similar USS MARK (ex-AKL 12, ex-AG 143, ex-U.S. Army FS 214) was transferred to Taiwan in 1971; she later served as the intelligence collection ship WU KANG.

1 MISSILE RANGE INSTRUMENTATION SHIP: FORMER T-AGOS

Number	Name	FY	Launched	In service	Status
T-AGM 24 (ex-T-AGOS 10)	INVINCIBLE	82	1 Nov 1986	30 Jan 1987	**MSC-P**

Builders:	Tacoma Boatbuilding, Wash.	Propulsion:	diesel-electric (4 Caterpillar D-398B diesel generators with
Displacement:	1,600 tons light		General Electric motors); 3,200 bhp; 2 shafts
	2,285 tons full load	Speed:	11 knots
Tonnage:	1,584 GRT	Range:	3,000 nm (5,556 km) at 11 knots
	786 DWT		+ 90 days on station at 3 knots
Length:	203⅔ feet (62.1 m) waterline	Personnel:	18 civilian + 9 technicians
	224 feet (68.3 m) overall	Helicopters:	no facilities
Beam:	43 feet (13.1 m)	Radars:	2 navigation
Draft:	15 feet (4.6 m)		missile tracking

The INVINCIBLE was converted from a STALWART-class ocean surveillance ship. She was taken out of service on 6 February 1995 and stricken on 9 May 1995. She was reactivated on 13 March 1998 for conversion to a T-AGM. The ship began operations in 2000.

The INVINCIBLE is employed in support of Air Force surveillance of Chinese and North Korean missile testing.

Classification: She was changed to T-AGM 24 on 4 April 2000.

The INVINCIBLE is one of only two missile range instrumentation ships now in naval service. Her radar tracking system is called Gray Star. She originally was a STALWART-class ocean surveillance ship; all ships of that class now are employed in other roles. The class had a short service life in the T-AGOS role. (U.S. Navy)

1 MISSILE RANGE INSTRUMENTATION SHIP: MARINER CLASS

Number	Name	Launched	Comm.	Status
T-AGM 23 (ex-AG 154)	OBSERVATION ISLAND	15 Aug 1953	5 Dec 1958	**MSC-A**

Builders:	New York Shipbuilding, Camden, N.J.	Speed:	20 knots
Displacement:	13,060 tons light	Range:	17,000 nm (31,500 km) at 13 knots
	16,076 tons full load	Personnel:	66 civilian + 60 technicians
Length:	563 feet (171.6 m) overall	Helicopters:	no facilities
Beam:	76 feet (23.2 m)	Radars:	Raytheon 1650/9X navigation
Draft:	29⅚ feet (9.1 m)		Raytheon 1660/12S navigation
Propulsion:	2 steam turbine (General Electric); 22,000 shp; 1 shaft		SPQ-11 missile tracking
Boilers:	2 600 psi (41.7 kg/cm2) (Combustion Engineering)		missile tracking

The OBSERVATION ISLAND is a former missile test ship now employed as a range instrumentation ship, primarily to monitor Russian missile tests in the Western Pacific. A replacement ship is being considered.

The ship was built for commercial cargo service, being completed in February 1954; after brief operation, she was laid up in the NDRF in November 1954. She was transferred to the Navy on 10 September 1956 for conversion to a missile test ship for the Polaris Submarine-Launched Ballistic Missile (SLBM) and was commissioned in 1958; she subsequently was modified to launch the Poseidon missile. After completion of the Poseidon development program, the ship was decommissioned on 25 September 1972 and again laid up in the NDRF.

The OBSERVATION ISLAND was reacquired for conversion to a missile range instrumentation ship on 18 August 1977. Converted in 1979–1981, she now is operated by the MSC with a civilian crew

in support of Air Force and NASA activities in the Pacific. She is the oldest ship on the NVR except for the relic CONSTITUTION.

Class: Five Mariner-class merchant ships were acquired by the Navy: three were converted to amphibious assault ships (AKA 112, APA 248, and APA 249) and two to support ships for the Polaris program, the COMPASS ISLAND (AG 153) and OBSERVATION ISLAND. A third Mariner was planned to support the Polaris effort (to become AG 155) but was not acquired. The COMPASS ISLAND was configured to test strategic missile submarine navigation systems; she was stricken in 1981.

Classification: The OBSERVATION ISLAND originally was classified YAG 57 for naval service; she was changed to AG 154 on 19 June 1956 and was listed as EAG 154 until 1 April 1968, when the ship was "reclassified" as AG 154 to avoid confusion caused by her "E" prefix. The ship was changed to T-AGM 23 on 1 May 1979.

Conversion: The ship was converted to the AGM configuration at Shipbuilding & Dry Dock Co., Baltimore, Maryland, from July 1977 to April 1981. She was fitted with the Cobra Judy phased-array radar (SPQ-11) aft, and two radar spheres were installed atop her superstructure.

The Cobra Judy operates in the 2900–3100 MHz band. The S-band array forms a large, octagonal structure approximately 23 feet (7 m) in diameter that is integrated into a mechanically rotated antenna structure. The entire system weighs about 250 tons and is more than 40 feet (12.2 m) in height.

In 1985, a 9-GHz X-band radar using a parabolic dish antenna was installed to complement the S-band phased array system. The five-story-high X-band dish antenna is installed between the funnel and the S-band array. It is known as the Cobra Gemini project.

Design: As an AG, she was fitted with two SLBM launch tubes.

Engineering: Two bow thrusters are fitted for precise position-keeping.

Names: Her merchant name was EMPIRE STATE MARINER.

The OBSERVATION ISLAND with the massive Cobra Gemini (left) and Cobra Judy missile tracking antenna systems. Like most research ships, missile range instrumentation ships are rarely photographed. (1993, Giorgio Arra)

The OBSERVATION ISLAND operates under a project named Cobra Judy, a program of tracking Chinese and Russian missile tests in the Western Pacific area. She is the oldest auxiliary ship in U.S. naval service, originally having been acquired as a Polaris missile test ship. (U.S. Navy)

MISSILE RANGE INSTRUMENTATION SHIPS: VICTORY CLASS

Number	Name	APA Comm.	T-AGM In service	Notes
T-AGM 22	Range Sentinel	1944	1971	OSIR 7 Sep 1995; str. 3 May 1999

The Range Sentinel was the former Navy attack transport Sherburne (APA 205), converted to a missile range instrumentation ship. She was the last of eight Victory-type ships to serve in that role (T-AGM 1, 3–8, and 22). She underwent conversion from October 1969 to October 1971 to a support ship for Poseidon and later Trident missile test firings.

See 16th Edition/pages 222–23 for characteristics.

Table 23-4. MISSILE RANGE INSTRUMENTATION SHIPS

Number	Name	In service	Notes
T-AGM 1	Range Tracker	1961	ex-AG 160; VC2-S-AP3 type
T-AGM 2	Range Recoverer	1962	ex-AG 161, ex-FS 278
T-AGM 3	Longview	1960	ex-AK 238; VC2-S-AP3 type
T-AGM 4	Richfield	1959	ex-AK 253; VC2-S-AP2 type
T-AGM 5	Sunnyvale	1960	ex-AK 256; VC2-S-AP3 type
T-AGM 6	Watertown	1961	VC2-S-AP3 type
T-AGM 7	Huntsville	1961	VC2-S-AP3 type
T-AGM 8	Wheeling	1964	VC2-S-AP3 type
T-AGM 9	Gen. H. H. Arnold	1963	ex-AP 139; C4-S-A1 type
T-AGM 10	Gen. Hoyt S. Vandenberg	1963	ex-AP 145; C4-S-A1 type
T-AGM 11	Twin Falls Victory	1964	VC2-S-AP3 type; to AGS 37
T-AGM 12	American Mariner	1964	EC2 type
T-AGM 13	Sword Knot	1964	C1-M-AV1 type
T-AGM 14	Rose Knot	1964	C1-M-AV1 type
T-AGM 15	Coastal Sentry	1964	ex-AK 212; C1-M-AV1 type
T-AGM 16	Coastal Crusader	1964	C1-M-AV1 type; to AGS 36
T-AGM 17	Timber Hitch	1964	C1-M-AV1 type
T-AGM 18	Sampan Hitch	1964	C1-M-AV1 type
T-AGM 19	Vanguard	1966	ex-AO 122; T2-SE-A2 type
T-AGM 20	Redstone	1966	ex-AO 114; T2-SE-A2 type
T-AGM 21	Mercury	1966	ex-AO 126; T2-SE-A2 type
T-AGM 22	Range Sentinel	1971	ex-APA 205; VC2-S-AP5 type
T-AGM 23	Observation Island	1981	ex-AG 154; C4-S-1a type
T-AGM 24	Invincible	2000	ex-T-AGOS 10

The in-service dates above are as Navy/Air Force missile range instrumentation ships. The Navy acquired 13 merchant and naval ships and the Air Force 10 ships (AGM 9–18) to support military and NASA missile/ space operations, providing a worldwide telemetry and communications network. All of the ships eventually were operated by the MSC for the Navy, Air Force, and NASA.

The ten Air Force ships initially were operated on the Atlantic Missile Range by contractor personnel under contract to that service; the ships were transferred to the MSC on 28 April 1964. Some immediately were taken out of service.

The conversion of the AGM 11 to a surveying ship (AGS 37) was canceled.

The submersible support ship Point Loma (AGDS 2) also served as a range instrumentation ship; see page 252.

OCEANOGRAPHIC RESEARCH SHIPS

Oceanographic research ships perform a broad range of basic ocean research. A major U.S. oceanographic research/surveying ship construction program to replace the large number of such ships procured in the 1960s recently has been completed. The older ships had reached the ends of their effective service lives and are technologically inadequate for modern oceanographic operations. Their replacement ships are multimission designs.

Navy AGORs carry out military research and also are part of the University-National Oceanographic Laboratory System (UNOLS). UNOLS is funded primarily by the National Science Foundation (approximately 75 percent) and the Office of Naval

Research (approximately 13 percent), with the remainder made up by other federal and state organizations. UNOLS, chartered in 1972, has 59 federal and state agencies as members, of which 20 operate oceanographic research ships. Table 23-6 lists the UNOLS ships of 100 feet (30.5 m) or greater, other than those of the Navy, Coast Guard, and National Oceanic and Atmospheric Administration (NOAA). The Coast Guard and NOAA ships, as well as those of the National Science Foundation, are listed in Chapters 32, 33, and 34.

All active Navy research ships are operated by civilian crews under the aegis of the MSC. Other oceanographic and surveying ships are operated by the NOAA (see Chapter 33).

The former oceanographic research ship Hayes (T-AGOR 16) has been converted to a sound trials ship and reclassified T-AG 195 (see page 249).

The unique, Navy-owned Floating Instrumentation Platform (FLIP) is described in Chapter 25.

Names: Kilo Moana is the Hawaiian term for "oceanographer," but it literally means "one who is looking for understanding of the deep sea."

1 OCEANOGRAPHIC RESEARCH SHIP: SWATH DESIGN

Number	Name	FY	Launched	In service	Status
AGOR 26	Kilo Moana	97	17 Nov 2001	Oct 2002	**Academic**

Builders:	Atlantic Marine Inc. (Lockheed Martin), Jacksonville, Fla.
Displacement	2,542 tons full load
Length:	186 feet (56.7 m) overall
	172 feet (52.43 m) waterline
Beam:	88 feet (26.83 m)
Draft:	25 feet (7.62 m)
Propulsion:	diesel-electric (4 Caterpillar 3508B SCAC diesel generators, 4,880 bhp; 2 Westinghouse electric motors, 4,024 shp); 2 shafts
Speed:	15 knots (12 knots sustained)
Range:	10,000 nm (18,530 km) at 11 knots
Personnel:	17 civilian + 31 scientists and technicians
Helicopters:	no facilities
Radars:	2 Raytheon Pathfinder navigation
Sonar:	various

This is a small, SWATH-configured research ship acquired to replace the Moana Wave. The Kilo Moana is operated by the University of Hawaii's School of Ocean and Earth Science and Technology.

The newest oceanographic research ship in the Navy's inventory is the Kilo Moana, *a catamaran platform operated by the University of Hawaii. Here she is on trials off the eastern coast of Florida. The* Kilo Moana *replaced the smaller* Moana Wave *as the university's Navy-owned research ship. (2003, U.S. Navy)*

3 OCEANOGRAPHIC RESEARCH SHIPS: "THOMPSON" CLASS

Number	Name	FY	Launched	In service	Status
AGOR 23	THOMAS G. THOMPSON	87	27 July 1990	8 July 1991	**Academic**
AGOR 24	ROGER REVELLE	93	20 Apr 1995	11 June 1996	**Academic**
AGOR 25	ATLANTIS	94	1 Feb 1996	3 Mar 1997	**Academic**

Builders:	Trinity/Halter Marine, Moss Point, Miss.
Displacement:	2,155 tons light
	3,250 tons full load
Length:	243 feet (74.09 m) waterline
	274 feet (83.5 m) overall
Beam:	53 feet (16.16 m)
Draft:	19 feet (5.79 m)
Propulsion:	diesel-electric (3 diesel generators/Caterpillar 3516TA,
	2 electric motors/General Motors CD6999); 6,000 shp;
	2 all-azimuth propellers
Speed:	15 knots
Range:	11,300 nm (20,940 km) at 12 knots
Personnel:	20 civilian + 35–40 scientists and technicians
Helicopters:	no facilities
Radars:	navigation
Sonar:	Krupp-Atlas seafloor mapping

These oceanographic research ships are especially suited to support Navy research laboratories, academic institutions, and commercial contractors involved in Navy projects (replacing the ROBERT D. CONRAD-class ships). The program was designated AGX during the design phase. A fourth ship of this class, the RONALD H. BROWN, was built for the NOAA; see Chapter 34.

The lead ship, the THOMAS G. THOMPSON, was laid down on 29 March 1989.

Classification: The RONALD H. BROWN was assigned hull number T-AGOR 26 while under construction.

Design: These ships were built to commercial standards. They are designed especially for extended at-sea operations and are fitted with a dynamic positioning system to maintain station during research activities. Four laboratory/accommodation vans can be carried on deck in addition to more than 4,000 square feet (372 m²) of laboratory space.

Their endurance is 60–70 days.

The AGOR 23 is configured for oceanographic research and coastal survey.

Engineering: In addition to three diesel generators for propulsion, the ships have three ship's service power generators (3508TA) and one emergency generator (3406TA).

The ships are fitted with azimuth or Z-drives with 360° rotating propellers; there also is a rotating 360°, 1,180-shp bow thruster to provide precise station keeping.

Names: The AGOR 23 initially was to be named EWING; the AGOR 24 originally was named REVELLE. The AGOR 25 remembers two previous oceanographic research ships operated by Woods Hole Oceanographic Institution (WHOI), the ATLANTIS I and ATLANTIS II.

Operational: The THOMAS G. THOMPSON is operated by the University of Washington, replacing her namesake, the former AGOR 9 (subsequently IX 517); the ROGER REVELLE is operated by the Scripps Institution of Oceanography in La Jolla, California; and the ATLANTIS by WHOI in Massachusetts.

OCEANOGRAPHIC RESEARCH SHIP: "GYRE" CLASS

Number	Name	FY	Launched	Delivered	Status
AGOR 21	GYRE	71	25 May 1973	14 Nov 1973	str. 17 Aug 1992
AGOR 22	MOANA WAVE	71	18 June 1973	16 Jan 1974	str. 30 May 1999

These were small "utility" research ships built specifically for use by academic research institutions. The GYRE was assigned to the Texas A&M University for operation. She was stricken in 1992 and transferred on the same date to the school.

The MOANA WAVE was operated for the Oceanographer of the Navy by the Hawaii Institute of Geophysics, having been assigned to that institution on completion. During the early 1980s, the MOANA WAVE was employed for at-sea testing of the T-AGOS/SURTASS towed sonar array. She was replaced by the KILO MOANA.

The ROGER REVELLE, the second of a new class of monohull oceanographic research ships, at San Diego. All Navy AGORs are operated by civilian academic institutions. This ship and many other AGORs have blue hulls. (1998, Leo Van Ginderen)

The ATLANTIS at San Diego. The NOAA ship RONALD H. BROWN (formerly named RESEARCHER) is similar; in official Navy documents she was listed as the AGOR 26, with that hull number subsequently being assigned to the KILO MOANA. (1999, W. Michael Young)

2 OCEANOGRAPHIC RESEARCH SHIPS: "MELVILLE" CLASS

Number	Name	FY	Launched	Comm.	Status
AGOR 14	MELVILLE	66	10 July 1968	27 Aug 1969	**Academic**
AGOR 15	KNORR	66	21 Aug 1968	14 Jan 1970	**Academic**

Builders:	Defoe Shipbuilding, Bay City, Mich.
Displacement:	1,915 tons standard
	2,670 tons full load
Tonnage:	2,100 GRT
Length:	279 feet (85.1 m) overall
Beam:	46½ feet (14.1 m)
Draft:	15 feet (4.6 m)
Propulsion:	diesel-electric (4 diesel generators); 3,000 shp; 3 azimuth propellers (1 forward retractable, 2 aft)
Speed:	14 knots
Range:	12,000 nm (22,224 km) at 12 knots
Personnel:	24 civilian + 34 scientists
Helicopters:	no facilities
Radars:	navigation

These ships are large research ships. The MELVILLE is operated by the Scripps Institution of Oceanography and the KNORR by the WHOI, both for the Office of Naval Research under the technical control of the Oceanographer of the Navy. They were assigned to those institutions on completion.

The MELVILLE was laid down on 12 July 1967 and the KNORR on 9 August 1967.

Class: The AGOR 19 and AGOR 20 of this design were authorized in the FY 1968 shipbuilding program, but their construction was canceled.

Design: SCB No. 710. Although these ships have the same SCB number as the ROBERT D. CONRAD class, they are quite different. A bow observation dome is fitted. Endurance is 35–40 days.

Engineering: These ships were built with a single diesel engine driving two cycloidal (vertical) propellers through long, internal shafts; the forward propeller is located just behind the bow observation dome and the after propeller is just in front of the rudder. The ships could hold a fixed position in heavy seas with winds up to 35 knots. Cycloidal propulsion—controlled by a "joystick"—allowed them to be propelled in any direction and to turn up to 360° in their own length. This type of propulsion also allowed precise station keeping and slow speeds without the use of auxiliary propulsion units.

The ships experienced transmission difficulties with their original propulsion plants. They were reengined in 1988–1991 to the configuration described above. They have azimuth or Z-drives with 360° rotating propellers.

Modernization: Both ships were extensively modernized when reengined, 1988–1991.

Operational: The KNORR helped to locate the wreck of the British liner TITANIC in the North Atlantic on 1 September 1985 using a remote-controlled search submersible.

The MELVILLE (left) and KNORR have an unusual configuration. The "mack"—combination mast and stack—structure is amidships, with an enclosed lookout position. These ships are well equipped for their academic research activities. (Scripps Institution of Oceanography)

Table 23-5. NAVY OCEANOGRAPHIC RESEARCH SHIPS

Number	Name	In service	Notes
AGOR 1	JOSIAH WILLARD GIBBS	1958	ex-AVP 51; to Greece
AGOR 2	H. U. SVERDUP	1960	built in Norway
AGOR 3	ROBERT D. CONRAD	1962	to NDRF 1989
AGOR 4	JAMES M. GILLISS	1962	to Mexico 1982
AGOR 5	CHARLES M. DAVIS	1963	to New Zealand 1970
AGOR 6	SANDS	1964	to Brazil 1974
T-AGOR 7	LYNCH	1965	decomm. 21 Oct 1991; str. 6 Nov 1991
T-AGOR 8	ELTANIN	1961	ex-T-AK 270; C1-ME2-13a type; to Argentina
AGOR 9	THOMAS G. THOMPSON	1965	to IX 517 in 1989
AGOR 10	THOMAS WASHINGTON	1965	decomm. 1 Aug 1992; to Chile 28 Sep 1992
AGOR 11	MIZAR	1962	ex-T-AK 272; C1-ME2-13a type
T-AGOR 12	DE STEIGUER	1969	decomm. 2 Nov 1992; to Tunisia (same date)
T-AGOR 13	BARTLETT	1969	decomm. 26 July 1993; to Morocco (same date)
AGOR 14, 15	MELVILLE class		
AGOR 16	HAYES	1971	to T-AG 195
AGOR 17	CHAIN	1958	ex-ARS 20; str. 1977
AGOR 18	ARGO	1960	ex-ARS 27; str. 1970
AGOR 19			canceled 1969
AGOR 20			canceled 1969
AGOR 21, 22	GYRE class		
AGOR 23–25	THOMAS G. THOMPSON class		
AGOR 26	KILO MOANA	2002	

The above in-service dates are as oceanographic research ships.

The AGOR 2 was built for the Norwegian government with U.S. offshore procurement funds. The nine ROBERT D. CONRAD-class ships (the AGOR 3–7, 9, 10, 12, and 13) were the U.S. Navy's first purpose-built oceanographic research ships. The highly capable ELTANIN and MIZAR were extensively converted from Arctic cargo ships.

Table 23-6. UNIVERSITY-NATIONAL OCEANOGRAPHIC LABORATORY SYSTEM

Name	Operating Agency*	Built	Length
ALPHA HELIX	NSF	1966	134 1/2 ft (41.0 m)
CAPE HATTERAS	NSF	1981	135 ft (41.15 m)
CAPE HENLOPEN	University of Delaware	1976	120 ft (36.6 m)
EDWIN LINK	Harbor Branch Oceanographic Institution	1982	168 ft (51.2 m)
ENDEAVOR	NSF	1993	183⅔ ft (56.0 m)
HEALY	USCG	1999	419⅝ ft (128.0 m)
LONGHORN	University of Texas	1971	105 ft (32.0 m)
MAURICE EWING	NSF	1983	239½ ft (73.0 m)
NEW HORIZON	Scripps Institution of Oceanography	1978	170 ft (51.8 m)
OCEANUS	NSF	1994	176 1½ ft (53.9 m)
PELICAN	Louisiana Universities Marine Consortium	1985	105 ft (32.0 m)
POINT SUR	NSF	1981	135 ft (41.15 m)
POLAR SEA	USCG	1978	399 ft (121.65 m)
POLAR STAR	USCG	1976	399 ft (121.65 m)
RONALD H. BROWN	NOAA (ex-AGOR 26)	1997	274 ft (83.5 m)
SEAWARD JOHNSON	Harbor Branch Oceanographic Institution	1994	203⅓ ft (62.0 m)

* NOAA (see Chapter 32) NSF = National Science Foundation (see Chapter 33); USCG = U.S. Coast Guard (see Chapter 31).

Only non-Navy-owned UNOLS ships of 100 feet (30.5 m) and larger are listed here; there are a few smaller, coastal research ships in service. The Coast Guard no longer operates specialized oceanographic cutters (WAGO); hence, only that service's three icebreakers are listed. Only NOAA's flagship, the RONALD H. BROWN, is listed as part of UNOLS; another 15 ships are in the NOAA fleet, most configured for nautical charting and fisheries research.

OCEAN SURVEILLANCE SHIPS

These ships are configured for operating the Surveillance Towed Array Sensor System (SURTASS), a submarine detection system intended to supplement the seafloor Sound Surveillance System (SOSUS). The ships were designed to operate where SOSUS coverage is inadequate or where the seafloor arrays are damaged or destroyed. The SURTASS data are sent via satellite link to shore facilities for processing and further transmission to Anti-Submarine Warfare (ASW) forces; however, the ships can provide "raw" acoustic data to ASW ships in the area. (The SURTASS concept differs from the Tactical Towed Array Sonar (TACTAS) system in that the latter consists of tactical hydrophone arrays towed by warships to supplement hull-mounted sonars.)

The SURTASS carried by the later ocean surveillance ships is being supplemented by a Low-Frequency Active (LFA) system, considered suitable for effective submarine detection in shallow/littoral areas as well as deep-ocean areas.

The initial Navy planning for the T-AGOS/SURTASS program called for 18 ships. This was later reduced to 12 because of fiscal constraints; however, because of the success of the early ships and the increasing Soviet submarine threat, in the late 1980s the Navy sought a force of 27 surveillance ships—the 18 monohull ships of the STALWART class, 4 SWATH-P ships, and 5 SWATH-A ships.

In January 1992, the Navy announced its intention to dispose of all monohull T-AGOS ships by 1997 because of budget constraints, although the decline of the Russian submarine threat usually is cited for this action.[5] Accordingly, the planned force level was reduced to nine SWATH-type ships. Contractual and construction problems with the first of the larger SWATH-P ships led to delays in procuring the five ships of this design.

The current Navy planning is for an eventual force of four to six ships, all in the Pacific.

These ships are not armed.

Costs: In 1992, as the Navy revised its T-AGOS force planning, it stated the cost of the SWATH acquisition program as $487 million for the first five SWATH ships (T-AGOS 19–23) and $674 million for the last four ships, i.e., a total of $1.2 billion.

At that time, annual operating costs were postulated as:

$6.3 million for monohull ships
$7.0 million for SWATH-P ships
$7.7 million for SWATH-A ships

Electronics: The UQQ-2 SURTASS array is a flexible, tube-like structure some 2,600-feet (793-m) long containing numerous hydrophones towed by a 6,000-foot (1,829-m) cable. It is neutrally buoyant when at depth, with the depth being varied to compensate for environmental conditions. Typical array operating depths are 500–1,500 feet (152 to 457 m).

Data from the hydrophone array are generated at a very high data rate. The information is "preprocessed" on board the T-AGOS

---

5 See *Undersea Surveillance: Navy Continues to Build Ships Designed for Soviet Threat* (Washington, D.C.: General Accounting Office, December 1992).

and sent at a much lower rate, reduced by a factor of ten, via satellite to shore stations. The data rate from ship to shore is about 32,000 bits (32 kilobits) per second.

Names: Surveillance ships have names that convey traits of capability or accomplishment.

Operational: The massive decommissioning of T-AGOS ships is taking place despite the Navy's inability to meet certain surveillance operational requirements. For example, early in 1994, Rear Admiral James Prout, the Deputy Chief of Staff for Resources, Requirements, and Assessment of the U.S. Pacific Fleet, told the Senate Armed Services Committee: "We were recently unable to support a U.S. Central Command request for full-time deployment of a T-AGOS ship to the Persian Gulf for surveillance purposes."[6]

(8) OCEAN SURVEILLANCE SHIPS

The Navy's 30-year shipbuilding plan presented to Congress in 2003 shows the construction of eight advanced ocean surveillance ships, designated T-AGOS, to be authorized in FY 2013–2023. No characteristics for these ships have been developed.

1 OCEAN SURVEILLANCE SHIP: SWATH-A DESIGN

Number	Name	FY	Launched	In service	Status
T-AGOS 23	IMPECCABLE	90	25 April 1998	20 March 2001	**MSC-P**

Builders:	Halter Marine, Moss Point, Miss.
Displacement:	5,362 tons full load
Length:	232 feet (70.73 m) waterline
	281½ feet (85.8 m) overall
Beam:	95¾ feet (29.2 m)
Draft:	26 feet (7.9 m)
Propulsion:	diesel-electric (4 diesel generators); 5,000 shp; 2 shafts
Speed:	12 knots sustained
Range:	8,000 nm (14,816 km) at 15 knots
Personnel:	25 civilian + 25 Navy technicians
Helicopters:	no facilities
Radars:	navigation
Sonars:	Low-Frequency Active (LFA)
	UQQ-2 SURTASS

This is an enlarged SWATH ship intended to conduct SURTASS missions in higher sea states, specifically for operations in high-latitude areas. It is intended to operate through sea state 6 on all headings and sea state 7 on best heading.

A class of four ships originally was planned. The IMPECCABLE was ordered from American Shipbuilding at Tampa, Florida, on 28 March 1991. However, work was halted due to contractual problems.[7] (She was to have been laid down in December 1993,

The IMPECCABLE *represents the "ultimate" U.S. Navy T-AGOS design. Delays in construction and reduced interest in the T-AGOS deep-ocean surveillance mission led to cancellation of three other ships of this design. No additional ocean surveillance ships now are planned. (U.S. Navy)*

launched in March 1994, and completed in January 1995.) The unfinished hull was transferred from the Tampa yard to Halter Marine for completion; she was placed on the ways at Halter Marine on 21 January 1996.

It is unlikely that additional ships of this class will be constructed in the near term.

Design: The SWATH form was evaluated in the research craft KAIMALINO (see Chapter 25). The SWATH concept differs from a catamaran, which has two conventional ship hulls joined together; the SWATH design provides two fully submerged underwater hulls with structures rising through the water to support the ship's superstructure.

The SWATH designs provides a high degree of ship stability in rough waters and a large deck space. The design was adopted because the monohull T-AGOS ships experienced seakeeping difficulties in northern latitudes during winter.

Endurance is planned to be 50–60 days.

Engineering: Fitted with two 360° thrusters for station keeping.

---

6 Barbara Starr, "SOSUS Suffers as USN Stretches Its Funding," *Jane's Defence Weekly* (26 March 1994), p. 3.
7 The American Shipbuilding Corps. also defaulted on the construction of two Navy oilers (T-AO 191 and 192).

The hunter and the hunted: The ocean surveillance ship ABLE *is flanked by the Colombian diesel-electric submarine* TAYRONA *(top) and the U.S. nuclear-propelled attack submarine* SPRINGFIELD *(SSN 761) while participating in the training exercise UNITAS 44-03. At the time, the multinational force was operating in the Caribbean Sea. (2003, U.S. Navy/Chantel M. Chapman)*

4 OCEAN SURVEILLANCE SHIPS: "VICTORIOUS" CLASS (SWATH-P)

Number	Name	FY	Launched	In service	Status
T-AGOS 19	VICTORIOUS	87	2 May 1990	13 Aug 1991	**MSC-P**
T-AGOS 20	ABLE	89	14 Feb 1991	24 Mar 1992	AR
T-AGOS 21	EFFECTIVE	89	26 Sep 1991	28 Jan 1993	**MSC-P**
T-AGOS 22	LOYAL	89	19 Sep 1992	1 July 1993	**MSC-A**

Builders:	McDermott, Morgan City, La.
Displacement:	2,676 tons light
	3,438 tons full load
Length:	190⅔ feet (58.1 m) waterline
	234½ feet (71.5 m) overall
Beam:	93½ feet (28.5 m)
Beam of "box":	80½ feet (24.5 m)
Draft:	25 feet (7.6 m)
Propulsion:	diesel-electric (4 Caterpillar-Kato 3512-TA diesel generators; 2 General Electric motors); 3,200 bhp; 2 shafts
Speed:	16 knots; 9.6 knots array towing speed
Range:	3,000 nm (5,556 km) at 10 knots
Personnel:	T-AGOS 19: 20 civilian + 5 Navy technicians
	T-AGOS 21: 18 civilian + 5 Navy technicians
	T-AGOS 22: 19 civilian + 5 Navy technicians
Helicopters:	no facilities
Radars:	navigation
Sonars:	Low-Frequency Active (LFA)
	UQQ-2 SURTASS

These are improved, SWATH-configured SURTASS ships.

A contract was awarded to McDermott in October 1986 for the detailed design and construction of the lead ship of this class, the VICTORIOUS, which was laid down on 12 April 1988.

The ABLE was taken out of service (OSIR) on 8 July 2003 and laid up in reserve at Philadelphia.

Design: These are the world's first operational military ships with the SWATH design. The design is based on the Navy's research/range support ship KAIMALINO.

Mission endurance is 90 days.

Engineering: The ships' steering system uses a pair of angled rudders aft and a pair of angled canards forward; two azimuth thrusters are fitted forward.

Operational: The SURTASS data are transmitted from the T-AGOS via satellite link to shore facilities for processing and further transmission to ASW forces; however, the ships can provide "raw" acoustic data to ASW ships in the area

AIR DEFENSE SHIP: FORMER T-AGOS

Number	Name	FY	Launched	In service	Status
T-AGOS 16	CAPABLE	86	28 Oct 1998	9 June 1989	to NOAA 2004

The CAPABLE was one of three STALWART-class ocean surveillance ships modified to serve as an air defense (radar) ship, the others being the STALWART and INDOMITABLE; they were fitted with the SPS-49(V)3 air surveillance radar. The INVINCIBLE has been converted to a missile range instrumentation ship (T-AGM 24).

These were the last STALWART-class ships in naval service. The CAPABLE is one of seven ships that have been transferred to the National Oceanic and Atmospheric Administration (NOAA).

The Coast Guard was to have acquired six of the ships; however, they were rejected by that service because of their slow speed and lack of helicopter facilities. Subsequently, 15 ships have gone to other U.S. government agencies, educational institutions, and foreign nations. The CONTENDER was transferred to the Merchant Marine Academy, Kings Point, New York, for service as a training ship and renamed KINGS POINTER. The PERSISTENT was assigned to the NDRF on 1 November 2001 for conversion to a training ship for the Great Lakes Maritime Academy; she went on loan effective 1 August 2002 and was renamed STATE OF MICHIGAN.

Some ships were employed briefly under the aegis of MSC in counterdrug operations.

The STALWART class suffered from significant cost overruns and equipment failures, resulting in a several-year delay beyond their original 1974 operational date. With the end of the Cold War the Navy rapidly disposed of all but the CAPABLE. She is employed in support of Air Force activities.

Class: This originally was a class of 18 ships (see Table 23-7). All were constructed by Tacoma Boatbuilding in Washington, and by Halter Marine, New Orleans.

The LOYAL demonstrates the catamaran hull adopted for the later T-AGOS ships, which provides stability for towing acoustic arrays in the high sea states of the North Atlantic and North Pacific. See 17th Edition/page 250 for photos of hull underwater configuration. (U.S. Navy)

Design: This T-AGOS hull is similar to that of the T-ATF 166 class. For MSC operation, a high degree of crew habitability is provided, including single staterooms for all crewmen and three single and four double staterooms for technicians. There are four additional berths in the T-AGOS 1–12 and seven additional berths in the later ships. The T-AGOS 13–18 also have a larger SURTASS operations center and modified machinery layout.

Endurance is rated at 98 days (see *Operational* notes).

Engineering: The four diesel generators drive two main propulsion motors. A bow-thruster powered by a 550-hp electric motor is fitted for station keeping. There are special features to reduce machinery noise.

Names: The T-AGOS 11 originally was named DAUNTLESS, T-AGOS 12 VIGOROUS, and T-AGOS 17 INTREPID. All three were renamed while under construction.

Operational: Early Navy planning provided for these ships to have 90-day patrol periods plus 8 days in transit, resulting in more than 300 days at sea per year. This intensity of operations was rejected by the MSC as impractical and unrealistic, and a patrol duration to 60–74 days subsequently was undertaken.

The last of the STALWART-class ships rated as a T-AGOS, was the CAPABLE is employed as a radar surveillance ship to support drug interdiction efforts. Her tripod mast supports an SPS-40 air search radar. The STALWART and INDOMITABLE were similarly employed. (U.S. Navy)

The EFFECTIVE at sea. Note the ship's twin funnels, angled lattice mast, and control station aft for handling towed acoustic arrays. The four surviving surveillance ships all will operate in Pacific Ocean areas.Their value in coastal or littoral areas is severely limited. (U.S. Navy)

Table 23-7. OCEAN SURVEILLANCE SHIPS

Number	Name	In Service	OSIR	Notes
STALWART class (18)				
T-AGOS 1	STALWART	1984	15 Nov 1984	str. 2 Dec 2002; to MarAd
T-AGOS 2	CONTENDER	1984	1 Oct 1992	str. 11 Dec 1992; to Merchant Marine Academy, Kings Point, N.Y.
T-AGOS 3	VINDICATOR	1984	30 Mar 1993	str. 30 June 1993; reactivated 26 Aug 1999; to OSIR/Coast Guard 15 May 2001; to NOAA 30 Oct 2001
T-AGOS 4	TRIUMPH	1985	20 June 1994	str. 6 Jan 1995; to MarAd
T-AGOS 5	ASSURANCE	1985	28 Mar 1994	str. 6 Jan 1995; to Portugal 1999
T-AGOS 6	PERSISTENT	1985	11 Oct 1994	str. 6 Jan 1995; reactivated 26 Aug 1999; OSIR/to Coast Guard 1 May 2001; to Great Lakes Maritime Academy
T-AGOS 7	INDOMITABLE	1985	6 Apr 1985	str. 1 May 2001; to civilian training ship (see notes); to NOAA 9 Dec 2002
T-AGOS 8	PREVAIL	1986	18 Apr 2003	to NOAA 18 Apr 2003
T-AGOS 9	ASSERTIVE	1986	1 Sep 2003	to NOAA 1 Sep 2002
T-AGOS 10	INVINCIBLE	1986	6 Feb 1995	str. 9 May 1995; reactivated 13 Mar 1998 for T-AGM conversion
T-AGOS 11	AUDACIOUS	1989	30 Nov 1995	str. 30 Nov 1995; to Portugal 1996
T-AGOS 12	BOLD	1989		str. 31 Mar 2004; to Environmental Protection Agency 31 Mar 2004
T-AGOS 13	ADVENTUROUS	1988	1 June 1992	str. 3 June 1992; to NOAA 5 June 1992
T-AGOS 14	WORTHY	1989	17 Mar 1993	to Geological Survey 17 Mar 1993; to U.S. Army 25 Mar 1993; str. 20 May 1993
T-AGOS 15	TITAN	1989	31 Aug 1993	to NOAA 31 Aug 1993; str. 3 Sep 1993
T-AGOS 16	CAPABLE	1989		to NOAA 13 Sep 2004; str. 14 Sep 2004
T-AGOS 17	TENACIOUS	1989	3 Feb 1995	str. 6 Feb 1997; to New Zealand 1996
T-AGOS 18	RELENTLESS	1990	17 Mar 1993	to NOAA 17 Mar 1993; str. 20 May 1993
T-AGOS 19–22	VICTORIOUS class			
T-AGOS 23	IMPECCABLE			

SURVEYING SHIPS

Surveying ships conduct ocean surveys and collect data in support of fleet operations and systems development. All Navy surveying ships are operated by the Military Sealift Command under the sponsorship of the Naval Oceanographic Command. They have civilian crews.

Names: Surveying ships generally are named for oceanographers and Navy oceanographic officers. The PATHFINDER commemorates the Coast and Geodetic Survey ship by that name that was operated by the Navy as AGS 1 during World War II.

6 OCEAN SURVEYING SHIPS: "PATHFINDER" CLASS

Number	Name	FY	Launched	In service	Status
T-AGS 60	PATHFINDER	90	4 Oct 1993	5 Dec 1994	**MSC**
T-AGS 61	SUMNER	90	28 Feb 1994	30 May 1995	**MSC**
T-AGS 62	BOWDITCH	90	15 Oct 1994	30 Dec 1995	**MSC**
T-AGS 63	MATTHEW HENSON	94	21 Oct 1996	20 Feb 1998	**MSC**
T-AGS 64	BRUCE C. HEEZEN	97	25 Mar 1999	13 Jan 2000	**MSC**
T-AGS 65	MARY SEARS	99	19 Oct 2000	17 Dec 2001	**MSC**

Builders:	Halter Marine, Moss Point, Miss.
Displacement:	2,800 tons light (see *Design* notes)
	5,100 tons full load
Length:	328 feet (100.0 m) overall
Beam:	58 feet (17.7 m)
Draft:	19 feet (5.8 m)
Propulsion:	diesel engines; 8,000 bhp; 2 azimuth propellers
Speed:	16 knots
Range:	
Personnel:	28 civilian + 27 scientists/technicians
Helicopters:	no facilities
Radars:	navigation

This is a new class of ships for long-range ocean survey and research. Research for a variety of ocean sciences can be conducted. Their design is based on the AGOR 23, with the BOWDITCH having special features for ice operations.

The PATHFINDER and SUMNER both were laid down on 30 January 1991. The MARY SEARS was laid down on 28 July 1999.

Design: Details differ. The ships have 3,500 square feet (325.5 m²) of deck working space and 4,000 square feet (372 m²) of laboratory space; in addition, four 20-foot (6.1-m) containers can be carried to provide additional laboratory spaces.

Engineering: These ships are propelled and steered through a Z-drive arrangement to all-azimuth thrusters. The elimination of conventional reduction gears and long propeller shafts frees space for other uses, and the Z-drive provides excellent maneuverability and station keeping for survey and research activities. Retractable bow thrusters are fitted.

The BOWDITCH is one of six PATHFINDER-class ocean surveying ships completed in the past decade. Despite major fleet reductions since the end of the Cold War, the Navy has maintained a viable and relatively modern fleet of research and surveying ships. (U.S. Navy)

1 COASTAL SURVEYING SHIP: "JOHN McDONNELL" CLASS

Number	Name	FY	Launched	In service	Status
T-AGS 51	JOHN McDONNELL	87	13 Dec 1990	15 Nov 1991	**MSC-A**
T-AGS 52	LITTLEHALES	87	14 Feb 1991	10 Feb 1992	to NOAA

Builders:	Trinity/Halter Marine, Moss Point, Miss.
Displacement:	2,000 tons full load
Length:	190 feet (57.9 m) waterline
	208⅙ feet (63.5 m) overall
Beam:	45 feet (13.7 m)
Draft:	14 feet (4.3 m)
Propulsion:	diesel engines; 1 shaft
Speed:	16 knots sustained
Range:	13,800 nm (25,535 km) at 16 knots
Complement:	23 civilian + 11 scientists
Helicopters:	no facilities
Radars:	navigation

Both of these coastal surveying ships were laid down on 10 November 1988. They were intended to collect bathymetric/hydrographic data in shallow and deep water. They carry small survey launches.

The LITTLEHALES was taken out of service and stricken from the NVR on 27 February 2003. The ship was transferred to NOAA on 8 July 2003.

1 OCEAN SURVEYING SHIP: "WATERS"

Number	Name	FY	Launched	In service	Status
T-AGS 45	WATERS	90	6 June 1992	26 May 1993	**MSC-P**

Builders:	Avondale Industries, New Orleans, La.
Displacement:	12,208 tons full load
Length:	442 feet (134.75 m) overall
Beam:	69 feet (21.0 m)
Draft:	21⅛ feet (6.45 m)
Propulsion:	diesel-electric; 7,400 shp; 2 shafts
Speed:	13.2 knots sustained
Range:	
Complement:	32 civilian + 60 civilian technicians
Helicopters:	no facilities
Radars:	navigation

This is a large, multifunction surveying ship constructed to replace the MIZAR (T-AGOR 11). The ship is capable of performing bathymetric, oceanographic, and hydrographic surveys and is able to launch and recover a variety of remotely operated vehicles.

The keel for the WATERS was laid down on 21 May 1991.

Design: The ship is fitted with bow and stern thrusters for precise maneuvering.

The JOHN McDONNELL (above), one of a two-ship class of surveying ships, is the smallest of the several AGOR/AGS ships in naval service. The ship is considered a coastal surveying ship, which should properly be designated AGSC. (U.S. Navy)

The WATERS is the largest Navy surveying/oceanographic research ship. She has a single square funnel-like structure aft for her diesel exhausts. The WATERS replaced the long-serving and highly effective deep-ocean survey ship MIZAR. (1993, Giorgio Arra)

OCEAN SURVEYING SHIPS: "MAURY" CLASS

Number	Name	In service	Notes
T-AGS 39	MAURY	1989	OSIR/str. 28 Oct 1994
T-AGS 40	TANNER	1990	OSIR/str. 14 Jan 1994

These were built-for-the-purpose ocean survey ships, acquired to replace the outdated BOWDITCH (AGS 21) and DUTTON (AGS 22). They were the largest purpose-built U.S. Navy research ships, designed to conduct primarily hydrographic, magnetic, and gravity surveys.

The MAURY and TANNER were discarded after unprecedentedly short service lives; they were taken out of service and stricken on the same dates. The TANNER suffered major engineering problems and was taken out of service after having steamed only 166,000 nm (307,600 km).

The MAURY was transferred to the California Maritime Academy on 4 May 1996 and renamed GOLDEN BEAR (in place of the H. H. HESS; see below). The TANNER was transferred to the Maine Maritime Academy on 6 October 1997 and renamed STATE of MAINE.

OCEAN SURVEYING SHIP: "H. H. HESS"

The large surveying ship H. H. HESS (T-AGS 38) was taken out of service on 5 February 1992, transferred to the NDRF on 21 February 1992, and stricken on 28 July 1992. She was to have been transferred to the California State Maritime Academy as a training ship, but was rejected because of a burned out boiler.

The HESS was built as a merchant ship and launched in 1964; she was acquired by the Navy in 1976 for conversion to an ocean surveying ship.

SURVEYING SHIPS: "SILAS BENT" CLASS

Number	Name	In service	Status
T-AGS 26	SILAS BENT	23 July 1965	OSIR/str. 28 Oct 1999; to Turkey 2000
T-AGS 27	KANE	19 May 1967	OSIR/str. 14 Mar 2001; to Turkey 2001
T-AGS 33	WILKES	28 June 1971	OSIR 9 Aug 1995; to Tunisia 1995
T-AGS 34	WYMAN	3 Nov 1971	OSIR 10 Mar 1997; str. 3 May 1999; to MarAd

These ships were designed specifically for surveying operations. They differ in detail. All four ships were operated by the MSC, with some supporting the Navy's SOSUS program.

See 17th Edition/page 256 for characteristics.

Class: The WILKES was transferred to Tunisia on 19 September 1995; the KANE was transferred to Turkey on 14 March 2001; and the SILAS BENT transferred to Turkey on 31 January 2000.

The WYMAN was assigned to the NDRF on 26 March 2001.

OCEAN SURVEYING SHIPS: "CHAUVENET" CLASS

Number	Name	In service	Notes
T-AGS 29	CHAUVENET	1970	OSIR 7 Nov 1992; str. 30 Nov 1992
T-AGS 32	HARKNESS	1971	OSIR/str. 15 Mar 1993

These British-built surveying ships were constructed for the U.S. Navy specifically for the research role. They were the U.S. Navy's first purpose-built surveying ships.

The CHAUVENET was transferred to the Texas State Maritime Academy and renamed TEXAS CLIPPER II. The HARKNESS was transferred to the NDRF on 29 March 1993 for retention as a "spare parts" store for the TEXAS CLIPPER II. On 8 January 2001, the HARKNESS was transferred to the New York State Maritime College as a nonoperational training ship; she was again transferred, this time to the Massachusetts State Maritime Academy, on 28 February 2001 for the same role.

Table 23-8. POST–WORLD WAR II SURVEYING SHIPS

Number	Name	In service	Notes
AGS 15	TANNER	1946	ex-AKA 34; S4-SE2-BE1 design
AGS 16	MAURY	1946	ex-AKA 36; S4-SE2-BE1 design
AGS 17	PURSUIT	1950	ex-MSF 108
AGS 18	REQUISITE	1950	ex-MSF 109
AGS 19	SHELDRAKE	1952	ex-AM 62
AGS 20	PREVAIL	1952	ex-MSF 107
AGS 21	BOWDITCH	1958	VC2-S-AP3 type
AGS 22	DUTTON	1958	VC2-S-AP3 type
AGS 23	MICHELSON	1958	VC2-S-AP3 type
AGS 24	SERRANO	1960	ex-ATF 112
AGS 25	KELLAR	1968	to Portugal 1972
AGS 26, 27	SILAS BENT class		
AGS 28	TOWHEE	1964	ex-MSF 388
AGS 29	CHAUVENET	1970	
AGS 30	SAN PABLO	1948	ex-AVP 30
AGS 31	S. P. LEE	1968	to AG 192 (see above)
AGS 32	HARKNESS	1971	
AGS 33, 34	SILAS BENT class		
AGS 35	SGT GEORGE D. KEATHLEY	1967	ex-APc 117; C1-M-AV1 type
AGS 36	COASTAL CRUSADER	—	ex-AGM 16; C1-M-AV1 type
AGS 37	TWIN FALLS	—	ex-AGM 11; VC2-S-AP3 type
AGS 38	H. H. HESS	1976	C4-S-1a type
AGS 39, 40	MAURY class		
AGS 41–44	not used		
AGS 45	WATERS	1993	
AGS 46–49	not used		
AGS 50	REHOBOTH	1948	ex-AVP 50
AGS 51	JOHN MCDONNELL	1992	
AGS 52	LITTLEHALES	1992	
AGS 53–59	not used		
AGS 60–65	PATHFINDER class		

The above in-service dates are as oceanographic surveying ships. World War II–era surveying ships reached hull number AGS 14. The designations AGSc 12–15 were used for coastal surveying ships (assigned in same series as the AGS type). The SAN PABLO and REHOBOTH retained their seaplane hull numbers as surveying ships, throwing the AGS numbering scheme out of sequence and leading to confusion.

The three former Victory-type merchant ships (the AGS 21–23) acquired by the Navy in 1957 and converted for seafloor charting and magnetic surveys to support the Navy's SSBN programs have been stricken.

The TWIN FALLS was never converted.

HOSPITAL SHIPS

The Department of Defense during the early 1980s decided to provide two hospital ships to support the deployment of U.S. forces overseas in conventional combat operations. Several alternatives were considered, including merchant ship conversions and new construction.

One of the candidates for conversion was the superliner UNITED STATES, laid up since her final transatlantic voyage in November 1969. The 990-foot (301.8-m) liner, completed in 1952, carried up to 2,000 passengers and was designed from the outset for conversion to a transport for 14,000 troops. In the AH role, she would have had 2,000–2,500 beds.

(The UNITED STATES attained 46.4 knots on her classified sea trials; she averaged 35.59 knots on her maiden transatlantic voyage—the fastest oceangoing merchant ship ever built. The ship, now privately owned, has been stripped and is immobilized in Philadelphia, although there are plans to rehabilitate her and place her back in commercial service.)

The hospital ships COMFORT and MERCY will be stricken in the near future. Under current planning, forward-deployed medical facilities afloat would be provided Maritime Prepositioning Future (MPF) ships; see Chapter 24.

Names: Hospital ships are assigned "benevolent" names.

2 HOSPITAL SHIPS: CONVERTED TANKERS

Number	Name	Launched	In service	Status
T-AH 19	MERCY	19 July 1975	15 Dec 1986	MSC-ROS-5
T-AH 20	COMFORT	12 Feb 1976	1 Dec 1987	MSC-ROS-5

Builders:	National Steel and Shipbuilding, San Diego
Displacement:	24,752 tons light
	69,360 tons full load
Length:	854⅚ feet (260.6 m) waterline
	894 feet (272.6 m) overall
Beam:	105¾ feet (32.25 m)
Draft:	32⅝ feet (10.0 m)
Propulsion:	1 steam turbine (General Electric); 24,500 shp; 1 shaft
Boilers:	2
Speed:	17.5 knots
Range:	13,400 nm (24,817 km) at 17.5 knots
Personnel:	ROS: 16 civilian + 58 Navy communications and support (6 officers + 52 enlisted)
	Active: 61 civilian + 58 Navy + 1,100 medical/dental (see *Personnel* notes)
Patients:	900+ beds (see *Conversion* notes)
Helicopters:	landing area
Radars:	navigation
	SPS-67 surface search

These ships are former commercial tankers that have been fully converted to support U.S. forward deployed troops. They were delivered as tankers to commercial customers on 19 February 1976 and 23 July 1976, respectively.

These are the first ships of the type in U.S. service since the SANCTUARY was decommissioned in March 1974; at that time, the SANCTUARY was serving as a naval dependents support ship. They are intended to be based at U.S. ports; in crisis or wartime they are assigned medical staffs from military hospitals and go to sea with five days' notice as part of the MSC ready reserve force/ROS. The MERCY is based at San Diego, California, and the COMFORT at Baltimore, Maryland. (The MERCY shifted her home port from Oakland, California, in 1997.) Both ships will be discarded in the near future.

Conversion: Both ships were converted at the National Steel and Shipbuilding yard in San Diego; the T-AH 19 conversion was authorized in FY 1983 (begun July 1984) and the T-AH 20 in FY 1984 (begun April 1985).

As hospital ships, they have 12 operating rooms, four X-ray rooms, a pharmacy, a blood bank, an 80-bed intensive care facility,

The hospital ship COMFORT *at the Hudson River piers in New York City, where she arrived on 17 September 2001 after the terrorist attacks on the World Trade Center. These ungainly ships are the largest hospital ships to ever enter naval service; they are significantly larger than the Soviet Navy's two* OB'-*class ships. (2001, U.S. Navy/Eric J.Tilford)*

and 920 other beds; up to 1,000 additional patients can be accommodated for limited care. The ships are designed to handle a peak admission rate of 300 patients in 24 hours with surgery required by 60 percent of the admissions and an average patient stay of five days.

They are designed to take aboard casualties primarily by helicopter; there is a limited capability for taking on casualties from boats on the port side.

There are facilities for preparing 7,500 meals daily and distilling 75,000 gallons (285,000 liters) of fresh water daily.

Design: Maritime Administration T8-S-100b type.

Names: The merchant names of the ships were WORTH and ROSE CITY, respectively.

Operational: The MERCY operated in the Philippines as a hospital facility from March to June 1987. She was staffed by 375 medical personnel from all the U.S. military services and the Public

The hospital ship COMFORT *operating in the Persian Gulf during Operation Iraqi Freedom. These ships are configured to receive casualties primarily by helicopter, with a limited capability for transfer from small craft. The ships should be modified to provide a second helicopter landing position. (2003, U.S. Navy/Shane T. McCoy)*

Health Service. The ship treated almost 63,000 patients during the three-month period.

Both ships were activated in August 1990 in response to the Kuwaiti crisis. They departed their respective home ports on 13 August; the COMFORT arrived in the Persian Gulf on 8 September and the MERCY on 14 September. They were manned by some 450 medical personnel from the naval hospitals at Oakland, California, and Bethesda, Maryland; this staff later was augmented by about 700 additional personnel from the hospitals who were flown to the Middle East to rendezvous with the ships. Both ships were in the Persian Gulf during Operations Desert Shield/Desert Storm.

The COMFORT was sent to Jamaica in June 1994 to support Haitian refugee processing; she subsequently sailed to the U.S. naval base at Guantanamo Bay, Cuba, to support Haitian and Cuban refugees interned there. She returned to Baltimore in July 1994.

The COMFORT was reactivated to take part in Baltic Challenge '98, an air–naval exercise conducted in July 1998 in the Baltic Sea as part of the NATO Partnership for Peace program. The United States and 11 European nations participated in the two-week exercise.

After the terrorist air attacks on the World Trade Center in New York, the COMFORT was reactivated. She sailed from Baltimore on 12 September 2001 for Earle, New Jersey, where she embarked Navy medical personnel. The ship arrived in New York City on 17 September to provide medical facilities for casualties of the terrorist attacks.

The COMFORT was again placed in MSC service on 27 December 2002 for Operation Iraqi Freedom and deployed to the war zone on 6 January 2003. She returned to Baltimore and was changed to MSC-ROS-5 status on 12 June 2003.

Both ships undertake periodic sea trials.

Personnel: The ships operate as Medical Treatment Facilities in the ROS status; on full mobilization, each ship would be manned by 1,156 Navy personnel.

The stern of the COMFORT as the ship docked at Rota, Spain, en route to support U.S. military operations in the Persian Gulf area. The Navy's two MSC-operated hospital ships have been very active since their completion. (2003, U.S. Navy/Timothy Comerford)

CARGO SHIPS

No cargo ships remain on the Naval Vessel Register except for sealift ships (see Chapter 24).

The last "straight" cargo ship on the NVR was the MIRFAK (T-AK 271), completed in 1957; she was stricken on 21 February 1992. The MIRFAK was one of three small cargo ships designed for Arctic operations (C1-ME2-13a type). Her sister ships ELTANIN (AK 270) and MIZAR (AK 272) were converted to the AGOR 8 and AGOR 11, respectively.

FLEET BALLISTIC MISSILE SUPPLY SHIPS

These cargo ships—usually referred to as AK(FBM)—were configured to support U.S. Polaris/Poseidon/Trident I submarines tenders. They carried strategic missiles, fuel oil (for tenders), diesel oil (for tenders and submarines), spare parts, and provisions to tenders at Holy Loch, Scotland; Rota, Spain; and Apra Harbor, Guam. The ships were manned by MSC civilian crews with Navy security detachments.

There was no further need for these supply ships after the concentration of U.S. Trident missile submarines at Kings Bay, Georgia, and Bremerton, Washington.

FBM SUPPLY SHIP: "VEGA"

Number	Name	In service	Notes
T-AK 286	VEGA	1983	OSIR 28 Apr 1994; str. 7 Nov 1998

The VEGA was a one-of-a-kind AK(FBM). Built for commercial service, she was launched in 1960 and, after brief merchant service, was laid up until acquired by the Navy in 1981. She was a C3-S-33a-type merchant ship. Two sister ships were to be converted to surveying ships (T-AGS 39 and 40), but Congress directed that new ships be constructed for that role. Accordingly, the two ships served instead as maritime prepositioning ships (NORTHERN LIGHT/T-AK 284 and SOUTHERN CROSS/T-AK 285; see Chapter 24).

FBM SUPPLY SHIPS: CONVERTED VICTORY TYPE

Number	Name	In service	Notes
T-AK 259	ALCOR	1952	str. 1968
T-AK 260	BETELGEUSE	1952	str. 1974
T-AK 279	NORWALK	1963	str. 1979
T-AK 280	FURMAN	1963	OSIR 1981; str. 13 Apr 1992
T-AK 281	VICTORIA	1965	str. 1986
T-AK 282	MARSHFIELD	1970	OSIR 1 Oct 1992; str. 30 Nov 1992

These are former VC2-S-AP3 merchant ships built during World War II; they were converted to support deployed FBM submarine tenders. The ALCOR and BETELGEUSE originally served as fleet supply ships carrying general cargo.

The FURMAN was further modified in 1982–1983 to transport undersea cable. The ship was operated by the MSC under the sponsorship of the Naval Space and Warfare Systems Command.

DRY CARGO/AMMUNITION SHIPS

The Navy is using the designation dry cargo/ammunition ship (AKE) for a new class of UNREP ships. These ships also carry liquid cargo for transfer to other ships, but in insufficient quantities to be designated as AOR. Rather, the designation of combat stores ships (AFS) would have been more appropriate. The invention of the AKE designation reflects the Navy's panacea of devising new designations to compensate for having fewer ships than are required.

(12) DRY CARGO/AMMUNITION SHIPS: "LEWIS AND CLARK" CLASS

Number	Name	FY	Launch	In service	Status
T-AKE 1	LEWIS AND CLARK	00	Feb 2005	May 2005	Building
T-AKE 2	SACAGAWEA	00		2006	Building
T-AKE 3	....	01		2006	Building
T-AKE 4	....	03		2007	Building
T-AKE	(2 ships)	04		2007	Building
T-AKE	(2 ships)	05		2008	Building
T-AKE	(2 ships)	06		2009	Planned
T-AKE	(1 ship)	07		2010	Planned
T-AKE	(1 ship)	08		2011	Planned

Builders:	National Steel and Shipbuilding, San Diego
Displacement:	35,400 tons full load
Length:	689 feet (210.0 m) overall
Beam:	105½ feet (32.16 m)
Draft:	28⅚ feet (9.1 m)
Propulsion:	diesel-electric; 1 shaft
Speed:	20 knots
Range:	14,000 nm (16,130 km) at 20 knots
Personnel:	123 civilian + 13 Navy + 36 aviation det.
Helicopters:	2 MH-60S Knighthawk or 2 UH-46 Seaknight
Guns:	none
Radars:	navigation

This is a planned class of 12 underway replenishment ships intended to operate independently to replenish naval ships with dry cargo, provisions, munitions, spare parts, and a limited amount of fuel. In this role, they would replace T-AE ammunition ships and T-AFS combat stores ships, having two-thirds the capacity of each of those UNREP ships. A T-AKE and an oiler of the HENRY J. KAISER class operating together could provide a carrier battle group with the replenishment capability of a single AOE fast combat support ship.

The program was initiated in 1997 and is significantly behind schedule. Several changes in authorization years have been made.

It is expected that the entire class will be constructed by a single shipyard.

Builders: Contract for the LEWIS AND CLARK was awarded to National Steel and Shipbuilding on 18 October 2001.

Classification: During planning, these ships were designated T-ADC(X), for replenishment/dry cargo ship. This was changed to T-AKE in the fall of 2000, although that designation still has not been added to the official classification list. The Naval Sea Systems Command's *Quarterly Progress Report* in 2004 continued to list these vessels as dry cargo ships (T-AKE).

Design: These ships are designed to carry 5,900 tons of dry cargo and 3,000 tons of fuel (18,000 barrels—10,500 barrels of ship fuel and 7,500 barrels of JP-5 aviation fuel). Some of the dry cargo holds are chill/freeze spaces. The ships have eight internal cargo elevators, and there are three port and two starboard STREAM kingposts for UNREP operations. Four 10-ton-capacity extending cranes also are fitted.

They are built to commercial standards.

Space and weight are reserved for two Phalanx Close-In Weapon Systems (CIWS) and the SLQ-25 Nixie torpedo countermeasures system.

Names: The Secretary of the Navy announced on 27 October 2000 that these ships would be named for "legendary explorers." The name LEWIS AND CLARK, previously assigned to the strategic missile submarine SSBN 644, honors explorers Army Captain Meriwether Lewis and Army Lieutenant William Clark.

The second ship honors the Shoshone woman living in North Dakota who served as guide and interpreter for Lewis and Clark during their 1804–1806 expedition into the northwest region of the United States.

Personnel: There is berthing space for 25 transient personnel.

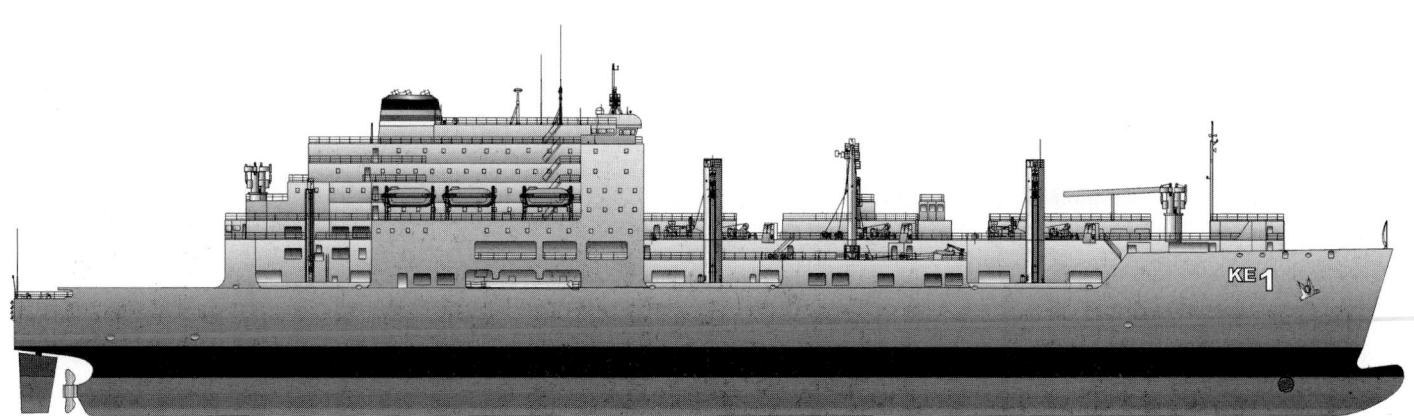

The new multiproduct replenishment ships of the LEWIS AND CLARK class will replace several existing AE/AFS ships, and in company with a fleet oiler, can replace AOE-type ships. The T-AKEs are designed for 40-year service lives. (U.S. Navy)

OILERS

Oilers—also referred to as fleet oilers—provide underway replenishment of naval forces. These ships differ from tankers, which provide point-to-point transfer of fuels, at times replenishing oilers at sea (see Chapter 24).

All active Navy oilers are operated by MSC civilian crews.

Names: Oilers historically have been named for rivers with Indian names. The lead ship of the latest class, the HENRY J. KAISER, is named for an American industrialist and World War II master shipbuilder; the next eight ships of the class are named for industrialists, engineers, and naval architects—after which Indian names resumed for the final nine ships.

(16) OILER-REPLENISHMENT SHIPS

The Navy's 30-year shipbuilding plan presented to Congress in 2003 shows the construction of 16 advanced oiler-replenishment ships, designated T-AO(X), to be authorized in FY 2018–2028. No characteristics for these ships have been developed.

16 FLEET OILERS: "HENRY J. KAISER" CLASS

Number	Name	FY	Launched	In service	Status
T-AO 187	HENRY J. KAISER	82	5 Oct 1985	19 Dec 1986	MSC-ROS-30
T-AO 188	JOSHUA HUMPHREYS	83	22 Feb 1986	3 Apr 1987	OSIR 29 June 1996
T-AO 189	JOHN LENTHALL JR.	84	9 Aug 1986	25 June 1987	**MSC-A**
T-AO 190	ANDREW J. HIGGINS	84	17 Jan 1987	22 Oct 1987	OSIR 6 May 1996
T-AO 191	BENJAMIN ISHERWOOD	85	15 Aug 1988	—	canceled 1993
T-AO 192	HENRY ECKFORD	85	14 Aug 1989	—	canceled 1993
T-AO 193	WALTER S. DIEHL	85	10 Oct 1987	13 Sep 1988	**MSC-P**
T-AO 194	JOHN ERICSSON	86	21 Apr 1990	19 Mar 1991	**MSC-P**
T-AO 195	LEROY GRUMMAN	86	3 Dec 1988	2 Aug 1989	**MSC-A**
T-AO 196	KANAWHA	87	22 Sep 1990	10 Dec 1991	**MSC-A**
T-AO 197	PECOS	87	23 Sep 1989	13 July 1990	**MSC-P**
T-AO 198	BIG HORN	88	2 Feb 1991	21 May 1992	**MSC-A**
T-AO 199	TIPPECANOE	88	16 May 1992	8 Feb 1993	**MSC-P**
T-AO 200	GUADALUPE	89	5 Oct 1991	25 Sep 1992	**MSC-P**
T-AO 201	PATUXENT	89	23 July 1994	22 June 1995	**MSC-A**
T-AO 202	YUKON	89	6 Feb 1992	25 Mar 1994	**MSC-P**
T-AO 203	LARAMIE	89	6 May 1995	7 May 1996	**MSC-A**
T-AO 204	RAPPAHANNOCK	89	14 Jan 1995	7 Nov 1995	**MSC-P**

Builders:	Avondale Shipyards, New Orleans, except T-AO 191 and 192 by Pennsylvania Shipbuilding (Pa.) and American Shipbuilding, Tampa, Fla	Speed:	20 knots	
		Range:	6,000 nm (11,112 km) at 20 knots	
		Personnel:	81 civilian, except 82 in T-AO 189, 194, 195, 203; 74 in T-AO 199, 200; 66 in T-AO 202 + 21 Navy (1 officer + 20 enlisted), except T-AO 197–200, 204 5 Navy (enlisted)	
Displacement	9,500 tons light			
	40,700 tons full load			
Tonnage:	26,500 deadweight			
Length:	649¾ feet (198.1 m) waterline	Helicopters:	landing area	
	677½ feet (206.6 m) overall	Guns:	none (see notes)	
Beam:	97 1/2 feet (29.7 m)	Radars:	2 navigation	
Draft:	36 feet (11.0 m)	EW systems:	(see *Electronics* notes)	
Propulsion:	2 diesel engines (Colt-Pielstick 10PC4.2V); 32,540 bhp; 2 shafts			

These fleet oilers/UNREP ships were built to civilian specifications. Although civilian manned, they operate regularly with forward deployed battle groups. This class provides the only fleet oilers currently in naval service.

The lead ship was laid down on 22 August 1984.

The HENRY J. KAISER previously was assigned as a Maritime Prepositioning Ship (MPS); from 31 January 1995, she carried JP-4 fuel for military aircraft and was assigned to Maritime Prepositioning Squadron 2, normally moored at Diego Garcia. Subsequently, she has been laid up in reserve, ready for reactivation within 30 days.

Builders: Contracts for the construction of T-AO 191, 192, 194, an 196 were awarded to Pennsylvania Shipbuilding in 1985–1986; those contracts were canceled on 31 August 1989 for default on construction. The first two ships were towed to the Philadelphia Naval Shipyard in October 1989 and subsequently were transferred to American Shipbuilding (Tampa) for completion; they were reordered on 16 November 1989. The T-AO 194 and 196, for which assembly had not yet begun, were awarded to Avondale for construction.

The two ships towed to the Tampa yard were, according to shipyard officials, "a mess." The yard sued the Navy, which argued it was forced to send the ships to the yard because of political pressure and that the yard did not have the trained workforce to complete them. Despite additional congressional funding to the Tampa yard, the ships were not completed and the Navy terminated the contract on 15 August 1993. The ships then were towed to the James River (Virginia) NDRF anchorage. The ISHERWOOD was 95.3 percent complete and the ECKFORD 84 percent complete when canceled.

The government had paid Pennsylvania Shipbuilding $331 million and American Shipbuilding $102 million for the two ships. They are not completed and there is no plan to finish them.

Design: These are midsize petroleum carriers with a 180,000-barrel cargo capacity; in addition, they can carry 25,000 gallons (95,000 liters) of lubrication oil as bulk cargo plus 105,000 gallons (399,000 liters) of potable water and 88,000 gallons (334,400 liters) of boiler feed water. The ships have seven UNREP stations.

The PATUXENT and later ships are the first "double hulled" oilers built for MSC operation.

The ships have a limited UNREP capacity for dry stores as well, with a tunnel for forklift trucks running through the superstructure to permit cargo to be carried aft to the helicopter deck. Crew requirements have been increased by about ten from the early designs, with space also provided for another ten transient personnel.

Electronics: Space and weight are reserved for the SLQ-25 Nixie torpedo countermeasures. However, no SLQ-32 installation is planned.

Guns: There are provisions to mount 20-mm Phalanx CIWS on the bow and after superstructure in wartime.

Names: The ANDREW J. HIGGINS honors the American industrialist who pioneered the development and construction of innovative landing craft in World War II. (The destroyer HIGGINS/DDG 76 honors a U.S. Marine, Colonel William Higgins, kidnapped by terrorists in Lebanon in 1988 and subsequently murdered.)

The fleet oiler PECOS refuels the aircraft carrier ABRAHAM LINCOLN (CVN 72) in the Pacific. Nuclear-propelled carriers require regular replenishment of aviation fuel for their air wings. (2004, U.S. Navy/Patrick Bonafede)

The KANAWHA shows the large helicopter deck of the HENRY J. KAISER-class fleet oilers. These ships lack the helicopter hangars found in AOE/AOR-type ships, relying on helicopters from other UNREP ships or aircraft carriers to move cargo. (2003, U.S. Navy/Tony C. Foster)

The LEROY GRUMMAN is typical of the Navy's only class of fleet oilers. Although these ships are unarmed, they conduct UNREP operations in forward areas, a role previously assigned to Navy-manned, armed AOE/AOR-type ships. (2003, U.S. Navy/Danny Ewing Jr.)

FLEET OILERS: "CIMARRON" CLASS

Number	Name	Comm.	Status
AO 177	Cimarron	1981	decomm./str. 15 Dec 1998; str. 3 May 1999
AO 178	Monongahela	1981	decomm./str. 30 Sep 1999
AO 179	Merrimack	1981	decomm./str. 18 Dec 1998
AO 180	Willamette	1982	decomm./str. 30 Apr 1999
AO 186	Platte	1983	decomm./str. 30 June 1999

These were the last U.S. Navy fleet oilers in active commission. They were a class of five ships, built to Navy (vice Maritime Administration) design. They could provide two complete refuelings to a conventional aircraft carrier and six to eight accompanying escort ships. All five ships were lengthened or "jumboized" from 1989 to 1992.

See 16th Edition/pages 237–39 for characteristics.

Classification: The hull numbers 182–185 were assigned to the Falcon-class transport tankers (T-AOT), and the USNS Potomac is T-AOT 181 (see Chapter 24).

FLEET OILERS: "NEOSHO" CLASS

Number	Name	Comm.	Notes
T-AO 143	Neosho	1954	OSIR 10 Aug 1992; str. 16 Feb 1994
T-AO 144	Mississinewa	1955	OSIR 30 July 1991; str. 16 Feb 1994
T-AO 145	Hassayampa	1955	OSIR 2 Oct 1991; str. 16 Feb 1994
T-AO 146	Kawishiwi	1955	OSIR 31 July 1992; str. 7 Nov 1994
T-AO 147	Truckee	1955	OSIR 21 Oct 1991; str. 18 July 1994
T-AO 148	Ponchatoula	1956	OSIR 1 Apr 1992; str. 31 Aug 1992

These were the first fleet oilers built for the U.S. Navy after World War II. They were large, graceful, heavily armed ships, built to a Navy (vice MarAd) design. They were configured as service squadron flagships.

All originally were active Navy-manned ships; they were transferred to the MSC for civilian manning in 1976–1980.

FLEET OILERS: "MISPILLION" CLASS

Number	Name	Comm.	Notes
T-AO 105	Mispillion	1945	OSIR 8 Feb 1990; str. 15 Feb 1995
T-AO 106	Navasota	1946	OSIR 2 Oct 1991; str. 2 Jan 1992
T-AO 107	Passumpsic	1946	OSIR/str. 17 Dec 1991
T-AO 108	Pawcatuck	1946	OSIR/str. 21 Sep 1991
T-AO 109	Waccamaw	1946	OSIR/str. 11 Oct 1989

These were the last of a large class of twin-screw naval oilers built during World War II as Navy fleet oilers (Maritime Administration T3-S2-A1/A3 design). The above five ships comprised the A3 series. They were jumboized in the mid-1960s to increase their cargo capacity. All five were transferred from the active Navy to the MSC with civilian manning in 1973–1975; they subsequently were taken out of service and transferred to the NDRF and later stricken.

Class: A total of 23 ships of the T3 designs were delivered to the Navy (AO 51–64, 68–72, 97–100, and 105–109). See the Cimarron class.

Designation: The Waccamaw was intended for conversion to a replenishment oiler (AOR 109); that was not undertaken.

FLEET OILERS: "CIMARRON" CLASS

Number	Name	Comm.	Notes
AO 51	Ashtabula	1943	decomm. 1982; str. 6 Sep 1991
T-AO 57	Marias	1944	OSIR 1982; str. 11 Dec 1992
T-AO 62	Taluga	1944	OSIR 1983; str. 21 Feb 1992
AO 98	Caloosahatchee	1945	decomm. 1989; str. 18 July 1994
AO 99	Canisteo	1945	decomm. 1989; str. 31 Aug 1992

These were fleet oilers of the T3-S2-A1 type. Three ships (Navy manned) were jumboized in the mid-1960s to increase their carrying capacity. Two ships were transferred to MSC operation in 1972–1973. All were assigned to the NDRF after being taken out of service.

The lead ship of this design was the Cimarron (AO 22).

POST–WORLD WAR II OILERS

War-built fleet oilers reached hull number AO 109. The ex-German submarine tender Dithmarschen (built in 1938) became the USS Conecuh (IX 301) after the war; her designation was changed to AO 110 and, subsequently, because of ordnance and stores capability, to AOR 110. (The AOR classification was established in 1952 as fleet replenishment tanker to provide "one stop" fuel and munitions replenishment. The classification AOR was reestablished as replenishment oiler in 1964.)

The AO 111–142 were Mission-class T2 merchant tankers operated by the MSTS/MSC. The Mission Capistrano (AO 112) was converted to a sonar trials ship (AG 162).

The AO 143–148 were the Neosho class, built specifically as naval fleet oilers (see above).

The AO 149–152 were large tankers of the Maumee class built specifically for MSTS/MSC service and subsequently designated AOT (see Chapter 23). The similar American Explorer was built for merchant use but on completion was acquired by the Navy as AO 165.

The AO 153–164 were commercial T2 tankers acquired during the 1956 Suez crisis for MSTS operations; they were stricken in 1957–1958.

Hull numbers AO 166 and 167 were reserved for planned Mission-class jumbo conversions (i.e., civilian merchant tankers).

The AO 168–176 were the Sealift-class tankers built for MSC operation (see Chapter 23).

The AO 177–180 and 186 are the Cimarron class, built specifically for naval service (see above).

Hull number AO 181 was assigned to the Potomac, which was constructed from portions of an earlier Potomac (AO 150) (see Chapter 23).

The AO 182–185 were merchant tankers taken over for naval use (see Chapter 23).

The AO 187–204 are the Henry J. Kaiser class (see above).

FAST COMBAT SUPPORT SHIPS

These ships are intended to operate as part of fast carrier battle groups, providing petroleum products, munitions, and other supplies to aircraft carriers and their screening surface combatants. In practice, they combine the functions of fleet oilers (AO) and ammunition ships (AE) and, to a limited extent, the combat stores ships (AFS).

Names: The AOE 1–4 are named for cities; the AOE 6–10 carry the names of earlier supply ships (AE/AF/IX types).

(8) FAST COMBAT SUPPORT SHIPS

The Navy's 30-year shipbuilding plan presented to Congress in 2003 includes the construction of eight T-AOE(X) replenishment ships to be authorized in FY 2009–2033. No characteristics for these ships have been developed.

Plans for a class of 16 improved fast combat support ships, designated AOE(V), were canceled in 1991. The first unit was to be requested in the FY 1993 budget and completed in 1997. These ships were to replace the ammunition ships (AE) of the Nitro and Suribachi classes and, subsequently, the combat stores ships (AFS) of the Mars and Lyness classes.

See 17th Edition/page 262 for characteristics.

4 FAST COMBAT SUPPORT SHIPS: "SUPPLY" CLASS

Number	Name	FY	Launched	Comm.	to MSC	Status
T-AOE 6	Supply	87	6 Oct 1990	26 Feb 1994	13 July 2001	**MSC-A**
T-AOE 7	Rainier	89	28 Sep 1991	1 Dec 1994	29 Aug 2003	**MSC-P**
T-AOE 8	Arctic	90	30 Oct 1993	11 Sep 1995	14 June 2002	**MSC-A**
T-AOE 10	Bridge	93	24 Aug 1996	31 Mar 1998	24 June 2004	**MSC-P**

Builders:	National Steel, San Diego, Calif.		Range:	
Displacement:	19,700 tons light		Personnel:	176 civilian + 27 Navy (2 officers + 25 enlisted)
	48,800 tons full load			+ helicopter det.
Length:	730 feet (222.56 m) waterline		Helicopters:	3 UH-46 Sea Knight
	754¾ feet (230.1 m) overall		Missiles:	removed
Beam:	107 feet (32.6 m)		Guns:	removed
Draft:	39 feet (11.9 m)		Radars:	SPS-64(V)9 navigation
Propulsion:	4 gas turbines (General Electric LM 2500); 100,000 shp;			SPS-67(V) surface search
	2 shafts		Fire control:	removed
Speed:	26 knots		EW systems:	removed

These are large, multiproduct replenishment ships. They are based on the SACRAMENTO design, the principal difference in the two classes being in their propulsion plants. Note that the later ships are smaller.

The lead ship, the SUPPLY, was laid down on 24 February 1989.

The first three ships suffered major delays, caused mainly by delays in the delivery of reduction gears, a major propulsion system component. All four ships were delivered behind schedule. Related to these delays was a major increase in cost. In August 1991, the Navy stated that the ships would cost 30 percent more than original estimates.

All four have been transferred to the Military Sealift Command for operations.

Class: The AOE 9 was authorized in FY 1992 and tentatively named CONECUH. Her construction was deferred and the funds were used to pay for shipbuilding cost overruns. The ship was reauthorized in FY 1993 as the AOE 10.

Design: Cargo capacity is 156,000 barrels of petroleum products plus 1,800 tons of munitions, 400 tons of refrigerated provisions, and 250 tons of dry stores.

This is the second class of U.S. Navy ships built with the so-called Level III collective protection features against Chemical-Biological-Radiological (CBR) attack; the first was the ARLEIGH BURKE (DDG 51)-class destroyers. Level III provides the maximum protection possible within a ship, including berthing, medical, and control spaces.

Electronics: When Navy manned, the ships had SLQ-25 Nixie and SLQ-32(V)3 electronic warfare systems.

Guns: At the time of their transfer to the MSC, each ship was armed with two 25-mm Bushmaster cannon Mk 38, two 20-mm Phalanx CIWS Mk 15, and four .50-cal machine guns; they also carried guided missiles (see below).

Missiles: When transferred to the MSC, each ship had one 8-cell NATO Sea Sparrow launcher Mk 29.

Names: The AOE 10 is named for the first U.S. Navy ship built from the keel up as a store ship, the BRIDGE (AF 1); she, in turn was named for Commodore Horatio Bridge, the first Chief of the Bureau of Provisions and Clothing, established in 1842, and a pioneer in fleet supply.

The AOE 7 originally was named PAUL HAMILTON; while under construction, that name instead was assigned to the destroyer DDG 60.

Personnel: In March 2000, the Navy announced that the SUPPLY would be assigned 17 civil service steward/utilitymen to carry out food service and laundry functions aboard the ship. This is believed to be the first time civilians have been assigned to the actual crew in a commissioned Navy ship (i.e., USS).

The program, which replaced 24 sailors normally assigned to the ship, evaluated the feasibility of such assignments in the future. During the year-long trial, the SUPPLY deployed for about six months with the GEORGE WASHINGTON (CVN 73) battle group to the Mediterranean area.

The SUPPLY replenishes the carrier GEORGE WASHINGTON while the flattop conducts flight operations in the North Atlantic. AOEs are the world's largest UNREP ships, having been designed with speed, armament, and cargo capacity to operate with forward deployed carrier battle groups. (2003, U.S. Navy/Summer M. Anderson)

The BRIDGE in the Western Pacific while still in Navy commission, armed with an array of small-caliber guns. A Phalanx CIWS mount is visible forward of the bridge. This class has been transferred to the MSC at the rate of one per year. (2003, U.S. Navy/Joshua K. Tyree)

An MH-60S Knighthawk assigned to Helicopter Combat Support Squadron (HCS) 6 lifts cargo from the SUPPLY during operations in the Persian Gulf. When a Navy helicopter detachment is embarked, about 30 additional Navy personnel come aboard the AOE. (2004, U.S. Navy/ Michael D. Blackwell II)

3 FAST COMBAT SUPPORT SHIPS: "SACRAMENTO" CLASS

Number	Name	FY	Launched	Comm.	Status
AOE 1	SACRAMENTO	61	14 Sep 1963	14 Mar 1964	AR; decomm. 1 Oct 2004
AOE 2	CAMDEN	63	29 May 1965	1 Apr 1967	**PA**
AOE 3	SEATTLE	65	2 Mar 1968	5 Apr 1969	**AA**
AOE 4	DETROIT	66	21 June 1969	28 Mar 1970	**AA**

Builders:	AOE 1, 3, 4: Puget Sound Naval Shipyard, Bremerton, Wash.
	AOE 2: New York Shipbuilding, Camden, N.J.
Displacement:	18,700 tons light
	53,600 tons full load
Length:	770 feet (234.75 m) waterline
	794¾ feet (242.4 m) overall
Beam:	107 feet (32.6 m)
Draft:	38 feet (11.6 m)
Propulsion:	2 steam turbines (General Electric); 100,000 shp; 2 shafts
Boilers:	4 600 psi (41.7 kg/cm²) (Combustion Engineering)
Speed:	27.5 knots (26 knots sustained)
Range:	10,000 nm (18,520 km) at 17 knots
	6,000 nm (11,112 km) at 26 knots

Personnel:	604 (28 officers + 576 enlisted)
Helicopters:	2 UH-46 Sea Knight
Missiles:	1 8-cell NATO Sea Sparrow launcher Mk 29
Guns:	2 20-mm Phalanx CIWS Mk 15 (2 multibarrel)
	4 .50-cal machine guns M2 (4 single)
Radars:	SPS-10F surface search
	SPS-40E air search in AOE 1, 2
	SPS-64(V)9
Fire control:	2 Mk 95 missile Fire Control System (FCS)
	1 Mk 23 Target Acquisition System (TAS) in AOE 3
EW systems:	SLQ-25 Nixie
	SLQ-32(V)2 or 5

These are the world's largest underway replenishment ships, designed to provide a carrier battle group with full fuels, munitions, dry and frozen provisions, and other supplies.

Plans to modernize (Service Life Extension Program/SLEP) these ships beginning about FY 2000 were dropped. The SACRAMENTO was decommissioned on 1 October 2004 and is expected to be stricken; all four ships will be discarded by FY 2007.

Class: The AOE 5 of this class was planned for the FY 1968 program but canceled on 4 November 1968.

Design: SCB No. 196. These ships can carry 156,000 barrels of fuels, 2,100 tons of munitions, 250 tons of dry stores, and 250 tons of refrigerated stores. They have highly automated cargo-handling equipment.

A large helicopter deck is fitted aft with a three-bay hangar for VERTREP helos. Each bay is 47–52-feet (14.3–15.85 m) long, 17–19-feet (5.2–5.8 m) wide, and 18–18½-feet (5.5–5.6 m) high.

Electronics: The hull has provision for SQS-26 sonar, but it has not been installed. The earlier WLR-1 Electronics Countermeasures (ECM) system has been replaced by the SLQ-32 system.

Engineering: The first two ships were provided with the main propulsion machinery produced for the canceled battleship KENTUCKY (BB 66).

Guns: As built, these ships were armed with eight 3-inch guns in twin mounts and associated Mk 56 GFCS. Armament was reduced in the mid-1970s, and a NATO Sea Sparrow launcher was installed forward. The remaining 3-inch guns have been removed, with two Phalanx CIWS being fitted to each ship.

The DETROIT at high speed in the North Sea shows the massive size of these UNREP ships. They can replenish major warships on both sides—aircraft carriers to port. Unlike the later SUPPLY class, these ships have stem and port side anchors. (2004, U.S. Navy/Alex J. Recalde Jr.)

The DETROIT in the Persian Gulf while simultaneously refueling an aircraft carrier and an Aegis cruiser. There is a NATO Sea Sparrow launcher forward of her bridge; the SLQ-32 electronic countermeasures antennas are visible atop her bridge structure. (2003, U.S. Navy/Douglas M. Pearlman)

The stern aspect of the DETROIT as she steams in the Persian Gulf shows her triple-hangar configuration. An MH-60S Knighthawk from HCS-6 is hovering above the flight deck, almost lost in the clutter of the hangar structure. Twin Phalanx CIWS mounts are on the after structure. (2004, U.S. Navy)

REPLENISHMENT OILERS

These ships combined the capability of a fleet oiler (AO) with a limited capability for the services of an ammunition ship (AE) and combat store ship (AFS).

REPLENISHMENT OILERS: "WICHITA" CLASS

Number	Name	Comm.	Notes
AOR 1	WICHITA	1969	decomm. 12 Mar 1993; str. 15 Feb 1995
AOR 2	MILWAUKEE	1969	decomm. 27 Jan 1994; str. 8 Apr 1997
AOR 3	KANSAS CITY	1970	decomm. 7 Oct 1994; str. 8 Apr 1997
AOR 4	SAVANNAH	1970	decomm. 28 July 1995; str. 29 Oct 1998
AOR 5	WABASH	1971	decomm. 30 Sep 1994; str. 8 Apr 1997
AOR 6	KALAMAZOO	1973	decomm. 16 Aug 1996; str. 29 Oct 1998
AOR 7	ROANOKE	1976	decomm./str. 6 Oct 1995

These are smaller variations of the AOE-type ships. All were decommissioned and stricken within a few years of the end of the Cold War. The SAVANNAH, KALAMAZOO, and MILWAUKEE (all in strike status) were assigned to the NDRF on 27 July, 3 August, and 7 August 2000, respectively.

The AORs were Navy-manned ships and were armed; all had hangars and flight decks to support two UH-46 Sea Knight cargo helicopters for vertical replenishment operations.

REPAIR SHIPS

These ships provided major repairs to ship hulls, machinery, and equipment. They did not carry the weapons and specialized stores and parts stocked on destroyer, submarine, and seaplane tenders.

The Navy planned a new class of repair ships to replace the VULCAN class, with the lead ship included in the FY 1994 shipbuilding program and then slipped to FY 1998. This class eventually also was to replace older destroyer tenders (AD).

In the event, the plan was canceled in the early 1990s when the Navy decided to dispose of all repair ships as well as most of the tenders. Only two large repair ships, the VULCAN and JASON, were in active U.S. Navy service in the 1990s.

Table 23-9. REPAIR SHIPS

Number	Name	Comm.	Notes
	VULCAN class (4)		
AR 5	VULCAN	1941	decomm. 30 Sep 1991; str. 28 July 1992
AR 6	AJAX	1943	decomm. 31 Dec 1986; str. 16 May 1989
AR 7	HECTOR	1944	decomm. 31 Mar 1987; to Pakistan 20 Apr 1989
AR 8	JASON	1944	decomm./str. 24 June 1995
AR 9–21	World War II program		
	Reclassified destroyer tenders (3)		
AR 22	KLONDIKE (ex-AD 22)	1945	str. 1974
AR 23	MARKAB (ex-AD 21)	1941	str. 1976
AR 24–27	not used		
AR 28	GRAND CANYON (ex-AD 28)	1946	str. 1978

World War II-era repair ships reached hull number AR 21. Three destroyer tenders were reclassified as repair ships after the war, indicating their employment in general repair and support work. Two retained their AD hull numbers.

The large VULCAN-class ships were highly capable repair ships, although they lacked the ability to support more sophisticated weapon and electronic systems. They served well into the Cold War era. The VULCAN class was one of three series of large tender-type ships begun in the late 1930s, the others being the DIXIE (AD 14) and FULTON (AS 11) classes. The JASON was completed as a heavy hull repair ship (ARH 1); she was reclassified as AR 8 in 1957.

Numerous specialized repair ships were built/converted during World War II; none remain on the NVR. They were:

ARB	battle damage
ARG	internal combustion engines
ARL	landing craft
ARV	aircraft
ARVA	aircraft—airframes
ARVE	aircraft—engines

Most of these ships were converted from LSTs.

CABLE REPAIR SHIPS

The Navy's cable ships support SOSUS and other underwater cable activities. In addition, cable ships conduct special oceanographic and acoustic surveys in support of the Naval Space and Warfare Systems Command under the Oceanographer of the Navy. (Commercial ships also are used under contract to support U.S. seafloor cable installations.)

Names: Cable ships are assigned names from mythology.

1 CABLE REPAIR SHIP: "ZEUS"

Number	Name	FY	Launched	In service	Status
T-ARC 7	ZEUS	79	30 Oct 1982	19 Mar 1984	**MSC-P**

Builders:	National Steel and Shipbuilding, San Diego, Calif.
Displacement:	8,297 tons light
	14,225 tons full load
Length:	454 feet (138.4 m) waterline
	502½ feet (153.2 m) overall
Beam:	73⅙ feet (22.3 m)
Draft:	23⅝ feet (7.3 m)
Propulsion:	diesel-electric (5 General Motors EMD diesel engines); 12,500 shp; 2 shafts
Speed:	15.8 knots
Range:	10,000 nm (18,520 km) at 15 knots
Personnel:	38 civilian + 6 Navy (enlisted) + 15 civilian technicians
Helicopters:	no facilities
Radars:	2 navigation

The ZEUS was the first cable ship built specifically for use by the U.S. Navy. Two ships of this type were planned to replace the now-stricken THOR and AEOLUS. The second ship of the class was planned for the FY 1986 budget but was not requested.

The ZEUS was delayed because of design and construction problems; her keel was laid down 1 June 1981. She is operated by the MSC under sponsorship of the Naval Space and Warfare Systems Command.

The Navy personnel are communications specialists.

Design: The ship can lay up to 1,000 miles (1,610 km) of cable in depths to 10 miles (16 km).

Electronics: The ZEUS is fitted with the SSN-2 precise seafloor navigation system.

Engineering: Two 1,200-hp bow and two 1,200-hp stern thrusters are fitted for station keeping while handling cables.

Table 23-10. CABLE REPAIR SHIPS

Number	Name	Comm.*	Notes
ARC 1	PROTUNUS (ex-LSM 275)	1952	to Portugal 1959
T-ARC 2	NEPTUNE	1953	OSIR 24 Sep 1991; str. 20 Aug 1992
T-ARC 3	AEOLUS (ex-AKA 47)	1955	str. 1985
T-ARC 4	THOR (ex-AKA 49)	1956	str. 1978
ARC 5	YAMACRAW (WARC 333)	1948	str. 1965
T-ARC 6	ALBERT J. MYER	1963	OSIR 13 Feb 1994; str. 7 Nov 1944

* Commission or in service as cable ships

A World War II-built landing ship completed in 1944, the ARC 1, after brief service as a cable ship, was transferred to Portugal, where she was converted to a diving tender.

Two war-built attack cargo ships (AKA 47 and AKA 49)were converted to cable ships and assigned new names. The NEPTUNE and MYER were built-for-the-purpose cable ships initially intended for Army use. Both were completed in 1946 and laid up in MarAd reserve. The MYER was acquired by the Navy in 1952 and the NEPTUNE in 1953 to support the SOSUS program; they were placed in Navy commission (ARC 2 and 6) and operated as commissioned ships (USS). The MYER was transferred outright to the

Navy and the NEPTUNE was on loan until permanently acquired in 1966. Both ships were transferred to MSC operation as T-ARCs in 1973.

The ex-Army MAJ GEN ARTHUR MURRAY was acquired by the Navy in 1945 as the USS TRAPPER (ACM 9). She was transferred to the Coast Guard in 1948 and renamed YAMACRAW (WARC 333), then retransferred to Navy in 1959, commissioned as ARC 5, and engaged largely as an underwater research ship.[8]

---

8 ACM = auxiliary minelayer.

The ZEUS *is the Navy's only cable ship and was the only ARC to be constructed specifically for U.S. naval service. Commercial cable ships also supported the Navy's SOSUS seafloor acoustic detection system, as well as Air Force missile impact sensors on the sea floor. (U.S. Navy)*

SALVAGE SHIPS

These ships are fitted for deep-sea salvage and towing operations. In addition to naval salvage activities, the Navy has a national responsibility for salvaging all U.S. ships, both government and private (Public Law 80-513).

These ships, as well as the ATS-type tugs, are the principal diver support ships of the Navy.

Names: Salvage ships are named for terms related to diving and salvage activities.

(4) SALVAGE SHIPS

The Navy's 30-year shipbuilding plan presented to Congress in 2003 includes the construction of four salvage ships, designated ARS(X), to be authorized in FY 2019–2024. No characteristics for these ships have been developed.

An earlier class of ARS-type ships to replace the older ARS/ASR-type ships was planned, with the lead unit scheduled for authorization in the FY 1994 shipbuilding program. However, that program was canceled in the early 1990s.

4 SALVAGE SHIPS: "SAFEGUARD" CLASS

Number	Name	FY	Launched	Comm.	Status
ARS 50	SAFEGUARD	81	12 Nov 1983	17 Aug 1985	**PA**
ARS 51	GRASP	82	21 Apr 1984	14 Dec 1985	**AA**
ARS 52	SALVOR	82	28 July 1984	14 June 1986	**PA**
ARS 53	GRAPPLE	83	8 Dec 1984	15 Nov 1986	**AA**

Builders:	Peterson Builders, Sturgeon Bay, Wisc.
Displacement:	2,725 tons light
	3,193 tons full load
Length:	240 feet (73.15 m) waterline
	254½ feet (77.7 m) overall
Beam:	51 feet (15.5 m)
Draft:	15⅝ feet (4.7 m)
Propulsion:	4 geared diesel engines (Caterpillar D399 BTA); 4,200 bhp;
	2 shafts (Kort-nozzle propellers)
Speed:	13.5 knots
Range:	8,000 nm (14,816 km) at 12 knots
Personnel:	106 (7 officers + 99 enlisted)
Helicopters:	VERTREP area
Guns:	2 .50-cal machine guns M2 (2 single)
Radars:	Raytheon 1900 navigation
	SPS-64(V)9 navigation

These ships replaced several of the long-serving salvage ships of the ESCAPE class in the salvage and towing roles.

The SAFEGUARD is homeported in Sasebo, Japan; the only other U.S. auxiliary ships currently homeported outside the continental

United States are the submarine tenders EMORY S. LAND and FRANK CABLE.

Design: The ships are fitted for towing and heavy lift, with a limited diving support capability. A 40-ton-capacity boom is fitted aft and a 7.5-ton boom is located forward.

Engineering: A 500-hp bow thruster is provided.

Operational: In July 1990, the GRASP salvaged an S-3B Viking anti-submarine aircraft off the coast of Virginia from a depth of more than 10,000 feet (3,049 m). The aircraft had crashed at sea

during a takeoff from the carrier JOHN F. KENNEDY (CV 67) on 7 October 1989.

Subsequently, the GRASP had a major role in the salvage of TWA Flight 800 (a Boeing 747) off Long Island, New York, in 1996 and the recovery of the plane and remains of John F. Kennedy Jr. off Martha's Vineyard, Massachusetts, on 16 July 1999.

The GRAPPLE helped to recover debris from EgyptAir Flight 990 (a Boeing 767), which crashed off Rhode Island on 31 October 1999.

The SAFEGUARD, homeported in Japan, entering Sattahip, Thailand. The four ships of this class are the only Navy-manned tug/salvage-type ships now in service. Commercial salvage ships would be used in emergency in peacetime—and in war if available. (2003, U.S. Navy/ Chuck Bell)

The GRASP, showing the simple layout of these most useful ships. There is a vertical replenishment position marked on the fantail. (2000, Camil Busquets i Vilanova)

SALVAGE AND RESCUE SHIPS: "EDENTON" CLASS

Number	Name	Comm.	Notes
ATS 1	EDENTON	1971	decomm. 29 Mar 1996; to Coast Guard 1997
ATS 2	BEAUFORT	1972	decomm. 8 Mar 1996; to South Korea 29 Aug 1996
ATS 3	BRUNSWICK	1972	decomm. 8 Mar 1996; to South Korea 29 Aug 1996

These British-built, oceangoing tugs had extensive salvage and diving capabilities. They are one of two classes of auxiliary ships to be constructed in British shipyards for the U.S. Navy, the other being the two-ship CHAUVENET (T-AGS 29) class. The more-recently acquired British-built store ships (T-AFS) were constructed for Royal Fleet Auxiliary service.

The EDENTON has been resurrected as the Coast Guard cutter ALEX HALEY (WMEC 39), being transferred to that service on 18 November 1997. The BEAUFORT and BRUNSWICK were transferred to South Korea on 29 August 1996; both were stricken on 12 December 1996. They were delivered in July 1997.

Classification: ATS originally indicated salvage tug; it was changed to salvage and rescue ship on 16 February 1971.

See 16th Edition/page 248 for characteristics.

SALVAGE SHIPS: "DIVER" AND "BOLSTER" CLASSES

Number	Name	Comm.	Notes
ARS 8	PRESERVER	1944	decomm. 7 Aug 1992; str. 16 Mar 1994
ARS 38	BOLSTER	1945	decomm./str. 24 Sep 1994
ARS 39	CONSERVER	1945	decomm./str. 1 Apr 1994
ARS 40	HOIST	1945	decomm./str. 30 Sep 1994
ARS 41	OPPORTUNE	1945	decomm. 30 Apr 1993/str. 5 Aug 1993
ARS 42	RECLAIMER	1945	decomm./str. 16 Sep 1994
ARS 43	RECOVERY	1946	decomm./str. 30 Sep 1994

Seven World War II-built ARS-type ships survived into the 1990s, testimony to the excellence of their design. Four were transferred to the Naval Reserve Force in 1979–1986 and manned by composite active–reserve crews—the PRESERVER, BOLSTER, HOIST, and

RECLAIMER. The PRESERVER and CONSERVER were decommissioned on 30 September 1986; both ships were recommissioned on 26 September 1987 for salvage and anti-drug patrol duties in the Caribbean. The PRESERVER then shifted to the NRF in exchange for the HOIST on 30 April 1989, with the latter returning to active service. The PRESERVER was again decommissioned in 1992.

The RECLAIMER (in strike status) was assigned to the NDRF on 6 October 2000, and the HOIST (in strike status) on 19 June 2001.

Class: Originally, these two similar classes included 21 ships: the ARS 5–9, 19–28, and 38–43 (plus the canceled ARS 44–49). The lead ship of this design was the DIVER (ARS 5); after she was sold in 1949, the Navy listed ESCAPE as the class name. The BOLSTER and later ships were considered a separate class, but the differences were minimal (e.g., beam, fuel capacity).

Two ships of these classes were converted to oceanographic ships, the CHAIN (AGOR 17, ex-ARS 20) and ARGO (AGOR 18, ex-SNATCH/ ARS 27). Three other ships served with the Coast Guard: the ESCAPE (ARS 6/WMEC 6), SHACKLE (ARS 9/WMEC 167), and SEIZE (ARS 26/WMEC 168).

SUBMARINE TENDERS

Submarine tenders have extensive maintenance shops for various submarine systems and equipment as well as considerable weapon and provision storage. Tenders also provide hospital facilities and extra berths for submarine relief personnel.

There are two submarine tenders in commission, the only tender-type ships now in active U.S. Navy service. They are expected to remain in service for some 50 years, i.e., until about 2030.

Names: Submarine tenders had a variety of name sources—mostly mythological (PROTEUS) and submarine pioneers (SIMON LAKE) and builders (EMORY S. LAND). The CANOPUS (AS 34) remembered an earlier CANOPUS (AS 9) lost in the Philippines in 1942.

3 SUBMARINE TENDERS: "EMORY S. LAND" CLASS

Number	Name	FY	Launched	Comm.	Status
AS 39	EMORY S. LAND	72	4 May 1977	7 July 1979	**AA**
AS 40	FRANK CABLE	73	14 Jan 1978	5 Feb 1980	**PA**
AS 41	McKEE	77	16 Feb 1980	15 Aug 1981	PR; decomm. 1 Oct 1999;

Builders:	Lockheed Shipbuilding and Construction, Seattle, Wash.
Displacement:	13,842 tons light
	22,650 tons full load
Length:	620 feet (189 m) waterline
	645⅔ feet (196.9 m) overall
Beam:	85 feet (25.9 m)
Draft:	25½ feet (7.8 m)
Propulsion:	1 steam turbine (De Laval); 20,000 shp; 1 shaft
Boilers:	2 650 psi (43.6 kg/cm²) (Combustion Engineering)
Speed:	20 knots (18 knots sustained)
Range:	7,600 nm (14,075 km) at 18 knots
Personnel:	AS 39: 581 (55 officers + 526 enlisted)
	AS 40: 604 (64 officers + 540 enlisted)
Flag:	69 (25 officers + 44 enlisted)
Helicopters:	VERTREP area
Guns:	4 20-mm cannon Mk 67 (4 single)
	2 40-mm grenade launchers Mk 19 (2 single)
Radars:	SPS-10 surface search
	1 navigation

These are improved versions of the L. Y. SPEAR-class tenders with the later ships fitted specifically to support the LOS ANGELES (SSN 688)-class attack submarines. Up to four SSNs can be supported alongside simultaneously.

The EMORY S. LAND is homeported at La Maddalena, Sardinia, supporting U.S. Sixth Fleet submarines operating in the Mediterranean; the CABLE is homeported at Apra Harbor, Guam, supporting U.S. ships assigned to the Seventh Fleet in the Western Pacific. The only other U.S. auxiliary ship homeported outside the continental United States is the salvage ship SAFEGUARD at Sasebo, Japan.

Design: SCB No. 737. These ships are fitted with a 30-ton-capacity crane and two 5-ton traveling cranes. Medical facilities include an operating room, dental clinic, and 23-bed ward.

The submarine tender EMORY S. LAND provides support to two mine countermeasures ships of the AVENGER (MCM 1) class at Souda Bay, Crete. The only two tender-type ships in U.S. Navy service, the LAND and the similar FRANK CABLE support a variety of ships. (2003, U.S. Navy/Benjamin D. Olvey)

The FRANK CABLE is approached by the attack submarine SALT LAKE CITY (SSN 716) at Apra Harbor, Guam. Guam is now home port to several SSNs serviced by the FRANK CABLE. The tender also supports other Seventh Fleet ships. (2002, U.S. Navy/Alan D. Monyelle)

The EMORY S. LAND, homeported at La Maddalena on Sardinia, maneuvers at Gaeta, Italy, home port of the Sixth Fleet flagship LA SALLE (AGF 3). Tenders have a helicopter deck but cannot accommodate helicopters. (2004, U.S. Navy/Jared Hill)

SUBMARINE TENDERS: "L. Y. SPEAR" CLASS

Number	Name	Comm.	Notes
AS 36	L. Y. SPEAR	1970	decomm. 6 Sep 1996; str. 31 May 1999
AS 37	DIXON	1971	decomm. 15 Dec 1995; str. 18 Mar 1996

These were the U.S. Navy's first submarine tenders designed specifically to support nuclear-propelled attack submarines. The DIXON was placed out of commission, special, on 7 August 1995 and out of commission, full, on the above date.

The DIXON was sunk as a target on 21 July 2003.

See 16th Edition/pages 248–50 for characteristics.

Class: The AS 38 of this design was authorized in the FY 1969 budget but was not built because of funding shortages in other ship programs; the ship was canceled on 27 March 1969.

1 SUBMARINE TENDER: "SIMON LAKE" CLASS

Number	Name	FY	Launched	Comm.	Status
AS 33	SIMON LAKE	63	8 Feb 1964	7 Nov 1964	AR; decomm. 31 July 1999
AS 34	CANOPUS	64	12 Feb 1965	4 Nov 1965	decomm. 30 Nov 1996; str. 30 May 1995

Builders:	Puget Sound Naval Shipyard, Bremerton, Wash.
Displacement:	12,000 tons light
	19,934 tons full load
Length:	643¾ feet (196.3 m) overall
Beam:	85 feet (25.9 m)
Draft:	28½ feet (8.7 m)
Propulsion:	1 steam turbine (De Laval); 20,000 shp; 1 shaft
Boilers:	2 650 psi (43.6 kg/cm²)(Combustion Engineering)
Speed:	18 knots
Range:	7,600 nm (14,080 km) at 18 knots
Personnel:	612 (62 officers + 550 enlisted)
Helicopters:	VERTREP area
Guns:	4 20-mm cannon Mk 67 (4 single)
Radars:	LN-66 navigation
	SPS-10 surface search

These were two of the four tenders constructed specifically to service fleet ballistic missile submarines (SSBNs). In addition, the World War II–built tender PROTEUS was converted to support SSBNs.

Class: The AS 35 of this design was authorized in FY 1965 but construction was deferred and the ship was not built. That ship would have meant one tender would be available for each of the five Polaris SSBN squadrons, with a sixth ship in overhaul or transit. However, the Polaris SSBN program was reduced from the proposed 45 to 41 submarines, and only four squadrons were formed, with four tenders built (AS 31–34) plus one conversion (AS 19).

Operational: The SIMON LAKE was the last submarine tender to be based at Holy Loch, Scotland, where the U.S. Navy maintained an SSBN base from 1961 until 1992. Subsequently, she was home-ported at La Maddalena as a tender for U.S. submarines operating in the Mediterranean (relieved by the EMORY S. LAND).

SUBMARINE TENDERS: "HUNLEY" CLASS

Number	Name	Comm.	Notes
AS 31	HUNLEY	1962	decomm. 30 Sep 1994; str. 30 May 1995
AS 32	HOLLAND	1963	decomm./str. 30 Sep 1996

These were the first tenders designed specifically to service fleet ballistic missile submarines. The HOLLAND was placed out of commission, special, on 13 April 1996 and out of commission, full, on the above date. The HOLLAND (in strike status) was assigned to the NDRF on 26 May 2000.

See 16th Edition/page 252 for characteristics.

The Navy retains two submarine tenders, including the SIMON LAKE (above), and two destroyer tenders laid up in reserve. The LAKE was one of four tenders built and one converted specifically to support ballistic missile submarines. (1995, Leo Van Ginderen)

Table 23-11. SUBMARINE TENDERS

Number	Name	Comm.	Notes
FULTON class (7)			
AS 11	FULTON	1941	decomm. 17 May 1991; str. 20 Dec 1991
AS 12	SPERRY	1942	str. 1982
AS 13, 15	converted cargo ships		
FULTON class (continued)			
AS 15	BUSHNELL	1943	str. 1980
AS 16	HOWARD W. GILMORE	1944	str. 1980
AS 17	NEREUS	1960	str. 1971
AS 18	ORION	1943	decomm./str. 30 Sep 1993
AS 19	PROTEUS	1944	to IX 518 (see notes)
AS 20–26	converted cargo ships		
AS 27–30	redesignated AD 30–33		
AS 31, 32	HUNLEY class		
AS 33–35	SIMON LAKE class		
AS 36–38	L. Y. SPEAR class		
AS 39–41	EMORY S. LAND class		

Submarine tenders reached hull number AS 30 during World War II. The long-serving FULTON-class tenders were similar to the contemporary DIXIE-class destroyer tenders and VULCAN-class repair ships. The ships had been modernized but had a limited capability to support nuclear-propelled attack submarines.

The PROTEUS was rebuilt and lengthened in 1959–1960 to service Polaris missile submarines and served in that role at Holy Loch, Scotland; Rota, Spain; and Apra Harbor, Guam. She then served as a general repair ship at Diego Garcia. She was decommissioned and stricken on 30 September 1992, but was reinstated on the Naval Vessel Register on 1 February 1994 as the IX 518 (see Chapter 25).

SUBMARINE RESCUE SHIPS

All submarine rescue ships have been stricken. These ships carried out general salvage and diving duties, and were configured to carry the McCann submarine rescue chamber (see Chapter 12). The large PIGEON and ORTOLAN also could each carry two of the Deep Submergence Rescue Vehicles (DSRV; see Chapter 12) and were fitted with the fleet's most advanced deep diving system (Mk II).[9]

SUBMARINE RESCUE SHIPS: "PIGEON" CLASS

Number	Name	Comm.	Notes
ASR 21	PIGEON	1973	decomm./str. 31 Aug 1992
ASR 22	ORTOLAN	1973	decomm./str. 30 Mar 1995

These large catamarans were constructed specifically to carry DSRV submarine rescue vehicles and to support deep-ocean diving operations with the Mk II deep-dive system. Their completion was delayed by problems in design, construction, and fitting out.

The PIGEON class was developed after the loss of the submarine THRESHER (SSN 593) in 1963 to provide an ASR/DSRV force for submarine rescue down to the collapse depth of contemporary submarines. Up to ten ASRs were planned, but delays and funding constraints reduced the program to two ships. (The DSRVs also are carried by SSNs.)

The PIGEON has been transferred to the NDRF and in 2001 was towed to the Naval Station San Diego, California, for use as a stationary training platform by the Chief of Naval Education and Training.

SUBMARINE RESCUE SHIPS: "CHANTICLEER" CLASS

Number	Name	Comm.	Notes
ASR 9	FLORIKAN	1943	decomm. 2 Aug 1991; str. 3 Sep 1991
ASR 13	KITTIWAKE	1946	decomm./str. 30 Sep 1994
ASR 14	PETREL	1946	decomm. 30 Aug 1991; str. 9 Oct 1991
ASR 15	SUNBIRD	1950	decomm./str. 30 Sep 1993

These were the last of a series of large, tug-type ships fitted for salvage and helium–oxygen diving operations. They had a limited submarine rescue capability employing the McCann chamber. The first ASRs were converted Bird-class minesweepers built in World War I, hence the fowl names for these ships.

The SUNBIRD was accepted by the Navy on 15 January 1947 and towed (inactivated) to the Charleston Naval Shipyard; she was not commissioned for three and a half years.

The FLORIKAN (in strike status) was assigned to the NDRF on 6 October 2000.

Class: There originally were seven ships in this class: the ASR 7–11, 13, and 14 (plus the canceled ASR 15–18). The ASR 12, 19, and 20 were converted fleet tugs (ATF 99, 164, and 165, respectively). The ASR 1–6 were converted World War I–built minesweepers.

OCEANGOING TUGS

The Navy uses primarily harbor tugs to handle port tug duties (see Chapter 25). The ATS-series salvage and rescue ships (formerly salvage tugs) are listed as salvage ships in this edition of *Ships and Aircraft*; see page 276.

Names: Tugs have American Indian tribe names.

(6) OCEANGOING TUGS

The Navy's 30-year shipbuilding plan presented to Congress in 2003 includes the construction of six oceangoing tugs, designated T-ATF, to be authorized in FY 2009–2018. No characteristics for these ships have been developed.

---

9 The only other U.S. Navy ship fitted with the DDS II system was the ELK RIVER (IX 501, ex-LSMR 501).

7 FLEET TUGS: "POWHATAN" CLASS

Number	Name	FY	Launched	In service	Status
T-ATF 166	POWHATAN	75	24 June 1978	15 June 1979	Loan
T-ATF 167	NARRAGANSETT	75	28 Nov 1978	9 Jan 1979	(see text)
T-ATF 168	CATAWBA	75	22 Sep 1979	28 May 1980	**MSC-P**
T-ATF 169	NAVAJO	75	20 Dec 1979	13 June 1980	**MSC-P**
T-ATF 170	MOHAWK	78	5 Apr 1980	16 Oct 1980	**MSC-A**
T-ATF 171	SIOUX	78	30 Oct 1980	12 May 1981	**MSC-P**
T-ATF 172	APACHE	78	20 Dec 1980	30 July 1981	**MSC-A**

Builders:	Marinette Marine, Wisc.
Displacement:	2,000 tons standard
	2,260 tons full load
Length:	225¹¹⁄₂ feet (68.9 m) waterline
	240½ feet (73.2 m) overall
Beam:	42 feet (12.8 m)
Draft:	15 feet (4.6 m)
Propulsion:	diesel-electric (2 General Motors EMD 20 645X7 diesel
	engines); 4,500 shp; 2 shafts (Kort-nozzle propellers)
Speed:	15 knots
Range:	10,000 nm (18,520 km) at 13 knots
Personnel:	16 civilian, except 17 in T-ATF 168, + 4 Navy (enlisted)
	+ 20 transients
Helicopters:	VERTREP area
Radars:	SPS-53 surface search
	Raytheon TM 1660/12S navigation

These are oceangoing tugs based on a commercial design. They have replaced the war-built ATFs in the active fleet. The new ATF lacks the salvage and diving equipment of the ASR and ATS ships and has a limited towing capability. A portable Mk 1 Mod 1 diving/decompression module can be loaded on the stern of these ships.

The POWHATAN was leased to a commercial salvage firm, the Donjon Marine Co. at Hillside, New Jersey, on 26 February 1999 for a period of five years. The wheelhouse was reconfigured for civilian use, and other, minor, modifications have been made.

The NARRAGANSETT was taken out of service (OSIR) on 30 September 1999; she was leased on 15 October to a commercial firm in support of Navy activities. She was officially stricken from the NVR on 5 June 2002 and transferred to the Naval Air Systems Command for further service in support of that agency.

Design: SCB No. 744. These craft are easily distinguished by their side-by-side funnels and low, open sterns. The Navy personnel are communications specialists; the transients are salvage and diving specialists. There is a 10-ton-capacity crane.

In wartime, two 20-mm guns and two .50-cal machine guns can be fitted.

Engineering: The ships have a 300-hp bow thruster.

The NAVAJO at speed. Most Navy towing services are provided by commercial tugs, both at sea and in ports. Note the twin funnels and open working area aft, with vertical replenishment spot marked. (2001, Brian Morrison)

The APACHE at sea in the North Atlantic. At the time, she was serving as a target for maritime boarding teams from warships in the ENTERPRISE carrier strike group. (2003, U.S. Navy/Aaron Peterson)

FLEET TUGS: "CHEROKEE" CLASS

Number	Name	Comm.	Notes
ATF 105	MOCTOBI	1944	decomm. 1985; str. 7 Feb 1995
ATF 110	QUAPAW	1944	decomm. 1985; str. 26 Jan 1995
ATF 113	TAKELMA	1944	decomm. 20 Feb 1992; str. 30 June 1992
ATF 149	ATAKAPA	1944	decomm. 1981; str. 21 Feb 1992
ATF 158	MOSOPELEA	1945	decomm. 1981; str. 21 Feb 1992
ATF 159	PAIUTE	1945	decomm. 7 Aug 1992; str. 14 Feb 1995
ATF 160	PAPAGO	1945	decomm. 28 July 1992; str. 14 Feb 1995

These were the last of a class of 48 large oceangoing tugs, many of which saw extensive combat service in World War II.

All of the above ships were laid up in the NDRF after being decommissioned except for the SENECA, which was reacquired from stricken status in 1985 and used as an immobilized trials craft at the David Taylor Research Center at Annapolis, Maryland. She was sunk as a target on 21 July 2003.

The PAIUTE and PAPAGO were decommissioned in 1985; they were recommissioned into active naval service for anti-drug patrols in the Caribbean on 23 August 1985 and 28 June 1985, respectively. They were again decommissioned in 1992.

Ships of this class served in the U.S. Coast Guard, as well as in several foreign navies.

Class: The AT 64–76 and 81–118 were built to the same basic design, the principal differences being in their engineering plants. The class was officially known as the CHEROKEE (ATF 66) after the loss of the NAVAJO (AT 64) in 1943 and the SEMINOLE (AT 65) in 1942. Later ships are unofficially referred to as the ABNAKI (ATF 96) class.

Classification: These ships all were ordered with the AT designation. The AT 66 and later ships were changed to ATF on 15 May 1944.

AVIATION LOGISTIC SHIPS

These ships provide maintenance and logistic support for aircraft in forward areas. The AVB 3 and 4 are operated by the MSC with civilian crews.

The AVB 1 and 2 were tank landing ships converted to support land-based patrol aircraft from unimproved airfields and seaplanes in the Mediterranean area; they were Navy manned in the AVB role. The ALAMEDA COUNTY (LST 32) became the AVB 1 and, after she was stricken in 1962, the TALLAHATCHIE COUNTY (LST 1154) became the AVB 2.

Names: The current aviation logistic ships are named for aviation pioneers. (The two LST/AVB conversions retained their landing ship names.)

2 AVIATION LOGISTIC SUPPORT SHIPS: "SEABRIDGE" CLASS

Number	Name	Built	In service	Status
T-AVB 3	WRIGHT	1970	14 May 1986	MSC-ROS-A
T-AVB 4	CURTISS	1969	18 Aug 1987	MSC-ROS-P

Builders:	Ingalls Shipbuilding, Pascagoula, Miss.
Displacement:	12,409 tons light
	27,580 tons full load
Length:	559⅝ feet (170.7 m) waterline
	600¹¹⁄₂ feet (183.2 m) overall
Beam:	90 feet (27.4 m)
Draft:	34 feet (10.4 m)
Propulsion:	2 steam turbines (General Electric); 30,000 shp; 1 shaft
Boilers:	2 (Combustion Engineering)
Speed:	23.6 knots
Range:	9,000 nm (16,668 km) at 23.6 knots
Personnel:	37 civilian
Troops:	300+
Helicopters:	landing area (forward)
Radars:	2 navigation

The CURTISS (above) and the WRIGHT provide extensive maintenance and parts stowage for Marine Corps fixed-wing aircraft and helicopters. The amidships cargo areas are stacked with aviation support containers. (U.S. Navy)

The CURTISS *under way. The planned sea base ships will replace the aviation logistics ships. (see Chapter 24). (U.S. Navy)*

These ships were converted from Roll-On/Roll-Off (RO/RO)-container ships to provide support for Marine aviation in forward areas. They normally are at ports in the United States, partially loaded with a Marine intermediate maintenance unit; the WRIGHT normally is based Baltimore, Maryland, and the CURTISS at San Diego, California. During war or crisis periods, the remainder of the unit and personnel are loaded on board and the ships deployed to forward areas to support Marine tactical aircraft.

The majority of the maintenance unit's facilities used ashore are packaged in standard freight containers. Access ladders, scaffolding, and shipboard electrical power and other services permit the unit to function while embarked in the ship.

Most of the embarked troops are with the maintenance unit; the remainder are communications and other support personnel.

Conversion: The WRIGHT underwent conversion from December 1984 to May 1986 and the CURTISS from December 1985 to August 1987; both ships were converted at Todd Shipyards in Galveston, Texas.

Design: MarAd C5-S-78a type. The ships are combination RO/RO and self-sustaining container ships. The conversion included fitting a helicopter deck above the two forward holds; the deck can be removed to permit full access to the holds with the use of offboard cranes.

There are seven cargo holds, with the No. 7 hold, aft, having troop berthing and mess facilities installed above it. As a maintenance ship, the AVB can embark 300 standard containers plus 52 access modules; in the resupply role, the ship can carry 684 containers. There are 35,000 square feet (3,150 m2) of vehicle storage space provided.

The ships are fitted with ten 30-ton-capacity booms (which can be joined to form 60-ton lifts); a single 70-ton Stuelcken boom also is installed.

Names: Their original merchant names were YOUNG AMERICA and GREAT REPUBLIC, respectively; these were changed when they were acquired by the Navy for conversion to AVB.

Operational: Both ships were placed in service for the Gulf War buildup and conflict in 1990–1991 and again for the Gulf War of 2003. For the latter, they were reactivated for MSC service on 13 January 2003; the CURTISS returned to MSC-ROS status on 11 June 2003 and the WRIGHT on 17 June 2003.

UNCLASSIFIED MISCELLANEOUS SHIPS

Unclassified miscellaneous ships (IX) were listed as auxiliary ships until 23 September 1970, when they were reclassified as service craft. Current IX ships and craft are listed in Chapter 25.

CHAPTER 24

Sealift Ships

Marines unload heavy vehicles from the fast sealift ship BELLATRIX at Mina Ash-Shu'aibah, Kuwait, as part of the rotation of U.S. troops in Iraq. All U.S. sealift ships are operated by the Military Sealift Command (MSC) with civilian crews, except for the High Speed Vessel (HSV) SWIFT (HSV 2), which is Navy manned. (2004, U.S. Navy/Eric L. Beauregard)

Sealift ships provide point-to-point transportation for cargo of all of the U.S. military services and Department of Defense agencies. Also included in this category are the forward-deployed or prepositioned cargo ships that carry guns, vehicles, munitions, provisions, fuels, field hospitals, and other supplies for U.S. troops who are to be flown into forward areas to "marry up" with the materiel; merchant ships that are laid up in reserve, but ready for rapid reactivation, also are included.

The Quadrennial Defense Review of 2001 stated:

The Secretary of the Navy will develop new concepts of maritime pre-positioning, high-speed sealift. . . . The Secretary of the Navy will develop options to shift some of the Marine Corps' afloat prepositioned equipment from the Mediterranean toward the Indian Ocean and Arabian Gulf to be more responsive to contingencies in the Middle East.[1]

All sealift ships except one are operated by civilian crews under the control of the Military Sealift Command (MSC). Navy-owned ships have the prefix USNS (U.S. Naval Ship); most of the other ships are under long-term charter from their owners and have the

prefixes GTS for Gas-Turbine Ship, MV for Motor Vessel (diesel propulsion), or SS for Steamship (steam turbines). The appropriate prefixes are indicated in the class/ship headings on the following pages.

A breakdown of the specific ships in various categories of sealift is provided in Chapter 8. Ships in this chapter are arranged in the following order:

> Maritime Prepositioning
> Ocean Transportation (Sealift)
> Ready Reserve Ships

Within these categories, ships are listed on the basis of size (length), except that all crane ships are listed together under the Ready Reserve Force (RRF) ships in the order of the Navy T-ACS designations.

The following status comments are used in the individual ship entries; bold face indicates active ships:

---

1 Department of Defense, *Quadrennial Defense Review Report* (Washington, D.C.: 30 September 2001), p. 27. Maritime Prepositioning Ship (MPS) Squadron 1 is in the Mediterranean.

AA	Atlantic Active
APS	Afloat Prepositioning Ship[2]
FSS	Fast Sealift Ships
LPS	Logistics Positioning Ship
MPF	Maritime Prepositioning Force
MPS	Maritime Prepositioning Ship[3]
NDRF	National Defense Reserve Fleet[4]
PA	Pacific Active
RRF	Ready Reserve Force
Sealift	ocean transportation (active)

Ship assignments to APS and MPS squadrons are indicated in the following entries under *Status*; those ships are fully operational. Ships assigned to the RRF are laid up in reserve, most in four- to ten-day readiness for reactivation. They have cadre crews of about ten personnel who maintain the ships. The number of days allocated to activation is indicated under *Status*.

Ships indicated by **Sealift** are active, engaged in point-to-point ocean transportation. In addition to the ships so indicated, several FSS and RRF ships periodically are activated and employed in this role for special operations and exercises.

Classification: There are two types of hull numbers used in this chapter: the four-digit Navy Ships and Aircraft Supplementary Data Tables (SASDT) numbers that are assigned for accounting purposes and are not actual hull numbers in the normal context, and the one- to three-digit traditional Navy hull numbers, assigned when the ship is ordered, that are part of the ship designation scheme that began in 1920.

The HSV designation is not an official Navy classification, although it is painted on the craft and appears in official Navy documentation.

The Maritime Administration (MarAd) code scheme for U.S.-built merchant ship designs is explained in Chapter 3. A few ships constructed in the United States to private designs do not have MarAd designations.

Design: Shipboard container capacity is measured in TEUs (Twenty-foot Equivalent Units), the standard container size, which are 8 x 8 x 20 feet (2.4 x 2.4 x 6.1 m).

Electronics: All ships listed here have one or (usually) two navigation radars of commercial types.

Guns/Missiles: Sealift ships normally are not armed. However, since the war on terrorism began, those ships being sent into forward areas have carried armed security detachments. The Navy-manned SWIFT (HSV 2) is armed with machine guns.

Helicopters: The prepositioning ships, Large Medium-Speed Roll-on/roll-off (LMSR) ships, and eight converted SL-7 fast sealift ships have helicopter landing decks, as does the SWIFT, which can hangar two H-60 series helicopters. Some other sealift ships have open areas that could be used in an emergency.

Operational: Maritime prepositioned materiel was used by all the U.S. military services in the Persian Gulf conflict of 1990–1991. The first U.S. ground combat units brought into Saudi Arabia with tanks, heavy artillery, etc., were two Marine Expeditionary Brigades (MEB) that married up with two MPS squadrons. The third MPS squadron followed. In addition, several Afloat Prepositioning Force (APF) ships were at Diego Garcia, loaded with field hospitals, Air Force and Army equipment, and potable water.

Both MPF and sealift ships also were used extensively in support of the second Gulf War (2003). The 45 RRF ships that were reactivated in 2002–2003 (and subsequently returned to laid up status) are indicated by an asterisk. The first to be reactivated was the BOB HOPE, on 16 October 2002.

Following the terrorist attacks on the destroyer COLE (DDG 67) and the United States, the Department of Defense became con-

A Guardian Mariner from the Puerto Rican Army National Guard test fires a .50-caliber machine gun M2 aboard the roll-on/roll-off ship PILILAAU. At the time, the ship was off the coast of Indonesia. (U.S. Navy)

cerned for the security of prepositioned sealift ships. However, it was not until March 2003 that security detachments were placed aboard MSC ships, which are otherwise unarmed, except for a few small arms normally kept under lock and key.

More than 1,600 troops of the Puerto Rican Army National Guard's 92nd Separate Infantry Brigade were called to active duty for the role of "Guardian Mariners." Following special training by Army and Marine Corps personnel at Fort A. P. Hill in Virginia, 165 teams of 12 men each were established and, in two phases, placed aboard sealift ships for force protection. They were used until June 2004, when they were relieved by Navy security teams.

Personnel: All sealift ships are manned by civilian mariners except for the SWIFT, which has two active-duty Navy crews. Several prepositioning ships are fitted as squadron flagships, able to carry a squadron commodore and small Navy planning/ communications staff. Some prepositioning ships have small numbers of civilian maintenance personnel to check equipment and handle embarked landing craft/pontoon barges.

Prepositioning ships also have facilities for embarking small numbers of troops (primarily maintenance and unloading personnel).

Status: In 1994 and again in 2004, a large number of RRF ships were transferred to the NDRF, under the aegis of MarAd, because of funding shortages. Their readiness is far lower than when in MSC/RRF status. Subsequently, older RRF ships were transferred to the NDRF or discarded as new ships became available. Table 24-1 lists sealift ships that have been discarded since 1 January 1990.

The NDRF ships would take considerably longer to reactivate than RRF ships. On a periodic basis, they are "broken out" of the RRF and "exercised" by employing them in cargo carrying for the Department of Defense.

---

2 Afloat Prepositioning Squadron is indicated, e.g., as APS-4.
3 Maritime Prepositioning Squadrons are indicated, e.g., as MPS-1.
4 Administered by the Maritime Administration, Department of Transportation.

HIGH SPEED VESSELS

The U.S. Navy, Marine Corps, and Army are evaluating several High Speed Vessels (HSV) to determine their effectiveness in several sealift and support roles. In particular, under the new Sea Basing concept, these craft can provide high-speed intratheater lift, especially from advance bases to sea bases (see below). While they also could be used as "high speed connectors" to the beach, they are not intended for assault operations and cannot be beached. The nominal range requirement for these craft is 2,000 nm (3,700 km) at high speed.

Four such craft have been evaluated by the U.S. military services. Two, listed below, currently are in naval service, under lease from their building firms. A third HSV, after being evaluated by the Navy and Marine Corps, has been transferred to the Army. That craft, the JOINT VENTURE (HSV X1), and the SPEARHEAD (TSV 1), which originally was leased for Army service, are listed in Chapter 34.

All four HSVs were constructed in Australia, three as commercial vessels that were leased by the U.S. government and one—the SWIFT—built specifically for the U.S. Navy. Congress subsequently has stipulated that all future HSV-type ships acquired by the U.S. military services be constructed in the United States; however, such an effort will require significant foreign expertise.

Both the Navy and Army plan the construction of such craft in large numbers.

HIGH SPEED VESSELS: IMPROVED INCAT TYPE

The Navy plans to construct additional INCAT-type HSVs beginning with Fiscal Year (FY) 2007 funds. These craft will be approximately 328 feet (100 m) in length.

The Navy is considering bow ramps for these ships.

1 HIGH SPEED VESSEL: IMPROVED INCAT TYPE (HSV)

Number	Name	Launched	In service	Status
HSV 2	SWIFT	29 July 2003	15 Aug 2003	AA

Builders:	Incat, Hobart, Tasmania (Australia)
Displacement:	
Tonnage:	approx. 700 Deadweight Tons (DWT)
Length:	301¾ feet (92.0 m) waterline
	318½ feet (97.22 m) overall
Beam:	87¼ feet (26.6 m)
Draft:	11¼ feet (3.43 m)
Propulsion:	4 diesel engines (Caterpillar 3618); 40,000 shp; 4 waterjets
Speed:	38 knots sustained loaded
	47 knots low sea state with light load
Range:	1,100 nm (1,270 km) at 35 knots
	4,000 nm (4,600 km) at 20 knots
Personnel:	39–42 (see *Personnel* notes)
Troops:	970 (see *Design* notes)
Helicopters:	landing area (see *Aircraft* notes)
Armament:	1 25-mm/87-cal Bushmaster cannon Mk 38
	8 .50-cal machine guns (4 twin)
	1 .50-cal machine Ex-45
	1 40-mm grenade launcher Mk 19
Radars:	navigation

The SWIFT was built specifically for the U.S. Navy, her design reflecting initial lessons learned in the construction of the HSV 1X and TSV 1X. The craft is operated jointly by the Atlantic Fleet and the Naval Mine Warfare Command on lease from INCAT. Thus, she has two home ports, Norfolk, Virginia, and Ingleside, Texas, and is manned by two, alternating crews.

Employed primarily to evaluate HSV technologies and operational capabilities, she has served as a high-speed transport and as a mine warfare command and support ship.

The SWIFT was built in record time—ten months from contract award to ship delivery. She departed on her maiden voyage 11 days after delivery.

She is the only sealift-type ship that is armed and manned by Navy personnel.

Aircraft: The SWIFT has a landing area that can accommodate H-60 and H-46 series helicopters; there is a twin helicopter hangar adjacent to the flight deck.

Design: She is a 98-meter, wave-piercing catamaran design of aluminum construction. The ship has no berthing for passengers but can transport 970 troops in airline style reclining seats on the upper deck. A combat information center is provided.

There are 28,730 square feet (2,670 m²) of vehicle cargo space. A stern ramp is fitted, and there is a 13-ton-capacity (11,795-kg) crane. Vehicles up to 70 tons (i.e., an M1 Abrams tank) can be accommodated.

Engineering: The propulsion plant is fully automated and requires no personnel in the engineering spaces when under way. The waterjets are used for ahead and reverse speeds and for steering. The SWIFT achieved 47 knots on trials.

Personnel: Personnel assigned varies with the role. There is berthing space for more than 107 personnel in addition to the troop seating.

The SWIFT glides through the Atlantic Ocean at high speed. Note the streamlined shape of the forward portion of her wave-piercing hulls. An H-60 series helicopter rests on her flight deck. She can hangar two of these aircraft. (2004, U.S. Navy/Michael Sandberg)

The SWIFT at Pearl Harbor—note the lattice mast of the battleship MISSOURI (BB 63) behind her—shows the wave-piecing catamaran design of these high-speed ships. Large numbers of similar HSVs are in commercial service. (2004, U.S. Navy/William R. Goodwin)

The SWIFT presents a strange beauty while under way in the Atlantic Ocean. Her helicopter deck is foreshortened from this angle. The SWIFT was built for U.S. naval service, unlike the other HSVs in U.S. service. (2004, U.S. Navy/Michael Sandberg)

The stern aspect of the SWIFT shows her open stern, with a crane on the port quarter and a folding ramp on the starboard quarter. She can carry additional troops, vehicles, or rigid hull inflatable boats in her large garage. (2004, U.S. Navy/ William R. Goodwin)

1 HIGH SPEED VESSEL: AUSTAL TYPE (HSV)

Number	Name	Launched	In service	Status
HSV 4676	WESTPAC EXPRESS	9 April 2001	11 July 2001	**PA**

Builder:	Austal, Freemantle (Australia)
Displacement:	
Tonnage:	750 DWT
Length:	290'1½ feet (88.7 m) waterline
	331 feet (100.91 m) overall
Beam:	87 feet (26.52 m)
Draft:	14 feet (4.27 m)
Propulsion:	4 diesel engines (Caterpillar 3618); 40,236 bhp; 4 waterjets
Speed:	36 knots (see *Engineering* notes)
Range:	1,320nm (2,445 km) at 32 knots
Personnel:	24 (civilian)
Troops:	970 (see *Design* notes)

A bow-on view of the wave-piercing catamaran WESTPAC EXPRESS. Her configuration is significantly different from the INCAT-design HSVs. This photo shows the WESTPAC EXPRESS entering the Korean Port of Pyongtaek carrying 610 Marines and 480 tons of cargo. (U.S. Marine Corps/Chris Korhonen)

The WESTPAC EXPRESS is assigned to support the III Marine Expeditionary Force in the Western Pacific. She was chartered by the MSC for Marine Corps use in July 2001.

She is based on Okinawa.

Design: She is listed as a 101-meter wave-piercing catamaran design of aluminum construction.

The ship has no berthing for passengers but can transport 970 troops in airline-style reclining seats on the upper deck. She has 32,000 square feet (9,756 m²) of stowage space for vehicles, loaded and unloaded over a stern ramp. She can carry 420 tons of cargo in addition to troops, or 531 tons without troops.

Engineering: Fully loaded, her maximum speed is 33 knots. The waterjets are used for ahead and reverse speeds and for steering.

Operational: During an exercise, the WESTPAC EXPRESS carried a 400-ton load, including 370 Marines and their gear, five AH-1W SeaCobra helicopters, two UH-1N Huey helicopters, and aviation ground support equipment from Japan to Guam in less than 40 hours. (The helicopters were carried as cargo and could not operate from the ship.)

HIGH SPEED VESSELS: INCAT TYPE

Two INCAT-built HSVs have been operated under lease by the U.S. Army. The JOINT VENTURE (IX 532, ex-HSV 1) was operated by the Navy prior to being transferred to the Army. The SPEARHEAD (TSV 1X) was leased from the outset by the Army. (See Chapter 33 for characteristics and details.)

Vehicles of the 1st Battalion, 2nd Marine Regiment are driven aboard the WESTPAC EXPRESS at Camp Butler, Okinawa. The HSVs have large vehicle decks and load/unload via stern ramps. Troops are transported in airline-type seats and have cafeteria-style mess facilities (U.S. Marine Corps/Stephen L. Standiford)

The WESTPAC EXPRESS is operated by the Military Sealift Command (MSC) in support of the III Marine Expeditionary Force, based on Okinawa and in Japan. The HSVs provide high-speed transport for personnel and vehicles, but not over great distances. (U.S. Navy)

MARITIME PREPOSITIONING FORCE

When this edition of *Ships and Aircraft* went to press, there were 33 ships in the prepositioning force: 16 Maritime Prepositioning Force ships loaded with equipment and supplies for the three Marine Corps brigades; 10 Combat Prepositioning Force (CPF) ships assigned to APS-4 to carry equipment and supplies for a U.S. Army heavy brigade and combat support/combat service support elements; and 7 Logistics Prepositioning Ships—four loaded primarily with Air Force munitions, one with Navy munitions, and two large tankers. (See Chapter 8 for details of the MPF squadrons.)

In the wake of the invasion of Iraq (2003), the ship assignments of MPS Squadrons 2 (at Diego Garcia) and 3 (at Guam) are being reconsidered. The latest squadron assignment information available is presented below.

In addition to the prepositioning ships listed below, the MSC lists three others ships as Logistics Prepositioning Force (LPF) components: the aviation logistics ships WRIGHT (T-AVB 3) and CURTISS (T-AVB 4) and the HSV WESTPAC EXPRESS. Because they are not prepositioned ships, as are the others in this category, the T-AVBs, which are part of the RRF (laid up in U.S. home ports), are listed with auxiliary ships in Chapter 23.

The ships listed in the MPF section of this chapter are in the following order:

T-AKR	Large Medium-Speed RO/RO ships
T-AK/AKR	Roll-On/Roll-Off (RO/RO) ships
T-AK	container ships

In addition to the ships listed in this section, the following RRF ships currently are active and employed in the maritime prepositioning role:

Number	Name	Type
T-ACS 3	GRAND CANYON STATE	crane ship C6-S-MA1qd
T-ACS 5	FLICKERTAIL STATE	crane ship C5-S-MA73c

T-ACS 9	GREEN MOUNTAIN STATE	crane ship C6-S-MA60d
T-AK 5029	CAPE JACOB	C4-S-1
T-AK 5051	CAPE GIBSON	C5-S-75a
T-AOT 5084	CHESAPEAKE	tanker
T-AOT 9101	PETERSBURG	tanker

Names: The specialized MPF ships are named for Marine Corps recipients of the Medal of Honor. Eighteen of the 20 LMSR ships are named for Medal of Honor recipients of the Army and Marine Corps; the BOB HOPE honors a great American comedian who long entertained U.S. troops throughout the world, and the MAJ BERNARD F. FISHER an Air Force hero who received the Medal of Honor for his actions in Vietnam in 1966.

MARITIME PREPOSITIONING FORCE (FUTURE)

A new series of MPF ships has been proposed by the Navy and Marine Corps that would be more flexible than the current MPF ships. According to the Chief of Naval Operations:

> MPF(F)'s transformational characteristics include significant improvements in force closure, sustainment, selective offload, command and control, and reconstitution. MPF(F) will be interoperable with current amphibious task force shipping via surface transport (LCAC and/or LCU), underwater replenishment stations, and compatible C4I systems.[5] MPF(F) has significant joint warfighting potential and will be interoperable with joint forces support capabilities. MPF(F) will transform naval logistics into a seamless and integrated system that will complement current Combat Logistics Forces by providing sea-based logistics to all naval forces. This ability could include cargo transshipment and intermodal shipping to other naval ships or ashore. While independent forcible entry is not a mission envisioned, MPF(F) will be able to support directly a committed expeditionary strike group and apply forces directly where required.[6]

---

5 C4I = Command, Control, Communications, Computers, and Intelligence.

6 Adm. Vern Clark, USN, Chief of Naval Operations, . . . *Vision . . . Presence . . . Power . . .* (Washington, D.C.: Department of the Navy, 2004), p. 106.

The maritime prepositioning ship 1ST LT JACK LUMMUS uses cranes in tandem to offload slide-loading warping tugs at Sattahip, Thailand, during Cobra Gold 2002, an exercise in conjunction with forces from Singapore and Thailand. (U.S. Navy/Jennifer A. Smith)

The proposed MPF(F) ships would have:
• selective off-load to enable Marines to select equipment tailored for specific operations with space on board for reconfiguring loads and marrying troops with equipment
• space for Marine planning and command staffs
• the ability to form a Maritime Prepositioning Group (MPG) to support a Carrier Strike Group (CSG) or Expeditionary Strike Group (ESG) with limited logistics support
• the capability to provide joint sustainment in direct support of joint forces
• the capability to reconstitute (i.e., reembark troops and equipment) in a forward area and redeploy to another area
• medical facilities eventually to replace the Navy's two specialized hospital ships (T-AH)

Under current Navy planning, a force of 12–18 MPF(F) ships is envisioned, with the lead ship authorized in FY 2009. These will be large ships, estimated at between 70,000 and 90,000 tons full-load displacement.

The high cost of such ships may limit MPF(F) procurement to sufficient ships to establish only two groups in place of the currently established three MPS squadrons. (The term *group* is used for these ships in place of squadron to indicate their ability to operate in conjunction with a CSG or ESG.) Each MPS group will be able to provide support for 20-plus days of combat for a Marine expeditionary brigade (three maneuver battalions), plus one or two Marine expeditionary units.

Another issue is whether the ships should all be similar in configuration (which would require larger ships) or have specialized configurations (e.g., only some with flight decks and support facil-

ities for MV-22 and successor heavy-lift aircraft). If the latter, the force could be more vulnerable to a single ship loss, but overall ship size and cost would be less. A compromise might be to have two ships of each type in a prepositioning group.

With "connectors"—high-speed surface craft and aircraft—to advance bases and the shore, the prepositioning group would form a sea base.

Another candidate for the sea base is the Afloat Forward Staging Base (AFSB) modified from a Maersk S-class container ship, described below. The ship is an MPF(F) candidate as well as a possible stand-alone ship to support U.S. Special Operations Forces (SOF).

AFLOAT FORWARD STAGING BASE (AFSB): S-CLASS CONVERSION

Builders:	Odense Staalskibsvaerf, Lindo (Denmark)
Displacement:	
Tonnage:	104,696 DWT (maximum container configuration)
Length:	1,138⅛ feet (347.0 m) overall
Beam:	140⅝ feet (42.8 m)
Draft:	47½ feet (14.5 m)
Propulsion:	diesel; 75,000 bhp; 1 shaft
Speed:	24.6 knots sustained
Range:	15,000 nm (27,800 km) at 24.6 knots
Personnel:	approx. 40 (see *Personnel* notes)
Aircraft:	see *Design* notes

Following the operation of the carrier KITTY HAWK (CV 63) as an SOF helicopter ship during the U.S. invasion of Afghanistan in late 2001, the Department of Defense examined the feasibility of a specialized SOF support ship, including full-size aircraft carriers, amphibious assault ships (LHA/LHD type), and converted merchant

A variety of preliminary ship designs are being considered for the MPF(F) program. Sufficient data on MPF(F) concepts of operations are not available to finalize the designs; also, political considerations—i.e., which yards will build the ships—will be a major factor in the selection. (U.S. Navy)

ships. After assessment of the various platforms, in February 2002 Maersk Line Ltd. received the sole commercial award for the AFSB design. The firm subsequently designed an AFSB conversion of its S-class container ship. Conversion would take 12 to 18 months.[7]

The Maersk S-class ships are the world's largest container ships. First completed in 1997, they are known as post-PANAMAX (Panama Maximum) ships because they are too large to transit the Panama Canal. The S-class ships are in worldwide service; 21 are operational and additional units are under construction. In commercial service they have a maximum capacity of 8,000 containers in an overload condition.

Design: In the AFSB configuration, the ships would have a flight deck forward and aft of the amidships island structure. They would have a full hangar deck, with two internal elevators carrying aircraft between the two decks.

The DoD requirement is for a flight deck capable of accommodating up to 15 large helicopters (H-53 series) or 12 MV-22 Osprey aircraft in a ready-to-fly condition. The hangar deck also must be able to support the AV-8B Harrier and F-35 Joint Strike Fighter (JSF). Various hangar deck configurations have been proposed: 28 Army helicopters (MH-60, MH-47, UH-1); or 72 Marine helicopters (CH-46); or 144 Hummvee vehicles.

The AFSB must have modular berthing, messing, laundry, and toilet facilities for up to 6,000 troops and support personnel.

An ammunition magazine also will be provided.

The original designs provided for side ramps to provide a RO/RO capability for unloading vehicles onto air cushion landing craft (LCAC) or conventional landing craft. However, in August 2004, the Naval Research Advisory Committee (NRAC) recommend instead fitting the ship with traverse side hull openings for LCACs to enter the ship and be loaded/unloaded in a stable environment during high sea states. The viability of the ramps in high sea states was questionable, at best.[8]

Personnel: In commercial service the S-class ships are manned by 14 operators, plus a small number of maintenance personnel; there also is berthing for merchant marine cadets. In naval service the ship would have an operating crew of about 40.

In addition, under Army requirements, there would be 43 support personnel (cooks, cleaning and laundry workers) for every 1,000 troops and air crew embarked.

---

7 See Stephen M. Carmel, "A Commercial Approach to Sea Basing—Afloat Forward Staging Bases," U.S. Naval Institute *Proceedings* (January 2004), pp. 78–80, and "Adaptability in Sea-Base Platform Design," *RUSI Defence Systems* (Summer 2004), pp. 54–55.

8 Drawings of an S-class AFSB ship showing the ramps appear in both of the articles by Mr. Carmel.

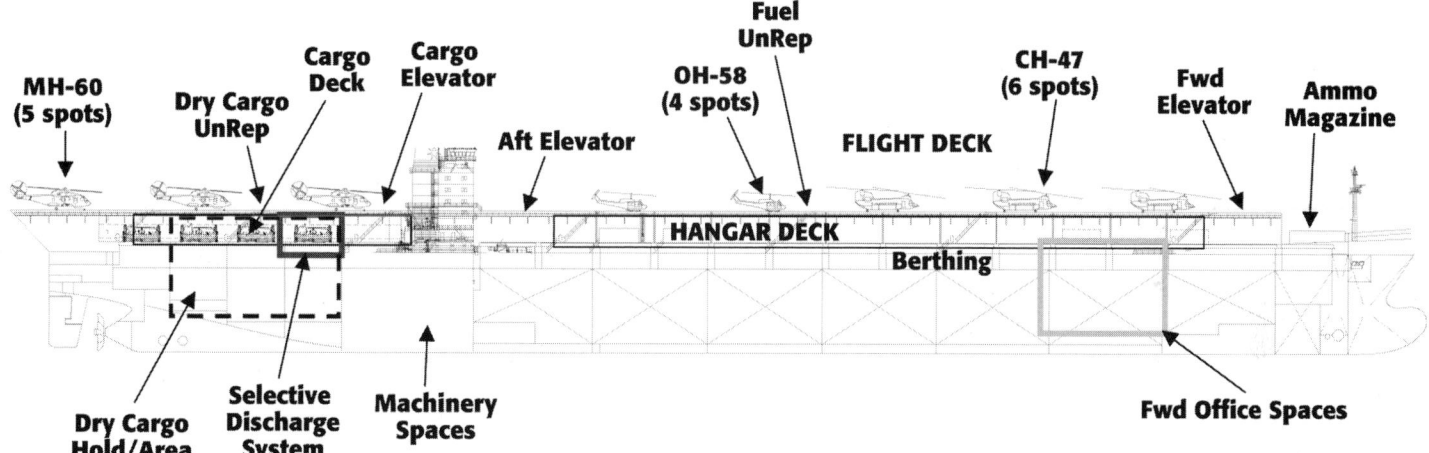

A drawing of a Maersk S-class container ship configured for Army helicopters. The "selective discharge" (ramp) system shown here would be replaced by a drive-through opening for LCAC operations, farther forward, as recommended by the Naval Research Advisory Committee. (Maersk)

An artist's concept of a Maersk S-class container ship configured for the Afloat Forward Staging Base role with Marine MV-22 Osprey aircraft on the flight deck. There is an aircraft elevator to starboard, forward of the bridge, and one at the forward end of the flight deck, to port. This illustration also shows the "drive-through" opening for LCAC operations. (Maersk–U.S. Navy)

8 LARGE MEDIUM-SPEED RO/RO SHIPS: "WATSON" CLASS (USNS)

Number	Name	FY	Launched	In service	Status
T-AKR 310*	WATSON	93	26 July 1997	23 June 1998	**CPF/APS-4**
T-AKR 311	SISLER	95	28 Feb 1998	1 Dec 1998	**CPF/APS-4**
T-AKR 312	DAHL	95	2 Oct 1998	13 July 1999	**CPF/APS-4**
T-AKR 313*	RED CLOUD	96	7 Aug 1999	18 Jan 2000	**CPF/APS-4**
T-AKR 314	CHARLTON	97	11 Dec 1999	23 May 2000	**CPF/APS-4**
T-AKR 315	WATKINS	97	28 July 2000	2 Mar 2001	**CPF/APS-4**
T-AKR 316	POMEROY	98	10 Mar 2001	14 Aug 2001	**CPF/APS-4**
T-AKR 317	SODERMAN	00	26 Apr 2002	24 Sep 2002	**CPF/APS-4**

Builders:	National Steel and Shipbuilding, San Diego
Displacement:	62,968 tons full load
Tonnage:	
Length:	889¾ feet (271.28 m) waterline
	951⁵⁄₁₂ feet (290.0 m) overall
Beam:	105¾ feet (32.24 m)
Draft:	34 feet (10.37 m)
Propulsion:	2 gas turbines (General Electric LM2500-30); 64,000 shp; 2 shafts
Speed:	24 knots
Range:	12,700+ nm (23,530+ km) at 24 knots
Personnel:	30 civilian (+ 5 maintenance personnel in the SISLER only)
Troops:	50
Helicopters:	landing area

These ships are similar to the BOB HOPE design but with gas turbine propulsion. They were designed and constructed based on lessons of the Gulf War of 1991.

The ships are assigned to the Army's APS-4, which normally is forward deployed to the Arabian Gulf and/or Diego Garcia. The squadron's nominal home port is Norfolk, Virginia, although the ships have no ties whatsoever to that port.

Design: These ships have approximately 394,000 square feet (36,642 m²) of vehicle cargo space. Two paired Hägglunds 55-ton-capacity cranes are fitted; each pair can operate together to lift more than 100 tons. More than 1,000 military vehicles can be carried, including about 60 M1 Abrams tanks.

Engineering: The original planned speed for these ships was 36 knots; however, that would have been prohibitively expensive.

These ships and the LCPL ROY M. WHEAT are the only prepositioning ships with gas turbine propulsion; most have diesel engines and a few have steam turbines. These are the world's largest gas turbine ships.

Names: The RED CLOUD remembers Army Corporal Mitchell Red Cloud Jr., who posthumously received the nation's highest military award for action in the Korean War.

The WATSON represents the "ultimate" conventional prepositioning ship. Future MPS/MPF ships will be configured to serve as a component of a sea base, as well as carrying Army and Marine Corps vehicles, stores, and equipment. (U.S. Navy)

The POMEROY at San Diego with her portside vehicle port open. These ships can load/unload vehicles through their side ports or over the stern ramp, or by crane into landing craft alongside or onto piers. (2001, W. Michael Young)

1 LARGE MEDIUM-SPEED RO/RO SHIP: DANISH BUILT (USNS)

Number	Name	Launched	In service	Status
T-AK 3017 (ex-T-AKR 299)	GYSGT FRED W. STOCKHAM (ex-PFC WILLIAM A. SODERMAN, LICA MAERSK)	1981	11 Nov 1997	**MPS-2**

Builders:	Odense Staalskibsvaerf, Lindo (Denmark)
Displacement:	54,298 tons full load
Tonnage:	43,325 Gross Registered Tons (GRT) (as built)
	53,000 DWT
Length:	850½ feet (259.32 m) waterline
	884¹¹⁄₁₂ feet (269.79 m) hull
	906¾ feet (276.45 m) overall
Beam:	105½ feet (32.2 m)
Draft:	34⅝ feet (10.62 m)
Propulsion:	1 diesel engine (Burmeister & Wain 12L90 GFCA);
	46,653 bhp; 1 shaft
Speed:	24 knots
Range:	12,000 nm (22,235 km) at 24 knots

Personnel:	30 civilian + 5 maintenance personnel
Troops:	50
Helicopters:	landing area

This is a conversion to the LMSR configuration. She was funded under the FY 1993 conversion program and converted at the National Steel yard in San Diego, beginning in April 1995.

Class: Two sister ships serve in the sealift role, the SHUGHART and YANO (see below).

Classification: The ship originally was designated AKR 299 in naval service.

Conversion: The ship was modified and lengthened at the Hyundai shipyard, Ulsan, in 1987. Cargo capacity is 312,461 square feet (29,059 m²). Bow and stern thrusters are fitted.

Names: The ship was renamed as GYSGT FRED W. STOCKHAM on 16 January 2001.

The GYSGT FRED W. STOCKHAM *leaving port. The ship's massive stern ramp is evident; she has two side ports on either side. (2001, Leo Van Ginderen)*

3 CONTAINER—RO/RO SHIPS: CONVERTED C7-S-133a (SS)

Number	Name	Launched	Start Conv.	In service	Status
T-AK 3005	SGT MATEJ KOCAK (ex-JOHN B. WATERMAN)	1981	Mar 1983	5 Oct 1984	**MPS-1**
T-AK 3006	PFC EUGENE A. OBREGON (ex-THOMAS HEYWOOD)	1982	Nov 1982	15 Jan 1985	**MPS-1**
T-AK 3007	MAJ STEPHEN W. PLESS (ex-CHARLES CARROLL)	1983	Mar 1983	1 May 1985	**MPS-1**

Builders:	Sun Shipbuilding and Dry Dock, Chester, Pa.,
	except T-AK 3007 by General Dynamics, Quincy, Mass.
Displacement:	15,000 tons light
	48,754 tons full load
Tonnage:	25,426 GRT
	22,910 DWT
Length:	770⅓ feet (234.85 m) waterline
	821 feet (250.24 m) overall
Beam:	105½ feet (32.2 m)
Draft:	32⅛ feet (9.8 m)
Propulsion:	2 steam turbines (General Electric); 30,000 shp; 1 shaft
Boilers:	2 (Combustion Engineering)
Speed:	20 knots
Range:	13,000 nm (24,076 km) at 20 knots
Personnel:	26 or 27 civilian + 3 maintenance personnel,
	except no maintenance personnel in T-AK 3007
Troops:	100
Helicopters:	landing area

These ships previously were commercial container ships operated by Waterman Corp. They were acquired under a 25-year charter specifically for conversion to the MPS role. They were designated T-AKX during the planning stage.

Conversion: As built, these ships were 695 feet (211.9 m) overall with a full load displacement of 38,975 tons. A 126-foot (38.4 m) midbody section was inserted, and the ships were reconfigured for 152,524 square feet (13,727 m2) of vehicle cargo space, 540 standard cargo containers, and 1,544,000 gallons (5.8 million liters) of bulk fuels and 94,780 gallons (360,164 liters) of potable water. The ships have paired 50-ton-capacity and paired 35-ton-capacity cranes, plus a 30-ton-capacity traveling gantry forward to handle containers.

All three were converted to the MPS role by the National Steel yard in San Diego, California.

Engineering: Sustained speed is 18 knots.

The PFC Eugene A. Obregon with an empty main deck. Two helicopter spots are marked on the raised helicopter deck, aft of the bridge. MPS ships cannot easily move cargo from their holds to the helicopter flight deck. (1989, Giorgio Arra)

The Sgt Matej Kocak anchored off Norfolk. These ships have two pairs of heavy cranes forward, as well as a traveling crane forward for handling containers. (1998, Giorgio Arra)

5 CONTAINER—RO/RO SHIPS: DANISH BUILT (MV)

Number	Name	Launched	Start Conv.	In service	Status
T-AK 3000	Cpl Louis J. Hauge Jr. (ex-Estelle Maersk)	3 Aug 1979	Jan 1984	7 Sep 1984	**MPS-2**
T-AK 3001	PFC William B. Baugh Jr. (ex-Eleo Maersk)	1979	Jan 1983	30 Oct 1984	**MPS-2**
T-AK 3002	PFC James Anderson Jr. (ex-Emma Maersk)	23 Mar 1979	Oct 1983	26 Mar 1985	**MPS-2**
T-AK 3003	1st Lt Alex Bonnyman Jr. (ex-Emilie Maersk)	3 Aug 1979	Jan 1984	26 Sep 1985	**MPS-2**
T-AK 3004	Pvt Franklin J. Phillips (ex-Pvt Harry Fisher, Evelyn Maersk)	12 Oct 1979	Apr 1984	12 Sep 1985	**MPS-2**

Builders:	Odense Staalskibsvaerf, Lindo (Denmark)	Propulsion:	1 diesel (Sulzer 7RND 76M); 16,800 bhp; 1 shaft
Displacement:	28,249 tons light	Speed:	17.5 knots
	46,484 tons full load	Range:	10,800 nm (20,000 km) at 17.5 knots
Tonnage:		Personnel:	25–27 civilian + 3 maintenance personnel,
Length:	705 feet (215.0 m) waterline		except 14 maintenance in T-AK 3004
	755½ feet (230.25 m) overall	Flag:	25 Navy in T-AK 3004
Beam:	90½ feet (27.5 m)	Troops:	77
Draft:	32½ feet (9.8 m)	Helicopters:	landing area

These are former Maersk Line combination container and RO/RO vehicle cargo ships acquired by the U.S. government specifically for conversion to the MPS role.

The Pvt Franklin J. Phillips is the flagship of MPS-3.

Conversion: During conversion, a 157½-foot (48-m) midsection was added to each ship (original length 598½ feet/ 182.3 m with a deadweight tonnage of 29,182 tons). In the MPS role, they have 120,080 square feet (10,807 m2) of vehicle storage space and can carry up to 332 standard containers, 1,283,000 gallons (4.8 million liters) of bulk fuels, and 65,000 gallons (247,000 liters) of potable water. Cranes are fitted.

The T-AK 3000, 3002, and 3004 were converted by the Bethlehem Steel yard at Sparrows Point, Maryland; the PFC William B. Baugh Jr. and 1st Lt Alex Bonnyman Jr. by the Bethlehem Steel yard in Beaumont, Texas.

Names: The 1st Lt Alexander Bonnyman Jr. was changed to 1st Lt Alex Bonnyman Jr. on 4 March 1986. The Pvt Harry Fisher was changed to Pvt Franklin J. Phillips, the former being the pseudonym Phillips used when he was awarded the Medal of Honor.

Note that the T-AKR 301 is named Fisher.

The C**PL** L**OUIS** J. H**AUGE** J**R.** *showing how the heavy lift cranes are paired in these ships for lifting heavy vehicles and landing craft. Military containers are stowed on the forward deck. (1991, Leo Van Ginderen)*

The PFC W**ILLIAM** B. B**AUGH** J**R.** *at Portsmouth, Virginia. The ship is riding high in the water even though a large amount of deck cargo is being carried. (1990, Leo Van Ginderen)*

5 CONTAINER—RO/RO SHIPS: CONVERTED C8-M-MA134j (MV)

Number	Name	Launched	In service	Status
T-AK 3008	2ND LT JOHN P. BOBO	19 Jan 1985	14 Feb 1985	**MPS-1**
T-AK 3009	PFC DEWAYNE T. WILLIAMS	18 May 1985	6 June 1985	**MPS-3**
T-AK 3010	1ST LT BALDOMERO LOPEZ	26 Oct 1985	21 Nov 1985	**MPS-3**
T-AK 3011	1ST LT JACK LUMMUS	22 Feb 1986	6 Mar 1986	**MPS-3**
T-AK 3012	SGT WILLIAM R. BUTTON	17 May 1986	18 May 1986	**MPS-3**

Builders:	General Dynamics, Quincy, Mass.
Displacement:	22,700 tons light
	40,846 tons full load
Tonnage:	44,543 GRT
	26,523 DWT
Length:	652¾ feet (199.0 m) waterline
	673 feet (205.18 m) overall
Beam:	105½ feet (32.2 m)
Draft:	29½ feet (9.0 m)
Propulsion:	2 diesels (Stork Werkspoor 18TM410V); 26,400 bhp; 1 shaft
Speed:	17.7 knots
Range:	11,100 nm (20,557 km) at 17.7 knots
Personnel:	29 or 30 civilian + 3 maintenance personnel, except 9 maintenance in T-AK 3008 and 3011
Flag:	20 Navy personnel in T-AK 3008 and 3011
Troops:	100
Helicopters:	landing area

These new-construction ships were classified T-AKX during planning stages. Each carries equipment and supplies for about a quarter of a Marine Amphibious Brigade for 20 days. They were built specifically for the MPS role.

The first two ships were laid down in 1983, the others in 1984.

The 2ND LT JOHN P. BOBO is flagship of MPS Squadron 1 and the 1ST LT JACK LUMMUS is the flagship of MPS Squadron 2.

Design: These ships have 162,500 square feet (14,625 m²) of vehicle deck space and can carry 1,605,000 gallons (6 million liters) of break-bulk petroleum products, plus 81,770 gallons (310,726 liters) of potable water. Up to 522 containers can be carried. A stern ramp is fitted for unloading vehicles into landing craft and onto piers, and five 39-ton-capacity cranes are fitted.

Engineering: These ships achieved 18.8 knots on trials; the speed noted in the data table is sustained speed. A 1,000-hp bow thruster is fitted to permit maneuvering alongside a pier without the aid of tugs.

The PFC DEWAYNE T. WILLIAMS at Norfolk. When forward deployed, the ship's hold are stuffed with munitions, vehicles, provisions, and equipment for Marine expeditionary forces. (1998, Jürg Kürsener)

The 1ST LT JACK LUMMUS is typical of the original 13 maritime prepositioning ships placed in MSC service in the 1980s. These ships have raised helicopter decks above their sterns. (1995, Giorgio Arra)

1 CONTAINER—RO/RO SHIP: FRENCH BUILT (MV)

Number	Name	Launched	In service	Status
T-AK 323	MERLIN	1978	Sep 2002	**LPS**

Builders:	Chanters Navigation de la Ciotat (France)
Displacement:	26,378 tons full load
Tonnage:	
Length:	670 feet (204.35 m) overall
Beam:	87 feet (26.54 m)
Draft:	34½ feet (10.52 m)
Propulsion:	1 diesel engine (Pielstick); 23,400 bhp; 1 shaft
Speed:	16 knots
Range:	
Personnel:	19 civilian

This is a medium-size container ship employed to carry Air Force munitions.

The MERLIN is one of several MSC cargo ships prepositioned to carry munitions for the Navy and Air Force. (U.S. Navy)

1 CONTAINER—RO/RO SHIP: UKRAINIAN BUILT (USNS)

Number	Name	Launched	In service	Status
T-AK 3016	LCPL ROY M. WHEAT (ex-BAZALIYA, VLADIMIR VASLAYAYEV)	1987	7 Nov 2003	**MPS-3**

Builders:	Chernomorskiy Zavod, Nikolayev (Ukraine)[9]
Displacement:	50,570 tons full load
Tonnage:	32,264 GRT
Length:	787½ feet (239.97 m) waterline
	863¾ feet (263.34 m) overall
Beam:	98⅓ feet (29.98 m)
Draft:	35½ feet (10.7 m)
Propulsion:	2 gas turbines (Mashproekt-Zorya M25); 46,000 shp; 2 shafts
Speed:	22 knots
Range:	11,000+ nm (20,380+ km) at 22 knots
Personnel:	30 civilian + 12 maintenance
Troops:	100

The LCPL ROY M. WHEAT and the 1ST LT HARRY L. MARTIN (below) are MPF(E)—Maritime Prepositioning Force (Enhancement)—assigned to support maritime prepositioning squadrons.

Conversion: This ship was converted by Bender Shipbuilding at Mobile, Alabama, beginning 18 July 1997. During conversion, a midbody section 118-feet (35.97-m) long was inserted; new Ukrainian-manufactured turbines also were installed. The ship has 127,000 square feet (11,811 m²) of deck space; 960 standard containers can be carried.

Bow and stern thrusters are installed.

Engineering: The M25 gas turbines each produce 18,000 shp; two waste-heat turbines each provide an additional 5,300 shp.

The LCPL ROY M. WHEAT as converted to the MPF(E) role. The WHEAT was built in one of the major shipyards of the USSR. (U.S. Navy)

1 CONTAINER—RO/RO SHIP: GERMAN BUILT (USNS)

Number	Name	Launched	In service	Status
T-AK 3015	1ST LT HARRY L. MARTIN (ex-TARAGO, NOSAC CEDAR, RABELAIS, LILIOOET)	1979	21 Apr 2000	**MPS-1**

Builders:	Bremer Vulkan, Bremen (Germany)
Displacement:	47,519 tons full load
Tonnage:	39,441 GRT (as built)
	34,100 DWT
Length:	688¹¹⁄₁₂ feet (210.04 m) waterline
	754 feet (229.88 m) overall
Beam:	105¾ feet (32.24 m)
Draft:	33⅗ feet (10.26 m)
Propulsion:	1 diesel engine (Bremer Vulkan-MAN K7-SZ-90/160); 25,700 bhp; 1 shaft
Speed:	17 knots
Range:	16,000 nm (29,650 km) at 17 knots
Personnel:	24 civilian + 12 maintenance
Troops:	100

The 1ST LT HARRY L. MARTIN was converted to the MPF(E) role at the Atlantic Drydock Co., Jacksonville, Florida.

Design: The ship has 127,000 square feet (11,811 m²) of vehicle deck space; 767 standard containers can be carried.

The 1ST LT HARRY L. MARTIN at less than full load. She has only one pair of cranes, just forward of the superstructure. Such ships with a combination container/vehicle payload are very useful for military operations. (U.S. Navy)

2 CONTAINER SHIPS: KOREAN BUILT (MV)

Number	Name	Launched	In service	Status
T-AK 4496	LTC JOHN U. D. PAGE	1985	2 Mar 2001	**CPF/APS-4**
	(ex-AMERICAN UTAH, IRENE D. UTAH, NEWARK BAY)			
T-AK 4544	SSGT EDWARD A. CARTER JR.	1985	14 June 2001	**CPF/APS-4**
	(ex-AMERICAN NEBRASKA, SUSAN NEBRASKA,			
	NEDLLOYD HUDSON, OOCL INNOVATOR)			

Builders:	Daewoo Shipbuilding (South Korea)
Displacement:	74,500 tons full load
Tonnage:	T-AK 4496: 57,075 GRT
	58,869 DWT
	T-AK 4544: 57,075 GRT
	57,939 DWT
Length:	915 feet (278.96 m) waterline
	949¾ feet (289.56 m) overall
Beam:	105¾ feet (32.24 m)
Draft:	35 feet (10.67 m)
Propulsion:	1 diesel engine; 28,000 bhp; 1 shaft
Speed:	18 knots
Range:	
Personnel:	22 civilian

These are massive container ships, two of eight of the type operated by the Military Sealift Command. Both ships were acquired by the MSC for conversion on 22 May 2000.

Design: These ships each can carry 2,500 standard containers. They have a limited self-unloading capability.

1 CONTAINER SHIP: KOREAN BUILT (MV)

Number	Name	Launched	In service	Status
T-AK 4296	CAPT STEVEN L. BENNETT	1984	19 Nov 1997	**LPS**
	(ex-TNT EXPRESS, MARTHA II, SEA PRIDE)			

Builders:	Samsung Shipbuilding, Koje (South Korea)
Displacement:	59,207 tons full load
Tonnage:	29,223 GRT
	41,151 DWT
Length:	656 feet (200.01 m) waterline
	687 feet (209.45 m) overall
Beam:	99¾ feet (30.41 m)
Draft:	38½ feet (11.74 m)
Propulsion:	1 diesel engine (Sulzer 6RLB76); 16,320 bhp; 1 shaft
Speed:	16.5 knots
Range:	
Personnel:	26 civilian

The CAPT STEVEN L. BENNETT is a large container ship acquired to preposition Air Force munitions. The ship can carry 1,922 containers.

Conversion: The BENNETT was converted for the MPF role at Bender Shipbuilding, Mobile, Alabama. Two 30-ton-capacity gantry cranes are provided.

Names: Some Navy lists refer to the ship as the STEVEN BENNETT; however, the full name and rank are on the ship.

The container ship LTC JOHN U. D. PAGE with cranes rigged outboard, indicating the ship is handling cargo. The earlier LTC JOHN U. D. PAGE was a large Army beach discharge lighter, taken out of service in 1989. (U.S. Navy)

The CAPT STEVEN L. BENNETT is one of several MSC-operated container ships that carry munitions. The "white" structures on these ships provide controlled temperature–humidity environments for their cargoes. (U.S. Navy)

1 CONTAINER SHIP: FRENCH BUILT (MV)

Number	Name	Launched	In service	Status
T-AK 4638	A1C WILLIAM H. PITSENBARGER (ex-THERESE DELMAS)	1983	12 Dec 2001	**LPS**

Builders:	Chanters d'Atlantique, St. Nazaire (France)
Displacement:	31,986 tons full load
Tonnage:	30,750 GRT
	32,709 DWT
Length:	575⅓ feet (175.42 m) waterline
	622 feet (189.71 m) overall
Beam:	106 feet (32.33 m)
Draft:	37½ feet (11.43 m)
Propulsion:	1 diesel engine (Sulzer 7RLB66); 13,800 bhp; 1 shaft
Speed:	17.5 knots
Range:	
Personnel:	23 civilian

This is a medium-size container ship employed for the prepositioning of Air Force munitions.

Design: The A1C WILLIAM H. PITSENBARGER can carry 885 standard containers and has a self-unloading capability. The ship has a bow thruster.

1 CONTAINER SHIP: DANISH BUILT (MV)

Number	Name	Launched	In service	Status
T-AK 4396	MAJ BERNARD F. FISHER (ex-SEA FOX, AMERICAN HAWAII)	1985	9 Sep 1999	**LPS**

Builders:	Odense Staalskibsvaerf, Lindo (Denmark)
Displacement:	48,000 tons full load
Tonnage:	34,318 GRT
	24,500 DWT
Length:	611½ feet (186.42 m) waterline
	652 feet (198.86 m) overall
Beam:	106 feet (32.33 m)
Draft:	36 feet (10.99 m)
Propulsion:	1 diesel engine (Sulzer 7RTA76); 23,030 bhp; 1 shaft
Speed:	19 knots
Range:	
Personnel:	21 civilian

The MAJ BERNARD F. FISHER carries Air Force munitions. This is a container ship capable of carrying 1,914 containers.

Class: The similar LT COL CALVIN P. TITUS (T-AK 5089) and SP5 ERIC G. GIBSON (T-AK 5091) have been discarded.

Design: Bow and stern thrusters are fitted.

The A1C WILLIAM H. PITSENBARGER also is employed to carry Air Force munitions. Like most MSC prepositioning ships, the PITSENBARGER is foreign built. (U.S. Navy)

The MAJ BERNARD F. FISHER often is confused with the USNS FISHER, one of the newer Large Medium-Speed Roll-on/roll-off (LMSR) ships. Ships carrying Air Force munitions carry the names of Air Force heroes. (U.S. Navy)

SEALIFT (OCEAN TRANSPORTATION) SHIPS

The Military Sealift Command operates approximately 30 ships of various types in the sealift (ocean transportation) role. These include a variety of ship types—LMSR, container, tankers, and break-bulk cargo ships.

2 LARGE MEDIUM-SPEED RO/RO SHIPS: DANISH BUILT (USNS)

Number	Name	Launched	In service	Status
T-AKR 296	GORDON (ex-JUTLANDIA)	1972	23 Aug 1996	**Sealift**
T-AKR 298*	GILLILAND (ex-SELANDIA)	1972	23 May 1997	**Sealift**

Builders:	Burmeister & Wain Skibsbyggeri, Kobenhavn (Denmark)
Displacement:	55,422 tons full load
Tonnage:	54,035 GRT (as built)
Length:	894¼ feet (272.65 m) waterline
	954 feet (290.85 m) overall
Beam:	105⅚ feet (32.25 m)
Draft:	35¾ feet (10.9 m)
Propulsion:	3 slow-speed diesel engines (1 Burmeister & Wain 12K84EF, 26,000 bhp; 2 Burmeister & Wain 9K84EF, 39,000 bhp); 3 shafts
Speed:	24 knots
Range:	12,000 nm (22,235 km) at 24 knots
Personnel:	30 civilian + 5 maintenance personnel
Troops:	50

These conversions to LMSR configurations, authorized in FY 1993, were undertaken at Newport News Shipbuilding, Virginia, both beginning in October 1993. The GILLILAND previously was assigned to the RRF.

Conversion: These ships were modified and lengthened at the Hyundai shipyard, Ulsan (South Korea), in 1984.

Cargo capacity is 334,055 square feet (31,067 m²).

A bow thruster is fitted.

Names: In MSC service, these ships initially were named MSGT GARY I. GORDON and CPL CHARLES L. GILLILAND; they subsequently were shortened to last names only.

7 LARGE MEDIUM-SPEED RO/RO SHIPS: "BOB HOPE" CLASS (USNS)

Number	Name	FY	Launched	In service	Status
T-AKR 300*	BOB HOPE	93	27 Mar 1997	18 Nov 1998	**Sealift**
T-AKR 301	FISHER	94	21 Oct 1997	4 Aug 1999	**Sealift**
T-AKR 302*	SEAY	94	25 June 1998	28 Mar 2000	**Sealift**
T-AKR 303	MENDONCA	96	25 May 1999	30 Jan 2001	**Sealift**
T-AKR 304*	PILILAAU	97	29 Jan 2000	24 July 2001	**Sealift**
T-AKR 305*	BRITTIN	98	11 Nov 2000	11 July 2002	**Sealift**
T-AKR 306	BENAVIDEZ	99	11 Aug 2001	10 Sep 2003	**Sealift**

Builders:	Northrop Grumman Ship Systems/Avondale, New Orleans
Displacement:	35,500 tons light
	62,069 tons full load
Tonnage:	26,569 DWT
Length:	889¾ feet (271.28 m) waterline
	950 feet (289.63 m) overall
Beam:	105⅚ feet (32.27 m)
Draft:	34⅔ feet (10.57 m)
Propulsion:	4 medium-speed diesel engines (Colt Pielstick 10 PC4.2V); 65,160 bhp; 1 shaft
Speed:	24 knots
Range:	12,000+ nm (22,235+ km) at 24 knots
Personnel:	30 civilian + 5 maintenance personnel
Troops:	50
Helicopters:	landing area

These ships are similar to the WATSON class but with diesel propulsion. The BOB HOPE was laid down on 31 May 1995. Several of these ships initially were assigned to the RRF.

Design: Approximately 380,000 square feet (35,340 m²) of vehicle cargo space is provided in these ships (i.e., more than 1,000 military vehicles, including about 60 M1 Abrams tanks). Two paired Hägglunds 58-ton-capacity cranes are fitted; each pair can operate together to lift 112 tons.

The GILLILAND under way shows the typical configuration of large RO/RO ships. The enormous number of vehicles in U.S. Army and Marine Corps units demands large numbers of these ships. (U.S. Navy)

The BOB HOPE, *lead ship for a new series of prepositioning and RO/RO sealift ships, has two side ports and a stern ramp for loading/unloading vehicles. (2004, U.S. Navy/Paul Farley)*

The BENAVIDEZ and other LMSR ships were a compromise of cost and speed, as many Department of Defense officials believe that a speed in excess of 24 knots is needed for modern sealift ships. (2003, U.S. Navy/Ron Elias)

The BENAVIDEZ at full speed while on sea trials. The ships can carry 60-plus-ton M1 Abrams tanks and even heavier military engineer vehicles. (2003, U.S. Navy/Ron Elias)

2 LARGE MEDIUM-SPEED RO/RO SHIPS: DANISH BUILT (USNS)

Number	Name	Launched	In service	Status
T-AKR 295*	SHUGHART (ex-LAURA MAERSK)	1981	7 May 1996	**Sealift**
T-AKR 297*	YANO (ex-LEISE MAERSK)	1981	8 Feb 1997	**Sealift**

Builders:	Odense Staalskibsvaerf, Lindo (Denmark)
Displacement:	54,298 tons full load
Tonnage:	43,325 GRT (as built) 53,000 DWT
Length:	850 7/12 feet (259.32 m) waterline 884 11/12 feet (269.79 m) hull 906¾ feet (276.45 m) overall
Beam:	105 7/12 feet (32.2 m)
Draft:	34⅚ feet (10.62 m)
Propulsion:	1 diesel engine (Burmeister & Wain 12L90 GFCA); 46,653 bhp; 1 shaft
Speed:	24 knots
Range:	12,000 nm (22,235 km) at 24 knots
Personnel:	30 civilian + 5 maintenance personnel
Troops:	50
Helicopters:	landing area

These ships are conversions to the LMSR configuration. Both were funded under the FY 1993 conversion program and then converted at the National Steel yard in San Diego, California; the SHUGHART began conversion in June 1994 and the YANO in December 1994.

Class: A third ship of this design, the PFC WILLIAM A. SODERMAN, is an MPS ship (described above).

Design: These ships were modified and lengthened at the Hyundai shipyard, Ulsan, in 1987. Their cargo capacity is 312,461 square feet (29,059 m^2).

Bow and stern thrusters are fitted.

Names: In MSC service these ships initially were named SFC RANDALL D. SHUGHART and SFC RODNEY J. T. YANO; these subsequently were shortened to last names only.

5 TRANSPORT OILERS: MODIFIED T5 TYPE (USNS)

Number	Name	Launched	In service	Status
T-AOT 1121	GUS W. DARNELL (ex-OCEAN FREEDOM)	10 Aug 1985	11 Sep 1985	**Sealift**
T-AOT 1122	PAUL BUCK (ex-OCEAN CHAMPION)	1 June 1985	11 Sep 1985	**Sealift**
T-AOT 1123	SAMUEL L. COBB (ex-OCEAN TRIUMPH)	2 Nov 1985	15 Nov 1985	**Sealift**
T-AOT 1124	RICHARD G. MATTHIESEN (ex-OCEAN SPIRIT)	15 Feb 1986	18 Feb 1986	**Sealift**
T-AOT 1125	LAWRENCE H. GIANELLA (ex-OCEAN STAR)	19 Apr 1986	22 Apr 1986	**Sealift**

Builders:	American Shipbuilding, Tampa, Fla.
Displacement:	9,000 tons light 39,624 tons full load
Tonnage:	19,037 GRT 30,150 DWT
Length:	587⅓ feet (179.1 m) waterline 614⅚ feet (187.45 m) overall
Beam:	90 feet (27.4 m)
Draft:	34 feet (10.4 m)
Propulsion:	1 diesel (Mitsubishi or Ishikawajima-Sulzer 5RTA-76); 15,300 bhp; 1 shaft
Speed:	16 knots
Range:	12,000 nm (22,224 km) at 16 knots
Personnel:	23 civilian

These are build-and-charter oilers constructed specifically for naval service, although they initially were contracted for commercial service. They were formally acquired by the MSC on 15 January 2003. The lead ship was laid down on 26 December 1983.

Builders: Major components for these ships were built by American Shipbuilding Co. at Lorain, Ohio, and Nashville, Tennessee.

Design: They are built to a modified T-5 design with ice-strengthened hulls. Cargo capacity is 238,400 barrels in the first three ships; 239,500 barrels in the last two units.

Engineering: Mitsubishi diesels are fitted in the first two ships; Ishikawajimas are in the others.

The SHUGHART was the first LMSR ship to enter U.S. naval service. The ship has two ports on each side, as well as a stern ramp. Here the ship moves slowly through San Diego harbor. (1999, Leo Van Ginderen)

The RICHARD G. MATTHIESEN is one of 13 government-owned tankers operated by the MSC in the sealift role, carrying liquid cargo for all of the military services. (U.S. Navy)

The LAWRENCE H. GIANELLA is one of the two T5-type tankers in MSC service provided with an underway replenishment capability. (1993, Leo Van Ginderen)

1 CONTAINER SHIP: GERMAN BUILT (MV)

Number	Name	Launched	In service	Status
T-AK 4729	AMERICAN TERN (ex-KARIBA)	1990	26 Dec 2002	**Sealift**

Builder:	Neptun Shipyard, Rostock (Germany)
Displacement:	17,350 tons full load
Length:	521 feet (158.91 m) overall
Beam:	76 feet (23.18 m)
Draft:	33 feet (10.06 m)
Propulsion:	1 diesel engine (Selzer 5RTA58); 1 shaft
Speed:	16 knots
Range:	
Personnel:	21 civilian

This is a container ship with ice-breaking capability. She is employed carrying cargo to U.S. activities in the Arctic and Antarctica, replacing the GREEN WAVE (T-AK 2050).

Design: She is built to Finnish Ice Class 1A specification for merchant ships and can carry 1,033 containers.

COMBINATION CARGO SHIP: GERMAN BUILT (MV)

The break-bulk/container ship GREEN WAVE (T-AK 2050) was discarded in March 2003 after almost 20 years of MSC service. She was employed primarily to support U.S. military and research facilities in Greenland and Antarctic. She was replaced in that role by the AMERICAN TERN.

The GREEN WAVE's near sister ship GREEN RIDGE (T-AK 9655) was discarded on 13 August 2000.

For characteristics see 17th Edition/pages 280–81.

1 TANKER: TURKISH BUILT (MTV)

Number	Name	Launched	In service	Status
(none)	MONTAUK (ex-BITTEN THERESA)			**Sealift**

Builders:	Tuzla Gemi, Tuzla (Turkey)
Displacement:	5,780 tons full load
Tonnage:	3,457 GRT
	4,780 DWT
Length:	326⅔ feet (99.60 m) waterline
	357¹¹⁄₁₂ ft (109.19 m) overall
Beam:	52½ ft (16.0 m)
Draft:	18⁷⁄₁₂ ft (10.54 m)
Propulsion:	1 diesel engine (M.A.N. B&W Alpha 8L28/32); 2,665 bhp; 1 shaft
Speed:	12 knots
Range:	
Personnel:	13 civilian

The MONTAUK is a small, shallow-draft tanker on long-term charter to the MSC for supporting small U.S. overseas bases.

Design: A bow thruster is fitted. Her cargo capacity is 30,000 barrels.

1 CONTAINER SHIP: TURKISH BUILT (MV)

Number	Name	Launched	In service	Status
(none)	SAGAMORE (ex-MINT ARROW, FAS RED SEA II)	1997		**Sealift**

Builders:	Yardimici Shipyard, Tuzla (Turkey)
Displacement:	7,100 tons
Tonnage:	3,838 GRT
	5,070 DWT
Length:	308⅓ feet (94.0 m) waterline
	330½ feet (100.76 m) overall
Beam:	52½ feet (16.0 m)
Draft:	20¼ feet (6.17 m)
Propulsion:	1 diesel engine (Wäartsila 8R32E); 1 shaft
Speed:	13 knots
Range:	
Personnel:	15 civilian

This is a small, self-loading container ship. She operates between Singapore and Diego Garcia.

Design: Her cargo capacity is 570 containers. Two 39.4-ton-capacity container cranes are fitted to her port side.

The MONTAUK is the smallest tanker in MSC service. She carries cargo to shallow-draft ports in South Korea and Japan. (U.S. Navy)

The small cargo ship SAGAMORE is employed carrying cargo to the U.S. military facility on Diego Garcia in the Indian Ocean. (U.S. Navy)

1 RANGE SUPPORT SHIP: "SEAMARK III" (MV)

Number	Name	Launched	In service	Status
(none)	SEAMARK III			**Sealift**

Builder:	
Displacement:	
Length:	150 feet (45.73 m) overall
Beam:	50 feet (15.24 m)
Draft:	9¼ feet (2.8 m)
Propulsion:	
Speed:	
Range:	
Personnel:	4 civilian

This is a small, open-deck cargo ship employed to support U.S. space tracking and research facilities on Caribbean islands.

READY RESERVE SHIPS

There are some 60 merchant ships laid up in U.S. ports, plus two gasoline tankers laid up in Japan. The number of days in which they can be reactivated is indicated in parentheses under *Status*.

These ships are listed in this section in the following order:

T-AKR	Fast Sealift Ships (FSS)
T-ACS	auxiliary crane ships
T-AK	Lighter Aboard Ship (LASH) ships
T-AKR	Sea Barge (SeaBee) ships
T-AK/AKR	Roll-On/Roll-Off (RO/RO) ships
T-AK	cargo (break-bulk) ships
T-AOT	tankers
T-AOG	gasoline tankers

8 FAST SEALIFT SHIPS: CONVERTED SL-7 TYPE (USNS)

Number	Name	Launched	In service	Status
T-AKR 287*	ALGOL (ex-SEA-LAND Exchange)	22 Sep 1972	19 June 1984	FSS
T-AKR 288*	BELLATRIX (ex-SEA-LAND TRADE)	30 Sep 1972	10 Sep 1984	FSS
T-AKR 289*	DENEBOLA (ex-SEA-LAND RESOURCE)	10 May 1973	7 Oct 1985	FSS
T-AKR 290*	POLLUX (ex-SEA-LAND MARKET)	18 May 1973	31 Mar 1986	FSS
T-AKR 291*	ALTAIR (ex-SEA-LAND FINANCE)	28 Apr 1973	13 Nov 1985	FSS
T-AKR 292*	REGULUS (ex-SEA-LAND COMMERCE)	18 Dec 1972	28 Aug 1985	FSS
T-AKR 293*	CAPELLA (ex-SEA-LAND McLEAN)	9 Sep 1971	1 July 1984	FSS
T-AKR 294*	ANTARES (ex-SEA-LAND GALLOWAY)	13 May 1972	12 July 1984	FSS

Builders:	T-AKR 287, 289, 293: Rotterdamsche Dry Dock Maats, Rotterdam (Netherlands)
	T-AKR 288, 291: Rheinstahl Nordseewerke, Emden (Germany)
	T-AKR 290, 292, 294: A.G. Weser, Bremen (Germany)
Displacement:	31,017 tons light
	55,425 tons full load
Tonnage:	T-AKR 287, 288: 25,915 DWT
	T-AKR 289: 25,169 DWT
	T-AKR 290: 24,212 DWT
	T-AKR 291, 292: 25,595 DWT
	T-AKR 293: 25,407 DWT
	T-AKR 294: 24,270 DWT
Length:	893 feet (272.26 m) waterline
	946¼ feet (288.5 m) overall
Beam:	105½ feet (32.2 m)
Draft:	36⅔ feet (11.2 m)
Propulsion:	2 steam turbines (General Electric); 120,000 shp; 2 shafts
Boilers:	2 (Foster-Wheeler)
Speed:	33 knots
Range:	12,200 nm (22,594 km) at 27 knots
Personnel:	42 civilian
Helicopters:	landing area

The SEAMARK III is employed carrying supplies and provisions to U.S. research and tracking stations in the Caribbean area. (U.S. Navy)

These are the world's fastest oceangoing cargo ships. Together they can carry almost all of the equipment of an Army mechanized division.

The ships are former high-speed merchant ships of the SL-7 class built for the SeaLand Corporation in European shipyards. They have been converted to fast sealift ships that can carry U.S. military cargoes with an extensive roll-on/roll-off capability. They are operated by civilian charter crews.

The ships were available because they were found to be uneconomic for commercial operation because of high fuel costs. The average cost per ship to the Navy was $34.6 million.

Classification: During the planning stage, these ships were designated T-AKRX. On acquisition, they were designated T-AK and assigned hull numbers in the cargo ship (AK) series; however, on conversion to RO/RO configuration, they were changed to T-AKR but retained the AK-series hull numbers.

The T-AK 287 changed to T-AKR on 19 June 1984; T-AK 288 to T-AKR on 10 September 1984; T-AK 289–292 to T-AKR on 1 November 1983; and T-AK 293 and 294 to T-AKR on 30 June 1984.

Conversion: Four ships were converted with FY 1982 funds and four with FY 1984 funds; the T-AKR 287, 288, and 292 at National Steel and Shipbuilding, San Diego; T-AKR 289 and 293 at Pennsylvania Shipbuilding, Chester, Pennsylvania; and T-AKR 290, 291, and 294 at Avondale Shipyards, New Orleans.

These ships have approximately 185,000 square feet (16,650 m²) of vehicle space. A major container capability remains aft, with provisions for special racks for loading heavy material, including trucks and tanks (being lifted on and off vice RO/RO). Side ports and heavy ramps are provided on both sides of the ship. Twin 35-ton-capacity cranes are fitted forward and twin 50-ton cranes aft. Through limited arcs, they can provide a combined lift of 70 and 100 tons, respectively.

A helicopter landing deck amidships can accommodate the largest U.S. military helicopters (Marine/Navy H-53E, Army CH-47 Chinook). The four cargo decks beneath the landing deck are connected by ramps and can accommodate helicopters, the first with a height of 19½ feet (5.95 m) and the others with 13½ feet (4.1 m).

In addition to the RO/RO and helicopter space, the ships each can each accommodate other vehicles, plus 78 35-foot (10.7-m) flat racks and 46 containers. There is a tunnel for trucks up to 5-ton capacity in the amidships deck structure to permit passage between the forward and after cargo areas.

Design: As built, the 33-knot SL-7s were the fastest cargo ships ever constructed for the U.S. merchant service.

Names: These ships are assigned traditional Navy cargo ship names (i.e., stars and constellations), reflecting their acquisition on bare-boat charter versus the time charter of maritime prepositioning ships. Most names previously were carried by store ships (AF).

Operational: All eight ships participated in Operations Desert Shield and Desert Storm in 1990–1991, being activated in August 1990. The ANTARES, which had suffered previous machinery problems, had an engine breakdown in the eastern Atlantic during the initial lift of Desert Shield, in August 1990. She was towed into a Spanish port and her cargo was shifted to other sealift ships.

All ships also participated in the second Iraq conflict of 2003.

The fast sealift ship POLLUX unloads cargo into small craft. Paired cranes amidships and aft can unload cargo, but stern and side ramps are the principal means of loading/unloading vehicles in these ships. (U.S. Navy)

The REGULUS at Norfolk with her starboard side port open. These are the world's fastest oceangoing cargo ships; they were too expensive for commercial service because of fuel costs. (2003, Jürg E. Kürsener)

The fast sealift ships CAPELLA (left) and ANTARES laid up at Baltimore, Maryland. Note their flat stern counter, after pair of cranes, and massive superstructure blocks. (1999, Kevin Clarke)

The ANTARES, *one of eight fast sealift ships in naval service. These ships were employed to great benefit in the Iraqi invasions of 1991 and 2003, as well as in numerous other military operations and exercises. (U.S. Navy)*

CRANE SHIPS

2 AUXILIARY CRANE SHIPS: C6-S-MA60d TYPE (SS)

Number	Name	Launched	To RRF	Status
T-ACS 9	GREEN MOUNTAIN STATE (ex-AMERICAN ALTAIR, MORMACALTAIR)	14 Jan 1965	31 July 1991	**MPS-3**
T-ACS 10	BEAVER STATE (ex-AMERICAN DRACO, MORMACDRACO)	14 Jan 1965	22 Dec 1993	RRF (5)

Builders:	Ingalls Shipbuilding, Pascagoula, Miss.
Displacement:	16,600 tons light
	22,900 tons full load
Tonnage:	14,000 GRT (as built)
	12,763 DWT (as built)
Length:	634⅚ feet (193.55 m) waterline
	665¾ feet (203.0 m) overall
Beam:	75½ feet (22.9 m)
Draft:	31½ feet (9.6 m)
Propulsion:	2 steam turbines (General Electric); 19,000 shp; 1 shaft
Boilers:	2 (Combustion Engineering)
Speed:	21 knots
Range:	17,000 nm (31,485 km) at 20 knots
Personnel:	64 civilian

These are converted container ships.

Conversion: The GREEN MOUNTAIN STATE was converted at Norfolk Shipbuilding Co. in February–March 1989. The BEAVER STATE began conversion to a crane ship on 28 February 1989 at the same yard, but slowed by lack of funding, the conversion was canceled on 12 January 1990 and she was transferred to MarAd for layup on 9 April 1990. The conversion was resumed in 1992 at the Charleston Naval Shipyard.

Both ships are fitted with three sets of twin 30-ton-capacity cranes.

Design: These ships are intended to provide an unloading capability for other sealift ships when port facilities are not available. Moored alongside a loaded merchant ship, a T-ACS can lift cargo onto a pier or into landing craft or barges alongside.

Each crane ship has two or three sets of 30-ton-capacity cargo cranes; the cranes can be paired to lift 60 tons. Thus, one crane can lift a fully loaded container; two cranes can lift an M1 Abrams main battle tank; and four cranes working together can lift a 105-ton floating causeway.

The C6-S-1 container ship AMERICAN BANKER was to have become the T-ACS 11 and another, undesignated ship was to have become the T-ACS 12.

Engineering: They are fitted with highly automated engineering plants. Several ships of this design exceeded 24 knots when new.

Names: These ships carry state nicknames.

The GREEN MOUNTAIN STATE, *like most auxiliary crane ships, is a converted C6-series cargo ship. The subtypes of these ships and three C5-type crane ships differ in dimensions and details. (1990, Leo Van Ginderen)*

2 AUXILIARY CRANE SHIPS: C6-S-MA1xb TYPE (SS)

Number	Name	Launched	To RRF	Status
T-ACS 7	DIAMOND STATE (ex-PRESIDENT TRUMAN, JAPAN MAIL)	8 Aug 1961	22 Feb 1989	RRF (5)
T-ACS 8	EQUALITY STATE (ex-AMERICAN BUILDER, PHILIPPINE MAIL, SANTA ROSA, PRESIDENT ROOSEVELT, WASHINGTON MAIL)	11 May 1962	24 May 1989	RRF (5)

Builders:	Todd Shipyards, San Pedro, Calif.
Displacement:	15,138 tons light
Tonnage:	16,518 GRT (as built) 19,871 DWT (as built)
Length:	63211/12 feet (192.95 m) waterline 667⅚ feet (203.6 m) overall
Beam:	76 feet (23.2 m)
Draft:	33¼ feet (10.1 m)
Propulsion:	2 steam turbines (General Electric); 22,000 shp; 1 shaft
Boilers:	2 (Combustion Engineering)
Speed:	20 knots
Range:	14,000 nm (25,930 km) at 20 knots
Personnel:	

These are former container ships converted to crane ships.

Conversion: The T-ACS 7 was converted in November 1987–December 1988 and the T-ACS 8 in January 1988–February 1989 at Tampa (Florida) Shipbuilding Co. They are fitted with three sets of twin 30-ton-capacity cranes.

The DIAMOND STATE, showing her massive, paired heavy-lift cranes. They can handle cargo, but only in low sea states. These ships can carry large amounts of cargo. (1999, Leo Van Ginderen)

2 AUXILIARY CRANE SHIPS: C5-S-MA73c TYPE (SS)

Number	Name	Launched	To RRF	Status
T-ACS 5	FLICKERTAIL STATE (ex-LIGHTNING)	11 May 1968	8 Feb 1988	**MPS-3**
T-ACS 6*	CORNHUSKER STATE (ex-STAGHOUND)	2 Nov 1968	12 Apr 1988	RRF (5)

Builders:	Bath Iron Works, Maine
Displacement:	15,060 tons light 25,000 tons full load
Tonnage:	16,445 DWT
Length:	581⅚ feet (177.35 m) waterline 609⅚ feet (185.9 m) overall
Beam:	91⅙ feet (27.8 m)
Draft:	30 feet (9.1 m)
Propulsion:	2 steam turbines; 17,500 shp; 1 shaft
Boilers:	2 (Babcock & Wilcox)
Speed:	20 knots
Range:	9,340 nm (17,300 km) at 20 knots
Personnel:	35 civilian

These are former container ships.

Class: The GOPHER STATE (T-ACS 4) of this type has been stricken. She was assigned to APS-4.

Conversion: Both ships were converted at Norfolk Shipbuilding Co. (Virginia)—the T-ACS 5 from December 1986 to February 1988, and the T-ACS 6 from March 1987 to April 1988. They were fitted with two sets of twin 30-ton-capacity cranes.

In 2003–2004, the FLICKERTAIL STATE evaluated an advanced, motion-compensating crane system intended for operation in conditions to sea state 4.

Operational: The T-ACS 4, as the mercantile EXPORT LEADER, served as test ship for the Arapaho project, exploring the feasibility of operating and supporting military helicopters from a merchant ship. The 1982 evaluation was totally successful, albeit conducted on a limited scale. (During a 40-hour at-sea period, 178 day and 45 night landings were logged by several helicopter types.)

In early 1990, the FLICKERTAIL STATE and GOPHER STATE were activated and fitted with collective protection spaces for defense against Chemical-Biological-Radiological (CBR) attacks. They then carried more than 100,000 artillery projectiles filled with nerve agents from Nordenham, Germany, to Johnston Island in the Pacific. The voyage, from 22 September to 6 November 1990 (via Cape Horn), was under the escort of two guided missile cruisers and was made without incident. The ships subsequently were employed in Desert Shield (1990–1991).

3 AUXILIARY CRANE SHIPS: C6-S-MA1qd TYPE (SS)

Number	Name	Launched	To RRF	Status
T-ACS 1	KEYSTONE STATE (ex-PRESIDENT HARRISON)	2 Oct 1965	7 May 1984	RRF (5)
T-ACS 2	GEM STATE (ex-PRESIDENT MONROE)	22 May 1965	31 Oct 1985	RRF (5)
T-ACS 3	GRAND CANYON STATE (ex-PRESIDENT POLK)	23 Jan 1965	27 Oct 1987	**MPS-3**

Builders:	National Steel and Shipbuilding, San Diego
Displacement:	28,660 tons full load
Tonnage:	17,128 GRT 13,600 DWT
Length:	632 11/12 feet (192.95 m) waterline 668½ feet (203.8 m) overall
Beam:	76⅙ feet (23.2 m)
Draft:	33 feet (10.1 m)
Propulsion:	2 steam turbines (General Electric); 19,250 shp; 1 shaft
Boilers:	2 (Foster Wheeler)
Speed:	20 knots
Range:	13,000 nm (24,075 km) at 20 knots
Personnel:	64 civilian

These ships each can accommodate 303 containers.

Conversion: The T-ACS 1 was converted by Bay Shipbuilding, Sturgeon Bay, Wisconsin, from March 1983 to May 1984; the T-ACS 2 by Continental Marine, San Francisco, from October 1984 to October 1985; and the T-ACS 3 from October 1985 to October 1987 by Dillingham Corp., San Francisco.

All are fitted with three sets of twin 30-ton-capacity cranes.

The GOPHER STATE*—now stricken—and other crane ships of the C5 type have their navigation bridge forward; their machinery is aft, with a helicopter landing deck on their fantails. (1994, Leo Van Ginderen)*

The GRAND CANYON STATE*, an early auxiliary crane ship. There are two sets of heavy-lift cranes forward of the superstructure and a third set aft. (1995, Leo Van Ginderen)*

SPECIALIZED CARGO SHIPS

2 LASH CARGO SHIPS: C9-S-81d TYPE (SS)

Number	Name	Launched	To RRF	Status
T-AK 5070	CAPE FLATTERY (ex-DELTA NORTE)	19 May 1973	5 June 1987	RRF (10)
T-AK 5073	CAPE FAREWELL (ex-DELTA MAR, AMERICAN MAR)	1973	2 Apr 1987	RRF (10)

Builders:	Avondale Shipyards, New Orleans
Displacement:	62,314 tons full load
Tonnage:	29,508 GRT
	41,363 DWT
Length:	797⅙ feet (243.0 m) waterline
	893⅓ feet (272.35 m) overall
Beam:	100 feet (30.56 m)
Draft:	40⅚ feet (12.4 m)
Propulsion:	2 steam turbines (De Laval); 32,000 shp; 1 shaft
Boilers:	2 (Combustion Engineering)
Speed:	22.75 knots
Range:	15,000 nm (27,780 km) at 22 knots
Personnel:	24 civilian

These LASH ships can carry 89 preloaded barges. A small tug also is embarked to help maneuver barges alongside. They are fitted with a 510-ton traveling crane.

Class: The GREEN VALLEY (T-AK 2049) of this type has been discarded. The DELTA SUD of this design was to have been acquired as the CAPE FEAR, but she suffered machinery damage during an overhaul prior to becoming an RRF ship and was returned to MarAd for disposal. Subsequently, that name was assigned to a C8-S-81b ship taken into naval service (see below).

Design: LASH ships carry large, fully loaded barges or lighters that can be floated or lifted on and off the ship. This scheme speeds up loading and unloading, and allows cargo to be handled at ports where piers or wharves are unavailable. The two principal barge-carrying designs are known as LASH and SeaBee; the former ships use cranes to lift barges to the cargo decks and the latter have large stern elevators.

The CAPE FLATTERY shows the long, clean lines of LASH ships. The containers on her deck actually are in lighters, moved and lowered over the stern by the massive overhead traveling crane. (1995, Leo Van Ginderen)

2 LASH SHIPS: C8-S-81b TYPE (SS)

Number	Name	Launched	To RRF	Status
T-AK 5061	CAPE FEAR	1971	30 Sep 1985	RRF (10)
	(ex-AUSTRAL LIGHTNING, LASH ESPAÑA)			
T-AK 5071	CAPE FLORIDA	10 Oct 1970	13 Feb 1987	RRF (10)
	(ex-AMERICAN CARIBE, DELTA CARIBE, LASH TURKIYE)			

Builders:	Avondale Shipyards, New Orleans
Displacement:	44,606 tons full load
Tonnage:	26,456 GRT
	29,820 DWT
Length:	723⅝ feet (220.7 m) waterline
	819⅝ feet (249.9 m) overall
Beam:	100 feet (30.5 m)
Draft:	40¾ feet (12.4 m)
Propulsion:	2 steam turbines (De Laval); 32,000 shp; 1 shaft
Boilers:	2 (Babcock & Wilcox or Combustion Engineering)
Speed:	22.5 knots
Range:	13,000 nm (24,076 km) at 22.5 knots
Personnel:	24 civilian

These are former LASH barge carriers modified (prior to MSC charter) to combination barge/container ships. They can carry 71–77 standard cargo barges or some 840 containers. A 30-ton-capacity traveling crane is fitted for handling containers, and a 446-ton-capacity traveling barge crane and two 5-ton cranes also are fitted.

These ships are similar to the larger C9-S-81d barge carriers.

Class: These were highly innovative ships; 11 were built. Several previously operated by the MSC have been laid up in the NDRF or returned to commercial service, including the AUSTRAL

RAINBOW (T-AK 1005) and GREEN HARBOUR (T-AK 2064), both of which served with the MPF.

2 SEABEE SHIPS: C8-S-82a TYPE (SS)

Number	Name	Launched	To RRF	Status
T-AKR 5063	CAPE MAY (ex-ALMERIA LYKES)	1972	21 July 1986	RRF (5)
T-AKR 5065	CAPE MOHICAN (ex-TILLIE LYKES)	1973	22 Aug 1986	RRF (5)

Builders:	General Dynamics, Quincy, Mass.
Displacement:	18,880 tons light
	57,290 tons full load
Tonnage:	21,667 GRT
	38,410 DWT
Length:	721⅓ feet (219.9 m) waterline
	873¾ feet (266.39 m) overall
Beam:	105⅝ feet (32.3 m)
Draft:	39½ feet (11.9 m)
Propulsion:	2 steam turbines (General Electric); 36,000 shp; 1 shaft
Boilers:	2 (Babcock & Wilcox)
Speed:	20.5 knots
Range:	14,300 nm (26,485 km) at 19.25 knots
Personnel:	39 civilian

These ships each can carry 38 cargo barges.

Class: The CAPE MENDOCINO (T-AKR 5064) of this class transferred from the RRF to the NDRF on 1 July 2004.

Design: Each ship is fitted with a 2,000-ton-capacity elevator at the stern for loading and unloading fully laden barges. In addition, these ships can carry 4,000 barrels (the CAPE MOHICAN can carry 11,000 barrels) of liquid cargo.

The now-discarded AUSTRAL RAINBOW shows the C8-type LASH configuration. These ships are significantly smaller than the C9-type LASH ships. There are two small lighter-handling tugs near the stern, carried as deck cargo. (U.S. Navy)

The Cape MOHICAN, a SeaBee ship, is similar in appearance to LASH ships. The bridge structure straddles the barge decks. The ship's propulsion machinery is in the sidewalls. (1991, Leo Van Ginderen)

The CAPE MAY at Norfolk, showing her heavy-lift elevator; the portside elevator machinery is visible in this view. (2003, Jürg Kürsener)

3 CONTAINER—RO/RO CARGO SHIPS: JAPANESE/NORWEGIAN BUILT (MV)

Number	Name	Launched	To RRF	Status
T-AKR 5066*	CAPE HUDSON (ex-BARBER TAIF)	1979	30 Oct 1986	RRF (4)
T-AKR 5067	CAPE HENRY (ex-BARBER PRIAM)	1979	Sep 1986	RRF (5)
T-AKR 5068*	CAPE HORN (ex-BARBER TØNSBERG)	1979	10 Dec 1986	RRF (4)

Builders:	T-AKR 5066: Mitsubishi, Nagasaki (Japan)
	T-AKR 5067: Kaldnes Mek., Versted Tønsberg (Norway)
	T-AKR 5068: Tangen Verft, Kragerø (Norway)
Displacement:	approx. 47,200 tons full load
Tonnage:	T-AKR 5066: 21,976 GRT
	T-AKR 5067: 21,747 GRT
	T-AKR 5068: 22,090 GRT
Length:	693¾ feet (211.5 m) waterline
	749½ feet (228.5 m) overall
Beam:	105⅚ feet (32.3 m)
Draft:	35⅚ feet (10.8 m)
Propulsion:	1 diesel engine (Mitsubishi-Sulzer in T-AKR 5067; Burmeister & Wain in others); 30,150 bhp (30,700 bhp in Norwegian-built ships); 1 shaft
Speed:	21 knots
Range:	24,300 nm (45,000 km) at 17 knots
Personnel:	27 civilian

All three of these large combination container-RO/RO ships were purchased on 1 June 1986. Their details vary. They can carry vehicles or 1,607–1,626 containers.

They all have one 40-ton-capacity crane forward (the superstructure is aft).

Status: All three ships were assigned to the Army's APS-4 on 30 September 1994; they subsequently were shifted to the RRF.

The CAPE HENRY, one of three specialized RO/RO–container ships operated by the MSC. The three ships were constructed in three different shipyards in two countries. (1994, Leo Van Ginderen)

The CAPE HORN at Antwerp. These ships have a massive, angled stern ramp. They are vital to U.S. military operations because of the huge numbers of vehicles in Army and Marine Corps units. (1994, Leo Van Ginderen)

2 CONTAINER—RO/RO CARGO SHIPS: POLISH BUILT (MV)

Number	Name	Launched	To RRF	Status
T-AKR 9961*	CAPE WASHINGTON (ex-HUAL TRANSPORTER)	1981	5 Apr 1994	RRF (5)
T-AKR 9962*	CAPE WRATH (ex-HUAL TRADER, HOEGH TRADER)	1982	30 Sep 1994	RRF (5)

Builders:	Stocznia imeni Komuny Paryskiej, Gdynia (Poland)
Displacement:	approx. 55,000 tons
Tonnage:	T-AKR 9961: 23,597 GRT
	32,695 DWT
	T-AKR 9962: 20,563 GRT
	32,722 DWT
Length:	642 feet (195.76 m) waterline
	697⅓ feet (212.6 m) overall
Beam:	105¹¹⁄₂ feet (32.28 m)
Draft:	38⅙ feet (11.63 m)
Propulsion:	1 diesel engine (Cegielski-Sulzer 6RND 90/155);
	17,400 bhp; 1 shaft
Speed:	17 knots
Range:	
Personnel:	

The CAPE WASHINGTON was acquired for the RRF on 7 April 1993, and the CAPE WRATH on 14 May 1993. Both initially were assigned to the Army's APS-4 on 30 September 1994.

These ships are former automobile carriers (capacity was 6,000 cars); they can carry vehicles (loaded/unloaded through side doors and quarter doors/ramps). Capacity is 1,203 containers or vehicles.

These ships have ice-strengthened hulls and are fitted with bow thrusters.

2 CONTAINER—RO/RO CARGO SHIPS: JAPANESE BUILT (MV)

Number	Name	Launched	To RRF	Status
T-AKR 5082*	CAPE KNOX (ex-NEDLLOYD ROUEN, ROUEN)	1978	15 July 1996	RRF (4)
T-AKR 5083*	CAPE KENNEDY (ex-NEDLLOYD RRFARIO, RRRFARIO)	1979	11 June 1996	RRF (4)

Builders:	Nippon Kokan, Tsurumi (Japan)
Displacement:	36,450 tons full load
Tonnage:	21,144 GRT
	29,218 DWT
Length:	695⅔ feet (212.1 m) overall
Beam:	105¹¹⁄₂ feet (32.29 m)
Draft:	35⅙ feet (10.72 m)
Propulsion:	1 diesel engine (Sumitomo-Sulzer 8RND90M); 25,400 bhp; 1 shaft
Speed:	19 knots
Range:	
Personnel:	

Both ships were acquired for the RRF in February 1995. They have a large stern door and two angled stern ramps and each can carry 1,550 standard containers or vehicles.

A bow thruster is fitted.

The CAPE WASHINGTON *(above) and her sister ship* CAPE WRATH *are among the most ungainly looking ships afloat. They have a high freeboard, low bridge structure, and short funnel aft. (1994, Leo Van Ginderen)*

The CAPE KENNEDY *(above) and* CAPE KNOX *have a large stern door with two vehicle ramps. The upper portion of the ship's bulbous bow is visible. (1997, Leo Van Ginderen)*

1 RO/RO CARGO SHIP: "CALLAGHAN" (GTS)

Number	Name	Launched	In service	Status
T-AKR 1001*	ADM WM. M. CALLAGHAN	17 Oct 1967	19 Dec 1967	RRF (4)

Builders:	Sun Shipbuilding and Dry Dock, Chester, Pa.
Displacement:	26,573 tons full load
Tonnage:	13,500 GRT
	24,471 DWT
Length:	633⅚ feet (193.12 m) waterline
	694¼ feet (211.66 m) overall
Beam:	92 feet (28.1 m)
Draft:	29 feet (8.8 m)
Propulsion:	2 gas turbines (General Electric LM2500); 40,000 shp; 2 shafts
Speed:	26 knots
Range:	12,000 nm (22,225 km) at 20 knots
Personnel:	28 civilian

The ADM WM. M. CALLAGHAN was an early RO/RO ship, and the first built for the U.S. Navy; however, she was operated under charter to the Military Sea Transportation Service (MSTS)/MSC rather than under outright Navy ownership. She was operated by the MSTS/MSC in that status for almost two decades, until purchased outright in 1986.

She was assigned to the RRF on 30 October 1985.

The ship has 167,537 square feet (15,078 m²) of vehicle storage space, with four side ports and a stern ramp for rapid loading and unloading. She can offload some 750 vehicles in 27 hours. She is fitted with two 120-ton-capacity booms and 12 booms with a capacity of 5–10 tons.

She was laid down on 17 October 1967.

Engineering: The CALLAGHAN was the first all-gas-turbine ship constructed for the U.S. Navy. The original engines were two Pratt & Whitney FT-4 (rated at 25,000 shp each); they were replaced in 1977 by the widely used LM 2500.

Name: The ship is named for Admiral William M. Callaghan, first commander of the Military Sea Transportation Service (predecessor to the MSC), from 1949 to 1952. He retired from the MSTS and was employed by American Export lines, which built the ship, when she was named in his honor by the firm.

Status: The ship was taken out of service and transferred to RRF status on 31 May 1987, after almost 20 years of continuous MSC service. Transferred to MarAd on 25 June 1987 for layup, she subsequently returned to RRF status. The ship has the prefix GTS for Gas Turbine Ship.

The long-serving ADM WM. M. CALLAGHAN—*the first RO/RO ship acquired by the U.S. Navy—has cargo holds forward. Vehicles are loaded/unloaded through side ports, as well as by the stern ramp. (1985, Leo Van Ginderen)*

4 RO/RO CARGO SHIPS: C7-S-95a TYPE (SS)

Number	Name	Launched	To RRF	Status
T-AKR 10*	Cape Island (ex-Mercury, Illinois)	21 Dec 1976	22 Nov 1993	RRF (4)
T-AKR 11*	Cape Intrepid (ex-Jupiter, Lipscomb Lykes, Arizona)	1 Nov 1976	2 May 1986	RRF (4)
T-AKR 5062*	Cape Isabel (ex-Charles Lykes, Nevada)	15 May 1976	23 May 1986	RRF (5)
T-AKR 5076*	Cape Inscription (ex-Tyson Lykes, Maine)	24 May 1975	2 Sep 1987	RRF (5)

Builders:	Bath Iron Works, Maine
Displacement:	14,222 tons light
	33,765 tons full load
Tonnage:	13,156 GRT
	19,172 DWT
Length:	639⅝ feet (195.1 m) waterline
	684¾ feet (208.8 m) overall
Beam:	102 feet (31.1 m)
Draft:	32½ feet (9.8 m)
Propulsion:	2 steam turbines (General Electric); 37,000 shp; 2 shafts
Boilers:	2 (Babcock & Wilcox)
Speed:	24 knots
Range:	12,600 nm (23,335 km) at 23 knots
Personnel:	36 civilian, except 41 in T-AKR 10

These ships were built for commercial service by the Lykes Brothers Steamship Co. They are RO/RO vehicle carriers, with side ports and a stern ramp for rapidly loading and unloading vehicles. They also can carry containers and 728 tons of liquid cargo.

The Mercury and Jupiter were acquired by the Navy on long-term charter in 1980 for use as prepositioning ships in the Indian Ocean. Note that they were assigned standard Navy hull designations. They were placed in service on 3 June 1980 and 7 May 1980, respectively.

The Mercury was taken out of service and transferred to the NDRF on 30 April 1993, renamed Cape Island and assigned to the RRF on 22 November 1993, and subsequently placed in MSC service. The Jupiter was transferred to MarAd (Suisun Bay) on 23 April 1986, was assigned to the RRF on 2 May 1986, and was renamed in 1993.

Status: The Mercury and Jupiter previously were classified as U.S. Naval Ships.

The Cape Intrepid—shown here as the USNS Jupiter—carries a deckload of military containers; below are vehicle stowage decks. (U.S. Navy)

The Cape Island—long the USNS Mercury—and her sister ships have a small crane forward; the larger crane visible here is on the adjacent pier. (1990, Leo Van Ginderen)

2 RO/RO CARGO SHIPS: CANADIAN BUILT (MV)

Number	Name	Launched	To RRF	Status
T-AKR 5077*	CAPE LAMBERT (ex-FEDERAL LAKES, AVON FOREST)	1973	23 Oct 1987	RRF (10)
T-AKR 5078*	CAPE LOBOS (ex-FEDERAL SEAWAY, LAURENTIAN FOREST, GRAND ENCOUNTER)	1972	31 Mar 1988	RRF (10)

Builders:	Port Weller Dry Dock, St. Catherines, Ontario (Canada)
Displacement:	30,375 tons full load
Tonnage:	15,005 GRT
	20,545 DWT
Length:	621⅓ feet (189.4 m) waterline
	681⅚ feet (207.9 m) overall
Beam:	75⅙ feet (22.9 m)
Draft:	30½ feet (9.3 m)
Propulsion:	2 diesel engines (Crossley-Pielstick); 18,000 bhp; 2 shafts
Speed:	19 knots
Range:	6,000 nm (11,112 km) at 17.5 knots
Personnel:	27 civilian

These ships were built as newsprint and vehicle carriers. They have side doors with two vehicle ramps and 189,937 square feet (17,094 m²) of vehicle space. They are fitted with a bow thruster.

They are ice strengthened for operations on the Great Lakes and were purchased on 5 June 1987.

5 RO/RO CARGO SHIPS: FRENCH-SWEDISH BUILT (MV)

Number	Name	Launched	To RRF	Status
T-AKR 5051*	CAPE DUCATO (ex-BARRANDUNA)	1972	5 Dec 1985	RRF (4)
T-AKR 5052*	CAPE DOUGLAS (ex-LALANDIA)	1973	15 Nov 1985	RRF (4)
T-AKR 5053*	CAPE DOMINGO (ex-TARAGO)	1973	30 Oct 1985	RRF (4)
T-AKR 5054*	CAPE DECISION (ex-TOMBARRA)	1973	15 Oct 1985	RRF (4)
T-AKR 5055*	CAPE DIAMOND (ex-TRICOLOR)	1972	15 Oct 1985	RRF (4)

Builders:	T-AKR 5051, 5052, 5054: Eriksberg M/V, Lindholmen (Sweden)
	T-AKR 5053, 5055: Ch. de France, Dunkerque (France)
Displacement:	35,173 tons full load
Tonnage:	23,972–24,437 GRT
	21,299–21,398 DWT
Length:	633⅝ feet (193.24 m) waterline
	680¼ feet (207.4 m) overall
Beam:	97 feet (29.57 m)
Draft:	31½ feet (9.59 m)
Propulsion:	French built: 3 diesel engines (Ch. d'Atlantic-Pielstick); 28,890 bhp; 1 shaft
	Swedish built: 3 diesel engines (Lindholmen-Pielstick); 27,000 bhp; 1 shaft
Speed:	22 knots
Range:	26,000 nm (48,180 km) at 20.6 knots
Personnel:	27 civilian

These are combination cargo ships, able to carry heavy vehicles as well as 1,327 containers. They are fitted with bow and stern thrusters.

The CAPE LOBOS riding high in the water. (1999, Leo Van Ginderen)

The CAPE DECISION at Antwerp. Large numbers of ventilators are fitted on her deck to clear exhaust fumes from the ship's vehicle decks. (1993, Leo Van Ginderen)

Status: The CAPE DECISION and CAPE DOUGLAS were assigned to the Army's APS-4 on 30 September 1994. (Beyond Army combat equipment, the CAPE DOUGLAS carries a 300-bed field hospital.) They subsequently were assigned to the RRF.

1 CONTAINER—RO/RO CARGO SHIP: SWEDISH BUILT (MV)

Number	Name	Launched	To RRF	Status
T-AKR 5069	CAPE EDMONT (ex-PARALLA)	1971	10 Apr 1987	RRF (4)

Builders:	Eriksberg M/V, Lindholmen (Sweden)
Displacement:	approx. 32,000 tons full load
Tonnage:	13,355 GRT 20,224 DWT
Length:	602½ feet (183.7 m) waterline 652 11/12 feet (199.02 m) overall
Beam:	94⅙ feet (28.7 m)
Draft:	31½ feet (9.6 m)
Propulsion:	3 diesel engines (Eriksberg-Pielstick 18PC2V 400); 25,920 bhp; 1 shaft
Speed:	19 knots
Range:	17,000 nm (31,500 km) at 19 knots
Personnel:	32 civilian

The CAPE EDMONT is a combination container and RO/RO ship; 1,212 containers can be carried. She was assigned to the RRF on 10 April 1987. The ship has 118,325 square feet (10,649 m^2) of vehicle space and is fitted with bow thruster.

3 CONTAINER—RO/RO CARGO SHIPS: JAPANESE BUILT (MV)

Number	Name	Launched	To RRF	Status
T-AKR 9678*	CAPE RISE (ex-SAUDI RIYADH, SEASPEED ARABIA)	1977	15 Nov 1994	RRF (5)
T-AKR 9679	CAPE Ray (ex-SAUDI MAKKAH, SEASPEED ASIA)	1977	17 Dec 1994	RRF (4)
T-AKR 9960*	CAPE RACE (ex-STENA AMERICA, G and G ADMIRAL, SEASPEED AMERICA)	1977	11 Sep 1994	RRF (4)

Builders:	Kawasaki Heavy Industries, Sakaide (Japan)
Displacement:	32,054 tons
Tonnage:	14,825 GRT 22,735 DWT
Length:	591 feet (180.22 m) waterline 647⅚ feet (197.52 m) overall
Beam:	105⅚ feet (32.26 m)
Draft:	32⅚ feet (10.0 m)
Propulsion:	2 diesel engines (Kawasaki-MAN 14V 52/55A); 28,000 bhp; 1 shaft
Speed:	19.75 knots
Range:	
Personnel:	

These ships are combination vehicle and container carriers. The CAPE RISE was acquired on 9 August 1993, the CAPE RAY on 20 April 1993, and the CAPE RACE on 28 April 1993. They each can carry 1,315 containers and are fitted with bow and stern thrusters.

1 CONTAINER—RO/RO CARGO SHIP: SWEDISH BUILT (MV)

Number	Name	Launched	To RRF	Status
T-AKR 2044*	CAPE ORLANDO (ex-AMERICAN EAGLE, ZENIT EAGLE, FINNEAGLE)	1981	12 Sep 1994	RRF (4)

Builders:	Kockums AB, Mälmo (Sweden)
Displacement:	approx. 30,000 tons full load
Tonnage:	15,632 GRT
Length:	593 feet (180.8 m) waterline 635¼ feet (199.2 m) overall
Beam:	91⅚ feet (28.0 m)
Draft:	29½ feet (9.0 m)
Propulsion:	2 diesel engines (Cegielski-Sulzer 6RND68M); 21,500 bhp; 1 shaft
Speed:	22 knots
Range:	16,800 nm (31,130 km) at 19 knots
Personnel:	20 civilian

The CAPE ORLANDO was acquired for the RRF as the AMERICAN EAGLE; on charter since 22 August 1983, she was purchased by the MSC in December 1992.

Class: Two other ships of this type have been discarded by the MSC, the AMERICAN CONDOR and AMERICAN FALCON (no hull numbers assigned).

Design: This is a large ship, with her bridge forward and twin funnels aft. The CAPE ORLANDO can carry 1,040 containers or vehicles, with 116,669 square feet (10,500 m^2) of vehicle parking area. Vehicles are loaded/unloaded via stern ramps.

There are two bow thrusters.

Names: The CAPE ORLANDO originally was chartered as the AMERICAN EAGLE; she was renamed in 1993.

The CAPE ORLANDO—as the AMERICAN EAGLE—showing the separate superstructure blocks of this unusual RO/RO ship. There is an open vehicle/cargo deck amidships; twin funnels are fitted aft. (U.S. Navy)

The Cape Orlando *at rest. The ship earlier was chartered by the British Ministry of Defence, at which time she was renamed* American Eagle. *(1997, Leo Van Ginderen)*

2 CONTAINER—RO/RO CARGO SHIPS: ITALIAN BUILT (MV)

Number	Name	Launched	To RRF	Status
T-AKR 9666*	Cape Vincent (ex-Taabo Italia, Merzario Italia)	1984	19 Aug 1994	RRF (4)
T-AKR 9701*	Cape Victory (ex-Merzario Britannia)	1984	2 Sep 1994	RRF (4)

Builders:	Fincantieri, Genoa (Italy)
Displacement:	28,215 tons full load
Tonnage:	22,423 GRT
	21,439 DWT
Length:	566¾ feet (172.8 m) waterline
	631¾ feet (192.6 m) overall
Beam:	87 feet (26.55 m)
Draft:	27¾ feet (8.47 m)
Propulsion:	1 diesel engine (GMT-Sulzer 6RNB 66/140); 11,850 bhp; 1 shaft
Speed:	16 knots
Range:	21,000 nm (38,900 km) at 16 knots
Personnel:	25 civilian

The Cape Vincent was acquired for the RRF on 13 May 1993 and Cape Victory on 2 April 1993. The ships can carry 1,306 containers or vehicles, loaded/unloaded via a stern ramp.

They are fitted with bow thrusters.

The Cape Vincent *(left) and* Cape Victory *are the only Italian-built ships in U.S. naval service. They are the slowest nontanker ships in the MSC inventory. (U.S. Navy)*

3 RO/RO CARGO SHIPS: GERMAN/JAPANESE BUILT (MV)

Number	Name	Launched	To RRF	Status
T-AKR 112*	CAPE TEXAS (ex-LYRA, REICHENFELS)	1977	19 Aug 1944	RRF (5)
T-AKR 113*	CAPE TAYLOR (ex-THEKWINI, CYGNUS, RABENFELS)		27 July 1994	RRF (5)
T-AKR 9711*	CAPE TRINITY (ex-SANTOS, CANADIAN FOREST, RADBOD, NOREFJORD, RHEINFELS)		21 Nov 1994	RRF (4)

Builders:	T-AKR 112, 9711: Howaldtswerke, Kiel (Germany) T-AKR 113: Sasebo Heavy Industries (Japan)
Displacement:	T-AKR 112: 9,870 tons light T-AKR 112: 24,555 tons full load others 26,455 tons full load
Tonnage:	14,174 GRT 15,075 DWT
Length:	583⅚ feet (178.0 m) waterline 627⅚ feet (191.29 m) overall, except T-AKR 112: 634⅙ feet (193.33 m)
Beam:	89¼ feet (27.2 m)
Draft:	28⅙ feet (8.6 m)
Propulsion:	2 diesel engines (MAN 9L 52/55A heavy-oil); 18,980 bhp; 1 shaft
Speed:	20.5 knots
Range:	22,600 nm (41,880 km) at 16.5 knots
Personnel:	49 civilian

These large container—RO/RO ships were purchased in December 1992 and acquired in 1993. The CAPE TEXAS initially operated in MSC service as the USNS LYRA.

These ships can accommodate 340 containers, plus vehicles. Their hulls are ice strengthened.

The CAPE TEXAS has a conventional RO/RO ship appearance, with superstructure aft, side ports, and a stern ramp. This design has twin funnels aft. (1994, Giorgio Arra)

1 RO/RO CARGO SHIP: C4-ST-67a TYPE (SS)

Number	Name	Launched	Comm.	Status
T-AKR 9*	METEOR (ex-SEA LIFT)	17 Apr 1965	19 May 1967	RRF (10)

Builders:	Lockheed Shipbuilding and Construction, Seattle
Displacement:	9,154 tons light 21,480 tons full load
Tonnage:	16,467 GRT 12,326 DWT
Length:	4991/2 feet (152.28 m) waterline 540 feet (164.7 m) overall
Beam:	83⅔ feet (25.5 m)
Draft:	29 feet (8.8 m)
Propulsion:	2 steam turbines (De Laval); 19,400 shp; 2 shafts
Boilers:	2
Speed:	22 knots
Range:	10,000 nm (18,520) at 20 knots
Personnel:	56 civilian

The METEOR was built specifically as a RO/RO ship for naval service. She has four side ramps and a stern ramp and 87,735 square feet (7,896 m^2) of vehicle space.

She was assigned to the Rapid Deployment Force (RDF) in 1980–1981, then placed in the RRF on 15 March 1985.

The ships was authorized in the FY 1963 naval shipbuilding program and laid down on 19 May 1964.

Classification: Authorized as T-AK 278 but changed to T-LSV 9 while under construction, the ship was changed again to vehicle cargo ship T-AKR 9 on 14 August 1969.

The LSV 1–6 were World War II–built vehicle landing ships, all of which served under other designations. The TAURUS (LSV 8) was the former AK 273; she had been begun as the FORT SNELLING (LSD 23). Note that the later SL-7 conversions to rapid response ships have AK-series hull numbers with the prefix AKR type designation.

Design: The METEOR was one of the few ships to have both an SCB (No. 236) and a MarAd design designation.

Names: Her name was changed from SEA LIFT to METEOR on 12 September 1975 to avoid confusion with the Sealift-class tankers (T-AOT 168–176).

Status: The METEOR was a U.S. Naval Ship until transferred to the RRF in 1985, when her prefix was changed to SS.

1 RO/RO CARGO SHIP: C3-ST-14a TYPE (SS)

Number	Name	Launched	In service	Status
T-AKR 7	COMET	31 July 1957	24 Jan 1958	RRF (10)

Builders:	Sun Shipbuilding and Dry Dock, Chester, Pa.
Displacement:	8,175 tons light 18,286 tons full load
Tonnage:	13,792 GRT 10,111 DWT
Length:	465 feet (141.77 m) waterline 499 feet (152.2 m) overall
Beam:	78 feet (23.8 m)
Draft:	29⅙ feet (8.9 m)
Propulsion:	2 steam turbines (General Electric); 13,200 shp; 2 shafts
Boilers:	2 (Babcock & Wilcox)
Speed:	18 knots
Range:	12,000 nm (22,235 km) at 18 knots
Personnel:	44 civilian

The COMET, laid down on 15 May 1956, was built specifically for naval service. She can accommodate some 700 vehicles in her two after holds; the two forward holds are intended for general cargo. Vehicle space totals 83,613 square feet (7,525 m^2).

She was assigned to the RRF on 15 March 1985.

Classification: The COMET originally was classified T-AK 269; she was changed to vehicle cargo ship T-LSV 7 on 1 June 1963 and again to T-AKR 7 on 1 January 1969.

Status: The COMET was a U.S. Naval Ship prior to transfer to MarAd on 15 March 1985, when her prefix was changed to SS.

CARGO SHIP: C5-S-78a TYPE

The CAPE NOME (T-AK 1014), a combination break-bulk/vehicle/container ship was transferred from the RRF to NDRF on 1 July 2004. See 17th Edition/pages 276, 278 for characteristics.

1 CARGO SHIP: C4-S-1 TYPE (SS)

Number	Name	Launched	To RRF	Status
T-AK 5029	CAPE JACOB (ex-CALIFORNIA)	28 July 1961	1986	**LPS**

Builders:	Newport News Shipbuilding, Va.
Displacement:	22,629 tons
Tonnage:	12,691 GRT
	14,321 DWT
Length:	528⁵⁄₁₂ feet (161.1 m) waterline
	565 feet (172.25 m) overall

Beam:	76 feet (23.2 m)
Draft:	32 feet (9.75 m)
Propulsion:	2 steam turbines (General Electric); 17,500 shp; 1 shaft
Boilers:	2 (Foster Wheeler)
Speed:	20.75 knots
Range:	12,600 nm (23,335 km) at 20 knots
Personnel:	47 civilian

The CAPE JACOB is the sole survivor of several break-bulk cargo ships built for the States Steamship Co. and More-McCormack Lines that were acquired for MSC service. The CAPE JACOB is employed as a prepositioning ship carrying Navy munitions.

Class: The most recent disposals are three ships transferred from the RRF to NDRF on 1 July 2004: the CAPE JOHN (T-AK 5022), CAPE JOHNSON (T-AK 5075), and CAPE JUBY (T-AK 5077). The CAPE JOHN earlier was assigned to MPS Squadron 2.

Design: One 60-ton-capacity boom, ten 20-ton cranes, two 10-ton cranes, and ten 5-ton cranes are fitted.

Engineering: Normal horsepower is indicated in the data table; the maximum is 19,200 shp.

The venerable METEOR, a combination cargo–RO/RO ship. The ship has small, twin funnels abreast the bridge structure. (1999, Leo Van Ginderen)

The COMET is another early cargo–RO/RO ship. Her two portside vehicle ports are clearly visible here. (1982, Leo Van Ginderen)

The recently discarded CAPE JOHNSON. Only the CAPE JACOB of this class remains on the Naval Vessel Register, as break-bulk cargo ships have less utility in moving U.S. military cargoes. (2001, Leo Van Ginderen)

The CAPE GIRARDEAU in reduced operating status. She is a versatile ship, combining break bulk, container, and liquid cargo capabilities. (Leo Van Ginderen)

2 CARGO SHIPS: C5-S-75a TYPE (SS)

Number	Name	Launched	To RRF	Status
T-AK 2039	CAPE GIRARDEAU	1968	12 Apr 1988	RRF (5)
	(ex-PRESIDENT ADAMS, ALASKAN MAIL)			
T-AK 5051	CAPE GIBSON	1968	1 Apr 1988	**MPF**
	(ex-PRESIDENT JACKSON, INDIAN MAIL)			

Builders:	Newport News Shipbuilding, Va.
Displacement:	31,995 tons full load
Tonnage:	15,949 GRT
	T-AK 2039: 22,273 DWT
	T-AK 5051: 22,216 DWT
Length:	582⅓ feet (177.55 m) waterline
	604⅚ feet (184.4 m) overall
Beam:	82⅙ feet (25.05 m)
Draft:	35 feet (10.7 m)
Propulsion:	2 steam turbines (General Electric); 24,000 shp; 1 shaft
Boilers:	2 (Babcock & Wilcox)
Speed:	21 knots
Range:	14,000 n.miles (25,928 km) at 20.8 knots
Personnel:	47 civilian

These break-bulk cargo ships can carry 409 containers as well as dry and refrigerated cargo and 17,000 barrels of liquid cargo. Accommodations are provided for 22 passengers.

One 70-ton-capacity boom and 20 20-ton and four 15-ton cranes are fitted.

Class: The CLEVELAND (T-AK 851) has been discarded.

Operational: The CAPE GIBSON is part of the RRF but is activated for service with the MPF.

2 TRANSPORT OILERS: "CHESAPEAKE" CLASS (SS)

Number	Name	Launched	To RRF	Status
T-AOT 5084	CHESAPEAKE	1964	20 July 1991	LPS
	(ex-HESS VOYAGER)			
T-AOT 9101	PETERSBURG	1963	1 Aug 1991	LPS
	(ex-SINCLAIR TEXAS, CHARLES KURZ, KEYSTONE)			

Builders:	Bethlehem Steel, Sparrows Point, Baltimore, Md.
Displacement:	approx. 65,000 tons full load
Tonnage:	T-AOT 5084: 27,015 GRT
	50,826 DWT
	T-AOT 9101: 27,469 GRT
	50,072 DWT
Length:	704⅚ feet (214.9 m) waterline
	736⅙ feet (224.4 m) overall
Beam:	102⅚ feet (31.2 m)
Draft:	39¾ feet (12.1 m)
Propulsion:	2 steam turbines (Bethlehem); 15,000 shp; 1 shaft
Boilers:	2
Speed:	15 knots
Range:	
Personnel:	38 civilian in T-AOT 9101

These are large merchant tankers, prepositioned overseas with fuels.

The PETERSBURG is fitted with the Offshore Petroleum Discharge System (OPDS) to transfer fuel ashore without pier facilities; both ships are fitted with a 4-mile (6.5-km) flexible floating pipeline.

Operational: These large tankers are part of the RRF, but currently are activated for duty with the Prepositioning Program. In the MPS role, they carry LCM(6) landing craft redesignated as utility boats (56UB series).

The tanker CHESAPEAKE with an Offshore Petroleum Discharge System (OPDS) loaded on her main deck, including a work barge. (U.S. Navy)

1 TRANSPORT OILER: "MOUNT WASHINGTON" (SS)

Number	Name	Launched	To RRF	Status
T-AOT 5076	MOUNT WASHINGTON	1963	30 Oct 1989	RRF (5)

Builders:	Bethlehem Steel, Sparrows Point, Baltimore, Md.
Displacement:	approx. 65,800 tons full load
Tonnage:	27,412 GRT
	47,751 DWT
Length:	706⅚ feet (215.5 m) waterline
	736⅙ feet (224.4 m) overall
Beam:	102⅚ feet (31.2 m)
Draft:	40¼ feet (12.3 m)
Propulsion:	2 steam turbines (Bethlehem); 21,500 shp; 1 shaft
Boilers:	2 (Foster Wheeler)
Speed:	17.5 knots
Range:	
Personnel:	

This is a large commercial tanker, similar to the CHESAPEAKE and PETERSBURG (see above), but with more powerful turbines. The ship is fitted with OPDS.

Status: The MOUNT VERNON (T-AOT 3009) of this design was discarded in 1994.

The tanker MOUNT WASHINGTON, ballasted down for unloading an OPDS during an exercise. She has a crane aft of the bridge structure to facilitate unloading. (2004, U.S. Navy)

The tanker MOUNT WASHINGTON, empty of cargo, at San Francisco. She has an OPDS on her deck. (2003, W. Michael Young)

TRANSPORT OILERS: FALCON CLASS

All four tankers of this class have been discarded. Three were returned to their owners in 1983–1984 after MSC service: the NECHES (T-AOT 183), HUDSON (T-AOT 184), and SUSQUEHANNA (T-AOT 185). The fourth ship acquired by MSC, the MISSION CAPISTRANO (T-AOT 5005), was transferred from RRF status to NDRF on 1 July 2004.

The MISSION CAPISTRANO was designated T-AO 182 on being chartered by the MSC; changed to T-AOT in 1979. She should not be confused with the earlier MISSION CAPISTRANO (AO 112), a World War II–built T2-SE-A2 fleet oiler, later employed as a Sound Surveillance System (SOSUS) test ship (AG 162).

See 17th Edition/page 313 for characteristics.

TRANSPORT OILER: "MISSION BUENAVENTURA"

The large tanker MISSION BUENAVENTURA (T-AOT 1012) was transferred from the RRF to NDRF on 1 July 2004. Only one ship of this type was acquired by the Navy.

See 17th Edition/page 313 for characteristics.

1 TRANSPORT OILER: "POTOMAC" (SS)

Number	Name	Launched	In service	Status
T-AOT 181	POTOMAC	(see notes)	12 Jan 1976	RRF

Builders:	Sun Shipbuilding and Dry Dock, Chester, Pa.
Displacement:	7,333 tons light
	34,800 tons full load
Tonnage:	15,739 GRT
	27,908 DWT
Length:	591⅙ feet (180.2 m) waterline
	619⅚ feet (189.0 m) overall
Beam:	83½ feet (25.5 m)
Draft:	33 7/12 feet (10.2 m)
Propulsion:	1 steam turbine (Westinghouse); 20,460 shp; 1 shaft
Boilers:	2 (Combustion Engineering)
Speed:	18.5 knots
Range:	18,000 nm (33,335 km) at 18 knots
Personnel:	37 civilian

The POTOMAC was constructed with the mid-body and bow sections built to mate with the stern section of an earlier tanker named

POTOMAC (T-AO 150). The "new" tanker was named SHENANDOAH and operated under commercial charter to the MSC for several years, until she was purchased on 12 January 1976. At that time, the ship was renamed POTOMAC and designated T-AO 181; her designation was changed to T-AOT 181 on 30 September 1978.

The ship was contractor operated by the MSC with a civilian crew. She was taken out of service on 26 September 1983, placed in the RRF on 5 March 1984, and subsequently was assigned to the MPF but again placed in the RRF.

(The original POTOMAC was launched on 8 October 1956; she was partially destroyed by fire on 3 October 1961, but the stern section and machinery were relatively intact. She was built as a T5-S-12a type.)

The ship's cargo capacity is 200,000 barrels, and she is fitted with OPDS (see entry for PETERSBURG/T-AOT 9101).

Class: Three other tankers of the original POTOMAC design have been discarded: the MAUMEE (T-AOT 149), SHOSHONE (T-AOT 151), and YUKON (T-AOT 152).

Status: The POTOMAC was a U.S. Naval Ship (USNS) prior to transfer to RRF, when her prefix was changed to SS.

1 GASOLINE TANKER: "TONTI" CLASS (T1-M-BT2)(MV)

Number	Name	Launched	To RRF	Status
T-AOG 78	NODAWAY (ex-BELRIDGE)	15 May 1945	30 Sep 1985	RRF (10)

Builders:	Todd Shipyards, Houston, Texas
Displacement:	2,060 tons light
	6,060 tons full load
Tonnage:	4,000 DWT
Length:	309 feet (94.21 m) waterline
	325⅙ feet (99.2 m) overall
Beam:	48⅙ feet (14.7 m)
Draft:	19 feet (5.8 m)
Propulsion:	2 diesels (Nordberg); 1,400 bhp; 1 shaft
Speed:	10 knots
Range:	5,500 nm (10,186 km) at 10 knots
Personnel:	45 civilian

The NODAWAY is the lone survivor of the large number of small gasoline tankers built during World War II for naval and merchant service. The ship originally was placed in MSTS service on 7 September 1950. She was taken out of naval service on 22 July 1984 and assigned to the RRF on 30 September 1985. She then was transferred to the NDRF on 7 October 1994, but was reacquired for RRF service on 1 October 1995. She is berthed at Tsuneishi, Japan.

Class: Five ships of this design were built as merchant tankers;

The POTOMAC, *her fuel tanks empty, riding high in the water. The OPDS is visible on her deck. The ship has a bridge-aft configuration. (1996, Leo Van Ginderen)*

The NODAWAY *is one of three gasoline tankers retained in U.S. naval service. During World War II, these AOGs transported aviation fuel for seaplane tenders, torpedo boat tenders, and shore bases. (U.S. Navy)*

all were acquired by the Navy in 1950 and assigned to the MSTS, later the Military Sealift Command, as the T-AOG 76–80. The AOG 64–75 were similar (T1-M-BT1 design); those were the last gasoline tankers in the Navy's World War II program.

Classification: The MSC on occasion lists these ships as standard tankers (T-AOT); however, they are carried on the Naval Vessel Register as T-AOG so that is their official designation.

Design: The AOG type was developed during World War II to carry gasoline and aviation fuels for aircraft, motor torpedo boats, and other special craft.

2 GASOLINE TANKERS: "ALATNA" CLASS (T1-MET-24a) (MV)

Number	Name	Launched	In Service	Status
T-AOG 81	ALATNA	16 Sep 1956	17 July 1957	RRF (10)
T-AOG 82	CHATTAHOOCHEE	4 Dec 1956	22 Oct 1957	RRF (10)

Builders:	Bethlehem Steel, Staten Island, N.Y.
Displacement:	2,367 tons light
	7,300 tons full load
Tonnage:	4,933 DWT
Length:	290 feet (88.41 m) waterline
	302 feet (92.1 m) overall
Beam:	61 feet (18.6 m)
Draft:	19 feet (5.8 m)
Propulsion:	diesel-electric (4 Alco diesels; Westinghouse electric motors); 4,000 shp; 2 shafts
Speed:	13 knots
Range:	5,760 nm (10,670 km) at 10 knots
Personnel:	24 civilian

This two-ship class was built specifically for the support of U.S. military activities in the Arctic. Both ships were operated by the MSTS from their completion until taken out of service on 8 August 1972 and laid up in the NDRF. The ships were reacquired by the Navy on 10 May 1979 and 24 May 1979, respectively, and reactivated for MSC service to replace older AOGs. The ALATNA was placed in MSC service on 3 February 1983 and the CHATTAHOOCHEE on 11 January 1982; they were assigned to the RRF on 30 September 1985.

They again were taken out of service on 25 January 1985 and placed in the MSC Ready Reserve Force in April 1985 and January 1985, respectively (berthed at Tsuneishi, Japan). Both ships were transferred from the RRF to the NDRF on 7 October 1994. They were reacquired for the RRF on 1 October 1995, remaining in Japan.

Design: These ships have ice-strengthened hulls and icebreaking prows and other features for Arctic operation (similar to the ELTANIN/T-AK 270 class). Their cargo capacity is 30,000 barrels of petroleum products plus some 2,700 tons of dry cargo. A small helicopter platform was fitted aft in their original configuration.

The long-serving gasoline tankers ALATNA *(left) and* CHATTAHOOCHEE *are laid up in Tsuneishi, Japan. They were built for Arctic operations, to support U.S. radar stations in remote areas. (U.S. Navy)*

MERCHANT MARINE ACADEMY TRAINING SHIPS

Several merchant marine academy training ships remain the property of the U.S. government and some are carried on MSC roles. In theory all are available for recall to government service in a national emergency.

The former sonar ship CONTENDER (T-AGOS 2) serves as a training ship for the U.S. Merchant Marine Academy at Kings Point, New York; she is named KING'S POINTER. The following ships are operated by state merchant and regional marine academies; all are former Navy ships except the EMPIRE STATE VI (she is the ex-OREGON, ex-MORMACTIDE).

Former		Institution	New Name
T-AGOS 6	PERSISTENT	Great Lakes	STATE OF MICHIGAN
T-AGS 29	CHAUVENET	Texas	TEXAS CLIPPER II
T-AGS 39	MAURY	California	GOLDEN BEAR
T-AGS 40	TANNER	Maine	STATE of MAINE
(none)	OREGON, MORMACTIDE	New York	EMPIRE STATE VI
T-AK 5059	CAPE BON	Massachusetts	ENTERPRISE

The ocean surveillance ship PERSISTENT was taken out of Navy/MSC service and transferred to the NDRF on 1 May 2001; she was transferred to the Great Lakes Maritime Academy on 1 August 2002. She is based at Traverse City, Michigan.

The INVINCIBLE, which served briefly as a missile range instrumentation ship, was transferred to the Southern Maine Technical College in South Port, Maine, as a school ship.

The EMPIRE STATE VI is carried on the Naval Vessel Register as the AP 1001 for accounting purposes; she and the ex-CAPE BON are the only state training ships on the list. She replaced the former USNS BARRETT (T-AP 196).

The CAPE BON was discarded by the Navy on 1 October 2000 and was changed to T-AP 1003 for accounting purposes while in service with the Massachusetts Maritime Academy for use as a training ship. She was placed in service on 22 May 2002, replacing the PATRIOT STATE II (Navy T-AP 1000).

The California state training ship GOLDEN BEAR. (2000, George Schneider)

The Maine state training ship STATE OF MAINE. (1999, Leo Van Ginderen)

The Massachusetts state training ship ENTERPRISE as the CAPE BON, prior to conversion. (1991, Peter Voss)

The New York state training ship EMPIRE STATE VI. (2000, Alexander George)

Table 24-1. MSC SHIPS DISCARDED SINCE 1 JANUARY 1995

Number	Name	Type	Discarded	Notes
(none)	AMERICAN CONDOR	RO/RO		
(none)	AMERICAN FALCON	RO/RO		
(none)	MARGARET B. CHOUEST	container		
T-ACS 4	GOPHER STATE	C5-S-MA73c		
T-AK 284	NORTHERN LIGHT	C3-S-33a		
T-AK 851	CLEVELAND	C5-S-75a		
T-AK 1005	AUSTRAL RAINBOW	C8-S-81b	Feb 2000	
T-AK 1014	CAPE NOME	C5-S-78a	1 July 2004	to NDRF
T-AK 2016	PIONEER COMMANDER	C4-S-57a	1 Oct 2000	
T-AK 2018	PIONEER CONTRACTOR	C4-S-57a	1 Oct 2000	
T-AK 2036	GULF TRADER	C3-S-37d		
T-AK 2049	GREEN VALLEY	C9-S-81d	2001	
T-AK 2050	GREEN WAVE	container	Mar 2003	
T-AK 2062	AMERICAN CORMORANT	FLO/FLO*	Sep 2002	
T-AK 2064	GREEN HARBOUR	C8-S-81b	2001	
T-AK 5008	BANNER	C3-S-46a	1 Oct 2000	
T-AK 5009	CAPE ANN	C4-S-58a	19 Dec 2002	to NDRF
T-AK 5010	CAPE ALEXANDER	C4-S-58a	31 Mar 2003	to NDRF
T-AK 5011	CAPE ARCHWAY	C4-S-58a	19 Dec 2002	to NDRF
T-AK 5012	CAPE ALAVA	C4-S-58a	1 Oct 2000	
T-AK 5013	CAPE AVINOF	C4-S-58a	31 Mar 2003	to NDRF
T-AK 5016	LAKE	C3-S-33a	1 Oct 2000	
T-AK 5018	SCAN	C3-S-33a	1 Oct 2000	
T-AK 5019	COURIER	C3-S-46a	1 Oct 2000	
T-AK 5036	CAPE CHALMERS	C3-S-37c	1 Oct 2000	to NDRF
T-AK 5039	CAPE CLEAR	C3-S-37c	4 Dec 1996	to NDRF
T-AK 5041	CAPE COD	C3-S-37c	1 Oct 2000	to NDRF
T-AK 5042	CAPE CARTHAGE	C3-S-37c	7 May 1998	to NDRF
T-AK 5044	GULF BANKER	C3-S-37d	1 Oct 2000	
T-AK 5045	GULF FARMER	C3-S-37d		
T-AK 5056	CAPE BRETON	C4-S-66a	19 Dec 2002	to NDRF
T-AK 5057	CAPE BOVER	C4-S-66a	28 Apr 2003	to NDRF
T-AK 5058	CAPE BORDA	C4-S-66a	28 Apr 2003	to NDRF
T-AK 5059	CAPE BON	C4-S-66a	1 Oct 2000	(see notes)
T-AK 5060	CAPE BLANCO	C4-S-66a	19 Dec 2002	to NDRF
T-AK 5064	CAPE MENDOCINO	C8-S-82a	1 July 2004	to NDRF
T-AK 5074	CAPE CATAWBA	C3-S-33a	1 Oct 2000	
T-AK 5075	CAPE JOHNSON	C4-S-1	1 July 2004	to NDRF
T-AK 5076	NOBLE STAR	cargo		
T-AK 5077	CAPE JUBY	C4-S-1	1 July 2004	to NDRF
T-AK 9204	JEB STUART	LASH	2001	
T-AK 9205	STRONG VIRGINIAN	FLO/FLO	Aug 2002	
T-AK 9302	BUFFALO SOLDIER	RO/RO	July 2001	
T-AK 9652	ADVANTAGE	cargo		
T-AK 9655	GREEN RIDGE	container	13 Aug 2001	
T-AKR 2053	MAERSK CONSTELLATION	cargo		
T-AKR 9670	STRONG TEXAN	RO/RO		
T-AKR 9718	LT COL CALVIN P. TITUS	RO/RO		
T-AKR 9966	SP5 ERIC G. GIBSON	RO/RO		
T-AOT 75	SAUGATUCK	T2-SE-A1	15 Feb 1995	(stricken)
T-AOT 94A	VALIANT	tanker		
T-AOT 168	SEALIFT PACIFIC	Sealift	15 Feb 1995	
T-AOT 169	SEALIFT ARABIAN SEA	Sealift	2 Mar 1995	
T-AOT 170	SEALIFT CHINA SEA	Sealift	18 Apr 1995	
T-AOT 171	SEALIFT INDIAN OCEAN	Sealift	2 May 1995	
T-AOT 172	SEALIFT ATLANTIC	Sealift	4 Apr 1995	
T-AOT 173	SEALIFT MEDITERRANEAN	Sealift	18 Apr 1995	
T-AOT 174	SEALIFT CARIBBEAN	Sealift	4 Apr 1995	
T-AOT 175	SEALIFT ARCTIC	Sealift	4 Apr 1995	
T-AOT 176	SEALIFT ANTARCTIC	Sealift	4 Apr 1995	
T-AOT 183	NECHES	Falcon		
T-AOT 184	HUDSON	Falcon		
T-AOT 185	SUSQUEHANNA	Falcon		
T-AOT 1001	PATRIOT	T6-M-98a		
T-AOT 1002	RANGER	T6-M-98a		
T-AOT 1006	ROVER	T6-M-98a		
T-AOT 1007	COURIER	T6-M-98a		
T-AOT 1201	ALLEGIANCE	tanker		
(none)	OMI CHAMPION	Overseas		
T-AOT 1012	MISSION BUENAVENTURA	tanker	1 July 2004	to NDRF
T-AOT 1203	OVERSEAS ALICE	Overseas		
T-AOT 1204	OVERSEAS VALDEZ	Overseas		
T-AOT 1205	OVERSEAS VIVIAN	Overseas		
T-AOT 5005	MISSION CAPISTRANO	Falcon	1 July 2004	to NDRF
T-AOT 5075	AMERICAN OSPREY	tanker	1 Apr 2000	to NDRF

*FLO/FLO = Float-On/Float-Off

Numerous older ships, mostly in RRF status, have been discarded or transferred to the NDRF as new prepositioning and sealift ships have become available.

The nine Sealift-class tankers (T-AOT 168–176) were built for naval service and were contractor operated under "bare-boat" charter for the MSC with civilian crews for a 20-year period. All were returned to their owners in 1995; by that time their condition was marginal for safe and efficient service. (Their designations were changed from T-AO to T-AOT on 30 September 1978.)

The SAUGATUCK (T-AOT 75), the last of the T2 fleet oilers operated by the Navy in World War II, was laid up in the NDRF on 5 November 1974. She was changed from T-AO to T-AOT on 30 September 1978 (while laid up).

The MISSION SANTA YNEZ (T-AOT 134) was the last survivor retained in reserve of the Mission series of merchant tankers built late in World War II and acquired by the Navy after the war. She was laid up in the NDRF on 6 March 1975 (and changed to from T-AO to T-AOT on 30 September 1978). She was stricken on 1 November 1990. The Mission class encompassed AO 111–137.

The two Float-On/Float-Off (FLO/FLO) ships previously operated by the MSC have been discarded. Those ships could be ballasted down to permit small ships and craft to be floated on and off. Foreign-flag ships now are used in this role and have been employed to bring back to the United States the damaged destroyer COLE (DDG 67) and frigate SAMUEL B. ROBERTS (FFG 58) and to transport minesweepers and Coast Guard cutters.

CHAPTER 25

Service Ships and Craft

A friendly nudge: The yard tug OPELIKA assists the command ship BLUE RIDGE (LCC 19) to her berth in Yokosuka, Japan. The number of harbor tugs in Navy service is declining precipitously, with civilian tugs taking their places at naval bases. (2004 U.S. Navy/Alan Warner)

The U.S. Navy operates a couple hundred service craft, both self-propelled and non-self-propelled, as well as a number of unclassified ships and craft (designated IX), test ships, and several operational support ships leased by the Military Sealift Command (MSC). This conglomeration of ships and craft is described in this chapter.

Two major test platforms are arbitrarily listed at the beginning of this chapter, the self-defense test ship PAUL F. FOSTER and the signature-reduction (stealth) research ship SEA SHADOW. They are followed by the large submarine support ships leased by the MSC and a similarly operated ocean surveillance ship.

Next are the Navy's miscellaneous unclassified ships (IX). They were classified as auxiliary ships until 23 September 1970, when they were reclassified as service craft. Although the relic CONSTITUTION has dropped her designation IX 21, she is included in sequential position for historical reasons. (The sailing corvette CONSTELLATION, formerly IX 20, is not listed in this volume. She is not owned by the U.S. government; see CONSTITUTION entry.)

These ships are followed by the traditional service craft, most designated in the Y-series (having once been considered yard craft). Only the self-propelled service craft are described below, with a few exceptions—all IX-series ships are provided to present a complete listing. The non-self-propelled units are indicated by *(NSP)*.

The Navy's manned submersibles and floating dry docks, officially classified as service craft, are listed in Chapters 12 and 26, respectively.

Classification: Most service craft have Y-series designations; some have hull registry numbers (length + type designation + serial); a few have both. For example, the TWR 821 has the hull registry number 120TR821.

Only Y-series service craft are listed in the Naval Vessel Register (NVR). All service craft are found in the Service Craft and Boat Accounting Report (SABAR).

Guns: Service craft are not armed. The Naval Academy's seamanship training craft (YP) can be armed with light weapons for use as harbor patrol craft, and some of the utility cargo carriers (YFU) and barracks ships (APB) were armed for service in the Vietnam War. The surface effects ship SES-200/IX 515 has carried out trials with a number of weapons.

Helicopters: The test ship PAUL F. FOSTER, the high-speed vessel JOINT VENTURE, the Small Waterplane Area Twin Hull (SWATH) research ships KAIMALINO and X-craft, and the "mini-carrier" BAY LANDER are the only service craft with a helicopter capability.

Operational: Most Y-series service craft are manned by Navy personnel. Those assigned to the Naval Space and Warfare Command (SPAWAR) Systems Center at San Diego, California, and a few other service craft are operated by civilian personnel.

SPECIAL TEST SHIPS

1 SELF-DEFENSE TEST SHIP: "SPRUANCE" CLASS

Number	Name	FY	Launched	Comm.	Decomm.	Status
DD 964	PAUL F. FOSTER	70	23 Feb 1974	21 Feb 1975	29 March 2003	Yard

The PAUL F. FOSTER was one of 31 Anti-Submarine Warfare (ASW) destroyers of the SPRUANCE (DD 963) class completed from 1975 to 1983 (see Chapter 15 for details and class notes). The FOSTER was sailed to Port Hueneme, California, site of the Naval Surface Warfare Center, which will operate the ship in the self-defense test ship role, arriving on 27 March 2003 and decommissioning two days later. She was stricken on 6 April 2004.

This ship is undergoing extensive modification prior to entering service as a test ship, which is planned for 2005. Like her predecessor, the ex-USS DECATUR, the FOSTER will present a "non-impact" target for incoming cruise missiles as the ship tests and evaluates missile defense systems. An impact target barge will be towed behind the ship. For tests with attacking missiles, the ship's crew is removed (by helicopter), and the ship operates under radio/remote control.

Classification: Some documents refer to the FOSTER in her test role as EDD 964; however, because the ship has been stricken, she cannot officially be redesignated. The DECATUR also was referred to (improperly) as EDD 31; at times, she had E-41 painted on her bow.

SELF-DEFENSE TEST SHIP: EX-"FORREST SHERMAN" CLASS

Number	Name	FY	Launched	Comm.	Status
(ex-DDG 31, DD 936)	DECATUR	54	15 Dec 1955	7 Dec 1956	Discarded

The former destroyer DECATUR served as a test ship for self-defense systems, both active and passive, from October 1994 until September 2003. In that role, she operated both manned and under radio control.

Originally completed as one of 18 all-gun destroyers of the FORREST SHERMAN (DD 931) class, the DECATUR was one of four ships converted to a guided missile configuration in 1965–1967. She was decommissioned on 30 June 1983 and stricken on 16 March 1988.

The DECATUR subsequently was converted to a test platform in 1989–1994 at the Puget Sound Naval Shipyard and at the Naval Surface Weapons Center at Port Hueneme, California. Her masts and superstructure were extensively modified, a helicopter plat-

The PAUL F. FOSTER at sea shortly before being decommissioned and stricken. She is being converted to a self-defense test ship to help develop defensive weapons and electronics for countering hostile missile attacks. As a test ship, she will retain several of her destroyer systems. (U.S. Navy/William H. Ramsey)

form was fitted aft, and an outboard drive system was installed. All original guns, torpedo tubes, and ASW weapons were deleted in favor of the latest available self-defense sensors, countermeasures, and weapons.

Classification: Originally DD 936, the DECATUR was changed to DDG 31 on 15 September 1966. The NVR lists the ship's designation as having been changed to EDDG 31 in 1996, the prefix *E* indicating experimental.

The ex-destroyer DECATUR showing the ship's configuration as a self-defense systems test ship. She has a NATO Sea Sparrow launcher amidships and a Phalanx Close-In Weapon System (CIWS) atop her after deckhouse, and a helicopter deck on her fantail plus several systems installed for her test role. (U.S. Navy)

1 CATAMARAN RESEARCH CRAFT: X-CRAFT

Number	Name	Launch	In service	Status
—	SEA FIGHTER	Feb 2005	2005	Building

Builders:	Nichols Bros. Boat Builders, Freeland (Whidbey Island), Wash.
Displacement:	
Length:	265 feet (80.97 m) overall
Beam:	73 feet (22.26 m)
Draft:	
Propulsion:	CODOG: 2 gas turbines (General Electric LM 2500); 67,200 shp + 2 diesel engines (MTU 16V595); 4 waterjets
Speed:	50 knots (sea state 4)
Range:	4,000 nm (7,400 km) at 20 knots
Personnel:	16 + 10 Coast Guard
Helicopters:	landing area

The X-craft—tentatively named SEA FIGHTER when this edition of *Ships and Aircraft* when to press—is being built to test concepts of mission modules, hull design, mechanical and electrical systems, tactics, techniques, and procedures for small, high-speed combat craft.

The craft was built because of congressional pressure on the Navy. The contract was with Titan Corp, which engaged Nicholas Brothers to construct the craft.

Th X-craft was laid down on 5 June 2003.

Design: The X-craft has a catamaran design and bears some resemblance to the earlier SEA SHADOW (see below). The main deck had landing spots for two H-60 series helicopters.

No armament initially will be fitted.

1 STEALTH RESEARCH SHIP: "SEA SHADOW"

Number	Name	In service	Status
IX 529	SEA SHADOW	1985	**Active**

Builders:	Lockheed Missiles and Space Co., Sunnyvale, Calif.
Displacement:	499 tons light 563 tons full load
Length:	118½ feet (36.0 m) waterline 164 feet (50.0 m) overall
Beam:	58 feet (17.68 m) waterline
Width:	68 feet (20.73 m) maximum
Draft:	14 feet (4.27 m)
Propulsion:	diesel-electric (2 General Motors diesel engines 12V149 TI); 1,600 shp; 2 shafts
Speed:	13 knots sustained 15 knots maximum
Range:	2,250 nm (4,170 km) at 9 knots
Personnel:	12 Navy and civilian + 12 technicians (see *Design* notes)

The SEA SHADOW was built as a test platform for several surface ship technologies, among them ship control, automation, structures, seakeeping, and—especially—signature reduction. The program was sponsored by the Navy, the Advanced Research Projects Agency (ARPA), and Lockheed.[1] Results of the signature reduction research have been used in the ARLEIGH BURKE (DDG 51) class and SWATH-configured ocean surveillance ships (T-AGOS 19–23). The SEA SHADOW was not intended as a prototype for a stealth warship.

Builders: The craft was designed and built by the Lockheed "Skunk Works," which developed the U-2 spy plane, SR-71 Blackhawk, and F-117A stealth fighter, among other projects. Construction began in 1983 inside the floating dock HMB-1.[2]

Classification: The SEA SHADOW was classified as IX 529 on 15 March 2000.

Cost: The Navy states the cost of the SEA SHADOW program as $195 million, including ship construction costs of $50 million.

Design: The SEA SHADOW has a SWATH configuration with twin submerged hulls. The diesel engines are fitted in the "fuselage" and the electric motors in the hulls.

The X-craft sponsored by the Office of Naval Research—unofficially named SEA FIGHTER—has been justified, in part, as a design for the Navy's Littoral Combat Ship (LCS). This model shows a combination Phalanx CIWS and Rolling Airframe Missile (RAM) launcher atop the control cockpit. (Nichols Bros. Boat Builders)

The SEA SHADOW entering the support platform HMB-1. The island structure of the carrier JOHN C. STENNIS (CVN 74) is off to starboard. The hull, island structure, and innumerable antennas of a modern aircraft carrier provide a massive radar cross section. (1993, U.S. Navy)

---

1 Subsequently renamed Defense Advanced Projects Agency (DARPA).
2 HMB-1 = Hughes Mining Barge. This dock was developed for use with the deep-ocean salvage ship GLOMAR EXPLORER (AG 193); see page 251. The HMB-1 is 5,800 tons full load with a length of 323¹¹⁄₂ feet (98.75 m), beam of 105 feet (32.0 m), and draft of 8 feet (2.44 m); when ballasted down to receive the SEA SHADOW, draft is increased to 42 feet (12.8 m).

The SEA SHADOW inside her support platform, HMB-1. The platform partially submerges for the stealth craft to enter or depart; it then can be pumped out to raise itself and the SEA SHADOW out of the water to provide access to the lower areas of the craft. (Lockheed Martin)

The angled fuselage and supports for the twin submerged hulls help deflect radar signals. Anechoic coatings have been used on the craft to further deter the reflection of radar waves.

A small, retractable radar is fitted atop the control station. There are no fixed projections from the hull.

Berthing is provided for 12.

Operational: The SEA SHADOW conducted exclusively nighttime test runs off the coast of Southern California in 1985–1986, after which funding shortages led the craft to be laid up. She then was stored in covered floating dock HMB-1 at Redwood City in the San Francisco Bay area.

At-sea testing was resumed in April 1993 off Santa Cruz Island and, subsequently, in San Francisco Bay, until she again was laid up in the HMB-1 in May 1995. The first daylight test run of the SEA SHADOW—with publicity—was made on 11 April 1993.

The ship was reactivated in February 1999 to test signature-reduction concepts for the DD 21 and subsequent DD(X) programs.[3]

---

3 See David Abel, "Navy Stealthy about Details of 'Sea Shadow' Ship," *Defense Week* (2 August 1999), p. 7.

The stealth test craft SEA SHADOW prepares to moor alongside the Embarcadero waterfront park at San Diego, California, for public tours. The craft was reactivated in 1999 to continue research into ship design and signature-reduction technologies. Her forward and after hatches are open and her radar "pot" is raised. (2004, U.S. Navy/Sheldon Archie)

The SEA SHADOW's support platform—and hangar—is the HMB-1, originally built to support the recovery of a Soviet missile submarine by the GLOMAR EXPLORER (AG 193). The designation HMB indicated Hughes Mining Barge, part of the cover for the GLOMAR EXPLORER as a seafloor mining operation by Howard Hughes. (1999, Leo Van Ginderen)

SUBMARINE/SUBMERSIBLE/DIVER SUPPORT VESSELS

The Military Sealift Command operates four submarine/submersible support vessels under charter. These ships are owned by Edison Chouest Offshore of Galliano, Louisiana. They differ in size and configuration, and have highly specialized facilities. Three carry the name CHOUEST, the fourth is the C COMMANDO. These ships do not have Navy classifications; they are prefixed MV for motor vessel (i.e., diesel propulsion).

The LANEY CHOUEST, 2,700 tons full load, no longer is under Navy charter; she supported the DSV 3 and DSV 4. (See 17th Edition/page 338 for characteristics.)

In addition, the Navy operates three converted LCUs as diver/submersible support craft.

1 SUBMERSIBLE SUPPORT SHIP: "C COMMANDO"

Number	Name	In service	Status
(none)	C COMMANDO	1997	**Active**

Builders:	North American Shipbuilding, Larose, La.
Displacement:	2,089 tons full load
Length:	220 feet (67.07 m) overall
Beam:	56 feet (17.07 m)
Draft:	16½ feet (5.03 m)
Propulsion:	2 diesel engines (Caterpillar 3516); 3,420 bhp; 2 shafts (Ulstein Z-drive)
Speed:	11 knots
Personnel:	9 civilian + 34 Navy and technical

This former oil field support ship supports Navy SEAL training with Swimmer Delivery Vehicles (SDVs), as well as with the Advanced SEAL Delivery System (ASDS).

The C COMMANDO is based at Pearl Harbor, Hawaii.

1 SUBMERSIBLE SUPPORT SHIP: "CAROLYN CHOUEST"

Number	Name	In service	Status
(none)	CAROLYN CHOUEST	1994	**Active**

Builders:	North American Shipbuilding, Larose, La.
Displacement:	1,599 tons full load
Length:	238 feet (72.56 m) overall
Beam:	50 feet (15.2 m)
Draft:	17 feet (5.18 m)
Propulsion:	2 diesel engines (Caterpillar D339TA); 2,440 bhp; 2 shafts
Speed:	12 knots
Personnel:	13 civilian + 40 Navy and technical

This former oil field support craft was chartered by the Navy to support the nuclear-propelled submersible NR-1. The CAROLYN CHOUEST provides berthing for NR-1 support personnel, as well as services for the submersible, and undertakes surface towing the submersible.

She is based at Groton, Connecticut.

The submersible NR-1 alongside the support ship CAROLYN CHOUEST. She is one of five support ships operated by the Chouest firm in support of Navy activities. (1999, Leo Van Ginderen)

The CAROLYN CHOUEST, support ship for the nuclear-propelled submersible NR-1, off key Largo, Florida. (1995, U.S. Navy/G. Hurd)

1 SUBMERSIBLE SUPPORT SHIP: "KELLIE CHOUEST"

Number	Name	Completed	In service	Status
(none)	KELLIE CHOUEST	1 Mar 1996	17 Mar 1996	**Active**

Builder:	North American Shipbuilding, Larose, La.
Displacement:	1,575 tons full load
Tonnage:	2,786 Gross Registered Tons (GRT)
	2,373 Deadweight Tons (DWT)
Length:	291½ feet (88.88 m) waterline
	309¹¹⁄₁₂ feet (94.48 m) overall
Beam:	52 feet (15.85 m)
Draft:	15 feet (4.57 m)
Propulsion:	2 diesel engines (General Motors); 3,900 bhp; 2 shafts
Speed:	13 knots
Personnel:	13 civilian + 40 Navy and technical

The KELLIE CHOUEST was built specifically for the submersible support role. The in service date above is the date of charter by the MSC.

She is based at San Diego, California.

Design: She can support various diving devices, including unmanned vehicles and the Deep Submergence Rescue Vehicle (DSRV). She has a four-point mooring system, to allow her to remain stationary over a hulk or disabled submarine, and dynamic positioning equipment.

A 68-ton-capacity stern lift is fitted for the launch and recovery of submersibles.

The rescue submersible MYSTIC *high and dry aboard the support ship* KELLIE CHOUEST. *(1998, Leo Van Ginderen)*

The KELLIE CHOUEST, *support ship for the Navy's remaining DSRV. (The superstructure of another craft is off her port quarter.) (1999, Leo Van Ginderen)*

The stern of the KELLIE CHOUEST *with the* MYSTIC *in her docking well. This civilian manned ship is one of several leased by the Military Sealift Command for special support roles. (U.S. Navy)*

1 SUBMERSIBLE SUPPORT SHIP: "DOLORES CHOUEST"

Number	Name	In service	Status
(none)	DOLORES CHOUEST	1978	**Active**

Builders:	North American Shipbuilding, Larose, La.
Displacement:	1,500 tons full load
Length:	240 feet (73.17 m) overall
Beam:	40 feet (12.2 m)
Draft:	11⅝ feet (3.64 m)
Propulsion:	2 diesel engines (Caterpillar D399-SCAC); 2,250 bhp; 2 shafts
Speed:	12 knots
Personnel:	7 civilian + 32 Navy and technical

A former oil field support ship, she is configured to support DSRV submersibles and other Navy submersible/underwater work.

She is based at Norfolk, Virginia.

Design: The DOLORES CHOUEST has an unusual configuration with twin, amidships funnels. She has a stern lift for the launch and recovery of submersibles.

3 AUXILIARY SWIMMER DELIVERY VESSELS: MODIFIED LCUs

Number	Built	Status
ASDV 1 (ex-LCU 1621)	1960	**Active**; Naval Amphibious Base Coronado (San Diego)
ASDV 2 (ex-LCU 1623)	1960	**Active**; Naval Special Warfare Group 2
ASDV 3 (ex-LCU 1628)	1967	**Active**; Special Boat Unit 12

Builders:	Southern Shipbuilding, Slidell, La.
Displacement:	approximately 210 tons light
	approximately 390 tons full load
Length:	134¾ feet (41.07 m) overall
Beam:	29¾ feet (9.07 m)
Draft:	6'1½ feet (2.08 m)
Propulsion:	4 diesel engines (General Motors 6-71); 1,200 bhp; 2 Kort-nozzle propellers, except vertical cycloidal on ASDV 1
Speed:	11 knots
Range:	1,200 nm (2,220 km) at 8 knots
Personnel:	10–14 (enlisted)
Guns:	removed
Radars:	1 SPS-69 navigation

These are modified utility landing craft of the LCU 1610 class; they are employed to support training operations for SEALs and other Navy swimmers.

As an ASDV, each is fitted with a decompression chamber and associated air compressors, storage flasks, and an electric generator. Manning varies from 10 to 14 enlisted personnel, depending on whether the training operation requires use of the decompression chamber. Sleeping accommodations are provided for embarked personnel. A crane is fitted for handling rubber boats.

Classification: ASDV does not appear on the current list of Navy ship classifications (see Chapter 3).

Operational: The ASDVs 2 and 3 are based at Little Creek (Norfolk), Virginia.

ACOUSTIC RESEARCH SHIPS

1 ACOUSTIC RESEARCH SHIP: "COREY CHOUEST"

Number	Name	Completed	In service	Status
(none)	COREY CHOUEST (ex-FAR COMET, TENDER COMET)	1974	14 Nov 1991	**Active**

Builders:	Ulstein Hatlo A/S, Ulsteinvik (Norway)
Displacement:	approx. 3,900 tons full load
Tonnage:	1,597 GRT
	1,800 DWT
Length:	250 feet (76.21 m) waterline
	265 1½ feet (81.08 m) overall
Beam:	59⅙ feet (18.04 m)
Draft:	14⅙ feet (4.32 m)
Propulsion:	2 diesel engines (Atlas-MaK 6M453AK); 4,000 bhp; 2 shafts
Speed:	13.75 knots
Personnel:	16 civilian + 41 Navy and technicians

A former offshore oil field cargo/pipe carrying ship, the COREY CHOUEST serves as an acoustic/ocean surveillance research platform. She is leased from Alpha Marine Services, Galliano, Louisiana, and operated by Edison Chouest Offshore.

Class: The COREY CHOUEST's sister ship AMY CHOUEST was chartered by the Military Sealift Command from 1990 to 1993 for acoustic research.

Design: The ship has a catamaran hull configuration similar to the Navy's later T-AGOS ocean surveillance ships.

Operational: The COREY CHOUEST is employed in research in the Hawaii area in the development of Low-Frequency Active (LFA) sonar systems. During 1997–1998, she conducted studies on the effects of low-frequency sound on marine mammals.

The DOLORES CHOUEST also can support the DSRV, as well as other Navy submersibles and underwater work. (1998, Leo Van Ginderen)

The Corey Chouest *is employed in acoustic research. The large superstructure, with stern openings, provides facilities for towed arrays and other gear for test and evaluation. (1996, W. Michael Young)*

1 SONOBUOY TRIALS CRAFT: "ACOUSTIC PIONEER"

Number	Name	Completed	Status
180WB8701	Acoustic Pioneer	1981	**Active**

Builders:	Halter Marine, Moss Point, La.
Displacement:	approx. 1,500 tons full load
Length:	179'1½ feet (54.86 m) overall
Beam:	40 feet (12.2 m)
Draft:	14 feet (4.3 m)
Propulsion:	2 diesel engines (General Motors 12-645-E6); 3,000 bhp; 2 shafts
Speed:	12 knots
Personnel:	

Formerly the oil field supply boat September Morn, the Acoustic Pioneer was acquired by the Navy in 1987 and employed by the Naval Avionics Development Center at St. Croix in the Virgin Islands for sonobuoy testing. She subsequently was transferred to Alaskan waters for sonobuoy research.

The Acoustic Pioneer *is employed as a support craft at the Naval Air Development Center's detachment in Key West, Florida. (U.S. Navy)*

The Acoustic Explorer *supports research at the Naval Avionics Detachment Center in the Virgin Islands. (1998, Leo Van Ginderen)*

1 SONOBUOY TRIALS CRAFT: "ACOUSTIC EXPLORER"

Number	Name	Completed	In service	Status
111NS8801	Acoustic Explorer	Dec 1981	1988	Active

Builder:	Eastern Marine, Panama City, Fla.
Displacement:	
Length:	125 feet (38.1 m) overall
Beam:	30 feet (9.14 m)
Draft:	4⅔ feet (1.42 m)
Propulsion:	2 diesel engines; 2 shafts
Speed:	
Personnel:	

The Acoustic Explorer is the former oil field supply boat Strong Brio, acquired by the Navy and employed by the Naval Avionics Development Center at St. Croix in the Virgin Islands for sonobuoy testing.

MISCELLANEOUS UNCLASSIFIED SHIPS

Unclassified ship designations reached hull number IX 235 at the end of World War II. The series was continued after the war, beginning with the designation IX 300, assigned to the German heavy cruiser Prinz Eugen. This left a gap in IX hull numbers, from 236 to 299.

The postwar IX series had reached hull number 310 when—in 1967—the extensively converted Elk River (ex-LSMR 501) was placed in this category and classified IX with her previous hull number. Subsequent craft were given 500-series designations, creating a second major sequential gap in IX hull numbers, from 311 to 500.

Thus, there has been an official disregard for the IX numerical series, which dated back to December 1941. (The IX symbol for unclassified vessels was used by the Navy from 1920, but without specific hull numbers assigned.)

The IX 521, 522, 524, 525, and 535 are floating dry dock sections; they are listed in Chapter 26. The other craft "missing" between hull numbers IX 501 and IX 532 are listed in Table 25-1.

The stealth research ship Sea Shadow (IX 529) is listed above.

1 TRAINING SUPPORT VESSEL: EX-OCEAN SURVEILLANCE SHIP

Number	Name	FY	Launched	In Service AGOS	Status
IX 537 (ex-T-AGOS 8)	PREVAIL	81	7 Dec 1985	5 Mar 1986	**Active**

Builders:	Tacoma Boatbuilding, Wash.
Displacement:	1,600 tons light
	2,285 tons full load
Tonnage:	1,584 GRT
	786 DWT
Length:	203⅔ feet (62.1 m) waterline
	224 feet (68.3 m) overall
Beam:	43 feet (13.1 m)
Draft:	15 feet (4.6 m)
Propulsion:	diesel-electric (4 Caterpillar D-398B diesel generators with General Electric motors); 3,200 bhp; 2 shafts
Speed:	11 knots
Range:	3,000 nm (5,556 km) at 11 knots
	+ 90 days on station at 3 knots
Personnel:	

The PREVAIL was employed as an escort ship for submarines undergoing trials after overhaul, replacing the GOSPORT (IX 517, ex-THOMPSON/AGOR 9) in that role. She now is employed as a training ship for maritime interdiction operations.

Class: The PREVAIL was one of 18 ocean surveillance ships of the STALWART (T-AGOS 1) class completed from 1984 to 1990 (see Chapter 24 for additional data).

Classification: The PREVAIL was reclassified from T-AGOS 8 to IX 537 on 17 October 2003. She is unofficially listed as a training support vessel (TSV 1).

1 AFLOAT LABORATORY: FORMER YP

Number	Launched	Completed	Status
IX 531 (ex-YP 679)	11 Dec 1984	3 June 1985	**Active**

Builder:	Peterson Builders, Sturgeon Bay, Wisc.
Displacement:	172 tons light
	176 tons full load
Length:	101⅔ feet (31.0 m) waterline
	108 feet (32.9 m) overall
Beam:	24 feet (7.3 m)
Draft:	5¾ feet (1.75 m)
Propulsion:	2 diesel engines (General Motors 12V71N); 875 bhp; 2 shafts
Speed:	12 knots
Range:	1,500 nm (2,778 km) at 12 knots
Personnel:	6 (2 officers + 4 enlisted)

This is a former seamanship training craft acquired by the Office of Naval Research (ONR) as an "afloat lab" both to evaluate technologies in the maritime environment and to serve as a public relations platform. The ship is based at the Naval Academy, Annapolis, Maryland, although when this edition of *Ships and Aircraft* went to press, there were discussions of basing her at the Naval Research Laboratory in Washington, D.C.

Sister ships continue to serve as YPs (see below).

Classification: She was changed from YP to IX on 7 August 2001.

Design: She has a wood hull with an aluminum deckhouse and pilothouse, and is fitted with a bow thruster.

Name: The name STARFISH has been unofficially assigned by the ONR.

The Office of Naval Research's floating laboratory has been officially redesignated IX 531, but carries her YP number. "Naval Research" is printed on the hull and "afloat lab" on the superstructure. (2004, U.S. Navy)

1 DIVING TENDER (NSP)

Number	Launched	Completed	Status
IX 530 (ex-YFND 5, YFN 268)	1 Dec 1940	1 Feb 1941	**Active**

Builder:	Associated Shipbuilders, Seattle
Displacement:	170 tons light
	590 tons full load
Length:	110 feet (33.53 m) overall
Beam:	35 feet (10.66 m)
Draft:	7 feet (2.13 m)
Propulsion:	non-self-propelled
Manning:	

This archaic craft—more than 60 years old—serves as a diving tender at San Diego. She was stricken on 25 June 1999 as the YFND 5, but reinstated as the IX 530 on 6 September 2000.

Classification: She was built as YFN 268 (non-self-propelled).

1 ACOUSTIC TEST BARGE (NSP)

Number	Launched	In service	Status
IX 528 (ex-YRDH 1, YR 55)	3 Sep 1943	2 Dec 1943	**Active**

Builder:	Associated Shipbuilding, Seattle
Displacement:	460 tons light
	750 tons full load
Length:	150 feet (45.73 m) waterline
	151 feet (46.0 m) overall
Beam:	34 feet (10.37 m)
Draft:	6 feet (1.83 m)
Propulsion:	non-self-propelled (diesel generator)
Personnel:	47 (1 officer + 46 enlisted)

Assigned to the Naval Surface Warfare Center's detachment at Ketchikan, Alaska, the IX 528 is employed to monitor submarine noise signatures.[4]

Class: Three sister barges are in service as floating workshops (YRDH).

Classification: Built as a non-self-propelled floating workshop (YR 55), she was changed to floating workshop (hull) (YRDH 1) during World War II and to IX 528 on 7 April 1999.

---

4 The actual acoustic measurement facility is at nearby Block Island in the Behn Canal.

1 SUPPORT CRAFT (NSP)

Number	In service	Status
IX 527 (ex-YFN 1259)	1 June 1982	**Active**

Builder:	Steel Style
Displacement:	174 tons light
	699 tons full load
Length:	94 feet (28.65 m) waterline
	110 feet (33.53 m) overall
Beam:	32 feet (9.76 m)
Draft:	8 feet (2.44 m)
Propulsion:	non-self-propelled (diesel generator)
Personnel:	

The IX 527 is assigned to the Naval Surface Warfare Center's detachment at Ketchikan, Alaska, for submarine monitoring.

Classification: It was changed from YFN 1259 to IX 527 on 7 April 1999.

1 TRAINING CRAFT

Number	Launched	In service	Status
IX 523 (ex-YOG 93)	8 Sep 1945	8 Feb 1946	**Active**

Builders:	R.T.C. Shipbuilding, Camden, N.J.
Displacement:	440 tons light
	1,390 tons full load
Length:	174 feet (53.0 m) overall
Beam:	32 feet (9.76 m)
Draft:	13 feet (4.0 m)
Propulsion:	1 diesel engine (General Motors); 640 bhp; 1 shaft
Speed:	11 knots
Personnel:	

This is a former self-propelled gasoline barge, assigned to the Fleet Training Group, Norfolk, Virginia.

Two sister ships, the last YOGs in Navy service, have been stricken, the YOG 78 in 1995 and the YOG 88 in 1997.

Classification: She was changed from YOG 93 to IX 523 on 25 November 1996.

Design: As a YOG, her cargo capacity was 6,570 barrels.

1 CLASSROOM BARGE (NSP)

Number	Built	In service	Status
IX 516 (ex-Matthew, Christina F)	1976	15 Apr 1988	**Active**

Builder:	McDermott Shipyard, Morgan City, La.
Displacement:	3,122 tons light
	3,476 tons full load
Length:	302¾ feet (92.28 m) overall
Beam:	90 feet (27.43 m)
Draft:	22 feet (6.7 m)
Propulsion:	non-self-propelled (diesel generator)
Personnel:	

The IX 516 is a classroom barge employed at the Trident ballistic missile submarine (SSBN) facility at Kings Bay, Georgia. There is a three-story deckhouse on the barge containing classrooms; the structure is 241 feet (73.5 m) long, 72 feet (21.95 m) wide, and 35 feet (10.7 m) high.

The craft was acquired by the Navy and converted by McDermott Shipyard, Morgan City, Louisiana.

1 LIFTING BODY RESEARCH SHIP: EX-SES

Number Name	Launched	In service	Status
IX 515 Sea Flyer (ex-USCGC Dorado)	Dec 1978	1 Sep 1980	**Active**

Builders:	Bell-Halter, New Orleans
Displacement:	270 tons light
	340 tons full load
Length:	167⁵⁄₁₂ feet (51.0 m) overall
Beam:	42⁷⁄₁₂ feet (13.0 m)
Draft:	18½ feet (5.64 m)
Propulsion:	2 diesel engines (VP 185); 2 waterjets
Speed:	30+ knots (see *Propulsion* notes)
Personnel:	

The Sea Flyer is hybrid lifting body research ship that combines the high speed of a hydrofoil and the rough-water stability of a Small Waterplane Area Twin-Hull (SWATH) ship.

The ship was built as a prototype Surface Effects Ship (SES), originally designated as SES-200 and, when evaluated by the Coast Guard, as WSES 1, with the name Dorado. Subsequently, the Coast Guard procured three similar craft for operational service. See *Operational* notes.

The Sea Flyer was converted to her present configuration from 2000 to 2004 by Navatek, Ltd., of Honolulu, a subsidiary of Pacific Marine and Supply, Ltd., with funding from the Office of Naval Research.

In addition to undertaking trials and demonstrations, she is being employed to train the crew of the Sea Fighter (X-craft)

Classification: The hull number IX 515 was assigned on 11 May 1987; previously, she was listed as "floating equipment."

Conversion: The Sea Flyer's conversion to a hybrid lifting body configuration included removing her SES air cushion system and installing a 170-ton lifting body. An after crossfoil was added for pitch stabilization and control. Also installed were a new propulsion system, including engines, drivetrain, gearboxes, shafts, and propellers.

The Sea Flyer at high speed in calm waters off the coast of San Diego. The craft combines two advanced hull technologies into a unique hybrid configuration that permits high speeds and stability in rough seas. (2004, U.S. Navy)

The rebuilt craft was launched in June 2003 and began sea trials in Hawaiian waters in 2004. She traveled to San Diego in July 2004 for additional trials and demonstrations.

See 17th Edition/page 325 for earlier configuration and modification data.

Propulsion: During sea trials in 8- to 14-foot seas with 40-knot winds (i.e., sea state 5), the SEA FLYER was able to maintain an average speed only 1 knot less than her calm water speed. The ship also demonstrated a high degree of maneuverability; in 12-foot seas she made a 360° turn at 27 knots while maintaining a 3° bank through all headings.

Operational: The Coast Guard operated the ship from January 1980 to September 1982, when she was transferred back to the Navy. The ship again was evaluated by the Coast Guard in late 1984.

Stern aspect of the SEA FLYER. The open stern mounts the ship's crossfoil, which provides stability and control. (2004, U.S. Navy)

The stern of the SEA FLYER showing the crossfoil. (2004, Navatek, Ltd.)

A broadside view of the SEA FLYER. Originally built as a prototype Surface Effects Ship (SES), she has undergone a massive conversion to her current configuration. (2004, U.S. Navy)

The 170-ton lifting body of the SEA FLYER. (2004, Navatek, Ltd.)

1 HELICOPTER TRAINING CRAFT: EX-YFU TYPE

Number	Name	In service	To IX	Status
IX 514 (ex-YFU 79)	BAY LANDER	1968	Mar 1986	**Active**

Builders:	Pacific Coast Engineering, Alameda, Calif.
Displacement:	220 tons light
	380 tons full load
Length:	125 feet (38.1 m) overall
Beam:	36 feet (11.0 m)
Draft:	7½ feet (2.3 m)
Propulsion:	2 diesel engines (General Motors 6-71); 1,000 bhp; 2 shafts
Speed:	8 knots
Personnel:	15 civilian + Navy helicopter control officers
Radars:	1 Decca navigation

The YFY 79 was converted in 1985–1986 for use as a helicopter landing ship to train helicopter pilots. Placed in service on 31 March 1986, she operates in the Gulf of Mexico, based at the Naval Air Station Pensacola, Florida.

Classification: She was changed from YFU 79 to IX 514 on 31 March 1986.

Helicopters: The flight deck landing area is 57⅚ (17.6 m) feet long and 28 feet (8.5 m) wide. There is no helicopter parking area or hangar on the craft, nor is refueling capability provided. Lighting is installed for night landings.

Operational: She operates at sea about 90 days per year and has approximately 350 deck landings per month at sea. Since 1985, she has accomplished more than 75,000 landings without an accident.

Army, Navy, Marine Corps, Air Force, Coast Guard, and other government agency pilots have made landings on her deck.

Personnel: The IX 514 was manned by Navy personnel until November 1999, when she was turned over to civilian manning.

RADIATION TEST BARGE (NSP)

The IX 513 was an unmanned barge used to produce electric pulse to evaluate ships' Electro-Magnetic Pulse (EMP) protection under a program called Empress II. A pulse of 7 million volts could be generated by the craft's two diesel generators. The IX 513 was disposed of on 20 November 1997.

The barge began pulse tests against warships in 1990 off the coast of North Carolina; she subsequently was moved to the Gulf of Mexico.

See 17th Edition/page326 for characteristics.

1 SONAR TEST BARGE (NSP)

Number	IX in service	Status
IX 310	1 Apr 1971	**Active**

Builders:	Wiley Manufacturing
Displacement:	1,070 tons light
	1,438 tons full load
Length:	195 feet (59.45 m) overall
Beam:	123 feet (37.5 m)
Draft:	5 feet (1.52 m)
Propulsion:	non-self-propelled

The IX 310 consists of two non-self-propelled barges moored in Lake Seneca, New York, for sonar research by the Naval Undersea Warfare Center at Newport, Rhode Island (formerly the Naval Underwater Sound Laboratory). Built in 1969–1971, the barges are connected, and each has a kingpost-crane for handling underwater sonar arrays.

The barges are constructed of steel.

The IX 310. (2000, U.S. Navy)

The helicopter landing training craft IX 514 off Pensacola, Florida. The TH-57C SeaRanger on her deck is practicing landings aboard the world's "smallest aircraft carrier." During the Vietnam War, smaller U.S. LCMs were fitted with flight decks. (Bell Helicopter Textron)

1 SAILING FRIGATE: "CONSTITUTION"

Number	Name	Launched	Comm.	Status
(ex-IX 21)	CONSTITUTION	21 Oct 1797	July 1978	Relic

Builders:	Hartt's Shipyard, Boston
Displacement:	2,200 tons standard
Length:	175 feet (53.35 m) waterline
	204 feet (62.2 m) billet head to taffrail
Beam:	43½ feet (13.3 m)
Draft:	22½ feet (6.85 m)
Masts:	fore: 198 feet (60.4 m)
	main: 220 feet (67.0 m)
	mizzen: 172 1/2 feet (52.6 m)
Speed:	13+ knots (under sail)
Personnel:	54 (2 officers + 52 enlisted) as relic;
	up to 500 as frigate (including 55 Marines)
Guns:	several smooth-bore cannon (see *Guns* notes)

The CONSTITUTION is the oldest ship in U.S. Navy commission and the oldest known warship still afloat. (The older HMS VICTORY, Admiral Lord Nelson's flagship at the battle of Trafalgar, is preserved in concrete at the naval dockyard in Portsmouth, England.) Her original commissioning date is not known; she first put to sea on 23 July 1798. She is now moored as a relic at the Charlestown Naval Shipyard in Boston.

The CONSTITUTION's keel was laid down on 1 November 1794.

No sails normally are fitted; her designed sail area was 42,710 square feet (3,844 m²).

Class: The CONSTITUTION was one of six sail frigates built under a 1794 act of Congress. The CONSTELLATION (38 guns), built under the same act and launched on 7 September 1797, was broken up at the Gosport shipyard (Norfolk), Virginia, in 1852–1853; almost simultaneously, a sailing corvette of that name was built in the same yard. That CONSTELLATION served in the Navy (designated IX 20 in 1941) until her transfer in 1954 to a private group in Baltimore, Maryland, where she is maintained.[5]

Classification: The CONSTITUTION was classified as an "unclassified" ship in 1920 (IX without a hull number). She became IX 21 on 8 December 1941 and carried that classification until 1 September 1975 when it was withdrawn because, according to Navy officials, the designation "tended to demean and degrade the CONSTITUTION through association with a group of insignificant craft of varied missions and configurations."

Design: A three-masted sail frigate designed by Joshua Humphreys, the ship was built at Edmond Hartt's shipyard in Boston. She was rebuilt several times, but her basic lines and configuration have been retained.

Guns: The CONSTITUTION was authorized as a 44-gun frigate, but was in fact completed with a larger gun battery. The ship was usually overgunned, with an early armament consisting of 30 long 24-pounders, 20–22 long 12-pounders, and 2 long 24-pounder chase guns. This heavy armament overloaded and strained the ship; still, she could have accommodated up to 60 guns.

The number and types of guns varied considerably during her service as a frigate.

Names: The ship was named OLD CONSTITUTION from 1 December 1917 until 4 July 1925, while the name CONSTITUTION was assigned to a battle cruiser (CC 5); the cruiser was never completed and the name reverted to this ship.

Operational: As a sail frigate, the CONSTITUTION fought in the Quasi-War with France, against the Barbary pirates, and in the War of 1812 against Great Britain. She has been rebuilt several times and is now restored as much as possible to her original configuration.

The ship has been at Boston since 7 May 1934, following a sailing tour of 90 ports on the U.S. Atlantic, Pacific, and Gulf coasts from 1931 to 1934. Once a year, usually on 4 July, she is taken out into Boston Harbor under tow and "turned around," so that her masts do not warp from the effects of sun and wind. At noon on 4 July, the CONSTITUTION traditionally fires a 21-gun salute from her forward 24-pounder long guns. She hosts more than one million visitors per year.

On 21 July 1997, the CONSTITUTION was towed from Boston to Marblehead, Massachusetts, a distance of 17 nm (31.5 km). There the tow lines were cast off and the ship set sail for the first time since 1881.

---

5 Until 1991 the preserving organization contended that the Baltimore CONSTELLATION was the frigate of 1797, despite extensive evidence to the contrary. The issue was decisively addressed and the Baltimore ship proved to be the 1853 vessel in an analysis published in 1991 by Dana M. Wegner, et al., of the Navy's David Taylor Research Center (*Fouled Anchors: The Constellation Questions Answered*, September 1991).

The CONSTITUTION in her normal habitat in Boston harbor. She is the world's oldest warship in commission and afloat. (1996, U.S. Navy/ David G. Schmidt)

The CONSTITUTION *under sail on her 200th anniversary—for the first time in 116 years. During her brief cruise, she was accompanied by the destroyer* RAMAGE *(DDG 61) and frigate* HALYBURTON *(FFG 40), with an overhead salute by the Blue Angels flight demonstration team. (1997, U.S. Navy/Todd Stevens)*

Table 25-1. MISCELLANEOUS UNCLASSIFIED SHIPS DISCARDED OR RECLASSIFIED SINCE 1 JANUARY 1990

Number	Former	Name	Type	Notes
IX 308	AKL 17	NEW BEDFORD	torpedo trials	str. 4 Apr 1995
IX 309	YW 87	MONOB ONE	sound trials	changed to YAG 61; discarded 2 Aug 1996
IX 501	LSMR 501	ELK RIVER	diving	str. 13 Aug 1999
IX 502	APB 39	MERCER	barracks	changed to APL 39
IX 503	APB 40	NUECES	barracks	changed to APL 40
IX 504	APB 37	ECHOLS	barracks	OSIR/str. 22 Dec 1995
IX 506	YFU 82	SEA LION	research	str.21 Aug 1997
IX 507	AP 121	GEN HUGH J. GAFFEY	barracks	str. 26 Oct 1993
IX 508	LCU 1618	ORCA	research	str. 19 June 2003
IX 510	AP 127	GEN WILLIAM O. DARBY	barracks	str. 26 Oct 1993
IX 512	Army BD 6651	(none)	missile test	str. 13 Dec 1995
IX 513		(none)	test barge	discarded 20 Nov 1997
IX 517	AGOR 9	GOSPORT	escort	OSIR 19 June 2003*
IX 518	AS 19	PROTEUS	barracks ship	str. 13 Mar 2001
IX 519	YC 1643	(none)	barge	fitted in USS La Salle (AGF 3)
IX 520	APL 19	(none)	barracks ship	str. 13 March 2001
IX 526	YRST 1, YDT 11	(none)	work barge	changed to YR 94

* Laid up at Philadelphia, Pa., pending being sunk as a target

The ex-submarine tender PROTEUS is described in the 17th Edition/page 323. The non-self-propelled barracks ship IX 520 was sunk as a target on 13 June 2002. The GOSPORT is the former oceanographic research ship THOMPSON; she has been replaced by the PREVAIL (ex-T-AGOS 8). The GOSPORT/THOMPSON is described in the 17th Edition/page 324. The ex-transports GEN HUGH J. GAFFEY and GEN WILLIAM O. DARBY, lately employed as barracks ships, are described in the 17th Edition/page 326.

The IX 519 was an open, steel barge carried by the Sixth Fleet flagship LA SALLE and employed as an alongside landing stage for small boats. In 1994, the barge was converted for use as a berthing and working space and welded into the well deck of the LA SALLE. The barge was formally stricken from the NVR on 16 February 2002 and is now considered "equipment."

The ELK RIVER, a test ship for the Deep Dive System Mk II, was sunk as a gunnery target on 24 February 2001. She had been used as a barracks hulk after the DDS Mk II was removed in 1986.

Y-SERIES SERVICE CRAFT

SOUND TRIALS SHIP: "DEER ISLAND"

The sound trials ship DEER ISLAND (YAG 62), a former oil field supply ship built in 1966, was stricken on 2 August 1996. She was acquired by the Navy on 15 March 1982, retaining her commercial name. The craft was used for sound testing by the Naval Surface Warfare Center (formerly David Taylor Research Center), operating from Port Everglades, Florida.

SOUND TRIALS SHIP: "MONOB ONE"

The MONOB ONE—so named for *Mobile Noise Barge*—was converted to a sound trials configuration (YAG 61) in 1969 and placed in service in 1970 for the David Taylor Research Center—later the Naval Surface Warfare Center—operating from Port Canaveral, Florida. She was stricken on 2 August 1996. The MONOB ONE was built as YW 87 and reclassified IX 309 and, subsequently, YAG 61.

She was discarded (as YAG 61) on 2 August 1996 and transferred to Mexico.

2 DIVING TENDERS

Number	Name	In service	Status
YDT 17	NEPTUNE	25 Feb 1999	**Active**
YDT 18	POSEIDON	19 May 1999	**Active**

Builders:	Swiftships, Morgan City, La.
Displacement:	275 tons full load
Length:	131 feet (39.93 m) waterline
	135 feet (41.15 m) overall
Beam:	27 feet (8.23 m)
Draft:	6 feet (1.83 m)
Propulsion:	diesel engines (Caterpillar 3508 DITA); 2,600 bhp; 2 shafts
Speed:	20 knots
Range:	540 nm (1,000 km) at 20 knots
Personnel:	8 + 7 instructors, 25 students
Radars:	1 Raytheon navigation
Sonars:	hull-mounted high-frequency

These craft are employed at the Naval Diving and Salvage Training Center in Panama City, Florida. They replaced the YDT 14 and YDT 15.

Design: They are of aluminum construction with state-of-the-art navigation equipment. A large decompression chamber is fitted and a rubber boat can be carried.

The NEPTUNE. *(1999, Skeets Photo Service/Swiftships)*

TORPEDO TRIALS CRAFT: "YF 852" CLASS

The KEYPORT (YF 885), the last survivor of several covered lighters converted to torpedo trials craft, was stricken on 11 December 2000. She had been laid up in reserve since 23 August 1990.

FERRYBOATS

Two Navy ferryboats are in service at Guantanamo Bay, Cuba. Several others have been stricken in the past few years. The WA'A HELE HONUA (YFB 83) and MOKU HOLO HELE (YFB 87), in service at Pearl Harbor, were stricken on 25 June 1999; they were rendered redundant by the construction of a bridge–causeway to Ford Island in the center of the harbor.

All former LCU 1610-class utility landing craft modified in 1969 for use as ferryboats have been stricken: YFB 89 (ex-LCU 1638), YFB 90 (ex-LCU 1639), and YFB 91 (ex-LCU 1640) on 9 October 1992; YFB 88 (ex-LCU 1636) on 30 June 1993. The YFB 94 (ex-Army LCU 1504) was stricken on 11 July 2000, and the YFB 95 (ex-Army LCU 1516) was stricken on 24 April 1996.

2 FERRYBOATS: "WINDWARD" CLASS

Number	Name	Launched	In service	Status
YFB 92	R. W. HUNTINGTON	Oct 1993	30 Jan 1995	**Active**
YFB 93	WILLIAM H. ALLEN	Dec 1993	30 Jan 1995	**Active**

Builder:	Bender Shipbuilding & Repair, Mobile, Ala.
Displacement:	200 tons light
Length:	136 feet (41.46 m) overall
Beam:	36 feet (10.98 m)
Draft:	11 feet (3.35 m)
Propulsion:	2 diesel engines (General Motors 12V-71); 720 bhp; 2 shafts
Speed:	10 knots
Personnel:	4 + 80 passengers

These craft were built specifically for use at the naval base at Guantanamo Bay. Each can carry 15 civilian automobiles or two M1 Abrams main battle tanks.

Names: They were renamed in 1996—YFB 92 is the ex-WINDWARD, YFB 93 the ex-LEEWARD.

TORPEDO TRIALS CRAFT: CONVERTED LIGHTERS

The POTENTIAL (YFRT 520, ex-YF 520), a torpedo trials craft, was stricken on 11 December 2000. She was converted from a YF-type lighter originally completed in 1943 to a torpedo trials configuration. She had been laid up in reserve on 21 June 1991.

The similar (unnamed) YFRT 451 was stricken on 15 November 1993 and YRFT 287 was stricken on 3 March 1998.

1 HARBOR UTILITY CRAFT: "YFU 71" CLASS

Number	Launched	Completed	Status
YFU 81	1 July 1968	1 Sep 1968	**Active**

Builders:	Pacific Coast Engineering Co., Alameda, Calif.
Displacement:	220 tons light
	380 tons full load
Length:	125 feet (38.1 m) overall
Beam:	38 feet (11.0 m)
Draft:	7 1/2 feet (2.4 m)
Propulsion:	2 diesel engines (General Motors 6-71); 1,000 bhp;
	2 shafts (Kort nozzles)
Speed:	8 knots
Personnel:	12 (2 officers + 10 enlisted)

This craft was constructed specifically for use as a coastal cargo craft in the Vietnam War. Twelve units, built to a modified commercial design, were completed in 1967–1968 (YFU 71–82). Cargo capacity is 300 tons.

The YFU 81 is based at Roosevelt Roads, Puerto Rico.

Class: The YFU 71–77 and 80–82 were transferred to the U.S. Army in 1970 for use in South Vietnam; they were returned to the Navy in 1973. The YFU 74 and YFU 75 were stricken in 1986. The

The YFU 81. (1999, Leo Van Ginderen)

YFU 71, 72, 76, and 77 were transferred to the Department of the Interior in 1984; the YFU 76 and 77 subsequently were transferred to the government of the Marshall Islands in 1987.

The YFU 82 became the IX 506 and the YFU 79 became the IX 512. The YFU 83 was stricken on 28 October 2002. The YFU 91 (ex-LCU 1608) was stricken on 28 October 2002.

Guns: During their service in Vietnam waters, these craft each had two or more .50-cal machine guns fitted.

SELF-PROPELLED DREDGES

All Navy self-propelled dredges have been stricken: the YM 32 on 17 January 1990, YM 35 on 31 July 1995, YM 17 on 13 December 1995, and YM 33 on 3 August 1998.

FUEL OIL BARGES

All self-propelled fuel oil barges have been stricken:

YO 46 class: The CASING HEAD (YO 47) was stricken on 21 August 1997.

YO 65 class: The YO 130 was immobilized and changed to YON 130 on 5 September 1990; the YO 203 was immobilized and changed to YON 320 on 1 February 1994. The YO 129 was stricken on 25 March 1994, the YO 220 and YO 223 on 19 May 1997, and the YO 230 on 9 October 1997.

YO 153 class: The YO 153 was stricken on 27 March 1992.

GASOLINE BARGES

All self-propelled gasoline barges have been stricken. The last units, of the YOG 5 class, were the YOG 78, stricken on 31 July 1995, and the YOG 88, stricken on 19 May 1997. The YOG 93 became the IX 523 in 1996.

(4) SEAMANSHIP TRAINING CRAFT: "YP 703" CLASS

Four new-construction YPs were authorized on 7 August 2003. They will be of an improved design, numbered YP 703–706.

23 SEAMANSHIP TRAINING CRAFT: "YP 676" CLASS

Number	Launched	Completed	Status
YP 676	9 Apr 1984	1 Nov 1984	**Active**
YP 677	23 June 1984	1 Dec 1984	**Active**
YP 680	23 Mar 1985	30 July 1985	**Active**
YP 681	1 June 1985	11 Oct 1985	**Active**
YP 682	3 Aug 1985	19 Nov 1985	**Active**
YP 683	19 June 1986	21 Oct 1986	**Active**
YP 684	14 Aug 1986	21 Oct 1986	**Active**
YP 685	25 Sep 1986	25 Nov 1986	**Active**
YP 686	25 Oct 1986	8 Dec 1986	**Active**
YP 687	17 Mar 1987	22 May 1987	**Active**
YP 688	13 Mar 1987	22 May 1987	**Active**
YP 689	20 Mar 1987	10 June 1987	**Active**
YP 690	17 Apr 1987	10 June 1987	**Active**
YP 691	19 May 1987	2 July 1987	**Active**
YP 692	18 June 1987	27 July 1987	**Active**
YP 694	21 Sep 1987	27 Oct 1987	**Active**
YP 695	26 Oct 1987	1 Dec 1987	**Active**
YP 696	31 Mar 1988	1 May 1988	**Active**
YP 697	1 Feb 1988	26 May 1988	**Active**
YP 698	29 Mar 1988	16 June 1988	**Active**
YP 700	12 May 1988	21 July 1988	**Active**
YP 701	14 June 1988	9 Aug 1988	**Active**
YP 702	19 July 1988	2 Sep 1988	**Active**

Builders:	YP 676–682 Peterson Builders, Sturgeon Bay, Wisc.
	YP 683–702 Marinette Shipbuilding, Marinette, Wisc.
Displacement:	172 tons full load
Length:	101⅔ feet (31.0 m) waterline
	108 feet (32.9 m) overall
Beam:	24 feet (7.3 m)
Draft:	5¾ feet (1.75 m)
Propulsion:	2 diesel engines (General Motors 12V71N); 875 bhp; 2 shafts
Speed:	12 knots
Range:	1,500 nm (2,778 km) at 12 knots
Personnel:	6 (2 officers + 4 enlisted) + 24 students

The YP 684 and YP 680 lead a line of seamanship training craft returning to the Naval Academy at Annapolis, Maryland, following a three-week summer training cruise. The YPs provide practical at-sea training to complement classroom sessions for the midshipmen. (2000, U.S. Navy/Ken Mierzejewski)

These are seamanship training craft, most serving at the Naval Academy in Annapolis, Maryland (based at the adjacent naval station). The YP 686 is fitted for oceanographic research by Academy midshipmen.

Class: The YP 678 and YP 679 were stricken on 20 November 1998; however, the YP 679 was reinstated on 25 June 1999 for use by the ONR and is listed separately as the IX 531. The YP 693 and YP 699 were stricken on 13 March 2001.

Design: These craft have a wood hull with an aluminum deckhouse and pilothouse.

Electronics: All are fitted with Navigation Satellite (NAVSAT) and Loran C receivers, as well as with navigation radar and fathometers.

Operational: All are active, and all but four units are employed for seamanship training at the Naval Academy. The YP 696 and YP 702 train officer candidates and are based at the Naval Air Station Pensacola, Florida, and the YP 697 and YP 701 are at the Naval Undersea Warfare Center at Keyport, Washington, employed to escort shipments of reactor compartments from dismantled submarines from the Puget Sound Naval Shipyard to temporary burial at Hanford, Washington.

A trio of YPs shows the simple lines of these craft. In theory, in wartime they could be armed for harbor patrol duties. A new YP class will be constructed. (1999, Leo Van Ginderen)

2 UTILITY CRAFT: "YP 654" CLASS

Number	Launched	Completed	Status
YP 663	12 Mar 1958	15 Nov 1958	**Active**
YP 665	27 Aug 1960	28 Nov 1960	**Active**

Builders:	YP 663: Stephens Bros., Stockton, Calif.
	YP 665: Elizabeth City Shipyard, N.J.
Displacement:	55 tons light
	65 tons full load
Length:	80⅚ feet (24.5 m) overall
Beam:	18¾ feet (5.72 m)
Draft:	5¼ feet (1.6 m)
Propulsion:	2 diesel engines (General Motors 6-71; 590 bhp; 2 shafts
Speed:	12.6 knots
Range:	400 nm (740 km) at 12 knots
Personnel:	10 (2 officers + 8 enlisted)

All craft of this class have been stricken except for these two units used as utility craft at Bremerton, Washington.

Class: The class originally consisted of 22 units, the YP 654–675. Seventeen units were reclassified as mine countermea-

sures craft under the Craft of Opportunity Program (COOP) (YP 654, 659–666, 668–675). The YP 655–658 were stricken on 12 February 1993, and the YP 667 on 4 February 1994.

Design: The craft have wood hulls and aluminum superstructures.

1 SEAPLANE WRECKING DERRICK: "YSD 11" CLASS

Number	Launched	Completed	Status
YSD 74	5 June 1943	15 July 1944	**Active**

Builders:	Pearl Harbor Navy Yard
Displacement:	240 tons light
	270 tons full load
Length:	104 feet (31.7 m) overall
Beam:	31⅙ feet (9.5 m)
Draft:	4 feet (1.2 m)
Propulsion:	2 diesels (Superior); 640 bhp; 2 shafts
Speed:	6 knots
Personnel:	16 (1 officer + 15 enlisted)

This is a small, self-propelled floating crane with a steel hull and fitted with a 10-ton-capacity crane. She is active at Pearl Harbor, Hawaii.

YSDs are called "Mary Anns."

Class: The YSD 53 was stricken in May 1991; the YSD 63 was stricken on 16 July 1993.

Design: Accommodations and galley facilities are provided within the craft's hull.

The "Mary Ann" YSD 63 chugging along. Only the YSD 74 of this once numerous class survives. Mary Anns of this class have been in the fleet since the early 1930s. (1977, Giorgio Arra)

HARBOR TUGS

Increasingly, the Navy employs commercial tugs in place of Navy-manned YTBs. These commercial craft are chartered by the Military Sealift Command. About 30 such tugs are currently under charter.[6]

---

6 See A.D. Baker III, *Combat Fleets of the World 2002-2003* (Annapolis, Md.: Naval Institute Press, 2002), pp. 1023–24.

27 LARGE HARBOR TUGS: "YTB 760" CLASS

Number	Name	Launched	Completed	Status
YTB 760	NATICK	28 Feb 1961	30 June 1961	str. 28 Mar 2003
YTB 761	OTTUMWA	30 May 1961	9 Oct 1961	str. 28 Oct 2002
YTB 763	MUSKEGON	8 Aug 1962	19 Apr 1963	**Active**
YTB 764	MISHAWAKA	3 Jan 1963	19 Apr 1963	str. 28 Oct 2002
YTB 765	OKMULGEE	18 Apr 1963	25 July 1963	Reserve 22 Nov 2000
YTB 766	WAPAKONETA	11 June 1963	25 July 1963	str. 16 Apr 2001
YTB 767	APALACHICOLA	26 Oct 1963	9 June 1964	str. 28 Oct 2002
YTB 769	CHESANING	5 Feb 1964	16 June 1964	Reserve 9 June 2000
YTB 770	DAHLONEGA	23 Mar 1964	4 Aug 1964	str. 13 Mar 2001
YTB 771	KEOKUK	21 May 1964	23 Aug 1964	**Active**
YTB 775	WAUWATOSA	19 May 1965	21 June 1965	str. 16 Feb 2002
YTB 776	WEEHAWKEN	8 June 1965	22 Oct 1965	str. 5 Jan 2001
YTB 777	NOGALESEN	24 June 1965	22 Oct 1965	str. 13 Mar 2001
YTB 779	MANHATTAN	15 July 1965	1 Dec 1965	**Active**
YTB 782	MANISTEE	20 Oct 1965	1 Feb 1966	**Active**
YTB 783	REDWING	12 Nov 1965	1 Feb 1966	str. 28 Mar 2003
YTB 784	KALISPEL	13 Dec 1965	4 May 1966	str. 16 Feb 2002
YTB 787	KITTANNING	29 Mar 1966	19 May 1966	**Active**
YTB 789	TOMAHAWK	5 May 1966	7 June 1966	**Active**
YTB 791	MARINETTE	10 Apr 1967	10 June 1967	Reserve 30 June 2000
YTB 793	PIQUA	25 Apr 1967	10 July 1967	str. 13 Mar 2001
YTB 794	MANDAN	30 Apr 1968	15 Oct 1968	str. 5 Jan 2001
YTB 795	KETCHIKAN	11 June 1968	6 Nov 1968	str. 5 Jan 2001
YTB 796	SACO	3 July 1968	8 Jan 1969	str. 9 June 2004
YTB 797	TAMAQUA	14 Aug 1968	26 Jan 1969	**Active**
YTB 798	OPELIKA	21 Aug 1968	30 Jan 1969	**Active**
YTB 806	TUSKEGEE	15 Apr 1970	2 Oct 1970	**Active**
YTB 807	MASSAPEQUA	27 May 1970	30 Nov 1970	**Active**
YTB 808	WENATCHEE	7 July 1970	21 Dec 1970	**Active**
YTB 810	ANOKA	15 Apr 1971	31 Aug 1971	str. 13 Mar 2001
YTB 812	ACCOMAC	8 June 1971	17 Nov 1971	**Active**
YTB 813	POUGHKEEPSIE	23 July 1971	27 Nov 1971	**Active**
YTB 814	WAXAHACHIE	9 Sept 1971	2 Jan 1971	**Active**
YTB 815	NEODESHA	6 Oct 1971	2 Jan 1972	**Active**
YTB 818	MECOSTA	23 Mar 1973	25 June 1973	str. Mar 2003
YTB 820	WANAMASSA	4 May 1973	12 July 1973	**Active**
YTB 821	TONTOCANY	16 May 1973	28 July 1973	str. 13 Mar 2001
YTB 822	PAWHUSKA	7 June 1973	10 Sep 1973	str. 28 Oct 2002
YTB 823	CANONCHET	10 July 1973	23 Sep 1973	**Active**
YTB 824	SANTAQUIN	13 Aug 1973	30 Sep 1973	**Active**
YTB 828	CATAHECASSA	29 May 1974	16 Aug 1974	**Active**
YTB 829	METACOM	19 June 1974	21 Sep 1974	str. 5 Jan 2001
YTB 831	DEKANAWIDA	12 Sep 1974	31 Oct 1974	**Active**
YTB 832	PETALESHARO	3 Oct 1974	17 Nov 1974	Reserve 12 June 1999
YTB 833	SHABONEE	29 Oct 1974	16 Dec 1974	str. 16 Feb 2002
YTB 834	NEGWAGON	27 Mar 1975	19 May 1975	**Active**
YTB 835	SKENANDOA	3 Apr 1975	10 June 1975	**Active**
YTB 836	POKAGON	9 Apr 1975	24 June 1975	**Active**

Builders:	YTB 763, 765: Southern Shipbuilding, Slidell, La.
	YTB 769, 771: Mobile Ship Repair, Ala.
	YTB 779–798: 820–836: Marinette Marine, Marinette, Wisc.
	YTB 806–815: Peterson Builders, Sturgeon Bay, Wisc.
Displacement:	283 tons light
	356 tons full load
Length:	109 feet (33.2 m) overall
Beam:	30 1/2 feet (9.3 m)
Draft:	13 1/2 feet (4.1 m)
Propulsion:	1 diesel engine (Fairbanks-Morse 38D8 1/8); 2,000 bhp; 1 shaft
Speed:	12.5 knots
Range:	2,000 nm (3,704 km) at 12 knots
Personnel:	10–14 (enlisted)

Twenty-three of these tugs are in active service; four are laid up in reserve. They are fitted with small commercial navigation radars.

Many units have been stricken during the past few years with commercial tugs taking their place.

Class: This class originally covered hull numbers YTB 760–836. The similar YTB 837 and YTB 838 were transferred to Saudi Arabia in 1975.

Disposals since 1990:

The Navy's oldest YTB, the MUSKEGON, assists the missile cruiser COWPENS (CG 63) getting under way at Shimoda, Japan. Navy-manned YTBs still are used in Japanese ports; other U.S. naval bases rely mainly on commercial tugs. (2004, U.S. Navy/Alan Warner)

The OPELIKA at Yokosuka, Japan. Note the roller-fenders on the starboard and port sides of the superstructure. (2004, U.S. Navy/Alan Warner)

Name/Number	Notes
EUFAULA (YTB 800)	to NDRF 9 November 1992
TONKAWA (YTB 786)	to NDRF 18 November 1992
NASHUA (YTB 774)	stricken 6 May 1994
ARCATA (YTB 768)	stricken 4 April 1995
PALATKA (YTB 801)	stricken 4 April 1995
TUSCUMBIA (YTB 762)	to NDRF 11 September 1995
PUSHMATAHA (YTB 830)	stricken 2 October 1995
AHOSKIE (YTB 804)	stricken 10 October 1995
NATCHITOCHES (YTB 799)	stricken 13 October 1995
IUKA (YTB 819)	stricken 19 October 1995
WINNEMUCCA (YTB 785)	stricken 20 December 1995
CHERAW (YTB 802)	stricken 29 February 1996
CHETEK (YTB 827)	stricken 29 February 1996
WAPATO (YTB 788)	stricken 25 April 1996
APOPKA (YTB 778)	stricken 26 June 1996
HYANNIS (YTB 817)	stricken 21 August 1997
WASHTUENA (YTB 826)	stricken 21 August 1997
SAUGUS (YTB 780)	stricken 28 October 1997
OCALA (YTB 805)	stricken 28 October 1997
WATHENA (YTB 825)	stricken 28 October 1997
MENOMINEE (YTB 790)	stricken 4 September 1998
HOUMA (YTB 811)	stricken 1 February 1999
ANTIGO (YTB 792)	stricken 25 June 1999
CAMPTI (YTB 816)	stricken 9 November 1999
NANTICOKE (YTB 803)	stricken 9 November 1999
AGAWAM (YTB 809)	stricken 9 November 1999
HOUMA (YTB 811)	stricken 9 November 1999

The YTB 817 and YTB 826 were transferred to the U.S. Fish

The Chesaning at Norfolk, Virginia. The YTBs have short, folding masts to facilitate their working under a ship's overhang. There is a large open working space aft. A small commercial navigation radar is fitted atop the bridge. (1999, Jürg Kürsener)

and Wildlife Service at Midway Island; the YTB 802 and YTB 827 were transferred to the Army Corps of Engineers; and the YTB 759 and YTB 778 were transferred to the Maritime Administration for use with the James River (Virginia) reserve group.

The large number of YTBs stricken since 2000 are listed in the class table.

The following were sunk as targets: YTB 776 on 24 April 2003; YTB 794 on 27 April 2003; YTB 795 on 25 April 2003; and YTB 777 on 26 April 2003.

Design: SCB No. 147A. These and other Navy harbor tugs are used for towing and for maneuvering ships in harbors. Their masts fold down to facilitate working alongside large ships.

Tugs also are equipped for firefighting.

Names: These tugs primarily are named for American Indian tribes.

LARGE HARBOR TUGS: "YTB 756" CLASS

All of these 109-foot (33.2-m), 409-ton harbor tugs have been stricken. Tugs stricken during the 1990s were: the PONTIAC (YTB 756) on 18 November 1992; the BOGALUSA (YTB 759) on 7 August 1996; the OSHKOSH (YTB 757) on 25 April 1996; and the PADUCAH (YTB 758) on 25 June 1999.

LARGE HARBOR TUGS: "YTB 752" CLASS

The last harbor tugs of this design, similar to the YTB 760 class, have been stricken: The MARIN (YTB 753) was stricken on 21 May 1991. The EDENSHAW (YTB 752) was stricken on 5 May 1994 and transferred to the Coast Guard that same year. She was stricken by the Coast Guard in 2001.

1 SMALL HARBOR TUG: "YTL 422" CLASS

Number	Launched	Completed	Status
YTL 602	26 July 1945	5 Oct 1945	**Active**

Builders:	Robert Jacob, City Island, N.Y.
Displacement:	70 tons light
	80 tons full load
Length:	62 feet (18.9 m) waterline
	66⅙ feet (20.2 m) overall
Beam:	17 feet (5.2 m)
Draft:	5 feet (1.5 m)
Propulsion:	1 diesel engine (Hoover); 375 bhp; 1 shaft
Speed:	10 knots
Personnel:	6 (enlisted)

The YTL 602 is the lone survivor in Navy service of several hundred small tugs built during World War II. Many served in foreign navies. The YTL 602 is active at the Pearl Harbor Naval Shipyard.

Classification: The YTLs initially were classified YT with the same hull number. YTL originally stood for harbor tug, *little*.

2 TORPEDO TRIALS CRAFT: "YTT 9" CLASS

Number	Name	Launched	Completed	Status
YTT 9	CAPE FLATTERY	5 May 1989	28 Sep 1990	str. 13 Aug 1999
YTT 10	BATTLE POINT	17 Aug 1989	11 Nov 1990	**Active**
YTT 11	DISCOVERY BAY	22 Feb 1990	19 Apr 1991	**Active**
YTT 12	AGATE PASS	6 Sep 1990	1 July 1991	str. 13 Aug 1999

Builders:	McDermott Shipyard, Morgan City, La.
Displacement:	1,000 tons light
	1,200 tons full load
Length:	176½ feet (53.83 m) waterline
	186½ feet (56.85 m) overall
Beam:	40 feet (12.19 m)
Draft:	10½ feet (3.23 m)
Propulsion:	diesel-electric (1 Cummins VTA-28 diesel engine);
	1,250 shp; 2 all-azimuth drives
Speed:	11 knots
Torpedoes:	2 21-inch (533-mm) tubes Mk 59 (fixed single; submerged)
	3 12.75-inch (324-mm) tubes Mk 32 (triple)
Personnel:	31 civilian + 9 technicians

These are specialized torpedo trials craft that were to replace the IX and YFRT craft previously employed in this role. They are assigned to the Naval Undersea Warfare Center, Keyport, Washington.

The AGATE PASS was never put in naval service, but was laid up in reserve at the Bremerton Naval Shipyard on completion; the

The BATTLE POINT with the CAPE FLATTERY moored astern at Keyport, Washington, the Navy's principal torpedo testing facility. The ships have cranes forward and aft for recovering torpedoes and carry specialized underwater recovery devices. (1990, U.S. Navy)

The now-stricken CAPE FLATTERY. The broad working area aft is flanked by the craft's twin engine exhausts. Two bar-type radar antennas sit atop the large deckhouse. (1990, U.S. Navy)

CAPE FLATTERY was stricken after only nine years of service. Thus, these two craft have provided the Navy with little return on its investment.

Classification: These craft were planned as YFRT type, but were built as YTT. The classification YTT originally indicated torpedo testing barge. The YTT 1–4 were built in 1912–1916; the YTT 5–7 were of World War II construction. All were non-self-propelled barges. The designation YTT 8 was not assigned.

Operational: The AGATE PASS was transferred to the National Oceanic and Atmospheric Administration (NOAA) in 2000 (see Chapter 33).

Engineering: A 350-hp bow thruster is fitted. Electric drive on batteries permits quiet operation for launching acoustic-homing torpedoes.

WATER BARGES

These craft were similar to the YO/YOG types, being employed to carry fresh water for ships. The last two units were the YW 98, stricken on 10 September 1991, and the YW 127, stricken on 18 April 1994.

The similar YW 87 was converted to the MONOB ONE (YAG 61, ex-IX 309).

MISCELLANEOUS SHIPS AND CRAFT

These craft do not have Y-series designations; some have hull registry numbers (length + type designation + serial). The ships and craft in this section are listed according to length.

Classification: The type designations used below are:
NS Non-Standard (commercial design)
UB Utility Boat
SB Sail Boat
ST Sail Trainer
WB Work Boat

The definition of the designation "C" does not appear in the SABAR directory.

1 FORMER SPACE BOOSTER RECOVERY SHIP: "INDEPENDENCE"

Number	Name	Launched	In service	Status
(none)	INDEPENDENCE	27 Feb 1985	1988	**Active**

Builders:	Halter Marine, Moss Point, Miss.
Displacement:	1,798 tons full load
Length:	182 feet (55.47 m) waterline
	199½ feet (60.96 m) overall
Beam:	40 feet (12.2 m)
Draft:	13½ feet (4.1 m)
Propulsion:	diesel (2 Cummins KTA 3067-M); 2,500 bhp; 2 shafts
	+ 2 all-azimuth thrusters (1,000 shp each)
Speed:	13 knots
Range:	8,500 nm (15,750 km) at 11 knots
	7,800 nm (14,450 km) at 13 knots
Personnel:	13 civilian + 14 scientists/technicians

Built for the U.S. Air Force to recover solid-propellant missile boosters from off Vandenberg Air Force Base, California, the INDEPENDENCE was transferred to the Navy in 1988 and is operated by the Naval Facilities Engineering Center at Port Hueneme, California. The ship is used to maintain underwater sensors and to support other specialized projects for the Navy and other government agencies.

Can carry 338 tons of deck cargo aft, including laboratory vans. Fitted with a 22-ton-capacity crane.

2 TRIALS SUPPORT CRAFT

Number	Name	Completed	Status
192UB8701	RANGER	1981	**Active**
	(ex-SEACOR RANGE, SEA LEVEL No. 27)		
192UB8702	NAWC 38	1981	**Active**
	(ex-SEA LEVEL No. 7)		

Builders:	McDermott Shipyard, New Iberia, La.
Displacement:	approximately 1,800 tons full load
Length:	191½ feet (58.52 m) overall
Beam:	40 feet (12.19 m)
Draft:	14 feet (4.27 m)
Propulsion:	2 diesel engines (General Motors 12-645-E6);
	3,000 bhp; 2 shafts
Speed:	12 knots
Range:	
Personnel:	NAWC 38: 8 civilian + 22 technicians/scientists

Both ships were acquired in 1986 to support ship trials. The NAWC 38 operates from Fort Lauderdale, Florida. The RANGER is employed on the Anglo-American Atlantic Undersea Test and Evaluation Center (AUTEC) range, Andros Island, Bahamas; she replaced the IX 306 (former U.S. Army FS 221).

The trials support craft NAWC 38. She previously had a crane fitted on her fantail. (1991, Giorgio Arra)

2 RESEARCH CRAFT: "ASHEVILLE" CLASS

Number	Name	Launched	PG Comm.	To DTRC*	Status
165NS761 (ex-PG 94)	ATHENA I	8 June 1968	8 Nov 1969	21 Aug 1975	**Active**
165NS762 (ex-PG 98)	ATHENA II	4 Apr 1970	5 Sep 1970	3 Oct 1977	**Active**
165NS763 (ex-PG 100)	LAUREN	19 June 1970	6 Feb 1971	1990	str. 2000

*David Taylor Research Center

Builders:	Tacoma Boatbuilding, Wash.
Displacement:	approx. 265 tons full load
Length:	164½ feet (50.2 m) overall
Beam:	23¾ feet (7.2 m)
Draft:	9½ feet (2.9 m)
Propulsion:	Combined Diesel or Gas Turbine (CODOG): 2 diesel engines (Cummins VT12-875M), 1,400 bhp; 1 gas turbine (General Electric LM 1500), 12,500 shp; 2 shafts
Speed:	16 knots on diesel engines; 40+ knot on gas turbines
Range:	2,400 nm (4,445 km) at 14 knots on diesel engines
	325 nm (602 km) at 37 knots on gas turbines
Personnel:	

These are former patrol combatants/gunboats of the ASHEVILLE (PG 84) class employed in the research role. They are the last of a class of 17 in U.S. naval service. These three ships were transferred on the dates indicated to the David Taylor Research Center (DTRC) for use in various offshore research projects; they are based at Panama City, Florida.

The DOUGLAS was stricken on 1 October 1977 for transfer to the DTRC to be placed in service as the ATHENA III. Instead, she was discarded in 1984 but retained in storage at Little Creek, Virginia, for possible foreign transfer. She was reacquired and converted in 1991–1992 for use as a test ship in the Athena program, but given the name LAUREN. The LAUREN was discarded in 2000.

The ATHENA I, showing the deckhouse extension forward of the bridge. The ATHENA I and II have orange hulls with white superstructures. The ATHENA I does not have the "I" painted after her name on the bow. (1991, Giorgio Arra)

The ATHENA II, with a rounded bridge face. All three craft have been employed for research and development work by the David Taylor Research Center. (1991, Giorgio Arra)

All weapons have been removed.

Class: This originally was a class of 17 gunboats (PGM/PG 84–101), completed from 1966 to 1970. (See 16th Edition/page 195 for class disposition.)

Classification: When assigned to the DTRC, these ships were reclassified as service craft without specific hull designations; the NVR lists the ATHENA I and ATHENA II as being reclassified as service craft on 1 August 1975 and 1 October 1977, respectively. The LAUREN is listed as having been stricken on 1 October 1977.

Design: These ships have aluminum hulls with fiberglass superstructures.

Names: Their names as gunboats were CHEHALIS (PG 94), GRAND RAPIDS (PG 98), and DOUGLAS (PG 100).

Operational: These ships have participated in a variety of research projects. Possibly the most unusual was one in which the ATHENA II, at maximum speed, towed an in-flight MH-53E helicopter backward to help assess flight envelope characteristics. Other trials have included sonars and mine countermeasures gear.

SALVAGE TENDER: "SOTOYOMO" CLASS

The KEYWADIN (142NS9201), a former auxiliary tug (ATA 213) employed for fire and salvage training by Mobile Diving and Salvage Unit 2 at Little Creek, Virginia, was sunk as a target on 3 June 2001. Completed in 1945, she had been officially stricken from the NVR on 1 June 1980 but was reacquired for naval service in 1992.

Several other ex-ATAs were used as salvage training hulks; they were sunk and salved in training exercises. The ex-ATA 203 used in that manner was sunk as a target on 10 February 2003.

Class: Originally the SOTOYOMO class consisted of 70 ships: ATA 121–125, 146, 170–213, and 219–238. (The KEYWADIN was the only one given a small craft number.)

1 HULL FORM RESEARCH SHIP: "SEA SLICE"

Number	Name	Launched	In service	Status
(none)	SEA SLICE	Nov 1996	1997	**Active**

Builder:	Honolulu Shipyard Division, Pacific Marine, Hawaii
Displacement:	180 tons full load
Length:	105 feet (32.01 m) overall
Beam:	55 feet (16.77 m)
Draft:	14 feet (4.27 m)
Propulsion:	2 diesel engines (MTU 16V396 TB 94); 6,850 bhp; 2 propulsion pods.
Speed:	23–27 knots cruise (varies with payload)
	31 knots maximum
Range:	850 nm (1,575 km) at cruise speed
	400 nm (740 km) at 30 knots
Personnel:	2 civilian + 4 trials technicians

The SEA SLICE is a multihull test platform for a variation of the SWATH (Small Waterplane-Area Twin Hull) configuration. Funded jointly by the Office of Naval Research and the Pacific Marine and Supply Co., the SEA SLICE is based on the design for an interisland ferry. The craft is capable of towing a "trailer" platform, also supported on four struts/pods.

A scaled-up SEA SLICE configuration was considered as a potential hull form for the Navy's Littoral Combat Ship (LCS) program (see Chapter 17).

Also see the QUEST entry (below).

Armament: The SEA SLICE has evaluated the Lockheed Martin/Oerlikon Contraves Millennium 35-mm rapid-fire cannon and a variety of short-range surveillance and gunfire control systems. (In her earlier configuration, the SEA SLICE could operate a helicopter.)

Design: The SEA SLICE has four supporting struts/pods that penetrate the air–water interface to provide lift at high speeds. The *forward* pods contain the diesel engines and are fitted with 7¼-foot

The quad-hull configuration of the SEA SLICE is seen clearly in this view. The twin propeller pods are forward; the after pods can carry fuel or ballast. There are inboard stabilizing fins attached to each pod. (U.S. Navy)

The hull is fabricated of aluminum.

Names: Initially called SLICE, she now is known as SEA SLICE.

Operational: The SEA SLICE participated in Fleet Battle Experiment Juliet off the West Coast from 24 July to 7 August 2002.

1 HULL FORM RESEARCH SHIP (SWATH): "KAIMALINO"

Number	Name	Launched	In service	Status
90WB8701	KAIMALINO	7 Mar 1973	1973	**Active**

Builder:	Coast Guard Yard, Curtis Bay, Md.
Displacement:	228 tons full load
Length:	88⅓ feet (26.9 m) overall
Beam:	46½ feet (14.2 m)
Draft:	15¼ feet (4.65 m)
Propulsion:	CODOG: 2 diesel engines (General Motors 6-71); 160 bhp; 2 gas turbines (General Electric T64-6B); 5,000 shp; 2 shafts
Speed:	22 knots
Range:	1,500 nm (2,778 km) at 5 knots on diesel engines 450 nm (833 km) at 17 knots on gas turbines
Personnel:	10 civilian + 6 technicians

(2.2-m) controllable-pitch propellers; the after pods carry fuel and/or ballast. A fifth strut could be fitted to provide a third propeller pod. The pods are 40 feet (12.20 m) in length and 8 feet (2.44 m) in diameter.

The SWATH configuration provides a large, open deck and considerable internal cargo volume, suitable for cargo or missiles. The design/propulsion system provides for low wake observability.

In her current configuration, the SEA SLICE's open well has been decked over and a structure has been installed on the helicopter deck; a lattice mast has been installed amidships.

The U.S. Navy's first SWATH/Semi-Submerged Platform (SSP) research ship, the KAIMALINO has had a long career as a test platform. She was taken out of service in 1994 after 20 years of operation testing the SWATH configuration and service as an underwater test range support ship. She was laid up at San Diego until reactivated in 1997 for trials in conjunction with the SEA SLICE program (see above).

The SWATH design subsequently was adopted for the SEA SHADOW stealth research ship and for later ocean surveillance ships (T-AGOS 19–23).

The SEA SLICE in her current configuration and paint scheme—an artistic combination of blues, gray, and yellow. "Lockheed Martin" is painted on the stern, below "Navy" with "Sea Slice" on the bow. (U.S. Navy)

The SEA SLICE at San Diego. There is a 35-mm gun fitted forward and a lattice mast and deckhouse amidships as she tests various sensor and fire control systems. Her twin hull is evident. (2002, W. Michael Young)

Conversion: The KAIMALINO was modified at the Dillingham Shipyard in Hawaii in 1980–1981. She was enlarged from 190 to 228 tons through the addition of fiberglass buoyancy modules. Plans to further enlarge the ship to some 600 tons were not carried out.

Design: The SWATH design provides for considerable stability and a large working/payload deck area. Different from a catamaran, which has two conventional ship hulls joined together, the KAIMALINO has two fully submerged, torpedo-shaped hulls, each 6 1/2 feet (2.0 m) in diameter, with vertical struts penetrating the water to support the superstructure and deck. The ship's flight deck area is 3,400 square feet (306 m²).

The KAIMALINO has a hull-stabilizing fin connecting the two submerged hulls and two small canard fins forward, one inboard on each hull. There is an opening in the craft's main deck for lowering search and recovery devices. (The opening is covered over for helicopter operations.) The beam listed in the data table is the maximum over both hulls.

Up to 16 tons of mission equipment can be carried.

Engineering: Two T64 aircraft-type gas turbine engines provide propulsion power. Two diesel engines (General Motors 8V-71T) are installed for auxiliary propulsion.

Helicopters: The KAIMALINO conducted tests in 1976 on the feasibility of landing helicopters on SSP/SWATH-type ships in high sea states at speeds up to 25 knots. The operations with an SH-2F LAMPS I were completely successful.

Torpedoes: In 1982, the KAIMALINO was fitted with triple Mk 32 torpedo tubes for tests of lightweight ASW torpedoes.

The KAIMALINO in dry dock, showing her underwater hulls. She served as a prototype for the SWATH T-AGOS designs (see Chapter 23). (1973, U.S. Navy)

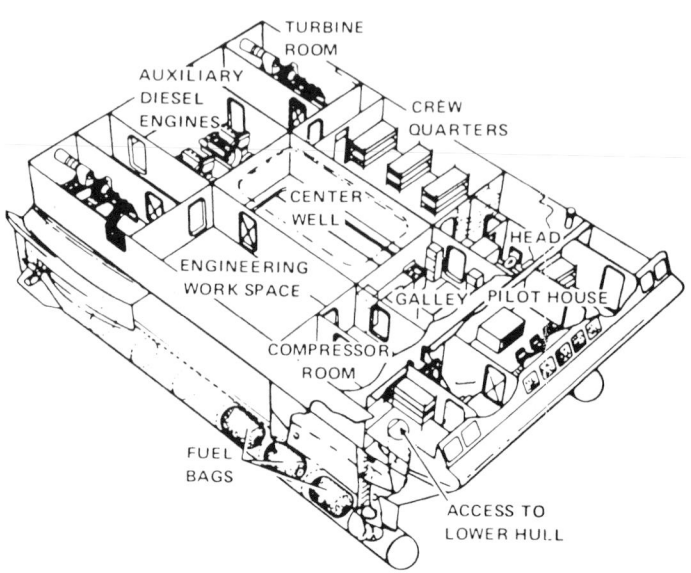

The interior arrangement of the KAIMALINO. SWATH configurations provide relatively high cube for a given displacement, as well as high stability in rough seas. (U.S. Navy)

The research ship KAIMALINO at San Diego. She has two torpedo-like hulls with two struts projecting from each hull to support her superstructure. A photo in the 17th Edition/page 343 shows the KAIMALINO with an SH-2F LAMPS I helicopter on her flight deck. (1997, W. William Young)

PATROL BOAT: EX-COAST GUARD CUTTER

Number	Name	USCG Comm.
95NS8801 (ex-WPB 95310)	Venture	15 Dec 1953

Builder:	Coast Guard Yard, Curtis Bay, Md.
Displacement:	87 tons standard
	105 tons full load
Length:	95 feet (29.0 m) overall
Beam:	19 feet (5.8 m)
Draft:	6 feet (1.8 m)
Propulsion:	4 diesel engines (Cummins VT-12-M-700); 2,300 bhp; 2 shafts
Speed:	20 knots
Range:	2,600 nm (4,820 km) at 9 knots
	460 nm (850 km) at 20 knots
Personnel:	8 (enlisted)
Radar:	SPS-64(V)1 navigation

Formerly the U.S. Coast Guard cutter CAPE WASH, this is the last of the 95-foot Cape class units in U.S. service. She was stricken from the Coast Guard on 1 June 1987 and transferred to the Navy for use as a patrol–escort ship for submarines going to and from sea from Bangor, Washington.

Class: Four cutters of this class were transferred to the Navy. The VANGUARD (ex-CAPE HEDGE/WPB 95311) was returned to the Coast Guard for transfer to Mexico in 1990; unnamed 95NS8902 (ex-CAPE JELLISON/WPB 95317) was transferred from the Navy to the Sea Scouts at San Diego in 1993; the unnamed 95NS8901 (ex-CAPE ROMAINE/WPB 95319) was discarded in 1993.

2 WEAPON TRIALS CRAFT: SEA SPECTRE TYPE

Number	Name	Launched	Comm.	Status
65PB734	Navy Prince	1975	1975	**Active**
65PB777	Plymouth	1979	1979	**Active**

Builder:	Peterson Builders, Sturgeon Bay, Wisc.
Displacement:	28 tons light
	36.7 tons full load
Length:	64¹¹⁄₂ feet (19.8 m) overall
Beam:	18¹⁄₂ feet (5.5 m)
Draft:	5⅝ feet (1.8 m)
Propulsion:	3 diesel engines (General Motors 8V71); 1,950 bhp; 3 shafts
Speed:	approximately 25 knots
Range:	2,000 nm at slow speeds
	450 nm (835 km) at 26 knots
Personnel:	9 (1 officer + 8 enlisted)
Guns:	(see notes)

These craft are the survivors of 22 Patrol Boats (PB) Mk III built for the U.S. Navy after the Vietnam War. (A slightly larger version

The PLYMOUTH *with a stabilized gun mount forward and related fire control equipment. (1996)*

also was built for the U.S. Navy.) Both are assigned to the Naval Surface Warfare Center at Dahlgren, Virginia.

The PLYMOUTH has been used in gun trials.

Design: The Mk III was adopted from a commercial design used to support offshore drilling rigs in the Gulf of Mexico. The craft are all-aluminum construction with their pilothouse offset to starboard to permit maximum deck space for mounting weapons.

Mission duration was up to five days.

Guns: These craft originally were fitted with an automatic 40-mm Bofors cannon or manually operated 20-mm cannon forward, and up to four .50-caliber machine guns on pintel mountings. Most later carried in their place a 20-mm Bushmaster cannon and several 7.62-mm machine guns. There were deck fittings for other guns, as well as missiles, mines, torpedoes, or minesweeping gear.

1 HULL TEST CRAFT: "QUEST"

Number	Name	Launched	Completed	Status
HYSWAS 1	Quest	7 July 1995	1995	**Active**

Builder:	Maritime Applied Physics, Laurel, Md.
Displacement:	12 tons full load
Length:	27 feet (8.22 m) overall
Beam:	10⅙ feet (3.1 m) over foils
Draft:	9⅗ feet (3.0 m) hullborne
	6⁷⁄₁₂ feet (2.0 m) foilborne
Propulsion:	2 diesel engines (Cummins); 1 shaft
Speed:	37 knots foilborne
Personnel:	

The QUEST is a small hull test platform, included here despite her diminutive size because of her unusual configuration. HYSWAS indicates Hydrofoil Small Waterplane-Area Ship. Unlike SWATH designs, which have twin hulls, she has a single hull.

Design: The QUEST has a single, centerline "hull" mounted on a tall pylon, with two sets of variable-incidence foils mounted on the "foot." The design is intended to maintain 35 knots in sea state 5.

The QUEST *high and dry on her monohull. (1995, Maritime Applied Physics)*

TORPEDO/WEAPON RETRIEVERS

These craft support torpedo testing and submarine practice torpedo launches. The designations TR, TWR (torpedo weapon retriever), and TRB (torpedo recovery boat) are used for these craft. The names listed are unofficial.

These craft have stern ramps for recovering torpedoes; some also have hydraulic cranes. They are listed according to size.

2 TORPEDO RETRIEVERS: EX-OIL FIELD SUPPORT CRAFT

Number	Name	Completed	In service
180NS8201	HUGO (ex-CRYSTAL PELHAM)	Jan 1982	3 July 1991
180NS8202	HUNTER (ex-NOLA PELHAM)	Jan 1981	3 July 1991

Builders:	8201: McDermott Shipyard, New Iberia, La.
	8202: Quality Shipbuilders, Moss Point, Miss.
Displacement:	approx. 1,500 tons full load
Length:	8201: 165 feet (50.32 m) overall
	8202: 180 feet (54.86 m) overall
Beam:	8201: 40 feet (12.19 m)
	8202: 38 feet (11.58 m)
Draft:	8201: 11 feet (3.35 m)
	8202: 13 feet (3.96 m)
Propulsion:	2 diesel engines (Caterpillar D399 SCAC); 2,250 bhp; 2 shafts
Speed:	12 knots
Range:	
Personnel:	

These are former oil field support vessels acquired for the torpedo recovery role and assigned to the Atlantic Fleet Weapons Training activity at Roosevelt Roads, Puerto Rico.

Details of the ships differ.

Class: A third craft of this type, the RANGE ROVER (180NS9201), previously served as a trials ship at the Anglo-American AUTEC range, Andros Island, Bahamas.

The torpedo recovery craft HUNTER *going to sea. The* HUGO *is similar. (1999, Leo Van Ginderen)*

2 DIVER SUPPORT TENDERS } 120-FOOT TYPE
4 TORPEDO RETRIEVERS

Number	Name	Launched	Completed
TWR 821	SWAMP FOX	17 Oct 1984	4 Nov 1985
TWR 823	PORPOISE	4 May 1985	6 Dec 1985
TWR 832		22 Mar 1986	3 July 1986
TWR 833		4 Apr 1986	3 July 1986
TWR 841		15 Aug 1986	18 Oct 1986
TWR 842	NARWHAL	22 Sep 1986	24 Dec 1986

Builders:	Marinette Marine, Marinette, Wisc.
Displacement:	174 tons standard
	213 tons full load
Length:	120 feet (36.6 m) overall
Beam:	25 feet (7.6 m)
Draft:	12 feet (3.65 m)
Propulsion:	2 diesel engines (Caterpillar D 3512); 2,350 bhp; 2 shafts
Speed:	16 knots
Range:	1,700 nm (3,150 km) at 16 knots
Personnel	15 (1 officer + 14 enlisted)
Radar:	Canadian Marconi LN-66 navigation

The SWAMP FOX *is typical of the later series of U.S. Navy torpedo recovery craft. She has several awards painted on her deckhouse, indicating outstanding performance. (1994, Giorgio Arra)*

These are improved torpedo retrievers capable of recovering and carrying up to 14 Mk 48 torpedoes. The TWR 833 and TWR 841 have been modified and serve as diver support tenders.

Class: This originally was a class of ten units: the TR 821–825, 831–833, 841, and 842. The TWR 824 and TWR 831 were severely damaged (not sunk) by Hurricane Hugo at Roosevelt Roads in 1990. The TWR 822 and TWR 835 were stricken in 1997.

Classification: These craft have SABAR designations consisting of the prefix 120 + TR + the above numbers; thus, TWR 821 has the SABAR designation 120TR821.

Design: A stern ramp and crane are provided for torpedo recovery. Endurance is seven days.

2 MISSILE RETRIEVERS: EX-AIR FORCE CRAFT

Number	Name	Completed
120NS8801 (ex-MR-120-8805)	SEADOG	1988
120NS8004 (ex-MR-120-8004)	SL-120	1988

Builders:	Swiftships, Morgan City, La.
Displacement:	91 tons light
	133 tons full load
Length:	117⅓ feet (35.78 m) overall
Beam:	24⅔ feet (7.51 m)
Draft:	6¾ feet (2.06 m)
Propulsion:	4 diesel engines (Detroit Diesel 16V92 MTA); 5,600 bhp; 4 shafts
Speed:	30 knots
Range:	600 nm (1,111 km) at 27 knots
Personnel:	10 (enlisted)

These retrieval craft are employed to recover practice missiles. They were built for the U.S. Air Force and transferred to the Navy in 1996. Most retain their Air Force numbers; the 8001 serves at Kadena Air base, Okinawa, and the 8004 at Port Hueneme. They can carry 20 tons of cargo and are of aluminum construction.

Class: Originally, five of these craft were transferred to the Navy.

The weapons recovery craft SL-120 *at Port Hueneme. (1995, George R. Schneider)*

1 TORPEDO AND DECOY RETRIEVER: "RANGEMASTER"

Number	Name	Completed
110WB8501	RANGEMASTER	1981

Builder:	Steiner Fabricators, Bayou LaBatre, Ala.
Displacement:	
Tonnage:	99 GRT
Length:	110 feet (33.53 m) overall
Beam:	26 feet (7.92 m)
Draft:	11½ feet (3.51 m)
Propulsion:	1 diesel engine; 1 shaft
Speed:	
Personnel:	

Built as a crewboat for RCA to support Navy contract work, the RANGEMASTER was purchased by the Navy in 1985 for use at the Anglo-American AUTEC range for torpedo and decoy recovery.

2 TORPEDO RETRIEVERS

Number	Name	Completed
110NS8701	TRANSPORTER (ex-SEACO TRANSPORTER; ALEXANDRA ROBIN)	1978
100NS8702	Retriever (ex-SEACO TRAVELLER, LORRAINE ROBIN)	1978

Builder:	Swiftships, Morgan City, La.
Displacement:	
Tonnage:	85 GRT
Length:	100 feet (30.48 m) overall
Beam:	20 feet (6.1 m)
Draft:	7 feet (2.13 m)
Propulsion:	3 diesel engines (General Motors 12V-71 T1); 1,650 bhp; 3 shafts
Speed:	20 knots
Range:	800 nm (1,480 km) at 18 knots
Personnel:	12 civilian

These former oil field crew boats were acquired in 1989. The TRANSPORTER is operated by the Naval Air Station Patuxent River (Maryland), and the RETRIEVER—also designated DLR 3—is operated by Fleet Composite Squadron (VC) 6 at Norfolk, Virginia.

Cranes are fitted.

The RETRIEVER, with signal flags strung up and a Chukar target on her deck. (2000, A. D. Baker III)

The PHOENIX, wearing several award insignia on her bridge, is another of these most-useful torpedo and weapon retrieval craft. The twin-funnel configuration permits a large area for torpedo recovery and stowage. A rubber raft is stowed aft. (1998, Leo Van Ginderen)

1 TORPEDO RETRIEVER: 100-FOOT TYPE

Number	(SABAR)	Name	Completed
TWR 771	(100TR771)	PHOENIX	Dec 1978

Builders:	Peterson Builders, Sturgeon Bay, Wisc.
Displacement:	110 tons light
	165 tons full load
Length:	102 feet (31.1 m) overall
Beam:	21 feet (6.4 m)
Draft:	7¾ feet (2.4 m)
Propulsion:	4 diesel engines (General Motors 12V-149); 1,600 bhp; 2 shafts
Speed:	17 knots
Range:	1,920 nm (3,556 km) at 10 knots
Personnel:	15 (enlisted)

The PHOENIX is the last of a series of torpedo retrievers based on the PGM 59-class motor gunboat design.

Class: Stricken units of this type are the CRAYFISH (TWR 682) in 1991, the unnamed TWR 711 and DIAMOND (TWR 1) in 1994, the LABRADOR (TWR 681) in 1995, the CONDOR (TWR 3) in 2000, and the FERRET (TWR 6) in 2001.

Design: The ship is of steel construction, is fitted with a stern recovery ramp, and can carry 17 tons of torpedoes.

2 TORPEDO RETRIEVERS: 85-FOOT TYPE

Number	SABAR	Name	Completed
TWR 7	(85TR762)	CHAPPARAL	1975
TWR 8	(85TR761)	ILIWAI	1975

Builders:	Tacoma Boatbuilding, Wash.
Displacement:	
Length:	85 feet (25.9 m) overall
Beam:	18⅔ feet (5.7 m)
Draft:	5⅔ feet (1.7 m)
Propulsion:	4 diesel engines (General Motors); 2 shafts
Speed:	18 knots
Personnel:	

The TWR 7 was laid up at San Diego in 1992, but returned to service in 1997; both craft are at Pearl Harbor, Hawaii.

These craft each can carry eight torpedoes, up to a total of 22,000 pounds (9,979 kg). They are of aluminum construction.

The HM 8, sole U.S. survivor of a class of weapon retrievers and patrol craft. (2001, George R. Schneider)

1 WEAPONS RETRIEVER: EX-AIR FORCE CRAFT

Number	Name	Completed
85NS681	HM 8	1967

Builders:	Swiftships, Morgan City, La.
Displacement:	90 tons full load
Length:	85 feet (25.91 m) overall
Beam:	18 feet (5.49 m)
Draft:	5⅙ feet (1.57 m)
Propulsion:	2 diesel engines (General Motors 16V-92); 2 shafts
Speed:	17 knots
Range:	400 nm (740 km) at 17 knots
Personnel:	8 (enlisted)

This is the last of a series of craft built for the U.S. Air Force as weapon retrievers and transferred to the Navy 1990–1996. The HM designation was assigned by Port Hueneme.

The HM 9 (85NS691) went aground and was lost on 21 January 1999; the TWR 4 (85NS9001) was stricken in 1999, and the 85NS9601 craft was stricken in 2001.

3 TORPEDO RETRIEVERS: 85-FOOT TYPE

Number	(SABAR)	Completed
TR 651	(85TR651)	July 1965
TR 653	(85TR653)	Dec 1966
TR 654	(85TR654)	Jan 1967

Builders:	Tacoma Boatbuilding, Wash.
Displacement:	61 tons full load
Length:	85 feet (25.9 m) overall
Beam:	18⅔ feet (5.69 m)
Draft:	5⅔ feet (1.73 m)
Propulsion:	2 diesel engines (General Motors 16V-71); 1,160 bhp; 2 shafts
Speed:	21 knots
Personnel:	8 (enlisted)

These craft each can carry eight torpedoes (up to 22,000 pounds/9,979 kg total) and are of aluminum construction.

One craft of this design has been stricken, the TR 761 (correction to previous edition). Two similar patrol craft, built without stern ramps, have the SABAR designations 85C14252 and 85C14253.

2 TORPEDO RETRIEVERS: 72-FOOT MK 2 TYPE

Number	(SABAR)	Completed
TRB 32	(72TR645)	Mar 1966
TRB 33	(72TR652)	Aug 1966

Builders:	
Displacement:	53 tons full load
Length:	72⅙ feet (22.0 m) overall
Beam:	17 feet (5.2 m)
Draft:	4⅓ feet (1.3 m)
Propulsion:	8 diesel engines; 1,300 bhp; 2 shafts
Speed:	18 knots
Range:	180 nm (333 km) at 18 knots
Personnel:	7 (enlisted)
Radar:	SPS-69 navigation

This series of torpedo recovery craft was to be replaced by the new, 120-foot craft but was retained because of the shortfall in TRs. These wooden-construction craft can carry 24,000 pounds (10,886 kg) of torpedoes.

They were built with SPS-53 radars, which subsequently were replaced by the SPS-69.

Four units have been stricken: the TRB 31 (72C3211) in 1995, TRB 10 (72TR653) in 1996, TRB 37 (72C9426) in 1999, and TRB 36 (72C4560) in 2001.

3 TORPEDO RETRIEVERS: 65-FOOT TYPE

Number	(SABAR)	Name	Completed
TR 671	(65TR671)		Oct 1967
TRB 5	(65TR675)	HARRIER	July 1968
TR 6	(65TR676)	PEREGRINE	July 1968

Builders:	
Displacement:	34.8 tons full load
Length:	65 feet (19.8 m) overall
Beam:	17¼ feet (5.25 m)
Draft:	3⅞ feet (1.2 m)
Propulsion:	2 diesel engines (General Motors 12V-71); 1,000 bhp; 2 shafts
Speed:	24 knots
Range:	280 nm (518 km) at 18 knots
Personnel:	6 (enlisted)

The HARRIER. (2000, Brian Morrison)

This basic 65-foot design also was used for Navy utility and air-sea rescue boats. These aluminum-construction craft can carry four Mk 48 torpedoes.

The TR 671 is at Roosevelt Roads, the TRB 5 is at Pearl Harbor, and the TR 6 is at Keyport.

Two units were stricken in 1996: the SEA HAWK (TR 673) and ALBATROSS (TR 4/65TR674); both were transferred for use by the Sea Scouts.

TARGET CRAFT

In addition to the two large afloat targets listed here, the Navy operates a number of small, radio-controlled target boats.

A 55-foot (16.7-m) SEPTAR radio-controlled target boat. The Navy operates a large number of similar craft. (2000, A.D. Baker III)

WEAPON SET-TO-HIT THREAT TARGET (NSP)

This unmanned submersible was acquired in 2004 to test ASW weapons and sensors. Designated as a Weapon Set-to-hit Threat Target (WSTTT), it can be raised and lowered from a tug-type support ship, but it has no self-propulsion capability. The craft is based at San Diego.

A tug prepares to tow the submersible WSTTT during operations off the coast of San Diego. The craft is painted bright yellow. (2004, U.S. Navy/Todd Reeves)

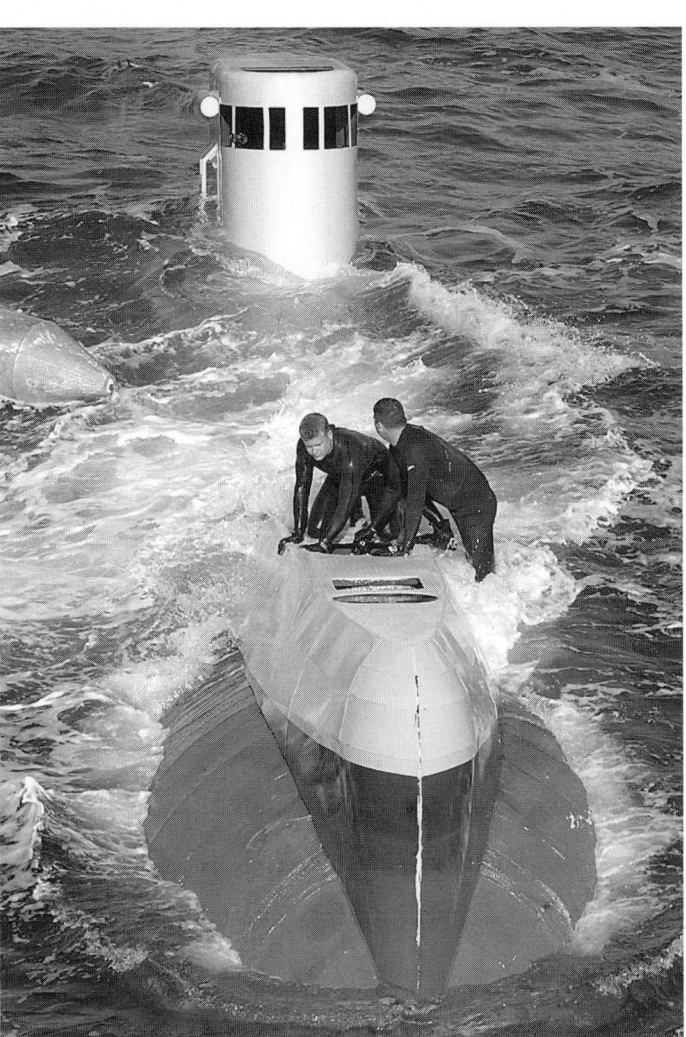

Navy divers work on the submersible target known as the WSTTT. (2004, U.S. Navy/Todd Reeves)

SURFACE SHIP TARGET

Builders:	Maritime Contractors, Bellingham, Wash.
Displacement:	850 tons full load
Length:	260 feet (79.25 m) overall
Beam:	26 feet (7.92 m)
Draft:	7 feet (2.13 m)
Propulsion:	2 diesel engines; 2 shafts
Speed:	15 knots

This is a large, unmanned target ship built in 1994. It operates under radio control with 20-foot (6-m) containers stacked on deck to provide various target signatures. The ship is based at Port Hueneme.

The radio-controlled SST. (1994, U.S. Navy)

MISCELLANEOUS SHIPS AND CRAFT

Several hundred small craft, including various launches, work boats, and ship's boats, are in service at various U.S. naval stations and bases and aboard ships. There also are numerous pollution control, patrol craft, and boom tenders. The boom tenders maintain protective booms around U.S. naval ships in harbors and shipyards to prevent the approach of small craft that might be a terrorist threat to those ships.

NON-SELF-PROPELLED SERVICE CRAFT

The following are the approximate numbers of various types of non-self-propelled service craft listed on the Naval Vessel Register; almost all are in service. The YCF transport railroad cars, and some of the YD floating cranes have maneuvering propulsion.

Only eight of these craft have names: the MERCER (APL 39), NUECES (APL 40), PHOEBUS (YDT 14), SUITLAND (YDT 15), TOM O'MALLEY (YDT 16), SEA TURTLE (YFNX 30), SPRUCE BARGE (YFNX 42), and THE BIG W (YSR 6).

The single car float YCF 16 is moored at Seneca Lake, New York, in support of the IX 310. The floating cranes (YD) include two units, on loan from the Japanese government since 1954, that are not numbered in the U.S. hull series; one is at Sasebo and Yokosuka to support U.S. naval ships homeported there.

The non-self-propelled craft are tallied below; units in reserve are indicated in parentheses (included in totals). For characteristics see, A. D. Baker III, *Combat Fleets of the World 2002–2003* (Annapolis, Md.: Naval Institute Press, 2002), pp. 1015–22.

17	APL	Barracks craft
48	SWOB	Ship waste oil barge
168	YC	Open lighters (9)
1	YCF	Car float
8	YCV	Aircraft transportation lighters
34	YD	Floating cranes (2)
4	YDT	Diving tenders
54	YFN	Covered lighters (6)
6	YFNB	Large covered lighters (1)
3	YFND	Dry dock companion craft
12	YFNX	Special-purpose lighters
1	YFP	Floating power barges
3	YGN	Garbage lighters
2	YLC	Salvage lift craft
1	YNG	Gate craft
9	YOGN	Gasoline barges
41	YON	Fuel oil barges
3	YOS	Oil storage barge
2	YPD	Floating pile drivers
16	YR	Floating workshops
3	YRB	Repair and berthing barges
39	YRBM	Repair, berthing and messing barge
3	YRDH	Floating dry dock workshops(hull)
2	YRDM	Floating dry dock workshops (machinery)
3	YRR	Radiological repair barges
2	YRST	Salvage craft tenders
4	YWN	Water barges (1)
2	. . . .	Reactor transport barges (1)

The barracks ships include the former self-propelled MERCER (APL 39, ex-IX 502, APB 39) and NUECES (APL 40, ex-IX 503, APB 40). They were reclassified from IX to APL on 7 March 2001. Built during World War II to a modified LST design, they have had their 40-mm anti-aircraft guns removed, and their propulsion plants no longer are operational. These are the only named APLs. (See 17th Edition/page 327 for characteristics.)

Two large APLs were delivered in 1997-1998, the APL 61 and APL 62. They are 4,680 tons full load, 360 feet (110 m) long, and can provide accommodations and mess facilities for 600. Office, training, and medical spaces also are provided in these craft.

The YFNX special-purpose lighters are constructed or modified from YC or YFN hulls for use in performing a specialized service, such as sonar research, deperming ships, and decontamination services. Thus, it is rare that two or more YFNXs have the same configuration.

The two reactor transport barges, the BARGE 40 (in reserve) and BARGE 60, do not have Navy hull numbers and are not on the NVR. They are employed to transport nuclear reactor hull sections cut from submarines from the Puget Sound Naval Shipyard to Hanford, Washington, for temporary burial.

The designations of these craft change periodically as they are modified or reassigned. For example, in July 2003, the YR 68 and YR 78 were changed to YRB 34 and YRB 35, respectively, because "the current hull designation as a floating workshop does not reflect the crafts' current mission."[7]

In addition to the non-self-propelled craft listed above, the Navy owns a unique oceanographic research craft known as FLIP that warrants description.

---

7 Office of the Chief of Naval Operations, OPNAV Notice 5030, Subj.: Reclassification of Naval Service Craft," ser N431L/ 3U573947, 11 July 2003.

Floating workshop YR 60. (1999, Leo Van Ginderen)

Barracks craft APL 5 at San Diego. (2000, W. Michael Young)

Open lighter YC 829. (1998, Leo Van Ginderen)

Landing barge YC 746. (1999, Leo Van Ginderen)

Covered lighter YFN 1266 at San Diego. (1998, W. Michael Young)

Barracks craft APL 15. (1999, Leo Van Ginderen

Floating dry dock workshop (machinery) YRDM 5. (1999, Leo Van Ginderen)

Repair, berthing, and messing barge YRBM 44. (1999, Leo Van Ginderen)

A waste disposal barge—designated SWOB—at San Diego. (1997, W. Michael Young)

Repair, berthing, and messing barge YRBM 38. (2000, Leo Van Ginderen)

Crane barge YD 251. (1999, Leo Van Ginderen)

1 FLOATING INSTRUMENTATION PLATFORM: "FLIP"

Number	Name	Launched	In service	Status
(none)	FLIP	22 June 1962	6 Aug 1962	**Academic**

Builder:	Gunderson Brothers, Portland, Ore.
Displacement:	700 tons full load
Length:	359½ feet (109.73 m) overall
Beam:	28 feet (8.53 m)
Draft:	12½ feet (3.81 m) horizontal
	280 feet (85.37 m) vertical
Propulsion:	non-self-propelled (see *Engineering* notes)
Personnel:	5 civilian + 11 technicians

The FLIP is a unique research craft—basically a long cylinder that can be "flipped" to a vertical position, with the upper portion above sea level and the lower portion providing sensors at various levels within the water column. It has a "ship bow" to facilitate towing (towing speed is up to 10 knots).

The FLIP was built to support Navy submarine/ASW research; subsequently, it has been used for a variety of ocean research projects. The craft is Navy owned and, since entering service, has been operated by the Scripps Institution of Oceanography's Marine Physical Laboratory, part of the University of California, in La Jolla.

The FLIP has an at-sea endurance of up to 30 days without replenishment.

The FLIP, ballasted down, has 55 feet of her "bow" above water. Note the radar reflector and bar-type search radar antenna fitted on the above-water portion of the FLIP. The horizontal waterline is visible on the bow. (Scripps Institution of Oceanography)

The FLIP in the horizontal position, for towing and mooring when in port. The 360-foot instrument has been in service for almost four decades. (Scripps Institution of Oceanography)

A similar, unmanned Navy project was the Seagoing Platform for Acoustic Research (SPAR), in use in the latter 1960s. This platform was 354 feet (107.93 m) in length, 16 feet (4.88 m) in diameter, displaced 1,370 tons in the horizontal position, and 1,720 tons ballasted in the vertical position; the platform operated with a draft of 302 feet (92.07 m).

Engineering: The craft is non-self-propelled but has a 60-horsepower thruster for station keeping. She is towed to operating areas and can drift free or be anchored to the ocean floor.

Names: FLIP stands for Floating Instrumentation Platform.

SAILING SHIPS AND CRAFT

The sailing craft listed below are used by the U.S. Naval Academy at Annapolis, Maryland, to support a four-part sailing program: plebe summer sail training; the Command, Seamanship, and Navigation Training Squadron; the Intercollegiate Sailing Team; and the Offshore Sailing Team.

The AMERICAN PROMISE while tacking. (U.S. Navy)

In addition to these seagoing craft, the Academy operates a larger number of small sailing "knockabouts."

The small sailing sloop CINNABAR of 13 tons full load has been discarded.

1 SAILING SLOOP: "AMERICAN PROMISE"

Number	Name	Completed
60SB8701	AMERICAN PROMISE	1985

Builders:	Little Harbor Boat Yard, Marblehead, Mass.
Displacement:	38.7 tons full load
Length:	60 feet (18.29 m) overall
Beam:	17⅙ feet (5.23 m)
Draft:	10¼ feet (2.12 m)
Masts:	
Propulsion:	1 auxiliary diesel; 1 shaft
Speed:	
Personnel:	
Radar:	navigation

The AMERICAN PROMISE was designed by naval architect Ted Hood specifically for a single-hand, nonstop, around-the-world cruise by Dodge Morgan. That circumnavigation, accomplished in 1985–1986, set several records.[8] The voyage was accomplished in just over 150 days at an average speed of 7.13 knots, averaging 171.1 nm (317 km) per day.

The ship was donated to the Naval Academy in 1987 and is employed in local and transatlantic sailing.

Design: The craft is of Glass-Reinforced Plastic (GRP) construction.

---

8 Morgan was the first American and the 13th person to complete a solo circumnavigation. See Dodge Morgan, *The Voyage of the American Promise* (Boston: Houghton Mifflin, 1989).

A pair of 44-foot sail training yawls at the U.S. Naval Academy maneuver in Chesapeake Bay under very light wind. (U.S. Navy)

The DAUNTLESS, a Navy 44 sail training yawl at the U.S. Naval Academy. These craft provide valuable training to future naval officers. Unfortunately, such an experience is not available to officers entering from non-Academy sources. (U.S. Navy)

21 SAIL TRAINING CRAFT: NAVY 44 DESIGN

Number	Name	Number	Name
NA-1	Audacious	NA-12	Vigilant
NA-2	Courageous	NA-13	Resolute
NA-3	Invincible	NA-14	Intrepid
NA-4	Valiant	NA-15	Frolic
NA-5	Active	NA-16	Restless
NA-6	Alert	NA-17	Dandy
NA-7	Dauntless	NA-18	Dash
NA-8	Fearless	NA-19	Bold
NA-9	Flirt	NA-20	Challenger
NA-10	Lively	NA-21	(none)
NA-11	Swift		

Builders:	Tillotson-Pearson, Warren, R.I.
Displacement:	14.35 tons full load
Length:	35¾ feet (10.91 m) waterline
	44 feet (13.41 m) overall
Beam:	11⅛ feet (3.4 m)
Draft:	7⁵⁄₁₂ feet (2.26 m)
Masts:	main: 62¼ feet (18.98 m) above waterline
Propulsion:	1 auxiliary diesel; 33 bhp; 1 shaft
Speed:	
Personnel:	8–10 officers and midshipmen
Radar:	SPS-66 navigation

Designed by the firm of McCurdy & Rhodes of Cold Spring, New York, the "Navy 44" design has, according to Naval Academy statements, "proven to be a very successful design, being seaworthy, strong, and stable in the worst weather; fast and comfortable and with the rig and interior arrangement planned to meet the single minded objective of midshipmen training."

These are successors to the famous Luders-designed 44-foot yawls that long served the Naval Academy.[9] The first eight were ordered in 1987, with options for another 20 units, of which 13 were ordered. The first unit was delivered on 21 May 1987, the last in 1989.

Classification: The NA-1 through NA-8 are designated 44ST8701–8708; the NA-9 through NA-20 are 44ST8901–8912.

Design: These craft are of GRP construction. The sail area is a maximum of 980 square feet (88 m2). The radar "pot" is supported on a 4-foot (1.2-m) pole aft of the mainmast.

---

9 The initial 12 Luders yawls, procured shortly after World War II, had wood hulls; after 25 years of service they were replaced by a similar Luders design with a fiberglass hull. The "Navy 44" design thus was procured as the third generation postwar Academy sailing craft.

CHAPTER 26

Floating Dry Docks

The ARCO at the Naval Submarine Base (Point Loma) in San Diego has an unimposing appearance. Still, dry docks—military and civilian, floating and fixed—are vital to the support of the operating fleet. The two cranes ride on tracks atop the dock's sidewalls. (2004, W. Michael Young)

The Navy operates floating dry docks at several bases in the continental United States, primarily for the repair and maintenance of submarines. These are non-self-propelled docks, but they have electrical generators to provide power for their lighting, tools, and equipment. Normally they operate with a flotilla of non-self-propelled barges that provide specialized services, such as messing and berthing, for the docks themselves and for ships being dry-docked.

Like the Navy's ships and service craft, the number of dry docks has been reduced in the post–Cold War era. The floating docks in this chapter are arranged according to their classifications. The docks in active Navy service have their locations indicated; several others are on lease from the Navy and operated by commercial firms. One ex-Navy dock, the former OAK RIDGE (ARDM 1, ex-ARD 19) is in Coast Guard service.

Floating dry docks officially are considered to be service craft; they are listed in both the Naval Vessel Register (NVR) and the Service Craft and Boat Accounting Report (SABAR).

Classification: IX 521, 522, 524, and 525 were assigned to AFDB dock sections in 1996–1997. The rationale for this change has not been given by the Navy, but it relates to the extensive modification of the IX 524 as a mobile at-sea sensor platform.

Many existing U.S. floating dry docks were reclassified on 1 August 1946, several of which remain on the NVR:

World War II	*Post–1946*
ABSD	AFDB
ARD	AFDL/ARD
ARDC	AFDL[1]
AFD	AFDL
YFD	AFDM and YFD

Design: All U.S. Navy floating dry docks are open-ended, through-type docks, except for the ARD series. The ARDs are distinctive in being closed at one end by a ship-shaped bow.[2]

The large ABSD/AFDB-series docks are sectional, to facilitate disassembly and towing. Mounted on their hull sections—which are called "pontoons"—are side or "wing" walls that fold down for storage or towing. These wing walls can be shifted easily between pontoons in the event of damage.

---

1 Initially, these were referred to as AFDL(C).

2 The ARD-type docks also are referred to as Camel docks, for a ship of that name that was gutted and fitted with a stern gate in 1700 to serve as a dock at the Russian harbor of Kronshtadt (near St. Petersburg/Leningrad). The project was undertaken by a captain in the Royal Navy because of the lack of docking facilities at Kronshtadt, which is now a major Russian naval base.

The lift capacities listed in this chapter are nominal; much heavier ships can be lifted if the distribution of ship weight is favorable.

Guns: No floating dry docks are armed, although some originally were fitted to mount light anti-aircraft guns.

Names: Floating dry docks were unnamed until the 1960s. Dry docks that service nuclear-propelled submarines have been given the names of towns and cities associated with nuclear power; most of the others that are named have positive trait names.

Operational: Operational docks are manned by Navy personnel.

LARGE AUXILIARY FLOATING DRY DOCKS

Seven of the floating dry docks in this category (AFDB 1–7) were built during World War II; the AFDB 8 and 9 were acquired much later.

The ABSD 1–7 (later changed to AFDB 1–7) were intended to be towed in sections to advance bases to be assembled and then to service the Navy's largest warships. The ABSD 1 and ABSD 2 were the largest, being ten-section docks intended to lift battleships of the Iowa (BB 61) class and aircraft carriers of the Midway (CVB 41) class; the ABSD 3 had nine sections, and the others were seven-section docks. The ABSD 1 was completed in 1943, the ABSD 2–6 in 1944, and the ABSD 7 in 1945. A planned eighth ABSD was canceled.

The following notes refer to the AFDB 1–7:

Classification: These docks originally were designated ABSD with the same hull numbers; they were reclassified AFDB in August 1946.

Design: All feature steel construction. The large wing walls can support cranes and, as built, anti-aircraft (AA) guns (authorized armament when built was a twin 40-mm Bofors AA mount on each section).

The ABSD 1–3 had the capacity to lift any World War II–era U.S. warship; the ABSD 4–7 could lift Iowa-class battleships and Essex (CV 9)-class aircraft carriers.

Dock	Sections	Lift capacity
ABSD 1, 2	10	90,000 tons
ABSD 3	9	81,000 tons
ABSD 4–7	7	55,000 tons

The following characteristics apply to standard dock sections:

Displacement:	15,400 tons
Length:	approx. 93 feet (28.35 m) overall
	approx. 82½ feet (25.15 m) on pontoon
Beam:	256 feet (78.05)
Width clear inside:	133⁷⁄₁₂ feet (40.73 m)
Draft:	9 feet (2.74 m) light surface
	68 feet (23.78 m) max submerged

Names: Names were assigned to two of these docks in the 1960s: AFDB 1 became the Artisan and AFDB 7 the Los Alamos.

Operational: AFDB 7 sections A-B-C-D were reactivated from the reserve fleet in 1961 and towed across the Atlantic in February–March 1961 for use at the Holy Loch (Scotland) SSBN refit base. AFDB 7 sections were in use at Holy Loch for 30 years, until the forward base there was disestablished in 1992.

AFDB 9

The unnamed AFDB 9 is a civilian-built, two-section dock acquired by the Navy in 1974. She has been on commercial lease since 14 June 1993, operated by Metro Machine Corp. in Norfolk, Virginia.

The AFDB 9 was taken over by the Navy and placed on the NVR effective 12 July 1990. The dock had been operated by Pennsylvania Shipbuilding Co. and was acquired by the Navy when that firm defaulted on Navy contracts.

See 16th Edition/page 327 for characteristics.

Two sections of an AFDB (top) and the Adept (foreground) at Subic Bay, Philippines. The wing walls of the AFDBs fold down for towing and storage. When this photo was taken, the AFDL 23 still had the gun tubes that held anti-aircraft guns during World War II. (U.S. Navy)

"MACHINIST" AFDB 8

The German-built floating dock MACHINIST (AFDB 8) is a single-piece dock acquired by the Navy in 1985. She was towed to Subic Bay in the Philippines for operation beginning in March 1986; with the withdrawal of U.S. forces from the Philippines, she was towed to Pearl Harbor in 1992. The MACHINIST was stricken for sale on 23 April 1997.

See 16th Edition/page 327–28 for characteristics.

"LOS ALAMOS" AFDB 7

Floating dock AFDB 7 sections A-B-C-D-E and G were loaned to the Brownsville Navigation District, Brownsville, Texas.

Section F was transferred to the Army's Corps of Engineers in 1966 for use as a floating power plant at Kwajalein atoll (Marshall Islands) in conjunction with anti-ballistic missile tests. The dock was fitted with two gas turbine generators (General Electric 7LM1500) to produce 22 megawatts. The Army named her ANDREW J. WEBER. The dock section subsequently was used in the Philippines from 1968 to 1972, when it was moved to Guam. It was then moved to Pearl Harbor for storage and later scrapped.

AFDB 6

The seven-section AFDB 6 was stricken on 1 January 1974 and sold to Industrial Investment Corp. of Bermuda. (Correction to previous edition.)

AFDB 5

The seven-section AFDB 5 was stricken on 1 December 1983 and transferred to the city of Port Arthur, Texas, in 1984 for use by Todd Shipyards Corp.

AFDB 4

The seven-section AFDB 4 was stricken on 15 April 1989 and transferred to the Port of Portland, Oregon.

AFDB 3

The nine-section AFDB 3 was stricken on 1 August 1981 and transferred to the state of Maine in 1982 for use by Bath Iron Works at Portland.

AFDB 2

Five of the ten sections of the AFDB 2 remain on the NVR and five have been sunk or sold:

Sections	Status
A, G	sold for scrap
B	sunk as target 2001
C	sunk as target 1987
D	to IX 522 on 16 Aug 1996
E, I	reserve 24 Mar 1987 (at Pearl Harbor)
F	to IX 524 on 25 Apr 1997
H	to IX 535 on 10 Oct 2002
J	sunk as target

The IX 524, an AFDB 2 section converted to a Mobile At-Sea Sensor (MATSS) to support ballistic missile intercept tests on the Pacific Missile Range (PMR). There are two small antennas set up on the vertical replenishment spots forward; a Missile Range Safety System (MRSS) is in the small structure immediately aft of the spots, and the large antenna aft is for the Wide-Band Coherent Signal Processor (WB-COSIP), an advanced tracking radar. (U.S. Navy)

The extensively modified IX 524/MATSS under tow in Hawaiian waters. She primarily provides support to the Department of Defense's Missile Defense Agency (formerly the Ballistic Missile Defense Office). (U.S. Navy)

The IX 524 was reclassified as an IX for use at the Pacific Missile Range Facility at Kekaha, Hawaii, and has been employed as a support platform for the Mobile Aerial Target Support System (MATSS). She is based at Pearl Harbor. She has been fitted as a tracking and communications platform and provided with crew accommodations. She is towed to sea for test operations.

"ARTISAN" AFDB 1

Of the ten sections of the AFDB 1, three remain on the NVR and seven have been sunk or sold:

Sections	Status
A, G, H, I, J	str. 27 Oct 1986; sold
C	to IX 525 on 2 Apr 1998
D	to IX 521 on 16 Aug 1996
E	reserve 1 Mar 1987 (at Pearl Harbor)
F	sunk as target

SMALL AUXILIARY FLOATING DRY DOCKS

1 SMALL AUXILIARY FLOATING DRY DOCK: "AFDL 1" CLASS

Number	Name	In service	Status
AFDL 6	DYNAMIC	Mar 1944	**Active**

Builders:	Chicago Bridge and Iron, Calif.
Sections:	1
Lift capacity:	1,000 tons
Length:	200 feet (61.0 m) overall
Width:	64 feet (19.5 m)
Width clear inside:	45 feet (13.7 m)
Draft:	3⅗₂ feet (1.0) light
	28½ feet (8.7) max submerged
Personnel:	24 (1 officer + 23 enlisted)

The AFDL 6 is the last dock of this type in Navy service. She is operational at Little Creek, Virginia.

Class: See Table 26-1 for class listing.

Design: Of one-piece, steel construction, the AFDL 1-type docks originally were intended to service minesweeper-size ships (AM/MSF/MSO).

Table 26-1. SMALL AUXILIARY FLOATING DRY DOCKS

Number	Name	In service	Lift (tons)	Notes
AFDL 1 class (28)				
AFDL 1	ENDEAVOR	1943	1,000	to Dominican Republic 1986
AFDL 2		1943	1,000	str. 15 Nov 1981
AFDL 3		1943	1,000	commercial lease
AFDL 4		1943	1,000	to Brazil 1966; purchased 1977
AFDL 5		1944	1,000	to China (Taiwan) 1948
AFDL 6	DYNAMIC	1944	1,000	active (see text)
AFDL 7 class (5)				
AFDL 7	ABILITY	1944	1,900	sold 1 July 1982 (scrapped)
AFDL 1 class (continued)				
AFDL 8		1944	1,000	str. 1 Dec 1981 (donated 1 Mar 1982 for sinking as an artificial reef)
AFDL 9		1943	1,000	str. 15 July 1982; sold 1 Oct 1982 (scrapped)
AFDL 10		1943	1,000	to Philippines 1978; str. 13 July 1987
AFDL 11		1944	1,000	to Cambodia (Khmer Republic) 1971
AFDL 12		1943	1,000	commercial lease (disposal 1 July 1984)
AFDL 13		1943	1,000	to South Vietnam; str. 1 Oct 1983
AFDL 14				not used
AFDL 15		1943	1,000	commercial lease; str. 18 Dec 1983
AFDL 16		1943	1,000	commercial lease; str. 15 Aug 1986; sold 1 June 1982 (scrapped)
AFDL 17		1943	1,000	sold Jan 1971 (scrapped)
AFDL 18		1944	1,000	sold Dec 1962
AFDL 19		1944	1,000	(disposal 1 Apr 1983)
AFDL 20		1944	1,000	to Philippines 1961; purchased 1980
AFDL 21		1944	1,000	commercial lease; str. 31 March 1989
AFDL 7 class (continued)				
AFDL 22		1944	1,900	to South Vietnam; str. 1 July 1985 (disposal same date; see text)
AFDL 23	ADEPT	1944	1,900	commercial lease; str. 15 July 1994
AFDL 1 class (continued)				
AFDL 24		1944	1,000	to Philippines 1948; purchased 1980
AFDL 25	UNDAUNTED	1944	1,000	str. 13 Mar 1996 (disposal 19 May 1997)
AFDL 26		1944	1,000	to Paraguay 1977; purchased 1977
AFDL 27		1944	1,000	sold May 1961 (scrapped)
AFDL 28		1944	1,000	to Mexico 1973; purchased 1978
AFDL 29		1944	1,000	commercial lease; str. 15 July 1885; sold 1 Aug 1983 (scrapped)
AFDL 30		1944	1,000	sold 1 June 1979 (scrapped)
AFDL 31		1943	1,000	loan to Coast Guard 1943–2002; listed as YFD 83 (see text)
AFDL 7 class (continued)				
AFDL 32		1944	1,900	scuttled 1945; str. 1946
AFDL 33		1944	1,900	to Peru 1959; purchased 1980
AFDL 34 class (13)				
AFDL 34		1944	2,800	to Taiwan 1959
AFDL 35		1944	2,800	sold 1 Jan 1974 (scrapped)
AFDL 36		1944	2,800	to China (Taiwan) 1947
AFDL 37		1944	2,800	commercial lease; sold 1 Dec 1981 (scrapped)
AFDL 38		1944	2,800	commercial lease (disposal 1 Oct 1981)
AFDL 39		1944	2,800	to Brazil 1966; purchased 1981
AFDL 40		1944	2,800	commercial lease; str. 30 June 1987; to Philippines 30 June 1990
AFDL 41		1944	2,800	sold 1983

Table continued on next page

Table 26-1. Continued

Number	Name	In service	Lift (tons)	Notes
AFDL 42		1944	2,800	sold 15 Jan 1975 (scrapped)
AFDL 43		1944	2,800	sold 29 May 1979 (scrapped)
AFDL 44		1944	2,800	to Philippines 1969; purchased 1980
AFDL 45		1945	2,800	commercial lease (disposal 1981)
AFDL 46		1945	2,800	target at Bikini 1946; scuttled 1946; str. 1947
AFDL 47 type				
AFDL 47	RELIANCE	1946	6,500	ex-ARD 33; commercial lease; 15 July 1991
AFDL 48 type				
AFDL 48	DILIGENCE	1956	4,000	commercial lease; str. 28 Aug 1986
AFDL 49 type				
AFDL 49				canceled 1958

Table 26-1 represents an attempt to list all AFDL-type floating docks. Navy records are incomplete; some docks were stricken and some were not; the term "disposal" is used in the NVR and is provided when no strike date is known.

The AFDL 1–6, 8–21, and 24–31 originally were designated AFD (mobile floating dry docks). The AFDL 34–46 originally were the ARDC 1–13. Seven of these docks were given names. All are one-piece steel docks except the AFDL 34–46 and the AFDL 48, which were built of reinforced concrete.[3] The AFDL 47 was the largest U.S. Navy single-piece through-type floating dock.

The AFDL 13 and AFDL 22 were taken over by Communist forces on 30 April 1975 with the fall of the South Vietnamese government. The AFDL 25 was taken back from commercial lease in June 1984, refitted, and towed to Guantanamo Bay to replace the AFDL 1; the dock was stricken in 1996.

2 MEDIUM AUXILIARY FLOATING DRY DOCKS: "AFDM 3" CLASS

Number	Name	In service	Status
AFDM 7 (ex-YFD 63)	SUSTAIN	Jan 1945	Reserve 21 Oct 1997
AFDM 10 (ex-YFD 67)	RESOLUTE	Jan 1945	Reserve 7 Nov 2003

Builders:	Everett Pacific Shipbuilding, Everett, Wash.
Sections:	3
Lift capacity:	18,000 tons
Length:	622 feet (189.6 m) overall
Width:	124 feet (37.8 m)
Width clear inside:	93–96 feet (28.35–29.27 m)
Draft:	6⅕ feet (l.9 m) light
	52¾ feet (16.1 m) maximum submerged
Personnel:	AFDM 7 143 (4 officers + 139 enlisted)
	AFDM 10 150 (6 officers + 144 enlisted)

These are three-piece, steel docks. The AFDM 7 was taken out of service on 21 October 1997 and laid up in the National Defense Reserve Fleet (NDRF) at Fort Eustis, Virginia; she was extensively overhauled in 1991–1992 by the Bethlehem Steel yard at Sparrows Point, Baltimore, Maryland. The AFDM 10 supported Submarine Squadron 8 at Norfolk, Virginia, until 2003.

Classification: These docks initially were classified as yard floating dry docks (YFD).

Design: These docks originally were intended to dock destroyers, light cruisers, and escort carriers.

---

3 Concrete was used in the construction of some ARDC and YFD floating dry docks because of the steel shortage during World War II.

The RESOLUTE at Norfolk serving the attack submarine OKLAHOMA CITY (SSN 723). The RESOLUTE had been at Norfolk for more than 20 years. During that period, she had dry docked 139 submarines and completed 55 shipyard restricted availabilities for Atlantic Fleet submarines, an impressive record. (1999, Jürg Kürsener)

1 MEDIUM AUXILIARY FLOATING DRY DOCK: "AFDM 1" CLASS

Number	Name	In service	Status
AFDM 2 (ex-YFD 4)	(unnamed)	1 Oct 1942	Reserve 16 May 1995

Builders:	Alabama Dry Dock and Shipbuilding
Sections:	3
Lift capacity:	15,000 tons
Length:	615⅔ feet (187.7 m) overall
Width:	116 feet (35.4 m)
Width clear inside:	87½ feet (26.7 m)
Draft:	5¾ feet (1.75 m) light
	49¾ feet (15.2 m) maximum submerged
Personnel:	

This is a three-section steel dock. She was leased to Halter Marine, Gulfport, Mississippi, on 1 September 1992. The dock was returned to Navy custody on 16 May 1995 and promptly placed in storage in the NDRF at Beaumont, Texas.

Design: The dock originally was intended to dock destroyers, light cruisers, and escort carriers.

These all were three-piece steel docks, originally designated YFD. Only six were given names.

Table 26-2. MEDIUM AUXILIARY FLOATING DRY DOCKS

Number	Name	In service	Lift (tons)	Notes
AFDM 1 class (2)				
AFDM 1 (ex-YFD 3)		1942	15,000	commercial lease; str. 1 Sep 1986 (scrapped)
AFDM 2 (ex-YFD 4)		1942	15,000	reserve (see above)
AFDM 3 class (11)				
AFDM 3 (ex-YFD 6)		1943	18,000	commercial lease 1983
AFDM 4		1943	18,000	
AFDM 5 (ex-YFD 21)	RESOURCEFUL	1943	18,000	str. 22 Aug 1997 (disposal 6 Apr 1997)
AFDM 6 (ex-YFD 62)	COMPETENT	1944	18,000	str. 21 Aug 1997
AFDM 7 (ex-YFD 63)	SUSTAIN	1945	18,000	reserve (see above)
AFDM 8 (ex-YFD 64)	RICHLAND	1944	18,000	str. 22 Aug 1997 (disposal 6 Apr 1997)
AFDM 9 (ex-YFD 65)		1945	18,000	commercial lease; str. 31 Dec 1987 (disposal 2 Aug 1989)
AFDM 10 (ex-YFD 67)	RESOLUTE	1945	18,000	active (see above)
AFDM 11				canceled 1945
AFDM 12				canceled 1945
AFDM 13 (ex-YFD 85)				canceled 1945
AFDM 14 type				
AFDM 14 (ex-YFD 71)	STEADFAST	1945	14,000	str. 7 Feb 1999 (disposal 25 Aug 1999)

The now-stricken STEADFAST shows the square lines of the YFD/AFDM-type dry docks. Note the twin cranes on the dock walls. (1997, W. Michael Young)

AUXILIARY REPAIR DOCKS

Two floating dry docks of this type remain on the NVR, the ARDM 4 and 5, which were constructed specifically to support nuclear-propelled submarines.

2 MEDIUM AUXILIARY REPAIR DOCKS: "ARDM 4" CLASS

Number	Name	In service	Status
ARDM 4	SHIPPINGPORT	27 Jan 1979	**Active**
ARDM 5	ARCO	27 Feb 1986	**Active**

Builders:	ARDM 4: Bethlehem Steel, Sparrows Point, Md.
	ARDM 5: Todd Shipyards, Seattle
Sections:	1
Lift capacity:	7,800 tons
Length:	492 feet (150.0 m) overall
Width:	96 feet (29.3 m)
Width clear inside:	64 feet (19.5 m)
Draft:	54½ feet (16.6 m) maximum submerged
Personnel:	ARDM 4: 131 (6 officers + 125 enlisted)
	ARDM 5: 130 (5 officers + 125 enlisted)

These were the first floating dry docks built for the U.S. Navy specifically to support nuclear-propelled submarines. The SHIPPINGPORT is operational at the Naval Submarine Base New London, and the ARCO is operational at the Naval Submarine Base (Point Loma) San Diego.

Class: The SHIPPINGPORT and ARCO were authorized in the Fiscal Year (FY) 1975 and 1983 naval shipbuilding programs, respectively. A third, similar dock planned for FY 1984 was not built.

MEDIUM AUXILIARY REPAIR DOCKS: CONVERTED "ARD 12" CLASS

The OAK RIDGE (ARDM 1, ex-ARD 19) was taken out of service on 10 August 2001 and stricken on 26 November 2001. Originally completed in 1944, she was one of three ARD 12-class docks converted in the 1960s to service Polaris/Poseidon missile submarines.

The OAK RIDGE was active at the Naval Submarine Base New London, Connecticut, until 2001. After being struck from the NVR, she was transferred to the Coast Guard Yard at Curtis Bay, Maryland, on 7 February 2002. Two sister docks also have been stricken; see Table 26-4.

The ARCO at San Diego, where she services submarines of Submarine Squadron 11. She was built specifically to service nuclear-propelled submarines. (2000, W. Michael Young)

FLOATING DRY DOCK CONFIGURATION

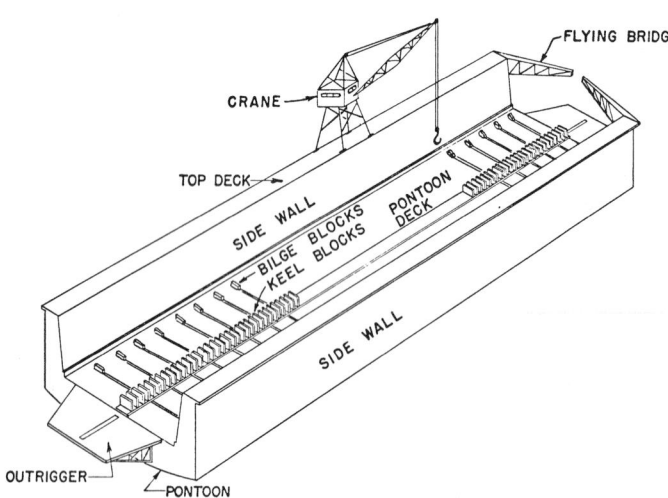

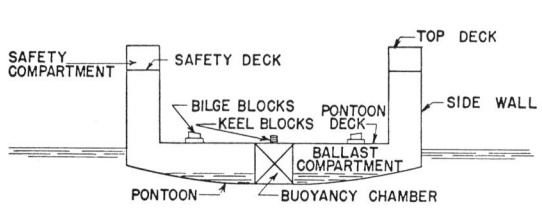

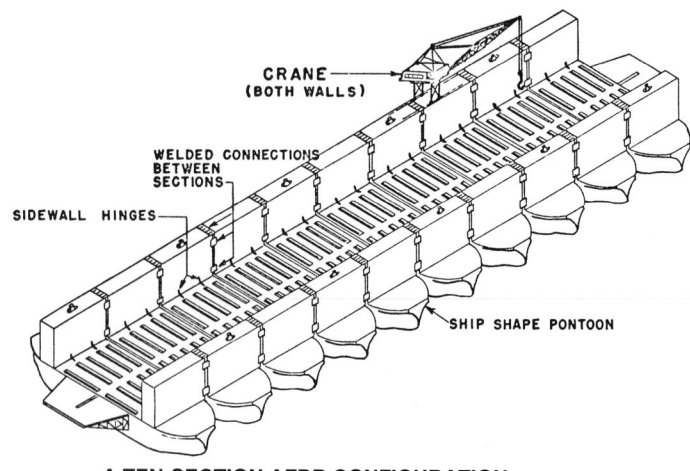

A TEN-SECTION AFDB CONFIGURATION

A SEVEN-SECTION AFDB CONFIGURATION

Table 26-3. AUXILIARY REPAIR DRY DOCKS

Number	Name	In service	Lift (tons)	Notes
ARD 2 class (8)				
ARD 2		1942	3,500	to Mexico 1963
ARD 3				canceled
ARD 4				canceled
ARD 5	WATERFORD	1942	3,500	str. 1 Oct 1997; to Chile 10 Mar 1999
ARD 6		1943	3,500	to Pakistan 1961; str. 24 Nov 1997
ARD 7	WEST MILTON	1943	3,500	str. 23 Aug 1990 (disposal 23 Jan 1992)
ARD 8		1943	3,500	to Peru 1961; purchased 1980
ARD 9		1943	3,500	to Taiwan 1977; purchased 1981
ARD 10		1943	3,500	str. 1972 (scrapped)
ARD 11		1943	3,500	to Mexico 1974
ARD 12 class (21)				
ARD 12		1943	3,500	to Turkey 1971; purchased 1987
ARD 13		1943	3,500	to Venezuela; purchased 1977
ARD 14		1943	3,500	to Brazil 1963; purchased 1980
ARD 15		1944	3,500	to Mexico 1971; purchased 1981
ARD 16		1944	3,500	sold 1 Mar 1973 (scrapped)
ARD 17		1944	3,500	to Ecuador 1951; purchased 1980
ARD 18		1944	3,500	converted to ARDM 3
ARD 19		1944	3,500	converted to ARDM 1
ARD 20		1944	3,500	
ARD 21		1944	3,500	to Taiwan
ARD 22	WINDSOR	1944	3,500	to Taiwan 1976; purchased 1995
ARD 23		1944	3,500	to Argentina; purchased 1993
ARD 24		1944	3,500	to Ecuador; purchased 1982
ARD 25		1944	3,500	to Chile 1960; purchased 2000
ARD 26		1944	3,500	converted to ARDM 2
ARD 27		1944	3,500	sold 1 Sep 1974 (scrapped)
ARD 28		1944	3,500	sold 1 Feb 1981 (scrapped)
ARD 29	ARCO	1944	3,500	to Iran 1977
ARD 30	SAN ONOFRE	1944	3,500	str. 21 Aug 1997; to Mexico 2000
ARD 31		1944	3,500	to U.S. Air Force
ARD 32		1944	3,500	to Chile 1970; str. 25 June 1992; purchased 2000
ARD 33			3,500	reclassified AFDL 47
ARD 34–36				cancelled 1945
ARD 37 type				
ARD 37				cancelled 1956

These were one-piece steel dry docks. All ARD-type docks have been stricken; the last in active U.S. Navy service was the SAN ONOFRE, inactivated on 29 September 1995.

The 2,200-ton-capacity ARD 1 was placed in service in 1934. All subsequent ARDs were of the same design. They were intended to dock World War II–era destroyers and submarines; the ARD 12 and later docks were slightly longer and could accommodate tank landing ships (LST). Three ARDs were converted to support Polaris/Poseidon missile submarines (and changed to ARDM).

Only five of these docks were named, all for sites associated with nuclear energy development. The same name source was used for ARDM-type docks.

Table 25-4. MEDIUM AUXILIARY REPAIR DRY DOCKS

Number	Name	In service	Lift (tons)	Notes
Converted ARD 12 class (3)				
ARDM 1	OAK RIDGE	1944	8,000	to Coast Guard (see text)
ARDM 2	ALAMOGORDO	1944	8,000	str. 23 Nov 1993
ARDM 3	ENDURANCE	1944	8,000	str. 31 July 1995
ARDM 4 class (2)				
ARDM 4	SHIPPINGPORT	1979	7,800	active (see above)
ARDM 5	ARCO	1986	7,800	active (see above)

These five docks were intended specifically to support nuclear-propelled submarines. The first three units were converted from ARD-type docks in the 1960s.

The OAK RIDGE was taken out of service and placed in reserve on 10 August 2001 and stricken from the Naval Vessel Register on 26 November 2001. She then was transferred to the Coast Guard on 7 February 2002 for service at the Coast Guard Yard at Curtis Bay, near Baltimore, Maryland.

YARD FLOATING DRY DOCKS

The Navy built 81 docks designated YFD from 1942 onward. (The YFD 1 and YFD 2 were completed in 1900 and 1905, respectively.[4]) The YFDs varied in size and type (one to six sections), and were constructed of steel, wood, and concrete to several different designs.

The unnamed YFD 83 (ex-AFDL 31) was on loan from the Navy to the Coast Guard from her completion on 1 December 1943 until 2002. She was in service at the Coast Guard yard at Curtis Bay. (She was reclassified AFDL 31 with other YFDs, but apparently reverted to YFD in Coast Guard service; see 17th Edition/page 357 for characteristics.)

Units disposed of since 1990 are listed below (lift capacity in parentheses):

YFD 69 (14,000 tons)   commercial lease 1 Feb 1995.
YFD 70 (14,000 tons)   commercial lease 16 Apr 1996
YFD 83 (1,000 tons)   discarded by Coast Guard in 2002

---

4 The YFD 1 was towed to Pearl Harbor in 1940; on 7 December 1941 she was sunk (with the destroyer SHAW/DD 373). Both were salvaged, and the YFD 1 continued to serve throughout the war. The YFD 2—unofficially named the DEWEY DRYDOCK—was towed to the Philippines in 1906; she served there until scuttled on 8 April 1942 at Mariveles to prevent her capture by the Japanese. The Japanese did raise the dock, but it soon sank without being rehabilitated.

CHAPTER 27

Naval Aviation

Flight deck personnel crouch—and a photographer (right) snaps their picture—as an F/A-18 Hornet is about to be catapulted from the carrier GEORGE WASHINGTON during operations off the Atlantic coast. (U.S. Navy/Sheryl Campbell)

U.S. naval aviation consists of the aviation organizations and activities of the Navy and Marine Corps. The naval air training organization also supports the Coast Guard and certain Air Force programs.

The strength and structure of U.S. naval aviation have been reduced at a precipitous rate since the end of the Cold War and this reduction continues.[1] U.S. naval aviation—the Navy and Marine Corps air arms—has almost 4,000 operational aircraft, in both active and reserve units. This includes just over 600 aircraft in the "pipeline" inventory, undergoing maintenance or conversion, or in transit to and from units. The current active aircraft inventory is listed in Table 27-2. (U.S. Coast Guard aircraft are listed separately; see Chapter 32.)

Also, in the post–Cold War era, the Navy's carrier air wings are being reshaped to meet changing operational requirements—and to compensate for the failure of the Navy to develop a long-range/all-weather attack aircraft. At the same time, according to the head of the Naval Strike and Air Warfare Center, "The challenges to Naval Aviation Readiness . . . are mounting with reduced forces—a higher percentage of assets at sea, a higher percentage deployed, a resultant compression of the management cycle, higher aircraft utilization rates, increased maintenance demands, and certainly a higher [personnel/operational tempo] accompanying the reduction in our turn-around time."[2]

The Navy currently operates 12 active carriers, following the aborted effort to employ the JOHN F. KENNEDY as an "operational reserve/training" ship. Flying from their flight decks are ten active

carrier air wings (CVW) and one reserve air wing (CVWR). The current force is based on the Department of Defense's Bottom-Up Review of 1993 and subsequent quadrennial reviews. (By comparison, during the 1980s, the Navy briefly had 14 active wings as part of the Reagan–Lehman naval buildup, with a 15th wing planned but not activated; in addition, there were two reserve air wings.)

To sustain ten active air wings and one reserve air wing, the Navy has restructured carrier aviation, reducing the number of fighter-attack aircraft per carrier and "necking down" the different types of aircraft within the wings.[3] With the change, each wing has a nominal 50 strike fighter aircraft: one fighter (VF) squadron with 14 F-14 Tomcats and three strike-fighter (VFA) squadrons with a combined total of 36 F/A-18 Hornets, or four VFA squadrons with a total of 48 aircraft.

Because of the shortage of Navy F/A-18 squadrons, Marine Corps F/A-18 squadrons (VMFA) are regularly assigned to Navy carrier wings. Under current Navy–Marine Corps planning, up to ten VMFA squadrons eventually will be part of carrier air wings. At

---

1 Details of current U.S. naval aviation structure are provided in the annual feature "The Year in Review," published in the July–August issue of *Naval Aviation News.*

2 Rear Adm. Bernard J. Smith, USN, statement before the Subcommittee on Military Readiness and Personnel, National Security Committee, House of Representatives, 4 March 1997.

3 "Neck down" is the naval aviation term for a fewer number of aircraft or missiles replacing a larger number of types.

the same time, the rapid demise of the F-14 squadrons results in their replacement, when available, by F/A-18 squadrons. This reduces the training time the Marine squadrons have for combined operations with ground combat forces, their primary purpose.

Periodically, a Marine electronic attack squadron (VMAQ) flying the EA-6B Prowler has been assigned to a carrier air wing when a Navy VAQ squadron is not available.

Carrier air wings also have a squadron of E-2C Hawkeye Airborne Early Warning (AEW) aircraft, a squadron of S-3B Viking "sea control" aircraft (which have no anti-submarine capability), and a composite squadron of HH-60/SH-60 Seahawk helicopters configured for a variety of missions, including Anti-Submarine Warfare (ASW).

The F-14 Tomcats and S-3 Vikings both will be retired over the next few years. Thus, by about 2010, all carrier air wings will have some 48 F/A-18 Hornets for the fighter and strike roles. Beyond the first decade of the 21st century, the Joint Strike Fighter (JSF), now designated F-35, is envisioned joining the fleet, providing a multirole, stealth aircraft to complement the F/A-18.[4] However, the JSF promises to be a controversial program, and the Navy may have all–F/A-18 air wings well into the 21st century.

Also scheduled for retirement during the next decade are the extensively employed EA-6B Prowler Electronic Countermeasures (ECM) aircraft. The Navy–Marine Corps team performs the ECM mission for the Air Force, as well as for the naval services. The replacement for that aircraft will be an EA-18G, given the interim name Growler, possibly complemented by Unmanned Aerial Vehicles (UAV).

The current composition of carrier air wings is described below. Reserve CVWR-20 and its squadrons are scheduled to be deactivated in 2005–2006 under current Navy planning.

Navy and Marine Corps wings and squadrons disestablished since 1 January 1990 are listed; official disestablishment dates are given, not the ceremonial dates, which usually differ by a few days. Note that, until 1998, Navy squadrons are "established" and "deactivated" (the official term) or "disestablished," not "commissioned" and "decommissioned." In 1998 and 2002, the Navy revised its policy on aircraft squadron lineage. Under the new policies:
• *Establishment*: A squadron's lineage and history begin on the date it is established.
• *Redesignation*: A squadron may be redesignated, such as VA-67, which later was redesignated VA-15 and then VFA-15. The history of VFA-15 began on the date it was established as VA-67.
• *Deactivation*: A squadron may be deactivated—not disestablished—by reassigning its aircraft and personnel. The designation remains on the record of inactive squadrons until it is reactivated.
• *Reactivation*: A squadron may be reactivated and placed in active operational service; at such time, it must use the last designation that was assigned prior to deactivation. To avoid confusion, a squadron cannot be reactivated and redesignated on the same date.

For simplicity and consistency, the term "disestablished" is used in this volume for Navy aircraft squadrons that have stood down both before and after the changes in terminology.

The Marine Corps uses the terms "activated" and "deactivated" for its aviation units.

NAVAL AIR ORGANIZATION

All naval aviation units belong to an administrative organization, and most units also belong to tactical organizations. For example, a strike-fighter squadron is administratively under a strike-fighter "type" wing commander while at its home base; when deployed on board a carrier, the squadron comes under the air wing commander embarked in that ship. Similarly, a patrol squadron is under the patrol "type" wing commander while in the United States, but if deployed in a forward area, would be under a fleet commander and his subordinate air commander.

The administrative organization is headed by the Director, Air Warfare Division, in the Office of the Chief of Naval Operations[5] and extends through the Commander, Naval Air Force Atlantic Fleet (NAVAIRLANT), and Commander, Naval Air Force Pacific Fleet (NAVAIRPAC), and their respective wing type commanders. (Details of naval air administrative organization are in Chapter 6.)

In addition to the numbered wings and squadrons described in this chapter, in 1995–1996 the aircraft at various test facilities were organized into two test wings:
• Naval Test Wing Atlantic with four squadrons, all based at Naval Air Station (NAS) Patuxent River, Maryland: Naval Rotary Wing Test Squadron, Naval Strike Aircraft Test Squadron, Naval Force Aircraft Test Squadron, and Naval Test Pilot School
• Naval Test Wing Pacific with two squadrons: Naval Weapons Test Squadron Point Mugu and Naval Weapons Test Squadron China Lake, both in California.

UNIT DESIGNATIONS

Naval air units are designated in two systems of abbreviations: pronounceable acronyms and simpler, letter–number combinations. Accordingly, Fighter Squadron 11 is known as both FITRON 11 and VF-11. The latter series is used in this volume.

All naval aviation units have the prefix *V* for heavier-than-air or *H* for helicopter. Previously, *Z* was employed for lighter-than-air (airship/blimp) units.

The *V* prefix for naval aircraft types and, subsequently, for aviation units dates from 1922. VF indicated fighter squadron, VA attack squadron, ZP airship patrol squadron, etc. (The last U.S. Navy airship, a Goodyear ZPG-2W, was taken out of service in 1962.) *H* was introduced as the helicopter type letter for aircraft (HNS-1) in 1943 and for squadrons in 1947 (the first naval helicopter squadron was Marine Corps HMX-1, followed in 1948 by Navy HU-1 and HU-2). Marine Corps units have the letter *M* added as the second letter of aviation unit designations.[6]

UNIT CODES

Most naval aviation organizations have two-letter identification codes that are displayed on aircraft tail fins and, in some marking schemes, on wings. Training wings have single-letter designations while air stations and other special organizations use a number–letter scheme.

In 1946, the Navy began using single-letter codes to identify the specific ships to which the planes were attached—e.g., *B* for BOXER (CV 21) and *F* for FRANKLIN D. ROOSEVELT (CVB 42)—with land-based units having two-letter codes. The system was revised in 1957 to provide the current fleet "split," with the first letter indicating the fleet assignment: A–M for Atlantic and N–Z for Pacific. The letters *I* and *O* are not used to avoid confusion with numerals. The unit code AF was dropped because of confusion with *Air Force* (previously it had been used by Carrier Air Group 6, which then took the code letters AE), but it now is assigned to reserve wing CVWR-20.

---

4 See N. Polmar, "Next Generation Strike Fighter," U.S. Naval Institute *Proceedings* (January 1997), pp. 89–90. The JSF program is successor to the Joint Advanced Strike Technology (JAST) program.

5 Prior to 1 January 1993, this position was the Assistant Chief of Naval Operations (Air Warfare). The position originally was established in 1944 as the Deputy Chief of Naval Operations (Air); it was a three-star billet from 1944 to 1992; it was changed to Assistant CNO (Air Warfare) in 1987 and again changed, to Director, Air Warfare Division, on 10 August 1992.

6 The H, V, and Z also were used for ship designations, hence CV for aircraft carrier, AV for seaplane tender, and AZ for airship tender. Subsequently, H was used for helicopter-carrying ships—CVHA, CVHE, LPH, LHA, and LHD.

Table 27-2. ACTIVE U.S. NAVAL AIRCRAFT (MID-2004)

Aircraft Type		Total	Navy Active	Naval Reserve	Marine Active	Marine Reserve	Pipeline
Attack							
AV-8B	Harrier	138	6	—	119	—	13
NAV-8B	Harrier	1	1	—	—	—	—
Fighter/Strike Fighter							
F-5E	Tiger II	30	—	15	—	11	4
F-5F	Tiger II	4	—	3	—	—	1
F-5N	Tiger II	1	—	—	—	—	1
F-14A	Tomcat	10	9	—	—	—	1
F-14B	Tomcat	58	56	—	—	—	2
F-14D	Tomcat	33	28	—	—	—	5
NF-14A	Tomcat	1	1	—	—	—	—
NF-14B	Tomcat	1	1	—	—	—	—
NF-14D	Tomcat	2	2	—	—	—	—
F-16A	Fighting Falcon	10	10	—	—	—	—
F-16B	Fighting Falcon	4	4	—	—	—	—
F/A-18A	Hornet	153	30	34	26	37	26
F/A-18B	Hornet	30	20	3	3	2	2
F/A-18C	Hornet	395	256	—	77	—	62
F/A-18D	Hornet	139	35	—	80	—	24
F/A-18E	Hornet	83	75	—	—	—	8
F/A-18F	Hornet	90	82	—	—	—	8
NF/A-18A	Hornet	1	1	—	—	—	—
NF/A-18C	Hornet	2	2	—	—	—	—
NF/A-18D	Hornet	2	1	—	—	—	1
Patrol-Anti-Submarine							
P-3B	Orion	1	—	—	—	—	1
P-3C	Orion	201	110	40	—	—	51
NP-3C	Orion	1	1	—	—	—	—
NP-3D	Orion	11	9	—	—	—	2
S-3B	Viking	95	82	—	—	—	13
Electronic-Special Purpose							
E-2C	Hawkeye	72	50	9	—	—	13
E-6B	Mecury	16	13	—	—	—	3
EA-6B	Prowler	119	50	3	12	—	54
EP-3E	Orion	11	7	—	—	—	4
DC-130	Hercules	1	1	—	—	—	—
Cargo-Transport							
C-2A	Greyhound	35	22	—	—	—	13
C-9B	Skytrain	17	—	8	1	—	8
DC-9	Skytrain	5	—	5	—	—	—
C-12C	Super King Air	4	4	—	—	—	—
C-20A	Gulfstream	1	1	—	—	—	—
C-20D	Gulfstream III	2	—	1	—	—	1
C-20G	Gulfstream IV	5	—	4	1	—	—
C-26D	Metroliner	7	7	—	—	—	—
C-37	Gulfstream	1	—	1	—	—	—
CT-39G	Sabreliner	8	—	—	2	—	6
C-40A	Clipper	6	—	6	—	—	—
DC-130A	Hercules	1**	1	—	—	—	—
KC-130F	Hercules	29	2	—	24	—	3
LC-130F	Hercules	1	1	—	—	—	—
NC-130H	Hercules	1***	1	—	—	—	—
KC-130J	Hercules	13	—	—	10	—	3
KC-130R	Hercules	13	—	—	10	—	3
C-130T	Hercules	28	—	—	—	21	7
KC-130T	Hercules	28	—	—	—	25	3
VP-3A	Orion	4	3	—	—	—	1

Aircraft Type		Total	Navy Active	Naval Reserve	Marine Active	Marine Reserve	Pipeline
Training							
T-2C	Buckeye	47	47	—	—	—	—
T-6A	Texan	36	32	—	—	—	4
T-34C	Mentor	305	271	—	2	—	32
NT-34C	Mentor	1	1	—	—	—	—
T-38A	Talon	11	9	—	—	—	2
T-39D	Sabreliner	1	1	—	—	—	—
T-39G	Sabreliner	8	3	—	—	—	5
T-39N	Sabreliner	15	15	—	—	—	—
T-44A	King Air	54	48	—	—	—	6
T-45A	Goshawk	74	64	—	—	—	10
T-45C	Goshawk	88	85	—	—	—	3
TAV-8B	Harrier	16	1	—	10	—	5
TC-12B	Huron	22	21	—	—	—	1
TE-2C	Hawkeye	2	1	—	—	—	1
Utility-Miscellaneous							
UC-12B	Huron	37	14	6	9	3	5
RC-12F	Huron	2	2	—	—	—	—
UC-12F	Huron	10	5	—	4	—	1
UC-12M	Huron	10	8	—	—	—	2
RC-12M	Huron	2	1	—	—	—	1
UC-35C	—	2	—	—	—	2	—
UC-35D	—	1	—	—	1	—	—
UP-3A	Orion	1	1	—	—	—	—
UP-3B	Orion	1	1	—	—	—	—
NU-1B	Otter	1	1	—	—	—	—
U-6A	Beaver	2	1	—	—	—	1
Rotary-wing							
MV-22B	Osprey	4	2	—	—	—	2
AH-1W	SeaCobra	186	5	—	121	35	25
HH-1N	Huey	27	16	—	9	—	2
UH-1N	Huey	87	1	—	55	18	13
VH-3D	Sea King	11	—	—	8	—	3
UH-3H	Sea King	46	32	6	—	—	8
NVH-3A	Sea King	1	1	—	—	—	—
TH-6B	Cayuse	6	6	—	—	—	—
CH-46D	Sea Knight	1	1	—	—	—	—
HH-46D	Sea Knight	17	11	—	6	—	—
CH-46E	Sea Knight	226	—	—	175	21	30
CH-53D	Sea Stallion	40	—	—	35	—	5
CH-53E	Super Stallion	149	1	—	100	18	30
MH-53E	Sea Dragon	37	23	7	—	—	7
TH-57B	SeaRanger	46	41	—	—	—	5
TH-57C	SeaRanger	77	69	—	—	—	8
OH-58C	Kiowa	3	3	—	—	—	—
SH-60B	Seahawk	149	123	4	—	—	22
SH-60F	Seahawk	72	55	7	—	—	10
HH-60H	Seahawk	39	23	10	—	—	6
UH-60L	Seahawk	4	4	—	—	—	—
VH-60N	Seahawk	8	—	—	—	6	2
MH-60R	Seahawk	7	6	—	—	—	1
MH-60S	Knighthawk	61	52	—	—	—	9
NSH-60B	Seahawk	2	2	—	—	—	—
Research-Experimental							
X-26A	—	2	2	—	—	—	—
Totals		3.982	2,004	265	906	193	614

* Includes Marine aircraft assigned to VX squadrons and training activities.
** DC-130A is a drone launching aircraft.
*** NC-130H is an AEW configuration.

able 27-1. NAVAL AVIATION ABBREVIATIONS*

AFB	Air Force Base
CVW	Carrier Air Wing
CVWR	Reserve Carrier Air Wing
FRS	Fleet Readiness Squadron
HC	Helicopter Combat Support Squadron
HCS	Helicopter Combat Search and Rescue/Special Warfare Support Squadron
HM	Helicopter Mine Countermeasures Squadron
HMAL	(Marine) Attack-Light Helicopter Squadron
HMH	(Marine) Heavy Helicopter Squadron
HMM	(Marine) Medium Helicopter Squadron
HMX	(Marine) Helicopter Squadron
HS	Helicopter Anti-Submarine Squadron
HSC	Helicopter Sea Combat Squadron
HSL	Light Helicopter Anti-Submarine Squadron
HSM	Helicopter Maritime Strike Squadron
HT	Helicopter Training Squadron
HX	Air Test and Evaluation Squadron
ISR	Intelligence, Surveillance, Reconnaissance
JRB	Joint Reserve Base
MAG	Marine Aircraft Group
MAW	Marine Aircraft Wing
MCAF	Marine Corps Air Facility
MCAS	Marine Corps Air Station
NAF	Naval Air Facility
NAS	Naval Air Station
SHARP	Shared Reconnaissance Pod
TARPS	Tactical Airborne Reconnaissance Pod System
TUAV	Tactical Unmanned Aerial Vehicle
UAV	Unmanned Aerial Vehicle
UCAV	Unmanned Combat Air Vehicle
VAQ	Electronic Attack Squadron
VAW	Carrier Airborne Early Warning Squadron
VC	Fleet Composite Squadron
VF	Fighter Squadron
VFA	Strike Fighter Squadron
VFC	Fighter Composite Squadron
VMAQ	(Marine) Tactical Electronic Warfare Squadron
VMFA	(Marine) Fighter-Attack Squadron
VMFA(AW)	(Marine) Fighter-Attack Squadron (All-Weather)
VMGR	(Marine) Refueler-Transport Squadron
VMMT	(Marine) Medium-Lift Tilt-Rotor Squadron
VMR	(Marine) Transport Squadron
VP	Patrol Squadron
VPU	Patrol Squadron—Special Projects Unit
VQ	Fleet Air Reconnaissance Squadron
VQ	Strategic Communications Squadron
VR	Fleet Logistics Support Squadron
VRC	Fleet Logistics Support (COD) Squadron**
VS	Sea Control Squadron
VT	Training Squadron
VX	Air Test and Evaluation Squadron
VXN	Oceanographic Development Squadron

* Marine squadrons add the letter *T* as a suffix for readiness/training units.
** Carrier On-board Delivery

F/A-18A Hornets of the Blue Angels flight demonstration team streak skyward over Topeka, Kansas, during an air show. The "Blues," composed of Navy and Marine Corps pilots and ground crewmen, present precision flying demonstrations for the public more than 70 times per year to help recruiting efforts. (U.S. Navy/Casey Akins)

The code letters AD and NJ are worn by several Fleet Readiness Squadrons (FRS). Those letters had been formally assigned to Combat Readiness Carrier Air Wing 4 and 12, respectively. Both of those wings were disestablished on 1 June 1970, but some of their squadrons survived in the Atlantic and Pacific Fleets.

Within carrier air wings, the squadrons are identified by blocks of numbers and colors, with the individual aircraft identified by numbers within the block. The block numbers (e.g., 100, 200) are aircraft flown by the wing commander, and the first of each series (e.g., 101, 201) is flown by the squadron commanding officer.

Side number	Squadron	Color code	Aircraft
1XX	VF or VFA	insignia red	F-14 or F/A-18
2XX	VFA	orange-yellow	F/A-18
3XX	VFA	light blue	F/A-18
4XX	VFA	international orange	F/A-18
50X	VAQ	light green	EA-6B
60X	VAW	black	E-2C
61X	HS	black	HH-60, SH-60
70X	VS	black	S-3B

Thus, the third E-2C Hawkeye assigned to the carrier CARL VINSON has NG (for CVW-9; see Table 27-3) on its tail and 603 on its forward fuselage and wings.

CARRIER AIR WINGS

The composition of carrier air wings continues to change. Into the 1980s, the standard wing had two fighter squadrons (24 F-14A), two light attack squadrons (24 A-7E), and one medium attack squadron (10 A-6E + 4 KA-6D tankers), in addition to specialized ASW, AEW, and ECM/electronic strike aircraft squadrons.

During the 1980s, with the introduction of the F/A-18 Hornet strike fighter, the Navy evaluated several air wing variations. For example, the so-called ROOSEVELT air wing (CVN 71) had double the number of A-6E Intruder aircraft, accommodated by reducing the numbers of fighters and strike fighters (the F/A-18 having replaced the A-7E). Under this plan, the A-6Es would have been succeeded in service by improved models of the Intruder (A-6F or A-6G) and, later, by the A-12 Avenger. The cancellation of the A-12 in early 1991 and overall budget reductions forced the Navy to drop this plan.

Subsequently, the Navy has gone to a smaller, but more flexible, strike fighter wing, with one F-14 squadron and three F/A-18 squadrons. As the F-14 is retired, a fourth F/A-18 squadron is embarked in place of the F-14 squadron. Thus, most carrier air wings consist of:

Units		Aircraft
1 VF	fighter squadron	14 F-4 Tomcat
3 VFA	strike fighter squadrons	36 F/A-18 Hornet
1 VAQ	electronic attack squadron	4 EA-6B Prowler
1 VAW	airborne early warning squadron	4 E-2C Hornet
1 VS	sea control squadron	8 S-3B Viking
1 HS	helicopter ASW squadron	6 HH-60H, SH-60 Seahawk

The VS squadrons are being disestablished. For those wings without S-3 Vikings, the aerial tanker role is performed by F/A-18E/F Hornets with "buddy stores."

On 13 January 1992, the Secretary of the Navy directed that the Navy and Marine Corps more closely integrate Marine tactical aviation into carrier air wings. The memorandum directed that the Navy and Marine Corps "undertake innovative measures to enhance the efficiency of naval aviation through . . . closer integration," especially of Marine fighter-attack and electronic warfare squadrons, to reduce Navy aircraft requirements by at least 140 planes in those categories.[7]

In addition to wing aircraft, forward-deployed carriers usually operate C-2A Greyhound Carrier On-board Delivery (COD) aircraft.

The Navy has no carrier-based Electronic Intelligence (ELINT) aircraft following retirement of the ES-3A Viking and its predecessor, the EA-3B Skywarrior. ELINT support of carrier groups now is provided by land-based EP-3E Orion maritime patrol aircraft and satellites.

The Navy has described an air wing envisioned for 2020–2025:[8]

40–50	strike fighters (F/A-18, F-35C)
12	Unmanned Combat Air Vehicles (UCAV)
4–6	Airborne Electronic Attack (AEA) aircraft (EA-18G)
4–6	advanced E-2C Hawkeye AEW aircraft
10	MH-60R/MH-60S helicopters

Historical: The designation "carrier air wing" (CVW) was established on 20 December 1963, in place of "carrier air group" (CVG).[9] Air group designations had reached No. 153 during World War II, albeit with several gaps in the series. The designation "ASW carrier air group" (CVSG) was established on 1 April 1960 for aircraft assigned to ASW carriers (CVS). Those ships were phased out in the late 1960s and early 1970s, and the last CVSG was disestablished on 30 June 1973. The ASW groups were numbered CVSG-50 to CVSG-62. When the ASW carrier air groups were phased out, the fixed-wing and helicopter ASW aircraft went aboard the larger attack aircraft carriers (which became CV/CVN vice CVA/CVAN).

The CV/CVN originally was intended as part of the "swing wing" concept, wherein a carrier could be loaded with an emphasis on fighter, attack, or ASW aircraft. In practice, this was not followed, and to the extent possible, standard wings were organized for all carriers. (However, in a demonstration of the swing-wing concept, in October 1971, the carrier SARATOGA operated 37 ASW aircraft—21 S-2E Trackers and 16 SH-3D Sea Kings—plus 20 fighters, 9 attack aircraft, and 8 special-mission aircraft.[10])

Replacement Air Groups (RAG) became Combat Readiness Air Wings (CRAW) in 1963, but those were phased out over the next few years, the last on 30 June 1973. Some of their squadrons survive, known as fleet readiness squadrons, and provide transition training to introduce pilots and air crewmen to fleet aircraft.

Specialized reconnaissance aircraft were phased off carrier decks in the late 1970s as the RA-5C Vigilante and RF-8G Photo Crusader were retired. The active fleet's last "recce" squadrons were RVAH-7, disestablished on 30 September 1979, and VFP-63, disestablished on 30 June 1982. Marine RF-4B Phantoms subsequently provided a limited photographic reconnaissance capability on some carriers pending the availability in the early 1980s of the Tactical Air Reconnaissance Pod System (TARPS) for the F-14 Tomcat on the larger carriers. (The Naval Air Reserve flew the RF-8G Photo Crusader until 1987.) The TARPS pod, however, flown by nonspecialized reconnaissance pilots, does not provide the quality or quantity of tactical reconnaissance that was possible with the RA-5C; this shortfall was keenly felt during Operation Desert Storm (1991). According to the U.S. Director of Naval Intelligence,

---

7 Marine tactical squadrons periodically have operated from aircraft carriers since November 1931, when Marine scouting squadron VS-15M went aboard the LEXINGTON/(CV 2) and VS-14M went aboard the SARATOGA/(CV 3) for fleet operations; they remained in those carriers until November 1934. Subsequently, in reaction to the Japanese kamikaze threat in late 1944, Marine F4U Corsair squadrons went aboard several fleet carriers. Toward the end of World War II and during the Korean War, the Marines embarked close air support squadrons in escort carriers (CVE) and light carriers (CVL), respectively.

8 Commander, Naval Air Forces, et al., *Naval Aviation Vision* (Washington, D.C.: Director, Naval Air Warfare [2003]), pp. 56-57.

9 CAG (Commander Air Group) is still used to refer to an air wing commander.

10 In 1960–1961, in an early example of a swing-wing concept in response to Soviet "saber-rattling," U.S. carriers in the Mediterranean and Far East unloaded their fighter aircraft to embark more nuclear strike aircraft.

TARPS "was totally inadequate" in providing sufficient and timely bomb damage assessment during that operation.[11]

The F-14/TARPS will be replaced by the Shared Reconnaissance Pod (SHARP) fitted to F/A-18 aircraft, as well as to UAVs. (See Chapter 28 for descriptions of SHARP and TARPS.)

Table 27-3. CARRIER AIR WINGS

Air Wing	Code	Carrier	Squadrons	
CVW-1	AB	Enterprise	VF-211 VFA-82 VFA-86 VMFA-312	VAQ-137 VAW-123 VS-32 HS-11
CVW-2	NE	Abraham Lincoln	VFA-2 VFA-137 VFA-151 VFA-82	VAQ-131 VAW-116 HS-2

Notes: CVW-2 made the last cruise of the carrier Constellation in 2003; planes from the wing were the first over Baghdad on 21 March 2003 in Operation Iraqi Freedom.

CVW-3	AC	Harry S. Truman	VF-32 VFA-22 VFA-37 VMFA-115	VAQ-130 VAW-126 VS-22 HS-7
CVW-4			Disestablished 1 June 1970	
CVW-5	NF	Kitty Hawk	VFA-27 VFA-102 VFA-192 VFA-195	VAQ-136 VAW-115 VS-21 HS-14

Notes: CVW-5 is based at Naval Air Facility (NAF) Atsugi, Japan. The wing flew from the carrier Midway (CV 41) from 1973 to 1991, when it was shifted in its entirety to the Independence; subsequently, the wing was transferred to the Kitty Hawk in 1998. While assigned to the Midway the wing did not have F-14 Tomcats or S-3 Vikings because of the ship's size and lack of an ASW command center. A detachment of three RF-4B Phantoms from Marine Photo-Reconnaissance Squadron (VMFP) 3 had provided the ship with a photo-reconnaissance capability until 1986, when the MIDWAY wing shifted from F-4 Phantom fighters to F/A-18 Hornets. On joining the "INDY" in 1991, CVW-5 gained two F-14 squadrons and an S-3 squadron, the last wing to receive those aircraft. The F-14 squadron (VF-154) was replaced by a fourth F/A-18 squadron (VFA-102) in 2003.

CVW-6	AE		Disestablished 1 Apr 1992	
CVW-7	AG	George Washington	VF-11 VF-143 VFA-131 VFA-136	VAQ-140 VAW-121 VS-31 HS-5
CVW-8	AJ	Theodore Roosevelt	VF-213 VFA-15 VFA-87 VFA-105	VAQ-141 VAW-124 VS-24 HS-3

Notes: The wing previously operated with reserve squadron VFA-201; see notes for CVWR-20.

CVW-9	NG	Carl Vinson	VFA-22 VFA-146 VFA-147 VFA-154 VMFA-314	VAQ-138 VAW-112 VS-33 HS-8
CVW-10	NM		Disestablished 1 June 1988	
CVW-11	NH	Nimitz	VFA-14 VFA-41 VFA-94 VFA-97	VAQ-135 VAW-117 HS-6
CVW-12	NJ		Disestablished 1 June 1970	
CVW-13	AK		Disestablished 1 Jan 1991	
CVW-14	NK	John C. Stennis	VF-31 VFA-25 VFA-113 VFA-115	VAQ-139 VAW-113 VS-35 HS-4
CVW-15	NL		Disestablished 31 Mar 1995	
CVW-16	AH		Disestablished 30 June 1971	
CVW-17	AA	John F. Kennedy	VF-103 VFA-34 VFA-81 VFA-83	VAQ-132 VAW-125 VS-30 HS-15
CVW-18			Not used	
CVW-19	NM		Disestablished 30 June 1977	
CVWR-20	AF	(Reserve)	VFA-201 VFA-203 VFA-204 VMFA-142	VAQ-209 VAW-77 VAW-78 HS-75

Notes: Reserve Carrier Air Wings 20 and 30 were established on 1 April 1970 to improve the readiness of reserve squadrons. A month later, on 1 May, two reserve ASW air groups were established, CVSGR-70 and CVSGR-80. VAW-77 is officially assigned to CVWR-20, but is employed in drug enforcement operations and does not operate from carriers. Similarly, land-based Fighter Composite Squadrons (VFC) 12 and 13 are assigned to the wing. Reserve squadron VFA-201 was recalled to active duty for one year in October 2002 to compensate for the shortfall in active fighter squadrons.

CVW-21	NP		Disestablished 12 Dec 1975	
CVW-22–29			Not used	
CVWR-30	ND	(Reserve)	Disestablished 31 Dec 1994	

11 Rear Adm. Thomas A. Brooks, USN, comments at a luncheon of Naval & Maritime Correspondents Circle, Washington, D.C., 15 July 1991.

With most of Air Wing 5 ashore, the Kitty Hawk operated Army special operations helicopters during the assault on Afghanistan in the fall of 2001. Here, an Army MH-47 Chinook rests on the Kitty Hawk's flight deck with S-3B Vikings in the background. (U.S. Navy/ Todd Frantom)

Personnel: Carrier air wings staffs average 16 officers plus 21 enlisted personnel, except Atsugi-based CVW-5 has 24 officers and 31 enlisted personnel assigned. See the specific squadron entries for their personnel strengths.

PATROL AND RECONNAISSANCE WINGS/FORCES

Patrol and Reconnaissance Wings (PATRECONWINGs) direct the operations of the Navy's patrol (VP), special projects patrol (VPU), and fleet air reconnaissance (VQ) squadrons.

East Coast wings are assigned to Commander, Patrol and Reconnaissance Force Atlantic (PATRECONFORLANT), at Norfolk, Virginia.[12] Squadrons assigned to the Atlantic Fleet are divided between two wings: PATRECONWING-5 at NAS Brunswick, Maine, and PATRECONWING-11 at NAS Jacksonville, Florida. PATRECONWING-5 also supports VQ-2 at Rota, Spain.

Until late 2003, the single West Coast wing was subordinate to Commander, Patrol and Reconnaissance Force Pacific, at Marine Corps Air Facility (MCAF) Kaneohe on the eastern coast of Oahu, Hawaii. That command also functioned as the wing commander for the four VP/VPU squadrons at Kaneohe Bay. On 15 October 2003, the Pacific Fleet's patrol/recon force was reorganized. The position of *Director*, Patrol and Reconnaissance Group Pacific (PATRECONGRUPAC), was established as the type command subordinate to Commander, Naval Air Force Pacific, and given command authority over the Pacific Fleet's PATRECONWINGs—the newly reactivated PATRECONWING-2 at MCAF Kaneohe Bay and PATRECONWING-10 at Whidbey Island, Washington. The group director was established at MCAF Kaneohe Bay, Hawaii.

Accordingly, the forward-deployed Pacific VP/VPU/VQ squadrons from the two patrol wings that deploy to the Western Pacific, Indian Ocean, and Persian Gulf come under the operational control of the Commander, Patrol and Reconnaissance Force Seventh Fleet, and the Patrol and Reconnaissance Force (PATRECONFOR) Fifth Fleet, both based at NAF Misawa, Japan.

PATRECONWING-1, previously at NAF Misawa, was deactivated. PATRECONFORPAC had been designated Patrol Wings Pacific Fleet, with its headquarters at NAS Moffett Field, south of San Francisco; that command moved to NAS Barbers Point, Hawaii, on 1 July 1993, and to MCAF Kaneohe on 1 July 1999.

Patrol Wing 2 in the Pacific was disestablished on 30 September 1993; the wing had been established at NAS Ford Island (Pearl Harbor) on 1 October 1937. The Navy had planned to reestablish the wing at Kaneohe Bay with the 1998–1999 move of VP squadrons to that base; in the event, the wing was reactivated on 15 October 2003. (Kaneohe Bay was a patrol plane base before and during World War II.)

Additional information on VP squadrons is provided below.

Historical: On 30 June 1973, Fleet Air Wings 1 and 2 were redesignated Patrol Wings 1 and 2. This was the end of the use of the fleet air wing designation and beginning of the patrol wing designation, which had been used prior to World War II.

NAVY SQUADRONS

ATTACK SQUADRONS

Squadron	Aircraft	Notes
VA-22	A-7E	to VFA-22 on 4 May 1990
VA-27	A-7E	to VFA-27 on 24 Jan 1991
VA-34	A-6E	to VFA-34 on 30 Sep 1996
VA-35	A-6E	disestablished 31 Jan 1995
VA-36	A-6E	disestablished 31 Mar 1994
VA-37	A-7E	to VFA-37 on 28 Nov 1990
VA-42	A-6E, TC-4C, T-34C	disestablished 30 Sep 1994
VA-46	A-7E	disestablished 30 Jun 1991
VA-52	A-6E	disestablished 31 Mar 1995
VA-55	A-6E	disestablished 1 Jan 1991
VA-65	A-6E	disestablished 31 Mar 1995
VA-72	A-7E	disestablished 30 Jun 1991
VA-75	A-6E	disestablished 31 Mar 1997
VA-85	A-6E	disestablished 20 Sep 1994
VA-94	A-7E	to VFA-94 on 28 June 1990
VA-95	A-6E	disestablished 31 Oct 1995
VA-97	A-7E	to VFA-97 on 24 Jan 1991
VA-105	A-7E	to VFA-105 on 17 Dec 1990
VA-115	A-6E	to VFA-115 on 30 Sep 1996
VA-122	A-7E	disestablished 31 May 1991
VA-128	A-6E, TC-4C	disestablished 30 Sep 1995
VA-145	A-6E	disestablished 1 Oct 1993
VA-155	A-6E	disestablished 10 Apr 1993
VA-165	A-6E	disestablished 30 Sep 1996
VA-176	A-6E	disestablished 30 Oct 1992
VA-185	A-6E	disestablished 30 Aug 1991
VA-196	A-6E	disestablished 28 Feb 1997

Table 27-4. PATROL AND RECONNAISSANCE FORCES

Commands	Wings	Location	Squadrons
PATRECONFORLANT		Norfolk, Va.	VP-30*
	PATRECONWING-5	Brunswick, Maine	VP-8
			VP-10
			VP-26
			VPU-1
	PATRECONWING-11	Jacksonville, Fla.	VP-5
			VP-16
			VP-45
		Rota, Spain	VQ-2
PATRECONGRUPAC		Kaneohe Bay, Hawaii	
	PATRECONWING-2	Kaneohe, Hawaii	VP-4
			VP-9
			VP-47
			VPU-2
	PATRECONWING-10	Whidbey Island, Wash.	VP-1
			VP-40
			VP-46
			VQ-1

* VP-30 is the P-3 Orion fleet readiness squadron.

The P-3 Orion squadrons and detachments of PATRECONFORLANT operate in the Atlantic, Caribbean, and Mediterranean areas. Pacific and Indian Ocean VP/VPU/VQ operations are directed by PATRECONFOR Seventh Fleet, and those in the Persian Gulf area are under PATRECONFOR Fifth Fleet.

The A-6E Intruder, the U.S. Navy's last specialized attack aircraft, was retired from the fleet in December 1996 when Attack Squadron (VA) 75 completed its final deployment, aboard the carrier ENTERPRISE. The disestablishment of the VA-75 "Sunday Punchers" marked the end of the plane's 34-year operational career.[13] With the demise of the Intruder the attack role has been taken over by bomb- and missile-carrying variants of the F-14 Tomcat fighter and the F/A-18 Hornet strike fighter.

Historical: U.S. carriers have operated attack aircraft since 15 November 1946, when the squadron designation VA was established to replace the previous carrier-based bombing (VB), bombing-fighting (VBF), and torpedo (VT) squadrons. The VA designation was used for "light" attack squadrons flying the A-1 Skyraider, A-4 Skyhawk, and A-7 Corsair, as well as for "medium" attack units flying the A-6 Intruder.

After 1991, all attack squadrons flew the A-6E Intruder, and two transition/readiness squadrons, VA-42 and VA-128, also flew specialized TC-4C trainers.

---

12 NAS Norfolk was officially changed to the Air Detachment Norfolk (Chambers Field) of NAS Oceana, Va., on 24 November 1998.

13 The last A-6E carrier landing occurred aboard the ENTERPRISE in February 1997.

All A-7E squadrons have been disestablished or converted to VFA units. VA-46 and VA-72 in the Atlantic were the Navy's last A-7E Corsair squadrons; their demise was delayed because of the Persian Gulf War (during which they flew from the JOHN F. KENNEDY). Both squadrons were disestablished in 1991, ending the 25-year career of the Corsair as a first-line Navy attack aircraft.[14] (It continued in service briefly in special-purpose roles; it was not flown by the Marine Corps.) VA-122, VA-125, and VA-174 were the A-7E readiness/transition squadrons.

14 The A-7D variant is still flown by the Air Force Reserve; several other countries also fly A-7 variants.

A pair of EA-6B Prowlers from VAQ-139, normally embarked in the carrier JOHN C. STENNIS, *on a training flight from NAS Whidbey Island. Navy and Marine Corps Prowlers provide electronic countermeasures for Air Force tactical aviation, as well as for Navy–Marine units. (U.S. Navy/Michael Watkins)*

14 ELECTRONIC ATTACK SQUADRONS

Squadron	Aircraft	Name/Notes*
VAQ-128	EA-6B	Fighting Phoenix (NL); established 1 Oct 1997; disestablished 30 Sep 2004
VAQ-129	EA-6B	Vikings (NJ)
VAQ-130	EA-6B	Zappers
VAQ-131	EA-6B	Lancers
VAQ-132	EA-6B	Scorpions
VAQ-133	EA-6B	Wizards (NL); disestablished 1 June 1992; again established 1 April 1996
VAQ-134	EA-6B	Garudas (NL)
VAQ-135	EA-6B	Black Ravens
VAQ-136	EA-6B	Gauntlets
VAQ-137	EA-6B	Rooks (NL); disestablished 30 Sep 1994; again established 1 Oct 1996
VAQ-138	EA-6B	Yellowjackets
VAQ-139	EA-6B	Cougars
VAQ-140	EA-6B	Patriots
VAQ-141	EA-6B	Shadowhawks
VAQ-142	EA-6B	Gray Wolves (NL); disestablished 1 July 1991; again established 1 Apr 1997
VAQ-143	EA-6B	establishment delayed (see notes)

* NJ = fleet readiness squadron; NL = land based

All front-line electronic attack (VAQ) squadrons have four EA-6B Prowlers. There are ten active and one reserve carrier-based squadron. In addition, there is one fleet readiness squadron (NJ) and four land-based VAQ squadrons (NL), the latter providing ECM support to Army, Navy, Air Force, and Marine air operations. (The Marine Corps has four VMAQ squadrons).

The formation of land-based VAQ squadrons was the result of the late 1995 decision by the Department of Defense to replace the Air Force's 24 EF-111A Raven ECM aircraft with Navy ECM aircraft. The Air Force retired its last EF-111 on 2 May 1998 and deactivated the 429th Electronic Combat Squadron at Cannon Air Force Base (AFB), New Mexico, on 19 June 1998, marking the transition to the EA-6B as the nation's only specialized ECM air-

craft. To meet this requirement, the Navy canceled the planned 30 September 1995 disestablishment of VAQ-134 and stood up three previously disestablished VAQ squadrons: VAQ-128, 133, and 142. These four Prowler squadrons each have the equivalent of one Air Force crew—a pilot and three ECM officers—and other Air Forces personnel on their staffs.

The EA-6B is expected to be replaced beginning in 2009 in Navy and Marine squadrons by the EA-18G Growler variant of the F/A-18F Hornet.

Plans to activate VAQ-143 as a fifth land-based squadron have been continually delayed because of the shortage of EA-6B aircraft. It was to have been established on 1 August 2002.

All Navy EA-6B units are based at NAS Whidbey Island, except for VAQ-136, based at NAF Atsugi. VAQ-129 provides EA-6B readiness training for Navy and Marine Prowler crews.

All Navy electronic attack squadrons report to Electronic Attack Wing Pacific Fleet (changed from Electronic Combat Wing Pacific Fleet on 30 March 1998).

Designation: VAQ formerly indicated tactical electronic warfare squadron; this was changed to electronic attack squadron on 30 March 1998.

Historical: VAQ-132 was the first squadron to receive the EA-6B, in July 1971. VAQ-129, 131, and 132 previously were heavy attack squadrons (VAH-10, 4, and 2, respectively); they were changed to VAQ in 1968–1970, when they shifted from EKA-3B Skywarriors to EA-6B aircraft. VAQ-130 is the former early warning squadron VAW-13, redesignated VAQ in 1968. Most of the other VAQs were built from EKA-3B detachments that operated from forward- deployed carriers.

Operational: During the Kosovo campaign of 1999, 10½ of 19 active and reserve Navy and Marine Corps electronic attack squadrons—each with four aircraft—were forward deployed (the half-squadron was a two-plane detachment from reserve squadron VAQ-209). At the height of the campaign, six squadrons were flying from Aviano, Italy, in support of Operation Allied Force, two were forward deployed aboard carriers, one was supporting the "no-fly" zone over southern Iraq from Saudi Arabia, and one was flying "no-fly" operations over northern Iraq from a base in Turkey. In addition, a Marine Prowler squadron was ashore in Japan.[15]

Personnel: Most VAQ squadrons have 28 officers and 163 enlisted personnel; VAQ-129 has 79 officers and 424 enlisted personnel.

In July 1990, VAQ-34 became the first U.S. military aviation squadron to be commanded by a woman.

11 AIRBORNE EARLY WARNING SQUADRONS

Squadron	Aircraft	Name/Notes
VAW-110	E-2C, C-2A	disestablished 30 Sep 1994
VAW-112	E-2C	Golden Hawks
VAW-113	E-2C	Black Hawks
VAW-114	E-2C	disestablished 31 Mar 1995
VAW-115	E-2C	Liberty Bells (ex-Sentinels)
VAW-116	E-2C	Sun Kings
VAW-117	E-2C	Wallbangers
VAW-120	E-2C, C-2A, TE-2C	Greyhawks (ex-Hummers) (AD)
VAW-121	E-2C	Bluetails
VAW-122	E-2C	disestablished 31 Mar 1996
VAW-123	E-2C	Screwtops
VAW-124	E-2C	Bear Aces
VAW-125	E-2C	Tigertails
VAW-126	E-2C	Seahawks
VAW-127	E-2C	disestablished 30 Sep 1991

The ten deploying AEW squadrons are assigned to carrier air wings, each with four E-2C Hawkeye aircraft. VAW-120 is the fleet readiness squadron.

The Pacific VAW squadrons are assigned to Strike Fighter Wing Pacific Fleet and are based at Naval Base Ventura County, California, except VAW-115, which is based at NAF Atsugi (it changed its name to the Liberty Bells on assignment to the INDEPENDENCE in 1991). The Atlantic squadrons are assigned to Airborne Early Warning Wing Atlantic at Norfolk. The West Coast VAQ units previously were based at NAS Miramar, California, which was changed to Marine Corps Air Station (MCAS) Miramar on 1 October 1997.

Designation: The two readiness AEW squadrons—VAW-110 and VAW-120—were designated RVAW until 1 May 1983, when they dropped the *R* prefix; they were the only readiness squadrons with that prefix.

Historical: The first carrier AEW squadrons were VAW-1 and VAW-2, commissioned in 1948 to provide aircraft detachments to Pacific and Atlantic carriers, respectively. (AEW aircraft had earlier flown from carriers, and a land-based squadron, VPW-1, had been established in 1948.)

The current VAW structure dates from 1967, when seven AEW squadrons numbered in sequence were established. Previously, VAW-11, 12, 13, and 33 provided AEW detachments to carriers, and Barrier Squadron Pacific and AEW Wing Atlantic operated land-based WV/EC-121 Warning Star aircraft as part of the North American air defense efforts until 1965.

Personnel: Most VAW squadrons have 29 officers and 134 enlisted personnel; VAW-120 has 89 officers and 366 enlisted men and women.

1 FLEET COMPOSITE SQUADRON

Squadron	Code	Aircraft	Name/Notes
VC-1	UA	F/A-18, CH-53A, VP-3A	disestablished 30 Sep 1992
VC-5	UE	F/A-18, SH-3G	disestablished 31 Aug 1992
VC-6	JG	RQ-2B (UAV)	Skeet of the Fleet (ex-Skeeters)
VC-8	GF	TA-4J, UH-3H	disestablished 1 Oct 2003
VC-10	JH	F/A-18	disestablished 14 Aug 1993

Composite squadrons historically provide utility services for the fleet, including noncombat photography, aerial target services, radar calibration, and transport. Two now-disestablished VC squadrons had combat missions: VC-1 and VC-10 had F/A-18 Hornets that had the additional role of air defense for Hawaii and Guantanamo Bay, Cuba, respectively. (They previously flew A-4E and TA-4J Skyhawks.)

---

15 See R. Holzer, "More Military Operations Keep Prowler Fleet Busier than Ever," *Navy Times* (3 May 1999), p. 10; and Capt. Lloyd E. Bonzo, USMC, "Parting with the Prowler," U.S. Naval Institute *Proceedings* (August 1999), pp. 36–37.

Fleet Composite Squadron 6 personnel aboard the frigate ROBERT G. BRADLEY *(FFG 49) launch a BQM-74 target drone during a multination UNITAS exercise in the South Atlantic. Another two of VC-6's target drones are visible on the ship's fantail. (U.S. Navy/Robert Taylor)*

VC-6 at Norfolk flies no aircraft, but operates air and surface target drones and the Navy's unmanned aerial vehicles. The aerial targets are BQM-74E drones and the UAVs are the U.S.–Israeli RQ-2B Pioneers. There are permanent VC-6 detachments at the Fleet Combat Training Center in Dam Neck, Virginia, and at the Naval Amphibious Base in Little Creek, Virginia. Five smaller, mobile detachments operate in the Atlantic–Mediterranean areas and periodically deploy with U.S. ships operating around South America in the UNITAS exercises.

VC-8 at Naval Station Roosevelt Roads, Puerto Rico, flew Sea Kings to provide services to Atlantic fleet training and weapon test activities. The squadron was disestablished with the closing of the Vieques Island training facility. The squadron also was the last to fly the TA-4J Skyhawk.

Historical: The current VC squadrons comprise the third series of composite squadrons in the fleet. From 1943 to 1945, the Navy had 83 composite squadrons that operated from escort carriers.

Beginning in 1948, six VC squadrons were formed with nuclear-strike aircraft (flying P2V-3C Neptunes and AJ Savages); those squadrons became heavy attack squadrons (VAH) in 1955–1956. At the same time, several ASW squadrons were formed but were redesignated VS. On 1 July 1965, the Navy's utility squadrons (VJ and later VU) were changed to VC, with VU-1, 5, 6, 8, and 10 being redesignated as fleet composite squadrons.

VC-2 (Oceana, Virginia) and VC-7 (Miramar) were disestablished in 1980, and VC-3 (North Island, California) was disestablished in 1981. The last squadron flew DC-130A Hercules to launch aerial drones.

Personnel: Including detachments, VC-6 has a total of 26 officers and 215 enlisted men.

6 FIGHTER SQUADRONS

Squadron	Aircraft	Name/Notes
VF-1	F-14	disestablished 30 Sep 1993
VF-2	F-14	to VFA-2 on 1 July 2003
VF-11	F-14B	Red Rippers
VF-14	F-14	to VFA-14 on 1 Dec 2001
VF-21	F-14	disestablished 31 Jan 1996
VF-24	F-14	disestablished 31 Aug 1996
VF-31	F-14D	Tomcatters
VF-32	F-14B	Swordsmen
VF-33	F-14	disestablished 1 Oct 1993
VF-41	F-14	to VFA-41 on 1 Dec 2001
VF-43	F-5E/F, A-4E, F-16N, F-21A, T--2C	disestablished 1 July 1994
VF-45	A-4E, TA-4J	disestablished 31 Mar 1996
VF-51	F-14	disestablished 31 Mar 1995
VF-74	F-14	disestablished 30 Apr 1994
VF-84	F-14	disestablished 1 Oct 1995
VF-101	F-14A/B/D, T-34C	Grim Reapers (AD)
VF-102	F-14	to VFA-102 on 1 May 2002
VF-103	F-14B	to VFA-103 in 2004
VF-111	F-14	disestablished 31 Mar 1995
VF-114	F-14	disestablished 30 Apr 1993
VF-124	F-14	disestablished 30 Sep 1994
VF-126	TA-4J, F-5E/F, F-16N	disestablished 1 Apr 1994
VF-142	F-14	disestablished 30 Apr 1995
VF-143	F-14B	World Famous Dogs (see *Historical* notes)
VF-154	F-14	to VFA-154 on 1 Oct 2003
VF-211	F-14D	to VFA-211 in 2004
VF-213	F-14D	Black Lions

There are five fighter squadrons (VF) assigned to carrier air wings plus one fleet readiness squadron, VF-101. All fly the F-14 Tomcat. Beginning with the arrival of the F/A-18E Hornet in the fleet in 2001, the number of F-14 squadrons has been reduced continuously, until most carriers no longer have F-14s. Several carriers have one squadron. The remaining F-14 squadrons will convert to the F/A-18 by 2008.

Each F-14 squadrons has 10–12 aircraft assigned; in each squadron, there are three aircraft wired for the TARPS reconnaissance package, which can be installed or removed in a few hours. VF-211 was the first squadron to deploy with TARPS, in early 1982 on board the CONSTELLATION. VF-211 transitioned from the F-14A to the F-14D in 2004, the last fleet squadron to fly the former aircraft.

All F-14 squadrons are assigned to Fighter Wing Atlantic Fleet and are based at NAS Oceana. VF-154, previously based at NAF Atsugi for the carrier KITTY HAWK, departed Japan in September 2003. Previously, West Coast fighter squadrons had been at NAS Miramar. F-14 readiness training is provided by VF-101. (The West Coast F-14 readiness unit—VF-124—was disestablished in 1994.)

The Naval Strike and Air Warfare Center, established in 1995 at Fallon, Nevada, replaced the Strike Warfare Center ("Strike University") and Fighter Weapons School ("Top Gun"). Top Gun had begun as a VF-121 detachment and became a separate command on 1 July 1972. The Strike and Air Warfare Center operates aircraft to help develop fleet tactics; "students" bring their own aircraft to the center. Currently assigned to the center are:

  8 F-16A Fighting Falcons
  4 F-16B Fighting Falcons
 19 F/A-18A Hornets
  3 F/A-18B Hornets
  2 SH-60F Seahawks

The F-16s are aircraft ordered by the Pakistani Air Force but withheld because of that nation's nuclear weapons program (see Chapter 28).

Historical: Squadrons VF-43 (Oceana), VF-45 (Key West, Florida), and VF-126 (Miramar) previously provided adversary training, with the last also providing instrument training. VF-45 was changed from VA-45 on 7 February 1985.

VF-191 and VF-194 were established in 1986 for the Navy's 14th carrier air wing, but were disestablished in 1988. Plans to establish "new" VF-191 and VF-194 as F-14D squadrons were canceled when VF-11 and VF-31 became available after CVW-6 was disestablished when the FORRESTAL was named as the training carrier. Those two VF squadrons were then shifted to the West Coast.

The MIDWAY flew the Navy's last two active Phantom squadrons (VF-151 and VF-161), which stood down as Phantom units in 1986. The squadrons then became VFA-151 and VFA-161 flying the F/A-18. The last Phantom fleet readiness squadron was VF-171, disestablished in 1984. All Navy–Marine readiness training in the Phantom was then being undertaken by Marine Fighter-Attack Training Squadron (VMFAT) 101 at MCAS Yuma, Arizona. (VF-121, the West Coast F-4 readiness squadron, was disestablished in 1980; it had been the Navy's first squadron to fly the F-4.)

Personnel: Most VF squadrons have 34 officers and about 240 enlisted personnel. VF-101, the FRS unit, has 63 officers and 565 enlisted personnel.

Names: VF-143 was the World Famous Pukin' Dogs from 1949 until 1994, when "Pukin'" was deleted, another casualty of political correctness.

An F/A-18F Super Hornet is catapulted from the carrier KITTY HAWK during Summer Pulse 2004, the exercise to surge as many carriers as possible to sea during a simulated crisis. The aircraft carries drop tanks, but no missiles or bombs. (U.S. Navy/Jonathan Chandler)

35 STRIKE FIGHTER SQUADRONS

Squadron	Aircraft	Name/Notes
VFA-2	F/A-18F	Bounty Hunters; former VF-2
VFA-14	F/A-18E	Tophatters; former VF-14
VFA-15	F/A-18C	Valions; former VA-15
VFA-22	F/A-18E	Fighting Redcocks; former VA-22
VFA-25	F/A-18C	Fist of the Fleet; former VA-25
VFA-27	F/A-18E	Chargers; former VA-27
VFA-34	F/A-18C	Blue Blasters; former VA-34
VFA-37	F/A-18C	Bulls; former VA-37
VFA-41	F/A-18F	Black Aces; former VF-41
VFA-81	F/A-18C	Sunliners; former VA-81
VFA-82	F/A-18C	Marauders; former VA-82
VFA-83	F/A-18C	Rampagers; former VA-83
VFA-86	F/A-18C	Sidewinders; former VA-86
VFA-87	F/A-18C	Golden Warriors; former VA-87
VFA-94	F/A-18C	Mighty Shrikes; former VA-94
VFA-97	F/A-18C	Warhawks; former VA-97
VFA-102	F/A-18F	Diamondbacks; former VF-102
VFA-103	F/A-18F	Sluggers; former VF-103
VFA-105	F/A-18C	Gunslingers; former VA-105
VFA-106	F/A-18B/C/D, T-34C	Gladiators (AD); former VA-106
VFA-113	F/A-18C	Stingers; former VA-113
VFA-115	F/A-18E	Eagles; former VA-115
VFA-122	F/A-18E/F	Flying Eagles (NJ); former VA-122
VFA-125	F/A-18B/C/D, T-34C	Rough Riders (NJ); former VA-125
VFA-127	A-4, F-5	former VA-127; disestablished 31 Mar 1996
VFA-131	F/A-18C	Wildcats
VFA-132	F/A-18A	disestablished 1 June 1992
VFA-136	F/A-18C	Knighthawks
VFA-137	F/A-18E	Kestrels
VFA-146	F/A-18C	Blue Diamonds; former VA-146
VFA-147	F/A-18C	Argonauts; former VA-147
VFA-151	F/A-18C	Fighting Vigilantes; former VF-151
VFA-154	F/A-18F	Black Knights; former VF-154
VFA-192	F/A-18C	World Famous Golden Dragons
VFA-195	F/A-18C	Dambusters; former VA-195
VFA-211	F/A-18F	Flying Checkmates; former VA-211

All carrier air wings have three or four strike fighter squadrons, each with 12 F/A-18 aircraft. With the retirement of the F-14 Tomcat, all carrier wings will have four F/A-18 squadrons. SHARP, a replacement for the F-14/TARPS capability, initially is being carried by F/A-18F aircraft.

VFA-97 is the last fleet squadron flying the F/A-18A, having been delayed in its update to the F/A-18C. It now will transition to the F/A-18E.

There are three F/A-18 readiness training squadrons, VFA-106 at NAS Oceana, and VFA-122 and VFA-125, both at NAS Lemoore, California. VFA-122 is the first Navy F/A-18E/F unit; it was established on 1 October 1998.

Shortfalls in fleet squadrons have been met by assigning Marine F/A-18 squadrons to carrier air wings. The Atlantic F/A-18 squadrons are assigned to Strike Fighter Wing Atlantic Fleet; all are based at NAS Oceana except for VFA-82 and VFA-86, which moved to MCAS Beaufort, South Carolina, in late 1999. All Pacific squadrons are under Strike Fighter Wing Pacific Fleet and based at NAS Lemoore, except for VFA-27, VFA-102, VFA-192, and VFA-195, based at NAF Atsugi.

VMFA-323 was to have deployed aboard the ABRAHAM LINCOLN in 2004 with CVW-2, but the squadron was not ready. VFA-82 filled in for it.

Designation: The Navy designation VFA indicated fighter attack squadron from 1980 to 1983; this was changed in 1983 to strike fighter squadron to emphasize the attack role.

Historical: The first F/A-18 squadron was VFA-125, established on 13 November 1980 as the F/A-18 readiness squadron for training Navy and Marine pilots and ground crews; VFA-125's first aircraft was delivered in February 1981. A second F/A-18 readiness squadron, VFA-106, subsequently was stood up in October 1985 at NAS Cecil Field (Jacksonville, Florida).

VFA-75 and VFA-113 were the Navy's first F/A-18 fleet squadrons, shifting from the A-7E Corsair to the F/A-18 in March–June 1983. Most F/A-18 squadrons are former A-7E Corsair units (VA); two F-14 squadrons (VF-151, VF-161) are transitioning to F/A-18s, and more VA and VF squadrons are scheduled to follow. VFA-161 was disestablished in 1987.

Personnel: Most VFA squadrons have 25 officers and about 210 enlisted personnel; including detachments, the three FRS units have:

Squadron	Officers	Enlisted
VFA-106	65	500
VFA-122	84	423
VFA-125	61	464

Operational: The Navy operates more F/A-18 Hornets than any other aircraft type. The aircraft had its combat debut in the 1986 carrier strikes against Libya; it has been active in subsequent U.S. peacekeeping and combat operations.

13 PATROL SQUADRONS

Squadron	Code	Aircraft	Name/Notes
VP-1	YB	P-3C	Screaming Eagles
VP-4	YD	P-3C	Skinny Dragons
VP-5	LA	P-3C	Mad Foxes
VP-6	PC	P-3C	disestablished 31 May 1993
VP-8	LC	P-3C	Tigers
VP-9	PD	P-3C	Golden Eagles
VP-10	LD	P-3C	Red Lancers
VP-11	LE	P-3C	disestablished 2 Aug 1997*
VP-16	LF	P-3C	Eagles
VP-17	ZE	P-3C	disestablished 31 Mar 1995
VP-19	PE	P-3C	disestablished 31 Aug 1991
VP-22	QA	P-3C	disestablished 31 Mar 1994
VP-23	LJ	P-3C	disestablished 28 Feb 1995*
VP-24	LR	P-3C	disestablished 30 Apr 1995*
VP-26	LK	P-3C	Tridents
VP-30	LL	P-3C, VP-3A	Pro's Nest
VP-31	RP	P-3C	disestablished 1 Nov 1993
VP-40	QE	P-3C	Fighting Marlins
VP-44	LM	P-3C	disestablished 28 June 1991
VP-45	LN	P-3C	Pelicans
VP-46	RC	P-3C	Grey Knights
VP-47	RD	P-3C	Golden Swordsmen
VP-48	SF	P-3C	disestablished 26 June 1991
VP-49	LP	P-3C	disestablished 1 Mar 1994
VP-50	SG	P-3C	disestablished 30 June 1992
VP-56	LQ	P-3C	disestablished 28 June 1991

* Corrections to 17th Edition

There are 12 active patrol squadrons, plus one P-3 Orion readiness training squadron. This is half the number of VP squadrons in the active fleet from the early 1970s until 1991. Most Atlantic Fleet squadrons have nine aircraft; the Pacific squadrons ten because of their greater operating area. VP-30, with 28 aircraft, serves as the FRS for all P-3 users. The Pacific Fleet readiness squadron was VP-31 at NAS Moffett Field. It was consolidated with VP-30 at NAS Jacksonville.

Patrol squadrons are assigned to Patrol Reconnaissance Force Atlantic and Patrol Reconnaissance Group Pacific; see Table 27-4.

Designation: VP indicated patrol squadron from 1922 to 1944, when patrol and multiengine land-based bombing squadrons were redesignated patrol bombing squadrons (VPB). The squadrons reverted to VP on 15 May 1946.

Historical: VP-8 was the first P3V/P-3 Orion squadron, receiving the aircraft in 1962. Previously, VP units flew P2V/P-2 Neptunes and P5M/P-5 Marlin flying boats.

Operational: VP squadrons—active and reserve—regularly deploy, whole or as detachments, to Guantanamo; Keflavik, Iceland; Sigonella, Sicily; Masirah, Oman; Diego Garcia; Misawa, Japan; and Kadena, Okinawa. (Deployments to Adak, Alaska; Bermuda; Lajes, Azores; Jidda, Saudi Arabia; Rota, Spain; Cubi Point, Philippines; and Agana, Guam, have ceased.)

Personnel: Most VP squadrons have 67 officers and 338 enlisted personnel. VP-30 has 130 officers and 638 enlisted personnel, including detachments.

2 SPECIAL PROJECTS PATROL SQUADRONS

Squadron	Code	Aircraft	Name/Notes
VPU-1	OB	P-3C	Ancient Order of the Buzzard
VPU-2	SP	P-3C	Wizards

These two squadrons fly specially modified electronic surveillance variants of the Orion. They often operate with the tail codes of other squadrons. VPU-1's unit code is unofficial, derived from "*O*rder of the *B*uzzard"; VP-2's code is derived from Special Projects.

VPU-1 is based at NAS Brunswick, Maine, and VPU-2 is at MCAF Kaneohe. They each are assigned five P-3C aircraft.

Designation: VPU was Patrol Squadron Special Projects Unit; VPU-1 was changed to Special Projects Patrol Squadron on 8 April 1988, and to VPU-2 on 14 April 1998.

Personnel: VPU-1 has 34 officers and 204 enlisted personnel; VPU-2 has 35 officers and 199 enlisted.

2 FLEET AIR RECONNAISSANCE SQUADRONS

Squadron	Code	Aircraft	Name/Notes
VQ-1	PR	P-3C, EP-3E, UP-3A/B	World Watchers
VQ-2	JQ	P-3C, EP-3E	Batmen
VQ-5	SS	S-3B, ES-3A	disestablished 30 July 1999
VQ-6	ET	ES-3A	disestablished 30 Sep 1999

VQ-1 and VQ-2 provide electronic surveillance in direct support of fleet operations and carry out special reconnaissance along the borders of foreign territory. They have five and six ELINT-configured EP-3E Orions, respectively, plus support and training aircraft.

VQ-1, based at NAS Whidbey Island, is under Patrol Wing 10; VQ-2, based at NAS Rota, Spain, is under Fleet Air Mediterranean (at Naples, Italy).

VQ-5 at NAS North Island (San Diego) and VQ-6 at NAS Jacksonville flew the ES-3A Sea Shadow as carrier-based ELINT aircraft.[16] The squadrons were established in 1991. The ES-3A succeeded the EA-3B Skywarrior ("Whale"), with one or two aircraft assigned to forward-deployed aircraft carriers. VQ-2 retired the last EA-3B operated by a VQ squadron in September 1991. (They were flown a while longer by VAQs.)

VQ-1 and VQ-2 and other electronic intelligence "assets" took over the collection role of the ES-3A aircraft.

Also see VQ-11 under Naval Air Reserve.

Designation: VQ was changed from Electronic Counter-measures Squadron to Fleet Air Reconnaissance Squadron on 1 January 1960.

Historical: VQ-1 was established as Electronic Counter-measures Squadron 1 at NAS Iwakuni, Japan, on 1 June 1955, initially flying P4M-1Q Mercator aircraft. VQ-2 was established as ECM Squadron 2 on 1 September 1955 at Port Lyautey, Morocco, first flying the P4M-1Q and the A3D-1Q (EA-3B) aircraft. Previously, PB4Y-2 Privateer and PBM Mariner aircraft were employed in the ELINT role.

Operational: VQ-2 flew both EP-3s and EA-3Bs in support of Desert Shield and Desert Storm in 1990–1991; the latter were the last operational combat-environment flights by the Skywarrior.

Personnel: VQ-1 has 102 officers and 421 enlisted personnel; VQ-2 has 90 officers and 405 enlisted personnel.

3 STRATEGIC COMMUNICATION SQUADRONS

Squadron	Code	Aircraft	Name/Notes
VQ-3	TZ	E-6B	Ironmen (ex-TACOMOPAC)
VQ-4	HL	E-6B	Shadows
VQ-7	(none)	Boeing 737	Roughnecks

VQ-3 and VQ-4, officially designated fleet air reconnaissance squadrons, fly the E-6A Mercury, a navalized version of the Boeing 707-320B airframe. They provide low frequency (LF)/very low frequency (VLF) communications relay to strategic missile submarines under a program known as TACAMO (Take Charge and Move Out); in addition, in the E-6B configuration, these aircraft replace the Air Force EC-135 "Looking Glass" strategic command post aircraft. The last EC-135 was retired on 25 September 1998.

---

16 Sea Shadow was an unofficial name; the aircraft retained the name Viking in official documentation. Note that the unit code ET also is assigned to Marine helicopter squadron HMM-262.

Fifteen E-6B aircraft are flown by the two squadrons, replacing 22 EC-130Q Hercules aircraft.

VQ-3 and VQ-4 are under Navy Strategic Communications Wing 1, which was established on 1 May 1992, the year both squadrons moved to Tinker Air Force Base (AFB), outside Oklahoma City, Oklahoma. Operationally, they are under the U.S. Strategic Command. (Previously, VQ-3 was at NAS Barbers Point and VQ-4 at NAS Patuxent River.)

The two squadrons "forward deploy" aircraft to Travis AFB, California, Offutt AFB, Nebraska, and NAS Patuxent River to fly operational patrols.

Two similar 707-320B aircraft designated TC-18F were operated by the Naval Training Support Unit at Tinker AFB to train E-6A pilots. The unit was redesignated VQ-7 on 1 November 1999. During 2000, structural problems were found in the TC-18Fs, and they were withdrawn from service. They were replaced by Air Force EC-18B, and the squadron was flying Boeing 737 aircraft when this edition went to press.

Historical: VQ-3 transitioned from the EC-130Q Hercules to the E-6A Hermes in 1989–1990, and VQ-4 in 1991–1992. The last EC-130Q TACAMO flight, by a VQ-4 "Herk," was on 7 May 1992.

Personnel: VQ-3 has 78 officers and 454 enlisted personnel; VQ-4 has 78 officers and 426 enlisted, including detachments.

2 FLEET LOGISTIC SUPPORT SQUADRONS

Squadron	Code	Aircraft	Name/Notes
VR-22	JL	C-130F, KC-130F	disestablished 31 Mar 1993
VR-24	JM	C-2A, CT-39G	disestablished 31 Jan 1993
VRC-30	RW	C-2A, UC-12B, RC-12F	Providers (ex-Truckin' Traders)
VRC-40	CD	C-2A	Rawhides
VRC-50	RG	C-2A, US-3A, C-130	disestablished 7 Oct 1994

The two surviving fleet logistic support squadrons (VRC) deliver passengers, mail, and high-priority parts to carriers at sea. The Navy's straight transport squadrons (VR) have been phased out, their role taken over by Naval Reserve VR units and the Air Force's Air Mobility Command (formerly the Military Airlift Command).

VRC-30 is at NAS North Island under AEW Wing Pacific Fleet, and VRC-40 is under AEW Atlantic Fleet at Norfolk. The assignment of the C-2A COD aircraft to the E-2C Hawkeye wings is based on the similarity of their aircraft.

The disestablishment of VRC-50 led the Navy to set up VRC-30 Detachment 5 at NAF Atsugi, to provide COD aircraft to support carriers in the Western Pacific. The turboprop C-2A is not normally based aboard carriers because of its large size.

The KC-130F Hercules of VR-22 were the Navy's only land-based tanker aircraft. VRC-50 flew the Navy's three US-3A Viking COD aircraft. VAW-110 and VAW-120 took over readiness training for the C-2 from VRC-30 and VRC-40; currently, VRC-30 and Naval Station Norfolk (formerly NAS Norfolk) provide transition and readiness training for the UC-12 Super Air King for the Navy.

Designation: The VR squadrons originally were transport squadrons, but were changed to fleet tactical support squadrons on 15 July 1957. They became fleet logistic support squadrons on 1 April 1976.

Historical: The first Navy transport squadron was VR-1. It was established on 9 March 1942; it was disestablished in October 1978.

The first COD squadron was VRC-40, established on 1 July 1960. The first COD aircraft were converted TBM Avengers, intended to fly nuclear bomb components from forward bases to aircraft carriers.

Personnel: VRC-30 has 54 officers and 346 enlisted personnel; VRC-40 has 47 officers and 313 enlisted personnel, including detachments.

An S-3B Viking from VS-30 flying from the carrier JOHN F. KENNEDY performing air-to-air refueling over the Persian Gulf. The coming demise of VS/S-3 units will place the carrier-based tanker burden on F/A-18 Hornet strike fighters. (U.S. Navy/Joshua Karsten)

9 SEA CONTROL SQUADRONS

Squadron	Aircraft	Name/Notes
VS-21	S-3B	Fighting Redtails
VS-22	S-3B	Checkmates
VS-24	S-3B	Scouts
VS-27	S-3B	disestablished 30 Sep 1994 (AD)
VS-28	S-3B	disestablished 1 Oct 1992
VS-29	S-3B	disestablished 30 Apr 2004
VS-30	S-3B	Diamond Cutters
VS-31	S-3B	Topcats
VS-32	S-3B	Maulers
VS-33	S-3B	Screwbirds
VS-35	S-3B	Blue Wolves
VS-37	S-3B	disestablished 31 Mar 1995
VS-38	S-3B	disestablished 30 Apr 2004
VS-41	S-3B	Shamrocks (NJ)

The Navy's eight operational sea control squadrons each fly eight S-3B Viking aircraft. During the 1980s, these units—then called ASW squadrons—had ten aircraft; during a short period in the 1990s, this was reduced to six.

These aircraft no longer are employed in ASW operations, but are used for surface surveillance, aerial refueling, and utility functions. All Vikings will be retired by 2009, possibly sooner. F/A-18E/F aircraft with "buddy stores" will carry out tanking functions for non-VS carrier wings.

VS-41 at NAS North Island provides readiness training for the S-3 community; previously, VS-27 at NAS Cecil Field, Jacksonville, Florida, provided S-3 readiness/transition services for the Atlantic Fleet. (VS-30 was an S-2 Tracker readiness training squadron; it became an operational squadron on transitioning to the S-3A in 1976.)

Viking squadrons and their respective fleet sea control wings operate out of North Island and Cecil Field, except VS-21 is based at NAF Atsugi.

Designation: The 13 VS units in service on 16 September 1993 were changed from anti-submarine squadrons to sea control squadrons, reflecting their more versatile operations.

Historical: Specialized carrier-based ASW squadrons were formed in World War II, most designated as composite squadrons (VC). In April 1950, eight VC squadrons were changed to air anti-submarine squadrons (VS); each flew 18 TBM-3E Avengers. Four of the squadrons previously had been attack units (VA) that had been changed to VC on 1 September 1948.

Operational: An S-3B from VS-35 flew President George W. Bush aboard the carrier ABRAHAM LINCOLN on 1 May 2003 off the coast of San Diego. The LINCOLN was returning from Operation Iraqi Freedom. For that flight, the aircraft was designated "Navy One."

Personnel: VS squadrons have 33 officers and 186 enlisted personnel. VS-41 has 73 officers and 392 enlisted personnel.

16 TRAINING SQUADRONS

	Squadron	Aircraft	Name	Training	Personnel*
TRAINING WING 1 (code A) NAS Meridian, Miss.					19 + 1
	VT-7	T-45C	Strike Eagles	Advanced jet	33 + 0
	VT-9**	T-45C	Tigers	Intermediate jet	31 + 0
TRAINING WING 2 (code B) NAS Kingsville, Texas					21 + 0
	VT-21	T-45A	Fighting Redhawks	Intermediate/advanced jet	26 + 0
	VT-22	T-45A	Golden Eagles	Intermediate/advanced jet	23 + 0
	VT-23	T-45C	Professionals	disestablished 30 Sep 1999	
TRAINING WING 3 (code C)				disestablished 31 Aug 1992	
	VT-24	TA-4J		disestablished 30 Oct 1992	
	VT-25	TA-4J		disestablished 30 Oct 1992	
	VT-26	T-2C		disestablished 29 May 1992	
TRAINING WING 4 (code G) NAS Corpus Christi, Texas					15 + 9
	VT-27	T-34C	Boomers	Primary flight	44 + 0
	VT-28	T-34C	Rangers	Primary flight	43 + 4
	VT-31	T-44A	Wise Owls	Advanced maritime	24 + 3
	VT-35	TC-12B	Stingrays	Advanced maritime	17 + 0
TRAINING WING 5 (code E) NAS Milton, Fla.					19 + 2
	VT-2	T-34C	Doer Birds	Primary flight	30 + 0
	VT-3	T-34C	Red Knights	Primary flight	11 + 0
	VT-6	T-34C	Shooters	Primary flight	30 + 0
	HT-8	TH-57B/C	Eight Ballers	Advanced helicopter	42 + 14
	HT-18	TH-57B/C	Vigilant Eagles	Advanced helicopter	43 + 14
TRAINING WING 6 (code F) NAS Pensacola, Fla.					19 + 0
	VT-4	T-1A, T-6A, T-34C	Mighty Warbucks	Advanced	39 + 0
	VT-10	T-1A, T-6A, T-34C	Wildcats	Advanced	42 + 0
	VT-86	T-2C, T-39G/N	Sabrehawks	Advanced NFO***	49 + 0

* Officer and enlisted personnel
** VT-19 was redesignated VT-9 on 1 October 1998.
*** NFO = Naval Flight Officer (i.e., the "backseater")

These 16 squadrons provide fixed-wing training for Navy, Marine Corps, Coast Guard, Air Force, and foreign pilots and aircrew under the direction of the Naval Air Training Command at NAS Corpus Christi, Texas. VT-3 provides primary flight training for U.S. Air Force pilots, and VT-31 and VT-35 train Navy, Marine, and Coast Guard pilots in multiengine turboprop aircraft; VT-31 also trains U.S. Air Force C-130 pilots.

There currently are three Air Force Flying Training Squadrons (FTS) that train Navy pilots:

Squadron	Aircraft	Training	Location
35th FTS	T-37	Primary	Reese AFB, Texas
32nd FTS	T-1A	E-6A	Vance AFB, Okla.
562nd FTS	T-43A	Advanced NFO	Randolph AFB, Texas

The T-45 is carrier capable and enables students to practice landings aboard aircraft carriers; the carrier-capable T-2C made its last carrier qualification flights aboard the HARRY S. TRUMAN in July 2003. VT-21 began operating the long-delayed T-45 Goshawk in early 1992; the plane finally replaced the TA-4J Skyhawk in

1999, with VT-9 being the last U.S. Navy training squadron to fly that long-serving aircraft.

VT-86 trains naval flight officers, as well as U.S. Air Force Weapon System Operators (WSO) for B-1, B-2, and F-15 bomber/strike aircraft. The T-39G/N aircraft of VT-86 are refurbished Sabreliners used to train NFOs. Flown and maintained by contractor personnel, they replaced T-47A aircraft that were operated under a similar arrangement.

Training aircraft are assigned by wing:

Training Wing	Aircraft
1	53 T-2C
	76 T-45C
2	73 T-45A
	2 T-45C
4	92 T-34C
	54 T-44A
	21 TC-12B
5	145 T-34C
	46 TH-57B
	72 TH-57C
6	15 T-2C
	51 T-34C
	8 T-39G
	15 T-39N
	15 T-6A

Designation: The letters *T* and *HT* (helicopter) have been used for naval aircraft designations since shortly after World War II; however, VT and HT were not used for squadron designations until 1 May 1960, when 17 training units were redesignated as training squadrons (VT). From the 1920s until 15 November 1946, the designation VT indicated torpedo squadron.

Note that HT squadrons are numbered in the same series as VT squadrons

Historical: VT-7 was the last U.S. military squadron to fly the A-4 Skyhawk. The diminutive and highly versatile aircraft had entered Navy service as the A4D-1 in September 1956; the TA-4J two-seat trainer entered service on 6 June 1969. The aircraft still is flown by several other countries.

HT-8 traces its history to HTU-1, established in 1950 and changed to HTG-1 in 1957 and to HT-8 in 1960. HT-18 was established in 1972.

Figure 27-1. NAVAL AVIATION PILOT TRAINING

FRS Aircraft

Preflight Introduction → Primary Training (23 weeks)
VT-2 VT-27
VT-3 VT-28
VY-6

→ Strike Training (44 weeks)
VT-21 VT-22
F-14
F/A-18
AV-8B
EA-6B
S-3B

→ Strike Training (25 weeks)
VT-9
→ Advanced Strike Training (35 weeks)
F-14
F/A-18
AV-8B
EA-6B
S-3B

→ C-2/E-2 Intermediate Training (16 weeks)
VT-31
→ C-2/E-2 Carrier Quals (26 weeks)
VT-9
E-2
C-2

→ Maritime Training (6 weeks)
VT-2 VT-27
VT-3 VT-28
VT-6
→ Maritime Multiengine Training (22 weeks)
VT-31 VT-35
P-3
EP-3
C-130
HU-25

→ TACAMO/E-6 Training (6 weeks)
VT-2 VT-27
VT-3 VT-28
VT-6
→ TACAMO/E-6 Training (26 weeks)
USAF
E-6B

→ Helicopter Training (6 weeks)
VT-2 VT-27
VT-3 VT-28
VT-6
→ Helicopter Training (25 weeks)
HT-8 HT-18
H-1
H-3
H-46
H-53
H-60
H-65

A T-45C Goshawk from VT-7 makes an arrested landing aboard the HARRY S. TRUMAN during carrier qualifications off the Atlantic coast. The Navy has no dedicated training carrier as was available during most of the Cold War. (U.S. Navy/Danny Ewing Jr.)

Figure 27-2. NAVAL AVIATION NFO TRAINING

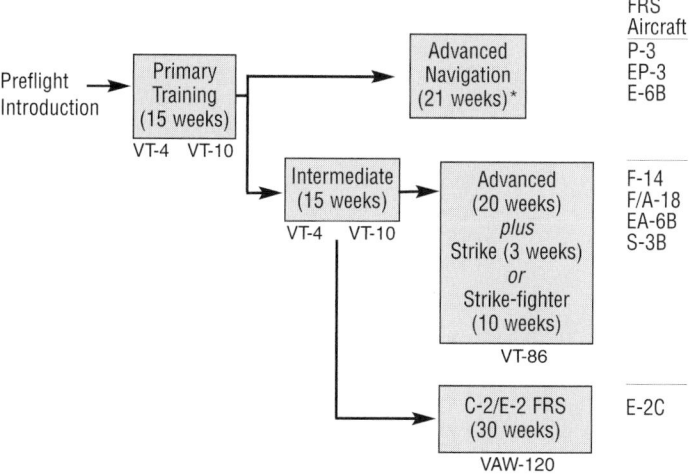

*Training at 562nd Flying Training Squadron, Randolf AFB, Texas

A bevy of TH-57 SeaRanger helicopters form Training Wing 5 based at Naval Air Station Whiting Field, Florida, tied down at Millington, Tennessee. They were among 300 naval training aircraft flown to Millington when Hurricane Ivan approached Florida in September 2004. (U.S. Navy/Joseph M. Bulivac)

1 FLIGHT DEMONSTRATION SQUADRON

Code	Aircraft	Name
BA	F/A-18A/B, C-130T	Blue Angels

The Blue Angels is the Navy–Marine Corps flight demonstration team, performing around the United States to encourage aviation recruiting. The unit currently flies early model F/A-18A Hornets—ten F/A-18A and one two-seat F/A-18B. The team's F/A-18s are not normally capable of carrier operations, have had their guns removed, and are provided with smoke generators, improved flight control systems, and additional navigation equipment.

A Navy C-130T Hercules is assigned to the team as a support aircraft; it replaced the Marine TC-130G in 2003. (A Marine "Herk" had been assigned to the unit since December 1970.)

The tail code BA is not shown on Blue Angels aircraft; they have blue-and-gold livery with large numerals indicating the aircrafts' places in formation.

Historical: The unit was established on 18 April 1946; it was named the Blue Angels soon afterward—for a New York City night club. The Blue Angels performed its first flight demonstration in June 1946 at its home base, NAS Jacksonville. The unit stood down in 1950–1951 for the start of the Korean War, with its pilots forming the cadre of VF-191 flying the F9F-2 Panther. Reestablished, the Blue Angels was formally designated the Flight Demonstration Squadron on 1 December 1973.

The "Blues" has flown a succession of first-line naval aircraft: F6F-5 Hellcat, F8F-1 Bearcat, F9F-2 and F9F-5 Panther, F9F-6 Cougar, F11F-1 Tiger, F-4J Phantom, A-4F Skyhawk, and, since November 1986, the F/A-18 Hornet.

Operational: The first carrier "trap" and launch by a Blue Angel aircraft occurred on 11 November 1998, when Commander Patrick Driscoll, the team leader, landed an F/A-18A aboard and took off from the HARRY S. TRUMAN.

The C-130T Hercules of the Blue Angels flight demonstration team—known as "Fat Albert"—performs a high-powered takeoff during an air show at NAS Oceana. Flown by a Marine crew, the aircraft has modified Blue Angels livery. (U.S. Navy/Danielle L. Hertlein)

7 AIR TEST AND EVALUATION SQUADRONS

Squadron	Code	Aircraft	Names/Notes
VX-1	JA	P-3C, MH-60R/SH-60B/F	ASW Pioneers
VX-4	XF	TA-4J, F-14A/D, F/A-18A	disestablished 30 Sep 1994
VX-5	XE	TA-4J, A-6E, EA-6B, AV-8B, F/A-18, AH-1W	disestablished 29 Apr 1994
VX-9	XE	AV-8B, EA-6B, F-14B/D, NF-14B, F/A-18C/D/E/F, AH-1W	Vampires (ex-Evaluators); established 30 April 1994
VX-20		KC-130F/J, NP-3C/D, P-3C, NT-34C, T-2C, T-6A, T-34C, C-2A, NC-130H, E-2C	Force; redesignated 1 May 2002
HX-21		MH-60R/S, NSH-60B, NVH-3A, SH-60B/F, UH-1N, X-49A	established 1 May 2002
VX-23	SD	EA-6B, F/A-18A/B/E/F, NF-18C/D, T-45A/C	Salty Dogs; redesignated 1 May 2002
VX-30	BH	F/A-18A/B, P-3C	Bloodhounds; redesignated 1 May 2002
VX-31		AV-8B, NAV-8B, F/A-18A/C/D/E/F, AH-1W, HH-1N, T-39D	Dust Devils; redesignated 1 May 2002

These squadrons test and evaluate air weapon systems and tactics; they fly a variety of aircraft. VX-1 at NAS Patuxent River, specializes in operational test and evaluation of airborne ASW under the cognizance of Naval Air Force Atlantic Fleet.

VX-9 at NAS China Lake specializes in fighter-attack aircraft, air-to-surface weapons and tactics, and electronic countermeasures programs. It is directly subordinate to Naval Air Force Pacific Fleet. VX-9 was established in 1994 by the merger of VX-4 at Point Mugu, California, and VX-5 at China Lake; their successor unit was appropriately designated VX-9.

Five other test "squadrons" were redesignated VX or HX in 2002: the Naval Force Warfare Aircraft Test Squadron at NAS Patuxent River became VX-20; the Naval Rotary-Wing Aircraft Test Squadron at "Pax River" became VX-21; the Naval Strike Aircraft Test Squadron at Pax River became HX-23; the Naval Weapons Test Squadron Pt. Mugu became VX-30; and the Naval Weapons Test Squadron China Lake became VX-31. Note that HX is designated as an "air" and not helicopter T&E squadron.

The Naval Test Pilot School at Patuxent River is considered a squadron, but does not have a VX designation.

Designation: Two specialized development squadrons—VXE-6 and VXN-8—were numbered in the basic VX series (see below).

Historical: VX-1 had two predecessors: The Aircraft Experimental and Development Squadron was established at NAS Anacostia in Washington, D.C., on 13 August 1942. On 1 April 1943, an Air Anti-Submarine Development Detachment was established at Quonset Point, Rhode Island, and subsequently was recommissioned as Anti-Submarine Development Squadron 1 in 1946. These units underwent several name changes, and their functions eventually were combined, with Air Test and Evaluation Squadron 1 adopted on 1 January 1969. The squadron was moved to Pax River on 15 September 1973.

Operational: The Navy's lone DC-13A Hercules drone-carrier was operated by VX-30 during Operation Iraqi Freedom in 2003; the aircraft launched BQM-34 Firebee drones over Baghdad to drop chaff and distract ground fire.

ANTARCTIC DEVELOPMENT SQUADRON

Squadron	Code	Aircraft	Notes
VXE-6	XD	LC-130F/R, UH-1N	disestablished 31 Mar 1999

The Navy's only squadron dedicated to aerial support of U.S Antarctic operations—VXE-6, long known as the "Puckered Penguins"—has been disestablished. (In its final days, the squadron was known as the "Ice Pirates.") Based at Point Mugu, it provided support to U.S. Antarctic programs sponsored by the National Science Foundation. The squadron flew from McMurdo, Antarctica, when operating in the Antarctic.

VXE-6's role has been taken over by the Air National Guard 109th Airlift Wing, Schenectady, New York. Flying ski-equipped LC-130 Hercules transports, the 109th Airlift Wing has operated in the northern and, subsequently, southern polar regions since 1975. It is now the only U.S. military aviation unit flying ski-fitted "Herks."

VXE-6 was flying two LC-130F and five LC-130R Hercules at the time it was disestablished; it was the last active-duty Navy squadron to fly the C-130 other than air test and evaluation squadrons (VX). Prior to February 1996, the squadron also flew UH-1N Huey helicopters equipped with skis. Helicopter support is now provided under contract by a commercial firm.

Designation: VXE-6 originally was established as Air Development Squadron 6 (VX-6) on 17 January 1955, specifically for Antarctic operations (Operation Deepfreeze); the squadron was redesignated VXE-6 on 1 January 1969.

Historical: The U.S. Navy has had aviation interests in the Antarctic since 1928, when retired Commander Richard E. Byrd took four civilian aircraft on his first expedition to the South Pole.[17] Major Navy support began with Byrd's 1939–1940 expedition, and on his 1947–1948 expedition, 19 Navy fixed-wing aircraft and four helicopters participated, including six R4D/C-47 transports that flew into Antarctica from the aircraft carrier PHILIPPINE SEA.

OCEANOGRAPHIC DEVELOPMENT SQUADRON

Squadron	Code	Aircraft	Notes
VXN-8	JB	RP-3D, UP-3A	disestablished 1 Oct 1993

VXN-8 at NAS Patuxent River operated five RP-3D Orion aircraft in support of worldwide research projects: Project Magnet was a gravity and geomagnetic study, Project Birdseye an ice reconnaissance and physical oceanography study, and Project Outpost Seascan an aerial oceanographic effort.

Some of the squadron's efforts have been taken over by aircraft sponsored by the Naval Research Laboratory (NRL) in Washington, D.C., which operates four research-configured NP-3D aircraft in support of worldwide scientific research projects. Based at Patuxent River, the NRL Orions are extensively modified P-3A/B/C models that support research into gravity and ocean floor spreading, basic and advanced electronic warfare, space sensing applications, spaceborne radar, laser projects, and optical systems. These aircraft have "NRL" and the American flag on their tail fins (no code letters); they are painted orange and white.

Historical: VXN-8 had its beginnings as Airborne Early Warning Training Unit Atlantic Fleet, which, in 1951, was assigned Project Magnet. Projects Birdseye and Outpost Seascan were assigned in 1962, and Project Jenny in July 1965. The last project was to provide radio and television broadcasts to South Vietnam

---

17 While Byrd was on the expedition, Congress promoted him, on 21 December 1928, to the rank of rear admiral on the retired list.

pending the completion of ground facilities. Subsequently, the unit became the Oceanographic Airborne Survey Unit and, on 1 July 1967, Air Development Squadron (VX) 8. It was changed to VXN-8 on 1 January 1969.

HELICOPTER SEA COMBAT SQUADRONS (PLANNED)

Current	Planned	Year	Current	Planned	Year
HC-2	HSC-2	2006	HS-3	HSC-9	2010
HC-3	HSC-3	2005	HS-4	HSC-4	2007
HC-5	HSC-25	2005	HS-5	HSC-5	2009
HC-6	HSC-26	2005	HS-6	HSC-6	2010
HC-8	HSC-28	2005	HS-7	HSC-7	2008
HC-11	HSC-21	2005	HS-8	HSC-8	2008
new	HSC-22	2007	HS-11	HSC-11	2011
new	HSC-23	2007	HS-14	HSC-14	2011
HS-2	HSC-12	2009	HS-15	HSC-15	2012

The "necking down" of most helicopter types to variants of the H-60 series led the Navy to decide in 2003 to reorganize all helicopter squadrons into two new types: helicopter sea combat (HSC) and helicopter maritime strike (HSM). The transition will begin in March 2005, with the six surviving helicopter combat support squadrons being redesignated HSC, followed by the ten helicopter ASW squadrons.

The planned transition schedule for HSC squadrons is indicated above. Two new squadrons are to be established in January 2007.

The HSC squadrons will report to the Commanders, Helicopter Sea Combat Wings Atlantic and Pacific, which are to be established in March 2005. They will succeed the Commanders, Helicopter Tactical Wings Atlantic and Pacific, respectively.

HELICOPTER MARITIME STRIKE SQUADRONS (PLANNED)

Current	Planned	Year	Current	Planned	Year
HSL-37	HSM-37	2014	HSL-45	HSM-75	2008
HSL-40	HSM-40	2010	HSL-46	HSM-76	2011
HSL-41	HSM-41	2005	HSL-47	HSM-77	2010
HSL-42	HSM-42	2014	new	HSM-78	2012
new	HSM-70	2008	new	HSM-79	2011
new	HSM-71	2009	HSL-48	HSM-48	2015
new	HSM-72	2009	HSL-49	HSM-49	2014
HSL-43	HSM-73	2007	HSL-51	HSM-51	2013
HSL-44	HSM-74	2010			

All light helicopter ASW squadrons are to be redesignated HSM, based on the above schedule. Five new squadrons will be established. The first HSM will be HSL-41, which will be redesignated in March 2005.

The HSM squadrons will report to the Commanders Helicopter Maritime Strike Wings Atlantic and Pacific. Those commands will succeed the Commanders Helicopter Anti-Submarine Wings (Light) Atlantic and Pacific, respectively. The reorganization took place in March 2003.

CH-46F Sea Knights of HC-11 transfer weapons from the ammunition ship KILAUEA (T-AE 26) to the carrier NIMITZ in the Pacific. These Sea Knights will be replaced by MH-60 series helicopters, as will most Navy rotary-wing aircraft. (U.S. Navy/Elizabeth Thompson)

7 HELICOPTER COMBAT SUPPORT SQUADRONS

Squadron	Code	Aircraft	Name/Notes
HC-1	UP	SH-3G/D/H, CH-53E	disestablished 29 Apr 1994
HC-2	HU	UH-3H	Circuit Riders
HC-3	SA	MH-60S	Packrats
HC-4	HC	MH-53E	Black Stallions
HC-5	RB	MH-60S	Providers (ex-Night Riders)
HC-6	HW	MH-60S	Chargers
HC-8	BR	MH-60S	Dragon Whales
HC-11	VR	UH-3H, MH-60S	Gunbearers
HC-16	BF	SH-3D, UH-1N	disestablished 1 Apr 1994

Most of these squadrons provide helicopter detachments for Search and Rescue (SAR) and Vertical Replenishment/Vertical On-board Delivery (VERTREP/VOD) operations in direct support of the fleet. Atlantic units report to Helicopter Tactical Wing Atlantic Fleet, Pacific units to Helicopter Tactical Wing Pacific Fleet

HC-2 at Norfolk is both an operational and fleet readiness squadron. It had the Navy's last remaining VH-3A Sea Kings for VIP transport, including ferry service between Norfolk and the Pentagon. It has UH-3H detachments at Bahrain and Naples to provide helicopters for the Commander, Fifth Fleet, and Commander, Sixth Fleet, respectively.

HC-3 and HC-11 are at NAS North Island, with HC-3 conducting all Navy readiness/transition training for the MH-60S Knighthawk. HC-11 operates a UH-3H for Commander Third Fleet.

HC-4 at NAS Sigonella, Sicily, provides logistics support for the Sixth Fleet with MH-53Es (it previously flew the CH-53E). The MH-53Es came from reserve squadrons HM-18 and HM-19 when those units combined with active Mine Countermeasures (MCM) units.

HC-5 at Anderson AFB on Guam provides detachments to the Seventh Fleet for VERTREP operations; the squadron, with 14 MH-60S Knighthawks, also flies a variety of secondary missions on Guam, including SAR, medical evacuation, VIP transport, and support of local police agencies. It was the first operational squadron to fly the MH-60S.

HC-6 and HC-8 at Norfolk support Atlantic Fleet ships, having completed transition to the MH-60S in 2003 and 2004, respectively. HC-8 and HC-11 flew the last Navy H-46 Sea Knight helicopters, which were retired in 2004.

HC-9 was a reserve unit when disestablished in 1990 (see below).

Historical: The progenitor of these squadrons was VX-3, the Navy's first helicopter squadron, established in 1947.[18] The following year, on 1 April 1948, VX-3 was split into helicopter utility squadrons HU-1 and HU-2, on the East and West Coasts, respectively. All helicopter utility squadrons were changed to combat support squadrons on 1 July 1965.

Personnel: In addition to personnel at their home bases, these squadrons have numerous detachments.

Squadron	Officers	Enlisted
HC-2	83	349
HC-3	51	333
HC-4	43	243
HC-5	77	366
HC-6	61	229
HC-8	61	235
HC-11	82	287

2 HELICOPTER MINE COUNTERMEASURES SQUADRONS

Squadron	Code	Aircraft	Name/Notes
HM-12	DH	CH/MH-53E	disestablished 30 Sep 1994
HM-14	BJ	MH-53E	Sea Stallions (ex-Vanguard)
HM-15	TB	MH-53E	Blackhawks

HM-14 at Norfolk and HM-15 at NAS Corpus Christi, Texas, are Airborne Mine Countermeasures (AMCM) squadrons, comprised of active and reserve personnel. Including detachments, HM-14 has 12 helicopters and HM-15 has 8. Both squadrons have reserve components, with that for HM-14 being assigned 3 MH-53E helicopters and that for HM-15 having 4 assigned. Thus, a total of 27 MH-53Es are assigned to the two squadrons.

The future of these helicopters is not clear; some Navy officials wish to transfer the MCM role to the MH-60S Knighthawk units.

Originally, HM-14 and HM-16 were established in 1978 for operational deployments, but HM-16 was disestablished in 1987, and HM-15 was established at NAS Alameda, California for Pacific-area MCM operations. (A four-helicopter detachment from HM-15 was deployed to Cubi Point in the Philippines until U.S. forces withdrew from that country.)

Both MCM squadrons are assigned to Helicopter Tactical Wing Atlantic Fleet.

HM-12 at Norfolk provided AMCM readiness training until disestablished in 1994; it was established in 1971 as the first U.S. dedicated MCM aviation squadron. From 1994 to 2001, Marine HMT-302 at MCAS New River, North Carolina, provided AMCM readiness training; that mission subsequently was assumed by HM-14.

Reserve squadrons HM-18 and HM-19 have been disestablished, and their aircraft and personnel were merged with HM-14 and HM-15 in 1995 and 1994, respectively. This was the first complete merger of active and reserve aviation squadrons in the U.S. Navy.

Historical: The Navy used helicopters for mine spotting in the Korean War (1950–1953), and beginning in September 1966, HC-6 and HC-7 provided RH-3A Sea King detachments for mine countermeasure operations. Those helicopters flew from the MCM support ships CATSKILL (MCS 1) and OZARK (MCS 2).

---

18 During World War II, the Coast Guard undertook helicopter development activities for the Navy.

A UH-3H SEA KING helicopter assigned to SAR duties at eh Naval Air Station, Oceana, Virginia, overflying the carrier piers at Norfolk. From left are the HARRY S. TRUMAN, GEORGE WASHINGTON, and ENTERPRISE. The Oceana SAR unit, which provided services to both the military and civilian communities, was disestablished shortly after this photo was taken in August 2004. (U.S. Navy/Anthony M. Koch)

HM-12 was established on 1 April 1971 as the world's first helicopter mine countermeasures squadron. Initially flying Navy and Marine CH-53A Sea Stallions and then the specialized RH-53D, HM-12 operated off North Vietnam in 1972 (Operation Endsweep), at the northern end of the Suez Canal in 1974 (Nimbus Star) and again in 1975 (Nimbus Stream), and in the Red Sea in 1984. HM-12, 14, and 15 flew MH-53E helicopters in the Persian Gulf area in the late 1980s (escorting Kuwaiti merchant ships) and in Operation Desert Storm and the subsequent mine cleanup.

Personnel: HM-14 has 38 officers and 464 enlisted personnel; HM-15 has 32 officers and 393 enlisted men and women.

11 HELICOPTER ANTI-SUBMARINE SQUADRONS

Squadron	Aircraft	Name\Notes
HS-1	SH-3G/H, SH-60F	disestablished 30 June 1997
HS-2	SH-60F, HH-60H	Golden Falcons
HS-3	SH-60F, HH-60H	Tridents
HS-4	SH-60F, HH-60H	Black Knights
HS-5	SH-60F, HH-60H	Night Dippers
HS-6	SH-60F, HH-60H	Indians
HS-7	SH-60F, HH-60H	Dusty Dogs (ex-Shamrocks)
HS-8	SH-60F, HH-60H	Eight Ballers
HS-9	SH-3H	disestablished 30 April 1993
HS-10	SH-60F, HH-60H	Task Masters (RA)
HS-11	SH-60F, HH-60H	Dragonslayers
HS-12	SH-3H	disestablished 30 Nov 1994
HS-14	SH-60F, HH-60H	Chargers
HS-15	SH-60F, HH-60H	Red Lions
HS-17	SH-3H	disestablished 30 June 1991

Helicopter ASW squadrons are assigned to all carrier air wings, with most of the ten carrier squadrons flying three or four SH-60F Seahawks and two or three HH-60H combat SAR variants. The squadrons provide combat search and rescue, vertical replenishment, passenger transfer, and support to special operations, as well as ASW. The multipurpose MH-60R will replace the SH-60F (as well as the SH-60B).

Atlantic squadrons are based at NAS Jacksonville under Helicopter Anti-Submarine Wing Atlantic Fleet; Pacific units are at NAS North Island under Helicopter Anti-Submarine Wing Pacific Fleet, except HS-14 is based at NAF Atsugi.

HS-10 has consolidated all SH-60F/HH-60 readiness/transition training for the Navy. It was the first squadron to receive the SH-60F, in June 1989. The first fleet squadron to receive the SH-60F was HS-2, taking delivery in March 1990; beginning with HS-6 in September 1990, these squadrons also were provided with two HH-60H combat SAR helicopters, a number subsequently increased.

Note that HS-8 and HT-8 have the same name.

Historical: Previously, HS units flew the SH-3H Sea King; HS-7 made the last SH-3H deployment, on the DWIGHT D. EISENHOWER in early 1995.

The Navy's first helicopter ASW squadron was HS-1, established on 3 October 1951, flying the Sikorsky HO4S-1 helicopter.

Personnel: Most HS squadrons have 24 officers and 180 enlisted personnel. HS-10 has 42 officers and 315 enlisted men and women.

12 LIGHT HELICOPTER ANTI-SUBMARINE SQUADRONS

Squadron	Code	Aircraft	Name/Notes
HSL-30	HT	SH-2F	disestablished 30 Sep 1993
HSL-31	TD	SH-2F	disestablished 31 July 1992
HSL-32	HV	SH-2F	disestablished 31 Jan 1994
HSL-33	TF	SH-2F	disestablished 29 Apr 1994
HSL-34	HX	SH-2F	disestablished 30 Nov 1993
HSL-35	TG	SH-2F	disestablished 4 Dec 1992
HSL-36	HY	SH-2F	disestablished 30 Sep 1992
HSL-37	TH	SH-60B	Easy Riders
HSL-40	HK	SH-60B	Airwolves
HSL-41	TS	SH-60B	Seahawks
HSL-42	HN	SH-60B	Proud Warriors
HSL-43	TT	SH-60B	Battlecats
HSL-44	HP	SH-60B	Swamp Foxes
HSL-45	TE	SH-60B	Wolfpack
HSL-46	HQ	SH-60B	Grand Masters
HSL-47	TY	SH-60B	Saberhawks
HSL-48	HR	SH-60B	Vipers
HSL-49	TX	SH-60B	Scorpions
HSL-51	TA	SH-60B, UH-3H	Warlords

An HH-60H Seahawk of HS-8 hovers above the flight deck of the carrier CARL VINSON. *There is a laser target designator in the helicopter's nose, and the weapons rack is mounted on the left side. (U.S. Navy/Inez Lawson)*

The HSL squadrons provide detachments of two ASW helicopters for deployments on board most cruisers, destroyers, and frigates. Each operational squadron has 10–13 aircraft. HSL-51 operates two UH-3H helicopters to support the Commander Seventh Fleet. HSL-40 and HSL-41 are readiness squadrons. The multipurpose MH-60R will replace the SH-60B (as well as the SH-60F).

Atlantic squadrons are based at Naval Station Mayport, Florida, under Helicopter Anti-Submarine Wing Light Atlantic Fleet; Pacific units are at NAS North Island under Helicopter Anti-Submarine Wing Light Pacific Fleet, except HSL-51 is at NAF Atsugi. HSL-51 was established in October 1991 to operate helicopters from Japan-based ships.

The seven squadrons flying the SH-2F Seasprite have been disestablished; those aircraft flew from active frigates of the KNOX (FF 1052) class and a few cruisers and destroyers. (Reserve squadrons HSL-84, HSL-94, and HSL-60 subsequently provided helicopters for reserve frigates of the OLIVER HAZARD PERRY/FFG 7 class.)

Historical: The first Seahawk squadron was HSL-41, established on 21 January 1983 at NAS North Island as the SH-60B readiness training squadron. The first SH-60B fleet squadrons were established the following year.

The first SH-2D LAMPS helicopters were assigned to helicopter combat support squadrons HC-4 and HC-5, which were redesignated HSL-30 and HSL-31, respectively, on 1 March 1972. The last SH-2F deployment was from HSL-33 in 1994.

Personnel: Most HSL squadrons have about 60 officers and some 185 to 220 enlisted personnel; HSL-51 has 60 officers and 248 enlisted personnel.

NAVAL AIR WARFARE CENTER

Squadron	Aircraft/Notes
Naval Force Warfare Aircraft Test Squadron	redesignated VX-20
Naval Rotary-Wing Aircraft Test Squadron	redesignated HX-21
Naval Strike Aircraft Test Squadron	redesignated VX-23
Naval Weapons Test Squadron Point Mugu	redesignated VX-30
Naval Weapons Test Squadron China Lake	redesignated VX-31
Naval Test Pilot School	F/A-18B, NP-3D, T-2C, T-38A, NU-1B, U-6A, U-21F, TH-6B, OH-58C, UH-60L, NSH-60B, X-26A, C-12C

The first three test squadrons were subordinate to the Naval Air Warfare Center and the Center's Aircraft Division at NAS Patuxent River. All three squadrons were established on 21 July 1995, and were changed to air test and evaluation squadrons in 2002.

The two latter test squadrons were under the Naval Air Warfare Center's Weapons Division. Those squadrons are based at NAS China Lake and NAS Point Mugu. Both were established on 8 May 1995; they were changed to air T&E squadrons in 2002.

The test pilot school supports all U.S. military services as well as the National Aeronautics and Space Administration (NASA) and other government agencies.

NAVAL AIR STATIONS/NAVAL SUPPORT ACTIVITIES

Code	Aircraft	Activity
7A	UC-12B, UH-3H	NAS Patuxent River, Md.
7B	UC-12B	NAS Atlanta, Ga.
7C	UC-12B/M	Naval Station Norfolk, Va.
7D	UC-12B	NAS Fort Worth, Texas
7E	UH-3H	NAS Jacksonville, Fla.
7F	UC-12B	NAS Brunswick, Maine
7G	UH-3H	NAS Whidbey Island, Wash.
7H	HH-1N	NAS Fallon, Nev.
7J	UC-12B	NAS Alameda, Calif.
7K	UC-12B	NAS Memphis, Tenn.; disestablished 30 Sep 1998
7L	UC-12B	NAS Pt. Mugu, Calif.
7M	UC-12B	NAS North Island, Calif.
7N	UC-12B	NAF Washington, D.C. (Andrews AFB, Md.)
7Q	UH-3H	NAS Key West, Fla.
7R	UC-12B,	NAS Oceana, Va.
7S	(no planes at this time)	NAS Lemoore, Calif.
7T	UC-12B	NARC Santa Clara, Calif.*
7V	UC-12B	NAS Glenview, Ill.
7W	UC-12B, UH-3H	NAS Willow Grove, Pa.
7X	UC-12B	NAS New Orleans, La.
7Y	UC-12B	Sefridge ANGB, Maine**
7Z	UC-12B	NAS South Weymouth, Mass.
8A	UC-12F	NAF Atsugi, Japan
8C	C-26D	NAS Sigonella, Sicily
8D	UC-12M	Naval Station Rota, Spain
8E	RC-12M, UC-12M	Naval Station Roosevelt Roads, P.R.; disestablished 31 Mar 2004
8F	UC-12B, RC-12M,	Naval Station Guantanamo, Cuba
8G	UC-12M	NAF Mildenhall, England
8H	UC-12FNAF	Kadena, Okinawa
8J	(none)	Anderson AFB, Guam***
8K	UC-12B/M	Sheikh Isa Air Base, Bahrain
8M	UC-12F	NAF Misawa, Japan
8N	(no planes at this time)	NAF El Centro, Calif.
8U	(none)	Naval Station Mayport, Fla.
(none)	C-26D	Naval Support Activity Naples, Italy
(none)	HH-1N, MH-53E	Naval Support Activity, Panama City, Fla.

* NARC = Naval Air Reserve Center
** ANGB = Air National Guard Base
*** AFB = Air Force Base

Utility and light transport aircraft and helicopters are assigned to the Navy and Marine bases in the United States and abroad. The Naval Coastal Systems Center at Panama City, Florida, responsible for the development of mine countermeasures systems, was renamed Naval Support Activity Panama City in 2003.

NAVAL AIR FORCE RESERVE

The Naval Air Force Reserve operates approximately 230 aircraft. These are organized primarily into one carrier air wing, seven maritime patrol squadrons, and several helicopter and transport squadrons. The carrier air wing—CVWR-20—and its squadrons are scheduled to be deactivated in 2005–2006.

All air reserve units are assigned to the Naval Air Reserve Force based at New Orleans. The major air reserve subordinate commands are Reserve Patrol Wing (Willow Grove, Pennsylvania), which controls the VP squadrons; Reserve Helicopter Wing (NAS North Island), which directs reserve HC, HCS, HSL, and HS squadrons; and Reserve Fleet Logistics Support Wing (Fort Worth, Texas), which controls VR squadrons.

Squadrons within the reserve carrier air wing are designated in sequence based on the wing designation, except for the AEW squadron. Non-carrier air wing squadrons have designations in the standard Navy squadron numerical series. The VF and VFA squadrons normally are assigned 12 aircraft each, the VAQ and VAW squadrons four each. There are no fixed-wing ASW aircraft (S-3 Vikings) assigned to the wing; an SH-60F Seahawk squadron could provide ASW helicopters.

The reserve HSL squadron flies the SH-60F, which operates from Naval Reserve Force (NRF) frigates. Three reserve HAL/HC squadrons have been merged to form two combat support squadrons (HCS).

Figure 27-3. NAVAL AIR FORCE RESERVE

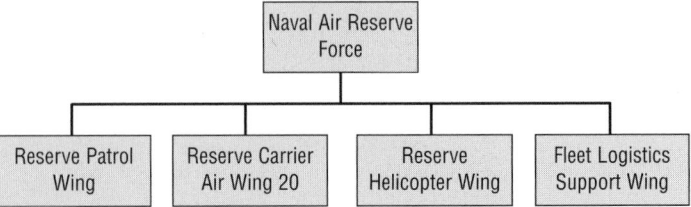

Table 27-5. RESERVE CARRIER AIR WINGS

Wing	Code	Squadron	Aircraft	Name	Base/Notes
CVWR-20	AF	VFA-201	F/A-18A	Hunters	JRB* Fort Worth, Texas
		VF-202	F-14A	Superheats	disestablished 31 Dec 1994
		VFA-203	F/A-18A/B	Blue Dolphins	disestablished 30 June 2004
		VFA-204	F/A-18A	River Rattlers	NAS New Orleans, La.
		VA-205	A-6E, KA-6D	Green Falcons	disestablished 31 Dec 1994
		VAQ-209	EA-6B	Star Warriors	NAF Washington, D.C.
		VAW-77	E-2C	Night Wolves	NAS Atlanta, Ga.
		VAW-78	E-2C	Fighting Escargots	Norfolk, Va.
		VFC-12	F/A-18A/B	Fighting Omars	NAS Oceana, Va.
		VFC-13	F-5E/F	Saints	NAS Fallon, Nev.
CVWR-30	ND				disestablished 31 Dec 1994
		VF-301	F-14A	Flying Infernos	disestablished 31 Dec 1994
		VF-302	F-14A	Stallions	disestablished 31 Dec 1994
		VFA-303	F/A-18A	Golden Hawks	disestablished 31 Dec 1994
		VA-304	A-6E, KA-6D	Firebirds	disestablished 31 Dec 1994
		VFA-305	F/A-18A	Lobos	disestablished 31 Dec 1994
		VAQ-309	EA-6B	Axemen	disestablished 31 Dec 1994
		VAW-88	E-2C	Compickers	disestablished 31 Dec 1994

* JRB = Joint Reserve Base

One reserve carrier air wing now exists. The second was a casualty of the end of the Cold War. CVWR-20 is planned for deactivation in September 2005, although when this edition of *Ships and Aircraft* went to press, it was expected that the action would be strongly opposed by Congress.

Note that land-based squadrons VAW-77, VFC-12, and VFC-13 are assigned to CVWR-20.

Historical: The two reserve carrier air wings (CVWR) were commissioned on 1 April 1970.

ATTACK SQUADRONS

All reserve VA squadrons have been disestablished. Six reserve VA squadrons—three per wing—flew the A-7E, the last was the VA-204, which became VFA-204 on 1 May 1991. VA-205 and VA-304 traded in their Hornets for A-6E and KA-6D Intruders; the four other squadrons shifted to F/A-18 Hornets (see below). Earlier, all six squadrons flew the trouble-plagued A-7B model, and before that the A-4 Skyhawk.

KA-6D tankers were assigned to these units to replace the KA-3B Skywarrior in the in-flight refueling role.

FIGHTER SQUADRONS

Four reserve fighter squadrons shifted in the 1980s to the F-14A Tomcat, which replaced the F-4 Phantom. The last naval squadron to fly the Phantom was VF-202, which transitioned from the F-4S to the F-14A in early 1987.[19]

All reserve fighter squadrons have been disbanded.

2 STRIKE FIGHTER SQUADRONS

VFA-201 was activated on 7 October 2002 for one year to deploy with CVW-8. The squadron took the place intended to be filled temporarily by VF-22, which took the place of VFA-102, which was in transition to the F/A-18F. VFA-201 was the first reserve "tail hook" squadron to deploy on board a carrier since the Korean War.

The F/A-18 Hornet replaced the A-7E Corsair in four attack squadrons, which became VFA. VA-303 became the first Naval Reserve squadron to fly the F/A-18 Hornet, acquiring its first aircraft in 1985. The two F/A-18 squadrons assigned to CVWR-30 have been disestablished, as has CVWR-20's VFA-203.

2 FIGHTER COMPOSITE SQUADRONS

The two reserve composite fighter squadrons—VFC-12 and VFC-13—are assigned to CVWR-20. They provide air combat maneuver training for reserve and active fighter and attack squadrons.

Both squadrons previously flew A-4F Skyhawks; they switched to F/A-18s in 1992–1993, and VFC-13 subsequently shifted to the nimble F-5E/F Tigers to simulate MiG-type fighter aircraft.

Prior to being assigned to CVWR-20, the squadrons were assigned tail codes AF and UX, respectively.

Designation: These squadrons previously were designated VC-12 and VC-13, respectively; they were changed to VFC on 22 April 1988 to reflect their emphasis on adversary training.

RECONNAISSANCE SQUADRONS

The last specialized Navy reconnaissance squadron, VFP-206, flying the RF-8G Photo Crusader, was disestablished on 1 April 1987. This was a light photo-reconnaissance squadron. The unit was based at NAF Washington, D.C., located at Andrews AFB in a nearby Maryland suburb. Subsequently, F-14 Tomcat fighters provided a photo-reconnaissance capability with TARPS pods, but that has been lost with the demise of the F-14/VF units.

1 ELECTRONIC ATTACK SQUADRON

VAQ-209 and VAQ-309 were established in 1977 and 1979, respectively, to provide the reserve air wings with an organic ECM capability. The reserve VAQ squadrons flew the EA-6A Intruder until 1989, when they shifted to the more-capable EA-6B Prowler.

Only VAQ-209 survives. With the disestablishment of active squadron VAQ-33, it also is assigned the Navy's electronic aggressor role.

VAQ-209 is based at NAF Washington. The squadron participated in combat operations in the Bosnia and Kosovo campaigns of Operational Allied Force in the late 1990s.

2 AIRBORNE EARLY WARNING SQUADRON

The first E-2C variant of the Hawkeye to be flown by the reserves was assigned to VAW-78 in 1983; VAW-88 began receiving the E-2C in 1986.

VAW-88 was later disestablished, and VAW-77 was established on 1 October 1995. Both VAW-77 and VAW-88 have assisted in U.S. drug enforcement surveillance efforts, as have active Navy AEW squadrons. VAW-77 is considered a land-based squadron, although it is assigned to CVWR-20 (it uses the tail code AF).

Designation: Note that VAW-78 and VAW-88, both established in 1970, were not numbered in the standard CVWR designation scheme.

---

19 The Phantom flew in the Marine air reserve into 1992.

7 PATROL SQUADRONS

Squadron	Code	Aircraft	Name	Location/Notes
VP-60	LS	P3-B	Cobras	disestablished 1 Sep 1994
VP-62	LT	P-3C	Broad Arrows	NAS Jacksonville, Fla.
VP-64	LU	P-3C	VR-64	18 Sep 2004
VP-65	PG	P-3C	Tridents	NB Ventura, Calif.*
VP-66	LV	P-3C	Liberty Bells	NAS Willow Grove, Pa.
VP-67	PL	P3-B	Golden Hawks	disestablished 30 Sep 1994
VP-68	LW	P-3C		disestablished 31 Dec 1996
VP-69	PJ	P-3C	Totems	NAS Whidbey Island, Wash.
VP-90	LX	P-3B	Lions	disestablished 30 Sep 1994
VP-91	PM	P-3C	Black Cats	disestablished 1 Apr 1999
VP-92	LY	P-3C	Minutemen	NAS Brunswick, Maine
VP-93	LH	P-3B	Executioners	disestablished 30 Sep 1994
VP-94	LZ	P-3C	Crawfish	NAS New Orleans, La.

* NB = Naval Base

These squadrons each fly six or seven Orion patrol aircraft (down from nine). The reserve P-3s regularly supplement active squadrons in U.S. and overseas operational deployments. The reserve VP strength has been reduced from its long-standing Cold War strength of 13 squadrons to 7.

All remaining squadrons fly the P-3C variant; the first to transition to the P-3C from the P-3B was VP-62. The last reserve-flown P-3A was retired by VP-69 in October 1990.

VP-66 received the two EP-3J aircraft previously flown by VAQ-33 in 1993. They flew worldwide operations to simulate enemy jamming aircraft in exercises against U.S. forces. In 1997, the aircraft and their flight and support personnel were assigned to reserve squadron VQ-11 (see below).

Two VP Master Augmentation Units (VP-MAU) were based at NAS Brunswick (code LB) and NAS Moffett Field (code PS). These units—with P-3C, UP-3A, and TP-3A Orions—trained crews to augment fleet VP squadrons and often operated detachments overseas; VP-MAU Moffett Field operated one aircraft and crew in Desert Storm. The two units were disestablished on 30 June 1991 and 30 September 1991, respectively.

A C-130T Hercules from VR-53 takes on cargo at Clark Field in the Philippines for U.S. forces participating in the exercise Balikatan 2004. Reserve logistics support squadrons continuously support active as well as reserve naval forces. (U.S. Navy/Lou Rosales)

FLEET AIR RECONNAISSANCE SQUADRON

Squadron	Code	Aircraft	Name	Location/Notes
VQ-11	LP	EP-3J	Bandits	disestablished 31 Mar 2000

This squadron was established on 2 August 1997 and disestablished less than three years later. It flew the two EP-3J "jammers" (P-3B Orions modified in 1992), providing worldwide support for fleet exercises; those aircraft previously were flown by (reserve) VP-66. One aircraft was severely damaged in a ground fire in 1998 and was not returned to service; the second EP-3J was retired in late 1999.

VQ-11 was based at NAS Brunswick.

15 FLEET LOGISTICS SUPPORT SQUADRONS

Squadron	Code	Aircraft	Name	Location/Notes
VR-1	JK	2 C-20D 1 C-37A	Starlifters	NAF Washington, D.C.; established 1 May 1997
VR-46	JS	3 C-9B	Peach Airlines	NAS Atlanta, Ga.
VR-48	JR	2 C-20G	Capital Skyliners	NAF Washington, D.C.
VR-51	RG	2 C-20G	Windjammers	MCAF Kaneohe, Hawaii; established 1 June 1997
VR-52	JT	4 C-9B	Taskmasters	NAS Willow Grove, Pa.
VR-53	AX	4 C-130T	Capital Express	NAF Washington, D.C.; established 1 Oct 1993
VR-54	CW	4 C-130T	Revelers	NAS New Orleans, La.; established 1 June 1991
VR-55	RU	5 C-130T	Bicentennial Minutemen	NAS Point Mugu, Calif.
VR-56	JU	4 C-9B	Globemasters	Norfolk, Va.
VR-57	RX	2 C-9B 2 DC-9	Conquistadors	NAS North Island, Calif.
VR-58	JV	3 C-40A	Sun Seekers	NAS Jacksonville, Fla.
VR-59	RY	3 C-40A	Lone Star Express	JRB Fort Worth, Texas
VR-60	RT	DC-9		disestablished 1 Apr 1995
VR-61	RS	3 DC-9 2 C-9B	Islanders	NAS Whidbey Island, Wash.
VR-62	JW	4 C-130T	Downeasters	NAF Brunswick, Maine
VR-64	LU	2 C-130T	Condors	NAS Willow Grove, Pa.

These squadrons provide transport support for active and reserve Navy activities within the United States and overseas. Reserve VR squadrons report to Fleet Logistics Support Wing at Fort Worth.

The C-9B Skytrain and similar (commercial) DC-9 provide long-range logistics support for naval activities; four squadrons fly the C-130T Hercules, the only Navy squadrons with "Herks" except for test and evaluation squadrons and the Blue Angels. The C-40A Clipper is replacing C-9B and DC-9 aircraft. VR-1 and VR-48 in the nation's capital provide a C-37A and four C-20D/G Gulfstreams for VIP flights. These squadrons have multiple crews for their aircraft.

Historical: VR-48 previously flew the C-131H Samaritan, the last one being retired in mid-1990.

Names: VR-62 was nicknamed "Mowtowners" while based at NAS Detroit, and then "Mass Transit" while at NAS South Weymouth, Massachusetts, before moving to NAS Brunswick.

1 HELICOPTER COMBAT SUPPORT SQUADRON

Squadron	Code	Aircraft	Location/Notes
HC-85	NW	UH-3H	NAS North Island, Calif.

HC-85 operates eight utility helicopters. Previously designated HS-85, the squadron moved from Alameda, California, to North Island in 1994 to replace HC-1 in providing target/torpedo recovery off San Clemente Island. The squadron received eight UH-3H Sea Kings specially modified for recovery operations and was redesignated HC-85 on 1 October 1994. The squadron is assigned to the Helicopter Reserve Wing.

HC-9, established in 1975, was the Navy's only active combat SAR unit, flying armed and armored HH-3A Sea Kings. The squadron was disestablished on 31 July 1990, and its mission passed to reserve squadrons HCS-4 and HCS-5.

Note that all reserve helicopter squadrons have the code letters NW for the now defunct reserve helicopter wing; no helicopter squadrons are assigned to reserve air wings.

Designation: HC-9 was numbered in the standard (active) Navy HC designation series.

2 HELICOPTER SAR/SPECIAL WARFARE SUPPORT SQUADRONS

Squadron	Code	Aircraft	Name	Location
HCS-4	NW	HH-60H, SH-60F	Red Wolves	Norfolk, Va.
HCS-5	NW	HH-60H, SH-60F	Firehawks	NAS North Island, Calif.

These squadrons were established in 1989 to provide combat SAR and special warfare support for both active and reserve operations. Each squadron flies eight HH-60H and two SH-60F Seahawk helicopters. During Operations Desert Shield and Desert Storm in 1990–1991, they deployed HH-60H helicopters as a joint unit into Saudi Arabia for combat SAR operations. Both squadrons also deployed to the Persian Gulf for Operation Iraqi Freedom in 2003.

The HH-60H is the Navy's only dedicated combat SAR helicopter; it also is integrated into active HS anti-submarine squadrons. (The Coast Guard flies the HH-60J SAR-configured version of the Blackhawk/Seahawk helicopter.)

The HCS squadrons took over the functions of reserve helicopter light attack squadrons HAL-4 and HAL-5, which flew the HH-1K Huey in support of riverine and special operations, and of helicopter composite squadron HC-9, which flew the HH-3A in the combat SAR role. The reserve HALs also had anti-terrorist support roles, working with SEAL units.

Historical: Reserve squadrons HAL-4 and HAL-5 were established in 1976–1977 as the Navy's first armed helicopter (gunship) units. The Navy's only active gunship unit was HAL-3, established in 1967 and disestablished in 1972 after extensive service in Vietnam. (The squadron never operated in the United States.)

HELICOPTER MINE COUNTERMEASURES SQUADRONS

Squadron	Code	Aircraft	Notes
HM-18	NW	RH-53D/MH-53E	disestablished 4 Mar 1995
HM-19	NW	RH-53D/MH-53E	disestablished 5 Nov 1994

Reserve mine countermeasure squadron HM-18 was established in 1986 and HM-19 in 1989. They initially flew the RH-53D Sea Stallion helicopter; they were transitioning to the MH-53E Sea Dragon when the Navy decided to merge them with active MCM squadrons HM-14 and HM-15, respectively.

1 HELICOPTER ANTI-SUBMARINE SQUADRON

Squadron	Code	Aircraft	Name	Location/Notes
HS-75	NW	SH-60F	Emerald Knights	NAS Jacksonville Fla.
HS-85	NW	SH-3H		changed to HC-85

HS-75 flies ASW helicopters capable of operating from carriers with the reserve carrier air wing. The squadron has six SH-60F helicopters.

The Navy plans to disestablish the squadron in 2005.

1 LIGHT HELICOPTER ANTI-SUBMARINE SQUADRON

Squadron	Code	Aircraft	Name	Location/Notes
HSL-60	NW	SH-60B	Jaguars	Naval Station Mayport, Fla.; established 7 Apr 2001
HSL-74	NW	SH-2F	Demon-Elves	disestablished 1 Apr 1994
HSL-84	NW	SH-2G	Thunderbolts	disestablished 30 June 2001
HSL-94	NW	SH-2G	Titans	disestablished 31 Mar 2001

The three reserve HSL squadrons flying the SH-2 LAMPS I helicopter have been disestablished. The remaining reserve frigate-based SH-60B Black Hawk helicopters are assigned to HSL-60, the squadron number being based on the SH-60 aircraft designation. The squadron, with only five aircraft assigned, is scheduled to be disestablished in 2005.

The three disestablished squadrons previously were designated HS and flew the SH-3G Sea King; HS-74 transitioned to HSL for LAMPS operations on 1 January 1985; HS-84 on 1 March 1984; and HS-94 on 1 October 1985. HSL-94 helicopters were fitted with the Magic Lantern laser mine-detection system beginning in December 1996.

Operational: HSL-60 provided an SH-60B detachment to the cruiser TICONDEROGA (CG 47) for a Caribbean counterdrug deployment in 2004. This was the first time that a reserve SH-60B detachment operated from an active warship.

CHIEF OF NAVAL AIR RESERVE

The Chief of Naval Air Reserve has several aircraft assigned, based at various air stations. They are listed above under the heading Naval Air Stations/Naval Aviation Support Activities.

MARINE CORPS AVIATION

The U.S. Marine Corps currently operates about 900 aircraft, most assigned to three active aircraft wings, plus just over 200 aircraft in a reserve wing. It is the only marine force in the world with a major air arm.[20]

During the 1990s, Marine aviation completed a major force upgrade, with the advanced AV-8B Harrier replacing the earlier AV-8A/C Short Take-Off/Vertical Landing (STOVL) aircraft, and variants of the F/A-18 Hornet strike-fighter replacing all A-4 Skyhawk, A-6 Intruder, and RF-4 and F-4 Phantom aircraft.[21] The F/A-18 has become the most numerous fixed-wing aircraft in the Marine Corps, as it has in the Navy.

The Marine Corps now is acquiring the long-delayed MV-22 Osprey tilt-rotor STOVL aircraft (which can land and take-off only in a vertical mode). Procurement of the improved F/A-18E/F is not now planned, pending availability of the F-35/Joint Strike Fighter (JSF).

In the longer-term, the Marine Corps will be a key participant in the F-35/JSF program, which is now the Marine Commandant's number one procurement priority. The F-35B STOVL variant of the JSF will replace the AV-8B, and is planned for acquisition by the Royal Navy to replace its carrier-based Harriers.

Operational: Marine aviation had a major role in the Gulf War during January–February 1991, with most Marine aircraft flying from shore bases in Saudi Arabia. In the 2003 conflict—Operation Iraqi Freedom—Marine aircraft operated from bases in Kuwait as

---

20 Britain's Royal Marines fly helicopters and light fixed-wing aircraft, while Russia's Naval Infantry has some helicopters assigned.

21 The term VSTOL for Vertical/Short Take-Off and Landing was used by the Marine Corps until early 1995, when the less accurate term STOVL was adopted by Headquarters, Marine Corps.

well as from aircraft carriers and amphibious ships. Marine aircraft also took part in enforcement of the "no fly" zones over northern and southern Iraq, and in the air campaign over Kosovo in 1999.

ORGANIZATION

Marine Aviation is under the Deputy Chief of Staff for Aviation, a lieutenant general at Marine Corps Headquarters.

The Marine Aircraft Wing (MAW) is the principal Marine aviation command. Marine fixed-wing and rotary-wing aircraft are assigned to three active wings, plus one reserve wing, for a few utility and cargo aircraft. The wings vary in size and composition; an active wing has a theoretical strength of 325 aircraft of all types. However, only the 2nd and 3rd MAW actually have full aircraft assignments.

The 1st MAW is based at Iwakuni, Japan, and Futenma, Okinawa, with most of its aircraft provided on six-month rotation from the other aviation commands, including the newly established Marine Aircraft Group (MAG) 24 (formerly 1st MAW Aviation Support Element), at MCAF Kaneohe Bay, Hawaii. Wing headquarters is at Camp Butler (Futenma), Okinawa.

The 2nd MAW, with headquarters at Cherry Point, North Carolina, has aircraft squadrons based on the East Coast, and the 3rd MAW, with headquarters at MCAS Miramar, California, has its squadrons on the West Coast and at Yuma, Arizona.

In addition to aircraft groups, a Marine aircraft wing contains:
• Marine Wing Headquarters Squadron: Provides command, administration, and camp facilities for the wing headquarters.

• Marine Air Control Group: Provides communications, air control, and air support squadrons for the operation of the wing; it also contains a light anti-aircraft missile battalion (with 16 Hawk missile launchers) and a low-altitude air defense battalion (with 90 Stinger missile teams). The air support squadron provides control and coordination for aircraft operating in direct support of Marine ground forces.
• Marine Wing Support Group: Provides fixed-wing and helicopter maintenance as well as mess, medical, supply, transportation, weather, and airfield services for the wing's components.

An aircraft wing generally is paired with a reinforced division to form a Marine Expeditionary Force (MEF), an aircraft group with a reinforced regiment to form a Marine Expeditionary Brigade (MEB), and a composite squadron with a reinforced battalion to form a Marine Expeditionary Unit (MEU) (see Chapter 7).

Marine aviation units—like ground units—have Navy chaplain, medical, and dental personnel assigned.

Unlike Navy aircraft wings, in which the principal subordinate command is the squadron, the Marine aircraft wings have several groups, as shown in Figure 27-4, which depicts a notional Marine aircraft wing with five aircraft groups. Each Marine aircraft group controls specific aircraft squadron types, i.e., fighter and attack, and helicopter. Several aircraft are attached to wing headquarters and support squadrons.

A composite squadron generally consists of 4 CH-53, 12 CH-46, 4 AH-1, and 2 UH-1N helicopters deployed on board an LHA/LHD and accompanying amphibious ships. In addition, AV-8B Harriers may be assigned to the squadron, depending on the mission and aircraft and ship availability.

Figure 27-4. NOTIONAL MARINE AIRCRAFT WING (i.e., 2nd or 3rd MAW)

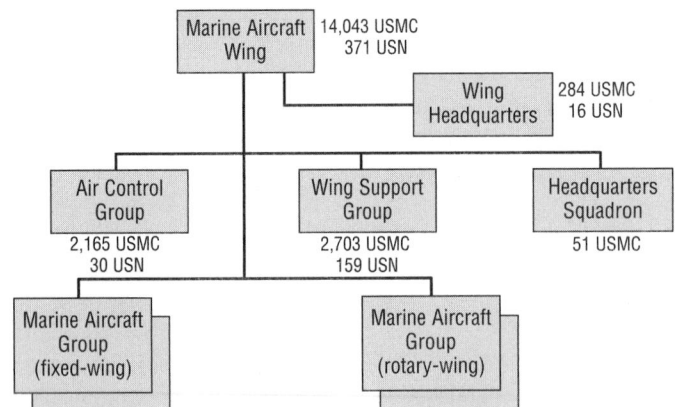

Figure 27-5. NOTIONAL MARINE AIRCRAFT GROUP (FIXED-WING)

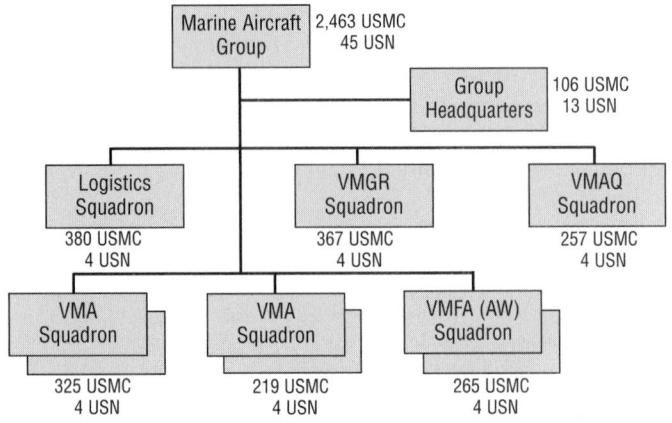

Figure 27-6. NOTIONAL MARINE AIRCRAFT GROUP (ROTARY-WING)

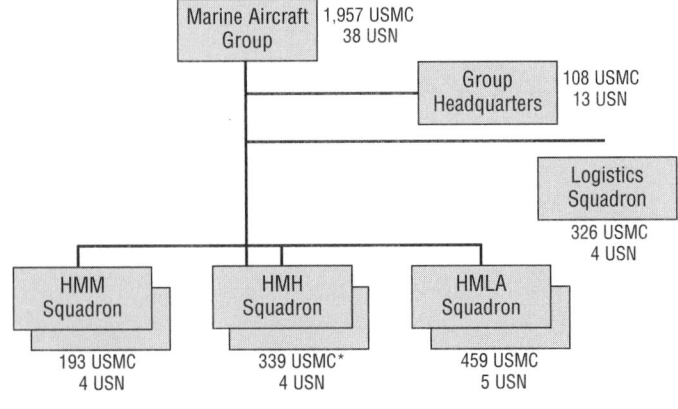

*For CH-53E squadron; CH-53D squadrons have 141 USMC

UNIT DESIGNATIONS

The Marine Corps uses the standard naval squadron designation scheme, except that the letter *M* is used in the second position to indicate Marine aviation squadrons; the suffix *T* indicates Marine readiness-transition squadrons.

Table 27-6. MARINE AIRCRAFT WINGS

Wing	Groups	Notes
1st	MAG-12 Iwakuni, Japan	Squadrons rotate from MAW-2 and MAW-3 except VMFA-212
	MAG-24 Kaneohe, Hawaii	
	MAG-36 Futenma, Okinawa	HMH and HMLA squadrons rotate from MAW-3 except VMGR-152, HMM-262, HMM-265
		A VMAQ squadron rotates to the wing from MAW-1/MAG-14.
2nd	MAG-14 Cherry Point, N.C.	
	MAG-26 New River, N.C.	
	MAG-29 New River, N.C.	
	MAG-31 Beaufort, S.C.	
3rd	MAG-11 Miramar, Calif.	
	MAG-13 Yuma, Ariz.	
	MAG-16 Miramar, Calif.*	
	MAG-39 Camp Pendleton, Calif.	

* Formerly at MCAS Tustin, Calif., which was closed in 1999.

8 MARINE ATTACK SQUADRONS

MAG	Squadron	Code	Aircraft	Name/Notes
14	VMAT-203	KD	AV-8B/TAV-8B	Hawks
13	VMA-211	CF	AV-8B	Wake Island Avengers
13	VMA-214	WE	AV-8B	Black Sheep
14	VMA-223	WP	AV-8B	Bulldogs
14	VMA-231	CG	AV-8B	Ace of Spades
13	VMA-311	WL	AV-8B	Tomcats
	VMA-322	QR	A-4M	deactivated 30 June 1992
	VMA-331	VL	AV-8B	deactivated 30 Sep 1992
13	VMA-513	WF	AV-8B	Flying Nightmares
14	VMA-542	CR	AV-8B	Flying Tigers

Marine attack squadrons have been reduced to seven units, plus a readiness squadron (VMAT-203), all flying the AV-8B Harrier. They converted from the A-4 Skyhawk and A-6 Intruder; other Marine attack squadrons that flew those two aircraft have been deactivated or converted to the F/A-18 Hornet.

By the late 1990s, most Harrier squadrons had 20 aircraft; the number is now standardized at 16, but varies considerably with the squadrons' deployment schedule, with six-plane detachments being assigned to LHA/LHDs in deployed amphibious groups.

Historical: VMA-513 was the first operational Harrier squadron, with AV-8A deliveries beginning in April 1971; all AV-8A/C models of the Harrier have been retired. VMA-331 was the first AV-8B squadron, established at Cherry Point on 30 January 1985.

The A-6 was flown by the Marine Corps from 1964 until 20 October 1993, when VMA(AW)-332 retired its last A-6E. (Six squadrons plus VMAT-202 flew the Intruder.)

The A-4 was flown by the Marine Corps from 1957 until 1992.

4 MARINE TACTICAL ELECTRONIC WARFARE SQUADRONS

MAG	Squadron	Code	Aircraft	Name
14	VMAQ-1	CB	EA-6B	Screaming Banshees
14	VMAQ-2	CY	EA-6B	Death Jesters
14	VMAQ-3	MD	EA-6B	Moon Dogs
14	VMAQ-4	RM	EA-6B	Seahawks

The Marine Corps formed four EW squadrons in 1992, replacing the single active-duty squadron (VMAQ-2 with code CY) and the reserve squadron VMAQ-4 (RM). VMAQ-1 and VMAQ-3 were established on 1 July 1992; VMAQ-4 was deactivated as a reserve unit on 1 October 1992 and reactivated as an active unit the following day. Each of the squadrons is authorized five EA-6B Prowlers.

All four squadrons are at MCAS Cherry Point and provide aircraft or detachments to the 1st and 3rd MAW.

Historical: The Marine Corps originally operated EW and photo-reconnaissance aircraft in three composite reconnaissance squadrons (VMCJ); they were deactivated in 1975 and their aircraft allocated to VMAQ-2 and VMFP-3. VMAQ-2 flew the EA-6A Intruder and then the EA-6B Prowler, providing detachments to the aircraft wings and occasionally to Navy carrier wings.

Names: VMAQ-2 was named The Playboys until 1999. The name change was another example of political correctness. Also given up was the squadron's historic and well-known Playboy bunny symbol. It was renamed Panthers and then Death Jesters.

15 MARINE FIGHTER-ATTACK SQUADRONS

MAG	Squadron	Code	Aircraft	Names/Notes
11	VMFAT-101	SH	F/A-18A/B/C/D T-34C	Sharpshooters
31	VMFA-115	VE	F/A-18A	Silver Eagles
11	VMFA(AW)-121	VK	F/A-18D	Green Knights; former VMA(AW)-121
31	VMFA-122	DC	F/A-18C	Crusaders
12	VMFA-212	WD	F/A-18C	Lancers
31	VMFA(AW)-224	WK	F/A-18D	Bengals
11	VMFA(AW)-225	CE	F/A-18D	Vikings; former VMFP-3
11	VMFA-232	WT	F/A-18C	Red Devils
	VMFA-235	DM	F/A-18C	deactivated 28 June 1996
11	VMFA(AW)-242	DT	F/A-18D	Bats; former VMA(AW)-242
31	VMFA-251*	DW	F/A-18C	Thunderbolts
31	VMFA-312*	DR	F/A-18A	Checkerboards
11	VMFA-314*	VW	F/A-18C	Black Knights
11	VMFA-323*	WS	F/A-18C	Death Rattlers
31	VMFA(AW)-332	EA	F/A-18D	Moonlighters
	VMFA-333	DM	F/A-18C	deactivated 31 Mar 1992
	VMFA-451	VM	F/A-18C	deactivated 31 Jan 1997
	VMFA-531	EC	F/A-18C	deactivated 31 Mar 1992
31	VMFA(AW)-533	ED	F/A-18D	Nighthawks; former VMA(AW)-533

The F/A-18 Hornet succeeded the F-4 Phantom in Marine fighter-attack squadrons. All remaining Marine fighter squadrons have made the transition to the F/A-18 Hornet, the first being VMFA-314, which shifted to the F/A-18 in January 1983. In addition to former VMFA and VMA squadrons that now fly the F/A-18C, five

Marine AV-8B Harriers of VMA-542 prepare to take off from the STOVL/helicopter carrier BATAAN *(LHD 5). There is an AAQ-28 Litening targeting pod under the right wing. These aircraft are "first cousins" to the Royal Navy's Harriers, which had an important role in the Falklands conflict of 1982. (U.S. Navy/John Taucher)*

An MV-22 Osprey STOVL aircraft rests on the Iwo Jima *(LHD 7) during at-sea tests of the aircraft, which will replace the CH-46 Sea Knight in Marine Corps service. The Air Force is procuring the Osprey as the CV-22 for special operations. (U.S. Navy/Peter Cline)*

A-6E (VMA[AW]) squadrons transitioned to the two-seat F/A-18D variant. These planes also replaced OA-4M and TA-4F Skyhawks in the tactical air control role.

Each squadron is authorized 12 aircraft. Asterisks indicate the four squadrons currently in the Navy's carrier rotation plan.

VMFA-212 is one of only two fixed-wing aircraft squadrons permanently assigned to the 1st MAW and based in Japan.

VMFAT-101 at MCAS Miramar provides readiness training. Beyond F/A-18 Hornets, it flies two T-34C Mentors, the only ones assigned to the Marine Corps.

Historical: Marine fighter squadrons flew the F-4 from 1961 to 1988. On 1 August 1962, the F-4 squadrons were changed from VMF(AW) to the current VMFA, for fighter-attack squadron. Plans to provide the F-14 Tomcat to at least four Marine squadrons were canceled in August 1975 at the request of the Marine Corps (freeing funds for the procurement of the AV-8A Harrier).

VMFA-314 was the first squadron to transition to the F/A-18 Hornet, trading in its F-4J Phantoms in 1982.

MARINE PHOTO-RECONNAISSANCE SQUADRONS

The last photo-reconnaissance squadron in service with the Navy or Marine Corps was VMFP-3, which was deactivated on 30 September 1990. It was the only Navy or Marine Corps squadron to fly the RF-4B Phantom (the U.S. Air Force and several foreign air forces flew other RF-4 variants).

VMFP-3 flew 21 of the reconnaissance-configured Phantoms. Detachments from the squadron were provided to the other wings (and to the carrier Midway's air wing).

4 MARINE REFUELER-TRANSPORT SQUADRONS

MAG	Squadron	Code	Aircraft	Names/Notes
36	VMGR-152	QD	KC-130F/R	—
14	VMGR-252	BH	KC-130F/J/R	Heavy Haulers
14	VMGRT-253	GR	KC-130F	—
11	VMGR-352	QB	KC-130F/R	Raiders

These squadrons fly KC-130 Hercules aircraft to provide transport for ground forces and in-flight refueling. Each VMGR squadron is authorized 12 aircraft.

VMGRT-253 provides readiness training.

VMGR-152 is one of only two fixed-wing aircraft squadrons permanently assigned to the 1st MAW based in Japan.

1 MARINE MEDIUM LIFT TILT-ROTOR TRAINING SQUADRON

MAG	Squadron	Code	Aircraft	Names/Notes
29	VMMT-204	GX	MV-22B	Raptors

VMMT-204 provides training for both Navy and Air Force MV-22/CV-22 Osprey pilots and crew. The squadron was established at MCAS New River, North Carolina, through the redesignation of HMT-204—previously the Marine CH-46 transition/training squadron—on 10 June 1999.

Operational MV-22B squadrons are planned at 12 aircraft; the squadrons are planned at 32 officers and 162 enlisted personnel.

MARINE OBSERVATION SQUADRONS

Squadron	Code	Aircraft	Names/Notes
VMO-1	ER	OV-10D	deactivated 31 July 1993
VMO-2	UU	OV-10D	deactivated 20 May 1993

The two Marine observation squadrons flew the Short Take-Off and Landing (STOL) OV-10 Bronco. Unlike previous Marine observation aircraft, the Bronco could be heavily armed. Twelve aircraft were assigned to each squadron. (The Navy's lone light attack squadron, VAL-4, flew Broncos during the Vietnam War.)

The VMO mission was taken over by the F/A-18D units.

Operational: OV-10 aircraft periodically operated from LHA/LHD helicopter carriers, as well as from large aircraft carriers. (They were not fitted with arresting hooks.)

1 MARINE TRANSPORT SQUADRON

Squadron	Code	Aircraft	Names/
VMR-1	5C	C-9B, UC-12B, HH-46D	Roadrunners

VMR-1 at MCAS Cherry Point, North Carolina, provides worldwide air transport for the Marine Corps with one Huron and two Skytrain II aircraft. The squadron has three Sea Knights configured for the SAR mission in support of the 2nd MAW. It previously was known as the Station Operations Engineering Squadron.

The aircraft wear the base's tail code.

All other Marine air stations and facilities place their SAR aircraft under local Headquarters Squadrons. VMR-2 was briefly in existence at MCAS Miramar, but was renamed Headquarters Squadron in 1999.

VMR-1 is assigned 11 officers and 119 enlisted personnel, plus a reserve contingent of 13 officers and 21 enlisted men and women.

1 MARINE EXPERIMENTAL SQUADRON

Squadron	Code	Aircraft	Names/Notes
VMX-22		MV-22	

The squadron was established at MCAS New River, North Carolina, on 28 August 2003, to provide operational testing and evaluation of the MV-22 Osprey.

10 MARINE HEAVY HELICOPTER SQUADRONS

MAG	Squadron	Code	Aircraft	Names/Notes
24	HMT-301	SU	CH-53D	Windwalkers
29	HMT-302	UT	CH-53E	Phoenix
16	HMH-361	YN	CH-53E	Pineapples
24	HMH-362	YL	CH-53D	Ugly Angels
24	HMH-363	YZ	CH-53D	Lucky Red Lions
24	HMH-366	HH	CH-53D	deactivated 1 Oct 2000
29	HMH-461	CJ	CH-53E	Sea Stallions
16	HMH-462	YF	CH-53E	Heavy Haulers
24	HMH-463	YH	CH-53D	Pegasus
26	HMH-464	EN	CH-53E	Condors
16	HMH-465	YJ	CH-53E	Warhorses
16	HMH-466	YK	CH-53E	Wolfpack

Three operational squadrons fly the two-engine CH-53D Sea Stallion (8 aircraft each), and six fly the three-engine CH-53E Supper Stallion (16 aircraft). In addition, there are two CH-53 transition squadrons, HMT-301 and HMT-302.

All CH-53D squadrons are assigned to the 1st MAW and based at MCAF Kaneohe. These squadrons formed MAG-24 until 30 September 1994, when the group was redesignated the 1st Marine Aircraft Wing Aviation Support Element; it was changed back to MAG-24 on 1 February 2002. HMT-302 was the CH/MH-53E readiness/transition squadron for both the Navy and Marine Corps, including Airborne Mine Countermeasures (AMCM); the Navy's MH-53E training shifted to HM-14 in 2002.

HMH-366 was activated on 30 September 1994 and closed down six years later.

Historical: The first CH-53E squadron was HMH-464, activated at New River, North Carolina, on 27 February 1981.

Operational: HMT-301 was assigned the code US according to official documents, but the squadron used SU on its aircraft.

7 MARINE UTILITY AND ATTACK HELICOPTER SQUADRONS

MAG	Squadron	Code	Aircraft	Names
29	HMLA-167	TV	AH-1W, UH-1N	Warriors
39	HMLA-169	SN	AH-1W, UH-1N	Vipers
39	HMLA-267	UV	AH-1W, UH-1N	Black Aces
26	HMLA-269	HF	AH-1W, UH-1N	Sea Cobras
39	HMT-303	QT	AH-1W, UH-1N	Atlas
39	HMLA-367	VT	AH-1W, UH-1N	Scarfaces
39	HMLA-369	SM	AH-1W, UH-1N	Gunfighters

Marine CH-53E Super Stallions operating from the ESSEX (LHD 2). Note the three-engine arrangement, the inflight refueling probe, and auxiliary fuel tanks. These helicopters have a greater lift capacity than any other Western helicopter. (U.S. Navy/Marvin Thompson)

The Marine light (HML) and attack (HMA) helicopter squadrons were combined beginning on 1 April 1986 to facilitate the afloat deployment of detachments of combined troop-carrying/command UH-1N Huey helicopters and AH-1W SeaCobra gunships. The last of these squadrons transitioned from the AH-1J/T to the AH-1W model in the early 1990s. Each unit has 18 AH-1W and 9 UH-1N helicopters.

HMT-303 provides helicopter readiness training for both helicopter types. With the disestablishment of Navy squadron HC-16 in 1994, all Navy–Marine HH-1N/UH-1N training was assigned to HMT-303.

15 MARINE MEDIUM HELICOPTER SQUADRONS

MAG	Squadron	Code	Aircraft	Names
16	HMM-161*	YR	CH-46E	The First
26	HMM-162	YS	CH-46E	Golden Eagles
16	HMM-163*	YP	CH-46E	Ridgerunners
39	HMMT-164	YT	CH-46E	Knightriders
16	HMM-165	YW	CH-46E	White Knights
16	HMM-166	YX	CH-46E	Sea Elk
29	HMM-261	EM	CH-46E	Bulls
36	HMM-262*	ET	CH-46E	Flying Tigers
26	HMM-263*	EG	CH-46E	Red Lions
29	HMM-264*	EH	CH-46E	Black Knights
36	HMM-265	EP	CH-46E	Dragons
29	HMM-266*	ES	CH-46E	Griffins
39	HMM-268	YQ	CH-46E	Red Dragons
39	HMM-364	PF	CH-46E	Purple Foxes
26	HMM-365	YM	CH-46E	Blue Knights

Each medium helicopter squadron flies 12 Sea Knight helicopters, down from 18 in some units. Six squadrons (indicated by asterisks) have CH-53E, AH-1W, and UH-1N helicopters assigned to provide the basis for Marine Expeditionary Unit (MEU) deployments aboard LHA/LHD-type carriers. HMMT-164 at Camp Pendleton, California, provides all CH-46E readiness/transition training. Previously, HMT-301 provided CH-46 training.

HMT-204 became VMMT-204 in 1999 for the MV-22 Osprey program. The CH-46 is scheduled for eventual replacement by the MV-22 Osprey tilt-rotor aircraft.

Due to an administrative oversight, HMM-262 and Navy squadron VQ-6 both had the same tail code—ET. VQ-6 was assigned the code after HMM-262 was inadvertently omitted from the official code assignment listing (VQ-6 has been disestablished).

Historical: HMM-161 was the first Marine tactical helicopter squadron, established on 15 January 1951, flying the Sikorsky HRS-1.

1 MARINE HELICOPTER SQUADRON

Squadron	Code	Aircraft
HMX-1	MX	VH-3D, VH-60A/N, CH-46E, CH-53E

This unique squadron, based at MCAS Quantico, Virginia, fulfills a variety of development and operational functions, including providing helicopter transport for the president and other senior government officials with the VH-3D Sea King and VH-60A/N Blackhawk.[22] The squadron has an "alert facility" at the Naval Station Anacostia in Southeast Washington, D.C. With the president embarked, a helicopter is designated "Marine One." The president normally flies in a Sea King.

HMX-1 is the only Marine Corps unit to operate the H-60 Black Hawk/ Seahawk and H-3 Sea King helicopters.

The squadron is one of the largest in the U.S. armed forces, with a Marine complement of 51 officers and 598 enlisted personnel and a Navy contingent of 4 officers aand 14 enlisted men and women.

Designation: HMX-1 is officially Marine Helicopter Squadron 1; the word "experimental" is not a part of its designation.

Historical: This squadron—originally designated Marine Helicopter Experimental Squadron 1 or Marine Development Squadron 1—was established on 1 December 1947 to develop helicopter assault tactics for the Marine Corps. HMX-1 began providing helicopter transportation for presidents in September 1957, when a HUS-1 (UH-34) from HMX-1 carried President Dwight D. Eisenhower from Newport, Rhode Island, to NAS Quonset Point, Connecticut. In 1976, the Marine Corps was given sole responsibility for the helicopter transport of the president, having previously shared that role with the Army.

2 UNMANNED AERIAL VEHICLE SQUADRONS

MAG	Squadron	Code	Aircraft	Notes
13	VMU-1	FZ	RQ-2B	—
14	VMU-2	FF	RQ-2B	—

Two Marine Unmanned Aerial Vehicle (UAV) squadrons were established on 15 January 1996, VMU-2 at MCAS Cherry Point and VMU-1 at MCAS Yuma. Previously, Marine UAVs were operated by remotely piloted vehicle companies. (Each company consisted of 10 Marine officers, 56 Marine enlisted personnel, and 1 Navy hospital corpsman.) The squadrons fly the RQ-2B Pioneer.

Earlier UAV platoons were the primary Marine Corps drone operating units.

Operational: Both squadrons deployed to Kuwait and Iraq during Operation Iraqi Freedom in 2003.

MARINE AIR RESERVE

The Marine Air Reserve consists of the 4th Marine Aircraft Wing. The wing, organized similarly to the active MAWs, has almost 200 aircraft in 13 squadrons. Several squadrons have detachments at other bases/airfields.

In addition to the aircraft squadrons indicated for the 4th MAW, there are various wing command and support aircraft, as well as a detachment of C-12 utility aircraft. (The wing headquarters has the tail code EZ.)

Table 27-7. 4th MARINE AIRCRAFT WING

MAG	Squadron	Code	Aircraft	Location
41				JRB Fort Worth, Texas
	VMFA-112	MA	F/A-18A	JRB Fort Worth, Texas
	VMGR-234	QH	KC-130T	JRB Fort Worth, Texas
42				NAS Atlanta, Ga.
	VMFA-142	MB	F/A-18A	NAS Atlanta, Ga.
	HMLA-773	MP	AH-1W, UH-1N	NAS Atlanta, Ga.
	HMM-774	MQ	CH-46E	Naval Station Norfolk, Va.
	HMLA-775	WR	AH-1W/UH-1N	NAS New Orleans, La.
46				MCAS Miramar, Calif.
	VMFA-134	MF	F/A-18A/B	MCAS Miramar, Calif.
	VMFT-401	WB	F-5E/F	MCAS Yuma, Ariz.
	HMM-764	ML	CH-46E	Edwards AFB, Calif.
	HMH-769	MS	CH-53E	Edwards AFB, Calif.
49				NAS Willow Grove, Pa.
	VMFA-321	MG	F/A-18A	NAF Washington, D.C.; deactivated 30 Sep 2004
	VMGR-452	NY	KC-130T	Stewart ANGB, N.Y.*
	HMH-772	MT	CH-53E	NAF Washington, D.C.

* ANGB = Air National Guard Base.

---

22 The Army name for the H-60A series is Black Hawk (two words).

MARINE ATTACK SQUADRONS

Reserve squadron VMA-131 was the last Navy–Marine Corps squadron to fly the single-seat A-4 Skyhawk, retiring its last A-4M "Scooter" in 1992. The squadron—still held in service by congressional edict—finally was deactivated in December 1998.

VMA-133 and VMA-322 flying the A-4M Skyhawk were deactivated in 1992.

MARINE TACTICAL ELECTRONIC WARFARE SQUADRONS

VMAQ-4 became an active EW squadron in 1992.

MARINE FIGHTER SQUADRONS

VMF-112 was the last U.S. Navy–Marine Corps squadron to fly the versatile Phantom, the F-4S variant in this instance. The squadron converted to F/A-18s in late 1992.

Fighter readiness training squadron VMFT-401 was activated in 1986 to provide adversary training aircraft for active and reserve Marine squadrons. The squadron initially flew 13 F-21A Kfir fighters leased from Israel Aircraft Industries from June 1987 until September 1989. They were replaced by 12 F-5E Tiger II and one F-5F aircraft for adversary training.

MARINE OBSERVATION SQUADRONS

The last Marine OV-10 Bronco unit, VMO-4, was deactivated on 30 July 1994.

MARINE REFUELER-TRANSPORT SQUADRONS

VMGR-234 and VMGR-452 were activated on 14 January 2003 in anticipation of combat operations against Iraq. They reverted to reserve status on 30 September 2003.

MARINE HEAVY HELICOPTER SQUADRONS

HMH-769 was activated on 1 April 1993 from Detachment A of HMH-772. Deactivated on the same date were HMH-769 and HMH-772, both flying ex-Navy RH-53D Sea Stallion mine countermeasures helicopters. HMH-769 was recalled to active duty on 27 January 2002 and released to reserve status on 27 June 2002; HMH-772 was recalled to active service on 12 February 2002.

MARINE UTILITY AND ATTACK HELICOPTER SQUADRONS

HMA-767 was changed to HMLA-767 on 1 August 1994; HMA-773 to HMLA-773 on 1 July 1994, and HMA-775 to HMLA-775 on 1 August 1994.

HML-771 at NAS South Weymouth, Massachusetts, flying the UH-1N, was deactivated on 1 August 1994, and HML-776 at NAS Glenview, Illinois, flying the UH-1N. was deactivated on 1 July 1994.

MARINE CORPS AIR STATION AIRCRAFT

Code	Aircraft	Activity
5A	UC-12B, UC-35C	NAF Washington, D.C. (Andrews AFB, Md.)
5B	UC-12B, HH-46D	MCAS Beaufort, N.C.
5C	UC-12B	MCAS Cherry Point, N.C.
5D	UC-12B	MCAS New River, N.C.
5F	UC-12B, UC-35D	MCAS Futenma, Okinawa
5G	UC-12F	MCAS Iwakuni, Japan
5Y	UC-12B, HH-1N	MCAS Yuma, Ariz.
—	UC-12B, UC-35C	NAS New Orleans, La.
—	UC-12B	JRB Fort Worth, Texas

Tail code 5T was assigned to MCAS El Toro, California.

Aircraft of Carrier Air Wing 11 crowd the forward flight deck of the carrier NIMITZ *as the flattop operates in the Middle East area. Carriers provide mobile and politically independent bases for these tactical aircraft. (U.S. Navy/Angel G. Hilbrands)*

CHAPTER 28

Naval Aircraft

Sailors and Marines stand by as the assault ship Belleau Wood *(LHA 3) departs for the Middle East. The "black boxes" on the tail pylons of the CH-46E Sea Knights are ALQ-157 Infrared (IR) jammers; the "buttons" under the tail are the APR-39 radar detectors and ALR-47 missile warning systems. (U.S. Navy/Steven L. Cooke)*

This chapter describes the aircraft flown by naval aviation—the U.S. Navy and Marine Corps—as well as the Coast Guard. The Unmanned Aerial Vehicle (UAV) programs, formerly referred to as Remotely Piloted Vehicle (RPV) or drone programs, are described in Chapter 29.

The procurement of naval aircraft, both types and numbers, was drastically reduced following the end of the Cold War. Severe budget constraints, technical problems, and the Navy's misman- agement of aircraft programs have caused the delay or cancellation of several aircraft. By the beginning of the 21st century, however, there had been a turnaround in aircraft procurement rates as part of the "recapitalization" of the Navy and Marine Corps.

Twelve manned aircraft currently are being procured by the Navy and Marine Corps:

A variety of naval aircraft have been flown by the Blue Angels flight demonstration team since its establishment almost 60 years ago. This is the squadron's single F/A-18B Hornet, wearing blue-and-gold livery. (U.S. Navy/Mark Rebilas)

Aircraft		Type	Prime contractor
F/A-18E	Hornet	strike fighter	Boeing
F/A-18F	Hornet	strike fighter	Boeing
E-2C	Hawkeye	AEW*	Northrop Grumman
EA-18G	Growler	electronic attack	Boeing
C-140A	Clipper	transport	Boeing
UC-35	—	utility–transport	Cessna Textron
KC-30J	Hercules	transport	Lockheed Martin
T-6A	Texan	trainer	Raytheon
T-45	Goshawk	trainer	British Aerospace and Boeing
MV-22B	Osprey	assault (STOVL)**	Bell-Boeing
MH-60R	Knighthawk	multimission helicopter	Sikorsky
MH-60S	Knighthawk	multimission helicopter	Sikorsky

*AEW = Airborne Early Warning
**STOVL = Short Take-Off/Vertical Landing

The T-6A was developed as the Joint Primary Aircraft Training System (JPATS). Both the T-6 and V-22 are joint programs with the Air Force. Beyond these new-procurement aircraft, in the near-term the Navy plans to procure the multimission F-35, known as the Joint Strike Fighter (JSF), and the Multimission Maritime Aircraft (MMA). The JSF is a joint Air Force–Navy–Marine Corps–Royal Navy program. The MMA is the long-awaited successor to the P-3 Orion.

The F-35/JSF and MV-22, and to a lesser degree the MMA, offer the promise of foreign procurement. However, the future of the JSF still is considered precarious by some observers. The Air Force seeks the continued production of its controversial F/A-22 Raptor stealth fighter, which can only detract from its interest in the JSF.[1] At the same time, the Air Force is seeking to increase the fighter capabilities of the JSF at the expense of its effectiveness as a strike aircraft. This could result in an aircraft so analogous to the F/A-22 that there would be insufficient rationale (and funds) for Air Force procurement of the JSF.

Similarly, the Navy's interest in the JSF is tempered by its desire to fully procure the F/A-18E and F aircraft, which have suffered technical problems, as well as increasing costs. Again, the acquisition of these improved F/A-18 variants could delay the JSF and dissipate Navy interest in the aircraft.

This is in stark contrast to the Marine Corps and Royal Navy, to whom the F-35/JSF is critical if those services are to continue fixed-wing aircraft operations from small carriers (i.e., LHA/LHD amphibious ships in the U.S. Navy). The various U.S. and British Harrier variants are aging and will need replacement within a decade.

Historically, the Marine Corps and Coast Guard have flown Navy aircraft; however, during the 1980s, both services sponsored the procurement of aircraft not acquired by the Navy, principally the AV-8 Harrier series for the Marine Corps and the HU-25 Guardian reconnaissance aircraft and HH-65 Dolphin helicopter for the Coast Guard. All of these procurement programs are completed. (The original AV-8A Harrier has been replaced in Marine service by the improved AV-8B.)

U.S. naval aircraft in service after 1990 are listed in this chapter, even if they subsequently have been discarded.

AIRCRAFT DESIGNATIONS

U.S. military aircraft are designated in a scheme adopted on 18 September 1962. It is relatively simple, with prefix and suffix letters providing extensive detail. Nevertheless, confusion persists as the old and new schemes are mixed or written incorrectly.

For example, the McDonnell Douglas F-4B Phantom often was written incorrectly as F4B—which was a Boeing fighter of the 1920s. Similarly, the F4F Wildcat of World War II fame often is written incorrectly as F-4F, which is the U.S. designation used for F-4 Phantoms configured for West Germany. The phasing out of most pre-1962 aircraft, however, is alleviating this problem.

There also have been major corruptions of the system by the services. The most numerous aircraft in the Navy–Marine Corps

---

1 The Air Force redesignated the F-22 Raptor fighter the F/A-22 in 2002. Gen. John P. Jumper, Air Force Chief of Staff, announced the change on 17 September. He told an audience at the Air Force Association's National Convention that the new designation more accurately describes the fighter's true role. "Secretary [of the Air Force James G.] Roche and I have decided to adopt the name F/A-22, using the A prefix to emphasize the multiple roles and many dimensions of the Raptor," he said. However, calling the F-22 an "attack" aircraft is ludicrous: it is a high-performance fighter, carrying air-to-air missiles and a 30-mm Gatling gun. Its "attack" capability will be two 1,000-pound Joint Direct Attack Munitions (JDAM), a capability that had not yet been demonstrated when this volume went to press, and it pales in comparison to the F/A-18, which can carry up to 17,000 pounds of weapons (plus two Sidewinder air-to-air missiles).

inventory—the F/A-18 Hornet—carries an unofficial designation that violates the prescribed designation scheme. In 1975—three years before the first Hornet flew—Vice Admiral William D. Houser, then Deputy Chief of Naval Operations (Air), determined that the designation F-18 would be used for the fighter variant and A-18 for the attack variant.[2] However, on 5 September 1978, Houser's successor, Vice Admiral Frederick C. Turner, wrote to the Commander, Naval Air Systems Command, stating his preference for the designation F/A-18, which did not follow the official aircraft designation guidance:

> My choice, F/A-18, would be based not so much on conformance with existing directives as with the necessity to designate this aircraft so that it truly reflects its multimission nature. Certainly the designation F-18 is in consonance with the tri-service instruction. . . . I prefer to continue [with F/A-18] even though it may be one that receives its legitimacy through use rather than directive.[3]

The F/A-18 designation is now "accepted," and appears in the Department of Defense directive on aircraft designators. The F/A designation has been further misused in the F/A-22.

The U.S. military services do not follow the 1962 designation system in other respects, as well. For example, they established a new helicopter series, beginning with H-1 (formerly the HU-1), but that series reached only H-6 before the services began adding to the abandoned Air Force series with H-54 and above. More severe violations have been made by the Air Force, with fighter-series numbers above F-111 being assigned despite the new series that had begun with the F-1 and carried through to the F-23.

Similarly, the 1962 system dictated that the "next" training aircraft be designated T-41. That was done, and successive training aircraft reached number T-47. Under the 1962 system, the Navy's T2V-1 Sea Star, a navalized version of the T-33, was the T-1. However, in 1992, the Air Force assigned T-1 to a new undergraduate pilot training aircraft (named Jayhawk). This probably was the most flagrant violation of the 1962 Department of Defense directive on designations.

Modifications to aircraft, which in the past have meant the addition of a suffix numeral or letter, now have such confusing designations as P-3C Update III, EA-6B ICAP, and EP-3E Aries II. Also, where under the original 1962 scheme, the prefix *M* meant missile-carrying aircraft, today it indicates multipurpose aircraft, as MH-53E Sea Dragon and MH-60S Knighthawk helicopters.

Perhaps most absurd deviation is the assignment of F-35 to the Joint Strike Fighter. Secretary of the Air Force James Roche announced in 2003 that the JSF would become F-35 because the technology demonstration aircraft was designated X-35. But that research aircraft was not a prototype JSF; rather, its experimental designation is akin to that of the XV-15 tilt-rotor aircraft, which was the technology demonstrator for the V-22 Osprey series. According to the Department of Defense aircraft designation procedure, the next U.S. fighter aircraft should have been designated F-24. (The F-23 was the McDonnell Douglas competitive design to the Lockheed F-22 Raptor high-performance fighter.)

Historical: From 1922 to 1962, the Navy had its own designation scheme that indicated the aircraft mission, sequence of that aircraft type produced by the manufacturer, manufacturer, and (after a hyphen) model, and modification. Thus AD-2N indicated the first series of attack (A) aircraft built by Douglas (D), the second model (2), modified for night operation (N); the second Douglas attack aircraft was A2D, the third A3D, and so on.

That scheme became unwieldy as the number of manufacturers of naval aircraft increased. For example, the letter *F* was used for Grumman (as in F9F) because *G* already was assigned to Gallaudet; *Y* for Consolidated (as in PBY) because *C* was used by Curtiss and, later, Cessna and Culver; *A* for Brewster (as in F2A)

because *B* previously was assigned to Boeing and, later, Beech and Budd Manufacturing. Also, the same aircraft flown by different services had different designations. The famed Boeing B-29 Superfortress had the Navy designation P2B; the North American B-25 was flown by the Marine Corps as the PBJ; and the McDonnell Phantom II entered service as the F4H in the Navy and F-110 in the Air Force.

The U.S. Air Force and Army used different designation schemes for their respective aircraft after the establishment of the Air Force as a separate service in 1947. (Previously, from 1941 to 1947, what became the U.S. Air Force was the U.S. Army Air Forces.)

Under the unified scheme of 1962, all existing and new naval aircraft were redesignated. The Navy-flown AD Skyraider became the first plane in the new attack series, the A-1; the Navy's TF Trader started the new cargo series as C-1; the FJ Fury became the F-1; the T2V Sea Star the T-1; and the UC-1 Otter the U-1.[4]

There was no P-1 or S-1, as the new system picked up the Navy's P2V Neptune and S2F Tracker as the P-2 and S-2, respectively. The improved P3V Orion was the obvious candidate for P-3 and the P5M Marlin, the Navy's last combat flying boat, for P-5. The designation P-4 was used, albeit briefly, for the drone versions of the Privateer (the P4Y-2K, formerly PB4Y-2). The designations P-4 and P-6 sometimes are cited as having been reserved for the P4M Mercator and the P6M Seamaster, but the last of the combination piston-turbojet Mercators were gone by 1962 and the turbojet Seamaster flying boat had been canceled in 1959. The next patrol aircraft was to be the P-7, which was the canceled Long-Range Air Anti-submarine Capable Aircraft (LRAACA).

The 1962 system also introduced the mission designation of special electronic E-series aircraft. The first two planes were the Navy's: the WF-2 Tracer became the E-1B and the W2F-1 Hawkeye the E-2A.

Variations of the previous Air Force *X* (for experimental) and *V* (for Vertical/Short Take-Off and Landing/VSTOL) designations remained, but official records differ as to which aircraft were part of the old or new series. The Marine AV-8 Harrier is officially in the V series, the designation A-8 being avoided apparently to reduce confusion. In the V series, the Ryan "flying jeep" already had been designated XV-8, but the program never took off; hence, the *8* spot is firmly held by the successful Harrier series.

Planes that were used by both services, such as the Albatross seaplane (Navy UF), generally took on the existing Air Force numerical designation (U-16, formerly SA-16). But the Phantom was recent enough to be given a new designation, the now-familiar F-4, and not the Air Force F-110.

Helicopters proved to be a more confusing issue because the Army had its own helicopter designation system before 1962 in addition to those of the Navy–Marine Corps and the Air Force. The Sea Knight was the Navy HRB, while the Army called the helicopter HC-1A (HC for helicopter–cargo). This became the H-46 in the new scheme. The Army's HU-1 Iroquois (HU for helicopter–utility) started the new helicopter series as H-1, and most of the Army and Air Force designations were merged to form the new H series. Navy helicopters were "stuck in" where there were gaps. The Kaman HU2K became the H-2 and the Sikorsky HSS-2 the H-3, but the Navy–Marine HSS-1/HUS, being similar to the Army–Air

2 Vice Adm. Houser, USN, "Memorandum for the Chief of Naval Operations," Memo 05/187 (30 Oct. 1975).

3 Vice Adm. Turner, USN, "Memorandum for the Commander, Naval Air Systems Command," ser. 506C5/781084, 5 Sep. 1978.

4 A full discussion of the designation issue is found in James P. Stevenson, *The Pentagon Paradox* (Annapolis, Md: Naval Institute Press, 1993). The U-2 spy plane was given a utility designation in an effort to hide its real purpose.

Force H-34, took on the H-34 designation. Further, after the new H-series reached H-6, the military reverted to adding to the larger numerical series, i.e., H-54 and above.

Figure 28.1 explains the current aircraft designation scheme.

Names: The U.S. military services assign popular names to aircraft. Those carrying a previously used name are assigned a Roman numeral suffix, although in reality, the suffix is meaningless because the earlier aircraft always has been discarded by the time the "II" aircraft enters service.

The following contemporary aircraft have such a suffix:

AV-8B   Harrier II
C-9B   Skytrain II
T-6   Texan II

AIRCRAFT MARKINGS

Unit markings: Indicative of wing, squadron, or base assignment, these consist of letters or letter–number combinations and appear on the tail fin or after body of the aircraft (see Chapter 27 for unit codes).

Side numbers: Generally painted on the fuselage and upper right and lower left wing surfaces, these indicate the aircraft position in a squadron or other unit. The side number sequence for carrier air wings is shown on page 369.

Bureau numbers: Assigned to all Navy and Marine Corps aircraft in the sequence of their procurement, these numbers are used on the aircraft's after fuselage or tail; on transports, the last three digits sometimes are used as their side numbers. "Bureau" refers to the Bureau of Aeronautics, which directed naval aircraft procurement from 1921 to 1959, when it became the Bureau of Naval Ordnance, and in 1966, the current Naval Air Systems Command. However, the term "bureau number" continues in use.

National insignia: The U.S. national insignia consists of a white star within a blue circle, with white rectangles on either side; the rectangles have a red horizontal stripe and blue border. All naval aircraft have the national insignia on both sides of the fuselage, and fixed-wing aircraft also have it on the upper left and lower right wing surfaces. Most U.S. tactical aircraft now have low-visibility national markings (i.e., no color).

Navy Carrier Onboard Delivery (COD) and other transport aircraft usually have the American flag on their tail fins. Coast Guard aircraft have the national insignia or American flag on their tail fins and the service's distinctive crest and orange-and-blue stripe on their noses. These aircraft have four-digit side numbers based on their (Coast Guard) procurement sequence.

ATTACK AIRCRAFT

Specialized attack aircraft have been phased out of naval aviation except for the AV-8B Harrier, which the Marine Corps will operate for several more years pending delivery of the F-35/JSF.

The last Navy "straight" attack aircraft was the A-6E Intruder, which was taken out of squadron service in 1996. Retirement of the A-6E ended the 50-year history of VA aircraft in the U.S. Navy. (TA-4J Skyhawks, two-seat variants of the famed A-4 light attack aircraft, remained in service until 2003.) Attack missions now are carried out by the multipurpose F/A-18 Hornet and the upgraded F-14 Tomcats.

Several efforts to develop a specialized successor to the A-6 Intruder have been aborted or stillborn. The last was the Navy's A/F-X program, initiated in the early 1990s after the demise of the AX. The A/F-X was a study effort that quickly fell victim to another paper airplane, the so-called Joint Attack Fighter (JAF), an Air Force–sponsored conceptual aircraft. The JAF was to have a range of about 575 miles (925 km) carrying a payload goal of four internal air-to-air missiles and up to four 2,000-pound (907-kg) air-to-surface weapons externally.

The previous attack aircraft program was the "stealth" A-12 Avenger, formally initiated in 1984, with the first of six A-12 prototypes originally scheduled to fly in June 1990. At the time the aircraft was canceled in 1991, the first flight was expected to occur in March 1992 and carrier trials were expected in late 1992 or early 1993, with an Initial Operational Capability (IOC) of 1996. Details of that convoluted program are given in the 17th Edition/pages 391–92.

AV-8B HARRIER

The AV-8B is a highly capable STOVL attack aircraft flown by Marine attack squadrons.[5] Since 1996, the Harrier has been the only straight attack aircraft (VA/VMA) in naval aviation. The air-

---

5 The designation STOVL for the AV-8B Harrier in place of VSTOL was made by the Deputy Chief of Staff/Aviation, Headquarters, U.S. Marine Corps, in March 1995.

An AV-8B Harrier assigned to HMM-365 on the deck of the assault ship Bataan *(LHD 5). Deployed Harriers have been assigned to medium helicopter squadrons to coordinate aircraft embarked in a forward-deployed LHA/LHD amphibious ship. (U.S. Navy/Johnny Bivera)*

craft normally operates from amphibious ships and land bases, but has flown from large aircraft carriers.

The AV-8B has replaced the A-4M Skyhawk and AV-8A Harrier aircraft in VMA squadrons. The Marines have operated the AV-8A version of the Harrier since 1971 (see below).

During the Carter administration (1977–1981), the Department of Defense sought to have the Marine Corps procure the F/A-18 Hornet as a replacement for the A-4M, but the Marines—with congressional support—held fast to the AV-8B program. In the event, during the Reagan administration (1981–1989), then-Secretary of the Navy John Lehman procured both the AV-8B and the F/A-18 for the Marine Corps.

The Marine Corps originally planned to procure 336 operational AV-8B aircraft plus four full-scale development aircraft in addition to the two YAV-8B prototypes that were converted from AV-8A aircraft. Procurement was revised downward to the actual production of 256 AV-8B models and 20 of the two-seat TAV-8B trainers, the last procurement being in Fiscal Year (FY) 1991.

Design: The AV-8B differs from the earlier AV-8A Harrier flown by the Marine Corps in having a supercritical wing shape, larger trailing-edge flaps, drooped ailerons, strakes under the gun pods, redesigned engine intakes, strengthened landing gear, and a more- powerful engine, providing twice the payload of the AV-8A with up to 9,200 pounds (4,173 kg) of external stores. The aircraft has one external 25-mm gun pack faired into the underfuselage, with one fuselage and six wing points available for bombs, rockets, missiles, or 300-gallon (1,140-liter) fuel tanks.

Compared to the AV-8A, the AV-8B wing has 15 percent greater area, and the aircraft can carry 75 percent more fuel in its wing tanks. The AV-8B also has six wing store stations compared to four on the AV-8A, plus an uprated engine, composite material in some fuselage areas, an elevated cockpit and canopy to improve visibility, redesigned engine intakes, and improved avionics.

AV-8B aircraft has the ASB-19(V)3 angle-rate bombing system. Those aircraft delivered after September 1989 are night-attack capable, being fitted with nose-mounted Forward-Looking Infrared (FLIR), pilot night-vision goggles, Head-Up Display (HUD), color head-down displays, and a digital moving-map system. Aircraft delivered from 1993 (Harrier II Plus) have the APG-65 multimode, synthetic-aperture radar and the improved Pegasus 408 engine; the aircraft also are 17 inches (0.43 m) longer in the forward fuselage and weigh some 900 pounds (408 kg) more than the basic radar-equipped AV-8B. Earlier AV-8B aircraft have been "remanufactured" to the "Plus" configuration.

Also fitted are the ALR-67 radar warning receiver and the pod-mounted ALQ-164 Electronic Countermeasures (ECM) system.

The two-seat TAV-8B differs from the standard AV-8B in having an enlarged forward fuselage and canopy and a vertical fin extension; the two aircraft have a 90 percent component commonality.

Operational: Marine AV-8B Harriers participated in Operation Desert Storm in 1991 and Operation Iraqi Freedom in 2003, operating from amphibious ships and land bases. (Earlier Harriers flown by Britain's Royal Navy and Royal Air Force from VSTOL carriers achieved remarkable results in both the fighter and attack roles in the 1982 Falklands conflict.)

Status: Operational. First flight of the YAV-8B occurred on 9 November 1978. The first flight of the AV-8B was on 5 November 1981, with IOC in January 1985 (with VMA-331). The Harrier II Plus first flew in September 1992; with IOC in June 1993 (with VMA-542).

(Britain's Royal Air Force procured essentially the same aircraft as the AV-8B, designated GR.Mk 5 and the night-attack GR.Mk 7 variants; the British T.Mk 10 variants are similar to the TAV-8B. AV-8B variants also are flown from VSTOL aircraft carriers by Italy and Spain; earlier Sea Harriers are flown from two Indian aircraft carriers.)

AV-8B "Plus"

Manufacturer:	McDonnell Douglas and British Aerospace
Crew:	(1) pilot (2 in TAV-8B)
Engines:	1 Rolls-Royce F402-RR-408 Pegasus turbofan; 23,800 lbst (10,795 kgst)
Weight:	empty: 12,922 lb (5,861 kg)
	gross: Vertical Take-Off (VTO) 19,550 lb (8,868 kg)
	Short Take-Off (STO) 31,000 lb (14,060 kg) with 1,200-ft (366-m) takeoff run
Dimensions:	length AV-8B: 46 ft 4 in (14.12 m)
	TAV-8B: 50 ft 3 in (15.32 m)
	wingspan: 30 ft 4 in (9.25 m)
	wing area: 230 ft² (21.37 m²)
	height: 11 ft 7¾ in (3.55 m)
Speed:	max. 668 mph (1,075 kmh) at sea level
Ceiling:	50,000 ft (15,244 m)
Range:	radius 173 miles (280 km) with 12 500-lb (227-kg) bombs with 1 hour loiter with STO takeoff
	radius 690 miles (1,111 km) with 7 500-lb bombs in STO mode
	ferry: 2,945 miles (4,741 km) with 4 300-gallon (1,140-liter) drop tanks
Armament:	1 25-mm cannon GAU-12/U (multibarrel; 300 rounds)
	11,920 lb (5,407 kg) bombs, missiles, drop tanks including Sidewinder AAMs
Radar:	APG-65

A two-seat TAV-8B Harrier at rest with both canopies open while on the tarmac at McDill Air Force Base, Florida. The after cockpit is raised above the forward, student cockpit. (John Bouvia)

An AV-8B Harrier makes a landing approach to the assault ship PELELIU (LHA 5). Note the bicycle landing gear configuration and the six store stations (plus the gun pod under the fuselage). (U.S. Navy/Terry Cosgrove)

AV-8B Harriers are parked on the after portion of the flight deck of the assault ship Nassau (LHA 4). Six-plane Harrier detachments normally are assigned to LHA/LHDs, although those ships have operated in excess of 20 Short Take-Off/Vertical Landing (STOVL) aircraft. (U.S. Navy/Michael Sandberg)

AV-8A HARRIER

The Harrier was the first VSTOL aircraft to enter first-line service with the U.S. armed forces. The British-developed aircraft initially was procured for three Marine Corps attack squadrons, and the Marines deemed it a success despite a high accident rate. Several surviving AV-8A aircraft were upgraded to the AV-8C, and two AV-8A Harriers were converted to YAV-8B prototypes for the Harrier II. All AV-8A/C aircraft have been discarded.

The Marine Corps took delivery of 102 single-seat AV-8A (British GR.Mk 50) and eight two-seat TAV-8A (British T.Mk 4) aircraft from 1971 to 1976, with McDonnell Douglas as the U.S. support contractor.

See 14th Edition/pages 403–4 for characteristics.

A-7 CORSAIR

The Corsair was a carrier-based, light attack aircraft in Navy service from 1966 to 1991. It saw extensive combat in the Vietnam War. The last two A-7E squadrons (VA-46 and VA-72) flew in the Gulf War; both were disestablished in May 1991. The last naval air reserve units to fly the A-7E traded in their Corsairs for the F/A-18 Hornet in April 1991. The Marine Corps did not fly the A-7.

The A-7E was replaced in Navy carrier air wings by the F/A-18. Production of the A-7 ended in 1983 with 1,551 Corsairs delivered—997 for the U.S. Navy, 459 A-7D and 30 two-seat A-7K for the U.S. Air Force, and 65 A-7H and TA-7H models for Greece. Two A-7D models were upgraded to YA-7F prototypes for an improved close air support aircraft, but no large-scale conversion followed. Many former U.S. Navy aircraft were modified for foreign use.

Sixty U.S. Navy versions were two-seat TA-7C with dual controls (converted from A-7A and A-7C aircraft). A proposed RA-7E with reconnaissance pods was dropped in favor of the F-14 with the Tactical Air Reconnaissance Pod System (TARPS), and a proposed twin-engine A-7 variant lost out in the concept stage to the F/A-18 as the new Navy attack aircraft.

See 14th Edition/pages 404-405 for characteristics.

A-6 INTRUDER

A highly capable attack aircraft, the Intruder was the U.S. Navy's most capable carrier-based aircraft with respect to weapons payload and was able to carry out all-weather, day/night strikes.

Navy and Marine Corps Intruders flew combat missions in the Vietnam War, as well as in the Persian Gulf conflict of 1991. The last Navy A-6E squadrons were disestablished in 1996; the last Marine A-6E squadrons were deactivated in 1993.

A total of 679 A-6 aircraft were produced, plus 5 A-6F prototypes and 191 electronic warfare variants (EA-6A, EA-6B). The KA-6D tankers (all converted from earlier aircraft) had avionics deleted from the after fuselage to provide space for a reel-and-drogue apparatus; up to five 300-gallon (1,140-liter) drop tanks could be carried to permit the transfer of up to 2,977 gallons of JP-5 fuel to other aircraft immediately after takeoff. Later modifications enabled some aircraft to carry 400-gallon (1,514-liter) drop tanks. A KA-6H tanker based on the enlarged EA-6B airframe was proposed as a successor to the KA-6D, but none was procured. (After the phaseout of the KA-6D aircraft, A-6Es were employed as tankers, being fitted with "buddy store" hose-and-drogue pods.)

The EA-6A Intruder and EA-6B Prowler electronic warfare variants were derived from the basic Intruder (see Electronic Aircraft).

Designation: The Intruder originally was designated A2F; it was changed to A-6 in 1962.

See 16th Edition/pages 366–67 for characteristics.

A-4 SKYHAWK

See TA-4J Skyhawk under Training Aircraft.

A-3 SKYWARRIOR

The Douglas A3D (later A-3) was developed as a long-range, carrier-based nuclear strike aircraft. The A3D was the largest aircraft to operate regularly from an aircraft carrier, the tanker version having a carrier takeoff weight of more than 80,000 pounds (36,288 kg).

The aircraft was used in the Vietnam War in a variety of roles, including conventional bombing attacks.

The Navy took delivery of 282 Douglas-built Skywarriors of all variants, including 25 A3D-2Q/EA-3B specialized Electronic Intelligence (ELINT) collection aircraft. Other straight attack variants subsequently were modified to EC configurations. The ELINT version was the last flown by the Navy, that variant of the "Whale" having been assigned to squadrons VQ-1 and VQ-2 from 1959 until 1991. (From 1987 until 1991, they were restricted to operations from land bases.)

The A3D survived its intended successor, the A3J (later A-5) Vigilante. The last Skywarrior was retired from VQ-2 in September 1991.

(The Air Force flew the B-66 Destroyer, derived from the A3D, in the bomber, electronic, reconnaissance, weather, and research roles; B-66 production totaled 206 aircraft.)

Designation: The aircraft originally was designated A3D; it was changed to A-3 in 1962.

See 14th Edition/pages 415-416 for characteristics.

FIGHTER/STRIKE FIGHTER AIRCRAFT

The Navy now flies the F-14 Tomcat in limited numbers in the fighter-attack role, and both the Navy and Marine Corps fly the multipurpose F/A-18 Hornet. The remaining F-14s will be discarded by 2010 at which time the F/A-18 will fill the fighter and strike roles for both services pending introduction of the F-35/JSF.

The proposed Naval Advanced Tactical Fighter (NATF) was essentially stillborn, being considered unaffordable by the Navy's leadership. Still, proposals were put forward for a carrier-capable variant of the Air Force's Advanced Technology Fighter (ATF), now the Lockheed/Boeing F/A-22 Raptor. The Navy's record for adopting non-Navy-developed aircraft for carrier use made it highly unlikely there would be a navalized version of that aircraft.

The JSF is being developed in place of the NATF for the Navy and Marine Corps.

F-35 JOINT STRIKE FIGHTER (JSF)

The Joint Strike Fighter is being developed as a multipurpose aircraft, initially for U.S. and British service. As currently configured, the program is planned to produce more than 2,500 aircraft for the U.S. Air Force (1,763), Navy and Marine Corps (680), and Royal Navy (60). (Procurement plans were reduced in January 2003; previously, the Air Force intended to procure about 2,000 aircraft, the Navy 300, and the Marine Corps 650.)

The JSF could replace up to eight aircraft types:

- F-15 Eagle
- F-16 Fighting Falcon   } F-35A conventional variant for U.S. Air Force
- F-117A stealth strike aircraft

- AV-8B Harrier   } F-35B STOVL variant for U.S. Marine
- RN Harrier   Corps and Royal Navy

- F-14 Tomcat
- F/A-18C Hornet   } F-35C carrier variant for U.S. Navy
- F/A-18D Hornet

The three principal variants are to have 90 percent commonality and only 10 percent differences for separate service needs.

The F-35B also may replace the Royal Air Force's GR.Mk 7 Harrier. In addition, several other air forces have expressed interest in the JSF program: Australia, Canada, Denmark, the Netherlands, and Norway. All these countries hope to have industrial participation in the JSF program.

A successful JSF program could result in the U.S. armed forces having only four fighter-type aircraft in service by the second decade of the 21st century: the F/A-18E and F Hornet, F/A-22 Raptor, and F-35 Joint Strike Fighter.

As now envisioned, JSF production—scheduled to begin in 2006—could be worth more than $150 billion to the firms that build the planes. This massive outlay will be the largest U.S. weapons procurement of the first decade of the 21st century.

Industrial teams led by Boeing and Lockheed Martin developed two competitive prototypes for the JSF, designated X-32 and X-35A, respectively. (A third team, led by McDonnell Douglas, in collaboration with Northrop Grumman and British Aerospace, was dropped from the competition in November 1996.) Each team produced one conventional JSF aircraft and one STOVL version for flight demonstrations. Following the Department of Defense selected the Lockheed Martin design. That firm's X-35A demonstrator first flew on 24 October 2000.

The Lockheed Martin JSF design has a traditional aircraft configuration, somewhat resembling existing fighter designs. The firm has extensive experience in stealth aircraft and won the Air Force's 1981 competition for the ATF, now the F/A-22. That aircraft has the F119 engine, to be used in the JSF, which some analysts believe gave Lockheed Martin a significant advantage in the contest. In addition, Lockheed Martin claimed two significant advantages over the Boeing entry: (1) an additional 100 nm (183 km) in radius, and (2) increased potential supply of electrical power to run sensor payloads or a laser weapon.

In late 2003, it was revealed that the JSF was approximately 1,000 pounds (454 kg) overweight, a situation that would extend development at least a year and increase costs.

The F-35 will not be a low-level attack aircraft, but will operate above the kill zones of small arms and shoulder-launched missiles. This tactic will require that the planes employ stand-off tactical missiles and guided bombs. The availability of data links to off-board sensors (unmanned aerial vehicles, satellites, other aircraft, ground forces) will provide the F-35 with precision targeting data for these stand-off weapons.

Design: The Lockheed Martin X-35 was chosen over the competing Boeing X-32 primarily because of Lockheed's lift-fan STOVL design, which is considered superior to Boeing's thrust-vectored approach. The lift fan, which is lowered by the aircraft engine through a clutched driveshaft, is technically feasible, and the Department of Defense concluded that Lockheed had the technology in hand to make it a reality. The lift fan has significant excess power that could be critical given the weight gain that all fighter aircraft tend to experience.

All three versions of the X-35 have the same fuselage and internal weapons bay, common outer mold lines, identical swept-back wings, and comparable tail configurations. All have the same core engine, based on the Pratt & Whitney F119 derived from the F-22 Raptor. The weapons bay will be an unusual feature for contemporary carrier-based aircraft; previous naval fighters and light/medium attack aircraft have carried their weapons on external pylons and attachment points. Only Air Force tactical strike aircraft—largely developed to carry nuclear weapons—tend to have internal weapon bays, which usually permit higher speeds and enhanced stealth. In the Marine Corps and British F-35C variant, the weapons bay may be smaller because of the STOVL requirement.

The aircraft is intended to have a Radar Cross Section (RCS) slightly larger than the radar signature of the F/A-22 Raptor at a fraction of the cost. The reduction is achieved through shaping, construction materials, and skin coatings. An equivalent signature is the radar reflection from a perfectly electrically conducting metal sphere the size of a golf ball.[6]

Historical: Past efforts to develop multiservice tactical aircraft have not been marked by success. The most notable example is the 1960s effort to produce the Tactical Fighter Experimental (TFX) for the Air Force, Navy, and Marine Corps, and, subsequently, for the strategic bomber role. The resulting F-111/FB-111 had a lack-luster career as a tactical strike (*not* fighter) and strategic bombing aircraft; the Navy rejected its F-111B variant as unsuitable for carrier operation, and that ended possible Marine Corps procurement. The proposed British F-111 was stillborn, although the Royal Australian Air Force acquired the F-111 and still flies that aircraft.[7]

Similarly, several land-based tactical aircraft proposed for naval (carrier) use also have been less than successful, with most such efforts having been British. In sharp contrast, carrier-based aircraft that have been adopted for land operation have had marked success, among them the F-4 Phantom, A-1 Skyraider, A-3 Skywarrior (as the B-66 Destroyer), A-4 Skyhawk, and A-7 Corsair. Indeed, the Phantom achieved the second highest production number of any Western combat aircraft since World War II, even though it was designed specifically for carrier operation. (Only the F-86 Sabre/FJ Fury was produced in larger numbers.)

Status: In development. IOC is planned for 2009–2010.

F-35B/C _____

Manufacturer:	Lockheed Martin
Crew:	(1) pilot
Engines:	1 Pratt & Whitney F119-PW-100 turbofan
Weight:	empty: 22,500–24,000 lb (10,206–10,886 kg)
	gross: F-35B 30,700 lb (13,925 kg)
	F-35C 30,600 lb (13,880 kg)
	max. Take-Off (T/O) approx. 50,000 lb (22,680 kg)
	from land
Dimensions:	length: F-35B 50 ft 6 in (15.4 m)
	F-35C 50 ft 10 in (15.5 m)
	wingspan: F-35B 34 ft 8 in (10.6 m)
	F-35C 43 ft (13.1 m)
	wing area:
	height: 15 ft 1 in (4.6 m)
Speed:	max. Mach 1.8
	cruise:
Range:	radius 690+ miles (1,110+ km)
Ceiling:	
Armament:	1 20-mm Vulcan cannon M61A1 in F-35C
	2 Advanced Medium Range Air-to-Air Missiles (AMRAAM)
	2 1,000-pound (454-kg) bombs or missiles
Radar:	Advanced Electronically Scanned Array (AESA)

---

6 See David A. Fulghum, "JSF Reflection Is Golf Ball-Sized," *Aviation Week & Space Technology* (15 February 1999), pp. 27, 30.

7 Major variants of the General Dynamics F-111 Aardvark were the EF-111 electronic countermeasures aircraft, FB-111 strategic bomber, and RF-111 reconnaissance aircraft. The EF-111 was the last variant flown by the U.S. Air Force, and was replaced by the Navy–Marine Corps EA-6B Prowler.

A head-on view of an F-35B STOVL prototype. The Royal Navy plans to procure this aircraft to replace its ship-based Harriers. The Royal Air Force, which also flies Harriers, may follow suit. (Lockheed Martin)

An F-35B STOVL prototype with the exhaust angled in the aircraft's vertical-landing configuration. One X-35B prototype aircraft is in the National Air and Space Museum at Dulles, Virginia. (Lockheed Martin)

The F-35C variant will replace the Navy's carrier-based F-14 Tomcat and F/A-18C/D Hornets, although the Tomcats probably will be gone before the F-35C goes aboard carriers. The large JSF buy should encourage other nations to consider the plane. (Lockheed Martin)

A prototype F-35C variant of the JSF intended for carrier operation. The last major U.S. effort to develop a single basic aircraft for Navy, Marine Corps, and Air Force use—the TFX/F-111—had limited success. (Lockheed Martin)

Another view of the F-35B STOVL aircraft showing the general similarity to the F-35A and F-35C configurations. If successful, this "family" of aircraft will greatly reduce the cost of aircraft maintenance and training. (Lockeed Martin)

SHARP

The Shared Reconnaissance Pod (SHARP) is a multifunction reconnaissance system fitted to the F/A-18 Hornet to provide afloat commanders with real-time intelligence. It replaces the F-14 Tomcat/Tactical Air Reconnaissance Pod System (TARPS) capability.

SHARP contains both electro-optical and infrared cameras, with a datalink to surface ships or other aircraft. The pod is designed to easily be reconfigured with other sensors. The initial SHARP system could be used at altitudes up to 50,000 feet (15,245 m) to provide photography of targets approximately 50 nm (93 km) from the aircraft.

The pod, carried on the aircraft centerline, is the same size as the standard 330-gallon (1,140-liter) fuel tank.

Initially, four SHARP systems will be provided to each F/A-18F squadron, although the system is compatible with the F/A-18C, D, and E aircraft as well. The first SHARP-equipped squadron was VFA-41, deployed aboard the carrier NIMITZ in 2003; the squadron participated in Operation Iraqi Freedom.

Sailors from VFA-41 move a SHARP on the hangar deck of the carrier NIMITZ on the way to a maintenance shop. SHARP will replace the long-used Tactical Air Reconnaissance Pod System (TARPS) for tactical reconnaissance by carrier planes. (U.S. Navy/Tiffini M. Jones)

F/A-18E/F SUPER HORNET

This advanced Hornet series—unofficially referred to as the Super Hornet—is being produced as the principal fighter-attack aircraft for the Navy and Marine Corps. The F/A-18E is a single-seat aircraft, and the F/A-18F is a two-seat variant; they are enlarged and more capable successors to the F/A-18C and F/A-18D, respectively. Both the E and F variants are now in production for the Navy and Marine Corps, with a buy of 548 aircraft planned (see chapter introduction).

Officials of Boeing point to several advantages of the F/A-18E/F over the previous C/D variants:
- increased range
- increased payload
- enhanced maneuverability
- 10-knot (18.5 km) slower speed on landing approach
- easier to fly

The requirement for an enhanced F/A-18 first was mentioned in a 15 July 1987 memorandum from then-Secretary of Defense Caspar Weinberger to the Secretaries of the Navy and Air Force noting that, because the next-generation Navy attack aircraft and a replacement for the Air Force's F-16 fighter could not be available "for many years," the Navy should conduct studies derivatives of the F/A-18 and the Air Force should study F-16 upgrades as interim replacements.

In selecting the F/A-18E as the next-generation carrier-based fighter over several alternatives, including resumed production of the F-14D, then-Secretary of Defense Dick Cheney, in a letter to Senator Christopher Bond dated 29 July 1991, said the F/A-18E "was the clear choice over the F-14" based on reliability, safety, ease of maintenance, and operating costs: "It is three times more reliable, twice as easy to maintain, and has a safety record which is 50 percent better, requires about 25 [percent] fewer maintenance personnel, and costs about 25 percent less to operate per flight hour." Cheney concluded, "When combined, these factors clearly show that the FA-18E/F is the more cost effective aircraft."

Subsequently, the F/A-18E/F program has encountered several delays and higher-than-expected costs while, according to the General Accounting Office (GAO),

The operational deficiencies in the F/A-18C/D that the Navy cited in justifying the F/A-18E/F either have not materialized or can be corrected with nonstructural changes to the C/D. Furthermore, E/F operational capabilities will only be marginally improved over the C/D model. In addition, although the E/F will have increased range over the C/D model, the C/D's range will exceed the range required by the E/F's system specifications and the E/F's range increase is achieved at the expense of its aerial combat performance. Also, modifications to increase the E/F's payload have created a problem when weapons are released from the aircraft that may reduce the E/F's potential payload capability.[8]

Separate from the problems identified in the lengthy GAO report, on the seventh flight of the first F/A-18E (4 March 1996), naval test personnel detected a "wing-drop" phenomena in the aircraft. During certain high-speed maneuvers, the aircraft's wing would dip uncontrollably, caused by turbulence in the air passing over the wing. It took almost two years to develop a correction to the problem—perforated panels 5 feet (1.52 m) in length and made of composite material were fitted in each wing. With the wing-drop fixed, Secretary of Defense William Cohen approved low-rate production of the F/A-18E/F in April 1998.

The original Navy–Marine Corps requirement was for 1,000 aircraft; however, by the mid-1990s, the E/F goal had been reduced to just under 800 aircraft. Procurement began with the FY 1998 budget, with all 800 aircraft to be acquired by 2015. The production number was based on a squadron requirement (including readiness units) of 630 aircraft, plus 60 pipeline aircraft and about 100 aircraft for attrition through 2020. In addition, five F/A-18E and two F/A-18F aircraft were built specifically for the flight test program.

In 2003, the proposed Navy and Marine Corps "merger" of certain aviation units further reduced the total E/F buy.

The EA-18G Growler variant of the F/A-18F has been selected as the Navy–Marine Corps next-generation electronic attack aircraft. (see Electronic Aircraft).

---

8 General Accounting Office, *Navy Aviation: F/A-18E/F will Provide Marginal Operational Improvements at High Cost* (NSIAD-96-98) (June 1996), pp. 4-5.

Design: The E/F models are based on an enlarged and upgraded F/A-18C/D design. Compared to the earlier series, the E/F variants have a center section plug, 25 percent larger wings, and improved engines with 35 percent more thrust. The F414 engine is a derivative of the F404 used in earlier F/A-18s. Two wing stores stations were added, for a total of 11 on the fuselage and wings, plus two wingtip stations for the Sidewinder Air-to-Air Missile (AAM).

The E/F aircraft are fitted with a towed missile countermeasures system, more expendable chaff, and flare countermeasures. They are able to accommodate an in-flight refueling pod to permit the aircraft to serve in a limited tanker role while carrying two 480-gallon (1,817-liter) drop tanks.

The "spotting factor" or footprint on the carrier deck is 23 percent larger for the F/A-18E than for the F/A-18C.

Status: In production. First flight of the F/A-18E occurred on 29 November 1995; of the F/A-18F on 1 April 1996. The F/A-18E IOC was in 2001.

F/A-18E

Manufacturer:	Boeing and Northrop Grumman
Crew:	(1) pilot in F/A-18E
	(2) pilot, bombardier/navigator in F/A-18F
Engines:	2 General Electric F414-GE-400 turbofan;
	22,000 lbst (9,979 kgst) each
Weight:	empty: 30,500 lb (13,835 kg)
	gross: 66,000 lb (29,937 kg)
Dimensions:	length: 60 ft 4 in (18.38 m)
	wingspan: 44 ft 8½ in (13.63 m) with Sidewinder AAMs fitted
	wing area: 500 ft² (45 m²)
	height: 15 ft 10 in (4.83 m)
Speed:	max. 1,185 mph (1,900 kmh) at 37,000 ft (11,280 m); Mach 1.8
Range:	radius 230 miles (370 km) in fighter role with 1.8 hours on station (2 Sidewinders + 4 AMRAAMs)
	radius 483 miles (778 km) in fighter escort role (2 Sidewinders + 2 AMRAAMs)
	radius 546 miles (880 km) in interdiction role (2 Sidewinders + 4 1,000-lb/454-kg bombs)
Ceiling:	50,000 ft (15,244 m)
Armament:	1 20-mm Vulcan cannon M61A1 (multibarrel; 400 rounds)
	up to 17,750 lb (8,051 kg) of bombs, rockets, missiles, and external fuel tanks
Radar:	APG-73

F/A-18C/D HORNET

The Hornet strike-fighter is flown by the Navy and Marine Corps in significantly larger numbers than any other naval aircraft. Aboard carriers, the F/A-18 replaced the F-14 Tomcat and A-7 Corsair; in the Marine Corps, it replaced the F-4S Phantom fighter, A-6E Intruder, and A-4M Skyhawk attack aircraft and the RF-4B Phantom and OA-4 Skyhawk special-purpose aircraft.

Development of the F/A-18 came as a result of congressional pressure on the Navy to obtain a lightweight fighter to complement the F-14 in carrier air wings. Congress originally had directed the Navy to select the winner of the Air Force's lightweight fighter competition of the mid-1970s between the General Dynamics YF-16 and Northrop YF-17 prototypes. In the event, the Air Force selected the F-16 for production, and the Navy selected the YF-17, but made major modifications, leading to the F/A-18, developed jointly by McDonnell Douglas and Northrop. The naval aircraft failed to fully achieve its range/payload goals in the attack role.

The original F/A-18 procurement plan was for 11 development aircraft and 1,366 production planes for 24 Navy attack and 6 Navy fighter squadrons and 12 Marine fighter squadrons, plus 332 aircraft in reserve units and 142 attrition and pipeline aircraft. Actual procurement was less (see *Status* on page 408).

An F/A-18E Super Hornet from VFA-115 carries out touch-and-go landings aboard the carrier JOHN C. STENNIS (CVN 74) during training exercises off the California coast. (U.S. Navy/Mark J. Rebilas)

An F/A-18E Super Hornet flown by CVW-14 wing commander approaches the JOHN C. STENNIS during Operation Summer Pulse 2004 in the Pacific. There is a Sidewinder missile on the left wingtip. (U.S. Navy/Jayme Pastoric)

An F/A-18E Super Hornet from VFA-14 aboard the carrier NIMITZ (CVN 68) streaks low over the water. At the time, the NIMITZ carrier strike group was returning from a deployment. (U.S. Navy/Christopher L. Jordan)

An F/A-18F Super Hornet from VFA-41 carrying a Shared Reconnaissance Pod (SHARP) catches the No. 3 wire on the carrier NIMITZ. The aircraft also carries two drop tanks. The B, D, and F variants of the F/A-18 are two-seat aircraft. (U.S. Navy/Yesenia Rosas)

An F/A-18F Super Hornet from VFA-41 aboard the NIMITZ refuels another "Black Ace" during operations over the Persian Gulf. With the pending demise of the S-3B Viking, F/A-18s will be employed with "buddy stores" to serve as carrier-based tankers—a distraction from their strike-fighter role. (U.S. Navy)

The Navy–Marine Corps Blue Angels flight demonstration team began flying the F/A-18 in 1987; its aircraft are early, development models of the Hornet not normally considered carrier capable.[9] However, in on 11 November 1998, Commander Patrick Driscoll, the Blue Angels team leader, landed an F/A-18A aboard and took off from the HARRY S. TRUMAN.

The F/A-18 has been a controversial program because of the initial Marine Corps decision to procure the AV-8B Harrier instead of the F/A-18 for the attack role and because of the aircraft's higher-than-predicted costs and shorter range compared with the A-7. However, the F/A-18's widespread use has had a positive impact on cost and support, and its performance in Operation Desert Storm (1991) fulfilled its manufacturer's performance promises.

Design: A twin-engine, single- or two-seat aircraft, the F/A-18 is characterized by high maneuverability, the ability to operate in either the fighter or attack role with the push of a button, and comparatively low maintenance requirements. The initial versions were the F/A-18A strike-fighter and the TF-18 two-seat trainer, the latter now referred to as the F/A-18B. The F/A-18C is an improved single-seat aircraft, and the F/A-18D is a two-seat aircraft with a weapons officer in the rear seat (no flight controls).

The twin-engine aircraft is distinguished by swept leading wing edges and twin tail fins. The F/A-18 has wingtip Sidewinder AAM positions, as well as three fuselage and four wing stations for weapons and sensor/guidance pods. A variety of bombs, missiles, and rockets can be carried, including up to four 2,000-lb (907-kg) bombs.

Initially, the F/A-18 flew with a pod-mounted FLIR developed specifically for the aircraft (AAS-38). The F/A-18C/D models delivered after October 1989 have a night-attack capability based on a FLIR sensor called TINS (Thermal Imaging Navigation Set) and designated ARR-50, and an improved HUD. The F/A-18s delivered through mid-1994 have the APG-65 multimode, synthetic-aperture radar.

A proposed Northrop F-18L land-based variant has not been procured.

Designation: The initial Navy order for 11 development aircraft used the designation YF-18. The designation F/A-18A was used for initial single-seat aircraft and F/A-18B for those with tandem seating. See page 398 for further discussion of the F/A-18 designation.

Operational: More F/A-18s participated in the Persian Gulf War (January–February 1991) and the liberation of Iraq (March–April 2003) than any other fixed-wing naval aircraft. The aircraft also participated in the Kosovo/Bosnian campaign of 1999.

On 17 January 1991, two Navy F/A-18C aircraft shot down two Iraqi MiG-21 fighters using Sparrow and Sidewinder missiles.[10]

An F/A-18C Hornet from VFA-97 with wings folded taxis to a catapult aboard the carrier NIMITZ in the Persian Gulf. The wingtip rails hold Sidewinder missiles; three drop tanks are mounted on fuselage and wing pylons. (U.S. Navy/Angel G. Hilbrands)

Status: Operational; in production. First flight of the F/A-18A occurred on 18 November 1978; the F/A-18C on 18 November 1978; and the F/A-18D on 6 May 1988. Navy–Marine Corps F/A-18A IOC (with VFA-125) was in February 1981; Marine Corps F/A-18A IOC (with VMFA-314) in March 1983; and F/A-18D IOC (with VMFA[AW]-121) in May 1991.

F/A-18 Hornets are flown by Australia, Canada, Finland, South Korea, Kuwait, Malaysia, Spain, and Switzerland. The aircraft has been coproduced with Aerospace Technologies of Australia.

Almost all F/A-18A/B models have been retired from U.S. service.

F/A-18C

Manufacturer:	McDonnell Douglas and Northrop
Crew:	(1) pilot in F/A-18A/C
	(2) pilot, bombardier/navigator in F/A-18D
Engines:	2 General Electric F404-GE-400 turbofan; 16,000 lbst (7,258 kgst) each; F404-GE-402 engines with 17,700 lbst (8,029 kgst) in FY 1992 and later aircraft
Weight:	empty: 23,050 lb (10,455 kg)
	fighter mission normal T/O: 36,710 lb (16,651 kg)
	attack mission normal T/O: 49,224 lb (22,328 kg)
Dimensions:	length: 56 ft (17.07 m)
	wingspan: 37 ft 6 in (11.43 m)
	40 ft 5 in (12.31 m) with Sidewinder AAMs fitted
	wing area: 400 ft² (37.16m²)
	height: 15 ft 3½ in (4.66 m)
Speed:	max. 1,185 mph (1,900 kmh) at 37,000 ft (11,280 m); Mach 1.8
Ceiling:	50,000 ft (15,240 m)
Range:	radius 230 miles (370 km) in fighter role with 1 hour on station (2 Sidewinders + 4 AMRAAMs)
	radius 350 miles (565 km) in fighter escort role (2 Sidewinders + 2 AMRAAMs)
	radius 320 miles (513 km) in interdiction role (2 Sidewinders + 4 1,000-lb/454-kg bombs)
Armament:	1 20-mm Vulcan cannon M61 (multibarrel; 570 rounds)
	2 Sidewinder + 4 Sparrow/AMRAAM AAMs in fighter role or 2 Sidewinder AAMs + 17,000 lb (7,711 kg) of bombs, missiles, rockets in attack role
Radar:	APG-65 or APG-73

F-16N FIGHTING FALCON

The Navy flew 26 modified F-16C Fighting Falcon fighters in the adversary training role (replacing the F-21A Kfir). It took delivery of 22 single-seat F-16N and 4 two-seat TF-16N aircraft in 1987–1988, but these aircraft were grounded beginning in 1991 because of structural cracking in the center fuselage. They subsequently were disposed of.

The F-16 is the standard U.S. Air Force lightweight fighter, and also is flown by several allied air forces. The Navy F-16Ns were identical to the Air Force F-16C variant, but did not have the M61 20-mm Vulcan cannon; in addition, the Navy planes were fitted with the APG-66 radar of the earlier Air Force F-16A/B and had a more advanced engine.

The F-16 evolved from the 1972 Air Force Lightweight Fighter (LWF) competition, which sought a low-cost, air-superiority day fighter with high performance and ease of maintenance. The Air Force selected the General Dynamic's YF-16 over the Northrop YF-17, and the latter design was used as the basis for the Navy's F/A-18 Hornet series.

Operational: The F-16N/TF-16Ns were flown by the Navy Fighter Weapons School (Top Gun) and VF-43, VF-45, and VF-126.

---

9 See page 379 for previous Blue Angel aircraft.

10 On 17 January 1991, two Navy F/A-18 Hornets from the carrier SARATOGA on a bombing mission, each carrying four 2,000-pound (907-kg) bombs, were able to engage two Iraqi MiG-21 fighters. Both Iraqi planes were shot down with air-to-air missiles, after which the F/A-18s were able to continue their bombing mission, not having had to jettison their bombs to engage the enemy planes.

Two F/A-18C Hornets from VFA-34 and an F-14B Tomcat from VF-103 (left) based aboard the JOHN F. KENNEDY (CV 67) fly on patrol over Iraq. The F/A-18s carry Maverick air-to-ground missiles, but no Sidewinders because of the lack of an air threat over Iraq. (U.S. Air Force/Lee O. Tucker)

VMFA-115 is one of the few squadrons still flying the F/A-18A Hornet. This "Silver Eagle" aircraft was photographed over Iraq during Operation Iraqi Freedom while the Marine squadron was embarked in the HARRY S. TRUMAN (CVN 75). By coincidence, Navy squadron VFA-115 is known as the "Eagles." (U.S. Navy)

Navy-flown F-16s sit on the tarmac at the Navy Fighter Weapons School in Fallon, Nevada. These aircraft are useful for "dissimilar" aerial combat training, pitting Navy and Marine fighter pilots against non-familiar aircraft. The older F-5 series of fighters also is useful in that role. (U.S. Navy)

F-16A/B FIGHTING FALCON

The Navy currently operates ten F-16A and four F-16B in the adversary training role with the Fighter Weapons School. These aircraft are from a batch of 28 F-16s ordered by the Pakistani Air Force in 1992 but canceled by the U.S. government late in the George H. W. Bush administration because of Pakistan's nuclear weapons program. Islamabad paid $658 million for the aircraft in 1989, and an agreement was reached in late 1998 for U.S. repayment of that amount to Pakistan. (Pakistan previously had procured F-16A/B aircraft from the United States, the first arriving in country in January 1983.)

The 28 Falcons were mothballed and kept for almost a decade at Davis-Monthan Air Force Base in Arizona. In June 2002, the George W. Bush administration decided that 14 of the aircraft would go to the U.S. Navy and the remainder to the Air Force, the latter to the 412th Test Wing as chase planes.

The Navy's planes are Block 15A/B models with HUD avionics and improved engines compared to earlier F-16A/B aircraft.

Design: The F-16B is a combat-capable, two-seat trainer version of the F-16A, essentially an A model with a second cockpit in place of internal fuel cells. The exterior dimensions of the two aircraft are identical.

The F-16 is a Mach 2 multipurpose aircraft capable of day/night operations. It is a mid-wing design with a blended wing/body; the flaring of the wing/body intersection provides lift at high angles of attack and increased internal fuel volume. There is a large, distinctive engine intake under the fuselage. The swept-back tail configuration is relatively conservative.

Wingtip missile rails are provided for the Sidewinder AAM (as in the F/A-18 Hornet).

With limited internal fuel, the aircraft can carry 15,200 pounds (6,894 kg) of stores on one fuselage and six wing stations; with full internal fuel, the aircraft can carry 10,500 pounds (4,763 kg).

Operational: The F-16 is flown by the U.S. Air Force in greater numbers than any other combat aircraft. Twenty-two other countries also fly the F-16. Approximately 4,000 F-16s are in service worldwide, with production continuing in the United States and in other countries.[11]

Status: First flight of the YF-16 occurred on 20 January 1974; the F-16A on 8 December 1976, with IOC in October 1980. First flight of the F-16B occurred on 8 August 1977, with production aircraft deliveries beginning in 1978.

F-16 A/B

Manufacturer:	General Dynamics
Crew:	(1) pilot in F-16A
	(2) pilot and student in F-16B
Engines:	1 Pratt & Whitney F100-PW-200 turbofan; 23,830 lbst (10,810 kgst) with afterburner
Weight:	empty:
	gross: 33,000 lb (13,608 kg)
Dimensions:	length: 47 ft 8 in (14.53 m)
	wingspan: 32 ft 10 in (10.0 m) with missiles
	30 ft (9.15 m) without missiles or rails
	wing area:
	height: 16 ft 5 in (5.0 m)
Speed:	max. 1,345 mph (2,165 kmh)
	cruise: 577 mph (930 kmh)
Ceiling:	55,000 ft (16,768 m)
Range:	1,400 miles (2,253 km)
Armament:	1 20-mm Vulcan cannon M61A1 (multibarrel; 500 rounds various combinations of bombs, missiles, and rockets (see text)
Radar:	APG-68

---

11 F-16s have been manufactured in South Korea and Turkey, and have been assembled in Belgium and the Netherlands.

TARPS

The Tactical Air Reconnaissance Pod System (TARPS) was the only manned tactical airborne reconnaissance capability in the U.S. fleet following the retirement of Marine-flown RF-4B Phantoms in 1992. Each carrier air wing had one squadron with three F-14 Tomcats wired to carry the TARPS pod. As the Tomcats are withdrawn from service, the F-14/TARPS capability is being drawn down and should disappear by about 2008.

The TARPS is fitted with a digital imaging and data link to provide near-real-time imagery to commanders ashore and aboard ship. (Early versions, first introduced in the early 1980s, had reconnaissance imagery that had to be downloaded after the aircraft returned to the carrier.) The TARPS package contains a KS-87 frame camera, KA-99 panoramic camera, and AAD-5 infrared line scanner. It can be fitted to or removed from a standard aircraft in a few hours.

The F-14/TARPS, flown by nonspecialized reconnaissance pilots, does not provide the quality or quantity of tactical reconnaissance that was possible with some earlier carrier-based aircraft. That shortfall was keenly felt during Operation Desert Storm in 1991. According to the U.S. Director of Naval Intelligence at the time, Rear Admiral Thomas A. Brooks, the TARPS "was totally inadequate" in providing sufficient and timely bomb damage assessment.

When the F-14/TARPS is retired the ship-based reconnaissance role will be taken over by the F/A-18 Hornet fitted with

Crewmen work on a TARPS attached to an F-14 Tomcat aboard the carrier GEORGE WASHINGTON. This system will be retired in the near future as the last F-14 squadrons are removed from carriers. (U.S. Navy/Brian Fleske)

the Shared Reconnaissance Pod (SHARP), as well as by unmanned aerial vehicles.

F-14 TOMCAT

The F-14 was the standard U.S. Navy carrier-based fighter of the 1970s and 1980s, with two squadrons normally assigned to each carrier air wing. The aircraft now is being phased out of service in favor of the F/A-18 Hornet, with the last F-14 squadron scheduled to convert to the newer aircraft in 2008.

Designed to intercept Soviet long-range strike aircraft, in several respects the F-14 remains the most-capable long-range, all-weather fighter in service with any air force.

The F-14 originally was planned for Marine Corps use, but that service turned it down, in part because of its decision to procure the AV-8A Harrier.

Design: A two-seat aircraft, the F-14 has variable-geometry wings that sweep back as the aircraft maneuvers during flight; they extend for long-range flight and landings and sweep back for high-speed flight (and carrier stowage). Normal sweep range is 20°–68°, with a 75° "oversweep" position provided for shipboard hangar stowage; sweep speed is 7.5° per second.

The F-14 has the long-range AWG-9 radar, which can detect hostile aircraft out to more than 100 miles (161 km) and simultaneously track up to 24 targets, and the Phoenix missile, which can engage targets more than 60 miles (96.5 km) away. The basic F-14 suite includes the ALR-45 and ALR-50 radar warning receivers, ALE-29 and ALE-39 chaff/flare dispensers, and ALQ-100 deception jamming pod. A forward-looking AXX-1 television camera is fitted for long-range visual detection.

All surviving F-14s are fitted with the AAQ-14 LANTIRN (Low Altitude Navigation and Targeting Infrared for Night) pod for aiming laser-guided munitions. (The first F-14 squadron to receive LANTIRN was VF 103, which deployed aboard the carrier ENTERPRISE in July 1996.)

Up to 14,500 pounds (6,577 kg) of external stores can be carried by the F-14. The aircraft originally had a total of four fuselage missile positions (four Sparrow or four Phoenix) and two wing missile positions (four Sidewinder or two Sparrow or two Phoenix); alternatively, fuel tanks or a TARPS could be carried with a reduced missile load. Subsequently, the F-14B/D have been fitted with racks for "iron bombs" and laser-guided bombs (GBU); the F-14D also has pylon adapters for HARM and Harpoon air-to-surface missiles.[12]

Only about 80 F-14A variants originally were to have been procured; subsequent aircraft were to have been the F-14B with F401-PW-400 engines and, later, the F-14C, also with an avionics upgrade. In the event, only the F-14A model was produced through the mid-1980s. (The Navy had planned an F-14 upgrade with improved engines and air-to-surface weapons in the 1970s, but those programs were halted for lack of funds.)

Engine problems plagued the F-14A, and the F-14A+ were fitted with F110-GE-400 engines (formerly F101 DFE), but otherwise were similar to the basic F-14A. The F-14A+ was changed to F-14B in 1991; previously, one F-14A had been reengined and designated F-14B. The follow-on F-14D has the APG-71 synthetic-aperture radar and other improvements, including a capability for the AMRAAM. The F-14B/D have F110-GE-400 engines, which provide an increased radius (deck-launched intercept) from 155 to 240 miles (250–390 km) and a maximum catapult weight increase from 59,000 pounds (26,762 kg) to 74,000 pounds (33,566 kg).

The Navy decided in early 1984 to procure 324 F-14D models with the F110 engines and upgraded avionics. In early 1989, however, the Department of Defense halted new procurement in favor of the "remanufacture" of 400 earlier F-14A aircraft. Subsequently, in 1991, the Navy decided to remanufacture only 104 F-14A to the F-14D configuration by 1997, in an unsuccessful effort to garner funds for new F-14D production. In the event, only 37 new F-14D aircraft and 18 F-14A upgrades to full F-14D configurations were procured.

The F-14C variant was to have been a development of the original (engine update) F-14B with improved avionics. Several research variants were designated NF-14D.

Operational: The first use of the Tomcat in the air-to-ground role in combat occurred on 5 September 1995, when an F-14A from the carrier THEODORE ROOSEVELT dropped two 2,000-pound (907-kg) bombs on Serb positions in Bosnia.

Status: Operational; no longer in production. First flight of the F-14A occurred on 21 December 1970; the F-14B (F-14A engine conversion) on 29 September 1986; and the F-14A+ on 24 November 1987. IOC for the F-14A (with VF-124) was in January 1973; for the F-14D in November 1990.

The last F-14 was delivered in May 1992. A total of 632 aircraft were produced for the U.S. Navy: 557 F-14A (including development models), 38 F-14A+ (redesignated F-14B), and 37 new F-14D variants. Subsequently, the following F-14A conversions were undertaken: 1 F-14A to F-14B (engine change only, in 1973); 32 to F-14A+; 3 to F-14D electronic test bed aircraft; and 18 to F-14D. The last F-14A was phased out of fleet squadrons in 2004.

An additional 80 F-14A aircraft were built for Iran; 79 were delivered in 1976–1979 with 1 retained by Grumman because of the Iranian revolution.

---

12 GBU = Guided Bomb Unit, referring to the guidance package fitted to Mk 82 (500-lb), Mk 83 (1,000-lb), and Mk 4 (2,000-lb) bombs.

An F-14B from VF-103 aboard the JOHN F. KENNEDY wearing flamboyant markings, including the Jolly Roger insignia previously worn by VF-84—the "Jolly Rogers." Shortly after this photo was taken in August 2004, the squadron began transitioning to the F/A-18F Super Hornet. (U.S. Air Force/Lee O. Tucker)

F-14D

Manufacturer:	Grumman
Crew:	(2) pilot, radar-intercept officer
Engines:	F-14A: 2 Pratt & Whitney TF30-P-414A turbofan; 20,900 lbst (9,480 kgst) each with afterburning
	F-14B/D: 2 General Electric F110-GE-400 turbofan; 27,000 lbst (12,150 kg) each with afterburning
Weight:	empty: 41,780 lb (18,951 kg)
	T/O with 4 Sparrow AAMs/AMRAAM: 59,714 lb (27,086 kg)
	T/O with 6 Phoenix AAMs: 70,764 lb (32,098 kg)
	max. T/O: 74,350 lb (33,725 kg)
Dimensions:	length: 62 ft 8 in (19.1 m)
	wingspan: 64 ft 1½ in (19.54 m) unswept
	38 ft 2½ in (11.65 m) swept back
	wing area: 565 ft² (52.49m²)
	height: 16 ft (4.88 m)
Speed:	max. 1,544 mph (2,485 kmh) at altitude
	912 mph (1,468 kmh) at low level
	max. cruise: 633 mph (1,019 kmh)
Ceiling:	56,000 ft (17,070 m)
Range:	radius approx. 575 miles (925 km) in strike role
	1,065 miles (1,715 km) in air intercept role
	ferry: 2,000 miles (3,220 km) with 2 267-gallon (1,015-liter) drop tanks
Armament:	1 20-mm Vulcan cannon M61 (multibarrel; 676 rounds)
	2 Phoenix + 3 Sparrow/AMRAAM + 2 Sidewinder AAMs + 2 267-gallon (1,015-liter) drop tanks
	or 4 Phoenix + 2 Sparrow/AMRAAM + 2 Sidewinder AAMs + 2 267-gallon drop tanks
	or 6 Phoenix + 2 Sidewinder AAMs + 2 267-gallon drop tanks
	or 6 Sparrow/AMRAAM + 2 Sidewinder AAMs + 2 267-gallon drop tanks
	max. 14,500 lb (6,575 kg) missiles, bombs, rockets, drop tanks
Radar:	F-14A: AWG-9
	F-14D: APG-71

The rear end of an F-14D Tomcat from VF-31. The F-14 is being retired, although it remains one of the world's most capable all-weather fighter-attack aircraft. (U.S. Navy/J. Scott Campbell)

An F-14D Tomcat from VF-31 makes an arrested landing aboard the JOHN C. STENNIS during an exercise in the Pacific. Note the large, rectangular air intakes with drop tanks attached. The F-14 was intended for the strike as well as the fighter role from its inception. (U.S. Navy/Mark J. Rebilas)

An F-14B Tomcat from VF-103 launches from the JOHN F. KENNEDY during operations in the Persian Gulf. The wings are fully extended; they "tuck in" for high-speed flight. The F-14 is one of the few successful swing-wing (variable-sweep) aircraft. (U.S. Navy/Michael Sandberg)

An F-14B Tomcat from VF-32 landing aboard the HARRY S. TRUMAN in a "dirty" condition with landing gear and arresting hook lowered. The F-14 was too large and required too much support to operate from carriers of the MIDWAY (CV 41) class. (U.S. Navy/Mark Gleason)

F-5E/F TIGER II

The F-5E/F variants of the F-5 lightweight fighter are flown by the Navy as air combat maneuvering/adversary training aircraft. They were the penultimate design in a long series of trainer/ fighter aircraft developed by Northrop, primarily for Third World markets. (The much-improved F-5G was redesignated F-20.)

Design: The F-5E Tiger is a single-seat aircraft, and the F-5F is the two-seat version, both with two turbojet engines. Sidewinder AAMs can be carried on wingtips, and there are four wing and one fuselage station for ordnance.

The aircraft are not carrier capable.

Status: Operational; no longer in production. First flight of the F-5A was on 30 July 1959; the F-5E on 11 August 1972.

More than 3,000 F-5 fighters and similar T-38 Talon trainers have been built for the U.S. Air Force and some 25 foreign nations. The U.S. Navy has 32 F-5E variants and 4 F-5F aircraft (plus 11 T-38s) to simulate Russian fighter aircraft in adversary training. The Marines previously flew the F-5E/F in reserve adversary training squadron VMFT-401.

F-5 E/F

Manufacturer:	Northrop
Crew:	(1)pilot
	(2) pilot and student in F-5F
Engines:	2 General Electric J85-GE-21B turbojet; 5,000 lbst (2,268 kgst) each with afterburning
Weight:	empty F-5E: 9,723 lb (4,410 kg)
	F-5F: 10,576 lb (4,797 kg)
	gross F-5E: 24,722 lb (11,214 kg)
	F-5F: 25,152 lb (11,409 kg)
Dimensions:	length F-5E: 47 ft 4¾ in (14.45 m)
	F-5F: 51 ft 4 in (15.65 m)
	wingspan: 26 ft 8 in (8.13 m)
	wing area: 186 ft² (17.3 m²)
	height F-5E: 13 ft 4 in (4.06 m)
	F-5F: 13 ft 1¾ in (4.01 m)
Speed:	max. Mach 1.64 at 36,000 ft (10,975 m)
Ceiling:	51,800 ft (15,790 m)
Range:	radius 655 miles (1,056 km) with 2 Sidewinder AAMs
	1,775 miles (2,861 km) with external tanks
Armament:	none
Radar:	APQ-159

In Navy markings, this F-5E Tiger II shows the stub wings and twin engines of this lightweight fighter. In naval service, these aircraft are camouflaged, reflecting the paint scheme of many Third World air forces. (Northrop/Michael Benolkin)

An F-5E Tiger II in Marine markings. Both the Navy and Marine Corps have flown the F-5E and two-seat F-5F to provide stand-ins for high-performance MiG-21 type aircraft, which still are flown by many Third World countries. (Northrop/Michael Benolkin)

F-4 PHANTOM

Long the principal all-weather, multipurpose fighters of the Navy and Marine Corps, all F-4 Phantoms have been retired from combat squadrons, replaced by the F-14 Tomcat in Navy fighter squadrons (VF) and by the F/A-18 Hornet in Marine Corps fighter-attack squadrons (VMFA).

A few Phantoms designated QF-4N/S still were in use as radio-controlled target drones in 2004.

McDonnell Douglas produced 5,211 Phantom aircraft for U.S. and foreign service, and Japan built 138 F-4EJ variants, including 11 from parts produced by McDonnell Douglas. Production ended in 1979; the last of 1,264 aircraft delivered to the Navy and Marine Corps were completed in December 1971 (including 46 of the RF-4B reconnaissance variant). The principal U.S. naval production versions were the F-4B and F-4J, which subsequently were upgraded to the F-4N and F-4S, respectively. The Phantom no longer is in service with the U.S. Air Force, but still is flown by several other nations.[13]

The last Navy squadron to fly the Phantom, reserve VF-202, retired its last F-4S in early 1987; the last Marine Corps unit, also flying the F-4S, was reserve VMFA-112, which phased out its last Phantoms in mid-1992. All RF-4B reconnaissance variants have been retired from Marine Corps service, the last in 1992.

Designation: The Phantom originally was designated F4H by the Navy and F-110 by the Air Force; both those designations were changed to F-4 in 1962.

See 14th Edition/pages 401–2 for characteristics.

MARITIME PATROL/ASW AIRCRAFT

For the first decade of the 21st century, the U.S. Navy has a requirement for 300 land-based maritime patrol aircraft for active and reserve patrol squadrons, plus special-purpose aircraft (EP-3, RP-3, etc.). This requirement compares to more than 400 P-3 aircraft in service in 1990 and 230 operational in 2000 (plus EP-3 electronic, NP-3D research, VP-3 transport, and UP-3 utility aircraft). However, in 2003, the Navy announced plans to reduce the number of patrol aircraft by about one-half because of the age of the existing P-3C force.

All first-line U.S. maritime patrol aircraft are P-3C variants, with various levels of the Update-series of modernizations.

Following cancellation of the P-7 LRAACA program in 1990, the Navy began examining options to meet future requirements for maritime patrol aircraft. After several false starts, the MMA will be the P-3 successor.

MULTIMISSION MARITIME AIRCRAFT

The MMA—which is expected to be designated P-8—is planned to replace the Navy's P-3C and possibly EP-3E Orion aircraft. A derivative of the Boeing 737-800 was selected for the MMA role on 14 June 2004, following a competition with Lockheed Martin's Orion 21, an upgrade of the P-3. The winning MMA design is being developed by a team comprised of Boeing, CFM International, Northrop Grumman, Raytheon, and Smiths Aerospace.

The 737-800, originally designated Boeing 737-400X Stretched, is in widespread commercial use—more than 1,000 have been ordered. Up to 162 passengers can be carried.

Navy planning provides for an IOC of about FY 2012 with 22 aircraft. A total program of 120–150 aircraft initially was proposed, but this was cut to 108 in 2003 (see above).

The MMA will have the APS-137 maritime surveillance radar, other sensors, advanced tactical data and communications systems, and an internal weapons bay for Anti-Submarine Warfare (ASW) torpedoes.

While an ELINT collection variant generally is discussed to replace the 11 EP-3Es, in 2003, the Chief of Naval Operations decided to pursue the Army's Aerial Common Sensor (ACS) as a successor to that aircraft.

Status: In development. The commercial Boeing 737-800 first flew on 31 July 1997, and the first commercial deliveries took place in 1998.

The following data are for the 737-800 commercial aircraft.

737-800	
Manufacturer:	Boeing
Crew:	(2) pilot, copilot + service personnel
Engines:	2 CFM International CFM56-7B27A turbofan; 27,300 lbst (12,380 kgst) each
Weights:	empty: 90,710 lb (41,145 kg)
	maximum T/O: 155,500 lb (70,535 kg)
Dimensions:	length: 138 ft 2 in (42.1 m)
	wingspan: 117 ft 5 in (35.8 m)
	wing area: 1,344 ft² (125.0 m²)
	height: 41 ft 2 in (12.5 m)
Speed:	maximum: approx. 575 mph (925 kmh)
	cruise:
Ceiling:	41,000 ft (12,500 m)
Range:	with 162 passengers: 2,290 miles (3,585 km)
	at maximum weight: 3,380 miles (5,445 km)

---

13 The Royal Navy flew Phantoms from aircraft carriers with the F-4K being Britain's last non-VSTOL carrier-based fighter-attack aircraft; all now discarded.

An artist's depiction of the Multimission Maritime Aircraft (MMA), the long-awaited replacement for the Lockheed P-3 Orion. Lockheed has produced a long line of Navy land-based patrol aircraft: the PBO Hudson, PV Ventura and Harpoon, P2V/P-2 Neptune, and P3V/P-3 Orion. (Boeing Company)

A Boeing 737 Business Jet 2 aircraft that was used to demonstrate the capabilities of the proposed Boeing 373 MMA to Navy officials. Note the aircraft's tall tail and winglets. (Boeing Company)

P-7A LRAACA

The P-7 Long-Range Air Anti-Submarine Warfare Capable Aircraft was intended as a replacement for the P-3 Orion in the maritime patrol and ASW roles. Development and procurement of the P-7 were canceled by the Navy on 20 July 1990 because the contractor, Lockheed, "failed to make adequate progress toward completion of all contract phases, which were to have resulted in the delivery of two prototype aircraft in April and December 1992."

The Navy held the competition for the P-3 replacement in the mid-1980s, with the Lockheed design, the Boeing 757, and the McDonnell Douglas MD-90 competing. The modified P-3 design submitted by Lockheed was selected in October 1988 on the basis of acquisition and life-cycle costs, according to the Navy.[14] The $3.5-billion program was badly needed at Lockheed, as the last P-3 Orion was scheduled to come off the production line in September 1991, and few other aircraft were on the order book.

Lockheed subsequently experienced major cost problems with the P-7 program, as well as some technical difficulties. In March 1989—shortly before cancellation—the estimated acquisition cost for 125 P-7A aircraft was about $7.9 billion, with an estimated production cost of $56.7 million per aircraft. The technical problems were particularly perplexing to observers because the Lockheed design was in several respects an enlarged P-3, with less technical innovation than the competitive designs.

The LRAACA bore a strong resemblance to the P-3 Orion; there was to be a large internal weapons bay, plus 12 wing hard points for weapons. The four GE-38 engines were estimated to have a 25

---

14 Boeing proposed a modified version of the 757 twin-engine commercial transport and McDonnell Douglas a modified MD-87 twin-engine transport, the latter with ultra-high-bypass-ratio engines. Gulfstream Aerospace also had proposed a twin-engine, wide-body Gulfstream 4 for the LRAACA program, but it was not accepted as a viable competitor.

percent lower fuel consumption over the aircraft operating envelope compared with the P-3's T56 engines. The improved performance was due in part to five-blade composite propellers.

Initial Navy planning was for 125 aircraft plus two prototypes, to be delivered from 1994 through 2001, but more aircraft were anticipated, in addition to eventual foreign orders. The German government in April 1988 announced that it planned to select the P-7 to replace its Dassault-Breguet Atlantic ASW aircraft for long-range maritime patrol duties.

See 16th Edition/pages 375–76 for characteristics.

P-3C ORION

The Orion is a long-range maritime reconnaissance and ASW aircraft, with the Harpoon anti-ship missile (ASM) providing a surface attack capability. The P-3C Orion serves in all active and reserve Navy patrol squadrons (VP/VPU), with several specialized ELINT, research, and utility variants also in naval service—a current total of some 240 aircraft.

The decision not to procure the P-7 necessitated further upgrades to the P-3 force. P-3s are expected to remain in U.S. Navy patrol squadrons at least through 2015, when they will be succeed by the MMA.

Design: The Orion was adapted from the commercial Electra transport, with a lengthened fuselage and other design modifications. It is powered by four turboprop engines. Up to 15,000 pounds (6,804 kg) of rockets, missiles, mines, ASW torpedoes, or nuclear depth bombs can be carried in the internal weapons bay and on ten wing pylons. The P-3C aircraft are fitted to carry the Harpoon. (In the early 1970s, some P-3B variants were fitted to carry the AGM-12 Bullpup missile.) The plane's ASW equipment includes radar, a tail-mounted ASQ-81 Magnetic Anomaly Detector (MAD) and 48 external (fuselage) sonobuoy chutes and four in-flight reloadable (internal) chutes; a total of 84 buoys normally are carried.

The P-3C variants have undergone a series of modernizations: Update I of the mid-1970s included a computer upgrade, the Omega navigation system, additional tactical displays, and a new tactical program for computer-aided analysis of incoming data. Update II, introduced in 1977, had additional navigation capabilities and provision for Harpoon. Update III, introduced in 1984, provided an IBM Proteus signal processor system and new avionics. An Update IV implemented in the 1990s primarily provided improvements in signal processing; the Raytheon APS-137(V) surveillance radar also was fitted. Plans to provide an in-flight refueling capability have not been pursued.

Several specialized P-3 variants are in U.S. Navy service. The EP-3E is listed separately under Electronic Aircraft. Thirteen NP-3C/D aircraft are flown in various research configurations by the Navy; these previously were designated RP-3A/D, EP-3A/B, and several UP-3A testbed variants. The Navy also flies three UP-3A and four VP-3A "bob-tailed" (sans MAD "stinger") aircraft as executive transports and support aircraft.

Two WP-3D are operated by the National Oceanic and Atmospheric Administration (NOAA), and several P-3A aircraft have been on loan to the Customs Service for anti-drug surveillance since October 1985 (those aircraft have been fitted with an APG-53 radar, as in the Air Force F-15 fighter, one with an APS-125 radar with rotodome antenna, as in the E-2C, and one with an APS-138 radar). NASA flies one P-3B.

A planned P-3G maritime patrol/ASW aircraft for the U.S. Navy was to have had new engines and updated avionics. (That aircraft was incorrectly identified as a P-3F in some official documents; six P-3F variants were produced for Iran.) Procurement of

125 of this model in FY 1990–1995 was envisioned; however, the Navy did not pursue the P-3G option because only Lockheed responded to the request for a proposal, and the P-7 LRAACA was developed in its place. Proposals also were being considered to reengine and upgrade the avionics of the P-3C force, with a possible enlargement of the weapons bay to carry extended-range Harpoon missiles internally, that upgrade being labeled the P-3H.

Designation: The Orion originally was designated P3V; it was changed to P-3 in 1962.

Status: Operational; no longer in production. First flight of the aerodynamic airframe occurred on 19 August 1958; the YP-3A on 25 November 1959; the P-3A on 15 April 1961; and the YP-3C on 18 September 1968. P-3A IOC (with VP-8) was in August 1962; P-3C IOC in 1969.

Lockheed facilities at Burbank and Palmdale, California, delivered a total of 551 Orions to the U.S. Navy. The last to be produced was a P-3C delivered on 17 April 1990.

More than 700 Orions were produced in the United States by Lockheed; the last Lockheed-Palmdale aircraft was a CP-140A for the Canadian Forces, completed in May 1991. Eight P-3C aircraft for South Korea were delivered by the Lockheed Martin facility at Marietta, Georgia, in 1995. Kawasaki in Japan assembled five airframes produced by Lockheed and, under license, built more than 100 P-3C, EP-3, UP-3C, and UP-3D aircraft for the Japanese Maritime Self-Defense Force.[15]

---

15 The single Japanese UP-3C is an in-flight electronic systems testbed aircraft; the UP-3D aircraft support fleet EW training.

A P-3C Orion demonstrates the aircraft's weapons capability: The weapons bay is open and mounted under the wings are two Sidewinder Air-to-Air Missiles (AAM) (outermost pylons) and four Harpoon Anti-Ship Missiles (ASM). The Orion can also carry Maverick ASMs in addition to ASW weapons and mines. (U.S. Navy)

Orions—new and ex-U.S. Navy—are flown by 15 other countries: Argentina, Australia, Canada, Chile, Greece, Iran, Japan, the Netherlands, New Zealand, Norway, Pakistan, Portugal, South Korea, Spain, and Thailand.

P-3C

Manufacturer:	Lockheed
Crew:	(10) command pilot, 2 pilots, flight engineer, navigator/communications officer, tactical coordinator, 3 systems operators; 1 technician; plus provisions for 2 additional observers
Engines:	4 Allison T56-A-14 turboprop; 4,910 shp each
Weight:	empty: 61,491 lb (27,892 kg)
	normal T/O: 35,000 lb (61,236 kg)
	max. T/O: 142,000 lb (64,411 kg)
Dimensions:	length: 116 ft 10 in (35.61 m)
	wingspan: 99 ft 8 in (30.37 m)
	wing area: 1,300 ft² (120.77 m²)
	height: 33 ft 8½ in (10.29 m)
Speed:	max. 473 mph (761 kmh) at 15,000 ft (4,573 m)
	cruise: 380 mph (611 kmh) at 25,000 ft (7,622 m)
	loiter: 230 mph (370 kmh) with two engines shut down
Ceiling:	28,300 ft (8,628 m)
Range:	radius 1,550 miles (2,493 km) with 13 hours on station

Armament:	weapons bay	wing points
	8 Mk 46/50 torpedoes	+ 4 Mk 46/50 torpedoes
or	2 2,000-lb mines	+ 4 Mk 46/50 torpedoes
or	4 1,000-lb mines	+ 4 Mk 46/50 torpedoes
or	8 Mk 46/50 torpedoes	+ 16 5-inch rockets
	or	HARM ASM, Maverick ASM

Radar:	EP-3B/E: APS-20
	P-3C: APS-115 or APS-137(V)

A P-3C Orion from VP-30—the Orion Replacement Air Group (RAG) squadron—shows the aircraft's open weapons bay, chutes of the sonobuoy dispenser, "bumps" of various electric antennas, and the Magnetic Anomaly Detection (MAD) boom, or "stinger." (U.S. Navy/Damon J. Moritz)

A P-3C Orion from VP-46 taxis prior to takeoff from Al Salam Air Base in Kuwait. The Orions regularly forward deploy in support of deployed fleets. In the Afghanistan and Iraq conflicts, the P-3s also provided extensive overland surveillance and communications relay. (U.S. Navy/Chris Otsen)

A P-3C Orion from VP-16 over the Mediterranean Sea. The aircraft was operating from the NATO airfield at Souda Bay, Crete, which is invaluable for supporting U.S. naval operations in the Med by providing a base for maritime patrol and transport aircraft. (U.S. Navy/Paul Farley)

S-3B VIKING

The S-3 Viking is a carrier-based surveillance/tanker aircraft, with one six-plane squadron serving on board most carriers. The Viking was built to replace the S2F/S-2 Tracker as the Navy's ship-based, fixed-wing ASW aircraft.

From 1993, the S-3B was considered a "sea control" rather than an ASW aircraft, and in the mid-1990s, the ASW equipment and operators were removed. Thus configured, they are employed in ocean surveillance, anti-shipping (with Harpoon and Maverick air-to-surface missiles/ASM), and aerial tanking (with external drogue pod and fuel tanks). The last role is particularly significant because of the demise of the KA-6D Intruder tanker aircraft and the relatively short range of the F/A-18 Hornet.

All surviving aircraft are the S-3B configuration. They will be discarded by 2009.

Design: The S-3 was designed to be within the approximate dimensions of the piston-engine Tracker, but to be faster and to carry more advanced ASW equipment. The internal weapons bay, sized to hold four lightweight ASW torpedoes, can carry 2,400 pounds (1,089 kg) of weapons or auxiliary fuel tanks. There also are two wing pylons, which in the S-3B are upgraded to carry Harpoon. The S-3B has an improved acoustic processor and the improved APS-137 Inverse Synthetic Aperture Radar (ISAR), and a major avionics upgrade program for 124 S-3B aircraft was begun in 1995. (ASW systems included the ASQ-81 MAD, FLIR, and 60 sonobuoys in fuselage chutes.)

The wings and tail fin fold for carrier stowage.

Five preproduction S-3A aircraft were modified to a US-3A cargo configuration for operation from carriers in the Western Pacific and Indian Ocean; those planes were taken out of service in the early 1990s (see 15th Edition/pages 414–15). A KS-3 tanker configuration was proposed, as well as pod tanks and a drogue system for the US-3A variant; however, no development of a specialized tanker was undertaken.

Sixteen S-3A aircraft were converted to the ELINT role and were designated ES-3A (see Electronic Aircraft).

Operational: S-3A/B aircraft served in the ground attack role in low-threat areas during Operation Desert Storm in 1991.

Status: Operational; no longer in production. First flight of the S-3A occurred on 21 January 1972. S-3A IOC (with VS-41) was in February 1974.

The last of 187 S-3A aircraft was completed in 1978. About 160 were upgraded to S-3B by 1994. Proposals for additional S-3 production have not come to fruition.

S-3B

Manufacturer:	Lockheed
Crew:	(2) pilot, copilot, plus 2 passengers
Engines:	2 General Electric TF34-GE-400 turbofan; 9,275 lbst (4,207 kgst) each
Weight:	empty: 26,783 lb (12,149 kg)
	gross: 52,539 lb (23,832 kg)
Dimensions:	length: 53 ft 4 in (16.26 m)
	wingspan: 68 ft 8 in (20.93 m)
	wing area: 598 ft² (55.56 m²)
	height: 22 ft 9 in (6.94 m)
Speed:	max. 506 mph (814 kmh) at sea level
	cruise: 400+ mph (644+ kmh)
	loiter: 240 mph (386 kmh) at 20,000 ft (6,098 m)
Ceiling:	40,000 ft (12,195 m)
Range:	patrol: 2,645+ miles (4,260+ km)
	ferry: 3,450+ miles (5,556+ km)
Armament:	*weapons bay* *wing points*
(ASW configuration)	4 Mk 46/50 torpedoes + 6 500-lb bombs
	or 4 500-lb bombs + 6 500-lb bombs
Radar:	APS-137 ISAR

An S-3B Viking from VS-29 flies low over the Pacific, ready to refuel other aircraft from the carrier NIMITZ. The Vikings are being phased out of service, having already lost their Anti-Submarine Warfare (ASW) capabilities. (U.S. Navy/Kristi J. Earl)

Close to its home base of NAS North Island, an S-3B Viking from VS-41 poses over downtown San Diego. VS-41 is the RAG squadron for the Viking. All Vikings will be gone from the fleet by 2009. SH-60F and MH-60R helicopters now are the only carrier-based ASW aircraft. (U.S. Navy/Tomothy Smith)

ELECTRONIC AIRCRAFT

U.S. naval electronic aircraft have two distinct types of designations: those with E-series designations that were designed specifically for an electronic mission (e.g., E-2C, E-6B), and those that have been adapted from other aircraft types and have an E prefix added to their original designations (e.g., EA-18G, EA-6B, EP-3E). In this subsection, all electronic aircraft are listed in alphabetical sequence by designation, which is not their chronological order.

In addition to the electronic aircraft discussed here, the Customs Service flies AEW-configured P-3 Orions and the Coast Guard evaluated an AEW-configured C-130 Hercules, as well as E-2 Hawkeyes. The Coast Guard's C-130 AEW aircraft is now flown by the Navy as an NC-130H.

AERIAL COMMON SENSOR PROGRAM

The Navy has joined the U.S. Army's Aerial Common Sensor (ACS) program. This decision will result in a common Army–Navy aircraft and airborne Intelligence, Surveillance, Reconnaissance (ISR) and target identification system. The ACS program will replace the Navy's EP-3E Orion/ARIES II aircraft, as well as the Army's Guardrail aircraft.

ACS will provide instantaneous access to decision-quality intelligence from manned, unmanned, and space-based ISR systems. It will provide Army and Navy commanders with persistent surveillance, allowing them to see a complete representation of the battle space, and help enable network-centric operations. A Navy official stated that the Army ACS program "ended up having all the attributes that we wanted on it." Rear Admiral Mark Fitzgerald, Director of Air Warfare, explained, "Instead of doing things we do on board the EP-3, you could [have] a smaller airplane with the capacity to do the important tactical things on board, and send the intelligence collections off-board through satellites back to a place where it could be processed."[16]

The aircraft component of the ACS will be the Brasilia Embraer ERJ 145, a twin turbofan passenger aircraft now flying in commercial as well as military electronic configurations for several countries. (The designation ERJ indicates Embraer Regional Jet.)

In August 2004, the Army awarded a contract to develop the ACS to the Lockheed Martin-led team, which includes Argon

Engineering, BAE Systems, General Dynamics, Harris, L-3 Communications and Raytheon. This team was selected following competition with a team led by Northrop Grumman, which would have used the Gulfstream G450 as the aircraft platform. (The Brasilia ERJ 145 aircraft had been selected earlier as the ACS platform.)

The ERJ 145/ACS system is planned for initial testing in 2006, with full-scale production expected to begin in 2009. Current Army plans are to procure 39 aircraft, and the Navy up to 19. Embraer will construct a plant in Jacksonville, Florida, to produce the ACS aircraft.

Design: The aircraft has a circular cross section fuselage, rear-mounted engine pods, low-mounted swept wings, and a T-tailplane. The commercial variants of the ERJ 145 accommodate approximately 50 passengers.

The AEW variants have the fixed, blade-type antenna for the Erieye pulse-Doppler radar developed by Ericsson Microwave Systems of Sweden. The Erieye is capable of 360° detection and tracking of air and sea targets; the instrumented range is 280 miles (450 km), and a typical detection range against a target the size of a fighter aircraft is in excess of 215 miles (350 km).

Status: The first flight of the ERJ 145 occurred on 11 August 1995; the first commercial delivery was made in December 1996. Several hundred commercial aircraft have been delivered or are on order.

Militarized versions of the ERJ 145 generally are known as the EMB 145. The Brazilian Air Force has taken delivery of five AEW variants and three remote sensing variants; the Greek Air Force has acquired four AEW variants; and Mexico has procured one surveillance aircraft. The first militarized version, for the Brazilian Air Force, was delivered in July 2002.

The following data reflect the EMB 145/AEW variant.

EMB 145

Manufacturer:	Brasilia Embraer
Crew:	(7) pilot, copilot, 5 mission systems specialists + 3 relief crewmen
Engines:	2 Allison AE3007A1S turbofan; 7,426 lbst (3,368 kg) each
Weights:	empty: maximum T/O: 45,415 lb (20,600 kg)
Dimensions:	length: 90 ft (29.87 m) wingspan: 65 ft 9 in (20.4 m) wing area: 550.9 ft² (51.2 m²) height: 22 ft 2 in (6.75 m)
Speed:	max. 520 mph (833 kmh) cruise: 415 mph (667 kmh)

Ceiling:	37,000 ft (11,278 m)
Range:	8-hour mission endurance
Radar:	navigation

AIRBORNE ELECTRONIC AIRCRAFT (AEA)

The Airborne Electronic Aircraft (AEA) is an "in-house" Navy term for the successor to the EA-6B Prowler ECM aircraft and possibly a platform for other electronic warfare missions. The EA-18G, unofficially named "Growler," is being procured by the Navy and Marine Corps as a replacement for the EA-6B.

E-6B MERCURY

This aircraft has replaced the EC-130 Hercules in the TACAMO (Take Charge And Move Out) role, providing Very Low Frequency (VLF) radio relay to strategic missile submarines at sea. In addition, in the late 1990s, these aircraft (upgraded to the E-6B configuration) replaced 27 Air Force EC-135 aircraft in the "Looking Glass" program, providing airborne control of U.S. land-based strategic weapons with the Airborne Launch Control System (ALCS). In this role, the aircraft carry joint Navy-Air Force operational teams.

The original E-6A was a modified Boeing 707-320B airframe, which also served as the airframe for the E-3 AWACS (Airborne Warning and Control System); the C-135, KC-135, VC-137, EC-18, and E-8A aircraft are similar.

This is the largest aircraft currently flown by the U.S. Navy.

Design: When seeking a replacement for the EC-130, the Navy had proposed a competition of available airframes; however, only the Boeing Company responded, proposing the modified 707-320B airframe. The E-6 has the familiar lines of the Boeing 707-series commercial transports, but is fitted with four large GE/SNECMA turbofan engines. (The engine oil tanks have been enlarged to provide for increased flight endurance.)

In the TACAMO role, the E-6 has essentially the same communications equipment as the EC-130Q, with two trailing-wire antennas, one almost 5,000 feet (1,524 m) and the other some 30,000 feet (9,146 m) in length. Only the shorter wire is electrically charged, with energy reradiating off the longer wire. Wingtip pods on the E-6 contain satellite communication antennas. The aircraft are hardened against Electro-Magnetic Pulse (EMP) effects.

---

16 Jason Sherman and Gail Kaufman, "U.S. Navy to Replace EP-3 with Army Aircraft," *Defense News* (13 October 2003), p. 26.

The planned Aerial Common Sensor (ACS) aircraft in Navy markings. The Brazilian-developed aircraft will be flown by the U.S. Air Force and Navy in the ELINT role. (Lockheed Martin)

The E-6s retain the in-flight refueling receptacle for the Air Force flying-boom refueling system. Normal mission duration is 16 hours; with in-flight refueling, that can be extended to 72 hours.

Status: Operational; no longer in production. First flight of the E-6A occurred in February 1987. IOC for the E-6A (with VQ-3) was in August 1989, and its first operational mission was completed on 31 October 1989. IOC for the E-6B was in October 1998.

The E-6 program consisted of one prototype aircraft, which has been upgraded to full operational capability, and 15 production aircraft. The prototype was delivered in 1987; after being reconfigured as a standard E-6A, it was "redelivered" in 1992. The last E-6A aircraft was delivered on 7 May 1992. Subsequently, all aircraft have been upgraded to the E-6B configuration, the last completed in 2003.

E-6B

Manufacturer:	Boeing
Crew:	(22) 3 pilots, 2 navigators, 2 flight engineers, 15 mission specialists
Engines:	4 General Electric/SNECMA CFM-56-2A-2 high-bypass turbofan; 24,000 lbst (10,886 kgst) each
Weight:	empty: 172,795 lb (78,380 kg)
	gross: 342,000 lb (155,131 kg)
Dimensions:	length: 150 ft 4 in (45.82 m)
	wingspan 148 ft 4 in (45.22 m)
	wing area 3,050 ft² (283.4 m²)
	height: 42 ft 5 in (12.93 m)
Speed:	cruise: 508 mph (817 kmh)
	max. 607 mph (977 kmh)
Ceiling:	42,000 ft (12,805 m)
Range:	7,590 miles (12,223 km)
	radius 1,150 miles (1,852 km) with 10.5 hours loiter on station
Radar:	APS-133 weather

An E-6B Mercury shows its origins in the Boeing 707 transport design. These aircraft are assigned to Navy Strategic Communications Wing 1 and its two subordinate squadrons, VQ-3 and VQ-4. (U.S. Navy)

The E-6B Mercury combines the historic Navy TACAMO role of communications relay with strategic missile submarines with the Air Force "Looking Glass" airborne launch control of strategic weapons. The "B" variant is readily identified by the dorsal hump, which houses electronic gear. (U.S. Navy)

E-2C HAWKEYE

The Hawkeye is an AEW aircraft developed specifically for carrier operation. The E-2C variant is considered by many authorities to be the most capable radar warning and aircraft control plane now in service. A four-plane squadron is provided to each carrier air wing, having replaced the piston-engine WF/E-1 Tracer in AEW squadrons.

Procurement will continue through at least the next few years at the rate of four aircraft per year. Previously planned rebuilding of the aircraft has been canceled in favor of new E-2C aircraft. In 2003, the Navy signed a $1.9-billion contract with Northrop Grumman to produce two prototypes of an advanced E-2C. Delivery is planned for 2007, with an IOC of production models in 2011.

A "hot" production line also will facilitate continued foreign sales.

Design: The Hawkeye's most distinctive feature is the 24-foot (7.3-m) diameter, saucer-like radome for the APS-125 or APS-145 Ultra-High Frequency (UHF) radar. The radome revolves freely in the airstream at the rate of six revolutions per minute. It provides sufficient lift to offset its own weight in flight and on board ship can be lowered to facilitate aircraft handling.

The E-2C represents primarily an avionics upgrade over the previous E-2A/B variants (which had the APS-96 radar). Beginning with the FY 1986 procurement, the E-2C is being upgraded to T56-A-427 engines, providing improved flight safety with some increase in aircraft weight.

The APS-120 radar with overland surveillance capability initially was installed in E-2C aircraft. Electronic upgrades have included the APS-125 radar, with an effective aircraft detection range of some 275 miles (444.5 km) and both an overland and overwater capability; the aircraft can simultaneously track more than 250 air targets and control up to 30 interceptors. The ALR-73 passive detection system also is installed. Subsequently, the more-capable APS-145 radar has been provided to E-2C aircraft.

Designation: Originally designated W2F, the Hawkeye was changed to E-2 in 1962.

Status: Operational; in production. First flight of the E-2A occurred on 21 October 1960; the E-2C on 20 January 1971. IOC for the E-2A (with VAW-11) was in January 1964; for the E-2C (with VAW-123) was in November 1973.

Fifty-nine E-2A aircraft were delivered from 1960 to 1967; all have been retired. The E-2B designation was assigned but not popularly used for E-2A aircraft with upgraded computers. Two E-2A development aircraft were modified to a YE-2C configuration; these and two early production E-2C aircraft later were employed as trainers (TE-2C).

The Navy has 72 E-2C and 2 TE-2C aircraft in service. Four E-2C aircraft were transferred to the Coast Guard in 1987 and one to the Customs Service in 1989 for anti-drug operations. One Coast Guard aircraft crashed, and the remainder were returned to the Navy in 2002.

The aircraft also is flown by Egypt, France, Israel, Japan, Mexico, Singapore, Taiwan, and the United Arab Emirates. The French Navy operates its E-2Cs from the carrier CHARLES DE GAULLE; the other nations fly the aircraft from land bases. Three ex-Israeli Hawkeyes were transferred to Mexico in 2004.

E-2C

Manufacturer:	Northrop Grumman
Crew:	(5) pilot, copilot, combat information center officer, air controller, radar operator or technician
Engines:	2 Allison T56-A-422 turboprop; 4,591 shp each
Weight:	empty: 37,678 lb (17,090 kg)
	gross: 51,569 lb (23,392 kg)
Dimensions:	length: 57 ft 7 in (17.56 m)
	wingspan: 80 ft 7 in (24.58 m)
	wing area: 700 ft² (65.03 m²)
	height: 18 ft 4 in (5.59 m)
Speed:	max. 375 mph (603 kmh)
	cruise: 310 mph (499 kmh)
Ceiling:	30,800 ft (9,390 m)
Range:	radius 230 miles (370 km) with 6 hours on station
	ferry: 1,755 miles (2,820 km)
Armament:	none
Radar:	APS-125 or APS-145

An E-2C Hawkeye from VAW-117 about to land aboard the NIMITZ during operations off the coast of California. The E-2C and the C-2A Greyhound are the only propeller-driven aircraft aboard carriers, albeit having turboprop engines. (U.S. Navy/Yesenia Rosas)

An E-2C Hawkeye from VAW-117 aboard the NIMITZ during operations in the Western Pacific. Airborne Early Warning (AEW) aircraft, which date to late in World War II, are vital for effective operations over sea and land. In some respects, the Hawkeye is more capable than the larger, land-based E-3 Airborne Warning and Control System (AWACS) aircraft. (U.S. Navy/Angel G. Hilbrands)

An upgraded E-2C Hawkeye, with eight-blade, digitally controlled propellers, makes its first carrier landing in late 2003 aboard the carrier JOHN F. KENNEDY. The new propellers have less vibration and produce less noise than the standard four-blade propellers now in use. (U.S. Navy/Christian Weibull)

EA-18G GROWLER

The EA-18G is a derivative of the F/A-18F Hornet being developed to replace the long-serving EA-6B as the Navy's electronic attack aircraft. An F/A-18 derivative has the advantages of being carrier capable and already in service with the Navy; however, the EA-18G will have room for only one ECM officer (plus pilot), compared with three ECM officers (plus pilot) in the EA-6B, requiring a high degree of automation in the ECM suite.[17]

Design: The Block 1 EA-18G—which is funded through FY 2009—will have the ICAP (Improved Capability) III features of the EA-6B: the ALQ-99 tactical jamming pods, ALQ-218 radar receiver, AESA (Airborne Electronically Scanned Array) multimode radar, and a communications receiver and jammer. The wingtip pods on the EA-6G will displace the AIM-9 Sidewinder air-to-air missiles carried by the F/A-18E/F. The EA-18G will be armed with AIM-120C AMRAAM and AGM-88 HARM missiles. No gun will be fitted.

The EA-18G will have space available for the ATFLIR (Advanced Tactical Forward-Looking Infrared) system. The planned

Block 2 and 3 EA-18Gs—not currently funded—are expected to be able to launch precision-guided weapons such as the AGM-154 Joint Stand-Off Weapon (JSOW) and AGM-158 Joint Air-to-Surface Stand-off Missile (JASSM). Sidewinders also will be carried. The Shared Reconnaissance Pod (SHARP) will not be fitted.

Names: The nickname "Growler" is a combination of the *G* from EA-18G and *Prowler*.

Status: IOC is planned for FY 2009. An initial procurement of 56 EA-18G aircraft is planned, with a unit cost (in FY 2003 dollars) of $66 million. Total Navy procurement is envisioned as 90 aircraft, to equip ten fleet squadrons (VAQ) and one readiness squadron with five aircraft per unit. The Marine Corps also will procure the EA-18G.

---

17 See Lt. Comdr. Hunter Ware, USN, "Military Off-the-Shelf Has Promise & Pitfalls," U.S. Naval Institute *Proceedings* (September 2004), pp. 32–35.

The EA-18G Growler prototype, shown here with two Sidewinder AAMs on wingtips, and two jamming pods and two drop tanks on wing pylons. While simplifying maintenance and training, the EA-18G may not be as capable in the Electronic Countermeasures (ECM) role as the EA-6B Prowler. (Boeing Company)

EA-6B PROWLER

The EA-6B is an electronic attack aircraft based on the now-discarded A-6 Intruder attack aircraft. The EA-6B has significantly more Electronic Warfare (EW) and ECM capabilities than previous carrier-based electronic aircraft and generally is considered to be the world's most capable, combat-proven tactical jamming aircraft. Four-plane VAQ squadrons flying the Prowler normally are assigned to each carrier air wing, and several additional Navy and Marine squadrons are land based.

The Prowler is the only U.S. fixed-wing electronic strike/countermeasures aircraft, having replaced previous naval aircraft, as well as the Air Force's EF-111A Aardvark, in that role.

The Prowler is scheduled for retirement about 2015, at which time VAQ/VMAQ squadrons will operate the EA-18G Growler.

Design: The Prowler has the basic Intruder configuration, with an enlarged cockpit for two additional crew members. There is a distinctive electronics pod mounted atop the tail fin, and up to five jamming pods and two fuel tanks can be carried on fuselage and wing pylons. The weight of internal avionics/EW equipment totals 8,000 pounds (3,636 kg), in addition to 950 pounds (431 kg) being carried on each of five pylons. Normally, five ALQ-99 pods are carried, each with two jamming transmitters, although a 300-gallon drop tank can be substituted for each pod. Beginning in 1986, EA-6B aircraft have been configured to carry the High-speed Anti-Radiation Missile (HARM), their first "hard kill" armament. (The Air Force EF-111A did not carry weapons.)

The EA-6B has undergone a number of EW system upgrades since the original configuration: EXCAP (Expanded Capability), in service from 1973 to 1985; ICAP (Improved Capability), first delivered in 1976; ICAP II, first delivered in 1984; and ADVCAP (Advanced Capability), which entered service in 1994. The ADVCAP was terminated in 1994, however, after examination of the ICAP II aircraft and predicted post–Cold War threats. These upgrades responded to changing foreign radar and surface-to-air

The dual cockpits of the EA-6B Prowler house the pilot and three ECM operators. This Prowler from VMAQ-2 was forward deployed at Souda Bay, Crete, during the 2003 buildup for the invasion of Iraq to support U.S. naval forces in the Mediterranean Sea. (U.S. Navy/ Paul Farley)

missile threats and have been incorporated into new-production EA-6B aircraft.

The ADVCAP upgrades were to have included adding the low-band ALQ-149 communications ECM, providing two additional ALE-39 chaff/flare dispensers (a total of four), and fitting the J52-P-409 engine to increase allowable landing weight by about 2,000 pounds (907 kg) and decrease stall speed. In addition, wing pylons were increased to seven, and a Global Positioning System (GPS) was provided. The jammer pods have been successively upgraded from the basic ALQ-99 to the A/B/C configurations, primarily to increase reliability.

Further upgrades are planned to enable Prowlers to serve through 2015.

Designation: Changed from A2F-1Q to EA-6B in 1962.

Names: The EA-6B name was changed from Intruder to Prowler in February 1972.

Status: Operational; no longer in production. First flight (of a converted A-6A) occurred on 25 May 1968; first flight of a production EA-6B was in November 1970. IOC (with VAQ-129) was in January 1971.

Grumman built 170 EA-6B aircraft for the U.S. Navy and Marine Corps through June 1991, when production ended. In addition, three A-6A Intruder airframes were modified to serve as development aircraft for the EA-6B program.

EA-6B

Manufacturer:	Grumman
Crew:	(4) pilot, 3 electronic countermeasures officers[18]
Engines:	2 Pratt & Whitney J52-P-408 turbojet;
	11,200 lbst (5,080 kgst) each
Weight:[19]	empty: 32,162 lb (14,589 kg)
	normal T/O: 54,461 lb (24,704 kg)
	max. T/O: 65,000 lb (29,480 kg)

Dimensions:	length: 59 ft 10 in (18.24 m)
	wingspan: 53 ft (16.15 m)
	wing area: 528.9 ft² (49.1 m²)
	height: 16 ft 3 in (4.95 m)
Speed:	max. 613 mph (986 kmh) at sea level
	cruise: 483 mph (777 kmh)
Ceiling:	41,000 ft (12,500 m)
Range:	805 miles (1,296 km)
Armament:	2 HARM
Radar:	APQ-129

18 The electronic countermeasures officer in the right forward seat (next to the pilot) also serves as navigator.
19 Normal takeoff weight, speed, ceiling, and range while carrying five jammer pods.

This EA-6B Prowler from VAQ-138 aboard the CARL VINSON (CVN 70) shows the basic A-6 Intruder/EA-6B Prowler configuration, with a bulbous nose, fixed refueling probe forward of the cockpit, swept wings, and tapered after fuselage. There is an ECM pod atop the tail fin. (U.S. Navy/Martin S. Fuentes)

An EA-6B Prowler from VAQ-139, normally assigned to the carrier JOHN C. STENNIS, operates near the Prowler master base at NAS Whidbey Island, Washington. VAQ-136 is based in Japan as part of the KITTY HAWK (CV 63) air wing; all other VAQ squadrons are at Whidbey Island. (U.S. Navy/ Michael Watkins)

EA-6A INTRUDER

This variant of the carrier-based Intruder had a built-in ECM suite to detect and jam hostile radars, primarily for suppressing anti-aircraft missile systems. The aircraft was developed specifically for Marine Corps use; it was succeeded in Marine Corps service by the more-capable EA-6B Prowler beginning in 1977. It was flown by the Navy only in the research and development and training roles.

The EA-6A differed from the later and larger EA-6B Prowler in having only one ECM operator (compared to three in the EA-6B) and significantly less ECM equipment.

Seven A-6A Intruder attack aircraft were converted to the EA-6A configuration, followed by the production of 21 EA-6A aircraft delivered by Grumman from 1965. In service from December 1965 (with VMCJ-2). The last EA-6A in service was a Navy aircraft (with VAQ-33), retired in 1993.

Designation: Originally designated A2F-1H, the aircraft was changed to EA-6A in 1962.

See 15th Edition/pages 419–20 for characteristics.

NC-130H HERCULES

The NC-130H Hercules, previously designated EC-130V, is an AEW conversion of an HC-130H Hercules aircraft developed for U.S. Coast Guard evaluation. It has a large rotating radome (rotodome) for the APS-125 radar of the type fitted in the E-2C Hawkeye, now updated with the Radar Modernization Program (RMP).[20]

Flight testing for the aircraft began in July 1991; it was handed over to the Coast Guard on 16 October 1991 for a one-year evaluation. The Coast Guard referred to the project as a High-Endurance Surveillance (HES) aircraft, given the nickname "Delphi." Initial funding for the project was based on the aircraft's potential value in anti-drug surveillance operations.

After Coast Guard tests, the aircraft was transferred to the Air Force. Subsequently, it was retransferred to the Navy and designated NC-130H; it is assigned to VX-20 at NAS Patuxent River, Maryland.

[ ]C-130J "HAIRY BUFFALO"

The Department of Homeland Security has proposed that the Coast Guard configure six C-130J Hercules aircraft to accommodate a roll-on/roll-off suite suitable for Command, Control, Communications, Computers, Intelligence, Surveillance, and Reconnaissance (C4ISR) to support a variety of homeland security and defense missions. The prototype system—known as Hairy Buffalo—was demonstrated on a modified Navy NP-3C Orion.

The Hairy Buffalo system includes radar, electro-optical, and electronic surveillance sensors. All could be data linked to other aircraft (manned or unmanned), as well as to ground or shipboard stations.

Under the Hairy Buffalo concept, the suite could be installed on any model C-130 within 24 hours without permanent physical modification of the aircraft. The suite would have up to four operator positions.

EC-130Q HERCULES

The EC-130Q aircraft were C-130 transports extensively modified for the TACAMO role of communications relay with strategic missile submarines (SSBN). These aircraft had the USC-13 airborne VLF communications suite with a trailing wire antenna. The E-6 Mercury replaced the 22 TACAMO "Herks" in VQ-3 and VQ-4.

EP-3J ORION

The Navy acquired two P-3B aircraft modified in 1992 to the EP-3J configuration to simulate hostile electric emissions for fleet exercises. They were fitted with the USQ-113 communications intrusion and deception system and could carry the ALE-43, ALQ-167, ALQ-170, and AST-4/6 pods.

The two EP-3Js initially were flown by reserve squadron VP-66 and, subsequently, by reserve squadron VQ-11. One aircraft was severely damaged in a ground fire in 1998 and was not returned to service; the second was retired in late 1999.

EP-3E ORION

These are P-3 Orions extensively modified for ELINT collection and designated ARIES (Airborne Reconnaissance Integrated Electronic System). The 11 aircraft in service are P-3C variants converted to the EP-3E ARIES II configuration, having replaced the earlier EP-3E ARIES I.

These aircraft—flown by squadrons VQ-1 and VQ-2—have automatic electronic and communication intercept/analysis equipment to provide fleet and task force commanders with real-time

---

20 The aircraft should properly have been redesignated EC-130H; however, that designation already is used for the U.S. Air Force "Compass Call" electronic jamming aircraft.

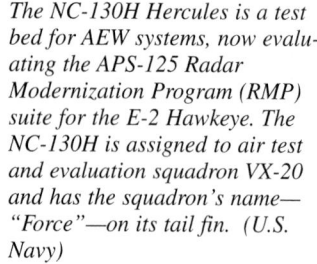

The NC-130H Hercules is a test bed for AEW systems, now evaluating the APS-125 Radar Modernization Program (RMP) suite for the E-2 Hawkeye. The NC-130H is assigned to air test and evaluation squadron VX-20 and has the squadron's name— "Force"—on its tail fin. (U.S. Navy)

intelligence. They are fitted with the ALR-52 multiband frequency measuring receiver and/or ALR-60 Deepwell communications intercept/ analysis system and the ALR-76 combined ESM/radar warning system.

(The Japanese Maritime Self-Defense Force acquired six Kawasaki-produced EP-3 variants for ELINT missions.)

See P-3C Orion for basic characteristics.

The successor to the EP-3E will be the Army's Aerial Common Sensor (ACS) aircraft.

Operational: During the Cold War, the EP-3E Orions flew reconnaissance flights along the periphery of the Soviet Union, China, and other target counties, carefully remaining beyond the 12-mile (19.3-km) territorial limit.

Periodically, the Orions were "buzzed" by foreign aircraft. This practice became particularly prevalent off the coast of China in the late 1990s, and on 1 April 2001, a pair of Chinese J-8 fighters approached an EP-3E off Hainan Island. One veered into the EP-3E. Heavily damaged, the fighter fell into the sea, killing its pilot. The EP-3E, also heavily damaged, turned toward Hainan Island. While the technicians hastily destroyed equipment and recordings, the pilots fought to control the aircraft and were able to bring it down at a Chinese airfield.

The 24 U.S. Navy personnel (21 men and 3 women) were detained—but well treated—by the Chinese. The EP-3E was searched but not ransacked. After 11 days, the crew was released. After lengthy negotiations, the United States was allowed to send technicians to Hainan to partially disassemble the aircraft, which then was flown out in a Russian An-124 cargo plane, as the Chinese refused permission for U.S. military aircraft to land on Hainan.

The aircraft was rehabilitated and returned to service, making its first flight on 15 November 2002.

An EP-3E Orion/ARIES II aircraft from VQ-1 showing blade-type antennas under the after fuselage, dorsal and ventral electronic canoes, radome under forward fuselage, and "bobbed" tail. The "PR" and a small bat symbol on the tail fin are the only unit markings. (U.S. Navy/ R. Hepp)

This EP-3E Orion/ARIES II intelligence collection aircraft from VQ-1 is at a base somewhere in the "Central Command area of responsibility." It probably was returning from a flight over Afghanistan in this 2002 photo. Note the underfuselage radome and ventral electronic "canoe." (U.S. Navy/Michael Sandberg)

A P-3B Orion extensively modified to an AEW configuration and redesignated NP-3D. This aircraft is flown under the auspices of the Naval Research Laboratory; other AEW-configured P-3s are operated by the Customs Service. This single Navy P-3/AEW aircraft has red trim markings. (U.S. Navy)

P-3 ORION AEW VARIANTS

Nine P-3 Orion aircraft were produced for U.S. service in AEW configurations, one for the Navy and eight for the Customs Service, the latter employed primarily to counter drug smuggling.

The first aircraft was a modified P-3B, acquired by Lockheed from the Royal Australian Air Force (RAAF) in exchange for a new-production P-3C Orion. Following Customs Service trials in 1988, that aircraft was acquired by Customs, as was a second modified P-3B AEW aircraft also acquired from the RAAF in exchange for a new-production P-3C.

Subsequently, the Customs Service acquired six additional P-3 AEW aircraft, the last two delivered by Lockheed Martin in 2000. The surveillance radars fitted in these aircraft—all of which are in service—are:

No. 1	APS-125
No. 2–4	APS-138
No. 5–8	APS-145

The Navy's AEW-configured aircraft is a rebuilt NP-3D operated by the Naval Research Laboratory in Washington, D.C. That aircraft, fitted with an extensively modified APS-145 radar, is based at NAS Patuxent River, Maryland.

See the P-3C Orion entry for basic characteristics.

ES-3A SHADOW

The Navy converted 16 S-3A Viking carrier-based ASW aircraft to an ES-3A configuration to serve as electronic surveillance aircraft. One or two planes normally operated from each forward-deployed aircraft carrier. Sometimes labeled TASES (Tactical Airborne Signal Exploitation System), the aircraft's missions were (1) electronic warfare reconnaissance (i.e, surveillance), (2) over-the-horizon targeting, and (3) airborne tactical command, control, communications, and intelligence.

The last ES-3A aircraft was taken out of service in 1999. A year earlier, the Navy had stated that the aircraft supported "all facets of Navy, Marine Corps, and joint operations," seeking out electronic emissions from potential hostile radars and intercepting communications, and that it had "already demonstrated tremendous reliability and safety, as well as a robust mission capability."[21] Shortly thereafter, the Navy decided to retire the aircraft to save operating funds.

The ES-3A aircraft, delivered to the fleet in 1995–1996 and operated by VQ 5 and 6, were long-delayed replacements for the

Navy's EA-3B Skywarrior. For more than a decade the Navy had sought a replacement to the EA-3B. Now, in place of the ES-3A, carrier battle group commanders employ land-based aircraft, primarily the EP-3E Aries II aircraft flown by squadrons VQ-1 and VQ-2.

Names: The ES-3A aircraft generally were called Shadow or Sea Shadow, although the names were not officially assigned.

Status: No longer operational. First flight of the prototype ES-3A conversion (NS-3A aerodynamic prototype) occurred on 7 September 1989 (the second conversion was the first with a full electronics suite; its first flight was on 21 January 1992). IOC was on 9 May 1992 (with VQ-5). All were delivered in 1992–1993 to squadrons VQ-5 and VQ-6.

NKC-135A STRATOTANKER

The Navy's two NKC-135A aircraft employed in the electronic warfare simulation/jamming role in support of weapons development and fleet exercises were discarded in 1992. They had replaced a pair of modified EB-47E Stratojet bombers previously flown in this role; the two NKC-135A aircraft entered Navy service in 1977–1978 and were contractor operated.

The aircraft were modified Boeing 707/Air Force KC-135A tankers, originally fitted with in-flight refueling equipment. They were modified by the Air Force for research work, with their refueling equipment removed. Further modifications by the Navy included removal of some of the body fuel cells to provide equipment bays, replacement of the weather track radar with a sea search unit, provision of wing pylons for electronic pods, and addition of an electronic warfare officer/navigator station in the cargo cabin area. Each carried about 12,500 pounds (5,670 kg) of electronic equipment on board and had two wing pylons, providing a greater jamming capability than any other aircraft then flying.

Operational: The two NKC-135A were operated by contractor personnel for the Fleet Electronic Warfare Support Group (FEWSG) to provide ECM training for naval forces. These planes had Navy markings but did not carry FEWSG's GD tail code. Squadrons VAQ-33, VAQ-34, and VAQ-35 also operated under FEWSG.

See 14th Edition/page 416 for characteristics.

---

21 Office of the Chief of Naval Operations, *Naval Aviation: Forward Air Power . . . From the Sea* (1988), p. 45.

OBSERVATION/RECONNAISSANCE AIRCRAFT

The Navy and Marine Corps no longer operate specialized reconnaissance or observation aircraft, other than ELINT collectors and UAVs. Carrier-based and land-based tactical reconnaissance now are performed by the F-14 Tomcat/TARPS and F/A-18 Hornet/SHARP systems.

RF-4B PHANTOM

The Marine Corps operated one squadron of RF-4B photo- reconnaissance aircraft. These aircraft were similar to the now-discarded F-4B version of the Phantom, and 46 were produced. All RF-4B reconnaissance variants have been retired from Marine Corps service, the last in 1992.

The U.S. Navy never flew the reconnaissance version of the Phantom, although Marine RF-4s flew from the carrier MIDWAY until 1986, when the ship's fighter and attack squadrons transitioned to the F/A-18 Hornet. Reconnaissance variants of the F-4 were flown by the U.S. Air Force and several foreign air forces.

Designation: Reconnaissance variants of the Phantom originally were designated F4H-1P; this was changed to RF-4B in 1962.

OV-10D BRONCO

The turboprop Bronco was developed for the Marine Corps during the Vietnam War as a multipurpose Counterinsurgency (COIN) aircraft. The Navy also flew the Bronco during the Vietnam War.

The Navy and Marine Corps took delivery of 114 aircraft from 1967 to 1969, with additional OV-10s going to the U.S. Air Force and foreign services. The last Marine observation squadrons flying the OV-10D Bronco were deactivated in 1993, and the last aircraft was transferred from the Marine Corps to the Bureau of Alcohol, Tobacco, and Firearms on 24 July 1994. Other ex-Marine Broncos have been transferred to the Bureau of Land Management and California Forestry Department.

The aircraft's STOL operating characteristics permitted limited flight operations from LHA/LPH-type ships without the use of catapults or arresting gear. (Trials also were flown from fleet carriers.)

See 15th Edition/page 424 for characteristics.

CARGO/TRANSPORT AIRCRAFT

C-40A CLIPPER

The Navy is procuring the Boeing 737-700 cargo/transport aircraft as the C-40A Clipper. The aircraft is a partial replacement for the C-9B/DC-9 Skytrain in naval service.

Design: The C-40A is a conventional, swept-wing aircraft with engines mounted under the wing and a conventional tail configuration. In the all-passenger role, the aircraft can accommodate 121 passengers; in the all-cargo role, it can carry eight standard cargo pallets. The C-40A also can be configured as a "combi" for 70 passengers and three cargo pallets.

Status: First flight of the 737-700 occurred on 9 February 1997; of the Navy C-40A on 14 April 1999. The first Navt aircraft was procured in the FY 2000 budget and delivered in April 2001 to squadron VR-59; eight aircraft were delivered by 2005.

The C-40B is flown by the Air Force and the C-40C by the Air National Guard; they are modifications of the C-40A. The aircraft is in production for commercial users.

C-40A

Manufacturer:	Boeing
Crew:	(4) pilot, copilot, 2 crewmen, plus 121 passengers (see *Design* notes)
Engines:	2 General Electric CFM56-7B high-bypass turbofan; 24,000 lbst (10,886 kgst) each
Weight:	empty: 84,100 lb (38,147 kg)
	gross: 171,000 lb (77,565 kg)
Dimensions:	length: 110 ft 4 in (33.63 m)
	wingspan: 112 ft 7 in (34.3 m)
	wing area: 1,344 ft² (125.0 m²)
	height: 41 ft 2 in (12.5 m)
Speed:	cruise: 585 mph (940 kmh)
	max. 615 mph (990 kmh)
Ceiling:	40,600 ft (12,370 m)
Range:	3,450 miles (5,555 km) in 121-passenger configuration
	40,000 lb (18,144 kg) in cargo configuration
Radar:	navigation/weather

A C-40A Clipper of squadron VR-59 shows the aircraft's large, left-side cargo door. The Naval Reserve VR squadrons provide transport services for active and reserve Navy and Marine Corps activities throughout the world. (Boeing Company)

The C-40A Clipper is being produced in small numbers—six have been delivered through 2004—to replace the C-9B Skytrains flown by reserve VR squadrons. The C-40A is the military version of the Boeing 737-700 and can operate in various cargo–passenger configurations. (Boeing Company)

C-37 GULFSTREAM V

This is an updated Gulfstream VIP aircraft (see page 431). The Naval Air Reserve flies a single C-37A in squadron VR-1. The Air Force operates several C-37A aircraft as VIP transports for senior government officials.

Design: This is the latest and largest of the Gulfstream line of corporate jet transports.

Status: Operational. First flight of the Gulfstream V was on 28 November 1995; first commercial delivery was in July 1997.

C-37	
Manufacturer:	Gulfstream Aerospace
Crew:	(4) pilot, copilot, 2 flight crewmen, plus 12 passengers
Engines:	2 BMW Rolls-Royce BR710A1-10 turbofan; 14,900 lbst (6,760 kgst) each
Weight:	empty: 46,800 lb (21,228 kg)
	max. T/O: 89,000 lb (40,370 kg)
Dimensions:	length: 96 ft 5 in (29.39 m)
	wingspan: 93 ft 4 in (28.50 m)
	wing area: 1,137 ft² (105.6 m²)
	height: 25 ft 10 in (7.87 m)
Speed:	max. 575 mph (930 kmh)
	cruise: 528 mph (851 kmh)
Ceiling:	51,000 ft (15,550 m)
Range:	7,485 miles (12,045 km); 14.5-hour mission
Radar:	navigation

UC-35

The UC-35 is a medium-range executive and priority cargo aircraft that the Navy has procured beginning in FY 2001. This is a Commercial-off-the-Shelf (COTS) buy of the Cessna Encore, with upgraded communications and navigation system. The UC-35C/D variants are flown by both the Navy and Marine Corps.

Design: The aircraft has a conventional, low-wing configuration with the engines fitted in pods on the after fuselage.

Status: Operational; in production.

UC-35	
Manufacturer:	Cessna Textron
Crew:	(2) pilot, copilot, plus 6 passengers
Engines:	UC-35C: 2 Pratt & Whitney JT15D-5D turbofan; 3,045 lbst (1,380 kgst) each
	UC-35D: 2 Pratt & Whitney 535A turbofan; 6,800 lbst (3,085 kgst) each
Weight:	empty: 9,977 lb (4,525 kg)
	gross: 16,500 lb (7,484 kg)
Dimensions:	length: 48 ft 1½ in (14.66 m)
	wingspan: 54 ft 1½ in (16.49 m)
	wing area: 322 ft² (29.93 m²)
	height: 15 ft 2½ in (4.63 m)
Speed:	max. 518 mph (833 kmh)
	cruise: 380 mph (610 kmh)
Ceiling:	45,000 ft (13,720 m)
Range:	2,070 miles (3,330 km)
Radar:	navigation

A Beech-Cessna Encore Ultra V aircraft in civilian markings. The few UC-35s flown by the Navy and Marine Corps are similar.

C-26D

The Navy flies several of these transport aircraft, which are a military version of the Fairchild Metro 23. The planes are used to delivery high-priority personnel and parts. Some are employed to conduct test range clearance.

C-26 and UC-26 variants also are flown by the Army and Air National Guards. The latter flies electronic-configured aircraft in counterdrug operations, as well as in the transport role.

Design: The C-26 is a high-performance, low-wing aircraft with turboprop engines.

Status: Operational. First flight of the basic Fairchild Metro design was on 26 August 1969.

C-26D	
Manufacturer:	Fairchild
Crew:	(2) pilot, copilot, plus 19 passengers
Engines:	2 Garrett TPE-331 turboprop; 1,100 shp each
Weight:	empty: 10,048 lb (4,558 kg)
	gross: 16,000 lb (7,258 kg)
Dimensions:	length: 59 ft 4½ in (18.09 m)
	wingspan: 57 ft (17.37 m)
	wing area: 309 ft² (28.71 m²)
	height: 16 ft 8 in (5.08 m)
Speed:	cruise: 275 mph (443 kmh)
	max. 285 mph (459 kmh)
Ceiling:	26,700 ft (8,140 m)
Range:	800 miles (1,290 km)
Radar:	navigation

C-20 GULFSTREAM

Gulfstream VIP transport aircraft are flown by the Navy (active and reserve) and Marine Corps as executive transports; the C-20A, D, and G variants are in naval service. The single Coast Guard VC-20B, which replaced a long-serving VC-11A Gulfstream II, was retired in January 2003.

The Navy planned to acquire three additional G variants configured for EW/ECM training, to have been designated EC-20F; that acquisition was canceled.

Gulfstream Aerospace has proposed a maritime patrol/anti-submarine warfare variant of the improved Gulfstream IV; the Royal Danish Navy flies the Gulfstream III in a maritime/fisheries patrol variant.

Design: Designed for the commercial market, the Gulfstreams are swept-wing, T-tail aircraft, with twin engine pods mounted on the after fuselage. Winglets are fitted (5 ft 4 1/4 in high).

Seats can be removed from the C-20G to carry up to 4,500 pounds (2,041 kg) of cargo, handled through a large cargo door on the right side, forward.

Status: Operational. First flight of the Gulfstream III occurred on 24 December 1979; Gulfstream IV on 19 September 1985. The Coast Guard's C-20B became operational in 1995. Variants of the C-20 also are flown by the Air Force and Army.

C-20D

Manufacturer:	Gulfstream Aerospace
Crew:	(2) pilot, copilot, plus 19 passengers
Engines:	2 Rolls-Royce Spey Mk 511-8 turbofan; 11,400 lbst (5,171 kgst) each
Weight:	empty: 32,000 lb (14,515 kg)
	gross: 69,700 lb (31,616 kg)
Dimensions:	length: 83 ft 1 in (25.32 m)
	wingspan: 77 ft 10 in (23.72 m)
	wing area: 934.6 ft² (86.83 m²)
	height: 24 ft 4½ in (7.43 m)
Speed:	max. 576 mph (927 kmh)
	cruise: 508 mph (817 kmh)
Ceiling:	45,000 ft (13,720 m)
Range:	4,800 miles (7,725 km)
Radar:	navigation

C-20G

Manufacturer:	Gulfstream Aerospace
Crew:	(4) pilot, copilot, 2 flight crewmen, plus 26 passengers
Engines:	2 Rolls-Royce Tay Mk 611-8 turbofan; 13,850 lbst (6,282 kgst) each
Weight:	gross: 74,600 lb (33,838 kg)
Dimensions:	length: 88 ft 4 in (26.92 m)
	wingspan: 77 ft 10 in (23.73 m)
	wing area: 934.6 ft² (86.83 m²)
	height: 24 ft 5 in (7.44 m)
Speed:	max. 563.5 mph (907 kmh) at 35,000 ft (10,670 m)
Range:	4,860 miles (7,820 km)
Ceiling:	45,000 feet (13,720 m)
Radar:	weather

A C-20G Gulfstream IV from VR-51 lands at MCAF Kaneohoe on Oahu, Hawaii, the squadron's home base. The unit's two C-20G aircraft primarily are used to transport the staff of the U.S. Central Command, primarily in the Middle East area. (U.S. Navy/William R. Goodwin)

A C-20G Gulfstream IV from VR-48, one of two Naval Reserve squadrons that fly the C-20G. The squadrons' aircraft primarily transport the staff of the U.S. Central Command's Navy and Marine Corps components. This C-20G sits under a rainbow at NAF Washington, D.C. (U.S. Navy)

The Coast Guard's C-20B Gulfstream IV streaks over the coast near Elizabeth City, North Carolina. The lone Coast Guard C-20B is a VIP transport used by that service and by officials of the Department of Homeland Security. (U.S. Coast Guard/ Telfair Brown)

C-12/UC-12/RC-12/TC-12 HURON

The Navy and Marine Corps fly large numbers of these military versions of the Super King Air 200 for transport, utility, and training purposes. They also are flown in a variety of configurations by the Army and Air Force.

Design: The aircraft's twin turboprop engines are mounted far forward on the low wing; the aircraft has a T-tail, as opposed to the conventional tail configuration of the smaller T-44A King Air trainer. Payload is 2,000 pounds (907 kg) of cargo or eight passengers.

Operational: More than 2,800 aircraft of this basic design have been produced, most for civilian use. This is the only fixed-wing aircraft flown by the U.S. Army, Navy, Marine Corps, and Air Force (plus the Army National Guard and Marine Corps Reserve). About 65 are flown by the Navy and Marine Corps in the C-12C, UC-12B/F/M, RC-12F/M, RC-12M, and TC-12B variants, with the UC-12B being the most widely used. The RC-12 variants are fitted with surface search radar to support test and exercise areas.

Status: Operational. First flight of the Super King Air 200 occurred on 27 October 1972.

UC-12B

Manufacturer:	Beech
Crew:	(2) pilot, copilot, plus 8 passengers
Engines:	2 Pratt & Whitney PT6A-41 turboprop; 850 shp each
Weight:	empty: 7,869 lb (3,569 kg)
	gross: 12,500 lb (5,670 kg)
Dimensions:	length: 43 ft 9 in (13.34 m)
	wingspan: 54 ft 6 in (16.61 m)
	wing area: 303 ft² (28.2 m²)
	height: 14 ft 6 in (4.42 m)
Speed:	max. cruise: 310 mph (500 kmh)
	cruise: 261 mph (420 kmh)
Ceiling:	31,000 ft (9,451 m)
Range:	2,025 miles (3,260 km)
Radar:	none

A UC-12B from squadron VRC-30 with its gear down coming in for a landing. Navy transport aircraft usually have the U.S. flag on their tail fin(s). The numerals 1327 are the last four digits of the aircraft's serial or "BuAer" number—161327. (U.S. Navy)

A Marine UC-12 Huron undergoes an engine check at an airfield in the Central Command area during Operation Iraqi Freedom. The aircraft usually are referred to by their civilian names—King Air or Super King. (U.S. Marine Corps/W. A. Napper Jr.)

A UC-12B Huron from NAS Jacksonville, Florida, is refueled at Norfolk. These aircraft are used to transport personnel and high-priority cargo. (Peter B. Mersky)

VC-11A GULFSTREAM II

The Coast Guard's single VC-11A, the only such aircraft in U.S. government service, was retired in 1995. It was flown in the executive transport role and based at Washington, D.C.

The Grumman-built aircraft had entered Coast Guard service in July 1968. It was suffering from structural integrity problems and communications limitations and lacked sufficient range and passenger capacity for current requirements. Accordingly, it was replaced by a VC-20B Gulfstream, which was, in turn, retired in January 2003.

See 15th Edition/page 427 for characteristics.

C-9B/DC-9 SKYTRAIN

The C-9B is the naval version of the commercial DC-9 series 30 medium-range passenger/cargo aircraft and is convertible to the cargo or passenger transport roles.

All Skytrains—both military (C-9B) and commercial (DC-9) versions—are flown by the Naval Air Reserve, except for two C-9Bs flown by Marine Corps squadron VMR-1. The C-9B/DC-9 replaced the long-serving C-118 Liftmaster (formerly R6D). The U.S. Air Force flies the C-9A Nightingale in the medical evacuation role and the VC-9C as an executive transport.

McDonnell Douglas has proposed a maritime patrol/anti-submarine warfare variant of the aircraft (company designation P-9D);

it would have General Electric Unducted Fan (UDF) turboprop-type engines.

Design: This sleek, swept-wing transport has a T-tail, with the turbofan engines in nacelles mounted on the after fuselage. The cargo compartment can accommodate eight standard 88-inch x 108-inch (2.2 m x 2.7 m) cargo pallets. Payload is 32,444 pounds (14,717 kg) or 90 passengers

Status: Operational. First flight of the DC-9 series 30 occurred on 1 August 1966. IOC in the Naval Air Reserve was in 1976.

C-9B/DC-9

Manufacturer:	McDonnell Douglas
Crew:	(5) pilot, copilot, crew chief, 2 attendants, plus 90 passengers
Engines:	2 Pratt & Whitney JT8D-9 turbofan; 14,500 lbst (6,577 kgst) each
Weight:	empty: 59,706 lb (27,083 kg) in cargo configuration 65,283 lb (29,612 kg) in transport configuration gross: 110,000 lb (49,896 kg)
Dimensions:	length: 119 ft 4 in (36.37 m) wingspan: 93 ft 5 in (28.47 m) wing area: 1,000.7 ft² (92.97 m²) height: 27 ft 6 in (8.38 m)
Speed:	max. 576 mph (927 kmh) cruise: 504 mph (811 kmh)
Ceiling:	37,000 ft (11,280 m)
Range:	2,920 miles (4,700 km) with 10,000 lb (4,536 kg) cargo
Radar:	navigation

A C-9B Skytrain from squadron VR-56 coming in for a landing at Naval Station Norfolk. These aircraft provide worldwide logistics support for the Navy and Marine Corps. (U.S. Navy/Daniel J. McLain)

A C-9B Skytrain from VR-57 seen over the Pacific on a training flight. All C-9Bs are assigned to Naval Reserve squadrons, except one aircraft currently assigned to Marine squadron VMR-1. These aircraft will mostly be replaced by the C-40 Clipper. (U.S. Navy/ Edward G. Martens)

A C-9B Skytrain from squadron VR-56 shows the aircraft's large cargo door. These aircraft are similar to commercial DC-9s, a few of which still are flown by the Naval Reserve. (Peter B. Mersky)

VC-4A GULFSTREAM

The Coast Guard operates a single VC-4A as an executive transport. The Navy and Marine Corps have discarded the several TC-4C trainers built on the same airframe that were employed to train A-6E Intruder bombardier/navigators.

Developed as a business executive aircraft, the Gulfstream I is a low-wing, twin turboprop aircraft with the long nacelles common to Rolls-Royce engines. The cabin is pressurized.

Status: Operational. First flight (Gulfstream I) occurred on 14 August 1958. VC-4A IOC was in March 1963. First flight of the TC-4C occurred on 14 June 1967.

Grumman produced 190 Gulfstream I commercial aircraft, plus the single Coast Guard VC-4A and nine TC-4C aircraft for the Navy and Marine Corps. The T-41A (later TC-4B) was a navigation training version of the Gulfstream I ordered by the Navy, but that entire program was canceled prior to deliveries.

A second VC-4A planned for the Coast Guard was not acquired.

VC-4A

Manufacturer:	Grumman
Crew:	(2) pilot, copilot, plus 10–14 passengers
Engines:	2 Rolls-Royce Dart Mk 529-8X turboprop; 2,210 shp each
Weight:	empty: 24,575 lb (11,147 kg)
	gross: 36,000 lb (16,330 kg)
Dimensions:	length: 63 ft 9 in (19.43 m)
	wingspan: 78 ft 6 in (23.92 m)
	wing area: 610.3 ft² (56.7 m²)
	height: 22 ft 9 in (6.94 m)
Speed:	max. 348 mph (560 kmh) at 25,000 ft (7,625 m)
	cruise: 288 mph (463 kmh) at 25,000 ft (7,625 m)
Ceiling:	33,600 ft (10,240 m)
Range:	2,540 miles (4,090 km)
Radar:	navigation

The Coast Guard's lone VC-4A Gulfstream I still flies as an executive transport. This is the only Gulfsteam I remaining in U.S. military service. The Navy previously had flown TC-4C Academe training aircraft. (U.S. Coast Guard)

C-2A GREYHOUND

The Greyhound is a second generation, built-for-the-purpose COD aircraft derived from the E-2 Hawkeye AEW aircraft. Nineteen C-2A models originally were procured.

In the late 1970s, the Navy developed a plan to produce 24 new COD aircraft beginning in FY 1983 to replace the existing C-1A and, eventually, early C-2A aircraft. The principal candidate—designated VCX for planning purposes—was a variant of the S-3A Viking, with several early aircraft having been modified to a US-3A COD configuration. The decision, however, was to procure 39 additional C-2As (with the first of these "reprocured" aircraft making its first flight on 4 February 1985); the principal difference in the later aircraft was uprated engines.

Design: The cargo aircraft has the E-2's wings, power plant, and tail configuration, but a larger fuselage and a rear-loading ramp. This last feature permits the carrying of high-cube cargo, including some aircraft engines. Cargo capacity is 675 cubic feet (20.25 m³); payload is 10,000 lbs (4,536 kg) of cargo or 26 passengers. The wings fold for carrier stowage, although these planes are not assigned to carrier wings.

Status: Operational. First flight of the C-1A occurred on 18 November 1964. IOC (with VRC-50) was in December 1966. Total C-2A production—both "batches"—was 58 aircraft. Thirty-five C-2A aircraft remain in Navy service.

C-2A

Manufacturer:	Grumman
Crew:	(3) pilot, copilot, flight engineer + 26 passengers or 20 litters
Engines:	2 Allison T56-A-425 turboprop; 4,910 shp each
Weight:	empty: 31,250 lb (14,175 kg)
	gross: 54,382 lb (24,668 kg)
Dimensions:	length: 56 ft 8 in (17.27 m)
	wingspan: 80 ft 7 in (24.57 m)
	wing area: 700 ft² (65.03 m²)
	height: 15 ft 11 in (4.85 m)
Speed:	max. 352 mph (566 kmh) at 30,000 ft (9,146 m)
	cruise: 296 mph (476 kmh) at 30,000 ft
Ceiling:	33,500 ft (10,210 m)
Range:	normal: 1,200 miles (1,930 km)
	max. 1,800 miles (2,890 km)
Radar:	navigation

A C-2A Greyhound from VRC-40 over the Persian Gulf en route from Bahrain to the carrier ENTERPRISE (CVN 65). Carrier Onboard Delivery (COD) aircraft range worldwide, wherever U.S. aircraft carriers are operating. (U.S. Navy/Aaron Peterson)

A C-2A Greyhound from squadron VRC-40 lands aboard the carrier GEORGE WASHINGTON (CVN 73). COD aircraft deliver people, mail, and high-priority supplies to carriers at sea. The first COD aircraft were modified TBM Avengers, adapted to carry nuclear bomb components to carriers. (U.S. Navy/Corey T. Lewis)

A pair of C-2A Greyhounds from squadron VRC-30 at rest on the flight deck of the carrier RONALD REAGAN (CVN 76). The aircraft in the foreground has its wings folded; the other plane has its tail ramp lowered. (U.S. Navy/Kitt Amaritnant)

C-130/KC-130 HERCULES

The Hercules, or "Herk," is the most widely flown military cargo/transport aircraft in the West. The Navy and Marine Corps—active and reserve components—operate more than 100 C-130 variants as tankers and cargo aircraft, plus one C-130T supporting the Blue Angels flight demonstration team, one DC-130A drone carrier, and one NC-130H in an AEW configuration.[22] The DC-130A and NC-130H are listed separately, the latter under Electronic Aircraft. The Coast Guard has 27 HC-130H aircraft configured for Search and Rescue (SAR) and has acquired six HC-130J SAR variants. The approximately 65 KC-130 variants assigned to Marine Corps refueler–transport squadrons (VMGR) are fitted for in-flight refueling, as well as for cargo/troop transport operations.

The latest C-130 variant entering naval service is the KC-130J. It is a "stretched" aircraft, with advanced avionics, cockpit display, and fight control systems and is flown by two pilots and two air crewmen. In the cargo configuration, the aircraft can lift loads up to 18½ tons or 72 litters, or 92 combat-equipped troops, or 64 paratroops; the KC-130R has a payload of 13½ tons or 92 troops. (See *Design* notes for the tanker configuration.)

The Navy has retired the ski-equipped LC-130F/R Hercules flown in support of Antarctic research programs (by squadron VXE-6), except for one for test and evaluation. The Navy's EC-130Q TACAMO aircraft have been retired from the strategic communications role, replaced by the E-6 Mercury.

Design: The C-130 is a high wing, four-engine cargo aircraft with the main landing gear in pods to provide a clear fuselage cargo space; a rear ramp provides access to the cargo compartment and can be opened in flight for parachuting troops or equipment.

The C-130J has Dowty six-blade, composite propellers that provide significantly enhanced performance over the standard, four-blade propellers in previous C-130s. The aircraft also has enhanced avionics and cockpit display.

The Marine Corps KC-130F/J/R/T aircraft can accommodate removable aluminum tanks for 3,600 gallons (13,680 liters) of fuel in the cargo area; two refueling drogues can be streamed simultaneously from wing-mounted pods.

The Coast Guard HC-130H aircraft—generally similar to the C-130R variant—carry air-dropped rescue and salvage gear; they are fitted with extra fuel tanks, flare launchers, and other improvements over the C-130B aircraft they replaced. The HC-130H aircraft have been retrofitted with the APS-137 ISAR radar; they also have APN-215 weather radar, and an external SAMSON sensor pod containing a FLIR can be fitted.

Designation: The Navy–Marine Corps variants of the Hercules originally were designated GV-1; this was changed to C-130 in 1962.

Operational: A KC-130F conducted carrier landings and take-offs from the FORRESTAL in 1963 without the use of arresting gear or catapults. C-130s also have been employed to evaluate aerial minelaying techniques.

More than 2,200 Hercules have been built for the U.S. military services and more than 60 other countries.

Status: Operational; in production. First flight of the YC-130 occurred on 23 August 1954. Production of KC-130J aircraft for the Navy and Marine Corps continues. The C-130J entered production in 1997.

KC-130J

Manufacturer:	Lockheed Martin
Crew:	(4) pilot, copilot, 2 crewmen + 92 troops
Engines:	4 Allison AE2100D3 turboprop; 4,591 shp each
Weight:	empty: 75,562 lb (34,275 kg)
	gross: 155,000 lb (70,307 kg)
	max. T/O: 175,000 lb (79,380 kg)
Dimensions:	length: 97 ft 9 in (29.81 m)
	wingspan: 132 ft 7 in (40.42 m)
	wing area: 1,745 ft² (162.12 m²)
	height: 38 ft 10 in (11.84 m)
Speed:	max. 402 mph (647 kmh)
	cruise: 390 mph (628 kmh)
Ceiling:	30,500 ft
Range:	3,260 miles (5,245 km)
Radar:	Northrop Grumman MODAR 4000 (weather/navigation)

22 The C-130T assigned to the Blue Angels is called "Fat Albert" for a characterization of comedian Bill Cosby.

KC-130R

Manufacturer:	Lockheed (Georgia)
Crew:	(5) pilot, copilot, navigator, flight engineer, radio operator/loadmaster + 92 troops
Engines:	4 Allison T56-A-15 turboprop; 4,591 shp each
Weight:	empty: 75,368 lb (34,187 kg)
	loaded: 109,744 lb (49,780 kg)
	gross: 155,000 lb (70,308 kg)
Dimensions:	length: 99 ft 5 in (30.32 m)
	wingspan: 132 ft 7 in (40.42 m)
	wing area: 1,745 ft² (162.12 m²)
	height: 38 ft 3 in (11.66 m)

Speed:	max. 348 mph (560 kmh) at 19,000 ft (5,790 m)
	cruise: 331 mph (533 kmh)
Ceiling:	25,000 ft (7,622 m)
Range:	radius 2,950 miles (4,749 km) with maximum payload
	radius 1,150 miles (1,852 km) in tanker role with 32,140 lb (14,579 kg) of fuel for transfer
Radar:	APN-59B

A Marine KC-130 Hercules in flight over the Philippine Sea prepares to refuel an approaching CH-53E Super Stallion helicopter. The KC-130s can refuel two aircraft simultaneously using the probe-and-drogue method. (U.S. Navy/James Davis)

A Marine KC-130 Hercules assigned to squadron VGMR-352 prepares for a mission at an undisclosed airfield—probably in Afghanistan—during Operation Enduring Freedom in 2002. Another KC-130, carrying Marines, is taking off for the airport at Kandahar. (U.S. Marine Corps/William D. Crow)

The HC-130H Hercules is the largest aircraft currently flown by the Coast Guard. This "Herk" is based at CGAS Barbers Point, Hawaii. These aircraft are employed for surveillance, as well as for search and rescue operations. (U.S. Navy/Keith W. DeVinney)

A C-130T Hercules from squadron VR-53 at Clark Field in the Philippines. Although the United States no longer has bases in the Philippines, U.S. troops and support activities are deployed there to help counter guerrillas. (U.S. Navy/Lou Rosales)

DC-130A HERCULES

The Navy operates a single DC-130A drone launch/control aircraft. It is assigned to squadron VX-30.

CT-39G SABRELINER

The few CT-39G aircraft employed to transport high-priority cargo and passengers for the Marine Corps and the Navy have been discarded. The T-39/CT-39 have long been used in the training and utility transport roles. As trainers, they have been employed to train bombardier/navigators and radar intercept officers. (See Training Aircraft.)

The Sabreliner also was flown in large numbers by commercial users.

Status: North American produced 12 of its Sabreliner 60 series as the CT-39G. The aircraft was also flown in large numbers by the Air Force. See 17th Edition/page 430 for characteristics.

UTILITY AIRCRAFT

HU-25 GUARDIAN

The Guardian is an all-weather, medium-range search and surveillance aircraft flown by the Coast Guard. It replaced the HU-16 Albatross and HC-131 Samaritan.

Design: This aircraft is a modification of the French- developed commercial Falcon 20G. It has two turbofan engines mounted in nacelles outboard of the after fuselage, an arrangement similar to the T-39 Sabreliner. In addition to crew and passengers, it can carry 3,200 pounds (1,452 kg) of rescue supplies. A galley and toilet are provided.

The ATF3-6 engines have been difficult and expensive to support.

Seven aircraft were modified with the AIREYE sensor system with infrared/ultraviolet line scanners in an under-wing pod and an APS-131 Side-Looking Airborne Radar (SLAR) in a fuselage pod, a television camera, and other equipment for pollution reconnaissance; these were redesignated HU-25B in 1989.

Nine other aircraft were fitted with the APG-66 multimode radar, to provide the capability to detect aircraft out to 80 nautical miles (148 km), and FLIR; they were redesignated HU-25C in 1989.

Status: Operational. Coast Guard IOC was in February 1982; the last of 41 aircraft were delivered in 1984. (Guardian Jet Corpor-

ation was a jointly owned subsidiary of Dassault-Breguet and Pan American.)

As part of the downsizing of Coast Guard fixed-wing aircraft, beginning in 1994, several of these aircraft were placed in storage. Similar French-built Mystére-Falcon aircraft are flown in a variety of roles by several air forces.

HU-25A

Manufacturer:	Dassault-Breguet and Guardian Jet
Crew:	(5) pilot, copilot, drop master, avionics man, air crewman, plus 3 passengers + 4 litters
Engines:	2 Garrett AiResearch ATF3-6-2C turbofan; 5,538 lbst (2,512 kgst) each
Weight:	empty: 19,000 lb (8,618 kg)
	gross: 33,510 lb (15,200 kg)
Dimensions:	length: 56 ft 3 in (17.15 m)
	wingspan: 53 ft 6 in (16.30 m)
	wing area: 450 ft² (41.80 m²)
	height: 17 ft 5 in (5.32 m)
Speed:	max. 531 mph (854 kmh) at 40,000 ft (12,195 m)
Ceiling:	42,000 ft (12,805 m)
Range:	2,590 miles (4,167 km) with 30 minutes on station
Radar:	APS-127 search/weather radar, except APG-66 in eight HU-25C aircraft plus APS-131 SLAR in eight HU-25B aircraft

An HU-25 Guardian at the Coast Guard's aviation training center in Mobile, Alabama. An HH-65 Dolphin helicopter sits on the flight line behind the HU-25. The Coast Guard also refers to the HU-25 as the Falcon, the aircraft's French name. (U.S. Coast Guard/Jeff Hall)

An HU-25B Guardian fitted with the Aireye sensor system to detect oil pollution. The antenna is mounted in a canoe-type pod under the fuselage. Russian aircraft have been similarly fitted. (U.S. Coast Guard)

An HU-25 Guardian at rest. The French-designed Guardians have been difficult and expensive to maintain. Just more than half of the Coast Guard's HU-25 inventory is in storage. (U.S. Coast Guard)

U-6A BEAVER

Two de Havilland DHC-2 aircraft are in service as U-6As at the Naval Test Pilot School at NAS Patuxent River, Maryland. This is a rugged aircraft, used largely in the Arctic region with wheels, floats, or skis.

These Beavers are the oldest aircraft type flown by the U.S. Navy.

Design: The DHC-2 has a straightforward design with a single radial engine, high-wing configuration, and fixed landing gear. The seats for seven passengers can be easily removed to provide space for carrying cargo.

Designation: These aircraft were flown by the Army, Navy, and Air Force with the designation L-20A until 1962, when it was changed to U-6A.

Status: Operational. The Beaver first flew in August 1947. A total of 1,631 aircraft were produced, of which 980 went to the U.S. armed forces.

One of two U-6A Beaver utility aircraft flown by the Naval Test Pilot School. Beavers continue in commercial service in remote areas. (Mike Wilson)

U-6A

Manufacturer:	de Havilland (Canada)
Crew:	(2) pilot, copilot + 7 passengers
Engines:	1 Pratt & Whitney R-985 radial piston; 450 hp
Weight:	empty: 2,850 lb (1,293 kg)
	gross: 5,099 lb (2,313 kg)
Dimensions:	length: 30 ft 3 in (9.22 m)
	wingspan: 48 ft (14.63 m)
	wing area: 250 ft² (23.2 m²)
	height: 9 ft (2.74 m)
Speed:	cruise: 163 mph (262 kmh)
Ceiling:	17,991 ft (5,485 m)
Range:	733 miles (1,180 km)
Radar:	none

One of the U-6A Beavers flown by the Naval Test Pilot School. The school operates a variety of utility and training aircraft in addition to high-performance aircraft. (U.S. Navy)

NU-1B OTTER

A single de Havilland DHC-3 Otter is in service at the U.S. Naval Test Pilot School with the designation NU-1B. This is a rugged aircraft, largely used in the Arctic region with wheels, floats, or skis.

Design: This is an enlarged version of the U-6A/DHC-2 (see above). Their appearance is similar.

Designation: Initially given the Navy designation UC-1; this was changed to U-1 in 1962.

Status: Operational. The Otter first flew on 12 December 1951. Almost half of the de Havilland production of some 460 aircraft went to the U.S. Air Force; a few went to the Navy as the U-1.

NU-1B

Manufacturer:	de Havilland (Canada)
Crew:	(2) pilot, copilot + 10 passengers
Engines:	1 Pratt & Whitney R-1340-S1H1-G radial piston; 600 hp
Weight:	empty: 4,431 lb (2,010 kg)
	gross: 8,000 lb (3,629 kg)
Dimensions:	length: 41 ft 10 in (12.75 m)
	wingspan: 58 ft (17.68 m)
	wing area: 375 ft² (34.84 m²)
	height: 12 ft 7 in (3.84 m)
Speed:	cruise: 138 mph (222 kmh)
Ceiling:	18,795 ft (5,730 m)
Range:	945 miles (1,520 km)
Radar:	none

A single NU-1B Otter utility aircraft also is flown by the Naval Test Pilot School. The school trains primarily Navy and Marine Corps pilots, but also pilots from other U.S. services, foreign air forces, and some civilian agencies. (U.S. Navy)

The first T-6A Texan trainers went to the Air Force, as this one shown in U.S. Air Force markings. The use of the same designation and name as a World War II-era aircraft will only confuse future aviation buffs, writers, and historians. (Raytheon/Beech)

TRAINING AIRCRAFT

T-6A TEXAN

The T-6A Texan is the aircraft component of the Joint Primary Aircraft Training System (JPATS), an Air Force–Navy program to develop a new training aircraft for production after 2000. The Air Force was the lead service for JPATS development.

In naval service, the T-6A is replacing the T-34, and in Air Force service it replaces the T-37. The service requirements are for 339 and 372 aircraft, respectively, for a total program of 711 aircraft, plus three prototypes. Production is expected to be completed about 2014.

Raytheon Aircraft Company's Beech Mk II was selected as the JPATS aircraft in June 1995. Six other aircraft types competed for the role.

Design: The T-6 is a single-engine, turboprop aircraft with tandem seating. It is derived from the Swiss-built Pilatus PC-9. It is a straight-wing aircraft with a pressurized cockpit and ejection seats.

Designation: The next designation in the trainer series at the time of the JPATS selection was T-48. However, the Air Force assigned the designation T-6 in remembrance of the North American AT-6/T-6 Texan trainer (also used as a limited attack aircraft); the Navy designation of the earlier trainer was SNJ. The Navy procured more than 4,000 SNJs during World War II, with the last being retired in 1968.

Status: In production for U.S. Navy and Air Force. First flight of the engineering prototype JPATS occurred in September 1992; first flight of the T-6A was on 15 July 1995. The Navy's IOC was in 2003, and the Air Force IOC in 2002.

T-6A

Manufacturer:	Beech (Raytheon)
Crew:	(2) pilot, student
Engines:	1 Pratt & Whitney PT6A-68 turboprop; 1,700 shp
Weight:	empty: approx. 4,707 lb (2,135 kg)
	max. T/O: approx. 6,500 lb (2,948 kg)
Dimensions:	length: 33 ft 4¾ in (10.175 m)
	wingspan: 33 ft 2½ in (10.12 m)
	wing area: 16.9 ft² (1.57 m²)
	height: 10 ft 8 in (3.29 m)
Speed:	310.5 mph (500 kmh) at sea level
Range:	approx. 1,020 miles (1,642 km)
Ceiling:	31,000 ft (9,450 m)
Armament:	none
Radar:	none

The Beech Mk II trainer, prototype for the T-6A Texan, shows the excellent visibility of this nimble aircraft. (Raytheon/Beech)

TC-4C ACADEME

The Navy previously operated several TC-4C trainers for A-6E Intruder bombardier/navigators. These aircraft were discarded in 1995 in anticipation of the A-6E being phased out of Navy service in 1996. The Marines transferred their TC-4s to the Navy, and the Coast Guard retired its single, long-servicing VC-4A Gulfstream VIP transport. (All variants of the aircraft in military service generally are referred to as Gulfstreams; the Coast Guard aircraft officially retained the name Gulfstream I.)

The TC-4C variants had a simulated A-6E cockpit, with pilot and bombardier/navigator positions in the after section of the cockpit, plus four identical bombardier/navigator training consoles. In addition to the A-6E radar (upgraded from the original APQ-92 and APQ-88 radars), these planes had the Target Recognition Attack Multiple-sensor (TRAM) and FLIR fitted in the A-6Es.

The T-41A (later TC-4B) was a navigation training version of the Gulfstream I; that program was canceled before delivery.

See 15th edition/pages 428–29 for characteristics.

T-47A CITATION

The Navy's T-47 trainers, built to a modified commercial Cessna Citation II Model 500 design, have been discarded. The Navy employed 15 T-47A aircraft in training squadrons VT-10 and VT-86 to train Naval Flight Officers (NFO). The T-47 replaced the T-39 Sabreliner in that role. The T-47 was contractor maintained and operated.

See 14th Edition/page 426 for characteristics.

T-45 GOSHAWK

The Goshawk is the Navy's basic undergraduate jet training aircraft, replacing the T-2C and TA-4J. It is a variant of British Aerospace's Hawk series 60 trainer. Employing the T-45 reduces flight training by about 15 hours per student compared to the previously used T-2C/TA-4J. Despite using an off-the-shelf aircraft, the first flight of a U.S. Navy Goshawk took place almost five years behind the original schedule. The first student pilots flew in the T-45A on 11 February 1994.

The Navy initially planned to procure 253 carrier-capable T-45A trainers and 54 land-based T-45B variants, but Congress directed that they all be T-45A "wet" models. Accordingly, the current program provides for a total of 234 training aircraft and two prototypes (plus 32 flight-simulation devices).

Developed by Hawker Siddeley Aviation before it was merged into British Aerospace, the Hawk entered Royal Air Force service in 1976 and also is flown by several other air forces as a trainer and light attack aircraft. (No other Hawk variants are carrier capable.) The U.S. Navy's program originally was designated VTX-TS, the VTX for new training aircraft and TS for Training System, i.e., the simultaneous development of simulators and related training equipment.

Initial T-45 flight tests revealed several shortcomings; among other changes, the original Adour Mk 861/F405-RR-400 engine was replaced in production aircraft with the Adour Mk 871/F405-RR-401.

Design: The T-45 is a low, swept-wing aircraft with relatively small air intakes beneath the cockpit. The vertical tail surface is forward of the horizontal surfaces.

The U.S. Navy's Goshawks differ from the British Hawk design in having a small ventral fin, an arresting hook, and modified wing, landing gear, and speed brakes. Endurance is approximately four hours. Leading-edge slats are fitted to bring carrier approach speeds within acceptable limits. A pylon is fitted under each wing for small bombs, rockets, or drop tanks; there also is a provision for a centerline store.

The wing and after fuselage sections of the T-45A are built in Britain by British Aerospace, and Rolls-Royce produces the engines in Britain. (The Hawk continues in production in Britain.)

Name: The name Goshawk previously was assigned to the Navy's Curtiss-built F11C fighter of the 1930s.

Status: Operational; in production. First flight of the British T.Mk 1 occurred on 21 August 1974; of the T-45A on 16 April 1988. IOC (with VT-21) was in 1994. The British Hawk is flown by ten other countries.

T-45

Manufacturer:	British Aerospace and Boeing
Crew:	(2) pilot, student
Engines:	1 Rolls-Royce Adour Mk 871/F405-RR-401 turbofan; 5,845 lbst (2,651 kgst)
Weight:	empty: 9,834 lb (4,461 kg)
	gross: 14,081 lb (6,387 kg)
Dimensions:	length: 35 ft 9 ft (10.89 m) + probe
	wingspan: 30 ft 9¾ in (9.39 m)
	wing area: 179.6 ft² (9.39 m²)
	height: 13 ft 6⅛ in (4.12 m)
Speed:	max. 609 mph (980 km) at 8,000 ft (2,439 m)
Ceiling:	42,500 ft (12,957 m)
Range:	805 miles (1,296 km)
	ferry: 1,840 miles (2,963 km) with external tanks
Radar:	none
Armament:	25-lb (11-kg) Mk 76 target bombs and 2.75-inch (70-mm) rockets

A T-45C Goshawk from Training Wing 1 comes aboard the GEORGE WASHINGTON. *Note the aircraft's twin nose wheels, tricycle landing gear, and tail hook. (U.S. Navy/Corey Lewis)*

A T-45C Goshawk from squadron VT-7 lands aboard the JOHN C. STENNIS. When this photo was taken in March 2003, the Navy was forced to move pilot carrier qualification training to the Pacific coast because of the deployment of Atlantic Fleet carriers for Operation Iraqi Freedom. (U.S. Navy/Joshua Word)

A T-45C Goshawk is about to be refueled on the flight deck of the HARRY S. TRUMAN during a training evolution off the East Coast. The T-45C is based on the British Hawk, a popular aircraft flown by several nations in the training and light attack roles. (U.S. Navy/ Craig Spiering)

T-44A KING AIR

The T-44A was procured as a replacement for the TS-2/US-2 Tracker employed in the multiengine training role.

Design: The aircraft is a modification of the commercial Air King 90, with a straight wing mounting twin turboprop engines relatively far forward and a conventional tail configuration. The aircraft can be configured as a transport to carry two pilots and three passengers. During development the military version was designated VTAM(X).

Status: Operational. First flight of the T-44A occurred in January 1977. From April 1977, the Navy took delivery of 61 T-44A aircraft, all being assigned to squadrons VT-21 and VT-31; only the latter squadron now flies the T-44A. The U.S. Army procured unpressurized versions as the U-21A, and the Air Force obtained one as the UC-6A for special missions and one VC-6 as a VIP transport.

T-44A

Manufacturer:	Beech
Crew:	(5) pilot, copilot, instructor, 2 students
Engines:	2 Pratt & Whitney of Canada PT-6A-34B turboprop; 550 hp each
Weight:	empty: 6,326 lb (2,869 kg)
	gross: 9,650 lb (4,377 kg)
Dimensions:	length: 35 ft 6 in (10.82 m)
	wingspan: 50 ft 3 in (15.32 m)
	wing area: 293.9 ft² (27.3 m²)
	height: 14 ft 3 in (4.33 m)
Speed:	cruise: 276 mph (444 km) at 15,000 ft (4,573 m)
Ceiling:	29,500 ft (8,994 m)
Range:	1,455 miles (2,343 km)
Radar:	navigation

A T-44A King Air and a T-34C Turbomentor from Training Wing 4 fly in formation over Corpus Christi, Texas. The King Air wears a rear admiral's flag; in an earlier aviation era, aircraft actually flew such flags when admirals were on board. (U.S. Navy)

T-39 SABRELINER

The Navy operates several of the long-serving T-39s to train NFOs who fly in F-14, P-3C, S-3B, and two-seat variants of the F/A-18 aircraft. The T-39N is a basic T-39A upgraded with advanced radar and engines. It is flown only by training squadron VT-86. A single T-39D also remains in service.

Design: The T-39 has a low, swept-wing configuration with two turbojet engine nacelles mounted on the after fuselage. The aircraft is not carrier capable.

The N variant is distinguished from the basic T-39A by its Westinghouse APG-66NT radar, a modification of the APG-68 currently installed in several combat aircraft. The T-39N also has engine thrust reversers.

Designation: Originally flown by the Navy as the T3J, it was changed to T-39 in 1962.

Status: Operational. First flight of a modified commercial Sabreliner occurred on 16 September 1958; T-39A in June 1960; T-39D in December 1962. The first of 17 T-39N aircraft were delivered in late 1991; these were converted civil Sabre 40 aircraft. The aircraft are flown by Tracor Flight Services, Inc., under contract to the Navy.

T-39N

Manufacturer:	North American Rockwell
Crew:	(6) pilot, 2 instructors, 3 students
Engines:	2 Pratt & Whitney J60-P-3A turbojet; 3,000 lbst (1,361 kgst) each
Weight:	empty:
	gross: approx. 24,000 lb (10,886 kg)
Dimensions:	length: 46 ft 11 in (14.30 m)
	wingspan: 50 ft 5 in (15.37 m)
	wing area:
	height: 16 ft (4.88 m)
Speed:	max. 530 mph (853 kmh)
	cruise: 501 mph (806 kmh)
	Ceiling: 45,000 ft (13,720 m)
Range:	3,350 miles (5,390 km)
Radar:	APG-66NT

A T-39G Sabreliner assigned to squadron VT-86. Training squadrons have wing tail-fin letters with the squadron designation in small characters on the after fuselage. Previously, T-39s also were employed as VIP transports. (U.S. Navy/Patrick Nichols)

One of the T-39N Sabreliners assigned to the training role for instructing Naval Flight Officers (NFOs). These aircraft are contractor flown and maintained for squadron VT-86. (U.S. Navy)

T-38A TALON

The T-38 is the standard U.S. Air Force trainer, flown in small numbers by the Navy for test-pilot proficiency and air combat maneuver training. It closely related to the design of the Northrop F-5 Freedom Fighter and F-5E/F/G (now F-20) Tiger II aircraft.

Status: The YT-38 first flew in April 1959. More than 1,200 were produced, most for the U.S. Air Force, which still flies almost 500 in the training role; others remain in foreign service. The Air Force also flew an AT-38B attack version. The U.S. Navy took delivery of 18 aircraft.

One of the T-38A Talons assigned to the Naval Test Pilot School. The Navy previously employed T-38s for adversary training with squadron VF-43. The Air Force flies several hundred T-38s in the training role. (Mike Wilson)

T-38A

Manufacturer:	Northrop
Crew:	(2) pilot, student
Engines:	2 General Electric J85-GE-5A turbojet; 3,850 lbst (1,746 kgst) each with afterburner
Weight:	empty: 7,594 lb (3,445 kg)
	gross: 12,000 lb (5,443 kg)
Dimensions:	length: 46 ft 10 in (14.13 m)
	wingspan: 25 ft 3 in (7.7 m)
	wing area: 170 ft² (15.80 m²)
	height: 12 ft 11 in (3.92 m)
Speed:	max. cruise: 630 mph (1,014 kmh) at 40,000 ft (12,195 m)
	economical cruise: 594 mph (956 kmh) above 40,000 ft
Ceiling:	53,600 ft (26,341 m)
Range:	1,310 miles (2,111 km)
Radar	none

T-34C TURBOMENTOR

The Turbomentor is the Navy's training aircraft for basic and primary flight training. A few T-34C aircraft are used for recruiting and utility activities.

The turboprop T-34C model has replaced the earlier piston-engine aircraft in Navy service. The plane is not carrier capable. The Navy selected the Beechcraft Model 45 as a primary trainer in 1953, leading to procurement of the T-34A/B/C series. Two T-34B aircraft were converted to YT-34C prototypes (with turboprop engines) in 1973.

Names: The piston-engine T-34 aircraft had the name Mentor.

Status: Operational. First flight of the YT-34C occurred on 21 September 1973. IOC for the T-34C was in July 1976. A total of 352 T-34C aircraft were delivered from 1976 to 1988. (The earlier, piston-engine T-34s have been retired.)

The T-34 no longer is flown by the U.S. Air Force.

The T-34C Turbomentor continues to serve in the Navy training role, soon to be replaced by the T-6A Texan. The T-34 was procured in several variants in large numbers by the Air Force and Navy; the early, piston-engine variants were called simply Mentors. (Beech)

T-34C

Manufacturer:	Beech
Crew:	(2) pilot, student
Engines:	1 Pratt & Whitney of Canada PT6A-25 turboprop; 400 shp
Weight:	empty: 2,940 lb (1,334 kg)
	gross: 4,300 lb (1,950 kg)
Dimensions:	length: 28 ft 8½ in (8.75 m)
	wingspan: 33 ft 3⅞ in (10.16 m)
	wing area: 179.6 ft² (16.69 m²)
	height: 9 ft 7 in (2.92 m)
Speed:	max. 257 mph (413 kmh) at 5,335 ft (1,627 m)
	cruise: 247 mph (397 kmh) at 5,335 ft
Ceiling:	30,000 ft (9,146 m)
Range:	850 miles (1,370 km)
Radar:	none

TC-18F

The two training versions of the Boeing 707-320B used to prepare air crewmen for the E-6B Mercury TACAMO aircraft were discarded after structural problems were discovered in 2000. Both TC-18F aircraft were flown in this role in 1987–1991 and again from 1993 by Navy Strategic Communications Wing 1. The break in service was caused by a lack of funding, when they were grounded.

The Air Force flies an EC-18 electronics aircraft.

T-2C BUCKEYE

The T-2C variant of the Buckeye has long been used by the Navy for undergraduate jet pilot training. Only training squadron VY-86 currently flies the T-2C in the advanced NFO training program. A few aircraft also are flown by fleet readiness squadrons (for spin recovery training), the Navy's aggressor training squadron, and the Naval Test Pilot School. It is being replaced by the T-45 Goshawk.

Design: The Buckeye has straight wings, generally with wingtip tanks fitted, with the twin engines buried in the bottom of the fuselage. Wing pylons can be fitted for carrying small bombs, rockets, or gun pods. The aircraft is carrier capable; the last Navy student carrier qualifications in the T-2C were conducted aboard the HARRY S. TRUMAN (CVN 75) on 15 July 2003.

The T-2A was a single-engine aircraft, and the T-2B/C were similar but with twin engines; all earlier aircraft have been phased out of U.S. naval service. A T-2D variant was developed from the T-2C for the Venezuelan Navy, and a T-2E attack variant for the Greek Air Force.

Designation: The Buckeye originally was designated T2J; it was changed to T-2 in 1962.

Status: Operational. The Navy took delivery of 217 T-2A and 97 T-2B aircraft before procuring 231 T-2C variants from 1969 to 1975. The aircraft's service life has been extended from 7,500 to 12,000 hours, at considerable cost, pending availability of the T-45.

T-2C

Manufacturer:	North American Rockwell
Crew:	(2) pilot, student
Engines:	2 General Electric J85-GE-4 turbojet; 2,950 lbst (1,338 kg) each
Weight:	empty: 8,115 lb (3,681 kg)
	gross: 13,191 lb (5,983 kg)
Dimensions:	length: 38 ft 3½ in (11.67 m)
	wingspan: 38 ft 1½ in (11.62 m) over wingtip tanks
	wing area: 255 ft² (23.69 m²)
	height: 14 ft 10 in (4.51 m)
Speed:	max. 530 mph (853 kmh) at 25,000 ft (7,622 m)
Ceiling:	45,500 ft (13,970 m)
Range:	1,045 miles (1,683 km)
Armament:	up to 640 lb (290 kg) of bombs or rockets on 2 wing stations + wingtip tanks
Radar:	none

A trio of T-2C Buckeyes from squadron VT-9 fly in close formation during a training flight over Florida. Only two Navy squadrons now fly the T-2C. The long-serving Buckeye is being replaced by the T-45 Goshawk. (U.S. Navy/Darin K. Russell)

A T-2C Buckeye from squadron VT-9 comes aboard the carrier GEORGE WASHINGTON during carrier qualifications off the Atlantic coast. The last T-2C "carquals" were flown in July 2003 aboard the carrier HARRY S. TRUMAN. (U.S. Navy/Brian Fleske)

TA-4J SKYHAWK

The Skyhawk was developed in the early 1950s as a lightweight, daylight-only, nuclear strike aircraft. It subsequently evolved into a highly versatile attack aircraft, widely used by the Navy and Marine Corps, as well as by several foreign air forces. It survived in Navy service in the TA-4J configuration as a training aircraft until 1998 and as a utility aircraft until 2003. The last Marine Corps A-4M aircraft were retired in 1992.

The TA-4J has been replaced by the T-45 Goshawk.

Designation: The Skyhawk originally was designated A4D; it was changed to A-4 in 1962.

Status: A total of 2,960 A-4s were built for U.S. and foreign use, of which 555 were two-seaters, including 293 TA-4J aircraft for the Naval Air Training Command. The last delivery was an A-4M for the Marine Corps, in 1979. This was one of the longest production runs of any combat aircraft in history. The last U.S. combat variants was the Marine Corps A-4M, retired in 1992. Many A-4s survive in foreign air forces.

See 16th Edition/pages 399–400 for TA-4J characteristics.

ROTARY-WING AIRCRAFT

PRESIDENTIAL HELICOPTER PROGRAM (VXX)

There is a competition under way to acquire a new presidential helicopter—designated VXX in the development stage—to replace the long-serving VH-3 Sea Kings flown by Marine squadron HMX-1. The newer VH-60N "white top" helicopters are too small to accommodate the president and his immediate party as well as the necessary communications and navigation equipment.

The candidates for the VXX aircraft are the Sikorsky-Vought team's S-92 and the Lockheed Martin–led team's US101, a variant of the Agusta-Westland EH-101. The latter helicopter already is in military use in several other counties.

The delay in selecting the VVX until after the U.S. presidential election in early November 2004 suggested the selection would be the foreign aircraft—the Agusta-Westland EH-101.

MV-22B OSPREY

The MV-22 Osprey is a high-speed, rotary-wing aircraft currently being produced for the Marine Corps assault role as a replacement for the CH-46E Sea Knight and CH-53D Sea Stallion. In addition, the Air Force is procuring the CV-22 as a special operations aircraft. The Navy had plans to procure the HV-22 for the Search-and-Rescue (SAR) role, but procurement of that variant has not been initiated.

The aircraft has the potential for both AEW and ASW missions. The AEW aircraft would loiter at about 15,000 feet (4,500 m), with a radius of some 230 miles (370 km) with 2.5 hours on station; in-flight refueling could extend the on-station time to 5.5 hours. That aircraft would carry the APS-138 or APS-145 radar. (Potential U.S. Navy AEW configurations also provide for conformal-array radars on the fuselage of the aircraft.) The proposed ASW variant would carry Mk 50 torpedoes and operate a number of anti-submarine sensors, including APS-137 radar, dipping sonar, sonobuoys, and FLIR. At this writing, the Navy has no development plans for either the ASW or AEW variant.

The Navy–Marine Corps had the lead in developing the aircraft under the project designation JVX. The Marine Corps initially planned to procure 552 aircraft for vertical assault and the Navy an additional 50 for combat SAR.[23] The other Navy missions could have added some 200–300 additional aircraft to the program. The Air Force at one point envisioned a buy of 80 aircraft for special operations and the Army about 230 for medical evacuation, as well as for Special Electronic Mission Aircraft (SEMA). Thus, the V-22 program could have reached 900–1,200 aircraft.

The Army and Air Force withdrew from the program in the late 1980s, and on 25 April 1989, Secretary of Defense Dick Cheney eliminated all funding for the Navy–Marine Corps program. At the time, his staff proposed an alternative force of 376 CH-53E and 590 H-60 helicopters. Department of Defense opposition to the V-22 continued as late as September 1994, but the Marine Corps opposed all alternatives and Congress continued to support and fund the V-22 program.

Production is now approved for a Marine Corps buy of 360 MV-22s, Air Force procurement of 50 CV-22s, and 48 HV-22s for the Navy—a total acquisition of 458 aircraft. The CV-22 will replace the HM-53J Pave Low helicopter and the HV-22 the HH-60 helicopter. To help compensate for the delays in procurement, the Marine Corps MV-22 buy was accelerated to 30 aircraft per year beginning in FY 2003.

Design: The V-22, developed from the XV-15A technology-demonstration aircraft, has twin rotor-engine nacelles mounted on a connecting wing. The nacelles rotate to a horizontal position for conventional aircraft flight and are vertical for vertical take-off and landing or hover. Conversion from the hovering mode to forward airplane flight takes 12 seconds.

The basic aircraft has an internal cargo capacity of 10,000 pounds (4,536 kg) and an external (slung) capacity of 15,000 pounds (6,804 kg). Rolling takeoffs and landings are the normal operating mode, although VTOL operations are feasible. Thus, the design has the advantages of both a conventional aircraft and a helicopter. An in-flight refueling probe is provided.

The wing-engine section rotates 90°, and the rotors fold (automatically) for shipboard stowage. The length in that configuration is 62 feet, 7 inches (19.08 m), with a width of 18 feet, 5 inches (5.61 m).

The Marine Corps has proposed a gunship variant of the MV-22 that could carry a variety of guns, rockets, and missiles.

Operational: The No. 4 development aircraft began shipboard flight trials on the USS WASP (LHD 1) on 4 December 1990; they were highly successful.

Status: In production. First flight of the MV-22 occurred on 19 March 1989; first full conversion flight was on 14 September 1989. MV-22 IOC is planned for 2005; CV-22 IOC is planned for 2009.

Six development aircraft have been built. (Two crashed.)

MV-22B

Manufacturer:	Bell-Boeing
Crew:	(3) pilot, copilot, crew chief + 24 troops or 12 litters
Engines:	2 Allison T406-AD-400 turboshaft; 6,150 shp each (continuous rating 5,890 shp)
Weight:	gross: 60,500 lb (27,443 kg)
Dimensions:	fuselage length: 57 ft 4 in (17.48 m)
	wingspan: 46 ft 6 in (14.18 m) over engine nacelles
	height: 21 ft 8 in (6.63 m)
	rotor diameter: 36 ft (10.98)
	aircraft width (including rotor blades): 83 ft 8 in (25.51 m)
Speed:	max. 316 mph (143 kmh)
	max. cruise: approx. 300 mph (483 kmh) at 18,000 ft (5,488 m)
Ceiling:	26,000 ft (7,925 m)
Range:	494 miles (224 km) with 24 troops or 6,000 lb (2,720 kg) cargo in VTOL mode
	253 miles (115 km) with 8,300 lb (3,765 kg) external cargo in VTOL mode
	ferry: 2,100 miles (3,890 km) without refueling
Armament:	1 12.7-mm cannon (nose turret)
Radar:	none

---

23 The original Marine requirement was based on:
   16 HMM squadrons x 15 aircraft = 240
   2 reserve squadrons x 15 aircraft = 30
   2 HMT squadrons x 20 aircraft = 40
   1 VMX squadron x 15 aircraft = 15
   RDT&E, pipeline, 20 year attrition = 227

A pair of MV-22 Ospreys fly in the "conventional" mode over Edwards Air Force Base, California. Their turboshaft engine nacelles are in the horizontal position. The aircraft have massive rotors/propellers. The Air Force will use the CV-22 variant for special operations. (U.S. Air Force)

Two MV-22 Osprey STOVL aircraft carry out tests aboard the assault ship Iwo Jima (LHD 7). The large size and rotor downdraft of the MV-22 have presented challenges to operating the aircraft aboard ship. The MV-22 can takeoff vertically or in a rolling-takeoff mode. (U.S. Navy/ Mike Jones)

An MV-22 Osprey aboard the assault ship Iwo Jima during shipboard flight tests that resumed in 2003 after a delay of two years while technical and operational difficulties were solved. The MV-22 will provide far greater assault capabilities than the CH-46 Sea Knight helicopters. (U.S. Navy/Peter Cline)

An MV-22 Osprey with rotors folded at NAS Patuxent River, Maryland. The "wing" rotates to reduce the aircraft's footprint aboard ship. Note the rear loading ramp; most cargo is slung externally from the aircraft. (U.S. Marine Corps/Kevin Gross)

MH-68A STINGRAY

The MH-68A is a light armed helicopter acquired by the Coast Guard, primarily for the drug-interdiction role. Since 11 September 2001, the aircraft also has been employed in the homeland security role.

The helicopter is a variant of the Agusta A109 Power. It was selected by the Coast Guard in April 2000, following a competition and a year-long trial employing two MH-90 Enforcer helicopters from cutters.

The eight helicopters procured by the Coast Guard were manufactured in Italy, with completion, delivery, and support by Agusta Aerospace Corp., the firm's wholly owned U.S. subsidiary in Philadelphia. At the time of the Coast Guard selection, more than 140 A109 helicopters had been sold worldwide for police, emergency, and military use.

Design: The A109 is a streamlined helicopter of conventional design with a pod-and-boom configuration and a four-blade main rotor. The tricycle landing gear is fully retractable. A weather radar is fitted, as are FLIR and Low-Light-Level Television (LLLTV). Maximum endurance is five hours.

The helicopters are armed with machine guns.

Designation: The Coast Guard designates the MH-68A as a "short-range armed interdiction helicopter."

An MH-68A Stingray, with wheels tucked in, moves fast during an exercise. There is a 7.62-mm machine gun M240 mounted in the open doorway. The helicopter—often referred to (incorrectly) as "Shark" or "Maco"—was acquired to intercept drug runners. (U.S. Coast Guard/Scott Carr)

Three MH-68A Stingrays from Helicopter Interdiction Tactical Squadron (HITRON), the only squadron organization within Coast Guard aviation. There is a rescue hoist on the right side of the fuselage, giving the helicopter a multimission capability. (U.S. Coast Guard/Dana War)

Operational: The MH-68As are operated by the Coast Guard's Helicopter Interdiction Tactical Squadron (HITRON), based at Jacksonville, Florida.

Status: Operational. The Agusta A109 first flew on 4 August 1971. These helicopters were delivered to the Coast Guard in 2000–2001.

MH-68A

Manufacturer:	Agusta (Italy)
Crew:	(2) pilot, flight crewman + 6 passengers
Engines:	2 Pratt & Whitney 206C turboshaft; 426 shp each
Weight:	empty: 4,000 lb (1,815 kg)
	gross: 6,613 lb (3,000 kg)
Dimensions:	fuselage length: 37 ft 7 in (11.46 m)
	overall length: 42 ft 8 in (13.01 m)
	height: 11 ft 5 in (3.48 m)
	main rotor diameter: 36 ft 1 in (11.0 m)
Speed:	max. 193 mph (311 kmh)
	cruise: 177 mph (285 kmh)
Ceiling:	19,600 ft (5,975 m)
Range:	
Radar:	weather

HH-65A DOLPHIN

The French-designed Dolphin is flown by the Coast Guard in the short-range SAR role, replacing the HH-52A. The HH-65A is flown in larger numbers than any other Coast Guard aircraft.

Developed by Aérospatiale as model SA 366G Dauphin, the helicopter was selected in a Coast Guard competition in 1979.

Engine problems forced the Coast Guard to restrict operations beginning in January 2004. In FY 2003, the Coast Guard reported 32 incidents involving loss of engine power, compared to the same number for the three-year period FY 2000–2002.

Design: This is a streamlined helicopter with fully retract-able landing gear, twin turboshaft engines, and a fan-in-fin *fenestron* tail rotor (i.e., an 11-blade tail rotor within a shroud). The original problem-plagued LTS101 engines were replaced by Allison-Garrett LHTEC T800-800 turboshafts, the first being changed in 1991.

In Coast Guard service, they have a 3.5-million candlepower searchlight, an infrared system, and droppable rescue equipment. Maximum mission endurance is four hours. Those HH-65A helicopters that embark in icebreakers are fitted with skis in addition to their standard landing gear, giving them more stability for snow and ice operations.

The HH-65B was a proposed variant with avionics upgrade, and the HH-65C would have had the avionics upgrade and an enhanced digital engine control system. Neither variant was pursued.

Status: First flight of the SA 360 occurred on 2 June 1972; the SA 366G/HH-65A (prior to installation of avionics) on 23 July 1980. Coast Guard IOC was in November 1984.

The Coast Guard has procured 96 Dolphins, with deliveries delayed from a planned IOC of late 1981 because of engine problems.

Several nations fly the helicopter in the military role, with some variants fitted with anti-ship missiles and ASW equipment. The Israeli Navy procured two H-65A helicopters for shipboard evaluation with funds provided by the United States; the procurement of 20 additional helicopters by Israel followed, all built by Aérospatiale to HH-65A standards.

HH-65A

Manufacturer:	Aérospatiale
Crew:	(3) pilot, copilot, crewman + 3 passengers
Engines:	2 Allison-Garrett LHTEC T800-800 turboshaft; 1,200 shp each
Weight:	empty: 5,992 lb (2,718 kg)
	gross: 9,200 lb (4,173 kg)
Dimensions:	fuselage length: 37 ft 6 in (11.43 m)
	overall length: 43 ft 9 in (13.33 m)
	height: 12 ft 9 in (3.89 m)
	main rotor diameter: 39 ft 2 in (11.9 m)
Speed:	max. 201 mph (324 kmh)
	cruise: 160 mph (257 kmh)
Ceiling:	7,510 ft (2,290 m) hover In Ground Effect (IGE)
	5,340 ft (1,627 m) hover Out of Ground Effect (OGE)
Range:	radius 175 miles (280 km) with 30 minutes loiter
	max. 470 miles (760 km)
Radar:	none

A hovering HH-65A Dolphin lowers a swimmer into the water during a Search And Rescue (SAR) demonstration. In flight, the landing gear retracts, unlike the all-service H-60 series helicopters. The rescue hoist on the right side of the fuselage is obvious. (U.S. Coast Guard/Matthew Belson)

An HH-65A Dolphin returns from a mission. The helicopter has the unusual fenestron in place of a conventional tail rotor. Coast Guard aircraft wear the service's "racing stripes," as do cutters and small craft. (U.S. Coast Guard/Harry C. Craft III)

An HH-65A Dolphin on the ground at the Iraqi port of Umm Qasr. The helicopter was embarked in the BOUTWELL (WHEC 719), one of several Coast Guard cutters operating in the Persian Gulf during Operation Iraqi Freedom in 2003. (U.S. Coast Guard/John Gaffney)

MH-60S KNIGHTHAWK

The MH-60S is the fleet combat support variant of the H-60 series, intended for Vertical Replenishment (VERTREP), SAR, and Mine Countermeasures (MCM) roles and to support special forces. The Navy is planning to procure 237 helicopters to replace its H-46 Sea Knight, UH-3 Sea King, and HH-1 Huey, and possibly its MH-53E MCM helicopters.

All MH-60S helicopters are new production; previous proposals to remanufacture earlier H-60s were dropped. More than 60 were delivered by mid-2004.

The principal competitor to the MH-60S was a Kaman single-engine helicopter designated K-MAX®, which had conducted VERTREP tests from Navy ships. (K-MAX® helicopters are in commercial service.)

Design: The prototype MH-60S was a modified UH-60L Black Hawk, transferred to Navy in 1997 and redesignated YCH-60. The production aircraft are based on the UH-60L airframe, with two T700 engines and certain SH-60 dynamic systems, including the gear box and flight controls. An External Stores Support System (ESSS), consisting of removable four-station pylons, can be fitted to the MH-60S; the ESSS can carry additional fuel tanks to increase ferry range.

The MH-60S has the common cockpit configuration also used in the MH-60R; the rotor heads and tail pylons of both helicopters fold for shipboard storage. Like the MH-60R, the MH-60S can carry Hellfire guided missiles, guns, rockets, and machine guns.

The MH-60S can lift 9,000 pounds (4,082 kg) of cargo externally by sling.

Designation: Originally designated CH-60S.

Names: The Army tends to use two-word names for its H-60 "Hawk" series helicopters, the Navy one word.

Status: The first MH-60S flight occurred on January 2000. IOC was in February 2002.

The U.S. Army and National Guard have more than 1,500 H-60 series helicopters in service; the helicopter also is flown by the Air Force, primarily for special operations, and in smaller numbers by the Marine Corps (VH-60N) and Coast Guard (HH-60J), as well as by the armed forces of several other nations.

MH-60S

Manufacturer:	Sikorsky
Crew:	(3–4) pilot, copilot, 1 or 2 crewmen + 13 passengers
Engines:	2 General Electric T700-GE-401C turboshaft; 1,900 shp each
Weight:	empty: 11,516 lb (5,224 kg)
	loaded: 17,432 lb (7,907 kg)
	max. T/O: 22,000 lb (9,979 kg)
Dimensions:	fuselage length: 50 ft 9 in (15.26 m)
	overall length: 64 ft 10 in (19.76 m)
	height: 12 ft 4 in (3.76 m)
	main rotor diameter: 53 ft 8 in (16.36 m)
Speed:	max.:
	cruise:
Ceiling:	
Range:	
Radar:	none

An MH-60S Knighthawk from squadron HC-6 prepares to take off from the carrier HARRY S. TRUMAN during an exercise off Morocco. The MH-60S is intended for a variety roles and is capable of carrying rockets, missiles, and machine guns. (U.S. Navy/Craig R. Spiering)

An MH-60S Knighthawk from squadron HC-6 carries cargo to the carrier GEORGE WASHINGTON operating in the Persian Gulf. The Navy operates more H-60 series helicopters than all other types, and, under current plans, eventually only H-60s will be in Navy helicopter squadrons. (U.S. Navy/Brien Aho)

MH-60R SEAHAWK

The MH-60R is a multipurpose variant of the Seahawk, intended primarily for the ASW role but also capable of surface surveillance and attack. Because the MH-60R is to be based aboard aircraft carriers, as well as on surface combatants, it also is employed in numerous other combat and support roles, supplementing the MH-60S Knighthawk.

The Navy plans to acquire 247 new-production MH-60R helicopters, plus seven aircraft remanufactured from existing SH-60s. Seven MH-60R helicopters were in service by mid-2004.

The MH-60R is fitted with the APS-147 Multi-Mode Radar (MMR), which includes ISAR imaging and periscope detection modes; AAS-44 FLIR; ALQ-210 electronic countermeasures; MAD; AQS-22 Airborne Low-Frequency Sonar (ALFS); and sonobuoys for submarine detection. In the attack role, the helicopter can carry ASW torpedoes (Mk 46, Mk 50), Penguin ASMs, and Maverick ASMs. As in the MH-60S, door-mounted .50-cal machine guns can be fitted.

Two external fuel tanks can be fitted.

Designation: Originally designated SH-60R.

Status: Operational. First flight of the SH-60R occurred on 9 July 2002.

MH-60R

Manufacturer:	Sikorsky
Crew:	(4) pilot, copilot, 2 systems operators
Engines:	2 General Electric T700-GE-401C turboshaft; 1,900 shp each
Weight:	empty:
	max. T/O: 22,500 lb (10,204 kg)
Dimensions:	fuselage length: 50 ft 9 in (15.26 m)
	overall length: 64 ft 10 in (19.76 m)
	height: 12 ft 4 in (3.76 m)
	main rotor diameter: 53 ft 8 in (16.36 m)
Speed:	max: 160 mph (257 kmh)
	cruise:
Ceiling:	
Range:	2.7-hour mission in ASW configuration
	3.3-hour mission in ASUW configuration
Radar:	APS-147 MMR surveillance

One of two MH-60R Seahawks assigned to the Naval Air Systems Command lowers an AQS-22 Airborne Low-Frequency Sonar (ALFS) at the Atlantic Undersea Test and Evaluation Center. The MH-60R is a multimission helicopter, replacing the specialized SH-60B/F anti-submarine aircraft. (U.S. Navy)

VH-60N "WHITE TOP"

The Marine Corps flies eight VH-60 variants of the H-60 series as executive transports. Assigned to squadron HMX-1 at Quantico, Virginia, these "white top" helicopters provide transportation for the president and other senior national officials. They replaced the VH-1A Hueys previously employed in this role. When the president is embarked in one of these helicopters, it is designated "Marine One."

Design: The VH-60N is fitted with weather radar, cabin sound-proofing, EMP hardening, and has a VIP interior configuration.

Name: These helicopters do not have an official name; they generally are referred to as "White Tops" (see *Operational* notes for VH-3 Sea King).

Status: IOC was on 30 November 1988.

VH-60N

Manufacturer:	Sikorsky
Crew:	(4) pilot, copilot, flight engineer, radio operator, plus passengers
Engines:	2 General Electric T700-GE-700 turboshaft; 1,560 shp each
Weight:	empty: 11,284 lb (5,118 kg)
	loaded: 16,994 lb (7,708 kg)
Dimensions:	fuselage length: 50 ft ¾ in (15.26 m)
	overall length: 64 ft 10 in (19.76 m)
	height: 16 ft 10 in (5.13 m)
	main rotor diameter: 53 ft 8 in (16.36 m)
Speed:	max. 184 mph (296 kmh)
	max. cruise: 167 mph (268 kmh)
Ceiling:	19,000 ft (5,790 m)
	9,500 ft (2,896 m) hover IGE
	10,400 ft (4,390 m) hover OGE
Range:	370 miles (600 km) with 30 minutes loiter
Radar:	weather

HH-60J JAYHAWK

The HH-60J is the Coast Guard's medium-range SAR variant of the ubiquitous Black Hawk/Seahawk helicopter series. The HH-60J replaced the HH-3F Pelican and CH-3E Sea King in Coast Guard service. The Jayhawk is second only to the HH-65A in number of aircraft in Coast Guard service.

Design: The HH-60J configuration is similar to the Navy's SH-60F variants, with generally the same characteristics, except that the HH-60J can be fitted with three external fuel tanks for long-range operations (see maximum range, below). The helicopter has an external lift of 4,000 pounds (1,814 kg).

Like all H-60 series helicopters, the HH-60J has a fixed, tail-wheel landing gear. It can operate on board the 12 Famous-class Coast Guard medium-endurance cutters and larger ships. The helicopter has FLIR and a large searchlight.

Standard SH-60F data apply, except as indicated below.

Designation: The Japanese Maritime Self-Defense Force flies the SH-60J and UH-60J helicopters, the former a copy of the U.S. SH-60B Seahawk ASW aircraft and the latter a utility variant. The J indicates Japanese, in an improper use of the suffix letter.

Status: Operational. First flight was in September 1986. HH-60J IOC was in July 1991. The Coast Guard procured 42 Jayhawks through 1995.

HH-60J

Manufacturer:	Sikorsky
Engines:	2 General Electric T700-GE-401C turboshaft; 1,900 shp each
Crew:	(4) pilot, copilot, 2 crewmen + 6 rescuees
Weight:	gross: 21,884 lb (9,927 kg)
Range:	radius 345 miles (556 km) with 45 minutes loiter
Radar:	Bendix RDR-1300C weather

A VH-60N "White Top" configured as an executive transport flown by Marine squadron HMX-1. Eight of these helicopters are available to transport the president and other VIPs. The VH-60N has a single tail-wheel, mounted far aft. (Sikorsky)

An HH-60J Jayhawk sits on the tarmac at CGAS Astoria, Oregon. These helicopters can fly rescue missions of up to seven hours. A radome protrudes from the nose. (U.S. Coast Guard/Sarah Foster-Snell)

An HH-60J Jayhawk flies over a 41-foot utility boat from the Coast Guard Reserve Training Center in Yorktown, Virginia. Coast Guard helicopter crews are well practiced in operating with small craft and non-helicopter-capable ships. (U.S. Coast Guard/Jacquelyn Zettles)

HH-60H SEAHAWK

The HH-60H is the Navy's combat SAR variant of the H-60 series, replacing the HH-3A Sea King in that role. The HH-60H variants are flown by reserve squadrons HCS-4 and HCS-5, and all carrier HS squadrons are assigned two HH-60H variants (in addition to four SH-60F helicopters).

These helicopters can carry eight SEALs and their equipment when operating in support of special operations.

Design: The HH-60H variants have the APR-39 radar warning receiver, ALE-39 chaff/flare dispenser, and ALQ-144 infrared jammer, as well as sophisticated communications gear. Although these helicopters initially were armed with machine guns, proposals are being considered also to provide them with 2.75-inch (70-mm) rockets and Hellfire missiles, with growth potential for air-to-air missiles.

Planned upgrades to the HH-60 include a FLIR/laser designator-range finder.

Standard SH-60B/F data apply, except as indicated below.

Status: Operational. First flight occurred on 17 August 1988. HH-60H IOC (with HCS-5) was in July 1989.

HH-60H

Manufacturer:	Sikorsky
Crew:	(3) pilot, copilot, crew chief + rescuees
Range:	radius 290 miles (465 km)
Armament:	2 7.62-mm machine guns M60D (8,000 rounds)
Radar:	none

*AN HH-60H from squadron HS-2 aboard the carrier C*ONSTELLATION *(CV 64) moves into a hover alongside the ship. The "Connie" was on her final deployment in May 2003 when this photo was taken; she was decommissioned less than three months later. (U.S. Navy/Daniel J. McLain)*

*Members of Explosive Ordnance Disposal (EOD) Mobile Unit 6 drop to the flight deck of the carrier H*ARRY S. T*RUMAN during an exercise off the Atlantic coast of Morocco. The HH-60H Seahawk was designed for combat SAR and to support special operations forces. However, it is used for Underway Replenishment (UNREP) and in other roles. (U.S. Navy/Craig R. Spiering)*

SH-60B/F SEAHAWK

In naval service, the Seahawk is primarily an ASW helicopter; the SH-60B is the helicopter component of the Navy's ship-based LAMPS III ASW and over-the-horizon targeting system, and the SH-60F is a carrier-based ASW aircraft. Seven helicopters of both types have been remanufactured to the multipurpose SH-60R variant (see above).

Forward deployed SH-60s are armed with M60 or M240 7.62-mm machine guns.

The SH-60B is embarked in active cruisers, destroyers, and frigates in two-plane detachments from HSL squadrons; four SH-

60Fs are combined with two HH-60H Seahawks in six-aircraft HS squadrons aboard aircraft carriers.

The following ships were configured to carry two SH-60B helicopters:

    25 CG 47 TICONDEROGA class
    24 DD 963 SPRUANCE class
    26 FFG 7 OLIVER HAZARD PERRY class

In addition, the improved ships of the ARLEIGH BURKE (DDG 51) class, beginning with the OSCAR AUSTIN (DDG 79), have accommodations for two helicopters.

A single SH-60F was converted to test the vectored-thrust ducted propeller; it was redesignated X-49A.

Design: The Seahawk is adapted from the UH-60A Black Hawk, the U.S. Army's basic transport/utility helicopter. The SH-60B carries 2,000 pounds (907 kg) of avionics, including the ALQ-142 Electronic Support Measures (ESM) sensor (similar to the SLQ-32 found on most U.S. surface warships); this system permits the helicopter to provide over-the-horizon detection and missile targeting for the launching ship. The SH-60B also has a 25-sonobuoy dispenser, APS-124 radar, FLIR, ASQ-81 MAD, and a UYS-1(V)2 Proteus acoustic processor. No dipping sonar is fitted in the SH-60B. Beginning in 1990, the SH-60B variants have been fitted to carry the Penguin anti-ship missile. Some helicopters will be further modified to fire the Hellfire missile.

From 1995, these helicopters also are being fitted to mount a 7.62-mm M60D machine gun, AAR-47 missile detection system, ALE-39 chaff/flare dispenser, and ALQ-144 infrared jammer.

A YSH-60B was modified in 1984 to test the AQS-13F active dipping sonar and automated flight control system for the SH-60F. The carrier-based SH-60F has AQS-13F dipping sonar with a 1,500-foot (457-m) cable; the radar, MAD, sonobuoys, and some other equipment of the SH-60B have been deleted. The UYS-1(V)2 acoustic processor is fitted in the F variants.

Early plans called for a crew of four in the SH-60B, but in the event, the aircraft has three crewmen. Although designed to carry nuclear depth bombs, the Seahawks have not been "wired" for this weapon. The IBM corporation was the prime contractor for the LAMPS III/SH-60B, the first time the airframe manufacturer did not perform this role for a U.S. Navy helicopter; Sikorsky is the prime contractor for the SH-60F variant.

Designation: LAMPS (Light Airborne Multi-Purpose System) is a term originally coined for the SH-2 LAMPS I helicopter (see below). The LAMPS II was a design study that did not reach fruition.

Status: Operational; no longer in production. First flight of the YUH-60 test bed occurred on 17 October 1974; prototype SH-60B on 12 December 1979. Navy SH-60B IOC (with HSL-41) was in September 1983; SH-60F IOC (with HS-10) was in June 1989.

Australia, Greece, Spain, and Turkey have purchased the SH-60B or the commercial-sale S-70 Seahawk, and Japan has produced the SH-60J for shipboard use and the UH-60J for land basing. (A total of 17 nations other than the United States fly military variants of H-60/S-70 helicopters.)

SH-60B/F

Manufacturer:	IBM/Sikorsky
Crew:	(3) pilot, copilot/airborne tactical officer, sensor operator
Engines:	2 General Electric T700-GE-401 turboshaft; 1,690 shp each; helicopters procured after 1988 have 2 T700-GE-401C turboshaft; 1,900 shp each
Weight:	empty: 13,648 lb (6,191 kg)
	loaded: 19,500 lb (8,845 kg) in ASW role
	18,000 lb (8,165 kg) in Harpoon targeting role
	21,000+ lb (9,526+ kg) in utility role
Dimensions:	fuselage length: 50 ft (15.26 m)
	overall length: 64 ft 10 in (19.76 m)
	height: 17 ft 2 in (5.23 m)
	main rotor diameter: 53 ft 8 in (16.36 m)
Speed:	max. cruise: 145 mph (233 kmh)
Ceiling:	19,000 ft (5,790 m)
	9,500 ft (2,896 m) hover IGE
	10,400 ft (4,390 m) hover OGE
Range:	radius 57.5 miles (92.5 km) with 3 hours loiter
	radius 172.5 miles (278 km) with 1 hour loiter
Armament:	2 Mk 46/50 ASW torpedoes or 2 Penguin ASMs
Radar:	APS-124 in SH-60B (none in SH-60F)

An SH-60F Seahawk from HS-8 aboard the carrier JOHN C. STENNIS overflies the ship during operations in the Persian Gulf during Operation Enduring Freedom. The SH-60B and SH-60F Seahawks will be replaced by the versatile MH-60R Seahawk. (U.S. Navy/Tina Lamb)

An SH-60B Seahawk from HSL-43 on a training flight off San Diego carries a Penguin ASM on its left side, just forward of the helicopter's sonobuoy dispenser. There is a circular radome fitted under the aircraft's nose. (U.S. Navy/Edward G. Martens)

All H-60 helicopters can be fitted with machine guns. Here, Chief Aviation Warfare Systems Operator "Rusty" Kane checks a .50-caliber machine gun in the door of an SH-60F Seahawk from HS-5 aboard the carrier GEORGE WASHINGTON operating in the Persian Gulf. (U.S. Navy/ Summer Anderson)

An SH-60B Seahawk from HSL-44 hovers over the GEORGE WASHINGTON as crewmen attach a sling to the helicopter. The circular object on the helicopter is the rear of the towed MAD antenna. SH-60s are regularly employed in UNREP and other non-ASW operations. (U.S. Navy/Robert Brooks)

OH-58C KIOWA

Three diminutive OH-58C helicopters are assigned to the Naval Test Pilot School. The H-58 series was the losing entry in the Army's 1961 Light Observation Helicopter (LOH) competition. Despite being beat out by the OH-6, the Bell 206/OH-58 design became a commercial success, and the Navy ordered 40 as TH-57 SeaRangers for basic helicopter flight training (see below). Subsequently, the Army reopened the LOH competition and placed an initial order for 2,200 OH-58s.

Design: This is a single-engine, light helicopter with landing skids, a two-blade main rotor, and an anti-torque tail rotor mounted on the left side of the tailboom.

Several hundred OH-58A helicopters were updated to the OH-58C configuration.

Status: Operational. First flight of the OH-58A occurred on 10 January 1966. IOC of the TH-57A was in 1968; this was the first

An early OH-58 Kiowa light observation helicopter of the type flown by the Naval Test Pilot School. The helicopter still is flown in large numbers by the U.S. Army. The TH-57 SeaRanger is similar. (Bell)

military procurement of the OH-58 design. About 300 OH-58 series helicopters remain in service with the U.S. Army. It is flown by numerous other countries.

OH-58C

Manufacturer:	Bell
Crew:	(2) pilot, copilot + 2 passengers
Engines:	1 Allison T63-8-720 turboshaft; 420 shp
Weight:	empty: 1,464 lb (664 kg)
	max. T/O: 3,200 lb (1,451 kg)
Dimensions:	length: 32 ft 7 in (9.93 m)
	height: 9 ft 61/2 in (2.91 m)
	rotor diameter 35 ft 4 in (10.77 m)
Speed:	max. 138 mph (222 kmh)
	cruise: 117 mph (188 kmh)
Ceiling:	18,500 ft (5,640 m)
Range:	300 miles (490 km)
Radar:	none

TH-57C SEARANGER

The SeaRanger is a training version of the commercial Bell 206 JetRanger series. See OH-58C (above) for program details.

Design: The TH-57 is fitted with dual controls. The TH-57C models have improved avionics and controls; these aircraft are upgraded TH-57A variants (their designation was changed to TH-57C in February 1983).

Status: TH-57A IOC was in 1968; TH-57C IOC was in November 1982.

The Navy purchased 40 off-the-shelf commercial aircraft as the TH-57A in 1968; subsequently, 89 improved TH-57C models were procured in the 1980s. The latter replaced the TH-1L Hueys in the training role.

TH-57

Manufacturer:	Bell
Crew:	(5) pilot, 4 students
Engines:	1 Allison T63-A-700 turboshaft; 317 shp
Weight:	empty: 1,464 lb (664 kg)
	gross: 3,000 lb (1,361 kg)
Dimensions:	fuselage length: 32 ft 7 in (9.94 m)
	overall length: 41 ft (12.5 m)
	height: 9 ft 7 in (2.91 m)
	main rotor diameter: 35 ft 4 in (10.78 m)
Speed:	max. 138 mph (222 km)
	cruise: 117 mph (188 km)
Ceiling:	18,900 ft (5,762 km)
	13,600 ft (4,146 m) hover IGE
Range:	345 miles (483 km)
Radar:	none

A TH-57 SeaRanger, the Navy's basic training helicopter. The Navy provides basic helicopter training for Navy, Marine Corps, and Coast Guard pilots, and on occasion, for pilots from other government agencies. (Bell)

A TH-57C SeaRanger flown by the Naval Test Pilot School at NAS Patuxent River, home of the school as well as several of the Navy's test and development squadrons. The SeaRanger also is flown in the training role by squadrons HT-8 and HT-18. (Mike Wilson)

CH-53X HEAVY LIFT HELICOPTER

The Navy and Marine Corps are developing a more powerful version of the H-53E helicopter, at this writing designated CH-53X. Initially, it was believed the existing CH-53E/MH-53E force could be modernized to provide increased capability and to replace those helicopter when they reached the end of their service lives. However, improvements in flight controls, engines, rotor transmissions, cockpit displays, and other features led the services' to decide to have Sikorsky/United Aircraft develop a follow-on version of the H-53E. The aircraft would be capable of carrying a slightly heavier load but in more arduous operating environments, especially in hotter temperatures.

It is proposed to have the aircraft powered by three Rolls-Royce AE11007C turboshaft engines rated at 6,000 shp each. This power plant should permit a CH-53X lift capacity of 20 tons (20,412 kg), with a radius of approximately 125 miles (201 km).

Other features being considered are a greater ferry range (with drop tanks) and a rapid disassembly/reassembly capability for air transport. The existing H-53E helicopters generally require two days each to disassemble and to reassemble, an important factor in rapid-deployment operations.

Designation: The next aircraft designation in the H-53 series is H-53H. The VH-53F was a VIP version of the CH-53D, and the CH-53G was a helicopter similar to the CH-53A built for West Germany with German-made components.

Status: In development. If properly funded, the CH-53X could have its first flight in 2009–2010, with a possible IOC of 2013.

CH-53E/MH-53E SUPER STALLION/SEA DRAGON

Developed specifically for the U.S. Navy and Marine Corps, the H-53E series is the heaviest lift helicopter in service outside Russia. The CH-53E is flown by the Marines in the assault/heavy cargo roles; the MH-53E is flown by the Navy in the mine countermeasures and VERTREP roles.

Design: The CH-53E can lift 16 tons (16,330 kg) of external load. These helicopters have the same basic configuration as the D-model Sea Stallion, but with three engines, a seven-blade main rotor (vice six in the CH-53A/D), larger rotor blades, an in-flight refueling probe, and improved transmission. Two 650-gallon (2,470-liter) external tanks can be fitted to the sponsons. The CH-53E can lift 93 percent of the heavy equipment in a Marine division, compared to 38 percent for the CH-53D.

The MH-53E can handle the Mk 103 moored sweep gear, Mk 104 acoustic sweep, Mk 105 magnetic sweep, Mk 106 magnetic/acoustic sweep, ALQ-166 Lightweight Magnetic Sweep (LMS), and AQS-14 towed mine-hunting sonar. The improved AQS-20 mine-hunting sonar will be provided for these helicopters in place of the AQS-14. The MH-53E is capable of night operations, with a six-hour mission capability. (The RH-53D can operate only in daylight.)

Designation: The M prefix indicates multimission capability.

Historical: The RH-3A Sea King was the first airborne MCM helicopter approved for U.S. Navy service. In the early 1970s, it was replaced by the CH-53A Sea Stallion, which was used during Operation End Sweep, the 1972–1973 clearance of mines from North Vietnamese ports.

The CH-53A was succeeded by the RH-53D in 1972; these new helicopters were deployed to the Suez Canal in 1974–1975 (Operations Nimbus Star/Stream); to the Red Sea/Gulf of Suez in 1984 (Operation Intense Look); and to the Persian Gulf in 1987 (Operation Earnest Will).

In turn, the RH-53D was succeeded in the MCM role by the MH-53E.

Operational: Six MH-53E Sea Dragons were air-lifted by C-5A Galaxy transports to the Persian Gulf in early October 1990 to participate in Desert Shield/Desert Storm. They then operated from the helicopter carrier TRIPOLI (LPH 10), displacing Marine helicopters and troops.

Status: Operational. First flight of the YCH-53E occurred on 1 March 1974; first flight of the CH-53E on 13 December 1980; first flight of the MH-53E on 1 September 1983 (a CH-53E in the MCM configuration flew on 23 December 1981). IOC for the CH-53E (with HMH-464) was in February 1981.

An MH-53E Sea Dragon from squadron HM-15 retrieves an AQS-14A side-looking sonar during mine countermeasure operations in the Persian Gulf. The MH-53E was part of the detachment based at Bahrain when the photo was taken in November 2003. (U.S. Navy/Christopher Mobley)

A Fabrique National .50-caliber M3M machine gun has been mounted on the rear ramps of CH-53E Sea Stallion helicopters of squadron HMH-461. Normally, CH-53E and other U.S. Navy and Marine Corps cargo heliopters carry door-mounted machine guns when in forward areas. (U.S. Marine Corps/Eric C. Ely)

H-53E

Manufacturer	Sikorsky
Crew:	(3) pilot, copilot, crew chief + 55 troops
Engines:	3 General Electric T64-GE-416 turboshaft; 4,380 shp each
Weight:	empty CH-53E: 33,685 lb (15,280 kg)
	MH-53E: 36,336 lb (16,482 kg)
	gross: 73,500 lb (33,340 kg)
Dimensions:	fuselage length: 73 ft 4 in (22.33 m)
	overall length: 99 ft ½ in (30.18 m)
	height: 27 ft 9 in (8.46 m)
	main rotor diameter 79 ft (24.08 m)
Speed:	max. 195 mph (315 kmh) at sea level
	cruise: 172 mph (278 kmh) at sea level
Ceiling:	18,500 ft (5,640 m)
	11,550 ft (3,520 m) hover IGE
	9,500 ft (2,895 m) hover OGE
Range:	radius: 57.5 miles (92.5 km) with 16 tons of external cargo
	radius: 575 miles (926 km) with 10 tons of external cargo
	ferry: 1,150 miles (1,852 km)
Radar:	none

Operating out of Camp Lemonier, Djibouti, a Marine KC-130 Hercules simultaneously refuels two CH-53E Super Stallions over the Gulf of Aden. Each CH-53E has two "hum-vee" vehicles on slings. The helicopters are from reserve squadron HMH-772. (U.S. Marine Corps/Paula M. Fitzgerald)

A CH-53E Super Stallion lifts a 155-mm howitzer M198 belonging to the 13th Marine Expeditionary Unit during a pre-deployment exercise. The CH-53E—the largest helicopter in the West—is the only helciopter that can lift the M198. (U.S. Marine Corps/M. C. Miller)

A pair of CH-53E Sea Stallion helicopters from squadron HMH-362 fly over the Pacific, returning to MCAS Iwakuni, Japan, after an exercise in the Philippines. These helicopters will be retired in the near future, replaced by the MV-22 Osprey STOVL aircraft. (U.S. Marine Corps/Ruben D. Calderon)

An MH-53E Sea Dragon from squadron HM-14 at Bahrain. The squadron deploys detachments to the Persian Gulf to support U.S. naval operations in the area. Note the combination wheel–fuel housings and the in-flight refueling probe. (U.S. Navy/Miachel Sandberg)

An MH-53E Sea Dragon—partially disassembled and with its after fuselage folded—is unloaded from a C-5 Galaxy transport at NAS Sigonella, Sicily, after being flown from the United States. The HM-15 helicopter was used to support U.S. naval operations in the Mediterranean. (U.S. Navy/Damon J. Moritz)

CH-53D SEA STALLION

The H-53 series has served as the Marine Corps's heavy assault helicopter and the Navy's mine countermeasures helicopter. Only the Marines now operate the CH-53D. It has been partially replaced in Marine Corps and Navy service by the CH-53E Super Stallion and MH-53E Sea Dragon, respectively.

All earlier Navy/Marine Marine CH-53A helicopters have been retired.

Design: The basic dimensions of the CH-53D variant are similar to the E, except that the later helicopter has a third engine and other propulsion improvements. The H-53s have a large cargo compartment with a rear ramp.

The Navy previously operated RH-53D mine countermeasures helicopters. They were succeeded by the MH-53E Sea Dragon.

Operational: Eight Navy RH-53D helicopters, flying from the carrier NIMITZ, were used in the aborted April 1980 attempt to rescue hostages from the U.S. embassy in Tehran; seven of those helicopters were destroyed in the operation.

Refueling in flight five times from KC-130 tankers, an RH-53D made an 18½-hour flight across the United States.

Status: Operational. First flight of the CH-53A occurred on 14 October 1964. Marine Corps IOC (with HMH-463) was in November 1966.

The Navy and Marine Corps took delivery of 384 H-53A/D series helicopters; others were flown by the U.S. Air Force and foreign services. In addition to the 30 RH-53D models delivered to the U.S. Navy, six more MCM versions went to Iran prior to the 1979 Islamic revolution.

CH-53D

Manufacturer:	Sikorsky
Crew:	(3) pilot, copilot, crewman + 38 troops
	or 24 litters + 4 attendants (7 crewmen in RH-53D)
Engines:	2 General Electric T64-GE-413 turboshaft; 3,925 shp each
Weight:	empty: 23,628 lb (10,718 kg)
	loaded: 34,958 lb (15,857 kg)
	gross: 42,000 lb (19,051 kg)
Dimensions:	fuselage length: 67 ft 2 in (20.48 m)
	overall length: 88 ft 3 in (26.92 m)
	height: 24 ft 11 in (7.59 m)
	main rotor diameter: 72 ft 3 in (22.04 m)
Speed:	max. 196 mph (315 kmh)
	cruise: 173 mph (278 kmh)
Ceiling:	21,000 ft (6,402 m)
	13,400 ft (4,085 m) hover IGE
Range:	620 miles (1,000 km)
	ferry: 1,020 miles (1,641 km)
Radar:	none

A CH-53D Sea Stallion from squadron MHM-463 is refueled on an airstrip on the Philippine island of Basco during an exercise with U.S. and Philippine forces. These helicopters have two turboshaft engines above the fuselage; the H-53E series has three. (U.S. Marine Corps/Josh Hauser)

CH-46E SEA KNIGHT

The CH-46E is the Marine Corps's principal assault helicopter. The CH-46D/HH-46D/UH-46D variants flown by the Navy in the VERTREP and SAR roles are being withdrawn from service. The Marine variant will be replaced by the long-delayed MV-22 Osprey tilt-rotor aircraft. The Navy is replacing the Sea Knights in the VERTREP role with the MH-60S, with the last Sea Knights being retired by 2004–2005.

Design: The Sea Knight has a tricycle landing gear and small, wheel-housing sponsons aft, distinguishing it from the similar, widely flown CH-47 Chinook cargo helicopter. It is a tandem-rotor helicopter with a rear ramp for the rapid loading and unloading of cargo, including small vehicles; the rotor blades fold for shipboard stowage. The H-46 series has demonstrated the capability to remain afloat for more than two hours in 2-foot (0.6 m) waves with the rotors stopped.

The Marines have upgraded 273 CH-46A/D troop helicopters to the CH-46E configuration. Provided in the upgrade are improved engines, crash attenuating seats for pilots, a more survivable fuel system, and an improved rescue winch. Subsequent upgrades have been undertaken to extend the service lives of these aircraft.

Designation: Originally designated HRB, the naval variants were changed to H-46 in 1962.

Status: Operational. First flight of the YHC-1A prototype occurred on 22 April 1958. Marine IOC (with HMM-265) was in June 1964.

The Navy took delivery of 264 Sea Knights and the Marine Corps received 360 helicopters from 1961 to 1977.

Marines from the 24th MEU rope from a hovering CH-46E Sea Knight on to the deck of the assault ship SAIPAN (LHA 2). The ship was operating off the Atlantic coast in April 2004 as she prepared for deployment to the Persian Gulf. (U.S. Navy/Garl L. Johnson III)

CH-46E

Manufacturer:	Boeing Vertol
Crew:	(3) pilot, copilot, crewman + 25 troops
	or 15 litters + 2 attendants
Engines:	2 General Electric T58-GE-16 turboshaft; 1,870 shp each
Weight:	empty: 15,198 lb (6,894 kg)
	gross: 24,300 lb (11,022 kg)
Dimensions:	fuselage length: 46 ft 8 in (13.92 m)
	overall length: 84 ft 4 in (25.72 m)
	main rotor diameter: 25 ft 6 in (7.81 m)
	height: 16 ft 8 in (5.08 m)
Speed:	max. 161 mph (259 kmh)
	cruise: 158 mph (254 kmh)
Ceiling:	9,400 ft (2,866 m)
Range:	radius: 86 miles (139 km) with payload
	ferry: 690 miles (1,111 km)
Radar:	none

TH-6B CAYUSE

The Naval Test Pilot School flies six TH-6B Cayuse helicopters. Previously, the school operated four OH-6B Cayuse helicopters, which have been discarded.

The Cayuse was developed by Hughes for the Army's 1961 Light Observation Helicopter (LOH) competition. The helicopter proved a highly versatile aircraft, and the commercial Model 500 set 23 international records for helicopters in 1966.

Design: The fuselage has a pod-and-boom structure with landing skids. The TH-6B has a two-blade main rotor and anti-torque rotor on the tail boom.

Designation: The OH-6 was designated HO-6 prior to 1962.

Status: Operational. First flight of the YHO-6 occurred on 27 February 1963. IOC with the U.S. Army was in 1966.

Soldiers from the 1st Battalion of the 1st Special Operations Airborne Unit parachute from a CH-46E Sea Knight from HMM-262 during exercises on Okinawa. The CH-46 and MV-22 can carry light vehicles, loaded through the rear ramp. (U.S. Navy/Kaitlyn Rae Vargo)

A CH-46E Sea Knight from squadron HMM-263 lifts off the assault ship KEARSARGE (LHD 3) as the ship supports the 24th Marine Expeditionary Unit (MEU) ashore in Iraq. The long-serving CH-46s are schedule to be replaced by the MV-22 Osprey STOVL aircraft. (U.S. Navy/Dave Nagle)

A TH-6B Cayuse helciopter assigned to the Naval Test Pilot School. A variety of aircarft are flown by the school to allow students to undergo flight in dissimilar aircarft with various flight characteristics. (U.S. Navy)

Several foreign military services fly variants of the 500/H-6 in a variety of roles, including ASW.

TH-6B

Manufacturer:	McDonnell Douglas
Crew:	(2) pilot, observer + 2 passengers
Engines:	1 Allison T63-A-5A turboshaft; 317 shp
Weight:	empty: 1,229 lb (557 kg)
	loaded: 2,400 lb (1,090 kg)
Dimensions:	length: 30 ft 3¾ in (9.24 m)
	height: 8 ft 1½ in (2.48 m)
	rotor diameter: 26 ft 4 in (8.03 m)
Speed:	max. cruise: 150 mph (241 kmh)
	cruise: 134 mph (216 kmh)
Ceiling:	7,300 ft (2,225 m) hover OGE
	11,800 ft (3,595 m) hover IGE
	15,800 ft (4,815 m) service
Range:	380 miles (611 km)
Radar:	none

UH-3/VH-3 SEA KING

The SH-3 Sea King was the U.S. Navy's standard carrier-based ASW helicopter from the early 1960s into the early 1990s. It has been replaced aboard aircraft carriers by the SH-60F Seahawk in the ASW role and in the SAR and utility roles by another variant of the H-60 series. The Sea King now is flown only in the VIP transport role, designated VH-3D.

Navy aircraft have had all ASW gear removed. The Marine Corps VH-3 aircraft are assigned to squadron HMX-1 to transport the president and other VIPs.

Design: The Sea King has a "boat" hull but does not normally alight on the water (unlike the Coast Guard HH-3F Pelican). The tail pylon and main rotor blades fold for carrier stowage. In the ASW role, the ultimate ASW-configured SH-3H had AQS-13B dipping sonar, sonobuoys, APN-130 Doppler radar, AQS-81 MAD, and an ALE-37 chaff dispenser. A total of 145 Sea Kings were converted to this configuration.

Two Sea Kings (designated YSH-3J) were used to test sensors for the SH-60B.

Earlier SH-3A/D ASW variants, the HH-3A rescue variant, and the RH-3A mine countermeasures versions all have been discarded.

Designation: Formerly the HSS-2, the Sea King was redesignated SH-3 in 1962. The HSS-1 was the original designation of the SH-34 Seabat, a very different helicopter.

SH-3H Sea Kings employed in the utility role with ASW equipment removed were changed to UH-3H in the late 1990s.

Operational: During Operations Desert Shield and Desert Storm in 1990–1991, SH-3H helicopters aboard participating aircraft carriers were fitted with a flexible 7.62-mm M60D machine gun, mounted in the (starboard) door opening.

Marine squadron HMX-1 provides VH-3D helicopters for the presidential transport mission. The VH-3D (as well as VH-60N) helicopters assigned to the Executive Flight Detachment of HMX-1 are painted a mix of Army brown and Marine green with white upper surfaces, the source of their nickname "White Tops."

A VH-3D from HMX-1 was used to transport Pope John Paul II during his October 1995 visit to the United States.

Status: First flight of the XHSS-2 occurred on 11 March 1959; first flight of the SH-3H in April 1972. Navy IOC (with HS-1) was in June 1961.

The helicopter is flown by several foreign services.

Hovering over San Diego Bay, a UH-3H Sea King from squadron HC-85 practices loading water buckets to help fight California fires. The bucket can hold 324 gallons, weighing 3,000 pounds. Several Navy helicopters helped fight the 2003 fires that ravaged the state. (U.S. Navy/Michael D. Kennedy)

UH-3H

Manufacturer:	Sikorsky
Crew:	(4) pilot, copilot, 2 systems operators
Engines:	2 General Electric T58-GE-10 turboshaft; 1,400 shp each
Weight:	empty: 13,465 lb (6,108 kg)
	gross: 21,000 lb (9,526 kg)
Dimensions:	fuselage length: 54 ft 9 in (16.69 m)
	overall length: 72 ft 8 in (22.15 m)
	height: 16 ft 10 in (5.13 m)
	main rotor diameter: 62 ft (18.9 m)
Speed:	max. 166 mph (267 kmh)
	cruise: 136 mph (219 kmh)
Ceiling:	10,500 ft (3,201 m) hover IGE
	14,700 ft (4,482 m) ceiling
Range:	620 miles (1,000 km)
	ferry: 745 miles (1,198 km)
Radar:	LN-66HP search

A VH-3D Sea King from Marine squadron HMX-1 overflies Washington, D.C. The president normally flies in a Sea King, which has more headroom than the VIP-configured VH-60N White Top helicopters. The presidential seal is on the nose of the helicopter. (U.S. Navy)

A UH-3H Sea King from squadron HC-2 hovers while members of EOD Mobile Unit 8 are recovered from the Persian Gulf. The remaining Sea Kings are scheduled to be replaced by MH-60S Knighthawk helicopters. (U.S. Navy/Johnny R. Wilson)

SH-2 LAMPS I

The SH-2 LAMPS I was an ASW helicopter previously flown in large numbers from surface combatants. All have been discarded from the U.S. Navy, although they still are flown by the navies of Australia, Egypt, New Zealand, Pakistan, and Portugal.

The last U.S. SH-2G helicopters were assigned to reserve squadron HSL-94; they were fitted with the Magic Lantern laser mine-detection system.

The Navy's need for ship-based ASW helicopters in the early 1970s led to the conversion of 20 single-engine HU2K/UH-2 Seasprite utility helicopters to the SH-2D configuration and another 85 conversions to the SH-2F variant; subsequently, 54 additional SH-2F helicopters were procured. The surviving D models later were upgraded to the F configuration, the last in 1983. Subsequently, a small number of SH-2s were upgraded to the SH-2G configuration for exclusive service aboard Naval Reserve Force

A prototype AH-1Z SeaCobra—sometimes referred to as a Super Cobra—takes off during flight trials. The Marine Corps has decided to acquire the AH-1Z instead of a larger, more capable helicopter gunship, like the Army's AH-56 Apache. (Bell)

(NRF) frigates, and six FY 1987 helicopters were built to the SH-2G configuration.

See 17th Edition/pages 454–55 for characteristics.

Designation: Originally designated HU2K; this was changed to UH-2 in 1962 and to SH-2 on their conversion to the ASW configuration.

Name: The name Seasprite was officially assigned to the HU2K/H-2 series, but it was rarely used.

AH-1Z SEACOBRA

The AH-1Z is a major upgrade of the AH-1W SeaCobra to provide the Marine Corps (and some foreign users) with an affordable helicopter gunship well into the 21st century. The Marine Corps plans to procure 180 remanufactured AH-1W/AH-1Z helicopters from Bell Helicopter Textron.

The principal changes are (1) provision of a four-blade, hinge-less, bearingless main rotor system in place of the two-blade, semi-rigid, teetering rotor system; and (2) an enhanced electronic warfare suite with the APR-39(XE2) radar warning device, APR-44 infrared detector, AVR-2A laser warning receiver, ALQ-144A Infrared (IR) countermeasures system, and ALE-39 chaff and IR flare dispenser.

The four-blade rotor provides an increase in the helicopter's flight envelope, maximum speed, and rate of climb and reduced rotor vibration.

See AH-1W SeaCobra for basic characteristics.

Status: First flight of the AH-1Z occurred on 7 December 2000; IOC is planned for 2007. Remanufacturing of AH-1W helicopters is under way.

AH-1W SEACOBRA

The SeaCobra is a specialized gunship helicopter that evolved from the widely used Huey series. It is flown by the Marine Corps's utility and attack helicopter squadrons (HMLA).

The AH-1G variant was the first specialized gunship of the Huey series, produced for both the Army and Marine Corps. (UH-1 series helicopters have been heavily armed, including Navy variants flown in the Vietnam War.)

Design: The SeaCobra has a narrow fuselage that provides minimal cross section, with stub wings for carrying rocket packs or gun pods, a nose turret with a 20-mm three-barrel cannon, and tandem seating for a gunner (forward) and pilot. The 20-mm cannon has a helmet-sight system.

All AH-1W helicopters are being fitted with the FLIR/laser designator–range finder and a video camera/recorder as part of a Night Targeting System (NTS).

The now-standard AH-1W has a weapons payload of 3,000 pounds (1,361 kg), including the Army-developed Hellfire missile, TOW anti-tank missile, Sidearm radar-homing missile, and Sidewinder AAM. Alternatively, drop tanks can be fitted to extend range. An ALE-39 chaff/flare dispenser is fitted. This helicopter can take off on a single engine and climb at more than 800 feet (244 m) per minute.

Surviving AH-1T helicopters were upgraded to the AH-1W configuration, with new procurement following.

Designation: The AH-1W originally was designated AH-1T+.

Status: Operational. First flight of the Army AH-1G occurred on 7 September 1965; first flight of the AH-1T+ on 16 November 1983. IOC of the AH-1G with the Marine Corps was in 1969; AH-1T in October 1977; AH-1W in March 1986.

The last AH-1W helicopters were delivered in 1999. Weapon and other upgrades are expected to provide for a service life through at least 2020, at which point it is planned to be replaced by the proposed Joint Rotary-wing Aircraft (JRA).

More than 2,500 Cobra gunships have been built for U.S. and foreign military services, with the AH-1S model coproduced by Mitsui in Japan.

AH-1W

Manufacturer	Bell
Crew:	(2) pilot, gunner
Engines:	2 General Electric T700-GE-401 turboshaft; 1,690 shp each
Weight:	empty: 10,200 lb (4,627 kg)
	gross: 14,750 lb (6,690 kg)
Dimensions:	fuselage length: 45 ft 6 in (13.87 m)
	overall length: 58 feet (17.68 m)
	height: 14 ft 2 in (4.32 m)
	main rotor diameter: 48 ft (14.63 m)
Speed:	max. 219 mph (352 kmh) at sea level
Ceiling:	17,500 ft (5,335 m)
	14,750 ft (4,497 m) hover IGE
	3,000 ft (915 m) hover OGE
Range:	330 miles (528 km)
Armament:	1 20-mm cannon M197 (750 rounds)
	8 TOW or Hellfire missiles
	or 38 2.75-inch rockets
	or 32 5-inch Zuni rockets
	plus 2 Sidewinder AAMs
Radar:	none

An AH-1W SeaCobra from squadron HMA/L-269 prepares to take off from the assault ship KEARSARGE. The gunship has Hellfire anti-tank missiles mounted on the right side of the fuselage. These missiles have been used in large numbers against targets in Iraq. (U.S. Navy/Finley Williams)

Flight deck personnel on the KEARSARGE service an AH-1W SeaCobra from squadron HMA/L-269. The twin turboshaft engines are visible atop the fuselage. More H-1 series helicopters have been produced than any other Western helicopter. (U.S. Navy/Finely Williams)

UH-1Y HUEY (IROQUOIS)

Bell is remanufacturing 100 UH-1N helicopters for the Marine Corps. The principal changes are provision of two General Electric T700-GE-401C turbine engines (1,546 continuous shp each) and a four-blade, hingeless, bearingless main rotor system in place of the two-blade, semirigid, teetering rotor system (as in the AH-1Z upgrade). The four-blade rotor provides an increase in the helicopter's flight envelope, maximum speed, and rate of climb, and reduced rotor vibration.

A FLIR with thermal imaging, TV camera, and laser designation system is provided. A variety of weapons can be fitted, with provision for a GAU-17A multibarrel machine gun to be mounted as well as flexible door-mounted .50-caliber GAU-16A or 7.62-mm M240D machine guns. The APR-39B(V)2 radar warning receiver and AAR-47(V)2 missile warning and laser detection system are provided, as well as the ALE-47 countermeasures dispenser.

See HH-1N/UH-1N entry for basic characteristics.

Status: First flight of the UH-1Y occurred in December 2001.

HH-1N/UH-1N HUEY (IROQUOIS)

The Huey series is the most widely used military helicopter in the West. The HH-1N and UH-1N are the only variants now flown by the Navy and Marine Corps, employed in the utility role from ships and ashore.

The Navy TH-1L training and HH-1K rescue variants have been discarded, as have the Marine Corps VH-1N variants used for VIP transport with HMX-1.

Designation: The Huey originally was designated XH-40 during development. It entered service with the Army as HU-1 and changed in 1962 to UH-1. In 1991, many of the UH-1Ns employed for SAR operations aboard amphibious ships and at air stations were redesignated HH-1N.

Name: Officially named Iroquois, in accord with the Army scheme of naming helicopters for American Indian tribes, the hel-

A Marine UH-1 Huey shown in August 2003 supporting a U.S. raid on a terrorist position in the city of Rashid, Iraq. The Navy is phasing out its few remaining Hueys. (U.S. Marine Corps/Colin Wyers)

Troops rappel from a UH-1Y Huey during flight trials of the updated helicopter. The Huey, which gained fame in the Vietnam War, has been replaced in the U.S. Army by the UH-60 Black Hawk helicopter, which the Marine Corps has rejected as a replacement for the CH-46 Sea Knight. (Bell)

icopter invariably is called *Huey*, derived from the earlier designation HU-1E.

Status: Operational. First flight of the XH-40 occurred on 22 October 1956. Marine IOC (with VMO-1) was in March 1964; UH-1N IOC was in 1971.

More than 16,000 Hueys have been produced for U.S. and foreign service since the Bell design won the U.S. Army's competition for a turbine helicopter in 1955.

UH-1N _____

Manufacturer:	Bell
Crew:	(3) pilot, copilot, crew chief + 12–15 troops
Engines:	2 United Aircraft of Canada PT6T turboshaft; 900 shp each
Weight:	empty: 5,549 lb (2,517 kg)
	gross: 10,500 lb (4,763 kg)
Dimensions:	fuselage length: 42 ft 5 in (12.93 m)
	overall length: 57 ft 3 in (17.47 m)
	height: 14 ft 5 in (4.39 m)
	main rotor diameter: 48 ft 2 in (14.7 m)
Speed:	126 mph (203 kmh)
Ceiling:	15,000 ft (4,573 m)
	12,900 ft (3,933 m) hover IGE
Range:	290 miles (463 km)
Armament:	various combinations of machine guns and rockets can be mounted
Radar:	none

A Marine UH-1 Huey is unloaded from the high-speed ship WESTPAC EXPRESS (HSV 4676) at the port of Chuk Su Met, Thailand. The HSVs can carry vehicles and light aircraft, as well as troops, but are limited in the distances they can transport troops. (U.S. Marine Corps/James P. Douglas)

A Marine UH-1 Huey over Iraq. These helicopters generally are armed with door-mounted machine guns when in forward areas. The Hueys and SeaCobras have distinctive skids. (U.S. Marine Corps/ J. A. Krusen)

SA 330J PUMA

The Navy's shortfall of UH-46 Sea Knight helicopters for VERTREP operations led the Military Sealift Command (MSC) to evaluate the commercial SA 330J Puma helicopter for that role. Following trials aboard the replenishment ship SIRIUS (T-AFS 8) in December 1999, MSC awarded an initial three-year, fixed-price contract to Geo-Seis Helicopters, Inc., to provide and operate two Pumas aboard the combat stores ships SIRIUS, SATURN (T-AFS 10), and CONCORD (T-AFS 5).

One of these ships operates the helicopters for six months, after which the Pumas are shifted to another ship about to forward deploy. Additional Pumas may be similarly employed, pending availability of the CH-60S for the VERTREP role.

The Puma was developed initially to meet a French Army requirement for an all-weather, day/night helicopter that could operate in all climates. In 1978 the SA 330J became the first commercial helicopter outside of the Soviet Union to be certified for all-weather operations.

Status: Operational. The SA 330J civil variant was introduced in 1976 (the SA 330L was the military configuration). The Puma is in service with the armed forces of more than 40 nations. It has been produced under license in Britain, Indonesia, and Romania, with production totaling about 700 helicopters.

SA 330J

Manufacturer:	Aérospatiale
Crew:	(2) pilot, flight crewman
Engines:	2 Turboméca Turmo IVC turboshaft; 1,575 shp each
Weight:	empty: 8,365 lb (3,766 kg)
	max T/O: 16,315 lb (7,400 kg)
Dimensions:	fuselage length: 46 ft 2 in (14.06 m)
	overall length: 59 ft 6 in (18.15 m)
	height: 16 ft 11 in (5.14 m)
	main rotor diameter: 49 ft 6 in (15.08 m)
Speed:	max. 162 mph (262 kmh)
Ceiling:	
Range:	342 miles (550 km)
Radar:	none

An SA 330J Puma carries cargo from the replenishment ship SATURN (T-AFS 10) to the carrier ENTERPRISE during a replenishment operation in the Indian Ocean. These French-designed aircraft have been leased to make up for a shortfall in Navy VERTREP helicopters. (U.S. Navy/Jason W. Pfiester)

Cargo aboard the replenishment ship SPICA (T-AFS 9) is picked up by an SA 330J Puma for delivery to the carrier HARRY S. TRUMAN as the ships steam off the Atlantic coast of Morocco. The SA 330Js have U.S. civil registration numbers (i.e., N prefix). (U.S. Navy/ Lilliana LaVende)

EXPERIMENTAL AIRCRAFT

X-49A

A single SH-60F has been converted to test the vectored-thrust ducted propeller; it was redesignated X-49A. The aircraft is assigned to HX-21.

X-31A ENHANCED FIGHTER MANEUVERABILITY DEMONSTRATOR

The two X-31A research aircraft intended to demonstrate the possibility of the high-angle-of-attack flight regime to enable a fighter to achieve tighter, faster turns and earlier weapon firing opportunities have been discarded.

Flight testing of the two X-31A aircraft was carried out by an international test organization made up of representatives from NASA, the Defense Research Projects Agency (DARPA), the U.S. Navy and Air Force, Germany, and Rockwell International and Messerschmitt-Bolkow-Blöhm (MBB).[24] DARPA has overall program management, with the Navy serving as DARPA's agent and providing on-site direction.

Two aircraft were built; one X-31 crashed at Edwards Air Force Force, California, on 19 January 1995.

See 16th Edition/pages 416–17 for characteristics.

Designation: The designation X-31 was assigned on 23 February 1987.

X-26A

The X-26 is a "quiet" observation research aircraft intended to develop stealth features for a target acquisition aircraft. Two X-26A are flown by the Navy. Details are classified.

The unpowered X-26A is a high-performance sailplane based on the all-metal Schweizer SGS 2-32 design. The X-26B uses a gasoline engine behind the pilot's compartment to drive a propeller mounted on a pylon atop the aircraft's nose.

The predecessor to the X-26 was the Lockheed QT-2PC, which was evaluated in Vietnam during the 1960s; on return to the United States, it was reconfigured as the X-26B. It subsequently was tested by the Army, Air Force, and Navy.

Two men can be carried in the large cockpit.

Status: First flight of the SGS 2-32 occurred on 3 July 1962. A total of 89 were built through January 1978, when production ended. The military X-26 program included three A and one B aircraft. All three X-26A variants are operated by the Navy.

X-26A

Manufacturer:	Schweizer
Crew:	(2) pilot, observer
Engines:	none
Weight:	empty:
	loaded: 1,430 lb
Dimensions:	length: 26 ft 9 in (8.15 m)
	wingspan: 57 ft 1 in (17.40 m)
	wing area: 180 ft² (16.72 m²)
	height: 9 ft 3 in (2.82 m)
Speed:	
Ceiling:	
Range:	
Radar:	none

An X-26A operated by the Naval Test Pilot School at NAS Patuxent River. The quiet research aircraft is another one of the unusual planes employed to train test pilots. (U.S. Navy)

XV-15A

The XV-15A is a tilt-rotor VTOL demonstration aircraft that served as a technology prototype for the V-22 Osprey series and the Bell Agusta 609 aircraft. Developed by Bell Helicopter Textron, the XV-15A demonstrated the ability of a rotary-wing aircraft to fully convert in flight to a conventional aircraft configuration.

Bell built two XV-15A aircraft under NASA and Army sponsorship. Subsequently, the Navy–Marine Corps gave support to the project. See 17th Edition/page 460 for characteristics.

Operational: In a key XV-15A evaluation, one aircraft flew 54 landings and takeoffs from the helicopter carrier TRIPOLI (LPH 10) in August 1982. Although the aircraft was not intended for shipboard operation, the tests succeeded with only minor difficulties. The XV-15A also has flown trials from a Coast Guard cutter.

Status: First flight occurred on 3 May 1957. One aircraft crashed while landing in 1993 and was not rehabilitated; the second continued in operation until 2003, when it was transferred to the new National Air and Space Museum at Dulles, Virginia.

LIGHTER-THAN-AIR

All Navy and Coast Guard Lighter-Than-Air (LTA), or airship, programs have been halted. The Navy's development of a surveillance airship was canceled in early 1992, shortly before completion of the first flight of a full-size prototype (the YEZ-2A/Sentinel 5000), and the Coast Guard's fully operational aerostat surveillance program was "grounded" on 31 December 1991 for transfer to the Army.[25] On that date, the five Coast Guard sea-based aerostat vessels were brought into the ports of Miami and Key West, Florida, pending completion of studies on the future of the program. Subsequently, the ships were briefly returned to service, operated by civilian contract crews and with uniformed Army personnel on board for technical duties.

---

24 Now part of Deutsche Aerospace.

25 Aerostat is the term for an unmanned airship.

The lack of defense funds in the post–Cold War era makes it unlikely that airship programs will be pursued by either the Navy or Coast Guard in the foreseeable future. Several Navy studies had supported airship development, primarily in an AEW/missile targeting role.

(See 15th Edition/pages 453–55 for characteristics of the Coast Guard program.)

The U.S. Customs Service and the Drug Enforcement Agency currently are using aerostats to carry surveillance radars aloft to assist in monitoring illegal activities along U.S. borders. Similar systems are deployed in foreign countries by other government agencies to monitor the movements of unfriendly forces in contiguous areas.

Navy and Marine Corps F/A-18 Hornet strike fighters crowd the flight deck of the HARRY S. TRUMAN as the carrier cruises in the Persian Gulf. Although air wings are "necking down" to fewer types of aircraft—primarily the F/A-18. E-2C Hawkeye, and variants of the H-60 helicopter, the wings still will provide a potent air capability. In the future, the air wings could be enhanced by UAVs. (U.S. Navy/Kristopher Wilson)

CHAPTER 29

Unmanned Aerial Vehicles

Airmen from the Air Force 57th Wing's Operations Group work on a Predator Unmanned Aerial Vehicle (UAV) at a base in Afghanistan. The Predator has been employed over Afghanistan and Iraq to provide intelligence to all the military services. (U.S. Marine Corps/ William D. Crow)

Unmanned Aerial Vehicles (UAV) hold the promise of dramatically changing the nature of naval warfare in the coming decades.[1] There currently are more than 100 UAV designs in development, in production, in evaluation, or in service for the U.S. armed forces. The UAVs listed below include those that can be considered as Navy–Marine Corps vehicles and other service vehicles that are employed in joint operations, especially the Global Hawk and Predator. Also listed are some research and development UAVs that hold promise for future Navy–Marine Corps roles.

Significantly, the U.S. Navy has been a leader in the UAV field. In the 1960s, it planned to have the Drone Anti-Submarine Helicopter (DASH) in service aboard more than 200 U.S. warships. In the 1980s, the Navy again led U.S. military development of UAVs with procurement of the Pioneer reconnaissance drone, derived from the highly successful Israeli Mistaff III. That "bird" was flown by the U.S. Army, as well as by the Navy and Marine Corps, and has seen extensive service in combat beginning with the Gulf War of 1991. It continues in U.S. service today with the Navy and Marine Corps, and the latter recently has been funded by Congress to update its Pioneer systems.

The Navy now is seeking to identify the next generation of UAVs to support naval operations. The Office of the Chief of Naval Operations has developed a UAV "road map" for future UAV development. These vehicles will be key components of the Navy's vision of FORCEnet, its future Command, Control, Communications, Computers (C4)/Intelligence, Surveillance, and Reconnaissance (ISR) network, as well as employed in specific combat roles.

Three categories of systems are proposed in the Navy's current UAV road map:

Long-dwell standoff ISR: Known by the term Broad-Area Maritime Surveillance (BAMS), this UAV would provide coverage of ocean or littoral areas from high altitudes for long periods (days or weeks). The BAMS would provide surveillance and reconnaissance, communications relay, and Signals Intelligence (SIGINT). Its sensors would be radar, infrared, and electro-optical systems. Communications relay could include line-of-sight communications for ships and aircraft, or satellite linking of naval and ground forces. The BAMS vehicle, flying above cloud cover, might employ laser communications to link up to a satellite, providing significantly increased bandwidth, and then employ radio frequencies to communicate with air, surface, and submarine forces.

---

1 Until the 1990s, UAVs generally were known as Remotely Piloted Vehicles (RPV).

Because of its large size, the BAMS vehicle would require land basing.

As recently shown by the Air Force's RQ-4 Global Hawk, such long-duration, high-altitude performance is feasible in operational situations. The Global Hawk has a demonstrated loiter of 24 hours at a range of 6,000 miles (9,655 km), a ceiling of 65,000 feet (19,817 m), and a relatively large payload. Its speed of 400 mph (644 kmh) gives it a respectable reaction time. An improved variant is under development.

A Global Hawk maritime demonstration is under way, with two of the Northrop Grumman vehicles being acquired and modified for maritime ISR missions.[2] Unfortunately, the two UAVs will not be delivered until about Fiscal Year (FY) 2005. Tests, demonstrations, and exercises are planned through FY 2009, when an operational capability could be possible.

There are other candidates for the BAMS vehicle, including the giant, high-flying Helios system. And in 2003, General Atomics Aeronautical and Lockheed Martin announced they would team to offer the Navy a maritime version of the Predator B vehicle for the BAMS role. That UAV—according to the firms—could be operational by late FY 2007 or early 2008. The firms have labeled the proposed UAV "Mariner"; its characteristics are listed below.

Penetrating surveillance/Suppression of Enemy Air Defenses (SEAD)/strike: These missions will be carried out by Naval Unmanned Combat Air Vehicles (UCAV-N). The UCAV-N is envisioned as a multimission vehicle that can undertake ISR, strike, and SEAD missions in a hostile environment. The Navy is putting initial emphasis on the ISR role, as target identification and precise location capability are considered the best leverages for its investment. Because the UCAV-N will operate in high-threat areas, it will be a low-observable (stealth) aircraft.

This vehicle will be carrier based.

Tactical surveillance and targeting: This Tactical UAV (TUAV) is a successor to the current Pioneer UAV, to be employed by the Marine Corps at the battalion level and by the Navy at the carrier strike group and expeditionary strike group levels. The TUAV could be used over sea and land and would be particularly important to the "networked" operations of the planned Littoral Combat Ship (LCS).

Like the Pioneer, the new TUAV would be land and sea based. It is a rotary-wing, Vertical Take-Off/Landing (VTOL) vehicle, which introduces certain stealth and other problems to the system. The Navy earlier had considered and rejected the Northrop Grumman RQ-8A Fire Scout as its next-generation TUAV (see below); but that vehicle was resurrected because of the urgent need to have a TUAV available for the LCS program.

The Navy has developed a broad, extensive road map for unmanned aerial vehicles. Unfortunately, delays, inattention, and lack of interest from the powerful aviation community have caused the Navy to lose its lead in this important area of naval operations.

The Marine Corps operates several smaller, tactical UAVs in addition to the Pioneer.

The U.S. Coast Guard has selected Bell Helicopter Textron's Eagle Eye, a VTOL aircraft that employs the tilt-wing/nacelle principal of the firm's XV-15 and V-22 Osprey. The Marine Corps probably will procure the Eagle Eye for several roles. Deputy Commandant for Aviation Lieutenant General Michael Hough told an industry conference at Panama City, Florida, in October 2004 he is seeking procurement of the UAVs to escort MV-22 Ospreys in hostile areas. He envisions the Eagle Eye being fitted with an imagery system and carrying guns or missiles. Weapons–sensor payload would be on the order of 200–300 pounds (90.7–136 kg).

The considerable success of the Navy-developed Pioneer, the Air Force-developed Global Hawk, and the Predator, developed by

the Air Force and Central Intelligence Agency (CIA), came after a long succession of program failures and cancellations, among them the Army's Aquila and the Department of Defense-sponsored Hunter, DarkStar, and Outrider. The Army's Aquila UAV program, started in 1979 and canceled in 1988, failed badly to meet its mission requirements, and its estimated cost increased by more than 700 percent.

The RQ-5A Hunter was an enlarged version of the highly successful Pioneer intended for use by the Army, Navy, and Marine Corps (see entry, below).

The RQ-3A DarkStar was a competitor to the Global Hawk. It was terminated on 29 January 1999, shortly after the third aircraft had been delivered. The first vehicle crashed on its second flight in April 1996. DarkStar was to have been a stealthy vehicle, whereas the Global Hawk has a more conventional design.

In the wake of the Hunter UAV termination, in 1995 the Department of Defense awarded a contract for 24 RQ-6 Outrider UAVs. The vehicle was intended for operation by Army brigades and battalions and Marine Corps expeditionary brigades and expeditionary units, as well as by Navy task forces. Technical problems, schedule delays, poor performance, and high costs plagued the program, although 185 flights eventually were made by the UAV through 1999. The Navy and Marine Corps withdrew from the program, and the Army rejected the Outrider in a UAV flyoff, selecting the RQ-7 Shadow 200 for the TUAV role.

The Hunter, DarkStar, and Outrider were developed under a Department of Defense multitier program established in the early 1990s. That program provided for:

Tier	Type	Altitude	Endurance	Payload
I		5,000–25,000 ft	24–40 hours	141 lb
		(1,524–7,620 m)		(64 kg)
II	MAE*	25,000 ft	24–40 hours	441 lb
		(7,620 m)		(200 kg)
II+	HAE	25,000+ ft		
		(7,620 m)		
III-		45,000 ft	8 hours	795 lb
		(13,720 m)		(360 kg)

* MAE = Medium-Altitude Endurance; HAE = High-Altitude Endurance

Tier I was a project directed by the Central Intelligence Agency. The Tier II MAE evolved into the Predator and was developed by the Air Force and CIA. These designations have been discarded.

Operational UAVs generally are components of systems that include four or more UAVs plus the ground control station and data/control links.

Designations: Q is the type designator for unmanned aircraft. The prefix letters indicate cargo (C), multipurpose (M), and reconnaissance (R).[3] FQM is a missile/rocket-series designation.

Historical: Since the 1950s, the U.S. armed forces have made extensive use of target and reconnaissance drones, the latter usually of a highly classified (black) nature. Reconnaissance drones were used in large numbers by the Air Force in the Vietnam War.[4] Also in the 1960s, the Navy had the large DASH program. Those

---

2 Schedules based on Chief of Naval Operations, *Vision, Presence, Power: A Program Guide to the U.S. Navy* (Washington, D.C.: Department of then Navy, 2003).

3 The Army-operated, Canadian-developed CQ-10 Snow Goose is the only U.S. UAV with the C-prefix.

4 From August 1964 through June 1975, the Air Force 100th Strategic Reconnaissance Wing flew 3,435 combat sorties over North Vietnam with the Teledyne Ryan-produced AQM-34 "Buffalo Hunter" drone. Adapted from a target drone, the vehicle was employed in photographic and electronic reconnaissance. Other reconnaissance drones used in that conflict included the Air Force projects 147 Fire Fly and Lightning Bug and 154 Compass Arrow programs. Those drones overflew North Vietnam, China, and North Korea during that period.

drones—designated DSN and, after 1962, QH-50—were successful aerial vehicles, but problems with training and operating procedures caused a large number of losses. The DASH project was short-lived (and U.S. Anti-Submarine Warfare [ASW] ships were left without helicopters until the LAMPS program was initiated in the early 1970s.) However, the Japanese Maritime Self-Defense Force continued to employ DASH vehicles after they were discarded by the U.S. Navy, and several were employed for gunfire spotting for the battleship NEW JERSEY (BB 62) during her brief service in the shore bombardment role off South Vietnam in 1968.

During the 1970s and early 1980s, the U.S. Navy resisted proposals for Remotely Piloted Vehicles (RPV)/drones except for use as target vehicles. But following the extensive use of RPVs by the Israelis in the 1982 invasion of Lebanon, especially against anti-air gun and missile systems in the Bekaa Valley, Secretary of the Navy John Lehman directed that the Navy look into the pilotless aircraft. As a result, in January 1984, the Navy ordered a Mistaff III drone system produced by Tadiran Israeli Electronics, Ltd., for gunfire spotting.

In June 1984, the Marine Corps established the 1st RPV Platoon at Camp Lejeune, North Carolina, to evaluate and operate the Mistaff RPVs in support of Marine requirements. The first launch of an Israeli Mistaff (a development of the Scout vehicle) from a U.S. warship occurred in March 1984 from the helicopter carrier GUAM (LPH 9), with Israeli controllers. Marine Corps trials were carried out in February 1986 on the helicopter carrier TARAWA (LHA 1).

Subsequently, the Navy awarded a contract to provide the fleet with the Israeli-developed Pioneer RPV. This vehicle was used extensively from ashore and from the battleships MISSOURI (BB 63) and WISCONSIN (BB 64) in the 1991 Gulf War. The Marine Corps deployed all three of its RPV companies to Saudi Arabia, and the Army deployed a UAV platoon to the theater. The Navy assigned detachments from composite squadron VC-6 to the two battleships to operate the Pioneers from those ships. Each of these six units had about five vehicles and 40 personnel assigned. According to the Department of Defense report to Congress on the Gulf conflict, "Pioneer proved to be valuable and appears to have validated the operational employment of UAVs in combat."[5]

Also during the 1991 Gulf conflict, at the start of air operations, the U.S. Air Force launched 38 Northrop BQM-74C "Chukar" target drones into Iraq and the Navy launched a number of ADM-141A Tactical Air-Launched Decoys (TALD) from aircraft. These were used to trick the Iraqis into turning on their radars so they could be attacked by U.S. radar-suppression aircraft—Air Force F-4G Wild Weasels and Navy EA-6B Prowlers armed with High-Speed Anti-Radiation Missiles (HARM). The BQM-74Cs were ground launched, and A-6E Intruders air-launched the TALDs.

On the ground, Marines flew a number of small, lightweight FQM-151 Pointer and BAI Exdrone vehicles during the Gulf War.

Subsequently, the Predator UAV was used in the Persian Gulf to support Operation Southern Watch.

U.S. UAV deployments to the Balkans in the late 1990s began with the deployment of Air Force Predators to Taszar, Hungary, to support NATO peacekeeping efforts in Bosnia. U.S., British, French, and German UAVs supported Operation Allied Force, the three months of massive NATO air operations against Serbian forces in Kosovo and strikes against Serbia in the spring of 1999. By a significant margin, the most sorties during Allied Force were flown, in order, by the U.S. Hunter and Predator and the German CL-289. In terms of hours flown, the Hunter and Predator gave the most impressive performance, with the Predators having an aver-

age flight endurance in excess of nine hours. The CL-289 sorties were short-duration operations, averaging 30 minutes. (See 17th Edition/page 465 for statistics on UAV operations during Operation Allied Force.)

Global Hawk and Predator UAVs were used extensively in Operation Iraqi Freedom, the second Gulf War, in 2003, as was the Navy's Silver Fox and the Marines' Pioneer. Several Air Force BQM-34 Firebee aerial targets were launched by the lone Navy DC-130A Hercules to force reactions by Iraqi air defenses.[6]

The Predator also was used by the Air Force and CIA in the invasion of Afghanistan in 2002, and by the CIA in Yemen in 2002.

DRAGON DRONE: see EXDRONE

EXDRONE BQM-147

This is a small, multipurpose TUAV developed by the Marine Corps. The drone is fitted with a television camera and laser range finder. Other payloads evaluated included an electronic countermeasures package.

In 1997-1998, the Marine Corps modified some 30 Exdrones into the heavier Dragondrone variant.

Design: The Exdrone has a flying-wing configuration with twin tail fins at the outer extremities of the wing. The UAV is stowed in a box and can be assembled using quick release fasteners, fueled, and readied for flight in less than 30 minutes.

---

5 Department of Defense, *Conduct of the Persian Gulf Conflict* (July 1991), pp. 6-8.
6 See David A. Fulghum, "Targets Become UAVs," *Aviation Week & Space Technology* (28 July 2003), p. 54.

A Dragondrone is catapulted from the amphibious ship DULUTH *(LPD 6). The TUAV is recovered into a net, similar to the procedure for the Pioneer UAV. The launch and recovery gear for the Dragondrone is relatively complicated. (U.S. Navy)*

It is launched from a pneumatic catapult and can land on its skids or be recovered in a net. Maximum endurance is three hours.

Exdrone was the BAI Aerosystems name for the UAV.

Operational: During the 1991 Gulf War, the Marine Corps operated some 30 Exdrones from Saudi Arabia and, subsequently, in Iraq in support of tactical operations.

During 1968, a Dragondrone was deployed with a Marine unit on board the amphibious ship DULUTH (LPD 6), demonstrating shipboard compatibility.

Status: Operational. More than 400 Exdrones have been produced, most for the U.S. Marine Corps.

Manufacturer:	BAI Aerosystems
	AeroVironment
Engines:	1 piston engine; 2 hp
Weights:	empty: 55 lb (24.95 kg)
	gross: 95 lb (43.09 kg)
Dimensions:	length: 5 ft (1.52 m)
	wingspan: 8 ft (2.44 m)
	height: 2 ft (0.61 m)
Speed:	max. 80 mph (129 kmh)
	cruise: 60 mph (96.5 kmh)
Range:	50 miles (80 km) with 1+ hour loiter
Ceiling:	10,000 ft (3,050 m)

A Dragon Eye Tactical UAV (TUAV) is assembled by Lieutenant (j.g.) David Potere during an exercise in Bahrain. The Dragon Eye can be unpacked and assembled in about five minutes. (U.S. Navy/Ted Banks)

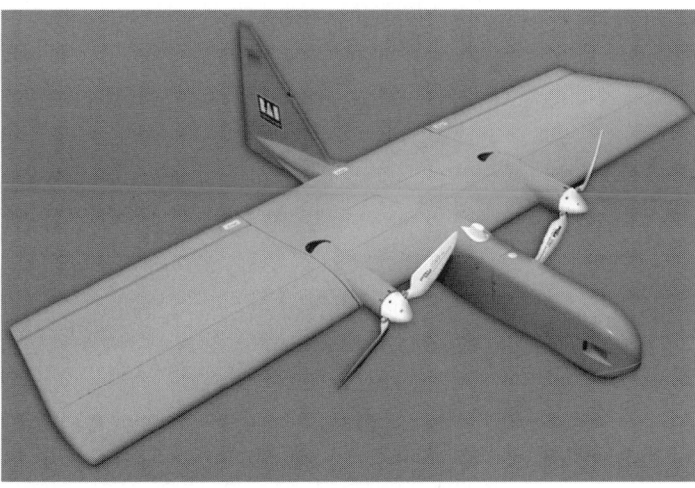

Dragon Eye TUAV.

DRAGON EYE

This is a small, multipurpose TUAV deployed by the Marine Corps. The drone is fitted with various day and night camera payloads with a video stream fed back to the monitor on a real-time basis.

Design: The Dragon Eye has a flying-wing configuration with a small tail fin but no horizontal tail surfaces. The UAV breaks down into five components and can be carried in backpacks. The vehicle is launched by hand or by bungee and is powered by a lithium (Li) battery.

The control range is limited to 6 miles (10 km), although it theoretically is possible the UAV could be passed from one controller to another, extending its operational radius. It has the radar cross section of a bird.

Status: Operational. Marine Corps evaluation occurred in June 2001. The Marine Corps plans to procure 311 operation systems through FY 2006; each system consists of three Dragon Eye UAVs and one portable ground control station and weighs a total of 12 pounds (5.44 kg).

Manufacturer:	AeroVironment and BAI Aerosystems
Engines:	2 piston engines with Li battery
Weights:	5 lb (2.3 kg)
Dimensions:	length: 3 ft (0.91 m)
	wingspan: 3 ft 9 in (1.4 m)
	height:
Speed:	40 mph (65 kmh)
Range:	endurance 1 hour
Ceiling:	300–500 ft (91–152 m)

The Dragon Eye TUAV is made with commercial, off-the-shelf components, making it one of the cheaper tactical vehicles now flying. The vehicle and control station can be carried in backpacks. (U.S. Navy)

EAGLE EYE

This is a tilt-rotor TUAV—based in part on XV-15/V-22 technology—developed for battlefield and shipboard use. A variety of sensors can be carried, including Forward-Looking Infrared (FLIR), synthetic aperture radar, and electro-optical sensors. It is being procured by the Coast Guard, that service having decided to acquire the TUAV on 8 February 2003.

A ⅝th scale UAV was used as a flight/technology demonstrator.

Design: The Eagle Eye is a tilt-rotor vehicle with twin engine nacelles that rotate to the vertical position for takeoff and landing and to the horizontal position for conventional flight; it has twin tail rudders angled inward. The bicycle landing gear is fully retractable.

The UAV is based partially on the Bell-Boeing Pointer UAV, which flew for the first time in November 1988.

Status: In production. First flight of a ⅝th scale model occurred on 10 July 1993; first full conversion flight was on 9 February 1994. Initial operational capability (IOC) is expected in 2005. The Coast Guard plans to procure 69 vehicles and 50 ground control stations for at least 46 ships.

Manufacturer:	Bell Helicopter Textron
Engines:	1 Allison 250-C20 GT recuperative turboshaft; 420 shp
Weights:	empty: 1,300 lb (590 kg)
	gross: 1,960 lb (889 kg)
	payload: 210 lb (95 kg)
	fuel: 750 lb (340 kg)
Dimensions:	length: 16 ft 6 in (5.03 m)
	wingspan: 14 ft 2½ in (4.33 m)
	height: 5 ft 2 in (1.58 m) with nacelles in vertical position
	rotor diameter: 8 ft 2½ in (2.5 m)
Speed:	max. approx. 230 mph (370 kmh)
	cruise: approx. 115 mph (185 kmh)
Range:	radius: 50 miles (80 km) with 8-hour endurance
	with 100 lb (45.4 kg) of sensors
Ceiling:	20,000+ ft (6,100+ m)

FIRE SCOUT RQ-8A

The Navy belatedly selected the Fire Scout UAV as a successor to the ship- and land-based Pioneer. It is to provide a platform for ISR and targeting using infrared/optical sensors and a laser target designator. The Navy also envisions an improved variant for search and rescue that could home on an emergency beacon and drop a line when over a man. The Fire Scout also could serve as a radio and data relay platform when equipped with three ARC-120 radios.

In February 2000, the Navy awarded Northrop Grumman a $93.7-million engineering and manufacturing development contract for the Fire Scout. That was followed in March 2001 by another contract for low-rate initial production. The Fire Scout was believed to have a low development risk because its design was similar to that of a conventional helicopter. (It was based on the commercial Schweizer 330 series helicopter with a sensor payload developed by the Taman Division of Israel Aircraft Industries.)

But critics immediately argued that the Fire Scout was too large, too noisy, and too slow to be survivable if flown close enough to hostile forces for its sensors to be effective; another criticism was its relatively small payload. The effort was terminated—although that word rarely was used—the Navy said, because its tactical UAV "requirements have changed." When pressed, service officials cited the earlier criticisms, although those limitations should have been known from the outset of the program.

The Navy resurrected the Fire Scout in 2003 because of the urgent need for a TUAV capable of operating from the LCS.

The Fire Scout was a component of a the Northrop Grumman Ryan Aeronautical Center's proposal in the Navy's TUAV competition, and was given that firm's designation—Model 379. The losing competitors were Bell Helicopter Textron's tilt-rotor Eagle Eye and Sikorsky's Cypher III. Although not a finalist in the competition, Bombardier Aéronautique's CL-327 Guardian was considered a viable candidate by many observers, having conducted trials at sea in U.S. Navy and Coast Guard ships. (The Cypher III and CL-327 Guardian are described in the 17th Edition/pages 466, 469.)

The Army and Marine Corps also plan to procure the Fire Scout. The Army's RQ-8B will be a more rugged vehicle with a four-blade rotor and increased payload.

Design: The Fire Scout is based on the Hughes/Schweizer 330 series helicopter. It resembles a small, conventional-configuration helicopter with a large, three-blade main rotor and a stabilizing rotor mounted on a tail boom. It rests on skids. There is a gimbaled sensor pod mounted under the nose.

Status: In production. The initial procurement of 23 systems will provide 12 to the Navy and 11 to the Marine Corps, with 3 of the latter to be carried in Maritime Prepositioning Ships (MPS). Each system consists of three aerial vehicles and two control stations. IOC is planned for 2007.

Manufacturer:	Northrop Grumman/Teledyne Ryan Aeronautical
Engines:	1 Allison Rolls-Royce 250-C20W turboshaft; 420 shp
Weights:	empty: 1,457 lb (661 kg)
	gross: 2,650 lb (1,157 kg)

The Eagle Eye technology demonstrator wearing Coast Guard livery. The Navy rejected the Eagle Eye for its shipboard TUAV, but the aircraft is being procured by the Marine Corps as well as by the Coast Guard for at least 46 cutters. (Bell Helicopter Textron)

A Fire Scout TUAV stands ready for flight testing. The U.S. Navy pioneered modern UAV development for the U.S. armed forces with the DSN/QH-50 DASH anti-submarine vehicle in the 1960s and the RQ-2 Pioneer reconnaissance UAV in the 1980s. (U.S. Navy/Kurt Lengfield)

A Fire Scout flies in the TUAV's test program at China Lake, California. Initially rejected by the Navy, Fire Scout will fly from the Littoral Combat Ship (LCS), as well as from other Navy platforms, and will be operated ashore by Marines. (U.S. Navy)

Dimensions:	length: 22 ft 10 in (6.97 m) fuselage
	rotor diameter: 27 ft 6 in (8.38 m)
	height: 9 ft 5 in (2.87 m)
Speed:	max. 144 mph (213 kmh)
	cruise:
Range:	125 miles (200 km) with 3 hour endurance
	max. endurance 6 hours
Ceiling:	20,000 ft (6,096 m)

GLOBAL HAWK RQ-4A

Global Hawk is a highly successful long-range surveillance UAV operated by the Air Force. It has been considered as a successor to the long-serving U-2 spy plane.

The Air Force developed the Global Hawk to meet the HAE Tier II+ requirements for a long-endurance UAV. It achieved an impressive record during extensive trials until one of two prototypes crashed on 29 March 1999 at China Lake, California. Subsequently, the remaining UAV resumed flight trials on 18 May 1999, leading to the decision later that year to procure the Global Hawk for operational service.

Global Hawk development has been managed by the Air Force. It will be employed in the Navy BAMS trials (see above).

Design: This is the largest and highest-flying UAV to become operational. Global Hawk has a conventional aircraft design, with minimal stealth characteristics, and a fully retractable landing gear. Employing conventional runways, the Global Hawk requires 3,700 feet (1,130 m) for takeoff and 5,000 feet (1,525 m) for landing.

Initially, the Global Hawk had electro-optical sensors and synthetic aperture radar; more advanced sensors subsequently have been provided as well as a communications relay capability.

Operational: During flight tests, on 19–20 October 1999, a Global Hawk flew from Edwards Air Force Base (AFB),

California, to Alaska and back—a 24-hour, unrefueled, nonstop flight.

On 22–23 April 2001, a Global Hawk flew from Edwards AFB to Adelaide, Australia, a distance of 8,600 miles (13,840 km), in 22 hours. That flight represented only about 60 percent of the UAV's potential range. That Global Hawk then participated in U.S.–Australian exercises. A minor problem on its fourth local flight was quickly fixed. On local flight No. 6—which lasted 25 hours—the Global Hawk reached 63,000 feet (19,210 m) and took 200 reconnaissance photos, which it downloaded to Australian ground stations and to the USS KITTY HAWK (CV 63).

The Global Hawk was used operationally in Operation Iraqi Freedom in 2003.

Status: Operational and in production. First flight occurred on 28 February 1998. The first production Global Hawk was delivered in August 2003; the units being used up to that time were prototype/engineering development aircraft. Current requirements are for 51 units.

Manufacturer:	Northrop Grumman/Teledyne Ryan Aeronautical
Engines:	1 Allison Rolls Royce AE3007H turbofan;
	7,050 lbst (3,200 kgst)
Weights:	empty: 9,200 lb (4,173 kg)
	gross: 25,600 lb (11,612 kg)
	payload: 1,900 lb (862 kg)
Dimensions:	length: 44 ft (13.41 m)
	wingspan: 116 ft 3 in (35.43 m)
	height: 15 ft 3 in (4.63 m)
Speed:	400 mph (644 kmh)
Range:	endurance: 38 hours
	6,000 miles (9,655 km) with 24 hours loiter
	15,525 miles (24,985 km) with no loiter
Ceiling:	65,000+ ft (19,820+ m)

A Global Hawk lands at Nordholz Air Base in Germany after a flight from Edwards Air Force Base in California on a demonstration of the UAV's transcontinental range. These vehicles can carry out some of the roles and missions of manned maritime patrol aircraft. (Northrop Grumman/Gene Yano)

The Global Hawk is a large, graceful, and highly capable aircraft. Although too large for carrier operation, it has demonstrated in exercises its value to a naval force commander at sea. (U.S. Air Force)

A newly completed RQ-4A. Global Hawk's large size is evident in this view of the Teledyne Ryan Aeronautical facility at Palmdale, California. The Navy will evaluate the Global Hawk for the planned Broad-Area Maritime Surveillance (BAMS) system. (Northrop Grumman)

HUNTER RQ-5A

This is an enlarged version of the highly successful Pioneer originally developed for the Army and Marine Corps, with some Navy interest. It was to undertake ISR and targeting missions at the division and corps levels ashore, and operate from helicopter carriers (LHA/LHD) in support of naval task forces.

The Hunter experienced technical problems in development and major cost increases, which led to the program being canceled by the Department of Defense on 1 February 1996.[7] However, the Army's need for a short-range UAV led to a subsequent decision to continue limited production and evaluation. Hunter was employed extensively in Bosnia in 1995 and again was flown in the Balkans in 1999.

The Army procured seven systems (eight aircraft each with four ground stations), with a total of 75 aircraft being built. The Marine Corps did not acquire or operate the Hunter, instead continuing to operate the Pioneer.

Designation: The Hunter originally was designated BQM-155.

MARINER (PREDATOR B–ER)

Mariner is the corporate name for a maritime version of Northrop Grumman's Predator B being proposed by General Atomics for the Navy's BAMS role. The vehicle, according to the firms, could be operational by late FY 2007 or early 2008.

The Predator B is larger, has a 50 percent increase in payload over the basic Predator, and has improved performance.

In 2003, the estimated cost of the Predator B–ER (Extended Range) was $4 million per vehicle, compared to Global Hawk's $16–$20 million; neither cost includes sensors.[8]

A Hunter UAV in flight; the light object behind the main landing gear is a booster rocket being jettisoned. Although the Hunter project was canceled, the Army has employed the UAV on an operational basis. The Marine Corps continues to monitor the program. (U.S. Navy)

7 The technical problems included: (1) it could not adequately transmit video images during relay operations, (2) it could not meet Army standards for artillery adjustments, (3) it was unreliable, and (4) the Hunter system was too large to be transported by the specified number of transport aircraft.

8 David A. Fulghum, "Navy Eyes Cheaper UAV," *Aviation Week & Space Technology* (8 December 2003), pp. 36-37.

Design: The Signal turboprop engine is to provide a 49-hour endurance at altitudes of 40,000–52,000 feet (12,195–15,850 m).

Status: Development.

Manufacturer:	General Atomics and Northrop Grumman
Engines:	1 Honeywell TPE-331-10T turboprop
Weights:	empty:
	gross: 10,500 lb (4,763 kg)
	payload internal: 800 lb (363 kg)
	payload external: 3,000 lb (1,361 kg)
Dimensions:	length: 36 ft (10.97 m)
	wingspan: 86 ft (26.21 m)
	height
Speed:	max. 250+ mph (400+ kmh)
	cruise:
Range:	endurance: 49 hours
Ceiling:	52,000 feet (15,855 m)

PIONEER RQ-2

The Pioneer TUAV is a highly effective unmanned, tactical reconnaissance vehicle flown by the Army, Navy, and Marine Corps. It was employed extensively in the Persian Gulf conflict of 1991 and in other subsequent operations. The Navy had planned to replace the Pioneer with a more advanced UAV by 2000; however, delays in UAV development have led the Navy and Marine Corps to retain the Pioneer (in small numbers) pending the belated introduction of the Fire Scout TUAV.

Impressed with Israeli successes using UAVs in the early 1980s, the Navy initiated a procurement effort. In January 1986, the Navy awarded contracts to AAI Corp. of Cockeysville, Maryland, and Mazlat, Ltd., the latter a joint venture of Israel Aircraft Industries (IAI) and Tadiran. The firms were able to skip the traditional development phase of the acquisition process because of Secretary of the Navy John Lehman's support of the program. They produced 72 Pioneer UAVs at a cost of $87.7 million.

The Pioneer encountered technical difficulties, including electromagnetic interference from other ship systems and recovery problems, and several crashed. Although the UAV has never met objective requirements, it has been used operationally with considerable success. Originally flown from battleships and shore launchers, with the demise of the battleship, the vehicles have been flown by Navy squadron VC-6 from a variety of amphibious ships.

Design: The Pioneer, modeled on the IAI Scout vehicle, carries its sensors and engines in a fuselage section fitted with twin tail booms. It is powered by a reciprocating engine with a small pusher propeller. The vehicle, which has a fixed landing gear, can be launched with rocket assistance and can be recovered on a runway or by a net. Metal and fiberglass construction presents a low radar cross section. The Pioneer is transported disassembled and can be put together rapidly with minimum tools.

At the time of the Gulf War (1991), the Pioneer was fitted with a daylight television camera or, alternatively, a FLIR sensor. The existing control/data link is a C-band system, resistant to jamming, with a range of 100 nautical miles (185 km).

Operational: The first shipboard trials of the Pioneer were conducted from the battleship IOWA (BB 61) in the Chesapeake Bay in December 1986. During subsequent "proof-of-concept" tests in the Caribbean in January–February 1987, the IOWA's 16-inch (406-mm) guns fired on targets detected by the vehicle. (In that exercise, four of the five embarked Pioneers were lost in accidents.) The Marine Corps evaluated the Pioneer in 1987, including operations from an LHA amphibious ship.

During the Gulf conflict, from 16 January to 27 February 1991, some 40 UAVs flew 552 sorties for a total mission duration time

Marines from squadron VMU-2 "walk" a Pioneer TUAV down the flightline prior to takeoff from Al Taqqadum, Iraq. During a three-month period in 2003, the Marines flew Pioneers for more than 1,000 hours in support of Operation Iraqi Freedom. (U.S. Marine Corps/ Matthew T. Rainey)

of 1,641 hours. *At least one Pioneer UAV was airborne at all times during Operation Desert Storm.* The vehicles were employed to adjust naval gunfire and to conduct battle damage assessment, reconnaissance, and force coordination. On 27 February, after a Pioneer detected two Iraqi patrol boats off Faylaka Island and naval aircraft were called in to destroy the craft, a large number of Iraqi soldiers on the island surrendered to a UAV launched by the battleship MISSOURI. Apparently, the soldiers knew their detection by the drone would be followed by air or naval gunfire attack. It was history's first known surrender of enemy troops to an unmanned vehicle.

For the Gulf War, the Pioneers were flown from two battleships, operated by VC-6 detachments, and from ashore by the Army and Marine Corps. The Department of Defense final report on the war (April 1992) stated: "The Navy Pioneer UAV system's availability exceeded expectations. Established sortie rates indicated a deployed unit could sustain 60 flight hours a month." (See 17th Edition/pages 471–72 for a summary of Pioneer operations during the conflict.)

In late 1992, the Navy operated Pioneers from the helicopter carrier NEW ORLEANS (LPH 11). During launch and recovery operations, two arresting wires were set up on the flight deck (as well as the standard recovery net), and the drones snagged the arresting wires, as done ashore. All shipboard recoveries previously had been made into nets.

The Pioneer was used in support of U.S. operations in Bosnia in 1996–1997. Marine squadron VMU-1 deployed with a Pioneer system that included seven UAVs, one ground control station, and four receiving stations.

Status: Operational. U.S. Navy IOC was in May 1986. A few UAVs are in Navy service with squadron VC-6; Marine squadrons VMU-1 and VMU-2 operate Pioneers.

Manufacturer:	AAI and Mazlat (Israel)
Engines:	1 Sachs 2-stroke piston; 26 hp
Weights:	max. launch: 430 lb (195 kg)
	payload: 100 lb (45.4 kg)
Dimensions:	length: 16 ft 3 in (4.96 m)
	wingspan: 16 ft 9½ in (5.12 m)
	height: 3 ft 3 in (1.0 m)
Speed:	max. 115 mph (185 kmh)
	cruise: 55–81 mph (89–130 kmh)
Range:	endurance: 8 hours
Ceiling:	15,000 ft (4,573 m)

A Pioneer TUAV taking off during a training flight at Laguna Army Air Field at Yuma, Arizona. The TUAV normally makes rocket-assisted take-offs, but it can be launched by catapult. This Pioneer belongs to Marine Corps squadron VMU-2. (U.S. Marine Corps/Kyle Davidson)

A Pioneer is recovered in a net aboard the battleship Iowa *(BB 61), the standard shipboard "landing" procedure. The Pioneer also can be landed, under radio control, on a runway or a flight-deck ship. (U.S. Navy)*

POINTER FQM-151

The Pointer is a small, very low cost, hand-launched UAV used by the Marine Corps. Resembling a model aircraft, it is man-portable, with the entire system carried in two backpacks—one carrying the air vehicle (45 lb/20.25 kg) and one containing the control unit (50 lb/22.5 kg).

The Pointer's sensor payload is a black-and-white television camera using an 8-mm video cassette or an infrared (night vision) camera. Alternatively, it can carry a chemical agent detector.

Design: The Pointer is a high-wing "model" airplane with a T-tail configuration. Power is provided by Nickel-Cadmium (NiCd) or Li batteries, resulting in a very quiet vehicle.

The system can be fully prepared for flight in about five minutes. For recovery, the Pointer is directed into a deep stall and falls to the ground. It normally is flown within line-of-sight of the ground operator.

Status: Operational. First flight occurred in 1986. In 1988, the Marine Corps purchased one unit for tests. The Department of Defense joint program office procured 24 Pointers in December 1989; several of these were deployed to Saudi Arabia with the Marines in 1991. In addition, the Pointer is used by the U.S. Army and Special Operations Command and is flown by the French Army.

Manufacturer:	AeroVironment
Engines:	1 Astro electric motor; 300 watts; 2-blade pusher propeller
Weights:	empty: 7 lb (3.2 kg)
	gross: 9 lb (4 kg)
	payload: 2 lb (0.9 kg)
Dimensions:	length: 6 ft (1.83 m)
	wingspan: 9 ft (2.74 m)
	height:
Speed:	max. approx. 45 mph (72 kmh)
	cruise: approx. 23 mph (37 kmh)
Range:	endurance: 1 hour with NiCd batteries
	2+ hours with Li batteries
Ceiling:	3,000 ft (915 m)

With a strong right arm, a Marine launches a Pointer UAV—in some respects the progenitor of the "mini" UAVs. (U.S. Marine Corps)

PREDATOR B MQ-9

This is an enlarged version of the highly successful MQ/RQ-1 Predator UAV. On armed missions, it can carry up to ten AGM-114 Hellfire missiles.

Status: In production. First flight occurred in February 2001.

Manufacturer:	General Atomics
Engines:	1 Honeywell TPF-331-10T turboprop
Weights:	empty: 6,000 lb (2,722 kg)
	gross: 10,000 lb (4,536 kg)
	payload internal: 800 lb (363 kg)
	payload external: 3,000 lb (1,361 kg)
Dimensions:	length: 36 ft (10.97 m)
	wingspan: 66 ft (20.12 m)
	height:
Speed:	max. 250+ mph (400+ kmh)
	cruise:
Range:	endurance: 30+ hours
Ceiling:	50,000 ft (15,245 m)

PREDATOR MQ-1/RQ-1

The Predator is a versatile UAV; in addition to performing reconnaissance missions, it has been used for strikes against terrorist targets, as well as for intelligence collection. It was developed for use at the theater commander and joint force commander level.

The same vehicle is designated RQ-1 when carrying sensors and MQ-1 when carrying air-to-surface weapons in addition to sensors.

The Predator has been operated by the Air Force over the Balkans, Afghanistan, and Iraq. It also was flown by the CIA in Afghanistan and Yemen, where it was used to launch Hellfire missiles against ground targets.

Design: The Predator is capable of day/night operations with a variety of sensors, including video and infrared (with ground link). It has retractable landing gear, being designed to takeoff and land on highways, airstrips, or other open areas. Normal operations require a 2,200-foot (670-m) runway for takeoff and a 1,100-foot (335-m) runway for landing. The UAV can be disassembled into six main components and transported in a container (referred to as a "coffin").

The use of the Predator over Bosnia has accelerated fitting the UAV with synthetic aperture radar, because flights there have been hampered by overcast and ground fog.

Two AGM-114 Hellfire missiles can be carried.

Designation: The change from RQ-1 to MQ-1 for armed variants was made in 2002.

Operational: The Predator began intelligence collection missions in July 1995, flying from Albania to observe targets in Bosnia and Herzegovina.[9] Four disassembled Predators were flown into Gjader Airfield near Tirana in C-130 Hercules. The UAVs were assembled and flown by civilian contract personnel.

One of the Predators was lost over Bosnia on 11 August 1995; a second was deliberately destroyed on 14 August after suffering an engine failure over Bosnia, which may have been caused by hostile ground fire.

A second Predator deployment to Bosnia began in March 1996. Subsequently, three UAVs, operating from Sarmellek, Hungary, were fitted with synthetic aperture radar, permitting more effective reconnaissance through clouds and fog.

In 1996, the Navy conducted tests with a submarine controlling a Predator UAV. The drone was launched from land, flew out to an ocean operating area, and then was controlled by the submarine, running submerged with an antenna raised above the surface for the data link to the Predator. (The data links can be direct or via satellite relay.)

In January 1999, UAVs returned to the Persian Gulf for the first time since the 1990–1991 war. The Air Force deployed a Predator system to Kuwait to fly reconnaissance flights over Iran as part of

The Predator B is an enlarged and more capable version of the MQ-1/RQ-1 Predator.

An armed MQ-1 Predator carries a single Hellfire missile under its right wing on a training flight over Nellis Air Force Base, Nevada. The UAV has been flown in the attack mode by the Air Force and by the Central Intelligence Agency. (U.S. Air Force)

In near darkness, airmen perform last-minute checks on a Predator UAV at a "forward-deployed location." These UAVs have proved highly successful in the reconnaissance and—armed with Hellfire missiles—attack roles. (U.S. Air Force/Jeremy T. Lock)

Operation Southern Watch, supporting United Nations sanctions. (One of these UAVs was an operational loss.)

Predator UAVs also participated in the air war over Kosovo in 1999. They subsequently were operated over Afghanistan, Iraq, and Yemen, flown by both the Air Force and the CIA.

Status: Operational and in production. First flight occurred in July 1994. The Department of Defense awarded General Atomics Aeronautical a $31.7-million contract in January 1994 to build ten Predator UAVs and three ground control stations; these were delivered by mid-1995. Subsequent contracts totaling $579 million were

9 The distance from Tirana to Sarajevo is approximately 200 miles (320 km).

awarded for the development and production of 13 Predator systems with 80 vehicles.

Manufacturer:	General Atomics
Engines:	1 Rotax 914 4-cylinder with fuel injection; 101 hp
Weights:	empty: 1,130 lb (512 kg)
	gross: 2,250 lb (1,020 kg)
	payload: 450 lb (204 kg)
Dimensions:	length: 26 ft 8 in (8.13 m)
	wingspan: 48 ft 8 in (14.84 m)
	height: 6 ft 11 in (2.11 m)
Speed:	max. 138 mph (222 kmh)
	cruise: 80 mph (129 kmh)
Range:	endurance: 40 hours
Ceiling:	25,000 ft (7,625 m)

SILVER FOX

This is a small, low-cost UAV developed by the Office of Naval Research. Originally for whale spotting, it is controlled from a laptop computer, and various cameras and infrared sensors can be fitted, with real-time transmission to the ground control station.

Design: The Silver Fox resembles a model airplane; it is launched by a compressed-air launcher and is powered by an Li battery.

The Silver Fox UAV was developed hastily by the Office of Naval Research to meet a Marine Corps operational requirement for Operation Iraqi Freedom. It has proved highly successful. (U.S. Navy)

Status: Operational. The Silver Fox was used by the Navy and Marine Corps in Operation Iraqi Freedom (2003) and subsequent operations in Iraq.

Manufacturer:	Advanced Ceramics Research
Engines:	1 piston 4-cycle
Weights:	empty: 16 lb (7.26 kg)
	gross: 20 lb (9.07 kg)
	payload: 4 lb (1.81 kg)
Dimensions:	length: 6 ft (1.83 m)
	wingspan: 8 ft (2.44 m)
	height:
Speed:	max.
	cruise:
Range:	line-of-sight (approx. 20 miles/32 km)
	endurance: 5 hours
Ceiling:	1,000 ft (305 m)

UNMANNED COMBAT AERIAL VEHICLES

The current efforts are part of the Joint Unmanned Combat Air Systems (J-UCAS) program, a Defense Advanced Research Projects Agency (DARPA)/Air Force/Navy endeavor to demonstrate the technical feasibility, military use, and operational value of a networked system of high-performance and weapons-capable air vehicles. The Navy hopes to have an operational UCAV-N capability about 2015. (The Air Force plans an operational UCAV in 2010.)

Obviously, the problem of such a joint effort—with the Air Force already flying the Boeing X-45 demonstration vehicle—is compatibility with the maritime/shipboard environment. The Northrop Grumman X-47 is a Navy/DARPA UCAV project. Both demonstration vehicles are described below.

Key technologies that will be required for the UCAV are:
- automatic target recognition
- secure communications
- adaptive autonomous operations
- onboard processing
- intervehicle communications
- cognitive aids

A portent: An artist's concept of a Naval Unmanned Combat Air Vehicle (UCAV-N) landing aboard an aircraft carrier. Navy planning calls for UCAV-Ns to be integrated into carrier air wings (see Chapter 27). (U.S. Navy)

X-47 PEGASUS

The X-47, given the corporate name Pegasus, is a joint DARPA/Navy UCAV-N demonstrator being developed under a $12-million contract with Northrop Grumman.

Design: The X-47 has a near-diamond shape flying-wing design, providing stealth configuration. Both the X-45 (below) and X-47 have two weapon bays; in the development process, one is a working weapons bay and the other holds an avionics pallet.

Operational: The X-47 is fitted with an arresting hook and has simulated arrested carrier landings on runways ashore.

Status: A single X-47 has been procured. First flight occurred in February 2003.

Manufacturer:	Northrop Grumman
Engines:	1 Pratt & Whitney JT15D-5C-TF turbofan; 3,190 lbst (1,447 kgst)
Weights:	empty: 3,835 lb (8,455 kg)
	gross: 5,500 lb (2,495 kg)
	payload
Dimensions:	length: 27 ft 11 in (8.51 m)
	wingspan: 27 ft (8.23 m)
	height: 6 ft 1 in (1.86 m)
Speed:	max.
	cruise:
Range:	endurance: 1+ hour
Ceiling:	

X-45

This is a UCAV demonstrator built under a $131-million DARPA/Air Force technology demonstration program to evaluate technologies and concepts for future UCAVs.

Design: The X-45 has a flying-wing configuration with a protruding forward section. It has stealth design characteristics. A fully retractable landing gear is provided.

Status: Two X-45s were built, designated X-45A and X-45B; first flights were in May and November 2002, respectively. The latter aircraft was modified to provide enhanced performance and redesignated X-45C. Three X-45C vehicles are being built with first flight planned for 2007.

Manufacturer:	Boeing	
Engines:	X-45A: 1 Honeywell F124-GA-100 turbofan; 6,300 lbst (2,858 kgst)	
	X-45B: 1 General Electric GE F404-102D turbofan	
Weights:	empty:	X-45A 8,000 lb (3,628 kg)
		X-45B 14,000 lb (6,350 kg)
		X-45C 36,530 lb (16,570 kg)
	gross:	X-45A 15,000 lb (6,804 kg)
		X-45B
		X-45C
	payload: 3,000 lb (1,360 kg)	
Dimensions:	length:	X-45A 27 ft (8.2 m)
		X-45B 32 ft (9.7 m)
		X-45C 32 ft (9.7 m)
	wingspan:	X-45A 34 ft (10.3 m)
		X-45B 47 ft (14.3 m)
		X-45C 49 ft (14.95 m)
	height: 7 ft (2.1 m)	
Speed:	max. Mach 0.85	
	cruise:	
Range:	endurance 3 hours	
Ceiling:	45,000 ft (13,720 m)	

An X-45 releases a GPS-guided bomb over China Lake, California, during flight testing. It was the first time tan unmanned aircraft dropped a precision-guided weapon from an internal weapons bay. The large object under the aircraft is the open weapons bay door. (Boeing Company)

The X-47A Pegasus is Northrop Grumman's entry in the UCAV-N competition for a future unmanned multimission aircraft for naval operations. UCAVs eventually will be able to fulfill most—but probably not all—roles and missions of manned aircraft. (Northrop Grumman)

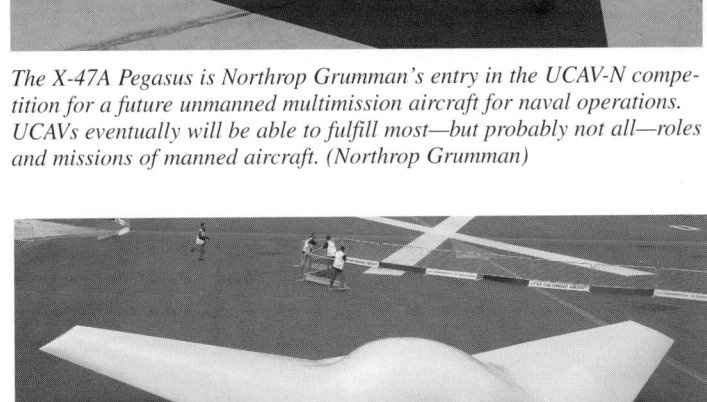

The Boeing X-45C variant of the UCAV reveals a very different configuration from the competitive Northrop Grumman X-47A design. Both designs are "stealthy," with an absence of vertical control surfaces. (Boeing Company)

An X-45A test vehicle in flight with landing gear lowered. (Boeing Company)

UNMANNED COMBAT ARMED ROTORCRAFT

DARPA and the U.S. Army have developed the Unmanned Combat Armed Rotorcraft (UCAR) program to demonstrate the technical feasibility and military utility of such a platform performing armed reconnaissance and attack missions, especially in urban environments. The UCAR program, if successful, will be of great interest to the Marine Corps.

A decision on which of two teams will develop the UCAR was to have been made in late 2004. DARPA and the Army funded preliminary efforts by Lockheed Martin, teamed with Bell Helicopter Textron, and Northrop Grumman, working with Kaman and Sikorsky. Earlier in the competition, McDonnell Douglas (a subsidiary of Boeing Company) and Sikorsky, teamed with Raytheon, were eliminated. DARPA and the Army plan to complete prototype development by about 2009 and have a UCAR system initial operational capability of about 2012.

The UCAR system will be capable of direct and autonomous collaboration with manned or unmanned air and ground systems, and will operate at low altitudes in close proximity to troops on the ground. The enabling technologies being developed under these contracts are:
• survivability
• autonomous operations
• command and control
• targeting/weapons delivery

One of the key features of the UCAR will be a three-beam laser radar (ladar) obstacle avoidance system. This system would detect other aircraft, ground structures, power lines, and other obstacles. The aerial vehicle would be highly maneuverable. DARPA program manager Don Wood has been quoted as saying both proposed vehicles display "really sporty performance."[11] The vehicles will have dash in excess of 200 mph (322 kmh), with a ceiling of about 20,000 feet (6,100 m).

The UCAR system will be controlled from existing command and control platforms, both ground based and airborne (aircraft) rather than from a dedicated mission control station.

LOCKHEED MARTIN DESIGN

The key features of this design include a propulsive anti-torque system and a small wing for high performance during forward flight to counteract blade stall by the rotor. There is a fan embedded in the fuselage that forces air down the tailboom to the exhaust nozzle.

A drawing of the proposed Lockheed Martin UCAR design.

Lockheed Martin's proposed UCAR configured for urban combat. The UCARs will be multipurpose vehicles, capable of reconnaissance and surveillance, as well as attack missions. (Lockheed Martin)

Manufacturer:	Lockheed Martin and Bell
Engines:	1 Allison-Garrett LHTEC T800-800 turboshaft
Weights:	empty:
	max. T/O:
Dimensions:	fuselage length:
	overall length:
	height:
	main rotor diameter:
Speed:	max: 200+ mph (322+ kmh)
	cruise:
Ceiling:	approx. 20,000 ft (6,100 m)
Range:	

NORTHROP GRUMMAN DESIGN

This UCAR will use intermeshing rotors, alleviating the need for a tail rotor or other stabilizing system in the tail.

Manufacturer:	Northrop Grumman, Kaman, and Sikorsky
Engines:	1 Allison-Garrett LHTEC T800-802 turboshaft
Weights:	empty:
	max. T/O:
Dimensions:	fuselage length:
	overall length:
	height:
	main rotor diameter:
Speed:	max: 200+ mph (322+ kmh)
	cruise:
Ceiling:	approx. 20,000 feet (6,100 m)
Range:	

11 Robert Wall, "Hot Performers," *Aviation Week & Space Technology* (6 September 2004), p. 48.

MICRO AIR VEHICLES

The Micro Air Vehicle (MAV) program was initiated by DARPA in 1996 to develop and test emerging technologies that could lead to small, inexpensive UAVs suitable primarily for surveillance and reconnaissance missions at the tactical level. The original requirement called for a maximum size of 6 inches (15 cm). To date, none of the proposals are known to have been accepted for production or operational use; however, there are rumors of highly classified (black) programs in this field being pursued.

A variety of designs have evolved from this DARPA sponsorship and from support from the Office of Naval Research (ONR). Among the smallest products are those developed by University of California (Berkeley) engineers who, inspired by the aerodynamic characteristics of flying insects, have produced a flying robot that weighs less than a paper clip. Labeled the Micromechanical Flying Insect (MFI), this effort is funded by ONR and DARPA. Another MFI program is the Robofly, a stealth robotic flyer about the size of a fly. Proponents envision squads of roboflies seeking out targets, providing damage assessment, or searching for chemical and biological warfare agents.

The following are some of the more promising MAV designs that have been publicized.

BLACK WIDOW

This is a disk-shaped vehicle carrying a camera and transmitter with a real-time, video down link. The color video camera is believed to be the smallest in existing, weighing 2 grams; the system has a transmission range of just more than 10½ miles (17 km). To extend the communications range of the system, the Black Widow is supported by an aerial relay installed on a Pointer UAV, which will fly higher to accomplish a non-line-of-sight relay for video transmissions.

The Black Widow has a 4-inch (101.5-mm) propeller. Two Li batteries provide 8 watts of power.

A possible derivative of the Black Widow known as the Microbat is in development. According to AeroVironment, that vehicle will weigh less than 15 grams.

Manufacturer:	AeroVironment
Engines:	electric motor with Li batteries
Weights:	2 ounces (57 grams)
Dimensions:	6 in (152 mm) disk platform
Speed:	33 mph (53 kmh)
Endurance:	30 minutes

HORNET

This MAV is believed to have made the worlds's first successful UAV flight powered entirely by a hydrogen fuel cell. The vehicle has a flying-wing configuration.

The fuel cell uses hydrogen, stored on board the aircraft, to react with oxygen collected from airflow over the wing to produce electricity. The fuel cell incorporates a metal mesh that also functions as a mechanical structure to strengthen the wing. The hydrogen is provided by a unique generator system in which the hydrogen is stored in a dry, solid, pellet form and released when combined with water, which also is carried in the vehicle. The system has the potential to provide 400 watt hours per kilogram (the fuel cell was developed by Lynntech).

The Hornet can carry a miniature color video camera.

The first flight was on 21 March 2003.

Manufacturer:	AeroVironment
Engines:	electric motor with fuel cell
Weights:	6 oz (170 grams)
Dimensions:	15 in (381 mm) span
Speed:	
Endurance:	

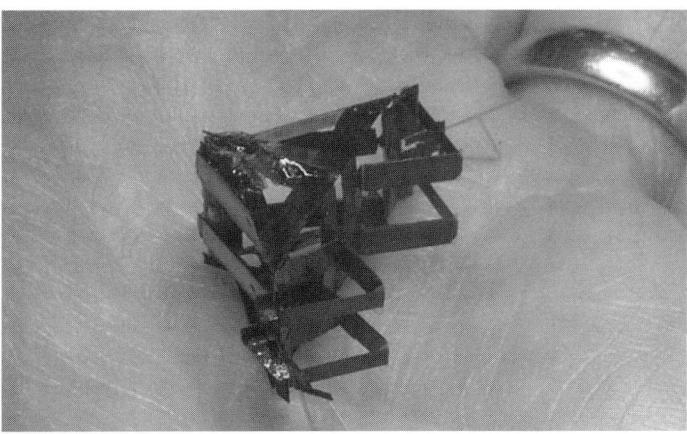

Inspired by the elegant aerodynamics of insects and sponsored by the Office of Naval Research, engineers at the University of California at Berkeley are developing a series of Micro Aerial Vehicles (MAVs) such as this "flying robo" about the weight of a paperclip. (University of California at Berkeley/© R. Fearing)

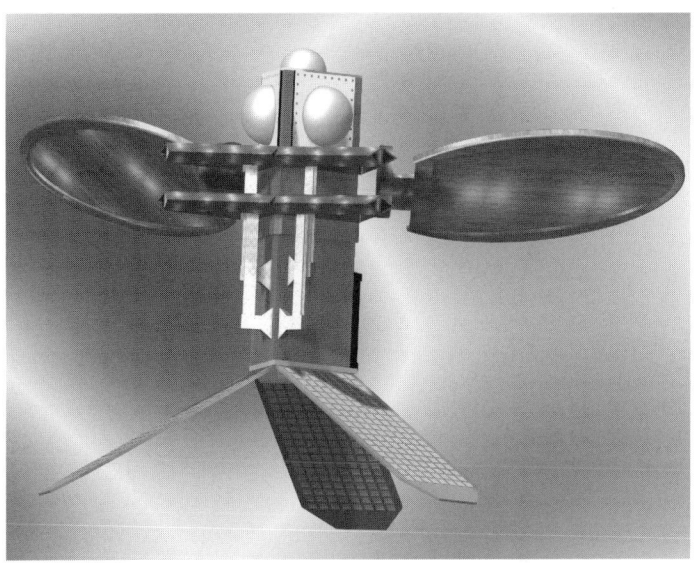

Another MAV design is the "robofly," about the size of a large insect. This flying device can carry a miniaturized sensor. According to the Office of Naval Research, "squads of roboflies may one day be sent to search out targets, collect and provide information damage assessment, or search for chemical and biological warfare agents." (University of California at Berkeley/© R. Fearing)

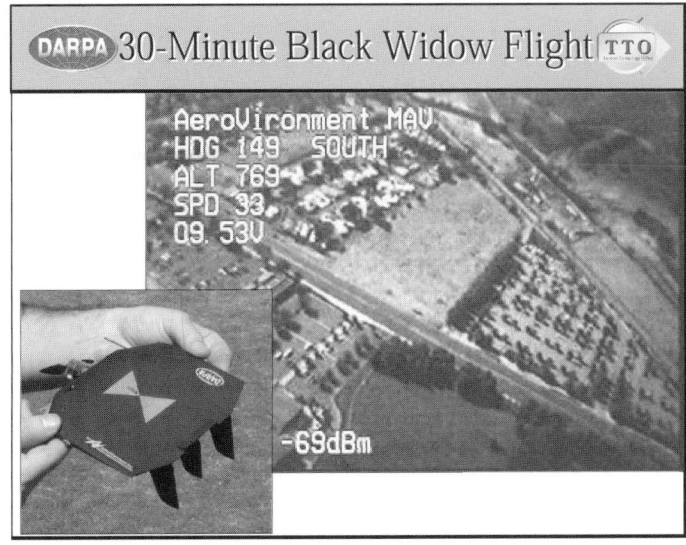

The Black Widow can downlink real time images to commanders on the ground or to other aerial vehicles. (Defense Advanced Research Projects Agency)

MOSQUITO 1

The saucer-shaped Mosquito 1 is Israel's entry into micro UAV development. The Mosquito is equipped with a video camera.

Its first flight occurred on 1 January 2003.

An improved Mosquito 1.5 is in development. It will weigh twice as much as the Mosquito 1, will be capable of 60-minute missions, and will be fitted with an enhanced video camera (two gimbals provide roll control with electronic image stabilization), and carry improved avionics.

Manufacturer:	Israel Aircraft Industries
Engines:	electric motor
Weights:	8.8 oz (250 grams)
Dimensions:	11⅞ in (300 mm) span
Endurance:	40 minutes

WASP

The Wasp is a "large" MAV with a flying-wing configuration. It is fabricated of plastic lithium-ion battery material that provides both electrical power and the wing structure for lift. The wing uses Telcordia synthetic battery material that generates an average output of more than 9 watts during flight.

Manufacturer:	AeroVironment
Engines:	electric motor with Li battery
Weights:	6 oz (170 grams)
Dimensions:	12⁷⁄₁₂ in (320 mm) span
Endurance:	1 hour, 47 minutes

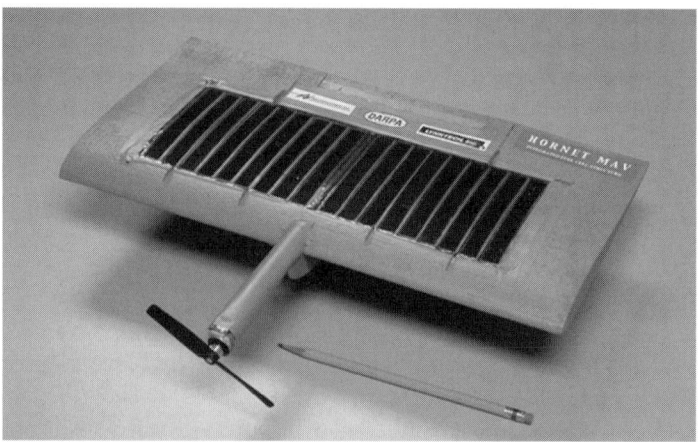

The Hornet MAV is a flying wing, with the wing structure being a hydrogen fuel cell. It was the first unmanned aerial vehicle to fly with power supplied entirely by a fuel cell. (AeroVironment)

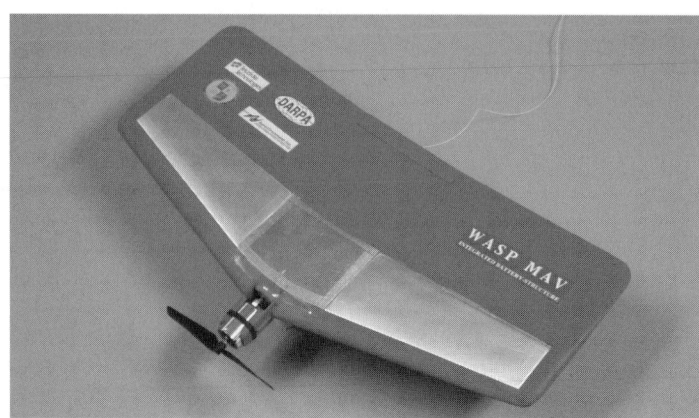

The Wasp established an endurance record of 1 hour, 47 minutes, three times the known endurance of previous MAV flights. Note the two-blade propellers on the MAVs illustrated here. (AeroVironment)

CHAPTER 30

Weapon Systems

A sailor stands watch on the flight deck "bomb park" of the carrier THEODORE ROOSEVELT (CVN 71) as the ship launches strikes in support of U.S. operations in Afghanistan (Operation Enduring Freedom). At bottom, he sits between a tractor and a Maverick missile; a score of laser guided bombs are visible. (U.S. Navy/Dela Torres)

The weapons fitted in U.S. ships and carried by naval aircraft are described in this chapter. Several new air-to-air and air-to-surface missiles are being introduced into the naval arsenal, all the products of joint Air Force–Navy programs. Two controversial programs are under way: The first is the ballistic missile intercept variant of the Standard surface-to-air missile. The ballistic missile defense program is discussed in Chapter 15.

The second addresses several weapons related to Naval Surface Fire Support (NSFS). The NSFS requirement—to provide fire support for amphibious landings and for inland combat operations by ground troops—is controversial because of (1) delays by the Navy and the Department and Defense in developing such weapons, (2) the long-running controversy over reactivating battleships of the IOWA (BB 61) class for this role, and (3) the question of whether non-shipboard weapons could carry out NSFS requirements, especially in competition with carrier- and land-based aircraft employing precision-guided munitions.

The current Marine Corps fire support requirement is for a naval gun similar to its own 155-mm artillery tubes, which have a range of 16 nm (29.6 km). Add that range to the *minimum* 25-nautical mile (46.3-km) ship standoff from land, and the gun must have a threshold range requirement of at least 41 nm (76 km). Thus, the 16-inch guns of the IOWA-class battleships do not have sufficient range to support Marine requirements.

The NSFS weapons now in U.S. Navy ships are the 5-inch (127-mm) gun and the Tomahawk Land-Attack Missile (TLAM); both weapons are fitted in all active U.S. cruisers and destroyers. Additional NSFS weapon systems are being developed for the near-term (through 2008) and long term (from 2009):

• The near-term weapons are the 5-inch gun firing the Autonomous Naval Support Round (ANSR), and the Tactical Tomahawk missile. An improved fire control system will be fitted in cruisers and destroyers to support these weapons. The previously planned Extended-Range Guided Munition (ERGM), which could be fired by the 5-inch/64-cal gun, was canceled in 2003.

• The long-term weapon is the 155-mm Advanced Gun System (AGS) firing advanced projectiles. That gun also was to have fired the ERGM round. The Land-Attack Standard Missile (LASM) and Advanced Land-Attack Missile (ALAM) have been canceled. Proposals to adopt the Army's Assault Ballistic Rocket System (ABRS) for surface ship and possible submarine launch also were stillborn, demonstrating the Navy's continuing lack of effort in this field.

Also under development is an Electro-Magnetic Gun (EMG) or "rail gun" that could be employed in the NSFS role.

BOMBS AND ROCKETS

U.S. naval aviation has shifted from "iron" or "dumb" bombs to the almost exclusive use of "smart" weapons—guided missiles and laser-guided bombs. The latter primarily are Mk 80-series bombs fitted with guidance kits to convert them to Laser-Guided Bombs (LGB).

An F-14D Tomcat of fighter squadron VF-2 with 1,000-pound GBU-16 laser-guided bombs loaded for a mission over Iraq during Operation Iraqi Freedom. The Tomcats normally carry four such weapons under the fuselage in addition to air-to-air missiles. (U.S. Navy/Daniel J. McLain)

Navy and Marine Corps aircraft carry Mk 80-series bombs and unguided Rockeye rockets. There are three Mk 80-series bombs in use. The Guided Bomb Unit (GBU) kits, Bomb Live Unit (BLU) kits, and miscellaneous kits (KMU) that convert bombs to LGB configurations are listed below.[1]

When fitted with LGB kits, these bombs can be guided to their targets by a laser designator fitted to the launching aircraft, another aircraft, or forces on the ground. (The last can include SEAL-type special forces operating behind enemy lines, as was done in the 1991 war in the Persian Gulf.) The kits consist of a laser

---

1 Bomb Live Unit indicates a bomb body filled with high explosives.

A sailor checks 2,000-pound GBU-32 Joint Direct Attack Munitions (JDAM) on the flight deck of the carrier JOHN F. KENNEDY (CV 67) during strikes in Afghanistan in support of Operation Enduring Freedom. There is an F-14B Tomcat in the background. (U.S. Navy/Jim Hampshire)

receiver, computer-control group, and an air-foil group (wing assembly and guidance fins).

The Navy and Marine Corps currently use the GBU-10/12/16/24 laser-guided bombs, collectively known as Paveway II weapons. Total procurement for the Navy–Marine Corps is planned at 21,814 laser-guided bombs, with production still ongoing (Raytheon and Lockheed Martin).

The Joint Direct Attack Munition (JDAM) is a joint Navy–Air Force program to provide guidance kits to Mk 80-series bombs. Guidance is from a GPS/inertial navigation package fitted to the tail that improves accuracy and all-weather capability. Accuracy is better than 10 feet (3 m), with a range up to 15 nm (28 km).

JDAM-fitted bombs were first used in the 1999 Kosovo campaign. Subsequently, they were used in operations in Afghanistan and Iraq. Delivery of strap-on kits to the Navy began in 1998. The total planned is for 87,496 kits for the Air Force and Navy. The prime contractor is Boeing (formerly Rockwell International and Martin Marietta).

An F-14B Tomcat releases a 1,000-pound GBU-16 laser-guided bomb during a live-fire exercise at Fallon, Nevada. The tail fins are deployed as the bomb seeks the laser "spot" on a ground target. (U.S. Navy/Andy Walton)

Bomb	Class	LGB kits	JDAM kits
Mk 82	500 lb (227 kg)	GBU-12	GBU-30
		KMU-388/B	
Mk 83	1,000 lb (454 kg)	GBU-16, BLU-110	GBU-31
		KMU-431/B	
Mk 84	2,000 lb (907 kg)	GBU-10, GBU-24/B	GBU-32
		BLU-109	
		KMU-351A/B	

The Mk 80 weapons have both standard (fixed) tail assemblies and low-drag tails, the latter extend on release to slow the bomb and enable a low-flying aircraft to escape the bombs' explosions.

Bombs also can be converted for use as naval mines (see Mines, below).

Nuclear bombs no longer are available to U.S. naval forces (see Nuclear Weapons, below).

ROCKEYE II

The Rockeye II Mk 20 is an unguided cluster bomb that dispenses bomblets to attack "soft" targets, such as anti-aircraft sites and lightly armored vehicles. Each bomb carries 247 bomblets with shaped-charge warheads; each bomblet weighs 1 pound (0.46 kg). On detonation, each releases a jet of superheated, pressurized gas that can penetrate up to 10 inches (254 mm) of steel or 30 inches (762 mm) of concrete.

The earlier Rockeye I was designated Mk 15.

The similar Anti-Personnel/Anti-Material (APAM) rocket, an improved munition carrying a bomblet dispenser, has been retired from service.

NAVAL GUNS

The reinstatement of two IOWA-class battleships on the Naval Vessel Register (NVR) has returned both 16-inch/50-cal (406-mm) and 5-inch/38-cal guns to the fleet, albeit in two ships laid up in reserve (see Chapter 14). The largest naval guns in active U.S. warships are 5-inch/54-cal and 5-inch/62-cal weapons; the former are fitted in all active cruisers and destroyers, and the longer-barrel guns are in the later ships of the ARLEIGH BURKE (DDG 51) class.

The Navy's shipboard firepower had increased dramatically in the 1980s with the reactivation of the four battleships of the IOWA class. Those ships each carried nine 16-inch guns and—as modernized in the 1980s—12 5-inch guns.[2] With the mothballing of the

Three Mk 20 Rockeye II cluster bombs are moved across the flight deck of a carrier. These and other unguided weapons still are useful in some situations, especially against lightly protected targets. (U.S. Navy/Marc M. Thurston)

---

2 As built, each IOWA-class battleship carried 20 5-inch/38-cal Dual Purpose (DP) guns in twin gun houses plus 80 40-mm Anti-Aircraft (AA) guns and up to 48 20-mm AA guns.

Advanced Munitions

The Navy is continuing its efforts to develop effective long-range, precision munitions to enable Naval Surface Fire Support (NSFS) systems to meet Marine Corps requirements. These efforts have been very convoluted, as different approaches have been taken to meet changing requirements and to overcome technical problems and cost increases. In early 2004, the programs were reconstructed to "provide a robust NSFS capability within existing resources," according to Navy statements.

These advanced munition programs now are being funded:

• *Long-Range Land-Attack Projectile (LRLAP)*. This 155-mm projectile is being developed for the Advanced Gun System (AGS) planned for installation in the DD(X). The LRLAP will be fitted with a Global positioning System (GPS) receiver and Inertial Measuring Unit (IMU) to provide a high degree of accuracy. The projectile is rocket assisted, carrying a high-explosive warhead, with a range in excess of 100 nm (185 km). The LRLAP projectile will be at least 84 inches (2.13 m) long. Projected cost is $35,000 per round.

• *Extended-Range Munition (ERM)*. This program supports the Mk 45 Mod 2/4 5-inch (127-mm) guns fitted in destroyers and cruisers. Designated Ex-171, the ERM is a rocket-assisted projectile capable of carrying a unitary blast-fragmentation warhead. The 110-pound (50-kg), aerodynamic projectile is 61 inches (1.55 m) in length and uses a GPS/Inertial Navigation System (INS) guidance system. The guidance is jamming resistant, enabling the ERM to attack targets in an Electronic Countermeasures (ECM) environment.

• *Extended-range Guided Munition (ERGM)*. The ERGM is being developed for the Mk 45 Mod 4 "long-barrel" 5-inch gun in ships of the ARLEIGH BURKE (DDG 51) class numbered DDG 81 and above. This rocket-assisted round can carry 72 M80 submunitions out to a range of some 40 nm (74 km), with GPS guidance providing an accuracy of 33–66 feet (10–20 m) at maximum range. The ERGM originally was designed for a range of 100 nm (185 km); in 2003, the Naval Sea Systems Command reported the round would have a range of 50 nm (92.65 km), and at about the same time, Raytheon reported a range of only 40 nm (74 km). The eight-year-old ERGM program originally was scheduled to have an initial operational capability in 2001 but is now expected to be 2006.

The M80 is a dual-purpose, Improved Conventional Munition (ICM) that incorporates a shaped charge capable of penetrating 2–3 inches (50.75–76 mm) of armor and a fragmenting steel case. The ERGM round is 5 feet (1.5 m) long and weighs 110 pounds (45.36 kg), compared to 3 feet (0.9 m) and 70 pounds (21.34 kg) for a conventional 5-inch round.

Funding was halted briefly in late 2003, but the Navy's February 2004 budget item justification cites a continuing program. The rounds are expected to cost $50,000 each.

• *Autonomous Naval Support Round (ANSR)*. This effort was undertaken as a "risk mitigation program" for the ERGM program. It can be fired from Mk 45 Mod 2/4 guns. Also known as the "barrage round," the ANSR does not have a rocket booster but achieves its high velocity and increased range through a system of sabot devices. Each device holds a smaller caliber shell within a larger container that falls away from the shell as it leaves the gun's muzzle; the round then rolls to achieve in-flight stability. When it detonates at its target, the barrage round dispenses a large number of flechettes—small metal arrows.

The ANSR carries 35 M46 submunitions to a maximum range of 50 nm (92.65 km) or 56 M46s to 30 nm (55.6 km). In firing tests, an ANSR reached a record 62 nm (114.9 km). The projectiles use a GPS/INS guidance system to achieve a Circular Error Probable (CEP) of 52½ feet (16 m).

MISSOURI (BB 63) in early 1992, all four of these behemoths again were laid up in reserve (and two subsequently were stricken). It is highly unlikely that the two remaining ships, the IOWA and WISCONSIN (BB 64), will or could be reactivated.

The Marine Corps requirement for naval gunfire support had led to a renewed interest in deployment of the 8-inch (203-mm) Major Caliber Lightweight Gun (MCLWG), which is suitable for installation in ships of cruiser and destroyer size, as well as several other naval gunfire support systems. However, austere budgets and the procurement of other gun systems essentially have ended consideration of the MCLWG; see 16th Edition/pages 427–28 for characteristics.

The principal rocket candidate for the naval fire support mission during the 1980s was the Assault Ballistic Rocket System (ABRS), an unguided rocket and launcher adopted from LTV Corporation's Multiple Launch Rocket System (MLRS) used by the U.S. Army and several NATO countries.[3] The ABRS had been proposed for installation on the IOWA-class battleships and landing ships of the NEWPORT (LST 1179) class. One proposal provided for full conversion of LSTs to "rocket monitors"; see 14th Edition/page 466 for ABRS/MLRS characteristics. Subsequently, the Army's Tactical Missile System (ATACMS) was proposed for the fire support role, but it was not pursued.[4]

In 2004, the issue of the MLRS and its successor Extended-Range (ER) MLRS system again was raised as a weapon system for some Littoral Combat Ships (LCS). A variant of that system was considered to provide limited NSFS for forces ashore, including SEAL and Marine raiding/reconnaissance operations. By that time, the MLRS/ER–MLRS rounds had increased significantly in range and had improved accuracy, the latter provided by the Global Positioning System (GPS) and an inertial navigation device.

A 1993 Cost and Operational Effectiveness Analysis (COEA) by the Center for Naval Analyses identified eight gun systems that—combined with missiles—were capable of attacking at least 95 percent of targets in postulated major regional conflicts. Five of these systems were 155-mm gun variants and three were 8-inch gun variants, with differing propellants, projectiles, and calibers. The analysis concluded that a 155-mm/60-cal gun system with an advanced propellant and precision guided munitions in combination with the Tomahawk missile was the most cost-effective option for naval gunfire support.

Beyond the retiring of the battleships, there has been a steady decline in naval guns as older cruisers and destroyers have been decommissioned; newer ships generally have fewer guns of smaller caliber. All cruisers armed with 8-inch and 6-inch (152-mm) guns have been retired, as have all pre-SPRUANCE (DD 963) destroyers, which carried up to six 5-inch guns. The last active U.S. ship with 8-inch guns was the heavy cruiser NEWPORT NEWS (CA 148), decommissioned in 1978, and the last active ship with 6-inch guns was the cruiser–flagship OKLAHOMA CITY (CG 5), retired in 1979; all mothballed cruisers with these guns have been stricken.

---

3 The U.S. Marine Corps planned to acquire the MLRS, but in the event, that was not pursued.

4 Fitting the MLRS to warships was proposed in the 1980s; see Scott C. Truver and Norman Polmar, "Naval Surface Fire Support and the IOWAs," U.S. Naval Institute *Proceedings* (November 1985), pp. 130–33.

(The only warships in service today in foreign navies with guns larger than 5-inch are the Russian Navy's later KIROV-class battle cruisers, SLAVA-class missile cruisers, and SOVREMENNYY-class destroyers, which mount 130-mm/70-cal dual-purpose guns. All cruisers of the SVERDLOV class, mounting from 6 to 12 152-mm guns, have been discarded.)

All active U.S. cruisers and destroyers have 5-inch/54-cal or 62-cal Mk 45 lightweight guns. All frigates armed with 5-inch/38-cal guns have been retired, and the Coast Guard cutters armed with 5-inch/38-cal guns have been retired or rearmed. The 5-inch guns in active cruisers and destroyers are considered primarily shore-bombardment weapons and have only a limited anti-air capability.

The 76-mm guns in Navy frigates and the larger Coast Guard cutters primarily are anti-aircraft weapons, but they do have an anti-surface capability. Most Navy surface warships and some fast combat replenishment ships (AOE) are armed with the Mk 15 20-mm Close-In Weapon System (CIWS) (in addition to Sea Sparrow and Rolling Airframe Missiles/RAM in some ships) for defense against anti-ship missiles. Various types of 25-mm and 20-mm cannon, and .50-cal and 7.62-mm machine guns also are fitted in naval ships, primarily for defense against small craft in restricted waters.

Classifications: Guns are classified by their inside barrel diameters and gun-barrel lengths. Diameters traditionally have been listed in inches for weapons larger than 1-inch diameter. Thus, a 5-inch/54-cal gun has a barrel length of 270 inches. The Italian-developed OTO Melara 76-mm gun retains its metric measurement in U.S. naval service.

Guns smaller than 1-inch diameter are measured in millimeters or calibers, the latter being fractions of an inch (e.g., .50 cal = _ inch).

Nomenclature: According to the Navy, "A mount is an assembled unit which includes the gun barrel (or barrels), housing(s), slide(s), carriage, stand, sight, elevating and training drives, ammunition hoists, and associated equipment." Guns from 20-mm caliber up to but not including 6-inch have mounts. A mount differs from a turret in that a mount does not necessarily have a barbette structure below, within the superstructure or hull.

Projectile weight: Weights vary with the type of projectile.

Saluting guns: U.S. aircraft carriers, cruisers, destroyers, amphibious ships, and some auxiliaries have the 40-mm Mk 11 saluting guns. This weapon has no combat capability.

The following entries are arranged by gun size (i.e., bore diameter), except that the Electro-Magnetic Gun is listed first.

ELECTRO-MAGNETIC GUN

The U.S. Army, Navy, and Defense Advanced Research Projects Agency (DARPA) have ongoing EMG or rail gun programs. The Fiscal Year (FY) 2004 defense authorization required that the Secretary of Defense establish a collaborative program among those organizations for the evaluation and demonstration of EMG technologies and concepts.

The Navy's program currently is oriented toward providing a long-range EMG as a fire support weapon.[5] It will be possible to install the weapon in the planned DD(X) and possibly CG(X) because those ships have electric-drive propulsion.

The propelling charge for the gun has an electrical energy output from 60 to 300 megajoules (MJ), and the projectile acceleration rate is 30,000–45,000 gs. (In contrast, the current 5-inch/54-cal gun has a muzzle energy of 10 MJ and a rocket-assisted projectile increases this to about 18 MJ; the planned 155-mm AGS will have a muzzle velocity in excess of 33 MJ.) The EMG would require a power supply of 15–30 megawatts, and approximately 6 gallons (22.7 liters) of ship's fuel would be required to fire each round.

"We hope to be on a technology development time line that would support integration into the second flight" of the DD(X) program, noted Fred Beach, the Navy's EMG manager.[6] He estimated

Remote Gun Mount

The Ex-45 stable gun mount is a remote-control mount that can be fitted with a 40-mm grenade launcher Mk 19, a .50-caliber machine gun M2, a 5.56-mm Squad Assault Weapon (SAW), or other automatic guns. The first two Ex-45 mounts provided to the fleet—fitted with .50-cal machine guns—were installed in the high-speed vessel SWIFT (HSV 2) and a Coast Guard cutter.

The stable gun mount, developed by the Office of Naval Research, is a three-axis, gyro-stabilized weapon mount coupled with a laser rangefinder and closed-circuit television. It can be fitted in ships and land vehicles, as well as in small combat craft, including the Marine Corps Small Unit Riverine Craft (SURC).

Afloat testing was conducted in 2004.

The Ex-45 remote gun mount fitted with a .50-cal machine gun as mounted on a Coast Guard cutter. (U.S. Navy)

that the first "full-up unit" of the weapon would have to be available by 2015.

In operational use, the rail gun would fire in bursts of ten rounds, using command-guided projectiles or conventional ammunition.

The EMG would fire an inert round, which would use kinetic energy to damage its target. A multiple "warhead" is possible. The round would have no propellant, as it will be propelled entirely by the electromagnetic process. GPS guidance is expected.

The EMG concept also is being considered for a shipboard terminal self-defense system against attacking cruise missiles. That system would be a totally different design from the NSFS weapon.

Also see 60-mm electrothermal technology demonstrator (below).

Status: Development.

Mount:	single
Gun barrel:	not applicable
Muzzle velocity:	Mach 6+
Weight:	undetermined
Rate of fire:	6–12 rounds/minute
Maximum range:	200+ n.miles (370+ km)
Projectile weight:	
Fire control:	undetermined
Crew:	undetermined
Ships:	*cruisers* CG(X)
	destroyers DD(X)

---

5 See Lt. Comdr. David Allan Adams, USN, "Naval Rail Guns Are Revolutionary," U.S. Naval Institute *Proceedings* (February 2003), pp. 34–37.

6 John T. Bennett, "Navy Wants Railguns Ready for Second Flight of DD(X) Destroyers," *Inside The Pentagon* (5 February 2004), p. 1.

The ammunition capacities of the IOWA-class magazines are 390 rounds for turret No. 1, 460 rounds for turret No. 2, and 370 rounds for turret No. 3. They were the world's largest guns fitted to fire nuclear projectiles and the only U.S. shipboard guns with that capability. Nuclear projectiles with a W23 gun-type warhead were available for these guns from December 1956 to October 1962.

Operational: The IOWA suffered an explosion in her No. 2 16-inch gun turret on 19 April 1989, while she was operating some 330 nm (610 km) off Puerto Rico. (See pages 129–30 for details.) The damaged gun—center gun of No. 2 turret—was not repaired before the ship was mothballed. The parts needed to rehabilitate the turret are available; the cost of the repairs was estimated at about $8 million at the time.

Status: Operational. None in active ships.

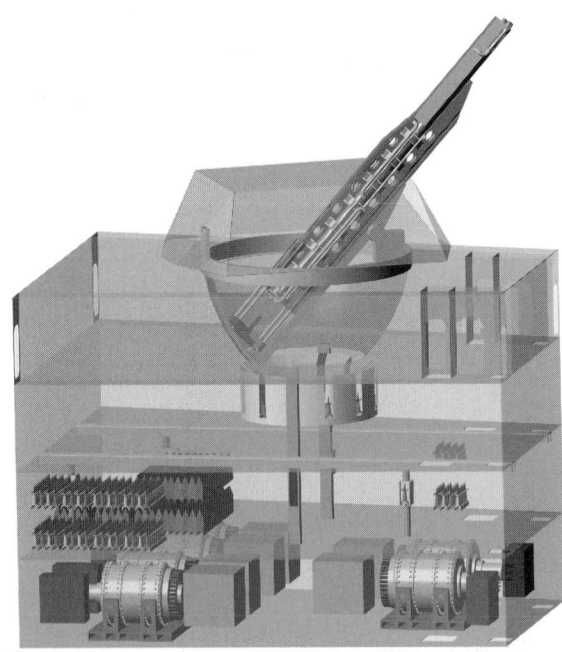

A drawing of a shipboard rail gun installation. The below decks section is about the size of the barbette for a 5-inch gun mount, including handling spaces and magazine. Note projectile stowage at lower left. (U.S. Navy)

16-INCH/50-CAL GUN

These guns, which are the main gun battery of the IOWA-class battleships, are the largest guns ever mounted in U.S. warships. They are surpassed by only the 18.1-inch (460-mm) guns of the Japanese YAMATO-class battleships of World War II and the single 18-inch (457-mm) gun of the British carrier FURIOUS of World War I.[7]

The 16-inch/50s also were intended for the five never-built battleships of the MONTANA (BB 67) class.

Mount:	triple
Gun barrel:	Mk 7 Mod 0
Muzzle velocity:	2,425 ft/sec (739 m/sec) Armor Piercing (AP)
	2,690 ft/sec (820 m/sec) High Capacity (HC) for shore bombardment
Weight:	1,700 tons (turret)
Rate of fire:	2 rounds/minute per barrel
Maximum range:	40,185 yds (36,755 m) AP at 45° elevation
	41,622 yds (38,069 m) HC at 45° elevation
Projectile weight:	2,700 lb (1,225 kg) AP
	1,900 lb (862 kg) HC
Fire control:	Mk 38 Gunfire Control System (GFCS)
Crew:	74 per turret: 27 in turret
	4 in machinery rooms
	15 in upper projectile room
	15 in lower projectile room
	13 in powder handling room
Ships:	*battleships* BB 61 class

7 The FURIOUS carried her single 18-inch gun from her completion, in April 1917, until installation of an after aircraft landing deck in November 1917.

The forward 16-inch/50-cal gun turrets of the battleship MISSOURI (BB 63). There is a Mk 56 gunfire control system (for 5-inch guns) atop the bridge structure. Quad 40-mm gun mounts previously adorned the top of No. 2 turret and the 01 level adjacent to the bridge. (Giorgio Arra)

Sixteen-inch projectiles are staged on the forecastle of the battleship IOWA (BB 61) as she sits at anchor at the Naval Weapons Station, Yorktown, Virginia, during her active service from 1984 to 1990. These "bullets" are about 6 feet long. (U.S. Navy)

Sailors transport a powder casing for the 16-inch guns aboard the battleship NEW JERSEY (BB 62). Within the casing are silk propellant bags; six of the bags, each 15½ inches long and 14¾ inches in diameter, normally are used to fire a 16-inch projectile. (U.S. Navy)

155-MM ADVANCED GUN SYSTEM

The AGS is planned for the Navy's DD(X) advanced destroyer. Previously, the weapon was intended for the land-attack destroyers (DD 21). It will be capable of firing both rocket-assisted and conventional 155-mm rounds. Two AGS weapons are to be fitted in each DD(X).

The objective for magazine capacity for the AGS is 750 rocket-assisted rounds per gun (i.e., 1,500 per ship). The gun will be capable of firing the Sense and Destroy Armor (SADARM) submunition, with two SADARM projectiles fitted to each 155-mm round.[8] The gun is planned for the ERGM round and the Long Range Land Attack Projectile (LRLAP). The magazines will be full automated.

The 155-mm mounts are designed with low radar cross sections and infrared signatures to help maintain the stealth characteristics of the DD(X). The AGS automated ammunition handling technology is based on the Army's 155-mm Crusader howitzer, which was canceled in 2003.

Status: Development. Initial Operational Capability (IOC) planned in 2011. United Defense Limited Partnership is the prime contractor.

Mount:	single
Gun barrel:	
Muzzle velocity:	
Weight:	
Rate of fire:	10–12 rounds/minute
Maximum range:	
Projectile weight:	
Fire control:	
Crew:	(unmanned mount and magazine)
Ships:	*destroyers* DD(X)

---

8 Each 155-mm SADARM projectile carries two submunitions, each of which uses a dual-mode millimeter-wave and infrared sensor and fires an explosively formed penetrator through the top of a target.

Two 155-mm AGS mounts will be fitted to the DD(X). These will be "disappearing guns," with fully retractable barrels to help maintain the ship's low radar cross section. The gun mounts and magazines will be fully automated. (United Defense)

155-MM/52-CAL VERTICAL GUN FOR ADVANCED SHIPS

The Vertical Gun for Advanced Ships (VGAS) was a proposal for the DD 21 land-attack destroyer. Twin 155-mm guns—with a range of about 100 nm (185 km)—and their magazines were to be fitted in a modular mounting that could replace Vertical Launching System (VLS) missile modules.

The gun system was to be fully automated, with 1,400 rounds per module (i.e., for two guns). Projectiles up to 6½ feet (1.9 m) long weighing 300 pounds (136 kg) could be handled by VGAS. The sustained rate of fire was to be 15 rounds per minute per barrel.

In the event, the Navy decided not to pursue development of VGAS because of potential operational limitations. See 17th Edition/page 481 for description.

The VGAS also might have been considered for the aborted arsenal ship program (see Appendix E).

5-INCH/62-CAL GUN MK 45 MOD 4

This is primarily a shore-bombardment weapon, designed specifically to fire ERGM rounds. The gun can fire all types of 5-inch rounds and can be used in an anti-aircraft mode.

The 5-inch/62-cal gun is being mounted in improved ARLEIGH BURKE-class destroyers beginning with the WINSTON S. CHURCHILL (DDG 81). The Navy had planned to rearm 22 improved TICONDEROGA-class cruisers (CG 52–73) with two guns each, but that program now is unlikely.

In 1996, the Navy awarded a contract for $49.6 million to United Defense to modify existing Mk 45 guns for extended range and enhanced performance. In addition to a longer barrel and capability for rocket-assisted projectiles, the Mod 4 gun has increased reliability and reduced maintenance requirements.

Each ship (single mount) has a magazine loadout of 225 rocket-assisted round and 210 conventional rounds. The ready service magazine holds 20 rounds (conventional size).

Status: Operational; in production (United Defense). The Mk 45 Mod 4 gun also is used by the Japanese Maritime Self-Defense Force.

Mount:	single
Gun barrel:	Mk 36 Mod 4
Muzzle velocity:	2,650 ft/sec (808 m/sec) conventional round
	2,800 ft/sec (853 m/sec) ERGM round
Weight:	63,767 lb (28,924 kg)
Rate of fire:	16–20 rounds/minute conventional round
Maximum range:	see Advanced Munitions sidebar
Projectile weight:	70 lb (31.75 kg) conventional round
	110 lb (50 kg) ERGM round
Fire control:	Mk 160 Mod 8 gun computing system
Crew:	6
Ships:	*destroyers* DDG 79

The destroyer PREBLE (DDG 88) fires a round (far right) from the ship's "long-barrel" 5-inch gun Mk 45 Mod 4. The gun house differs from that of the Mod 2 5-inch guns of the earlier ARLEIGH BURKE-class ships. These are the only U.S. destroyers built with a single main gun mount. (U.S. Navy/Ramon Preciado)

5-INCH/54-CAL GUN MK 45 Mod 2

The Mk 45 Mod 2 is the principal gun in U.S. cruisers and destroy-ers. It is capable of engaging air or surface targets. The gun mount is unmanned, with the gun crew stationed below deck, and stows up to 20 rounds of ready service ammunition that can be fired quickly by a single man at the below-deck control console. The magazine can be reloaded while the gun is firing without interrupt-ing the firing sequence. Maximum rate of fire is 16–20 rounds per minute with fixed ammunition. Firing rocket-assisted projectiles and other separated ammunition reduces the firing rate.

The gun is installed in all ARLEIGH BURKE-class ships prior to the WINSTON S. CHURCHILL, as well as in the TICONDEROGA-class cruisers and SPRUANCE-class destroyers. The three 5-inch Mk 45 guns have been removed from the large amphibious ships of the TARAWA (LHA 1) class; the successor WASP (LHD 1) class mounts only the 20-mm CIWS and lighter weapons. Magazine capacity in destroyers is 475–500 rounds per mount.

The Mk 45 was first deployed in U.S. ships in 1971.

Status: Operational. No longer in production.

The Mk 45 gun also is used in warships of Australia, Greece, New Zealand, Thailand, and Turkey.

Mount:	single
Gun barrel:	Mk 19 Mod 2
Muzzle velocity:	2,500 ft/sec (762 m/sec)
Weight:	47,820 lb (21,691)
Rate of fire:	16–20 rounds/minute
Maximum range:	25,909 yds (23,697 m) at 47° elevation
	48,700 ft (14,848 m) at 85° elevation

Projectile weight:	70 lb (31.75 kg)	
Fire control:	Mk 86 GFCS or Mk 160 gun computing system	
Crew:	6	
Ships:	*cruisers*	CG 47
	destroyers	DDG 51
		DD 963

Gunner's Mate 2nd Class Shermel Howard cleans the barrel of the 5-inch gun Mk 45 Mod 2 on the destroyer HOPPER (DDG 70). The gun mount is unmanned. (U.S. Navy/Johnny R. Wilson)

The cruiser LEYTE GULF (CG 55) fires her forward 5-inch gun Mk 45 Mod 2. Aegis cruisers—origi-nally classified as destroyers—are armed with two 5-inch guns. The amphibious ships of the TARAWA (LHA 1) class also were armed with Mk 45 guns when completed; they have been removed. (U.S. Navy/David K. Simmons)

5-INCH/38-CAL GUN MK 28

These 5-inch guns are fitted as the secondary battery in IOWA-class battleships. When these ships were reactivated during the 1980s, the original battery of ten 5-inch twin mounts was reduced to six mounts per ship.

The 5-inch/38 was the world's first 5-inch gun capable of effec-tively engaging both air and surface targets. It was first fitted in U.S. destroyers and the aircraft carrier RANGER (CV 4) in the early 1930s. Subsequently, it became the main armament for U.S. air-craft carriers, destroyers, anti-aircraft cruisers (CLAA), amphibi-ous ships, and fleet auxiliaries through the end of World War II. The 5-inch/38 was mounted as the secondary battery in all U.S. cruisers and battleships. It was fitted in both single and twin mounts.

The 5-inch/38 was succeeded in U.S. destroyers and a few other ships by the 5-inch/54-cal gun.

Status: Operational. None in active ships.

Mount:	twin	
Gun barrel:	Mk 12 Mod 1	
Muzzle velocity:	2,500 ft/sec (762 m/sec)	
Weight:	53,000–169,000 lb (69,400–76,658 kg) (varies with Mod)	
Rate of fire:	18 rounds/minute per barrel	
Maximum range:	17,306 yds (15,829 m) at 45° elevation	
	32,250 ft (9,832 m) at 85° elevation	
Projectile weight:	55 lb (25 kg)	
Fire control:	Mk 56 GFCS	
Crew:	27	
Ships:	*battleships*	BB 61

A twin 5-inch gun mount Mk 28 on the battleship IOWA. The white dome above the mount is a Phalanx CIWS on the next level up. Now 5-inch/38-cal guns are found only in the two mothballed IOWA-class battleships. (Giorgio Arra)

A pair of twin 5-inch gun mounts Mk 28 on the battleship MISSOURI. As reactivated in the 1980s, the IOWA-class dreadnoughts retained six of their original ten 5-inch mounts. There is a Phalanx Close-In Weapon System (CIWS) and a Mk 56 gunfire control director above the mounts. (Giorgio Arra)

76-MM/62-CAL GUN MK 75

The OLIVER HAZARD PERRY (FFG 7)-class frigates and numerous Coast Guard cutters are fitted with the 76-mm/62-cal Mk 75 gun mount. The gun also was fitted in the now-discarded PEGASUS (PHM 1) hydrofoil missile combatants. Designed by OTO Melara SpA of Italy, the system generally is identified by the firm's name.

The 76-mm gun is designed specifically for use in ships as small as 200 tons and is capable of engaging air and surface targets. It is remotely controlled with a small, unmanned mount. The ready magazine holds 70 rounds, plus 6 rounds in the hoist and 4 in the drum, permitting a single operator to fire 80 rounds without reloading.

The Mk 75 gun also is used by several foreign navies.

Status: Operational. No longer in production.

Mount:	single
Gun barrel:	Mk 75
Muzzle velocity:	3,000 ft/sec (915 m/sec)
Weight:	16,400 lb (7,439 kg)
Rate of fire:	approx. 80 rounds/minute
Maximum range:	approx. 21,000 yds (19,207 m) at 45° elevation
	approx. 39,000 ft (11,890 m) at 85° elevation
Projectile weight:	14 lb (6.29 kg)
Fire control:	Mk 92 GFCS
Crew:	3
Ships:	*frigates* FFG 7
	cutters WHEC 715
	WMEC 901

The frigate SIDES (FFG 14) fires her 76-mm gun Mk 75 during a live firing exercise off the California coast; the target was the destroyer TOWERS (DDG 9). Note the shell slide under the gun barrel. The frigate guns have severely limited arcs of fire. (U.S. Navy/Andrew Betting)

The CURTS (FFG 38) fires her 76-mm gun during a multinational exercise off Singapore. The gun is the principal weapon in frigates following removal of their Mk 13 missile launchers. The STIR radar antenna is visible forward of the gun mount. (U.S. Navy/Bruce Cummins)

3-INCH/50-CAL (76-MM) GUN MK 33

Large numbers of 3-inch/50-cal anti-aircraft guns were fitted from the early 1950s onward in numerous classes of surface combatants, amphibious ships, and fleet auxiliaries. The only U.S. Navy ships that now mount the guns are five amphibious cargo ships laid up in reserve.

The guns generally were ineffective and difficult to maintain. Most amphibious ships and auxiliaries were refitted with the Phalanx CIWS and/or Sea Sparrow point-defense missiles in place of some or all 3-inch mounts.

These are open or shielded (unarmored) mounts. They have two open, drum-type magazines for each barrel, which are hand loaded.

Status: Operational. None in active ships.

Mount:	twin
Gun barrel:	Mk 22
Muzzle velocity:	2,650 ft/sec (808 m/sec)
Weight:	approx. 33,000 lb (14,969 kg)
Rate of fire:	50 rounds/minute per barrel
Maximum range:	14,041 yds (12,842 m) at 45° elevation
	29,367 ft (8,953 m) at 85° elevation
Projectile weight:	7 lb (3.2 kg)
Fire control:	local control only
Crew:	12
Ships:	*amphibious* LKA 113

A dated but unusual photo shows the loading procedures and mechanism for the 3-inch gun Mk 33 twin mount. There are rotating ready ammunition racks adjacent to the gun breeches. These hand-loaded guns had limited effectiveness against aerial targets. (U.S. Navy)

A twin 3-inch gun Mk 33 mount fitted with a shield. The only U.S. ships still with the Mk 33 gun mounts are mothballed amphibious cargo ships of the CHARLESTON (LKA 113) class. The mounts were installed in hundreds of ships from the late 1940s into the 1970s. (U.S. Navy)

60-MM ELECTROTHERMAL TECHNOLOGY DEMONSTRATOR

This was a technology demonstration model of a 60-mm Electrothermal (ET) gun intended for shipboard use in the CIWS role. After initial ET testing, the gun was delivered to the Naval Surface Warfare Center at Dahlgren, Virginia, in 1993. Testing ended in 1995.

The ET gun and automatic loader were mounted on a Mk 15 CIWS trunnion assembly. The barrel length was 16 feet, 11 inches (5.16 m).

See 17th Edition/pages 485–86 for characteristics.

Status: Testing completed.

57-MM/70-CAL GUN MK 110

This is an adaptation of the Bofors 57-mm/60-cal Mk 3 rapid-fire gun intended for use on the U.S. Coast Guard's Maritime Security Cutter (MSC) and possibly on the Navy's LCS.

The original Bofors 57-mm weapon entered service in 1966 and has undergone continual upgrading (i.e., from Mk 1 to Mk 3). The Mk 110 weapon uses "smart" ammunition, and the above-deck mount has a low radar cross section.

The (unmanned) mount holds 120 rounds, and there are 1,000 rounds in the magazine. Several types of ammunition are fired. The U.S. Navy has test fired 3P (Pre-fragmented, Programmable,

Proximity-fuzed) all-target programmable ammunition that allows three proximity fuzing options, as well as settings for time, impact, and armor-piercing functions.

Originally designated Ex-57 and, subsequently Ex-110, the gun was developed by Bofors Defence AB of Sweden, a subsidiary of United Defense. Known throughout the world as the Bofors Mk 3/57-mm, this family of naval guns is in use in ships of 15 countries. On 30 September 2003, United Defense was awarded a contract by Northrop Grumman Ship Systems for production and ship integration engineering support of the gun for the new Coast Guard cutter.

Status: Development.

Gun barrel:	
Muzzle velocity:	3,360 feet/second (1,025 meters/second)
Weight:	approx. 14,960 lb (6,800 kg)
Rate of fire:	220 rounds/minute
Maximum range:	18,600 yards (17,000 m) against surface targets (45° elevation)
	24,930 feet (7,600 m) in proximity fuze mode against aerial targets
Projectile weight:	13.4–14.3 lb (6.1–6.5 kg)
Fire control:	
Crew:	(mount unmanned)
Ships:	*cutters* Maritime Security Cutter

The Mk 110 is the first 57-mm gun to be fitted in U.S. ships, although it is a popular caliber in other navies. In the littoral combat ship, the Mk 110 would have a "disappearing barrel," similar to the 155-mm AGS. The gun fires a round 27 inches in length. (United Defense)

40-MM GRENADE LAUNCHER MK 47

The Mk 47 Advanced Lightweight Grenade Launcher (ALGL)—called the Striker—is a replacement for the long-serving grenade launcher Mk 19. Initiated primarily for U.S. special forces and the Marine Corps, the ALGL also will be used for Navy small craft and possibly for the close-in defense of large ships.

The new weapon has a built-in laser rangefinder and ballistic computer. It will fire standard 40-mm belted grenades in addition to the Preprogrammed High-Explosive (PP-HE) round, which is designed for air bursts.

Development of the Mk 47 began in 1988.

Status: In development. The ALGL is being developed by the Naval Surface Warfare Center at Crane, Indiana. General Dynamics has been selected as the systems integrator for the weapon.

Muzzle velocity:	
Weight:	38 lb (17.24 kg)
Rate of fire:	250–300 rounds/minute
Maximum range:	
Projectile weight:	
Fire control:	optical/laser
Crew:	1
Ships:	various

40-MM GRENADE LAUNCHER MK 19 MOD 3

Numerous Navy auxiliaries and small combatants and Coast Guard cutters and small craft have 40-mm Mk 19 grenade launchers.

The launcher is blowback-operated, air-cooled, manually fired, and shoots high-velocity 40-mm grenades from linked belts. The rounds are configured in an armor-piercing shape, having been initially designed to counter lightly armored vehicles. The anti-armor round can penetrate 2 inches (51 mm) of armor.

The Mk 19 can fire several types of metallic-link, belted 40-mm grenades: M430 and M430A1 High-Explosive, Dual-Purpose (HEDP); M383 high-explosive; and M385I and M918 training. The M383 is the heaviest round at 12⅓ ounces (350 grams).

Effective range generally is cited as 1,650 yards (1,509 m). Sustained rate of fire is about 40 rounds per minute. The Mk 19 barrel is 43 inches (1.1 m) long. A night-vision sight is provided.

For ground use, the Mk 19 is fitted on a tripod weighing 44 pounds (20 kg). The Mk 19 is mounted on land vehicles, helicopters, and AAV7assault vehicles, as well as aboard ship.

Historical: Development of an automatic grenade launcher began in 1963. The first version was the Mk 18 hand-cranked launcher. In 1966, the need for more firepower inspired the development of a self-powered 40-mm machine gun, the Mk 19 Mod 0. This model was neither reliable enough nor safe enough for military use.

Improvements resulted in the 1972 Mod 1, of which only six were produced. The Mod 1 performed effectively in Navy riverine patrol craft, and broader applications for the Mk 19 were found. In 1973, the Navy developed the Mod 2, which featured improved reliability, safety, and maintainability. In 1976, a complete redesign resulted in the Mk 19 Mod 3, which the Army adopted in 1983.

Status: Operational. The Mod 3 entered U.S. Army service in 1983. It is in use in more than 20 countries.

Muzzle velocity:	790 ft/sec (240 m/sec)
Weight:	72.5 lb (32.9 kg)
Rate of fire:	325–375 rounds/minute
Maximum range:	2,400 yds (2,195 m) for area target
Projectile weight:	see text
Fire control:	open sight
Crew:	1
Ships:	various

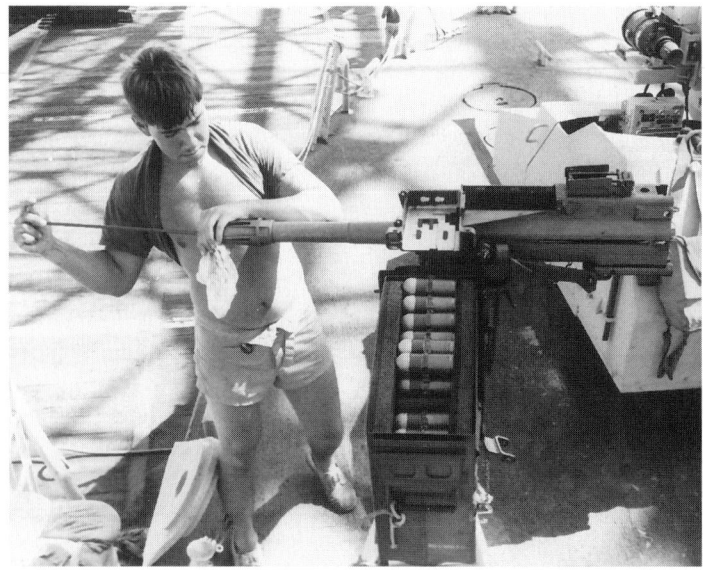

Marines in Kuwait pose with a 40-mm grenade launcher Mk 19. The 40-mm "machine gun" is fitted on Navy ships, as well as on small craft, AAV7 assault amphibious vehicles, ground vehicles, and helicopters. The belt-fed cartridges are evident here. (U.S. Marine Corps/Erik S. Hansen)

A sailor cleans the barrel of a 40-mm grenade launcher Mk 19 aboard a PB Mk III patrol boat. The craft was in the Persian Gulf at the time, resting high and dry aboard a support barge. (U.S. Navy)

30-MM GUN MK 44

This is a 30-mm version of the 25-mm Bushmaster, referred to as the Bushmaster II (see below). It is proposed by Boeing as a successor to the 25-mm weapon in U.S. Navy ships.

Unlike the Mk 38 gun, this weapon would have a stabilized mount to permit firing in rough seas. It also would have greater range. It has 70 percent commonality with the M242 gun and 90 percent commonality in gunner and maintenance training.

The Bushmaster II is being fitted in the U.S. Marines Corps's Advanced Amphibian Assault Vehicle (AAAV) and is being produced for the Norwegian and Swiss armies. The gun was proposed for ships of the SAN ANTONIO (LPD 17) class; however, the Mk 38 25-mm gun is being fitted in those ships.

A 35-mm version—referred to as the Bushmaster III—is being developed.

25-MM/87-CAL GUN MK 38

This is a rapid-fire cannon known as the Bushmaster or Chain Gun®. It provides close-in defense in a number of Navy ships and is the main armament of the CYCLONE (PC 1) class and smaller Coast Guard cutters. In the larger Navy surface combatants (up to cruisers) and in amphibious ships, the guns are installed to protect against attacks by small craft.

The Mk 38 was acquired by the Navy to replace the older 20-mm anti-aircraft guns. The older guns were developed from the 20-mm Oerlikon-developed guns first acquired by the U.S. Navy in late 1941.

The term "chain" is derived from the unusual mechanism of the externally powered endless roller chain riding in a "racetrack" around one driven and three idling sprockets. A chain drive slider mounted on the master link travels back and forth in a transverse slot on the underside of the bolt carrier. This reciprocal action opens and closes the breech on the single barrel at a rapid rate. This design is simpler and more reliable than other external-power gun mechanisms.

The gun has an M242 single barrel fitted on the M88 mounting. It can be selected to different rates of fire. The Mk 88 mount is not stabilized, and the gun is manually aimed. The weapon also is fitted in the Army's Bradley Armored Fighting Vehicle (AFV) and the Marine Corps Light Armored Vehicle (LAV).

Status: Operational. In production. IOC was in 1983; IOC in the Navy was in 1986. The first Bushmaster guns were delivered to the U.S. Army in 1972; more than 10,500 guns have been produced for all users.

Mount:	single
Gun barrel:	M242
Muzzle velocity:	3,610 ft/sec (1,100 m/sec)
Weight:	1,250 lb (567 kg)
Rate of fire:	variable; single shot or 175 rounds/minute
Maximum range:	2,500 yds (2,287 m) effective range
Projectile weight:	1.1 lb (0.5 kg)
Fire control:	optical
Crew:	2
Ships:	various

A Bushmaster 25-mm cannon Mk 38 is manned aboard the frigate INGRAHAM *(FFG 61) during an exercise in the Philippine Sea. A variety of large Navy ships are fitted with the weapon for defense against small craft. It is the main battery of the coastal patrol ships of the* CYCLONE *(PC 1) class. (U.S. Navy/Jeremie Kerns)*

An ordnanceman checks out a 25-mm cannon Mk 38 on the amphibious assault ship KEARSARGE *(LHD 3). The Mk 38 provides greater range and more killing power than the machine guns also fitted in large ships for defense against hostile small craft. (U.S. Navy/Kenny Swartout)*

20-MM GUN MK 67 and MK 68

These older, single-barrel weapons have been replaced aboard U.S. Navy and Coast Guard ships and craft by the 25-mm Mk 38 Bushmaster and machine guns. See 17th Edition/pages 487–88 for characteristics.

20-MM/76-CAL CLOSE-IN WEAPON SYSTEM MK 16

The Phalanx CIWS is intended to defeat attacking anti-ship missiles. Its installation followed by several years the appearance of similar rapid-fire gun systems, of larger caliber, in Soviet surface warships.

The Phalanx Block 0 underwent initial at-sea tests in the destroyer KING (DDG 41, then–DLG 10) from August 1973 to March 1974, with operational suitability tests in the destroyer BIGELOW (DD 942) from November 1976 to 1978. Production was initiated in December 1977, with first installations in the carrier CORAL SEA (CVA 43) in 1980.

The Block 1 provided high-angle capability against incoming missiles, with a new radar search antenna and increased gun elevation. It was first mounted in battleship WISCONSIN in 1988.

The Block 1B upgrade provides an improved capability against small, fast-moving surface craft with improved computational capability and electro-optical/Forward-Looking Infrared (FLIR) sensors. The OLIVER HAZARD PERRY-class frigates are the first U.S. ships to be fitted with the Block 1B upgrade; the UNDERWOOD (FFG 36) carried out trials in 1999.

It was first operationally installed in the frigate TAYLOR (FFG 50) in September 2000.

The Phalanx CIWS is a totally integrated weapon system that includes the VPS-2 search and track radar, gun, magazine, weapon control unit, and associated electronics, all fitted in a single unit 15 feet (4.6 m) high and weighing about 6 tons. Thus, it is suitable for small combat craft (and is fitted in Saudi Arabian and Israeli missile craft), as well as for larger warships; also, it can be rapidly installed—in 24 hours in an emergency situation. More than 400 mounts have been delivered to the U.S. Navy, from single guns in frigates to four mounts in IOWA-class battleships and some aircraft carriers. Several hundred additional Phalanx CIWS mounts are in ships of some 20 other navies.

The CIWS is designated both Mk 15 and Mk 16 by the U.S. Navy, with the 20-mm gun subsystem designated Mk 26. The gun is a six-barrel Gatling gun, adopted from the Air Force M61A1 Vulcan gun series used in several aircraft and ground mounted for airfield defense.

The gun is hydraulically powered, with a theoretical firing rate of 3,000 rounds per minute, a very low dispersion rate, and initially a 989-round magazine. The Block 1 guns have a 1,550-round magazine, and the earlier weapons are being upgraded. The diameter of the penetrator is only 12.75 mm, and it is fired in a nylon sabot with an aluminum pusher that imparts spin to the projectile. The sabot and pusher break away after the round leaves the muzzle with a velocity of 1,000 feet (305 m) per second. The projectile

The forward Phalanx CIWS mount on the replenishment ship RAINIER (now T-AOE 7) in 2003, prior to the ship's transfer to the Military Sealift Command. The Phalanx is found on all active U.S. aircraft carriers, cruisers, destroyers, frigates, and amphibious ships, as well as on the Navy-manned AOEs. (U.S. Navy/Brian Kirkwood)

Crewmen load ammunition in a Phalanx CIWS aboard the carrier GEORGE WASHINGTON (CVN 73). The weapon fires in few-second bursts. The built-in radar provides a shoot–look–shoot capability against incoming cruise missiles. (U.S. Navy/Konstandinos Goumenidis)

originally was a depleted-uranium penetrator; it was changed to tungsten in 1988.

The mount's built-in Ku-band radar combines several functions and follows the bullets in flight to make corrections for the next burst being fired. Early Navy analyses indicated that about 200 rounds would be fired per gun in each engagement against a cruise missile.

All engagement functions are performed automatically with a high-speed digital computer. When active, the CIWS will engage any incoming, high-speed target unless the operator holds fire. Reaction time is less than two seconds from the threat being detected and identified.

Designation: The Phalanx CIWS is designated Mk 15 and consists of one to four CIWS Weapon Groups Mk 16. The latter is the designation of the above-deck portion of the system, consisting of the actual gun, magazine, radar, and weapons control unit. The below-deck components of the Mk 15 are control panels.

Status: Operational.

In 1981, the Japanese destroyer KURAMA became the first foreign ship to mount the Phalanx; it also is fitted in ships of Australia, Canada, Great Britain, Greece, Israel, Portugal, Saudi Arabia, and Taiwan.

Mount:	single
Gun barrel:	Mk 26
Muzzle velocity:	3,720 ft/sec (1,135 m/sec) with Mk 149 ammunition, except Block 1B 3,650 ft/sec (1,110 m/sec)
Weight:	approx. 12,000 lb (5,443 kg)
Rate of fire:	Block 0: 3,000 rounds/minute
	Block 1: 4,500 rounds/minute
Maximum range:	1,625 yds (1,486 m)
Projectile weight:	0.22 lb (0.11 kg)
Fire control:	self-contained Ku-band search and track radars; digital Moving Target Indicator (MTI) electro-optical/FLIR sensors added in Block 1B
Crew:	(mount unmanned)
Ships:	various

.50-CAL (12.7-MM) MACHINE GUN M2HB AND MK 95

This machine gun and the 7.62-mm M60 (see below) are mounted in large surface combatants and amphibious ships for close-in protection against small craft and swimmers. They are the principal armament on various Navy and Coast Guard small craft.

The M2 is a relatively heavy, recoil-operated, air-cooled weapon. Its effective range is approximately 2,200 yards (2,000 m). Ball, tracer, incendiary, and armor-piercing ammunition are available.

The shipboard weapons are pintel mounted. Ashore, it normally is fired from a tripod mount weighing 44 pounds (20 kg) or is fitted to vehicles. It has an anti-aircraft capability. The aircraft pod version is the GAU-16. A updated version is designated Mk 56.

Historical: In service since the 1920s, it also is known as the Browning machine gun. In the 1930s and 1940s, the Navy also used a water-cooled version of the M2.

Status: Operational. The twin-mount gun system is designated Mk 95.

Muzzle velocity:	2,910 ft/sec (885 m/sec)
Weight:	84 lb (38 kg)
Rate of fire:	550 rounds/minute
Maximum range:	7,400 yards (6,770 m)
Projectile weight:	0.255 lb (0.116 kg)
Fire control:	open sight
Crew:	1 or 2
Ships:	various

7.62-MM MINIGUN GAU-17/A AND MK 44

The 7.62-mm minigun is a Gatling-type weapon that has long been used on a variety of U.S. Army, Navy, and Air Force helicopters. Late in 2000, the Navy Surface Warfare Center at Crane, Indiana, was tasked to provide a shipboard version of the GAU-17/A to several ships scheduled for near-term deployment. In less than 45 days, the Crane facility procured, assembled, and delivered to ships of the NIMITZ (CVN 68) and HARRY S. TRUMAN (CVN 75) battle groups.

A crewman stands watch with a .50-cal machine gun M2 aboard the frigate NICHOLAS (FFG 47) during a training evolution in the Mediterranean. The M2 series dates to World War II and was the most widely used machine gun in the West. (U.S. Navy/Corey Barker)

A twin .50-cal machine gun Mk 95 fitted on the frigate CROMMELIN (FFG 37) is manned as the ship departs Colon, Panama, to participate in a multi-navy exercise simulating a terrorist threat to the Panama Canal. In World War II and the Korean War, the U.S. Army used quad .50-cal gun mounts. (U.S. Navy/Ligia Cohen)

The GAU-17/A was designed to provide a lightweight, high-rate-of-fire armament for helicopters and light fixed-wing aircraft. The gun is a simplified and redesigned version of the widely used M61 Vulcan cannon (basis for the Phalanx CIWS); it also was modified to fire percussion primed 7.62-mm ammunition.

The gun is used on UH-1, H-3, and H-60 series helicopters. It is an electrically driven, six-barrel weapon with a maximum firing rate of 6,000 rounds per minute. In most helicopter applications, the rate of fire is selectable at either 2,000 or 4,000 rounds per minute. The helicopter storage system has a capacity of 4,000 rounds of linked ammunition.

The GAU-17/A also has been fitted in patrol ships of the CYCLONE (PC 1) class and the high-speed vessel JOINT VENTURE (HSV X1).

Designation: Although designated Mk 44, the shipboard weapon generally is referred to in the fleet as the GAU-17/A. The Air Force uses the designation GAU-2B/A and the Army M134.

Status: Operational. The system entered Navy service in 2001.

Muzzle velocity:	
Weight:	35 lb (15.88 kg)
Rate of fire:	2,000–4,000 rounds/minute
Maximum range:	1,640 yds (1,500 m) effective
Projectile weight:	
Fire control:	optical
Crew:	1
Ships:	various

7.62-MM MACHINE GUN M240

This machine gun—the successor to the M60—is mounted in large surface combatants and amphibious ships for close-in protection and is the principal armament in various Navy small craft and helicopters.

It is a gas-operated, air-cooled weapon and provides higher reliability and requires less maintenance than the M60 series.

The shipboard weapons are pintel mounted. The M242 is mounted in helicopters and on combat vehicles, as well as being used as a ground weapon (with tripod mount). The ground version of the M240 provides a common medium machine gun throughout the U.S. Marine Corps.

Status: Operational. Entered U.S. Army service in 1997.

Muzzle velocity:	2,800 ft/sec (855 m/sec)
Weight:	27.6 lb (12.5 kg)
Rate of fire:	200–600 rounds/minute
	100 rounds/minute sustained
Maximum range:	4,075 yards (3,725 m) maximum
	1,970 yards (1,800 m) against area targets
	875 yards (800 m) against point targets
Projectile weight:	
Fire control:	optical
Crew:	1 or 2
Ships:	various

7.62-MM MACHINE GUN M60

This machine gun is mounted in large surface combatants and amphibious ships for close-in protection and is the principal armament in various Navy and Coast Guard small craft and helicopters.

This is a lightweight, gas-operated, air-cooled weapon. It fires the standard NATO 7.62-mm round. Various types of ammunition are available including M61 armor-piercing, M62 tracer, and M80 ball. The realistic sustained rate of fire is 100 rounds per minute.

The shipboard weapons are pintel mounted.

The M60 has been the U.S. military services' general purpose machine gun since 1950. It is being replaced by the M240 machine gun. The M60D is fitted in several helicopter types.

Status: Operational.

Muzzle velocity:	2,800 ft/sec (850 m/sec)
Weight:	18.75 lb (8.5 kg)
Rate of fire:	550 rounds/minute
Maximum range:	4,070 yds (3,725 m)
Projectile weight:	
Fire control:	open sight
Crew:	1
Ships:	various

A 7.62-mm Gatling gun GAU-17/A (Mk 44) aboard the cruiser PHILIPPINE SEA *(CG 58) is fired during an exercise in the Persian Gulf by a Marine from the 1st Fleet Anti-terrorism Security Team (FAST). The gun is fitted with a flash suppressor and night-vision sight. (U.S. Navy/Jeffrey Lehrberg)*

A Marine sights a 7.62-mm machine gun M240G on the flight deck of the amphibious ship FORT MCHENRY *(LSD 43) in Philippine waters. U.S. military assistance to the Philippine effort against terrorism has included several exercises involving U.S. naval forces. (U.S. Marine Corps/Daniel Yarnall)*

Crewmen practice firing a 7.62-mm machine gun M60 on a bridge wing of the cruiser VINCENNES (CG 49) while under way in the Pacific Ocean. Since the terrorist attack on the destroyer COLE (DDG 67) the Navy has increased shipboard security with additional weapons and enhanced training. (U.S. Navy/Brandon A. Teeples)

An F/A-18 Hornet releases Mk 63 Quickstrike mines during an evaluation mission. The last major U.S. naval mining operation was flown in 1972 against Haiphong and other North Vietnamese ports; it was executed by carrier-based aircraft. Naval mines were used against land targets and for mining river approaches during the Persian Gulf War of 1991. (Rabdy Hepp)

NAVAL MINES

The U.S. Navy has a significant inventory of mines; however, all of these weapons are rapidly reaching obsolescence and have limited effectiveness against modern, quiet submarines. The Quickstrike mines do have some effectiveness against surface ships, a secondary target. The CAPTOR (Encapsulated Torpedo), the U.S. Navy's only deep-water mine, i.e., suitable for use to depths of some 3,000 feet (915 m), has been discarded.

The Navy's existing mines are based largely on technology of the 1950s and 1960s. The Quickstrike and Destructor mines were revolutionary at the time of their development in that they permitted the rapid adaptation of standard aircraft bombs for use as mines. In addition, standard bomb-handling facilities on aircraft carriers can ready the mines, and standard carrier-based and maritime patrol aircraft can carry them.

The Quickstrike mines—with the exception of the Mk 65—are Mk 80-series aircraft bombs with kit conversions that enable them to be used as shallow-water bottom mines. They can be activated by one or more influence firing mechanisms and are fitted with Target Detection Devices (TDD) prior to being laid. These weapons are effective against surface ships, as well as against submarines. Further, the Mk 57 TDD enables them to be dropped on land targets.

The Mk 65 was the only weapon of the Quickstrike series designed specifically for use as a mine.

The Destructor (DST) mine series was developed during the Vietnam War in response to the need for large numbers of mines. These mines also are converted from the standard Mk 80-series aircraft bombs, with the insertion of the Mk 42 firing mechanism and Mk 32 safety/arming device. The Destructors have been succeeded by the Quickstrike weapons.

See 16th edition/pages 436–37 for characteristics of Destructor mines (Mk 36, 40, and 41).

No mines currently are being procured pending development of the so-called 2010 Mine. The planned Improved Submarine-Launched Mobile Mine was not developed. The last mine procurement by the U.S. Navy was the CAPTOR in FY 1986.

Aircraft. The principal U.S. means of minelaying is by aircraft. The Navy's carrier-based S-3B Viking sea control aircraft and the land-based P-3 Orion maritime patrol/Anti-Submarine Warfare

The Destructor (above) and Quickstrike mines were developed by inserting a fusing device into "iron bombs," converting them into relatively simple but, in some situations, effective bottom mines in shallow water. (U.S. Navy)

(ASW) aircraft are configured for minelaying, although the former is being removed from service. The F/A-18 Hornet also can carry mines, but the availability of that aircraft for the offensive mine mission is questionable and its mine payload is limited.

The U.S. Air Force operates 183 strategic bombers that can carry mines: 21 B-2A Spirit (stealth), 78 B-1B Lancer, and 84 B-52H Stratofortress aircraft. The B-52H can carry all air-dropped naval mines currently in inventory. Again, the availability of those aircraft for minelaying missions is questionable.

The F/A-18 Hornet carries mines externally; the P-3C Orion and S-3B Viking carry them in their weapons bays and on wing pylons. The B-1B, B-2A, and B-52H carry mines internally, and the last aircraft also has wing pylons for bombs/mines.

The Department of Defense has evaluated the feasibility of employing C-130, C-141, and C-5 cargo aircraft in the minelaying role under a program called CAML (Cargo Aircraft Minelaying). A C-130 Hercules with the CAML rig fitted could carry 16 2,000-pound (907-kg) mines.

Table 30-1. AIRCRAFT MINE CAPACITIES

	F-14	F/A-18	S-3B	P-3C	B-1B	B-2	B-52H
Quickstrike Mk 65	—	4	2	6	8	—	18
Quickstrike Mk 63	—	5	4	11	—	—	18
Quickstrike Mk 62	4	10	10	18	84	80	51
Mine Mk 56	—	4	2	6	—	—	20

Submarines. U.S. submarines of the improved LOS ANGELES (SSN 751 and later) and SEAWOLF (SSN 21) classes are configured to launch CAPTOR mines.[9] However, mines can be carried by submarines only at the expense of torpedoes or tube-launched Tomahawk missiles. Submarines at sea when a mining decision is made would have to return to port, unload some or all of their other weapons, and load mines before they could undertake the mining mission. Depending on how many mines were carried, they could be required to return to port and rearm before undertaking anti-submarine or anti-shipping operations. Alternatively, during a period of crisis, some submarines could be preloaded with mines, again at the expense of other weapons.

Surface ships. No U.S. surface ships are employed to lay mines except in exercises for minesweepers or swimmers. Only the CAPTOR mine can be laid from surface ships.

In the following listings, shallow mines are those intended for use in water depths to a maximum of approximately 600 feet (182 m) and medium-depth mines down to about 1,000 feet (305 m). Deepwater mines are considered to be useful down to about 3,000 feet.

Operational: The Destructor mine series was used in large numbers during the Vietnam War, being dropped in coastal waters, river deltas, and rivers, as well as along roads and trails.

During the Persian Gulf War in 1991, naval aircraft employed bombs modified with Destructor kits in attacking Iraqi airfields. An aerial mining operation also was undertaken in an attempt to isolate Iraqi naval craft in the northern Persian Gulf from the port facilities and naval bases at Al-Basrah, Az-Zubayr, and Umm Qasr, and to prevent Iraqi naval craft from leaving those bases. On 18 January 1991, that operation was flown against the mouth of the Khawr Az-Zubayr River.

The mission consisted of 18 aircraft from the carrier RANGER (CV 61), including four A-6E Intruders carrying a total of 48 Destructor Mk 36 mines. Forty-two of the mines were dropped successfully at four separate locations in the river. (Six mines on one aircraft failed to release; the plane was diverted to an airfield in Bahrain, where the mines were offloaded before the A-6E returned to the RANGER. One A-6E was lost to enemy fire during the mission.)

2010 MINE

The so-called 2010 Mine is being developed as a replacement for the Mk 65 mine. Planned to become operational in FY 2010, the 2010 Mine will be capable of use against littoral threats, especially slow, quiet, non-nuclear submarines, high-speed patrol craft, and air cushion vehicles. This variety of targets presents a considerable technological challenge.

The weapon will be designed primarily for aircraft delivery, but it will be capable of being laid by surface ships and submarines.

Engineering development is scheduled to begin in FY 2005.

IMPROVED SUBMARINE-LAUNCHED MOBILE MINE (ISLMM)

Mobile mines permit the covert mining by submarines in waters inaccessible to other means of mine delivery. The Improved Submarine-Launched Mobile Mine (ISLMM) was intended to replace the SLMM Mk 67, which is outdated and will be phased out of service over the next few years. The ISLMM was based on early model Mk 48 torpedoes (see Torpedoes for characteristics).

The ISLMM was to be developed as a joint U.S.–Australian program. (The Royal Australian Navy employs the Mk 48 torpedo from its COLLINS-class diesel-electric submarines.) Due to funding limitations, the Australian Navy chose not to go forward with the program. The U.S. Navy did not have sufficient funds to develop the ISLMM and so redirected its half of the program to support an SLMM service life extension program. The program decision was made in 2002.

SUBMARINE-LAUNCHED MOBILE MINE (SLMM) MK 67

Based on the Mk 37 torpedo, the SLMM is a shallow-water bottom mine for use against surface ships and submarines. It is the U.S.

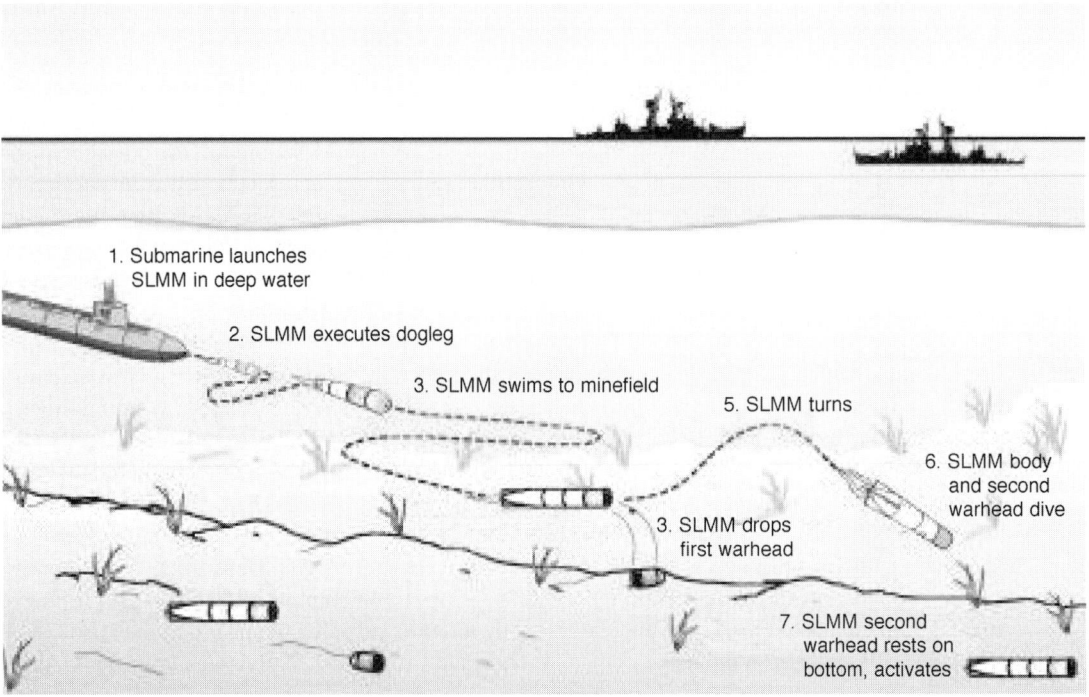

The Submarine-Launched Mobile Mine (SLMM) takes advantage of the range and payload of the Mk 48 heavy torpedo. The SLMM provides a long-range, two-warhead mining capability, as shown in this sketch of the "flight path" of the SLMM. (U.S. Navy)

1. Submarine launches SLMM in deep water
2. SLMM executes dogleg
3. SLMM swims to minefield
3. SLMM drops first warhead
5. SLMM turns
6. SLMM body and second warhead dive
7. SLMM second warhead rests on bottom, activates

Navy's only self-propelled mine; its electric motor provides a range of up to 17,500 yards (16,000 m). The SLMM is obsolescent but has been extended in service for several more years, using U.S. Navy funds originally intended to develop the ISLMM.

Status: Operational.

Type:	self-propelled, shallow/bottom
Targets:	submarines, surface ships
Weight:	1,765 lb (800 kg)
Length:	13⅖ ft (4.1 m)
Diameter:	19 in (485 mm)
Warhead:	515 lb (233.6 kg) PBXN-103 high explosive
Depth:	max. 328 ft (100 m)
Sensor:	Mod 0: TDD Mk 57 magnetic/seismic
	Mod 1: TDD Mk 58 magnetic/seismic/pressure
	Mod 2: Mk 42 magnetic/seismic
Delivery platforms:	submarines

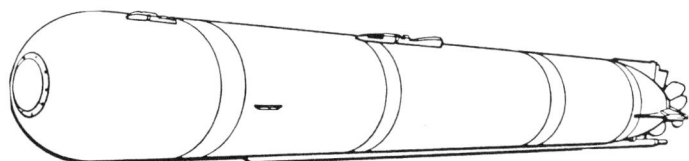

SLMM Mk 67

QUICKSTRIKE MK 65

The only weapon in the Quickstrike series designed specifically as a mine, the Mk 65 is the U.S. Navy's largest mine. With a thin-wall mine casing in lieu of the thick-wall casing of the Mk 80-series bombs, the Mk 65 is compatible with several naval aircraft, as well as with the Air Force B-1B.

Arming takes place at a preset time after the mine enters the water.

Status: Operational. IOC in 1983.

Type:	shallow/bottom
Targets:	submarines, surface ships
Weight:	2,390 lb (1,086 kg)
Length:	9⅙ ft (2.8 m)
Diameter:	20.9 in (531 mm)
Warhead:	HBX high explosive
Depth:	maximum 300 ft (91.5 m)
Sensor:	Mod 0: TDD Mk 57 magnetic/seismic
	Mod 1: TDD Mk 58 magnetic/seismic/pressure
	Mod 3: TDD Mk 71 magnetic/seismic/pressure
Delivery platforms:	aircraft

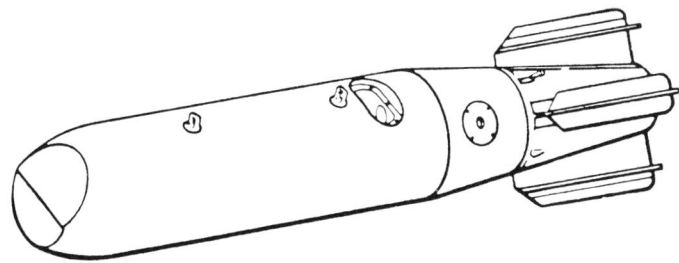

Quickstrike Mk 65

QUICKSTRIKE MK 63

This is a modified Mk 83 1,000-pound, low-drag bomb fitted with various target detection devices. Because a kit is used to convert the Mk 83 and Mk 82 bombs to mines, the competition for magazine space aboard aircraft carriers is reduced.

Arming occurs at a preset time after the mine enters the water.

Status: Operational.

Type:	shallow/bottom
Targets:	submarines, surface ships
Weight:	985 lb (447 kg) Conical Fixed (CF) tail assembly
	1,105 lb (501 kg) extending Low Drag (LD) tail assembly
Length:	9⅖ ft (2.9 m)
Diameter:	14 in (355.5 mm)
Warhead:	450 lb (204 kg) H-6 high explosive
Depth:	maximum 300 ft (91.5 m)
Sensor:	TDD Mk 57 magnetic/seismic
	TDD Mk 71 magnetic/seismic/pressure
Delivery platforms:	aircraft

Carrier-based aircraft are the Navy's primary minelaying platforms. Here, on the flight deck of the carrier JOHN C. STENNIS *(CVN 74), ordnancemen prepare a Quickstrike mine Mk 63 for loading on an F/A-18C Hornet. This mine has extending low-drag fins. (U.S. Navy/ Tyler Orsburn)*

A mineman of Mobile Mine Assembly Unit (MOMAU) 8 on Guam checks the loading of a Quickstrike mine Mk 65 into a transport dolly. The Mk 65, the U.S. Navy's largest mine, resembles a large bomb with folding stabilizing fins. (U.S. Navy/Nathanael T. Miller)

QUICKSTRIKE MK 62

This is a modified Mk 82 500-pound bomb fitted with various target detection devices. See Mk 63 for additional data.

Status: Operational.

Type:	shallow/bottom
Targets:	submarines, surface ships
Weight:	531 lb (241 kg) FC
	570 lb (258.5 kg) LD
Length:	7½ ft (2.3 m)
Diameter:	10.8 in (274 mm)
Warhead:	196 lb (89 kg) H-6 high explosive
Depth:	maximum 300 ft (91.5 m)
Sensor:	Mod 0: TDD Mk 57 magnetic/seismic
	Mod 3: TDD Mk 71 magnetic/seismic/pressure
Delivery platforms:	aircraft

A Quickstrike Mk 62 mine falls from a P-3C Orion of squadron VP-46 during a 2004 minelaying exercise in the Gulf of Thailand. The mine's retardation fins are opening. The U.S. Navy's offensive mine capability is limited. (U.S. Navy/Joseph Krypel)

CAPTOR MK 60

The CAPTOR (Encapsulated Torpedo) was the U.S. Navy's only deep-water mine. It was an anti-submarine mine that could be laid by aircraft, surface ship, or submarine. (Aircraft-laid mines are lowered to the water by parachute.)

On entering the water, the CAPTOR released an anchor that moored it to the ocean floor. The mine armed itself at a preset time. The Mk 60 had a passive acoustic transducer that listened for potential targets. When one was detected, after determining that the noise was "man-made," the sensor would emit "pings" that dis-

criminated against surface ships. Once satisfied the target was a submarine, the torpedo casing was flooded and the torpedo activated to swim out of the canister and home on the submarine.

The torpedo was a Mk 46 Mod 4. Mine life in the water could be several months; detection range was credited as 1,093 yards (333 m). The anchoring system maintained the torpedo–sensor canister at a maximum depth of approximately 1,000 feet (305 m).

The CAPTOR IOC was in September 1979. It suffered from significant development and operational problems, which led to several production delays. Also, the mine had the relatively small warhead of the Mk 46 torpedo.

Although in many respects the U.S. Navy's most capable ASW mine, the CAPTOR has been phased out of service, the last having been discarded in 2001. The Navy cited "affordability" issues, especially the rising costs to maintain the CAPTOR mines in inventory.

MINE MK 56

This is an air-dropped mine capable of being used against surface ships and submarines. It was designed specifically for use against high-speed, deep-operating submarines of the 1960s. It is the oldest mine in U.S. Navy use and the only U.S. mine now in service suitable for medium-depth water.

When laid, the mine sinks to the bottom, where the anchor separates from the case. Should the mine become embedded in the bottom sediment before the case/anchor separation and mooring take place, a slow-burning propellant in the anchor is ignited to free the mine. As the case rises, a hydrostat senses the preset mooring depth and arrests the cable payout.

At the end of its service life, the mine will either self-destruct or scuttle, depending on which feature is selected.

The Mk 56 is being phased out of service.

Status: Operational. IOC in 1966.

Type:	medium/moored
Targets:	submarines, surface ships
Weight:	2,135 lb (968 kg)
Length:	9½ ft (2.9 m)
Diameter:	23.4 in (594 mm)
Warhead:	357 lb (162 kg) HBX-3 high explosive
Depth:	maximum 1,200 ft (366 m)
Sensor:	magnetic
Delivery platforms:	aircraft

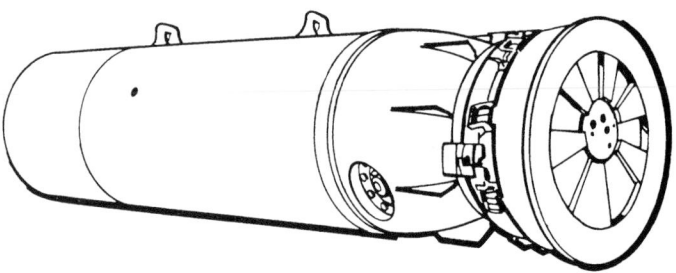

Mine Mk 56

Minemen of MOMAU 8 attach the warhead to a mine Mk 56 on Guam. This weapon is being phased out of service. Only the promised 2010 Mine program will give the U.S. Navy an offensive mining capability after about 2010. (U.S. Navy/Nathanael T. Miller)

Four surface combatants launch missiles from their Vertical Launching Systems (VLS), demonstrating the system's efficacy. The VLS provides great speed and flexibility. From left are the cruiser VICKSBURG (CG 69), and the destroyers ROOSEVELT (DDG 80), CARNEY (DDG 64), and THE SULLIVANS (DDG 68). (U.S. Navy)

MISSILE LAUNCHING SYSTEMS

Several types of missile launchers are fitted in U.S. warships. There are four general types: (1) traditional above-deck launchers, wherein missiles are pushed upward from below-deck magazines onto the launcher, which then is trained and elevated; (2) various "box"-like launchers, such as the NATO Sea Sparrow launcher; (3) the below-deck Vertical Launching System (VLS); and (4) Harpoon missile canisters, which are fitted in a variety of U.S. Navy and foreign warships. Only VLS and Harpoon canisters currently are installed in new U.S. surface combatants, i.e., the ARLEIGH BURKE-class destroyers and the planned DD(X) destroyer.

The new Mk 49 RAM box-type launcher is being backfitted in a few surface combatants and amphibious ships.

The VLS provides a high degree of missile launch flexibility, more rapid launching, and reduced maintenance requirements and requires fewer crewmen in comparison with earlier above-deck surface-to-air missile launch systems. The Mk 41 VLS can accommodate Standard and Tomahawk missiles and the Vertical-Launch Anti-Submarine Rocket (VLA). It can be configured for a four-pack container with the Evolved Sea Sparrow Missile (ESSM).

The Mk 57 Advanced Vertical Launch System (AVLS) is under development as a candidate for the DD(X).

The VLS and AVLS have total flexibility in missile selection, rapid reselection if a weapon fails to launch (without having to unload or jettison the missile), some protection for the missile from weather and shrapnel in comparison with an above-deck launcher, and more efficient use of shipboard space.

The basic Mk 41 VLS consists of a series of eight-cell launch modules, plus launch control units. The missile loading/strikedown module has been removed from U.S. ships; the strikedown module had taken the space of three missile cells. The Mk 41 launchers, developed specifically to replace the Mk 26 missile launcher and 88-round missile magazine in Aegis cruisers, have a modular, centerline "footprint." Twenty-two of the 27 ships of the TICONDEROGA class have the Mk 41 VLS, with 61-cell launchers forward and aft, in place of Mk 26 systems. Subsequently, 61-cell launchers also were installed forward in 24 destroyers of the SPRUANCE class, replacing the Anti-Submarine Rocket (ASROC) box launcher and magazine in those ships.

This modularity gives the Navy the potential to replace the Mk 41 VLS battery by a more-advanced weapons "module" when one becomes available. In the electric-drive DD(X) and CG(X), for example, a Mk 41 VLS battery could be replaced by the electro-magnetic rail gun or a laser weapon system. This could not be done with the peripheral AVLS, which will consist of rows of missiles cells along the sides of the ship.

In the following entries, the system weight generally does not include missiles or hydraulic fluids, except that missiles are included for the Mk 16, Mk 25, Mk 29, and Mk 141 launchers.

The only U.S. warships that retain Armored Box Launchers (ABL) for the Tomahawk missile are the mothballed IOWA-class battleships.

SEARAM LAUNCHER

The SeaRAM is a Phalanx CIWS mount fitted with an 11-missile launcher for the Rolling Airframe Missile. The launcher employs the standard CIWS radar and the electro-optical system of the Block 1B CIWS.

The system is not being procured by the U.S. Navy at this time. Raytheon is the prime contractor.

LAUNCHER Mk 143

The armored box launcher was fitted in several non-Aegis cruisers, seven destroyers of the SPRUANCE class, and the four IOWA-class battleships.[10] Each box held four Tomahawk missiles; the entire structure elevated for firing.

---

10 The other 24 SPRUANCE-class destroyers were fitted with the Mk 41 VLS for launching Tomahawk missiles.

SeaRAM is a proposed combination of the Phalanx Close-In Weapon System and the Rolling Airframe Missile (RAM). The Soviets developed a similar system, called Combined Air Defense System (CADS) 1 by NATO; it has eight SA-N-11 missiles and two 30-mm Gatling guns. The mount is fitted with autonomous search and track radars (similar to the Phalanx and SeaRAM). (Raytheon)

A Tomahawk Land-Attack Missile (TLAM) is launched from an ABL on the stern of a cruiser. These quad launchers now are found only on the two mothballed IOWA-class battleships, eight fitted in each ship, amidships on the 01 level. (U.S. Navy)

The cruiser NORMANDY (CG 60) fires her after 5-inch Mk 45 gun on a training range; the ship's Mk 141 Harpoon canister launchers are on the fantail, facing port and starboard. Note there are only two canisters facing port, although the launch mount can hold four missiles. Similar launchers are fitted to smaller ships. (U.S. Navy/Shane McCoy)

Details of the Mk 141 Harpoon canisters in the cruiser MOBILE BAY (CG 53). These canisters contain sealed "wooden rounds" that require no preparation for firing. The canisters are used to ship, store, and launch the Harpoon missiles. (Giorgio Arra)

Two ABLs were fitted in each cruiser and SPRUANCE-class destroyer; eight ABLs were fitted in each battleship. In the SPRUANCE class, the launchers, mounted forward to the bridge, were an alternative to the 61-cell VLS.

IOC:	1980
Type:	ABL
Missiles:	4 Tomahawk
System weight:	
Ships:	*battleships* BB 61

LAUNCHER Mk 141 Mod 1

These are Harpoon missile canisters, fitted in quad mountings on numerous U.S. and foreign warships. They have been removed from Coast Guard cutters of the HAMILTON (WHEC 715) class, those having been the first missile launching systems installed in U.S. Coast Guard ships.

The Mk 141 Mod 0 was fitted in the PEGASUS-class hydrofoil missile combatants.

IOC:	1977	
Type:	canister	
Missiles:	4 Harpoon	
System weight:	13,000 lb (5,897 kg)	
Ships:	*battleships*	BB 61
	cruisers	
	destroyers	

ADVANCED VERTICAL-LAUNCH SYSTEM (AVLS) Mk 57

The AVLS is being developed by Northrop Grumman, United Defense, and Raytheon as a candidate for the next-generation large surface combatant, the DD(X). Sometimes called the peripheral VLS, the system is intended to launch Tomahawk cruise missiles, Standard SM-2 surface-to-air missiles, and the Evolved Sea Sparrow point-defense missile. The AVLS differs from the tradi-

tional VLS in having four-cell modules installed along the perimeter of the ship's deck rather than in the standard, centrally placed VLS battery. According to the AVLS development team, this arrangement would reduce the ship's vulnerability to a single missile, shell, or bomb hit, with any AVLS missile detonations blowing outward.

The 28-inch cell of the AVLS will require mechanical adapters to accommodate the 25-inch VLS canisters now used for all U.S. vertical-launch missiles.

IOC:		
Type:	VLS	
Missiles:	Standard/Tomahawk/VLA/ESSM	
System weight:		
Ships:	*destroyers*	DD(X) (proposed)

LAUNCH SYSTEM Mk 49

This is an advanced box-type launcher developed specifically for the Rolling Airframe Missile (RAM); it also is being fitted in German patrol boats. Early proposals also called for firing the RAM from a modified Mk 29 NATO Sea Sparrow launcher (i.e., configured for both weapons).

IOC:	1992		
Type:	box		
Missiles:	21 RAM		
System weight:	12,736 lb (5,777 kg)		
Ships:	*carriers*	CV/CVN	
	destroyers	DD 963	
	amphibious	LHD 1	LHA 1
		LPD 17	LSD 41
		LSD 49	

Sailors aboard the amphibious ship KEARSARGE load Rolling Airframe Missiles into one of the ship's two Mk 49 RAM launchers. The missiles are in sealed, wooden-round canisters that are loaded into the 21-round launcher, a lengthy, labor-intensive procedure. (U.S. Navy/Kenny Swartout)

VERTICAL LAUNCH SYSTEM Mk 41 (32 cell)

The various Mk 41 VLS configurations of eight-cell modules are shown in Table 30-2. To date, the U.S. Navy uses only the standard/strike configuration, in 64- or 32-missile batteries.

The loadout options for the standard/strike version are discussed below. The tactical VLS can accommodate Standard MR-2 (Block II and III), VLA, Sea Sparrow RIM-7, and ESSM Quad Pack missiles. The self-defense VLS can accommodate only the Sea Sparrow missiles.

This originally was a 29-cell launcher with a loading/strikedown module; that module has been deleted from U.S. ships.

Mk 41 launchers also are fitted in warships of Australia, Canada, Germany, Japan, the Netherlands, New Zealand, Norway, South Korea, Spain, and Turkey.

IOC:	1991
Type:	VLS
Missiles:	32 Standard/Tomahawk/VLA/ESSM
System weight:	approx. 94,000 lb (42,638 kg)
Ships:	*destroyers* DDG 51

VERTICAL LAUNCH SYSTEM Mk 41 (64 cell)

This originally was a 61-cell launcher with a loading/strikedown module; that module has been deleted from U.S. ships.

IOC:	1986	
Type:	VLS	
Missiles:	61 Standard/Tomahawk/VLA/ESSM	
System weight:	approx. 188,000 lb (85,277 kg)	
Ships:	*cruisers* CG 52	
	destroyers DDG 51	DD 963

Table 30-2. VLS MK 41 CONFIGURATIONS

	Standard/Strike	Tactical	Self-Defense
Weight	32,000 lb (14,515 kg)	29,800 lb (13,517 kg)	26,800 lb (12,156 kg)
Deck size	134 x 100 in (3.4 x 2.54 m)	134 x 100 in (3.4 x 2.54 m)	134 x 100 in (3.4 x 2.54 m)
Height	303 in (7.7 m)	266 in (6.76 m)	209 in (5.31 m)

LAUNCH SYSTEM Mk 29 Mod 0

All active U.S. aircraft carriers have two or three Mk 29 launchers; other ships have one. The Navy-manned SACRAMENTO (AOE 1) replenishment ships are the Navy's only auxiliary ships to mount missiles.

The launcher box is designated Mk 132. It was derived from the Mk 16 ASROC launchers. Missiles are reloaded "by hand."

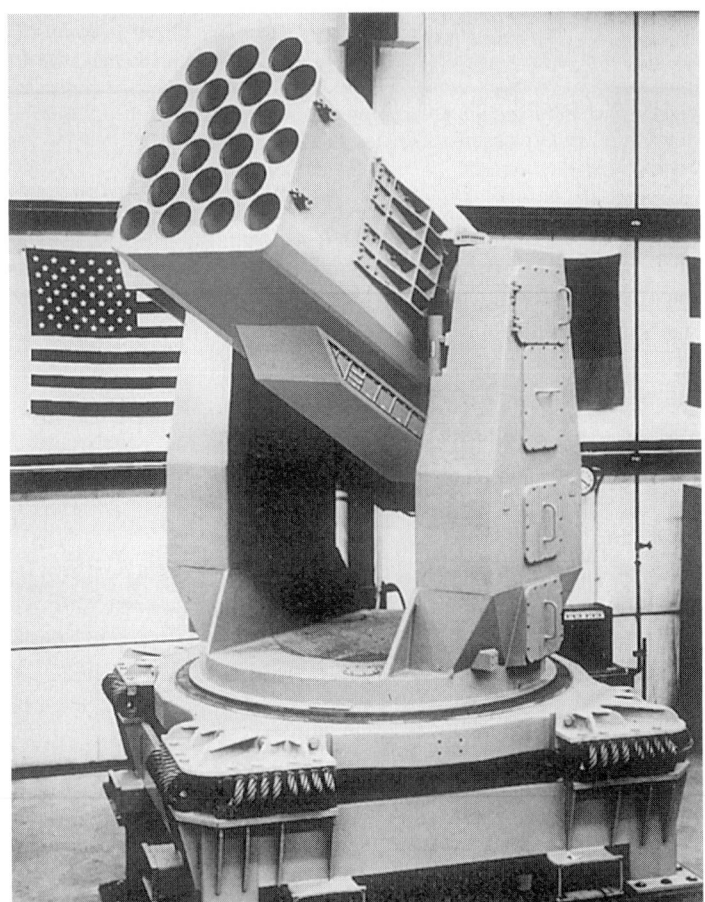

The Mk 49 RAM launcher provides more firepower than the Sea Sparrow missile launchers previously used in U.S. ships for close-in defense against anti-ship missiles. The Mk 49 also was fitted in destroyers of the SPRUANCE (DD 963) class. (General Dynamics/Pomona)

This weapon launcher is fitted in numerous foreign warships.

In U.S. ships, the Mk 29 is being replaced by the Mk 49 RAM launcher.

IOC:	1974	
Type:	box	
Missiles:	8 NATO Sea Sparrow	
System weight:	24,000–28,000 lb (10,886–12,700 kg)	
Ships:	*carriers* CV/CVN	
	amphibious LHD 1	
	auxiliary AOE 1	

An eight-cell VLS module is lowered into a destroyer of the ARLEIGH BURKE class. Each cell can launch a variety of missiles, providing more flexibility and a faster rate of fire than conventional, above-deck missile launchers. (General Dynamics/Raytheon)

Looking up at an eight-cell VLS module being slid into an ARLEIGH BURKE-class destroyer. The modules can be assembled into different size missile batteries. Initially, three cells in each battery were devoted to a reloading crane, since deleted. (General Dynamics/Raytheon)

A Mk 29 NATO Sea Sparrow launcher on the carrier KITTY HAWK (CV 63) is reloaded. The missiles are extracted from the shipping canisters and slid into the eight launch cells of the "pepper box"-type launcher. These launchers succeeded the Mk 25 Basic Point Defense Missile System (BPDMS) firing the Sea Sparrow. (U.S. Navy/Jason R. William)

LAUNCH SYSTEM Mk 26 Mod 1

A flexible conventional missile launcher, the Mk 26 was fitted in several cruiser classes and in destroyers of the KIDD (DDG 993) class. It is fitted forward and aft in the first five ships of the TICONDEROGA class, which are being discarded in 2004–2005.

IOC:	1976
Type:	twin-arm
Missiles:	44 Standard SM-2 MR/ASROC
System weight:	208,373 lb (94,518 kg)
Ships:	*cruisers* CG 47 (CG 47–51)

The after Mk 26 Standard-MR missile launcher on the cruiser VALLEY FORGE (CG 50); these are Standard SM-1 missiles, derivatives of the Tartar SAM. The only U.S. ships with these launchers are the first five ships of the TICONDEROGA (CG 47) class, which are being retired. (Jürg Kürsener)

LAUNCH SYSTEM Mk 25 Mod 0

The Basic Point Defense Missile System (BPDMS), derived from the Anti-Submarine Rocket (ASROC) launcher, has been removed from all U.S. Navy ships. It has been succeeded by the Mk 29 NATO Sea Sparrow launcher and the Mk 49 RAM launcher.

The last U.S. Navy ships to carry the Mk 25 were amphibious ships of the TARAWA class. Previously, the systems were fitted primarily in aircraft carriers and amphibious ships.

The launcher box was designated Mk 112.

See 17th Edition/pages 497–98 for launcher characteristics.

LAUNCH SYSTEM Mk 16 Mods 1–6

This is the standard ASROC box launcher introduced in the U.S. fleet in 1961. During the 1960s, 1970s, and into the 1980s, this weapon was fitted in all ASW-capable U.S. cruisers, destroyers, and frigates. Some ASROC box launchers were modified also to fire Standard-ARM and Harpoon surface-to-surface missiles.

There are no ASROC box launchers remaining in the U.S. fleet. The last ships to carry them were the CALIFORNIA (CGN 36) and SPRUANCE classes; they were deleted in the early 1990s. The box launcher still is in use in several other navies.

ASROCs also could be launched from the forward Mk 26 twin-arm launcher of cruisers and destroyers, as well as from vertical launching systems (VLA in the latter ships).

See 15th Edition/page 476 for launcher characteristics.

LAUNCH SYSTEM Mk 13 Mod 4

This was the last conventional missile launcher fitted in U.S. warships, except for the Mk 26 system. The Mk 13 was developed specifically for frigate-type ships and was mounted in all U.S. and foreign frigates of the OLIVER HAZARD PERRY class, as well as in the later guided missile destroyers of the CHARLES F. ADAMS (DDG 2) class and several DD/DDG conversions.

The launcher, with a 40-round magazine, could launch Standard/Tartar surface-to-air missiles, as well as Harpoon anti-ship missiles. Deletion of the Mk 13 launchers from the remaining PERRY-class ships in 2003–2004 left those ships with a 76-mm gun Mk 75 and Phalanx CIWS Mk 15 as their only anti-air/anti-missile/anti-ship capability.

See 17th Edition/pages 498–99 for launcher characteristics.

MISSILES

The missiles currently in service or under development for the Navy and Marine Corps for use from aircraft, surface ships, and submarines are listed below. (Ground- and vehicle-launched missiles used by the Marine Corps are not listed.)

The missiles are arranged alphabetically by name. All missiles in U.S. service or advanced development have letter–number designations, which are explained in Figure 30-1.

The term "anti-radiation" is used officially for missiles that home on enemy radar emissions; however, because of the popular confusion over the term "radiation," which normally is associated with nuclear weapons, the term "anti-radar" is used throughout this volume.

Most new air-launched missiles—in procurement and under development—are joint Navy–Air Force programs.

ALAM (ADVANCED LAND ATTACK MISSILE)

The ALAM was to be a fire support weapon to succeed the Land Attack Standard Missile (LASM). It was planned as a supersonic or possibly hypersonic missile with a "family" of warheads of various types. The IOC was planned for 2009.

With a solid-propellant rocket, the ALAM had an objective range of 300 nm (556 km) with a threshold of 200 nm (371 km). Global Positioning System (GPS) and inertial guidance were planned.

Status: Canceled.

Figure 30-1. Explanation of Symbols

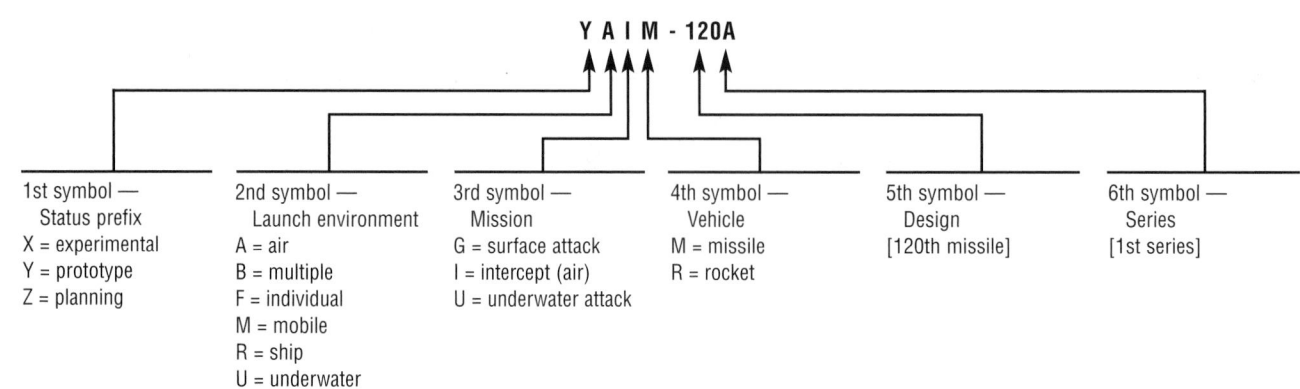

*AMRAAM (ADVANCED MEDIUM-RANGE AIR-TO-AIR MISSILE) AIM-120

The AMRAAM is a joint Navy–Air Force weapon developed to succeed the Sparrow and, subsequently, Phoenix Air-to-Air Missiles (AAMs). It thus will become the only Medium/Beyond Visual Range (M/BVR) missile used by Navy and Marine aircraft.

The F-14D can carry the AMRAAM, as can the F/A-18 Hornet and F-35 Joint Strike Fighter.

Design: The AMRAAM is smaller than the Sparrow and, instead of the Sparrow's semiactive radar guidance, uses a midcourse inertial reference system with a sophisticated monopulse radar seeker for terminal guidance. Maximum speed is approximately Mach 4. The radar-guided AMRAAM has a high resistance against enemy Electronic Countermeasures (ECM) and a "snapdown" capability to engage low-flying aircraft and possibly antiship missiles.

The AIM-120B has infrared guidance, and the AIM-120C adds improved aerodynamic performance. The latter has smaller control surfaces to increase the missile loadout of the Air Force F/A-22 Raptor aircraft.

Operational: A small number of AMRAAMs were available to U.S. Air Force F-15 fighter-attack aircraft during the 1991 Gulf War, although none was used. In December 1992, an F-16 Fighting Falcon fired the first AMRAAM used in combat, shooting down an Iraqi MiG-25 Foxbat during a confrontation over southern Iraq.

Status: Operational. In production. IOC was in 1991. AIM-120C Navy IOC was in 1996. The missile also is used by Germany, Great Britain, Israel, and the United Arab Emirates.

Total production of the missile is anticipated at 15,450 weapons for Air Force and Navy–Marine requirements with about a 75/25 percent split between the two services, plus allied requirements. European coproduction is planned.

Hughes Aircraft Company also proposed the possible use of the missile from surface ships (called Sea AMRAAM), but that concept has not been pursued. However, in 1997 the Marine Corps tested a ground-launched configuration with a five-missile launcher fixed on a "Humvee" vehicle.

Three AMRAAMs wait on a bomb cart before an F/A-18C Hornet aboard the carrier ABRAHAM LINCOLN (CVN 72). The missiles' small fins have not yet been fitted. AMRAAM replaces the definitive Sparrow III missile, which entered service in 1958 and was first used in combat in the Vietnam War. (U.S. Navy/Philip A. McDaniel)

Prime contractor:	Raytheon	
Weight:	335 lb (152 kg)	
Length:	12 ft (3.65 m)	
Span:	1 ft 8 3/4 in (526 mm)	
Diameter:	7 in (178 mm)	
Propulsion:	solid-propellant rocket	
Range:	approx. 40 nm (74 km)	
Guidance:	inertial + active terminal radar homing	
Warhead:	50 lb (22.7 kg) high explosive	
Platforms:	*aircraft*	F-14D
		F/A-18
		F-35 Joint Strike Fighter (JSF)

An F/A-18C Hornet shown carrying ten AMRAAMs mounted on wing pylons and two fuselage hard points. Two Sidewinder missiles are mounted on the aircraft's wingtips, and a drop tank is fitted under the fuselage. The AMRAAM is the successor to the radar-guided Sparrow AAM. (Hughes)

ASROC (ANTI-SUBMARINE ROCKET) RUR-5A

The ASROC was a ship-launched, ballistic ASW weapon that could be fitted with a conventional Mk 46 homing torpedo. From the early 1960s until the advent of the OLIVER HAZARD PERRY-class frigates, ASROC was fitted to all U.S. Navy cruisers, destroyers, and frigates. The ASROC was a short-range weapon; almost continuous proposals for an extended-range ASROC have been deferred. The weapon was phased out of U.S. Navy service in the early 1990s.

A Vertical-Launch ASROC (VLA) has been developed for use in warships with VLS; see separate entry below.

The standard ASROC was fired from an eight-tube box launcher (Mk 16) and from the Mk 26 surface-to-air missile launcher. It has been employed by 11 other navies with Mk 44/46 torpedoes.

As delivered to the U.S. Navy, the ASROC could carry a W44 nuclear depth bomb as an alternate payload to a conventional homing torpedo. The surviving nuclear warheads were removed from the fleet in the late 1980s. (The ASROC was tested on only one occasion with a nuclear warhead, fired from the destroyer AGERHOLM/DD 826 on 11 May 1962 in a Pacific weapons test.)

Designation: RUR-5A was a rocket, not missile, designation.

See 15th Edition/pages 482–83 for characteristics.

ATACMS (ARMY TACTICAL MISSILE SYSTEM)

The ATACMS is a long-range tactical semiballistic missile. The Navy considered the employment of ATACMS from surface ships (surface combatants with VLS and amphibious ships) and possibly submarines as a battlefield/naval fire support weapon for the Marine Corps. (The missile would have been launched from VLS.)

The Navy has instead opted for the ALAM, LASM, and Tactical Tomahawk (TACTOM) missiles. In the event, the first two weapons were not procured.

Proposed upgrades for a Navy ATACMS would have incorporated the GPS guidance package, increasing the missile's range to more than 150 nm (280 km).

The ATACMS has an M74 warhead that dispenses 950 M42 Anti- Personnel/Anti-Material (APAM) submunitions. The Army also plans to fit the missile with the BAT (Brilliant Anti-Tank) submunition.

See 16th Edition/page 44 for characteristics.

Operational: A standard Army tracked M270 two-missile ATACMS launcher was placed on the dock landing ship MOUNT VERNON (LSD 39) for missile test firings on 12 February 1995.

Status: Operational and in production for the U.S. Army. Army IOC was in 1990.

ERAM (EXTENDED-RANGE ACTIVE MISSILE)

This is a Standard SM-2 derivative using active-seeker technology to counter anticipated air and missile threats in the 2010+ period. The use of an active seeker reduces the missile's reliance on Aegis radar illuminators and provides improved performance against "stream" raids and targets employing advanced kinematics and ECM characteristics. The "fire-and-forget" missile will have a range of some 200 nm (370 km) employing over-the-horizon surveillance systems such as the E-2C Advanced Hawkeye aircraft.

The ERAM's active radar seeker is derived from that of the AIM-120 AMRAAM. The missile will have the SM-2 Block IVA propulsion system.

The ERAM replaces the now-defunct Navy Area Wide (NAW) Theater Ballistic Missile Defense (TBMD) missile program, which was canceled on 14 December 2001. That weapon, also based on the SM-2 Block IVA missile, was intended for both air defense and the NAW/TBMD program.

The ERAM/SM-6 system will be provided to the ARLEIGH BURKE destroyer and Improved TICONDEROGA cruiser classes, as well as to the new DD(X) and CG(X) warships.

In September 2004, Raytheon was awarded a contract for the system's development and demonstration, including the design, development, fabrication, assembly, integration, test, and delivery of test missiles.

FASTHAWK

Fasthawk was a proposed low-cost, high-speed (Mach 4) land-attack cruise missile intended to destroy time-critical and hardened targets. The Navy's decision to procure ALAM halted development of this weapon, although the ALAM subsequently was canceled.

Proposed by Boeing, Fasthawk was a wingless, finless missile with combination ramjet/rocket propulsion, with a solid-propellant rocket booster and an air-breathing, hydrocarbon ramjet sustainer engine. Thrust vector control provided flight control (and reduced drag compared with conventional missiles). The missile could have carried a warhead of 700 pounds (317.5 kg) at a cruise altitude of 70,000 feet (21,340 m) to a range of 700 nm (1,300 km) and would have been compatible with shipboard VLS.

GRAND SLAM

See SLAM entry.

HARM (HIGH-SPEED ANTI-RADIATION MISSILE) AGM-88

The HARM is the only anti-radar, defense-suppression missile in U.S. service. It is the only weapon carried by the EA-6B Prowler electronic jamming aircraft, which provide ECM/electronic attack capabilities for the Air Force, Navy, and Marine Corps.

Developed by the Naval Weapons Center at China Lake, California, HARM is the successor to the Shrike AGM-45A and Standard-ARM AGM-78D missiles. It provides greater range, increased velocity, greater frequency coverage, and additional flexibility in reacting to threats through an onboard computer. With respect to the last, HARM can automatically calculate threat priorities and engage the one that poses the greatest threat to friendly aircraft. It also can engage radiating targets detected at any angle from the aircraft.

The AGM-88B Block III and AGM-88C Block IV are being upgraded to the Block IIA and Block V, respectively, to provide increased capability against target radar shutdown, blanking, and "blinking." The Block V also has a capability to home on hostile jamming devices. The AGM-88D Block VI is in testing with a FY 2004–2005 IOC.

The HARM had been criticized for high costs, and in early 1986, the Navy briefly stopped accepting the missile because of manufacturing flaws.

Operational: HARM was first employed in combat in the 1986 Gulf of Sidra (Libya) operations. In the 1991 Gulf War, a total of 895 HARMs were launched by Navy and Marine aircraft—more than any other missile used by U.S. naval forces in the conflict. The Tactical Air Launched Decoy (TALD) was employed in conjunction with HARMs to entice Iraqi forces to use their radars against the decoys, marking them as HARM targets; 137 TALDs were used in this manner by naval aircraft during the conflict. In addition, TALDs were launched by S-3B Vikings working in conjunction with HARM-armed aircraft to attack Iraqi radar sites.

Subsequently, HARM missiles were used in the 1999 Kosovo campaign and to attack Iraqi radars in the no-fly zones prior to the 2003 invasion of Iraq.

Status: Operational. IOC was in 1984; AGM-88C IOC was in 1993. The last new-production HARM was delivered to the Navy

HARM missiles are moved inside the forward weapons magazine of the carrier ABRAHAM LINCOLN following an underway replenishment. Such missiles are stowed without fins, which are installed when the missiles are loaded onto the aircraft. HARM is the only anti-radar missile in U.S. service. (U.S. Navy/Michael S. Kelly)

A HARM missile mounted on a wing pylon of an EA-6B Prowler is checked on the flight deck of the carrier KITTY HAWK. The missile's fins have been attached. More than 2,000 HARM missiles were fired during Operation Desert Storm in 1991, and many more enforcing the subsequent "no-fly zones" over northern and southern Iraq prior to Operation Iraqi Freedom. (U.S. Navy/Todd Frantom)

in 1997. Some 21,000 missiles were delivered, plus more than 1,000 guidance packages for upgrading earlier missiles.

HARM also is used by several foreign air forces.

Prime contractor:	Raytheon (formerly Texas Instruments)
Weight:	796 lb (361 kg)
Length:	13 ft 7 in (4.17 m)
Span:	3 ft 8 in (1.13 m)
Diameter:	10 in (253 mm)
Propulsion:	solid-propellant rocket
Range:	approx. 80 nm (148 km)
Guidance:	radar homing
Warhead:	145 lb (65.8 kg) high explosive
Platforms:	*aircraft* F/A-18
	EA-6B
	EA-18G

HARPOON AGM/RGM/UGM-84A

The Harpoon is a versatile, widely used anti-ship missile. It is the first U.S. Navy missile designed for shipboard launch against surface targets since the Regulus I, which was deployed in the 1950s, albeit primarily for the strategic, land-attack role. The Harpoon initially was conceived for aircraft use against surfaced Soviet Echo-class (Project 675) cruise missile submarines. Subsequently, the missile was developed for air, surface, and submarine launch against surface targets. (It was taken off U.S. submarines in 1997.)

Harpoon is carried in most U.S. surface combatant classes, launched from stand-alone canisters (Mk 141). For shipboard launch, the missile has a rocket booster fitted. (Submarines could launch encapsulated Harpoons from standard 21-inch torpedo tubes; the capsule rose to the surface and the missile ignited, leaving the canister.) The F/A-18, P-3C, and S-3B aircraft also can carry the Harpoon.

(The Air Force modified B-52G bombers to carry up to 12 Harpoon AGM-84D missiles; those aircraft are out of service.)

Design: Starting in 1982, the U.S. Navy took delivery of the Block 1B Harpoon with improved radar guidance and a lower flight altitude. The subsequent 1C version, first delivered in 1984, had improved guidance and burned a higher-density fuel, resulting in an increase in range, to almost 80 nm (148.2 km).

The Block 1D improvements, backfit in earlier missiles starting in 1992, allow the missile to reattack a target by flying a cloverleaf pattern if it does not acquire the target on its first approach. The 1D variant also has a 23-inch (0.6-m) fuel tank extension to almost double the missile's range. The Block II has improved guidance.

The maximum Harpoon speed is Mach 0.85. For surface ship and submarine launch, the booster burn is approximately three seconds, after which the rocket booster falls off and the sustaining engine starts. Flight reliability is in excess of 93 percent.

The Harpoon forms the basis for the Standoff Land Attack Missile (SLAM).

Operational: The first combat use of the Harpoon was by U.S. naval forces against Libyan missile craft in the Gulf of Sidra in 1986.

The only known use of the Harpoon during the 1991 campaign in the Persian Gulf occurred when the Saudi Arabian missile craft FAISAL launched a single missile to sink an Iraqi minelayer. The engagement took place early on 23 January, with the detection and missile launch made by radar in the predawn darkness; the target ship was identified by Iraqi survivors.

Status: Operational. IOC was in 1977 for surface ships and submarines; 1979 in land-based aircraft (P-3C); and 1981 in carrier-based aircraft (A-6E).

Twenty other nations employ the Harpoon from surface ships and submarines (the submarine-launched Harpoon is called Sub-Harpoon in foreign navies). The Coast Guard briefly had Harpoon launchers on its larger cutters, and the U.S. Air Force has carried

Harpoon missiles on B-52G and F-111C bombers in the anti-shipping role.

More than 7,000 Harpoon and SLAM missiles have been produced for the United States and 24 other countries.

Data below are for the Harpoon Block 1D, unless otherwise indicated.

Prime contractor:	McDonnell Douglas
Weight:	1,390 lb (631.8 kg) for air launch
	1,757 lb (798.6 kg) for surface launch
Length:	14 ft 7 in (4.4 m) for air launch
	17 ft 2 in (5.2 m) for surface launch
Span:	3 ft (0.9 m)
Diameter:	13½ in (343 mm)
Propulsion:	turbojet (Teledyne CAE J402-CA-400); 600 lbst
	(272 kgst) + solid-propellant booster of
	12,000 lbst (5,443 kgst) for surface launch
Range:	75+ nm (105.6 km)
Guidance:	active radar
	GPS/inertial + active radar in Block II
Warhead:	510 lb (231 kg) high explosive
Platforms:	*aircraft* F/A-18
	P-3C
	S-3B
	cruisers CG 47/52
	destroyers DDG 51
	DD 963

HELLFIRE AGM-114

The Hellfire (its name derived from the term Helicopter-launched Fire and Forget) is an anti-tank missile launched from Marine attack helicopters. It also has been launched by Predator Unmanned Aerial Vehicles (UAVs). It is a free-flight weapon intended to replace the wire-guided TOW (Tube-launched, Optically tracked, Wire-guided missile), with a longer- range that permits launch-and-leave tactics.

When the Army initiated development of the Hellfire in the mid-1970s, Rockwell International was the prime contractor for the sole-source program, and Martin Marietta provided the laser seeker. However, from the mid-1980s, Martin became a second production source for the missile.

Design: The Hellfire is a modular missile, allowing a variety of sensors to be fitted. The Marines use the laser-guided variant. The target can be designated for helicopters by ground-based or airborne laser designators; it affords additional survivability to the launching helicopter by a lock-on-after-launch feature. A ground-launched version has been developed.

Operational: Hellfire missiles fired by Army AH-64 Apache helicopters against Iraqi radar sites were the first coalition weapons launched in Operation Desert Storm in January 1991.

Beginning in 2003, Hellfire missiles have been launched by MQ-1 Predator UAVs. The Central Intelligence Agency made the first operational use of UAV-launched Hellfires in Afghanistan and Yemen. (The Predator can carry two missiles; the enlarged MQ-9 Predator-B can carry up to ten. See Chapter 29.)

Status: Operational. IOC for the U.S. Army was in 1985. It is used by more than ten other nations. A ground-based version of the missile also has been developed, and there is an anti-ship variant designated RB-17.

Prime contractor:	Boeing (formerly Rockwell International and Martin Marietta)
Weight:	99.6 lb (45.2 kg)

An aviation ordnanceman prepares a Harpoon under the wing of a P-3C Orion maritime patrol aircraft. The Harpoon originally was developed for aircraft to attack surfaced Soviet cruise missile submarines. (McDonnell Douglas)

A Harpoon blasts out if its canister after being launched by a submarine. The springloaded fins and stub wings are fully deployed in this photo. U.S. submarines have beached the Harpoon; others navies still use it, labeled as the Sub-Harpoon. (McDonnell Douglas)

Length:	5 ft 4 in (1.625 m)	
Span:	1 ft 1 in (0.33 m)	
Diameter:	7 in (178 mm)	
Propulsion:	solid-propellant rocket	
Range:	3+ nm (5.55+ km)	
Guidance:	laser tracking	
Warhead:	20 lb (9 kg) high explosive	
Platforms:	*helicopters*	AH-1W/Z
		HH-60H
		MH-60R/S
		SH-60B/R

A pair of Hellfire missiles are mounted on the left side of an HH-60H Seahawk during operations in the Persian Gulf. These missiles have been used extensively by U.S. and Israeli helicopters against terrorist targets. Although mounted on a Navy helicopter from the carrier DWIGHT D. EISENHOWER (CVN 69), the missiles have "USMC" painted on their sides. (U.S. Navy)

An SH-60B Seahawk launches a Hellfire missile during an exercise. The markings "HQ" on the helicopter's tail identify Light Helicopter ASW Squadron (HSL) 46. The sonobuoy dispenser panel on the left side is clearly visible in this view. (U.S. Navy/James F. Slaughenhaupt)

JASSM (JOINT AIR-TO-SURFACE STANDOFF MISSILE) AGM-158

This is a totally autonomous ground-attack cruise missile being developed by the Air Force to provide a precision strike capability against highly defended targets. It will be used by Air Force, Navy, and Marine Corps aircraft, with the Navy–Marine F/A-18E/F Hornets carrying the missile.

The JASSM will employ a J-1000 penetrator warhead capable of destroying above-ground and shallow-buried point targets. It is designed specifically to survive in a high-threat environment (i.e., anti-aircraft guns and missiles). Range will be in excess of 200 nm (370 km).

Status: In development. Navy IOC is planned for FY 2009. The Navy's procurement budget provides for 30 missiles in FY 2008 and 110 in both FY 2009 and FY 2010.

Lockheed Martin is the prime contractor.

An artist's concept of a JASSM in flight. Lockheed Martin is looking into the possibility of an extended-range version that could reach up to 500 nm (925 km) and a configuration that could be launched from shipboard VLS installations. (Lockheed Martin)

Prime contractor:	Lockheed Martin
Weight:	2,250 lb (1,020 kg)
Length:	14 ft (4.27 m)
Span:	
Diameter:	18 in (457 mm)
Propulsion:	
Range:	300 nm (555 km)
Guidance:	GPS/inertial + Infrared (IR) terminal homing
Warhead:	approx. 1,000 lb (454 kg)
Platforms:	*aircraft* F/A-18E/F

JCM (JOINT COMMON MISSILE)

The JCM is a follow-on, precision-guided missile planned to replace the Hellfire, Maverick, and TOW ground-attack missiles. It is intended to kill moving and short-dwell-time targets. The JCM will be launched from both fixed-wing aircraft and helicopters.

It will have a precision, multimode seeker with a fire-and-forget capability. Range is approximately 15 nm (28 km).

The JCM initially will be used by the U.S. Army, Navy, and Marine Corps and by the British services.

Status: In development. JCM is scheduled to achieve IOC in FY 2008. The Navy has programmed the procurement of 22 missiles in FY 2008 and 88 in FY 2009. The U.S. Army is the lead service and Lockheed Martin the prime contractor

JSOW (JOINT STAND-OFF WEAPON) AGM-154

The JSOW is an advanced stand-off missile developed jointly by the Navy and Air Force. It will replace several of the two services' other air-to-surface missiles—the Maverick, Rockeye, Skipper, and Walleye—as well as laser-guided bombs. Also see JCM (above).

Design: JSOW has GPS/inertial guidance and can carry a variety of warheads. The AGM-154A is armed with the BLU-97 general-purpose submunition; the canceled AGM-154B was to carry the BLU-108, a "smart" anti-armor submunition; and the AGM-154C has a single, 500-pound BLU-111 warhead to provide blast fragmentation for use against bunkers and other hardened targets. The C variant has an infrared seeker and a man-in-the-loop data link to provide additional precision. The B variant was canceled because the Air Force pulled out of the program and the Navy could not afford to fund it.

The wings fold atop the missile; the tail fins do not fold.

Some 23,800 weapons are planned for Navy–Air Force procurement. Consideration also is being given to employing the missile in an electronic jamming role.

Operational: The JSOW was employed for the first time on 25 January 1999, when F/A-18C aircraft launched three missiles against targets in Iraq.[11] The missile also was used in the 1999 Kosovo campaign.

A pair of prototype JCMs is shown under the wing of an F/A-18F Hornet. A replacement for the widely used Hellfire, Maverick, and TOW missiles, the JCM will have a greater range and a trimode seeker to provide users with considerable strike flexibility. (Boeing Company)

Status: Operational. In production. AGM-154A IOC was in 1999 and AGM-154C in 2003.

Prime contractor:	Raytheon
Weight:	1,000 or 1,500 lb (454 or 680 kg); varies with warhead
Length:	13 ft 4 in(4.06 m)
Span:	8 ft 10 in (2.69 m)
Diameter:	
Propulsion:	solid-propellant rocket
Range:	35 nm (65 km)
Guidance:	GPS/inertial + seeker
Warhead:	AGM-154A: cluster bomb dispenser with 145 BLU-97/B Combined Effects Munition (CEM) bomblets, 3.4 lb (1.54 kg) each
	AGM-154C: multistage blast-fragmentation/penetrator
Platforms:	*aircraft* AV-8B
	F/A-18

11 The missiles were flown to the Middle East and transferred by air to the carrier CARL VINSON (CVN 71).

The JSOW missile is one of the first weapons developed specifically for multiservice use. These missiles were being prepared for aircraft aboard the carrier ABRAHAM LINCOLN as the ship was steaming in the Persian Gulf during Operation Iraqi Freedom. (U.S. Navy/Michael S. Kelly)

An artist's view of a JSOW in flight, with wings extended. Raytheon has announced plans for the development of a JSOW variant with a BLU-111/B 500-pound (225-kg) unitary warhead as its payload. (U.S. Navy)

LASM (LAND ATTACK STANDARD MISSILE)

The LASM was to be a near-term weapon for the naval fire support role, launched from VLS ships. It was based on the Standard surface-to-air missile, which was considered the most cost-effective way to provide such a weapon to the fleet. The program was initiated in 1998 and was to provide an interim weapon until the ALAM becomes available about 2009.

The LASM was to make maximum use of existing Standard missile components, hence the LASM rounds would have been "remanufactured" surface-to-air missiles with different guidance and the Mk 125 blast-fragmentation warhead. This was a supersonic missile.

Status: Canceled. Planned IOC was to be 2003. The procurement objective was 800 missiles.

MAVERICK AGM-65

This is an air-to-surface missile derived from an Air Force anti-tank missile for use by Marine Corps aircraft in the close air support role and by the Navy in the anti-ship role.

The Marines have the AGM-65E laser-guided version, compatible with air- and ground-based laser designators; the Navy's AGM-65F combines the Imaging Infrared (I2R) of the Air Force AGM-65D missile with the warhead and propulsion sections of the AGM-65E.

Design: The Maverick is a modular missile produced in several variants employing one of three guidance packages (television, laser, infrared), one of two warheads, and the same rocket motor. The Navy–Marine Corps variants have a 300-pound (136-kg) penetrating blast warhead in place of the 125-pound (57-kg) shaped charge used for attacking tanks in the Air Force versions.

Operational: Maverick missiles were used in the 1999 Kosovo campaign.

Status: Operational. IOC for the AGM-65E was in 1985. Eighteen other nations employ the Maverick.

Prime contractor:	Hughes
Weight:	AGM-65F: 645 lb (293 kg)
Length:	8 ft 2 in (2.49 m)
Span:	2 ft 4½ in (0.72 m)
Diameter:	12 in (300 mm)
Propulsion:	solid-propellant rocket
Range:	12 nm (22 km)
Guidance:	infrared
Warhead:	300 lb (136 kg) high explosive
Platforms:	*aircraft* AV-8B
	F/A-18
	P-3C
	helicopters A-1W/Z

PENGUIN Mk 3 AGM-119B

The Penguin Mk 3 (originally designated Mk 2 Mod 7) is an anti-ship missile developed by the Norwegian Navy that is in use by U.S. Navy SH-60/MH-60 helicopters. The missile also has undergone U.S. Navy evaluation for use on small craft, but that application is not being pursued; the missile was considered too heavy for that role.

The Navy announced in 2003 that the Penguin was being removed from service; however, congressional concern has caused the Navy to reevaluate that decision.

Design: The missile is a "fire-and-forget" weapon with several unusual features, including an indirect flight path to the target. On board ship, the Penguin is fired from a storage/launcher container that weighs 1,100 pounds (499 kg). The Mk 3 has a greater weight but a smaller wingspan than the Mk 2 that was evaluated for shipboard use; see 13th Edition/page 441.

The Penguin carries a Bullpup ASM warhead.

Maximum missile speed is approximately Mach 1.2.

An Air Force F-16 launching a Maverick air-to-surface missile. (Raytheon)

A Maverick air-to-surface missile is loaded onto the wing of a P-3C Orion at a forward base during Operation Iraqi Freedom. The Maverick and other non-ASW weapons carried by the Orion coupled with their communications relay and surveillance capabilities have largely diverted the aircraft from ASW missions and training. (U.S. Navy/Brad C. Dillon)

Status: Operational. IOC for the Mk 3 in Norwegian Air Force was in 1987. IOC in U.S. Navy was in April 1994.

The original Penguin became operational on Norwegian fast attack boats in 1972; it also is used by the Australian, Greek, Spanish, Swedish, and Turkish navies. The improved Mk 2 became operational in 1979, and the Mk 3 has been developed for launch from F-16 strike fighters of the Norwegian Air Force.

Current U.S. Navy procurement is 101 missiles.

Prime contractor:	Kongsberg Vaapenfabrikk (Norway) and Grumman
Weight:	820 lb (372 kg)
Length:	10 ft 6 in (3.2 m)
Span:	3 ft 3 in (1.0 m)
Diameter:	11 in (280 mm)
Propulsion:	solid-propellant rocket + solid-propellant booster
Range:	30+ nm (55+ km) air launch mode
Guidance:	inertial + infrared homing
Warhead:	265 lb (120 kg) high explosive
Platforms:	*helicopters* SH-60B/F
	MH-60R

A Penguin missile falls away from an SH-60F Seahawk during a test launch. The missile's wings still are folded, and the rocket engine has not yet ignited. Penguins are in use on several nations' warships. The U.S. Navy evaluated the missile aboard small combatants. (U.S. Navy/Danny Lee)

A Penguin missile ignites seconds after release by an SH-60B Seahawk during an exercise off the coast of Okinawa. The helicopter, from HSL-51, has begun to bank to the right. The ubiquitous H-60 series is flown in large numbers by four of the U.S. military services; the Marine Corps flies only eight of the VH-60N variant. (U.S. Navy/Lisa Aman)

Hail and farewell: An F-14 Tomcat from VF-103 aboard the carrier GEORGE WASHINGTON releases a Phoenix missile during a Mediterranean exercise. This was one of the last launches of the weapon, which was officially retired on 30 September 2004. The F-14 follows shortly. (U.S. Navy/Dana Potts)

PHOENIX AIM-54

The Phoenix was developed for long-range fleet air defense against attacking Soviet bomber aircraft. The missile was removed from service in 2004 in anticipation of the retirement of the F-14 Tomcat from the fleet. It was the most sophisticated and longest-range AAM in service with any nation.

The missile could be carried only by the F-14 using the AWG-9 radar/fire control system. The AWG-9 is capable of simultaneously guiding all six Phoenix missiles that could be carried by an F-14, although six-missile loadouts were rare.

Design: The AIM-54A, with analog electronics, was replaced by the AIM-54C/C+ models. The C/C+ had a digital system to allow software programming for more rapid target discrimination, improved beam attack, better resistance to electronic countermeasures, longer range, increased altitude, and increased reliability. The previously used expanding, continuous-rod warheads of the early Phoenix missiles were replaced by controlled fragmentation warheads (entering production in FY 1983). The AIM-54B was an interim model, similar to the AIM-54A but without the earlier missile's liquid cooling system; it did not go into production. The missile's designed range was 60 nm (111 km); intercepts had been made out to at least 110 nm (204 km). Maximum speed was approximately Mach 5.

Production ended with the FY 1992 order.

Status: Operational. IOC was in 1974. More than 2,500 AIM-54A missiles were produced by Hughes, as were more than 1,000 AIM-54C/C+ models.

RAM (ROLLING AIRFRAME MISSILE) RIM-116A

The RAM is a rapid-reaction, short-range missile for shipboard defense that uses off-the-shelf components. It is the first U.S. Navy shipboard fire-and-forget missile and the only Navy missile that rolls during flight (i.e., is not stabilized in flight).

Design: The RAM has the infrared seeker from the Army's Stinger missile and the rocket motor, fuze, and warhead from the Sidewinder AAM; it is provided with multimode guidance. The missile is supersonic.

The complete RAM round consists of the RIM-116A missile and the Ex-8 sealed canister; together they are designated Ex-44. The RAM missile is fired from the 21-missile Mk 49 launcher, which uses the mount and elevation/train assemblies from the Phalanx CIWS. The launcher is reloaded by hand.

It had been proposed to also fire the missile from two of the eight cells of the NATO Sea Sparrow launcher (five missiles per cell).

Status: Operational. In production. IOC was in 1992.

The Ex-31/Mk 49 launcher was evaluated in the destroyer DAVID R. RAY (DD 971) in the late 1980s. The first two production launchers were installed in the helicopter carrier PELELIU (LHA 5) in 1992 (with her Sea Sparrow launchers being removed). The Navy plans to provide approximately 80 ships with one or two launchers.

Early in 2000, the Navy revealed plans to provide frigates of the OLIVER HAZARD PERRY class with Mk 29 RAM launchers in place of the ships' Mk 13 launchers for Standard-MR/Harpoon missiles. In the event, their Mk 13 launchers were deleted without replacement.

About 1,400 RAM missiles currently are planned for procurement by the U.S. Navy.

The missile also is fitted in German, Greek, and South Korean warships.

Prime contractor:	Raytheon	
Weight:	162 lb (73.5 kg)	
Length:	9 ft 2 in (2.79 m)	
Span:	1 ft 5 in (434 mm)	
Diameter:	5 in (127 mm)	
Propulsion:	solid-propellant rocket	
Range:	approx. 5 nm (9 km)	
Guidance:	passive Radio Frequency (RF) acquisition + mid-course guidance with IR terminal or passive RF all the way	
Warhead:	25 lb (11.3 kg) high explosive	
Platforms:	*carriers*	CV/CVN	
	amphibious	LHD 1	LHA 1
		LPD 17	LSD 41
		LSD 49	

A RAM streaks skyward from a Mk 49 launcher aboard a carrier. RAM is a relatively simple surface-to-air weapon that can be fitted easily to a broad range of warships, replacing the Sea Sparrow missile in some and the Phalanx CIWS in others. (Raytheon)

Sailors aboard the carrier KITTY HAWK load a RAM launcher Mk 49. The missiles are loaded into the launcher in their stowage/shipping canisters. Although the missiles still are hand loaded, this is faster and more efficient than reloading Sea Sparrow "box" launchers. (U.S. Navy/Jo Wilbourn)

The destroyer STUMP (DD 978) launches a NATO Sea Sparrow missile during a UNITAS exercise off the coast of Argentina in October 2003, one year before the ship became one of the last SPRUANCE-class destroyers to be decommissioned. There is a RAM launcher Mk 49 on the ship's fantail. (U.S. Navy/Robert Taylor)

SEA SPARROW RIM-7/RIM-162

The Sea Sparrow is a modification of the Sparrow AAM employed as an anti-ship missile defense system; it was developed in the 1960s to counter the threat from Soviet anti-ship weapons. The missile is fired from the eight-cell Mk 25 box launcher of the BPDMS and the Mk 29 launcher of the NATO Sea Sparrow Missile (NSSM). The Mk 25/29 launchers are not automatically reloaded, and many ships do not have reloads on board. The RIM-7M and RIM-7P missiles currently are used in the anti-ship missile defense role.

The RIM-162 (formerly RIM-7R) Evolved Sea Sparrow Missile was developed for use in the VLS in U.S. ships. A four-pack ESSM canister can be fitted in each Standard missile tube. The ESSM configuration has a dual-mode guidance, combining the RIM-7P semiactive seeker with improved infrared guidance.

The Sea Sparrow launchers are not fitted in ships that have Standard missile capabilities.

Several foreign navies use vertical launching systems for the Sea Sparrow. In this configuration, a compact jet vane control unit is attached to the rear of the missile for launching. This device has four independent jet vanes that interact with the rocket exhaust plume to provide initial pitch-over, roll, and slew of the missile. Once the missile has achieved the proper heading for intercept and speed for normal fin control, the vane unit is jettisoned through the activation of four explosive bolts.

The Sea Sparrow is being succeeded in U.S. warships by the RAM.

Design: The Sea Sparrow launchers are derived from the ASROC box launcher.

The Mk 91 missile Fire Control System (FCS) is used with the NSSM, and the Mk 115 is used with the BPDMS. Beginning in 1980, the Mk 23 Target Acquisition System (TAS) was added to the NSSM on U.S. ships, making the missile a self-contained system (TAS provides a dual-mode radar and digital processor for automatic threat detection).

The RIM-7P has a combined semiactive radar homing and infrared seeker package.

Operational: More than 50 U.S. Navy ships are armed with the Sea Sparrow missile.

The carrier SARATOGA (CV 60) accidentally launched two Sea Sparrow missiles during an exercise in the Aegean Sea on 1 October 1992. One missile struck the Turkish destroyer MAUVENET, killing 5 men (including the commanding officer) and injuring at least 14 others. Initial reports cited personnel failures as the cause of the accidental launches. There were no U.S. casualties.

Status: Operational. IOC of the RIM-7 was in 1969; IOC RIM-7M was in 1983. The Sea Sparrow launchers have been removed from several U.S. amphibious and command ships. It is the only missile fitted in U.S. auxiliary ships (i.e., SACRAMENTO/AOE 1 class).

Thirteen other navies employ the Sea Sparrow in the missile-defense role, with some ships having vertical launchers.

The following data apply to the RIM-7M. See the listing for the Sparrow missile for additional data.

Prime contractor:	Raytheon
Weight:	450 lb (204 kg)
Length:	12 ft (3.7 m)
Span:	3 ft 4 in (1.0 m)
Diameter:	8 in (203 mm)
Propulsion:	solid-propellant rocket
Range:	approx. 10 nm (18.5 km)
Guidance:	radar homing
Warhead:	90 lb (40.8 kg) high explosive
Platforms:	*aircraft carriers* CV/CVN
	destroyers DDG 51 Flight IIA (VLS launcher)
	amphibious LHD 1
	auxiliaries AOE 1

A containerized Evolved Sea Sparrow Missile (ESSM) is lowered into a forward VLS cell of the missile destroyer MCCAMPBELL (DDG 85) at the Naval Air Station North Island (San Diego). The MCCAMPBELL was the first U.S. warship to deploy with the ESSM, in 2004. (U.S. Navy/Joel Jackson)

A NATO Sea Sparrow missile is launched from a Mk 29 box launcher on the carrier HARRY S. TRUMAN (CVN 75). Note how the missile penetrates the "soft" outer cover of the launcher. Relatively few U.S. Navy ships still mount these box launchers. (U.S. Navy/H. Dwain Willis)

SIDEARM AGM-122A

The Sidearm is an anti-radar missile developed to counter ground-based air-defense weapons at short ranges. It is based on the outdated AIM-9C Sidewinder AAMs that were taken out of service in the 1970s. It is used on Marine Corps AH-1 Sea Cobra helicopters and Army AH-64 Apache helicopters.

Design: The Sidearm missiles have been fitted with a relatively broad band, passive-only, radar-homing plus active optical target-detection device from AIM-9 missiles. The AIM-9s, in turn, have been refitted with newer, in-production rocket motors, warhead, and fins.

On launch, the Sidearm executes a pitch-up maneuver that permits launch from very-low altitudes, an important feature for helicopters flying in the nap-of-the-earth mode. The missile can be used by essentially all fixed-wing fighter and aircraft. Maximum speed is Mach 2.3.

The Sidearm was developed by the missile-prolific Naval Weapons Center at China Lake, California. Motorola of Tempe, Arizona, converted several hundred AIM-9 missiles to the Sidearm configuration; future new production is envisioned. An improved AGM-122B version was canceled because of funding problems. The first production/remade Sidewinders were funded in FY 1986, and more than 700 missiles have been delivered to the Marine Corps.

Status: Operational.

Prime contractor:	see text
Weight:	approx. 200 lb (90.7 kg)
Length:	9 ft 6 in (2.9 m)
Span:	2 ft 1 in (635 mm)
Diameter:	5 in (127 mm)
Propulsion:	solid-propellant rocket motor
Range:	18,000 yds (16,463 m)
Guidance:	radar homing + electro-optical
Warhead:	10 lb (4.5 kg) high-explosive fragmentation
Platforms:	*helicopters* AH-1W/Z

SIDEWINDER AIM-9

The Sidewinder is the most widely used missile outside Russia. Several hundred thousand have been produced for 37 nations, in addition to the United States.[12] The air-to-air weapon was used extensively by the U.S. Navy in the Vietnam War, as well as by allied forces in other conflicts. In the 1991 Persian Gulf War, it was responsible for 24 percent of the air-to-air kills (see *Operational* notes).

The latest variant is the AIM-9X, with improved guidance and kinematics and increased resistance to infrared countermeasures.

P-3 Orion maritime patrol/ASW aircraft have carried Sidewinders in exercises.

Design: Developed by the Naval Weapons Center at China Lake, California, the Sidewinder is a simple, effective, infrared-homing missile. The AIM-9M version currently is in production in the United States, and the AIM-9L is being built by a European consortium and by Mitsubishi in Japan. The AIM-9M features improved resistance to electronic countermeasures and can engage targets against hot backgrounds; the guidance includes digital electronics, electronic reprogramming for future software upgrades, imaging, and autotracking. In 1991, the Department of Defense approved full-scale development of the AIM-9R until additional upgrades become available in the AIM-9X.

The AIM-9X has an imaging infrared seeker, improved rocket motor, and enhanced maneuverability.

Missile speed is approximately Mach 2.5.

An AIM-9C with a modified anti-radar seeker is called Sidearm; see separate entry.

Operational: The Sidewinder scored most of the air-to-air kills by U.S. Navy and Air Force aircraft in the Vietnam War and by the

A Sidearm anti-radar missile fitted on a Marine AH-1 SeaCobra helicopter. The little-known, little-publicized Sidearm also has been used by U.S. Army helicopters. It can be launched from any aircraft that can carry the Sidewinder. (U.S. Navy)

An ordnance specialist "makes safe" a Sidewinder missile on an F/A-18C Hornet from Strike Fighter Squadron (VFA) 131 that has just landed aboard the carrier JOHN F. KENNEDY. Below the Sidewinder can be seen a laser-guided bomb and a drop tank with VFA-131's nickname, "Wildcats." (U.S. Navy/Aren Alseth)

Israeli Air Force in the 1967 and 1973 wars in the Middle East. During the 1982 fighting over Lebanon's Bekaa Valley, Israeli aircraft used Sidewinders to shoot down 51 of the 55 Syrian-flown MiG aircraft destroyed in aerial combat. The Sidewinder also was highly successfully when used by British Harrier aircraft in the 1982 Falklands conflict.

In the 1991 Gulf War, Sidewinders were responsible for ten air-to-air kills against Iraqi aircraft, two by Navy fighters: on 17 January 1991, a Navy F/A-18 Hornet downed a MiG-21,[13] and on

---

12 The AIM-132 Advanced Short Range Air-to-Air Missile (ASRAAM) was developed as a competitor for the AIM-9X Sidewinder. Both the AIM-9X and ASRAAM are fitted with the same [Raytheon-Hughes] infrared seeker. ASRAAM was initiated jointly by Britain and Germany, but the two nations were unable to agree on details. Germany left the project in the early 1990s and, subsequently, initiated development of an improved Sidewinder designated IRIS-T (Infrared Imagery Sidewinder–Tail controlled). The British government continued development of the ASRAAM, with the first delivery to the Royal Air Force late in 1998. Subsequently, a British–French consortium has undertaken production of the missile. The U.S. Air Force and Navy have carried out tests with ASRAAM, but no U.S. procurement was undertaken.

13 This F/A-18 also shot down a second MiG-21 on the same mission with a Sparrow missile.

6 February 1991, a Navy F-14A Tomcat downed a helicopter. (In addition, eight Iraqi high-performance aircraft were downed by U.S. Air Force F-15C Eagles firing Sidewinder missiles.)

Status: Operational. IOC for the AIM-9 was in 1956; AIM-9M in 1983; AIM-9X in 2003. More than 125,000 Sidewinder missiles have been produced for users in more than 40 countries. At least 5,080 AIM-9X missiles are planned for procurement by the Air Force and 5,000 by the Navy and Marine Corps.

The data below are for the AIM-9L variant, except where noted.

Prime contractor:	Raytheon and Ford Aerospace (Raytheon for AIM-9X)
Weight:	88 lb (40 kg) for AIM-9H
	86½ lb (39 kg) for AIM-9L/M
Length:	9 ft 6 in (2.87 m)
Span:	2 ft ¾ in (0.63 m) for AIM-9H
	2 ft 1 in (0.635 m) for AIM-9L/M
Diameter:	5 in (127 mm)
Propulsion:	solid-propellant rocket
Range:	approx. 10 nm (18.5 km)
Guidance:	infrared passive homing
Warhead:	25 lb (11.3 kg) high explosive for AIM-9H
	20.8 lb (9.4 kg) high explosive for AIM-9L/M
Platforms:	*aircraft* AV-8B
	F-14
	F/A-18
	P-3C
	helicopters AH-1W/Z

An aviation ordnanceman checks a wingtip-mounted Sidewinder on an F/A-18C Hornet of VFA-115 aboard the carrier ABRAHAM LINCOLN. The squadron now flies the F/A-18E and is embarked in the carrier JOHN C. STENNIS. The missile has a protective yellow cap on its nose. (U.S. Navy/Michael S. Kelly)

An F/A-18C Hornet from VFA-113 aboard the carrier JOHN C. STENNIS launches an AIM-9M Sidewinder missile during an exercise in the Indian Ocean. The long-serving Sidewinder has scored more aerial kills than any other air-to-air missile of any nation. (U.S. Navy/Mark J. Rebilas)

SLAM (STAND-OFF LAND-ATTACK MISSILE) AGM-84

The SLAM is a derivative of the Harpoon anti-ship missile. It is intended for use by carrier-based aircraft in "surgical strikes" against high-value fixed targets or enemy ships at sea and is considered the most accurate air-to-surface weapon in the Navy's arsenal.

SLAM has the airframe, propulsion, and control systems of the Harpoon missile, with a combination of existing missile guidance systems: the Maverick IIR (Imaging Infrared) seeker, Walleye II data link, and GPS receiver/processor. The missile's inertial guidance system is updated in flight by GPS fixes to ensure the infrared seeker is pointed directly at the target. When the infrared seeker is activated, it sends a video image to the launching aircraft, which selects the specific aim point for the missile. After the target is locked in, the missile steers to the target. The missile can be controlled by an aircraft other than the launching plane.

The SLAM-ER AGM-84H variant is listed separately.

SLAM is intended for aerial launch, as well as for shipboard launch from canisters or VLS installations.

SLAM-ER kits are being used to upgrade all existing SLAM weapons. A further improvement of the Harpoon/SLAM weapon has been proposed by McDonnell Douglas, whose officials call it the "Grand Slam." The range of this variant is on the order of 185 nm (300 km) carrying a 1,000-pound (453.6-kg) warhead.

The data provided below are for the air-launched configuration for SLAM-ER; a solid-propellant rocket booster is added for shipboard launch.

Operational: The SLAM's first use in combat was from A-6E Intruder and F/A-18 Hornet aircraft, controlled by A-7E Corsair attack aircraft using AAW-9 pods. The seven SLAMs used in the 1991 Persian Gulf War all struck their targets, with the infrared video providing verification of their accuracy. This was achieved despite the unreliability of the AAW-9 data-link pods (since replaced by the improved AAW-13 pods).

In a March 1995 test, four SLAM missiles were launched simultaneously by four F/A-18C Hornet; all struck the single target.

Status: Operational. IOC was in 1991. The missile was procured through FY 1995.

Prime contractor:	Boeing (formerly McDonnell Douglas)
Weight:	1,385 lb (628 kg)
Length:	14 ft 4 in (4.37 m)
Span:	3 ft (0.9 m)
Diameter:	13½ in (343 mm)
Propulsion:	turbojet (Teledyne CAE J402-CA-400); 600 lbst (272 kgst)
Range:	approx. 50 nm (92.65 km)
Guidance:	inertial + infrared/video command homing
Warhead:	510 lb (231 kg) high explosive
Platforms:	*aircraft* F/A-18
	P-3C

An F/A-18E Hornet from the carrier CARL VINSON (CVN 70) releases a SLAM-ER missile over the Naval Air Weapons Station at China Lake, California. The SLAM-ER also can be launched from ship-mounted canister launchers. (U.S. Navy/Dana Potts)

An ATM-84H training version of the SLAM-ER missile mounted on an F/A-18E Hornet. The stand-off missile is one of several in the Navy's inventory that will be replaced by a family of joint-service weapons. (U.S. Navy/Dana Potts)

A SLAM missile is launched from a shipboard canister. A derivative of the Harpoon missile, SLAM—like Harpoon—originally was developed for air launch. A section with fins is added to the missile for shipboard launch. (McDonnell Douglas)

SLAM-ER (STAND-OFF LAND-ATTACK MISSILE–EXPANDED RESPONSE) AGM-84H

The SLAM-ER (Expanded Response—*not* Extended Range) variant has a 50 percent increase in range over the SLAM (accomplished by planar wings), an improved warhead for penetrating hardened targets, and an improved data link that increases the stand-off range of the controlling aircraft by 100 percent and enhances resistance to jamming. It has a speed of Mach 0.8.

The SLAM-ER+ incorporates Automatic Target Acquisition (ATA), making it an autonomous weapon, enhancing its effectiveness against small targets and targets in urban environments. ATA uses a matching algorithm to recognize both the aim point and the surrounding scene.

The SLAM-ER is fitted with a GPS update receiver. It is intended for adverse-weather targeting amid clutter, especially in urban areas, with an on-board reference imaging system.

Operational: The first use of SLAM-ER was by Navy F/A-18C

aircraft in the Iraqi southern no-fly zone in late 1999. In 2004, the Navy announced the missile also would be carried by P-3C Orion maritime patrol aircraft.

Status: Operational. In production. IOC was in 1999. Some 700 existing SLAM missiles will be upgraded to the ER configuration, with additional new production of SLAM-ER continuing at least through 2004.

Prime contractor:	Boeing
Weight:	1,600 lb (727 kg)
Length:	14 ft 4 in (4.37 m)
Span:	7 ft 11½ in (2.4 m)
Diameter:	13½ in (343 mm)
Propulsion:	turbojet (Teledyne CAE J402-CA-400); 600 lbst (272 kgst)
Range:	approx. 150 nm (278 km)
Guidance:	GPS/inertial + infrared/video command homing
Warhead:	510 lb (231 kg) high explosive
Platforms:	*aircraft* F/A-18
	P-3C

SPARROW III AIM-7

The Sparrow is an all-weather, medium-range AAM. It has been adapted for surface launch as the Sea Sparrow for use in the anti-ship missile defense role (see page 520). It is being replaced rapidly in naval service by the AMRAAM.

Design: The AIM-7M combines the heavy warhead and large rocket motor introduced in the AIM-7F with an advanced monopulse seeker, better look-down/shoot-down capability, and improved resistance to ECM. The early, expanding continuous-rod warhead of these missiles has been replaced by a fragmentation warhead.

The AIM-7R is the latest variant, combining infrared terminal guidance with semiactive radar guidance (the latter fitted in earlier versions).

Missile speed reportedly is in excess of Mach 4.

A Marine ordnance specialist checks a Sparrow III missile fitted on an F/A-18C Hornet from VMFA-314 aboard the carrier NIMITZ *(CVN 68) during operations in the Persian Gulf. Such weapons are fully interchangeable between Navy and Marine Corps F/A-18s. (U.S. Navy)*

Operational: The weapon had minimal use in air-to-air engagements until the 1991 war in the Persian Gulf, when it was credited with 68 percent of the air-to-air kills—28 of the 41 air-to-air kills against Iraqi aircraft, although only one was by naval aircraft. On 17 January 1991, an Iraqi MiG-21 was shot down by a Sparrow from a Navy F/A-18 Hornet, which in the same engagement also used a Sidewinder to kill a second MiG-21. (U.S. Air Force F-15C Eagles used Sparrows to shoot down 22 high-performance Iraqi aircraft and 3 helicopters; one Saudi F-15C Eagle used Sparrows to kill two Iraqi fighters in the same engagement.[14]) The U.S. Air Force hit rate for Sparrows fired in the Gulf War was nearly triple the rate in the Vietnam War.

Status: Operational. IOC for the AIM-7 was in 1958; AIM-7F in 1976; AIM-7M in 1983.

The AIM-7E/F/M variants are in U.S. Marine Corps and Navy service, although production has ended.

The missile has been produced for U.S. and foreign air forces. In addition to the two U.S. producers, Mitsubishi in Japan manufactures the Sparrow. The data given below are for the AIM-7M model, except where indicated.

Prime contractor:	Raytheon and General Dynamics/Pomona
Weight:	450 lb (204 kg)
Length:	12 ft (3.7 m)
Span:	3 ft 4 in (1.1 m)
Diameter:	8 in (203 mm)
Propulsion:	solid-propellant rocket
Range:	approx. 30 nm (55.5 km)
Guidance:	semiactive radar homing (plus infrared in AIM-7R)
Warhead:	90 lb (40.1 kg) high explosive with continuous rod
Platforms:	*aircraft* F-14
	F/A-18

14 In addition to the 28 Sparrow and 10 Sidewinder air-to-air kills, one Iraqi MiG-29 crashed while maneuvering to escape a U.S. Air Force F-15C, and two Iraqi helicopters were shot down by U.S. Air Force A-10 Thunderbolt (Warthog) attack aircraft using 30-mm Gatling guns, for a total of 41 air-to-air kills in the Gulf War.

A Sparrow III missile is launched by an F/A-18C Hornet from VFA-131. The Sparrow has been used in relatively few combat actions in comparison with the Sidewinder missile because of the visual-range limitations often imposed by rules of engagement. (U.S. Navy)

STANDARD SM-1 MR (MEDIUM RANGE) RIM-66B

The Standard series of missiles was the principal surface-to-air weapon of U.S. cruisers, destroyers, and frigates. The series was developed as replacement for the three "T" missiles—the Talos, Terrier, and Tartar. Initially, the MR (Medium Range) missiles were to replace the Tartar and the ER (Extended Range) missiles the Terrier and Talos. However, various modifications and Standard missile production blocks with varying characteristics have blurred model distinctions.

Standard missiles currently are in use by the U.S. Navy and nine other navies.

The single-stage SM-1 MR replaced the Tartar SAM. It has been phased out of U.S. service with the removal of the Mk 13 missile launcher from the OLIVER HAZARD PERRY-class frigates in 2003–2004.

See 17th Edition/page 518 for characteristics.

Status: IOC was in 1970. Retired from U.S. Navy service in 2004.

STANDARD SM-2 MR RIM-66C

This surface-to-air missile has greater range than the SM-1 MR, as well as the addition of mid-course guidance and enhanced resistance to electronic countermeasures. It was intended specifically for use on Aegis missile ships.

Design: The Block IV variant provides significantly increased performance over all previous versions of the Standard. It is launched with a solid-propellant booster rocket.

The traditional expanding, continuous-rod warheads of the Standard missiles have been succeeded by controlled fragmentation warheads.

The Block IVA missile is configured for use in the ballistic missile defense role; see the entry for the SM-3 missile (below).

Also see the entry for the SM-6 ERAM (Extended-Range Active Missile).

Status: Operational. IOC was in 1981. The first at-sea firing of the SM-2 Block IV occurred in July 1994 from the LAKE ERIE (CG 70), with IOC in 1999 (see below). Block III entered production in 1988; Block IV production has ended with final deliveries in FY 2003.

Blocks III/IIIA/IIIB currently are deployed in U.S. warships.

The Standard SM-2 ER (RIM-67B), used with the Mk 26 launcher of the KIDD class, has been discarded.

Diameter:	13½ in (342 mm) missile
	21 in (533 mm) rocket booster
Propulsion:	solid-propellant rocket + solid-propellant rocket booster
Range:	100+ nm (185+ km)
Guidance:	semiactive radar homing
Warhead:	blast-fragmentation high explosive
Platforms:	cruisers CG 47
	CG(X)
	destroyers DDG 51
	DD(X)

Data for Blocks III/IIIA/IIIB

Prime contractor:	Raytheon
Weight:	1,558 lb (708 kg)
Length:	15 ft 6 in (4.72 m)
Wing span:	3 ft 6 in (1.08 m)
Diameter:	13½ in (342 mm)
Propulsion:	solid-propellant rocket
Range:	40–90 nm (74–167 km)
Guidance:	semiactive radar homing, except infrared in Block IIIB
Warhead:	blast-fragmentation high explosive
Platforms:	cruisers CG 47
	destroyers DDG 51

Data for Blocks II/III

Prime contractor:	Raytheon
Weight:	3,225 lb (1,466 kg)
Length:	21 ft 6 in (6.55 m) including rocket booster
Wing span:	3 ft 6 in (1.08 m)

A Standard-MR SM-2 missile is launched from the VLS of an Improved TICONDEROGA-*class cruiser. The retirement of the first five* TICONDEROGAS *and the removal of the Mk 13 launchers from the* OLIVER HAZARD PERRY-*class frigates will leave only VLS-fitted ships to launch Standard missiles. (United Defense/FMC)*

The missile cruiser LAKE ERIE *(CG 70) launches a Standard SM-3 missile on 13 June 2002 during a test of the Aegis/Standard ballistic missile defense program. This effort has been canceled in favor of the Extended-Range Active Missile (ERAM) SM-6 program. (U.S. Navy)*

STANDARD SM-3

The SM-3 was to be a variant of the Standard Block IVA missile configured to provide exoatmospheric, theater-wide defense against theater and tactical ballistic missiles. Also known as the Lightweight Exo-Atmospheric Projectile (LEAP), the missile was in development for use from the Improved TICONDEROGA-class cruisers fitted with VLS. This program was canceled on 14 December 2001 and is being replaced by the Extended Range Active Missile (ERAM) SM-6; see page 512.

An earlier proposal for a Standard SM-3 was to provide a very-long-range missile for intercepting Soviet stand-off jamming aircraft and possibly missile-carrying aircraft at ranges greater than possible with the SM-2 ER. This was similar in concept to the Long Range Dual Mission Missile; a concept called Thor also was similar. These missiles were not pursued. An IOC of late 2005 or 2006 was planned.

STINGER FIM-92

The Stinger is an advanced, shoulder-held surface-to-air missile that resembles the World War II–era bazooka rocket launcher. The missile was placed aboard several U.S. naval ships in the eastern Mediterranean beginning in the winter of 1983–1984 in reaction to threatened terrorist attacks against U.S. ships; it subsequently was carried in Navy ships operating in the Persian Gulf area. (The Russian Navy similarly uses the shoulder-held SA-7 Grail missile, formerly Strela, in various ships.)

Stinger missiles also are mounted in the gyro-stabilized Avenger turret, which holds eight missiles. The turret normally is mounted on a High Mobility Multipurposed Wheeled Vehicle (HMMWV), but it can be mounted on a variety of other military vehicles or operate in a stand-along configuration. The Avenger–"Humvee" is used by the U.S. Army and Marine Corps, as well as by the armed forces of Egypt and Taiwan.

The Stinger replaced the Redeye missile in U.S. service. (The later missile originally was designated Redeye II.)

An improved Stinger–POST (for Passive Optical Seeker Technique), with increased resistance to countermeasures, entered production in FY 1984. Subsequent upgrades are designated Stinger–RMP (Reprogrammable Microprocessor).

Design: The missile is tube launched, with four pop-out vanes at the front and four folding fins at the rear.

Status: Operational. IOC was in 1981. The Stinger is used by the U.S. Marine Corps, Army, and Air Force, as well as by several foreign services.

Prime contractor:	General Dynamics/Pomona
Weight:	34½ lb (15.7 kg)
Length:	5 ft (1.5 m)
Span:	8 in (203 mm)
Diameter:	2¾ in (70 mm)
Propulsion:	solid-propellant rocket
Range:	approx. 3 nm (5.5 km)
Guidance:	infrared homing
Warhead:	high explosive
Platforms:	see text

Marines fire a Stinger missile during an exercise on Okinawa. These weapons periodically have been placed aboard non-missile-armed U.S. Navy ships operating in forward areas where they could be exposed to hostile air threats. (U.S. Marine Corps/Jason Gallentine)

The Marine Corps also uses Stingers launched from the eight-missile Avenger weapon system, shown here mounted on a HMMWV. There is a radio-controlled target flying near the "Humvee." (U.S. Marine Corps/John A. lee II)

A Stinger missile launcher is demonstrated by Corporal Jason B. Carnahan of the 1st Stinger Battery, Marine Air Control Group 18, on Okinawa. These weapons also are referred to as MANPADs—Man-Portable Air Defense. (U.S. Marine Corps/M. A. Zeid)

TACTOM (TACTICAL TOMAHAWK) BGM-109/UGM-109

This is the Block IV Tomahawk (see below).[15] It is an improved missile for the land-attack role.

TACTOM provides:
• in-flight retargeting
• loiter capability
• monitoring of missile "health" and status in flight via satellite data link
• improved anti-jam GPS

In addition, the missile carries a camera to provide a "snapshot" of the battlefield via a satellite data link.

See page Tomahawk entry for basic characteristics.

Design: TACTOM originally was to have been propelled by the Teledyne Continental Motors J402-CA-402 engine, which also is being used in the JASSM. However, on 9 December 1999, Raytheon announced a stop-work order on the engine as part of a risk-reduction effort for TACTOM. Williams International has proposed the smaller version of its F-122 engine, which is being used in the German–Swedish Taurus missile. (Williams lost to Teledyne in the original TACTOM engine competition.)

The TACTOM carries either a unitary warhead (109C) or submunitions (109D).

Status: Operational. IOC was in 2004. The first TACTOM ship launch was from the USS STETHEM (DDG 63) in October 2002. The prime contractor is Raytheon.

TOMAHAWK BGM-109

The Tomahawk is a long-range cruise missile developed for both surface and submarine launch against both surface ship and land targets. It initially was known as the Sea-Launched Cruise Missile (SLCM), but in 1979, the Navy began using the terms Tomahawk Land-Attack Missile (TLAM) and Tomahawk Anti-Ship Missile (TASM) to distinguish the principal variants.

The TASM is being phased out of the fleet in favor of the Block IV Tomahawk Multi-Mission Missile, which was to have a common terminal sensor capable of attacking targets both on land and at sea. That weapon has been redesignated Tactical Tomahawk (TACTOM); see separate entry.

The Tomahawk was deployed in armored box launchers on four battleships, five cruisers, and seven SPRUANCE-class destroyers; it is carried in the vertical launchers (Mk 41) of later TICONDEROGA-class cruisers and ARLEIGH BURKE-class destroyers. (The SPRUANCE-class destroyers that had VLS also carried Tomahawk missiles.) It also can be fired from 21-inch submarine torpedo tubes and, in the SAN JUAN (SSN 751) and later LOS ANGELES-class submarines and the VIRGINIA (SSN 774) class, from vertical launch tubes.

Design: The Block III, the last production variant, features a smaller but more lethal warhead and an extended range, permitted by additional fuel; these missiles also have a GPS receiver for improved accuracy and time-of-arrival control to permit coordinated missile or aircraft and missile strikes. That variant also has a Williams 402 turbofan engine, with a 19 percent increase in thrust and a 2 percent decrease in fuel consumption.

About 100 Block IID missiles are being converted into a submunition variant called Block IIID; the remaining 525 Tomahawks are being upgraded to Block IIIC, with a unitary warhead.

The Navy variants were:

Model[16]	Launch mode	Type	Warhead
BGM-109A	ship/submarine	TLAM(N)	nuclear (W80 warhead)
BGM-109B	ship/submarine	TASM	conventional (1,000-lb Bullpup)
BGM-109C	ship/submarine	TLAM-C	conventional (1,000-lb Bullpup)
BGM-109D	ship/submarine	TLAM-D	conventional (bomblets)
BGM-109E	ship/submarine	TLAM/TASM	conventional (unitary)

The TLAM-D dispenses 166 BLU-97 bomblets, weighing 3.4 pounds (1.5 kg) each, in packets of 24; these submunitions can be armor-piercing, fragmentation, or incendiary. They are able to attack multiple targets; for example, in 1991, a submarine-launched TLAM-D struck three separate targets in Iraq and then performed a terminal dive to strike a fourth target.

In April 1992, the Department of Defense revealed that a warhead containing carbon-fiber spools also had been developed for the Tomahawk. Several of the 116 missiles fired on the first day of the Gulf War carried the still-experimental warheads, which, on detonation, disrupted Iraqi electric power, helping to blind air-defense and command and control activities. The warhead, developed under a highly classified "black" program, carries thousands of roles of very fine carbon fibers. When released by the Tomahawks, the fiber spools unwind in the wind, and the fibers then drop onto power lines and outdoor switching areas and transformers, causing massive short circuits but not permanent damage. (They are not "dispensed" as the are the BLU-97 bomblets.)

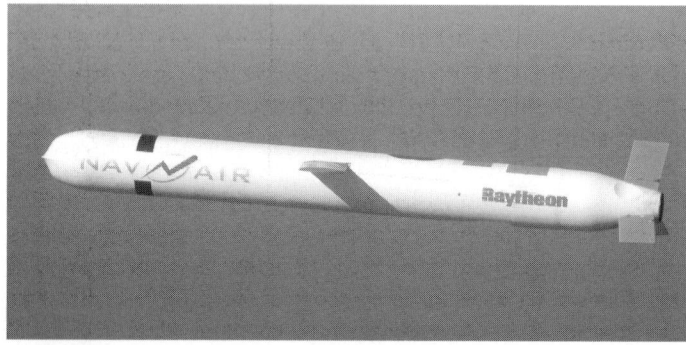

A TACTOM—Tactical Tomahawk Block IV cruise missile—on a test flight over the Naval Air Weapons Station China Lake. This version of the TLAM provides considerable flexibility in targeting options to commanders. However, the Block IV missile, like its predecessors, suffers from having a subsonic speed. (U.S. Navy)

The TACTOM achieved initial operational capability aboard the missile destroyer STETHEM (DDG 63) on 27 May 2004. This (unarmed) TACTOM was placed on display at the Pentagon on 29 September 2004 at a "fleet introduction" ceremony. TACTOM has a slightly different external, as well as internal, configuration from earlier TLAMs. (U.S. Navy/Daniel J. McLain)

---

15 In 1999, the Navy registered the names TACTOM and Tomahawk with the U.S. Patent Office, the first known effort to "protect" the names of weapons by the U.S. government. The absurdity of the action is evident, considering the name Tomahawk—the missile—has been in common usage for almost three decades, and the name Tomahawk—the hatchet—has been in the English language for almost 400 years!

16 Submarine-launched variants are UGM-109.

There are several subvariants of these missiles.

The accuracy of the early TLAM is on the order of 33 feet (10 m); later missiles—employing GPS—have considerably better accuracy. Speed is approximately 550 mph (880 kmh).

General Dynamics proposed an ASW variant of the Tomahawk as an alternative to the Sea Lance project (for both surface ship and submarine use).

An air-launched Tomahawk competed unsuccessfully with the Boeing Air-Launched Cruise Missile (ALCM) for use on B-52 strategic bombers. The BGM-199G Ground-Launched Cruise Missile (GLCM) was selected as a theater nuclear weapon for deployment in Western Europe under Air Force control, but those weapons were discarded under the Intermediate-range Nuclear Forces (INF) treaty.

The TLAM(N) fitted with the W80 nuclear warhead has been removed from ships; see page 533.

Operational: The first operational use of the Tomahawk was in the 1991 Gulf War (Operation Desert Storm). The U.S. Navy fired 288 Tomahawks—276 from surface combatants and 12 from submarines. Of those 288 missiles, approximately 80 percent were daylight attacks. All 288 transitioned to a cruise profile, for a successful launch rate of 98 percent. Reportedly, the Iraqis recovered one Tomahawk virtually intact.

According to the official Department of Defense report on the Gulf War, the Tomahawk's "demonstrated accuracy was consistent with results from precombat testing. The observed accuracy of TLAM, for which unambiguous target imagery is available, met or exceeded the accuracy mission planners predicted." (During the conflict, an estimated 477 TLAMs were available in theater.)

On 17 January 1993, three destroyers launched 45 missiles at targets in Iraq (plus one that failed to launch), and on 26 June 1993, an additional 23 missiles were fired at Iraqi targets (plus one that failed to launch) by a cruiser and a destroyer. Again, in December 1998 (Operation Desert Fox), U.S. ships fired approximately 325 TLAMs against targets in Iraq.

Tomahawk missiles first were used in the Bosnian conflict on the night of 10 September 1995, when the cruiser NORMANDY (CG 60) fired 13 TLAMs against Serbian air defense positions around Banja Luka. One missile did not function properly. (The NORMANDY launch came after another surface ship and the submarine OKLAHOMA CITY/SSN 723 were unable to fire Tomahawks because of equipment malfunctions.)

Additional TLAMs were fired in the lengthy Balkans confrontations and conflict. During the 1999 campaign to free Kosovo, a total of 202 TLAMs were fired by U.S. surface ships (approximately 75 percent) and submarines (approximately 25 percent). Additional TLAMs were fired by the British submarine SPLENDID.

Earlier in 1999, U.S. surface ships and submarines carried out missile strikes against reported terrorist targets in Sudan (30+ missiles) and Afghanistan (60+ missiles).

U.S. surface ships and U.S. and British SSNs again fired TLAMs into Iraq during the March–April 2003 invasion.

Status: Operational. Only the TLAM variant is operational; the TLAM(N) is in storage. IOC for the TASM in surface ships was in 1982; TASM in submarines in 1983; TLAM in surface ships in 1984; TLAM(N) in 1987; TLAM Block III in 1994. TASM IOC in HMS SPLENDID was in 1998.

A Tomahawk cruise missile was launched successfully from the submarine BARB (SSN 696) on 1 February 1978; the GUITARRO (SSN 665) was the first submarine armed with Tomahawk. The MERRILL (DD 976) was fitted with the first Tomahawk installation in October 1982 for at-sea evaluation; the battleship NEW JERSEY (BB 62) was the second ship, receiving the Tomahawk in March 1983.

The Royal Navy originally procured 65 TLAMs in 1998, with the submarine SPLENDID firing the first British missile on 18 November 1998. Subsequently, additional TLAMs were procured.

Prime contractor:	Raytheon
Weight:	2,650 lb (1,200 kg) + 550-lb (250-kg) booster + 1,000-lb (454-kg) capsule for submarine launch
Length:	18 ft 3 in (5.565 m) 2 ft (0.6 m) booster
Span:	8 ft 9 in (2.67 m)
Diameter:	20½ in (520 mm)
Propulsion:	turbofan (Williams F107-WR-402) + solid-propellant booster
Range:	TLAM 1,000+ nm (1,850+ km)
Guidance:	inertial and TERCOM (Terrain Contour Matching); GPS in Block III
Warhead:	1,000 lb (454 kg) high explosive or multiple payload
Platforms:	*cruisers* CG 47 (later ships with VLS)
	destroyers DDG 51
	DD(X)
	submarines SSN 21
	SSN 774
	SSN 751

The missile destroyer MILIUS (DDG 69) launching a Tomahawk on 22 March 2003 during Operation Iraqi Freedom. The Aegis cruisers and destroyers must carry a mix of Standard AAW and Tomahawk TLAM missiles; the SPRUANCE-class destroyers fitted with VLS could carry 61 TLAMs. (U.S. Navy/Thomas Lynaugh)

A Tomahawk land-attack missiles in flight with wings and air-intake scoop fully extended. The TLAM has become a weapon of choice, offering the advantages of range, accuracy, unmanned flight, and high survivability for attacking distant targets. (U.S. Navy)

TOW BGM-71

The TOW—for Tube-launched, Optically tracked, Wire-guided—missile is an anti-tank weapon fired from Army and Marine Corps helicopters, as well as from ground and vehicle mounts. However, Marine Ah-1W/Z helicopters carry the Hellfire missile almost exclusively. (The Marine Corps still uses TOW missiles on the ground.)

Design: Improved versions, designated Improved TOW (ITOW) and TOW 2, have an upgraded warhead and a higher impulse motor, respectively. The missile has a high subsonic speed.

Status: Operational. IOC was in 1970. Advanced variants are being produced by Raytheon, especially the TOW 2B Aero (formerly TOW 2B ER [Extended Range]).

Prime contractor:	Hughes and Raytheon
Weight:	54 lb (24.5 kg)
Length:	3 ft 8 in (1.1 m)
Span:	3 ft 9 in (1.1 m)
Diameter:	6 in (152 mm)
Propulsion:	solid-fuel rocket + solid-fuel booster
Range:	1.5 nm (2.8 km); 2 nm (3.7 km) for TOW 2
Guidance:	optical/wire
Warhead:	8 lb (3.6 kg) high explosive (shaped charge)
Platforms:	*helicopters* AH-1W/Z

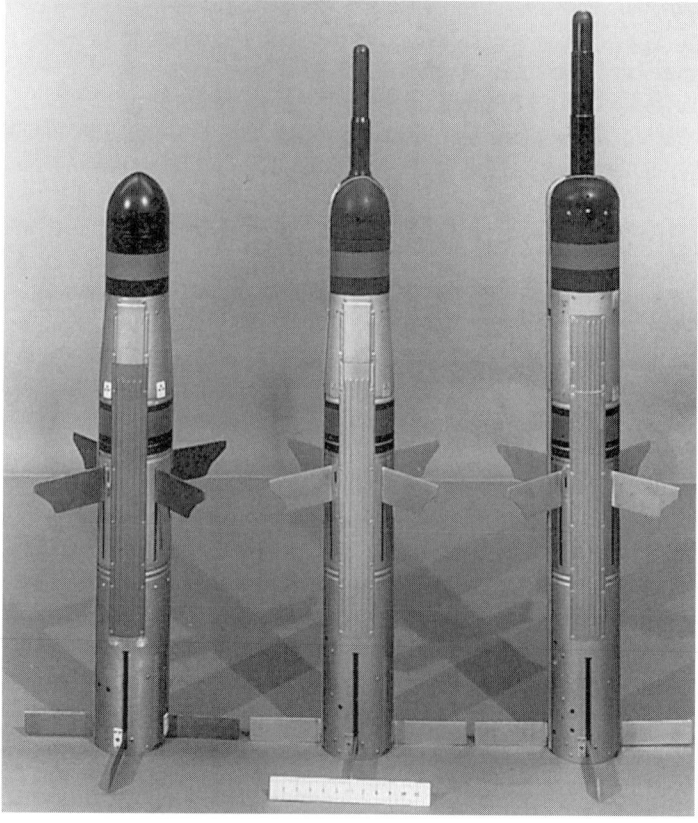

TOW missiles—from left: the basic TOW, Improved TOW, and TOW 2. There are further subtype improvements. The TOW and ITOW have 5-inch (127-mm) warheads; the TOW 2 series has a 6-inch (152-mm) warhead. The spikes provide armor penetration. (Hughes)

TRIDENT C-4 UGM-96A

The Trident I, or C-4, Submarine-Launched Ballistic Missile (SLBM) was fitted in the first eight submarines of the OHIO (SSBN 726) class as built and was backfitted in 12 submarines of the LAFAYETTE (SSBN 616) class. Of the OHIO class, four ships (SSBN 726–729) are being converted to cruise missile submarines (SSGNs) and four (SSBN 730–733) have been refitted with the Trident II/D-5 missile. The LAFAYETTEs have been stricken.

This classic photo of a TOW anti-tank missile being launched from a light truck shows the weapon in great detail, including the guidance wires. The wings and tail fins have not fully deployed. A wireless variant of the TOW was developed but did not enter production. The missile can be launched from helicopters. (U.S. Marine Corps)

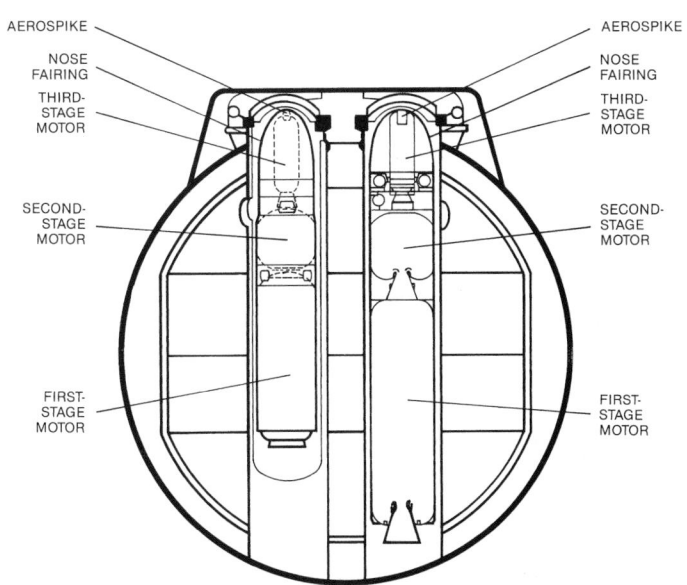

A comparison of the Trident C-4 (left) and Trident D-4 missiles is shown within a cross section of a submarine of the OHIO (SSBN 726) class. (U.S. Navy)

The Trident I SLBM evolved from the Department of Defense STRAT-X study of the late 1960s, which proposed an advanced SLBM with a range of 6,000 nm (11,120 km) to be carried in a new class of submarine. Subsequently, the Navy proposed a two-phase program: the Trident C-4 based on an Extend-range Poseidon (EXPO) missile with a range of some 4,000 nm (7,410 km) and the more-capable Trident D-5, to be developed at a later date with the longer range.

Status: The Trident C-4 IOC was on 20 October 1979 with deployment of the FRANCIS SCOTT KEY (SSBN 657), a former Poseidon-armed submarine. The OHIO first deployed with the Trident C-4 missile on 6 September 1982.

The last C-4 missile deployment was in the USS MICHIGAN (SSBN 727), which completed her last patrol as a strategic missile submarine on 15 December 2003. She now is undergoing conversion to an SSGN.

TRIDENT (D-5) UGM-133A

The Trident II, or D-5, is the U.S. Navy's sea-based strategic missile. It provides greater range and accuracy than the earlier Trident C-4 SLBM. In addition, the D-5 can deliver 75 percent more payload than the C-4, carrying eight of the Mark 5 reentry bodies, each fitted with a W88 nuclear warhead with an explosive force of about 300–475 kilotons. (Only some 400 W88 warheads have been produced; the remaining missiles are to be fitted with the W76 warhead, which has a yield of about 100 kilotons.)

Rear Admiral Kenneth Malley, Director, Strategic Systems Program, stated that you could draw a circle around the ends of a Trident submarine (i.e., of 560 feet [170.7 m] diameter) and a D-5 could put all its warheads in that circle from 4,000 nm (7,400 km) away.[17]

In the future, the D-5 missiles will be downloaded to only four warheads, reflecting the arms control limit of 1,728 warheads in submarines.

Design: This is a three-stage, solid-propellant, submarine-launched missile.

The D-5 version of the Trident missile was approved for development by the Secretary of Defense in October 1981 and fitted in the ninth and subsequent submarines of the OHIO class. The first eight submarines of that class were to be retrofitted to fire the D-5 missile, but those plans were canceled in 1991 because of fiscal

A Trident D-5 missile breaks the surface during a test launch. The D-5 has emerged as the principal U.S. strategic weapon; it now is fitted in all 14 U.S. strategic missile submarines and, with British warheads, in the Royal Navy's four SSBNs. (U.S. Navy)

constraints. Currently, four submarines are being converted to cruise missile ships (SSGNs) and four are being provided the D-5 missiles.

Designation: The missile formerly was designated UGM-96B.

Operational: The first test flight of the Lockheed D-5 missile from Cape Canaveral, Florida, on 21 March 1989 was a failure, as was the third launch on 15 August 1989. (The failures were due to a design flaw; water pressure on the missiles' nozzles caused them to tumble after leaving the water.) The second, fourth, and later launches were successful. The first submarine-launch occurred on 22 March 1989 from the TENNESSEE (SSBN 734); that test launch also failed. Following a series of successful test launches, the missile became operational.

The TENNESSEE began the first Trident D-5 patrol on 29 March 1990.

The D-5 missile eventually will be fitted to the 14 submarines of the OHIO class that are being retained for the foreseeable future.

Status: Operational. In production. The original inventory objective was 425 missiles for the 14 Trident II/D-5 submarines. An additional 115 missiles are being produced to maintain an ade-

---

17 Rear Admiral G. P. Nanos, USN, "Strategic Systems Update," *The Submarine Review* (April 1997), p. 12.

quate inventory for the extended service life planned for the OHIO-class SSBNs.

The D-5 is fitted in the Royal Navy's four VANGUARD-class SSBNs.

Prime contractor:	Lockheed Martin
Weight:	approx. 130,000 lb (58,968 kg)
Length:	44 ft (13.4 m)
Span:	(ballistic)
Diameter:	83 in (2.1 m)
Propulsion:	3-stage solid-propellant rocket
Range:	approx. 4,000 nm (7,400 km)
Guidance:	inertial
Warhead:	nuclear Mk 5 with 8 W88 or W76 Multiple Independently targetable Reentry Vehicles (MIRVs)
Platforms:	*submarines* SSBN 734–743

TSSAM (TRI-SERVICE STANDOFF ATTACK MISSILE) AGM-137

Formerly a highly classified "black" program, the TSSAM was revealed by the Department of Defense in June 1991, in part to help justify procurement of the B-2 "stealth" bomber. TSSAM was to provide a precision stealth weapon for the suppression of enemy air defenses; however, the Northrop-development weapon was canceled in January 1995 because of higher than expected costs.

In development since 1986, the low-observable TSSAM was intended to provide precision guidance with a conventional warhead to ranges of more than 100 nm (185 km). Apparently, a variety of warheads was to be available, including penetrating, multiple submunitions, and conventional high explosive.

The missile was to be compatible with the Army–Marine Corps Multiple Launch Rocket System (MLRS), the Air Force's B-2, B-52, and F-16 Fighting Falcon aircraft, and the Navy's F/A-18 Hornet and A-6E Intruder aircraft.

The procurement of 9,050 missiles was planned—2,250 for the Navy, 1,800 for the Army, and 5,000 for the Air Force.

In June 1991, the Department of Defense estimated a TSSAM procurement of 8,650 missiles for all services at a cost of $15.1 billion, or an average of $1.7 million per round, including research, tooling, support, etc. Subsequently, the unit cost increased to $2 million.

In place of the TSSAM, the Navy is procuring additional SLAM/SLAM-ER missiles.

VLA (VERTICAL LAUNCH ASROC) RUM-139A

This is a short-range ASW weapon, the vertical-launch successor to the ASROC RUR-5A ASW rocket for use in later TICONDEROGA-class cruisers and the ARLEIGH BURKE-class destroyers. Only small numbers of the weapon are being procured.

Design: The VLA has more than double the basic ASROC range. It also would be suitable for launch from modified ASROC launchers. The VLA carries a Mk 50 ASW torpedo as its warhead, although tests were conducted with the earlier Mk 46 Mod 5 torpedo.

The Navy originally had sought to combine the replacement for ASROC and SUBROC in a single weapon. This proved too difficult, however, and so the VLA was to be surface launched only and the Sea Lance ASW stand-off weapon was to fill the requirement for a submarine-launched weapon. In the late 1980s, the VLA was labeled as an interim weapon (with only 300 to be produced), and another an attempt was made to develop the Sea Lance as a common surface/submarine ASW weapon. In the event, Sea Lance was not produced.

Status: Operational. Congress approved a one-time procurement of 300 missiles in FY 1987 and 1989. The Japanese Aegis

destroyers of the KONGO class and latter classes with VLS also are VLA capable.

Prime contractor:	Loral	
Weight:	1,409 lb (634 kg)	
Length:	16 ft (4.9 m)	
Span:	2 ft 3.4 in (0.7 m)	
Diameter:	14 in (356 mm)	
Propulsion:	solid-propellant rocket	
Range:	approx. 15 nm (27.8 km)	
Guidance:	ballistic; terminal acoustic homing with Mk 50 torpedo	
Warhead:	Mk 50 torpedo	
Platforms:	*cruisers*	CG 47 (in VLS ships)
	destroyers	DDG 51

NUCLEAR WEAPONS

All nuclear weapons have been removed from U.S. Navy warships, except for submarine-launched ballistic missiles, and from naval air squadrons ashore. This unilateral nuclear weapons and readiness reduction and the similar large-scale cutback of Army and Air Force tactical and strategic nuclear weapons were announced in a dramatic television speech by President George H. W. Bush on 27 September 1991. (At the time, the president also proposed the elimination of all multiple warheads on land-based missiles by both the United States and the Soviet Union.)

The president's announcement was hailed by then-Secretary of Defense Dick Cheney, who said the initiative was, "in my opinion, the biggest single change in the deployment of U.S. nuclear weapons since they were first integrated into our forces."[18]

The U.S. action followed by a month the abortive Soviet right-wing, political-military coup. The victory of democratic forces in the Soviet Union had, said Cheney, permitted a "sweeping package" of nuclear arms reductions by the United States.

At the time of President Bush's statement, the Navy had the following nuclear weapons in service:

• *Strategic missiles*: 656 SLBMs in 35 strategic missile submarines.
    176 Poseidon C-3 in 11 LAFAYETTE class
    192 Trident C-4 in 12 LAFAYETTE class
    192 Trident C-4 in 8 OHIO class
    96 Trident D-5 in 4 OHIO class

• *Land-attack missiles*: Approximately 100 Tomahawk TLAM(N). These missiles were in attack submarines, cruisers, and destroyers; all were placed in storage ashore. The Navy's inventory goal for TLAM(N) prior to the president's statement was reported as 637, with 399 already funded through FY 1991; no additional missiles were to be procured beyond FY 1991.

• *Bombs*: Some 400 nuclear strike bombs (B57 and B61) and anti-submarine depth bombs (B57) embarked in aircraft carriers. All were to be withdrawn; most of the B61s were to be placed in storage and the B57s eliminated. Additional B57 weapons were at shore bases for use by P-3 Orion maritime patrol aircraft; these weapons were to be eliminated. Development of the advanced B90 dual-purpose bomb was halted. With its cancellation, no nuclear weapons remained under development for naval use.

(There were similar, far-reaching cuts of U.S. Army and Air Force tactical nukes. The only tactical nuclear weapons left with U.S. operational forces in 1991 were B57 and B61 bombs with Air Force fighter-bomber squadrons. The only U.S. tactical nuclear modernization program under way at the time of the president's speech, the Air Force's Short-Range Attack Missile–

---

18 Secretary of Defense Dick Cheney, Pentagon press briefing, 28 September 1991.
19 The follow-on SRAM II strategic weapon also had been terminated by President Bush's action.

Tactical/SRAM-T, also was terminated by the president's action.[19])

Department of Defense officials contend that in the future the Tomahawks and B61 bombs could be taken out of storage and returned to the fleet within a very short time—perhaps days. However, with the ongoing personnel reductions and severe budget constraints, it is unlikely the capability could be retained to rapidly bring nuclear weapons back aboard submarines and surface ships and use them effectively.

The only nuclear weapons that remain in the U.S. fleet are Trident C-4 and D-5 SLBMs. This force was reduced to 336 D-5 missiles on board 14 submarines by 2004.

The other strategic weapons in the U.S. arsenal in 2004 are 500 Minuteman III missiles (with 1,200 warheads), 40 MX Peacekeeper missiles (with 500 warheads), and 21 B-2 stealth bombers. Long-term plans call for the "de-MIRVing" of all land-based strategic missiles, i.e., downloading the 500 Minuteman IIIs and 50 MX Peacekeepers to one reentry vehicle per missile.[20]

Historical: The U.S. Navy had a theoretical nuclear strike capability as early as 1948 with the Mk 4 atomic bomb and a dozen land-based P2V-3C Neptune bombers. The twin-engine piston Neptunes could fly from airfields in Europe or North Africa, or be loaded by cranes aboard carriers for shipboard launch. It was a primitive force of questionable capability. At the time, atomic bombs had to be assembled by teams of up to 40 men, and it required several hours to "glue" them together.

Beginning in 1951, with the Mk 6 atomic bomb and AJ-1 Savage piston-engine attack aircraft, the Navy has had a continuous nuclear weapons capability on board surface ships, although the early carrier deployments were made without certain nuclear materials. In a crisis (or war), they would have been flown by B-47 jet bomber from storage sites in the United States to airfields in the Mediterranean area, and then flown aboard carriers by Carrier-On-board Delivery (COD) aircraft for bomb assembly. Subsequently, surface combatants and submarines were fitted with nuclear-armed anti-ship and anti-air missiles; land-attack and anti-ship cruise missiles; and anti-submarine torpedoes and rockets. A 16-inch (406-mm) nuclear projective also was developed for the IOWA-class battleships.

The 1991 decision to remove the remaining tactical weapons from warships followed the 1989 decision to dismantle the surviving ASROC anti-submarine rockets and Terrier-BTN (Beam-riding

Terrier Nuclear) anti-aircraft missiles fitted with nuclear warheads. Those weapons, like some of the bombs later taken out of service, were overage, and their remaining "shelf life" was severely limited and their effectiveness questionable.

Table 30-4 lists all nuclear weapons that were available to the U.S. Navy.

Table 30-4. NAVAL NUCLEAR WEAPONS

Warhead	Weapon*	Type	In stockpile
Mk 4	bomb	strike	1948–1953
Mk 5	Regulus missile	strike/ASUW**	1952–1963
Mk 6	bomb	strike	1951–1962
W7	Betty depth bomb	ASW	1955–1963
W7	BOAR bomb***	strike	1956–1963
Mk 8	bomb	strike	1951–1956
W23	16-inch shell	strike	1956–1961
W27	Regulus missile	strike/ASUW	1958–1965
W30	Talos missile	AAW	1958–1979
W34	Lulu depth bomb	ASW	1958–1971
W34	ASTOR torpedo	ASW	1958–1977
B43	bomb	strike	1961–1991
W44	ASROC	ASW	1961–1989
W45	Terrier missile	AAW	1962–1989
W47	Polaris missile	strike	1960–1975
W55	SUBROC	ASW	1964–1989
B57	bomb	strike/ASW	1963–1992
W58	Polaris missile	strike	1964–1982
B61	bomb	strike	1966–1992
W68	Poseidon missile	strike	1970–1991
W76	Trident I missile	strike	1979–present
W80	Tomahawk missile	strike	1984–1992
W81	SM-2 Standard	AAW	not developed
W88	Trident II missile	strike	1990–present
B90	bomb	strike/ASW	not developed

* Artillery shells and Atomic Demolition Munitions (ADM) used by the Marines not included
** ASUW = Anti-Surface Warfare; AAW = Anti-Air Warfare
*** Bureau of Ordnance Atomic Rocket

TORPEDOES

The U.S. Navy has two series of torpedoes in service: the lightweight Mk 46 and Mk 50, used by aircraft and surface ships and in

---

20 The surviving B-1B Lancers no longer are fitted for carrying nuclear weapons.

Mk 32 torpedo tubes on the destroyer HIGGINS (DDG 76) are checked by Torpedoman Seaman Norall Jackson. These tubes provide cruisers and destroyers with a very limited ASW capability in view of the ranges of contemporary submarine-launched torpedoes and cruise missiles. (U.S. Navy/Lance Kirk)

the CAPTOR mine; and the heavyweight Mk 48 ADCAP, carried in all submarines. These torpedoes are intended primarily for the anti-submarine role, although the Mk 48 can be used against surface ships.

The Mk 54 lightweight torpedo is in development. That weapon is intended for use against a variety of targets in littoral waters.

No torpedoes currently are being procured. Mk 48 torpedoes are being upgraded to later ADCAP configuration.

Both the heavyweight and lightweight torpedo programs have encountered major problems, most related to the nature of Soviet/Russian submarines. By some criteria, U.S. torpedoes have lagged behind the potential threat since the appearance of the first Soviet nuclear-powered submarines in 1958.

The problems with U.S. torpedoes have been identified publicly. In a 1981 congressional colloquy between a senator and Deputy Chief of Naval Operations (Surface Warfare) Vice Admiral William H. Rowden, the senator noted that then-new Soviet submarines of the Project 705/Alfa class, with titanium hulls and advanced hydrodynamic design, could travel at "40-plus knots and could probably outdive most of our anti-submarine torpedoes." He then asked what measures were being taken to redress this particular imbalance.[21]

The admiral replied, "We have modified the Mark 48 torpedo . . . to accommodate to the increased speed and to the diving depth of those particular submarines." He was less confident of the Mark 46 used by aircraft, helicopters, and surface ships: "We have recently modified that torpedo to handle what you might call the pre-Alfa."

Soviet undersea craft were difficult targets for several reasons. Their large size, double hulls, and multiple compartments reduced the effectiveness of the small Mk 46 and Mk 50 warheads. Both heavy and light torpedo effectiveness also suffered from the Soviet use of anechoic coatings, which degrade torpedo acoustic guidance, and their extensive use of acoustic decoys. Finally, the Mk 48's capability is reduced in the under-ice environment of the Arctic ice pack.

Subsequently, in the mid-1990s, with the demise of the Soviet Union and the rapid decline of the Soviet submarine threat, U.S. naval forces were reoriented toward operations in the littoral waters of the Third World. In this environment, too, there are major problems with the Navy's primary ASW weapons. The relatively shallow environment of the littorals can cause severe problems for torpedo homing sonars. The Mk 50 "is really challenged," and the Mk 48 is "stressed," according to a U.S. Navy official.

Accordingly, the Mk 54 Lightweight Hybrid Torpedo (LHT) was initiated to counter quiet, non-nuclear submarines operating in the shallow-water environment.

Submarines carry the Mk 48 torpedo. The Los Angeles-class SSNs have a capacity of some 25 tube-launched weapons (4 tubes + 22 reload spaces, with at least one rack left free to facilitate weapons handling). The later, improved Los Angeles-class submarines also have 12 vertical-launching tubes for TLAMs, making more reload spaces available within the submarine. The Seawolf class has space for 50 weapons (8 tubes + 42 reload spaces). The Virginia class returns to a 25-torpedo internal capacity, plus 12 vertical-launch tubes for TLAMs.

Surface ships have the Mk 46 or Mk 50 torpedo as an ASW weapon, launched by (1) over-the-side Mk 32 torpedo tubes, (2) SH-60 LAMPS helicopters, or (3) VLA for the Mk 50.

Until the late 1950s, U.S. surface combatants had torpedo tubes for heavy anti-ship torpedoes. For a brief period in the 1960s, the Mk 48 was intended for tube launch from surface warships to provide a long-range, wire-guided ASW torpedo. Several surface warships were fitted with torpedo handling gear and 21-inch tubes

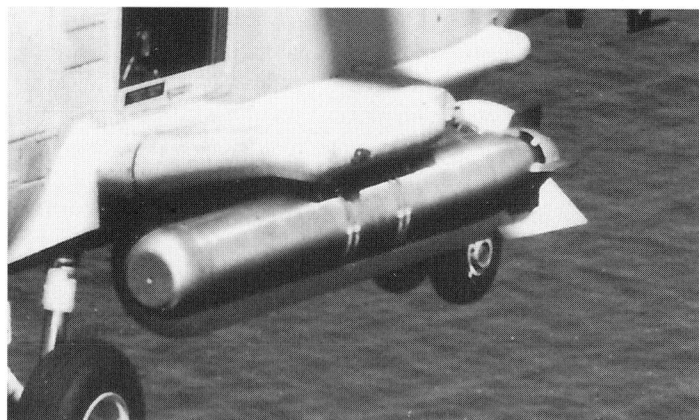

A Mk 50 torpedo fitted on an SH-60 helicopter. Two Mk 50 torpedoes can be carried by H-60 series aircraft. The Mk 50 has a "shrouded" propeller system in comparison with the open, contrarotating propellers of the Mk 46. (Alliant Techsystems)

in their stern counter or after deckhouse; however, this aspect of the Mk 48 program was canceled, and U.S. cruisers, destroyers, and frigates retain only Mk 32 tubes for lightweight torpedoes.

ASW aircraft and helicopters carry the Mk 46 or Mk 50 torpedo, externally on the SH-60 and MH-60 helicopters and in an internal weapons bay in the P-3C fixed-wing aircraft. (The S-3B Viking no longer is used in the ASW role.)

MK 54 LIGHTWEIGHT HYBRID TORPEDO (LHT)

The Mk 50 lightweight ASW torpedo is expensive and the number available is limited. Accordingly, the Navy is developing a Lightweight Hybrid Torpedo that combines the Mk 50 guidance package with the Mk 46 propulsion system and Commercial-off-the-Shelf (COTS) electronics. The Mk 54 is designed to have enhanced performance in shallow water against quiet, non-nuclear submarines.

The incorporation of COTS and open architecture will facilitate periodic upgrades of the Mk 54 in an effort to counter future non-nuclear submarine developments. According to Chief of Naval Operations Admiral Vern Clark, these features "will leverage the spiral acquisition process to synergistically introduce new hardware and software updates that will provide step-like increases in probability of kill while reducing life-cycle cost and allowing the torpedo to remain ahead of the evolving littoral submarine fleet."[22]

It is similar in size to the Mk 50 and will be air and surface ship launched.

Status: Development. IOC is planned for FY 2005. Procurement is planned through FY 2011, with an acquisition goal of 1,000 torpedoes. Raytheon is the prime contractor.

MK 50 LIGHTWEIGHT TORPEDO

The Mk 50—formerly known as the Advanced Lightweight Torpedo (ALWT)—is the successor to the Mk 46 for use by maritime patrol/ASW aircraft and helicopters and by surface warships (It also was intended for the aborted submarine-launched Sea Lance ASW missile.) The torpedo has enhanced kill capability compared to the Mk 46, but it still suffers from some of the shortcomings of the older torpedo, such as the small size of its warhead.

The ALWT program was initiated in August 1975, with a design

---

21 The Alfa SSN, with six operational units completed from 1979 to 1982, had a submerged speed of 43 knots and an operating depth estimated at the time by Western intelligence to be 2,000–2,500 feet (610–760 m). In realty, the Alfa operating depth was 1,300 feet (400 m); however, other Soviet submarines could dive significantly deeper.

22 Adm. Clark, *Vision . . . Presence . . . Power . . .* , p. 71.

A Mk 50 lightweight torpedo is launched from the Mk 32 tubes on the destroyer BULKELEY *(DDG 84) during an exercise in the Arabian Gulf in 2004. (U.S. Navy/Brien Aho)*

competition subsequently being held between Honeywell (Ex-50 design) and McDonnell Douglas (Ex-51). The former firm was selected to develop the torpedo. During the competition, the torpedo also was designated Mk XX. Concept development began in 1975 and advanced development was approved in 1979; limited production began in March 1989.

Design: Special features of the Mk 50 include the AKY-14 programmable digital computer.

The torpedo can be used by all Mk 46 launchers/attachment points without platform modification.

Name: The Mk 50 is referred to as Barracuda by the producer.

Status: Operational. Manufactured by Alliant Techsystems (formerly Honeywell) and Westinghouse Electric Corp.

Weight:	750 lb (340 kg)
Diameter:	12¾ in (324 mm)
Length:	9 ft 6 in (2.9 m)
Propulsion:	Stored Chemical Energy Propulsion System (SCEPS)
Speed:	50+ knots
Range:	
Guidance:	active/passive acoustic homing
Warhead:	approx. 100 lb (45 kg) conventional-shaped high explosive charge

Platforms:	*aircraft*	P-3C
		SH-60B/F/R
		MH-60R
	ships	cruisers
		destroyers
		frigates

MK 48 ADCAP TORPEDO

This is the U.S. Navy's only submarine-launched torpedo. The Mk 48 ADCAP (Advanced Capability) version of the Mk 48 heavy torpedo has been in production since FY 1985 as successor to the standard Mk 48. Developed from 1978 to counter the high-speed, deep-diving Project 705/Alfa SSN and other advanced Soviet submarines, its performance requirements were: (1) improve target acquisition range, (2) reduce the effect of enemy countermeasures, (3) minimize shipboard constraints such as warm-up and reactivation time, and (4) enhance effectiveness against surface ships.

Upgrades—hardware and software—to the ADCAP torpedoes are continuing in an effort to counter shallow-water, non-nuclear submarines. The Mod 6 ADCAP currently is in fleet service. The follow-on Mod 7 hardware upgrade known as Common Broadband Advanced Sonar System (CBASS) began development in FY 1998 to further enhance the torpedo's performance against SSNs and non-nuclear submarines employing advanced countermeasures.

Also see Improved Submarine-Launched Mobile Mine

(ISLMM) under Mines.

Design: The principal changes from the baseline Mk 48 to the ADCAP configuration were made to the torpedo's acoustic transducer (guidance) and control system. A higher-powered active sonar enables the torpedo to search a much greater volume of water to attain a target submarine. And the sonar is electrically steered, reducing the need for the torpedo to maneuver while searching. The torpedo retains the Gould (swashplate) motor, but with a larger fuel capacity. In November 1986, however, the Navy began seeking proposals for developing a quieter, closed-cycle propulsion system for the ADCAP, an apparent requirement in view of Soviet submarine quieting efforts.

The ADCAP program has suffered both delays and severe cost increases. In 1982, Chief of Naval Operations Admiral Thomas B. Hayward said the problems included (1) significant underestimation of the original research and development program, (2) the increasing scope of effort because of the evolving Soviet submarine threat, (3) an attempt to accelerate the IOC, (4) too little emphasis on cost control, and (5) the prime contractor (Hughes) being new to torpedo business and underestimating the effort required.

Reliability problems with the ADCAP surfaced in early 1991 but, according to Navy officials, were solved the following year. An under-ice capability has been provided in the ADCAP upgrade.

In 1995, the Navy proposed an upgrade to the ADCAP propulsion program to enhance the torpedo's effectiveness against diesel-electric submarines operating in littoral or shallow water. The upgrade would have quieted the torpedo's engine sounds and thus reduced the range at which an adversary would be alerted to an attack and able to undertake evasive action or counterfire. An analysis by the General Accounting Office stated:

> because of the short ranges at which diesel submarines are likely to be detected in littoral or shallow water, the technological improvement to be contributed by the propulsion upgrade—that is, torpedo quieting—will neither improve the performance of the ADCAP nor reduce the vulnerability of the launching submarine to enemy attack. Moreover, the Commander, Operational Test and Evaluation Force, already considers the current ADCAP operationally suitable and effective in shallow water, and the Navy did not establish a requirement to improve the ADCAP's propulsion system for use in open ocean, deep water in its operational requirements document for the upgrade.[23]

Status: Operational. IOC was in 1988. The Mk 48 ADCAP orig-

23 General Accounting Office, *Navy Torpedo Programs: MK-48 ADCAP Upgrades Not Adequately Justified*, GAO/NSIAD-95-104, June 1995, p. 1.

inally was manufactured by Westinghouse and Hughes Aircraft. Upgrades are continuing (Raytheon); Mod 7 CBASS modifications are scheduled for implementation on 513 torpedoes from FY 2005 to FY 2009.

Weight:	3,450 lb (1,564 kg)
Diameter:	21 in (533 mm)
Length:	19 ft 2 in (5.8 m)
Propulsion:	piston engine (liquid monopropellant fuel); pump-jet
Speed:	max. 55 knots
Range:	approx. 35,000 yds (32,012 m)
Guidance:	wire + active/passive acoustic homing
Warhead:	approx. 650 lb (295 kg) PBXN-103 high explosive
Platforms:	*submarines* SSN/SSBN

Mk 48 HEAVY TORPEDO

This was the latest weapon in a long series of heavy torpedoes, 21 inches (533 mm) in diameter with a length of up to 21 feet (6.4 m). Successor to the Mk 37, which remains in foreign naval service, the Mk 48 also replaced the Mk 45 ASTOR (Anti-Submarine Torpedo), the U.S. Navy's only nuclear torpedo, which was in service from 1958 to 1977 with a W34 warhead. The long range and improved guidance of the Mk 48 made it as effective with a large conventional warhead as the Mk 45 in most situations. In addition, the Mk 48's anti-surface-ship capability was considered sufficient to enable cancellation of the purely anti-surface Mk 47 torpedo.

Development of the Mk 48 began in the early 1960s as the Navy-sponsored Research Torpedo Configuration (RETORC) project of the Applied Research Laboratory of Pennsylvania State University and Westinghouse Electric Corp. (Baltimore, Maryland). The project initially was designated Ex-10. This effort led to the Mk 48 Mod 0 torpedo with a turbine propulsion system, which subsequently was refined into the Mk 48 Mod 2.

In 1967, Gould Corp. of Cleveland, Ohio, and the Naval Surface Warfare Center (White Oak, Maryland) began developing the Mod 1 with a redesigned acoustic homing guidance and a piston (swash-plate) engine. This torpedo uses an Otto fuel that contains its own oxidizer for combustion. After evaluation of the two versions, the Mod 1 was selected for production by Gould for fleet use.

Design: The Mk 48 had a guidance wire that spun out simulta-

neously from the submarine and the torpedo to permit the submarine to exercise control over the "fish," at least during the initial stages of its run. The Mod 3 introduced several improvements, including TELECOM (Telecommunications) to provide two-way data transmissions between submarine and torpedo; thus, the torpedo could transmit acoustic data back to the submarine for processing. See the Mk 48 ADCAP listing for basic characteristics.

The Mod 4 version was an upgrade to provide more capability against the Alfa-class and other advanced Soviet SSNs.

The Mk 48 is used in Australian, Canadian, and Dutch submarines.

Status: The Mk 48 has been succeeded in U.S. service by the Mk 48 ADCAP. IOC was in 1972.

Mk 46 LIGHTWEIGHT TORPEDO

The Mk 46 is a lightweight torpedo intended for use against submarines by helicopters, aircraft, and surface ships. It also was fitted in the CAPTOR deep-water mine.

The lightweight torpedo concept dates to the late 1940s, when it was envisioned that future convoys would be protected from submarine attack by helicopters with dipping sonar and airships (blimps) with towed sonar. For this application, light weight (initially a maximum of 350 pounds/159 kg) became a primary consideration. In addition, because the concept would require large num-

The basic Mk 48 torpedo, showing the shrouded propeller or "propulsor" configuration. The Mk 48 torpedo is in service with Australian, Canadian, and Dutch submarines. (Gould)

A Mk 48 ADCAP heavy torpedo "in flight" as it is being loaded into a submarine. It is the only torpedo now carried in U.S. submarines. (U.S. Navy)

bers of torpedoes, cost also was an important factor.

Subsequently, surface combatants were fitted with "short" torpedo tubes for launching these weapons and the ASROC was fitted with the lightweight torpedo. The first lightweight ASW torpedo to enter fleet service was the Mk 43 Mod 1 (260 lb/118 kg) in 1951, followed by the Mod 3, then the Mk 44 Mod 0 (425 lb/193 kg) introduced in 1957, and later the Mk 44 Mod 1. The Mk 46 is thus the third generation of lightweight ASW torpedoes.

The Navy procured kits to convert 172 Mk 46 torpedoes to function as anti-torpedo weapons as part of the Surface Ship Torpedo Defense (SSTD) project.

The Mk 46 was developed by the Naval Ordnance Test Station (Pasadena, California) and Aerojet General (Azusa, California). Subsequent production was undertaken at the Naval Ordnance Plant (Forest Park, Illinois) and Honeywell, as well as at Aerojet. The Mk 46 has a higher speed, twice the range, deeper operating depth, and better acoustic performance than its predecessor, the Mk 44.

Design: Mk 46 propulsion is provided by a thermal piston engine, with the Mod 0 using a solid propellant grain and the Mod 1 having a liquid monopropellant fuel, the latter providing improved performance. The Mod 2 introduced the PBXN-103 warhead (providing 27 percent more explosive power over the Mods 0/1). There was no Mod 3 torpedo.

The Mod 4 version of the Mk 46 was especially configured for the CAPTOR naval mine. In 1981, Secretary of Defense Harold Brown stated that "because the existing Mk 46 torpedo will not meet the submarine acoustic and countermeasures threat through the early 1980s, we have budgeted for a new version called the Near-Term Torpedo Improvement Program (NEARTIP)." This program included modification kits for earlier Mk 46s, as well as new torpedo procurement. The NEARTIP, or Mod 5, has an improved sonar transducer, new guidance and control group, and engine upgrades. Overall performance and shallow-water effectiveness are enhanced with these changes.

Status: Operational. IOC of the Mod 0 was in October 1965; Mods 1 and 2 in 1967. The last Mk 46 Mod 5 torpedoes were delivered to the U.S. Navy in 1992; they were produced by Alliant Techsystems, which was part of the defense-product spinoff from Honeywell in October 1990. In addition, Alliant produced several hundred conversion kits for the Navy to upgrade earlier Mod 1 and Mod 2 torpedoes to the Mod 5 configuration, which now is in U.S. service. The data below are for the Mod 5.

The U.S. Navy plans to retire the Mk 46 about 2015. It is used by numerous other countries.

Weight:	517.65 lb (234.8 kg)	
Diameter:	12¾ in (324 mm)	
Length:	8 ft 6 in (2.6 m)	
Propulsion:	reciprocating external combustion engine (liquid monopropellant)	
	contrarotating propellers	
Speed:	approx. 45 knots maximum	
Range:	approx. 8,000 yd (7.3 km)	
Guidance:	active/passive acoustic homing	
Warhead:	approx. 95 lb (43 kg) PBXN-103 high explosive	
Platforms:	Mod 4	CAPTOR mine
	Mod 5 *aircraft*	P-3C
		MH-60R
		SH-60B/F
	ships	cruisers
		destroyers
		frigates

ANTI-SURFACE WARFARE TORPEDO

The Navy promulgated a requirement for a low-cost, anti-surface ship torpedo on 2 December 1985 at the urging of then-Secretary of the Navy John Lehman. The torpedo was intended for use

A VLA rising from a VLS cell of the destroyer ELLIOT (DD 967). The exhaust is being vented at left. Vertical launch provides many advantages over conventional, above-deck missile launchers. The ASROC box launchers that long adorned U.S. warships have been discarded. (Loral)

The portside Mk 32 torpedo tubes on the destroyer ARLEIGH BURKE. These triple tubes, which rotate outboard for launching, can fire the Mk 46, Mk 50, or Mk 54 lightweight torpedo. The tubes are reloaded by hand. (Stephan Terzibaschitsch)

The contrarotating propellers of the Mk 46 lightweight torpedo are clearly visible in this view of the weapon fitted to an SH-3D Sea King helicopter. (U.S. Navy)

Mk 46 torpedoes rest side by side in the weapons bay of a P-3 Orion maritime patrol/ASW aircraft. Parachute packs are fitted to the rear of the torpedoes to slow their entry into the water. (U.S. Navy)

The destroyer PREBLE (DDG 88) launches a Mk 46 Mod 5 light-weight torpedo during an exercise. These weapons are far more effective when launched from an H-60 series helicopter or P-3C Orion maritime patrol/ASW aircraft than from a destroyer's deck. (U.S. Navy/ Ramon Preciado)

against surface ships that did not require the more complex (and higher cost) Mk 48 ADCAP torpedo, which was developed specifically for attacking maneuvering submarines, a much more difficult target.

Known as the "no frills" torpedo, the ASUW weapon encountered delays primarily because of contractual requirements for potential contractors, such as each finalists having to provide seven test torpedoes at its own expenses for a "swim-off" competition. The torpedo also was opposed by the submarine community, which questioned the utility of such a weapon, especially as it would have displaced Mk 48 torpedoes and other weapons in the limited reload space in attack submarines.

The ASUW torpedo had a program goal of 2,000 weapons at a cost of $200,000 each (compared to the $2.43 million unit cost for the Mk 48 ADCAP torpedo in the FY 1988 budget, plus continuing research and development costs). The initial procurement was set for FY 1987 with 34 torpedoes, but the program was canceled after Mr. Lehman's departure from office in 1986.

CHAPTER 31

Electronics Systems

Modern warships are inundated with electronic antennas, as those shown here on an Aegis missile cruiser. These electronic systems provide numerous capabilities to warships, but also create significant vulnerabilities. (N. Polmar)

The U.S. Navy is heavily dependent on electronic systems for navigation, communications, reconnaissance, surveillance, and, most especially, combat operations. The last includes both offensive and defensive operations. This chapter lists the principal electronic warfare systems, radars, sonars, torpedo countermeasures, and weapon control systems now fitted in U.S. surface ships and submarines. Helicopter-carried sonars employed in Anti-Submarine Warfare (ASW) and Mine Countermeasures (MCM) are listed, as they are extensions of shipboard systems. Sonobuoys and seafloor surveillance systems are listed as sub-sets of the sonar entries.

ELECTRONIC DESIGNATIONS

Most U.S. Navy electronic systems are identified by the joint electronics type designation system shown in Figure 31-1. This scheme previously was called the joint Army–Navy nomenclature system, and the three-letter-plus-number designations still are prefixed by

the AN/ of the World War II era. In this volume, the AN/ is omitted, except in the entry headings. The electronic systems designated in various mark (Mk) series do not have the AN/ prefix.

Variants of basic electronic equipment generally are indicated by suffix letters or (V)-series numbers.

SHIPBOARD ELECTRONIC WARFARE SYSTEMS

Electronic Warfare (EW) consists of efforts to detect, locate, exploit, reduce, or prevent an enemy's use of the electromagnetic spectrum and actions that retain one's own use. There are several categories of electronic warfare:

- Electronic Support Measures (ESM)
- Signals Intelligence (SIGINT)
- Electronic Countermeasures (ECM)
- Electronic Counter-Countermeasures (ECCM)

Figure 31-1. Explanation of Symbols

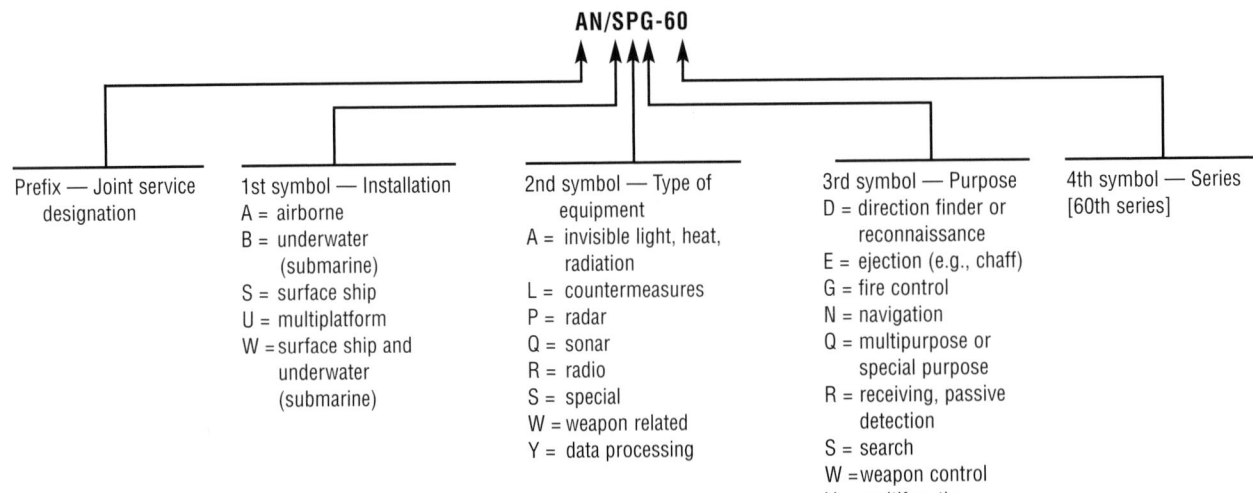

Because EW deals with electromagnetic energy and not just electronics, also included are infrared, laser, and optical systems. However, radiation produced by nuclear weapons usually is classified as nuclear effects and not EW.

Electronic Support Measures. ESM activities are the portion of EW that seeks to detect, intercept, locate, record, and analyze enemy electromagnetic radiations. Thus, ESM provides the information required to conduct electronic countermeasures and counter-countermeasures for immediate threat recognition. Generally passive, ESM seeks to detect the enemy by "listening" to his radio and radar emissions.

ESM systems are fitted in ships, submarines, aircraft, and ashore. Being passive, ESM offers a number of obvious tactical advantages: it permits the collection platform to remain electronically silent, and it can detect a hostile radar transmission beyond the radar's detection range because the radar requires much of its power to return a signal to the transmitter after it detects a target.

There are highly specialized—and highly classified—ESM systems, such as the ALR-series receivers in the Navy's EP-3E Orion aircraft that support fleet operations.

ESM capabilities also are incorporated into multifunction systems. For example, according to published Navy manuals, a submarine of the LOS ANGELES (SSN 688) class has the following equipment for the collection of Electronic Intelligence (ELINT), including Acoustic Intelligence (ACINT) and Communications Intelligence (COMINT):

• BQQ-5/BQQ-10 sonar systems, which have passive classification processors that can continuously evaluate low-frequency acoustic transmissions from other sonars
• BLD-1 radio direction finder
• BRD-7 radio direction finder
• WLR-8 receiver, which can detect enemy fire control radars, as well as radio communication frequencies (reportedly having a 50 MHz to 18 GHz frequency range)
• WLR-9 acoustic intercept receiver, which can detect active search sonars and acoustic-homing torpedoes
• WLR-10 countermeasures

Several of these systems are multipurpose, especially the BQQ-5/BQQ-10, which are the submarine's tactical sonars, having both active and passive modes. Additional ESM equipment can be installed in submarines for special collection missions.

Electronic surveillance and collection equipment have special design characteristics, among them:

• *Wide spectrum or bandwidth capability*—Because the frequency of a foreign radar may not be known before it is detected, a wide bandwidth should be covered. With modern technology, this means a frequency spectrum from 30 MHz to 50 GHz. This range is too large for a single receiver; thus, systems must use several receivers with different frequency ranges or a single receiver in which different tuning units can be inserted to cover the frequency range.

• *Wide dynamic range*—The ESM receiver must be able to receive both very weak and very strong signals. The receiver may be at different distances from different signals at the same time, and widely dissimilar signals could impair both collection and analysis unless the equipment is designed specifically for the role.

• *Unwanted signal rejection*—This characteristic, also called narrow band pass, enables the receiver to discriminate between the target frequency and signals at other, nearby frequencies.

• *Good angle-of-arrival measurement*—The ability of a receiver to accurately take bearings on a distant transmitter permits different

Figure 31-2. Frequency Spectrum

Current Frequency Designations Used by USA and NATO	A	B	C	D	E	F	G	H	I	J	K	L	M	
Wavelength (cm)	300	200 150	100 75 60 50 40	30	20 15	10	6 5	3.75 3	2	1.5	1 0.75	0.6 0.5 0.4	0.3	
Frequency (GHz)	0.1 0.15 0.2	0.3 0.4 0.5 0.6 0.75	1	1.5	3	5 6 8.0	10	15	20	30	40	50 60 70	100	
Previous Frequency Designations*	VHF	UHF	L	S	C	X	Ku	K	Ka	Millimeter				
Frequency Designations (WW II)	P	L	S	C	X	K	Q	V						

bearings (taken by the same or several surveillance platforms) to be plotted to give the precise location of the transmitter. Airborne, shipboard, or ground-based digital computers can be programmed to perform this function rapidly.

The receiver should be designed to immediately alert the operator to the presence of a signal of possible interest, to sort out the signal of interest, and to analyze it. The alerting and sorting are particularly important for airborne ESM because the platform may be exposed to the signal for a short time compared to a ship or shore facility, or the signal may be on the air for only a very short time. The current trend in ESM is to automatically record the intercepted signal for later analysis and, if appropriate, for reproduction for use in EW libraries.

The submarine is an excellent ESM platform because it is difficult to detect by conventional radar and visual means, and even by acoustic sensors under some conditions. And, of course, a submarine is not impeded by surface weather conditions. Submarines are particularly useful in gaining acoustic intelligence on enemy submarines.

The Navy's seafloor Sound Surveillance System (SOSUS) also provides an ACINT capability. In addition to being a peacetime warning system of submarine movements, the SOSUS networks in the Atlantic, Pacific, and regional seas can record data on surface ship and submarine noise characteristics. Most of the Cold War–era SOSUS network has been dismantled during the past decade.

There have been several programs to expand such acoustic surveillance into areas where SOSUS was not available. During the Cold War, the U.S. Navy initiated a major program of ocean surveillance ships (designated T-AGOS) to tow acoustic arrays into remote areas (see Chapter 23). More recently, the Navy has undertaken development of rapidly deployable acoustic systems, including the Advanced Deployable System (ADS), which can be rapidly emplaced in crisis areas.

Specialized electronic reconnaissance aircraft have long conducted ESM missions along the peripheries of the Soviet Union (and now Russia), China, and North Korea. The current U.S. naval aircraft in this category is the EP-3E Orion, flown by Fleet Air Reconnaissance Squadrons (VQ) 1 and 2.[1] These aircraft also provide electronic surveillance of surface ships and submarines for fleet commanders. The primary advantage of ESM aircraft is their altitude, which permits them to detect distant electronic emissions, including those originating inside enemy territory.

Aircraft—and surface ships—also are used to stimulate enemy radars and communications near enemy territory. This stimulation enables the aircraft or ship to then record the electromagnetic responses of an enemy, i.e., which of their radars they turn on and which communications channels they use.

Signals Intelligence. SIGINT includes the collection of intelligence information for Navy and national requirements, including all COMINT, ELINT, ACINT, and Telemetry Intelligence (TELINT). The National Security Agency (NSA) is the national program manager for the collection, analysis, and dissemination of SIGINT; however, the platforms and personnel involved in SIGINT collection belong to the armed services, and some systems obviously have both ESM and SIGINT collection capabilities. Thus, the actual operation of SIGINT activities is conducted by the services, and in wartime, the operational control of some dedicated SIGINT platforms would be assigned to tactical commanders.

Surface warships are used extensively for SIGINT activity. Two U.S. destroyers engaged in SIGINT, the TURNER JOY (DD 951) and MADDOX (DD 731), on the so-called DeSoto patrols off the North Vietnamese coast in August 1964 were involved in incidents in the Gulf of Tonkin that led to a dramatic escalation of U.S. involvement in the Vietnam conflict.[2] Because of the hostile nature

of the North Vietnamese and the guerrilla war then going on, destroyers were deemed the appropriate ESM platforms.

In the supposedly more benign international waters off North Korea, the U.S. Navy carried naval and NSA teams on board the "passive" SIGINT surveillance ships BANNER (AGER 1) and PUEBLO (AGER 3), and the LIBERTY (AGTR 5) was used in 1967 to monitor Israeli communications during the Six-Day War. The United States and Soviet Union had long believed that such ships operated by the two superpowers were immune to hostile actions by the Third World. However, attacks on the PUEBLO and LIBERTY—the latter made mistakenly by Israeli air and naval forces—demonstrated otherwise. The U.S. Navy has ceased to operate such passive intelligence ships, although many of these intelligence collectors still are active in the Russian Navy. (They are designated AGI by NATO.)

Land-based aircraft, satellites, and ground intercept facilities also provide SIGINT collection of foreign naval activities.

Electronic Countermeasures. ECM are intended primarily to (1) detect threats to friendly forces and (2) inhibit or degrade the effectiveness of enemy weapons and sensors. Most surface warships, submarines, and combat aircraft have ECM systems to help protect them against hostile detection and attack. In addition, there are specialized ECM aircraft that assist other aircraft in penetrating heavily defended areas.

Different ECM techniques are used to reduce the effectiveness of enemy radars. The three basic techniques are to (1) interfere with the radar through jamming and deception; (2) change the electrical properties of the air between the radar and the (friendly) target, mainly through the use of chaff; and (3) change the reflective properties of the (friendly) target through radar-absorbing materials or paint or through electronic and mechanical echo (blip) enhancers or decoys.

Although the above discussion concentrates on ECM techniques against radar, to some extent these concepts are useable against electromagnetic communications and sonar. For example, the properties of shipboard noise can be reduced. Modern U.S. surface warships use the PRAIRIE (Propeller Air Ingestion Emission) and Masker systems, creating small air bubbles around the ship's hull and wake to reduce her acoustic signature. Advanced submarine hull designs reduce the noise created by submarine movement, and special internal mountings ("rafts") dampen propulsion and auxiliary machinery noises. Russian submarines also use anechoic coatings—which are intended to reduce the effectiveness of hostile acoustic homing torpedoes but also can reduce submarine-generated noises, as can polymers discharged from a submarine—and active noise-cancellation systems. Of course, surface ships, and especially submarines can slow or stop to reduce their self-generated noises.

There are a large number of threat warning and countermeasure systems in U.S. surface ships and submarines, most numbered in the SLQ and WLR series.

The U.S. Navy and Marine Corps fly the EA-6B Prowler in the ECM role; these aircraft support Air Force as well as naval operations. The EA-6B carries up to five ALQ-99 tactical jammer pods on its wings and fuselage. These pods each have an exciter/processor and a minicomputer to detect, identify, and jam a broad spectrum of hostile radars. The aircraft also has the ALQ-100 multiband

1 The ES-3A Shadow, a carrier-based aircraft that also flew in this role, was taken out of service in 1998; see Chapter 28.
2 On the night of 2-3 August 1964, the destroyer MADDOX was attacked by North Vietnamese motor torpedo boats; there was no attack made against the two U.S. destroyers on the night of 5-6 August 1964, although U.S. naval commanders thought the destroyers again were under torpedo boat attack.

Electronics-laden aircraft are indispensable for contemporary naval operations. These include this E-2C Hawkeye from Carrier Airborne Early Warning Squadron 123 and EA-6B Prowler from Electronic Attack Squadron 137, both embarked in the carrier ENTERPRISE (CVN 65). (U.S. Navy/Joshua E. Helgeson)

track breaking system and the ALQ-92 communications jammer. The EA-6B probably is the most capable EW aircraft in the West (Grumman had provided these systems in the Air Force EF-111A, but it has been retired). The basic EA-6B has had its frequency coverage extended through a series of updates (see Chapter 28). It is officially considered an "electronic attack" aircraft and can carry the AGM-88 High-speed Anti-Radiation Missile (HARM).

The EA-6B aircraft are flown by Marine Corps electronic attack squadrons (VMAQ) and by Navy carrier-based electronic attack (VAQ) squadrons. In 1995, the Navy and Air Force reached an agreement whereby the Navy would assume responsibility for all airborne ECM. This led to the retirement of the Air Force's 40 EF-111A Raven aircraft that were in service in 1995.[3]

The EA-6B is scheduled to be replaced in Navy and Marine Corps, and probably Unmanned Aerial Vehicles (UAVs).

Electronic countermeasures are costly, not only in resources (especially for research and development, as well as for production), but also because of tactical uncertainties and the limitations they impose. For example, it may be undesirable to employ ECM against an enemy's communications, for by doing so, one denies communications intercept to one's own side. Or by firing chaff and decoys to defend against a possible enemy missile attack, one can degrade one's own radar effectiveness.

In addition, ECM produces "soft kills," meaning it is not always possible for the ECM operator to determine if his efforts are successful. Those who allocate resources are not always anxious to spend funds on an ECM system that may, for example, be a counter to a threat the intelligence community predicts *may* have a certain capability. Somehow, it seems easier to buy a new ship, missile, or aircraft rather than a new "black box."

Electronic Counter-Countermeasures. ECCM are actions taken to retain the effectiveness of one's own use of the electromagnetic spectrum against hostile electronic warfare efforts.

A variety EW systems are fitted in aircraft, surface ships, and submarines.

AIEWS (ADVANCED INTEGRATED ELECTRONIC WARFARE SYSTEM)

The AIEWS is being developed as the Navy's next-generation integration EW system to counter 21st-century threats. Consisting of block upgrades to the SLQ-32(V) series, AIEWS is intended to detect, correlate, and identify threat emitters, and then to automatically employ shipboard countermeasures.

AIEWS has an "open architecture" that will allow technology insertion and facilitate the use of Commercial-off-the-Shelf (COTS) components. The block upgrades include improved control and display (employing the standard Navy UYQ-70 dual-display console), computer processing improvements, the ability to launch the Super Rapid Blooming Offboard Chaff (SRBOC), Nulka, and other decoys on radar track data, and the capability to incorporate high-gain sensitivity enhancements to improve SLQ-32 performance against evolving threats.[4]

The advanced SLY-2(V) antenna is associated with the AIEWS upgrades. That antenna initially was installed in the cruiser PHILIPPINE SEA (CG 58).

AIEWS also has been identified with the designation SLQ-54.

Prime contractor: Lockheed Martin

AN/APR-39A(V)1 PRIVATEER RADAR WARNING

The AN/APR-39 is a omnidirectional Radar Warning Receiver (RWR) fitted in the coastal patrol ships of the CYCLONE (PC 1) class. It was designed for helicopters and fixed-wing aircraft, including several types of Navy–Marine Corps helicopters.

The system can determine the frequency, Pulse Repetition Frequency (PRF), pulse width, persistence, and threshold power level of missiles and radars.

The APR-39(V)1 consists of a blade antenna, four spiral antennas in hemispheric radomes, two dual video receiver units, an indicator unit, an analog comparator, and a control unit.

Prime contractor:	E-Systems
Ships:	PC 1

ASTECS (ADVANCED SUBMARINE TACTICAL ESM COMBAT SYSTEM)
See AN/ULR-21 Classic Troll.

AN/BLD-1 RADIO DIRECTION FINDER

This is a mast-mounted radio direction finder. The BLD-1 and BRD-7 will be replaced by the Integrated ESM Mast (IEM) under development for submarines of the VIRGINIA (SSN 774) class. It is being backfitted in SSN 21 and those SSN 688 submarines fitted with Vertical Launching Systems (VLS).

Prime contractor:	Litton Amecon
Ships:	SSN 21
	SSN 774
	SSN 688

---

3 Grumman converted 42 EF-111A ECM aircraft from standard F-111A strike aircraft. This aircraft was developed and produced by General Dynamics under the controversial TFX program.

4 The existing Mk 36 SRBOC Decoy Launching System (DLS) in U.S. warships has been modified to launch Nulka decoys, being redesignated as the Mk 53 DLS.

AN/BLQ-SERIES ACOUSTIC COUNTERMEASURES

These are submarine systems that provide a variety of SIGINT and ECM capabilities against hostile sonars.

The BLQ-3 is a low-frequency acoustic jammer, BLQ-4 a high-frequency acoustic jammer, BLQ-5 a low-frequency acoustic repeater, BLQ-6 a high-frequency acoustic repeater, and BLQ-8 acoustic countermeasures.

The BLQ-10 is an advanced SIGINT system being installed in all SSN/SSBNs to replace older systems. It is configured for operations in littoral waters, as well as in the open ocean environment. This system also serves as a link to disseminate all submarine SIGINT to onboard and off-board networks.

The Engineering Development Model (EDM) of the BLQ-10 completed an operational deployment on the ANNAPOLIS (SSN 760) in 2000. The first production set was installed in the TUCSON (SSN 770) in 2001. It is scheduled to be fitted in all deploying SSNs by Fiscal Year (FY) 2008 and in all SSN/SSBNs by FY 2012.

Prime contractor:	General Electric, except BLQ-8 Bendix/Aerojet, BLQ-10 Lockheed Martin
Ships:	submarines

AN/BLR-SERIES RADAR WARNING RECEIVERS

Mast mounted, these systems provide warning of hostile radar emissions from aircraft, surface ships, or (surfaced) submarines.

The BLR-14 is known as the Submarine Acoustic Warfare System (SAWS). It provides an integrated receiver, processor, display, and countermeasure launch system.

Prime contractor:	BLR-1–10: various
	BLR-13: Kollmorgen
	BLR-14: Sperry
	BLR-15: Kollmorgen
Ships:	submarines

AN/BRD-7 RADIO DIRECTION FINDER

This is a mast-mounted radio direction finding system. In VLS-configured submarines, it is comounted with the BLD-1 antenna. Previous models have been phased out of U.S. Navy service.

Prime contractor:	Sanders
Ships:	SSN 688

AN/SLQ-32(V) ELECTRONIC COUNTERMEASURES

The principal U.S. surface ship ECM system is the SLQ-32 "design- to-cost" EW suite, currently installed in more than 170 U.S. Navy ships and Coast Guard cutters. Variations of this system are fitted in most surface combatant and amphibious ships, as well as in four fast combat support ships (AOE 1–4). The SLQ-32 is considered a short-range, omnidirectional, self-defense system that evaluates electronic emissions and can, in some versions, initiate countermeasures.

The several versions of the SLQ-32 are based on modular "building blocks" for different types of ships: The (V)1 provides warning, identification, and bearing of radar-guided cruise missiles and their launch platforms; the (V)2 has the (V)1 capability and expanded ESM capabilities. An add-on ECM transmitter called "Sidekick" is fitted to destroyers of the SPRUANCE (DD 963) class and frigates of the OLIVER HAZARD PERRY (FFG 7) class to augment the SLQ-32(V)2, creating the (V)5 version. The Sidekick is an active ECM system intended to confuse enemy threats. (It was designed, produced, and delivered by Raytheon within 11 weeks of the Navy request for the system.)

The (V)3 configuration combines the (V)1 and (V)2 capabilities and the means to counter or deceive missile guidance radars. The (V)3 has a quick-reaction mode that permits the initiation of jamming against a target signal before its characteristics are fully analyzed. This feature could be particularly useful against "pop-up"

submarine-launched missiles or those fired by missile craft hiding in coastal shore "clutter."

The (V)4 combines most features—active and passive—into a set intended for aircraft carriers, which had not initially been intended for SLQ-32 installation. These sets are provided in all aircraft carriers, as well as in the battleship WISCONSIN (BB 64). The other battleship remaining on the Naval Vessel Register (NVR), the IOWA (BB 61), has the SLQ-32(V)3.

The SLQ-32 antennas are fitted in two box-like enclosures, to port and starboard, high in the ship's superstructure. The (V)2 and (V)3 are fitted with twin Rotman lens direction-finding receiving antennas. The SLQ-32 systems employ UYK-19 computers.

The proposed follow-on system to the SLQ-32 series is the Advanced Integrated Electronic Warfare System (AIEWS). The AIEWS upgrades are planned to counter hostile threats of the early 21st century. (See separate entry.)

The SLQ-32 and other ECM systems are used in conjunction with SRBOC and Nulka launchers that fire either semiautomatically or on manual direction from a ship's ECM operators. Large ships have four Mk 36 launchers and smaller ships have two, each consisting of six fixed barrels. (Infrared decoys and flares also can be fired in response to detections by threat warning devices.)

The ALQ-142 fitted in SH-60B helicopters is similar to the SLQ-32, with two Rotman lens antennas; data are transmitted via data link to ships fitted with the SLQ-32.

The bands covered by the SLQ-32 are:
- (V)1   H/I/J
- (V)2/5 B through J
- (V)3/4 B through J; countermeasures in H/I/J

Prime contractor:	Raytheon		
	Hughes		
Ships:	(V)1	LPD 4	LKA 113
		LSD 41	AOE 1 (some ships)
	(V)2	DDG 51–67	AGF 11
		LSD 49	FFG 7 (some ships)
	(V)3	BB 61	LCC 19
		CG 47	AGF 3
		DDG 79	LHD 1
		DDG 68+	LHA 1
		DDG 963	LPD 17
	(V)4	CV/CVN	
	(V)5	FFG 7 (some ships)	
		AOE 1 (some ships)	

Antenna for the SLQ-32(V)3 ECM suite on the cruiser GETTYSBURG (CG 64). The SLQ-32 systems are fitted in all active cruisers, destroyers, frigates, amphibious ships, and the Navy-manned fast combat support ships (AOE), as well as aircraft carriers. (N. Polmar)

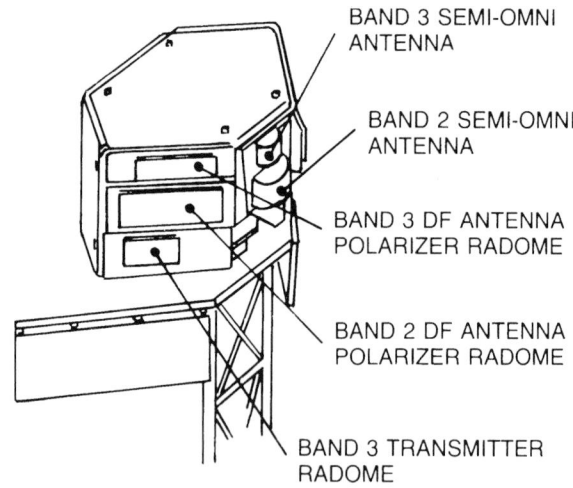

BAND 3 SEMI-OMNI ANTENNA

BAND 2 SEMI-OMNI ANTENNA

BAND 3 DF ANTENNA POLARIZER RADOME

BAND 2 DF ANTENNA POLARIZER RADOME

BAND 3 TRANSMITTER RADOME

SLQ-32(V)5 ECM system antenna in a frigate of the OLIVER HAZARD PERRY (FFG 7) class. There is an SLQ-32(V)2 antenna mounted on a pedestal above the smaller "Sidekick" antenna. The latter is an add-on ECM transmitter that enhances the SLQ-32's capabilities. (Raytheon)

AN/SLQ-25A NIXIE TORPEDO COUNTERMEASURES

See page 567.

AN/SLR-25(V)2 SSEE (SHIP SIGNAL EXPLOITATION EQUIPMENT)

The SLR-25(V)2 SSEE is Phase 2 of a program to provide surface ships with threat identification information. SSEE also provides cuing to radio direction finding assets. When paired with a Transportable–Radio Direction Finding (T-RDF) system, SSEE gives the supported ship commanding officer or embarked unit commander a comprehensive and complete SIGINT capability.

SSEE is a COTS program that is easily reconfigured and therefore able to respond rapidly to changes in threat tasking.

SSEE Phase 1 is installed in the command ship MOUNT WHITNEY (LCC 20) and three amphibious assault ships (LHA).

SSEE Increment B is installed in 14 Aegis cruisers of the TICONDEROGA (CG 47) class, the command ship BLUE RIDGE (LCC 19), and one LHD amphibious assault ship. SSEE Increment D(2) is on board the other 11 TICONDEROGAS and one command ship (AGF). Additional ships are to be fitted with Increment D(3). Previously, it was fitted in 13 destroyers of the SPRUANCE (DD 963) class.

Prime contractor:	Navy Space and Warfare Systems Command (SPAWAR)
Ships:	see text

AN/SLR-25(V)1 ACCESS (ADVANCED CRYPTOLOGIC CARRY-ON EXPLOITATION SYSTEM)

ACCESS is a "carry-on" cryptologic exploitation capability for ships not equipped with a permanent cryptologic capability. ACCESS hardware and software are similar to those of the SLR-25(V)2 SSEE system (see above), with minor hardware differences to facilitate rapid shipboard installation and removal.

The SLR-25(V)1 provides front-end sensor (receiver) and controls/monitors for tactical surveillance and targeting, as well as passive detection, classification, and tracking of selected targets at extended range. It also provides tools for the interpretation and reporting of intercepted data, geographic plot and analysis, and track correlation. When ACCESS is paired with a T-RDF system, the supported ship commanding officer or embarked unit commander has a comprehensive SIGINT capability.

The ships listed below have been modified to be fitted with ACCESS.

Prime contractor:	SPAWAR
Ships:	DDG 51 (some ships)
	LPD 4
	LSD 41 (some ships)

AN/SLR-24 TORPEDO COUNTERMEASURES

See page 567.

AN/SLR-23 RADIO DIRECTION FINDER

Associated with the WLR-1 and SLQ-32 systems, the SLR-23 intercepts signals in the D/E/J bands.

Prime contractor:	Southwest Research
Ships:	surface ships

AN/SRS-1 COMBAT DIRECTION-FINDING RECEIVER

A less-capable version of the SSQ-108 Classic Outboard system, the SRS-1 is intended to detect anti-ship missiles; it also is a component of Classic Outboard.

The basic SRS-1 is designated Block 0; the Block 1 (SRS-1A) incorporates the automated digital acquisition subsystem to enable the exploitation of unconventional and low-probability-of-intercept signals.

Several shore sites also are fitted with the Block 1 system.

Prime contractor:	Lockheed Sanders
Ships:	DDG 72
	LHD 1

AN/SSQ-108(V) CLASSIC OUTBOARD SIGINT SYSTEM

Classic Outboard was a Navy shipboard direction-finding system that provided signals acquisition and direction-finding systems (SRS-1) with the capability to detect, locate, and identify hostile targets at long-range and to input this data into the ship's tactical data system. This widely deployed system consists of a Very High Frequency (VHF) Adcock direction-finding antenna and 24 small, deck-edge antennas for low/medium/high-frequency band direction finding.

The SSQ-108 succeeded the older SSQ-72 and SSQ-74 Classic Outboard systems.

It was mounted on several destroyers of the SPRUANCE class.

The SRD-19 was associated with the SSQ-72 system.

AN/ULR-21 CLASSIC TROLL

Formerly known as the Advanced Submarine Tactical ESM Combat System (ASTECS), the ULR-21 is an ESM system for detection, identification, and direction finding for radar and communication signals emanating from ships, aircraft, and submarines. It is being developed for submarines of the VIRGINIA class. Reportedly, it provides broader ESM functions than the WLR-8 in the LOS ANGELES class or the WLQ-4 in the SEAWOLF (SSN 21) class.

The ULR-21 will be a component of the Integrated ESM Mast developed for the VIRGINIA class.[5]

Prime contractor:	Lockheed Martin
Ships:	SSN 774

AN/WLQ-4(V)1 SEA NYMPH

This submarine ESM system identifies the type and source of radar and communications signals. It can operate fully or semiautomatically; in the semiautomatic mode, an operator can direct the correlation of signals detected by the WLQ-4 with data collected by other sensors.

The WLQ-4 has up to six operator positions; it uses the UYK-44 (formerly UYK-20) computer.

Prime contractor:	GTE
Ships:	SSN 21

AN/WLR-13 INFRARED/ELECTRO-OPTICAL WARNING

This system is intended to warn surface ships of attack by anti-ship missiles fitted with infrared and electro-optical guidance systems.

Prime contractor:	
Ships:	surface ships

AN/WLR-11 RADAR WARNING/SIGINT SYSTEM

Prime contractor:	ARGO Systems
Ships:	surface ships

AN/WLR-10 RADAR WARNING RECEIVER

This is a submarine radar warning receiver fitted to a retractable mast in missile and attack submarines; it is collocated with the WLR-8. It is a modified version of the WLR-10 previously fitted in ballistic missile submarines of the LAFAYETTE (SSBN 616) class.

Prime contractor:	Astro Labs
Ships:	SSBN 726
	SSN 688

AN/WLR-9 SONAR WARNING RECEIVER

Prime contractor:	Norden (United Technologies)
Ships:	submarines

AN/WLR-8(V) RADAR WARNING RECEIVER

This receiver provides coverage of 0.5–18 GHz frequencies. A surface ship version was canceled in 1983, although it was installed in the ENTERPRISE (CVN 65) and subsequently removed. Trident missile submarines have the (V)5 and LOS ANGELES-class submarines have the (V)2 version.

Prime contractor:	GTE-Sylvania
Ships:	SSBN 726
	SSN 688

AN/WLR-6 WATERBOY RADAR WARNING, SIGNAL COLLECTION

Prime contractor:	GTE-Sylvania
Ships:	submarines
	surface ships

AN/WLR-1 RADAR WARNING

This is a widely used radar warning receiver fitted in surface ships and submarines. It originally covered the 50 MHz to 10.75 GHz frequency range; most sets now in use are WLR-1H versions and cover 0.55–20 GHz. It is employed with the WLR-11.

The WLR-1H(V)5 performs Over-the-Horizon (OTH) cued detection, classification, and targeting, as well as area surveillance and threat warning. This version has a single package antenna to replace the original suite of four antennas used with the WLR-1H(V)3 version. The new suite offers improved reliability and a significant reduction in mast weight.

Prime contractor:	
Ships:	SSN 688
	surface ships
	Coast Guard cutters

AN/WLY-1

The WLY-1 acoustic interception and countermeasures system provides the OHIO (SSBN 726)-class ballistic missile submarines with an automatic response against torpedo attack. The system is proposed as a replacement for the WLR-9A/12 acoustic intercept system fitted in the LOS ANGELES-class SSNs.

In addition to providing the detection, classification, and tracking of torpedo threats, the WLY-1 includes a control subsystem for the launch management of torpedo countermeasures.

It may be retrofitted into attack submarines.

Prime contractor:	Norden/Allied Signal
Ships:	SSBN 726

MK 70 MOSS (MOBILE SUBMARINE SIMULATOR)

MOSS is a torpedo-like decoy launched from submarine torpedo tubes to simulate the acoustic signatures of a submarine. Although MOSS has been out of service for several years, 310 units are in long-term storage at Keyport, Washington.

MOSS is a 10-inch (254-mm) diameter projectile that is packed in tandem racks for launching from 21-inch torpedo tubes.

Prime contractor:	Gould Electronics
Ships:	SSBN 726

---

5 The IEM is to replace the BLD-1 and BRD-7/8 mast-mounted electronic systems.

A pair of Mk 70 MOSS acoustic decoys are loaded into an attack submarine. These decoys, now in storage, were developed for use by ballistic missile submarines. (U.S. Navy)

MK 23 TORPEDO DECOY

This device is launched from submarine signal ejection tubes.

Prime contractor:	
Ships:	SSN

SHIPBOARD RADARS

U.S. Navy shipboard radars are used for surface and air search, height finding, weapons fire control, target illumination, navigation, and aircraft control. In a few radars, two functions can overlap, with the advanced SPY series providing multiple radar functions in a single system.

The small combatants of the CYCLONE class have commercial radars and sonar; see Chapter 21.

Aircraft control radars are unique to aviation ships (CV/CVN/LHA/LHD) and are designated in the SPN series, informally referred to as "spin" radars. They are used to guide aircraft into the proper approach pattern or glide path to the ship. The SPN radars are listed in Table 31-1.

Table 31-1. AIR CONTROL RADARS

Radar	Role	Frequency	Ships
SPN-35A	aircraft marshalling	X	LHA/LHD
SPN-42A*	Carrier Controlled Approach (CCA)	K	CV/CVN
SPN-43B/C	air control	S	CV/CVN/LHA/LHD
SPN-44	landing aid	X	CVN 68, CV 63
SPN-46	CCA	Ka/X	CV/CVN
SPN-47	CCA/Precision Approach Landing System (PALS)		LHD

Designations: Fire control radars were assigned mark (Mk) numbers beginning in 1941. This series ran through Mk 47, with the next radar initiating the SPG series. Subsequently, later versions of some earlier radars were given the SPG prefix; thus, the Mk 35 and SPG-35 were the same radar.

AN/BPS-16 RADAR

This is an advanced submarine search and navigation radar. It was evaluated in the ATLANTA (SSN 712) in 1991–1992. The BPS-16 has an outer "sleeve" that mounts the radar and reduces problems with retraction equipment and leakage. It also has multiple frequencies, which reduces the unique signature common to previous BPS-series radars that enabled a hostile ESM system to easily identify submarine radar emissions.

The system has been in service since 1991.

Prime contractor:	Sperry
Band:	X
Ships:	SSBN 726 (some ships)
	SSN 21
	SSN 688 (some ships)

AN/BPS-15 RADAR

This is a submarine search and navigation radar. The BPS-15 has replaced all older radars in U.S. submarines, except for later units of the OHIO class and the SEAWOLF class. The principal differences among the various BPS-series radars are their different pedestal mountings. Peak power is 35 kW.

Prime contractor:	Sperry
Band:	X
Ships:	BPS-15A/E/H: SSN 688 (some ships)
	BPS-15B: SSBN 726–740

MFR (MULTI-FUNCTION RADAR)

See SPY-3 MFR, page 551.

Sailors aboard the carrier HARRY S. TRUMAN (CVN 75) perform maintenance on the ship's SPN-43 aircraft traffic control/marshalling radar. (U.S. Navy/Andrea Decanini)

A technician aboard the amphibious assault ship BATAAN (LHD 5) performs a check on the massive antenna for the SPN-43B aircraft control radar. This radar is found on all U.S. aircraft carriers and LHA/LHD-type ships. (U.S. Navy/M. Dennis Timms)

A BPS-series radar fitted in the attack submarine TOLEDO *(SSN 769). The antenna retracts into the submarine's sail, forward of the open cockpit. The sub is rigged for surface running with plug-in instruments visible in the cockpit; a portable radar screen is at left. (U.S. Navy/David C. Lloyd)*

AN/SPG-62 RADAR

This is the illumination radar for the Standard SM-2 missile in Aegis warships. The Aegis ships have three (DDG 51 class) or four (CG 47 class) Mk 99 missile control directors that use the SPG-62 illumination channel to provide radar reflections for Standard missiles. They are "slaved" to the SPY-1 radar. The antenna is 7½ feet (2.3 m) wide. Peak power is 10 kW.

The system has been operational since 1983.

Prime contractor:	Raytheon
Band:	X
Ships:	CG 47/52
	DDG 51

AN/SPG-60 RADAR

The SPG-60 radar both provided gun control data and permitted Standard-MR missile tracking with the addition of an illuminator to the Mk 86 Fire Control System (FCS). The SPG-60 was a monopulse, pulse-Doppler radar combined with the SPQ-9A in the Mk 86 weapon control system; it could illuminate targets for Standard and Sea Sparrow missiles. Thus, this single fire control system could serve several functions. The X-band SPG-60 was credited with a nominal range of some 50 nm (92.5 km) and is able to track Mach 3 targets out to 100 nm (185 km). (The Mk 86 system can simultaneously track up to 120 incoming targets in a track-while-scan mode.)

It was fitted in SPRUANCE-class destroyers.

The Separate Target Illumination Radar (STIR) using the SPG-60 antenna mount is found in the OLIVER HAZARD PERRY-class frigates to provide two missile control channels for the Mk 86.

AN/SPG-53E RADAR

This is a fire control radar fitted in some IOWA-class battleships for use with the Mk 37 gunfire director for their 5-inch (127-mm) dual-purpose guns. Most directors in these ships had the Mk 25 radar (see below).

Range is about 120,000 yards (110 km). Peak power is about 250 kW.

Prime contractor:	Western Electric
Band:	X
Ships:	BB 61

AN/SPG-51D RADAR

The SPG-51 was a C/X-band pulse-Doppler tracking/illumination radar used with the Standard-MR in cruisers and destroyers armed with that missile. (It originally was developed for use with the Tartar missile). It was associated with the Mk 74 missile FCS. (The two operating modes shared a common antenna.)

Operational since 1960, the SPG-51 has been phased out of service with the retirement of older missile-armed ships.

The two after SPG-62 illumination radars in the destroyer ROSS *(DDG 71); there is another SPG-62 forward. Aegis missile cruisers have four SPG-62s. The top of the ship's after Phalanx Close-In Weapon System (CIWS) is visible in the foreground. (Leo Van Ginderen)*

The forward mast of the destroyer PETERSON *(DD 969) shows the ship's SPQ-9B radome mounted beneath the circular SPG-60 fire control radar. Several electronic intercept and countermeasures antennas are mounted above the radars. (Leo Van Ginderen)*

SPG-53 radar antenna. The SPG-53E radar is used in place of the Mk 25 radar on the forward Mk 37 Gunfire Control System (GFCS) in battleships of the IOWA (BB 61) class. The 53E version has shell-splash and missile-launch alarm systems. (Giorgio Arra)

AN/SPQ-9B RADAR

This is a slotted, phased-array, rotating radar that provides a significant capability to detect and track low-altitude anti-ship cruise missiles in heavy sea-clutter environments. The SPQ-9B is a high-resolution, track-while-scan, pulse-Doppler system.

It was developed by the Navy with preproduction "kits" ordered from Westinghouse-Norden. The basic SPQ-9A reflector was replaced by a larger unit with multiple feeds, a new processor and receiver/exciter were provided, and the transmitter was replaced by an APG-68 radar transmitter as used in the F-16 Fighting Falcon aircraft.

A shore-based SPQ-9B Advanced Development Model (ADM) was tested at Wallops Island, Virginia, and subsequently was installed for at-sea tests in the ex-destroyer DECATUR (DD 936/DDG 31), which also served as a test hulk for the Ship Self-Defense System (SSDS). Subsequently, in 2002, the system was installed in the carrier NIMITZ (CVN 68) and the destroyer OLDENDORF (DD 972).

Prime contractor:	Northrop Grumman (Westinghouse-Norden)
Band:	X
Ships:	carriers
	LHD 1

AN/SPQ-9A RADAR

The SPQ-9A is the fire control radar associated with the Mk 86 Gunfire Control System (GFCS). It provides surface search functions, as well as weapons control, operating in a high-resolution, pulse-Doppler, track-while-scan mode. The SPQ-9A operates from a minimum of 150 yards (137 m) out to 20 nautical miles (37 km) to detect aircraft-size targets. The high scan rate of 60 revolutions per minute can detect and track incoming missiles, as well as aircraft and surface targets. The Mk 86 system with the SPG-60/SPQ-9 is found in new missile cruisers, the SPRUANCE-class destroyers, and the TARAWA (LHA 1)-class helicopter ships. The battleship IOWA mounted the SPQ-9A without the Mk 86 system.

The antenna is housed in a 120-inch (3-m) diameter plastic radome. Peak power is 1.2 kW.

The system has been operational since 1970.

Prime contractor:	Lockheed Electronics
Band:	X
Ships:	BB 61
	CG 47
	DD 963
	LHA 1

AN/SPS-69 RADAR

This solid-state radar is a modification of the commercial Raytheon R41X small craft navigation radar. Maximum power is 4 kW.

The Coast Guard has several hundred sets in service. It no longer is fitted in Navy ships.

The radar has been operational since 1990.

Prime contractor:	Raytheon
Band:	X
Ships:	Coast Guard cutters and craft

AN/SPS-67(V) RADAR

This is a surface search/navigation radar, developed as a successor to the long-serving and widely used SPS-10. The SPS-67 has a high degree of automation and can distinguish instantly between moving and stationary targets. It has solid-state electronics.

The (V)1 uses the SPS-10 antenna; (V)2 introduced a new antenna; and (V)3 adds automatic tracking and gunfire control. The (V)4 is a lightweight version with a bar-type antenna.

The SPS-67 has been operational since 1982.

Prime contractor:	DRS Systems (formerly AIL, Norden [United Technologies])	
Band:	C	
Ships:	aircraft carriers	LSD 41
	BB 61	LSD 49
	DDG 51	AH 19
	LCC 19	AOE 6
	LHD 1	

The SPS-67(V)4 bar-type radar antenna on the missile destroyer Ross. This radar is found on scores of U.S. ships of all military services. (Leo Van Ginderen)

AN/SPS-64(V) RADAR

This is a surface search/navigation radar. It uses a bar-type antenna; the size of the four available antennas vary from 4 feet (1.2 m) to 12 feet (3.7 m), depending on the capability and size of the system. Versions have different frequency bands and operating characteristics.

The commercial versions have a four-digit number following the letters RM. Its commercial name is Raypath.

The SPS-64 can automatically track up to 20 targets. The versions are listed below. All U.S. aircraft carriers, the IOWA-class battleships, and TICONDEROGA-class cruisers have the (V)9 version.

Version	Band	Transmitter	User
(V)1	S	single 20 kW transmitter	Coast Guard
(V)2, 3	S	two 20 kW transmitters	Coast Guard
(V)4	S/X	two 20 kW transmitters	Coast Guard
(V)5	X	single tunable 20 kW transmitter	Army
(V)6	X	single 50 kW transmitter	Coast Guard
(V)7, 8	S		Coast Guard
(V)9	X		Navy
(V)10, 11	S		Coast Guard
(V)12–14	X		Army
(V)15	X		Navy
(V)16, 17	X		Army
(V)18	X		Navy

Prime contractor:	Raytheon	
Band:	S and X	
Ships:	CVN 65	LPD 17
	CVN 68	LSD 41
	BB 61	LSD 49
	CG 47	MHC 51
	DDG 51	MCM 1
	DD 963	
	LCC 19	AE 26
	AGF 3	AOE 1
	AGF 11	AOE 6
	LHA 1	ARS 50
	LHD 1	

SPS-64(V)9 antenna. This search/navigation radar is used widely on Army, Navy, and Coast Guard ships and small craft. (Raytheon)

AN/SPS-59 RADAR

SPS-59 is the Navy designation for the LN-66 commercial navigation radar; both designations are used. This is a short-range navigation radar, adopted from a commercial design. It has been installed in a variety of U.S. ships, from battleships to small riverine craft. (The radar also was fitted in the now-discarded SH-2G LAMPS I ASW helicopter.)

The SPS-59 is being replaced by the SPS-69 and other, more-modern radars.

Prime contractor:	Canadian Marconi	
Band:	X	
Ships:	AD 37	AFS 1
	LKA 113	AO 177
	LCAC	

AN/SPS-55 RADAR

This surface search radar was developed as a replacement for the widely used SPS-10. The SPS-55 has a slotted-array antenna six feet (1.8 m) across.

Prime contractor:	Cordion	
Band:	X	
Ships:	CG 47	FFG 7
	DDG 51	MCM 1
	DD 963	AO 177

AN/SPS-49(V) RADAR

The most effective rotating two-dimensional (2-D) air search radar in the U.S. Navy is the SPS-49, a lower-L-band radar. It is the principal air search radar in most large U.S. warships and is a complementary radar to the SPY-1 in the TICONDEROGA class. The ARLEIGH BURKE (DDG 51) class does not have the SPS-49; it was deleted from the design primarily because of cost constraints.

The last SPRUANCE-class destroyer, the HAYLER (DD 997), had the SPS-40 replaced by an SPS-49 radar. The surveillance ship STALWART (T-AGOS 1) was fitted with an SPS-49(V)3 prior to being taken out of service.

The SPS-49 was evaluated in 1965 on board the experimental destroyer GYATT (DD 712), and an advanced version was installed in the guided missile cruiser DALE (CG 19) in 1975.

The SPS-49 is a very long range radar and has a narrow beam, which helps to counter hostile jamming efforts. Its large, 24 x 14 foot (7.3 x 4.3 m) antenna is easily identified, with a large, lower feed horn (the similar-looking SPS-40 antenna has an overhead feed horn). Frequency range is 851–942 MHz. This radar has high reliability.

The SPS-50 was a modified SPS-49 intended to replace the earlier SPS-6 and SPS-12 radars; it failed its operational evaluation.

The system has been operational since 1975.

Prime contractor:	Raytheon	
Band:	L	
Ships:	(V)1: LSD 41 (some ships)	
	(V)4: FFG 7 (some ships)	
	(V)5: carriers	
	BB 61	LHD 1
	LPD 17	LSD 41 (some ships)
	FFG 7 (some ships)	
	(V)6/7/8: CG 47	

The SPS-49 long-range search radar antenna on an Aegis missile cruiser of the TICONDEROGA (CG 47) class. This radar is an important complement to the ship's multifunction SPY-1 radar system. (N. Polmar)

AN/SPS-48 RADAR

The SPS-48 is a 3-D FRESCAN radar used for aircraft control in carriers and command ships and to support the air defense role of missile ships. The older SPS-48A sets were upgraded with Automatic Detection and Tracking (ADT) features and are designated SPS-48C. This radar is more capable than the SPS-52 and can support the longer-range Standard missiles.

The rectangular antenna is 17 × 17½ feet (5.2 × 5.3 m). The radar's frequency band is 2900–3100.5 MHz, and maximum range is about 220 nm (407 km).

The SPS-48 has been operational since 1962.

Prime contractor:	ITT Gilfillan
Band:	S
Ships:	SPS-48C: LCC 19
	SPS-48E: carriers
	LHA 1
	LPD 17
	LHD 1

The SPS-48E is the basic 3-D air search radar in several major ship classes. It also was fitted in several classes of now-retired guided missile ships. Note the asymmetrical configuration of the antenna; the bar above the main antenna is the radar's Identification Friend or Foe (IFF) antenna; the radar above it is an SPS-67. (Stephan Terzibaschitsch)

The SPS-49(V)5 antenna on the carrier JOHN C. STENNIS (CVN 74). Most aircraft carriers have the SPS-67 mounted on a pedestal aft of the island structure, although the KITTY HAWK (CV 63) and JOHN F. KENNEDY (CV 67) have their SPS-48E antennas mounted on the pedestal. (U.S. Navy/Brian D. Forsmo)

Rear aspect of an SPS-48E antenna. (Stephan Terzibaschitsch)

AN/SPS-40 RADAR

The SPS-40 is a widely used 2-D air search radar capable of very long detection ranges. It previously was fitted in about 125 cruisers, destroyers, and frigates, plus amphibious and auxiliary ships.

The only fleet auxiliary ships now carrying the SPS-40 are the replenishment ships SACRAMENTO (AOE 1) and CAMDEN (AOE 2). (The surveillance ship CAPABLE /T-AGOS 16 also was fitted with the SPS-40.)

The radar's frequency range is 400–450 MHz (UHF), and range against medium-size aircraft is 150–200 nm (280–370 km). The SPS-40B has been upgraded to the SPS-40C, with higher power and improved ECCM. The SPS-40E is an updated SPS-40B/C/D with a solid-state transmitter and very low failure rate. It rotates at six revolutions per minute.

The SPS-40 was developed from the SPS-31.

The system has been operational since 1961. It is being phased out of U.S. Navy service.

Prime contractor:	SPS-40B:	Norden (United Technologies)	
	SPS-40E:	Westinghouse	
Band:	B		
Ships:	DD 963		
	LPD 4	LCC 19	
	AGF 3	AGF 11	
		LHA 1	

The SPS-40 long-range air search radar is fitted in command and amphibious ships that do not have the later SPS-49 radar. It can be easily identified by the overhead feed-horn. (Leo Van Ginderen)

The SPS-10 has been aboard U.S. Navy ships for more than a half century, albeit in improved variants. (Giorgio Arra)

AN/SPS-10 RADAR

The most widely used post–World War II radar in the Navy was the SPS-10 surface search, found in most surface combatants, amphibious ships, and auxiliaries. Its 11-foot (3.35-m) wide antenna has been a familiar sight on U.S. and allied ships since late 1953. It generally is considered a horizon-range radar, although significantly longer-range detections are routinely made.

A few of the SPS-10E/F versions remain in U.S. Navy service, all in amphibious-type ships and fleet auxiliaries. The improved I-band SPS-55, similar to the SPS-10 but with higher resolution, and the solid-state SPS-67, using the same antenna, have replaced the SPS-10.

The SPS-10 has been operational since 1953.

Prime contractor:	GTE-Gilfillan	
	Raytheon	
Band:	C	
Ships:	AGF 3	AGF 11
	LKA 113	AS 39

AN/SPY-3 MFR (MULTI-FUNCTION RADAR)

The SPY-3 is an X-band solid-state, phased-array (fixed-antenna) radar planned to meet all horizon search and fire control requirements for 21st-century major warships. The radar is being designed from the outset to detect advanced low-observable anti-ship cruise missiles and to support fire-control illumination requirements for the Evolved Sea Sparrow Missile (ESSM), Standard SM-2/SM-3 missiles, and future missiles.

The MFR also supports new ship-design requirement for reduced radar cross section, reduced manning, and total ownership cost reduction. In particular, the SPY-3 is being engineered to preserve the low-observable (stealth) features of the DD(X). For that ship, the SPY-3 will have three "faces" to provide 360o coverage.

The SPY-3 is planned for introduction in the CVN 78 next-generation aircraft carriers and the DD(X) destroyers. It may be back-fitted into the NIMITZ-class carriers.[6]

A development contract for an MFR prototype was awarded to Raytheon in July 1999. The Engineering Manufacturing Development (EMD) model was delivered to Wallops Island, Virginia, in 2003 for continued contractor testing with Navy testing beginning in 2004. Planned fleet introduction is about 2013 in the DD(X).

Prime contractor:	Raytheon
Band:	X
Ships:	CVN 78
	DD(X)
	LHA (R)

---

6 Several efforts to backfit the SPY-1 radar into NIMITZ-class carriers were rejected based on cost.

A model of the SPY-3 Multi-Function Radar being developed for the next-generation major surface warships. The flat-array antennas will be fitted to all four sides of the ships' superstructure. (U.S. Navy)

SS-SPY (SOLID-STATE SPY) RADAR

The U.S. Navy revised its plan for advanced radars during 2004. The Solid-State SPY (SS-SPY) is being developed as the primary air and surface radar for the Navy's next-generation cruiser, the CG(X). It replaces the development effort previously designated SPY-2.

The SS-SPY is a multifunction, phased-array radar capable of search, detection, and tracking of air and surface targets and of supporting missile engagement. Employing the Extended-Range Active Missile (ERAM) SM-6, the radar will not be required to remain active during the intercept phase. The SS-SPY program is leveraging the considerable investment in the Army's Terminal High-Altitude Air Defense (THAAD), employing that system's technologies, especially software.[7]

The new radar is being developed competitively through two research and development programs: the S-band advanced radar prototype and the active S-band radar program for the Cobra Judy effort, which is developing a replacement platform for the USS OBSERVATION ISLAND (T-AGM 23); see Chapter 23.

Down select for the SS-SPY program is planned for 2009.

S-VSR (S-BAND VOLUME SEARCH RADAR)

This is an S-band phased-array radar designed to meet all above-horizon detection and tracking requirements for 21st century ships without primary air-defense missions. It will provide long-range "situational awareness" with detection and tracking of air and surface targets and provide for aircraft control (marshalling).

The S-VSR will be a nonrotating, phased-array radar with the necessary track and "revisit" times to counter fast, low/very-low observable, and high-diving missile threats. With these capabilities, it also will provide cuing for the SPY-3 MFR.

It will replace or succeed the current SPN-43, SPS-48E, and SPS-49 radars.

The S-VSR EDM will be integrated with the SPY-3 MFR and tested at the Wallops Island facility. The S-VSR's initial operational capability is planned for 2013.

Prime contractor:	Northrop Grumman Ship Systems
Band:	S
Ships:	CVN 78
	DD(X)
	LHA(R)

AN/SPY-1 MFR (MULTI-FUNCTION RADAR)

The SPY-1 multifunction, phased-array radar is the heart of the Aegis Anti-Air Warfare (AAW) system. It combines the azimuth and height search, target acquisition, classification, and tracking functions and can provide command guidance to ship-launched missiles. The replacement of several different radars with the single SPY-1 results in the reduction or elimination of several complex interfaces between specialized radars, speeds all functions, and provides a very large target-handling capability.

The SPY-1 radar—consisting of the antenna, transmitter, signal processor, control groups, and auxiliary equipment—employs four fixed antennas ("faces") and operates in the F (formerly S) band. Each antenna contains 4,480 separate radiating elements in an octagonal face only 12½ feet (3.7 m) across. This small size facilitates ship design: the TICONDEROGA has two antennas on a forward deckhouse (facing forward and to starboard) and two on an after deckhouse (facing aft and to port); the ARLEIGH BURKE has four antennas fitted on a single deckhouse. These four antennas each cover a 90° quadrant from the horizon to zenith for total scanning around the ship.

The SPY-1 has a wide frequency bandwidth that randomly radiates different frequencies on a pulse-to-pulse basis, with very low sidelobes in comparison with its main lobe, and extremely complex signal structures. All these characteristics present great challenges to anti-radar missiles. The SPY-1 radar also is highly resistant to electronic countermeasures because of its frequency diversity, and it can "sense" jamming and automatically shift to different frequencies where less interference is present. In addition, digital signal-processing techniques are employed to counter or suppress jamming and sea clutter. This latter feature is vital for effective defense against sea-skimming missiles, whose radar return often is lost to conventional radars because sea clutter can mask the target's signal.

Control of the SPY-1 is exercised by four UYK-7 digital computers in the CG 47–64 and the UYK-43/UYK-44 series in the CG 65–74 and the DDG 51 class. These computers are used to schedule and direct the beams, because the SPY-1 can project hundreds of pencil-thin radar beams in rapid sequence—far too many for manual control or coordination. Beam steering is a mathematical problem that requires the calculations of a computer system. Computer capacity is a practical limitation on the number of targets the SPY-1 can handle at one time. Within a second of a target being detected, the computers automatically schedule several more beams to "dwell" on the target, initiating a track. Hundreds of targets can be identified and tracked simultaneously, out to ranges on the order of 200 nm (370 km).

In earlier missile ships, the surface-to-air missiles had to be guided all the way from launch to the target. Missile ships thus

---

7 THAAD previously indicated *Theater* High-Altitude Air Defense; the "T" was changed to *Terminal* in February 2004.

Shipyard workers at Pascagoula, Mississippi, install a SPY-1D radar antenna on an Aegis missile destroyer. The size of the antennas is relatively small considering their capabilities vis-á-vis conventional, rotating antennas. (Lockheed Martin)

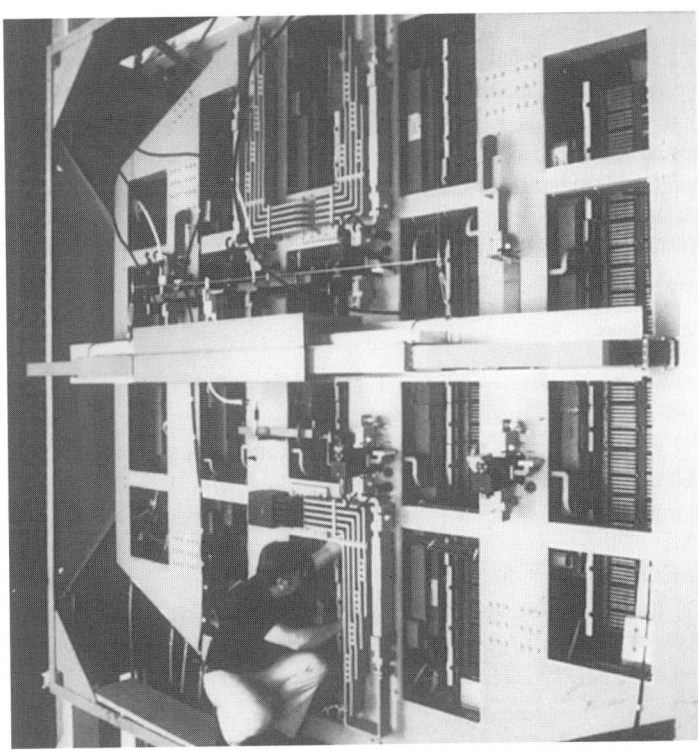

The reverse side of a SPY-1 radar during assembly. There is a technician working at the bottom of the radar. (RCA)

A rare photo of a SPY-1 radar being assembled, showing a technician inserting electronic elements into the face of the radar. (RCA)

could be characterized by the number of guidance channels, i.e., separate guidance radars, available. The later Standard missiles have an "autopilot" that is set at the moment of launch. The SPY-1 continuously tracks both the missiles in flight and targets, and the missile guidance can be updated in flight. Specific radar guidance is required only for the last few seconds before the missile detonates. Under this concept, the TICONDEROGA's four guidance radars can handle perhaps 20 separate targets simultaneously. This is a vast improvement over previous AAW ship capabilities.

The SPY-1 F-band covers 3100–3500 MHz with a beam measuring 1.7 x 1.7°. Its peak power is 4–6 MW, with an average power of 58 kW.

The production versions of the SPY-1 are:
- SPY-1A—initial design (CG 47–58)
- SPY-1B—an upgraded antenna, improved transmitter and signal processor for increased effectiveness against low-flying and small radar-cross-section missiles, and low sidelobe levels for enhanced ECM resistance (CG 59–73)
- SPY-1C—designation not used
- SPY-1D—single deckhouse version in the ARLEIGH BURKE class
- SPY-1D(V)—littoral operations upgrade fitted in DDG 92–112
- SPY-1E[8]—antenna upgrade of earlier radars to enhance bandwidth and sensitivity to increase effectiveness against ballistic missiles
- SPY-1F—lightweight version for frigates

There have been proposals to install the SPY-1 radar in the carriers of the NIMITZ class, primarily for aircraft control, and in the later nuclear-propelled guided missile cruisers (CGN). However, no installations were undertaken—for fiscal reasons in the carriers, and because the Navy's nuclear propulsion community, which sought the construction of nuclear-propelled Aegis ships, opposed installation in the cruisers.

The SPY-1 was developed from the SPG-59 phased-array radar intended for the aborted Typhon missile frigate (DLGN) program. Development began in the late 1960s. The SPY-1 (one radar face)

began operation at the RCA development facility in Cherry Hill, New Jersey, in 1973, followed a year later by a single face being installed in the missile test ship NORTON SOUND (AVM 1).

The SPY-1D radar is fitted in the destroyers of the Japanese KONGO class and the subsequent DDG designs and in the Spanish ÁLVARO de BAZÁN-class frigates. SPY-1F is being installed in frigates of the Norwegian FRIDTJOF NASSEN class. Taiwan expressed interest in obtaining the SPY-1 system for their future warships; however, the Clinton administration in 2000 rejected the request as being too provocative to China.

The SPY-1 has been operational since 1983.

Prime contractor:	Lockheed Martin (formerly General Electric-RCA)
Band:	S
Ships:	CG 47
	DDG 51

AN/VPS-2 RADAR

The VPS-2 radar is fitted in the Mk 15 Phalanx gun system, with a single transmitter supporting separate search and tracking radars mounted above the actual Gatling gun. The radar tracks both incoming targets and outgoing bullets, detects the angular error between them, and automatically corrects gun aim. It has a Moving Target Indicator (MTI) with the ability to track very high speed targets and has a very rapid reaction capability. (The radar also is used with the U.S. Army's Vulcan air-defense gun system.)

The radar's search range is approximately 5,500 yards (5,030 m). Its frequency range is 9200–9250 MHz with a peak power of 1.4 kW.

The system has been operational since 1980.

Prime contractor:	Lockheed
Band:	Ku and X
Ships:	various

---

8 Originally, the E suffix was for a SPY-1D upgrade to provide greater effectiveness against sea-skimming missiles and low-observable targets.

An artist's cutaway view of a Phalanx CIWS mounting shows the VPS-2 radar antenna fitted just above the weapon's six 20-mm barrels (within the white radome); IFF antennas are fitted at the top of the radome. (General Dynamics/Pomona)

MK 95 MISSILE FIRE CONTROL RADAR

This is the fire control radar component of the Mk 91 fire control system for the Sea Sparrow Surface-to-Air Missile (SAM). (See entry for Mk 91.)

MK 26 RADAR

This is a range-only fire control radar associated with the Mk 40 gun director in the IOWA-class battleships. Adapted from the Mk 11, the Mk 26 radar has a 36-inch (914-mm) paraboloid antenna. Its effective range is 10,000 yards (9,200 m) against a large aircraft and 16,000 yards (14,635 m) against a large warship. Peak power is 40–60 kW.

The system has been operational since 1944.

Prime contractor:	GE
	RCA
Band:	
Ships:	BB 61

MK 25 RADAR

The Mk 25 is the fire control radar associated with the Mk 37 GFCS in the IOWA-class battleships for use with their 5-inch dual-purpose guns. Some ships had the SPG-53E radar on their forward Mk 37 directors. (The Mk 25 Mod 7 was the first U.S. shipboard missile guidance radar.)

Its maximum range is 100,000 yards (91 km), and its peak power is 250 kW. The radar has a 60-inch (1.5-m) conical scanning "dash."

The Mk 25 has been operational since 1948.

Prime contractor:	Western Electric
Band:	X
Ships:	BB 61

MK 13 RADAR

This is the fire control radar in the IOWA-class battleships that provides range and bearing data for the Mk 38 and Mk 34 gun directors for the ships' main batteries. It previously was mounted in gun cruisers, as well as in the battleships.

The Mk 13's tracking range is 50,000 yards (45,730 m), and peak power is 50 kW. The bar-type antenna is 8 feet (2.4 m) long and 2 feet (0.6 m) in diameter. It is mounted atop the Mk 38 director in IOWA-class ships.

The after Mk 37 GFCS with the 60-inch (1.52-m) circular antenna of the Mk 25 radar (left) and the massive Mk 38 GFCS with the cylindrical antenna for the Mk 13 radar on the battleship IOWA. The Mk 37 GFCS was long found on numerous U.S. surface combatants, as well as amphibious and auxiliary ships, to direct 5-inch (127-mm) guns; the Mk 37 GFCS is for the main battery of 16-inch guns. (Giorgio Arra)

It has been operational since World War II.

Prime contractor:	Western Electric
Band:	X
Ships:	BB 61

STIR (SEPARATE TARGET ILLUMINATION RADAR)

The STIR is a modified SPG-60 radar for use with the Mk 92 gun/missile fire control system in the OLIVER HAZARD PERRY-class frigates.

It has been operational since 1974.

Prime contractor:	FMC
Band:	X
Ships:	FFG 7

The STIR in a OLIVER HAZARD PERRY-class frigate uses the SPG-60 antenna. The antennas is mounted immediately forward of the Mk 75 76-mm gun, mounted on the ship's 01 level. (Giorgio Arra)

SHIPBOARD SONARS

Sonar is the U.S. Navy's principal means for detecting and targeting submarines. All active U.S. surface warships except aircraft carriers and all submarines are fitted with sonars. Anti-submarine aircraft employ expendable sonobuoys, and the SH-60F and MH-60R ASW helicopters also use "dipping" sonar. Mine countermeasure forces use sonars to detect mines; and ASW forces make extensive use of seafloor Sound Surveillance Systems (SOSUS) and related seafloor acoustic systems.

Submarine sonars. Contemporary U.S. submarine sonars are derived principally from the German-developed passive array sonars of the World War II period. These sonars have a series of fixed transducers that form beams in various directions by the electrical phasing of the transducer inputs.[9] In the early years of nuclear-propelled submarines, U.S. submarines traditionally operated in the passive mode, generally being able to detect relatively noisy Soviet nuclear submarines before they themselves could be detected. However, the appearance in the early 1980s of quiet Soviet nuclear submarines, of which the Project 971/Akula class was the harbinger, resulted in new U.S. Navy interest in active sonar techniques. The Soviet Navy's modern diesel-electric submarines—when operating submerged on electric propulsion—had a very low acoustic signature. (Of course, operating techniques, environmental conditions, and other factors can make even relatively noisy submarines difficult to detect.)

Although the towed array sonars were developed by the U.S. Navy primarily for use in surface ships, they quickly were adapted to submarine use and now have been fitted in all current SSN and SSBN types.

Surface ship sonars. Surface ship sonars vary considerable in type and installation. The principal hull-mounted sonars in the U.S. Navy today are the SQS-53 and SQS-56 series. The SQS-53 and its predecessor SQS-26 sonars had their origins in the early 1950s, when the first Soviet post–World War II submarines began going to sea in large numbers; these are relatively large sonars, with long-range passive and some active capabilities.

During the later 1950s, the U.S. Navy developed two additional types of surface ship sonars: Variable Depth Sonar (VDS) and Towed Array Sonar (TAS). The VDS is lowered over the stern of the ship to place the sonar dome below the near-surface thermal layers that reflect sonar beams. Towed array development has led to the highly successful Tactical Towed Array Sonar (TACTAS), which consists of a passive (hydrophone) system in a cable towed behind the ship. By using convergence zone detection techniques, TACTAS has long-range capabilities against submarines, especially when employed by screening ships away from the noisy task force center. (If the ocean depth is sufficient, sound will travel down and back to the surface at an annular about 30 nm/55.5 km away, i.e., to the first convergence zone. An advanced passive sonar system can be effective out to three convergence zones or some 90–100 nm/ 167–185 km.)

A further development of the towed array concept is the Surveillance Towed Array Sonar System (SURTASS), which is a longer, more capable hydrophone array. While the TACTAS is carried by combatant ships (cruisers, destroyers, and frigates), the SURTASS is an area surveillance system, towed by slow-speed, tug-type ships designated T-AGOS (see Chapter 23). The SURTASS/T-AGOS concept is intended for use in areas where the seafloor SOSUS detection system has been destroyed or does not exist (see below).

In the post–Cold War era, the SOSUS, related seafloor systems, and SURTASS/T-AGOS systems have been cut back precipitously.

The SURTASS AN-series designation is UQQ-2.

Mine countermeasure sonars. Sonar also is used in mine countermeasures, with high-resolution sonars fitted in surface minesweepers and mine-hunting Unmanned Underwater Vehicles (UUV).

ADVANCED MINE DETECTOR SONAR (AMDS)

This is an active submarine sonar intended for mine detection. The "chin"-mounted sonar underwent trials in the ASHEVILLE (SSN 758). It will be fitted in the LOS ANGELES and later SSNs.

AN/BQG-5 WIDE APERTURE ARRAY SONAR

The Wide Aperture Array (WAA) sonar enhances submarine fire control solutions against hostile submarines. The first BQG-5 was installed in the submarine AUGUSTA (SSN 710) in 1992 for at-sea evaluation. WAA components also were evaluated in the research ship GLOVER (T-AGFF 1). The BQG-5 antenna arrangement consists of three rectangular panels mounted on each side of the submarine.

The SEAWOLF class is fitted with the BQG-5D version, and the VIRGINIA class has the lightweight BQG-5A. The BQG-5D has been backfitted in the Improved LOS ANGELES-class submarines (SSN 751–773).

Prime contractor:	Lockheed Martin
Ships:	SSN 21
	SSN 751

9 The first "modern" array sonar installations were fitted in German submarines and surface ships beginning in the late 1930s. After the war, the first U.S. array sonar developed for operational use was the BQR-4 fitted in the hunter-killer submarine *K-1* (SSK 1) in 1951.

AN/BQQ-10 A-RCI SONAR

The BQQ-10 Acoustic Rapid COTS Insertion (A-RCI) is an extensive program to replace four legacy sonars with the more flexible COTS-based open-systems-architecture system that will be common to all U.S. combat submarines. The BQQ-10 is replacing the BQQ-5 in the LOS ANGELES class, the BQQ-6 in the OHIO class, the BY-1 in the Improved LOS ANGELES class, and the BSY-2 in the SEAWOLF class.

The BQQ-10 allows for the development and use of complex algorithms that were previously beyond the capabilities of legacy sonars. Further, COTS and open-systems architecture permits future upgrades to sonar software and hardware with little or no impact on submarine scheduling.

This sonar includes the Precision Underwater Mapping and Navigation (PUMA) upgrade, which provides submarines with the capability to map the ocean floor and register geographic and object features, including mine-like detection for minefield surveillance and avoidance. These digital maps can be electronically compressed and transmitted to other naval forces.

Prime contractor:	Lockheed Martin
Ships:	SSBN 726
	SSN 21
	SSN 688

AN/BQQ-9 TASPE SONAR

The Towed Array Signal Processing Equipment (TASPE) is a passive sonar fitted in OHIO-class ballistic and cruise (SSGN) missile submarines. It supports the BQR-15 sonar.

Prime contractor:	Rockwell
Ships:	SSBN 726

AN/BQQ-6 SONAR

This sonar system was adapted from the BQQ-5 for use in strategic missile submarines of the OHIO class. It is primarily a passive system, with a limited active capability in the BQS-13; the BQQ-6 includes a large bow sphere with 944 hydrophones, plus flank arrays and a towed array.

Prime contractor:	IBM
Ships:	SSBN 726

AN/BQQ-5 SONAR

This active/passive sonar system is fitted in the LOS ANGELES-class attack submarines. The BQQ-5 originally was provided in submarines of the LOS ANGELES class and was backfitted in the PERMIT (SSN 594) and STURGEON (SSN 637) classes, replacing their original BQQ-2.

The BQQ-5 is a digital system that integrates the bow-mounted array, the conformal (hull-mounted) array, and the towed array. A computer-driven signal processor is used to select the hydrophones and steer the beams. With this method, the number of beams that can be formed is limited only by computer capacity. In addition, the digital BQQ-5 suffers far less from internal noise than the BQQ-2, with its manual switching, thus enhancing the detection of weaker acoustic signals. The BQQ-5 digital computer's processing also allows a reduction in the normal number of watch standers.

Developed from the BQQ-2 system, the BQQ-5 has a large spherical bow array fitted in a 15-foot (4.6-m) sphere mounting 1,241 transducers (the BQS-11, 12, or 13), a chin array with 104 hydrophones, and a TB-series towed array (see below).

Later BQQ-5 versions have provided improved display consoles, as well as integrated towed array processing. The latest version is the BQQ-5E modification, being fitted in all surviving LOS ANGELES-class submarines and the SEAWOLF class; this sonar and the TB-29 towed array sonar are components of the Combat Control System (CCS) Mk 2. The BQQ-5E is referred to as the "QE-2" system.

Submarines of the Improved LOS ANGELES class have the BQQ-5 integrated in their BSY-1 system.

The BQQ-5 is being upgraded to the BQQ-10 system.

Prime contractor:	Lockheed Martin (previously IBM, Loral)
Ships:	SSN 688

AN/BQR-15 TOWED SONAR ARRAY

The BQR-15 is a passive towed sonar array (with BQR-23 sonar processor). It consists of a 156-foot (47.7-m) passive array towed by a 2,200-foot (670-m) cable.

Prime contractor:	
Ships:	SSBN 726
	SSN 688

AN/BQS-24 SONAR

This is a high-frequency active array for under-ice operations fitted in the sail structure of the SEAWOLF.

Prime contractor:	
Ships:	SSN 21

AN/BQS-15 SONAR

This is a short-range sonar for under-ice and mine-avoidance operations. It has a cylindrical transducer housing and operates in both high- and low-frequency ranges.

Prime contractor:	
Ships:	SSBN 726
	SSN 688
	AGSS 555

AN/BQS-13 SONAR

This narrow-band, active search sonar is an active element of BQQ-5/6 systems.

Prime contractor:	Raytheon
Ships:	SSBN 726
	SSN 688

AN/BSY-2 COMBAT SYSTEM

The BSY-2 will detect, classify, track, and launch weapons against hostile submarine targets and permit SEAWOLF-class SSNs to detect and locate targets faster, allow operators to perform multiple tasks and address multiple targets concurrently, and—ultimately—reduce the time between detecting a threat and launching weapons. The principal antennas of the BSY-2 are a large spherical array, a conformal hull array, a separate active transmitter, a high-frequency mine/under-ice sonar, towed arrays, and wide aperture arrays. The last consist of three large, flat arrays mounted along each side of the submarine; they employ low-frequency, passive sensing capabilities to rapidly determine the locations of targets in both azimuth and depth to provide more accurate target range and tracking data. (The BSY-1 is similar in concept, although the configuration is different; see below.)

Formerly known as the Submarine Advanced Combat System (SUBACS)/FY 1989, the BSY-2 is an advanced sonar and fire control system for attack submarines of the SEAWOLF class. See BSY-1 entry for background information.

The BSY-2 has been plagued by a number of problems, including increasing costs and technical problems associated with the UYS-2 Enhanced Modular Signal Processor (EMSP), database management system, and computer network. Of particular concern was the unprecedented number of lines of computer (software) code required for the system—some 3.2 million lines, of which more than 2 million are in the new Ada language, for which there were inadequate numbers of experienced programmers available.[10] The BSY-2 computer code requirement is about twice the amount

---

10 The only Department of Defense program known to exceed the SEAWOLF in lines of Ada code is the F-22 Advanced Tactical Fighter.

needed for the BSY-1. An investigation by the Government Accounting Office into the BSY-2 concluded:

> The risks that the Navy has allowed in the development of its BSY-2 combat system are serious. . . .
>
> In its endeavor to meet BSY-2 delivery schedules, tied closely to the submarine's delivery, the Navy is not following some sound management principles and practices, and is pushing forward not only with development of the first three systems but also for approval of three additional systems. By doing so, the Navy could find itself with combat systems that fall short of their promised capability and could cost millions to enhance.[11]

The delays in completion of the first submarine of the class, however, did permit time to remedy some or all of these problems, many of which can be traced directly to its predecessor, the BSY-1.

The estimated cost of the BSY-2 program actually has *decreased* over the years, from about $16 billion to some $14 billion. The reduction mainly was the result of the Navy eliminating

one base at which SEAWOLFs would operate (with an associated reduction in BSY-2 spares, training equipment, personnel, etc.). Those costs, however, were based on the procurement of 29 sets; only 3 have been procured for the truncated SEAWOLF program.

BSY-2 component systems include the BQS-24 high-frequency active array in the sail, the BQG-5 WAA (three per side), and the TB-12X and TB-16D towed array sonars.

The BSY-2 is being upgraded to the BQQ-10 configuration.

The system has been operational since 1996.

Prime contractor:	Lockheed Martin (formerly General Electric)
Ships:	SSN 21

11 General Accounting Office, *Submarine Combat System: BSY-2 Development Risks Must Be Addressed and Production Schedule Reassessed* (Washington, D.C.: August 1991), p. 2.

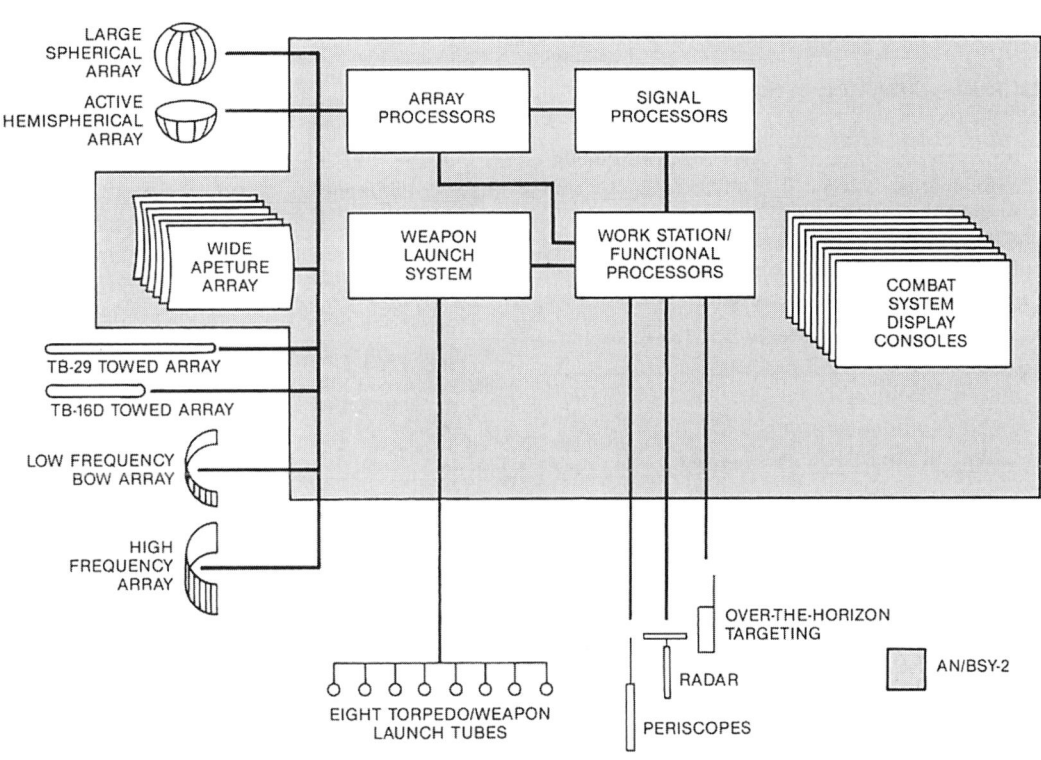

BSY-2 Combat System (William Clipson)

The spherical, bow-mounted array that mounts components of the BSY-2 sonar/combat system. Despite the massive development costs of the BSY-2 (originally part of SUBACS), the BSY-2 is being fitted only in the three submarines of the SEAWOLF class. (Newport News Shipbuilding)

AN/BSY-1 COMBAT SYSTEM

The BSY-1—known as the Submarine Advanced Combat System until 1986—is an advanced sonar and fire control system intended for installation in 20 Los Angeles-class submarines, beginning with the SSN 751. Early in 1986, the Secretary of Defense told Congress that SUBACS "will maintain our [submarine] force's edge in undersea detection and targeting." Employing advanced computer hardware and software, the system is intended to exploit advanced acoustic sensors—such as WAAs—to analyze acoustic detection data, identify targets, and make fire control calculations.

When SUBACS was conceived in the early 1980s, there were to be three versions: the *Basic* version for the SSN 751–759, the *B* version for the SSN 760 (FY 1986) and later Los Angeles-class submarines, and the *B-prime* version for the SSN 21 class. Subsequent restructuring because of major problems led to a two-part program: the BSY-1 for the Improved Los Angeles class (SSN 751–773) and the BSY-2 for the Seawolf.

The SUBACS/BSY-1 program was one of the most poorly run programs in recent Navy history. It suffered severe technical, cost, and management problems. The planned optical data bus—using fiber-optic technology to transmit data—encountered difficulties, requiring a redesign using more-conventional electronic technology. Next, there were difficulties in producing the multilayer computer circuit boards. And there were management problems, both on the part of IBM, which had been contracted to develop and produce SUBACS, and the Navy. A late 1985 congressional report stated: "severe technical and management problems have significantly increased costs, delayed schedules, and degraded planned system capability." Navy and other government agency reviews of SUBACS indicated that research and development for the system would cost $2.4 billion, and shipbuilding costs for the submarines already authorized were estimated to be 40 percent more than appropriated. The House and Senate armed services committees at the time reported: "the constrained capability of the SUBACS is no longer worth the investment."

The problems led the Secretary of the Navy and the Chief of Naval Operations to personally take over management of the contract and renegotiate it. In late 1985, the Navy restructured the program to provide a two-track BSY-1/BSY-2 approach. In January 1986, the Navy renegotiated the IBM contract to complete seven sets at a fixed-price of $1.3 billion. Admiral James Watkins, then Chief of Naval Operations, spoke in his February 1986 testimony to Congress of the "restructured" and "relabeled" SUBACS program: "The middle step was not deemed necessary; it was very expensive and there was no way we could have managed the transition from step 2 to 3, which is to the SSN 21 class suite."

When installation of the first BSY-1 set began on the San Juan (SSN 751) late in 1986, it was found that the cabling would not fit into the spaces allocated for the equipment in the submarine. This situation further increased costs and delayed completion of that submarine. In addition, the first four systems (in the SSN 751–754) were not complete when fitted in submarines, leaving them with only limited self-defense capabilities; they were upgraded to provide full BSY-1 capabilities after the submarines went to sea.

The BSY-1 became operational in 1989.

Prime contractor:	Lockheed Martin (formerly IBM, General Electric, Lockheed Missile and Space, Loral)
Ships:	SSN 751–773

AN/SQQ-89(V) ASW COMBAT SYSTEM

The SQQ-89 is the first integrated ASW combat system for surface combat ships, combining sensors and weapons control systems with sophisticated data processing and display. Known as the "Squeak 89," the system correlates and manages acoustic sensor input from hull-mounted sonar and towed array and forwards track data to the ship's combat direction system.

There are several variants of the SQQ-89 now in use:
- (V)3 in the CG 54 class
- (V)4 in the DDG 51 class
- (V)10 in the DDG 79 class
- SQQ-89A(V)15 backfit in the CG 47 class

The (V)4 system was planned for the Perry-class frigates, but the installation was canceled in 1990 because of budget constraints. That variant also was known as SQQ-98I—the suffix indicated "improved"—and subsequently was designated SQY-1. The (V)2 was to have been installed in both active and Naval Reserve Force (NRF) frigates of the Perry class. In those ships, the limited-capability SQS-56 sonar was to be integrated with the SQQ-89. In the event, only the FFG 7, 9, 20, and 48–52 were fitted with the (V)4.

The large, SQS-53B/C sonars of the cruisers and destroyers are integrated into the SQQ-89, as are the SQR-19 towed arrays, SQQ-28 shipboard acoustic processing component of the LAMPS III (helicopter) system, and the ships' ASW weapons control system.

The current SQQ-89 system consists of the following subsystems:
- Mk 116 ASW fire control system
- SQQ-28 sonobuoy processor
- SQQ-89( )-T On-Board Trainer (OBT)
- SQR-19 TACTAS
- SQS-53C/D hull-mounted sonar (CG/DDG/DD)[12]
- SQS-56 hull-mounted sonar (FFG 7)
- SRQ-4 MH-60R/SH-60 helicopter data link
- USQ-132 Tactical Display Support System (TDSS)
- UYQ-25B Sonar In-Situ Mode Assessment System (SIMAS)

Submarines carry a number of sensors, with several mast-mounted Electronic Surveillance Systems (ESM) visible in this view of the fairwater or sail of the submarine Toledo *(SSN 769). However, a submarine's most important sensors are sonars, which are integrated by a combat system. The* Toledo *has the controversial BSY-1 combat system. (U.S. Navy/Michael Sandberg)*

---

12 The SQS-53A/B sonars are being upgraded to the SQS-53D configuration.

The destroyer MOOSBRUGGER (DD 980) was the first ship to have the SQQ-89 installed. The system became operational in 1985.

Prime contractor:	Lockheed Martin (General Electric and Westinghouse)
Ships:	CG 47
	DDG 51
	FFG 7 (some ships)

AN/SQQ-32 SONAR

This is a high-resolution mine detection and classification sonar. Provided in all MCM ships, the sonar antenna is a "towed" body lowered through the hull of the carrying ship (the SQQ-14/SQQ-30 arrangement is similar). The sonar can be employed in a hull-mounted (retracted) mode for shallow-water operation. There are 48 acoustic arrays in a "stave" arrangement around the barrel-like towed body, with the bar-type classification antenna at the bottom of the body. The towed body weighs 7,845 pounds (3,530 kg).

The SQQ-32 has been in service since 1991; its first operational use was by the AVENGER (MCM 1) in the Persian Gulf. The system provided successful mine detections in the Gulf operations; however, the AVENGER suffered problems with her sonar, as well as with her engines.

Prime contractor:	Raytheon/Thomson CSF
Ships:	MCM 1 (6 ships)
	MHC 51

AN/SQQ-30 SONAR

This mine detection and classification sonar was developed from the SQQ-14. The antenna is cable-lowered from under the minesweeper. The SQQ-30 has limited capabilities and is being succeeded in service by the SQQ-32.

Prime contractor:	General Electric
Operational:	1987
Ships:	MCM 1 (8 ships)

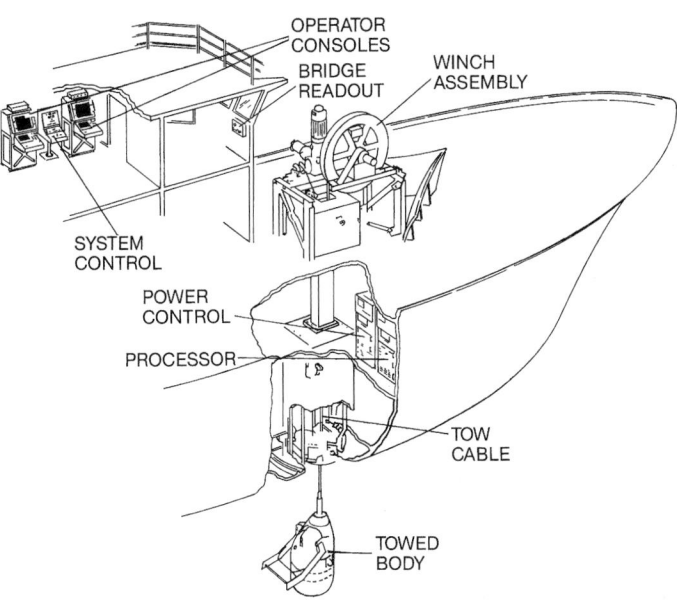

SQQ-32 minehunting sonar configuration in MCM/MHC-type ships. (William Clipson)

An SQQ-32 towed body prior to being installed in a mine countermeasures ship. (Raytheon)

An artist's view of the towed sensor body of the SQQ-32 minehunting sonar examining a seafloor object. The "hunting" technique is necessary to detect and identify objects on the sea floor that could be bottom mines. (Raytheon)

AN/SQQ-28 SONAR PROCESSOR

The SQQ-28 is the shipboard acoustic processor and data link for the SH-60B/R LAMPS III and MH-60R anti-submarine helicopter. It is being replaced by later systems.

Prime contractor:	
Ships:	CG 47
	DDG 51
	FFG 7

AN/SQR-19A/B TACTAS

The Tactical Towed Array Sonar is a passive hydrophone array deployed from the TICONDEROGA-class cruisers, the ARLEIGH BURKE and SPRUANCE destroyer classes, and the active OLIVER HAZARD PERRY-class frigates. The towed array, or "tail," locates the sonar away from ship-generated noises that could otherwise mask a target's acoustic signals. The modular construction of the array permits hydrophone components that fail or are damaged to be replaced aboard ship.

The SQR-19 can be effective at relatively high ship's speed and in sea states up to 4. The array has a nominal diameter of 3¼ inches (82.5 mm) and is towed at the end of a 5,600-foot (1,700-m) cable. The array section weighs about 10,000 pounds (4,536 kg).

The "wet end" (cable systems) of the SQR-19 also is fitted in Canadian and Spanish frigates.

Prime contractor:	Gould Electronics
Ships:	CG 47
	DDG 51
	FFG 7 (some ships)

AN/SQR-18A(V) TACTAS

This version of the TACTAS is a passive hydrophone system employed by frigates. Similar to the SQR-19, the SQR-18A(V)2 is streamed from the PERRY-class ships assigned to the NRF. The array—which is 730-feet (223-m) long—is towed with a 5,000-foot (1,525-m) cable rather than from the VDS towed body as in the earlier frigates of the KNOX (FF 1052) class. The system can be effective in sea states up to 4.

The SQR-18A is fitted in Japanese ASW ships.

The basic SQR-18 was an interim towed array that evolved into the SQR-18A TACTAS.

Prime contractor:	Gould Electronics
Ships:	FFG 7 (NRF ships)

AN/SQR-17A ACOUSTIC PROCESSOR

This was the acoustic processor for sonobuoys and the related display for use with SH-2G LAMPS I helicopters. It has been succeeded in newer ships by the SQQ-89. In 1986, Congress voted funds for the procurement of 20 SQR-17A sets for NRF frigates. The system has been discarded with retirement of the SH-2G helicopters from U.S. Service.

AN/SQS-56 SONAR

The SQS-56 is an active/passive sonar with severely limited capabilities. Ships fitted with this sonar are expected to detect submarines primarily with their towed array sonar.

The severe cost and size constraints imposed by the Chief of Naval Operations when the PERRY-class frigates were designed led to the small, higher-frequency—and thus shorter-range—SQS-56 being employed in this class. Raytheon had developed the SQS-56 as a totally company-funded project to provide a modern, lightweight sonar to smaller warships. The use of the SQS-56 saved perhaps 600 tons of displacement in the FFG 7, and required far less electrical power than the 66 kilowatts need for the SQS-53. The cost is effective range, with the SQS-56 being capable of direct path detections only on the order of 5 miles (8 km)—far too little for effective use with ship-based ASW helicopters. The SQS-56 operates at 5.6, 7.5, and 8.4 kHz.

During the 1980s, the set was modified to provide a capability for short-range mine detection; the modification is known as the "Kingfisher."

(Other factors in the decision to reduce the PERRY-class sonar effectiveness were the availability of large numbers of SQS-26/SQS-53 sonars in other ASW ships and the potential of towed array sonars.)

SQS-56 sonars have been fitted in the warships of several other navies, some with the Raytheon commercial designations DE-1160B/C.

This system has been operational since 1977.

Prime contractor:	Raytheon
Ships:	FFG 7

AN/SQS-53 SONAR

This is a large active/passive sonar. An improved SQS-26CX sonar, the SQS-53 became the bow-mounted sonar of the SPRUANCE variations (DD 963/DDG 993/CG 47 classes), as well as of the subsequent ARLEIGH BURKE-class destroyers.

The principal difference between the SQS-26CX and the SQS-53 is the digital interface with the Mk 116 ASW weapon control system in the latter sonar. The SQS-53B has an improved, digital, solid-state display; the SQS-53C has improved active performance, multiple target capability, automatic target tracking, and a higher systems availability.

The SQS-53B is fitted in the TICONDEROGA class (beginning with CG 56) and was backfitted in the SPRUANCE class (beginning with DD 980). The SQS-53C is being procured for the BURKE-class destroyers. The surviving SQS-53A/B sonars are being updated to an improved digital capability by the use of COTS processors and are redesignated SQS-53D.

The SQS-53 became operational in 1975.

Prime contractor:	General Electric and Hughes
Ships:	CG 47
	DD 963

An SQS-53 transducer housing as fitted in a SPRUANCE-class destroyer. (Litton/Ingalls Shipbuilding)

The missile cruiser COWPENS (CG 63) in dry dock at Yokosuka, Japan, shows the large bow sonar dome of the SQS-53 sonar. The ship has a stem anchor as well as a starboard anchor; the former provides some protection for the dome from the anchor chain. (U.S. Navy/Alan Warner)

AN/SQY-1 ASW COMBAT SYSTEM

This was to be an integrated ASW combat system for major ASW ships as the successor to the SQQ-89. It was to integrate all ASW sensors and fire control systems in surface combatants.

The SQY-1 was terminated by the Department of Defense in January 1992 as a cost-saving measure, appropriate in view of the demise of the Soviet Union and the reduced threat from its submarine force. Accordingly, there were be some changes in the SQQ-89 modernization program to reflect the SQY-1 cancellation.

The initial operational capability originally was planned for the mid-1990s, but it was delayed until after 2000 funding issues, before the entire program was cancelled. The system was intended for the 51 frigates of the PERRY class, as well as for cruisers and destroyers. The subsequent decision not to provide the system to ASW frigates reduced the program to some 80 ships, with a related increase in unit costs.

Like the BSY-2, the SQY-1 was to incorporate the UYS-2 EMSP to handle the large amount of data processing required for the system. (When developed, the EMSP also will be used for an upgrade of the SURTASS and other ASW systems.)

The system previously was designated SQQ-89 Improved (SQQ-89I).

TB-SERIES TOWED ARRAY SONARS

Submarine towed array sonars are designated in the TB- series (for Towed Body). These passive arrays are fully retractable into "sleeves" mounted on submarine decks.

The original TB-16 "fat-line" array was 240 feet (73 m) long and 3½ inches (89 mm) in diameter. It mounted 50 hydrophones that weighed 1,400 pounds (635 kg), and it was neutrally buoyant. The acoustics package was towed at the end of a 2,600-foot (793-m) cable that was 0.37 inches (9.4 mm) in diameter and weighed 450 pounds (204 kg).

Later versions have longer arrays, with the TB-16D being an early "thin-line" array.

The TB-23 is a thin-line passive array approximately 1,500 feet (457 m) long and is towed by a 2,600-foot (793-m) cable. It has 98 hydrophones, the smaller diameter of the array permitting the greater length to be accommodated by the submarine.

The TB-29 thin-line array has succeeded older TB-series arrays on submarines. In turn, the TB-29A, a COTS version of the towed array, is being fitted in all active submarines, as well as in the surviving surface surveillance ships (T-AGOS). The later version is less expensive while providing superior performance. Coupled with the BQQ-10 system, the TB-29A is expected to produce a 400–500 percent increase in detection of quiet submarines in both the blue-water and shallow-water (littoral) environments, according to Navy statements.[13] The first TB-29A arrays were delivered to the fleet in 2002.

Prime contractor:	Lockheed Martin	
Ships:	TB-16D: SSN 21	
	TB-16 or TB-23: SSN 688	
	TB-29 or TB-29A: SSBN 726	SSN 21
		SSN 688 (some ships)
	TB-29A: SSN 774	T-AGOS

AN/UQQ-2 SURTASS

The Surveillance Towed Array Sensor System is a submarine detection system towed by slow surface ships to supplement the SOSUS. These ships—designated T-AGOS—are to operate where SOSUS coverage is inadequate or where the seafloor arrays are damaged or destroyed. The SURTASS data are sent via satellite link to shore facilities for processing and further transmission to ASW forces; however, the ships can provide "raw" acoustic data to ASW ships in the area. The SURTASS concept differs from TASS/TACTAS in that the latter are tactical hydrophone arrays towed by warships to supplement hull-mounted sonars.

SURTASS employs either a long-line passive acoustic array or a shorter, twin-line array. The two-line array is superior for operations in littoral areas, as it can be towed in waters as shallow as 180 feet (55 m). The T-AGOS also are being fitted with the TB-29A twin-line arrays.

The oceanographic research ship MOANA WAVE (AGOR 22) conducted sea trials of the UQQ-2 in 1979–1984; the ex-missile submarine SAM HOUSTON (SSBN/SSN 609) was employed in the mid-1980s as an underwater test platform for the UQQ-2.

So-called block upgrades improved the compatibility of SURTASS for the T-AGOS 23 ships.

13 Adm. Clark, *Vision... Presence... Power...* , p. 80.

The system has been operational since 1984.

Prime contractor:	Raytheon (Hughes and Lockheed-Sanders)[14]
Ships:	T-AGOS 19
	T-AGOS 23

AN/WQT-2 LFA (LOW-FREQUENCY ACTIVE) SONAR

The WQT-2 is an improved LFA towed array sonar for later T-AGOS surveillance ships. At-sea tests in 2003 demonstrated tactically significant increases in submarine detection ranges that are unmatched by any other sensor.

The system was tested aboard the support ship COREY CHOUEST (see Chapter 25) and is being fitted in the USNS IMPECCABLE (T-AGOS 23).

Development of the system has been hampered by law suits that contend the sonar interferes with marine life.

The system also is designated UQQ-2 LFA.

Prime contractor:	Lockheed Martin (Saunders) and Raytheon
Ships:	T-AGOS 23

HELICOPTER SONARS

The Navy's SH-60F/MH-60R Seahawk ASW helicopters are fitted with active/passive "dipping" sonar. Dipping sonar is necessary for sonar detection in the vicinity of surface ships because the ship-generated noises inhibit the use of passive air-launched sonobuoys.

The MH-53E Sea Dragon MCM helicopter and MH-60R can employ mine-detection sonars. In addition, mine-detection sonars are fitted on the WLD-1 Remote Minehunting System (RMS), which is deployed from surface ships.

AN/AQS-22 ALFS (AIRBORNE LOW-FREQUENCY SONAR)

The AQS-22 ALFS is a variant of the Folding Light Acoustic Sonar (FLASH) developed by Thomson-CSF in France for the ASW role.

ALFS will be used by the U.S. Navy's MH-60R Seahawk multirole helicopters.

Compared to earlier dipping sonars, the AQS-22 features:
• improved deep- and shallow-water detection
• expanded search rate
• multifunction capabilities including environmental measuring and underwater communications
• mixed-mode operations

The transducer can be lowered into the water by a cable 2,550 feet (777 m) long; the transducer is 4⅙ feet (1.27 m) long and weighs 176 pounds (80 kg). There are 12 hydrophone stave arrays (each mounting two hydrophones) that expand when the transducer is deployed.

The FLASH system was chosen over several competitive U.S. helicopter sonars. It is being produced under a subcontract from Hughes Aircraft Co., now part of Raytheon. The prototype systems were delivered in the late 1990s, and low-rate production was initiated in October 2002.

(The FLASH system also is used in ASW helicopters of Britain, France, and the United Arab Emirates.)

The original ALFS program provided for 429 systems to be acquired at a production cost of $1.2 billion, which includes the costs of spares, training, and fitting the system to MH-60R helicopters.

A towed version of this array has been proposed; such a system could be employed from airships, as well as from small craft.

---

14 Developers included Johns Hopkins University, Applied Physics Laboratory; Raytheon; and Digital Systems Resources.

The AQS-22 ALFS dipping sonar being lowered by an SH-60F Seahawk helicopter during trials of the submarine-hunting device. It also is being fitted in the multimission MH-60R Seahawk helicopter. (Raytheon)

The sonar head of the AQS-22 ALFS system being fitted in Navy ASW/multimission helicopters. The staves open when the sonar head is at detection depths. (Raytheon)

AN/AQS-20A MINE-HUNTING SONAR

The AQS-20A is a mine-detection sonar that employs an electro-optical identification sensor to locate and identify bottom, close-tethered, and moored mines. The system is being deployed with MH-60S Knighthawk and MH-53E Sea Dragon helicopters and from the WLD-1 RMS, an unmanned device carried by later ships of the ARLEIGH BURKE class (see Chapter 22).

The towed body contains an active, high-resolution, multibeam, side-looking sonar fitted in a lightweight, hydrodynamically stable vehicle. It can be towed at speeds up to 12 knots.

On board the deploying helicopter, an operator can view the underwater image and identify objects on a video monitor, while recording the data on VHS digital tapes for post–mission analysis. An operator actually "flies" the device underwater, actively controlling the depth, or altitude, of the device in the water column.

Initial helicopter trials were conducted by an MH-53E in September 2000. By the end of 2003, there were ten systems on order, with a fleet operational capability planned for 2005.

The AQS-20A is produced by Raytheon.

An AQS-13 dipping sonar being lowered from an SH-3 Sea King ASW helicopter. This dipping sonar is being replaced by the AQS-22 ALFS. (U.S. Navy)

Aviation Electrician's Mate 2nd Class Tony Lio prepares to lower an AQS-20 mine detection sonar from an MH-53E Sea Dragon helicopter. The MH-53E is a highly capable mine countermeasures helicopter; it is scheduled to be replaced by the MH-60 series multimission helicopter. (U.S. Navy/Bradley J. Sapp)

AN/AQS-14 MINE-HUNTING SONAR

The AQS-14 is a helicopter-towed sonar employed by the MH-53E Sea Dragon MCM helicopters.

The AQS-14 towed body weighs 555 pounds (251 kg). The system's control console and winch are mounted on pallets and can be rapidly installed or removed from a helicopter. The system also can also be fitted to small surface craft.

The proposal to use LCAC landing craft for the MCM role called for employment of the AQS-14 as a towed array. That project was not pursued.

The AQS-14 was produced by Westinghouse.

AN/AQS-13 ASW DIPPING SONAR

Most of the Navy's SH-60F and MH-60R Seahawk ASW helicopters are fitted with the AQS-13 active dipping sonar. The latest version to be fitted in these helicopters is the AQS-13F. It is being replaced by the AQS-22 ALFS.

The AQS-13F has a 1,500-foot (457-m) cable.

SONOBUOYS

Naval aircraft employ expendable, short-duration sonobuoys for the localization of submarines. Sonobuoys generally are employed after an initial submarine contact is gained by other means; however, there are sonobuoy barrier tactics in which a string of sonobuoys periodically is planted ahead of a task force. The Navy's P-3C Orion and SH-60B and MH-60R Seahawk aircraft all can launch and monitor sonobuoys.

The principal types of sonobuoys now in U.S. Navy service are listed in Table 31-2. The data are for the latest production models, unless a version is indicated; "depth" indicates the level to which the buoy's hydrophone (or Expendable Bathythermograph [XBT] sensor) is lowered by cable.

When released by an aircraft, the buoy falls to the water, slowed by a parachute or retardation device. On reaching the water, the buoy's battery is activated, the transmission antenna extends, and the hydrophone is lowered by cable; buoys activate either on hitting the water or on command. After a specified number of minutes or hours, the buoy canister floods and sinks.

Most current sonobuoys are of a standard "A" size that fits launch chutes on board ASW aircraft—3 feet (0.9 m) in length and 4⅞ inches (122 mm) in diameter. However, the SSQ-75 is larger—7½ feet (2.3 m) in length, with a diameter of 10 inches (254 mm). Efforts are under way to reduce sonobuoy size; a dwarf "B" versions of the SSQ-53/77/79 is being developed that will permit three sonobuoys to be carried in a standard "A"-size aircraft launcher.

Ice-penetrating sonobuoys also have been developed for use in the Arctic to detect Russian submarines operating under ice. These air-launched buoys are known to have penetrated ice up to 10 feet (3 m) thick. At least one concept for such a buoy employs a 2-pound (0.9-kg) lithium nose cone for penetrating the ice cover. Housed in an A-size sonobuoy, the ice-penetrator has an oversized parachute and shock absorber to reduce impact on landing. Once on the ice, the lithium nose cone melts through; the sensor deploys through the hole in the ice, the nose cone falls away, and the antenna, which remains above the ice, extends and the sonobuoy becomes operational.

Sonobuoys are used in a complementary manner, with some being laid to attain initial detection of a possible submarine target and others providing shorter-range, more precise data on the target's depth and bearing. The SSQ-36 XBT is used to determine the acoustic conditions of the water column, vital data in ASW operations. The principal buoys currently used in air ASW operations are the SSQ-53 Directional Low-Frequency Acquisition and Ranging

Table 31-2. SONOBUOYS

Designation	Type	Manufacturer	Weight	Depth	Frequency range	Endurance
SSQ-36	bathythermograph (water temperature profile)	Sparton		1,000 ft (305 m)	—	few minutes
SSQ-41B	omnidirectional passive detection; LOFAR (Jezebel)	Hermes, Magnavox, Sparton	29 lbs (13 kg)	60 or 1,000 ft (18 or 305 m)	10 Hz to 10 kHz	hours
SSQ-53D	passive directional (DIFAR)	Canadian Commercial, Magnavox, Sparton	22 lbs (10 kg)	100, 400, or 1,000 ft (30.5, 122 or 305 m)	10 Hz to 2.4 kHz	1, 3, or 8 hours
SSQ-57B	passive for restricted waters	Hermes, Sparton	14 lbs (6.35 kg)	60 or 400 ft (18 or 122 m)		1, 3, or 8 hours
SSQ-62B	DICASS	Raytheon	34 lbs (15.4 kg)	90, 400, or 1,500 ft (27, 122, or 457 m)		30 hours
SSQ-77B	passive VLAD	Sparton, Magnavox	29 lbs (13 kg)	1,000 ft (305 m)	10 Hz to 2.4 kHz	1 or 8 hours
SSQ-79	SVLA	Hazeltine		1,000 ft (305 m)		4 or 8 hours
SSQ-102	Air-Deployed Active Receiver Tactical Surveillance Sonar*					

* Can operate in bistatic or multistatic mode, with a shipboard sonar providing the active signal.

(DIFAR) and the SSQ-62 Directional Command Activated Sonobuoy System (DICASS). The SSQ-77 passive Vertical-Line Array DIFAR (VLAD) is a deep-searching sonobuoy with a long-line array, as is the SSQ-79 Steered Vertical Line Array (SVLA). The SSQ-57 is a small, passive-detection sonobuoy intended for relatively shallow waters; the current U.S. Navy interest in regional naval operations could lead to renewed attention to this type of buoy.

The earlier SSQ-50 Command Activated Sonobuoy System (CASS) buoy has been succeeded by the SSQ-62. The SSQ-73 was an experimental deep-DIFAR buoy based on the SSQ-53; the SSQ-73 passive VLAD was procured in its place.

A large, 103-pound (46-kg) active pinging buoy designated SSQ-90 is in limited production for the Navy.

The SSQ-101 is a Horizontal-Line Array (HLA) sonobuoy that holds promise of long-range submarine detections. If development is successful, the buoy would be used for long-range detections ahead of surface naval forces. Development began in the mid-1980s (as did development of the TSS and LCS buoys) in response to the emergence of several Soviet quiet submarine classes.

An advanced submarine detection program known as the SSQ-102 Tactical Surveillance Sonobuoy (TSS) was canceled in late 1991 because of the reduced Soviet/Russian submarine threat. The TSS was to have an onboard minicomputer to analyze and record probable submarine noises and then transmit them to ASW aircraft when so directed. This transmit-on-command was necessary because of the expected service life of TSS, on the order of five to seven days.

An unusual photo of a sonobuoy falling away from an SH-2F LAMPS I helicopter. The retardation fins are open to slow its descent to the water. Note the 15 sonobuoy chutes fitted in the left side of the helicopter. There is a Mk 46 torpedo mounted below the sonobuoy chutes. (U.S. Navy)

Aviation Ordnanceman 3rd Class Herbert G. Chappell loads an SSQ-62 DICASS sonobuoy into a P-3C Orion aircraft at the Naval Air Facility Misawa, Japan. In addition to these external launch chutes, the P-3C has an internal sonobuoy launcher that can be reloaded from inside the aircraft. (U.S. Navy/Nicholas Fry)

Although TSS has been canceled, some of the technologies developed under the program will be applicable to other ASW projects.

Also under development is the SSQ-103 Low-Cost Sonobuoy (LCS), an A-size buoy that would field six minibuoys, each of which would suspend a hydrophone 300 feet (91 m) below the surface. The individual buoys would be 5½ inches (140 mm) in length and 4½ inches (114 mm) in diameter. The LCS system would seek out submarine flow noises, i.e., the water flow over a submarine's hull, which is a gross, broadband noise. This requires less sophisticated sensors and analyses than are needed for narrow-band noises (produced by a submarine's machinery and propellers), but because of its very short range, is effective only against slow-moving submarines.

The SSQ-58A is a moored surveillance buoy used by the Navy's Mobile Inshore Undersea Warfare units to form surveillance barriers to detect swimmers or small craft. The buoy itself is a fiberglass float 24 inches (0.6 m) in length and 36 inches (0.9 m) in diameter, carrying a standard, omnidirectional hydrophone, up-link transmitter, antenna, etc. It can be recovered and its battery recharged; it does not sink at a predetermined time as do other buoys discussed here. (The designation SSQ-58 previously was applied to a Low-Frequency Acquisition and Ranging [LOFAR] buoy.)

The U.S. Navy also employs several communication buoys for submarine use: The BRC-6 Expendable Submarine Tactical Transceiver (XSTAT) is a two-way expendable buoy for Ultra-High-Frequency (UHF) communications between a submarine and an aircraft; the BRT-1 Submarine-Launched One-way Transmitter (SLOT) is ejected by a submarine to broadcast, with a preset delay, a four-minute taped message; the BRT-3/4/5 buoys transmit a signal to identify a submarine at night/in bad weather; the BRT-6 is a one-way transmission buoy, to uplink prerecorded UHF transmissions to a communications satellite; and the SSQ-71 and SSQ-86 are A-size two-way aircraft–submarine communications buoys carried in aircraft sonobuoy dispensers.

SEAFLOOR ACOUSTIC SYSTEMS

Seafloor acoustic systems—both fixed and deployable—are intended to detect hostile submarines. These acoustic systems are to be linked into the Integrated Undersea Surveillance System (IUSS).

SOSUS (SOUND SURVEILLANCE SYSTEM)

The U.S. Navy has installed several seafloor SOSUS arrays in various parts of the Atlantic and Pacific, as well as across the Strait of Gibraltar and off North Cape (north of Norway). In the late 1960s, then-Secretary of Defense Robert S. McNamara first publicly acknowledged the existence of SOSUS, although installation had begun in the 1950s and the system was known to the Soviets shortly after emplacements began.[15] SOSUS is used to detect transiting submarines and, in wartime, to direct air, surface, and submarine ASW forces to their targets. However, the SOSUS arrays are vulnerable to active and passive (i.e., jamming) attacks by hostile naval and possibly merchant forces.

During World War II, the U.S. and British (and Soviet) navies installed limited-capability acoustic arrays on the ocean floor in shallow waters, especially near harbors. Immediately after the war, the U.S. Navy began development of deep-ocean arrays. By 1948, arrays were being tested at sea, and by 1951, the first SOSUS arrays were being implanted. Also termed Project Caesar, the first set of operational hydrophones was installed at Sandy

Hook, New Jersey, south of Manhattan, followed in 1952 by a deep-water (1,200-foot/365.85-m) installation off Eleuthra in the Bahamas. That year, the Chief of Naval Operations directed the establishment of six arrays in the Western Atlantic, all to be ready by the end of 1956. The first arrays in the Pacific were operational in 1958. Installations in other areas followed.

Initially, a number of Naval Facilities (NAVFAC) were established as the shore terminals for SOSUS; they were located along both U.S. coasts and in the Caribbean, Iceland, and Japan, as well as at other overseas locations. The seafloor hydrophones have since been replaced, and the NAVFACs in the United States and Caribbean have been consolidated as more-capable arrays and computers have been developed.

SOSUS and the SURTASS (T-AGOS) ships are integrated into the so-called Integrated Undersea Surveillance System. Acoustic data from the NAVFACs and Regional Evaluation Centers (REC) are provided through the Ocean Surveillance Information System (OSIS) to the Atlantic, Pacific, and European area Fleet Command Centers (FCC) and to the Naval Ocean Surveillance Information Center (NOSIC), in Suitland, Maryland, near Washington, D.C., as well as to national leaders. Thus, SOSUS information is provided at several levels—to tactical as well as theater and national commanders, and for technical evaluation.

Published sources cite detection ranges of "hundreds" of miles by SOSUS, with arrays reported in the Atlantic and Pacific areas, as well as in some regional seas. Several update programs have been announced, especially related to increased computer capability to more rapidly provide data with an improved signal-to-noise ratio. Current upgrades to SOSUS include transitioning from single-beam paper displays to multibeam CRT-based displays and the provision of improved communication links.

In the post–Cold War period, the size of the SOSUS network has been cut severely, as has the T-AGOS program. A minimal fixed surveillance system now is maintained.

FDS (FIXED DISTRIBUTED SYSTEM)

An improved SOSUS-type system known as the Fixed Distributed System (FDS) was intended to detect quiet, deep-running Soviet/Russian submarines. A shallow-water version was being developed, with greater emphasis on fiber-optics than SOSUS-type systems and possible integration of nonacoustic sensors, but the program was canceled following congressional reductions in funding, although one system is in service (see below).

The FDS-C is a developmental, COTS version of the FDS system. Both the FDS and FDS-C consist of a series of arrays deployed on the ocean floor in deep-ocean areas, across straits and other choke points, or in strategic shallow-water littoral areas. Both also are made up of two components: the Underwater Segment (UWS), which performs the detection, and the Shore Signal and Information Processing Segment (SSIPS), which handles the processing, display, and communication functions.

The FDS was in advanced development in the early 1990s, when massive reductions in defense funding began. Despite its traditional support for major ASW programs, Congress began cutting the funding for the IUSS and FDS programs. At the same time, the Navy began examining the feasibility of employing FDS in coastal and shallow-water areas.

The FDS program was canceled in 1993 following the deployment of the Engineering Development Model, designated FDS-1, which remains in fleet operation. FDS-C subsequently was developed by taking advantage of advances made in commercial indus-

---

15 The locations of U.S. SOSUS arrays have long been identified in Soviet magazine articles and books.

try that will provide a much more cost-effective system to meet the fleet's ongoing needs for long-term undersea surveillance.

FDS-C will provide threat location information to tactical forces and will contribute to a reliable maritime picture for the joint force commander. It will be deployed in strategic locations where surveillance is needed to maintain undersea battle space dominance. Because of its strategic positioning and long lifetime, FDS-C can provide indications and warning of hostile maritime activity prior to hostilities. Development of the all-fiber-optic hydrophone passive array will increase system reliability and performance and also reduce costs.

The system testing and evaluation of FDS-C is complete. When this edition of *Ships and Aircraft* went to press, the FDS-C was in the design verification and source-selection stage of development.

The FDS-C is being developed/manufactured by Lucent and Lockheed Martin.

ADS (ADVANCED DEPLOYABLE SYSTEM)
ADS is a rapidly deployable, short-term, large-area undersea surveillance system currently under development. It is designed to detect nuclear-propelled and quiet conventional (diesel-electric and air-independent propulsion) submarines operating in shallow-water littoral areas. The system also will have some capability to detect mine-laying activity and to track surface contacts.

ADS will provide threat location information directly to tactical forces and contribute to a reliable maritime picture for the joint force commander. It will be forward positioned in a standardized, modular, van configuration to allow on-scene forces to deploy it rapidly to areas where surveillance is needed to maintain undersea battle space dominance.

The system consists of a processing and analysis segment, which is connected to the ADS sensor array by a shore cable and contained in reusable, transportable vans; and the underwater segment, which is an expendable, battery-powered, large-area field of passive undersea surveillance arrays. Existing Undersea Surveillance System (USS) processing software and display formats form the core of the ADS shore signal-processing segment. COTS technologies are being emphasized to maximize cost effectiveness.

ADS is in the EMD phase. In May 1999, an ADS prototype completed a highly successful fleet exercise test. It is planned for fleet operations beginning in FY 2009.

The obvious vulnerabilities of SOSUS in wartime, as well as its coverage limitations, have led to the T-AGOS/SURTASS program and to proposals for smaller arrays that could be planted by surface ships or aircraft. The latter has been an on-again, off-again program, identified by such acronyms as MSS (Moored Surveillance System) and RDSS (Rapidly Deployable Surveillance System). The RDSS was canceled by the Navy on 26 December 1984.

ADS is being developed and manufactured by Lockheed Martin, Raytheon, DSR, and ORINCON.

TORPEDO COUNTERMEASURES

Torpedo countermeasures include electronic systems and decoys to reduce the effectiveness of enemy torpedoes or to "replace" the ship or submarine target in the torpedo's target-acquisition process. U.S. surface warships, amphibious ships, and certain auxiliary ships have the SLQ-25 Nixie.

U.S. attack submarines are reported to carry the Mk 23 acoustic countermeasure device to decoy homing torpedoes, and ballistic missile submarines also can launch the Mk 70 MOSS from torpedo tubes to simulate a full-size submarine to hostile sonar.

SURFACE SHIP TORPEDO DEFENSE
After several false starts, the Surface Ship Torpedo Defense (SSTD) project is providing U.S. ships with a limited hard-kill torpedo defense system, using modified Mk 46 torpedoes launched from Mk 32 torpedo tubes (see chapter 30).

On 26 October 1988, the U.S. and British governments signed a Memorandum of Understanding (MOU) to establish a four-phase, joint research effort, SSTD project. At the time, the MOU was hailed by a U.S. Navy spokesman as providing "an excellent opportunity to improve mutual defense capabilities, reduce development and acquisition costs and to provide for increased compatibility and interoperability between the U.S. and Royal navies."[16] However, the joint program immediately ran into shoal water. While the U.S. Navy pushed for a hard-kill approach, the British believed soft-kill would be more viable for SSTD. The British feared that a convoy escort firing weapons to intercept an incoming torpedo would put other ships in the convoy at risk.

More threatening to the joint effort, the U.S. House Appropriations Committee subsequently killed funding for several Anglo-American projects, among them SSTD. The House report stated that the "committee does not consider such a joint project to be feasible given the security consideration regarding the sharing of acoustic signal data and countermeasure development, which the program would ultimately require."[17] Such language was highly inflammatory and counterproductive given the close technical and operational relationship of the U.S. and British submarine communities and the large amount of acoustic data on Soviet/Russian undersea craft provided to the United States by the Royal Navy.

Three American-led consortia were formed to develop SSTD systems: General Electric teamed with Alliant Techsystems (formerly defense products of Honeywell) and Marconi Underwater

---

16 Caleb Baker, "U.S., Royal Navy to Explore Torpedo Defense Systems," *Navy Times* (19 December 1988), p. 26.
17 "House Cites 'Security Concerns' in Cutting U.K. from SSTD," *Navy News* (21 August 1989), p. 8.

A sailor holds the towed "fish" of the SLQ-25 Nixie torpedo countermeasures system; the towing cable is in the foreground. The Nixie was used in a combat environment by the Royal Navy in the 1982 Falklands conflict. (Aerojet General)

Systems; Westinghouse joined with AT&T, Dowty Maritime, and Ferranti; and Martin Marietta worked with Hughes Ground Systems, British Aerospace Dynamics, and Frequency Engineering Laboratories (USA). After a series of initial contracts in the torpedo defense area, in early 1992 the first two teams were awarded contract extensions for the program.

The U.S. Navy has converted 172 Mk 46 ASW torpedoes to active anti-torpedo systems for carrier defense against Russian wake-homing torpedoes.

AN/SLQ-39 DECOY LAUNCH BUOY

This is a chaff-dispensing buoy carried by some Navy surface combatants.

| Prime contractor: | Raytheon |
| Ships: | surface ships |

AN/SLQ-25A NIXIE

A towed torpedo countermeasures systems, Nixie is found on most U.S. Navy surface combatants and in many other ships, including four Navy-manned replenishment ships that normally would operate with surface warships.

Nixie is an electro-acoustic device that attempts to decoy the incoming torpedo away from the target ship. The acoustic projector that transmits the decoying signal is in a TB-14 towed "fish." The signal is generated aboard ship and transmitted to the towed body through the towing cable.

The Navy procured the original SLQ-25 and, subsequently, an improved SLQ-25A version. In all, the Navy acquired more than 400 sets.

The system has been in service since 1972. The effectiveness of Nixie was demonstrated in the 1982 war in the Falklands, when a Nixie being towed by the British carrier HERMES attracted and was blown up by a British ASW torpedo that had been launched against a suspected Argentine submarine contact.

Prime contractor:	Aerojet	
Ships:	CV/CVN	LCC 19
	BB 61	LHA/LHD/LPD/LSD
	CG 47	LKA 113 (1 ship)
	DD/DDG	AOE 1
	FFG 7	

AN/SLR-24 TORPEDO COUNTERMEASURES SYSTEM

In the mid-1990s, the Navy planned to procure the SLR-24 system. The contractor was to design, fabricate, produce, test, and deliver the system making maximum use of existing and COTS components.

The procurement subsequently was canceled.

WEAPON CONTROL SYSTEMS

Weapon control systems are designated in several series, with several mark series also being used. The major systems are identified in this section.

CCS-SERIES COMBAT CONTROL SYSTEMS

This is a multiple-function control system for weapons in LOS ANGELES-class submarines. The original Mk 1 CCS has been replaced in some units by the upgraded Mk 2 CCS (see Chapter 12). The system integrates the submarine's torpedo fire control system (Mk 117) with the central computer complex.

The original CCS Mk 1 was the Mod 0; the Mod 1 (using UYK-7 computers) integrated the Tomahawk missile; the Mod 2 (using UYK-44 computers) added a vertical-launching capability; the

Mod 3 added the Mk 48 ADCAP capability; and the Mods 4 and 5 added the capability for the (now canceled) Sea Lance missile.

The CCS Mk 2 has improved displays and work stations over the Mk 1. The Mod 0 was succeeded rapidly by the Mod 1, which included provisions for over-the-horizon targeting (Tomahawk and Harpoon missiles); the Mod 2, intended for Trident submarines, has modified consoles and controls.

The software is modular, facilitating adaptation for various submarine/weapon configurations.

Prime contractor:	Raytheon
Ships:	SSBN 726
	SSN 688

AN/SYS-SERIES INTEGRATED AUTOMATIC DETECTION AND TRACKING SYSTEMS

The SYS-1(V)2 and SYS-2(V) Integrated Automatic Detection and Tracking (IADT) systems integrate various radars in non-Aegis guided missile ships and large amphibious ships to facilitate command and control in high-threat environments. Each shipboard radar is fitted with a video converter, from which the images are passed through a processor and then integrated for display in the ship's combat information center.

The SYS-1 was developed specifically for destroyers of the CHARLES F. ADAMS (DDG 2) class and the SYS-2 for guided missile cruisers. The latter also was selected for the PERRY-class frigate upgrade and is installed in the WASP-class amphibious ships. (The SYS-3 system is provided in the Israeli SA'AR V-class missile corvettes, which were built in the United States.)

The follow-on Integrated Radar Detection and Identification System (IRDIS) will integrate nonradar data (e.g., ESM).

SYS-1 became operational in 1977.

Prime contractor:	Norden (United Technologies)
Ships:	FFG 7 (some ships)
	LHD 1

MK 160 GFCS

This is an advanced gunfire control system. It has been operational since 1991.

| Prime contractor: | |
| Ships: | DDG 51 |

MK 118 TORPEDO FCS

An all-digital torpedo fire control system developed for the Trident SSBNs, the Mk 118 controls both torpedo launches and the release of 3-inch (76-mm) and 6-inch (152-mm) torpedo countermeasures, as well as the Mk 70 MOSS target simulators.

It became operational in 1981.

| Prime contractor: | |
| Ships: | SSBN 726 |

MK 117 TORPEDO FCS

The U.S. Navy's first all-digital torpedo fire control system, the Mk 117 initially was installed in submarines of the THRESHER (SSN 593)/ PERMIT (SSN 594) class. Installation of the digital Mk 117 prevented use of the analog SUBROC missile; although there was an attempt to correct this interface, the missile had only limited use.

The Mk 117 Mods 6 and 7 are compatible with the Tomahawk missile; the Mod 8 is compatible with the Tomahawk and SUBROC, and it could have handled the Sea Lance, had that missile been developed.

Prime contractor:	
Ships:	Mod 0: SSN 700–715
	Mod 8: SSN 716–720

MK 116 ASW FCS

The Mk 116 is an advanced ASW weapons control system for surface ships. The all-digital system is linked to the SQS-53 sonar and controls ship-launched weapons (Mk 32 torpedo tubes); it also interfaces with the LAMPS helicopter (SH-2G and SH-60B/F).

Mods 1 through 4 are for various ship types; Mod 5 integrates the SQQ-89 sonar system; Mod 6 integrates Vertical-Launch ASROC (VLA) potential for later TICONDEROGA-class cruisers; and Mods 7, 8, 9, and 10 introduced the UYK-43B computer and are for use in ARLEIGH BURKE-class destroyers, as well as non-VLS ships.

Prime contractor:	Librascope	
Ships:	CG 47	DDG 51

MK 115 FIRE CONTROL SYSTEM

The Mk 115, associated with the Sea Sparrow Basic Point-Defense Missile System (BPDMS), is a director/ illuminator adopted from the older Mk 51 gun director mount. It also has side-by-side antennas. Tracking is manual.

Prime contractor:	
Band:	X
Ships:	LHA 1

MK 99 MISSILE FCS

These are fire control directors associated with the Aegis weapon system (Mk 7); they are operated in conjunction with the SPG-62 radar. Mods 0 and 3 were fitted in the missile test ship NORTON SOUND; Mod 1 was the prototype for the TICONDEROGA class; Mod 2 the production model for that class; and Mod 4 was a production model. The Mk 99 has been operational since 1983.

Prime contractor:		
Band:	X	
Ships:	CG 47	DDG 51

MK 98 MISSILE FCS

This is the missile control system for Trident missile submarines. It has been operational since 1981.

Prime contractor:	
Ships:	SSBN 726

MK 92/94 WEAPON DIRECTION SYSTEMS

The Mk 92 and Mk 94 are combined tracking and illuminating systems incorporating two antennas, one for air and one for surface target tracking. The Mod 2, in PERRY-class frigates, is combined with STIR to provide a second missile guidance channel; Mods 0 and 2 can control guns or missiles. Mods 1, 3, 4, and 5 are for gun control only; the Mod 1 was fitted in the PEGASUS (PHM 1) class, except for the lead ship, and the Coast Guard's BEAR (WMEC 901) and modernized HAMILTON classes. The Mk 94 prototype is fitted in the PEGASUS and the PERRY-class frigates. In the latter ships, those refitted with the Mk 92 Mod 6 system with a Coherent Radar Transmitter (CORT) in conjunction with the SYS-2(V)2 automatic target tracking system have increased weapons control capabilities.

Prime contractor:	Sperry
Band:	X
Ships:	FFG 7
	Coast Guard cutters

MK 91 WEAPON DIRECTION SYSTEM

This is the weapon direction system for the NATO Sea Sparrow missile system. It has side-by-side receiving and transmitting antennas; typically, targets are designated automatically by the SPS-58/ SPS-65 radars or Mk 23 TAS. It uses the Mk 95 fire control radar.

Prime contractor:		
Band:	X	
Ships:	carriers	LHD 1
	AOE 1	

MK 90 FIRE CONTROL SYSTEM

This is the fire control system for the Phalanx Close-In Weapon System (CIWS). See VPS-2 radar.

MK 86 GUN/MISSILE FCS

The Mk 86 weapons control system is fitted with the SPQ-9A radar. The complete system includes an electro-optical sensor (closed-circuit low-light-level television) and SPG-60 tracker-illuminator radar. Reportedly, up to 120 target tracks can be monitored simultaneously.

The Mk 86 was evaluated in 1965 in the destroyer BARRY (DD 933). Mods 0 through 10 were developed with various target/tracking capabilities for various ship/radar/computer configurations.

The system has been operational since 1970.

Prime contractor:		
Band:	X	
Ships:	CG 47	DD 963
	LHA 1	

MK 74 MISSILE FCS

The weapons control system associated with Tartar/Standard-MR missiles was fitted with the SPG-51D radar. All the cruisers and destroyers that carried the Mk 74 have been stricken.

MK 40 GUN DIRECTOR

The Mk 40 gun director is fitted with Mk 27 radar. It is employed as a standby director for the Mk 38 GFCS.

Prime contractor:	
Band:	
Ships:	BB 61

MK 38 GFCS

This is the large main battery gun director for battleships and gun cruisers.

Prime contractor:	
Band:	
Ships:	BB 61

MK 37 GFCS

The Mk 37 was a widely used World War II–era GFCS fitted with the Mk 25 radar. It was succeeded by the Mk 67 and Mk 68 systems and now is found only in the mothballed IOWA-class battleships.

Prime contractor:	
Band:	
Ships:	BB 61

MK 23 TAS (TARGET ACQUISITION SYSTEM)

The Mk 23 TAS supports the NATO Sea Sparrow launcher Mk 29; the Mk 92/Mk 94 weapon FCS adopted from the Dutch M28 system; and the Mk 115 director/illuminator for the basic Sea Sparrow launcher Mk 25.

The Mk 23, intended for automatic reaction/target designation of incoming sea-skimming missiles, has a maximum range of almost 100 nm (185 km) and a minimum designation range of 20 nm (37 km). It incorporates pulse-Doppler radar. Designed to operate in high-clutter environments, it can simultaneously track up to 54 targets with a two-second scan rate.

The Mk 23 first went to sea on an operational basis in the frigate DOWNES (FF 1070) in 1975.

Prime contractor:	Hughes	
Band:	L	
Ships:	CVN 65	LHD 1
	CV 67	LHA 1 (1 ship)
	CVN 68	LPD 17
	AOE 1 (1 ship)	

CHAPTER 32

Coast Guard

Coast Guardsmen, long involved in port and harbor defense, have had their homeland security duties greatly expanded in World War III—the war against fundamental Muslim terrorists. Here, the cutter BAINBRIDGE ISLAND patrols New York Harbor, keeping watch over the Statue of Liberty, a major symbol of U.S. democracy. (U.S. Coast Guard/Mike Lutz)

The U.S. Coast Guard is a military, multimission, maritime service within the Department of Homeland Security. It is one of the five U.S. military services (the only one outside of the Department of Defense). The Coast Guard provides unique benefits to the nation because of its distinctive blend of humanitarian, civilian law enforcement, and military capabilities.

The Coast Guard's missions are to protect the public and the environment and to support U.S. economic, security, and defense interests. It is responsible for the enforcement of U.S. laws in coastal waters and on the high seas subject to the jurisdiction of the United States. Following the events of 11 September 2001, it was assigned a major role in U.S. homeland security and, subsequently, on 1 March 2003, was transferred to the newly established Department of Homeland Security.

Federal statute states that, in the national security role, the Coast Guard "shall maintain a state of readiness to function as a specialized service in the Navy in time of war, including the fulfillment of Maritime Defense Zone command responsibilities."

Admiral Thomas H. Collins, USCG, Commandant of the Coast Guard since May 2002. (USCG/ John Gaffney)

At the direction of the president, the Coast Guard can become a part of the Navy (as it did during World Wars I and II). Alternatively, it can operate in a war zone while remaining an independent service (as it did during the Korean and Vietnam Wars, the 1991 conflict in the Persian Gulf, and the 2003 invasion of Iraq).

The principal nonmilitary activities of the Coast Guard are: (1) enforcing recreational boating safety; (2) conducting search and rescue operations; (3) maintaining aids to navigation (three manned and some 450 unmanned lighthouses, approximately 13,000 minor navigational lights, plus other navigation aids); (4) implementing merchant marine safety; (5) carrying out environmental protection; (6) being responsible for port safety; and (7) enforcement of laws and treaties. The last comprises enforcement of the nation's customs and immigration laws, including the prevention of drug smuggling and illegal immigration, and fisheries laws, including international treaties related to the 200-nm (370-km) offshore Exclusive Economic Zone (EEZ).

Historical: The Coast Guard was established on 4 August 1790 as the Revenue Marine of the Department of the Treasury. Subsequently, it became the Revenue Cutter Service and, from 1915, the Coast Guard. The service incorporated the Lighthouse Service in 1939. The Coast Guard was a component of the Treasury Department from its formation until its transfer to the newly established Department of Transportation in 1967.

With the establishment of the Department of Homeland Security in late 2002, the Coast Guard again was marked for transfer, and it moved to the new agency the following year.[1] It was the largest organization to be assigned to the department and, with the Secret Service, is protected by congressional directive from being broken up or parceled out to other agencies within the department. (The Department of Homeland Security is the third-largest U.S. cabinet department, after Defense and Veterans Affairs.)

ORGANIZATION

Coast Guard Headquarters, located in Washington, D.C., provides overall supervision and support for the operating districts. The headquarters has seven major directorates and several lesser directorates and offices (see Figure 32-1). The senior uniformed officer of the Coast Guard is the Commandant, currently Admiral Thomas H. Collins.[2]

The major U.S. Coast Guard operating commands are the Atlantic Area (headquartered in Portsmouth, Virginia) and the Pacific Area (headquartered in San Francisco, California), with nine subordinate district commands. Both area commands, in addition to their assigned districts, also have a Maintenance and Logistics Command (MLC).

Each area commander also commands a district (i.e., Atlantic Area/5th Coast Guard District and Pacific Area/11th Coast Guard District). The two areas commanders are vice admirals, as are the Vice Commandant and the Chief of Staff.

The district commanders are rear admirals, as are the MLC commanders and the assistant commandants. The district commanders control all shore, air, and sea activities in their areas of responsibility.

In 1985–1986, the commanders of the Coast Guard Atlantic and Pacific Areas were designated as commanders of the newly established Maritime Defense Zone (MDZ) Atlantic and Pacific, respectively.[3] In this role, they report to their respective Navy fleet commanders and are responsible for: (1) planning, conducting, and coordinating wartime operations in and around U.S. harbors and coasts; (2) ensuring an integrated defense plan for the MDZs' areas of responsibility; and (3) protecting coastal and nearby sea lines of communication. Within each MDZ are operating sectors, which are commanded by Coast Guard district or base commanders.

The MDZ organization sought to rectify a long-standing shortfall in U.S. defense policy—that of defending U.S. harbors and coastal waters from hostile activity, particularly submarine operations, in wartime. However, the threat from submarine mining and the use of Coast Guard forces in forward crisis and combat areas do raise the question of whether the Coast Guard also should be given control of the surface mine countermeasures forces, which now are, of course, a Navy activity.[4] (Proposals in the late 1990s to transfer some or all of the patrol craft of the CYCLONE/PC 1 class to the Coast Guard came to naught at that time.)

Beyond its cutters and aircraft, the Coast Guard operates several Port Security Units (PSUs) and Maritime Safety and Security Teams (MSSTs) that can operate in the United States and overseas.

Port Security Units. Coast Guard PSUs are deployable units organized for sustained operations to provide protection to pier areas, naval or merchant ships, and other waterfront assets. They can operate under the direction of a Coast Guard or MDZ commander or as a component of a forward-deployed naval or joint command structure.

Each PSU is assigned approximately 5 active-duty and 140 reserve personnel. They train during weekend drills and two weeks of annual active duty.

The PSUs are assigned six Transportable Port Security Boats (TPSBs), along with the necessary trucks and trailers to transport men, mess and berthing equipment, weapons, and the boats. The units normally have sufficient spares to sustain operations for 30 days. All of the equipment and vehicles are air transportable.

The current PSUs are:
- PSU-301 Cape Cod, Massachusetts
- PSU-302 Cleveland, Ohio
- PSU-303 Milwaukee, Wisconsin
- PSU-305 Fort Eustis, Virginia
- PSU-307 St. Petersburg, Florida
- PSU-308 Gulfport, Mississippi
- PSU-309 Port Clinton, Ohio
- PSU-311 San Pedro, California
- PSU-313 Tacoma, Washington

1 The Department of Homeland Defense was established with the presidential signing of the Homeland Security Act on 25 November 2002.
2 The Coast Guard Commandant was a rear admiral until 10 March 1942, when the incumbent, Russell R. Waesche, was promoted to vice admiral. Waesche was promoted to full admiral on 4 April 1945. His successors have had four-star rank, except for the period 1950–1960.
3 A more-detailed description of the Maritime Defense Zones is found in Comdr. Lawson W. Brigham, USCG, "U.S. Coast Guard in 1985," U.S. Naval Institute *Proceedings* [Naval Review] (May 1986), pp. 42–49.
4 This issue is examined in N. Polmar, "Mine Warfare Problems . . . and a Solution," U.S. Naval Institute *Proceedings* (December 1991), pp. 105–6.

In addition, there is a PSU Training Detachment at Camp Lejeune, North Carolina.

The first PSU to deploy overseas was PSU-303, sent to ad-Damman, Saudi Arabia, in September 1990. Additional units subsequently have been forward deployed to the Mediterranean and Middle East.

Maritime Safety and Security Teams. The MSSTs are Coast Guard anti-terrorism/force protection teams established after the events of 11 September 2001. Modeled after the existing PSUs, the MSSTs will respond to terrorist threats or incidents at ports and in waterways. The teams are able to deploy anywhere within the United States within 12 hours by road or C-130 Hercules aircraft.

The first MSST was commissioned on 3 July 2002 in Seattle, Washington. Twelve teams currently are planned.

Each MSST is assigned approximately 100 active duty and reserve Coast Guardsmen. They are organized into a headquarters element, two boat detachments, and two land security detachments. The MSSTs operate the new Defender-class fast response boats. The teams also have vehicles and other equipment to support their rapid deployment and operations; however, they have less sustainability in forward areas than the PSUs.

Table 32-1. COAST GUARD DISTRICTS

District	Headquarters	Area	Personnel*
1st District	Boston, Mass.	northeast	2,936
5th District	Portsmouth, Va.	middle Atlantic	2,417
7th District	Miami, Fla.	southeast	3,714
8th District	New Orleans, La.	central-Gulf Coast	3,231
9th District	Cleveland, Ohio	northern-Great Lakes	2,182
11th District	Alameda, Calif.	southwest	1,859
13th District	Seattle, Wash.	northwest	1,590
14th District	Honolulu, Hawaii	Hawaii	798
17th District	Juneau, Alaska	Alaska	1,246
MLC Atlantic	Norfolk, Va.	Atlantic	1,898
MLC Pacific	Alameda, Calif.	Pacific	1,327

* Active-duty Coast Guard men and women

PERSONNEL

Uniformed Coast Guard personnel operate all cutters and boats, as well as aircraft. Medical personnel are provided by the U.S. Public Health Service on assignment to the Coast Guard.

Active-duty Coast Guard strength in mid-2004 totaled 40,066 men and women:

  6,181 officers
  1,530 chief warrant officers
  31,284 enlisted
  992 cadets (Coast Guard Academy[5])
  79 Officer Candidate School

At the same time, 160 Public Health Service personnel were serving with the Coast Guard.

Women comprise about 11.5 percent of the Coast Guard's active-duty personnel. The Coast Guard was the first U.S. military service to accept women at its service academy and the first to assign women as commanding officers of armed vessels (WPB patrol boats).

The Coast Guard has 7,900 selected reservists, who attend periodic drills, as well as summer active-duty training. There also is a civilian auxiliary of 35,600 volunteer men and women. The Coast Guard Auxiliary, created in 1939, consists of expert boaters, amateur radio operators, and licensed aircraft pilots who use their own equipment to support Coast Guard activities. Their efforts include conducting free courtesy marine inspections of recreational boats, teaching a variety of boating courses, and assisting the Coast Guard in search and rescue.

Figure 32-1. COAST GUARD ORGANIZATION

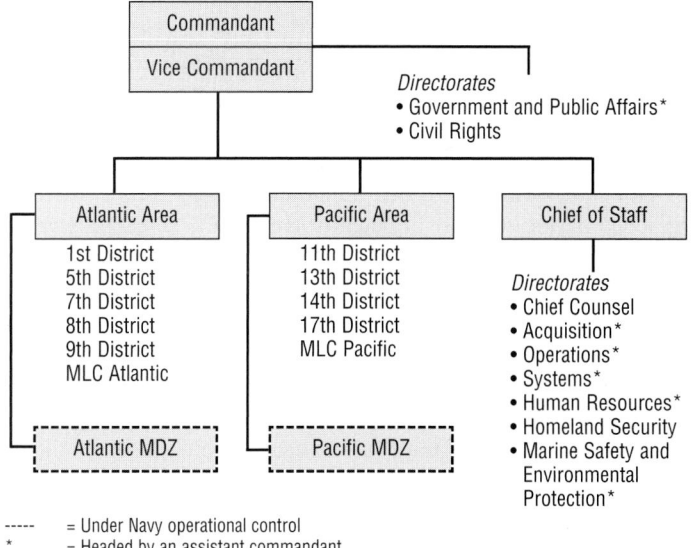

----- = Under Navy operational control
* = Headed by an assistant commandant
MDZ = Maritime Defense Zone
MLC = Maintenance and Logistics Command

Coast Guard personnel have Navy-style ranks, with the Commandant and Deputy Commandant normally having the rank of full admiral. As of mid-2004, the Coast Guard had 39 active-duty flag officers:

  1 admiral
  4 vice admirals
  16 rear admirals
  18 rear admirals (lower half)

In addition, there are two Coast Guard reserve rear admirals.

OPERATIONS

Coast Guard forces operate worldwide, though primarily in U.S. waters, with "black-hull" ships and craft maintaining inland and coastal aids to navigation. Offshore operations extend well into oceanic waters, with emphasis off the U.S. West Coast and Caribbean, to deter illegal migrants and drug smuggling.

In the Western Hemisphere, the Coast Guard is a major participant in drug interdiction. Beyond operations by its cutters and aircraft, the Coast Guard regularly provides small Law Enforcement Detachments (LEDET) on board Navy ships to carry out the boarding of vessels suspected of carrying contraband cargoes to Iraq, as well as for anti-drug patrols by Navy ships in the Caribbean.

In addition, during crises and conflicts, other Coast Guard units—active and reserve—support forward U.S. military operations. For example, during Operations Desert Shield/Desert Storm in 1990–1991, three U.S. Coast Guard reserve port security units, each with some 100 men and women, with patrol craft, were deployed in the Persian Gulf.[6] No Coast Guard cutters were deployed to the Gulf area. (In 1987—during the so-called tanker war between Iraq and Iran—the Coast Guard proposed to deploy 110-foot patrol craft to the Gulf, but the idea quickly was abandoned in the face of Navy opposition.)

During Operation Iraqi Freedom in the spring of 2003, the Coast Guard deployed six 110-foot patrol craft to the Persian Gulf

---

5 The Coast Guard Academy is located in Groton, Connecticut.

6 These units, which were flown to the Gulf with their boats, served as port security forces in Bahrain and Saudi Arabia. It was the first time in the 50-year history of the Coast Guard Reserve that its personnel had served outside the United States. The units were No. 301 from Buffalo, New York, No. 302 from Cleveland, Ohio, and No. 303 from Milwaukee, Wisconsin.

and another four to the Mediterranean, the latter to protect merchant ships transporting cargo for U.S. forces in the Middle East.[7] In addition, the 327-foot high endurance cutter DALLAS was sent to the Mediterranean and the BOUTWELL to the Persian Gulf, and the buoy tender WALNUT was deployed into the Gulf to repair and replace navigation aids. Port security units were sent to both areas, and LEDETs were placed aboard Navy ships.

Thus, the Coast Guard had important roles as well as forward presence during the first turbulent events of the so-called war on terrorism.

The end of the Cold War and the subsequent campaigns against terrorism have seen an expansion of Coast Guard responsibilities and areas of activity. Increasingly, Coast Guard assets are sought for overseas operations by U.S. government and military leaders.[8] These activities include, but are not limited to, training Third World naval and coast guard forces; carrying out liaison and joint operations with foreign navies and coast guards in the areas of law enforcement, pollution control, resource protection, and anti-terrorism; and providing direct support of U.S. military operations.

The Coast Guard is especially suited for working with Third World and developing countries, whose navies are more analogous to the U.S. Coast Guard in terms of men, ships, and missions than they are to the U.S. Navy. In many of those countries, the naval/coast guard missions are identical to those of the U.S. Coast Guard: the enforcement of resource and fisheries regulations, law enforcement, search and rescue, river and waterways management, port security, maritime safety, etc. Thus, the U.S. Coast Guard—a military service—can work directly with those countries on a non-military basis. As then-Coast Guard Commandant Admiral Robert Kramek noted in 1997, "We know the people, we know the geography, and, most importantly, we understand the maritime challenges that the Caribbean nations face."[9]

---

7 The patrol craft deployed in 2003 were:

WPB 1304	WPB 1332	WPB 1347
WPB 1309	WPB 1333	WPB 1348
WPB 1318	WPB 1338	
WPB 1326	WPB 1343	

8 This situation continues despite the expressed views of Secretary of Defense Donald Rumsfeld that the Coast Guard should shed its military roles; see Chapter 1.

9 Quoted in Dr. Scott C. Truver, "The World Is Our Coastline!" U.S. Naval Institute *Proceedings* (June 1998), p. 46.

Coast Guard aviation is fully integrated with surface operations. Here, a Coast Guard maritime security team fast-ropes from an HH-60J Jayhawk to the deck of the cutter SENECA during a training exercise. An armed MH-68A Stingray hovers close by to provide fire support if needed. (2004, U.S. Coast Guard/Mike Hvozda)

Coast Guardsmen in a 25-foot transportable security boat patrol the waters of Ash Shuaiba, Kuwait. These men are from Port Security Unit 307, based at St. Petersburg, Florida. In the background is a large U.S. military cargo ship, unloading equipment for U.S. operations in Iraq. (2004, U.S. Coast Guard/Matthew Belson)

CUTTERS AND BOATS

The Coast Guard operates a large number of oceangoing, coastal, and inland ships and small craft for a variety of purposes.

A major procurement program for oceangoing cutters, patrol boats, aircraft, and Command, Control, Communications, Computers and Intelligence (C^{4}I) systems is under way, known as the Integrated Deepwater System (IDS). This is the largest procurement program in Coast Guard history (see below). In addition, as part of IDS, some older patrol boats are being modernized.

The large HAMILTON-class high endurance cutters have undergone extensive modernization that will permit them to serve effectively into the early 21st century. Unfortunately, the program included removal of the ships' 5-inch/38-cal Dual-Purpose (DP) guns, which were most useful weapons. Their Anti-Submarine Warfare (ASW) weapons also were removed, and installation of Harpoon anti-ship missiles was halted. Several other cutter and boat classes have undergone upgrade programs, as well.

Most cutters are painted white; the larger icebreakers are painted red; and buoy tenders and harbor tugs are painted black (their superstructures remain white). The Coast Guard "racing stripes" insignia—a narrow blue and a wide orange stripe, angled 64°, with the Coast Guard shield superimposed on the latter—is carried on the bows of all cutters and boats. The words "U.S. Coast Guard" are painted on the sides of all ships and boats.

Decommission and strike dates are the same for patrol boats and "black-hull" cutters.

The former Navy ocean surveillance ship PERSISTENT (T-AGOS 6) was transferred to the Coast Guard on 1 May 2001, but was not activated because of a lack of funding; instead, she was transferred to the National Defense Reserve Fleet (NDRF) on 1 November 2001 for further service at the Great Lakes Maritime Academy. Other T-AGOS transfers were planned.

Designations: The Coast Guard uses the term "vessel" for all watercraft operated by the service. Within that classification, the term "cutter" is used for ships that have "an assigned personnel allowance and that [have] installed habitability features for the extended support of a permanently assigned crew." In practice, this includes 65-foot tugs and larger vessels. The term "cutter" comes from the early British revenue service ships that were cutter-rigged sailing vessels, although the original U.S. revenue cutters were sailing schooners.

Craft less than 65 feet in length are considered "boats," and the first two digits of their hull numbers indicate their length overall. However, the designation "patrol boat" (WPB) is used for craft up to 123 feet.

The Coast Guard classifies all its ships and small craft by length (in this chapter, shown in parentheses after the class name). Its vessel classification scheme is derived from that of the U.S. Navy (see Chapter 3), a system the Coast Guard adopted in February 1942, with each cutter assigned a two- or three-letter designation and sequential hull number. Previously, only small, unnamed cutters and former U.S. Navy destroyers in Coast Guard service had hull numbers. (Building numbers often were used to distinguish the larger cutters.)

To differentiate them from their Navy counterparts, all Coast Guard cutters were given the prefix letter *W* at that time. There is no definitive explanation for the W prefix. A bureaucratic argument is that W was used during the 1930s as the routing symbol on Treasury Department correspondence to designate the Coast Guard; another is that it indicated "weather patrol," one of the major tasks assigned to the Coast Guard. The theory also was put forth that the W indicated white-painted ships, although by February 1942 all Coast Guard vessels had been seconded to naval service and were painted gray.

In 1965, the Coast Guard adopted its own designation system for larger cutters and for specialized vessels, e.g., buoy tenders (WAGL). The larger cutters were designated on the basis of their range/sea-keeping qualities: high endurance (WHEC) and medium endurance (WMEC). Smaller cutters retained their Navy-type designations, e.g., WPC, WPB.

In 2004, the Coast Guard established a new series of designations for the cutters being developed under IDS:[10]

WMSL   Maritime Security Cutter (Large)
WMSM   Maritime Security Cutter (Medium)
WPC   Maritime Patrol Coastal
WPB   Maritime Patrol Boat

Cutter and patrol boat names are prefixed by USCGC, for U.S. Coast Guard Cutter.

---

10 Memorandum from Rear Adm. D. S. Belz and Rear Adm. P. M. Stillman, USCG, subj.: "Deepwater Cutter Designators and Hull Numbers," 24 March 2004.

Table 32-2. COAST GUARD CUTTERS AND PATROL BOATS

Number	Class/Ship	Length	Comm.	Active	Building/Converting	Notes
WHEC 715	HAMILTON	378	1967–1972	12	—	
WMEC 901	BEAR	270	1983–1990	13	—	
WMEC 615	RELIANCE	210	1964–1969	14	—	
WMEC 39	HALEY	288	1971	1	—	ex-Navy ATS
WMEC 38	STORIS	230	1942	1	—	ex-WAGB type
WMEC 6	ACUSHNET	213	1944	1	—	ex-Navy ARS
WPC 1	CYCLONE	170	2000–2004*	5	—	ex-Navy PC
WPB 1301	Modernized Island	123	2004–**	1	4	
WPB 1301	Island	110	1986–1990	44	—	
WPB 87301	PROTECTOR	87	1998–2005	56	8	
WAGB 20	HEALY	420	2000	1	—	
WAGB 10	Polar	399	1976–1978	2	—	
WAGB 83	MACKINAW	290	1944	1	—	Great Lakes
WIX 327	EAGLE	295	1936	1	—	sailing bark
WLB 201	JUNIPER	225	1996–2005	5	1	Keeper class
WLB 62	BALSAM	180	1942–1944	1	—	
WLM	coastal buoy tenders			14	—	
WLI	inland buoy tenders			6	—	
WLIC	inland construction tenders			14	—	
WLR	river buoy tenders			15	—	
WTGB	icebreaking tugs			9	—	
WYTL	small harbor tugs			11	—	

* U.S. Navy commission
**Matagorda completion of modernization

AVIATION

The Coast Guard air arm has more than 200 aircraft in service and in storage. They are based at 23 Coast Guard Air Stations (CGAS) in the continental United States and at 1 station in Puerto Rico, 1 in Hawaii, and 2 in Alaska. Coast Guard aviators are trained by the Navy, with specialized training being given at the Coast Guard's Aviation Training Center in Mobile, Alabama.

Historically, the Coast Guard has flown the same aircraft types as operated by the U.S. Navy. However, in the 1980s, the Coast Guard procured two French-designed aircraft: 41 HU-25 Guardian fixed-wing aircraft, to replace the HU-16 Albatross amphibian and HC-131 Samaritan; and 96 HH-65A Dolphin Short-Range Recovery (SRR) helicopters, to replace the HH-52A Sea Guard helicopters. The HU-25 and HH-65 are not flown by other U.S. military services. Both have suffered engineering problems and have been expensive to maintain; half of the Guardians are in storage, and the Dolphins are being reengined.

More recently, the Coast Guard has procured the MH-68A Stingray, a derivative of the Agusta Westland (of Italy) A109E helicopter. That acquisition decision followed a 1999–2000 Coast Guard evaluation of two MH-90 Enforcer helicopters during Operation New Frontier. Operating from the cutters GALLATIN and SENECA in the Caribbean area, the helicopters were highly effective in making several drug busts, leading to the Coast Guard competition for a helicopter of this type for service use. During the Caribbean operation, the helicopters were owned by MD Helicopters and leased to the Coast Guard. (Production rights for the helicopter had been sold to MD Helicopters by Boeing in 1999.)

The MH-68A Stingray helicopters are assigned to the Helicopter Interdiction Tactical Squadron (HITRON) based at Jacksonville, Florida. The armed-helicopter unit previously was designated HITRON-10. This is the only squadron structure in Coast Guard aviation and the only airborne law enforcement unit trained and authorized to employ airborne use of force.

The cutters of the HAMILTON and BEAR classes, as well as the three large icebreakers, regularly embark helicopters, and some of the other cutter classes have landing decks but cannot support helicopters. It had been intended that, in wartime, the HAMILTON and BEAR classes would embark Navy SH-2F LAMPS I anti-submarine helicopters. However, there were no towed-array sonars available for the cutters, and the ASW data links were removed from the HAMILTONS. In the end, the disposal by the Navy of the last SH-2 LAMPS helicopters in 2001 made that planned capability a moot point.

The Coast Guard had considered the use of Short Take-Off Vertical Landing (STOVL) and Vertical/Short Take-Off and Landing (VSTOL) aircraft for future cutter operations. The Bell XV-15 tilt-rotor aircraft, which was the prototype for the V-22 Osprey, was evaluated during May 1999 trials off Key West, Florida. The Bell-Boeing 609 model, which is smaller than the V-22, was being proposed to the Coast Guard for the Search and Rescue (SAR) role. The Coast Guard did not pursue the concept.

The Coast Guard is procuring the Bell Eagle Eye Vertical Take-Off and Landing (VTOL) Unmanned Aerial Vehicle (UAV) under the Deepwater program. The current funding plan envisions the acquisition of 69 Eagle Eyes and 50 ground/shipboard control sta-

An artist's concept showing a CASA 235-300M maritime patrol aircraft in Coast Guard markings. The procurement of the Spanish-developed aircraft continues the Coast Guard's propensity for procuring non-U.S. aircraft. (U.S. Coast Guard)

The Coast Guard has selected Bell Helicopter Textron's Eagle Eye for its ship-based UAV. Eagle Eye is a VTOL aircraft that employs the tilt-wing/nacelle principal of the firm's XV-15 and V-22 Osprey aircraft. The Marine Corps also will procure the Eagle Eye, which was rejected by the Navy in favor of the Fire Scout. (Bell Helicopter Textron)

tions, at a cost of more than $1 billion. Deliveries are scheduled to begin in 2006.

The largest Coast Guard aircraft currently in service is the four-engine HC-130H Hercules, flown in relatively large numbers as a long-rang search aircraft. An additional HC-130J Hercules is being procured. It will be supplemented by the twin-engine CASA 235-300M maritime patrol aircraft for medium range patrol. Lockheed Martin and European Aeronautic Defence and Space Company (EADS) will produce the CASA 235-300M. Two are under contract, with options in place for six additional planes. The first of these will be delivered in 2007.

The Coast Guard also flies two VIP transport aircraft, a C-37A Gulfstream V and a long-serving VC-4A Gulfstream I.

The Coast Guard has discarded its single EC-130V Hercules configured for Airborne Early Warning (AEW) and the three E-2C Hawkeye AEW aircraft it operated. (The fourth E-2C crashed in 1990.) These radar surveillance aircraft were intended primarily for anti-drug operations. The EC-130V was transferred to the Air Force in 1993 and, subsequently, to the Navy, where it now serves as a test aircraft designated EC-130H. The three surviving E-2Cs were returned to the Navy.

Of the Coast Guard's two RG-8 motorized gliders, one crashed at sea and was lost. The other was scrapped after an effort to modify its power plant.

The Coast Guard pioneered the U.S. development of unmanned airships, or aerostats, for ocean surveillance. A 1985 agreement between the Navy and Coast Guard gave responsibility for development of manned airships to the Navy and unmanned airships to the Coast Guard. Subsequently, the Coast Guard operated a series of aerostats and support ships. That program was transferred to the Army in 1992 and promptly disbanded. (See 15th Edition/pages 603–5 for characteristics of the aerostat tenders.)

Table 32-3. COAST GUARD AIRCRAFT

Type		Mission	Total	Active	Storage
Fixed-Wing Aircraft					
HC-130H	Hercules	long-range search	27	22	5
C-37A	Gulfstream V	transport	1	1	—
VC-4A	Gulfstream I	executive transport	1	1	—
HU-25A	Guardian	medium-range search	25	9	16
HU-25B	Guardian	pollution surveillance	7	3	4
HU-25C	Guardian	"interceptor"	9	8	1
Rotary-Wing Aircraft					
MH-68A	Stingray	short-range armed interdiction	8	8	—
HH-65A	Dolphin	medium-range recovery	94	80	14
HH-60J	Jayhawk	medium-range recovery	42	35	

INTEGRATED DEEPWATER SYSTEM

The greatest challenge confronting the Coast Guard is that large portions of its cutters, patrol boats, and aircraft rapidly are becoming technologically obsolete. As a result, these platforms have excessive operating and maintenance costs, lack essential capabilities in speed, sensors, and interoperability, and consequently, limit overall deep-water mission effectiveness and efficiency.

In addition, their outdated technology places greater demands on the Coast Guard's logistics infrastructure. Approximately two-thirds of the operating costs of a current major cutter goes to personnel costs. In the 30 years since some of these cutters were designed, advances have been made in automated shipboard systems and maintenance reduction.

Another challenge is that many system and component manufacturers no longer are able to provide support for equipment and parts. As a result, the overall logistics effort demands more labor

hours, and maintenance costs increase while cutter/aircraft operational availability decreases.

Accordingly, the Integrated Deepwater System has been initiated to ensure the timely acquisition of appropriate platforms and systems to satisfy deep-water mission needs. The project is using commercial and military technologies and innovation to develop a completely integrated, multimission, and highly flexible force at the lowest total ownership cost. The program is being executed by a joint venture—Integrated Coast Guard Systems—formed by the megafirms Lockheed Martin and Northrop Grumman as equal partners.

The major ship/craft programs being developed under Deepwater are: (1) maritime security cutter (large), formerly called the national security cutter; (2) maritime security cutter (medium), formerly the offshore patrol cutter; (3) maritime patrol coastal, formerly the fast response cutter; and (4) maritime patrol boat, which are modernized Island-class WPCs.

Deepwater also is supervising the acquisition of the CASA 235-300M maritime patrol aircraft, as well as the service's UAV procurement.

The IDS effort has received strong endorsement from the Department of Homeland Security and from Congress. The Fiscal Year (FY) 2005 budget request by President George W. Bush identifies $678 million in funding for Deepwater programs, an increase of 35 percent over the president's budget request for FY 2004. Coast Guard Commandant Admiral Collins, in a speech at the Naval War College in January 2004, stated,

> Deepwater will provide the means to extend our layered maritime defenses from our ports and coastlines many hundreds of miles to sea to increase maritime domain awareness. We must move forward to execute the program aggressively so that its modern, more capable platforms and systems are delivered with an appropriate sense of urgency.[11]

The original IDS funding profile was for a 20-year, $17 billion acquisition plan. The increased funding currently being requested by the executive branch and probable congressional "plus-ups" could accelerate the schedule if that sense of urgency continues. Fifteen- and even 10-year programs have been proposed, the latter by Senator Olympia Snowe (Maine).[12]

However, in April 2004, the General Accounting office (GAO) advised a congressional committee that IDS would cost about $2.2 *billion* more than the estimated cost in 2002, when the program was initiated, i.e., a 13 percent increase on the basis of a 20-year procurement program.[13] A more-rapid acquisition would cost more.

MARITIME SECURITY/HIGH ENDURANCE CUTTERS

These are the largest ships operated by the Coast Guard, except for icebreakers. The maritime security cutter (large) is a product of IDS and will replace the HAMILTON-class cutters.

All high endurance cutters prior to the HAMILTON class have been stricken.

With the cutback in active Navy frigates, it has been suggested on several occasions that the Navy transfer at least one frigate of the OLIVER HAZARD PERRY (FFG 7) class to the Coast Guard to

---

11 "Deepwater Funding Increases in FY05 Budget," *Deepwater News* (February 2004), on line at www.uscg.mil/deepwater. This is a Web site specifically addressing IDS issues.

12 Hunter C. Keeter, "Coast Guard Mulls Major Changes to Deepwater Program Requirements," *Sea Power* [Navy League] (April 2004), p. 24.

13 GAO Highlights, "Coast Guard: Key Management and Budget Challenges for Fiscal Year 2004 and Beyond" (6 April 2004); also see GAO Highlights, "Contract Management: Coast Guard's Deepwater Program Needs Increased Attention to Management and Contractor Oversight" (4 March 2004).

serve as a training cutter. Proposals for the Coast Guard to operate variants of the FFG 7 design as high endurance cutters were made as early as 1981.[14] Among the modifications put forward for Coast Guard use were removal of the (modular) Mk 13 Standard/Harpoon launcher and modification of the two-bay hanger to provide space for specialized SAR equipment while retaining the capability to operate one large helicopter (i.e., H-60 type).

There has been no action taken on these proposals, primarily because of the large manning requirements for frigates.

(8) MARITIME SECURITY CUTTERS—LARGE (425)

Number	Name	Builder	Comm.	Status
WMSL 750	....	Northrop Grumman, Pascagoula, Miss.	2006	Planned
WMSL 751–757		Northrop Grumman, Pascagoula, Miss.		Planned

Displacement:	3,206 tons light
	4,112 tons full load
Length:	390 ft (118.87 m) waterline
	421¾ ft (128.33 m) overall
Beam:	54 ft (16.46 m)
Draft:	21½ ft (6.42 m)
Propulsion:	Combination Diesel and Gas turbine (CODAG):
	1 gas turbine; 30,565 shp + 2 diesel engines; 19,310 bhp;
	2 shafts
Speed:	28 knots
Range:	12,000 nm (22,235 km)
Personnel:	approx. 150, including 20 in aviation detachment
Helicopters:	1 HH-65A Dolphin + Vertical Take-Off UAV (VTUAV)
	or 2 HH-65A Dolphin
	or 4 VTUAV
Guns:	1 57-mm/70-cal cannon Mk 110
	1 20-mm Phalanx Close-In Weapon System (CIWS) Mk 15
	(multi-barrel)
	4 .50-cal machine guns M2
Radar:	air search (3-D)
	navigation
	surface search
Fire control:	1 SPQ-9B radar
	1 Mk 46 electro-optical/infrared sensor
EW systems:	SLQ-32

These are high endurance cutters being procured under the Deepwater project as successors to the HAMILTON class.

The WMSL will be specially configured for transoceanic oper-

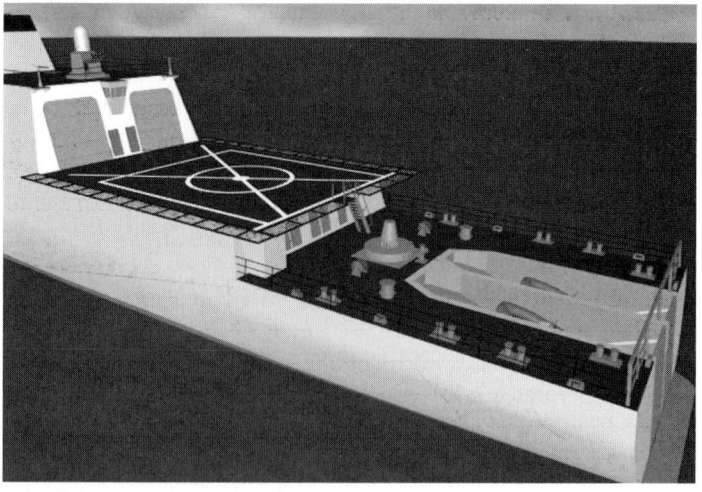

The stern of the maritime security cutter—large will have special facilities for rapidly launching and recovering two Rigid Hull Inflatable Boats (RHIBs), as shown here. (U.S. Coast Guard)

ations. The design provides for twin helicopter hangars and a flight deck capable of operating H-60-size helicopters, as well as UAVs. There will be ramps and handling facilities aft to accommodate two large Rigid Hull Inflatable Boats (RHIB).

The cutters will have a high standard of accommodations, with four-person staterooms for enlisted personnel.

Builders: Northrop Grumman Corporation's Ship Systems sector (Pascagoula, Mississippi) has been awarded a $129 million contract for the detail design and long-lead material procurement as the first step in the development and delivery of this new class of cutters.

Classification: During the design stage, these ships were designated national security cutters.

Engineering: These cutters will have a bow thruster.

Guns: It is expected that the WMSL will be armed with the 57-mm/70-cal cannon Mk 110. This is an adaptation of the Bofors 57-mm/60-cal Mk 3 rapid-fire gun.

Operational: These cutters will have a 60-day endurance.

---

14 For example, *Analysis of FFG-7 Variants for Naval Reserve and Coast Guard Operation* (Alexandria, Va.: Maritime Publications, Ltd., May 1981).

The maritime security cutter—large (WMSL) is planned as the successor to the outstanding but outdated HAMILTON-class high-endurance cutters. The WMSL will have greatly updated Command, Control, and Communications (C³) capabilities, a vital factor in modern, integrated security and defense operations. (U.S. Coast Guard)

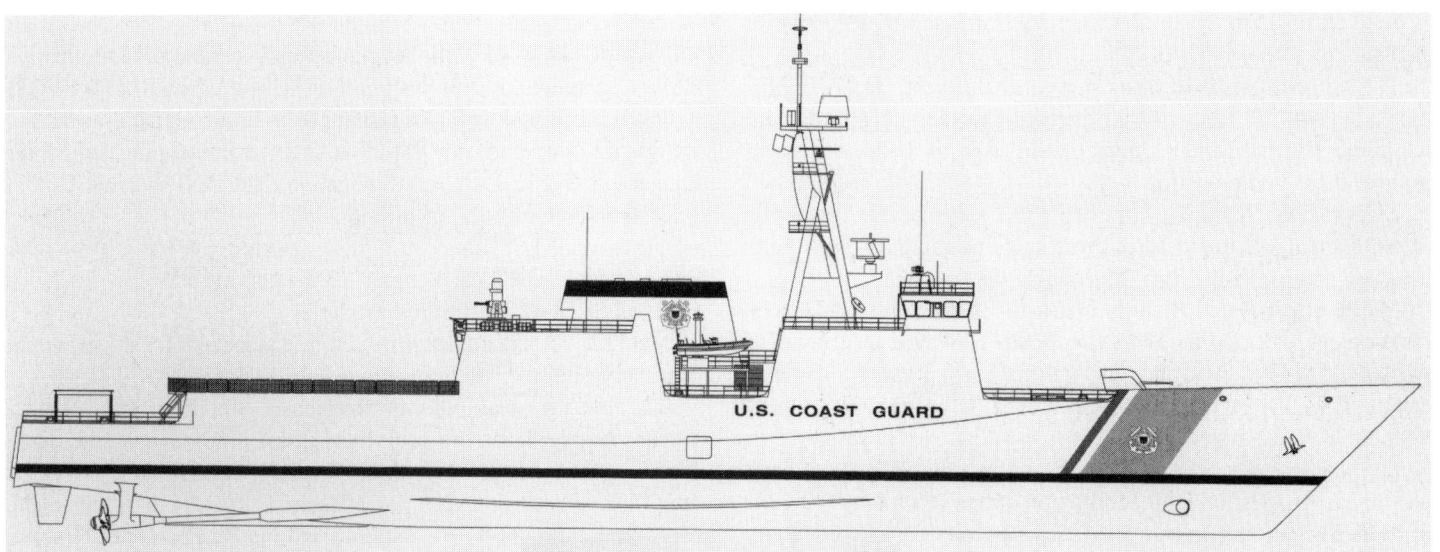

Maritime Security Cutter—Large

12 HIGH ENDURANCE CUTTERS: "HAMILTON" CLASS (378)

Number	Name	Builder	Laid down	Launched	Comm.	Modernized	Status
WHEC 715	HAMILTON	Avondale Shipyards, New Orleans	4 Jan 1965	18 Dec 1965	20 Feb 1967	Oct 19855–Nov 1988	**PA**
WHEC 716	DALLAS	Avondale Shipyards, New Orleans	7 Feb 1966	1 Oct 1966	1 Oct 1967	Nov 1986-Dec 1989	**AA**
WHEC 717	MELLON	Avondale Shipyards, New Orleans	25 July 1966	11 Feb 1967	22 Dec 1967	Oct 1985–June 1989	**PA**
WHEC 718	CHASE	Avondale Shipyards, New Orleans	15 Oct 1966	20 May 1967	1 Mar 1968	July 1989–Mar 1991	**PA**
WHEC 719	BOUTWELL	Avondale Shipyards, New Orleans	12 Dec 1966	17 June 1967	14 June 1968	Mar 1989–Apr 1991	**PA**
WHEC 720	SHERMAN	Avondale Shipyards, New Orleans	13 Feb 1967	23 Sep 1967	23 Aug 1968	May 1986–Feb 1990	**PA**
WHEC 721	GALLATIN	Avondale Shipyards, New Orleans	17 Apr 1967	18 Nov 1967	20 Dec 1968	Mar 1990–Jan 1992	**AA**
WHEC 722	MORGENTHAU	Avondale Shipyards, New Orleans	17 July 1967	10 Feb 1968	14 Feb 1969	Nov 1989–Dec 1991	**PA**
WHEC 723	RUSH	Avondale Shipyards, New Orleans	23 Oct 1967	16 Nov 1968	3 July 1969	July 1989–Sep 1991	**PA**
WHEC 724	MUNRO	Avondale Shipyards, New Orleans	18 Feb 1970	5 Dec 1970	10 Sep 1971	Dec 1986–Nov 1989	**PA**
WHEC 725	JARVIS	Avondale Shipyards, New Orleans	9 Sep 1970	24 Apr 1971	30 Dec 1971	Mar 1991–Dec 1992	**PA**
WHEC 726	MIDGETT	Avondale Shipyards, New Orleans	5 Apr 1971	4 Sep 1971	17 Mar 1972	Jan 1991-Mar 1992	**PA**

Displacement:	2,716 tons standard	Guns:	1 76-mm/62-cal DP Mk 75
	3,050 tons full load		2 40-mm grenade launchers Mk 19 (2 single)
Length:	350 ft (106.7 m) waterline		2 25-mm Bushmaster cannon Mk 38 (2 single)
	378⅝ ft (115.4 m) overall		1 20-mm Phalanx Close-In Weapon System (CIWS) Mk 15
Beam:	42¾ ft (13.0 m)		(multibarrel)
Draft:	20⅓ ft (6.2 m) over sonar dome		4 .50-cal machine guns (4 single)
Propulsion:	Combination Diesel or Gas (CODOG): 2 gas turbines	ASW weapons:	removed
	(Pratt & Whitney FT4-A6); 28,000 shp + 2 diesel engines	Missiles:	removed
	(Fairbanks Morse 38TD8 1/8), 7,200 bhp; 2 shafts	Radar:	1 SPS-40B air search
Speed:	29 knots		2 SPS-64(V)6 navigation
Range:	2,400 nm (4,445 km) at 29 knots	Sonars:	SQS-38 keel-mounted
	9,600 nm (17,790 km) at 19 knots (gas turbines)	Fire control:	1 Mk 92 Mod 1 Gunfire Control System (GFCS)
	14,000 nm (25,930 km) at 11 knots (diesel)	EW systems:	WLR-1C
Personnel:	178 (20 officers + 158 enlisted)		WLR-3
Helicopters:	1 HH-60J Jayhawk		

These are the largest cutters ever operated by the Coast Guard except for icebreakers. They are capable of long-range operations. All have been upgraded under a Fleet Rehabilitation and Modernization (FRAM) program (dates indicated above).

Class: Originally, 36 ships of this class were planned. The additional ships were deferred in favor of retaining older cutters and then were dropped with construction of the smaller BEAR-class cutters.

Design: These cutters were designed to operate as frigates in wartime, being provided from the outset with Anti-Submarine Warfare (ASW) weapons—low-frequency sonar, an ASW fire control system, and Mk 32 torpedo tubes for Mk 44/46 torpedoes. The first few ships also were fitted with hedgehogs. Subsequently, their ASW capabilities were upgraded, with provisions for operating an SH-2 LAMPS I helicopter with an SQR-4 and SQR-17 sonobuoy datalink and analysis equipment (fitted during the FRAM upgrade).

In 1992, Commandant Admiral J. William Kime directed that all ASW weapons and sensors be removed from these cutters:

The requirement to maintain the WHEC ASW mission/capability was reviewed by the Navy–Coast Guard Board (NAVGARD) on 23 July 1992. The Board determined that ASW should be retained as a mission for WHECs, but in [the] absence of a global ASW threat, the requirement to maintain an ASW capability can be eliminated. The Navy has sufficient assets to respond to regional contingencies requiring ASW and there will be enough warning time to regenerate the WHEC capability if needed for future global scale conflicts. . . .

The decision to eliminate the ASW capability requirement . . . was a hard one. The Coast Guard has been effectively prosecuting the ASW mission in defense of our country since before World War II. However, the world has changed and we must change with it.[15]

---

15 Message from Commandant, Coast Guard to All Coast Guard, 31 July 1992, COMDTNOTE 1430.

Also removed in this period were the Harpoon anti-ship missile canisters (see *Missile* notes).

The superstructures of these ships are fabricated largely of aluminum. They are fitted with oceanographic and meteorological facilities. The helicopter hangars were used as balloon shelters prior to their modernization.

Electronics: Beginning in 1967, the original keel-mounted SQS-36 sonar was replaced in these ships by the SQS-38, a hull-mounted version of the SQS-35 variable-depth sonar.

Mk 36 Super Rapid Bloom Off-Board Chaff (SRBOC) launchers were fitted during the FRAM upgrade. However, the previously planned SLQ-32(V)2 and SLQ-25 Nixie installations were canceled. (Thus, the BEAR-class cutters are the only Coast Guard units with the SLQ-32 system.)

Engineering: These were the largest U.S. combat ships to have gas-turbine propulsion until completion of the SPRUANCE (DD 963) in 1975. The gas turbines are FT-4A, marine versions of the J75 aircraft engine. The propulsion machinery is Combination Diesel or Gas (CODOG). A 350-hp bow propeller pod is fitted.

Guns: These were the last active ships in U.S. service to mount 5-inch (127-mm)/38-cal DP guns. (The last active U.S. Navy ships with this weapon were the frigates of the BROOKE/DEG 1 and GARCIA/FF 1040 classes.) The 5-inch gun mount was replaced during the FRAM upgrade.

Missiles: On 16 January 1990, the MELLON became the first Coast Guard cutter to fire a guided missile, launching a Harpoon Surface-to-Surface Missile (SSM). Five cutters were fitted with Harpoon through 1992, with all of the ships scheduled for eventual installation.

Modernization: The major armament/sensor/electronics upgrades to this class were:

1967–1987 ASW upgrade
• 6 Mk 32 12.75-inch (324-mm) torpedo tubes for Mk 44/46 torpedoes (hedgehogs deleted)
• Mk 309 torpedo control panel
• SQS-38 sonar (hull-mounted version of SQS-35 variable-depth sonar)

1985–1992 FRAM
• 76-mm OTO Melara Mk 76 (replacing 5-inch/38-cal DP gun)
• Mk 92 Gunfire Control System (GFCS) (replacing Mk 56 GFCS)
• SPS-40 air search radar (replacing SPS-29 air search radar)
• flight deck upgrade for SH-2F LAMPS I telescoping helicopter hangar and Tactical Aircraft Navigation (TACAN) system
• communications equipment upgrade
• Harpoon SSM
• SQR-4 and SQR-17 helicopter ASW support links
• Mk 36 SRBOC chaff/flare launchers

With the FRAM update, the manning standards for these cutters was increased from 152 (15 officers + 137 enlisted) to 171.

The FRAM work was undertaken at the Bath Iron Works, Maine, shipyard for the four East Coast ships and at the Todd Pacific yard in Seattle, Washington, for the eight West Coast ships (see *Operational* notes). A large deck structure was fitted to the forecastle to mount the 76-mm gun and the Harpoon canisters; the Phalanx CIWS mount is fitted aft of the flight deck.

The FRAM upgrades experienced major delays and cost increases over original estimates. The original cost of $30 million per ship increased to between $50 million and $70 million per ship.

Names: The first nine ships were named for Secretaries of the Treasury; the last three ships honor heroes of the Coast Guard. (Signalman 1st Class Douglas A. Munro posthumously received the Medal of Honor for bravery under fire while supporting Marines on Guadalcanal in 1942; he is the only Coast Guardsman to receive the nation's highest military honor.) Accordingly, the cutters have been referred to as the Hero class.

Operational: The HAMILTON and CHASE were transferred from the East Coast (Boston) to the West Coast (San Pedro, California) in late 1991, bringing 10 of the 12 ships of this class to the Pacific. The DALLAS and GALLATIN remain on the East Coast. They were based at Governor's Island in New York harbor until 1995, when both shifted their home port to Charleston. South Carolina.

The DALLAS deployed to the Mediterranean in July 1995 for a three-month assignment as a fully integrated unit of the U.S. Sixth Fleet. This is believed to have been the first time such an assignment occurred during peacetime.

The big sister: The high-endurance cutter DALLAS escorts the motor vessel BBC SPAIN as she transports four 110-foot Coast Guard cutters to the Mediterranean in support of Operation Enduring Freedom. The smaller craft were sent to the Med to provide security for U.S. shipping supporting Middle East actions. (2003, U.S. Coast Guard)

The BOUTWELL *operating in the northern Persian Gulf, one of several Coast Guard cutters and security units deployed to the Middle East region in support of U.S. operations in Iraq. The* HAMILTON-*class cutters are large, graceful ships, although in several respects they are outdated for contemporary operations. (2003, U.S. Coast Guard/John Gaffney)*

The MIDGETT, *the last of the* HAMILTON-*class cutters. Modernization programs have placed a deckhouse forward of the bridge structure, which supports the ship's 76-mm gun mount. Previously, these ships carried a 5-inch/38-caliber gun forward. (2004, U.S. Coast Guard)*

The BOUTWELL, *like other* HAMILTON-*class cutters, mounts a 20-mm Phalanx Close In Weapon System (CIWS) on the stern, after of the helicopter flight deck and hangar. The SPS-40B air search radar dominates her masts. (2003, U.S. Coast Guard/John Gaffney)*

Maritime Security Cutter— Medium

MEDIUM SECURITY/MEDIUM ENDURANCE CUTTERS

The new medium security cutters (WMSM) will carry an adaptable mission module, similar in concept to the Navy's Littoral Combat Ship (LCS). At times during development of the WMSM, the Coast Guard and Navy considered some degree of commonality between the two ships; however, such considerations were superficial and were unfulfilled because of the differing service requirements. For example, the Navy's LCS has a 50-knot requirement, far in excess of Coast Guard needs.

25) MARITIME SECURITY CUTTERS—MEDIUM (341)

Builder:	
Displacement:	
Length:	341 feet (103.96 m) overall
Beam:	
Draft:	
Propulsion:	2 diesel engines; 2 shafts
Speed:	23 knots
Range:	9,000 nm (16,675 km)
Personnel:	approx. 95
Helicopters:	1 HH-65 Dolphin or 2 VTUAV
Guns:	1 57-mm/70-cal cannon Mk 110

The WMSM cutters are being developed under the Deepwater program to replace the BEAR and RELIANCE classes.

These cutters will begin with hull number WMSM 915.

Classification: During the design stage, these ships were designated offshore patrol cutters.

Engineering: The WMSMs are to be fitted with bow thrusters.

Operational: These cutters will have a 45-day endurance.

1 MEDIUM ENDURANCE CUTTER: EX-NAVY SALVAGE SHIP (288)

Number	Name	Launched	Navy Comm.	USCG Comm.	Status
WMEC 39 (ex-ATS 1)	ALEX HALEY	15 May 1968	23 Jan 1971	10 July 1999	**PA**

Builders:	Brooke Marine, Lowestoft (England)
Displacement:	2,650 tons standard
	3,200 tons full load
Length:	264 ft (80.5 m) waterline
	288⅔ ft (88.0 m) overall
Beam:	50 ft (15.25 m)
Draft:	15⅙ feet (4.6 m)
Propulsion:	4 diesel engines (Caterpillar 3516); 6,800 bhp; 2 shafts
Speed:	16 knots
Range:	10,000 nm (18,520 km) at 13 knots
Personnel:	99 (7 officers + 92 enlisted)
Helicopters:	1 HH-65A Dolphin
Guns:	2 25-mm Bushmaster cannon Mk 38 (2 single)
	2 .50-cal machine guns M2 (2 single)
Radars:	SPS-64(V) navigation
Sonars:	none

This is the former EDENTON (ATS 1), a U.S. Navy tug-type ship with extensive salvage and diving capabilities. Most of these features have been removed for her role as a medium endurance cutter.

The ship was decommissioned from the Navy on 29 March 1996 and transferred to the Coast Guard on 18 November 1997. She was modified for Coast Guard service at the Coast Guard Yard at Curtis Bay, Maryland.

The HALEY is homeported in Kodiak, Alaska.

Class: The EDENTON was one of a class of three ships (ATS 1–3); see Chapter 23.

Design: Navy SCB No. 719. The ATS design provided for large, open work spaces forward and aft, with extensive salvage, diving, and towing facilities. (The diving system was limited to compressed air, not helium–oxygen.)

The ship has been reengined and rearmed in Coast Guard service. A helicopter hangar also has been installed.

Engineering: The ship has a through-bow thruster for precise maneuvering.

Names: All ships of this class originally were named for cities in both Britain and the United States. The ALEX HALEY remembers the late Pulitzer Prize-winning author, who had served in the Coast Guard from 1939 to 1959, retiring as a chief journalist.

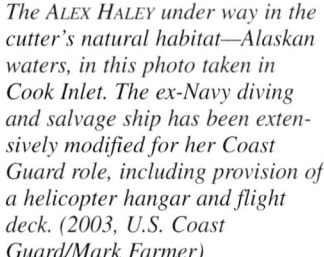

The ALEX HALEY under way in the cutter's natural habitat—Alaskan waters, in this photo taken in Cook Inlet. The ex-Navy diving and salvage ship has been extensively modified for her Coast Guard role, including provision of a helicopter hangar and flight deck. (2003, U.S. Coast Guard/Mark Farmer)

13 MEDIUM ENDURANCE CUTTERS: "BEAR" CLASS (270)

Number	Name	Builder	Laid down	Launched	Comm.	Status
WMEC 901	BEAR	Tacoma Boatbuilding, Tacoma, Wash.	23 Aug 1979	25 Sep 1980	4 Feb 1983	**AA**
WMEC 902	TAMPA	Tacoma Boatbuilding, Tacoma, Wash.	2 Apr 1980	19 Mar 1981	16 Mar 1984	**AA**
WMEC 903	HARRIET LANE	Tacoma Boatbuilding, Tacoma, Wash.	15 Oct 1980	6 Feb 1982	20 Sep 1984	**AA**
WMEC 904	NORTHLAND	Tacoma Boatbuilding, Tacoma, Wash.	9 Apr 1981	7 May 1982	17 Dec 1984	**AA**
WMEC 905	SPENCER (ex-SENECA)	Robert E. Derecktor, Middletown, R.I.	26 June 1982	17 Apr 1984	28 June 1986	**AA**
WMEC 906	SENECA (ex-ESCANABA)	Robert E. Derecktor, Middletown, R.I.	16 Sep 1982	17 Apr 1984	4 May 1987	**AA**
WMEC 907	ESCANABA (ex-TAHOMA)	Robert E. Derecktor, Middletown, R.I.	1 Apr 1983	2 June 1985	27 Aug 1987	**AA**
WMEC 908	TAHOMA (ex-SPENCER)	Robert E. Derecktor, Middletown, R.I.	28 June 1983	2 June 1985	6 Apr 1988	**AA**
WMEC 909	CAMBELL (ex-ARGUS)	Robert E. Derecktor, Middletown, R.I.	10 Aug 1984	29 Apr 1986	19 Aug 1988	**AA**
WMEC 910	THETIS (ex-TAHOMA)	Robert E. Derecktor, Middletown, R.I.	24 Aug 1984	29 Apr 1986	30 June 1989	**AA**
WMEC 911	FORWARD (ex-ERIE)	Robert E. Derecktor, Middletown, R.I.	11 July 1986	19 Aug 1987	4 Aug 1990	**AA**
WMEC 912	LEGARE (ex-McCULLOCH)	Robert E. Derecktor, Middletown, R.I.	11 July 1986	19 Aug 1987	4 Aug 1990	**AA**
WMEC 913	MOHAWK (ex-EWING)	Robert E. Derecktor, Middletown, R.I.	18 June 1987	18 May 1988	20 Mar 1990	**AA**

Displacement:	1,200 tons light	Personnel:	100 (11 officers + 89 enlisted) + 16 aircrew
	1,820 tons full load	Helicopters:	1 HH-65A Dolphin
Length:	255 ft (77.8 m) waterline	Guns:	1 76-mm/62-cal AA Mk 75
	270 ft (82.3 m) overall		2 .50-cal machine guns M2 (2 single)
Beam:	38 ft (11.6 m)	ASW weapons:	none
Draft:	14 ft (4.3 m)	Radars:	2 SPS-64(V)1/6 navigation
Propulsion:	2 geared diesel engines (Alco 18V-251E); 7,200 bhp; 2 shafts	Sonars:	none
Speed:	19.5 knots	Fire control:	Mk 92 Mod 1 GFCS
Range:	3,850 nm (7,130 km) at 19.5 knots	EW systems:	SLQ-32(V)1
	9,900 nm (18,335 km) at 12 knots		

These are multipurpose cutters. However, their lack of ASW weapons and sensors makes them unsuitable for employment in the ASW role without extensive modification. They have been criticized for their slow speed, and they ride poorly in heavy seas.

The first four ships were ordered from Tacoma Boatbuilding, with the remainder planned for procurement from the Tacoma yard; however, the Coast Guard was forced into competitive bidding. The subsequent ships were then awarded to the Derecktor yard.

The BEAR was not delivered to the Coast Guard for service until late in 1983.

Aircraft: A landing deck and expanding hangar permit these cutters to handle any of the Coast Guard's helicopters, as well as the Navy's SH-2F LAMPS I. It was intended in wartime that an SH-2F would be assigned to each ship for convoy escort, but such helicopters no longer are available for deployment aboard these ships. The ESCANABA conducted trials with a Navy SH-60B LAMPS III helicopter in 1988.

The Recovery Assistance and Traversing System (RAST) is fitted to facilitate helicopter operations in rough seas.

Class: The lead ship was authorized in FY 1976, WMEC 902–904 in FY 1977, and WMEC 905–913 in FY 1980. The class is known officially as the Famous class, but generally is referred to as the BEAR class.

Design: Design criteria for this class included the ability to conduct 14-day law enforcement patrols in areas out to 400 nm (740 km) from base. Maximum normal at-sea endurance is 21 days.

These ships have a very short forecastle with a large, two-level superstructure that gives them a humpback shape. Active fin stabilizers are fitted.

These were the first Coast Guard cutters to be completed with a contemporary Electronic Warfare (EW) suite after World War II. They are designed to be fitted with the following military systems in wartime: SH-2F LAMPS I anti-submarine helicopter, two Harpoon anti-ship quad missile canisters, one 20-mm Phalanx

The TAMPA passes near Fort Monroe, Virginia, showing her partially open helicopter hangar and her flight deck. The BEAR-class cutters have received "mixed reviews," as their service has revealed several shortcomings. (2004, U.S. Coast Guard/Jason R. Zalasky)

CIWS, the Tactical Towed Array Sonar (TACTAS), and chaff launchers. The ships seem unlikely, however, to be able to accommodate simultaneously all of these systems, in part because of the number of additional personnel required, as well as because of the probable shortage of available systems during a conflict.

Accommodations are provided for 109 personnel.

Guns: Six positions are provided for installing machine guns or 40-mm grenade launchers Mk 19.

Names: The Coast Guard named all 13 ships of the class at the beginning of the procurement cycle. Subsequently, the prematurely awarded names for WMEC 905 and later ships were withdrawn,

and those cutters were renamed, as indicated above.

The BEAR honors a long-serving Navy and Coast Guard screw steamer. Built in Scotland in 1874 as a sealing vessel, she was purchased by the U.S. Navy in 1884 and operated successively in the Navy, Revenue Cutter Service, and Coast Guard, and again in the Navy (designated AG 29). The BEAR was employed extensively in Arctic operations and was used by Rear Admiral Richard E. Byrd during his Antarctic expedition of 1933–1935. She was decommissioned in 1944 and transferred to the Maritime Commission in 1948.

Operational: The entire class is based on the Atlantic coast.

The TAMPA *off the coast of Colombia, operating with U.S. naval forces during the multination UNITAS exercise. Her helicopter hangar is expanded. Note the short forecastle and the location of her 76-mm gun mount. (2002, U.S. Coast Guard)*

14 MEDIUM ENDURANCE CUTTERS: "RELIANCE" CLASS (210)

Number	Name	Launched	Comm.	Modernized	Status
A series (5)					
WMEC 615	RELIANCE	25 May 1963	20 June 1964	Apr 1987–Jan 1989	**AA**
WMEC 616	DILIGENCE	20 July 1963	31 Aug 1964	July 1990–Dec 1991	**AA**
WMEC 617	VIGILANT	24 Dec 1963	1 Oct 1964	Feb 1989–June 1990	**AA**
WMEC 618	ACTIVE	21 July 1965	17 Sep 1966	Oct 1984–Feb 1987	**PA**
WMEC 619	CONFIDENCE	8 May 1965	19 Feb 1966	Oct 1986–June 1988	**AA**
B series (9)					
WMEC 620	RESOLUTE	30 Apr 1966	8 Dec 1966	Aug 1994–Sep 1996	**PA**
WMEC 621	VALIANT	14 Jan 1967	28 Oct 1967	Dec 1991–May 1993	**AA**
WMEC 623	STEADFAST	24 June 1967	7 Oct 1968	June 1992–Feb 1994	**PA**
WMEC 624	DAUNTLESS	21 Oct 1967	10 June 1968	Aug 1993–Feb 1995	**AA**
WMEC 625	VENTUROUS	11 Nov 1967	16 Aug 1968	Feb 1994–Oct 1995	**AA**
WMEC 626	DEPENDABLE	16 Mar 1968	22 Nov 1968	Feb 1995–Aug 1997	**AA**
WMEC 627	VIGOROUS	4 May 1968	23 Apr 1969	June 1991–Nov 1992	**AA**
WMEC 629	DECISIVE	14 Dec 1967	23 Aug 1968	Sep 1996–May 1998	**AA**
WMEC 630	ALERT	19 Oct 1968	28 July 1969	Dec 1992–Sep 1994	**PA**

Builders:	WMEC 615–617: Todd Shipyards, Houston, Texas	Speed:	18 knots	
	WMEC 618: Christy Corp., Sturgeon Bay, Wisc.	Range:	A series: 2,100 nm (3,890 km) at 18 knots	
	WMEC 619, 625, 629: Coast Guard Yard, Curtis Bay, Md.		6,100 nm (11,300 km) at 13 knots	
	WMEC 620, 621, 623, 624, 624, 626, 627, 630: American		B series: 2,700 nm (5,000 km at 18 knots	
	Shipbuilding, Lorain, Ohio		6,100 nm (11,300 km) at 13 knots	
Displacement:	950 tons standard	Personnel:	75 (12 officers + 63 enlisted)	
	1,007 tons full load, except WMEC 616–619 970 tons	Helicopters:	landing area	
Length:	200 ft (60.96 m) waterline	Guns:	1 25-mm Bushmaster cannon Mk 38	
	210½ ft (64.2 m) overall		2 .50-cal machine guns M2 (2 single)	
Beam:	34 ft (10.4 m)	ASW weapons:	none	
Draft:	10½ feet (3.2 m)	Radars:	2 SPS-64(V)1 navigation	
Propulsion:	2 turbocharged diesel engines (Alco 251B); 5,000 bhp;	Sonars:	none	
	2 shafts			

These are search-and-rescue ships. They can land helicopters but have no hangars.

Armament: No ASW armament is provided in these cutters, although their design included space and weight provisions for hedgehogs and, subsequently, Mk 32 ASW torpedo tubes. Also see *Guns* notes.

Class: Originally a class of 16 ships; the DURABLE (WMEC 628) was decommissioned and stricken on 20 September 2001 and the COURAGEOUS (WMEC 622) on 27 September 2001.

Classification: These ships originally were classified as patrol craft (WPC); they were changed to WMEC, with the same hull numbers, on 1 May 1966. The RELIANCE was changed to WTR 615 on June 1975 (the TR indicating Training of Reserves); she reverted to WMEC 615 on 16 August 1982.

Design: The RELIANCE design has a small island superstructure with 360° visibility from the bridge to facilitate helicopter operations and towing. The ALERT was fitted with the Canadian-developed "Beartrap" helicopter hauldown system.

Engineering: The WMEC 615–619 were built with CODAG turbine plants to give the Coast Guard experience in operating mixed propulsion plants. Those cutters had a high acceleration rate from all stop; with their engines shut down, they could be at full speed in a few minutes. They could make 15.25 knots on gas turbines alone. The cost factor influenced the decision to make the remaining ships all-diesel.

The first five ships were reengined to all-diesel during their mid-life modernization.

Guns: As built, the armament consisted of a single, open-mount 3-inch/50-cal gun Mk 22 forward of the bridge. During the ships' modernization, the 3-inch weapon was replaced by the 25-mm Bushmaster.

Modernization: These cutters were upgraded under a Mid-life Maintenance Availability (MMA) program. The upgrade included an enlarged superstructure, installation of a larger, improved engine exhaust (funnel), improved living spaces, a redesigned engine room, an upgraded firefighting system, new refrigeration and air conditioning units, a new electronics suite, and a new primary gun mount.

The MMA required approximately 18 months and cost about $20 million per cutter. The work was done at the Coast Guard Yard. The ACTIVE was the first cutter to be modernized and the DECISIVE was the last, the total 14 ship-program having taken almost 14 years to complete.

The ACTIVE *is typical of the long-serving* RELIANCE*-class cutters. They have been extensively modernized. These cutters have a platform for a helicopter but cannot support one. They have a large radio direction-finding antenna forward of the bridge. (2002, W, Michael Young)*

The DILIGENCE *escorts the Disney cruise ship* WONDER *off Cape Canaveral, Florida. At the time, several members of President George W. Bush's family were vacationing on board the cruise ship. (2002, U.S. Coast Guard)*

1 MEDIUM ENDURANCE CUTTER: "STORIS" (230)

Number	Name	Launched	Comm.	Status
WMEC 38	STORIS	4 Apr 1942	30 Sep 1942	**PA**

Builders:	Toledo Shipbuilding, Ohio
Displacement:	1,715 tons standard
	1,925 tons full load
Length:	230 feet (70.1 m) overall
Beam:	43 feet (13.1 m)
Draft:	15 feet (4.6 m)
Propulsion:	diesel-electric (3 Fairbanks Morse 38D 8¼ diesel engines);
	1,800 shp; 1 shaft
Speed:	14.5 knots
Range:	12,000 nm (22,225 km) at 14.5 knots
	22,000 nm (40,745 km) at 8 knots
Personnel:	86 (11 officers + 75 enlisted)
Helicopters:	no facilities
Guns:	1 25-mm Bushmaster cannon Mk 38
	4 .50-cal machine guns M2 (4 single)
Radars:	2 SPS-64 navigation

The STORIS was built specifically for offshore icebreaking and patrol in the Greenland area. She has been employed in Alaskan service for search and rescue and law enforcement since 1949. She is homeported in Kodiak, Alaska.

The oldest Coast Guard cutter in active service, the STORIS is entitled to have gold hull numbers.

Classification: The STORIS originally was classified as WAGL 38 and then WAG 38; she was changed to WAGB 38 on 1 May 1966. Subsequently, she was reclassified as a medium endurance cutter (WMEC) on 1 July 1972 to emphasize her role in law enforcement off the Alaskan fishing grounds.

Design: The ship was designed specifically for operation in northern waters and for icebreaking, although she generally is similar to the Coast Guard's 180-foot (54.9-m) buoy tenders. During World War II, the STORIS carried a single J2F Duck biplane scouting aircraft.

Guns: As built, the STORIS was armed with two 3-inch guns and four 20-mm guns, plus ASW weapons. A single 3-inch gun was retained into the 1980s, but eventually was replaced by the 25-mm Bushmaster.

Names: The ship initially was named ESKIMO, but that was changed during construction to STORIS at the request of the State Department, which feared the former name might offend the natives of Greenland. The name STORIS is derived from a Scandinavian word that means "blue ice," a reference to very hard ice.

Operational: During World War II, the STORIS served in the North Atlantic as an ocean escort ship.

The STORIS and the seagoing buoy tenders BRAMBLE and SPAR carried out the first circumnavigation of the North American continent and transited the Northwest Passage in 1957, departing from Unimak Pass, Alaska, on 1 July and reaching Argentia, Newfoundland, on 19 September.

1 MEDIUM ENDURANCE CUTTER: FORMER SALVAGE SHIP (213)

Number	Name	Launched	Navy ARS Comm	USCG Comm	Status
WMEC 167 (ex-ARS 9)	ACUSHNET	1 Apr 1943	5 Feb 1944	23 Aug 1946	**PA**

Builders:	Basalt Rock, Napa, Calif.
Displacement:	1,557 tons standard
	1,745 tons full load
Length:	213½ feet (65.1 m) overall
Beam:	39 feet (12.8 m)
Draft:	15 feet (4.9 m)
Propulsion:	diesel-electric: 4 diesel engines (Fairbanks-Morse);
	3,460 shp; 2 shafts
Speed:	15.5 knots
Range:	9,000 nm (16,670 km) at 15.5 knots
	20,000 nm (37,040 km) at 7 knots
Personnel:	72 (7 officers + 65 enlisted)
Helicopters:	no facilities
Guns:	removed
Radars:	2 SPS-64 navigation

This is the last of eight former Navy salvage ships and oceangoing tugs (ATF) operated by the Coast Guard after World War II. Formerly the Navy salvage ship SHACKLE (ARS 9), the ACUSHNET was permanently transferred to the Coast Guard on 29 June 1946.

Class: Two sister ships previously operated by the Coast Guard have been stricken. The ESCAPE (ARS 6) was transferred to the Coast Guard on 4 December 1980 and redesignated WMEC 6 (retaining her Navy name); she was decommissioned for disposal on 29 June 1995.

The SEIZE (ARS 26) was transferred to the Coast Guard on 28 June 1946 and redesignated WMEC 168 (renamed YOCONA); she was decommissioned for disposal on 30 May 1996.

Classification: On transfer to the Coast Guard, the ATF 167 was reclassified as a tug (WAT). She was changed to WMEC on 1 May 1966. On modification to handle environmental data buoys, the ACUSHNET was changed to oceanographic cutter (WAGO 167) in 1969; she was redesignated WMEC in 1978.

Engineering: The ship was reengined in Coast Guard service.

The STORIS is the longest-serving Coast Guard cutter on active service. Operating in the Alaska–Aleutians area, she carries out search-and-rescue and law enforcement operations. When built, she carried a seaplane. (2002, U.S. Coast Guard)

The ACUSHNET is the last of eight ex-Navy salvage ships and fleet tugs that have long served in Coast Guard markings. After Wold War II, the Coast Guard operated large numbers of ex-Navy destroyer escorts (DE) and seaplane tenders (AVP), as well as these eight ships. (Naval Institute Photo Archives)

MEDIUM ENDURANCE CUTTERS: FORMER FLEET TUGS (205)

Number	Name	Navy Comm.	USCG Comm.	Notes
WMEC 76 (ex-ATF 76)	UTE	1942	1980	str. 26 May 1988
WMEC 85 (ex-ATF 85)	LIPAN	1943	1980	str. 9 June 1988
WMEC 153 (ex-ATF 153)	CHILULA	1945	1956	str. 27 June 1991
WMEC 165 (ex-ATF 66)	CHEROKEE	1940	1946	str. 28 Feb 1991
WMEC 166 (ex-ATF 95)	TAMAROA	1943	1946	str. 1 Feb 1994

These are former Navy fleet tugs that were transferred to the Coast Guard and employed as medium endurance cutters. (The TAMAROA was named ZUNI in Navy service; the others retained their Navy names.)

All were returned to Navy custody for disposal; the TAMAROA was transferred to the INTREPID (CV 11) Sea-Air-Space Museum in New York City.

Classification: These ships were classified ATF by the Navy; on transfer to the Coast Guard, the ex-ATF 66, 95, and 153 became WAT, with two being assigned new hull numbers. All three were changed to WMEC on 1 May 1966.

MARITIME PATROL COASTAL CUTTERS

(58) MARITIME PATROL COASTAL CUTTERS (130)

Builder:	
Displacement:	
Length:	130 feet (39.63 m) overall
Beam:	
Draft:	
Propulsion:	2 diesel engines; 2 shafts
Speed:	30 knots
Range:	5,000 nm (9,265 km)
Personnel:	approx. 15
Guns:	1 57-mm/70-cal cannon Mk 110

These cutters are planned as replacements for the Island-class WPBs. The lead cutter will be designated WPC 1101.

Classification: During the design stage, these craft were designated as fast response cutters.

Operational: These cutters will have an endurance of seven days.

5 COASTAL PATROL CUTTERS: "CYCLONE" CLASS (170)

Number	Name	FY	Laid down	Launched	Navy Comm.	CG Comm.	Status
WPC 12 (ex-PC 1)	CYCLONE	90	22 June 1991	1 Feb 1992	7 Aug 1993[17]	29 Jan 2000	to Philippines
WPC 2 (ex-PC 2)	TEMPEST	90	30 Sep 1991	4 Apr 1992	21 Aug 1993	2005	**AA**
WPC 4 (ex-PC 4)	MONSOON	90	15 Feb 1992	10 Oct 1992	22 Jan 1994	2005	**PA**
WPC 8 (ex-PC 8)	ZEPHYR	90	6 Mar 1993	3 Dec 1993	15 Oct 1994	2005	**PA**
WPC 13 (ex- PC 13)	SHAMAL	91	22 Sep 1994	3 Mar 1995	27 Jan 1996	6 Dec 2004	**AA**
WPC 14 (ex- PC 14)	TORNADO	96	25 Aug 1998	7 June 1999	24 June 2000	2005	**AA**

Builders:	Bollinger Shipyards, Lockport, La.		Range:	2,000 nm (3,700 km) at 12 knots
Displacement:	331 tons full load		Personnel:	
Length:	157⅚ feet (48.0 m) waterline		Guns:	2 25-mm Bushmaster cannon Mk 38 (2 single)
	170½ feet (52.0 m) overall			2 .50-cal machine guns M2HB (2 single)
Beam:	25 feet (7.6 m)			2 7.62-mm machine guns M60 (2 single)
Draft:	7⅞ feet (2.4 m)			2 40-mm grenade launchers Mk 19 (2 single)
Propulsion:	4 diesel engines (Paxman Valenta 16VRP-200);13,400 bhp;		Radars:	2 Sperry RASCAR 2500 surface search (S and X bands)
	4 shafts		Sonars:	Wesmar side-scanning (HF)
Speed:	35 knots		EW systems:	APR-39A(V)1 radar warning receiver

These are former Navy coastal patrol ships. The lead ship of the class was transferred to the Coast Guard in early 2000, but not placed in service because of personnel shortages. That ship subsequently was transferred to the Philippines on 6 March 2003 without having seen Coast Guard service.

Following the terrorist attacks of 11 September 2001, the Coast Guard provided law enforcement teams and assumed tactical control of five additional Navy PCs for homeland defense operations. After lengthy discussions, those units were loaned to the Coast Guard in 2004. The Navy had sought to transfer the ships earlier, but it was prevented from doing so by the U.S. Special Operations Command, which previously had operational control of the CYCLONE-class ships.

The Navy retains eight of these ships.

See Chapter 21 for additional data.

Class: The CYCLONE was the lead ship for the class; see Chapter 21 for class notes. With completion of the last ship of the class, the TORNADO (PC 14), the CYCLONE was decommissioned on 28 January 2000 and transferred to the Coast Guard the following day at the Coast Guard Yard at Curtis Bay, Maryland. Prior to transfer to the Philippines, the CYCLONE was modified with a lengthened stern to facilitate launching and taking aboard RHIBs.

The THUNDERBOLT (PC 12) was transferred to the Coast Guard on a temporary basis from March 2000 to July 2000, to further determine the feasibility of operating these ships on Coast Guard missions. Her crew was assigned temporarily to Navy Special Boat Squadron 2 while the ship was operated by the Coast Guard.

Classification: The Coast Guard retained the designator PC and the Navy hull numbers for these ships, adding the Coast Guard prefix W, except that the CYCLONE was redesignated WPC 12. However, the CYCLONE was never placed in service with that designator.

Coast Guardsmen prepare to launch a RHIB from the stern ramp of the SHAMAL. This arrangement, being provided in numerous Coast Guard ships and patrol boats, permits rapid launching and recovery of RHIBs. (2004, U.S. Coast Guard/Barry Lane)

The THUNDERBOLT is another Navy CYCLONE-class coastal patrol ship on loan to the Coast Guard. Although designed for special forces operations, these ships have a large radar cross section and other signatures that detract from "stealth" activities. (U.S. Coast Guard/David Schuerholz)

The Coast Guard cutter SHAMAL cruises the Potomac River, one of five Navy CYCLONE-class coastal patrol ships on loan to the Coast Guard. Long shunned by the Navy, these ships are finding gainful employment by the Coast Guard. Their new missions are homeland security and the interdiction of illegal migrants and drug traffic. (2004, U.S. Coast Guard/Joseph P. Cirone)

SURFACE EFFECTS SHIPS

SURFACE EFFECTS SHIP CUTTERS: "SEA HAWK" CLASS

Number	Name	Comm.	Status
WSES 2	SEA HAWK	1982	
WSES 3	SHEARWATER	1982	decomm. 28 Jan 1994
WSES 4	PETREL	1983	

All three Surface Effects Ships (SES) acquired by the Coast Guard, primarily for use in the drug enforcement role, have been decommissioned and discarded. They were acquired after evaluation of a prototype ship, the DORADO (designated WSES 1), which was commissioned in the Coast Guard in 1981 and, after extensive trails, transferred back to the Navy. She survives in Navy service as the (unnamed) IX 515; see Chapter 25.

See 15th Edition/page 563 for characteristics.

PATROL BOATS

1+ 4 PATROL BOATS: MODERNIZED ISLAND CLASS (123)

Number	Name	Launched	Comm.	Modernized	Status
A series					
WPB 1303	MATAGORDA	15 Dec 1985	25 Apr 1986	Feb 2003–Mar 2004	**AA**
WPB 1306	NUNIVAK	15 Mar 1986	4 July 1986	2003–2005	Yard
B series					
WPB 1317	ATTU	4 Dec 1987	9 May 1988	2003–2005	Yard
WPB 1325	METOMKIN	16 Sep 1988	12 Jan 1989	2003–2005	Yard
WPB 1328	PADRE	6 Jan 1989	24 Feb 1989	2003–2005	Yard

Displacement:	A series: 175 tons full load
	B series: 170 tons full load
	C series: 170 tons full load
Length:	123 feet (37.5 m) overall

These are modernized Island-class WPBs. The number of WPBs that will be modernized has not been determined, in part because of the poor condition of some units and the rate of construction of new WPBs.

Their modernization includes renewed hull plating; significantly improved habitability; renovations to the pilothouse to provide 360° visibility; and a 13 foot (3.96 m) lengthening of the hull, primarily to provide a RHIB recovery capability in the stern.

Except for displacement and length, other characteristics remain the same as for the standard Island-class cutters (see below).

44 PATROL BOATS: ISLAND CLASS (110)

Number	Name	Launched	Comm.	Status
A series (15)				
WPB 1301	FARALLON	27 Aug 1985	21 Feb 1986	AA
WPB 1302	MANITOU	9 Oct 1985	28 Feb 1986	AA
WPB 1304	MAUI	13 Jan 1986	9 May 1986	AA
WPB 1305	MONHEGAN	15 Feb 1986	16 June 1986	AA
WPB 1307	OCRACOKE	12 Apr 1986	4 Aug 1986	AA
WPB 1308	VASHON	10 May 1986	15 Aug 1986	AA
WPB 1309	AQUIDNECK	14 June 1986	26 Sep 1986	AA
WPB 1310	MUSTANG	11 July 1986	29 Aug 1986	PA
WPB 1311	NAUSHON	22 Aug 1986	3 Oct 1986	PA
WPB 1312	SANIBEL	3 Oct 1986	14 Nov 1986	AA
WPB 1313	EDISTO	21 Nov 1986	7 Jan 1987	PA
WPB 1314	SAPELO	9 Jan 1987	24 Feb 1987	PA
WPB 1315	MATINICUS	26 Feb 1987	16 Apr 1987	AA
WPB 1316	NANTUCKET	17 Apr 1987	4 June 1987	AA
B series (21)				
WPB 1318	BARANOF	15 Jan 1988	20 May 1988	AA
WPB 1319	CHANDELEUR	19 Feb 1988	8 June 1988	AA
WPB 1320	CHINCOTEAGUE	25 Mar 1988	8 Aug 1988	AA
WPB 1321	CUSHING	29 Apr 1988	8 Aug 1988	AA
WPB 1322	CUTTYHUNK	3 June 1988	15 Oct 1988	PA
WPB 1323	DRUMMOND	8 July 1988	19 Oct 1988	AA
WPB 1324	KEY LARGO	12 Aug 1988	24 Dec 1988	AA
WPB 1326	MONOMOY	21 Oct 1988	16 Dec 1988	AA
WPB 1327	ORCAS	25 Nov 1988	14 Apr 1989	PA
WPB 1329	SITKINAK	10 Feb 1989	31 Mar 1989	AA
WPB 1330	TYBEE	17 Mar 1989	9 May 1989	PA
WPB 1331	WASHINGTON	21 Apr 1989	9 June 1989	PA
WPB 1332	WRANGELL	26 May 1989	24 June 1989	AA
WPB 1333	ADAK	30 June 1989	17 Nov 1989	AA
WPB 1334	LIBERTY	4 Aug 1989	22 Sep 1989	PA
WPB 1335	ANACAPA	8 Sep 1989	13 Jan 1990	PA
WPB 1336	KISKA	13 Oct 1989	1 Dec 1989*	PA
WPB 1337	ASSATEAGUE	17 Nov 1989	1 Jan 1990*	PA
C series (12)				
WPB 1338	Grand ISLE	1989	14 Dec 1990*	AA
WPB 1339	KEY BISCAYNE		27 Apr 1991	AA
WPB 1340	JEFFERSON ISLAND	1991	16 Aug 1991	AA
WPB 1341	KODIAK ISLAND	8 Feb 1991	21 June 1991	AA
WPB 1342	LONG ISLAND	19 Mar 1991	27 Aug 1991	PA
WPB 1343	BAINBRIDGE ISLAND	19 Apr 1991	14 June 1991*	AA
WPB 1344	BLOCK ISLAND		19 July 1991*	AA
WPB 1345	STATEN ISLAND		23 Aug 1991*	AA
WPB 1346	ROANOKE ISLAND		27 Sep 1991*	PA
WPB 1347	PEA ISLAND		1 Nov 1992*	AA
WPB 1348	KNIGHT ISLAND	6 Sep 1991	6 Dec 1991*	AA
WPB 1349	GALVESTON ISLAND	15 Nov 1991	17 Jan 1992*	PA

* Delivery date vice commissioning date

Builders:	Bollinger Shipyard, Lockport, La.
Displacement:	136 tons standard
	A series: 163 tons full load
	B series: 157 tons full load
	C series: 153 tons full load
Length:	110 feet (33.5 m) overall
Beam:	21 feet (6.4 m)
Draft:	7⅓ feet (2.2 m)
Propulsion:	2 diesel engines (Alco-Paxman Valenta 16 RP200, except C series Caterpillar 3526); 5,820 bhp, except C series 5,460 bhp; 2 shafts
Speed:	29.7 knots, except C series 28 knots
Range:	A series: 900 nm (1,670 km) at 30 knots
	2,700 nm (5,000 km) at 12 knots
	B and C series: 840 nm (1,555 km) at 30 knots
	2,400 nm (4,445 km) at 12 knots

The MATAGORDA after her modernization. She has an all-around view from her bridge, a RHIB ramp in her stern, and several internal upgrades. Unfortunately, the material condition of the Island class may restrict additional modernizations. (2004, U.S. Coast Guard)

The MATAGORDA recovering a RHIB while at speed. Her reconfigured bridge is evident in this view. (2004, U.S. Coast Guard)

Personnel:	16–18 (2 officers + 14–16 enlisted)
Guns:	1 25-mm Bushmaster cannon Mk 38
	2 7.62-mm machine guns M60 or M240 (2 single)
Radar:	1 SPS-64(V)1 navigation

The Coast Guard acquired this class of patrol boats for offshore surveillance and search and rescue operations, to replace the 95-foot (29-m) and 82-foot (25-m) WPBs. Unfortunately, some ports that had been able to accept those craft could not accommodate the larger Island-class WPBs.

The contract for these boats originally was awarded in May 1984 to Marine Power and Equipment Co., Seattle, Washington, for 16 boats; however, a U.S. District Court set aside the award because of irregularities in the procurement process. Subsequently, Bollinger received the contract for the first 16 units in August 1984.

The design was 20 years old when the contract was awarded, and critics have claimed that more-capable designs were available. In addition, early operational experience with the Island-class WPBs revealed hull problems, i.e., cracks developing in heavy seas.

The FARALLON was delivered on 15 November 1985, and the remainder were completed through 1992.

The five modernized/lengthened units are listed separately.

Class: Forty-nine cutters of this class were built.

Design: The design is based on an existing patrol boat developed by Britain's Vosper-Thornycroft to minimize cost and reduce technical risks. The craft have steel hulls with aluminum decks and superstructures; they have flush-deck, round-bilge hulls with some bow sheer, and low bow coamings. The WPB 1317 and later units have heavier bow plating to correct the hull-cracking problem. A quadruped mast is fitted.

Guns: The WPB 1301–1337 originally mounted a 20-mm gun Mk 67; all units now have the Bushmaster "chain gun."

Personnel: The VASHON undertook a historic manning experiment in 1994–1995, employing Naval Reserve personnel to help provide shore support and maintenance for the patrol boat; the reservists also undertook their at-sea drills on board for 12 to 17 days.[16] (The VASHON is based at Roosevelt Roads, Puerto Rico.) The concept was not pursued.

Operational: The Island-class units in the Caribbean area normally conduct 10–12-day patrols, followed by an in-port period.

16 See Lt. Joe DiRenzo III, USCG, "The Ultimate Odd Couple," U.S. Naval Institute *Proceedings* (June 1995), pp. 65–67.

The Island-class patrol boat ADAK on patrol in the Persian Gulf. The Coast Guard deployed six 110-foot patrol boats to the Persian Gulf during Operation Iraqi Freedom to interdict illegal arms smuggling and other terrorist-related activities. (2004, U.S. Coast Guard/Matthew Belson)

A "flying" Island-class patrol boat: The MONOMOY is off-loaded from a merchant ship at Bahrain as part of the Coast Guard's support of Operation Iraqi Freedom. These craft have been highly useful for interdiction operations because of the vast amount of indigenous ships and small craft in the Persian Gulf and Arabian Sea. (2004, U.S. Coast Guard/Zachary A. Crawford)

The AQUIDNECK in the Persian Gulf shows the crane used by the non-modernized Island-class boats to handle RHIBs. The lattice mast and other obstructions prevent looking directly aft from the craft's bridge. (2004, U.S. Coast Guard/Matthew Belson)

PATROL BOATS: HERITAGE CLASS (120)

This class of Coast Guard patrol boats was intended to replace the older and smaller Cape and Point classes. The Heritage-class design was to be faster, longer-lived, and less expensive to build and maintain than the Island class.

The lead unit—the LEOPOLD (WPB 1400)—was ordered in March 1989 and was laid down on 27 August 1990 at the Coast Guard Yard. Series production of 35 follow-on units was expected to begin in 1992, if the prototype proved successful; long-range plans called for a total of up to 96 units. However, the Coast Guard halted work on the LEOPOLD on 25 November 1991 because of the rapidly changing world situation. A Coast Guard spokesman stated: "The reason that we're suspending it at this point—and most likely it will be canceled—is basically times have changed."

The Coast Guard decision came four months after a GAO report questioned the need for the craft. The report summary stated: "There were weaknesses in identifying mission needs and the capabilities the replacement vessels [the Heritage class] would require to meet these needs. The Coast Guard also could not support its decision for the number of patrol boats needed because agency officials could not provide support for the calculations of the computer model used to determine the need for 96 vessels."[17] The GAO report also noted that the Coast Guard underestimated the time and cost required to acquire the Heritage class.

See 16th Edition/page 511 for characteristics.

Classification: The class was rated at 120 feet, although the actual length was 118 feet.

Names: These ships were to be named for former Coast Guard cutters that were part of the service's heritage.

56 + 8 COASTAL PATROL BOATS: PROTECTOR CLASS (87)

Number	Name	Comm.	Status
WPB 87301	BARRACUDA	1998	PA
WPB 87302	HAMMERHEAD	1998	AA
WPB 87303	MAKO	1998	AA
WPB 87304	MARLIN	1999	AA
WPB 87305	STINGRAY	1999	AA
WPB 87306	DORADO	1999	PA
WPB 87307	OSPREY	1999	PA
WPB 87308	CHINOOK	1999	AA
WPB 87309	ALBACORE	1999	AA
WPB 87310	TARPON	1999	AA
WPB 87311	COBIA	1999	AA
WPB 87312	HAWKSBILL	1999	PA
WPB 87313	CORMORANT	1999	AA
WPB 87314	FINBACK	2000	AA
WPB 87315	AMBERJACK	2000	AA
WPB 87316	KITTIWAKE	2000	PA
WPB 87317	BLACKFIN	2000	PA
WPB 87318	BLUEFIN	2000	AA
WPB 87319	YELLOWFIN	2000	AA
WPB 87320	MANTA	2000	AA
WPB 87321	COHO	2000	PA
WPB 87322	KINGFISHER	2000	AA
WPB 87323	SEAHAWK	2000	AA
WPB 87324	STEELHEAD	2000	AA
WPB 87325	BELUGA	2000	AA
WPB 87326	BLACKTIP	2000	PA
WPB 87327	PELICAN	2000	AA
WPB 87328	RIDLEY	2001	AA
WPB 87329	COCHITO	2001	AA
WPB 87330	MANOWAR	2001	AA
WPB 87331	MORAY	2001	AA
WPB 87332	RAZORBILL	2001	AA
WPB 87333	ADELIE	2001	PA
WPB 87334	GANNET	2001	AA
WPB 87335	NARWHAL	2001	PA
WPB 87336	STURGEON	2001	AA
WPB 87337	SOCKEYE	2001	PA
WPB 87338	IBIS	2001	AA
WPB 87339	POMPANO	2001	AA
WPB 87340	HALIBUT	2001	PA
WPB 87341	BONITO	2001	AA
WPB 87342	SHRIKE	2002	AA
WPB 87343	TERN	2002	PA
WPB 87344	HERON	2002	AA
WPB 87345	WAHOO	2002	PA
WPB 87346	FLYING FISH	2002	AA
WPB 87347	HADDOCK	2002	PA
WPB 87348	BRANT	2002	AA
WPB 87349	SHEARWATER	2002	AA
WPB 87350	PETREL	2002	AA
WPB 87352	SEA LION	2003	PA
WPB 87353	SKIPJACK	2003	AA
WPB 87354	DOLPHIN	2003	AA
WPB 87355	HAWK	2003	AA
WPB 87356	SAILFISH	2003	AA
WPB 87357	SAWFISH	2003	AA
WPB 87359	TIGER SHARK		Building
WPB 87360	BLUE SHARK		Building
WPB 87361	SEA HORSE		Building
WPB 87362	SEA OTTER		Building
WPB 87363	MANATEE		Building
WPB 87364	DIAMONDBACK		Building
WPB 87365	PIRANHA		Building
WPB 87366	SKATE		Building

Builders:	Bollinger Shipyard, Lockport, La.
Displacement:	89.5 tons full load
Length:	80⅚ feet (24.87 m) waterline
	87 feet (26.52 m) overall
Beam:	19⅓ feet (5.92 m)
Draft:	5⅔ feet (1.74 m)
Propulsion:	2 diesel engines (MTU 8V 396 TE94), 1,500 bhp; 2 shafts
Speed:	25 knots; patrol speed 10 knots
Range:	approx. 1,225 nm (2,270 km)
Personnel:	10 (enlisted)
Guns:	2 7.62-mm machine guns M60 or M240 (2 single)
Radars:	navigation

17 General Accounting Office, *Coast Guard: Adequacy of the Justification for Heritage Patrol Boats* (Washington, D.C.: 12 July 1991), pp. 1–2.

These are coastal patrol boats procured to replace the 82-foot WPBs and complement the 110-foot WPBs of the Island class as the principal Coast Guard patrol craft after 2000.

Bollinger was awarded a contract on 22 March 1996 to design and construct the lead unit. Series production contracts followed.

The WPB 87351 was built for transfer to Malta.

Classification: The Coast Guard initially used the designation CPB, for coastal patrol boat, in lieu of the standard WPB for these craft; subsequently, they officially were designated WPB.

Design: The 87-foot WPBs have improved habitability, intended for mixed-gender crews. Accommodations consist of two- and three-person berths (with one spare berth). The craft have aluminum hulls.

A single Rigid Inflatable Boat (RIB) is carried, with a stern ramp replacing the usual crane needed to launch and recover the RIB.

Provisions can be carried for five-day missions.

Engineering: Range is calculated at 15 hours at 25 knots and 85 hours at 10 knots.

The PETREL *bow-on. (2004, W. Michael Young)*

The PETREL *stern-on showing her RHIB handling ramp. (2004, W. Michael Young)*

The PETREL *at San Diego. The 87-foot patrol boat is based at Cape May, New Jersey. Her armament of two .50-caliber machine guns is mounted on her bow. The crew also has small arms for boarding operations. (2004, W. Michael Young)*

PATROL BOATS: CAPE CLASS (95)

Number	Name	Notes
WPB 95302	CAPE HIGGON	decomm. 5 Jan 1990; to Uruguay 1990
WPB 95305	CAPE HATTERAS	decomm. 14 Mar 1991; to Mexico 1991
WPB 95309	CAPE CARTER	decomm. 19 Jan 1990; to Mexico 1990
WPB 95321	CAPE CROSS	decomm. 20 Mar 1990; to Micronesia 1990
WPB 95322	CAPE HORN	decomm. 25 Jan 1990; to Uruguay 1990
WPB 95326	CAPE CORWIN	decomm. 6 Apr 1990; to Micronesia 1990

All 95-foot steel-hull patrol boats of the Cape class have been discarded. The above units are those decommissioned since 1990.

See 14th Edition/page 544 for characteristics.

Class: Thirty-five WPBs of this class were completed from 1953 to 1959.

Units of this class have been transferred to the Bahamas, Costa Rica, Ethiopia, Haiti, the Marshall Islands, Mexico, Micronesia, Saudi Arabia, South Korea, Thailand, and Uruguay.

The CAPE HEDGE (WPB 95311) was transferred to the Navy on 7 January 1987 and served as a pilot boat in 1987–1989 (renamed VANGUARD); she subsequently was transferred to Mexico in January 1990. The CAPE ROMAIN (WPB 95319) went to the U.S. Navy as a pilot boat on 11 August 1989.

These craft originally were intended primarily for harbor patrol and coastal ASW. Plans to discard this class in the 1970s in favor of new construction were dropped, and all surviving units were modernized. Subsequently, they were replaced from the mid-1980s by the Island-class WPBs.

PATROL BOATS: POINT CLASS (82)

Number	Name	Notes
WPB 82302	POINT HOPE	decomm. 3 May 1991; to Costa Rica 1991
WPB 82311	POINT VERDE	decomm. 12 June 1991; to Mexico 1991
WPB 82312	POINT SWIFT	decomm. 30 Mar 1995 (stored)
WPB 82314	POINT THATCHER	decomm. 13 Mar 1992 (hulk)
WPB 82318	POINT HERRON	decomm. 27 July 1991; to Mexico 1998
WPB 82332	POINT ROBERTS	decomm. Feb 1992
WPB 82333	POINT HIGHLAND	decomm. 14 July 2001; to Trinidad and Tobago 2001
WPB 82334	POINT LEDGE	decomm. 30 Aug 1998; to Venezuela 1998
WPB 82335	POINT COUNTESS	decomm. 29 June 2000
WPB 82336	POINT GLASS	decomm. 9 Apr 2001
WPB 82337	POINT DIVIDE	decomm. 30 Mar 1995; to Washington Maritime Academy
WPB 82338	POINT BRIDGE	decomm. 28 Sep 2001
WPB 82339	POINT CHICO	decomm. 14 June 2001
WPB 82340	POINT BATAN	decomm. 22 Dec 1999
WPB 82341	POINT LOOKOUT	decomm. 24 Mar 1994; scuttled 1997
WPB 82342	POINT BAKER	decomm. 12 Feb 2002
WPB 82343	POINT WELLS	decomm. 13 Oct 2000
WPB 82344	POINT ESTERO	decomm. 8 Feb 2001
WPB 82345	POINT JUDITH	decomm. 15 Jan 1992; to Venezuela 1992
WPB 82346	POINT ARENA	decomm. 30 Mar 1995 (storage)
WPB 82347	POINT BONITA	decomm. 14 Nov 2000; to Trinidad and Tobago 1999
WPB 82348	POINT BARROW	decomm. 7 June 1991; to Panama 1991
WPB 82349	POINT SPENCER	decomm. 12 Dec 2000
WPB 82350	POINT FRANKLIN	decomm. 23 June 1998; to Venezuela 1998
WPB 82351	POINT BENNETT	decomm. 12 Feb 1999; to Trinidad and Tobago 1999
WPB 82352	POINT SAL	decomm. 24 May 2001
WPB 82353	POINT MONROE	decomm. 19 Aug 2001
WPB 82354	POINT EVANS	decomm. 16 Nov 1999
WPB 82355	POINT HANNON	decomm. 11 Jan 2001
WPB 82356	POINT FRANCIS	decomm. 9 Mar 1999; to Panama 1999
WPB 82357	POINT HURON	decomm. 21 Apr 1999; to Panama 1999
WPB 82358	POINT STUART	decomm. 3 May 2001
WPB 82359	POINT STEELE	decomm. 9 July 1998; to Antigua-Barbuda 1998
WPB 82360	POINT WINSLOW	decomm. 20 Sep 2000
WPB 82361	POINT CHARLES	decomm. 13 Dec 1991; to Texas A&M University 1991
WPB 82362	POINT BROWN	decomm. 30 Sep 1991
WPB 82363	POINT NOWELL	decomm. 19 Oct 1999
WPB 82364	POINT WHITEHORN	decomm. 30 Mar 1995
WPB 82365	POINT TURNER	decomm. 3 Apr 1998; to St. Lucia 1998
WPB 82366	POINT LOBOS	decomm. 13 Oct 2001
WPB 82367	POINT KNOLL	decomm. 11 Sep 1991; to Venezuela 1991
WPB 82368	POINT WARDE	decomm. 29 June 2000
WPB 82369	POINT HEYER	decomm. 11 Dec 1998; to Trinidad and Tobago 1999
WPB 82370	POINT RICHMOND	decomm. 30 Sep 1997; to Ecuador 1997
WPB 82371	POINT BARNES	decomm. 12 Jan 2000
WPB 82372	POINT BROWER	decomm. 12 Sep 2001
WPB 82373	POINT CAMDEN	decomm. 12 Dec 1999
WPB 82374	POINT CARREW	decomm. 22 Aug 2000
WPB 82375	POINT DORAN	decomm. 22 Mar 2001
WPB 82376	POINT HARRIS	decomm. 12 Apr 1992
WPB 82377	POINT HOBART	decomm. 8 July 1999
WPB 82378	POINT JACKSON	decomm. 30 May 2000
WPB 82379	POINT MARTIN	decomm. 24 Aug 1999

All 82-foot steel-hull patrol boats of the Point class have been discarded. The above units are those decommissioned since 1990.

See 17th Edition/pages 583–84 for characteristics.

Class: This originally was a class of 79 units, completed from 1960 to 1970; 26 units were transferred to South Vietnam in 1969–1970. Decommissioning since 1990 are listed above.

The POINT CHARLES was transferred to Texas A&M University and the POINT BROWN to Kingsborough Community College, Brooklyn, New York, as school ships.

The POINT HARRIS was heavily damaged by Hurricane Iniki at Kauai, Hawaii, on 11 September 1992 and subsequently stricken.

The POINT MONROE and POINT LOBOS were transferred to the National Oceanographic and Atmospheric Agency (NOAA) for further service on the decommission date.

ICEBREAKERS

Coast Guard icebreakers operate in the Arctic and Antarctic regions in support of U.S. national requirements for military and scientific activities. The Coast Guard currently has three large icebreakers in service, two of the Polar class and the recently completed HEALY.

The Coast Guard had long planned to construct two additional Polar-class icebreakers to replace the GLACIER (WAGB 4, ex-AGB 4) and the two surviving Wind-class icebreakers, to provide a force of four modern icebreakers to meet national requirements. But those older ships were decommissioned without replacements.

In late 1986, the Coast Guard expressed interest in leasing two large polar icebreakers as an alternative to building and operating government-owned ships. Such a build-and-charter concept is similar to that used by the Navy for tankers and maritime pre-positioning ships. The concept, however, was rejected in favor of a single new-construction ship. Named HEALY, the new ship is larger and more powerful than the Polar-class icebreakers.

The icebreakers have extensive research laboratory facilities.

All Coast Guard icebreakers are based at Seattle, Washington.

Historical: Icebreakers were operated by the U.S. Navy and Coast Guard until 1966; at that time, the Navy's five active icebreakers were transferred to the Coast Guard:

Navy	Coast Guard	Name
AGB 1 (ex-AG 88)	WAGB 283	BURTON ISLAND
AGB 2 (ex-AG 89)	WAGB 284	EDISTO
AGB 3	WAGB 280	ATAK
AGB 4	WAGB 4	GLACIER
AGB 5	WAGB 278	STATEN ISLAND

The AGB 1–3 and 5 were Wind-class ships built during World War II; the GLACIER was the first U.S. icebreaker built after the war (completed in 1955).

Two-thirds of the U.S. Coast Guard's polar icebreakers are in this photograph: The POLAR SEA *(left) and* POLAR STAR *were operating together in the ice channel near McMurdo, Antarctica. The three large Coast Guard icebreakers support a variety of U.S. military and all-nation scientific activities. (2002, U.S. Coast Guard/Rob Rothway)*

1 ICEBREAKER: "HEALY" TYPE (420)

Number	Name	FY	Launched	Comm.	Status
WAGB 20	HEALY	93	15 Nov 1997	21 Aug 2000	**PA**

Builders:	Avondale Industries, New Orleans
Displacement:	16,400 tons full load
Length:	397⅔ feet (121.23 m) waterline
	419⅝ feet (128.0 m) overall
Beam:	82 feet (25.0 m)
Draft:	29½ feet (8.91 m)
Propulsion:	diesel-electric: 4 diesel engines (Sulzer-Westinghouse 12 ZA40S); 10,600 bhp + 4 electric motors; 30,000 shp; 2 shafts
Speed:	17 knots; 12.5 knots cruise
Range:	16,000 nm (29,650 km) at 12.5 knots
	37,000 nm (68,560 km) at 9.25 knots
Personnel:	75 (12 officers + 63 enlisted) + 35 scientists
Helicopters:	2 HH-65A Dolphin
Guns:	2 .50-cal machine guns M2 (2 single)
Radars:	2 navigation

This is the largest icebreaker to be built in a U.S. shipyard and the largest operated by the U.S. government.

Congress voted $275 million in the FY 1990 budget for construction of this ship; the remainder of the necessary funding, $60 million, was authorized in FY 1992. However, the Naval Sea Systems Command lists the ship in the FY 1993 program.

Naval Sea Systems Command, procurement agent for Coast Guard icebreakers, canceled the procurement of the ship on 20 March 1992 because the responses received from shipyards were in excess of appropriated funds. The Coast Guard and Navy stated that they would "continue to examine alternatives for procuring the icebreaker." Subsequently, the Navy awarded the contract to Avondale on 15 July 1993.

The HEALY's keel was laid down on 16 September 1996. Construction cost was estimated at $340 million.

Class: A second ship was planned but not authorized.

Design: The original design was revised and the ship reduced in size and power because of cost constraints.

The ship can break 4½-foot (1.4-m) ice at a continuous speed of 3 knots, or ice up to 7⅞ feet (2.4 m) by backing and ramming.

Engineering: A 2,000-shp bow thruster is fitted.

The USCGC HEALY *is the nation's largest and newest icebreaker. Here, the ship is entering ice for the first time in the Strait of Belle Isle, between Newfoundland and Labrador. Coast Guard icebreakers have red hulls. (2000, U.S. Coast Guard/Jamie Bigelow)*

While being completed at the Avondale Industries shipyard in New Orleans, the HEALY *displays the icebreaker's configuration, with a large block superstructure with a hangar and helicopter deck aft. (1999, U.S. Coast Guard/David Brimblecom)*

Operational: In September 2002, the HEALY became the second U.S. ship to reach the North Pole. (See entry for POLAR SEA.)

*Appearing like a weird ice-walk-
ing insect, the HEALY stretches
out the icebreaker's cranes while
crewmen work on the ice. The
ship has a limited cargo capacity.
An HH-65A Dolphin rests on the
ship's helicopter deck. (2000,
U.S. Coast Guard/Jamie
Bigelow)*

2 ICEBREAKERS: POLAR CLASS (399)

Number	Name	Launched	Comm.	Status
WAGB 10	POLAR STAR	17 Nov 1973	19 Jan 1976	**PA**
WAGB 11	POLAR SEA	24 June 1975	23 Feb 1978	**PA**

Builders:	Lockheed Shipbuilding, Seattle
Displacement:	10,863 tons standard
	13,623 tons full load
Length:	337⅙ feet (102.78 m) waterline
	399⅚ feet (121.91 m) overall
Beam:	83½ feet (25.45 m)
Draft:	33½ feet (10.2 m)
Propulsion:	CODOG: 6 diesel engines (Alco), 18,000 bhp + 3 gas
	turbines (Pratt & Whitney), 60,000 shp; 3 shafts
Speed:	18 knots
Range:	16,000 nm (2,963 km) at 18 knots
	28,275 nm (52,400 km) at 13 knots
Personnel:	142 (15 officers + 127 enlisted) + 33 scientists
Helicopters:	2 HH-65A Dolphin
Guns:	2 .50-cal machine guns M2 (2 single)
Radars:	2 SPS-64 navigation

These two large icebreakers were constructed as replacements for the Wind-class icebreakers.

When the Polar class was begun in the early 1970s, the Coast Guard operated seven oceangoing icebreakers, the GLACIER (WAGB 4) and six Wind-class ships (WAGB 279–284, 278). Several additional Polar-class ships were envisioned, but none was built, in part because of the higher-than-anticipated construction costs.

Both Polar-class icebreakers are homeported at Seattle, Washington.

Design: These ships have conventional icebreaker hull forms. A hangar and flight deck are fitted aft, and two 15-ton-capacity cranes are abaft the hangar. Arctic and oceanographic laboratories are provided.

Engineering: CODOG propulsion is provided, with diesel engines for cruising and rapid-reaction gas turbines for surge-power requirements. Controllable-pitch propellers allow propeller thrust to be reversed with reversing the direction of shaft rotation.

*The POLAR STAR breaks a path
through the ice of McMurdo
Sound, Antarctica. She has the
traditional icebreaker bow,
rounded for riding up onto the
ice and then using the ship's
weight to break through. These
ships have funnels of uneven
height. (2002, U.S. Coast Guard)*

Both ships have experienced problems with their controllable-pitch propellers and control systems. The POLAR SEA has been docked at Seattle, Washington, with two of her three main engines "condemned." Repairs will require more than two years and, because of previous problems with the ships, it is questionable whether she will be repaired.

The original design provided for a speed of 21 knots; it has not been achieved in service.

Operational: The POLAR SEA circumnavigated the North American continent in 1985. The icebreaker departed Seattle, Washington, on 6 June, transited the Panama Canal, sailed up the East Coast to Greenland and through the Northwest Passage into the Bering Sea and then into the Pacific, returning to Seattle on 2 October. The ship required just under seven days, including a brief stop at the village of Resolute Bay, to transit the 850-nm (1,575-m) Northwest Passage.

The POLAR SEA reached the geographic North Pole on 26 July 1994 in company with the Canadian icebreaker LOUIS S. ST. LAURENT. This was the first U.S. surface ship to reach the pole.[18] (The Coast Guard icebreaker WESTWIND/WAGB 281 came within 375 nm/690 km of the North Pole in 1970.)

1 ICEBREAKER: "MACKINAW" (290)

Number	Name	Launched	Comm.	Status
WAGB 83	MACKINAW	4 Mar 1944	20 Dec 1944	**GL**

Builders:	Toledo Shipbuilding, Ohio
Displacement:	5,320 tons full load
Length:	290 feet (88.4 m) overall
Beam:	75 feet (22.9 m)
Draft:	19 feet (5.8 m)
Propulsion:	diesel-electric (Fairbanks Morse diesel engines, Westinghouse electric motors); 10,000 shp aft + 3,000 shp forward; 2 shafts aft + 1 shaft forward
Speed:	18.7 knots
Range:	10,000 nm (18,520 km) at 18.7 knots
	41,000 nm (75,930 km) at 9 knots
Personnel:	75 (8 officers + 67 enlisted)
Helicopters:	landing area
Guns:	none

The MACKINAW was designed and constructed specifically for Coast Guard use on the Great Lakes. The ship is homeported in Cheboygan, Minnesota. Under terms of U.S.–Canadian treaty, neither nation can placed armed ships on the Great Lakes.

The ship is scheduled to be retired in 2006.

Classification: The ship originally was classified WAG 83; she was changed to WAGB on 1 May 1966.

Design: The MACKINAW has many features of the contemporary Wind class; however, being designed for the Great Lakes, she is longer and wider than the oceangoing ships, with significantly less draft. Two 12-ton-capacity cranes are fitted. The ship has a clear deck aft for a helicopter, but no hangar is provided.

Name: She originally was named MANITOWOC.

---

18 The Soviet nuclear-propelled icebreaker ARKTIKA was the first surface ship in history to reach the geographic North Pole, doing so on 17 August 1977. The ARKTIKA spent 15 hours at the North Pole. Her sister ship SIBIR' reached the North Pole in May 1987 and their sister ship YAMAL in August 1994.

This starboard quarter view of the POLAR STAR clearly shows the hangar and helicopter deck of the Polar-class icebreakers. Ships that operate in polar areas also have enclosed, heated crows nests. There were rumors that a third ship was considered—to be named "Polar Bear." (2002, U.S. Coast Guard, Rob Rothway)

The MACKINAW is another World War II–era cutter still in active Coast Guard service. Shown here breaking ice in the St. Mary's River, the MACKINAW was built specifically for operations on the Great Lakes. (2004, U.S. Coast Guard/Jeff Hall)

TRAINING CUTTERS

1 TRAINING BARK: "EAGLE" TYPE

Number	Name	Launched	USCG Comm.	Status
WIX 327	EAGLE	13 June 1936	15 May 1946	**TRA-A**

Builders:	Blohm and Voss, Hamburg (Germany)
Displacement:	1,784 tons full load
Length:	231 feet (70.43 m) waterline
	295 feet (89.9 m) over bowsprit
Beam:	39½ feet (11.9 m)
Draft:	17 feet (5.2 m)
Masts:	fore and main: 150½ feet (45.7 m)
	mizzen: 132 feet (40.2 m)
Propulsion:	auxiliary diesel engines (MAN); 700 bhp; 1 shaft
Speed:	up to 18 knots under sail
	10.5 knots on auxiliary diesel engines
Personnel:	50 (12 officers + 38 enlisted) + 150–175 cadets
Guns:	none
Radars:	1 SPS-64(V)1 navigation

The EAGLE is based at the Coast Guard Academy in New London, Connecticut; she is employed to train Coast Guard cadets on summer practice cruises.

She is the former German naval training bark HORST WESSEL. Taken by the United States as a reparation after World War II, she was acquired in January 1946 at Bremerhaven and assigned to the Coast Guard.

Class: The similar ALBERT LEO SCHLAETER (launched in 1937) also was taken over by the United States in 1945, but she was sold to Brazil in 1948 and then resold to Portugal in 1962 (she now is in service as the SAGRES). A third ship of this basic design, the GORCH FOCK (1933), was taken over by the Soviet Union in 1946 and renamed the TOVARISH; she remains in Russian service.[19]

---

19 The TOVARISH is employed as a sail training ship for the Russian merchant marine; see N. Polmar, *Guide to the Soviet Navy*, 5th ed. (Annapolis, Md.: Naval Institute Press, 1991), pp. 332–33.

The bark EAGLE, the Coast Guard Academy's sail-training ship and the only U.S. government "tall ship." This photo shows her in New York Harbor, a frequent port of call for the graceful ship. (2004, U.S. Coast Guard/Mike Lutz)

The similar MIRECA was built for Romania and also remains in service.

A later ship of the same general design, also named the GORCH FOCK, was built at the same German yard for the West German Navy (launched in 1958).

Classification: A three-masted bark is a square-rigged vessel on her fore and main masts, and fore-and-aft rigged on the mizzenmast. The Coast Guard currently uses the term *barque* for the EAGLE, which is the French spelling of the term. The English (and German) spelling is *bark*.

Design: The EAGLE is steel hulled. She carries up to 21,350 square feet (1,921.5 m²) of sail.

BUOY TENDERS

These ships maintain aids to navigation in U.S. coastal waters as well as on inland waterways.

All tenders are "black-hull" ships. No tenders are armed.

The EAGLE's figurehead is the fourth to be fitted in the ship. This is a mahogany replica of the original, which was installed in 1976 for the U.S. bicentennial celebrations. Here, the EAGLE is in Boston with the cutter ESCANABA during a training cruise. (2004, U.S. Coast Guard/C. T. O'Neil)

15 + 1 SEAGOING BUOY TENDERS: "JUNIPER" CLASS (225)

Number	Name	Launched	Comm.	Status
WLB 201	JUNIPER	24 June 1995	5 July 1996	**AA**
WLB 202	WILLOW	15 June 1996	12 Apr 1997	**AA**
WLB 203	KUKUI	3 May 1997	1 Jan 1998	**PA**
WLB 204	ELM	24 Jan 1998	1 July 1998	**AA**
WLB 205	WALNUT	22 Aug 1998	12 July 1999	**PA**
WLB 206	SPAR	12 Aug 2000	3 Aug 2001	**PA**
WLB 207	MAPLE	16 Dec 2000	19 Oct 2001	**PA**
WLB 208	ASPEN	21 Apr 2001	24 Jan 2002	**PA**
WLB 209	SYCAMORE	28 July 2001	3 July 2002	**PA**
WLB 210	CYPRESS	27 Oct 2001	11 Oct 2002	**AA**
WLB 211	OAK	26 Jan 2002	7 Mar 2003	**AA**
WLB 212	HICKORY	11 May 2002	3 July 2003	**PA**
WLB 213	FIR	18 Aug 2002	8 Nov 2003	**PA**
WLB 214	HOLLYHOCK	25 Jan 2003	30 Apr 2004	**GL**
WLB 215	SEQUOIA	23 Aug 2003	15 Oct 2004	**GL**
WLB 216	ALDER	7 Feb 2004	June 2005	Building

Builders:	Marinette Marine, Wisc.
Displacement:	2,000 tons full load
Length:	206 feet (62.79 m) waterline
	225 feet (68.58 m) overall
Beam:	46 feet (14.0 m)
Draft:	13 feet (4.0 m)
Propulsion:	2 diesel engines (Caterpillar 3608); 6,20 bhp; 1 shaft
Speed:	15 knots
Range:	6,000 nm (11,110 km) at 15 knots
Personnel:	40 (6 officers + 34 enlisted)
Guns:	see notes
Radars:	1 SPS-64(V)1 or 2 Decca BridgeMaster-E 340 ARPA navigation

These are the first seagoing buoy tenders built for the U.S. Coast Guard since the BALSAM class of World War II, which they are intended to replace. In 1991, the Coast Guard awarded contracts for the design of the new craft to several shipyards. In August 1992, the Marinette Marine yard was chosen to construct the lead tender.

Sixteen tenders currently are planned; previous estimates were for 28 units. The increased capabilities will enable them to replace a larger number of BALSAM-class tenders.

Design: These ships are highly automated, being significantly larger than the previous BALSAM class but with a much smaller crew.

The tenders have a 30,000-pound (13,605-kg) lift capacity, a large deck area for handling buoys, and the ability to work buoys in 8-foot (2.4-m) seas. They are fitted with a dynamic positioning system.

Engineering: A 440-shp bow thruster and a 550-shp stern thruster are fitted. At sea endurance is 45 days.

Guns: Space and weight are reserved for installation of a 25-mm Bushmaster cannon.

Names: The WLB 206 originally was to be named DOGWOOD. Her name was changed to SPAR while the tender was under construction, to honor the Coast Guard's women volunteers in World War II—called SPARs, a term derived from the Coast Guard motto, *Semper Paratus* ("Always Ready").

Operational: Many buoy tenders listed as Atlantic or Pacific are based on rivers and inland waterways.

The JUNIPER is the lead ship of a long-awaited new class of seagoing buoy tenders. Like all ships of that type, she has a black hull. Buoy tenders are distinguished by cranes and large open deck area for handling navigation aids, their chains, and anchors. (2000, U.S. Coast Guard)

The buoy tender OAK is side-launched at the Marinette shipyard. This procedure often is used at shipyards on the Great Lakes and on rivers where a conventionally launched ship could run aground. Her open buoy handling space is clearly seen here. (2002, U.S. Coast Guard/Val Ihde)

1 SEAGOING BUOY TENDER: "BALSAM" CLASS (180)

Number	Name	Launched	Comm.	Status
WLB 406	ACACIA	7 Apr 1944	1 Sep 1944	**GL**

Builders:	Zenith Dredge, Duluth, Minn.
Displacement:	935 tons standard
	1,025 tons full load
Length:	180 feet (54.9 m) overall
Beam:	37 feet (11.3 m)
Draft:	13 feet (4.0 m)
Propulsion:	diesel-electric (2 General Motors 8-645E6A diesel engines); 1,200 shp; 1 shaft
Speed:	13 knots
Range:	4,500 nm (8,335 km) at 13 knots
	13,500 nm (25,000 km) at 7.5 knots
Personnel:	49 (7 officers + 42 enlisted)
Guns:	removed
Radars:	SPS-73 navigation

The ACACIA is the last of a class 39 180-foot buoy tenders that served the Coast Guard for some 60 years. They were highly versatile ships, having served as convoys escorts, in the SAR role, in constructing and servicing LORAN navigation stations, and as salvage ships; some have a light icebreaking capability.

Class: Thirty-nine ships of this design were completed in 1942–1944.

Disposals since 1990 are listed below; see Appendix C for foreign transfers.

Number	Name	Decomm.
WLB 277	COWSLIP	24 Jan 2003
WLB/WIX 290	GENTIAN	1 June 1998
WLB 291	LAUREL	31 Dec 1999
WLB/WMEC 292	CLOVER	1 June 1990
WLB/WAGO/WMEC 295	EVERGREEN	13 June 1990
WLB 296	SORREL	20 June 1996
WLB 297	IRONWOOD	6 Oct 2000
WLB/WMEC 300	CITRUS	1 Sep 1994
WLB 301	CONIFER	23 June 2000
WLB 302	MADRONA	12 Apr 2002
WLB 306	BUTTONWOOD	30 June 2001
WLB 307	PLANETREE	19 Mar 1999
WLB 308	PAPAW	23 July 1999
WLB 309	SWEETGUM	15 Feb 2002
WLB 388	BASSWOOD	4 Sep 1998
WLB 389	BITTERSWEET	8 Aug 1997
WLB 390	BLACKHAW	26 Feb 1993
WLB 392	BRAMBLE	22 May 2003
WLB 393	FIREBUSH	30 June 2003

The recently retired seagoing buoy tender MADRONA, a sister ship of the ACACIA, the only cutter of this class remaining in service with the U.S. Coast Guard. These were long-serving and versatile ships. Several survive in foreign service. (2001, U.S. Coast Guard/Telfair H. Brown)

WLB 394	HORNBEAM	30 Sep 1999
WLB 395	IRIS	8 Aug 1997
WLB 396	MALLOW	15 May 1997
WLB 397	MARIPOSA	31 Mar 2000
WLB 400	SALVIA	12 Apr 1991
WLB 401	SASSAFRAS	31 Oct 2003
WLB 402	SEDGE	21 Dec 2002
WLB 403	SPAR	28 Feb 1997
WLB 404	SUNDEW	25 May 2004
WLB 405	SWEETBRIER	27 Aug 2001
WLB 407	WOODRUSH	28 Apr 2001

After being stricken, on 17 April 2000, the MARIPOSA was transferred to the Navy for use as a nonoperational training platform for ship boarding and damage control.

The COWSLIP was decommissioned 24 January 2003 but not stricken until two days later.

Classification: Several ships were temporarily reclassified as medium endurance cutters (WMEC) and engaged in patrol work during the 1970s and 1980s. The EVERGREEN (WLB 295) was refitted as an oceanographic cutter in 1973 and reclassified WAGO; she was changed to WMEC on 1 May 1982 and served in that role until decommissioned in 1990. The CITRUS served as a WMEC from June 1979 until decommissioned in 1994. (As WMECs and WAGO, they had white hulls.)

Design: The WLB 404 and other units have strengthened hulls for icebreaking. All ships of the class are fitted with a 20-ton-capacity boom. In ships that underwent the Service Life Extension Program (SLEP), a hydraulically powered system replaces the electrically powered boom. These ships are highly effective for breaking through light ice.

Guns: As completed, these tenders had one 3-inch/50-cal Anti-Aircraft (AA) gun and four 20-mm AA guns (two in A-series ships—WLB 277–309); the 3-inch gun was fitted in a raised "tub" aft of the funnel. They also carried depth charges, with some ships having ahead-throwing Mousetrap ASW projectors.

Names: The ACACIA originally was named THISTLE; her name was changed in 1944 because, at that time, that name also was carried by an Army hospital ship.

Operational: The GENTIAN (WLB 290) was recommissioned on 27 September 1999 as a Caribbean Support Tender (CST) to provide training and maintenance assistance to Caribbean nations engaged in anti-drug operations. In the CST role, her crew numbered 45 officers and enlisted personnel, including representatives from seven Caribbean-area nations in addition to her core U.S. Coast Guard crew.[20] She was redesignated WIX 290.

14 COASTAL BUOY TENDERS: KEEPER CLASS (175)

Number	Name	Launched	Comm.	Status
WLM 551	IDA LEWIS	14 Oct 1995	11 Apr 1997	AA
WLM 552	KATHERINE WALKER	14 Sep 1996	1 Nov 1997	AA
WLM 553	ABBIE BURGESS	5 Apr 1997	31 July 1998	AA
WLM 554	MARCUS HANNA	23 Aug 1997	19 May 1998	AA
WLM 555	JAMES RANKIN	25 Apr 1998	1 May 1998	AA
WLM 556	JOSHUA APPLEBY	8 Aug 1998	7 May 1999	AA
WLM 557	FRANK DREW	5 Dec 1998	5 Apr 2000	AA
WLM 558	ANTHONY PETIT	30 Jan 1999	18 May 2000	PA
WLM 559	BARBARA MABRITY	27 Mar 1998	20 Nov 1999	AA
WLM 560	WILLIAM TATE	8 May 1999	3 June 2000	AA
WLM 561	HARRY CLAIBORNE	12 June 1999	31 Mar 2000	AA
WLM 562	MARIA BRAY	28 Aug 1999	26 July 2000	AA
WLM 563	HENRY BLAKE	20 Nov 1999	12 Oct 2000	PA
WLM 564	GEORGE COBB	18 Dec 1999	27 Oct 2000	PA

Builders:	Marinette Marine, Wisc.
Displacement:	845 tons full load
Length:	155 feet (47.24 m) waterline
	175 feet (53.34 m) overall
Beam:	36 feet (10.98 m)
Draft:	7½ feet (2.41 m)
Propulsion:	2 diesel engines (Caterpillar 3508 TA); 1,710 bhp; 2 Z-drive propulsion units (see *Engineering* notes)
Speed:	12 knots
Range:	2,000 nm (3,700 km) at 10 knots
Personnel:	18 (1 officer + 17 enlisted)
Radars:	1 SPS-64(V)1 or SPS-73 navigation

These are advanced-capability coastal buoy tenders, built to replace the BALSAM-class WLBs.

Originally 28 tenders of this class were planned.

Design: The ships are fitted with 10-ton-capacity cranes. They can break ice of about 1 inch (25 mm) thickness at 3 knots. Six spare bunks are provided in each ship.

Engineering: Maximum brake horsepower is 1,998; sustained bhp is shown above. The ships are fitted with 400-hp bow thrusters.

Names: The class name reflects the fact that all units are named for lighthouse "keepers." The lead tender is named for Idawalley Zorada Lewis, a lighthouse keeper who, in 1858 at age 16, single-handedly saved four young boys.

The WLM 553 originally was named ABIGAIL BURGESS.

---

20 See Eric Miller, "Coast Guard Is a Partner in Caribbean Security," U.S. Naval Institute *Proceedings* (December 1999), pp. 58–61.

The JOSHUA APPLEBY is one of the new coastal buoy tenders named for lighthouse keepers, hence the name of this class. The ships are in some respects scaled down versions of the JUNIPER-class seagoing buoy tenders. (2000, U.S. Coast Guard/Harry Craft III)

The KATHERINE WALKER *breaking ice on the Hudson River. The seagoing and coastal buoy tenders are versatile ships; they could be armed for coastal patrol duties. Note the cutter's square stern counter. (2000, U.S. Coast Guard/Robert Lanier)*

COASTAL BUOY TENDERS: RED CLASS (157)

All five of these buoy and navigation aid tenders have been stricken. They were completed from 1964 to 1971.

See 16th Edition/page 522 for characteristics.

Number	Name	Stricken
WLM 685	RED WOOD	1 June 1999
WLM 686	RED BEECH	18 June 1997
WLM 687	RED BIRCH	9 June 1998
WLM 688	RED CEDAR	30 Mar 1999
WLM 689	RED OAK	28 Mar 1996

COASTAL BUOY TENDERS: WHITE CLASS (133)

All seven buoy and navigation aid tenders of this class have been discarded. They were converted from Navy self-propelled lighters (YF) and were transferred to the Coast Guard in August–September 1947. Disposals since 1990 are listed below.

See 17th Edition/page 595 for characteristics.

Number	Name	Stricken
WLM 540	WHITE SUMAC	9 July 1999
WLM 543	WHITE HOLLY	8 July 1998
WLM 544	WHITE SAGE	28 June 1996
WLM 545	WHITE HEATH	31 Mar 1998
WLM 546	WHITE LUPINE	28 Feb 1998
WLM 547	WHITE PINE	31 June 1999

4 INLAND CONSTRUCTION TENDERS: "PAMLICO" CLASS (160)

Number	Name	Number	Name
WLIC 800	PAMLICO	WLIC 802	Kennebec
WLIC 801	HUDSON	WLIC 803	Saginaw

Builders:	Coast Guard Yard, Curtis Bay, Md.
Displacement:	413 tons light
	459 tons full load
Length:	160 feet (48.8 m) overall
Beam:	30 feet (9.1 m)
Draft:	4 feet (1.2 m)
Propulsion:	2 diesel engines (Cummins); 1,000 bhp, 2 shafts
Speed:	10 knots
Personnel:	14 (1 officer + 13 enlisted)

These large inland tenders were completed in 1976–1977.

The inland construction tender HUDSON *under way on an inland waterway. She has a large crane forward, a pilothouse with all-around vision, and short, twin funnels. (1992, Giorgio Arra)*

The one-of-a-kind inland buoy tender BUCKTHORN. *The river and inland buoy tenders are rarely photographed as they conduct their arduous labors. (1989, Leo Van Ginderen)*

1 INLAND BUOY TENDER: "BUCKTHORN" (100)

Number	Name	Launched	Comm.
WLI 642	BUCKTHORN		17 July 1964

Builders:	Mobile Ship Repair, Mobile, Ala.
Displacement:	188 tons light
	196 tons full load
Length:	100 feet (30.5 m) overall
Beam:	24 feet (7.3 m)
Draft:	4 feet (1.2 m)
Propulsion:	2 diesel engines; 600 bhp; 2 shafts
Speed:	11.9 knots
Personnel:	15 (1 officer + 14 enlisted)

The BUCKTHORN, a single-ship design, operates on the Great Lakes. She is fitted with a five-ton-capacity boom.

1 INLAND CONSTRUCTION TENDER: "COSMOS" CLASS (100)

Number	Name	Launched	Comm.
WLIC 315	SMILAX	18 Aug 1944	1 Nov 1944

Builders:	WLI 313 Birchfield Boiler, Tacoma, Wash.
	WLIC 315 Dubuque Boat & Boiler, Iowa
Displacement:	178 tons full load
Length:	100 feet (30.5 m) overall
Beam:	24 feet (7.3 m)
Draft:	5 feet (1.5 m)
Propulsion:	2 diesel engines; 600 bhp; 2 shafts
Speed:	10.5 knots
Range:	1,400 nm (2,600 km) at 10.5 knots
	2,700 nm (5,000 km) at 7 knots
Personnel:	14 (1 officer + 13 enlisted)

The SMILAX is the last of a class of eight 100-foot inland construction tenders (WLI); she was changed to inland construction tender (WLIC) on 1 October 1979.

Design: The tender is fitted with a five-ton-capacity crane.

Names: Inland tenders were named in 1963.

*The inland buoy tender
BLUEBELL; the SMILAX, the last
craft of this design, is similar.
(1993, George R. Schneider)*

9 INLAND CONSTRUCTION TENDERS: "ANVIL" CLASS (75)

Number	Name	Number	Name
A series		*C series*	
WLIC 75301	ANVIL	WLIC 75306	CLAMP
WLIC 75302	HAMMER	WLIC 75307	WEDGE
B series		WLIC 75309	HATCHET
WLIC 75303	SLEDGE	WLIC 75310	AXE
WLIC 75304	MALLET		
WLIC 75305	VISE		

Builders:	WLIC 75301, 75302: Gibbs Shipyard, Jacksonville, Fla.
	WLIC 75303–75305: McDermott, Morgan City, Mich.
	WLIC 75306, 75307: Sturgeon Bay Shipbuilding, Wisc.
	WLIC 75309, 75310: Dorchester Shipbuilding, N.J.
Displacement:	129 tons light
	145 tons full load
Length:	75 feet (22.9 m) overall,
	except C series 76 feet (23.2 m) overall
Beam:	22 feet (6.7 m)
Draft:	4 feet (1.2 m)
Propulsion:	2 diesel engines; 600 bhp; 2 shafts
Speed:	A series: 8.6 knots
	B series: 9.1 knots
	C series: 9.4 knots
Range:	A series: 1,300 nm (2,400 km) at 9 knots
	2,400 nm (4,450 km) at 5 knots
	B series: 1,000 nm (1,850 km) at 9 knots
	2,200 nm (4,075 km) at 5 knots
	C series: 1,050 nm (1,950 km) at 9 knots
	2,500 nm (4,630 km) at 5 knots
Personnel:	13 (enlisted)

These tenders were completed in 1962–1966.

*The inland construction tender ANVIL on the Cooper River pushing a con-
struction barge. (2004, U.S. Coast Guard/Scott Carr)*

2 INLAND BUOY TENDERS: IMPROVED BERRY CLASS (65)

Number	Name	Launched	Comm.
WLI 65400	BAYBERRY	2 June 1954	28 June 1954
WLI 65401	ELDERBERRY	2 June 1954	28 June 1954

Builders:	Reliable Welding Works, Olympia, Wash.
Displacement:	68 tons light
	71 tons full load
Length:	65 feet (19.8 m) overall
Beam:	17 feet (5.2 m)
Draft:	4 feet (1.2 m)
Propulsion:	2 diesel engines (General Motors 6-71); 400 bhp; 2 shafts
Speed:	11.3 knots
Range:	800 nm (1,480 km) at 11.3 knots
	1,700 nm (3,150 km) at 6 knots
Personnel:	8 (enlisted)

These tenders are similar to the basic Berry-class design but
with a more powerful propulsion plant. Originally designed for
freshwater operation, they have been modified for saltwater operation.

*The inland buoy tender BAYBERRY. These craft have blunt bows with fend-
ers fitted for pushing barges. (1999, U.S. Coast Guard/Tiffany Powell)*

1 INLAND BUOY TENDER: BERRY CLASS (65)

Number	Name	Launched	Comm.
WLI 65303	BLACKBERRY		24 Aug 1946

Builders:	Dubuque Boat & Boiler, Iowa
Displacement:	50 tons light
	68 tons full load
Length:	65 feet (19.8 m) overall
Beam:	17 feet (5.2 m)
Draft:	4 feet (1.2 m)
Propulsion:	1 diesel (General Motors); 220 bhp; 1 shaft
Speed:	9 knots
Range:	1,500 nm (2,780 km) at 5 knots
Personnel:	8 (enlisted)

This originally was a class of three tenders.

RIVER BUOY TENDER: "SUMAC" (115)

The one-of-a-kind tender SUMAC (WLR 311), completed in 1944, was decommissioned in 1999.

See 16th Edition/page 524 for characteristics.

The inland buoy tender CHOKEBERRY, now discarded; the BLACKBERRY is similar. (U.S. Coast Guard)

2 RIVER BUOY TENDERS: "KANKAKEE" CLASS (75)

Number	Name	Launched	Comm.
WLR 75500	KANKAKEE	8 July 1989	Jan 1990
WLR 75501	GREENBRIER	1989	12 Apr 1990

Builders:	Avondale Industries, New Orleans
Displacement:	172 tons full load
Length:	75 feet (22.9 m) overall
Beam:	24 feet (7.3 m)
Draft:	5 feet (1.5 m)
Propulsion:	2 diesel engines (Caterpillar 3412-DIT); 1,080 bhp; 2 shafts
Speed:	12 knots
Range:	600 nm (1,110 km) at 11 knots
Personnel:	19 (enlisted)

These improved GASCONDE-class river tenders push 130-foot (96.6-m) work barges. Three additional units were planned but not constructed.

9 RIVER BUOY TENDERS: "GASCONADE" CLASS (75)

Number	Name	Number	Name
WLR 75401	GASCONADE	WLR 75406	KICKAPOO
WLR 75402	MUSKINGUM	WLR 75407	KANAWHA
WLR 75403	WYACONDA	WLR 75408	PATOKA
WLR 75404	CHIPPEWA	WLR 75409	CHENA
WLR 75405	CHEYENNE		

Builders:	WLR 75401: St. Louis Shipbuilding & Dry Dock, Mo.
	WLR 75402–75405: Maxon Construction, Tell City, Ind.
	WLR 75406–75409: Halter Marine, New Orleans
Displacement:	127 tons light
	141 tons full load
Length:	75 feet (22.9 m) overall
Beam:	22 feet (6.7 m)
Draft:	4 feet (1.2 m)
Propulsion:	2 diesel engines (Caterpillar); 600 bhp; 2 shafts
Speed:	7.6 or 8.7 knots
Personnel:	19 (enlisted)

These tenders were completed from 1964 to 1970. They work in tandem with a 90-foot (27.4-m) barge.

The river buoy tender CHEYENNE with a buoy barge. (U.S. Coast Guard)

The river buoy tender GREENBRIER, somewhat resembling a houseboat, makes her way up the Mississippi River near Natchez, Mississippi. There are twin engine exhausts on the upper deck, abaft the bridge. The mast is offset to port. (2004, U.S. Coast Guard/Jonathan McCool)

6 RIVER BUOY TENDERS: "OUACHITA" CLASS (65)

Number	Name	Number	Name
WLR 65501	OUACHITA	WLR 65504	SCIOTO
WLR 65502	CIMARRON	WLR 65505	OSAGE
WLR 65503	OBION	WLR 65506	SANGAMON

Builders:	Gibbs Shipyard, Jacksonville, Fla., except WLR 66501, 66502 by Platzer Shipyard, Houston, Texas
Displacement:	143 tons
Length:	65½ feet (20.0 m) overall
Beam:	21 feet (6.4 m)
Draft:	5 feet (1.5 m)
Propulsion:	2 diesel engines; 600 bhp; 2 shafts
Speed:	10.5 knots
Range:	3,500 nm (6,485 km) at 6 knots
Personnel:	12 (enlisted)

These tenders were completed in 1960-1962. They were designed specifically to operate with work barges on western rivers.

TUGS

8 ICEBREAKING TUGS	}	BAY CLASS (140)
1 TRAINING SHIP		

Number	Name	Launched	Comm.	Status
WTGB 101	KATMAI BAY	8 Apr 1978	8 Jan 1979	**GL**
WTGB 102	BRISTOL BAY	22 July 1978	5 Apr 1979	**GL**
WTGB 103	MOBILE BAY	11 Nov 1978	6 May 1979	**GL**
WTGB 104	BISCAYNE BAY	3 Feb 1979	8 Dec 1979	**GL**
WTGB 105	NEAH BAY	2 Feb 1980	18 Aug 1980	**GL**
WTGB 106	MORRO BAY	11 July 1980	25 Jan 1980	**AA**
WTGB 107	PENOBSCOT BAY	27 July 1984	2 Jan 1985	**AA**
WTGB 108	THUNDER BAY	15 Aug 1985	4 Nov 1985	**AA**
WTGB 109	STURGEON BAY	12 Sep 1987	20 Aug 1988	**AA**

Builders:	Tacoma Boatbuilding, Wash., except WTGB 107, 109 by Bay City Marine, Tacoma, Wash.
Displacement:	662 tons full load
Length:	140 feet (42.7 m) overall
Beam:	37 feet (11.3 m)
Draft:	12 feet (3.7 m)
Propulsion:	diesel-electric (2 Fairbanks Morse 38D8 1/8 diesel engines); electric drive (Westinghouse); 2,500 shp; 1 shaft
Speed:	14.7 knots
Range:	1,800 nm (3,333 km) at 14.7 knots 4,000 nm (7,410 km) at 12 knots
Personnel:	17 (3 officers + 14 enlisted)
Radar:	SPS-64(V)1 navigation

These are the largest tugs to be constructed specifically for Coast Guard service. They are designed to provide general towing and support services and can break through ice up to 20 inches (0.5 m) thick.

The MORRO BAY is employed as an enlisted training ship at the Coast Guard Academy in Groton, Connecticut; she is painted white. She was decommissioned in September 1998; however, with the increased Coast Guard training requirements following the 11 September 2001 attacks, she was rehabilitated and recommissioned on 25 November 2002 for general service, as well as for use as a training craft at the Academy. During her reactivation, she received an extensive engineering overhaul.

A planned tenth unit was not built.

Classification: These tugs originally were designated WYTM. The KATAMI BAY was changed to WTGB on 5 February 1979; the others were changed to WTGB on completion.

Design: These ships are fitted with a hull air-lubrication system to enhance icebreaking capability.

The river buoy tender OSAGE; she has twin funnels. (U.S. Coast Guard)

The icebreaking tug STURGEON breaking ice in the Hudson River between New York and New Jersey. These tugs are invaluable in keeping rivers and bays open to barge and shipping traffic during winters in the northeastern United States and on the Great Lakes. (2003, U.S. Coast Guard/Bill Barry)

The STURGEON doing what icebreaking tugs do in winter. (2003, U.S. Coast Guard/Bill Barry)

11 SMALL HARBOR TUGS (65)

Number	Name	Comm.	Status
WYTL 65601	CAPSTAN	19 July 1961	**AA**
WYTL 65602	CHOCK	12 Sep 1962	**AA**
WYTL 65604	TACKLE	1962	**AA**
WYTL 65607	BRIDLE	3 Apr 1963	**AA**
WYTL 65608	PENDANT	Aug 1963	**AA**
WYTL 65609	SHACKLE	7 May 1963	**AA**
WYTL 65610	HAWSER	17 Jan 1963	**AA**
WYTL 65611	LINE	21 Feb 1963	**AA**
WYTL 65612	WIRE	19 Mar 1963	**AA**
WYTL 65614	BOLLARD	10 Apr 1967	**AA**
WYTL 65615	CLEAT	10 May 1967	**AA**

Builders:	WYTL 65601, 65602, 65604: Gibbs Shipyard, Jacksonville, Fla.
	WYTL 65607–65612: Barbour Boat Works, New Bern, N.C.
	WYTL 65614, 65615: Western Boatbuilding, Tacoma, Wash.
Displacement:	62 tons light
	72 tons full load
Length:	65 feet (19.8 m) overall
Beam:	19 feet (5.8 m)
Draft:	7 feet (2.1 m)
Propulsion:	1 diesel engine; 400 bhp; 1 shaft
Speed:	10.5 knots, except WYTL 65607–65609 9.8 knots
Range:	3,600 nm (6,670 km) at 6 knots, except WYTL 65607–65609 2,700 nm (5,000 km) at 5.8 knots
Personnel:	8 (enlisted)

These are steel-hull tugs. All are based on the U.S. East Coast.

Class: This originally was a class of 15 tugs. The BITT (WYTL 65613) was decommissioned on 4 October 1982; the SWIVEL (WYTL 65603), TOWLINE (WYTL 65605), and CATENARY (WYTL 65606) were stricken on 1 May 1995.

Engineering: Their diesel engines are being upgraded to 500 bhp.

The small harbor tug CHOCK at anchor in the Washington, D.C., channel. These tugs carry out a variety of functions, including port security. (2004, U.S. Coast Guard/Joseph P. Cirone)

SMALL HARBOR TUG: EX-ARMY TUG

The small harbor tug MESSENGER (WYTM 85009), the former U.S. Army tug ST 710, was discarded in 1995 after 49 years of Coast Guard service. She was based at the Coast Guard Yard.

Completed on 9 May 1944 (correction to previous edition), the tug was transferred to the Coast Guard on 26 September 1946 and renamed. She ceased operations at Curtis Bay on 17 November 1995, having spent her entire Coast Guard career at that yard.

See 17th Edition/page 599 for characteristics.

SMALL CRAFT

The Coast Guard operates several hundred small craft in the patrol, search and rescue, oil cleanup, and navigation support roles.

Several DEPLOYABLE PURSUIT BOATS: 38-FT TYPE

Builder:	Fountain Powerboats, Washington, N.C.
Displacement:	
Length:	38 feet (11.59 m) overall
Beam:	9 feet (2.74 m)
Draft:	
Propulsion:	2 diesel engines (Yanmar); 840 bhp; 2 propellers
Speed:	48+ knots
Range:	250 nm (465 km)
Personnel:	4–6 (enlisted)
Guns:	small arms
Radar:	Raytheon RL 70RC navigation

These craft are being acquired to counter high-speed drug-smuggling craft. They are intended for operations off the U.S. West Coast and in the Caribbean area and are being based at San Diego and Portsmouth, Virginia.

The first unit was delivered in 2002.

Design: The craft are based on the Fabio Buzzi RIB design, with rigid, inflatable hulls.

Called "go-fasts," the Coast Guard's Deployable Pursuit Boats (DPB) are deployed from large cutters to counter high-speed craft engaged in drug smuggling. These photos shows DPBs during an exercise on the Elizabeth River, Virginia. (1999, U.S. Coast Guard/Dionne Short)

Deployable pursuit boats. (1999, U.S. Coast Guard/Dionne Short)

150 + APPROX. 550 RESPONSE BOATS: DEFENDER CLASS (25)

Builder:	SAFE Boats International, Port Orchard, Wash.
Displacement:	
Length:	25 feet (7.62 m) overall
Beam:	8½ feet (2.6 m)
Draft:	3¼ feet (1.0 m)
Propulsion:	2 outboard gasoline engines (Honda); 550 hp
Speed:	40+ knots
Range:	150 nm (280 km)
Personnel:	
Guns:	2 7.62-mm machine guns M240 (2 single)
Radar:	navigation

The Coast Guard is procuring approximately 700 of these craft to replace some 300 older boats of various types and to provide a standardized craft for the Coast Guard's Maritime Safety and Security Teams.

The first unit—No. 25400—was delivered in July 2003. The program is expected to take about seven years, i.e., a delivery rate of two boats per week. Estimated unit cost is $180,000.

The craft were designed to be carried by C-130 Hercules aircraft.

44 PORT SECURITY BOATS: GUARDIAN CLASS (25)

Displacement:	
Length:	24⅞ feet (7.49 m) overall
Beam:	8 feet (2.44 m)
Draft:	3¼ feet (1.0 m)
Propulsion:	2 outboard gasoline engines
Speed:	40+ knots
Range:	
Personnel:	3 or 4 (enlisted)
Guns:	1 .50-cal machine gun M2
	2 7.62-mm machine guns M60 or M240 (2 single)
Radar:	navigation

These craft are designated TPSB.

One of the hundreds of Defender security boats being acquired by the Coast Guard patrols New York Harbor, with the Staten Island ferry passing to port. (2004, U.S. Coast Guard/Kelly Newlin)

A Defender streaks toward Catalina Island off the coast of Southern California during a training exercise. (2004, U.S. Coast Guard/Dave Hardesty)

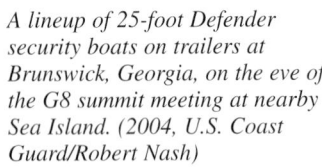

A lineup of 25-foot Defender security boats on trailers at Brunswick, Georgia, on the eve of the G8 summit meeting at nearby Sea Island. (2004, U.S. Coast Guard/Robert Nash)

A 55-foot aids-to-navigation boat, filled with civilian guests, off Mobile, Alabama. (2002, U.S. Coast Guard/Chad Saylor)

A Transportable Security Boat (TSB) from Port Security Unit 307 patrols Ash Shuaiba, Kuwait, with the 110-foot cutter BARANOF in the background. (2004, U.S. Coast Guard/Matthew Belson)

24 PATROL CRAFT: 22-FT RAIDER TYPE

Builders:	NAPCO International, Hopkins, Minn.
Displacement:	1.5 tons light
	2 tons full load
Length:	22⅓ feet (6.8 m) overall
Beam:	7 5/12 feet (2.25 m)
Draft:	
Propulsion:	2 outboard gasoline engines; 360 hp
Speed:	40 knots
Range:	165 nm (305 km) at 40 knots
Personnel:	3 (enlisted)
Guns:	1 .50-cal machine gun M2
	2 7.62-mm machine guns M60 (2 single)
	small arms
Radar:	1 navigation

These are modified Boston Whalers built of Glass-Reinforced Plastic (GRP). They were delivered to the Coast Guard from 1987 to 1989 and are numbered 233510–233524.

They are craft operated by reserve port security units; several were airlifted to the Persian Gulf during Operation Desert Shield (1990).

25 AIDS-TO-NAVIGATION BOATS: 55-FT TYPE

Builder:	Robert E. Derecktor, Mamaroneck, N.Y.
Displacement:	28.8 tons light
	31.25 tons full load
Length:	55 feet (16.77 m) overall
Beam:	17 feet (5.2 m)
Draft:	5 feet (1.5 m)
Propulsion:	2 diesel engines (General Motors 12V71 T1); 1,080 bhp;
	2 shafts
Speed:	22 knots
Range:	350 nm (650 km) at 18 knots
Personnel:	4 (enlisted)
Radar:	1 Raytheon 1900 navigation

These are aluminum-hull craft that support navigation aids on inland waterways. They are numbered 55101–55125. They were placed in service in 1976–1977.

Their cargo capacity is 4,000 pounds (1,814 kg), and they have a 1,000-pound (453-kg) crane fitted aft.

A swarm of Raider security boats—modified Boston Whalers—demonstrate their maneuverability off Yorktown, Virginia, as the missile cruiser NORMANDY (CG 60) passes by. (2000, U.S. Coast Guard/Stephen Baker)

4 MOTOR LIFEBOATS: 52-FT TYPE

Number	Name	Number	Name
52312	VICTORY	52314	TRIUMPH II
52313	INVINCIBLE	52315	INTREPID

Builders:	Coast Guard Yard, Curtis Bay, Md.
Displacement:	35 tons
Length:	52 feet (15.85 m) overall
Beam:	14½ feet (4.4 m)
Draft:	6¼ feet (1.9 m)
Propulsion:	2 diesel engines (General Motors 6-71); 340 bhp; 2 shafts
Speed:	11 knots
Range:	495 nm (920 km) at 11 knots
Personnel:	5 (enlisted) + 35 survivors
Radar:	1 navigation

These are "self-righting" lifeboats with steel hulls and aluminum superstructures. The VICTORY was built in 1956, the others in 1960–1961. Highly capable craft, they can operate in heavy sea conditions and are fitted with firefighting pumps.

These are the only Coast Guard small craft with names assigned.

1 SEARCH AND RESCUE BOAT: 50-FT TYPE

Builder:	Munson Manufacturing, Edmonds, Wash.
Displacement:	26 tons full load
Length:	50⁵⁄₁₂ feet (15.37 m) overall
Beam:	16⅓ feet (4.97 m)
Draft:	4 feet (1.2 m)
Propulsion:	2 diesel engines (General Motors 8V92 TI); 1,300 bhp; 2 shafts
Speed:	26 knots
Range:	300 nm (555 km) at 18 knots
	200 nm (370 km) at 26 knots
Personnel:	4 or 5 (enlisted) + survivors

The 502001 is a small SAR craft, procured in record time by the Coast Guard to evaluate the potential for a live-aboard boat to replace small shore stations. The craft was placed in service on 1 May 1992 at Station Taylors Island in the Chesapeake Bay, Maryland. With the availability of the 502001, the station's number of assigned personnel was reduced from 19 to 8.

The craft was adapted from a commercial design.

17 AIDS-TO-NAVIGATION BOATS: 49-FT TYPE

Builders:	Coast Guard Yard, Curtis Bay, Md.
	Maritime Contractors, Bellingham, Wash.
Displacement:	31.65 tons light
Length:	49¼ feet (15.02 m) overall
Beam:	16⅞ feet (5.13 m)
Draft:	6⅞ feet (2.08 m)
Propulsion:	1 diesel engine; 305 bhp; 1 shaft
Speed:	10.5 knots
Range:	300 nm (555 km) at 10 knots
Personnel:	4 (enlisted)

These craft, designated 49401–49417, were completed in August 1994 at Maritime Contractors. Additional units are planned.

The boats have a stern crane for handling buoys.

Approx. 200 MOTOR LIFEBOATS: 47-FT TYPE

Builder:	Textron Marine Systems, New Orleans
Displacement:	approx. 20 tons full load
Length:	47¹¹⁄₁₂ feet (14.6 m) overall
Beam:	14 feet (4.3 m)
Draft:	4½ feet (1.37 m)
Propulsion:	2 diesel engines (General Motors 6V92); 870 bhp; 2 shafts
Speed:	25 knots
	22 knots sustained
Range:	200 nm (370 km) at 22 knots
Personnel:	4 (enlisted) + 5 survivors
Radars:	1 SPS-69 navigation

These craft are numbered in the 47200 series. Constructed of aluminum, they are self-righting lifeboats, capable of flipping end-

The INVINCIBLE, one of the few small Coast Guard craft to be named. Here she, passes the Cape Disappointment lighthouse in Washington state. (2003, U.S. Coast Guard/Kurt Fredrickson)

The one-of-a-kind search-and-rescue boat 502001 at high speed in Chesapeake Bay, Maryland. (1992, U.S. Coast Guard)

A 49-foot aids-to-navigation boat working off Muskegon, Michigan. (2001, U.S. Coast Guard/Harry C. Craft III)

A 47-foot motor lifeboat off Galveston, Texas. These craft have a remark-able self-righting capability, illustrated in the 16th Edition/page 531. (2002, U.S. Coast Guard/Robert D. Wyman)

A 46-foot buoy serving boat based in New York City. (1991, Giorgio Arra)

over-end or rolling up to 360o and self-righting in less than 10 seconds. They can withstand 20-foot (6.1-m) breaking waves.

The lead boat was delivered in August 1990; about 200 units were built through the end of 2004.

9 BUOY SERVICING BOATS: 46-FT TYPE

Builders:	46301–46306: Hunt Shipyard
	46307–46309: Coast Guard Yard, Curtis Bay, Md.
Displacement:	20 tons light
	27 tons full load
Length:	46½ feet (14.1 m) overall
Beam:	16⅙ feet (4.9 m)
Draft:	5⅔ feet (1.7 m)
Propulsion:	1 diesel engine (General Motors 6-71); 180 bhp;
	Schottel rudder-propeller unit
Speed:	9 knots
Range:	440 nm (815 km) at 9 knots
Personnel:	4 (enlisted)

These craft have steel hulls and superstructures. The above data are for later units; the 46301–46306 have reduced fuel capacities and a range of only 320 nm (590 km). They were delivered in 1966 (Hunt units) and 1969 (Coast Guard units).

Cargo capacity is 7¼ tons of buoys and navigation aids; there is a 4,000-pound (1,800-kg) lifting frame mounted on the stern.

32 AIDS-TO-NAVIGATION BOATS: 45-FT TYPE

Builder:	Coast Guard Yard, Curtis Bay, Md.
Displacement:	21.5 tons light
	31.27 tons full load
Length:	45¼ feet (13.8 m) overall
Beam:	15 feet (4.6 m)
Draft:	3 feet (0.9 m)
Propulsion:	1 diesel engine (General Motors 6-71); 150 bhp; 1 shaft
Speed:	8.5 knots
Range:	550 nm (1,020 km) at 8.5 knots
Personnel:	4 (enlisted)

The 45-foot aids-to-navigation boat 45306. (1998, Leo Van Ginderen)

These are steel-hull craft with steel superstructures. The above characteristics relate to units 45302–45312; the similar 45313–45316 carry less fuel, but their GM 6-71 engine is rated at 180 bhp, with a range reduction to 520 nm (960 km).

These boats can carry about 9½ tons of buoys and navigation aids.

A 44-foot motor lifeboat in heavy seas off Cape Disappointment, Washington. (1997, U.S. Coast Guard/Chris Rose)

A 41-foot utility boat performing security duties at Belle Isle, Michigan. (2001, U.S. Coast Guard/Harry C. Craft III)

2 MOTOR LIFEBOATS: 44-FT TYPE

Builder:	Coast Guard Yard, Curtis Bay, Md.
Displacement:	14.9 tons light
	17.7 tons full load
Length:	44 feet (13.4 m) overall
Beam:	12⅔ feet (3.9 m)
Draft:	3¹¹⁄₁₂ feet (1.2 m)
Propulsion:	2 diesel engines (General Motors 6-71); 372 bhp; 2 shafts
Speed:	14 knots
	11.8 knots sustained
Range:	185 nm (340 km) at 11.8 knots
Personnel:	4 (enlisted) + survivors
Radars:	1 navigation

These are "unsinkable" lifeboats. The series originally was numbered 44300–44409; they were delivered from 1961 to 1973.

These craft are being replaced by the 47-foot design.

Eight of these craft were transferred to the Yemen Coast Guard Authority in 2004 for the startup of that force.

172 UTILITY BOATS: 41-FT TYPE

Builder:	Coast Guard Yard, Curtis Bay, Md.
Displacement:	13–14 tons full load
Length:	40⅔ feet (12.4 m) overall
Beam:	13½ feet (4.1 m)
Draft:	4 feet (1.2 m)
Propulsion:	2 diesel engines (Cummins V903M or VT903M); 560 or 636 bhp; 2 shafts
Speed:	22–26 knots (see notes)
Range:	300 nm (555 km) at 18 knots
Personnel:	3 (enlisted)
Radars:	1 Raytheon 1900 navigation

These are aluminum utility craft completed from 1973 to 1982. Hull numbers begin with 41300. The 41400 and later units have vanes on the propeller shafts, adding 2.5 knots to their maximum speed.

Their rescue equipment includes a fire pump.

The 38-foot utility boat 380502 against the New York City skyline. (1991, Giorgio Arra)

2 UTILITY BOATS: 38-FT TYPE

Builder:	Munson Manufacturing, Edmonds, Wash.
Displacement:	11 tons full load
Length:	38 feet (11.58 m) overall
Beam:	12½ feet (3.8 m)
Draft:	2⅗₂ feet (0.7 m)
Propulsion:	2 diesel engines (Caterpillar 3208 TA); 750 bhp; 2 shafts
Speed:	30 knots
Personnel:	4 (enlisted) + 8 passengers
Radars:	1 navigation

The 380501 and 380502 were placed in Coast Guard service in April 1991. They are based in New York City and patrol against the illegal dumping of hazardous materials.

365 PORT AND WATERWAYS BOATS: 32-FT TYPE

Builder:	
Displacement:	7.5 tons light
	8.6 tons full load
Length:	33⅓ feet (10.2 m) overall
Beam:	11¾ feet (3.6 m)
Draft:	2⅝ feet (0.9 m)
Propulsion:	2 diesel engines (Caterpillar 3208); 406 bhp; 2 shafts
Speed:	25 knots
Personnel:	3 (enlisted)
Radars:	1 Raytheon 1900 navigation

Built in the late 1970s, these craft are of GRP construction. They are equipped for firefighting.

28 PORT SECURITY BOATS: 31-FT TYPE

Builders:	31001–31004: Bertram Boat, Miami
	31005–31028: Coast Guard Yard, Curtis Bay, Md.
Displacement:	7.4 tons full load
Length:	30⁵⁄₁₂ feet (9.27 m) overall
Beam:	11½ feet (3.5 m)
Draft:	3¹¹⁄₁₂ feet (1.2 m)
Propulsion:	1 diesel engine (General Motors); 197 bhp; 1 shaft
Speed:	14 knots
Range:	165 nm (305 km) at 12.5 knots
Personnel:	3 (enlisted)
Radars:	1 navigation

These are GRP craft numbered from 31001. Completed in the 1960s, they are used primarily for training.

19 SURF RESCUE BOATS: 30-FT TYPE

Builder:	Coast Guard Yard, Curtis Bay, Md.
Displacement:	4.6 tons full load
Length:	30⅓ feet (9.25 m) overall
Beam:	9⅓ feet (2.8 m)
Draft:	3⅔ feet (1.1 m)
Propulsion:	2 diesel engines (General Motors 6VT92T); 375 bhp; 1 shaft
Speed:	31 knots
Range:	150 nm (280 km) at 25 knots
Personnel:	2 (enlisted) + survivors
Radar:	none

These rescue boats are employed in short-distance operations. Their hull numbers begin with 30201. They were placed in service in 1986–1990.

1 LAKE CHAMPLAIN PATROL BOAT: 28-FT TYPE

Builder:	SeaArk Boat, Monticello, Ark.
Displacement:	
Length:	28½ feet (8.69 m) overall
Beam:	11⅔ feet (3.56 m)
Draft:	1⅚ feet (0.56 m)
Propulsion:	2 diesel engines (Volvo AQAD 41/290); 400 bhp;
	2 outboard drives
Speed:	38 knots
Personnel:	3 (enlisted) + survivors

Based at Burlington, Vermont, this boat is used for search and rescue on Lake Champlain.

Several PATROL CRAFT: 27-FT VIGILANT TYPE

Builder:	Boston Whaler, Edgewater, Fla.
Displacement:	2.27 tons light
	4 tons full load
Length:	26⁷⁄₁₂ feet (8.10 m) overall
Beam:	10 feet (3.05 m)
Draft:	1⁷⁄₁₂ feet (0.48 m)
Propulsion:	2 outboard gasoline engines; 350 hp
Speed:	34 knots
Personnel:	4 (enlisted) + 8 passengers
Radars:	1 navigation

These GRP craft are for harbor patrol duties and were delivered in the 1990s. Similar units have been transferred to Kazakhstan and Romania with Coast Guard training assistance.

The 32-foot port and waterways boat 32328 based in New York City. (1990, Giorgio Arra)

The port and waterways boat 32328. (1990, Giorgio Arra)

1 HONOLULU PERSONNEL LAUNCH: 26-FT TYPE

Builder:	Munson Manufacturing, Edmonds, Wash.
Displacement:	3.2 tons full load
Length:	26 feet (7.9 m) overall
Beam:	10 feet (3.05 m)
Draft:	2 feet (0.61 m)
Propulsion:	1 diesel engine (Volvo AQAD 41/200); 1,200 bhp;
	1 outboard drive
Speed:	25 knots
Personnel:	1 + 12 passengers

This personnel launch is used in Honolulu, Hawaii, to transport Coast Guardsmen. She is assigned hull number 266200.

A 30-foot surf rescue boat going to sea. (U.S. Coast Guard)

The Coast Guard's unique Honolulu harbor launch. (Munson)

A 28-foot Lake Champlain patrol boat. (1987, SeaArk)

The 25-foot patrol boat 253503. The black markings on the bow are non-skid material. (1996, Leo Van Ginderen)

Several PATROL BOATS: CHALLENGER 25-FT TYPE

Builder:	Boston Whaler, Edgewater, Fla.
Displacement:	1.86 tons light
	3.2 tons full load
Length:	24⅝ feet (7.50 m) overall
Beam:	8 feet (2.45 m)
Draft:	1⅓ feet (0.4 m)
Propulsion:	2 outboard gasoline engines (Johnson); 300 bhp
Speed:	30+ knots
Crew:	3 (enlisted) + 9 passengers

These patrol craft, numbered from 253501, were delivered in the 1990s. They are constructed of GRP.

200+ SURF BOATS ⎫
41 CARGO BOATS ⎭ 25-FT TYPE

Builder:	Coast Guard Yard, Curtis Bay, Md.
Displacement:	2.3 tons light
	3.4 tons full load
Length:	25⅔ feet (7.8 m) overall
Beam:	7 feet (2.16 m)
Draft:	2 feet (0.61 m)
Propulsion:	1 diesel engine (General Motors 3-53); 80 bhp; 1 shaft
Speed:	11 knots
Range:	60 nm (110 km) at 11 knots
Personnel:	surf boats: 2 (enlisted) + survivors
	cargo boats: 3 (enlisted)

More than 200 surf boats of this design, plus 41 similar cargo craft, entered Coast Guard service from 1969 to 1983. Hull numbers 253301–253517 are assigned. They are of GRP construction.

One of two Hammerhead 24-foot patrol craft based on Lake Tahoe. (Munson)

72 HAMMERHEAD PATROL CRAFT: 24-FT TYPE

Builder:	Munson Manufacturing, Edmonds, Wash.
Displacement:	2.8 tons full load
Length:	24 feet (7.3 m) overall
Beam:	8½ feet (2.6 m)
Draft:	2 feet (0.61 m)
Propulsion:	2 outboard gasoline engines (Evinrude V-6)
Speed:	45 knots
Personnel:	

These craft are employed for search and rescue on Lake Tahoe, on the California–Nevada state line.

SEVERAL PATROL BOATS: SENTRY 22-FT TYPE

Builder:	Boston Whaler, Edgewater, Fla.
Displacement:	1.29 tons light
	2.5 tons full load
Length:	22⅓ feet (6.8 m) overall
Beam:	7½ feet (2.3 m)
Draft:	1⅙ feet (0.36 m)
Propulsion:	2 outboard gasoline engines (Johnson); 160 hp
Speed:	30+ knots
Personnel:	
Radar:	1 navigation

18 PATROL BOATS: 21-FT TYPE

Builder:	SeaArk Boat, Monticello, Ark.
Displacement:	1.9 tons full load
Length:	21 feet (6.4 m) overall
Beam:	8 feet (2.44 m)
Draft:	1⅚ feet (0.56 m)
Propulsion:	2 outboard gasoline engines (Evinrude)
Speed:	32 knots
Personnel:	

These are trailer-transportable patrol craft for use on inland waterways. They are of aluminum construction.

58 AIDS-TO-NAVIGATION BOATS: 21-FT TYPE

Builder:	SeaArk Boat, Monticello, Ark. [run-in]
Displacement:	1.6 tons light
	3.17 tons full load
Length:	21½ feet (6.56 m) overall
Beam:	7⅓ feet (2.24 m)
Draft:	1⅙ feet (0.36 m)
Propulsion:	1 outboard gasoline engine; 228 bhp
Speed:	28 knots
Range:	100 nm (328 km) at 20 knots
Personnel:	

These are transported on trailers for use in inland waterways.

The 21-foot aid-to-navigation craft 21489 in the St. Johns River, Florida. (2003, U.S. Coast Guard/Crystal K. Norman)

MISCELLANEOUS

1 CABLE REPAIR CRAFT: CONVERTED NAVY LCM(6)

Builder:	
Displacement:	50 tons full load
Length:	56 feet (17.07 m) overall
Beam:	14⅓ feet (4.37 m)
Draft:	3⅚ feet (1.17 m)
Propulsion:	2 diesel engines (General Motors 6-71); 330 bhp; 2 shafts
Speed:	10 knots
Range:	130 nm (240 km) at 10 knots
Personnel:	5 (enlisted)

Now designated 560500, this is the former Navy landing craft 56CM6841 converted in 1986 at the Coast Guard Yard for service at South Portland, Maine. A pilothouse has been added aft, and the bow has been modified. The 560500 has a black hull.

SEVERAL SAIL TRAINING CRAFT

The Coast Guard operates several sail training craft at the Coast Guard Academy. These include four 44-foot (13.41-m) sail training craft identical to the 44-foot yawls at the Naval Academy (see Chapter 25). The four yawls are the ARCTIC TERN, BLUE GOOSE, SHEARWATER, and STORMY PETREL.

1 FLOATING DRY DOCK: EX-NAVY

The former Navy dry dock OAK RIDGE (ARD 1) is in service at the Coast Guard Yard at Curtis Bay, Maryland.

The OAK RIDGE was in service at the Naval Submarine Base New London, Connecticut, until 2001. After being struck from the Naval Vessel Register on 26 November 2001, she was transferred to the Coast Guard on 7 February 2002. The OAK RIDGE replaced the unnamed YFD 83 (ex-AFDL 31), which was on loan from the Navy to the Coast Guard from her completion on 1 December 1943 until 2002.

See Chapter 26 for OAK RIDGE characteristics.

The cutters (from left) BARANOF, WALNUT, and BOUTWELL steam in the Persian Gulf, where they were supporting U.S. military activities in the Middle East. Although not placed under the Navy Department since World War II, the Coast Guard has had major roles in several U.S. conflicts. (2003, U.S. Coast Guard/John Gaffney)

CHAPTER 33

National Oceanic and Atmospheric Administration

Studying the oceans: NOAA undertakes oceanographic surveys and studies in support of the U.S. government. Here, a seaman aboard the NOAA ship MILLER FREEMAN prepares a specialized net-towing rig. (NOAA)

The National Oceanic and Atmospheric Administration (NOAA), an agency within the Department of Commerce, conducts ocean surveys and other environmental research activities for the U.S. government. NOAA conducts nonmilitary research operations in U.S. coastal waters as well as overseas; however, its maps and charts are used by the armed forces, and during time of war or national emergency, the president may transfer NOAA ships, aircraft, shore stations, and personnel to the Navy or to other military services.

NOAA's National Ocean Survey currently has 17 active ships, with the fleet planned for expansion to 19 ships in Fiscal Year (FY) 2006 and 21 ships in FY 2007, before older ships begin to be retired. Within this fleet will be seven former Navy ocean surveillance ships (T-AGOS) built in the late 1980s as long-endurance ships to tow sonar arrays to detect Soviet submarines in areas where the Navy's Sound Surveillance System (SOSUS) was not available or had been destroyed. Two other recent transfers from the Navy are the surveying ship LITTLEHALES (T-AGS 52), completed in 1992, and the torpedo trials ship AGATE PASS (YTT 12), completed in 1991.

NOAA has received only one new ocean research ship constructed specifically for it in the past decade, the RONALD H. BROWN. That ship was part of the Navy procurement of the THOMAS G. THOMPSON (AGOR 23) class, with three other ships being built for Navy-sponsored civilian research activities (see Chapter 23).

Construction of additional ocean research and surveying ships for NOAA, long delayed for budgetary reasons, now is not likely because of the former Navy units becoming available for service. However, NOAA does have a program under way to construct four relatively large fisheries research ships of the OSCAR DYSON class.

Several older survey ships have been disposed of in the past few years.

NOAA also operates 12 research and surveying aircraft, ranging from modified P-3 Orion maritime patrol aircraft to small helicopters.

Historical. An act of Congress on 10 February 1807 established the Survey of the Coast as a U.S. government agency. Its name was changed to the Coast Survey in 1834 and to the Coast and Geodetic Survey in 1878. The commissioned officer corps of the agency was established in 1917.

The Coast and Geodetic Survey was made a component of the Environmental Science Services Administration (ESSA) on 13 July 1965, when that agency was established within the Department of Commerce. ESSA subsequently became the National Oceanic and Atmospheric Administration on 3 October 1970, with the Coast and Geodetic Survey being renamed the National Ocean Survey, which now is the ship-operating branch of NOAA.

PERSONNEL

The NOAA administrator is retired Navy Vice Admiral Conrad C. Lautenbacher, who is "double-hatted" as Under Secretary of Commerce for Oceans and Atmosphere.

His direct subordinate, the director of NOAA, is Samuel De Bow Jr., a rear admiral (upper half) of the NOAA commissioned officer corps. He also is director of NOAA's Marine and Aviation Operations, which controls the agency's ships and aircraft.

NOAA has approximately 300 commissioned officers, about one-half of whom are assigned to shipboard duty. Ninety licensed civil service personnel and some 625 unlicensed mariners also man NOAA ships. Personnel assigned to ships include women; Evelyn J. Fields was the first woman to command a NOAA ship, the MCARTHUR. (She subsequently became director of the NOAA officer corps with the rank of rear admiral, serving in that position from May 1990 to August 2004. She was the first woman and the first black to serve in that position.)

Medical officers from the U.S. Public Health Service are assigned to NOAA ships when necessary.

SHIPS

The status of NOAA ships varies from year to year, with research and survey operations dependent on specific budget allocations. These ships are supported by the NOAA Atlantic Marine Center at Norfolk, Virginia, and the Pacific Marine Center at Puget Sound, Washington.

Rear Admiral Samuel P. De Bow Jr., Director, NOAA Officer Corps and Director, Office of Marine and Aviation Operations, since August 2004. (NOAA)

All 18 oceangoing NOAA ships are in active service.

Previously, most of the larger NOAA ships were built to Maritime Administration designs (designations shown in parenthesis). The smaller NOAA ships mostly are adopted from commercial designs.

In World War II, six of the larger Coast and Geodetic Survey ships were transferred to the Navy and designated as surveying ships (AGS). They were Navy manned, armed, and most were in combat. Another ten ships remained under the Coast and Geodetic Survey during the war; some of these were armed.

NOAA ships are painted white, with the NOAA insignia and acronym and the ship's number painted on the bow.

Designations: All NOAA ships are designated by a three-digit number preceded by the letter *R* for Research and *S* for Survey, with the first digit indicating the Horsepower Tonnage (HPT) class. The HPT is the numerical sum of the vessel's shaft horsepower plus her gross tonnage.

Table 33-1 lists the NOAA research and survey ships—their current hull numbers and previous designations.

Guns: NOAA ships are unarmed.

Helicopters: Only the DAVID STARR JORDAN has a helicopter platform.

Table 33-1. NOAA SHIPS

Class	Number	Name	Former	Mission/notes
I	R 104	RONALD H. BROWN	—	oceanographic-atmospheric research
II	S 220	FAIRWEATHER	—	nautical charting
II	S 221	RAINIER		nautical charting
II	S 222	THOMAS JEFFERSON	T-AGS 52	hydrographic survey
II	R 223	MILLER FREEMAN	—	fisheries research
III	R 333	KA'IMIMOANA	T-AGOS 15	oceanographic-atmospheric research
III	R 334	HI'IALAKAI	T-AGOS 3	multiple programs
III	R 335	OSCAR ELTON SETTE	T-AGOS 13	multiple programs
III	R 336	GORDON GUNTER	T-AGOS 18	fisheries research
III	R 337	MCARTHUR II	T-AGOS 7	multiple programs
III	R ..	(ex-Navy ASSERTIVE)	T-AGOS 9	fisheries research
III	R ...	(ex-Navy CAPABLE)	T-AGOS 16	ocean exploration
III	R 332	OREGON II	—	fisheries research
III	R 342	ALBATROSS IV	—	fisheries research
III	R 352	NANCY FOSTER	YTT 12	coastal oceanography
IV	R 444	DAVID STARR JORDAN	—	fisheries research
IV	R 445	DELAWARE II	—	fisheries research
V	R 552	JOHN N. COBB	—	fisheries research
V	S 590	RUDE		nautical charting

1 RESEARCH SHIP: "THOMAS G. THOMPSON" CLASS

Number	Name	FY	Launched	Comm.	Status
R104	RONALD H. BROWN	94	30 May 1996	19 July 1997	**AA**

Builders:	Trinity/Halter Marine, Moss Point, Miss.
Displacement:	2,100 tons light
	3,250 tons full load
Length:	274 feet (83.5 m) overall
Beam:	52 feet (15.85 m)
Draft:	17 feet (5.2 m)
Propulsion:	diesel-electric (3 diesel generators/Caterpillar 3516TA;
	2 electric motors/General Motors CD6999); 6,000 shp;
	2 azimuth propellers
Speed:	15 knots
Range:	11,300 nm (20,940 km) at 12 knots
Manning:	24 (4 officers + 20 mariners) + 35 scientists
Radars:	2 Sperry RASCAR navigation
	1 Enterprise WSR-74C weather
Sonar:	Nautronix RS916 positioning
	Ocean Data profiler
	Sea Beam 2112A seafloor mapping

The RONALD H. BROWN is one of four ships of this class, the others being built for operation by academic institutions on behalf of Navy research projects (see Chapter 23). The BROWN is the largest ship in the NOAA fleet and the only Class I ship at this time. She replaced both the DISCOVERY (R 102) and the MALCOLM BALDRIGE (R 103).[1]

The BROWN was laid down on 21 February 1995. This was the first keel laying of a built-for-the-purpose NOAA ship since 1980. She carries out worldwide oceanographic and atmospheric research.

Classification: The hull number AGOR 26 was assigned for Navy accounting purposes.

Design: The ship is built to commercial standards and is designed for extended at-sea operations. Four laboratory/accommodation vans can be carried on deck, in addition to more than 4,000 square feet (372 m²) of laboratory space.

Endurance is 60–70 days.

Engineering: In addition to three diesel generators for propulsion, the ship has three ships' service power generators (3508TA) and one emergency generator (3406TA).

She is fitted with azimuth or Z-drives with 360° rotating propellers; there also is a rotating 360°, 1,180-shp bow thruster to provide precise station keeping.

Names: The ship originally was named RESEARCHER, a name previously assigned to a NOAA research ship that had been renamed MALCOLM BALDRIGE in 1988. The R104 was renamed RONALD H. BROWN when christened to honor the Secretary of Commerce killed in a plane crash in Bosnia on 3 April 1996.

---

1 The SURVEYOR (S 132) was longer than the BROWN but displaced slightly less; see page 615.

RONALD H. BROWN (NOAA/Robert Embley)

RONALD H. BROWN at San Diego; the large radome atop the lattice mast has since been removed. (2000, W. Michael Young)

RESEARCH SHIPS: "OCEANOGRAPHER" CLASS

Number	Name	Comm.	Notes
R 101	OCEANOGRAPHER	1966	str. 1996
R 102	DISCOVERER	1967	str. 16 Aug 1996

These graceful Class I oceanographic research ships were the largest ships operated by NOAA (4,033 tons full load). They were built to maritime design S2-MET-MA62a.

See 16th Edition/page 540 for characteristics.

RESEARCH SHIP: "MALCOLM BALDRIGE" (S2-MT-MA7a)

The Class I research ship MALCOLM BALDRIGE (R 103), commissioned in 1970, was stricken on 23 August 1996.

See 16th Edition/page 541 for characteristics.

SURVEY SHIP: "SURVEYOR" (S2-S-RM28a)

The large, Class I survey ship SURVEYOR (S 132), commissioned in 1960, was stricken in 1995.

See 15th Edition/page 589 for characteristics.

(4) FISHERIES SURVEY VESSELS: "OSCAR DYSON" CLASS

Number	Name	Launched	Comm.	Status
R 224	OSCAR DYSON	17 Oct 2003	2005	trials
R 225	HENRY B. BIGELOW		2006	building
R 226	......		2006	building
R 227	......		2007	building

Builders:	VT Halter Marine, Moss Point, Miss.
Displacement:	1,840 tons light
	2,479 tons full load
Length:	208½ feet (63.6 m) overall
Beam:	48½ feet (14.9 m)
Draft:	19⁵⁄₁₂ feet (5.9 m) (see *Design* notes)
Propulsion:	diesel-electric; 4 diesel engines (2 Caterpillar 3512B DITA); 3,650 bhp + (2 Caterpillar 3508B); 2,440 bhp; 1 shaft
Speed:	14 knots
Range:	
Personnel:	45 (4 officers + 22 mariners) + 19 scientists

These are large Fisheries Survey Vessels (FSV). Their construction was delayed by lack of adequate funding by Congress, design problems, and the financial problems of the builder.

The lead ship was authorized in FY 1999 and ordered on 18 January 2001. Subsequent ships were requested in FY 2002–2004.

The ships are to be based, respectively, at Kodiak, Alaska; Woods Hole, Massachusetts; Pascagoula, Mississippi; and Newport, Oregon. They will replaced outdated fisheries research ships.

Design: These will be somewhat multipurpose ships, although all planned equipment will not be available when they are completed. They will be able to operate Remotely Operated Vehicles (ROVs).

The ships have a retractable center board; with the board lowered, their draft is 29⅔ feet (9.05 m).

Endurance will be 40 days.

Engineering: A bow thruster is provided.

2 SURVEY SHIPS: "FAIRWEATHER CLASS" (S1-MT-MA72a)

Number	Name	Launched	Comm.	Status
S 220	FAIRWEATHER	15 Mar 1967	2 Oct 1968	**PA**
S 221	RAINIER	15 Mar 1967	2 Oct 1968	**PA**
S 222	MT. MITCHELL	29 Nov 1966	23 Mar 1968	str. 1995

Builders:	Aerojet-General Corp., Jacksonville, Fla.
Displacement:	1,798 tons full load
Length:	231 feet (70.4 m) overall
Beam:	42 feet (12.8 m)
Draft:	13⅚ feet (4.2 m)
Propulsion:	2 diesel engines; 2,400 bhp; 2 shafts
Speed:	14.5 knots
Range	7,000 nm (12,965 km) at 13 knots
Personnel:	49 (10 officers + 39 mariners) + 4 scientists

These Class II ships are outfitted primarily for hydrographic surveys involving charting operations. The RAINIER operates off the Pacific coast of the United States.

The FAIRWEATHER was deactivated (stricken) in 1989, but the critical backlog of surveys for nautical charts of Alaskan waters led to the decision to recommission her. After being upgraded with new survey equipment, she was again placed in commission on 18 August 2004.

Design: Six aluminum survey launches are carried by each ship.

Engineering: These ships have a 200-hp through-bow thruster.

FAIRWEATHER (NOAA/Grady Tuell)

RAINIER in Alaskan waters.
(NOAA/Michael Riddle)

1 COASTAL SURVEYING SHIP: FORMER SURVEYING SHIP

Number	Name	FY	Launched	In service	to NOAA	NOAA Comm.	Status
S 222 (ex-T-AGS 52)	THOMAS JEFFERSON (ex-LITTLEHALES)	87	14 Feb 1991	10 Feb 1992	3 Mar 2003	8 July 2003	**AA**

Builders:	Trinity/Halter Marine, Moss Point, Miss.
Displacement:	2,000 tons full load
Length:	190 feet (57.9 m) waterline
	208⅙ feet (63.5 m) overall
Beam:	45 feet (13.7 m)

Draft:	14 feet (4.3 m)
Propulsion:	1 diesel engine (V12); 2,550 bhp; 1 shaft
Speed:	16 knots sustained
Range:	13,800 nm (25,535 km) at 16 knots
Personnel:	31 (8 officers + 23 mariners) + 11 scientists

The THOMAS JEFFERSON is the former LITTLEHALES, one of a two-ship class of small Navy surveying ships. With the JOHN McDONNELL (T-AGS 51), this ship was laid down on 10 November 1988. The McDONNELL remains in Navy service, civilian manned by the Military Sealift Command. The class was intended to collect bathymetric/hydrographic data in shallow and deep water.

The LITTLEHALES was taken out of Military Sealift Command (MSC) service and stricken on 27 February 2003 for transfer to NOAA. She replaced the WHITING, which was in NOAA service for almost 40 years.

Design: The THOMAS JEFFERSON has a 45-day endurance.

The THOMAS JEFFERSON *(ex-USNS* LITTLEHALES*) at Norfolk. (2003, NOAA/Albert E. Theberge)*

1 RESEARCH SHIP: "MILLER FREEMAN"

Number	Name	Launched	Comm.	Status
R 223	MILLER FREEMAN	1967	June 1967	**PA**

Builders:	American Shipbuilding, Lorain, Ohio
Displacement:	1,920 tons full load
Length:	216 1/2 feet (66.0 m) overall
Beam:	41 feet (12.5 m)
Draft:	20 feet (6.1 m)
Propulsion:	1 diesel engine (General Motors); 3,200 bhp; 1 shaft
Speed:	14 knots
Range:	13,800 n.miles (25,560 km) at 14 knots
Personnel:	39 (7 officers + 32 mariners) + 11 scientists

The MILLER FREEMAN is a fisheries research ship. She was scheduled to be replaced during the 1990s, but is being retained pending completion of the OSCAR DYSON class. The FREEMAN operates off the U.S. Pacific coast.

Design: She is a Stern-trawler design. Endurance is 31 days.

Engineering: A 400-hp Schottel bow thruster can be lowered for precision station keeping.

MILLER FREEMAN (NOAA)

5 + 2 RESEARCH AND SURVEY SHIPS: FORMER OCEAN SURVEILLANCE SHIPS

Number	Name	FY	Launched	USN in service	to NOAA	NOAA comm.	Status
R 333 (ex-T-AGOS 15)	KA'IMIMOANA (ex-TITAN)	86	18 June 1988	8 Mar 1989	31 Aug 1993	26 Apr 1996	**PA**
R 334 (ex-T-AGOS 3)	HI'IALAKAI (ex-VINDICATOR)	80	1 June 1984	21 Nov 1984	30 Oct 2001	3 Sep 2004	**PA**
R 335 (ex-T-AGOS 13)	OSCAR ELTON SETTE (ex-ADVENTUROUS)	85	23 Sep 1987	19 Aug 1988	5 June 1992	22 Jan 2003	**PA**
R 336 (ex-T-AGOS 18)	GORDON GUNTER (ex-RELENTLESS)	87	12 May 1989	12 Jan 1990	17 Mar 1993	28 Aug 1998	**AA**
R 337 (ex-T-AGOS 7)	MCARTHUR II (ex-INDOMITABLE)	81	16 July 1985	1 Dec 1985	9 Dec 2002	20 May 2003	**PA**
R ... (ex-T-AGOS 9)	...... (ex-ASSERTIVE)	82	20 June 1986	12 Sep 1986	1 Sep 2002	—	laid up
R ... (ex-T-AGOS 16)	...... (ex-CAPABLE)	86	28 Oct 1988	9 June 1989	13 Sep 2004	—	laid up

Builders:	ex-T-AGOS 3, 7, 9: Tacoma Boatbuilding, Wash.	Speed:	11 knots	
	ex-T-AGOS 13, 15, 16, 18: Trinity/Halter Marine, New Orleans	Range:	3,000 nm (5,556 km) at 11 knots	
Displacement:	1,600 tons light		+ 90 days on station at 3 knots	
	2,301 tons full load, except ex-ADVENTUROUS 2,285 tons	Personnel:		

	Officers	Mariners	Scientists
KA'IMIMOANA	5	16	12
HI'IALAKAI	6	18	23
OSCAR ELTON SETTE	4	16	12
GORDON GUNTER	4	14	15
MCARTHUR II	5	17	15

Tonnage:	1,584 Gross Registered Tonnage (GRT)
	786 Deadweight Tonnage (DWT)
Length:	203⅔ feet (62.1 m) waterline
	224 feet (68.3 m) overall
Beam:	43 feet (13.1 m)
Draft:	15 feet (4.6 m)
Propulsion:	diesel-electric (4 Caterpillar D-398B diesel generators with General Electric motors); 3,200 bhp; 2 shafts
Sonars:	removed

These ships were built for the Navy's Surveillance Towed Array Sensor System (SURTASS) program. With the massive cutbacks in that program, seven ships are being transferred to NOAA, with some not placed in service until after delays of several years as modifications have been made and operating funds identified.

The PREVAIL (T-AGOS 8) also was scheduled at one point for transfer to NOAA, but she was instead reclassified as a service craft and designated IX 537.

The WORTHY (T-AGOS 14) was transferred from the Military Sealift Command to NOAA on 30 September 1993; subsequently, she was laid up at Redwood City, California. She then was planned for operation by the U.S. Geological Survey, but instead was loaned to the U.S. Army in 1995 for use as a range instrumentation ship to support ballistic missile defense tests at Kwajalein Atoll (see Chapter 34).

Five ships are now in active NOAA service.

The above characteristics are as Navy surveillance ships, except for personnel data.

Class: The STALWART class originally consisted of 18 ships (T-AGOS 1–18).

The T-AGOS 3 was stricken from the Naval Vessel Register (NVR) on 30 June 1993 and transferred on 15 May 2001 to the Coast Guard, where she was briefly in service (designated WMEC 3). She was transferred to NOAA in November 2001. She has been fitted with a three-person, double-lock decompression chamber to support SCUBA diving operations.

The T-AGOS 7 was stricken from the NVR on 2 December 2002.

The T-AGOS 9 was stricken from the NVR on 3 March 2004. She is to be converted for NOAA use in FY 2007 and is scheduled to replace the DAVID STARR JORDAN in FY 2008.

The T-AGOS 13 was stricken from the NVR on 5 June 1992. In an "unmanned" status, she was employed for training NOAA officers in 1993–1994, then was laid up in the James River Reserve Fleet in Virginia until recalled for NOAA service. She was a replacement for the TOWNSEND CROMWELL.

The T-AGOS 15 was stricken from the NVR on 31 August 1993.

The T-AGOS 16 was stricken from the NVR in late 2004.

The T-AGOS 18 was stricken from the NVR on 20 May 1993. She was modified for fisheries research and now has 1,490 square feet (138.6 m²) of dedicated laboratory space, including a "wet lab" of 480 square feet (44.6 m²). She replaced the CHAPMAN.

Design: The T-AGOS hull is similar to that of the Navy's T-ATF 166 fleet tug design. A high degree of crew habitability is provided; as built, there were 19 single staterooms for the ships' civilian (MSC) crew and 3 single and 4 double staterooms for the ten Navy technicians; several additional berths were available.

Endurance is rated at 30 days in NOAA service.

Engineering: The four diesel generators drive two main propulsion motors. A bow-thruster powered by a 550-hp electric motor is fitted for station keeping. There are special features to reduce machinery noise during research operations.

Names: Ka'Imimoana is Hawaiian for "the ocean seeker"; Hi'Ialakai is Hawaiian for "embracing pathways to the sea" and has a second meaning of "guiding leaders of the seas."

GORDON GUNTER (ex-USNS RELENTLESS) in the Gulf of Mexico. (2000, NOAA/D. Drass)

KA'IMIMOANA (ex-USNS TITAN).
(NOAA)

SURVEY SHIPS: "PEIRCE" CLASS (S1-MT-59a)

The two ships of this class, which conducted hydrographic surveys of the 200-nm (237-km) exclusive economic zone for bathymetric maps and nautical charts, have been stricken. The PEIRCE (S 328), completed in 1963, was laid up in 1993 and transferred to New York City for use as a school ship; she was renamed ELIZABETH A. FISHER. The WHITING (S 329), also completed in 1963, was stricken on 2 May 2003.

See 17th Edition/page 614 for characteristics.

SURVEY SHIPS: "McARTHUR" CLASS (S1-MT-MA70a)

Both oceanographic research ships of this design, which operated primarily in the exclusive economic zone off the U.S. Pacific coast, have been stricken. The McARTHUR (S 330), completed in 1966, was stricken on 20 May 2003, and the DAVIDSON (S 331), completed in 1967, was stricken in 1997.

See 17th Edition/page 614 for characteristics.

OREGON II; the crow's nest subsequently was deleted from the forward mast. (NOAA)

1 RESEARCH SHIP: "OREGON II"

Number	Name	Launched	Comm.	Status
R 332	OREGON II	Feb 1967	17 Mar 1977	**AA**

Builders:	Ingalls Shipbuilding, Pascagoula, Miss.
Displacement:	952 tons full load
Length:	169¹¹⁄₂ feet (51.8 m) overall
Beam:	34½ feet (10.4 m)
Draft:	14½ feet (4.3 m)
Propulsion:	2 diesel engines (Fairbanks Morse); 1,600 bhp; 1 shaft
Speed:	12 knots
Range:	9,500 nm (17,600 km) at 12 knots
Personnel:	17 (3 officers + 14 mariners) + 14 scientists

The OREGON II is a far-ranging fisheries research ship, operating primarily off the U.S. Atlantic coast, in the Gulf of Mexico, and in the Caribbean area. She was delivered for service in August 1967, but was not formally commissioned until ten years later.

ALBATROSS IV. (NOAA)

1 RESEARCH SHIP: "ALBATROSS IV"

Number	Name	Launched	Comm.	Status
R 342	ALBATROSS IV	Apr 1962	May 1963	**AA**

Builders:	Southern Shipbuilding, Slidell, La.
Displacement:	1,089 tons full load
Length:	187 feet (57.0 m) overall
Beam:	32⅝ feet (10.0 m)
Draft:	16 feet (4.9 m)
Propulsion:	2 diesel engines (Caterpillar); 1,130 bhp; 1 Kort nozzle propeller
Speed:	12 knots
Range:	4,300 nm (7,965 km) at 12 knots
Personnel:	20 (4 officers + 16 mariners) + 14 scientists

The ALBATROSS IV is a fisheries research ship.

Engineering: The ship has a 125-hp bow thruster.

The ALBATROSS IV was one of four specialized torpedo trials craft built by the Navy to replace the older IX and YFRT craft previously employed in this role (see Chapter 25). Named AGATE PASS (YTT 12), the ship was laid up in reserve at the Bremerton Naval Shipyard on completion and was never placed in naval service; she was stricken from the NVR on 13 August 1999 and subsequently acquired by NOAA.

1 RESEARCH SHIP: FORMER TORPEDO TRIALS CRAFT

Number	Name	Launched	Completed	to NOAA	NOAA comm.	Status
R 352	NANCY FOSTER	6 Sep 1990	1 July 1991	31 Jan 2000	5 Oct 2004	**AA**

Builders:	McDermott Shipyard, Morgan City, La.	Draft:	10 1/2 feet (3.23 m)
Displacement:	1,000 tons light	Propulsion:	diesel-electric (1 Cummins VTA-28 diesel engine);
	1,200 tons full load		1,250 shp; 2 all-azimuth drives
Length:	176 1/2 feet (53.83 m) waterline	Speed:	11 knots
	186 1/2 feet (56.85 m) overall	Torpedoes:	removed
Beam:	40 feet (12.19 m)	Personnel:	

The FOSTER began operations in May 2003 as a coastal oceano-graphic research vessel. She was to have been formally commissioned by NOAA in September 2003, but the ceremony was canceled because of Hurricane Isabel.

She replaced the FERREL.

Classification: Originally planned as YFRT type, the ships was built as YTT. The classification YTT originally indicated torpedo testing barge.

Engineering: A 350-hp bow thruster is fitted. Electric drive on batteries permits quiet operation.

NANCY FOSTER (ex-USS AGATE PASS) at San Diego. (2003, W. Michael Young)

RESEARCH SHIP: "TOWNSEND CROMWELL"

The 652-ton TOWNSEND CROMWELL (R 443) was decommissioned on 10 October 2002. The ship was built in 1963 and had served in NOAA since 1975. She was turned over to American Samoa.

1 RESEARCH SHIP: "DAVID STARR JORDAN"

Number	Name	Launched	Comm.	Status
R 444	DAVID STARR JORDAN	19 Dec 1964	8 Jan 1966	**PA**

Builders:	Christy, Sturgeon Bay, Wisc.
Displacement:	993 tons full load
Length:	170 11/12 feet (52.1 m) overall
Beam:	36 3/4 feet (11.2 m)
Draft:	15 3/4 feet (4.8 m)
Propulsion:	2 diesel engines (White Superior); 1,086 bhp; 2 shafts
Speed:	11.5 knots
Range:	8,560 nm (15,850 km) at 11.5 knots
Personnel:	18 (4 officers + 14 mariners) + 15 scientists

A fisheries research ship, the DAVID STARR JORDAN operates off the U.S. Pacific coast.

Design: She is a modified stern-trawler. A bow observation chamber is fitted.

Engineering: A retractable 200-hp Schottel bow thruster is installed.

DAVID STARR JORDAN about to recover the NOAA McDonnell Douglas MD500D helicopter. (NOAA)

1 RESEARCH SHIP: "DELAWARE II"

Number	Name	Launched	Comm.	Status
R 445	DELAWARE II	Dec 1967	Oct 1968	**AA**

Builders:	South Portland Engineering, Maine
Displacement:	758 tons full load
Length:	154 5/6 feet (47.2 m)
Beam:	30 1/6 feet (9.2 m)
Draft:	14 3/4 feet (4.5 m)
Propulsion:	1 diesel engine (General Motors); 1,230 bhp; 1 shaft
Speed:	11.5 knots
Range:	6,600 nm (12,220 km) at 11.5 knots
Personnel:	16 (2 officers + 14 mariners) + 14 scientists

A fisheries research ship, the DELAWARE II operates off the Atlantic coast.

DELAWARE II. (NOAA)

RESEARCH SHIP: "CHAPMAN"

The Class IV fisheries research ship CHAPMAN (R 446), commissioned in 1980, was decommissioned on 2 June 1998 and subsequently transferred to the University of Puerto Rico.

See 16th Edition/page 544 for characteristics.

1 RESEARCH SHIP: "JOHN N. COBB"

Number	Name	Launched	Comm.	Status
R 552	JOHN N. COBB	Jan 1950	18 Feb 1950	**PA**

Builders:	Western Boatbuilding, Tacoma, Wash.
Displacement:	250 tons full load
Length:	92 5/6 feet (28.3 m) overall
Beam:	25 11/12 feet (7.9 m)
Draft:	10 5/6 feet (3.3 m)
Propulsion:	1 diesel engine (Fairbanks Morse); 325 bhp; 1 shaft
Speed:	9.3 knots
Range:	2,900 nm (5,370 km) at 9.3 knots
Personnel:	7 (2 officers + 5 mariners) + 4 scientists

The JOHN N. COBB is a fisheries research ship. She is the oldest active NOAA research vessel and the only wood-hulled ship in the NOAA fleet. The COBB conducts fishery and living marine resource research in southeastern Alaska and in U.S. Pacific coastal waters, supporting the research of the Auke Bay Laboratory of the National Marine Fisheries Service in Juneau, Alaska.

Design: The design is based on West Coast purse-seiners, modified for improved seakeeping. The COBB is capable of conducting bottom trawls to depths of more than 1,800 feet.

Endurance is rated at 13 days.

JOHN N. COBB in Alaskan waters. (1992, NOAA)

SURVEY SHIP: "FERREL" (S1-MT-MA83a)

The FERREL (S 492), employed in near-shore and estuarine-current surveys, was stricken on 21 November 2002. She was a modified offshore oil-rig supply boat completed in 1968; she employed data collection buoys in her work.

1 SURVEY SHIP: "RUDE" CLASS (S1-MT-MA71a)

Number	Name	Launched	Comm.	Status
S 590	RUDE	17 Aug 1966	29 Mar 1967	**AA**
S 591	HECK	1 Nov 1966	29 Mar 1967	str. 1995

Builders:	Jakobson Shipyard, Oyster Bay, N.Y.
Displacement:	214 tons full load
Length:	90 feet (27.4 m) overall
Beam:	22 feet (6.7 m)
Draft:	7 feet (2.1 m)
Propulsion:	2 diesel engines (Cummins); 800 bhp; 2 Kort-nozzle propellers
Speed:	11.5 knots
Range:	800 nm (1,480 km) at 10 knots
Personnel:	11 (4 officers + 7 mariners)

RUDE (NOAA)

A surveying ship, the RUDE previously operated in conjunction with her sister ship, the HECK, using wire drags to locate underwater navigational hazards. Under that construct, one commanding officer was assigned to the two ships; he normally rode one ship and the executive officer was aboard the other. The RUDE now operates independently, with a commanding officer.

She operates off the Atlantic coast.

The long-range NOAA plan calls for replacement of the RUDE by a Small Waterplane Area Twin-Hull (SWATH) ship, to become operational in FY 2008.

Engineering: The propellers on the ships are protected by shrouds, similar to Kort nozzles. Auxiliary propulsion provides 70 hp to each propeller for slow-speed dragging operations.

Operational: The RUDE used towed underwater sensors to locate the wreckage of the aircraft flown by John F. Kennedy Jr. when he crashed off Martha's Vineyard, Massachusetts, on 16 July 1999.[2]

RESEARCH CRAFT

NOAA laboratories operate some 20 small research craft that are 65 feet (19.8 m) or less in length.

AVIATION

NOAA operates ten fixed-wing aircraft and two helicopters. Its air operations are based at MacDill Air Force Base, Tampa, Florida.

The largest aircraft are two extensively modified WP-3D Orion

weather reconnaissance aircraft. The Hughes MD 500D often is deployed aboard the fisheries research ship DAVID STARR JORDAN.

Table 33-2 NOAA AIRCRAFT

Number	Type	Crew*	Engines	Notes
2	Lockheed WP-3D Orion	20	4 turboprop	
1	Gulfstream IV SP	8	2 turbojet	
1	Cessna Citation II	6	2 turbojet	
1	Gulfstream Turbo Commander	8	2 turboprop	
2	de Havilland DHC-6 Twin Otter	8	2 turboprop	
2	Rockwell Aero Commander	5	2 piston	
1	Lake Seawolf	4	1 piston	amphibious
1	Bell UH-1N (Bell 212)	15	2 turboshaft	helicopter
1	Hughes MD 500D	4	1 turboshaft	helicopter

* Total flight crew and scientists/technicians

WP-3D ORION

The two NOAA Orions participate in a variety of national and international meteorological, oceanographic, and environmental research programs. They were acquired from the Lockheed production line in the mid-1970s and extensively modified for NOAA service. Special features include a ventral C-band weather surveil-

---

2 The towed sensors consist of a side-scan sonar and multibeam bathymetric sonar, housed in a torpedo-shaped container referred to as a "fish." They provide an accurate acoustic image (sonogram) of the ocean floor extending up to 1,970 feet (600 m) on either side of the fish.

An NP-3D Orion; note the tail radome in place of the Magnetic Anomaly Detection (MAD) boom of Navy anti-submarine warfare variants. (NOAA)

lance radar, plus nose and tail radar installations, extensive instrumentation, and sonobuoy-type launch chutes for expendable instrument packages.

Up to 12 scientific personnel can be carried, in addition to a crew of seven or eight.

GULFSTREAM IV SP (SPECIAL PERFORMANCE)

The Gulfstream Aerospace IV SP aircraft, acquired in 1996, is configured to collect and process atmospheric soundings in support of the National Hurricane Center.

It has a crew of eight.

CITATION II (MODEL 550)

The NOAA Cessna Citation II has been modified for collecting coastal remote sensing imagery. These data are used for updating shoreline and shore features on NOAA's nautical charts.

The aircraft has a crew of two and carries up to four scientists.

TURBO COMMANDER (AC-690)

The Gulfstream Aerospace Turbo Commander carries out a variety of missions related to remote sensing. These surveys support coastal mapping, airport obstruction charting, photobathymetry, photogeodesy, and boundary determination.

The aircraft has a crew of three (including a photographer), and up to five scientists can be carried.

One of the two NOAA NP-3D Orion research aircraft; note the large radome fitted under the forward fuselage and the nose probe. (NOAA)

Gulfstream IV-SP (NOAA)

Cessna Citation II (NOAA)

TWIN OTTER (DHC-6)

The two de Havilland Twin Otters flown by NOAA are instrumented for low-level, slow-speed aerial surveys of marine mammals and coastal erosion and for various remote sensing missions, including atmospheric sampling.

The aircraft are flown by a crew of two, with up to six scientists on board.

AERO COMMANDER (AC-500S)

NOAA operates two Rockwell Aero Commander aircraft primarily as aerial survey platforms for visual verification of aeronautical charts and for high-resolution aerial photography. The aircraft also have been used in biological investigations.

They normally are flown by a crew of two, with three scientists on board.

SEAWOLF (LA-27)

The single NOAA Lake Seawolf is an amphibian employed for low-level surveys of near-shore areas.

The aircraft is flown by a pilot, and three scientists can be accommodated.

UH-1N HUEY (BELL 212)

The single Bell Huey-type helicopter operated by NOAA since 1986 is employed in a variety of scientific endeavors, among them aerial survey, nautical charting using laser hydrography, tracking polar bears for tagging, and filming. It also is used for moving base camps in the Arctic.

It normally is flown by one or two pilots, with a few scientific personnel on board, the number depending on the mission and installed equipment. Without equipment, seating for up to 13 personnel can be installed.

MD 500D

The Hughes MD 500D helicopter is the smallest NOAA aircraft but also one of the most versatile. It serves as a visual observation and photographic platform, often operating from the research ship DAVID STARR JORDAN, the only NOAA ship that can land a helicopter.

The MD 500D has a single pilot and can carry up to three scientists.

Gulfstream Turbo Commander (NOAA)

Bell UH-1N (Bell 212) using LIDAR sounding system off Cancun, Mexico. (NOAA)

Hughes MD500D operating from the DAVID STARR JORDAN during a study of marine mammals. (NOAA)

CHAPTER 34

Miscellaneous Ships and Craft

A U.S. Army BESSON-class landing ship pulls alongside an elevated causeway at Camp Patriot, Kuwait, during Operation Iraqi Freedom. These large Army LSVs are used for intratheater lift and do not have the long range of earlier LSTs and LSMs. (U.S. Navy/Joseph Krypel)

The U.S. Navy, Coast Guard, and National Oceanic and Atmospheric Administration are "maritime" services. Additional ships are operated by the U.S. Army and the agencies described in this chapter.

U.S. ARMY

The U.S. Army operates a large number of ships and small craft, although *not*—as often reported—more than the U.S. Navy. Army vessels are operated by three organizations: (1) Transportation Corps, (2) Kwajalein Range Services, and (3) Corps of Engineers.

The Transportation Corps provides waterborne intratheater logistics. For this mission, the Army has joined the Navy and Marine Corps in the evaluation of Australian-built High Speed Vessels

(HSVs). The Army leased the SPEARHEAD of this type, designated as a Theater Support Vessel (TSV 1); subsequently, the Navy-leased JOINT VENTURE (HSV X1) was transferred to Army control. The Army had participated in the earlier evaluation of the JOINT VENTURE. (Two HSVs are operated by the Navy; see Chapter 24.)

Kwajalein atoll in the Marshall Islands is used to test ballistic missile defense systems.[1] Under the aegis of the Army Space and Strategic Defense Command, the Army maintains several ships and small craft at Kwajalein to support the tests.

The Corps of Engineers is responsible for the construction and maintenance of channels (i.e., dredging) and infrastructure (locks

---

1 The Marshall Islands became independent in 1986, except for defense, which remains a U.S. responsibility..

and dams) of the nation's inland waterways. The Corps employs Army-owned dredges and small craft, as well as contractor-operated craft, in those roles.

Designations. The Army uses a ship and craft designation series derived in part from the Navy's designation scheme.

The Army designations are:

BC	barge, dry cargo (non-self-propelled)
BCDX	barge, deck enclosure
BD	floating crane
BDL	beach discharge lighter
BG	barge, liquid cargo (non-self-propelled)
BK	barge, dry cargo (non-self-propelled)
BPL	barge, pier, self-elevating
BR	barge, refrigerated (non-self-propelled)
FMS	floating marine repair shop (non-self-propelled)
FS	freight and supply vessel (over 100 ft/30.48 m)
FSR	freight and supply vessel, refrigerated
J	work boat (under 50 ft/15.24 m)
LARC	lighter, amphibious, resupply, cargo (amphibious)
LCM	landing craft, mechanized
LCU	landing craft, utility
LCV	landing craft, vehicle
LSV	landing ship, vehicle
LT	large tug (over 100 ft/30.48 m)
Q	work boat (over 50 ft/15.24 m)
ST	small tug (under 100 ft/30.48 m)
T	small freight and supply vessel (under 100 ft/30.48 m)
TSV	theater support vessel
Y	liquid cargo vessel

Historical: The U.S. Army claims to have operated ships and small craft since the crossing of the Delaware River by General George Washington's colonial troops for the attack on the Hessian garrison at Trenton on 25 December 1776.

The Army operated large numbers of ships and small craft during the Civil War and both World Wars. After World War II, on 1 October 1949, the Military Sea Transportation Service (MSTS) was established under the Navy to consolidate all military shipping. On 1 March 1950, the Water Transportation Division of the Army Transportation Corps (ATC) was assigned to MSTS and 71 large Army ships were transferred to MSTS and assigned Navy hull numbers. These ships included cargo ships, refrigerated cargo ships, aircraft cargo ships, transports, and one landing ship, the ex-Navy LST 694. (MSTS was renamed Military Sealift Command [MSC] in 1970.)

Subsequently, the Army has acquired specialized ships and small craft, as described below.

Names: Army ships and craft generally are named for campaigns and battles in which the Army participated, except that the LT 130-series large tugs are named for signers of the U.S. Constitution who had military affiliations. Several battle names are carried by both Navy ships and Army craft.

Personnel: Army Transportation Corps ships and craft are manned by Army personnel; ships and craft at Kwajalein are manned by civilian mariners, as are the dredges of the Corps of Engineers.

TRANSPORTATION CORPS

The Army Transportation Corps currently has three types of tactical organizations for operating small craft.

Figure 34-1. Transportation Floating Craft Company

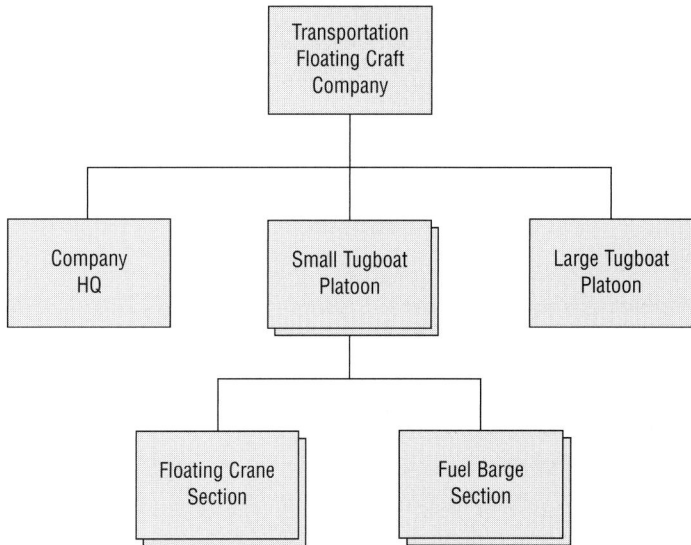

Figure 34-2. Transportation Heavy Watercraft Company

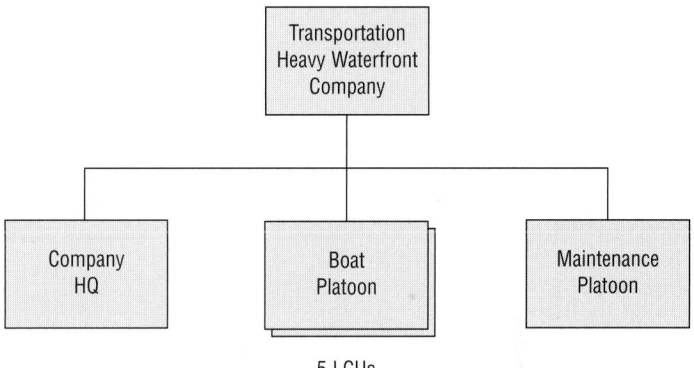

5 LCUs

Figure 34-3. Transportation Medium Boat Company

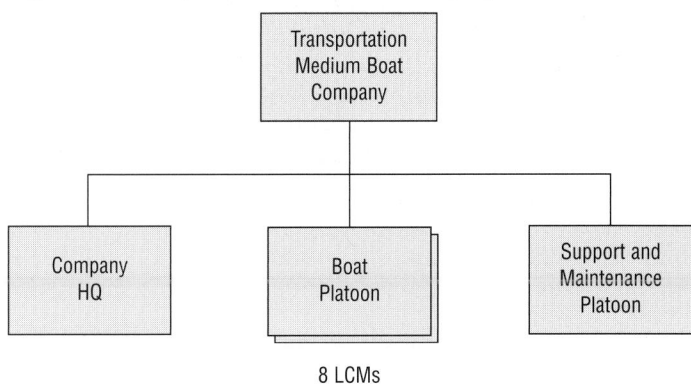

8 LCMs

(12) THEATER SUPPORT VESSELS: NEW CONSTRUCTION

The Army plans to construct up to 12 HSV-type ships. Whereas the four HSVs now in U.S. Army and Navy service on long-term lease were built in Australia, the new ships would be built in the United States. The design is being developed on the basis of the current HSV trials and operations.

These vessels are to be capable of carrying more than 350 troops, their vehicles and equipment. Speed will be 40-plus knots, with a range of 4,725 nm (7,925 km).

1 HIGH SPEED VESSEL: INCAT TYPE

Number	Name	Launched	Completed	In service
IX 532	JOINT VENTURE (ex-INCAT 050, TOP CAT, DEVIL CAT)	7 Nov 1998	21 Nov 1998	25 July 2001

Builders:	Incat, Hobart, Tasmania (Australia)
Displacement:	940 tons light
	1,668 tons full load
Length:	282 feet (86.0 m) hull
	319 feet (97.22 m) overall
Beam:	81⅓ feet (26.0 m)
Draft:	11¼ feet (3.43 m)
Propulsion:	4 diesel engines (Caterpillar 3618); 30,000 bhp; 4 waterjets
Speed:	35 knots sustained
	37.5 knots maximum loaded
	50 knots maximum light
Range:	4,000 nm (7,410 km) at 20 knots
	1,100 nm (1,850 km) at 35 knots
Personnel:	30 (5 officers + 25 enlisted)
Troops:	approx. 600
Helicopters:	landing area
Guns:	several .50-cal machine guns
Radars:	navigation

The JOINT VENTURE is being employed by the U.S. armed forces in a series of evaluations, primarily as a fast-deploying transport for troops and vehicles. Although she has a Navy IX-series hull number, she has "HSV X1," for High Speed Vessel– Experimental 1." painted on her hull.

Classification: The JOINT VENTURE was instated on the Naval Vessel Register (NVR) as the IX 532 on 23 July 2001. This is the only HSV/TSV with a Navy hull number.

Design: This is a wave-piercing catamaran design. She is similar to the Navy's SWIFT (HSV-2) and WESTPAC EXPRESS (HSV 4676).

The troops are provided with commercial, aircraft-style seating. In U.S. service, the ship is fitted with a helicopter platform and has a ramp aft for launching and recovering Rigid Hull Inflatable Boats (RHIBs).

Operational: During a transatlantic trip, the JOINT VENTURE made the crossing in 5 days, 17 hours, at an average speed of 27 knots.

1 THEATER SUPPORT VESSEL: INCAT TYPE

Number	Name	Launched	Completed	In service
TSV 1	SPEARHEAD	2002	19 Nov 2002	19 Nov 2002

Builders:	Incat, Hobart, Tasmania (Australia)
Displacement:	1,875 tons full load
Length:	315 feet (96.0 m) overall
Beam:	88½ feet (27.0 m)
Draft:	12 feet (3.66 m)
Propulsion:	4 diesel engines; 30,000 bhp; 4 waterjets
Speed:	40+ knots
Range:	
Manning:	31
Troops:	approx. 600
Helicopters:	landing area
Guns:	several .50-cal machine guns
Radars:	navigation

The SPEARHEAD was leased from INCAT by the Army for evaluation in the theater logistics role.

She is operated by the 469th Transportation Detachment at Fort Eustis, Virginia.

The stern of the JOINT VENTURE with a Rigid Hull Inflatable Boat (RHIB) being recovered at the ship's open stern; the vehicle ramp is stowed on the starboard quarter. (U.S. Navy/Michael J. Pusnik Jr.)

The JOINT VENTURE speeding off the coast of California. She is one of two high-speed vessels currently operated by the U.S. Army. Another ship of this basic design is the SWIFT (HSV 2), operated by the Navy. The Military Sealift Command operates the WESTPAC EXPRESS (HSV 4676) for the Marine Corps. (U.S. Navy/Frederick McCahan)

The Army's SPEARHEAD under way at slow speed in the Middle East. The Army plans to procure up to 12 similar ships, to be constructed in a U.S. shipyard. (U.S. Navy/Brien Aho)

SPEARHEAD (U.S. Navy/Brien Aho)

Class: The SPEARHEAD is similar to the Navy-leased JOINT VENTURE (see above) and SWIFT.

Design: The troops are provided with commercial, aircraft-style seating. There is a stern ramp for loading/unloading up to 800 tons of cargo, including M1 Abrams tanks (i.e., 60-plus tons).

Propulsion: The ship's self-deployment range (empty) is 4,730 nm (8,765 km).

7 + 2 VEHICLE LANDING SHIPS: "BESSON" CLASS

Number	Name	Launched	In service
LSV 1	GEN FRANK S. BESSON JR.	30 June 1987	20 Jan 1988
LSV 2	CW3 HAROLD C. CLINGER[2]	16 Sep 1987	20 Apr 1988
LSV 3	GEN BREHON B. SOMERVELL	18 Nov 1987	26 July 1988
LSV 4	LT GEN WILLIAM B. BUNKER	11 Jan 1988	1 Sep 1988
LSV 5	MAJ GEN CHARLES P. GROSS	11 July 1990	30 Apr 1991
LSV 6	SP4 JAMES A. LOUX[3]	7 Apr 1994	5 July 1995
LSV 7	SSGT ROBERT T. KURODA	21 May 2003	Feb 2004
LSV 8	MGEN ROBERT SMAILS		building
LSV 9	......		building

Builders:	Halter-Moss Point Marine, Escatawpa, Miss.
Displacement:	1,612 tons light
	4,199 tons full load
Tonnage:	1,800 Deadweight Tons (DWT)
Length:	256 feet (78.03 m) waterline
	272⅔ feet (83.14 m) overall
Beam:	60 feet (18.28 m)
Draft:	12 feet (3.66 m)
Propulsion:	2 diesel engines (General Motors EMD 16-645-E2);
	3,900 bhp; 2 shafts
Speed:	12 knots
Range:	5,500 nm (10,185 km) at 11 knots
Manning:	29 (6 officers + 23 enlisted)
Radars:	2 SPS-64(V) navigation

These are small LST-type ships based on the Australian roll-on/roll-off ship FRANCES BAY. The U.S. ships transport vehicles and standard containers (48 TEU) or 1,815 tons of vehicles or other cargo.[4]

The LSV 8 and LSV 9 are expected to be completed in 2005.

Design: These ships have an LST-like design, with a superstructure aft; there is a tunnel under the superstructure to permit vehicles to drive through from the stern ramp into the open cargo well. A bow ramp is fitted. They are built to commercial shipbuilding standards.

Endurance is 38 days.

Names: General Besson was named first Army Chief of Transportation in March 1958. He was promoted to full (four-star) general in 1964 and retired in 1970 after more than 37 years of commissioned service, 25 of them as a general officer.

Operational: The LSV 3 is assigned to the Army Reserve at Tacoma, Washington; the LSV 7 is assigned to the Army Reserve at Pearl Harbor, Hawaii.

HEAVY LIFT SHIP: C1-MT-123a TYPE

The JAMES McHENRY, a unique heavy lift ship employed by the Army primarily as a training ship for cargo handlers at Fort Story, Virginia, has been laid up since September 1993 in reserve with the James River (Virginia) National Defense Reserve Fleet. The ship was placed in service in 1978.

See 16th Edition/page 547 for characteristics.

---

2 CW = Chief Warrant.

3 SP4 = Specialist 4th Class.

4 TEU = Twenty-foot (6.1-m) Equivalent Unit.

BEACH DISCHARGE LIGHTER

The large beach discharge lighter LT COL JOHN D. PAGE was taken out of service in 1989 and discarded in March 1992. The ship was configured for unloading vehicles from large cargo ships onto landing craft or causeways.

CW3 HAROLD C. CLINGER at Pearl Harbor. (W. Michael Young)

A BESSON-class LSV with an empty tank deck. These are the largest ships in U.S. military service with a bow-ramp configuration. (U.S. Navy)

35 UTILITY LANDING CRAFT: LCU 2000 TYPE

Number	Name	Launched	In service
LCU 2001	RUNNYMEDE	14 Aug 1987	21 Feb 1990
LCU 2002	KENESAW MOUNTAIN	6 Oct 1987	28 Feb 1990
LCU 2003	MACON	1 Feb 1988	23 Mar 1990
LCU 2004	ALDIE	Apr 1989	23 Feb 1990
LCU 2005	BRANDY STATION	May 1989	7 Mar 1990
LCU 2006	BRISTOE STATION	31 July 1989	30 Mar 1990
LCU 2007	BROAD RUN	28 Aug 1989	4 May 1990
LCU 2008	BUENA VISTA	10 Sep 1989	18 Apr 1990
LCU 2009	CALABOZA	9 Feb 1990	13 July 1990
LCU 2010	CEDAR RUN	12 Mar 1990	17 Aug 1990
LCU 2011	CHICKAHOMINY	16 Apr 1990	21 Sep 1990
LCU 2012	CHICKAWAY BAYOU	26 May 1990	26 Oct 1990
LCU 2013	CHURUBUSCO	25 June 1990	Oct 1990
LCU 2014	COAMO	28 July 1990	4 Jan 1991
LCU 2015	CONTRERAS	9 Mar 1990	8 Feb 1991
LCU 2016	CORNITH	Oct 1990	15 Mar 1991
LCU 2017	EL CANEY	Nov 1990	19 Apr 1991
LCU 2018	FIVE FORKS	17 Dec 1990	24 May 1991
LCU 2019	FORT DONELSON	Jan 1991	28 June 1991
LCU 2020	FORT MCHENRY	Feb 1991	2 Aug 1991
LCU 2021	GREAT BRIDGE	1 Apr 1991	6 Sep 1991
LCU 2022	HARPERS FERRY	May 1991	11 Oct 1991
LCU 2023	HOBKIRK	June 1991	15 Nov 1991
LCU 2024	HORMIGUEROS	15 July 1991	20 Dec 1991
LCU 2025	MALVERN HILL	Aug 1991	24 Jan 1992
LCU 2026	MATAMOROS	Sep 1991	28 Feb 1992
LCU 2027	MECHANICSVILLE	Oct 1991	3 Apr 1992
LCU 2028	MISSIONARY RIDGE	Nov 1991	8 May 1992
LCU 2029	MOLINO DEL REY	7 Nov 1991	11 May 1992
LCU 2030	MONTERREY	5 Dec 1991	15 May 1992
LCU 2031	NEW ORLEANS	10 Jan 1992	1 June 1992
LCU 2032	PALO ALTO	6 Feb 1992	9 July 1992
LCU 2033	PAULUS HOOK	5 Mar 1992	18 Sep 1992
LCU 2034	PERRYVILLE	2 Apr 1992	4 Aug 1992
LCU 2035	PORT HUDSON	30 Apr 1992	1 Sep 1992

Builders:	LCU 2001-2003: Lockheed Shipbuilding, Savannah, Ga.
	LCU 2004-2035: Trinity-Moss Point Marine, Escatawpa, Miss.
Displacement:	672 tons light
	1,102 tons full load
Tonnage:	596 Gross Registered Tons (GRT)
Length:	156 feet (47.55 m) waterline
	174 feet (53.03 m) overall
Beam:	42 feet (12.8 m)
Draft:	8½ (2.6 m)
Propulsion:	2 diesel engines (Cummins KTA-50M); 2,500 bhp;
	2 Kort nozzle propellers
Speed:	11.5 knots
Range:	4,500 nm (8,333 km) at 11.5 knots empty
Manning:	12 or 13 (2 officers + 10 or 11 enlisted)
Radars:	1 SPS-64(V)2 navigation

These are large landing craft with a deckhouse aft; they are too large to be carried by Navy amphibious ships with docking wells (as can be the smaller LCU designs). They have replaced the LCU 1466-class landing craft.

LCU 2000-class landing craft. (U.S. Army)

These craft have a bow ramp for unloading onto the beach (beaching draft forward is 4 feet (1.2 m).

The first three units were completed at Trinity Marine after the demise of the Lockheed shipbuilding yard.

Class: LCU 2001–2007 were ordered in 1986; LCU 2008–2017 in 1987; LCU 2018–2023 in 1988; and LCU 2024–2035 in 1989. Two additional craft were authorized but not ordered; they were to have been named SACKETT'S HARBOR (LCU 2036) and SAYLER'S CREEK (LCU 2037).

Design: These LCUs were built to commercial shipbuilding standards specifically for the U.S. Army. All other U.S. LCU/LSU types were built to Navy designs.

Engineering: These craft have 300-shp bow thrusters.

Names: The LCU 2009 originally was named CALABOZA.

Operational: The GREAT BRIDGE is assigned to Kwajalein Range Services.

13 UTILITY LANDING CRAFT: "LCU 1610" CLASS

Number	Name	Number	Name
LCU 1667	MANASSAS	LCU 1674	ST. MICHIEL
LCU 1668	BELLEAU-WOOD	LCU 1675	COMMANDO
LCU 1669	MARSEILLES	LCU 1676	BIRMINGHAM
LCU 1670	SAN ISIDORO	LCU 1677	BRANDYWINE
LCU 1671	CATAWBA FORD	LCU 1678	NAHA
LCU 1672	BUSH MASTER	LCU 1679	CHATEAU-THIERRY
LCU 1673	DOUBLE EAGLE		

Builders:	General Ship & Engine Works, East Boston, Mass.
Displacement:	190 tons light
	390 tons full load
Tonnage:	396 GRT
Length:	134¾ feet (41.1 m) overall
Beam:	29¾ feet (9.1 m)
Draft:	6⅛½ feet (2.1 m)
Propulsion:	4 diesel engines (General Motors Detroit 6-71); 1,200 bhp;
	2 Kort-nozzle propellers
Speed:	11 knots
Range:	1,200 nm (2,222 km) at 11 knots empty
	1,200 nm (2,222 km) at 8 knots loaded
Personnel:	6 (enlisted)
Troops:	8
Radars:	1 LN-66 or SPS-53 navigation

These are Navy-designed LCUs completed in 1976–1978.

The COMMANDO has been modified to serve as a diver support ship; she is assigned to the Army's 558th Transportation Company at Fort Eustis, Virginia.

Class: This class originally consisted of hull numbers LCU 1610–1624 and 1627–1681; many still serve in the Navy (see Chapter 20).

Design: These craft have vehicle unloading ramps forward and aft.

Names: The Army spells BELLEAU-WOOD with a hyphen; the Navy's LHA 3 of the same name does not have a hyphen.

Operational: The LCU 1667 is assigned to the Kwajalein Range Services.

The SAN ISIDORO showing the starboard-side bridge structure of this design, which is used by the Army, as well as by the U.S. Navy and several foreign nations. (Leo Van Ginderen)

1 UTILITY LANDING CRAFT: "LCU 1466" CLASS

Number	Name	Completed
LCU 1509	Antietam	Apr 1954

Builders:	Avondale, New Orleans
Displacement:	180 tons light
	347 tons full load
Length:	119 feet (39.0 m) overall
Beam:	34 feet (10.4 m)
Draft:	6 feet (1.8 m)
Propulsion:	3 geared diesel engines (Gray Marine 64 YTL); 675 bhp;
	3 shafts
Speed:	8 knots
Range:	700 nm (1,300 km) at 7 knots with payload
Personnel:	6 (enlisted)
Troops:	8
Guns:	removed
Radars:	navigation

All but one of the 42 landing craft of this class built for the U.S. Army have been discarded. These were the survivors of a large class of Navy-designed LCUs.

Class: This class covered hull numbers LCU 1466–1609, with 14 units constructed in Japan. Numerous units were transferred to other nations; others became Navy service craft (YFU).

Three Army craft of this class have been converted to floating cranes: DELAWARE (LCU 1514) converted to BD 6804, CASABLANCA (LCU 1466) converted to BD 6805, and BULL RUN (LCU 1579) converted to BD 6806.

94 MECHANIZED LANDING CRAFT: LCM(8) MOD 1 TYPE

Weight:	varies 34–36.5 tons light
	111–121 tons full load
Length:	73½ feet (22.4 m) overall
Beam:	21 feet (6.4 m)
Draft:	4½ feet (1.4 m) aft
Propulsion:	2 diesel engines (General Motors Detroit 6-71); 600 bhp;
	2 shafts (see notes)
Speed:	12 knots empty
	9.2 knots loaded
Range:	150 nm (278 km) at 12 knots empty
	150 nm (278 km) at 9.2 knots loaded
Personnel:	2–4 (enlisted)

These are standard landing craft intended to carry vehicles and cargo. Capacity is about 60 tons of cargo. No accommodations are provided, although for short trips they can be fitted with a passenger ferry module to carry up to 170 troops. Some, with minimal modifications, are employed as pish-tugs.

Completed 1954–1972, these craft are deployed at Army bases around the world, with four currently at Kwajalein; some are in reserve. The LCM 8614 at Kwajalein is fitted with a ferry module.

LANDING AIR CUSHION VEHICLE CRAFT

The Army's LAMP-H enlarged, advanced prototype vehicle capable of carrying 89 tons of cargo was canceled on 18 October 1991, prior to completion. The craft had been ordered in 1990.

Subsequently, the 26 LACV in Army service were offered for sale in 1994.

LCM(8)-type landing craft. (Leo Van Ginderen)

The Army's air cushion landing craft were based at Fort Story, Virginia, and were intended for the ship-to-shore movement of troops and equipment. The Army used the term Logistics-over-the-Shore (LOTS) for this evolution.

See 15th Edition/page 601 for characteristics.

22 LARC LX TYPE AMPHIBIOUS VEHICLES

Weight:	88 tons empty
	190 tons loaded
Length:	62½ feet (19.07 m) overall
Beam:	26½ feet (8.1 m)
Propulsion:	4 diesel engines; 6,600 bhp; 2 propellers
Speed:	6.5 knots water
	15 mph land
Range:	75 nm (140 km) water at 6 knots
Personnel:	8 (enlisted)
Troops:	125

These four-wheel/propeller-driven vehicles are the successors to the DUKW "duck" amphibious trucks of World War II fame. They were introduced into amphibious landings by the U.S. Army in Operation Huskey, the 1943 Allied landings on Sicily.

The vehicles retained by the Army are designated LX-06, 18, 16–18, 20, 27, 37, 38, 40, 41, 43, 46–50, and 52–57; all are based in California.

These LARCs have a 60-ton normal load; 100 tons maximum. They have limited mobility.

All other amphibious wheeled vehicles have been discarded.

LARC LX 16 carrying a fuel truck. (U.S. Army)

6 LARGE HARBOR TUGBOATS: LT 130 CLASS

Number	Name	Launched	In service
LT 801	MAJ GEN NATHANAEL GREEN	4 July 1989	6 Mar 1994
LT 802	MAJ GEN HENRY KNOX	Oct 1989	7 May 1994
LT 803	MAJ GEN ANTHONY WAYNE	2 Aug 1990	7 May 1994
LT 804	BRIG GEN ZEBUON PIKE		30 Sep 1994
LT 805	MAJ GEN WINFIELD SCOTT		30 Sep 1994
LT 806	COL SETH WARNER	16 Dec 1993	15 Nov 1994

Builders:	Trinity/Halter Marine, Moss Point, Miss.
Displacement:	924 tons full load
Length:	128 feet (39.01 m) overall
Beam:	36 feet (10.97 m)
Draft:	15½ feet (4.73 m)
Propulsion:	2 diesel engines (General Motors EMD 12-645 FM8);
	5,100 bhp; 2 shafts
Speed:	12 knots
Range:	5,000 nm (9,260 km) at 12 knots
Manning:	
Radars:	navigation

This series of large tugs has been delayed, and several units have been canceled (see below).

Builders: Contracts for these tugs were awarded by the Navy beginning in 1988 to the Robert E. Derecktor yard at Middletown,

LT 130-class large tug (U.S. Army)

LT 100-class large harbor tug (U.S. Army)

Rhode Island, on behalf of the Army. The lead unit was "conditionally" delivered to the Army on 30 August 1991, with the yard responsible for correcting certain deficiencies. Subsequently, on 3 January 1992, the Derecktor yard filed for Chapter 11 bankruptcy protection. The contract then was transferred to the Trinity/Marine yard, which completed all six units.

Class: The Army originally envisioned a class of 13 tugs of this design. Two additional ships were named, the SGT MAJ JOHN CHAMPE (LT 807) and the MAJ GEN JACOB BROWN (LT 808).

17 LARGE HARBOR TUGBOATS: LT 100 CLASS

Number	Name	Number	Name
LT 1937	SGT WILLIAM W. SEAY	LT 1977	ATTLEBORO
LT 1953	SALERNO	LT 2076	NEW GUINEA
LT 1956	FREDERICKSBURG	LT 2081	SAN SAPOR
LT 1960	LUNDY'S LANE	LT 2085	ANZIO
LT 1970	OKINAWA	LT 2088	PETERSBURG
LT 1971	NORMANDY	LT 2090	SP4 LARRY G. DAHL
LT 1972	GETTYSBURG	LT 2092	NORTH AFRICA
LT 1973	SHILOH	LT 2096	VALLEY FORGE
LT 1974	CHAMPAGNE-MARNE		

Builders:	
Displacement:	295 tons light
	390 tons full load
Length:	107 feet (32.61 m) overall
Beam:	26½ feet (8.08 m)
Draft:	12⅛ feet (3.71 m)
Propulsion:	1 diesel engine (Fairbanks Morse); 1,200 bhp; 1 shaft
Speed:	12.75 knots
Range:	3,325 nm (6,160 km) at 12 knots
Manning:	16 (enlisted)

Sixty-five tugs of this design were built in the 1950s (LT 1936–1977, 2202, and 2075–2096). The survivors will be discarded during the next few years.

Engineering: Seven units (indicated by asterisks) were re-engined at Hythe (Kent), England, from 1995 to 1998, being fitted with a single General Electric EMD 12V-645-E7 diesel engine (2,350 bhp); those tugs have enhanced towing capability.

12 + 4 SMALL TUGBOATS: ST 900 CLASS

Number	Name	Launched	Completed
ST 901	DORCHESTER HEIGHTS	Apr 1998	Sep 1998
ST 902	PELHAM POINT	May 1998	Dec 1999
ST 903	FORT STANWIX	Aug 1998	Dec 1999
ST 904	GREEN SPRINGS	Oct 1998	Dec 1999
ST 905	SCHOLARIE	Jan 1999	Mar 2000
ST 906	SAG HARBOR	Apr 1999	Mar 2000
ST 907	Appomattox	Nov 1999	Mar 2000
ST 908	SACKETS HARBOR	Jan 2000	2000
ST 909	BUNKER HILL	2000	2000
ST 910	SANTIAGO		Aug 2001
ST 911	ENDURING FREEDOM		Dec 2001
ST 912	FORT MOULTRIE		2002
ST 912–915			building

Builders:	Orange Shipbuilding, Texas
Displacement:	110 tons light
Length:	59⅔ feet (18.19 m) overall
Beam:	22⅔ feet (6.90 m)
Draft:	6⅔ feet (2.03 m)
Propulsion:	2 diesel engines (Cummins KTA 19-M3); 1,280 bhp; 2 shafts (with Kaplan swiveling propellers)
Speed:	8 knots (see *Engineering* notes)
Range:	
Personnel:	5 or 6 (enlisted)

The Army's small tug FORT STANWIX, showing the compact design of these highly maneuverable craft. They are designed specifically to be carried aboard larger ships to forward areas. (Orange Shipbuilding)

These are small pusher tugs, carried aboard Lighter Aboard Ship (LASH) vessels for forward-area operations and for use on rivers and inland waterways.

Three additional units are under construction (funds were released in 2000), and three more are planned pending the availability of funds.

Design: Reinforced steel is provided in watertight bulkheads to enhance survivability if hit by small-arms fire. A stowage locker for M16 rifles is provided and, when forward deployed, the crews will be armed.

Engineering: Designed speed was eight knots; the DORCHESTER HEIGHTS reached 10.5 knots on trials.

Names: All but the LT 908 carry the names of discarded Army tugs.

11 SMALL TUGBOATS: ST 65 CLASS

Number	Name	Number	Name
ST 1988	BEMIS HEIGHTS	ST 2124	QUAKER HILL
ST 1990	MOHAWK VALLEY	ST 2126	STONY POINT
ST 1993	COWPENS	ST 2130	FORT MIFFLIN
ST 2104	MONMOUTH	ST 2199	VALCOUR ISLAND
ST 2118	GUILFORD COURT HOUSE	ST 2201	FALMOUTH
ST 2123	NINETY-SIX		

Builders:	
Displacement:	100 tons light
	122 tons full load
Length:	69¹¹⁄₁₂ feet (21.31 m) overall
Beam:	19½ feet (5.94 m)
Draft:	8¼ feet (2.5 m)
Propulsion:	1 diesel engine; 600 bhp; 1 shaft
Speed:	12 knots
Range:	3,500 nm (6,480 km) at 12 knots
Personnel:	6 (enlisted)

These are the survivors of a large class of Army tugs built in the 1950s. Some units stricken in the early 1990s were in storage at Hythe, England.

The MOHAWK VALLEY *high and dry for maintenance. (Leo Van Ginderen)*

2 SMALL TUGBOATS

Number	Number
ST 2154	ST 3000

Builders:	National Steel, San Diego, Calif.
Displacement:	25.2 tons light
	29 tons full load
Length:	45¼ feet (13.77 m) overall
Beam:	12⅝ feet (3.91 m)
Draft:	6 feet (1.83 m)
Propulsion:	1 diesel engine; 170 bhp; 1 shaft
Speed:	10 knots
Range:	700 nm (1,300 km) at 10 knots
Personnel:	4 (enlisted)

These are small, unnamed tugs built in the 1950s.

SMALL AND NON-SELF PROPELLED CRAFT

The Army Transportation Corps operates a large number of small craft, floating cranes, and barges. The largest of the floating cranes are listed below.

4 FLOATING CRANES: "KEYSTONE STATE" CLASS

Number	Name	Launched	Delivered
BD 6801	KEYSTONE STATE	June 1997	May 1998
BD 6802	SALTILLO	June 1998	Apr 1999
BD 6803	SPRINGFIELD	Jan 1999	Mar 2000

Builders:	Bollinger Shipyards, Lockport, La.
Displacement:	2,000 tons full load
Length:	200 feet (60.98 m) overall
Beam:	80 feet (24.39 m)
Draft:	14¼ feet (4.34 m)
Propulsion:	non-self-propelled (see *Design* notes)
Personnel:	15 (2 officers + 13 enlisted)

These are massive derricks intended to lift heavy cargo from ships in ports that do not have heavy lift facilities. Their secondary role is salvage and harbor and channel clearance in forward areas.

Design: These craft have three cranes with lift capacities of 115 tons, 25 tons, and 5 tons.

There are accommodations for a crew of two warrant officers and 13 enlisted men; the craft have berthing, galley, mess hall, medical, and laundry facilities, plus communications equipment.

Power is supplied by a 1,200-bhp diesel engine.

10 FLOATING CRANES

Number	Name	Number	Name
BD 6070	QUI NHON	BD 6659	WILDERNESS
BD 6072	ALGIERS	BD 6660	PRAIRIE FIRE
BD 6073	PINE RIDGE	BD 6661	DIAMOND HEAD
BD 6074	NAPLES	BD 6700	BIG SWITCH
BD 6658	MINDANAO	BD 6701	BIG BETHEL

Builders:	
Displacement:	1,630 tons full load
Length:	200 feet (42.67 m) overall
Beam:	80 feet (21.34 m)
Draft:	14¼ feet (1.91 m)
Propulsion:	non-self-propelled
Personnel:	

These floating cranes are being retired. The DB 6073 is in storage at Hythe, England.

Design: Lift capacity is up to 89 tons.

KEYSTONE STATE-*class floating crane under tow. (U.S. Army)*

KEYSTONE STATE-class floating crane under tow. (U.S. Army)

The largest oceangoing ship in the Army's fleet other than the BESSON-class landing ships is the WORTHY, a former Navy ocean surveillance ship. She now is configured as an instrumentation ship for the Army's Kwajalein Missile Range. (U.S. Army)

KWAJALEIN RANGE SERVICES

A total of 14 self-propelled ships and small craft are assigned to Kwajalein. In addition to the ships and craft listed below, the following craft from the above classes are assigned to Kwajalein Range Service:

LCUs 1667, 2021
LCMs 8601, 8605, 8609, 8614, 8615

1 RANGE SUPPORT SHIP: FORMER OCEAN SURVEILLANCE SHIP

Number	Name	FY	Launched	USN in service	USA in service
(ex-T-AGOS 14)	WORTHY	85	6 Feb 1988	7 Apr 1989	1995

Builders:	Trinity/Halter Marine, New Orleans
Displacement:	1,600 tons light
	2,285 tons full load
Tonnage:	1,584 GRT
	786 Deadweight Tons (DWT)
Length:	203⅔ feet (62.1 m) waterline
	224 feet (68.3 m) overall
Beam:	43 feet (13.1 m)
Draft:	15 feet (4.6 m)
Propulsion:	diesel-electric (4 Caterpillar D-398B diesel generators with General Electric motors); 3,200 bhp; 2 shafts
Speed:	11 knots
Range:	3,000 nm (5,556 km) at 11 knots
Personnel:	15 + 13 technicians
Guns:	none
Sonars:	removed

This is a modified surveillance ship of the STALWART (T-AGOS 1) class, built for the Navy's Surveillance Towed Array Sensor System (SURTASS) program. With the huge cutbacks in that program, several ships have been transferred to other government agencies.

The WORTHY was stricken from the NVR on 20 May 1993 and transferred to the National Oceanic and Atmospheric Administration on 30 September 1993; subsequently, she was laid up at Redwood City, California. She was planned for operation by the U.S. Geological Survey, but instead was loaned to the U.S. Army for use as a range instrumentation ship to support ballistic missile defense tests at Kwajalein Atoll.

RANGE SUPPORT SUBMERSIBLE

The two-man submersible PC-14C-2, previously operated by the Kwajalein Range Service, was discarded in 2001. The craft—painted yellow—provided deep-water search and surveillance during recovery operations on the missile range. It was especially useful in supporting the Army's "clean lagoon" policy, under which all debris from reentry vehicles is removed from the lagoon floor.

This is one of a long series of Perry Cubmarines (PC), built by the successor to the firm by that name established in 1962. The firm was sold to Martin Marietta, which, in turn, became part of Lockheed Martin. This is believed to be the only PC-series submersible used by the U.S. government. See 17th Edition/page 619.

2 LARGE HARBOR TUGBOATS: LT 100 CLASS

Number	Name	Number	Name
LT 101	GULF CONDOR	LT 102	MYSTIC

Builders:	Quality Shipyard, Houma, La.
Displacement:	
Length:	120 1½ feet (36.86 m) overall
Beam:	34 feet (10.37 m)
Draft:	14 feet (4.27 m)
Propulsion:	2 diesel engines (EMD 12-645-E6); 4,200 bhp; 2 shafts
Speed:	12 knots
Range:	8,800 nm (16,300 km)
Personnel:	7

These large tugs are used primarily to dock and undock large ships and to provide towing on the Kwajalein range. Both were completed in 1981.

2 PASSENGER FERRIES

Number	Name	Number	Name
FB 816	JERA	FB 817	JELANG K

Builders:	Nichols Brothers, Freeland, Wash.
Displacement:	
Length:	75½ feet (22.87 m) overall
Beam:	28½ feet (8.7 m)
Draft:	5½ feet (1.68 m)
Propulsion:	2 diesel engines (DDEC 16V-92); 1,980 bhp; 2 shafts
Speed:	28 knots light
	22 knots loaded
Range:	220 nm (465 km)
Personnel:	4 with up to 120 passengers
	5 with up to 200 passengers
Passengers:	200 short-duration trips
	175 long-duration trips

These high-speed passenger ferries operate between atoll harbors. Both were completed in 1988.

They are constructed of aluminum.

CORPS OF ENGINEERS

The Army Corps of Engineers operates numbers small, inland craft, as well as several large, non-self-propelled dredges.

13 DREDGES

Name	Builder	Gross Tonnage	Completed
CURRITUCK			
ESSAYONS	Bath Iron Works	12,000 tons	1982
FRY			
HURLEY	Halter Marine		1983
JADWIN			
MARKHAM	Avondale	5,400 tons	1960
MCFARLAND	Bethlehem	6,000 tons	1966
MERRITT			
POTTER			
SCHWEIZER			
THOMPSON			
WHEELER	Avondale	12,000 tons	1982
YAQUINA	Norshipco	1,960 tons	1981

Some of these dredges are laid up.

ESSAYONS at San Diego. (W. Michael Young)

AIR FORCE

The Air Force previously operated a large number of small craft, all managed by the San Antonio Air Logistics Center at Kelly Air Force Base in Texas. Most of these were missile and drone recovery boats, also used for rescue, up to 117⅓ feet (35.78 m) in length. They have been discarded or transferred to other agencies, with few small craft remaining in Air Force service.

See 16th Edition/pages 552–53 for data on these craft.

ENVIRONMENTAL PROTECTION AGENCY

The Environmental Protection Agency (EPA) operates two major research ships and numerous small craft to monitor environmental conditions in inland waterways and off the U.S. coasts.

1 RESEARCH SHIP: "LAKE GUARDIAN"

Number	Name	Launched	Completed	To EPA
—	LAKE GUARDIAN		1981	1988

Builders:	
Displacement:	850 tons light
Length:	180 feet (54.88 m) overall
Beam:	40 feet (12.2 m)
Draft:	
Propulsion:	diesel
Speed:	13 knots
Range:	6,000 nm (11,120 km) at 11 knots
Personnel:	14 (civilian) + 27 scientists

The LAKE GUARDIAN operates on the Great Lakes in support of EPA research and monitoring activities. She is based at Bay City, Michigan.

Design: The ship has three permanent laboratories plus four 20-foot (6.1-m) modular laboratories secured on deck.

1 RESEARCH SHIP: EX-NAVY GUNBOAT

Number	Name	FY	Launched	USN Comm.	To EPA
(ex-PG 86)	PETER W. ANDERSON	63	18 June 1966	4 Nov 1967	17 Jan 1978

Builders:	Tacoma Boatbuilding, Wash.
Displacement:	approx. 250 tons full load
Length:	164½ feet (50.2 m) overall
Beam:	23 ¾ feet (7.28 m)
Draft:	9½ feet (2.9 m)
Propulsion:	2 diesel engines (Cummins VT12-875M); 1,400 bhp; 2 shafts
Speed:	16 knots
Range:	2,400 nm (4,445 km) at 14 knots on diesel engines
	325 nm (602 km) at 37 knots on gas turbines
Manning:	30 (civilian contractor)

The PETER W. ANDERSON is a former ASHEVILLE-class patrol combatant/gunboat now employed in the pollution research role. Three sister ships serve as Navy research ships with the David Taylor Research Center (see Chapter 24).

This ship was decommissioned as a Navy gunboat on 1 October 1977 and transferred to EPA in 1978. She operates off the U.S. Atlantic coast.

All weapons have been removed.

Class: Originally a class of 17 units. The CROCKETT (PG 88), previously operated by the EPA, is now a museum at Muskegon, Michigan.

Design: This craft has an aluminum hull with a fiberglass superstructure. For the research role the ship has been fitted with three laboratories and a computer center.

Names: The ANDERSON was named ANTELOPE (PG 86) in naval service.

Operational: Under the EPA, the ship originally operated on the Great Lakes; she now is based at Annapolis, Maryland.

Propulsion: Originally she was a Combined Diesel or Gas (CODOG)-propelled ship; the gas turbine has been removed.

PETER W. ANDERSON (EPA/Stelian Codaracea)

PETER W. ANDERSON (Giorgio Arra)

RESEARCH SHIP: Ex-COAST GUARD BUOY TENDER

The former Coast Guard buoy tender MAPLE (WAGL 234), employed since 1974 by the EPA as the research ship ROGER R. SIMONS, was discarded in 1989. Based at Cleveland, Ohio, on Lake Erie, she carried out monitoring activities on the Great Lakes.

GEOLOGICAL SURVEY

The Geological Survey of the Department of Interior previously operated one major research ship, the former Navy survey ship S. P. LEE (ex-U.S. Navy AG 192, T-AGS 31). She was returned to the Navy on 1 August 1992; the ship was stricken from the NVR on 1 October 1992 and transferred to Mexico on 7 December 1992.

The LEE was built as a naval surveying ship and placed in service with the Military Sealift Command (USNS prefix) on completion in 1968. The ship was reclassified as a miscellaneous research ship (AG 192) on 25 September 1970. She was taken out of naval service on 29 January 1973 and transferred on loan to the National Geological Survey on 27 February 1974.

Under the Geological Survey the LEE conducted deep-sea seismic surveys, seafloor coring, and seafloor bottom sampling.

NATIONAL SCIENCE FOUNDATION

The National Science Foundation (NSF)—an independent government agency to "promote the progress of science" including in the area of national defense—operates two large polar research and support ships.

1 POLAR RESEARCH SHIP: "NATHANIEL B. PALMER"

Number	Name	Launched	Completed
(none)	NATHANIEL B. PALMER	1991	May 1992

Builders:	North American Shipbuilding, Larose, La.
Displacement:	6,800 tons full load
Length:	308 feet (93.9 m) overall
Beam:	60 feet (18.29 m)
Draft:	22½ feet (6.86 m)
Propulsion:	4 diesel engines (Caterpillar); 12,720 bhp; 2 shafts
Speed:	15 knots
Range:	
Personnel:	22 + 37 scientists

This ship was built specifically for NSF operations in the Antarctic. Both the NATHANIEL B. PALMER and the LAURENCE M. GOULD (below) have a very high standard of habitability and food service.

The NATHANIEL B. PALMER in Arctic waters. This ship and the LAURENCE M. GOULD have red hulls, as do the Coast Guard's oceangoing icebreakers. The PALMER's funnel is offset to port; an enclosed crow's nest is provided. (NSF/Stuart Klipper)

NATHANIEL B. PALMER

Design: The ship has an icebreaking hull with a rating of 3 feet (0.9 m) breaking capability. A helicopter deck and hangar are provided.

At-sea endurance is 75 days.

1 POLAR RESEARCH AND SUPPLY SHIP: "LAURENCE M. GOULD"

Number	Name	Launched	Completed
(none)	LAURENCE M. GOULD	1997	1997

Builders:	North American Shipbuilding, Larose, La.
Displacement:	2,755 tons standard
	3,780 tons full load
Length:	212 feet (64.7 m) waterline
	230 feet (70.2 m) overall
Beam:	46 feet (14.0 m)
Draft:	25¾ feet (5.8 m)
Propulsion:	2 diesel engines (Caterpillar 3606); 4,575 bhp; 2 shafts
Speed:	
Range:	
Personnel:	.... + 26 scientists

The LAURENCE M. GOULD was constructed specifically to support NSF operations in the Antarctic, replacing the POLAR DUKE in that role.

Design: The ship has an icebreaking hull. Endurance is 75 days at sea.

ARCTIC RESEARCH SHIP: "POLAR DUKE"

The POLAR DUKE, a Norwegian-built research ship launched in 1983, was built specifically for the National Science Foundation. She was in NSF service from 1985 to 1997, being replaced by the more-capable LAURENCE M. GOULD.

LAURENCE M. GOULD

Navy Force Levels, 1945–2005

The following are ships in active commission as of the end of the fiscal year indicated; beginning in 1965, operational Naval Reserve/Naval Reserve Force (NRF) ships manned by composite active–reserve crews are indicated by the plus (+) symbol.

Large frigate-type ships (DL/DLG/DLGN) are listed separately prior to 1975; from that year, they are included with missile cruisers and destroyers based on their reclassification in that year (see Chapter 15).

Ship Type	1945	1950	1953[a]	1955	1960	1965	1970	1975	1980	1985	1990	1995	2000	2005
Submarines–conventional														
SS-SSK-SSR	237	73	122	121	131	83	59	11	6	4	—	—	—	1[n]
SSG	—	—	1	2	4	—	—	—	—	—	—	—	—	—
auxiliary[b]	—	—	7	18	20	15	26	2	1	1	1	1	1	1
Submarines–nuclear														
SSN-SSRN	—	—	—	1	7	22	48	64	73	94[c]	87	77	54	54
SSGN	—	—	—	—	1	—	—	—	—	—	—	—	—	—
SSBN	—	—	—	—	2	29	41	41	40	37	34	16	18	14
auxiliary[d]	—	—	—	—	—	—	—	—	—	2	2	2	1	—
(total submarines)	(237)	(73)	(130)	(142)	(165)	(149)	(174)	(118)	(120)	(138)	(124)	(96)	(74)	(70)
Aircraft carriers														
CVB-CVA-CVAN-CV-CVN	20	7	17	16	14	16	15	15	13	13	12	11+1[e]	12	12
CVS	—	—	—	5	9	9	4	—	—	—	—	—	—	—
CVL	8	4	5	1	—	—	—	—	—	—	—	—	—	—
CVE	70	4	17	3	—	—	—	—	—	—	—	—	—	—
Battleships														
BB	25[f]	1	4	3	—	—	—	—	—	2	3	—	—	—
Cruisers														
CAG-CG-CLG-CGN	—	—	—	—	6	12	10	27	27	30	43	32	27	24
CA (8-inch guns)	24	9	15	10	6	2	2	—	—	—	—	—	—	—
CL (6-inch guns)	42	3	3	3	—	—	—	—	—	—	—	—	—	—
CLAA (5-inch guns)	6	1	1	—	—	—	—	—	—	—	—	—	—	—
Frigates[g]														
DL	—	—	—	5	5	5	—	—	—	—	—	—	—	—
DLG-DLGN	—	—	—	—	4	20	20	—	—	—	—	—	—	—
Destroyers														
DD-DDE-DDK-DDR	372	142	246	244	211	189+17	122	32	43	31+1	31	31	24	2
DDG	—	—	—	—	1	33	37	38	37	37	22	17	31	45
Escort Ships/Frigates														
DE-DER/FF-FFR[i]	365	11	89	64	41	39+21	41	58	59	53+6	36+12	—	—	22+8[o]
DEG/FFG	—	—	—	—	—	—	6	6	13	47+4	35+16	15+14	27+8	—
Flagships/Command Ships														
AGC-CC-CLC-LCC-AGF	18[k]	6				7	3	3	3	4	4	4	4	4
Amphibious Ships	~3,300	83				132	95	62	58+5	58+2	59+3	37+3	37+2	33

[a] End of Korean War (June 1953)
[b] Does not include the nuclear-propelled research vehicle NR-1, completed in 1969, but does include two SSNs employed as special operations transports.
[c] Beginning in 1983, SSNs were armed with Tomahawk anti-ship and land-attack missiles (TASM and TLAM, respectively).
[d] Includes transport submarines
[e] The NRF carrier was the JOHN F. KENNEDY (CV 67).
[f] The 1945 force included two large cruisers (designated CB); they often were referred to as battle cruisers (armed with 12-inch guns).
[g] Frigates (DL-DLG-DLGN) were reclassified as CG-CGN-DDG in 1975.
[h] Additional destroyer-type ships were employed as mine warfare ships (DM-DMS-MMD) until 1958; they retained most of their guns and some anti-submarine weapons.
[i] Includes one AGDE-AGFF from 1966 until classified as an FF in 1975.
[k] In addition, six large Coast Guard cutters were configured as amphibious force flagships.
[m] Includes amphibious force flagships (AGC)
[n] Swedish GOTLAND-class submarine on loan for ASW training
[o] These are FFG-type ships but their missile systems have been removed.

Navy Shipbuilding Programs, Fiscal Years 1947–2005

This appendix lists U.S. Navy shipbuilding programs since World War II. Only those ships constructed are listed, except where noted; ships transferred to other navies on completion are not included.

The Ships Characteristics Board (SCB) numbers are sequential for Navy ship designs reaching the advanced planning stage; they were numbered in a single series from 1947 (SCB No. 1 was the Norfolk/CLK 1, later DL 1) through 1964 (SCB No. 252 was the Flagstaff/PGH 1). From 1964 on, the SCB used numbered blocks: 001–099 for cruisers, 100–199 for carriers, 200–299 for destroyers/frigates (DL), 300–399 for submarines, 400–499 for amphibious vessels, 500–599 for mine warfare vessels, 600–699 for patrol ships and craft, 700–799 for auxiliary ships, 800–899 for service craft, and 900–999 for special purpose vessels. The later number series have a suffix of the fiscal year of the first ship, as 303.70 for the Los Angeles (SSN 688)—the first submarine under the new system ordered in fiscal year 1970.

Number		Class name	SCB No.	Notes
Fiscal Year 1947				
2	SS 563, 564	Tang	2	
Fiscal Year 1948				
2	SS 565, 566	Tang	2	
1	SSK 1	K-1	35	
(1)	CVA 58	United States	6A	construction canceled
1	CLK 1	Norfolk	1	completed as DL 1
(1)	CLK 2	Norfolk	1	construction canceled
4	DD 927–930	Mitscher	5	completed as DL 2–5
Fiscal Year 1949				
2	SS 567, 568	Tang	2	
2	SSK 2, 3	K-1	35	
Fiscal Year 1950				
1	AGSS 569	Albacore	56	
1	MSO 421	Agile	45A	
Fiscal Year 1951				
1	SSN 571	Nautilus	64	
1	SST 1	Mackerel	68	
28	MSO 422–449	Agile	45A	
Fiscal Year 1952				
1	SSN 575	Seawolf	64A	
2	SSR 572, 573	Salmon	84	changed to SS
1	SST 2	Mackerel	68	
1	CVA 59	Forrestal	80	changed to CV/AVT 59
1	DE 1006	Dealey	72	
1	IFS 1	Carronade	37	changed to LFS 1
4	LSD 28–31	Thomaston	75	
15	LST 1156–1170	Terrebonne Parish	9	
20	MSO 455–474	Agile	45A	
2	MSC 121, 122	Bluebird	69	
1	AGB 4	Glacier	11A	changed to WAGB 4
6	AO 143–148	Neosho	82	
Fiscal Year 1953				
1	SSG 574	Grayback	161	changed to LPSS 574
1	CVA 60	Forrestal	80	changed to CV 60
3	DD 931–933	Forrest Sherman	85	
2	DE 1014, 1015	Dealey	72	
9	MSO 488–496	Agile	45A	

Number		Class name	SCB No.	Notes
20	MSC 190–199, 201, 203–209, 289, 290	Bluebird	69	
2	AF 58, 59	Rigel	97	
Fiscal Year 1954				
1	SS 576	Darter	116	
1	CVA 61	Forrestal	80	changed to CV 61
3	DD 936–938	Forrest Sherman	85	
2	DE 1021, 1022	Dealey	72	
2	LSD 32, 33	Thomaston	75	
1	LST 1171	De Soto County	119	
1	MHC 43	Bittern	109	
4	MSO 508–511	Acme	45A	
2	AE 21, 22	Suribachi	114	
Fiscal Year 1955				
1	SSG 577	Grayback	161	
2	SSN 578, 579	Skate	121	
1	CVA 62	Forrestal	80	changed to CV 62
5	DD 940–944	Forrest Sherman	85	
8	DE 1023–1030	Dealey	72	
2	LSD 34, 35	Thomaston	75	
6	LST 1173–1178	De Soto County	119	
2	T-AOG 81, 82	Alatna	—	
Fiscal Year 1956				
3	SS 580–582	Barbel	150	
2	SSN 583, 584	Skate	121	
1	SSN 585	Skipjack	154	
1	SSRN 586	Triton	132	changed to SS 586
1	SSGN 587	Halibut	137A	changed to SS 587
1	CVA 63	Kitty Hawk	127	changed to CV 63
6	DLG 6–11	Coontz	142	changed to DDG 37–42
7	DD 945–951	Forrest Sherman	85	
2	DE 1033, 1034	Claud Jones	131	
2	AE 23, 24	Suribachi	114A	
Fiscal Year 1957				
5	SSN 588–592	Skipjack	154	
1	SSN 593	Thresher	188	
1	CVA 64	Kitty Hawk	127A	changed to CV 64
1	CLGN 160	Long Beach	169	completed as CGN 9
4	DLG 12–15	Coontz	142	changed to DDG 43–46
8	DD 952–959	Charles F. Adams	155	completed as DDG 2–9
2	DE 1035	Claud Jones	131	
1	AE 25	Suribachi	114A	
Fiscal Year 1958				
3	SSN 594–596	Thresher[a]	188	originally ordered as SSGN 594–596 (SCB No. 166A)
1	SSN 597	Tullibee	178	
3	SSBN 598–600	George Washington	180A	
1	CVAN 65	Enterprise	160	changed to CVN 65
3	DLG 16–18	Leahy	172	changed to CG 16–18
5	DDG 10–14	Charles F. Adams	155	
1	LPH 2	Iwo Jima	157	
Fiscal Year 1959				
2	SSBN 601, 602	George Washington	180A	
5	SSN 603–607	Thresher	188	1 unit originally planned as SSGN (SCB No. 166A)

Number	Class name	SCB No.	Notes
4 SSBN 608–611	Ethan Allen	180	
6 DLG 19–24	Leahy	172	changed to CG 19–24
1 DLGN 25	Bainbridge	189	changed to CGN 25
5 DDG 15–19	Adams	155	
1 LPD 1	Raleigh	187	
1 LPH 3	Iwo Jima	157	
Fiscal Year 1960			
4 SSN 612–615	Thresher	188	
3 DDG 20–22	Adams	155	
2 DE 1037, 1038	Bronstein	199	changed to FF 1037, 1038
1 PCH 1	High Point	202	
1 LPD 2	Raleigh	187	
1 LPH 7	Iwo Jima	157	
2 AGOR 3, 4	Conrad	185	academic ships
1 AS 31	Hunley	194	
Fiscal Year 1961			
1 SSBN 618	Ethan Allen	180	
4 SSBN 616, 617, 619, 620	Lafayette	216	
1 SSN 621	Thresher	188	
5 SSBN 622–626	Lafayette	216	FY 1961 supplemental
1 AGSS 555	Dolphin	207	
1 CVA 66	Kitty Hawk	127B	changed to CV 66
3 DLG 26–28	Belknap	212	changed to CG 26–28
2 DDG 23, 24	Adams	155	
2 DE 1040, 1041	Garcia	199A	changed to FF 1040, 1041
1 LPD 3	Raleigh	187	changed to AGF 3
1 AG 163	Glover	198	completed as AGDE 1; changed to FF 1098/ AGFF 1
1 AFS 1	Mars	208	
2 T-AGOR 5, 6	Conrad	185	academic ships
1 AOE 1	Sacramento	196	
Fiscal Year 1962			
3 SSN 637–639	Sturgeon	188A	
10 SSBN 627–636	Lafayette	216	
6 DLG 29–34	Belknap	212	changed to CG 29–34
1 DLGN 35	Truxtun	222	changed to CGN 35
3 DE 1043–1045	Garcia	199A	changed to FF 1043–1045
3 DEG 1–3	Brooke	199B	changed to FFG 1–3
1 LPD 4–6	Austin	187B	
1 LPH 9	Iwo Jima	157	
1 AFS 2	Mars	208	
1 AGEH 1	Plainview	219	
1 T-AGOR 7	Conrad	185	
1 T-AGS 25	Kellar	214	
1 AS 32	Hunley	194	
Fiscal Year 1963			
8 SSN 646–653	Sturgeon	188A	
6 SSBN 640–645	Lafayette	216	
1 CVA 67	John F. Kennedy	127C	
5 DE 1047–1051	Garcia	199A	changed to FF 1047–1051
3 DEG 4–6	Brooke	199B	changed to FFG 4–6
4 LPD 7–10	Austin	187B	
1 LPH 10	Iwo Jima	157	
1 T-AK 278	Meteor	236	changed to T-LSV/T-AKR 9
2 PGM 84, 85	Asheville	229	changed to PG 84, 85
2 AGOR 9, 10	Conrad	185	academic ships
1 T-AGS 26	Silas Bent	226	
1 AOE 2	Sacramento	196	
1 AS 33	Simon Lake	238	
Fiscal Year 1964			
5 SSN 660–664	Sturgeon	188A	
1 SSN 671	Narwhal	245	
6 SSBN 654–659	Lafayette	216	
10 DE 1052–1061	Knox	199C	changed to FF 1052–1061
3 LPD 11–13	Austin	187C	LPD 11 changed to AGF 11
2 PGM 86, 87	Asheville	229	changed to PG 86, 87
1 AD 37	Samuel Gompers	244	
1 AFS 3	Mars	208	
1 T-AGS 27	Silas Bent	226	
1 AS 34	Simon Lake	238	
Fiscal Year 1965			
6 SSN 665–670	Sturgeon	188M	
16 DE 1062–1077	Knox	200	new SCB series; changed to FF 1062–1077
Number	Class name	SCB No.	Notes
1 AGC 19	Blue Ridge	400	changed to LCC 19
4 AKA 113–116	Charleston	403	changed to LKA 113–116
2 LPD 14, 15	Austin	402	new SCB series
1 LPH 11	Iwo Jima	157	
1 LSD 36	Anchorage	404	new SCB series
1 LST 1179	Newport	405	new SCB series
3 PGM 88–90	Asheville	600	new SCB series; changed to PG 88–90
1 AD 38	Samuel Gompers	700	new SCB series
2 AE 26, 27	Kilauea	703	new SCB series
2 AFS 4, 5	Mars	705	new SCB series
2 T-AGOR 12, 13	Conrad	710	new SCB series
1 AGS 29	Chauvenet	723	built in Scotland
1 T-AGS 31	Kellar	709	
1 AOE 3	Sacramento	196	
2 AOR 1, 2	Wichita	707	
(1) AS 35	Simon Lake	738	*canceled*
1 AS 36	L. Y. Spear	702	
Fiscal Year 1966			
6 SSN 672–677	Sturgeon	188M	
10 DE 1078–1087	Knox	200	changed to FF 1078–1087
1 AGC 20	Mount Whitney	400	changed to LCC 20
1 LKA 117	Charleston	403	changed to LKA 117
1 LPH 12	Iwo Jima	157	
3 LSD 37–39	Anchorage	404	
8 LST 1180–1187	Newport	405	
2 PGH 1, 2	Flagstaff/Tucumcari	601	competitive prototypes
10 PGM 92–101	Asheville	600	changed to PG 92–101
2 AE 28, 29	Kilauea	703	
1 AFS 6	Mars	705	
2 AGOR 14, 15	Melville	710	academic ships
1 T-AGS 32	Chauvenet	723	built in Scotland
1 AOE 4	Sacramento	196	
2 AOR 3,4	Wichita	707	
1 AS 37	L. Y. Spear	702	
1 ATS 1	Edenton	719	built in England
Fiscal Year 1967			
5 SSN 678–682	Sturgeon	188M	
1 CVAN 68	Nimitz	102	changed to CVN 68
1 DLGN 36	California	241	changed to CGN 36
10 DE 1088–1097	Knox	200	changed to FF 1088–1097
1 LSD 40	Anchorage	404	
11 LST 1188–1198	Newport	405	
2 AE 32, 33	Kilauea	703	
1 AFS 7	Mars	705	
1 T-AGOR 16	Hayes	726	changed to T-AG 195
1 T-AGS 33, 34	Silas Bent	725/728	
2 AOR 5, 6	Wichita	707	
1 ASR 21	Pigeon	721	
2 ATS 2, 3	Edenton	719	built in England
Fiscal Year 1968			
2 SSN 683, 684	Sturgeon	188M	
1 SSN 685	Glenard P. Lipscomb	302	new SCB series
1 DLGN 37	California	241	changed to CGN 37
(10) DE 1098–1107	Knox	200	*canceled;* hull no. 1098 assigned to the Glover
2 AE 34, 35	Kilauea	703	
(2) AGOR 19, 20	Melville	710	*canceled*
1 ASR 22	Pigeon	721	
Fiscal Year 1969			
2 SSN 686, 687	Sturgeon	188M	
1 LHA 1	Tarawa	410	
Fiscal Year 1970			
3 SSN 688–690	Los Angeles		
1 CVAN 69	Nimitz	102	changed to CVN 69
1 DLGN 38	Virginia	246	changed to CGN 38
3 DD 963–965	Spruance	224	
2 LHA 2, 3	Tarawa	410	
Fiscal Year 1971			
4 SSN 691–694	Los Angeles	303	
1 DLGN 39	Virginia	246	changed to CGN 39
6 DD 966–971	Spruance	224	
2 LHA 4, 5	Tarawa	410	
2 AGOR 21, 22	Gyre	734	academic ships
Fiscal Year 1972			
5 SSN 695–699	Los Angeles	303	
1 DLGN 40	Virginia	246	changed to CGN 40

Number	Class name	SCB No.	Notes
7 DD 972–978	SPRUANCE	224	
1 AOR 7	WICHITA	707	
1 AS 39	EMORY S. LAND	737	
Fiscal Year 1973			
6 SSN 700–705	LOS ANGELES	303	
1 PF 109	OLIVER HAZARD PERRY	261	changed to FFG 7
1 PHM 1	PEGASUS	602	
(1) PHM 2	PEGASUS	602	*canceled;* reauthorized in FY 1976
1 AS 40	EMORY S. LAND	737	
Fiscal Year 1974			
5 SSN 706–710	LOS ANGELES	303	
1 SSBN 726	OHIO	304	
1 CVN 70	NIMITZ	102	
7 DD 979–985	SPRUANCE	224	
Fiscal Year 1975			
3 SSN 711–713	LOS ANGELES	303	
2 SSBN 727, 728	OHIO	304	
1 CGN 41	VIRGINIA	246	
7 DD 986–992	SPRUANCE	224	
3 FFG 8–10	PERRY	261	
4 PHM 3–6	PEGASUS	602	
1 AD 41	SAMUEL GOMPERS	700	
Fiscal Year 1976			
2 SSN 714, 715	LOS ANGELES	303	
1 SSBN 729	OHIO	304	
6 FFG 11–16	PERRY	226	
1 PHM 2	PEGASUS	602	
1 AD 42	SAMUEL GOMPERS	700	
2 AO 177, 178	CIMARRON	739	
3 T-ATF 166–169	POWHATAN	744	
Fiscal Year 1977			
3 SSN 716–718	LOS ANGELES	303	
1 SSBN 730	OHIO	304	
8 FFG 19–26	PERRY	261	
1 AD 43	SAMUEL GOMPERS	700	
1 AO 179	CIMARRON	739	
1 AS 41	MCKEE	737	
Fiscal Year 1978			
1 SSN 719	LOS ANGELES	303	
2 SSBN 731, 732	OHIO	304	
1 DDG 47	TICONDEROGA	226	changed to CG 47
1 DD 997	SPRUANCE[b]	224	
8 FFG 27–34	PERRY	261	
2 AO 180, 186	CIMARRON	739	
3 T-ATF 170–172	POWHATAN	744	
Fiscal Year 1979			
1 SSN 720	LOS ANGELES	303	
4 DDG 993–996	KIDD[c]	—	
8 FFG 36–43	PERRY	261	
1 AD 44	SAMUEL GOMPERS	700	
2 T-AGOS 1, 2	STALWART	—	
1 T-ARC 7	ZEUS	—	
Fiscal Year 1980			
2 SSN 721, 722	LOS ANGELES	303	
1 SSBN 733	OHIO	304	
1 CVN 71	NIMITZ	102	
1 CG 48	TICONDEROGA	226	
5 FFG 45–49	PERRY	261	
1 T-AGOS 3	STALWART	—	
Fiscal Year 1981			
2 SSN-723, 724	LOS ANGELES	303	
1 SSBN 734	OHIO	304	
2 CG 49, 50	TICONDEROGA	226	
6 FFG 50–55	PERRY	261	
1 LSD 41	WHIDBEY ISLAND	—	
1 ARS 50	SAFEGUARD	—	
5 T-AGOS 4–8	STALWART	—	
Fiscal Year 1982			
3 SSN 725, 750	LOS ANGELES	303	
3 CG 51–53	TICONDEROGA	226	
3 FFG 56–58	PERRY	261	
1 LSD 42	WHIDBEY ISLAND	—	
1 MCM 1	AVENGER	—	
4 T-AGOS 9–12	STALWART	—	
1 T-AO 187	HENRY J. KAISER	—	
2 ARS 51. 52	SAFEGUARD	—	

Number	Class name	SCB No.	Notes
Fiscal Year 1983			
1 SSBN 735	OHIO	304	
2 SSN 751, 752	LOS ANGELES	303	improved design
2 CVN 72, 73	NIMITZ		
3 CG 54–56	TICONDEROGA	226	
2 FFG 59, 60	PERRY	261	
1 LSD 43	WHIDBEY ISLAND	—	
1 MCM 2	AVENGER	—	
1 T-AO 188	HENRY J. KAISER	—	
1 ARS 53	SAFEGUARD	—	
Fiscal Year 1984			
1 SSBN 736	OHIO	304	
3 SSN 753–755	LOS ANGELES	303	improved design
3 CG 57–59	TICONDEROGA	226	
1 FFG 61	PERRY	261	
1 LHD 1	WASP	—	
1 LSD 44	WHIDBEY ISLAND	—	
(1) SWCM 1	(Sea Viking class)	—	*canceled*
3 MCM 3–5	AVENGER	—	
(1) MSH 1	CARDINAL	—	*canceled*
2 T-AO 189, 190	HENRY J. KAISER	—	
Fiscal Year 1985			
1 SSBN 737	OHIO	304	
4 SSN 756–759	LOS ANGELES	303	improved design
3 CG 60–62	TICONDEROGA	226	
1 DDG 51	ARLEIGH BURKE	—	
2 LSD 45, 46	WHIDBEY ISLAND	—	
4 MCM 6–9	AVENGER	—	
2 T-AGOS 13, 14	STALWART	—	
2 T-AGS 39, 40	MAURY	—	
3 T-AO 191–193	HENRY J. KAISER	—	
Fiscal Year 1986			
1 SSBN 738	OHIO	304	
4 SSN 760–763	LOS ANGELES	303	improved design
3 CG 63–65	TICONDEROGA	226	
1 LHD 2	WASP	—	
2 LSD 47, 48	WHIDBEY ISLAND	—	
2 MCM 10, 11	AVENGER	—	
1 MHC 51	OSPREY	—	
2 T-AGOS 15, 16	STALWART	—	
2 T-AO 194, 195	HENRY J. KAISER	—	
Fiscal Year 1987			
1 SSBN 739	OHIO	304	
4 SSN 764–767	LOS ANGELES	303	improved design
3 CG 66–68	TICONDEROGA	226	
2 DDG 52, 53	ARLEIGH BURKE	—	
(1) SWCM 1	(Sea Viking class)	—	*canceled*[d]
1 AOE 6	SUPPLY	—	
1 AGOR 23	THOMAS G. WASHINGTON	—	academic ship
2 T-AGOS 17, 18	STALWART	—	
1 T-AGOS 19	VICTORIOUS	—	
2 T-AO 196, 197	HENRY J. KAISER	—	
Fiscal Year 1988			
1 SSBN 740	OHIO	304	
3 SSN 768–770	LOS ANGELES	303	improved design
2 CVN 74, 75	NIMITZ	102	
5 CG 69–73	TICONDEROGA	226	
1 LHD 3	WASP	—	
1 LSD 49	HARPERS FERRY	—	
3 MCM 12–14	AVENGER	—	
2 T-AO 198, 199	HENRY J. KAISER	—	
Fiscal Year 1989			
1 SSBN 741	OHIO	304	
1 SSN 21	SEAWOLF	—	
2 SSN 771, 772	LOS ANGELES	303	improved design
5 DDG 54–58	ARLEIGH BURKE	—	
1 LHD 4	WASP	—	
2 MHC 52, 53	OSPREY	—	
3 T-AGOS 20–22	VICTORIOUS	—	
5 T-AO 200–204	HENRY J. KAISER	—	
1 AOE 7	SUPPLY	—	
Fiscal Year 1990			
1 SSBN 742	OHIO	304	
1 SSN 773	LOS ANGELES	303	improved design
5 DDG 59–63	ARLEIGH BURKE	—	
1 LSD 50	HARPERS FERRY	—	

Number	Class name	SCB No.	Notes
8 PC 1–8	CYCLONE	—	
2 MHC 54, 55	OSPREY	—	
1 T-AGOS 23	IMPECCABLE	—	
3 T-AGS 60–62	PATHFINDER	—	
1 AOE 8	SUPPLY	—	
Fiscal Year 1991			
1 SSBN 743	OHIO	304	last ship authorized in basic SCB series
1 SSN 22	SEAWOLF	—	
4 DDG 64–67	ARLEIGH BURKE	—	
1 LHD 5	WASP	—	
1 LSD 51	HARPERS FERRY	—	
5 PC 9–13	CYCLONE	—	
2 MHC 56, 57	OSPREY	—	
Fiscal Year 1992			
(1) SSN 23	SEAWOLF	—	*canceled* in January 1992; reauthorized as an FY 1996 ship
5 DDG 68–72	ARLEIGH BURKE	—	
3 MHC 58–60	OSPREY	—	
(1) AOE 9	SUPPLY	—	*canceled;* reauthorized as an FY 1993 ship
Fiscal Year 1993			
4 DDG 73–76	ARLEIGH BURKE	—	
1 LHD 6	WASP	—	
1 LSD 52	HARPERS FERRY	—	
2 MHC 61, 62	OSPREY	—	
1 AGOR 24	THOMAS G. WASHINGTON	—	academic ship
1 AOE 10	SUPPLY	—	
1 WAGB 20	HEALY	—	for Coast Guard operation
Fiscal Year 1994			
2 DDG 77, 78	ARLEIGH BURKE	—	
1 DDG 79	ARLEIGH BURKE	—	improved design
2 AGOR 25, 26	THOMAS G. WASHINGTON	—	1 academic ship; 1 NOAA ship
1 T-AGS 63	PATHFINDER	—	
Fiscal Year 1995			
1 CVN 76	NIMITZ	—	
3 DDG 80–82	ARLEIGH BURKE	—	improved design
Fiscal Year 1996			
1 SSN 23	SEAWOLF	—	
2 DDG 83, 84	ARLEIGH BURKE	—	improved design
1 LHD 7	WASP	—	
1 LPD 17	SAN ANTONIO	—	
1 PC 14	CYCLONE	—	
1 T-AGS 64	PATHFINDER	—	
Fiscal Year 1997			
4 DDG 85–88	ARLEIGH BURKE	—	improved design
1 T-AGS	PATHFINDER	—	
Fiscal Year 1998			
1 SSN 774	VIRGINIA	—	
4 DDG 89–92	ARLEIGH BURKE	—	improved design
1 LPD 18	SAN ANTONIO	—	
Fiscal Year 1999			
1 SSN 775	VIRGINIA	—	
3 DDG 93–95	ARLEIGH BURKE	—	improved design
1 LPD 19	SAN ANTONIO	—	

Number	Class name	SCB No.	Notes
Fiscal Year 2000			
3 DDG 96–98	Improved ARLEIGH BURKE	--	
2 LPD 19, 20	SAN ANTONIO	--	
2 T-AKE 1, 2	LEWIS AND CLARK	--	
Fiscal Year 2001			
1 SSN 776	VIRGINIA		
1 CVN 77	NIMITZ	--	
3 DDG 99–101	Improved ARLEIGH BURKE	--	
1 T-AKE 3	LEWIS AND CLARK	--	
Fiscal Year 2002			
1 SSN 777	VIRGINIA	--	
3 DDG 102–104	Improved ARLEIGH BURKE	--	
1 LHD 8	WASP		
Fiscal Year 2003			
1 SSN 778	VIRGINIA	--	
2 DDG 105, 106	Improved ARLEIGH BURKE	--	
1 LPD 21	SAN ANTONIO		
1 T-AKE 4	LEWIS AND CLARK	--	
Fiscal Year 2004			
1 SSN 779	VIRGINIA	--	
3 DDG 107–109	Improved ARLEIGH BURKE	--	
2 T-AKE 5, 6	LEWIS AND CLARK	--	
1 LPD 22	SAN ANTONIO	--	
Fiscal Year 2005			
1 SSN 780	VIRGINIA	--	
3 DDG 110–112	Improved ARLEIGH BURKE	--	
1 LCS	littoral combat ship	--	
2 T-AKE 7, 8	LEWIS AND CLARK	--	
1 LPD 23	SAN ANTONIO	--	

[a] Class renamed for PERMIT (SSN 594) after loss of THRESHER in April 1963.

[b] Congress authorized two improved SPRUANCE-class destroyers with enhanced aviation capabilities; in the event, the Navy ordered only one ship, to a standard SPRUANCE configuration.

[c] Taken over while under construction for Iran.

[d] The SWCM/Sea Viking program was restructured in 1987, with the lead ship reordered in 1987; no ships of the design were completed.

Note: As this edition went to press, it was learned that the lead DD(X), although funded in FY 2005, would not be authorized until FY 2007 (see page 9, Table 1-3, and page 145). This delay will further threaten the viability of the program and some subsystems, especially the Advanced Gun System (AGS).

The first two littoral combat ships, as well as the lead DD(X), are being constructed with research and development funding, not shipbuilding funds.

APPENDIX C

Foreign Ship Transfers, 2000–2005

Number	Name	Recipient	Transfer date	Type	Number	Name	Recipient	Transfer date	Type
Destroyers					*Coast Guard Cutters*				
DDG 993	KIDD	Taiwan	30 May 2003	Sale	WMEC 622	COURAGEOUS	Sri Lanka	24 June 2004	Grant Aid
DDG 994	CALLAGHAN	Taiwan	30 May 2003	Sale	WMEC 628	DURAGLE	Colombia	3 Sep 2003	Gift
DDG 995	SCOTT	Taiwan	30 May 2003	Sale	WPB 82333	POINT HIGHLAND	Trinidad & Tobago	24 July 2001	Sale
DDG 996	CHANDLER	Taiwan	30 May 2003	Sale	WPB 82335	POINT COUNTESS	Georgia	29 June 2000	Gift
Frigates					WPB 82338	POINT BRIDGE	Costa Rica	23 Sep 2001	Sale
FF 1041	BRADLEY	Brazil	24 Jan 2001	Sale	WPB 82339	POINT CHICO	Costa Rica	22 June 2001	Sale
FF 1045	DAVIDSON	Brazil	24 Jan 2001	Sale	WPB 82342	POINT BAKER	Georgia	12 Feb 2002	Gift
FF 1048	SAMPLE	Brazil	24 Jan 2001	Sale	WPB 82343	POINT WELLS	Colombia	13 Oct 2000	Sale
FF 1050	ALBERT DAVID	Brazil	24 Jan 2001	Sale	WPB 82344	POINT ESTERO	Colombia	6 Feb 2001	Sale
FF 1068	VREELAND	Greece	9 Feb 2001	Sale	WPB 82347	POINT BONITA	Trinidad & Tobago	14 Nov 2000	Sale
FF 1075	TRIPPE	Greece	9 Feb 2001	Sale	WPB 82349	POINT SPENCER	Dom. Republic	12 Dec 2000	Sale
FF 1080	PAUL	Turkey	9 Jan 2000	Grant Aid	WPB 82352	POINT SAL	Colombia	29 May 2001	Sale
FF 1094	PHARRIS	Mexico	2 Feb 2000	Sale	WPB 82355	POINT HANNAN	Panama	11 Jan 2001	Sale
FFG 9	WADSWORTH	Poland	28 June 2002	Grant Aid	WPB 82358	POINT STUART	El Salvador	27 Apr 2001	Sale
FFG 11	CLARK	Poland	15 Mar 2000	Sale	WPB 82360	POINT WINSLOW	Panama	30 Sep 2000	Sale
FFG 12	GEORGE PHILIP	Portugal	2005	Sale	WPB 82368	POINT WARDE	Colombia	29 June 2000	Sale
FFG 13	SAMUEL ELIOT MORISON	Turkey	10 Apr 2002	Grant Aid	WPB 82371	POINT BARNES	Jamaica	9 Jan 2000	Sale
FFG 14	SIDES	Portugal	2005	Sale	WPB 82372	POINT BROWER	Azerbaijan	28 Jan 2003	Gift
FFG 15	ESTOCIN	Turkey	3 Apr 2003	Sale	WPB 82374	POINT CARREWA	Argentina	22 Aug 2000	Sale
FFG 19	JOHN A. MOORE	Turkey	1 Sep 2000	Sale	WPB 82375	POINT DORAN	Philippines	22 Mar 2001	Sale
Patrol Ships					WPB 82378	POINT JACKSON	Turkmenistan	30 May 2000	Gift
PC 1*	CYCLONE	Philippines	6 Mar 2003	Grant Aid	WLB 277	COWSLIP	Nigeria	23 Jan 2003	Gift
Amphibious Ships					WLB 302	MADRONA	El Salvador	12 Apr 2002	Grant Aid
LSD 33	ALAMO	Brazil	24 Jan 2001	Sale	WLB 306	BUTTONWOOD	Dom. Republic	23 June 2001	Grant Aid
LSD 34	HERMITAGE	Brazil	24 Jan 2001	Sale	WLB 309	SWEETGUM	Panama	15 Feb 2002	Grant Aid
LST 1179	NEWPORT	Mexico	23 May 2001	Sale	WLB 393	FIREBUSH	Nigeria	30 June 2003	Gift
LST 1180	MANITOWOC	Taiwan	29 Sep 2000	Sale	WLB 401	SASSAFRAS	Nigeria	30 Oct 2003	Gift
LST 1181	SUMTER	Taiwan	29 Sep 2000	Sale	WLB 402	SEDGE	Nigeria	21 Dec 2002	Grant Aid
LST 1184	FREDERICK	Mexico	5 Oct 2002	Lease	WLB 405	SWEETBRIER	Ghana	27 Aug 2001	Gift
LST 1184	FREDERICK	Mexico	22 Nov 2002	Sale	WLB 407	WOODRUSH	Ghana	4 May 2001	Gift
LST 1186	CAYUGA	Brazil	19 Sep 2000	Sale					
LST 1196	HARLAN COUNTY	Spain	27 Apr 2000	Sale					
LST 1197	BARNSTABLE COUNTY	Spain	27 Apr 2000	Sale					
Auxiliaries									
T-AGS 27	KANE	Turkey	14 Mar 2001	Sale					
Service Craft									
ARD 30	SAN ONOFRE	Mexico	20 Mar 2001	Sale					

* Also WPC 12.

Beyond ships and cutters, the U.S. Navy and Coast Guard transfer "boats" and other craft to foreign navies. Here, the ex-U.S. Coast Guard 44-foot (13.4-m) motor lifeboat No. 44367 is laden with U.S. and Yemeni officials as the craft—one of eight 44-footers—is formally transferred to the Yemeni Coast Guard in 2004. (U.S. Navy/Matthew Belson)

APPENDIX D

Navy and Coast Guard Ships Preserved as Memorials and Museums

These ships are arranged alphabetically by name, and by hull number if unnamed. Also of significance, the U.S. nuclear-propelled merchant ship SAVANNAH is located at Patriot's Point, Charleston, South Carolina. The world's first civilian nuclear ship, she was launched in 1959 and went to sea in 1962 to demonstrate peaceful uses for nuclear power. She was retired from service in 1971.

Efforts are under way to preserve the first Aegis cruiser, the TICONDEROGA (CG 47), which was decommissioned in 2004. While the Washington (D.C.) Navy Yard has been mentioned, that site, on the Anacostia River, would require a major dredging operation for the ship to be moored there.

The Confederate submersible HUNLEY, which is credited with the first submarine sinking of a warship, the Union sloop-of-war HOUSATONIC in 1864, was salvaged in 2000. She also is planned for exhibition in Charleston. (The HUNLEY sank twice on trials and was lost immediately after sinking the HOUSATONIC).

The nuclear-propelled attack submarine NARWHAL (SSN 671), decommissioned and stricken in 1999, is planned as a museum–memorial at Newport-on-Levee (Cincinnati) on the Ohio River. She will be placed on a floating barge, with opening scheduled for 2007.

The battleship IOWA (BB 61) is planned as a museum–memorial at San Francisco. Although two of the four IOWA-class ships remain on the Naval Vessel Register, all are or soon will be museums.

The Coast Guard buoy tender BRAMBLE (WLB 392) is planned for installation as a museum at the Port Huron Museum of Arts and History in Michigan.

The destroyer BARRY (DD 933), long at the Washington (D.C.) Navy Yard, has been saved after developing major material problems in fall 2000. She is again in service as a memorial–museum.

And, more than 50 years after the end of World War II, three tank landing ships (LST) have been acquired as memorial–museums—the BOWMAN COUNTY (LST 391) and the unnamed LST 325 and LST 393. These were the ships of which Prime Minister Winston Churchill recorded in 1943:

> In this period of the war all the great strategic combinations of the Western Powers were restricted and distorted by the shortage of tank landing-craft [sic] for the transport, not so much of tanks, but of vehicles of all kinds. The letters "L.S.T." (Landing Ship, Tank) are burnt in upon the minds of all those who dealt with military affairs in this period.

Several German, Italian, and Japanese World War II-era manned torpedoes are at various locations in the United States.

Number	Name	Completed	Location/Notes
BB 60	ALABAMA	1942	Battleship Memorial Park, Mobile, Ala.
AGSS 569	ALBACORE	1953	Portsmouth, N.H.
BB 39	ARIZONA	1916	sunken remains and memorial off Ford Island, Pearl Harbor, Hawaii
DD 933	BARRY	1956	Navy Yard, Washington, D.C.
SS 310	BATFISH	1943	Muskogee War Memorial, Okla.
SS 319	BECUNA	1944	Independence Seaport Museum, Philadelphia
SS 581	BLUEBACK	1959	Oregon Museum of Science and Industry, Portland
SS 287	BOWFIN	1943	Submarine Memorial Park, Honolulu, Hawaii
LST 391	BOWMAN COUNTY	1942	LST Ship Memorial, Oregon, Ohio
	CAIRO	1862	Vicksburg National Park, Vicksburg, Miss.; Union Navy ironclad, paddle-Wheel gunboat.
DD 793	CASSIN YOUNG	1943	Boston Historical National Park, Mass.
SS 244	CAVALLA	1944	U.S. Submarine Veterans, Galveston, Texas
	CHATTAHOOCHEE	1862	Confederate Naval Museum, Columbus, Ga.; Confederate Navy gunboat.
SS 343	CLAMAGORE	1945	Patriot's Point, Charleston, S.C.
WAL 538	CHESAPEAKE (WLV 116)	1930	Baltimore Maritime Museum, Md.; lightship
SS 245	COBIA	1944	Manitowoc Maritime Museum, Wisc.
SS 224	COD	1943	Cleveland, Ohio
WATA 202	COMANCHE	1934	Patriots Point, Charleston, S.C.
IX 20	CONSTELLATION	1853	CONSTELLATION Dock, Baltimore; not the original ship built in 1797, but a ship constructed at the Gosport (Norfolk) Navy Yard (Va.) in 1853

Number	Name	Completed	Location/Notes
IX 21	CONSTITUTION	1798	Boston National Historical Park, Mass.; the only ship in this appendix still in full commission as a U.S. Navy ship
SS 246	CROAKER	1944	Buffalo Naval and Servicemen's Park, Buffalo, N.Y.
PG 88	CROCKETT	1967	Great Lakes Naval and Maritime Museum, Muskegon, Mich.
SS 228	DRUM	1941	Battleship Memorial Park, Mobile, Ala.
SSG 577	GROWLER	1958	Sea-Air-Space Museum, New York, N.Y.
MSF 240	HAZARD (AM 240)	1944	Omaha Military Historical Society, Omaha, Neb.
	HIDDENSEE	1985	Battleship Cove, Fall River, Mass.; former East German Tarantul I-class missile ship; built in the Soviet Union
CVS 12	HORNET	1943	NAS Alameda, Oakland, Calif.
MSF 242	INAUGURAL (AM 242)	1944	Gateway Arch, St. Louis, Mo.
WMEC 35	INGHAM (WPG 35)	1936	Patriot's Point, Charleston, S.C.
CVS 11	INTREPID	1943	Sea-Air-Space Museum, New York, N.Y.
	INTELLIGENT WHALE	1863	Army National Guard Museum, Sea Girt, N.J.; submersible.
	JACKSON	1864	Confederate Naval Museum, Columbus, Ga.; Confederate Navy ironclad ram
DD 850	JOSEPH P. KENNEDY JR.	1945	Battleship Cove, Fall River, Mass.
	Juliett (pennant 484)		Saratoga Museum Foundation, Providence, R.I.; ex-Soviet Project 651 SSG.
DD 661	KIDD	1943	Louisiana War Memorial, Baton Rouge
DD 724	LAFFEY		Patriot's Point, Charleston, S.C.

Number	Name	Completed	Location/Notes
AVT 16	LEXINGTON (CV 16)	1943	Corpus Christi, Texas
SS 297	LING	1945	Submarine Memorial, Hackensack, N.J.
SS 298	LIONFISH	1944	Battleship Cove, Fall River, Mass.
CLG 4	LITTLE ROCK (CL 92)	1945	Buffalo Naval and Serviceman's Park, Buffalo, N.Y.
LSM 45	(unnamed)	1944	Omaha Military Historical Society, Neb.
LST 325	(unnamed)	1943	National D-Day Museum, New Orleans
LST 393	(unnamed)	1942	Muskegon, Minn.
SST 2	MARLIN	1953	Omaha Military Historical Society ,Neb.
BB 59	MASSACHUSETTS	1942	Battleship Cove, Fall River, Mass.
WMEC	146 McLANE (WPC 146)	1927	Great Lakes Naval and Maritime Museum, Muskegon, Mich.
CV 41	MIDWAY	1945	San Diego, Calif.
BB 63	MISSOURI	1944	Ford Island, Pearl Harbor, Hawaii
WMEC 78	MOHAWK (WPG 78)	1934	City Piers, Wilmington, Del.
MSB 5	(unnamed)		Pate Museum of Transportation, Fort Worth, Texas
SSN 571	NAUTILUS	1954	Naval Submarine Base, Groton, Conn.
	NEUSE	1864	Caswell-Neuse State Historic Site, Kingston, N.C.; Confederate Navy ironclad ram
	NIAGARA	1813	Erie, Pa.; U.S. brig from Battle of Lake Erie
BB 6	NEW JERSEY	1943	Camden, N.J.
BB 55	NORTH CAROLINA	1941	NORTH CAROLINA Battleship Memorial, Wilmington, N.C.
C 6	OLYMPIA	1895	Independence Seaport Museum, Philadelphia
SS 383	PAMPANITO	1943	Fisherman's Wharf, San Francisco
PCF 1	(unnamed)	1965	Navy Museum, Navy Yard, Washington, D.C.
	PHILADELPHIA	1776	National Museum of American History Washington, D.C.; gondola gunboat built Lake Champlain during the American Revolution
	PIONEER	1862	New Orleans; Confederate Navy submersible

Number	Name	Completed	Location/Notes
AG 25	POTOMAC	1934	Oakland, Calif.; delivered to the Coast Guard in 1934 as the USCGC ELECTRA; transferred to the Navy in 1935 and placed in commission in 1936 as the presidential yacht (AG 25)
PT 309	(unnamed)	1944	Admiral Nimitz Museum, Fredericksburg, Texas
PT 617	(unnamed)	1945	Battleship Cove, Fall River, Mass.
PT 796	(unnamed)	1945	Battleship Cove, Fall River, Mass.
PTF 17	(unnamed)	1968	Buffalo Naval and Servicemen's Park, Buffalo, N.Y.
SSR 481	REQUIN	1945	Carnegie Science Center, Pittsburgh
CA 139	SALEM	1949	Fore River Shipyard, Quincy, Mass.
SS 573	SALMON	1956	Fore River Shipyard, Quincy, Mass.
SS 236	SILVERSIDES	1941	Great Lakes Naval and Maritime Museum, Muskegon, Mich.
DE 766	SLATER	1944	Albany, N.Y.
ARL 24	SPHINX (LST 963)	1944	Veterans' Park Museum, Dunkirk, N.Y.
DE 238	STEWART	1943	U.S. Submarine Veterans, Galveston, Texas
WPG 37	TANEY	1936	Baltimore Maritime Museum, Md.
BB 35	TEXAS	1914	Battleship TEXAS State Historical Park, Laporte, Texas
DD 537	THE SULLIVANS		Buffalo Naval and Servicemen's Park, Buffalo, N.Y.
SS 423	TORSK	1944	Baltimore Maritime Museum, Md.
	TRIESTE I	1953	Navy Museum, Navy Yard, Washington, D.C.; bathyscaph.
	TRIESTE II		Naval Undersea Museum, Keyport, Wash.; bathyscaph.
DD 951	TURNER JOY	1959	Puget Sound Naval Shipyard, Bremerton, Wash.
	U-505	1941	Museum of Science and Industry, Chicago; former German submarine
AG 16	UTAH (BB 31)	1911	sunken remains off Ford Island, Pearl Harbor, Hawaii; target ship.
BB 64	WISCONSIN	1944	Nauticus, Norfolk, Va.
SSX 1	X-1	1955	Naval Submarine Base, New London, Conn.; midget submarine
CV 10	YORKTOWN	1943	Patriots Point, Charleston, S.C.

The nuclear-propelled attack submarine NARWHAL (SSN 671) as planned for a museum on the Ohio River at Newport, Kentucky. The submarine will be permanently installed out of the water. The only other preserved U.S. nuclear submarine is the NAUTILUS (SSN 571), which is afloat in the Thames River at the Naval Submarine Base New London, Connecticut. (National Submarine Science Discovery Center)

APPENDIX E

Arsenal Ship Program

The so-called Arsenal Ship was one of the most innovative and controversial U.S. Navy ship programs of the 1990s. The concept died shortly after the death of Chief of Naval Operations Admiral M. J. Boorda in 1996.

A joint program was established by the Navy and the Defense Advanced Research Projects Agency (DARPA) to develop the Arsenal Ship, based in part on the findings of a DARPA study panel in late 1995.[1]

As envisioned, the Arsenal Ship would be fitted with more than 500 vertical-launch missile cells and would have a sustained speed of 22 knots; have provisions for future installation of the 155-mm Vertical Gun for Advanced Ships (VGAS), a 155-mm/52-cal gun with a range of about 100 nm (185 km); and have minimal manning requirements. No operational helicopters would be embarked, although a helicopter landing area would be provided.

A program of six such ships was proposed, with the lead ship to be a "high-tech" demonstrator, which would be a fully capable warship. The technology demonstrator was to:
- evaluate the advanced multiple weapon launcher system
- demonstrate the flexible adaptive fire control system
- transition Arsenal Ship technologies to the SC 21/DD 21

advanced surface combatant (initially the land-attack destroyer) In addition, the demonstrator would be used to evaluate the high degree of automation sought in the Arsenal Ship, new materials, welding techniques, and other features.

DARPA's participation in the project would permit an accelerated design, development, and procurement schedule, making maximum use of developing technologies. The joint Navy–DARPA program was formally established in 1996, with the lead ship (demonstrator) to carry out a fleet evaluation in Fiscal Year (FY) 2001 and all six Arsenal Ships to be delivered by FY 2010.

The Arsenal Ship concept was based on two factors. First, during Operation Desert Storm—as in all ground conflicts—massive amounts of ordnance, weapons to fire it, and vehicles, fuel, and people to move and guard the ordnance were landed in Saudi Arabia, almost all by ship. For example, a single armored division in the Gulf War had stockpiled in Saudi Arabia more than 25,000 tons of munitions. Not only did the ordnance have to be landed, moved to supply dumps, and then brought up to the front lines, but throughout that period it also was potentially vulnerable to Iraqi Scud missile and air attacks, as well as to anti-Coalition guerrilla or Iraqi commando strikes.

The Arsenal Ship could have provided much of that ordnance on target from the sea. The ships that brought the ordnance (missiles) into the area also could have launched the ordnance, resulting in great savings in shipping space, vehicles, and people.

Second, U.S. cruisers and destroyers of the TICONDEROGA (CG 47), ARLEIGH BURKE (DDG 51), and SPRUANCE (DD 963) classes fitted with vertical launch systems cannot reload their missile cells during underway replenishment. Rather, when their missiles are expended, they must withdraw from the combat area to a secure harbor or other sheltered waters to effectively replenish, depriving

An artist's view of an Arsenal Ship launching strike missiles against land targets. (Lockheed Martin)

the local force commander of ships with highly capable radar, weapons control, anti-submarine, and helicopter capabilities.

---

1 The members of the DARPA panel were Gen. Al Gray, USMC, former Commandant of the Marine Corps; Vice Adm. Joseph Metcalf, USN, former Deputy Chief of Naval Operations (Surface Warfare); Rear Adm. Wes Jordan, USN, former DARPA project manager of the SEA SHADOW; and Norman Polmar.

The Arsenal Ship could provide additional missiles on scene in an economical and effective manner. In this role, it could be compared to existing underway replenishment ships, i.e., ammunition ships (AE) or fast combat support ships (AOE). But the AE and AOE deliver their missiles to the combat area in a horizontal position, and they must be transferred to a warship to be launched. The Arsenal Ship, on entering the area, could immediately begin firing missiles—anti-air, land-attack, or even anti-ship weapons—with the missiles controlled by another warship, by an aircraft, or by a controller ashore.[2]

Would the Arsenal Ship have been vulnerable to enemy attack? Yes, but much less so than the AE/AOE. Stealth features could have helped it reach the combat area; once there, the cruisers and destroyers, some with empty magazines, would have provided defense of the missile ship.

Initially, the Navy and DARPA considered a semisubmerging hull configuration, with the ship partially submerging to reduce its radar signature. That configuration was abandoned early in the Arsenal Ship's development; instead, shaping and anechoic materials were to be employed to provide stealth. The ship also was to incorporate advanced survivability features to minimize both above- and below-water damage.

Some terminal/point-defense weapons could have been mounted, as well as large numbers of decoys and jammers to counter enemy weapons. However, the principal defense of the Arsenal Ship would have come from cruisers and destroyers in the area—possibly employing the Arsenal Ship's missiles.

A crew as small as 25 to 30 was considered to be practical for the ship through the use of advanced materials, automation, and other features. A small crew also was possible because the ship would have no combat information center or fire direction requirements, those functions being undertaken by offboard combat/control centers. Indeed, the director of DARPA at the time raised the issue of developing a completely unmanned Arsenal Ship. The minimal manning developed by the DARPA study team is listed in Table E-l.

The Arsenal Ship had a rapid demise following the death of Admiral Boorda. Three disparate groups took up the opposition:

TABLE E-1. ARSENAL SHIP MINIMAL MANNING

1 Commanding Officer
1 Executive Officer
Operations
  1 Operations Officer
  3 Quartermasters
  1 Cook
  1 Mess Specialist
  3 Communications Technicians
Engineering
  1 Engineer Officer
  1 Damage Control/Maintenance Officer
  3 Enginemen
  2 Maintenance Technicians
  2 Electricians
  1 Fireman
Weapons Support
  1 Weapons Officer
  1 Fire Control Technician
  2 Missile Technicians

supporters of reactivation of the mothballed battleships of the IOWA (BB 61) class, air power advocates who believed long-range bomber aircraft could effectively deliver missiles, and the submarine community, which sought instead "submarine arsenal ships" in the form of converted Trident missile submarines (see Chapter 11). The Arsenal Ship gave promise of providing effective long-range support for troops ashore, a role earlier fulfilled by battleships, while air power advocates saw its strike missiles as competition to manned strategic bombers.

Without the support of Admiral Boorda, the Arsenal Ship concept quickly died. During the 2000 presidential campaign, then-candidate George W. Bush stated that if elected, he would give consideration to resurrecting the project.

---

2 Aircraft controllers could be in the E-2C Hawkeye Airborne Early Warning (AEW) aircraft, E-3 Sentry Airborne Warning and Control System (AWACS) aircraft, or E-8 J-STARS (Joint Surveillance and Target Acquisition Radar System) aircraft.

APPENDIX F

Understanding Transformation

The term "transformation" has been adopted by the U.S. Department of Defense and the military services as a catchword for the change or evolution of the U.S. armed forces from a Cold War posture to being able to effectively engage the terrorism generated by Muslim fundamentalism—i.e., World War III.

Unfortunately, many military officials—civilian and uniformed—have adopted the term to justify the continued funding of their programs, regardless of their relationship to change. Similarly, opponents to programs often call them "nontransformational" in their efforts to curtail funding.

Accordingly, this appendix provides a realistic and current definition of the term, using the words of General Richard B. Myers, Chairman of the Joint Chiefs of Staff, in his article "Understanding Transformation," which appeared in the U.S. Naval Institute's Proceedings *(February 2003), pp. 38–41.*

General Richard B. Myers, Chairman Joint Chiefs of Staff since 1 October 2001

When the bombs fell on Pearl Harbor in 1941, they shattered more than the silence of a peaceful Sunday morning; they destroyed the illusion that U.S. military forces were safe at home. During the three-and-a-half years that followed, a world war transformed the U.S. armed forces into a first-rate military. The urgency of fighting a global conflict propelled the genius of Americans to make this transformation a reality.

In a similar manner, the events of 11 September 2001 shattered the illusion that Americans are safe at home. Today, we have the same imperative to transform our military forces to defeat the new threats of the 21st century and protect our nation. Transformation cannot wait—it must take place as we wage the war on terrorism. In his 11 December 2001 remarks at the Citadel, President George W. Bush summed up this challenge: "It's like overhauling an engine while driving 80 miles per hour. Yet we have no choice."

If the U.S. armed forces are to meet the President's expectations, those of us in uniform must have a common understanding of what transformation is and what it is not. Transformation is a process and a mind-set. Adopting a transformational mind-set means applying current fielded capabilities—in the current environment—to accomplish any assigned mission. In today's dynamic world, no armed service's core competencies can accomplish the mission alone. Transformation unites unique service capabilities into a seamless joint framework to accomplish the joint force commander's objectives.

To achieve transformation, the war fighters must understand its intellectual, cultural, and technological elements. The most important breakthroughs will take place between the ears of war fighters and planners. Soldiers, sailors, airmen, Marines, Coast Guardsmen, and Department of Defense civilians must know their units' technical and operational capabilities. Joint leaders must comprehend the joint force commander's intent and adapt their capabilities—sometimes in an unanticipated environment—to fulfill that intent. They must understand the probable employment of their unit and appre-

ciate its possible employment. In some cases, transformation may mean reaching beyond doctrine—because doctrine may not have described the specific scenario faced by the war fighter. As a result, transformation involves taking operational risks.

Military professionals should not be reckless, however. Commanders and leaders must weigh the options in the context of the ultimate objective. Transformation also means encouraging and rewarding subordinates to take educated and calculated risks. Key to this process is the obligation not to punish subordinates when creative initiatives fail.

During World War II, General George Kenney personified transformation's intellectual element. He adapted the capabilities of the 5th Air Force in the Southwest Pacific Theater to meet General Douglas MacArthur's objectives. In one example, during August 1943, General Kenney employed B-25 bombers to strafe the Japanese airfield at Nadzab in advance of an airborne assault. He then used A-20 Havoc attack aircraft to lay a smokescreen to shield the paratroopers as they descended on the airfield. This innovative use of bombers and attack aircraft allowed U.S. forces to quickly seize the airfield. General Kenney comprehended the potential of his forces and employed them in an imaginative way. He matched his forces' capabilities to the mission and environment—rather than trying to make the environment fit his preconceived notions.

Transformation's second element involves the operating culture within and among military units and services. U.S. military cultures are reinforced by tested checklists and proven tactics, techniques, and procedures. It is a comfortable environment of known quantities, familiar faces, and common verbal shorthand. Transforming the U.S. military means operating in new ways and sometimes with untested procedures. When a new idea surfaces, we first should evaluate its merits. The new idea may not work, but it never should be dismissed because it has not been considered before. Success in embracing the required cultural change will be driven by the joint war fighters' trust and confidence in each other.

In the past, trust and confidence among service components made the difference in combat. In World War II, Generals Joseph Lawton ("Lightning Joe") Collins and Elwood R. ("Pete") Quesada demonstrated what is possible when warriors extend trust across component boundaries. Following the breakout at St Lo, France, Generals Collins and Quesada created a shortcut in the targeting procedures to support VII Corps' exploitation of the fluid battlefield. General Quesada gave some of his pilots FM radios and had them ride with the lead Army tanks. In the process, they reduced the role of the upper chain of command. Generals Collins and Quesada delegated the target approval to the lowest level—to the warriors facing the enemy.

No one told these soldiers they had to do this. These commanders assumed risk. Without approved procedures or prescriptive doctrine, Generals Quesada and Collins demonstrated flexibility and adaptability. They succeeded because they trusted each other's judgment and experience. As a result, they accomplished the mission and saved American lives. As Army combat historian S. L. A. Marshall wrote in his 1947 Men against Fire, "Improvisation is the essence of initiative in all combat." To succeed in the crucible of combat often requires warriors to adopt innovative approaches.

Technology is the third element of transformation. For fiscal year 2003, the Department of Defense has requested nearly $128 billion for current and future weapon systems and capabilities. The department must invest in the right capabilities that reinforce its ability to perform the unexpected and master emerging challenges of the 21st century. To be successful, these capabilities must allow joint commanders to integrate our service capabilities.

In the past, joint warfare was segregated warfare. Desert Storm is an example of a successful campaign that had sectored operations. Air operations kicked things off and lasted 38 days. When ground combat began, U.S. Marines attacked in a path along the Kuwait coast; the Arab Coalition forces assaulted the middle sector; and the U.S. VII Corps and XVIII Airborne Corps swept around the western flank. Close air support sorties during the ground war were employed beyond the sight of the troops they supported. These are a few examples of how we segregated and sequenced our efforts. Instead of integration, it was deconfliction.

In the future, the joint war fighters must meld component capabilities into a seamless joint framework. The key to this effort will be shared information among the components. That is what Generals Quesada and Collins did by having an aviator with a radio accompany the lead tanks. Transformational technologies are an area of great promise for integrated information sharing across service boundaries. Still, such technological solutions must be applied in an environment of trust.

Interoperable and integrated command, control, communication, computer, intelligence, surveillance, and reconnaissance (C4ISR) suites are critical. Joint ISR will allow our commanders to "watch" the enemy. Enhanced joint command and control will allow joint commanders to make decisions faster with other members of the joint force. Horizontal and vertical integration of plans and operations will occur at all levels. Moving data faster is no longer the issue—getting the right data to the right people is. When this is achieved, components gain the insight needed to fulfill the commander's intent in an unpredictable environment. Improved joint C⁴ISR will allow U.S. forces to exploit a decision cycle—to observe, decide, and act—faster than an adversary. And as history documents, the side that does this faster, wins.

Improved C⁴ISR connectivity is more than a military issue. It must extend to information and knowledge sharing with other federal agencies and with U.S. coalition partners. The war on terrorism has demonstrated that all instruments of national power perform best when they have access to the best available and the most complete information.

Investing in the right new capabilities requires the Defense Department to ensure that new systems are "born joint" to share information with the other services' systems. Acquisition of service-centric technologies risks segregating the battlefield. To ensure that the systems are born joint, the Joint Chiefs of Staff are developing a Joint Capstone Concept to better describe how we will operate across the range of military operations and to better evaluate how individual service capabilities fit into the joint operational framework.

The Way Ahead

Joint Professional Military Education (JPME) is an ideal facilitator for the intellectual, cultural, and technological mind-set changes we need to inspire our transformation efforts. JPME must reinforce within the U.S. military—both in the officer and senior noncommissioned ranks—the mental agility to understand service and unit capabilities and match them with the mission at hand. A revamped JPME system must foster an ability and a desire to look forward and anticipate future conflict. This requires an approach much different from one that develops the ability to look back and recite past solutions. A transformed JPME system must teach our leaders not what to think, but how to think, and it must foster a culture that accepts intelligent, calculated risk. Most important, JPME must inculcate a culture of understanding and trust among the leaders of the services and agencies.

A transformed JPME requires reforming our intermediate and senior service schools, incorporating new and focused education

---

Planning Reflects 21st–Century Threats

The 2001 Quadrennial Defense Review marked a complete departure from Cold War planning. In this document, the Defense Department articulated a more sophisticated appreciation of the 21st-century strategic environment, the challenges to U.S. interests, and what military capabilities are needed.

Today, the threats to U.S. interests go beyond Iraq and North Korea. Political, ethnic, social, and historical factors have given rise to a range of conflict and crisis—from ethnic fighting to mass starvation and massacres—and disparities in resources and populations remain powerful motivators for future intra- and interstate strife. In addition, religious and cultural differences, some reflecting ancient hatreds, can cause additional crises around the globe.

Belligerents motivated by this wide array of influences now have access to modern conventional arms markets, a sophisticated industrial production infrastructure, and advanced communications. Advanced production capabilities also mean that hostile nations and agents might have access to weapons of mass destruction—nuclear, chemical, biological, and radiological. In addition, the global $3-trillion communications network allows previously isolated groups to communicate instantly worldwide and to access a wide array of information and intelligence, at little relative cost.

The past U.S. monopoly on the latest and most sophisticated capabilities is gone.

What Transformation Is Not

Transformation is not just about technology. It is not about wheeled versus tracked vehicles, stealthier aircraft, or the types of missiles on submarines. It is not about 20th-century forces being renamed with 21st–century titles. Such approaches risk reducing important concepts to a budget drill. These mind-sets inspire service program managers to declare their programs "transformational" and therefore safe in the budget process. This singular mentality reduces transformation efforts to rearguard actions to defend rice bowls.

Transformation is not just about seeking revolutionary changes in the conduct of warfare. Sudden and dramatic changes do occur. Nuclear weapons and stealth technology are examples of previous remarkable changes. Silver-bullet solutions, however, are rare and should not be our sole focus.

for our general and flag officers, and offering joint educational and training opportunities for junior officers and senior noncommissioned officers who have not received them before. These reforms will proceed beyond formal education and training opportunities and include how the U.S. armed forces "grow" senior general and flag officers. Joint task force commanders and regional combatant commanders must have an array of leaders with a full understanding of how to integrate the joint team prior to a crisis, when the lives of servicemen and women are at risk and the mission's success hangs in the balance.

The idea that education must match the demands of the security environment is not new. When President Theodore Roosevelt accelerated the transformation of the U.S. armed forces from a frontier army and coastal navy at the turn of the 20th century, he and his Secretary of War, Elihu Root, placed a premium on the education of the officers who would lead the new forces. Roosevelt's administration matched the procurement of 16 new battleships by expanding West Point and starting the Army War College to educate the officers who would lead the armed forces. Following this model, we know that current and future commanders must have the same intellectual capital to match the technological marvels this nation provides for its defense.

Because of the terrorist attacks in September 2001, we must accelerate our efforts to gain transformation's potential for our new security environment. We cannot wait until the war on terrorism is finished. The joint team needs transformation's agility and responsiveness to defeat those who threaten our nation, our citizens, and our liberties. The United States no longer has the luxury of time to prepare.

I challenge the readers of *Proceedings* to build on what I have presented. Share your ideas of how transformation applies to our nation's maritime and joint forces. If you think you know a better way to define the potential and promise of transformation, enter the forum. If you send copies of what you write to me, I will get back to you. Do not sit on the sidelines and think that others are responsible for transforming our forces to meet the challenges of the 21st century. Your ideas can and will make a difference. Transformation's result is a dramatically better joint force.

General Index

Ranks shown are the highest used in text. The appendixes are not indexed.

The island structure of the carrier JOHN F. KENNEDY *has two visible antennas for the Mk 91 weapon direction systems mounted atop the bridge (upper right). There is an SLQ-32(V)4 ECM antenna. Also shown are the ship's SPS-49 long-range air search radar and, below the funnel, a Phalanx CIWS mount. (U.S. Navy)*

Ship Name and Class Index

Named landing craft and Y-series service craft are not indexed unless they appear in photographs. The appendixes are not indexed.

About the Author

NORMAN POLMAR is an analyst, author, and historian specializing in naval issues. Since 1980, he has been a consultant to several senior officials in the Navy and Department of Defense and has directed several studies for U.S. and foreign shipbuilding and aerospace firms. From 1982 to 1986, and again from December 2002, he has been a member of the Secretary of the Navy's Research Advisory Committee (NRAC). In December 2004, he also was appointed to the Secretary of the Navy's Advisory Committee on Naval History.

Mr. Polmar has consulted to three U.S. senators and two members of the House of Representatives. He also has served as a consultant or advisor to three Secretaries of the Navy and two Chiefs of Naval Operations.

Mr. Polmar has written or coauthored 40 books and numerous articles on naval, aviation, and intelligence subjects. From 1967 to 1977, he was editor of the U.S. and several other sections of the annual *Jane's Fighting Ships*. The first American to hold an editorship with that publication, he was responsible for almost one-third of the volume in that period. He subsequently became author of the U.S. Naval Institute reference books *Guide to the Soviet Navy* and *Ships and Aircraft of the U.S Fleet*. He also writes a regular columns for *Proceedings* and *Naval History*, both published by the Naval Institute.

He has appeared on numerous radio and television news shows to discuss contemporary military– naval events and is featured regularly in documentaries and other features on the History, Discovery, and A&E television channels.

Mr. Polmar has visited Russia on several occasions and has traveled extensively in Europe, the Middle East, and the Far East.

The Naval Institute Press is the book-publishing arm of the U.S. Naval Institute, a private, nonprofit, membership society for sea service professionals and others who share an interest in naval and maritime affairs. Established in 1873 at the U.S. Naval Academy in Annapolis, Maryland, where its offices remain today, the Naval Institute has members worldwide.

Members of the Naval Institute support the education programs of the society and receive the influential monthly magazine *Proceedings* and discounts on fine nautical prints and on ship and aircraft photos. They also have access to the transcripts of the Institute's Oral History Program and get discounted admission to any of the Institute-sponsored seminars offered around the country. Discounts are also available to the colorful bimonthly magazine *Naval History*.

The Naval Institute's book-publishing program, begun in 1898 with basic guides to naval practices, has broadened its scope to include books of more general interest. Now the Naval Institute Press publishes about one hundred titles each year, ranging from how-to books on boating and navigation to battle histories, biographies, ship and aircraft guides, and novels. Institute members receive significant discounts on the Press's more than eight hundred books in print.

Full-time students are eligible for special half-price membership rates. Life memberships are also available.

For a free catalog describing Naval Institute Press books currently available, and for further information about joining the U.S. Naval Institute, please write to:

Membership Department
U.S. Naval Institute
291 Wood Road
Annapolis, MD 21402-5034
Telephone: (800) 233-8764
Fax: (410) 269-7940
Web address: www.navalinstitute.org